London Overview

P9-DEG-013

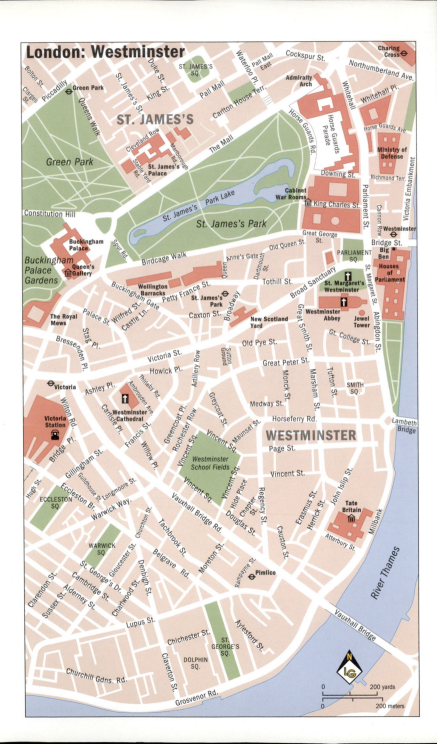

London: Westminster

Charing Cross

Cockspur St.

Northumberland Ave.

Bolton St.

Clarges St.

Piccadilly

Green Park

Queens Walk

Duke St.

St. James's St.

King St.

ST. JAMES'S SQ.

Pall Mall East

Waterloo Pl.

Pall Mall

Carlton House Terr.

Admiralty Arch

Whitehall

Whitehall Pl.

ST. JAMES'S

Cleveland Row

Marlborough Rd.

The Mall

Horse Guards Parade

Horse Guards Rd.

Horse Guards Ave.

Green Park

St. James's Palace

Stable Yard Rd.

Ministry of Defense

Downing St.

Richmond Terr.

Victoria Embankment

Constitution Hill

St. James's Park Lake

St. James's Park

Cabinet War Rooms

King Charles St.

Parliament St.

Cannon Row

Westminster

Buckingham Palace

Spur Rd.

Birdcage Walk

Queen Anne's Gate

Old Queen St.

Great George St.

PARLIAMENT SQ.

Big Ben

Buckingham Palace Gardens

Queen's Gallery

Dartmouth St.

Queen

Tothill St.

Broad Sanctuary

St. Margaret's Westminster

St. Margaret St.

Houses of Parliament

Wellington Barracks

Buckingham Gate

Petty France St.

St. James's Park

Broadway

Westminster Abbey

Jewel Tower

Abingdon St.

The Royal Mews

Palace St.

Wilfred St.

Castle Ln.

Caxton St.

New Scotland Yard

Great Smith St.

Gt. College St.

Bressenden Pl.

Stag Pl.

Victoria St.

Old Pye St.

Great Peter St.

Victoria

Ashley Pl.

Thirleby Rd.

Ambrosden Ave.

Howick Pl.

Artillery Row

Sutton Ground

Greycoat St.

Monck St.

Medway St.

Marsham St.

Tufton St.

SMITH SQ.

Wilton Rd.

Carlisle Pl.

Westminster Cathedral

Francis St.

Willow Pl.

Greencoat Pl.

Rochester Row

Vincent Sq.

Maunsel St.

Horseferry Rd.

WESTMINSTER

Victoria Station

Bridge Pl.

Gillingham St.

Guildhouse St.

Longmoore St.

Warwick Way.

Vincent Sq.

Westminster School Fields

Hide Place

Page St.

Vincent St.

Hugh St.

Eccleston Br.

ECCLESTON SQ.

Churchton St.

Vauxhall Bridge Rd.

Chapter St.

Regency St.

Douglas St.

Erasmus St.

Herrick St.

John Islip St.

Tate Britain

Millbank

Lambeth Bridge

WARWICK SQ.

St. George's Dr.

Cambridge St.

Gloucester St.

Denbigh St.

Belgrave Rd.

Tachbrook St.

Moreton St.

Rampayne St.

Causton St.

Atterbury St.

Pimlico

Clarendon St.

Sussex St.

Alderney St.

Charlwood St.

Lupus St.

Chichester St.

Claverton St.

Aylesford St.

ST. GEORGE'S SQ.

River Thames

Churchill Gdns. Rd.

DOLPHIN SQ.

Grosvenor Rd.

Vauxhall Bridge

N

0   200 yards

0   200 meters

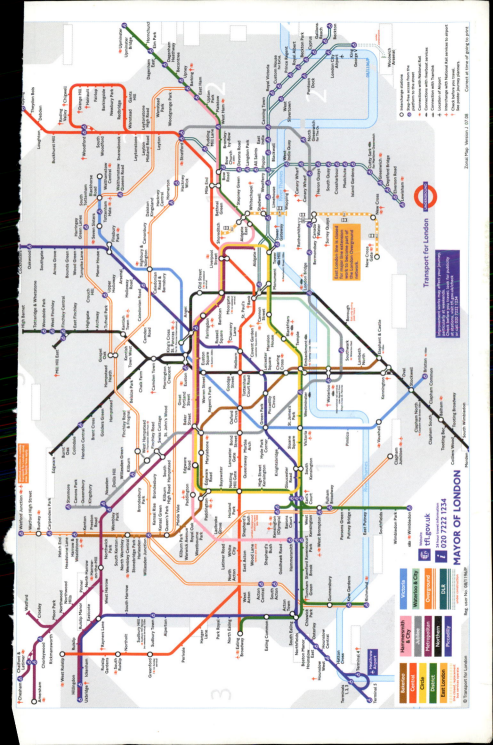

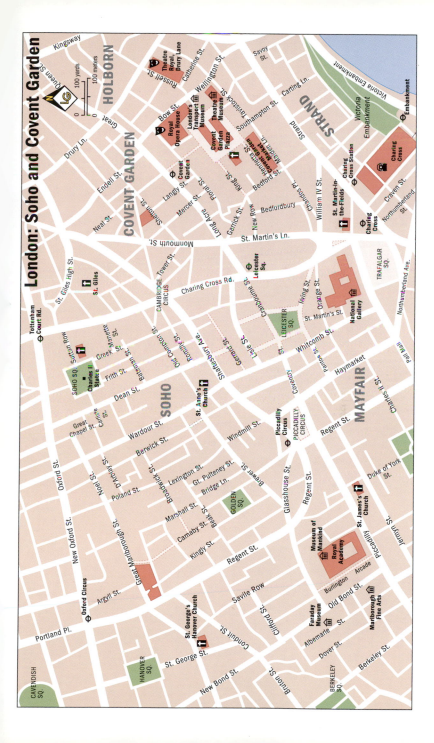
London: Soho and Covent Garden

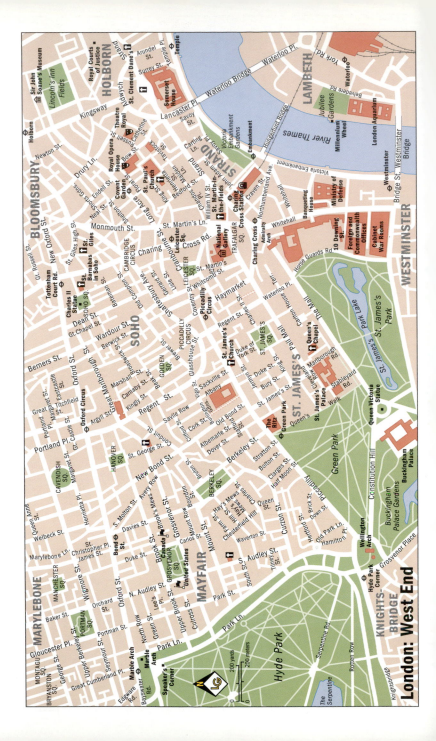

London: West End

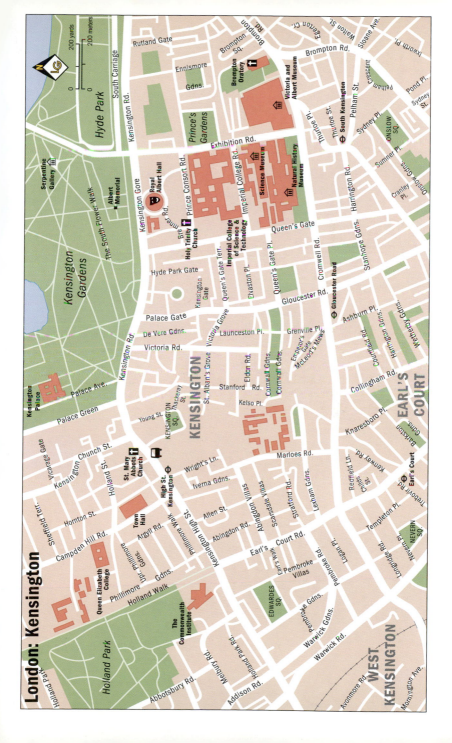

London: Kensington

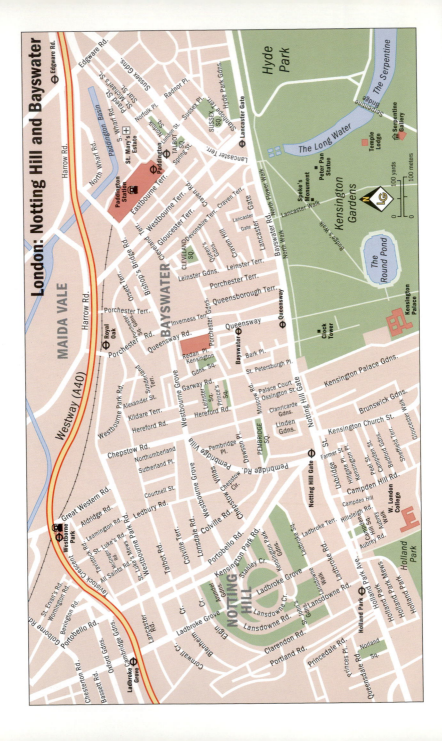

London: Notting Hill and Bayswater

LET'S GO

PAGES PACKED WITH ESSENTIAL INFORMATION

"Value-packed, unbeatable, accurate, and comprehensive."

—*The Los Angeles Times*

"The guides are aimed not only at young budget travelers but at the independent traveler; a sort of streetwise cookbook for traveling alone."

—*The New York Times*

"Unbeatable; good sight-seeing advice; up-to-date info on restaurants, hotels, and inns; a commitment to money-saving travel; and a wry style that brightens nearly every page."

—*The Washington Post*

THE BEST TRAVEL BARGAINS IN YOUR BUDGET

"All the dirt, dirt cheap."

—*People*

"Let's Go follows the creed that you don't have to toss your life's savings to the wind to travel—unless you want to."

—*The Salt Lake Tribune*

REAL ADVICE FOR REAL EXPERIENCES

"The writers seem to have experienced every rooster-packed bus and lunar-surfaced mattress about which they write."

—*The New York Times*

"[Let's Go's] devoted updaters really walk the walk (and thumb the ride, and trek the trail). Learn how to fish, haggle, find work—anywhere."

—*Food & Wine*

"A world-wise traveling companion—always ready with friendly advice and helpful hints, all sprinkled with a bit of wit."

—*The Philadelphia Inquirer*

A GUIDE WITH A SPIRIT AND A SOCIAL CONSCIENCE

"Lighthearted and sophisticated, informative and fun to read. [Let's Go] helps the novice traveler navigate like a knowledgeable old hand."

—*Atlanta Journal-Constitution*

"The serious mission at the book's core reveals itself in exhortations to respect the culture and the environment—and, if possible, to visit as a volunteer, a student, or a teacher rather than a tourist."

—*San Francisco Chronicle*

LET'S GO PUBLICATIONS

TRAVEL GUIDES

Australia
Austria & Switzerland
Brazil
Britain
California
Central America
Chile
China
Costa Rica
Eastern Europe
Ecuador
Egypt
Europe
France
Germany
Greece
Hawaii
India & Nepal
Ireland
Israel
Italy
Japan
Mexico
New Zealand
Peru
Puerto Rico
Southeast Asia
Spain & Portugal with Morocco
Thailand
USA
Vietnam
Western Europe

ROADTRIP GUIDE

Roadtripping USA

ADVENTURE GUIDES

Alaska
Pacific Northwest
Southwest USA

CITY GUIDES

Amsterdam
Barcelona
Boston
Buenos Aires
London
New York City
Paris
Rome
San Francisco
Washington, DC

POCKET CITY GUIDES

Amsterdam
Berlin
Boston
Chicago
London
New York City
Paris
San Francisco
Venice
Washington, DC

LET'S GO

BRITAIN

2009

KIMBERLY HAGAN EDITOR
CHARLIE RIGGS ASSOCIATE EDITOR

RESEARCHER-WRITERS

RACHEL BANAY   **LESLIE LEE**
SHOSHANNA FINE **ALANNA WINDSOR**
ATHENA JIANG   **DIANA C. WISE**

ILLIANA QUIMBAYA MAP EDITOR
NATHANIEL RAKICH MANAGING EDITOR

ST. MARTIN'S PRESS ✿ NEW YORK

Maps by Let's Go copyright © 2009 by Let's Go, Inc.
Maps by David Lindroth copyright © 2009 by St. Martin's Press.

Distributed outside the USA and Canada by Macmillan.

ISBN-13: 978-0-312-38709-9
ISBN-10: 0-312-38709-1

First edition
10 9 8 7 6 5 4 3 2 1

Let's Go: Britain is written by Let's Go Publications, 67 Mount Auburn St., Cambridge, MA 02138, USA.

Let's Go® and the LG logo are trademarks of Let's Go, Inc.

ABOUT LET'S GO

NOT YOUR PARENTS' TRAVEL GUIDE

At Let's Go, we see every trip as the chance of a lifetime. If your dream is to grab a machete and forge through the jungles of Costa Rica, we can take you there. If you'd rather bask in the Riviera sun at a beachside cafe, we'll set you a table. We write for readers who know that there's more to travel than sharing double deckers with tourists and who believe that travel can change both themselves and the world—whether they plan to spend six days in Bangkok or six months in Europe. We'll show you just how far your money can go, and prove that the greatest limitation on your adventures is not your wallet but your imagination.

BEYOND THE TOURIST EXPERIENCE

To help you gain a deeper connection with the places you travel, our fearless researchers scour the globe to give you the heads-up on both world-renowned and off-the-beaten-track attractions, sights, and destinations. They dive into the local culture only to emerge with the freshest insights on everything from festivals to regional cuisine. We've also opened our pages to respected writers and scholars to hear their takes on the countries and regions we cover, and asked travelers who have worked, studied, or volunteered abroad to contribute first-person accounts of their experiences. In addition, each guide's Beyond Tourism chapter shares ideas about responsible travel, study abroad, and how to give back while on the road.

FORTY-NINE YEARS OF WISDOM

Let's Go got its start in 1960, when a group of creative and well-traveled students compiled their experience and advice into a 20-page mimeographed pamphlet, which they gave to travelers on charter flights to Europe. Almost five decades later, we've expanded to cover six continents and all kinds of travel—while retaining our founders' adventurous attitude. Laced with witty prose and total candor, our guides are still researched and written entirely by students on shoestring budgets, experienced travelers who know that train strikes, stolen luggage, food poisoning, and marriage proposals are all part of a day's work.

THE LET'S GO COMMUNITY

More than just a travel guide company, Let's Go is a community. Our small staff comes together because of our shared passion for travel and our desire to help other travelers see the world the way it was meant to be seen. We love it when our readers become part of the Let's Go community as well—when you travel, drop us a postcard (67 Mt. Auburn St., Cambridge, MA 02138, USA), send us an e-mail (feedback@letsgo.com), or sign up online (http://www.letsgo.com) to tell us about your adventures and discoveries.

For more information, visit us online: www.letsgo.com.

HOW TO USE THIS BOOK

COVERAGE LAYOUT. *Let's Go: Britain* launches out of **London** and follows with a tour through **England**. From the idyllic **South,** venture to the criminally picturesque **Southwest,** through the storybook **Heart of England,** to the fens of **East Anglia** and the countryside of the **Midlands.** Cross the cities and lakes of the **Northwest** (with a quick hop to the Isle of Man) and the moors of the **Northeast.** Your travels restart in **Wales,** sweeping from Cardiff, through the beaches of **South Wales,** into mountainous **North Wales.** In **Scotland,** wheel from Edinburgh to **Southern Scotland** to Glasgow, then track north to the castles and lochs of **Central Scotland.** Continue to the rugged, remote **Highlands and Islands.** Next, it's across the sea to **Northern Ireland.** Begin in Belfast and then tour the Giant's Causeway. Through it all, you will encounter extensive coverage of Britain's 14 **national parks,** spread across the island and along the coastline.

TRANSPORTATION INFO. For connecting between destinations, info is listed under the Transportation section of the departure city. Parentheticals usually provide the trip duration, the frequency, and the price, in that order. For general information on travel, consult the **Essentials** (p. 11) section.

COVERING THE BASICS. The first chapter, **Discover Britain** (p. 1), contains highlights of Britain and **Suggested Itineraries.** The **Essentials** (p. 11) chapter contains practical information on planning a budget, making reservations, and staying safe. The **Life and Times** sections introduce each country **(England,** p. 74; **Wales, p. 460; Scotland,** p. 535; **Northern Ireland,** p. 688) and sum up its history, culture, and customs. The **Appendix** (p. 719) has climate information, conversations, and a glossary. For information on studying, volunteering, or working in Britain, consult the **Beyond Tourism** (p. 60) chapter.

SCHOLARLY ARTICLES. Two contributors with unique insight wrote articles for *Let's Go: Britain.* Columbia University professor and renowned British art historian **Simon Schama** discusses his favorite ruins (p. 401), and actor **David Ingber** sheds light on performing at the Edinburgh Fringe Festival (p. 73).

TIP BOXES AND FEATURES. *Let's Go*'s tip boxes and features are meant to guide you to the very best deals, the very best sights, and the very best places to splurge. Other features give you insight into local lore, small-scale city tours, or stories from the *Let's Go* researchers.

PRICE DIVERSITY. Our researchers list establishments in order of value, from best to worst. Our favorites are denoted by the *Let's Go* thumbs-up (◉). Since the lowest price does not always mean the best value, we have incorporated a system of price ranges for food and accommodations; see p. XII.

PHONE CODES AND TELEPHONE NUMBERS. Phone codes for each city appear opposite the name, denoted by the ☎ icon. For more on dialing, see p. 42.

A NOTE TO OUR READERS. The information for this book was gathered by Let's Go researchers from May through August of 2008. Each listing is based on one researcher's opinion, formed during his or her visit at a particular time. Those traveling at other times may have different experiences since prices, dates, hours, and conditions are always subject to change. You are urged to check the facts presented in this book beforehand to avoid inconvenience and surprises.

CONTENTS

RESEARCHER-WRITERS

Rachel Banay   *Northern Ireland*

Stomping her feet at Irish trad sessions or chatting with Derry cabdrivers, Rachel kept tremendous enthusiasm and energy along her route. Her earnest curiosity was apparent to everyone she met; Rachel charmed her way into a Belfast burlesque show and even into the VIP capsule of the Belfast Wheel. After adding loads of valuable new coverage to *Let's Go: Britain*, Rachel tirelessly moved on to the Republic of Ireland to research for *Let's Go: Europe*.

Shoshanna Fine   *Midlands, Heart of England, SW and N. England*

Shosh blazed across England, making friends in every city and burrow along the way. A fearless and determined researcher, she hiked between Cotswold villages, braved intense rains in Dartmoor, and candidly covered nightlife from Bournemouth to Manchester. Shosh's sunny disposition shone through; between 6am ferries and late-night club coverage, she still found time to savor cheese in Cheddar and enjoy the Southwest's best vegetarian eats.

Athena Jiang   *Glasgow, Central Scotland, Highlands and Islands*

Getting lost in a peat field on the Isle of Skye, stranded without public transportation in the Outer Hebrides, and caught in a storm out hiking in the Cairngorm Mountains—none of these things slowed Athena down. She navigated a route that had never been accomplished without a car, and improvised transportation like an old hand. Along the way, she fell in love with Scotland, from puffins in the Shetland Islands to laid-back pubs in St. Andrews.

Leslie Lee   *NE England, Southern and Central Scotland*

Whether she was befriending locals in a Helmsley pub, traipsing around Edinburgh, or sampling Scotch whisky at an Isle of Islay distillery, Leslie was always having a good time. And her writing showed as much—it was fun, spirited, and always opinionated. All summer, she kept her editors entertained with a steady stream of witty and irreverent commentary.

RESEARCHER-WRITERS

Alanna Windsor   *Wales, NW England, Isle of Man*

Alanna unleashed her impressive writing skills and meticulous research habits on every town she visited. With a keen eye for cheap prices and trendy decor, she sent back reams of pristine copy and exhaustive notes. The route was a perfect fit for Alanna, whose odd penchant for quirky museums (and ones featuring large industrial equipment) was more than satisfied in almost every town from Ironbridge to Cardiff.

Diana C. Wise   *NE and S. England, Midlands, East Anglia, London*

Diana finished her Medieval Studies final exam just in time to rush off to medieval Europe. Her love for history was apparent in her detailed observations and impeccable writing. From York Minster to Westminster Abbey, Diana put England's most famous and historic sites into prose, all the while entertaining her editors with humorous anecdotes of life on the road.

CONTRIBUTING WRITERS

Simon Schama is an author and a professor at Columbia University. He has written for *The New Yorker* and was recently the writer and host of the BBC's *History of Britain*.

David Ingber has a degree in English and American Literature and Language from Harvard University. He is an actor and comedian living in New York City.

PRICE RANGES
BRITAIN

Our researchers list establishments in order of value from best to worst, honoring our favorites with the *Let's Go* thumbs-up (👍). Because the best value is not always the cheapest price, we have incorporated a system of price ranges based on a rough expectation of what you will spend. For accommodations, we base our range on the cheapest price for which a single traveler can stay for one night. For dining establishments, we estimate the average amount one traveler will spend in one sitting. The table below tells you what you'll typically find in Britain and the corresponding price range, but keep in mind that no system can allow for the quirks of individual establishments.

ACCOMMODATIONS	RANGE	WHAT YOU'RE *LIKELY* TO FIND
1	under £15	Campgrounds and dorm rooms, both in hostels and actual universities. Expect bunk beds and a communal bath. You may have to provide or rent towels and sheets.
2	£15-25	Upper-end hostels and lower-end B&Bs. You may have an ensuite bath or communal facilities. Breakfast and some amenities, like TVs, may be included.
3	£26-35	A small room with a private bath. Should have decent amenities, such as phones and TVs. Breakfast may be included.
4	£36-60	Should have bigger rooms than a 3, with more amenities or in a more convenient location. Breakfast probably included.
5	over £60	Large hotels, upscale chains, nice B&Bs, and even castles. If it's a 5 and it doesn't have the perks you want, you've paid too much.

FOOD	RANGE	WHAT YOU'RE *LIKELY* TO FIND
1	under £6	Mostly street-corner stands, food trolleys, sandwiches, takeaway, and tea shops. Rarely a sit-down meal.
2	£6-10	Sandwiches, pizza, appetizers at a bar, or low-priced entrees. Most ethnic eateries are a 2. Either takeaway or sit-down, but only slightly more fashionable decor than a 1.
3	£11-15	Mid-priced entrees, good pub grub, and more upscale ethnic eateries. Since you'll likely have the luxury of a waiter, tip will set you back a little extra.
4	£16-24	A somewhat fancy restaurant. Entrees tend to be heartier or more elaborate, but you're really paying for decor and ambience. Few restaurants in this range have a dress code, but some may look down on T-shirts and sandals.
5	over £24	Your meal might cost more than your room, but there's a reason—it's something fabulous, famous, or both. Nicer outfits may be expected. Don't come here expecting a PB&J!

ACKNOWLEDGMENTS

TEAM BRITAIN THANKS: The whole office, for its general enthusiasm. The AUK pod, for its general lack of enthusiasm. Jun, for repping Britain in the Europe guide. Sheep. Batman. Mandy Gable, the proofer who spoke Welsh. Britain herself. Cheers.

KIMBERLY THANKS: Charlie, for late-night laughs and unimpeachable editorial judgment. Researchers, for brilliant copy. Nathaniel, for humor, precision, and guidance. Ills, for witty tearsheets and conversations in Mapland. Viet, for love, support, and meals at midnight. Roommates, for your travel stories. My family, for encouragement and visits to Boston. Mexico.

CHARLIE THANKS: Kimberly, for running things, pulling ridiculous hours, and always keeping a level head. My RWs, for allowing me to vicariously spend my summer along your routes. Illiana, for many, many entertaining Discuss posts. Nathaniel, for exacting standards, uncanny competence, and unfailing good cheer. Dan, for good times in 20-33. Mom, Dad, Nina, John, and Freddy, for putting up with work during vacation. And Julia for everything else.

ILLIANA THANKS: Yo Kim for her constant good cheer and hard work. Charlie for his amazing dedication to making sure that every inch of every map was perfect. All the Brit RWs for visiting every last pub (and sampling every brew!). Mapland for their humor, sighs, 4 o'clock dance parties, rolls, and Disney sing-alongs. And Nemo, for keeping me sane through the summer.

LET'S GO

Publishing Director
Inés C. Pacheco
Editor-in-Chief
Samantha Gelfand
Production Manager
Jansen A. S. Thurmer
Cartography Manager
R. Derek Wetzel
Editorial Managers
Dwight Livingstone Curtis,
Vanessa J. Dube, Nathaniel Rakich
Financial Manager
Lauren Caruso
Publicity and Marketing Manager
Patrick McKiernan
Personnel Manager
Laura M. Gordon
Production Associate
C. Alexander Tremblay
Director of IT & E-Commerce
Lukáš Tóth
Website Manager
Ian Malott
Office Coordinators
Vinnie Chiappini, Jennifer Q. Wong
Director of Advertising Sales
Nicole J. Bass
Senior Advertising Associates
Kipyegon Kitur, Jeremy Siegfried,
John B. Ulrich
Junior Advertising Associate
Edward C. Robinson Jr.

Editor
Kimberly Hagan
Associate Editor
Charlie Riggs
Managing Editor
Nathaniel Rakich
Map Editor
Illiana Quimbaya
Typesetter
Jansen A. S. Thurmer

President
Timothy J. J. Creamer
General Manager
Jim McKellar

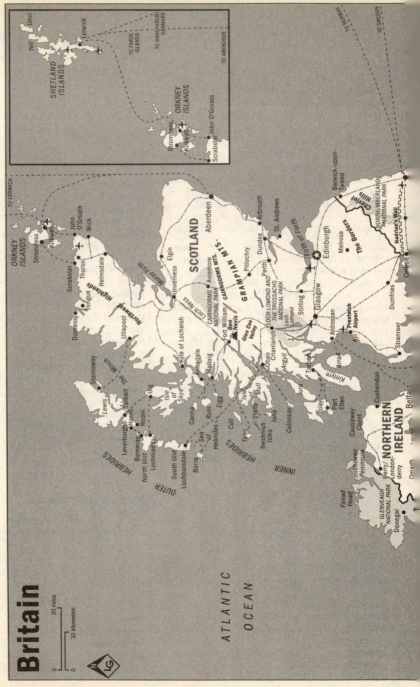

Britain

0   30 miles

0   30 kilometers

ATLANTIC OCEAN

SHETLAND ISLANDS

Unst
Yell
Lerwick

TO FAROE ISLANDS
TO HANSHOLM, DENMARK
TO ABERDEEN

ORKNEY ISLANDS
Stromness
Kirkwall
John O'Groats
Scrabster

TO NORWAY
TO SWEDEN

TO LERWICK

ORKNEY ISLANDS
Stromness
Kirkwall
John O'Groats
Wick
Scrabster
Thurso
Helmsdale
Tongue
Durness

Northern Highlands

Ullapool
Moray Firth
Elgin
Inverness
Loch Ness

SCOTLAND

Aberdeen
Arbroath
St. Andrews
Dundee
Pitlochy
Aviemore
CAIRNGORMS NATIONAL PARK
CAIRNGORMS MTS.
GRAMPIAN MTS.
Fort William
Ben Nevis
Glen Coe Valley

Perth
LOCH LOMOND AND THE TROSSACHS NATIONAL PARK
Loch Lomond
Stirling
Firth of Forth
Edinburgh
Melrose
The Borders
Berwick-upon-Tweed
CHEVIOT HILLS
NORTHUMBERLAND NATIONAL PARK
Hadrian's Wall
Carlisle

Stornoway
Lewis
The Minch
Tarbert
Harris
Rodel
Leverburgh
Berneray
North Uist
Lochmaddy
OUTER HEBRIDES
South Uist
Lochboisdale
Barra

Uig
Isle of Skye
Kyle of Lochalsh
Armadale
Mallaig
Canna
Rum
Eigg
Sea of the Hebrides
Coll
Tiree
Staffa
Iona
Treshnish Isles
Isle of Mull
Colonsay
INNER HEBRIDES

Oban
Crianlarich
Argyll
Jura
Islay
Port Ellen

Glasgow
Ayr
Prestwick Airport
Ardrossan
Arran
Tarbert
Kintyre
Cushendun
Causeway Coast
Londonderry
Derry/Londonderry
Inishowen Peninsula
Fanad Head
Donegal
GLENVEAGH NATIONAL PARK
NORTHERN IRELAND
Belfast
Omagh

Dumfries
Stranraer

XIV

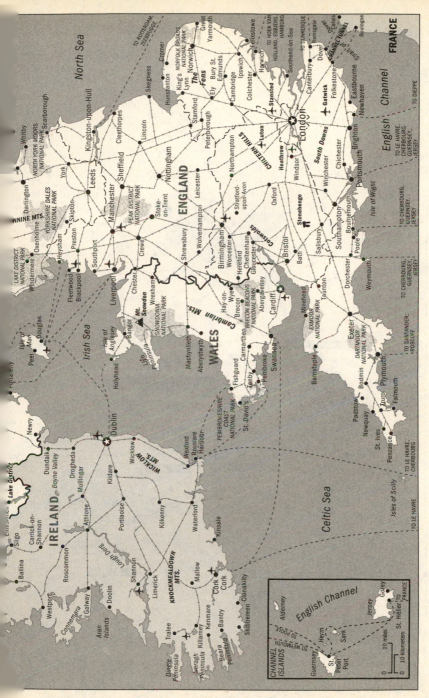

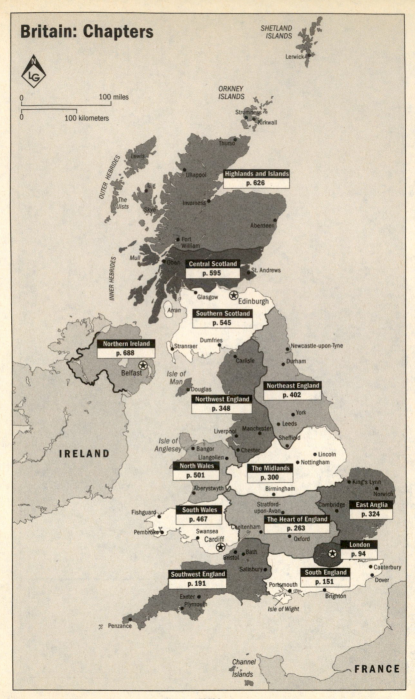

Britain: Chapters

N

0 ——— 100 miles
0 ——— 100 kilometers

SHETLAND ISLANDS

Lerwick

ORKNEY ISLANDS

Stromness
Kirkwall

Thurso

OUTER HEBRIDES

Lewis

Ullapool

Uig

The Uists

Skye

Inverness

Aberdeen

INNER HEBRIDES

Mull

Fort William

Oban

Highlands and Islands
p. 626

St. Andrews

Central Scotland
p. 595

Glasgow ✪ Edinburgh

Arran

Southern Scotland
p. 545

Dumfries

Stranraer

Newcastle-upon-Tyne

Northern Ireland
p. 688

✪ Belfast

Isle of Man

Carlisle

Durham

Douglas

Northeast England
p. 402

Northwest England
p. 348

York

IRELAND

Isle of Anglesey

Liverpool Manchester

Leeds

Sheffield

Bangor

Chester

Lincoln

North Wales
p. 501

Llangollen

The Midlands
p. 300

Nottingham

Aberystwyth

Birmingham

King's Lynn

Norwich

South Wales
p. 467

Stratford-upon-Avon

Cambridge

East Anglia
p. 324

Fishguard

The Heart of England
p. 263

Pembroke

Swansea

Cheltenham

Oxford

London
p. 94

✪ Cardiff

Bristol Bath

✪

Salisbury

Canterbury

Southwest England
p. 191

Portsmouth

South England
p. 151

Dover

Exeter

Brighton

Plymouth

Isle of Wight

Penzance

Channel Islands

FRANCE

DISCOVER BRITAIN

*There once was a country made up of great islands
with peat bogs and moors, great rivers and highlands.
Its people built castles and churches with spires
and started a powerful, global empire.
Meanwhile, the hills, filled with white sheep and crofters,
inspired great artists, bold monarchs, and authors.
Today, on a belly of bangers and mash,
the British continue their long, storied past
with Wimbledon, cricket, golf tourneys, and football,
festivals, dubstep, and cold pints on pub crawls.
It's time to discover and leave what you know—
boot up in your wellies, grab your pack, and let's go!*

FACTS AND FIGURES

POPULATIONS: England, 50.7 million; Wales, 3 million; Scotland, 5.1 million; Northern Ireland, 1.7 million.

PATRON SAINTS: George (England), David (Wales), Andrew (Scotland).

MONARCHS: Kings: 35. Queens: 7. Longest reign: 64 years (Victoria). Shortest reign: 9 days (Lady Jane Grey).

MOST COMMON NAMES: Jack (it's a boy!), Olivia (it's a girl!), Max (it's a dog!), The Red Lion (it's a pub!).

#1 SINGLES BY THE BEATLES: 17.

#1 SINGLES BY THE SPICE GIRLS: 9.

ANNUAL TEA CONSUMPTION PER PERSON: 860 cups.

ANNUAL BEER CONSUMPTION PER PERSON: 228 pints.

FIRST SIGHTING OF THE LOCH NESS MONSTER: 565AD. Hoaxes since then: over 1000.

HEIGHT OF A QUEEN'S GUARD BEARSKIN HAT: 18 in.

WHEN TO GO

Britain's popularity as a tourist destination makes it wise to plan around high season (June-Aug.). Spring or autumn (Apr.-May and Sept.-Oct.) are appealing alternatives, offering pleasant weather and cheaper flights. If you intend to visit the cities and spend time indoors, the low season (Nov.-Mar.) is cheapest. Keep in mind, however, that sights and accommodations often run reduced hours or close completely, especially in rural areas.

"Rain, rain, go away" is less a hopeful plea than an exercise in futility. No matter when you go, it will rain. Have warm, waterproof clothing on hand at all times. Relatively speaking, April is the driest month. The mild weather has few extremes—excluding Highland altitudes, temperatures average around 15-20°C (the mid-60s on the Fahrenheit scale) in summer and 5-7°C (low 40s) in winter. During the winter, snow often causes roads to close in Scotland and in the northern regions of England and Wales. The British Isles are farther north than you may think: Newcastle is on the same latitude as Moscow. In Scotland, the sun shines almost all day in summer and in winter sets as early as 3:30pm.

DISCOVER

THINGS TO DO

With Manchester's clubs only an hour from the Lake District peaks and Land's End only 16hr. from John O'Groats by car, Britain provides countless opportunities within an amazingly compact space. For more specific regional attractions, see the **Highlights** box at the start of each chapter.

ALL NATURAL

Britain's natural landscapes are surprisingly diverse and generally accessible via the country's **national parks**. Discover your inner romantic (or Romantic) among the gnarled crags and crystalline waters of the peaceful **Lake District** (p. 383). The **South Downs Way** (p. 163) ambles through the hills and along the shores of Southern England. Limestone cliffs hang over the Irish Sea in **Pembrokeshire Coast National Park** (p. 491), where coasteering and cliff jumping are popular. **Loch Lomond and The Trossachs** (p. 601), now part of Scotland's first national park, lie along the **West Highland Railway,** which travels north from Glasgow, past Loch Lomond and **Ben Nevis** (p. 645). Farther north, the misty peaks of the **Isle of Skye** (p. 655) and the **Northwest Highlands** (p. 667) lend themselves to postcard-perfect snapshots. Embrace the solitude of the windy **Orkney Islands** (p. 671), filled with wildlife, geological phenomena, and Iron Age monuments. Even more isolated and remote vistas characterize the **Shetland Islands** (p. 680). In Northern Ireland, the honeycomb columns of the **Giant's Causeway** (p. 717) contrast with Antrim's rocky outcrops and pristine white beaches.

EARLY RISERS

Britain was a popular destination long before the arrival of William the Conqueror and the Normans. Walk through a perfectly preserved Neolithic village at **Skara Brae** (p. 676) in the Orkneys. **Stonehenge** (p. 202) is the best-known marker of Bronze Age inhabitants and pagan revelry, while nearby **Avebury** (p. 203) is a bigger, less touristed site. On Scotland's Isle of Lewis, the **Callanish Stones** (p. 664) reveal the ancient Celtic tribes' knowledge of astronomy, while the burial tomb of Wales's **Bryn Celli Ddu** (p. 529) rises from the middle of a modern farm. Britain's first empire (the Roman one) left its mark all over the landscape. Fabulous mosaics and a theater have been excavated at **Saint Albans** (p. 263), once the capital of Roman Britannia, while **Bath** (p. 209) provided a regenerative retreat for Roman colonists. **Hadrian's Wall** (p. 456) marks an emperor's frustration with rebellious tribes to the north, and the nearby site of **Vindolanda** (p. 457) allows visitors to take part in an ongoing archaeological dig. Finding the light in the Dark Ages, early Christianity got its start in Canterbury, where the **Church of Saint Martin** (p. 155) is Britain's oldest house of worship. But a new era of British history was inaugurated that fateful day in 1066 when William trounced the Saxons at **Hastings** (p. 162).

CHURCH AND STATE

Restraint was not a popular concept among early Britons. They never held back when a fortress, castle, or cathedral could be defiantly built or defiantly razed. Edward I of England had a rough time containing the Welsh; his "iron ring" of massive fortresses—like **Caernarfon** (p. 525) or **Caerphilly** (p. 474)—mark the northwestern Welsh coast. Two castles top extinct volcanoes in Scotland, one ringed with gargoyles in **Stirling** (p. 595), the other perched high above **Edinburgh** (p. 545). **Dover Castle** (p. 160) has protected the southern coast since England ruled half of France. You can't leave Scotland without visiting **Dunnottar Castle** (p. 632); it's even more astounding on a stormy day. On your way south, stop by the ruined **Saint Andrews Castle** (p. 606) and scurry through Britain's only surviving countermine tunnel. In central England, get the full medieval experience at **Warwick Castle** (p. 301), complete with banquets and jousts. Stay in the university dorms at **Durham Castle** (p. 439). The sumptuous **Castle Howard** (p. 413) and **Alnwick Castle** (p. 452) both afford a taste of how the other 0.001% lives.

In northeast England, **York Minster** (p. 411), the country's largest Gothic house of worship, competes with **Durham Cathedral** (p. 439) for most jaw-dropping, while **Canterbury Cathedral** (p. 154) has attracted pilgrims since even before the time of Geoffrey Chaucer. **Salisbury Cathedral** (p. 200) holds the record for England's tallest spire. In London, thousands flock to **Westminster Abbey** (p. 116) and **Saint Paul's Cathedral** (p. 117), where Poets' Corner and the Whispering Gallery inspire appropriately quiet reverence. Up in Scotland, the ruined Border Abbeys—**Jedburgh** (p. 569), **Melrose** (p. 566), **Kelso** (p. 570), and **Dryburgh** (p. 567)—draw fewer visitors but offer greater vistas of the surrounding valleys.

LITERARY LANDMARKS

Even if you've never been to Britain, you've probably read about it. Jane Austen grew up in **Winchester** (p. 185), vacationed in **Lyme Regis** (p. 209), and wrote in **Bath** (p. 209), enabling future generations of romantic comedies and even a few chick flicks. Farther north, the brooding Brontës—Charlotte, Emily, and Anne—lived in the parsonage in **Haworth** (p. 420) and captured the wildness of the **Yorkshire Moors** (p. 427) in their novels. Thomas Hardy was a **Dorchester** (p. 206) man who perfectly captured Southwest England in the imaginary county of Wessex. Sir Arthur Conan Doyle set Sherlock Holmes's house on 221B Baker St. in **London** (p. 94), but even super-sleuths won't find the precise address—it's fictional. Virginia Woolf often vacationed in **Cornwall** (p. 238) and drew inspiration for her novel *To the Lighthouse* from **Saint Ives** (p. 254) and the **Isle of Skye** (p. 655). Long after shuffling off his mortal coil, William Shakespeare's legendary spirit lives on in **Stratford-upon-Avon** (p. 280). William Wordsworth grew up in the **Lake District** (p. 383) and spent much of his time roaming its surrounding mountain ridges with his poetic buddy Samuel Taylor Coleridge. JRR Tolkien and CS Lewis crafted wizards and wardrobes over pints at The Eagle and Child in **Oxford** (p. 268). Welshman Dylan Thomas was born in **Swansea** (p. 486) and was famous for his Welsh lilt. Scotland's national poet is Robert Burns, and every (really, every) town in **Dumfries and Galloway** (p. 571) pays tribute to him. **Edinburgh** (p. 545) cherishes its own favorite Scott, Sir Walter.

A SPORTS FAN'S PARADISE

Football (soccer, if you must) fanatics are everywhere: the queen is an Arsenal fan, and the police run a national hooligan hotline. In **London,** become a gunner for a day at Highbury, chant for the Spurs at White Hart Lane, or don the Chelsea blue. Pay homage at **Old Trafford** (p. 367), Manchester United's hallowed turf on Sir Matt Busby Way, or move west to the stadiums of bitter rivals **Everton** and **Liverpool** (p. 354). Rugby scrums are tangled in gaping Millennium Stadium in **Cardiff** (p. 467). Tree-trunk throwers and kilt wearers reach their own rowdy heights annually at the Highland Games in **Braemar** (p. 632) and other Scottish

BRITAIN FOR UNDER £5

1. Bask in Britain's (manicured) natural beauty in London's **Regent's Park** (p. 125), originally designed for the wealthy but now open to the public. Free.

2. Skip the lines at the London Eye and climb the narrow staircase at the **Monument** (p. 122) for stunning views of the city. £2.

3. Considered the finest Norman cathedral in the world, **Durham Cathedral** (p. 439) houses a bishop's throne that stands 3 in. higher than the pope's in Rome. Suggested donation £4.

4. See a world-class play as a groundling at **Shakespeare's Globe** theater (p. 126). £5.

5. Often billed as the eighth wonder of the world, the **Giant's Causeway** in Northern Ireland (p. 717) comprises 38,000 basalt columns. Free.

6. Get lost among the 50,000 items on display at London's **British Museum** (p. 133). Free.

7. Built in AD 122, **Hadrian's Wall** (p. 456) was created to protect the farthest borders of the Roman Empire. The best ruins are along the western portion. Free.

8. A daytrip from Cardiff, **Caerphilly Castle** (p. 474) is a masterpiece of defensive castle design, with concentric fortified walls, two parapets, and a moat. £3.50.

9. The expanses and seclusion of Gower Peninsula's **Rhossili Beach** (p. 490) reward visitors willing to make the trek. Free.

10. South of Aberdeen, the ruins of **Dunnottar Castle** (p. 632) cling to Scotland's coastline. £5.

towns. Cricket is more refined—the men in white play (and play, and play) their interminable games at London's Lords grounds. The world's longest cricket marathon was played by the Cheriton Fitzpaine Club in Devon for 27hr. and 34min. At the hallowed grounds of Wimbledon, huge crowds and fiercely competitive tennis are set against a garden-party backdrop. The Royal Ascot horse races and the Henley regatta draw Britain's blue-bloods, but the revered coastal "links" golf courses of **Saint Andrews** (p. 603) attract enthusiasts from all over. Surfers catch Atlantic waves at alternative **Newquay** (p. 243), secluded **Rhossili Beach** (p. 490), and hard-core **Lewis** (p. 662). Go canyoning or whitewater rafting at **Fort William** (p. 645) or try more tranquil punting in **Oxford** (p. 268) or **Cambridge** (p. 325). **Snowdonia National Park** (p. 516) and the **Cairngorm Mountains** (p. 634) challenge hikers and bikers. Any town will offer spontaneous kick-abouts: go forth and seek your game.

FEELING FESTIVE?

Britons love to party. The concurrent **Edinburgh International** and **Fringe Festivals** (p. 562) take over Scotland's capital each summer with a head-spinning program of performances. Torch-lit Viking revelry ignites the Shetlands during **Up Helly Aa** (p. 682), and all of Scotland hits the streets to welcome the new year for **Hogmanay.** Back in London, things turn fiery during the **Chinese New Year,** while the summer **Notting Hill Carnival** blasts the neighborhood with Caribbean color. Manchester's Gay Village hosts **Mardi Gras** (p. 366), the wildest of street parties, and the three-day **Glastonbury Festival** (p. 217) is Britain's biggest homage to rock, drawing banner names year after year. **T in the Park, Reading Festival, Leeds Festival, V Festival,** and the **Isle of Wight Festival** all bring massive musical acts and crowds, selling over a million tickets annually. The **International Musical Eisteddfod** is Wales's version of the mega-fest, swelling modest **Llangollen** (p. 507) to nearly 30 times its normal size. For a celebration of all things Welsh, check out the **National Eisteddfod** (p. 466). Grab a ferry to Northern Ireland on **Saint Patrick's Day** for a countrywide carnival of concerts, fireworks, street theater, and Guinness-soaked madness. More information on British festivals can be found in the sections for English (p. 93), Welsh (p. 466), and Scottish (p. 544) events.

⬛LET'S GO PICKS

BEST PLACE FOR A PINT: In Penzance, the **Admiral Benbow** (p. 254) adorns its walls with shipwreck relics. Students prowl **The Turf** (p. 277) in Oxford. Tradition mandates a pub crawl in **Edinburgh** (p. 545). Nottingham's **Ye Olde Trip to Jerusalem** (p. 318), carved from rock and established in 1189, claims to be England's oldest pub and still serves a mean pint. London brims with pubs: **Fitzroy Tavern** (p. 145) is perfect for sipping a pint on the street with your pals.

BEST LIVESTOCK: Don't pet Northumberland's psychotic **Wild Cattle**, inbred for seven centuries (p. 453). They aren't really livestock, but the tailless **Manx cats** on the Isle of Man (p. 393) are still pretty rad. Famous **seaweed-eating sheep** sustain themselves on the beaches of North Ronaldsay (p. 679).

BEST PLACE TO FEEL LIKE ROYALTY: For the ultimate regal experience, book the Bishop's Suite in **Durham Castle** (p. 439). Fend off the ghost at **Chillingham Castle** (p. 453) during a stay in a private apartment. Get lost in the hedge maze at the **Chatsworth House** (p. 382). The hidden sea cave beneath Northern Ireland's **Dunluce Castle** (p. 718) makes for stealth escapes back into the commoner's life outside.

BEST NIGHTLIFE: Brighton (p. 167) does native son Fatboy Slim proud as a legendary naughty town. Hip travelers command most of **Newcastle** (p. 441), while funkier folks try Oldham St. in **Manchester** (p. 362)—home of the famous Factory Records club nights—or Broad St. in **Birmingham** (p. 303).

BEST PLACE TO BE A ROCKSTAR: Rock gods like Oasis cut their teeth at the **Water Rats** in London (p. 141). Find three friends and strut the crosswalk in front of **Abbey Road Studios** (p. 131) in St. John's Wood. Channel The Beatles in the **Cavern Club** (p. 362), Liverpool's tourist mecca. Radiohead played its debut gig in 1984 at **Oxford's Jericho Tavern** (p. 279). See rock legends take the stage in **Pilton** (p. 215) at the Glastonbury Festival.

BEST SUNSETS: The walled Welsh city of **Caernarfon** (p. 524) sits on the water, full on facing the western horizon. The extreme northern location of the **Shetland Islands** (p. 680) makes for breathtaking skies, while **Arthur's Seat** (p. 557) grants 360° views of the Edinburgh skyline. Get even closer to the sun on an evening hot-air balloon ride in **Bristol** (p. 193).

BEST QUIRKY MUSEUMS: In Boscastle, the **Museum of Witchcraft** (p. 241) confirms the hocus pocus with biographies of living witches. The **Dog Collar Collection** in Leeds Castle (p. 158) displays medieval pooch attire. London's **Sir John Soane's Museum** (p. 135) contains the mummified corpse of the architect's wife's dog, among other fun oddities.

BEST WAY TO TEMPT FATE: According to legend, nappers on Snowdonia's **Cader Idris** (p. 519) will awake either as poets or madmen, although the two aren't mutually exclusive. Also in Snowdonia, mountaineers celebrate reaching the summit of **Tryfan** (p. 519) by jumping between its two peaks. Go coasteering in **Saint David's** (p. 497), or—for the truly courageous—root for Arsenal at a Manchester United (p. 367) football match.

BEST OF THE MACABRE: Lay down the law at the gallows at Nottingham's **Galleries of Justice** (p. 318). Some 250,000 bodies supposedly slumber around Edinburgh's **Greyfriars Tolbooth and Highland Kirk** (p. 557), while relics of the infamous Red Barn Murder spook visitors at **Moyse's Hall Museum** (p. 346) in Bury St. Edmund's. Watch your head at the **Tower of London** (p. 116).

BEST WAY TO TIME TRAVEL: Listen to the **town crier** announce the secession of the American colonies in Chester (p. 348). Near Shrewsbury, the **Land of Lost Content** (p. 310) salvages souvenirs of popular culture from trash cans.

BEST PLACE TO BE POSH: Shop till you drop in **Birmingham** (p. 303), the shopping capital of England. Hit up the **Victoria Quarter** (p. 413) in Leeds, where designer stores are housed in grand, stately Victorian buildings.

THE BEST OF BRITAIN (4 WEEKS)

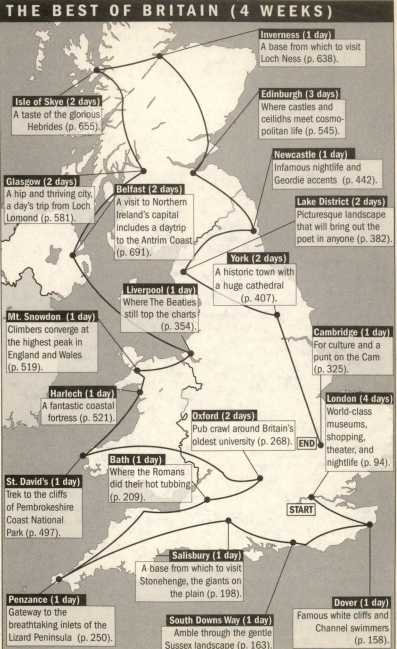

Inverness (1 day)
A base from which to visit Loch Ness (p. 638).

Isle of Skye (2 days)
A taste of the glorious Hebrides (p. 655).

Edinburgh (3 days)
Where castles and ceilidhs meet cosmopolitan life (p. 545).

Newcastle (1 day)
Infamous nightlife and Geordie accents (p. 442).

Glasgow (2 days)
A hip and thriving city, a day's trip from Loch Lomond (p. 581).

Belfast (2 days)
A visit to Northern Ireland's capital includes a daytrip to the Antrim Coast (p. 691).

Lake District (2 days)
Picturesque landscape that will bring out the poet in anyone (p. 382).

York (2 days)
A historic town with a huge cathedral (p. 407).

Liverpool (1 day)
Where The Beatles still top the charts (p. 354).

Mt. Snowdon (1 day)
Climbers converge at the highest peak in England and Wales (p. 519).

Cambridge (1 day)
For culture and a punt on the Cam (p. 325).

Harlech (1 day)
A fantastic coastal fortress (p. 521).

London (4 days)
World-class museums, shopping, theater, and nightlife (p. 94).

Oxford (2 days)
Pub crawl around Britain's oldest university (p. 268).

END

Bath (1 day)
Where the Romans did their hot tubbing (p. 209).

St. David's (1 day)
Trek to the cliffs of Pembrokeshire Coast National Park (p. 497).

START

Salisbury (1 day)
A base from which to visit Stonehenge, the giants on the plain (p. 198).

Penzance (1 day)
Gateway to the breathtaking inlets of the Lizard Peninsula (p. 250).

South Downs Way (1 day)
Amble through the gentle Sussex landscape (p. 163).

Dover (1 day)
Famous white cliffs and Channel swimmers (p. 158).

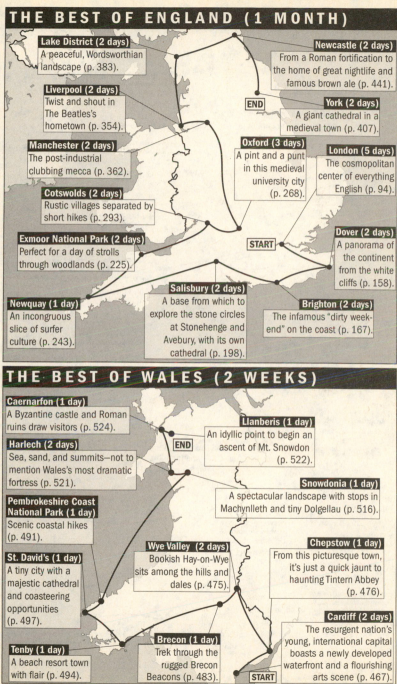

THE BEST OF ENGLAND (1 MONTH)

Lake District (2 days)
A peaceful, Wordsworthian landscape (p. 383).

Newcastle (2 days)
From a Roman fortification to the home of great nightlife and famous brown ale (p. 441).

Liverpool (2 days)
Twist and shout in The Beatles's hometown (p. 354).

END

York (2 days)
A giant cathedral in a medieval town (p. 407).

Manchester (2 days)
The post-industrial clubbing mecca (p. 362).

Oxford (3 days)
A pint and a punt in this medieval university city (p. 268).

London (5 days)
The cosmopolitan center of everything English (p. 94).

Cotswolds (2 days)
Rustic villages separated by short hikes (p. 293).

Exmoor National Park (2 days)
Perfect for a day of strolls through woodlands (p. 225).

START

Dover (2 days)
A panorama of the continent from the white cliffs (p. 158).

Newquay (1 day)
An incongruous slice of surfer culture (p. 243).

Salisbury (2 days)
A base from which to explore the stone circles at Stonehenge and Avebury, with its own cathedral (p. 198).

Brighton (2 days)
The infamous "dirty week-end" on the coast (p. 167).

THE BEST OF WALES (2 WEEKS)

Caernarfon (1 day)
A Byzantine castle and Roman ruins draw visitors (p. 524).

Llanberis (1 day)
An idyllic point to begin an ascent of Mt. Snowdon (p. 522).

END

Harlech (2 days)
Sea, sand, and summits—not to mention Wales's most dramatic fortress (p. 521).

Snowdonia (1 day)
A spectacular landscape with stops in Machynlleth and tiny Dolgellau (p. 516).

Pembrokeshire Coast National Park (1 day)
Scenic coastal hikes (p. 491).

Wye Valley (2 days)
Bookish Hay-on-Wye sits among the hills and dales (p. 475).

Chepstow (1 day)
From this picturesque town, it's just a quick jaunt to haunting Tintern Abbey (p. 476).

St. David's (1 day)
A tiny city with a majestic cathedral and coasteering opportunities (p. 497).

Cardiff (2 days)
The resurgent nation's young, international capital boasts a newly developed waterfront and a flourishing arts scene (p. 467).

Tenby (1 day)
A beach resort town with flair (p. 494).

Brecon (1 day)
Trek through the rugged Brecon Beacons (p. 483).

START

THE BEST OF HISTORY (4 WEEKS)

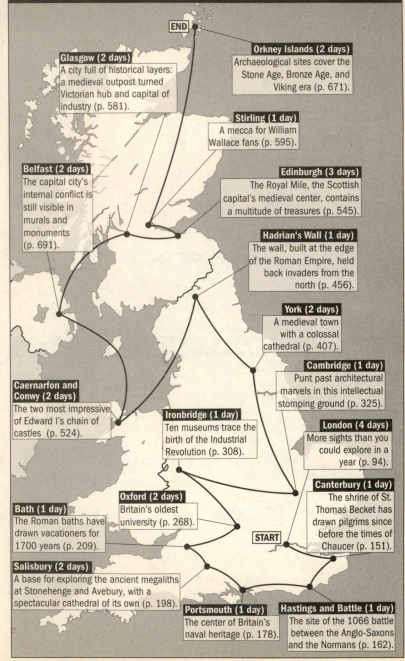

END

Glasgow (2 days)
A city full of historical layers: a medieval outpost turned Victorian hub and capital of industry (p. 581).

Orkney Islands (2 days)
Archaeological sites cover the Stone Age, Bronze Age, and Viking era (p. 671).

Stirling (1 day)
A mecca for William Wallace fans (p. 595).

Belfast (2 days)
The capital city's internal conflict is still visible in murals and monuments (p. 691).

Edinburgh (3 days)
The Royal Mile, the Scottish capital's medieval center, contains a multitude of treasures (p. 545).

Hadrian's Wall (1 day)
The wall, built at the edge of the Roman Empire, held back invaders from the north (p. 456).

York (2 days)
A medieval town with a colossal cathedral (p. 407).

Cambridge (1 day)
Punt past architectural marvels in this intellectual stomping ground (p. 325).

Caernarfon and Conwy (2 days)
The two most impressive of Edward I's chain of castles (p. 524).

Ironbridge (1 day)
Ten museums trace the birth of the Industrial Revolution (p. 308).

London (4 days)
More sights than you could explore in a year (p. 94).

Canterbury (1 day)
The shrine of St. Thomas Becket has drawn pilgrims since before the times of Chaucer (p. 151).

Bath (1 day)
The Roman baths have drawn vacationers for 1700 years (p. 209).

Oxford (2 days)
Britain's oldest university (p. 268).

START

Salisbury (2 days)
A base for exploring the ancient megaliths at Stonehenge and Avebury, with a spectacular cathedral of its own (p. 198).

Portsmouth (1 day)
The center of Britain's naval heritage (p. 178).

Hastings and Battle (1 day)
The site of the 1066 battle between the Anglo-Saxons and the Normans (p. 162).

BRITAIN FOR BOOKWORMS (3 WEEKS)

Edinburgh (3 days)
The Fringe and International Festivals bring scripts to stage (p. 545).

Strangford Lough (2 days)
The Mountains of Mourne inspired CS Lewis's *The Chronicles of Narnia* (p. 706).

Melrose (1 day)
Sir Walter Scott surrounded himself with 9000 rare books in his country estate (p. 566).

Dumfries (2 days)
A town devoted to all things Robert Burns (p. 571).

END

Tintern (1 day)
Behold the view that inspired William Wordsworth's "A Few Miles Above Tintern Abbey" (p. 476).

Haworth (1 day)
The childhood home of the Brontë sisters (p. 420).

Stratford-upon-Avon (2 days)
The birthplace of the Bard (p. 280).

London (5 days)
Charles Dickens's house, Bloomsbury Group haunts, and Platform 9¾ all find a place in literary London (p. 94).

Swansea (1 day)
Proud host of the annual Dylan Thomas festival (p. 486).

START

Winchester (1 day)
Where Jane Austen wrote polite novels and John Keats retreated from his London mistress (p. 185).

Dorchester (2 days)
Thomas Hardy's fictional Casterbridge is based on this quaint town (p. 206).

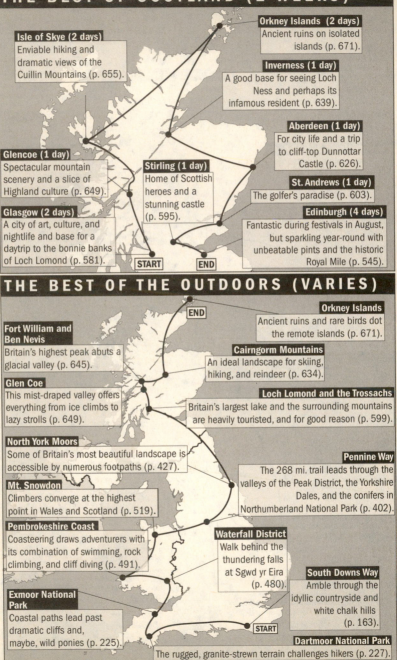

THE BEST OF SCOTLAND (2 WEEKS)

Isle of Skye (2 days)
Enviable hiking and dramatic views of the Cuillin Mountains (p. 655).

Orkney Islands (2 days)
Ancient ruins on isolated islands (p. 671).

Inverness (1 day)
A good base for seeing Loch Ness and perhaps its infamous resident (p. 639).

Aberdeen (1 day)
For city life and a trip to cliff-top Dunnottar Castle (p. 626).

Glencoe (1 day)
Spectacular mountain scenery and a slice of Highland culture (p. 649).

Stirling (1 day)
Home of Scottish heroes and a stunning castle (p. 595).

St. Andrews (1 day)
The golfer's paradise (p. 603).

Glasgow (2 days)
A city of art, culture, and nightlife and base for a daytrip to the bonnie banks of Loch Lomond (p. 581).

Edinburgh (4 days)
Fantastic during festivals in August, but sparkling year-round with unbeatable pints and the historic Royal Mile (p. 545).

START   END

THE BEST OF THE OUTDOORS (VARIES)

END

Orkney Islands
Ancient ruins and rare birds dot the remote islands (p. 671).

Fort William and Ben Nevis
Britain's highest peak abuts a glacial valley (p. 645).

Cairngorm Mountains
An ideal landscape for skiing, hiking, and reindeer (p. 634).

Glen Coe
This mist-draped valley offers everything from ice climbs to lazy strolls (p. 649).

Loch Lomond and the Trossachs
Britain's largest lake and the surrounding mountains are heavily touristed, and for good reason (p. 599).

North York Moors
Some of Britain's most beautiful landscape is accessible by numerous footpaths (p. 427).

Pennine Way
The 268 mi. trail leads through the valleys of the Peak District, the Yorkshire Dales, and the conifers in Northumberland National Park (p. 402).

Mt. Snowdon
Climbers converge at the highest point in Wales and Scotland (p. 519).

Pembrokeshire Coast
Coasteering draws adventurers with its combination of swimming, rock climbing, and cliff diving (p. 491).

Waterfall District
Walk behind the thundering falls at Sgwd yr Eira (p. 480).

South Downs Way
Amble through the idyllic countryside and white chalk hills (p. 163).

Exmoor National Park
Coastal paths lead past dramatic cliffs and, maybe, wild ponies (p. 225).

START

Dartmoor National Park
The rugged, granite-strewn terrain challenges hikers (p. 227).

ESSENTIALS

PLANNING YOUR TRIP

ENTRANCE REQUIREMENTS

Passport (p. 12). Required of all foreign nationals, although they may not be checked for citizens of the EU.

Visa (p. 13). Not required for short-term travel for citizens of Australia, Canada, New Zealand, the US, and many other Western countries. If you are unsure, call your local embassy or complete an inquiry at www.ukvi-sas.gov.uk. Students planning to study in the UK for six months or more must obtain a student visa.

Inoculations (p. 23). No specific inoculation, vaccination, certificate, or International Certificate of Vaccination (ICV) is required, but check to see if an ICV is required upon re-entry into your own country.

Work Permit (p. 14). Required for all foreigners planning to work in Britain.

EMBASSIES AND CONSULATES

UK CONSULAR SERVICES ABROAD

For addresses of British embassies in countries not listed here, consult the **Foreign and Commonwealth Office** (☎020 7008 1500; www.fco.gov.uk). Some cities have a British consulate that can fulfill most functions of an embassy.

Australia: Commonwealth Ave., Yarralumla, ACT 2600 (☎+61 2 6270 6666; http://bhc.britaus.net). Consular Section (UK passports and visas), Piccadilly House, 39 Brindabella Circuit, Brindabella Business Park, Canberra Airport, Canberra ACT 2609 (☎+61 1902 941 555). **Consulates General** in Brisbane, Melbourne, Perth, and Sydney; **Consulate** in Adelaide.

Canada: 80 Elgin St., Ottawa, ON K1P 5K7 (☎+1-613-237-1530; www.britainin-canada.org). **Consulate General,** 777 Bay St., Ste. 2800, Toronto, ON M5G 2G2 (☎416-593-1290). Other offices in Montreal and Vancouver; **Honorary Consuls** in Quebec City, St. John's, and Winnipeg.

Ireland: 29 Merrion Rd., Dublin 4 (☎+353 1 205 3700; www.britishembassy.ie).

New Zealand: 44 Hill St., Thorndon, Wellington 6011 (☎+64 4 924 2888; www.britain.org.nz); mail to P.O. Box 1812, Wellington 6140. **Consulate General:** 151 Queen St., Auckland (☎+64 9 303 2973); mail to Private Bag 92014, Auckland.

US: 3100 Massachusetts Ave. NW, Washington, DC 20008 (☎+1-202-588-7800; www.britainusa.com). **Consulate General:** 845 3rd Ave., New York City, NY 10022 (☎+1-212-745-0200). Other offices in Atlanta, Boston, Chicago, Houston, Los Angeles, and San Francisco. **Consulates** in Dallas, Denver, Miami, and Seattle.

CONSULAR SERVICES IN THE UK

Australia: Australia House, The Strand, London WC2B 4LA (☎020 7379 4334; www. australia.org.uk). Passport office (☎020 7887 5816; www.uk.embassy.gov.au).

Canada: 38 Grosvenor Sq., London W1K 4AA (☎020 7258 6600; www.canada.org.uk).

Ireland: See **Irish Consular Services Abroad** (above).

New Zealand: 80 Haymarket, London SW1Y 4TQ (☎020 7930 8422).

US: 24 Grosvenor Sq., London W1A 1AE (☎020 7499 9000; www.usembassy.org.uk). **Consulates** in Belfast, Cardiff, and Edinburgh.

TOURIST OFFICES

VISITBRITAIN

Formerly known as the British Tourist Authority (BTA), VisitBritain oversees UK tourist boards and solicits tourism. The main office is located at Thames Tower, Blacks Rd., London W6 9EL (☎020 8846 9000; www.visitbritain.com).

Australia: 15 Blue St., Level 2, North Sydney, NSW 2060 (☎+61 1300 858 589; www. visitbritain.com/au). Open M-F 9am-4pm.

Canada: 5915 Airport Rd., Ste. 120, Mississauga, ON L4V 1T1 (☎+1-888-847-4885; www.visitbritain.com/ca). Open M-F 9am-5pm.

New Zealand: IAG House, 17th fl., 151 Queen St., Auckland 1 (☎+64 9 309 1899; www. visitbritain.com/nz). Open M-F 10am-6pm.

US: 551 5th Ave., Ste. 701, New York City, NY 10176 (☎+1-212-986-1188; www.visit-britain.com/us). Open M-F 9am-5pm. Other offices in Chicago and Los Angeles.

WITHIN THE UK

Britain Visitor Centre, 1 Lower Regent St., Haymarket, London SW1Y 4XT (☎020 8846 9000). Open June-Sept. M 9:30am-6:30pm, Tu-F 9am-6:30pm, Sa 9am-5pm, Su 10am-4pm; Oct.-May M 9:30am-6:30pm, Tu-F 9am-6:30pm, Sa-Su 10am-4pm.

Northern Ireland Tourist Board, 59 North St., Belfast BT1 1NB (☎028 9023 1221; www.discovernorthernireland.com). Open M-F 9am-5:15pm.

VisitScotland, Ocean Point One, 94 Ocean Dr., Leith, Edinburgh EH6 6JH (☎0131 472 2222; www.visitscotland.com). Open M-Sa 9:30am-6pm.

Welsh Tourist Board, Brunel House, 2 Fitzalan Rd., Cardiff CF24 0UY (☎08701 211 251; www.visitwales.com). Open daily 9am-5pm.

DOCUMENTS AND FORMALITIES

PASSPORTS

REQUIREMENTS

Citizens of Australia, Canada, New Zealand, and the US need valid passports to enter Britain and to re-enter their home countries. EU citizens should carry their passports, although they may not be checked. Britain does not allow entrance if the holder's passport expires in under six months; returning home with an expired passport is illegal and may result in a fine.

ESSENTIALS

NEW PASSPORTS

Citizens of Australia, Canada, New Zealand, and the US can apply for a passport at any passport office or at selected post offices and courts of law. Citizens of these countries may also download passport applications from the official website of their country's government or passport office. Any new passport or renewal applications must be filed well in advance of the departure date, though most passport offices offer rush services for a very steep fee. Note, however, that "rushed" passports still take up to two weeks to arrive.

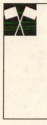

BRITAIN AND EUROPE. The EU's policy of freedom of movement means that most border controls have been abolished and visa policies harmonized under a treaty called the Schengen Arrangement. Most EU states are already members of Schengen, but Ireland and the UK are not, and travel to these countries may still require you to present a visa or passport, depending on your home country and the length of your stay. Together, however, Britain and Ireland have formed a common travel area, abolishing passport controls between the two island nations.

PASSPORT MAINTENANCE

Photocopy the page of your passport with your photo as well as your visas, traveler's check serial numbers, and any other important documents. Carry one set of copies in a safe place, apart from the originals, and leave another set at home. Consulates also recommend that you carry an expired passport or a copy of your birth certificate in a part of your baggage separate from other documents.

If you lose your passport, immediately notify the local police and your home country's nearest embassy or consulate. To expedite its replacement, you must show ID and proof of citizenship; it also helps to know all information previously recorded in the passport. A replacement may take anywhere from two to 15 business days to process, and it may be valid only for a limited time. Some countries charge an extra fee for lost or stolen passports. Any visas stamped in your old passport will be lost forever. In an emergency, ask for immediate temporary traveling papers that will permit you to re-enter your home country.

VISAS AND WORK PERMITS

VISAS

Visa requirements vary by country, and citizens of certain countries will need a visa merely to pass through Britain. Find a full list of countries whose citizens require visas online at www.ukvisas.gov.uk or contact your embassy for info.

EU citizens, as well as citizens of Iceland, Liechtenstein, Norway, and Switzerland, do not need a visa. Citizens of Australia, Canada, New Zealand, and the US do not need a visa for stays of up to 90 days, but this three-month period begins upon entry into any of the countries that belong to the EU's **freedom of movement** zone. For more information, see **Britain and Europe** (above). Those staying longer than 90 days may purchase a visa from British consulates. A visa costs £65 and allows the holder to spend six months in the UK.

A long-term multiple-entry visa usually costs £205 and allows visitors to spend a year or more in Britain. The British government, however, is currently revamping the entire visa and immigration system. If you plan to work or study in Britain, these policy changes may affect your plans. Under the new visa policy, all visa applicants are divided into five tiers, with priority given to skilled workers. Introduced in February of 2008, the new visa system will be implemented on a staggered basis. Consult the UK Visa Bureau website (www. visabureau.com/uk) to determine your visa eligibility.

US citizens can take advantage of the **Center for International Business and Travel** (**CIBT; ☎**+1-800-929-2428; www.cibt.com), which secures visas for stays longer than six months for a variable service charge. If you need a **visa extension** while in the UK, contact the Home Office, Immigration and Nationality Directorate (☎0870 606 7766; www.ind.homeoffice.gov.uk). Double-check entrance requirements at the nearest British embassy or consulate (see **UK Consular Services Abroad,** p. 11) for up-to-date info before departure. US citizens can also consult the State Department's website at http://travel.state.gov.

Entering Britain to study requires a special visa. For more information, see the **Beyond Tourism** chapter (p. 60).

WORK PERMITS

Entry to the UK as a traveler does not include the right to work, which comes only with a work permit. For details, see the **Beyond Tourism** chapter (p. 60)

IDENTIFICATION

When you travel, always carry at least two forms of identification on your person, including a photo ID. A passport and a driver's license or birth certificate will usually suffice. Never carry all of your IDs together; split them up in case of theft or loss and keep photocopies in your luggage and at home.

STUDENT, TEACHER, AND YOUTH IDENTIFICATION

The **International Student Identity Card (ISIC),** the most widely accepted form of student ID, provides discounts on some sights, accommodations, food, and transportation; access to a 24hr. emergency help line; and insurance benefits for US cardholders (see **Insurance,** p. 23). ISIC cardholders in London, for example, can gain free entry into some museums and discounts at the Shakespeare Globe Theatre or the London Zoo. Applicants must be full-time secondary- or post-secondary-school students at least 12 years old to qualify for a card. Because of the proliferation of fake ISICs, some services (particularly airlines) require additional proof of student identity.

The **International Teacher Identity Card (ITIC)** offers teachers the same insurance coverage as the ISIC and similar but more limited discounts. To qualify for the card, teachers must be currently employed and have worked a minimum of 18hr. per week for at least one school year. For travelers who are under 26 years old but are not students, the **International Youth Travel Card (IYTC)** also offers many of the same benefits as the ISIC.

Each of these identity cards costs US$22. ISICs, ITICs, and IYTCs are valid for one year from the date of issue. To learn more about ISICs, ITICs, and IYTCs, try www.myisic.com. Many student travel agencies (p. 28) issue the cards; for a list of issuing agencies or more information, see the **International Student Travel Confederation (ISTC)** website (www.istc.org).

The **International Student Exchange Card (ISE Card)** is a similar identification card available to students, faculty, and ages 12 to 26. The card provides discounts, student airfare prices, and access to a 24hr. emergency help line. An ISE Card costs US$25; call **☎**+1-800-255-8000 (in North America) or **☎**+1-480-951-1177 (from all other continents) for more info or visit www.isecard.com.

CUSTOMS

Upon entering Britain, you must declare certain items from abroad and pay a duty on the value of those articles if they exceed the allowance established by

Britain's customs service. Goods and gifts purchased at duty-free shops abroad are not exempt from duty or sales tax; "duty-free" means that you won't pay tax in the country of purchase. Duty-free allowances were abolished for travel between EU member states on June 30, 1999, but still exist for those arriving from outside the EU. Upon returning home, you must likewise declare all articles acquired abroad and pay a duty on the value of articles in excess of your home country's allowance. In order to expedite your return, make a list of any valuables brought from home and register them with customs before traveling abroad. It's a good idea to keep receipts for all goods acquired abroad.

If you're leaving Britain for a non-EU country, you can claim back any **value added tax** paid (see **Taxes,** p. 18). For information about traveling with pets, consult the **UK Department for Environment, Food, and Rural Affairs** (www.defra.gov.uk/ animalh/quarantine/index.htm) or call the **PETS Helpline** (☎0870 241 1710).

MONEY

CURRENCY AND EXCHANGE

The **pound sterling** is the unit of currency in the United Kingdom. Northern Ireland and Scotland have their own bank notes; the money is of equal value but may not be accepted outside Northern Ireland and Scotland.

The currency chart below is based on August 2008 exchange rates between pounds sterling and Australian dollars (AUS$), Canadian dollars (CDN$), European Union euro (EUR€), New Zealand dollars (NZ$), and US dollars (US$). Check the currency converter on websites like www.xe.com or www. bloomberg.com for the latest exchange rates.

POUNDS (£)		
AUS$1 = £0.47		£1 = AUS$2.14
CDN$1 = £0.49		£1 = CDN$2.04
EUR€1 = £0.79		£1 = EUR€1.26
NZ$1 = £0.37		£1 = NZ$2.71
US$1 = £0.51		£1 = US$1.95

As a general rule, it's cheaper to convert money in Britain than at home. While currency exchange will probably be available in your arrival airport, it's wise to bring enough foreign currency to last for at least 24-72hr.

When changing money abroad, try to go only to banks or bureaux de change that have at most a 5% margin between their buy and sell prices. Since you lose money with every transaction, it makes sense to **convert large sums** at one time (unless the currency is depreciating rapidly).

If you use traveler's checks or bills, carry some in small denominations (the equivalent of US$50 or fewer) for times when you have to exchange money at poor rates, but bring a range of denominations since charges may be applied per check cashed. Store your money in a variety of forms; at any given time you will be carrying some cash, some traveler's checks, and an ATM or credit card.

TRAVELER'S CHECKS

Traveler's checks are one of the safest and most convenient means of carrying funds. American Express and Visa are the best-recognized brands. Many banks and agencies sell them for a small commission. Check issuers provide refunds if the checks are lost or stolen, and many provide additional services,

ESSENTIALS

such as toll-free refund hotlines abroad, emergency message services, and assistance with lost and stolen credit cards or passports. Traveler's checks are readily accepted in the UK, though some hostels and B&Bs accept only cash. Many travelers choose to exchange traveler's checks at the bank for cash rather than spending them directly at stores and establishments. Ask about toll-free refund hotlines and the location of refund centers when purchasing checks and always carry emergency cash.

American Express: Checks available with commission at select banks, at all AmEx offices, and online (www.americanexpress.com; US residents only). AmEx cardholders can also purchase checks by phone (☎+1-800-528-4800). Checks available in American, Australian, British, Canadian, European, and Japanese currencies, among others. AmEx also offers the Travelers Cheque Card, a prepaid reloadable card. Cheques for Two can be signed by either of 2 people traveling together. For purchase locations or more information, contact AmEx's service centers: in Australia ☎+61 2 9271 8666, in New Zealand +64 9 367 4567, in the UK 01273 696 933, in the US and Canada +1-800-221-7282; elsewhere, call the US collect at +1-336-393-1111.

Travelex: Visa TravelMoney prepaid cash card and Visa traveler's checks available. For information about Thomas Cook MasterCard in Canada and the US, call ☎+1-800-223-7373, in the UK 0800 622 101; elsewhere, call the UK collect at +44 1733 318 950. For information about Interpayment Visa in the US and Canada, call ☎+1-800-732-1322, in the UK 0800 515 884; elsewhere, call the UK collect at +44 1733 318 949. For more information, visit www.travelex.com.

Visa: Checks available (generally with commission) at banks worldwide. For the location of the nearest office, call the Visa Travelers Cheque Global Refund and Assistance Center: in the UK ☎0800 895 078, in the US +1-800-227-6811; elsewhere, call the UK collect at +44 20 7937 8091. Checks available in American, British, Canadian, European, and Japanese currencies, among others. Visa also offers TravelMoney, a prepaid debit card that can be reloaded online or by phone. For more information on Visa travel services, see http://usa.visa.com/personal/using_visa/travel_with_visa.html.

CREDIT, DEBIT, AND ATM CARDS

Where they are accepted, credit cards often offer superior exchange rates—up to 5% better than the retail rate used by banks and other currency-exchange establishments. Credit cards may also offer services such as insurance or emergency help and are sometimes required to reserve hotel rooms or rental cars. **MasterCard** and **Visa** are the most frequently accepted; **American Express** cards work at some ATMs and at AmEx offices and major airports.

The use of ATM cards is widespread in Britain. Depending on the system that your home bank uses, you can most likely access your personal bank account from abroad. ATMs get the same wholesale exchange rate as credit cards, but there is often a limit on the amount of money you can withdraw per day (usually around US$500). There is also typically a surcharge of US$1-5 per withdrawal. Your own bank may also charge a transaction fee. **Barclays** banks around the UK offer withdrawals without a surcharge.

Debit cards are as convenient as credit cards but withdraw money directly from the holder's checking account. A debit card can be used wherever its associated credit-card company (usually MasterCard or Visa) is accepted. Debit cards often also function as ATM cards and can be used to withdraw cash from associated banks and ATMs throughout Britain.

The two major international money networks are **MasterCard/Maestro/Cirrus** (for ATM locations ☎+1-800-424-7787 or www.mastercard.com) and **Visa/PLUS** (for ATM locations ☎+1-800-847-2911 or www.visa.com).

PINS AND ATMS. To use a cash or credit card to withdraw money from a cash machine (ATM) in Europe, you must have a four-digit Personal Identification Number (PIN). If your PIN is longer than four digits, ask your bank whether you can just use the first four or whether you'll need a new one. Credit cards don't usually come with PINs, so, if you intend to hit up ATMs in Europe with a credit card to get cash advances, call your credit-card company before leaving to request one. Travelers with alphabetic, rather than numerical, PINs may also be thrown off by the lack of letters on European cash machines. The following are the corresponding numbers to use: 1 = QZ; 2 = ABC; 3 = DEF; 4 = GHI; 5 = JKL; 6 = MNO; 7 = PRS; 8 = TUV; and 9 = WXY. Note that if you mistakenly punch the wrong code into the machine three times, it will swallow your card for good.

GETTING MONEY FROM HOME

If you run out of money while traveling, the easiest and cheapest solution is to have someone back home make a deposit to your bank account. Otherwise, consider one of the following options.

WIRING MONEY

It is possible to arrange a **bank money transfer,** which means asking a bank back home to wire money to a bank in the UK. This is the cheapest way to transfer cash, but it's also the slowest, usually taking from three to five business days. Note that some banks may only release your funds in local currency, potentially sticking you with a poor exchange rate; inquire about this in advance. Money transfer services like **Western Union** are faster and more convenient than bank transfers—but also much pricier. Western Union has many locations worldwide. To find one, visit www.westernunion.com or call in Australia ☎1800 173 833, in Canada and the US 800-325-6000, or in the UK 0800 833 833. To wire money using a credit card, call in Canada and the US ☎800-CALL-CASH, in the UK 0800 833 833. Money transfer services are also available to **American Express** cardholders and at selected **Thomas Cook** offices.

US STATE DEPARTMENT (US CITIZENS ONLY)

In serious emergencies only, the US State Department will forward money within hours to the nearest consular office, which will then disburse it according to instructions for a US$30 fee. If you wish to use this service, you must contact the Overseas Citizens Services division of the US State Department (☎+1-202-501-4444, from US ☎888-407-4747).

COSTS

The cost of your trip will vary considerably, depending on where you go, how you travel, and where you stay. The most significant expenses will probably be your round-trip (return) airfare to Britain (see **Getting to the UK: By Plane,** p. 27) and a railpass or bus pass. Accommodations are also a big expense. Before you go, spend some time calculating a reasonable daily budget.

STAYING ON A BUDGET

To give you a general idea, a bare-bones day in Britain (camping or sleeping in hostels/guesthouses, buying food at supermarkets) would cost about US$65

(£33); a slightly more comfortable day (sleeping in hostels/guesthouses and the occasional budget hotel, eating one meal per day at a restaurant, going out at night) would cost US$110 (£56); and, for a luxurious day, the sky's the limit. Don't forget to factor in emergency reserve funds (at least US$200) when planning how much money you'll need.

TIPS FOR SAVING MONEY

Some simpler ways to avoid spending too much cash include searching out opportunities for free entertainment, splitting accommodation and food costs with trustworthy fellow travelers, and buying food in supermarkets rather than eating out. Bring a **sleepsack** (opposite page) to save on sheet charges in hostels and do your **laundry** in the sink (unless you're explicitly prohibited from doing so). Museums often have certain days once a month or once a week when admission is free; plan accordingly. If you are eligible, consider getting an ISIC or an IYTC (p. 14); many sights and museums offer reduced admission to students and youths. For getting around quickly, bikes are the most economical option. Renting a bike is cheaper than renting a moped or scooter. Don't forget about walking, though; you can learn a lot about a city by seeing it on foot. Drinking at bars and clubs quickly becomes expensive. It's cheaper to buy alcohol at a supermarket and imbibe before going out. That said, don't go overboard. Though staying within your budget is important, don't do so at the expense of your health or a great travel experience.

CONCESSIONS. Some sights offer admission at reduced prices for students, seniors, and the unemployed. These discounted prices are known in Britain as concessions and appear throughout *Let's Go*.

TIPPING

Tips in restaurants are often included in the bill (sometimes as a "service charge"). If gratuity is not included, you should tip your server about 12.5%. Taxi drivers should receive a 10% tip, and bellhops and chambermaids usually expect £1-3. To the great relief of many budget travelers, tipping is not expected at pubs and bars in Britain.

TAXES

The UK has a 17.5% **value added tax (VAT),** a sales tax applied to everything but food, books, medicine, and children's clothing. The tax is included in the amount indicated on the price tag. The prices stated in *Let's Go* include VAT. Upon exiting Britain, non-EU citizens can reclaim VAT (minus an administrative fee) through the **Retail Export Scheme,** although the complex procedure is probably only worthwhile for large purchases. You can obtain refunds only for goods you take out of the country (not for accommodations or meals). Participating shops display a "Tax-Free Shopping" sign and may have a minimum purchase of £50-100 before they offer refunds. To claim a refund, fill out the form you are given in the shop and present it with the goods and receipts at customs upon departure (look for the Tax-Free Refund desk at the airport). At peak times, this process can take up to an hour. You must leave the country within three months of your purchase in order to claim a refund, and you must apply before leaving the UK.

PACKING

Pack lightly: lay out only what you absolutely need, then take half the clothes and twice the money. The **Travelite FAQ** (www.travelite.org) is a good resource for tips on traveling light. The online **Universal Packing List** (http://upl.codeq.info) will generate a customized list of suggested items based on your trip length, the expected climate, your planned activities, and other factors. If you plan to do a lot of hiking, also consult **The Great Outdoors**, p. 49. Some frequent travelers keep a bag packed with all the essentials: passport, money belt, hat, socks, etc. Then, when they decide to leave, they know they haven't forgotten anything.

Luggage: If you plan to cover most of your trip on foot, a sturdy **internal-frame backpack** is unbeatable. (For the basics on buying a pack, see p. 51.) Unless you are staying in 1 place for a large chunk of time, a suitcase or trunk will be unwieldy. In addition to your main piece of luggage, a **daypack** (a small backpack or courier bag) is useful.

Clothing: No matter when you're traveling, it's a good idea to bring a warm jacket or wool sweater, sturdy shoes or hiking boots, thick socks, and, especially in Britain, a rain jacket (Gore-Tex® is both waterproof and breathable). Flip-flops or waterproof sandals are must-haves for grubby hostel showers, and extra socks are always a good idea. You may also want 1 outfit for going out and maybe a nicer pair of shoes. If you plan to visit religious or cultural sites, remember that you will need modest and respectful dress.

Sleepsack: Some hostels require that you either provide your own linen or rent sheets from them. Save cash by making your own sleepsack: fold a full-size sheet in half the long way, then sew it closed along the long side and one of the short sides.

Converters and Adapters: Electricity is 230 volts AC in Britain, enough to fry any 120V North American appliance. 220/240V electrical appliances won't work with a 120V current, either. Americans and Canadians should buy an adapter (which changes the shape of the plug; US$5) and a converter (which changes the voltage; US$10-30). Consider purchasing a converter-adapter in one (US$10-30). Don't make the mistake of using only an adapter (unless appliance instructions explicitly state otherwise, as for many laptops). Australians and New Zealanders (who use 230V at home) won't need a converter but will need a set of adapters to use anything electrical. For more on all things adaptable, check out http://kropla.com/electric.htm.

Toiletries: Condoms, deodorant, and tampons are available, but it may be difficult to find your preferred brand; bring extras. Contact lenses are likely to be expensive and difficult to find, so bring enough extra pairs and solution for your entire trip. Also bring your glasses and a copy of your prescription in case you need emergency replacements.

First-Aid Kit: For a basic first-aid kit, pack bandages, a pain reliever, antibiotic cream, a thermometer, a multifunction pocketknife, tweezers, moleskin, decongestant, motion-sickness remedy, diarrhea or upset-stomach medication (Pepto Bismol® or Imodium®), an antihistamine, sunscreen, insect repellent, and burn ointment.

Film: Developing film in Britain is expensive (about US$12 for a roll of 24 color exposures), so consider bringing along enough film for your entire trip and developing it at home. If you don't want to bother with film, consider using a **digital camera.** Although it requires a steep initial investment, a digital camera means you never have to buy film again. Just be sure to bring along a large enough memory card and extra (or rechargeable) batteries. Less serious photographers may want to bring a few disposable cameras. Airport security X-rays can fog film, so buy a lead-lined pouch at a camera store or ask security to hand-inspect it. Always pack film in your carry-on luggage, since higher-intensity X-rays are used on checked luggage.

Other Useful Items: For safety purposes, you should bring a **money belt** and a small **padlock.** Basic **outdoors equipment** (plastic water bottle, compass, waterproof matches, pocketknife, sunglasses, sunscreen, hat) may also be handy. Quick repairs of torn garments can be done on the road with a needle and thread; also consider bringing electrical tape for patching tears. Other things you're liable to forget include an umbrella, sealable **plastic bags** (for damp clothes, soap, food, shampoo, and other spillables), an **alarm clock,** safety pins, rubber bands, a flashlight, earplugs, garbage bags, and a small calculator. A **cell phone** can be a lifesaver (literally) on the road; see p. 45 for information on acquiring one that will work in Britain.

Important Documents: Don't forget your passport, traveler's checks, ATM and/or credit cards, adequate ID, and photocopies of all of the aforementioned in case these documents are lost or stolen (p. 13). Also check that you have any of the following that might apply to you: a hosteling membership card (p. 47); driver's license (p. 39); travel insurance forms (p. 23); ISIC (p. 14); and/or railpass or bus pass (p. 34).

SAFETY AND HEALTH

GENERAL ADVICE

In any type of crisis, the most important thing to do is **stay calm.** Your country's embassy abroad (p. 12) is usually your best resource in an emergency; registering with that embassy upon arrival in the country is a good idea. The government offices listed in the **Travel Advisories** box (opposite page) can provide information on the services they offer their citizens in case of emergencies.

LOCAL LAWS AND POLICE

Police presence in cities is prevalent, and most small towns have police stations. There are three types of police officers in Britain: regular officers with full police powers, special constables who work only part-time but have full police powers, and police community support officers (PCSO) who have limited police power and focus on community maintenance and safety. The national emergency numbers are ☎999 or ☎112. Numbers for local police stations are listed under each individual city or town.

DRUGS AND ALCOHOL

Remember that you are subject to the laws of the country in which you travel. It's your responsibility to know these laws before you go. If you carry insulin, syringes, or **prescription drugs** while you travel, it is vital to have a copy of the prescriptions and a note from your doctor. The Brits love to drink, and the pub scene is unavoidable. In trying to keep up with the locals, keep in mind that the **Imperial pint** is 20 oz., as opposed to the 16 oz. US pint. The drinking age in the UK is 18 (14 to enter, 16 for beer and wine with food). **Smoking** is banned in all enclosed public spaces in Britain, including pubs and restaurants.

SPECIFIC CONCERNS

DEMONSTRATIONS AND POLITICAL GATHERINGS

Sectarian violence in Northern Ireland has diminished dramatically in the past decade, but some neighborhoods and towns still experience unrest. It's best to remain alert and cautious while traveling in Northern Ireland, especially during **Marching Season** (the weeks leading up to July 12) and on August 12, when the **Apprentice Boys** march in Derry/Londonderry. The most common form of violence is property damage, and tourists are unlikely targets (but beware leaving a car unsupervised if it bears a Republic of Ireland license plate). In general, if traveling in Northern Ireland during Marching Season, prepare for transportation delays and for some shops and services to be closed. Vacation areas like the Glens and the Causeway Coast are less affected. Use common sense and, as in dealing with any issues of a different culture, be respectful of locals' religious and political perspectives.

Border checkpoints have been removed, and armed soldiers and vehicles are less visible in Belfast and Derry than they were ten years ago. Do not take **photographs** of soldiers, military installations, or vehicles; the film will be confiscated, and you may be detained for questioning. Taking pictures of political murals is not a crime, although many people feel uncomfortable doing so in residential neighborhoods. Unattended luggage is always considered suspicious and is liable to confiscation.

TERRORISM

The Anti-Terrorism Crime and Security Act 2001, passed in the aftermath of the September 11, 2001, attacks, strengthens the 2000 Terrorism Act, which outlaws certain terrorist groups and gives police extended powers to investigate terrorism. Britain is committed to an extensive program of prevention and prosecution. More information is available from the Foreign and Commonwealth Office (see box below) and the Home Office (☎020 7035 4848; www.homeoffice.gov.uk). Britain raised its terrorist alert level to "elevated" after the London tube bombings of July 7, 2005, and the city stepped up security considerably in order to deter future attacks. In August 2006, the UK raised its threat assessment level again after government authorities thwarted an attack on planes departing from UK airports. In the immediate aftermath, airport security was bolstered, and liquids and many electronics were banned in aircraft cabins.

The US State Department website (www.state.gov) provides information on the current situation and on developing flight regulations. To have advisories emailed to you, register with your home embassy or consulate when you arrive in Britain. If you see a suspicious unattended package or bag at an airport or other crowded public place, report it immediately at ☎999 or the **Anti-Terrorism Hotline** (☎0800 789 321). The box below lists offices to contact to get the most updated list of your home country's government's advisories about travel.

TRAVEL ADVISORIES. The following government offices provide travel information and advisories by telephone, by fax, or via the web:
Australian Department of Foreign Affairs and Trade: ☎+61 2 6261 1111; www.dfat.gov.au.
Canadian Department of Foreign Affairs and International Trade (DFAIT): ☎+1-800-267-8376; www.dfait-maeci.gc.ca. Call for their free booklet, *Bon Voyage...But.*
New Zealand Ministry of Foreign Affairs: ☎+64 4 439 8000; www.mfat.govt.nz.
United Kingdom Foreign and Commonwealth Office: ☎020 7008 1500; www.fco.gov.uk.
US Department of State: ☎+1-888-407-4747; http://travel.state.gov. Visit the website for the booklet, *A Safe Trip Abroad.*

PERSONAL SAFETY

EXPLORING AND TRAVELING

To avoid unwanted attention, try to blend in as much as possible. Respecting local customs may ward off would-be hecklers. Familiarize yourself with your surroundings before setting out and carry yourself with confidence. Check maps in shops and restaurants rather than on the street. If you are traveling alone, be sure someone at home knows your itinerary and never tell anyone you meet that you're by yourself. When walking at night, stick to busy, well-lit streets and avoid dark alleyways. If you ever feel uncomfortable, leave the area as quickly and directly as you can.

There is no surefire way to avoid all the threatening situations that you might encounter while traveling, but a good **self-defense course** will give you concrete ways to react to unwanted advances. **Impact, Prepare,** and **Model Mugging** can refer you to local self-defense courses in Australia, Canada, Switzerland, and the US. Visit www.modelmugging.org for a list of nearby chapters.

If you are using a **car,** learn local driving signals and wear a seat belt. Children under 40 lb. should ride only in specially designed car seats, available for a small fee from most car-rental agencies. Study route maps before you hit the road and, if you plan on spending a lot of time driving, consider bringing spare parts. For long drives in desolate areas, invest in a cell phone and a roadside assistance program (p. 40). Park your vehicle in a garage or well-traveled area and use a steering-wheel locking device in larger cities. Sleeping in your car is the most dangerous way to get your rest, and it's also illegal in parts of Britain. For info on the perils of **hitchhiking,** see p. 41.

POSSESSIONS AND VALUABLES

Never leave your belongings unattended; crime can occur in even the most safe-looking hostel or hotel. Bring your own padlock for hostel lockers and don't ever store valuables in a locker. Be particularly careful on **buses** and **trains;** horror stories abound about determined thieves who wait for travelers to fall asleep. Carry your bag or purse in front of you where you can see it. When traveling with others, sleep in alternate shifts. When alone, use good judgment in selecting a train compartment: never stay in an empty one and use a lock to secure your pack to the luggage rack. Use extra caution if traveling at night or on overnight trains. Try to sleep on top bunks with your luggage stored above you and keep important documents and other valuables on you at all times.

There are a few steps you can take to minimize the financial risk associated with traveling. First, **bring as little with you as possible.** Second, buy a few combination **padlocks** to secure your belongings either in your pack or in a hostel or train-station locker. Third, **carry as little cash as possible.** Keep your traveler's checks and ATM/credit cards in a **money belt**—not a "fanny pack"—along with your passport and ID cards. Fourth, **keep a small cash reserve separate from your primary stash.** This should be about £25 sewn into or stored in the depths of your pack, along with your traveler's check numbers, photocopies of your passport, your birth certificate, and other important documents.

In large cities, **con artists** often work in groups and may involve children. Beware of certain classics: sob stories that require money, rolls of bills "found" on the street, mustard spilled (or saliva spit) onto your shoulder to distract you while they snatch your bag. Never let your passport and your bags out of your sight. Hostel workers will sometimes stand at bus and train-station arrival points to recruit tired and disoriented travelers to their hostel; never believe strangers who tell you that theirs is the only hostel open. Beware of **pickpockets** in city crowds, especially on public transportation. Also, be alert in public telephone booths: if you must say your calling-card number, do so very quietly; if you punch it in, make sure no one can look over your shoulder.

If you will be traveling with electronic devices, such as a laptop computer or a PDA, check whether your homeowner's insurance covers loss, theft, or damage when you travel. If not, you might consider purchasing a low-cost separate insurance policy. **Safeware** (☎ +1-800-800-1492; www.safeware.com) specializes in covering computers and charges US$90 for 90-day comprehensive international travel coverage up to US$4000.

PRE-DEPARTURE HEALTH

In your passport, write the names of any people you wish to be contacted in case of a **medical emergency** and list any allergies or medical conditions. Matching a prescription to a foreign equivalent is not always easy, safe, or possible, so, if you take **prescription drugs,** consider carrying up-to-date prescriptions or a note from your doctor stating the medication's trade name, manufacturer, chemical name, and dosage. While traveling, be sure to keep all medication with you in your carry-on luggage. For tips on packing a **first-aid kit** and other health essentials, see p. 19.

IMMUNIZATIONS AND PRECAUTIONS

While no injections are required for entry to the UK, travelers over two years old should make sure that the following vaccines are up to date: MMR (for measles, mumps, and rubella); DTaP or Td (for diphtheria, tetanus, and pertussis); IPV (for polio); Hib (for *haemophilus influenzae* B); and HepB (for Hepatitis B). For recommendations on immunizations and prophylaxis, consult the Centers for Disease Control and Prevention (CDC; p. 24) in the US or the equivalent in your home country and check with a doctor for guidance.

INSURANCE

Travel insurance covers four basic areas: medical/health problems, property loss, trip cancellation/interruption, and emergency evacuation. Though regular insurance policies may well extend to travel-related accidents, you may consider purchasing separate travel insurance if the cost of potential trip cancellation, interruption, or emergency medical evacuation is greater than you can absorb. Prices for travel insurance purchased separately generally run about US$50 per week for full coverage, while trip cancellation/interruption may be purchased separately at a rate of US$3-5 per day, depending on length of stay.

Medical insurance (especially university policies) often covers costs incurred abroad; check with your provider. **Homeowners' insurance** (or your family's coverage) often covers theft during travel and loss of travel documents (passport, plane ticket, railpass, etc.) up to US$500.

ISIC and **ITIC** (p. 14) provide basic health insurance benefits to American cardholders, including US$100 per day of in-hospital sickness for up to 100 days and US$10,000 of accident-related medical reimbursement (see www.isicus.com for details). Cardholders have access to a toll-free 24hr. help line for medical, legal, and financial emergencies while traveling overseas. **American Express** (☎ +1-800-338-1670) grants most cardholders automatic collision and theft car-rental insurance on rentals made with the card.

USEFUL ORGANIZATIONS AND PUBLICATIONS

The American **Centers for Disease Control and Prevention** (**CDC**; ☎+1-877-FYI-TRIP; www.cdc.gov/travel) maintains an international travelers' hotline and an informative website. Consult the appropriate government agency of your home country for consular information sheets on health, entry requirements, and other issues for various countries (see the listings in the box on **Travel Advisories,** p. 21). For quick information on health and other travel warnings, call the **Overseas Citizens Services** (from overseas ☎+1-202-501-4444, from US 888-407-4747; line open M-F 8am-8pm EST) or contact a passport agency, embassy, or consulate abroad. For information on medical evacuation services and travel insurance firms, see the US government's website at http://travel.state.gov/travel/abroad_health.html or the **British Foreign and Commonwealth Office** (www.fco.gov.uk). For general health information, contact the **American Red Cross** (☎+1-202-303-4498; www.redcross.org).

STAYING HEALTHY

Common sense is the simplest prescription for good health while you travel. Drink lots of fluids to prevent dehydration and constipation and wear sturdy, broken-in shoes and clean socks. The British Isles are in the Gulf Stream, so temperatures are mild. In the Scottish highlands and mountains, temperatures reach greater extremes. When in areas of high altitude, be sure to dress in layers that can be peeled off as needed. Allow your body a couple of days to adjust to decreased oxygen levels before exerting yourself.

ONCE IN BRITAIN

ENVIRONMENTAL HAZARDS

Heat exhaustion and dehydration: Heat exhaustion leads to nausea, excessive thirst, headaches, and dizziness. Avoid it by drinking plenty of fluids, eating salty foods (e.g., crackers), abstaining from dehydrating beverages (e.g., alcohol and caffeinated beverages), and wearing sunscreen. Continuous heat stress can eventually lead to heatstroke, characterized by a rising temperature, severe headache, delirium, and cessation of sweating. Victims should be cooled off with wet towels and taken to a doctor.

High Altitude: Allow your body a couple of days to adjust to less oxygen before exerting yourself. Note that alcohol is more potent and UV rays are stronger at high elevations.

Hypothermia and frostbite: A rapid drop in body temperature is the clearest sign of overexposure to cold. Victims may also shiver, feel exhausted, have poor coordination or slurred speech, hallucinate, or suffer amnesia. Do not let hypothermia victims fall asleep. To avoid hypothermia, keep dry, wear layers, and stay out of the wind. When the temperature is below freezing, watch out for frostbite. If skin turns white or blue, waxy, and cold, do not rub the area. Drink warm beverages, stay dry, and slowly warm the area with dry fabric or steady body contact until a doctor can be found.

INSECT-BORNE DISEASES

Many diseases are transmitted by insects—mainly mosquitoes, fleas, ticks, and lice. Be aware of insects in wet or forested areas, especially while hiking and camping. Wear long pants and long sleeves, tuck your pants into your socks, and use a mosquito net. Use insect repellents such as DEET and soak or spray your gear with permethrin. **Mosquitoes**—responsible for malaria, dengue fever, and yellow fever—can be particularly abundant in wet, swampy, or wooded areas like those in national parks. **Ticks**—which can carry Lyme and other diseases—can be particularly dangerous in rural and forested regions.

Tick-borne encephalitis: A viral infection of the central nervous system transmitted during the summer by tick bites (primarily in wooded areas) or by consumption of unpasteurized dairy products. The risk of contracting the disease is relatively low, especially if precautions are taken against tick bites.

Lyme disease: A bacterial infection carried by ticks and marked by a circular bull's-eye rash of 2 in. or more. Later symptoms include fever, headache, fatigue, and aches and pains. Antibiotics are effective if administered early. Left untreated, Lyme can cause problems in joints, the heart, and the nervous system. If you find a tick attached to your skin, grasp the head with tweezers as close to your skin as possible and apply slow, steady traction. Removing a tick within 24hr. greatly reduces the risk of infection. Do not try to remove ticks with petroleum jelly, nail polish remover, or a hot match. Ticks usually inhabit moist, shaded environments and heavily wooded areas. If you are going to be hiking in these areas, wear long clothes and DEET.

FOOD- AND WATER-BORNE DISEASES

Prevention is the best cure: be sure that your food is properly cooked and the water you drink is clean. Watch out for food from markets or street vendors that may have been cooked in unhygienic conditions. Other culprits are raw shellfish, unpasteurized milk, and sauces containing raw eggs. Buy bottled water or purify your own water by bringing it to a rolling boil or treating it with **iodine tablets;** note, however, that boiling is more reliable. Further information is available through the CDC (www.cdc.gov/travel) and the **British Department for Environment, Food and Rural Affairs** (www.defra.gov.uk).

Bovine spongiform encephalopathy (BSE): Better known as **mad cow disease,** BSE is a chronic degenerative disease affecting the central nervous system of cattle. The human variety is called new variant Creutzfeldt-Jakob disease (nvCJD). Both forms involve fatal brain damage. NvCJD is thought to be caused by consuming infected beef. The risk is extremely small (around 1 case per 10 billion meat servings). Milk and milk products are not believed to pose a risk.

Foot and mouth disease (FMD): The UK and Western Europe experienced a serious outbreak of FMD in 2001. Easily transmissible between cloven-hoofed animals (cows, pigs, sheep, goats, and deer) but does not pose a threat to humans, causing mild symptoms, if any. In January 2002, the UK regained **international FMD-free status.** Restrictions on rural travel have been removed.

Giardiasis: Transmitted through parasites and acquired by drinking untreated water from streams or lakes. Symptoms include diarrhea, cramps, bloating, fatigue, weight loss, and nausea. If untreated, it can lead to severe dehydration. Giardiasis occurs worldwide.

OTHER INFECTIOUS DISEASES

The following diseases exist all over the world. Travelers should know how to recognize them and what to do if they suspect they have been infected.

AIDS and HIV: For detailed information on Acquired Immune Deficiency Syndrome (AIDS) in the UK, call the 24hr. National AIDS Hotline at ☎+1-800-342-2437.

Rabies: Transmitted through the saliva of infected animals; fatal if untreated. By the time symptoms (thirst and muscle spasms) appear, the disease is in its terminal stage. If you are bitten, wash the wound, seek immediate medical care, and try to have the animal located. A rabies vaccine, which consists of 3 shots given over a 21-day period, is available, but it is only semi-effective.

ESSENTIALS

Sexually transmitted infections (STIs): Gonorrhea, chlamydia, genital warts, syphilis, herpes, HPV, and other STIs are easier to catch than HIV and can be just as serious. Though condoms may protect you from some STIs, oral or even tactile contact can lead to transmission. If you think you may have contracted an STI, see a doctor immediately.

OTHER HEALTH CONCERNS

MEDICAL CARE ON THE ROAD

Medical aid is readily available and of excellent quality. For minor ailments, **chemists** (pharmacies) are easy to find. The ubiquitous Boots chain has a blue logo. **Late-night pharmacies** are rare even in big cities. Most major hospitals have a **24hr. emergency room** (called a "casualty department" or "A&E," short for Accident and Emergency). Call the numbers listed below for assistance.

In Britain, the state-run **National Health Service (NHS)** encompasses the majority of health-care centers (☎020 7210 4850; www.doh.gov.uk/nhs.htm). Cities may have private hospitals, but these cater to the wealthy and are not often equipped with full surgical staff or complete casualty units. Access to free care is based on residence, not on British nationality or payment of taxes; those working legally or undertaking long-term study in the UK may also be eligible. Health insurance is a must for all other visitors.

If you are concerned about obtaining medical assistance while traveling, you may wish to employ special support services. The **MedPass** from **Global-Care, Inc.,** 6875 Shiloh Rd. E., Alpharetta, GA 30005, USA (☎+1-800-860-1111; www.globalcare.net), provides 24hr. international medical assistance, support, and medical evacuation resources. The **International Association for Medical Assistance to Travelers** (**IAMAT;** US ☎+1-716-754-4883, Canada 519-836-0102; www.iamat.org) has free membership, lists English-speaking doctors worldwide, and offers detailed info on immunization requirements and sanitation. If your regular insurance policy does not cover travel abroad, you may wish to purchase additional coverage (see **Insurance,** p. 23).

Those with medical conditions (such as diabetes, allergies to antibiotics, epilepsy, or heart conditions) may want to obtain a **MedicAlert** membership (US$40 per year), which includes among other things a stainless-steel ID tag and a 24hr. collect-call number. Contact the MedicAlert Foundation International, 2323 Colorado Ave., Turlock, CA 95382, USA (☎+1-888-633-4298, outside US 209-668-3333; www.medicalert.org).

WOMEN'S HEALTH

Women traveling are vulnerable to **urinary tract** and **bladder infections,** common and uncomfortable bacterial conditions that cause a burning sensation and painful (sometimes frequent) urination. Vaginal yeast infections are known in Britain as **thrush** and can be treated with over-the-counter medicines like Diflucan One or Vagisil. **Tampons, pads,** and **contraceptive devices** are widely available in urban areas, although your favorite brand may not be stocked. If you are camping, remember to pack enough for your trip, as pharmacies are rare in rural areas; also be prepared to pack your used feminine hygiene products to dispose outside the park. Women who need an abortion or emergency contraception while in the UK should contact the **Family Planning Association (FPA;** ☎0845 122 8690; www.fpa.org.uk; available M-F 9am-6pm).

GETTING TO THE UK

BY PLANE

When it comes to airfare, a little effort can save you a bundle. Courier fares are the cheapest for those whose plans are flexible enough to deal with the restrictions. Tickets sold by consolidators and standby seating are also good deals, but last-minute specials, airfare wars, and charter flights often beat these fares. The key is to hunt around, be flexible, and ask about discounts. Students, seniors, and those under 26 should never pay full price for a ticket.

AIRFARES

Airfares to the UK peak between June and September; holidays are also expensive. The cheapest times to travel are November to February. Midweek (M-Th morning) round-trip flights run US$40-50 cheaper than weekend flights, but they are generally more crowded and less likely to permit frequent-flier upgrades. Not fixing a return date ("open return") or arriving in and departing from different cities ("open-jaw") can be pricier than round-trip flights. Patching one-way flights together is the most expensive way to travel. Flights between London, Dublin, and Belfast will tend to be cheaper.

If the UK is only one stop on a more extensive globe-hop, consider a round-the-world (RTW) ticket. Tickets usually include at least five stops and are valid for about a year; prices range US$1200-5000. Try **Northwest Airlines/KLM** (☎+1-800-225-2525; www.nwa.com) or **Star Alliance,** a consortium of 16 airlines including United Airlines (www.staralliance.com).

Fares for round-trip flights to London from the US or Canadian east coast cost US$500-1200, US$300-700 in the low season (Nov.-Feb.); from the US or Canadian west coast US$700-1500/500-900; from Australia AUS$1800 and up; from New Zealand NZ$1600 and up.

FLIGHT PLANNING ON THE INTERNET. The Internet may be the budget traveler's dream when it comes to finding and booking bargain fares, but the array of options can be overwhelming. Many airline sites offer special last-minute deals on the web. Try Virgin Atlantic (www.virgin-atlantic.com), BMI (www.flybmi.com), or British Airways (www.ba.com). **STA** (www.statravel.com) and **StudentUniverse** (www.studentuniverse.com) provide quotes on student tickets, while **Orbitz** (www.orbitz.com), **Expedia** (www.expedia.com), and **Travelocity** (www.travelocity.com) offer full travel services. **Priceline** (www.priceline.com) lets you specify a price and obligates you to buy any ticket that meets or beats it; **Hotwire** (www.hotwire.com) offers bargain fares but won't reveal the airline or flight times until you buy. Other sites that compile deals include www.bestfares.com, www.flights.com, www.lowestfare.com, www.onetravel.com, and www.travelzoo.com. **SideStep** (www.sidestep.com) and **Booking Buddy** (www.bookingbuddy.com) are online tools that can help sift through multiple offers; these two let you enter your trip information and search multiple sites. **Air Traveler's Handbook** (www.faqs.org/faqs/travel/air/handbook) is an indispensable resource on the Internet; it has a listing of links to everything you need to know before you board a plane.

BUDGET AND STUDENT TRAVEL AGENCIES

While knowledgeable agents specializing in flights to Britain can make your life easy, they may not spend the time to find you the lowest possible fare—they get paid on commission. Travelers holding ISICs and IYTCs (p. 14) qualify for big discounts from student travel agencies. Most flights from budget agencies are on major airlines, but in peak season some may sell seats on other cheaper but less reliable chartered aircraft.

The Adventure Travel Company, 124 MacDougal St., New York City, NY 10021, USA (☎+1-800-467-4595; www.theadventuretravelcompany.com). Offices across Canada and the US including New York City, San Diego, San Francisco, and Seattle.

STA Travel, 5900 Wilshire Blvd., Ste. 900, Los Angeles, CA 90036, USA (24hr. reservations and info ☎+1-800-781-4040; www.statravel.com). A student and youth travel organization with over 150 offices worldwide (check their website for a listing of all their offices), including US offices in Boston, Chicago, Los Angeles, New York City, Seattle, San Francisco, and Washington, DC. Ticket booking, travel insurance, railpasses, and more. Walk-in offices are located throughout Australia (☎+61 3 9207 5900), New Zealand (☎+64 9 309 9723), and the UK (☎08701 630 026).

COMMERCIAL AIRLINES

The commercial airlines' lowest regular offer is the **APEX (Advance Purchase Excursion)** fare, which provides confirmed reservations and allows "open-jaw" tickets. Generally, reservations must be made seven to 21 days ahead of departure, with seven- to 14-day minimum-stay and up to 90-day maximum-stay restrictions. These fares carry hefty cancellation and change penalties (fees rise in summer). Book peak-season APEX fares early. Use **Expedia** (www.expedia.com) or **Travelocity** (www.travelocity.com) to get an idea of the lowest published fares, then use the resources outlined here to try to beat those fares. Low-season fares should be appreciably cheaper than the high-season (June-Sept.) ones listed here. *Let's Go* treats **budget airlines** (p. 30) separately from commercial airlines. For travelers who don't place a premium on convenience, we recommend these no-frills airlines as the best way to jet around Europe. Even if you live outside the continent, you can save a lot of money by hopping onto the absolute cheapest flight to Europe you can find and then using budget airlines to reach your final destination.

TRAVELING FROM NORTH AMERICA

The most common ways to cross the pond are those you've probably heard of. Standard commercial carriers like **American** (☎+1-800-433-7300; www.aa.com), **United** (☎+1-800-538-2929; www.ual.com), and **Northwest** (☎+1-800-447-4747; www.nwa.com) will probably offer the most convenient flights, but they may not be the cheapest. Check **Lufthansa** (☎+1-800-399-5838; www.lufthansa.com), **British Airways** (☎+1-800-247-9297; www.britishairways.com), **Air France** (☎+1-800-237-2747; www.airfrance.us), and **Alitalia** (☎+1-800-223-5730; www.alitaliausa.com) for cheap tickets from destinations throughout the US to all over Europe. You might find an even better deal on one of the following airlines, if any of their limited departure points is convenient for you.

Aer Lingus: ☎0870 876 2020; www.aerlingus.com. Cheap round-trips from Boston, Chicago, Los Angeles, New York City, and Washington, DC to Birmingham, Bristol, London, Manchester, Glasgow, Dublin, and Shannon.

Icelandair: ☎+1-800-223-5500; www.icelandair.com. Stopovers in Iceland for no extra cost on most transatlantic flights. US$650-900; Oct.-May US$500-700. For last-minute offers, subscribe to Lucky Fares.

Finnair: ☎+1-800-950-5000; www.finnair.com. Cheap round-trips from San Francisco, New York City, and Toronto to Helsinki; connections throughout Europe.

TRAVELING FROM AUSTRALIA AND NEW ZEALAND

Air New Zealand: New Zealand ☎+64 800 737 000; www.airnz.co.nz. Flights from Auckland to Dublin and London.

Qantas Air: Australia ☎+61 13 13 13, New Zealand +64 800 808 767; www.qantas.com.au. Flights from Australia and New Zealand to London for around AUS$2800.

Singapore Air: Australia ☎+61 13 10 11, New Zealand +64 800 808 909; www.singaporeair.com. Flights from Auckland, Sydney, Melbourne, and Perth to London.

Thai Airways: Australia ☎+61 1300 65 19 60, New Zealand +64 9 377 3886; www.thaiair.com. Auckland, Sydney, and Melbourne to London, all through Bangkok.

BUDGET AIRLINES

Low-cost carriers are the latest big thing in Europe. With their help, travelers can often snag tickets for illogically low prices (i.e., less than the price of a meal in the airport food court), but you get what you pay for: namely, minimalist service and no frills. In addition, many budget airlines fly out of smaller regional airports several kilometers out of town. You'll have to buy shuttle tickets to reach the airports of many of these airlines, so plan on adding an hour or so to your travel time. After round-trip shuttle tickets and fees for services that might come standard on other airlines, that €1 sale fare can suddenly jump to €20-100. Prices vary dramatically; shop around, book months ahead, pack light, and stay flexible to nab the best fares. For a more detailed list of these airlines by country, check out www.whichbudget.com.

bmibaby: UK ☎0871 224 0224, elsewhere +44 870 126 6726; www.bmibaby.com. Departures from throughout the UK. London to Cork (£60) and Prague (£50).

easyJet: ☎871 244 2366, 10p per min.; www.easyjet.com. London to Athens, Barcelona, Madrid, Nice, Palma, and Zurich (£72-141).

Ryanair: Ireland ☎0818 30 30 30, UK 0871 246 0000; www.ryanair.com. From Glasgow, Liverpool, London, and to Dublin and Shannon (from £10).

SkyEurope: UK ☎0905 7222 747, elsewhere +421 2 3301 7301; www.skyeurope.com. 40 destinations in 19 countries around Europe. London to Prague (£50).

Transavia: UK ☎020 7365 4997; www.transavia.com. Short hops from Glasgow to Amsterdam (from £43 one-way) and London to Rotterdam (from £36 one-way).

Wizz Air: UK ☎0904 475 9500, 65p per min.; www.wizzair.com. London to Sofia (from £20 one-way).

AIR COURIER FLIGHTS

Those who travel light should consider courier flights. Couriers help transport cargo on international flights by using their checked luggage space for freight. Generally, couriers are limited to carry-ons and must deal with complex flight restrictions. Most flights are round-trip only, with short fixed-length stays (usually 1 week) and a limit of one ticket per issue. Most of these flights also operate only out of major gateway cities, mostly in North America. Generally, you must be over 18 (in some cases 21). In summer, the most popular destinations usually require an advance reservation of about two weeks (you can usually book up to 2 months ahead). Super-discounted fares are common for "last-minute" flights (3-14 days ahead).

FROM NORTH AMERICA

Round-trip courier fares from the US to Britain run about US$130-600. Most flights leave from Los Angeles, Miami, New York City, or San Francisco in the US and from Montréal, Toronto, or Vancouver in Canada. The organizations below provide members with lists of opportunities and courier brokers for an annual fee. Prices quoted below are round-trip.

Courier Travel (www.couriertravel.org). Searchable online database. Multiple departure points in the US to various European destinations.

International Association of Air Travel Couriers (IAATC; www.courier.org). From 7 North American cities to European cities, including London. 1-year membership US$45.

FROM AUSTRALIA, AND NEW ZEALAND

The **International Association of Air Travel Couriers** (www.courier.org; above) often sells courier flights from London to Tokyo, Sydney, and Bangkok and from Auckland to London. **Courier Travel** (above) also flies from London to Sydney.

STANDBY FLIGHTS

Traveling standby requires considerable flexibility in arrival and departure dates. Companies dealing in standby flights sell vouchers rather than tickets, along with the promise to get you to your destination (or near your destination) within a certain window of time (typically 1-5 days). You call in before your specific window of time to hear your flight options and the probability that you will be able to board each flight. You can then decide which flights you want to try to catch, show up at the appropriate airport at the appropriate time, present your voucher, and board if space is available. Vouchers can usually be bought for both one-way and round-trip travel. You may receive a monetary refund only if every available flight within your date range is full; if you opt not to take an available (but perhaps less convenient) flight, you can only get credit toward future travel. To check on a company's service record in the US, contact the **Better Business Bureau** (☎+1-703-276-0100; www.bbb.org). It is difficult to receive refunds, and clients' vouchers will not be honored when an airline fails to receive payment in time.

TICKET CONSOLIDATORS

Ticket consolidators, or **"bucket shops,"** buy unsold tickets in bulk from commercial airlines and sell them at discounted rates. The best place to look is in the Sunday travel section of any major newspaper (such as *The New York Times*), where many bucket shops place tiny ads. Call quickly, as availability is extremely limited. Not all bucket shops are reliable, so insist on a receipt that gives full details of restrictions, refunds, and tickets and pay by credit card (in spite of the 2-5% fee) so you can stop payment if you never receive your tickets. For more info, see www.travel-library.com/air-travel/consolidators.html.

ESSENTIALS

TRAVELING FROM CANADA AND THE US

Some consolidators worth trying are **Rebel** (☎+1-800-732-3588; www.rebel-tours.com), **Cheap Tickets** (www.cheaptickets.com), **Flights.com** (www.flights.com), and **TravelHUB** (www.travelhub.com). *Let's Go* does not endorse any of these agencies. As always, be cautious and research companies before you hand over your credit-card number.

CHARTER FLIGHTS

Tour operators contract charter flights with airlines in order to fly extra loads of passengers during peak season. These flights are far from hassle-free. They occur less frequently than major airlines, make refunds particularly difficult, and are almost always fully booked. Their scheduled times may change, and they may be canceled at the last moment (as late as 48hr. before the trip, and without a full refund). In addition, check-in, boarding, and baggage claim for them are often much slower. They can, however, be much cheaper.

Discount clubs and fare brokers offer members savings on last-minute charter and tour deals. Study contracts closely; you don't want to end up with an unwanted overnight layover. **Travelers Advantage** (☎+1-800-835-8747; www.travelersadvantage.com; US$90 annual fee includes discounts and cheap flight directories) specializes in **European travel** and tour packages.

BY CHUNNEL

Traversing 31 mi. under the sea, the Channel Tunnel (a.k.a. the **Chunnel**) is the fastest, most convenient, and least scenic route between Britain and France.

Trains: Eurostar, Eurostar House, Waterloo Station, London SE1 8SE (UK ☎08705 186 186, elsewhere +44 1233 617 575; www.eurostar.com). Frequent trains between London and the continent. Destinations include Paris (3½hr., UK£30-170), Lille, and Calais. Book online, at major rail stations in the UK, or at the office above.

Buses: Eurolines (www.eurolines.com) provides bus-ferry combinations to the UK.

Cars: Eurotunnel, Ashford Rd., Folkestone, Kent CT18 8XX (☎08705 35 35 35; www.eurotunnel.co.uk). Shuttles cars and passengers between Kent and Nord-Pas-de-Calais. Return fares range UK£50-200 for a car, depending on length of stay. Book online or via phone. Travelers with cars can also look into sea crossings by ferry (below).

BY FERRY

The fares below are one-way for adult foot passengers unless otherwise noted. Though standard return fares are usually just twice the one-way fare, fixed-period returns (usually within 5 days) are almost invariably cheaper. Ferries run year-round unless otherwise noted. Bikes are usually free, although you may have to pay up to UK£10 in high season. For a camper/trailer supplement, you will have to add UK£20-140 to the "with car" fare. If more than one price is quoted, the quote in pounds is valid for departures from the UK, etc. A directory of ferries in this region can be found at www.seaview.co.uk/ferries.html.

Brittany Ferries: ☎0871 244 0744, France +33 8 25 82 88 28; www.brittany-ferries.com. Between Plymouth and Roscoff, FRA, and Santander, ESP; Portsmouth and St-Malo, FRA and Caen, FRA; Poole and Cherbourg, FRA; Cork and Roscoff, FRA.

DFDS Seaways: ☎08702 520 524; www.dfdsseaways.co.uk. Between Harwich and Cuxhaven, DEU (19½hr., £29-49), and Esbjerg, DNK (18hr., £29-49). Between Newcastle and Amsterdam, NTH (16hr., £19-39), Kristiansand, NOR (18¼hr., £19-59); and Gothenburg, SWE (26hr., £19-59).

Fjord Line: ☎08701 439 669; www.fjordline.no. Between Newcastle and Stavanger, NOR (19½hr., £30-40), and Bergen, NOR (26hr., £30-40).

Irish Ferries: ☎08705 171 717, France +33 1 56 93 43 40, Ireland +353 818 300 400; www.irishferries.ie. Between Rosslare and Cherbourg, FRA, Roscoff, FRA, and Pembroke; Holyhead and Dublin.

Norfolkline, Norfolk House, Eastern Docks, Dover CT16 1JA (☎0870 870 1020; www. norfolkline-ferries.com). Between Dover and Calais, FRA and Dunkerque, FRA (equally convenient but less busy). Also between Liverpool and Dublin.

P&O Ferries: ☎08716 645 645; www.poferries.com. Daily ferries between Hull and Rotterdam, NTH and Zeebrugge, BEL; Dover and Calais, FRA; Portsmouth and Le Havre, FRA, and Bilbao, ESP; and several Britain-Ireland routes.

SeaFrance: France ☎+33 8 25 08 25 05; www.seafrance.com. Between Dover and Calais, FRA (1½hr., 15 per day, £7-11).

Stena Line: ☎08705 707 070; www.stenaline.co.uk. Between: Harwich and Hook of Holland, NTH; Fishguard and Rosslare; Holyhead and Dublin and Dún Laoghaire.

GETTING AROUND IN THE UK

Fares are either **one-way** or **round-trip.** "Period returns" require you to return within a number of days; "day return" means you must return on the same day. Unless stated otherwise, *Let's Go* always lists single one-way fares. Round-trip fares on trains and buses in the UK are simply double the one-way fare.

BY PLANE

Good sources of offers are the travel supplements of newspapers and the airline websites. The **Air Travel Advisory Bureau** in London (☎0189 255 3500; www. atab.co.uk) provides referrals to travel agencies and consolidators that offer discounted airfares out of the UK.

COMMERCIAL AIRLINES

For small-scale travel on the continent, *Let's Go* suggests ✈**budget airlines** (below) for budget travelers, but more traditional carriers have made efforts to keep up with the revolution. The **Star Alliance Europe Airpass** offers economy-class fares as low as US$65 for travel within Europe to 216 destinations in 44 countries. The pass is available to non-European passengers on Star Alliance carriers, including British Midland Airways. See www.staralliance.com for more information. In addition, a number of European airlines offer discount coupon packets. Most are only available as tack-ons for transatlantic passengers, but some are stand-alone offers. Most must be purchased before departure, so research in advance.

AirBerlin: ☎0871 500 0737, 10p per min.; www.airberlin.com. Departures from London, Southampton, and Manchester to over 60 European cities.

Aer Lingus: ☎0870 876 5000, Ireland +353 818 365 000; www.aerlingus.com. Services between Cork, Dublin, Galway, Kerry, Shannon, and many cities in Europe. Departures from Birmingham, Edinburgh, Glasgow, London, and Manchester in the UK.

EuropeByAir: ☎+1-888-321-4737; www.europebyair.com. FlightPass allows you to hop between 500 cities in Europe and North Africa. Most flights US$99.

Iberia: ☎+1-800-772-4642; www.iberia.com. EuroPass allows Iberia passengers flying from the US to the UK to tack on a minimum of 2 additional destinations in Europe. US$125-155 each.

BUDGET AIRLINES

The recent emergence of no-frills airlines has made hopscotching around Europe by air increasingly affordable. Though these flights often feature inconvenient hours or serve less popular regional airports, with ticket prices often dipping into single digits, it's never been faster or easier to jet across the continent. The following resources and the ones on p. 30 will be useful not only for crisscrossing Britain but also for those ever-popular weekend trips to nearby international destinations.

British Midland Airways: ☎08706 070 555; www.flybmi.com. Services between Aberdeen, Belfast, Dublin, Edinburgh, Glasgow, Inverness, and London. London to Brussels, Paris, and Frankfurt.

easyJet: ☎0871 244 2366; www.easyjet.com. 210 routes between 63 European cities. Departures from Aberdeen, Belfast, Bristol, Edinburgh, East Midlands, Glasgow, Inverness, Liverpool, London, and Newcastle. Frequent specials; online tickets.

KLM: ☎08705 074 074; www.klmuk.com. Round-trip tickets from London and other cities in the UK to Amsterdam, Brussels, Düsseldorf, Frankfurt, Milan, Paris, and Rome.

Ryanair: ☎0871 246 0000, 10p per min.; Ireland +353 818 30 30 30 (national rate); www.ryanair.ie. From Dublin, London, and Glasgow to destinations in France, Ireland, Italy, Scandinavia, and elsewhere. As low as £1 on specials; book far in advance.

 TRAVELINE. An essential resource, Traveline (☎0871 200 2233; www.traveline.org.uk) offers comprehensive and impartial information for travel planning throughout the UK—whether by train, bus, or ferry.

BY TRAIN

Britain's train network crisscrosses the length and breadth of the island. In cities with more than one train station, the city name is given first, followed by the station name (for example, "Manchester Piccadilly" and "Manchester Victoria" are Manchester's two major stations). In general, traveling by train costs more than by bus. Railpasses covering specific regions are sometimes available from local train stations and may include bus and ferry travel. Prices and schedules often change; find up-to-date information from **National Rail Inquiries** (☎08457 484 950) or online at www.nationalrail.co.uk.

TICKET TYPES

The array of tickets available for British trains is bewildering, and prices aren't always set logically—buying an unlimited day pass to the region may cost less than buying a one-way ticket. Prices rise on weekends and may be higher before 9:30am. Purchase tickets before boarding, except at unstaffed train stations, where tickets are bought on the train. There are several types of **discount** tickets. **APEX (Advance Purchase Excursion)** tickets must be bought at least seven days in advance (2 days for ScotRail); **SuperAdvance** tickets must be purchased before 6pm the day before you travel. **Saver** tickets are valid anytime with return trips within a month but may be restricted to certain trains at peak times; Super-Saver tickets are similar but are only valid at off-peak times (usually M-Th, Su, and holidays). It may seem daunting, but the general rule of thumb is simple: planning a week or more in advance can make a £30-60 difference.

BRITRAIL PASSES

If you plan to travel a great deal on trains within Britain, the **BritRail Pass** can be a good buy. Eurail Passes are not valid in Britain, but there is often a discount on Eurostar passes if you have proof of Eurail purchase at the ticket office. BritRail Passes are only available outside Britain; you must buy them before traveling there. They allow unlimited train travel in England, Wales, and Scotland, regardless of which company is operating the trains, but they do not work in Northern Ireland or on Eurostar. Unless noted, travelers under 26 should ask for a **Youth Pass** for a 25% discount on standard and first classes; **seniors** (over 60) should ask for a 15% discount on first class only. **Children** from ages five to 15 can travel free with each adult pass, as long as you ask for the **Family Pass** (free). All children under five travel free. The **Party Discount** gets the third through ninth travelers in a party a 50% discount on their railpasses. Check with BritRail (☎ +1-866-BRIT-RAIL; www.britrail.com) or one of the distributors for details on other passes. Prices listed do not include shipping costs (around US$15 for delivery in 2-3 days, US$25 for priority delivery).

BritRail + Ireland Pass: Includes all trains in Britain, Northern Ireland, and the Republic of Ireland, plus a round-trip Stena or Irish Ferries sea crossing. No discounts apply. Travel within a 1-month period. Any 5 days standard class US$462, 1st class US$636; any 10 days US$733/1040.

BritRail Scottish Freedom Pass: Includes all Scottish trains, the Glasgow Underground, and Caledonian MacBrayne and Strathclyde ferry services. No discounts apply. Standard class only. Travel within a 15-day period. Any 4 days US$217; any 8 days US$292.

Consecutive Pass: For consecutive-day travel. 4 days standard class US$232, 1st class US$349; 8 days US$332/499; 15 days US$499/748; 22 days US$631/950; 1 month US$748/1124.

England Consecutive: Travel for consecutive days, only in England. 4 days standard class US$185, 1st class US$279; 8 days US$265/399; 15 days US$399/599; 22 days US$505/760; 1 month US$599/898.

England Flexipass: Travel within a 2-month period, only in England. Any 4 days standard class US$235, 1st class US$349; any 8 days US$340/510.

Flexipass: For travel within a 2-month period. Any 4 days standard class US$293, 1st class US$436; any 8 days US$425/638; any 15 days US$644/960.

London Plus Pass: Travel between London and several popular daytrip locations, including Cambridge, Oxford, and Windsor. Travel within an 8-day period. Any 2 days standard-class US$74, 1st class US$113; any 4 days US$140/187; any 7 days within a 15-day period US$187/249.

BRITRAIL DISTRIBUTORS

The distributors listed below will either sell you passes directly or tell you where to buy them; you can also ask travel agents for more information.

Australia: Rail Plus, 10-16 Queen St., Level 4, Melbourne, Victoria 3000 (☎+61 3 9642 8644; www.railplus.com.au). Concorde International Travel, 403 George St., Sydney, NSW 2000 (☎+61 1300 656 777; www.concorde.com.au).

Canada and the US: Rail Europe, 44 South Broadway, White Plains, NY 10601 (☎+1-800-361-7245 or 877-257-2887; www.raileurope.com), is the North American distributor for BritRail.

Ireland: USIT, 19-21 Aston Quay, O'Connell Bridge, Dublin 2 (☎+353 1 602 1904; www.usit.ie).

New Zealand: Holiday Shoppe, 66 Wyndham St., 5th fl., Auckland (☎+64 800 80 84 80; www.holidayshoppe.co.nz). Locations throughout New Zealand.

RAIL DISCOUNT CARDS

Unlike BritRail passes, these can be purchased in the UK. Passes are valid for one year and generally offer one-third off standard fares. They are available for young people (£20; must be 16-25 or a full-time student), seniors (£20; must be over 60), families (£20), and people with disabilities (£18). Visit the **Railcards** website (www.railcard.co.uk) for details.

IN NORTHERN IRELAND

Northern Ireland Railways (☎028 9066 6630; www.nirailways.co.uk) is not extensive but covers the northeastern coast. The major line connects Dublin to Belfast and then splits, with one branch ending at Bangor and one at Larne. There is also service from Belfast and Lisburn west to Derry and Portrush, stopping at three towns between Antrim and the Causeway Coast. BritRail passes are not valid here, but Northern Ireland Railways offers its own discounts. A valid **Translink Student Discount Card** (£7) will get you up to 33% off all trains and 15% discounts on bus fares over £1.80 within Northern Ireland. The **Freedom of Northern Ireland** ticket allows unlimited travel by train and Ulsterbus (7 consecutive days £50, 3 out of 8 days £34, 1 day £14).

BY BUS AND COACH

The British distinguish between **buses** (short local routes) and **coaches** (long distances). *Let's Go* uses the term "buses" for both. Regional **passes** offer unlimited travel within a given area for a certain number of days; these are often called Rovers, Ramblers, or Explorers, and they usually offer cost-effective travel. Plan ahead and book tickets online to take advantage of discounts.

BUSES

In Britain, long-distance bus travel is extensive and cheap. **National Express** (☎08705 808 080; www.nationalexpress.com) is the principal operator of long-distance bus services in Britain, although **Scottish Citylink** (☎08705 505 050; www.citylink.co.uk) has extensive coverage in Scotland. Discounts are available for seniors (over 50), students, and youths (16-25). The **Brit Xplorer** passes offer unlimited travel for a set number of days (7 days £79, 14 days £139, 28 days £219; www.nationalexpress.com). For those who plan far ahead, the best option is National Express's **Fun Fares,** only available online, which offer a limited number of seats on buses from London starting at, amazingly, £1. A similar option is **Megabus** (☎0900 160 0900; www.megabus.com), which also offers the £1 price but has fewer buses. Tourist Information Centres carry timetables for regional buses and will help befuddled travelers decipher them.

Ulsterbus (☎028 9066 6630; www.ulsterbus.co.uk) runs extensive and reliable routes throughout Northern Ireland. Pick up a free regional timetable at any station. The Emerald Card, designed for travel in the Republic of Ireland as well as Northern Ireland, offers unlimited travel on Ulsterbus. The card works for eight days out of 15 (£115, under 16 £58) or 15 of 30 (£200/50).

BUS TOURS

Staffed by young, energetic guides, these tours cater to backpackers and stop right at the doors of hostels. They are a good way to meet other independent travelers and to get to places unreachable by public transportation; most ensure a stay at certain hostels. "Hop-on, hop-off" tours allow you to stay as long as you like at each stop.

Celtic Connection, 7/6 Cadiz St., Edinburgh EH6 7BJ (☎0131 225 3330; www.thecelt-icconnection.co.uk). 2- to 9-day tours of Scotland, Wales, and Ireland (£25-225).

HAGGIS, 60 High St., Edinburgh EH1 1TB (☎0131 558 3738; www.haggisadventures. com). Specializes in 1-, 3-, 4-, 6-, and 8-day prearranged tours of Scotland with small groups and witty guides (from £24). Sister tours HAGGiS Britain (same contact info) runs 3-8 days through England and Wales.

Karibuni (☎01202 661 865; www.karibuni.co.uk). Runs daytrips, weekend trips, and adventure tours in England and Wales from London, including biking, kayaking, surfing, horseback riding, and camping (£50-225). Longer tours available for groups of 8+.

MacBackpackers, 105 High St., Edinburgh EH1 1SG (☎0131 558 9900; www.macback-packers.com). Hop-on, hop-off flexitour (£75) of Scotland and 2- to 9-day tours.

BY CAR

Cars offer speed, freedom, and access to the countryside, but they introduce the hassle of driving, parking, traffic, and the high cost of petrol (gasoline). Although a single traveler won't save by renting a car, four usually will. If you can't decide between train and car travel, you may benefit from a combination of the two; BritRail and other railpass vendors sell combination rail-and-drive packages (p. 35). Fly-and-drive packages are also often available from travel agents or airline/rental agency partnerships.

Before setting off, know the rules of the road in the UK (e.g. remember to drive on the left). For a primer on British road signs and conventions, check out www.direct.gov.uk/en/TravelAndTransport/Highwaycode. The **Association for Safe International Road Travel (ASIRT),** 11769 Gainsborough Rd., Potomac, MD 20854, USA (☎+1-301-983-5252; www.asirt.org), can provide more specific information about road conditions. ASIRT considers road travel (by car or bus) to be relatively safe in the UK. Britons use **unleaded gas** almost exclusively.

RENTING A CAR

Since the public transportation system in Britain is so extensive and punctual, travelers should consider opting out of a rental. However, for longer trips, journeys to small, rural destinations, or into the farthest reaches of the Scottish Highlands and islands of the north and west, the convenience of a car can mean the difference between an amazing trip and a tiresome trek punctuated by long waits for infrequent buses and trains. Bear in mind that British agencies refer to rental as "car hire."

RENTAL AGENCIES

You can generally make reservations before you leave by calling major international offices in your home country. It's a good idea to cross-check this information with local agencies as well. The local desk numbers are included in town listings; for home-country numbers, call your toll-free directory.

To rent a car from most establishments in the UK, you need to be at least 21 years old. Some agencies require renters to be 25, and most charge those 21-24 an additional insurance fee (around £10-15 per day). Small local operations occasionally rent to people under 21, but be sure to ask about the insurance coverage and deductible and always check the fine print.

Arnold Clark (☎0845 607 4500; www.arnoldclarkrental.co.uk).

Auto Europe (☎+1-888-223-5555 or 207-842-2000; www.autoeurope.com).

Avis (UK ☎08700 100 287; www.avis.com).

Budget (US ☎800-472-3325, UK ☎8701 565 656; www.budgetrentacar.com).

easyCar (☎09063 333 333, 60p per min.; www.easycar.co.uk).

Europe by Car (☎+1-800-223-1516 or 212-581-3040; www.europebycar.com).

Hertz (☎+1-800-654-3001; www.hertz.com).

Kemwel (☎+1-877-820-0668 or 800-678-0678; www.kemwel.com).

COSTS AND INSURANCE

Rental-car prices start at around £25-30 per day. Expect to pay more for larger cars and for four-wheel-drive. Cars with automatic transmission can cost up to £10 per day more than cars with manual transmission (stick shift), and, in some places, automatic transmission is hard to find in the first place. It is often difficult to find an automatic four-wheel-drive.

Remember that, if you are driving a conventional rental vehicle on an unpaved road in a rental car, you are almost never covered by insurance; ask about this before leaving the rental agency. Be aware that cars rented on an **American Express** or **Visa/MasterCard Gold** or **Platinum** credit card in the UK might not carry the automatic insurance that they would in some other countries; check with your credit-card company. Insurance plans from rental companies almost always come with an **excess** (deductible) of around £500 for conventional vehicles; excess ranges up to around £650 for younger drivers and for four-wheel-drive. This means that the insurance bought from the rental company only applies to damages over the excess; damages up to that amount must be covered by your existing insurance plan. The excess can often be reduced or waived entirely if you pay an additional charge (£1-10 per day). Many British rental companies will require you to buy a **Collision Damage Waiver (CDW),** which will waive the excess in the case of a collision. **Loss Damage Waivers (LDWs)** do the same in the case of theft or vandalism.

National chains (see **Arnold Clark,** above) often allow one-way rentals (picking up in one city and dropping off in another). There is usually a minimum hire period and sometimes an extra dropoff charge of several hundred pounds.

LEASING A CAR

For longer than 17 days, leasing can be cheaper than renting; it is often the only option for those aged 18 to 21. The cheapest leases are agreements to buy the car and then sell it back to the manufacturer at a prearranged price. As far as you're concerned, though, it's a lease and doesn't entail enormous financial transactions. Leases generally include insurance coverage and are not taxed. Expect to pay around £150-300 (depending on size of car) per month. Contact Auto Europe, Europe by Car, or Kemwel (above) before you go.

BUYING A CAR

If you're brave and know what you're doing, buying a used car or van in Britain and selling it just before you leave can provide the cheapest wheels for longer trips. Check with consulates for import-export laws concerning used vehicles, registration, and safety and emission standards.

DRIVING PERMITS AND CAR INSURANCE

INTERNATIONAL DRIVING PERMIT (IDP)

If you plan to drive a car while visiting the UK, you must be over 17 and have a **valid foreign driver's license.** An **International Driving Permit (IDP)** is also advisable. Your IDP, valid for one year, must be issued in your own country before you depart. An application for an IDP usually requires one or two photos, a current local license, an additional form of identification, and a fee. To apply, contact your home country's automobile association. Be vigilant when purchasing an IDP online or anywhere other than your home automobile association. Many vendors sell permits of questionable legitimacy for higher prices.

CAR INSURANCE

Most credit cards cover standard insurance. If you rent, lease, or borrow a car, you will need a **green card,** or **International Insurance Certificate,** to certify that you have liability insurance and that it applies abroad. Green cards can be obtained at car-rental agencies, car dealers (for those leasing cars), some travel agents, and some border crossings. Rental agencies may require you to purchase theft insurance in countries that they consider to have a high risk of auto theft.

ON THE ROAD

You must be 17 to drive in the UK. Be sure you can handle **driving on the left side** of the road and driving **manual transmission** ("stick shift" is far more common than automatic). Be particularly cautious at **roundabouts** (rotary interchanges) and remember to give way to traffic from the right. Road atlases for the UK are available in travel bookshops and from many Tourist Information Centres. Seat belts are required by law. **Petrol** (gasoline) prices vary, but they average about £1.10 per liter and increase during the summer and in urban areas like London. The country is covered by a high-speed system of **motorways** ("M-roads," some of them toll) that connect London with major cities around the country. These are supplemented by a tight web of "A-roads" and "B-roads" that connect towns: A-roads are the main routes, while B-roads are narrower but often more scenic. Distances on road signs are in miles (1 mi. = 1.6km). **Speed limits** are 70 mph (113km per hr.) on motorways (highways) and dual carriageways (divided highways), 60 mph (97km per hr.) on single carriageways (non-divided highways), and usually 30 mph (48km per hr.) in urban areas. Speed limits are marked at the beginning of town areas; upon leaving, you'll see a circular sign with a slash through it, signaling the end of the restriction. Drivers and all passengers are required to wear **seat belts** in the UK. Since a controversial 2003 reform, driving in central **London** is taxed at a stiff £8 per day during weekday working hours. Parking in London can be nightmarish. The **Highway Code,** which details Britain's driving regulations, is accessible online (www.highwaycode. gov.uk) or can be purchased at most large bookstores or newsstands.

ESSENTIALS

> **DRIVING PRECAUTIONS.** When traveling in the summer, bring substantial amounts of water (a suggested 5L of water per person per day) for drinking and for the radiator. You should always carry a spare tire and jack, jumper cables, extra oil, flares, a flashlight, and heavy blankets (in case your car breaks down at night or in the winter). If you don't know how to change a tire, learn before heading out, especially if you are planning on traveling in deserted areas. If your car breaks down, stay in your vehicle.

DANGERS

Driving in rural areas often requires caution on single-lane roads, many of which are scarcely wide enough for two cars to pass. These roads have occasional "passing places," which cars use to make way for passing vehicles. Cars flash their lights to signal that they will pull aside; the other car should take the right of way. The Scottish Highlands, Northumberland, Yorkshire, the Lake District, and parts of Wales all have roads on steep inclines, which drivers should take slowly in a low gear. Beware livestock along remote countryside roads.

CAR ASSISTANCE

In the event of a breakdown, contact the **Automobile Association** (**AA;** ☎0161 495 8945, emergency breakdown 08457 887 766; www.theaa.com) or the **Royal Automobile Club** (☎08705 722 722; www.rac.co.uk). Call ☎**999** in an emergency.

BY FERRY

Many of Britain's northern and western islands are inaccessible except by ferry. Ticket fares vary but almost always increase for automobiles. Be sure to board at least 15min. prior to departure.

Caledonian MacBrayne, The Ferry Terminal, Gourock PA19 1QP (☎01475 650 100; www.calmac.co.uk). The MacDaddy of Scottish ferries, with routes in the Hebrides and along the west coast of Scotland. Sells various combo packages for convenient and cost-effective island-hopping in the Scottish Islands.

Isle of Man Steam Packet Company serves the Isle of Man; see p. 393 for details.

Norfolkline, Norfolk House, Eastern Docks, Dover CT16 1JA (☎0870 870 1020; www.norfolkline-ferries.com). Between Liverpool and Dublin and Belfast.

Northlink Ferries, Stromness, Orkney, KW16 3BH (☎01856 885 500, reservations 0845 600 0449; www.northlinkferries.co.uk). Sails between Aberdeen, Lerwick, Kirkwall, Stromness, and Scrabster.

P&O Ferries, Channel House, Channel View Rd., Dover CT17 9TJ (☎08716 645 645; www.poferries.com). Operates ferries between Britain, Ireland, and the continent.

Stena Line, Stena House (☎08705 707 070; www.stenaline.co.uk). Stranraer to Belfast and Fleetwood to Larne.

BY BICYCLE

With a mountain bike, you can do some serious natural sightseeing. Some airlines will count your bike as your second free piece of luggage; others charge extra (around US$80-160 one-way). Rules vary by airline, but usually bikes must be packed in a cardboard box with the pedals and front wheel detached; many airlines sell bike boxes at the airport (at least US$15). Most ferries let you take your bike for free or for a nominal fee, and you can always ship your bike on trains. Renting a bike beats bringing your own if you plan to stay in one or two regions. Some youth hostels **rent** ("hire") bicycles for low prices. In addition to **panniers** (US$40-150) to hold your luggage, you'll need a good **helmet** (US$10-40) and a sturdy **lock** (from US$30). British law requires a white light at the front and a red light and red reflector at the back. For a good guide to biking through the UK, try **Mountaineers Books,** 1001 SW Klickitat Way, Ste. 201, Seattle, WA 98134, USA (☎+1-206-223-6303; www.mountaineersbooks.org).

The **National Cycle Network** encompasses 10,000 mi. of biking and walking trails in the UK. Information and maps are available through Sustrans (☎0845 113 0065; www.sustrans.org.uk). The **Cyclists Touring Club,** Parklands, Railton Rd., Guildford, Surrey GU2 9JX (☎0844 736 8450; www.ctc.org.uk), provides maps and books. Membership costs £35 (under 18 and students under 26 £12, over 65 £21) and includes a magazine. **Bicycle Beano** (☎01982 560 471; www.bicycle-beano.co.uk) runs vegetarian tours in Wales and England; **Cycle Scotland** (☎0131 556 5560; www.cyclescotland.co.uk) operates "Scottish Cycle Safaris."

BY FOOT

Walking and hiking are favorite pastimes of the British. Well-marked and well-maintained long-distance paths cover Britain, from the rolling paths of the **South Downs Way** (p. 163) to the rugged mountain trails of the **Pennine Way** (p. 402). Ordnance Survey maps mark almost every house, barn, standing stone, graveyard, and pub. The **Ramblers' Association,** Camelford House, 87-90 Albert Embankment, 2nd fl., London SE1 7TW (☎020 7339 8500; www.ramblers.org.uk), publishes a *Walk Britain* yearbook (£6, free to members; membership £27) on walking and places to stay as well as free newsletters and magazines. The Ramblers' website abounds with information. The **National Cycle Network** (see **By Bicycle,** opposite page) includes walking trails. **Contours Walking Holidays** (☎0176 848 0451; www.contours.co.uk) provides both guided and self-guided walking expeditions in England, Scotland, Wales, and Ireland.

BY THUMB

! LET'S NOT GO. *Let's Go* urges you to consider the risks before you choose to hitch. We do not recommend hitching as a safe means of transportation, and none of the information presented here is intended to do so.

No one should hitch without careful consideration of the risks involved. Hitching means entrusting your life to a random person who happens to stop beside you on the road, and hitchers always risk theft, assault, sexual harassment, and unsafe driving. Some travelers report that hitchhiking allows them to meet local people and travel in areas where public transportation is sketchy. The choice, however, remains yours.

Hitchhiking at night can be particularly dangerous; experienced hitchers stand in well-lit places. For women traveling alone, hitching is just too dangerous. A man and a woman are a safer combination, two men will have a harder time, and three will go nowhere. Experienced hitchers pick a spot outside of built-up areas where drivers can stop, return to the road without causing an accident, and have time to look over potential passengers as they approach. Hitching or even standing on motorways is illegal; one may only thumb at rest stops or at the entrance ramps to highways. Finally, success will depend on appearance. Drivers prefer hitchers who are neat and wholesome-looking.

Hitching is most common in rural parts of Scotland. **Safety** precautions are always necessary, even for those not hitching alone. Safety-minded hitchers will not get into a car that they can't get out of again in a hurry (especially the back seat of a 2-door car) and never let go of their backpacks. If they feel threatened, they insist on being let off, regardless of location. Acting as if they are going to open the car door or vomit usually gets a driver to stop.

KEEPING IN TOUCH

BY EMAIL AND INTERNET

Internet access is ubiquitous in big cities, common in towns, and sparse in rural areas. You can find access in the cybercafes; in coffee shops, particularly chains such as Caffe Nero and Starbucks; and in public libraries. Sneaky travelers use computers in media shops like PC World to check email quickly.

WARY WI-FI. Wireless hot spots make Internet access possible in public and remote places. Unfortunately, they also pose **security risks.** Hot spots are public, open networks that use unencrypted, unsecured connections. They are susceptible to hacks and "packet sniffing"—ways of stealing passwords and other private information. To prevent problems, disable ad hoc mode, turn off file sharing and network discovery, encrypt your email, turn on your firewall, beware of phony networks, and watch for over-the-shoulder creeps.

Although in some places it's possible to forge a remote link with your home server, in most cases this is a much slower (and thus more expensive) option than taking advantage of free **web-based email accounts** (e.g., ![icon]www.gmail.com). **Internet cafes** and the occasional free Internet terminal at a public library or university are listed in the **Practical Information** sections of major cities. For lists of additional cybercafes in Britain, check out **www.cybercaptive.com.**

Increasingly, travelers find that taking their **laptop computers** on the road with them can be a convenient option for staying connected. Laptop users can call an Internet service provider via a modem using long-distance phone cards specifically intended for such calls. They may also find Internet cafes that allow them to connect their laptops to the Internet. Lucky travelers with wireless-enabled computers may be able to take advantage of an increasing number of Internet "hot spots," where they can get online for free or for a small fee. Newer computers can detect these hot spots automatically; otherwise, websites like www.jiwire.com, www.wififreespot.com, and www.wi-fihotspotlist.com can help you find them. *Let's Go* notes establishment with free wireless. For information on insuring your laptop while traveling abroad, see p. 23.

BY TELEPHONE

CALLING HOME FROM BRITAIN

Prepaid phone cards are a common and relatively inexpensive means of calling abroad. Each one comes with a **Personal Identification Number (PIN)** and a toll-

free access number. You call the access number and then follow the directions for dialing your PIN. To purchase prepaid phone cards, check online for the best rates; www.callingcards.com is a good place to start. Online providers generally send your access number and PIN via email, with no actual "card" involved. You can also call home with prepaid phone cards purchased in Britain (see **Calling Within Britain,** below).

PLACING INTERNATIONAL CALLS. To call Britain from home or to call home from Britain, dial:

1. The **international dialing prefix.** To call from **Australia,** dial 0011; **Canada** or the **US,** 011; **Ireland, New Zealand,** or the **UK,** 00.
2. The **country code** of the country you want to call. To call **Australia,** dial 61; **Canada** or the **US,** 1; **Ireland,** 353; **New Zealand,** 64; the **UK,** 44.
3. The **city/area code.** *Let's Go* lists the city/area codes for cities and towns in Britain opposite the city or town name, next to a ☎, as well as in every phone number. If the first digit is a zero (e.g., 020 for London), **omit the zero** when calling from abroad (e.g., dial 20 from the US).
4. The **local number.**

Examples: To call the US embassy in London from New York City, dial ☎011 44 20 7499 9000. To call the British embassy in Washington from London, dial ☎00 1 202 588 7800. To call the US embassy in London from London, dial ☎020 7499 9000.

Another option is to purchase a **calling card,** linked to a major national telecommunications service in your home country. Calls are billed collect or to your account. To call home with a calling card, contact the operator for your service provider in the UK by dialing the appropriate toll-free access number (listed below in the third column). Occasionally, major credit cards can also be used for direct international calls. In-room **hotel calls** invariably include an arbitrary, sky-high surcharge (as much as £6); the rare B&B with in-room phones tends to as well. See the box below for directions on how to place a direct international call. Placing a **collect call** through an international operator is even more expensive. The number for the **international operator** in Britain is ☎155. Placing a collect call through an international operator can be expensive but may be necessary in case of an emergency. You can frequently call collect without even possessing a company's calling card just by calling its access number and following the instructions.

COMPANY	TO OBTAIN A CARD:	TO CALL ABROAD:
AT&T (US)	☎+1-800-364-9292 or www.att.com	☎0800 890 011 or 0500 890 011
Canada Direct	☎+1-800-561-8868 or www.infocanadadirect.com	☎0800 599 3141 or 0800 096 0634
MCI (US)	☎+1-800-777-5000 or www.minutepass.com	☎0800 2790 5088
Telecom New Zealand Direct	www.telecom.co.nz	☎0800 890 064
Telstra Australia	☎1800 676 638 or www.telstra.com	☎0800 890 061

CALLING WITHIN BRITAIN

The most straightforward way to call within the country is to use a **coin-operated phone,** but be prepared to carry a hefty pocketful of change to feed the machine during your call. **Prepaid phone cards** (available at newspaper kiosks, train stations, and convenience stores) usually save time and money in the long run.

Phone rates tend to be highest in the morning, lower in the evening, and lowest on Sunday and late at night. On some public phones, you can swipe the magnetic strip on your phone card, or even your credit card, to pay for calls.

To make a call within a city or town, dial the phone code and the number. For **directory inquiries,** call ☎118 500 (or any of the myriad other 118 services, such as ☎118 118 or 118 888). The services normally charge a 50p connection fee and cost 15p per minute. Northern Ireland is part of the UK phone network.

PHONE CODES

The first three numbers of a British phone code identify the type of number being called. **Premium rate calls,** costing about 50p per minute, can be identified by the ☎090 phone code. **Freephone** (toll-free) numbers have a ☎080 code. Numbers that begin with an ☎084 code incur the **local call rate,** while the ☎087 code incurs the **national call rate** (these two rates are not significantly different for short calls). Calling a **mobile phone** (cell phone) is more expensive than a regular phone call. Mobile phone numbers carry ☎077, 078, or 079 codes, and pager numbers begin with ☎076.

PUBLIC PHONES

Public pay phones in Britain are mostly run by **BT Group** (formerly British Telecom). Public phones charge a minimum of 30p for calls and don't accept 1p, 2p, or 5p coins. The dial tone is a continuous purring sound; a repeated double-tone means the line is ringing. A series of harsh beeps will warn you to insert more money when your time is up. For the rest of the call, the digital display ticks off your credit. You may use any remaining credit on a second call by pressing the "follow on call" button (often marked "FC"). Otherwise, once you hang up, your remaining phone-card credit is rounded down to the nearest 10p. Pay phones do not give change, so use your smallest coins.

CELLULAR PHONES

Cell phones ("mobile phones") are everywhere in Britain. Competitive, low prices and the variety of calling plans make them accessible even for short-term, low-budget travelers. For most visitors to the UK, a **pay-as-you-go plan** is the most attractive option. Pick up an eligible mobile (from £25) and recharge, or top up, with a card purchased at a grocery store, online, or by phone. Incoming calls and incoming text messages are always free. **Vodaphone** (www.vodafone.co.uk) and **T-Mobile** (www.t-mobile.co.uk) are among the biggest providers.

> **TIP**
>
> **GSM PHONES.** Just having a GSM phone doesn't mean you're necessarily good to go when you travel abroad. The majority of GSM phones sold in the US operate on a different frequency (1900) than international phones (900/1800) and will not work abroad. Tri-band phones work on all three frequencies (900/1800/1900) and will operate through most of the world. Additionally, some GSM phones are SIM-locked and will only accept SIM cards from a single carrier. You'll need a SIM-unlocked phone to use a SIM card from a local carrier when you travel.

The international standard for cell phones is **Global System for Mobile Communication (GSM).** To make and receive calls in Britain, you will need a GSM-compatible phone and a **SIM (Subscriber Identity Module) card,** a country-specific, thumbnail-size chip that gives you a local phone number and plugs you into the local network. Many SIM cards are prepaid, and incoming calls are frequently free. You can buy additional cards or vouchers (usually available at convenience stores) to **"top up"** your phone. For more information on GSM phones, check out www.telestial.com, www.orange.co.uk, or www.roadpost.com. Companies like **Cellular Abroad** (www.cellularabroad.com) rent cell phones that work in a variety of destinations around the world.

TIME DIFFERENCES

Britain is on **Greenwich Mean Time (GMT)** and observes **Daylight Saving Time** between the last Sunday of March and the last Sunday of October: in March, the clock moves 1hr. later; in October, the clock moves 1hr. earlier.

4AM	5AM	6AM	7AM	8AM	NOON	10PM*
Vancouver Seattle Los Angeles	Denver	Chicago	Lima New York Toronto	New Brunswick	**London Belfast Cardiff Edinburgh**	Sydney Canberra Melbourne

*Australia observes **Daylight Saving Time** from October to March, the opposite of the Northern Hemisphere. Therefore, it is 9hr. ahead of Britain from March to October and 10hr. ahead from October to March, for an average of 10hr.

BY MAIL

SENDING MAIL TO BRITAIN

To ensure timely delivery, mark envelopes "airmail" or "par avion" in large letters. In addition to the standard postage system whose rates are listed below, **Federal Express** (Australia ☎+61 13 26 10, Canada and the US +1-800-463-3339, Ireland +353 800 535 800, New Zealand +64 800 733 339, the UK 08456 070 809; www.fedex.com) handles express mail services between the UK and most other countries. Sending a postcard within Britain costs 24p, while sending letters (up to 100g) domestically requires 27p. In general, mail service is more prompt in large cities than in Britain's rural areas.

There are several ways to arrange pickup of letters sent to you while you are abroad. Mail can be sent via **Poste Restante** (General Delivery) to almost any city or town in Britain with a post office. Address Poste Restante letters like so:

William SHAKESPEARE

Poste Restante

2/3 Henley St.

Stratford-upon-Avon CV37 6PU

United Kingdom

The mail will go to a special desk in the central post office, unless you specify a post office by street address or postal code. It's best to use the largest post office, since mail may be sent there regardless. Bring your passport (or other photo ID) for pickup; if the clerks insist that there is nothing for you, ask them to check under your first name as well. *Let's Go* lists post offices in the **Practical Information** section for each city and most towns.

American Express's travel offices throughout the world offer a free **Client Letter Service** (mail held up to 30 days and forwarded upon request) for cardholders who contact them in advance. Some offices provide these services to non-cardholders (especially AmEx Travelers Cheque holders), but call ahead to make sure. *Let's Go* lists AmEx locations and financial servicesfor most large cities in **Practical Information** sections; for a complete list, call ☎+1-800-528-4800 or check out www.americanexpress.com/travel.

SENDING MAIL HOME FROM BRITAIN

Airmail is the best way to send mail home from Britain. Just write "Par Avion—By Airmail" on the top-left corner of your envelope or swing by any post office and get a free "Airmail" label. **Aerogrammes,** printed sheets that fold into envelopes and travel via airmail, are available at post offices. Most post offices will charge exorbitant fees or simply refuse to send aerogrammes with enclosures. For priority shipping, ask for **Airsure;** it costs £4.20 on top of the actual postage, but your letter will get on the next available flight. **Surface mail** is by far the cheapest and slowest way to send mail, although letters and postcards to Europe can only be sent by airmail. Surface mail takes one to two months to cross the Atlantic and one to three to cross the Pacific—good for heavy items you won't need for a while, such as souvenirs that you've acquired.

Royal Mail has taken great care to standardize their international rates. To check how much a shipment will cost, surf to the Royal Mail Postal Calculator at www.royalmail.com. Allow five days for regular airmail home to Australia, Canada, and the US. Postcards/aerograms cost 56p, as do letters up to 20g.

ACCOMMODATIONS

HOSTELS

If you want to save money, stay in a hostel. In Britain, hostels are generally clean and friendly places, and in larger cities many students even choose to live in them for extended periods of time while enrolled. Many of them are laid out dorm-style, often with large single-sex rooms and bunk beds, although private rooms that sleep two to four are becoming more common. They sometimes have kitchens and utensils for your use, bike or moped rentals, storage areas, transportation to airports, breakfast and other meals, laundry facilities, and Internet. However, there can be drawbacks: some hostels close during certain daytime "lockout" hours, have a curfew, don't accept reservations, impose a maximum stay, or, less frequently, require that you do chores. In Britain, a dorm bed in a hostel will average around £12-15 in rural areas, £15-20 in larger cities, and £20-35 in London. Make reservations at least a week in advance, especially in more touristed areas on weekends and during the summer.

> **A HOSTELER'S BILL OF RIGHTS.** There are certain standard features that we do not include in our hostel listings. Unless we state otherwise, you can expect that every hostel has no lockout, no curfew, free hot showers, some system of secure luggage storage, and no key deposit.

HOSTELLING INTERNATIONAL

Joining the youth hostel association in your own country (listed below) automatically grants you membership privileges in **Hostelling International (HI),** a federation of national hosteling associations. Non-HI members may be allowed to stay in some hostels, but they will have to pay an extra £3 to do so. HI's umbrella organization's website (www.hihostels.com), which lists the web addresses and phone numbers of all national associations, can be a great place to begin researching hosteling in a specific region. Other comprehensive hosteling websites include www.hostels.com and www.hostelplanet.com.

ESSENTIALS

Most HI hostels also honor **guest memberships**—you'll get a blank card with space for six validation stamps. Each night you'll pay a nonmember supplement (one-sixth of the membership fee) and earn one guest stamp; six stamps make you a member. A new membership benefit is the FreeNites program, which allows hostelers to gain points toward free rooms. Most budget and student travel agencies (p. 28) sell HI cards, as do all of the national hosteling organizations listed below. All prices listed below are valid for a one-year membership unless otherwise indicated.

An Óige (Irish Youth Hostel Association), 61 Mountjoy St., Dublin 7 (☎+353 1 830 4555; www.anoige.ie). EUR€20, under 18 EUR€10.

Australian Youth Hostels Association (AYHA), 422 Kent St., Sydney, NSW 2000 (☎+61 2 9261 1111; www.yha.com.au). AUS$52, under 18 AUS$19.

Hostelling International-Canada (HI-C), 205 Catherine St., Ste. 400, Ottawa, ON K2P 1C3 (☎+1-613-237-7884; www.hihostels.ca). CDN$35, under 18 free.

Hostelling International Northern Ireland (HINI), 22-32 Donegall Rd., Belfast BT12 5JN (☎028 9032 4733; www.hini.org.uk). £15, under 25 £10.

Scottish Youth Hostels Association (SYHA), 7 Glebe Cres., Stirling FK8 2JA (☎01786 891 400; www.syha.org.uk). UK£8, student and under 16 free.

Youth Hostels Association of New Zealand Inc. (YHANZ), Level 1, 166 Moorhouse Ave., P.O. Box 436, Christchurch (☎+64 3 379 9970, in NZ 0800 278 299; www.yha.org.nz). NZ$40, under 18 free.

Youth Hostels Association (England and Wales), Trevelyan House, Dimple Rd., Matlock, Derbyshire DE4 3YH (☎08707 708 868; www.yha.org.uk). £16, under 26 £10.

Hostelling International-USA, 8401 Colesville Rd., Ste. 600, Silver Spring, MD 20910 (☎+1-301-495-1240; www.hiayh.org). US$28, under 18 free.

BED AND BREAKFASTS (B&BS)

For a cozy alternative to impersonal hotel rooms, B&Bs (private homes with rooms available to travelers) range from acceptable to sublime. B&B owners sometimes go out of their way to be accommodating, giving personalized tours, helping with travel plans, or serving home-cooked meals. Some B&Bs, however, do not provide private bathrooms **(ensuite)** and most do not provide phones. Some do provide wireless Internet access. A **double** room has one large bed for two people; a **twin** has two separate beds. *Let's Go* lists B&B prices by room type. You can book B&Bs by calling directly or asking the local Tourist Information Centre (TIC) to help you find accommodations; most can also book B&Bs in other towns. TICs usually charge a 10% deposit on the first night's or the entire stay's price, deductible from the amount you pay the proprietor. Occasionally a flat booking fee of £1-5 is added. Rooms in B&Bs generally cost £25-40 for a single and £45-60 for a double. Many websites provide B&B listings; check out **InnFinder** (www.inncrawler.com), **InnSite** (www.innsite.com), or **BedandBreakfast.com** (www.bedandbreakfast.com). The British tourist boards operate a B&B **rating system,** using a scale of one to five diamonds (in England) or stars (in Scotland and Wales). Rated accommodations are part of the tourist board's booking system, but it costs money to be rated and some perfectly good B&Bs choose not to participate. Tourist-board approval is legally required of all Northern Ireland accommodations.

OTHER TYPES OF ACCOMMODATIONS

HOTELS AND GUESTHOUSES

Hotel singles in Britain cost about US$140 (£70) per night, doubles US$190 (£95). Smaller guesthouses are often cheaper than hotels. If you make **reservations** in writing, indicate your night of arrival and the number of nights you plan to stay. The hotel will send you a confirmation and may request payment for the first night's stay. Some hotels have a 24hr. cancellation policy.

UNIVERSITY DORMS

Many **colleges** and **universities** open their residence halls to travelers when school is not in session; some do so even during term time. Getting a room may take a couple of phone calls and require advanced planning, but rates tend to be low and many offer free local calls and Internet access. Many dorm accommodations do not include breakfast options. Dorm information is included in the **Accommodations** section of many larger cities and can usually be found in large university towns like Durham, Cardiff, and Glasgow.

HOME EXCHANGES AND HOSPITALITY CLUBS

Home exchanges allow travelers various types of homes (houses, apartments, condominiums, villas, even castles in some cases), plus the opportunity to live like a native and to cut down on accommodation fees. For more information, contact **HomeExchange.com Inc.**, P.O. Box 787, Hermosa Beach, CA 90254, USA (☎+1-310-798-3864 or toll-free 800-877-8723; www.homeexchange.com) or **Intervac International Home Exchange** (☎0845 260 5776; www.intervac.com).

   Hospitality clubs link their members with individuals or families abroad who are willing to host travelers for free or for a small fee to promote cultural exchange and general good karma. In exchange, members usually must be willing to host travelers in their own homes; a small fee may also be required. **The Hospitality Club** (www.hospitalityclub.org) is a good place to start. **Servas** (www.servas.org) is an established, more formal, peace-based organization and requires a fee and an interview to join. An Internet search will find many similar organizations, some of which cater to special interests (e.g., women, GLBT travelers, or members of certain professions). As always, use common sense when planning to stay with or host someone you do not know.

LONG-TERM ACCOMMODATIONS

Travelers planning to stay in Britain for extended periods of time may find it most cost-effective to rent an **apartment** (or **"flat"**). Besides the rent itself, prospective tenants usually are also required to front a security deposit (frequently 1 month's rent) and sometimes the last month's rent. Rent in London is usually about £400-600 per month, elsewhere in the UK about £200-400 per month. **Housepals UK** (www.housepals.co.uk) and **Gumtree** (www.gumtree.co.uk) both have extensive listings of available apartments and rooms for sublet. Many students opt to stay in hostels instead of flats (see **Hostels**, p. 47).

THE GREAT OUTDOORS

Great Britain's mild (if rainy) weather and beautiful landscape make it a wonderful place to hike and camp. Newly instituted laws, established by the

Countryside and Rights of Way Act of 2000, have given hikers and walkers access to open land even if it is privately held. Common-sense restrictions remain, and **camping** on common land can be frowned upon; always ask the landowner before pitching a tent and be respectful of the grounds. Campgrounds are often privately owned, with basic sites costing £3 per person and more upscale ones with amenities costing up to £10 per person. **Camping barns,** farm buildings converted to provide basic accommodations, usually cost £5-10 per person to rent. They can be difficult to reach without a car, and campers must bring their own sleeping bag and sturdy shoes. The **Great Outdoor Recreation Page** (www.gorp.com) provides excellent general information for travelers planning on camping or enjoying the outdoors.

LEAVE NO TRACE. *Let's Go* encourages travelers to embrace the "Leave No Trace" ethic, minimizing their impact on natural environments and protecting them for future generations. Trekkers and wilderness enthusiasts should set up camp on durable surfaces, use cookstoves instead of campfires, bury human waste away from water supplies, bag trash and carry it out with them, and respect wildlife and natural objects. For more detailed information, contact the **Leave No Trace Center for Outdoor Ethics,** P.O. Box 997, Boulder, CO 80306, USA (☎+1-800-332-4100 or 303-442-8222; www.lnt.org).

USEFUL RESOURCES

A variety of publishing companies offer guidebooks to meet the educational needs of novice or expert hikers. For information about camping, hiking, and biking, write or call the publishers listed below to receive a free catalog. Campers heading to Europe should consider buying an **International Camping Carnet.** Similar to a hostel membership card, it's required at a few campgrounds and sometimes provides discounts. It is available in North America from the **Family Campers and RVers Association** and in the UK from **The Caravan Club** (below).

Automobile Association, Contact Centre, Lambert House, Stockport Rd., Cheadle SK8 2DY (☎08706 000 371; www.theaa.com). Publishes the useful guide *Caravan and Camping Europe* and *Britain & Ireland* (£10) as well as road atlases for Europe, Britain, France, Germany, Ireland, Italy, Spain, and the US.

Association of National Park Authorities, 126 Bute St., Cardiff CF10 5LE (☎029 2049 9966; www.nationalparks.gov.uk). Has lists of and introductions to all British national parks, camping and hiking advice, and information on events and festivals.

The Camping and Caravanning Club, Greenfields House, Westwood Way, Coventry CV4 8JH (☎0845 130 7632; www.campingandcaravanningclub.co.uk). Offers online booking for campsites and travel and technical advice. Membership £35 per year.

The Caravan Club, East Grinstead House, East Grinstead, West Sussex, RH19 1UA, (☎01342 326 944; www.caravanclub.co.uk). For £34, members receive access to sites, insurance services, equipment discounts, maps, and a monthly magazine.

The Mountaineers Books, 1001 SW Klickitat Way, Ste. 201, Seattle, WA 98134, USA (☎+1-206-223-6303; www.mountaineersbooks.org). Over 600 titles on hiking, biking, mountaineering, natural history, and conservation.

Ordnance Survey, Customer Service Centre, Romsey Rd., Southampton SO16 4GU (☎08456 050 505; www.ordsvy.gov.uk). Britain's national mapping agency (also known as the OS) publishes excellent topographical maps, available at TICs, National Park

Information Centres (NPICs), and many bookstores. Their excellent Explorer map series (£8) covers the whole of Britain in detailed 1:25,000 scale.

Sierra Club Books, 85 2nd St., 2nd fl., San Francisco, CA 94105, USA (☎+1-415-977-5500; www.sierraclub.org). Publishes general resource books on hiking and camping.

NATIONAL PARKS

Britain has a series of gorgeous national parks. The parks are in large part privately owned, but they generally provide expansive areas for public use. Maps outline which areas are open to visitors. There are 15 national parks in England and Wales. The Trossachs, Loch Lomond, and the Cairngorms were named Scotland's first national parks in 2002. Each park is administered by its own National Park Authority, charged with preserving and maintaining the parks. Northern Ireland doesn't currently have any national parks designated, although a number of Areas of Outstanding Natural Beauty (AONBs) have been identified. Be sure to check out the local **National Park Information Centre** (NPIC) of the park in order to find out about various outdoor activities popular in Britain, including hiking, cycling, mountaineering, coasteering, and surfing.

WILDERNESS SAFETY

TIP

TOWNS WITHIN PARKS? Unlike many countries in which government-owned parks do not include manmade settlements, the national parks in Britain often cover large tracts of privately owned land and contain many individual towns and villages. *Let's Go* organizes these sections by centralizing the listings of tourist information centers and hostel accommodations at the beginning of each national park section; B&Bs, food, and other budget options within descriptions of individual towns.

Staying **warm, dry,** and **well hydrated** is key to a happy and safe wilderness experience. For any hike, prepare yourself for an emergency by packing a first-aid kit, a reflector, a whistle, high-energy food, extra water, raingear, a hat, mittens, and extra socks. For warmth, wear wool or insulating synthetic materials designed for the outdoors. Avoid wearing cotton, which dries slowly.

Check **weather forecasts** often and pay attention to the skies when hiking, as weather patterns can change suddenly. Always let someone—a friend, your hostel, or a park ranger—know when and where you are going. See **Safety and Health,** p. 20, for information on outdoor medical concerns. If you are in trouble and can reach a phone, call ☎999. If not, six blasts on a whistle are standard to summon help (three are the reply); a constant long blast indicates distress.

CAMPING AND HIKING EQUIPMENT

WHAT TO BUY

Good camping equipment is both sturdy and light. North American suppliers tend to offer the most competitive prices.

Sleeping Bags: Most sleeping bags are rated by season; "summer" means 30-40°F (around 0°C) at night; "4-season" or "winter" often means below 0°F (-17°C). Bags are made of **down** (warm and light, but expensive, and miserable when wet) or of **synthetic**

material (heavy, durable, and warm when wet). Prices range from US$50-250 for a summer synthetic to US$200-300 for a good down winter bag. **Sleeping bag pads** include foam pads (US$10-30), air mattresses (US$15-50), and self-inflating mats (US$30-120). Bring a **stuff sack** to store your bag and keep it dry.

Tents: The best tents are freestanding (with their own frames and suspension systems), set up quickly, and only require staking in high winds. Low-profile dome tents are the best all around. Worthy 2-person tents start at US$100, 4-person tents at US$160. Make sure yours has a rain fly and seal its seams with waterproofer. Other useful accessories include a **battery-operated lantern,** a plastic **ground cloth,** and a nylon **tarp.**

Backpacks: Internal-frame packs mold well to your back, keep a lower center of gravity, and flex adequately to allow you to hike difficult trails, while **external-frame** packs are more comfortable for long hikes over even terrain, as they carry weight higher and distribute it more evenly. Make sure your pack has a strong, padded hip belt to transfer weight to your legs. There are models designed specifically for women. Any serious backpacking requires a pack of at least 4000 cu. in. (16,000cc), plus 500 cu. in. for sleeping bags in internal-frame packs. Sturdy backpacks cost anywhere from US$125 to US$420—your pack is an area where it doesn't pay to economize. On your hunt for the perfect pack, fill up prospective models with something heavy, strap it on correctly, and walk around the store to get a sense of how the model distributes weight. Either buy a rain cover (US$10-20) or store all of your belongings in plastic bags inside your pack.

Boots: Be sure to wear hiking boots with good **ankle support.** They should fit snugly and comfortably over 1-2 pairs of **wool socks** and a pair of thin **liner socks.** Break in boots over several weeks before you go to spare yourself blisters.

Other Necessities: Synthetic layers, like those made of polypropylene or polyester, and a pile jacket will keep you warm even when wet. A **space blanket** (US$5-15) will help you to retain body heat and doubles as a **ground cloth.** Plastic **water bottles** are vital; look for shatter- and leak-resistant models. Carry **water-purification tablets** for when you can't boil water. Although most campgrounds provide campfire sites, you may want to bring a small **metal grate** or **grill.** For those places (including virtually every organized campground in Britain) that forbid fires or the gathering of firewood, you'll need a **camp stove** (starts at US$50) and a propane-filled fuel bottle to operate it. Also bring a **first-aid kit, pocketknife, insect repellent,** and **waterproof matches** or a **lighter.**

WHERE TO BUY IT

The online and mail-order companies listed below offer lower prices than many retail stores. A visit to a local camping or outdoors store will give you a good sense of the look and weight of certain items before you buy.

Blacks, Mansard Close, Westgate, Northampton NN5 5DL (☎0800 665 410; www.blacks.co.uk).

Campmor, 400 Corporate Dr., P.O. Box 680, Mahwah, NJ 07430, USA (☎+1-800-525-4784; www.campmor.com).

Cotswold Outdoor, Unit 11 Kemble Business Park, Crudwell, Malmesbury Wiltshire SN16 9SH (☎08704 427 755; www.cotswoldoutdoor.com).

Eastern Mountain Sports (EMS), 1 Vose Farm Rd., Peterborough, NH 03458, USA (☎+1-888-463-6367; www.ems.com).

Gear-Zone, 17 Westlegate, Norwich, Norfolk NR1 3LT (☎01603 765 551; www.gear-zone.co.uk).

L.L.Bean, Freeport, ME 04033, USA (US and Canada ☎800-441-5713, UK 0800 891 297; www.llbean.com).

Mountain Designs, 443A Nudgee Rd., Hendra, Queensland 4011, Australia (☎+61 7 3114 4300; www.mountaindesigns.com).

OutdoorGB, Nene House, Sopwith Way, Daventry NN11 8PB (☎0845 120 4500; www.outdoorgb.com).

Recreational Equipment, Inc. (REI), Sumner, WA 98352, USA (US and Canada ☎800-426-4840, elsewhere +1-253-891-2500; www.rei.com).

CAMPERS AND RVS

Renting an RV costs more than tenting or hosteling but less than staying in hotels while renting a car (see **Rental Cars,** p. 37). The convenience of bringing along your own bedroom, bathroom, and kitchen makes RVing an attractive option, especially for older travelers and families with children.

Rates vary widely by region, season (July and Aug. are the most expensive months), and type of RV. Rental prices for a standard RV are around £400 per week. Try **Vivanti Motorhomes** (☎08707 522 225; www.vivanti.co.uk) or **Just Go** (☎0870 240 1918; www.justgo.uk.com).

ORGANIZED ADVENTURE TRIPS

Organized adventure tours offer another way of exploring the wild. Activities include hiking, biking, skiing, canoeing, kayaking, climbing, and archaeological digs. Tourism bureaus often can suggest parks, trails, and outfitters. Organizations that specialize in camping and outdoor equipment like REI and EMS (above) are also good sources for info. To find an organized tour, consider contacting the **Specialty Travel Index,** P.O. Box 458, San Anselmo, CA 94979, USA (US ☎888-624-4030, elsewhere +1-415-455-1643; www.specialtytravel.com).

SPECIFIC CONCERNS

SUSTAINABLE TRAVEL

As the number of travelers on the road rises, the detrimental effect they can have on natural environments is an increasing concern. With this in mind, *Let's Go* promotes the philosophy of sustainable travel. Through a sensitivity to issues of ecology and sustainability, today's travelers can be a powerful force in preserving and restoring the places they visit.

Ecotourism, a rising trend in sustainable travel, focuses on the conservation of natural habitats—mainly, on how to use them to build up the economy without exploitation or overdevelopment. Travelers can make a difference by doing advance research, by supporting organizations and establishments that pay attention to their carbon "footprint," and by patronizing establishments that strive to be environmentally friendly. Preserving Britain's open land is a governmental priority, passed down to the individual National Park Authorities of each national park. For UK-specific low-impact eco-tours, visit www.earthfoot.org/uk.htm. The largest organization in Britain for environmental conservation is the **British Trust for Conservation Volunteers,** which is listed along with other conservation opportunities in the **Beyond Tourism** chapter (p. 60).

ECOTOURISM RESOURCES. For more information on environmentally responsible tourism, contact one of the organizations below:

Conservation International, 2011 Crystal Dr., Ste. 500, Arlington, VA 22202, USA (☎+1-800-406-2306 or 703-341-2400; www.conservation.org).

Green Globe 21, Green Globe vof, Verbenalaan 1, 2111 ZL Aerdenhout, the Netherlands (☎+31 23 544 0306; www.greenglobe.com).

International Ecotourism Society, 1333 H St. NW, Ste. 300E, Washington, DC 20005, USA (☎+1-202-347-9203; www.ecotourism.org).

United Nations Environment Program (UNEP), 39-43 Quai André Citroën, 75739 Paris Cedex 15, France (☎+33 1 44 37 14 50; www.uneptie.org/pc/tourism).

RESPONSIBLE TRAVEL

Your tourist dollars can make a big impact on the destinations you visit. The choices you make during your trip can have powerful effects on local communities—for better or for worse. Travelers who care about the destinations and environments they explore should make themselves aware of the social and cultural implications of their choices. Simple decisions such as buying local products, paying fair prices for products or services, and attempting to speak a few words in the local language (Welsh, Scots, Scottish Gaelic, or Irish) can have a strong, positive effect on the community.

Community-based tourism aims to channel tourist dollars into the local economy by emphasizing tours and cultural programs that are run by members of the host community. This type of tourism also benefits the tourists themselves, as it often takes them beyond the traditional tours of the region. *The Ethical Travel Guide* (£13), a project of **Tourism Concern** (☎020 7133 3330; www.tourismconcern.org.uk), is an excellent resource for information on community-based travel, with a directory of 300 establishments in 60 countries. The UK is filled with open-air historic sites like cathedral ruins, Bronze Age settlements, and other ancient monuments. It is rare that such testaments to the multicultural heritage of the British Isles survive today, and it is a privilege to be able to walk up, in, and among them. It is up to tourists to treat these sights respectfully and responsibly by not taking anything or leaving anything behind. For more information on how to positively interact with Britain's historic landmarks, see **Beyond Tourism,** p. 60.

TRAVELING ALONE

Traveling alone can be extremely beneficial, providing a sense of independence and a greater opportunity to connect with locals. On the other hand, solo travelers are more vulnerable targets of harassment and street theft. If you are traveling alone, look confident, try not to stand out as a tourist, and be especially careful in deserted or very crowded areas. Stay away from areas that are not well lit. If questioned, never admit that you are traveling alone. Maintain contact with someone at home who knows your itinerary and always research your destination before traveling. For more tips, pick p *Traveling Solo* by Eleanor Berman (Globe Pequot Press; US$18), visit www.travelaloneandloveit.com, or subscribe to **Connecting: Solo Travel Network,** 689 Park Rd., Unit 6, Gibsons, BC V0N 1V7, Canada (☎+1-604-886-9099; www.cstn.org; membership US$30-48).

WOMEN TRAVELERS

Women exploring on their own inevitably face some additional safety concerns. Single women can consider staying in hostels that offer single rooms that lock from the inside or in religious organizations with single-sex rooms. It's a good idea to stick to centrally located accommodations.

Avoid solitary late-night walks or Tube rides and choose train or Tube compartments occupied by other women or couples. Carry extra cash for a phone call, bus, or taxi. **Hitchhiking** is never safe for lone women or even for two women traveling together. Look as if you know where you're going and approach older women or couples for directions if you're lost or feeling uncomfortable in your surroundings. Generally, the less you look like a tourist, the better off you'll be. Dress conservatively, especially in rural areas. Wearing a conspicuous **wedding band** sometimes helps to prevent unwanted advances.

Your best answer to verbal harassment is no answer at all; feigning deafness, sitting motionless, and staring straight ahead at nothing in particular will usually do the trick. The extremely persistent can sometimes be dissuaded by a firm, loud, and very public "Go away!" Don't hesitate to seek out a police officer or a passerby if you are being harassed. Memorize the emergency numbers in places you visit and consider carrying a whistle on your keychain. Mace and pepper sprays are illegal in Britain.

The national emergency number is ☎999. **Rape Crisis UK and Ireland** (a full list of helplines can be found at www.rapecrisis.org.uk, www.rapecrisisscotland. org.uk in Scotland) provides referrals to local rape crisis and sexual abuse counseling services throughout the UK. A self-defense course will both prepare you for a potential attack and raise your level of awareness of your surroundings (see **Personal Safety**, p. 22). Also, it might be a good idea to talk with your doctor about the health concerns that women face when traveling (p. 24).

GLBT TRAVELERS

Large cities, notably London, Dublin, Edinburgh, Manchester, and Brighton, are more open to GLBT culture than rural Britain. The magazine *Time Out* (p. 58) has gay and lesbian listings, and numerous periodicals make it easy to learn about the current concerns of Britain's gay community. The *Pink Paper* (☎020 7424 7400; www.pinkpaper.com) is available free from newsstands in larger cities. **Planet Out** (www.planetout.com) offers information and a comprehensive site addressing gay travel concerns. Listed below are contact organizations, mail-order catalogs, and publishers that offer materials addressing some specific concerns. **Out and About** (www.planetout.com) offers a weekly newsletter addressing travel concerns and a comprehensive site addressing gay travel concerns. The online newspaper **365gay.com** also has a travel section (www.365gay.com/travel/travelchannel.htm).

Gay's the Word, 66 Marchmont St., London WC1N 1AB (☎020 7278 7654; http://freespace.virgin.net/gays.theword). The largest gay and lesbian bookshop in the UK, with both fiction and non-fiction titles. Mail-order service available.

Giovanni's Room, 345 S. 12th St., Philadelphia, PA 19107, USA (☎+1-215-923-2960; www.queerbooks.com). An international lesbian and gay bookstore with mail-order service (carries many of the publications listed below).

International Lesbian and Gay Association (ILGA), Avenue des Villas 34, 1060 Brussels, Belgium (☎+32 2 502 2471; www.ilga.org). Provides political information, such as homosexuality laws of individual countries.

London Lesbian and Gay Switchboard (☎020 7837 7324; www.llgs.org.uk). Confidential advice, information, and referrals. Open 24hr.

▼ **ADDITIONAL RESOURCES: GLBT**
Spartacus International Gay Guide 2008. Bruno Gmunder Verlag (US$33).
Damron Men's Travel Guide, Damron Road Atlas, Damron Accommodations Guide, Damron City Guide, and *Damron Women's Traveller.* Damron Travel Guides (US$18-24). For info, call ☎+1-800-462-6654 or visit www. damron.com.
The Gay Vacation Guide: The Best Trips and How to Plan Them, by Mark Chesnut. Kensington Books (US$15).
Gayellow Pages USA/Canada, by Frances Green. Gayellow Pages (US$20). They also publish regional editions. Visit Gayellow pages online at http://gayellowpages.com.

TRAVELERS WITH DISABILITIES

Those with disabilities should inform airlines and hotels of their disabilities when making reservations; some time may be needed to prepare special accommodations. Call ahead to restaurants, museums, and other facilities to find out if they are wheelchair-accessible. Guide-dog owners should inquire as to the quarantine policies of each destination country.

Rail is probably the most convenient form of travel for disabled travelers in Britain: many stations have ramps, and some trains have wheelchair lifts, special seating areas, and specially equipped toilets. The National Rail website (www.nationalrail.co.uk) provides general information for travelers with disabilities and assistance phone numbers; it also describes the **Disabled Persons Railcard** (£18 for one year), which cuts one-third off most fares and guarantees other benefits at participating hotels. Most **bus** companies will provide assistance if notified ahead of time. All National Express coaches entering service after 2005 must be equipped with a wheelchair lift or ramp; call the **Additional Needs Help Line** (☎0121 423 8479) for information or consult www.nationalexpress.com. The London **Underground** is slowly improving accessibility, and all of London's public buses became wheelchair-accessible in January 2006; **Transport for London: Access and Mobility** (☎020 7222 1234) can provide more information on public transportation throughout the city.

Some major **car-rental** agencies (e.g., Hertz), as well as local agencies, can deliver hand-controlled cars. In addition, **Lynx** hand controls may be used with many rental cars; contact Lynx, 80 Church Ln., Aughton, Ormskirk, Lancashire L39 6SB (☎01695 422 622; www.lynxcontrols.com).

The British Tourist Boards rate accommodations and attractions using the **National Accessible Scheme (NAS),** which designates three categories of accessibility. Look for the NAS symbols in Tourist Board guidebooks or ask a sight directly for their ranking. Many **theaters** and performance venues have space for wheelchairs; some larger theatrical performances include special facilities for the hearing-impaired. Book ahead to guarantee special provisions.

USEFUL ORGANIZATIONS

Accessible Journeys, 35 W. Sellers Ave., Ridley Park, PA 19078, USA (☎+1-800-846-4537; www.disabilitytravel.com). Designs tours for wheelchair users and slow walkers. The site has tips and forums for all travelers.

Flying Wheels Travel, 143 W. Bridge St., Owatonna, MN 55060, USA (☎+1-507-451-5005; www.flyingwheelstravel.com). Specializes in escorted trips to Europe for people with physical disabilities; plans custom trips worldwide.

The Guided Tour, Inc., 7900 Old York Rd., Ste. 114B, Elkins Park, PA 19027, USA (☎+1-800-783-5841; www.guidedtour.com). Organizes travel programs for persons with developmental and physical challenges in Ireland and the UK.

Mobility International USA (MIUSA), P.O. Box 10767, Eugene, OR 97440, USA (☎+1-541-343-1284; www.miusa.org). Provides a variety of books and other publications containing information for travelers with disabilities.

Society for Accessible Travel and Hospitality (SATH), 347 5th Ave., Ste. 610, New York City, NY 10016, USA (☎+1-212-447-7284; www.sath.org). An advocacy group that publishes free online travel information. Annual membership US$49, students and seniors US$29.

MINORITY TRAVELERS

Minorities make up about 10% of Britain's population and are concentrated in London. Rural Scotland and Wales remain predominantly white. Minority travelers should expect reduced anonymity in rural regions, but onlookers are usually motivated by curiosity rather than ill will and should not cause you to alter your travel plans. For information on measures to combat racism, contact the **Commission for Racial Equality (CRE),** 3 More London, Riverside Tooley St., London, SE1 (☎020 3117 0235; www.equalityhumanrights.com).

DIETARY CONCERNS

Vegetarian travelers should not have any trouble finding meals in Britain. Virtually all restaurants, even pubs, have vegetarian selections, and many cater specifically to vegetarians or to organic-food diets. *Let's Go* notes restaurants with good vegetarian selections. Good resources include www.veggieheaven.com, for comprehensive listings and reviews of UK restaurants, and the **Vegetarian Society of the UK** (☎0161 925 2000; www.vegsoc.org).

The travel section of **The Vegetarian Resource Group's** website, at www.vrg.org/travel, has a comprehensive list of organizations and websites that are geared toward helping vegetarians and vegans traveling abroad. For more information, visit your local bookstore or health-food store and consult *The Vegetarian Traveler: Where to Stay if You're Vegetarian, Vegan, Environmentally Sensitive,* by Jed and Susan Civic (Larson Publications; US$16). *Vegetarian Britain 2006,* edited by Alex Bourke, lists restaurants and veggie-friendly markets throughout the UK, the Isle of Man, and parts of Ireland. Vegetarians will also find numerous resources on the web; try www.vegdining.com, www.happycow.net, and www.vegetariansabroad.com, for starters.

The prevalence of South Asian and Middle Eastern communities has made **halal** restaurants, butchers, and groceries common in large cities. Your own mosque or Muslim community organization may have lists of Muslim institutions or halal eateries. Travelers looking for halal food may find the **Halal Food Authority** (www.halalfoodauthority.co.uk) and www.zabihah.com useful.

Travelers who keep **kosher** should contact synagogues in larger cities for information on kosher restaurants. Your own synagogue or college Hillel should have access to lists of Jewish institutions across the nation. Check http://shamash.org for a detailed database of kosher restaurants around the world, including major cities in the UK. If you are strict in your observance, you may have to prepare your own food on the road, although orthodox communities in North London (in neighborhoods such as **Golders Green** or **Stamford Hill**), Leeds, and Manchester provide a market for kosher restaurants and grocers. A good resource is the *Jewish Travel Guide*, edited by Michael Zaidner (Vallentine Mitchell; US$18).

OTHER RESOURCES

Let's Go tries to cover all aspects of budget travel, but we can't put everything in our guides. Listed below are books and websites that can serve as jumping-off points for your own research.

USEFUL PUBLICATIONS

Backpax, Unit 19, The Coach House, 2 Upper York St., Bristol BS2 8QN (☎0117 924 1600; www.backpaxmag.com). "The backpacker's mag," free at most TICs, lists up-to-date information about backpacking and working in Great Britain and Europe.

The List, 14 High St., Edinburgh EH1 1TE (☎0131 550 3050; www.thelist.co.uk). Excellent biweekly magazine on the happenings of Scotland's major cities.

Time Out, Universal House, 251 Tottenham Court Rd., London W1T 7AB (☎020 7813 3000; www.timeout.com). The absolute best weekly guide to what's going on in London, Edinburgh, and Dublin. The magazine is sold at every newsstand in those cities, and the website is a virtual hub for the latest on dining, entertainment, and discounts.

Rand McNally, P.O. Box 7600, Chicago, IL 60680, USA (☎+1-800-275-7263; www.randmcnally.com). Publishes road atlases.

WORLD WIDE WEB

Almost every aspect of budget travel is accessible via the web. In 10min. at the keyboard, you can make a hostel reservation, get advice on travel hot spots from other travelers, or find out how much a train from London to Edinburgh costs. Listed here are some region-specific and travel-related sites to start off your surfing; other relevant websites like regional tourism webpages are listed throughout the book. Because website turnover is high, use search engines (e.g., www.google.com) to strike out on your own.

LET'S GO ONLINE. Plan your next trip on our newly redesigned website, **www.letsgo.com.** It features the latest travel info on your favorite destinations as well as tons of interactive features: make your own itinerary, read blogs from our trusty researcher-writers, browse our photo library, watch exclusive videos, check out our newsletter, find travel deals, and buy new guides. We're always updating and adding new features, so check back often!

THE ART OF TRAVEL

Backpacker's Ultimate Guide: www.bugeurope.com. Tips on packing, transportation, and where to go. Also tons of country-specific travel information.

BootsnAll.com: www.bootsnall.com. Numerous resources for independent travelers, from planning your trip to reporting on it when you get back.

How to See the World: www.artoftravel.com. A compendium of great travel tips, from cheap flights to self-defense to interacting with local culture.

Travel Intelligence: www.travelintelligence.net. A large collection of travel writing by distinguished travel writers.

Travel Library: www.travel-library.com. A fantastic set of links for general information and personal travelogues.

World Hum: www.worldhum.com. An independently produced collection of "travel dispatches from a shrinking planet."

INFORMATION ON BRITAIN

CIA World Factbook: www.odci.gov/cia/publications/factbook/index.html. Tons of vital statistics on Britain's geography, government, economy, and people.

Geographia: www.geographia.com. Highlights, culture, and people of Britain.

PlanetRider: www.planetrider.com. A subjective list of links to the "best" websites covering the culture and tourist attractions of Britain.

TravelPage: www.travelpage.com. Links to official tourist office sites in Britain.

Visit Britain: www.visitbritain.com. Exhaustive listing of British tourist sites, from the smallest Stone Age hut to Windsor Castle.

ESSENTIALS

BEYOND TOURISM

A PHILOSOPHY FOR TRAVELERS

> **HIGHLIGHTS OF BEYOND TOURISM IN BRITAIN**
>
> **JOIN** the movement for peace in Northern Ireland (p. 62).
>
> **EXCAVATE** Roman settlements near Hadrian's Wall (p. 63).
>
> **HARVEST** gooseberries on one of Britain's organic farms (p. 70).
>
> **FLIP** to our "Giving Back" sidebar feature for even more regional Beyond Tourism opportunities (p. 648).

As a tourist, you are always a foreigner. Sure, hostel-hopping and sightseeing can be great fun, but connecting with a foreign country through studying, volunteering, or working can extend your travels beyond tourist traps. We don't like to brag, but this is what's different about a *Let's Go* traveler. Instead of feeling like a stranger in a strange land, you can understand the United Kingdom like a local. Instead of being that tourist asking for directions, you can be the one who gives them (and correctly!). All the while, you get the satisfaction of leaving Britain in better shape than you found it (after all, it's being nice enough to let you stay here). It's not wishful thinking—it's Beyond Tourism.

As a **volunteer** in Britain, you can unleash your inner superhero with projects from saving seal pups in Cornwall to fighting poverty in London. This chapter is chock-full of ideas to get involved, whether you're looking to pitch in for a day or run away from home for a whole new life in British activism.

The powers of **studying** abroad are beyond comprehension: it actually makes you feel sorry for those poor tourists who don't get to do any homework while they're here. You can study everything from folklore to physics at some of the oldest universities in the English-speaking world: Cambridge, Oxford, and St. Andrews. British universities are also known for their strength in area studies like African Studies or Asian Studies. If economics is your cup of tea, spend a summer or a year studying accounting, finance, or management at the famed London School of Economics.

Working abroad immerses you in a new culture and can bring some of the most meaningful relationships and experiences of your life. Yes, we know you're on vacation, but these aren't your normal desk jobs. (Plus, it doesn't hurt that it helps pay for more globetrotting.) Visitors can find work teaching, farming, or lending a hand in local pubs. British nannies may not actually carry carpetbags or ride umbrellas over London (like PL Travers's Mary Poppins), but working as a live-in au pair provides an opportunity to become close to a family and a particular place.

SHARE YOUR EXPERIENCE. Have you had a particularly enjoyable volunteer, study, or work experience that you'd like to share with other travelers? Post it to our website, www.letsgo.com!

VOLUNTEERING

Feel like saving the world this week? Volunteering can be a powerful and fulfilling experience, especially when combined with the thrill of traveling in a new place. Although the UK is considered wealthy by world standards, there are countless aid organizations that need volunteers. Civil strife continues to plague Northern Ireland, large urban communities suffer from poverty and housing shortages, and the landscapes and wildlife of northern England face threats of deforestation and species depopulation.

Most people who volunteer in Britain do so on a short-term basis at organizations that make use of drop-in or once-a-week volunteers. The best way to find opportunities that match your interests and schedule may be to check with local or national volunteer centers. **CharitiesDirect.com** offers extensive listings and profiles on thousands of charities in the UK and can serve as an excellent tool for researching volunteering options. **Volunteering England** provides links to local charities and sponsors **Volunteer's Week,** which recognizes and recruits volunteers throughout Britain. (☎0845 305 6979; www.volunteering.org.uk.) Northern Ireland's **Volunteer Development Agency** (☎028 9023 6100; www.volunteering-ni.org) responds to inquiries concerning volunteer opportunities. Their Freephone (☎0800 052 2212) connects callers to local volunteer bureaus. The **Wales Council for Voluntary Action** (www.volunteering-wales.net) has a searchable database of opportunities organized by region and project type. **Volunteer Development Scotland** (☎01786 479 593; www.vds.org.uk) lets you connect with other volunteers in the area to share your experiences and learn about new opportunities. Glasgow's **Volunteer Centre,** 84 Miller St., 4th floor (☎0141 226 3431; www.volunteerglasgow.org), provides useful volunteer listings and contact information. As always, read up before heading out.

Those looking for longer, more intensive volunteer opportunities usually choose to go through a parent organization that takes care of logistical details and often provides a group environment and support system—for a fee. There are two main types of organizations—religious and secular—although there are rarely restrictions on participation for either. Websites like **www.volunteerabroad.com, www.servenet.org,** and **www.idealist.org** allow you to search for volunteer openings both in your country and abroad.

I HAVE TO PAY TO VOLUNTEER? Many volunteers are surprised to learn that some organizations require large fees or "donations," but don't go calling them scams just yet. While such fees may seem ridiculous at first, they often keep the organization afloat, covering airfare, room, board, and administrative expenses for the volunteers. (Other organizations must rely on private donations and government subsidies.) If you're concerned about how a program spends its fees, request an annual report or finance account. A reputable organization won't refuse to inform you of how volunteer money is spent. Pay-to-volunteer programs might be a good idea for young travelers who are looking for more support and structure (such as pre-arranged transportation and housing) or anyone who would rather not deal with the uncertainty of creating a volunteer experience from scratch.

PEACE PROCESS

The conflict in Northern Ireland has caused tensions in Britain and Ireland for centuries, resulting in violence on both sides and all over the UK. Over the past 30 years, the peace process has become an issue of increasingly international awareness. Although the tensions have relaxed since the Good Friday Agreement of 1998, reconciliation is still an ongoing project. Volunteering with the organizations listed below is a good opportunity for foreigners looking to advance political and social change in Northern Ireland.

Corrymeela Community, Corrymeela Centre, 5 Drumaroan Rd., Ballycastle BT54 6QU (☎028 9050 8080; www.corrymeela.org). A residential Christian community designed to bring Protestants and Catholics together to work for peace. Openings from 1 week to 1 year with 8-week summer programs. Ages 18-30 preferred for long-term positions.

Kilcranny House, 21 Cranagh Rd., Coleraine BT51 3NN (☎028 7032 1816; www.kilcrannyhouse.org). A residential center that provides a safe space for Protestants and Catholics to explore nonviolence and conflict resolution. Volunteering opportunities from 1 month to 2 years. Food and accommodations provided.

Ulster Quaker Service Committee, 541 Lisburn Rd., Belfast BT9 7GQ (☎028 9020 1444; www.ulsterquakerservice.com). Runs programs for Protestant and Catholic children from inner-city Belfast. Accommodations and small allowance provided. 6- to 8-week summer posts and 1- to 2-year posts available. Short-term volunteers 17+, long-term volunteers 21+.

Volunteers Centres: Northern Ireland, 34 Shaftesbury Sq., Belfast BT2 7DB (☎028 9020 0850; www.volunteernow.co.uk). A central search agency for volunteer opportunities throughout Northern Ireland from arts to anti-poverty work.

Volunteers for Peace, 1034 Tiffany Rd., Belmont, VT 05730, USA (☎+1-802-259-2759; www.vfp.org). Arranges 2- or 3-week placements in a variety of different service projects from environmental protection to historical preservation. Most programs 18+. Registration fee US$300; some programs have additional costs.

CONSERVATION AND ARCHAEOLOGY

The UK's national parks and natural landscapes provide scenic venues for community service opportunities, from trail maintenance to archaeological expeditions. The largest organization in Britain for environmental conservation is the **British Trust for Conservation Volunteers (BTCV),** Sedum House, Mallard Way, Potteric Carr, Doncaster DN4 8DB (☎01302 388 888; www2.btcv.org.uk). Their counterpart in Northern Ireland is **Conservation Volunteers Northern Ireland,** Beech House, 159 Ravenhill Rd., Belfast BT6 0BP (☎028 9064 5169; www.cvni.org). Many national parks have volunteer programs—the Association of National Park Authorities can contact individual park offices. Below is a list of other conservation agencies:

Earthwatch Europe, 267 Banbury Rd., Oxford OX2 7HT (☎01865 318 838; www.earthwatch.org/europe). Arranges 1- to 3-week programs to promote conservation of natural resources, awareness of endangered animal populations (such as the Eagles of Mull), and the study of archaeological remnants (like dinosaur footprints in Yorkshire). Fees range from US$500 to over US$3500, plus airfare.

Groundwork, 5 Scotland St., Birmingham B1 2RR (☎0121 236 8565; www.groundwork.org.uk). Local Trusts throughout England and Wales work toward green communities and sustainable development. Volunteer opportunities vary by Trust and project, but most are short-term (1 day to 1 month).

Hebridean Whale and Dolphin Trust, 28 Main St., Tobermory, Isle of Mull PA75 6NU (☎01688 302 620; www.whaledolphintrust.co.uk). Arranges marine education courses and runs 2- to 12-day programs for basic whale research on board its boat. 18+.

Hessilhead Wildlife Rescue Trust, Gateside, Beith KA15 1HT (☎01505 502 415; www. hessilhead.org.uk). Volunteers rehabilitate wild birds and mammals in Scotland.

National Seal Sanctuary, Gweek, near Helston, Cornwall, TR12 6UG (☎01326 221 361; www.sealsanctuary.co.uk). Volunteers clean pools, feed pups, nurse injured seals to health, and help with the running of the Sanctuary, a major Cornwall sight. 18+.

Royal Society for the Protection of Birds (RSPB), UK Headquarters, The Lodge, Sandy, Bedfordshire SG19 2DL (☎01767 680 551; www.rspb.org.uk). Volunteer opportunities range from a day constructing birdhouses in East Anglia to several months monitoring invertebrates in the Highlands.

The National Trust, Volunteering and Community Involvement Office, P.O. Box 39, Warrington WA5 7WD (☎0870 458 4000; www.nationaltrust.org.uk/volunteering). Arranges numerous volunteer opportunities, including volunteer work on holidays.

The Wildlife Trusts, The Kiln, Waterside, Mather Rd., Newark, Nottinghamshire NG24 1WT (☎0870 036 7711; www.wildlifetrusts.org). Includes volunteer openings in conjunction with their 47 local Wildlife Trusts. Durations vary greatly.

Vindolanda Trust, Hexham, Northumberland NE47 7JN (☎01434 344 277; www.vindolanda.com). Work on archaeological excavation at Roman forts and settlements near Hadrian's Wall. Site open Apr. to mid-Sept. 1-week min. stay. £50 excavation fee for up to 2 weeks, £10 per additional week.

YOUTH AND THE COMMUNITY

There are countless social service opportunities in the UK, including mentoring youths, working in homeless shelters, and promoting mental health.

Barnardo's, Tanner's Ln., Barkingside, Ilford, Essex IG6 1QG (☎020 855 08822; www. barnardos.co.uk). Volunteers work with abused and underprivileged children.

Christian Aid: Central Office, 35 Lower Marsh, Waterloo, London SE1 7RL (☎020 7620 4444; www.christian-aid.org.uk). **Northern Ireland,** 30 Wellington Park, Belfast BT9 6DL (☎028 9038 1204). **Scotland,** 41 George IV Bridge, Edinburgh EH1 1EL (☎0131 220 1254). **Wales,** 5 Station Rd., Radyr, Cardiff CF15 8AA (☎029 2084 4646). Work in various fundraising and administrative roles, occasionally for a small stipend.

Citizens Advice Bureau, Myddelton House, 115-123 Pentonville Rd., London N1 9LZ (☎020 7833 2181, volunteer hotline 0845 126 4264; www.citizensadvice.org.uk). Volunteers help address issues from employment to finance to personal relationships.

Community Service Volunteers, 237 Pentonville Rd., London N1 9NJ (☎020 7278 6601; www.csv.org.uk). Part- and full-time volunteer opportunities with the homeless, the disabled, and underprivileged youth. 16+.

Habitat for Humanity Great Britain, 46 West Bar St., Banbury OX16 9RZ (☎01295 264 240; www.habitatforhumanity.org.uk). Volunteers build houses for low-income families. Other offices in Liverpool, Southwark, Birmingham, Eastbourne, and Belfast.

International Voluntary Service (IVS), Old Hall, East Bergholt, Colchester CO7 6TQ (☎01206 298 215; www.ivs-gb.org.uk). Arranges placement in projects from building an ecologically sustainable "ecovillage" to working with young people. 18+.

DISABILILITES AND SPECIAL NEEDS

In 2002, the Disability Rights Commission launched an Educating for Equality campaign in Britain designed to ensure the equal rights of individuals with disabilities in the education system. Despite this progressive measure and increasing attitudes of acceptance and tolerance, those possessing physical and mental handicaps continue to face discrimination in the UK. Volunteers can work with one of the multiple organizations concerned with aiding the special needs of these individuals and fostering a culture of mutual respect. More volunteer opportunities related to disability arts and culture are also available with the upcoming London 2012 Olympic and Paralympic Games (opposite page).

Association of Camphill Communities, 55 Cainscross Rd., Stroud GL5 4EX (☎01453 753 142; www.camphill.org.uk). Christian, private communities cater to both children and adults with special needs. Volunteers generally work for at least 6 months. Food, accommodations, and stipend provided. 18+.

International Volunteer Program (IVP), 678 13th St., Ste. 100, Oakland, CA 94612, USA (☎+1-510-433-0414; www.ivpsf.org). Lists 4- to 12-week volunteer programs working with the disabled, the elderly, and underprivileged youth. US$1550 and up; includes food, travel within country, and accommodations. 18+.

The Share Centre, Smith's Strand, Lisnaskea, Co. Fermanagh BT92 0EQ (☎028 6772 2122; www.sharevillage.org). Volunteers work as outdoors and arts activities leaders for 1 week to 1 year. Food and accommodations provided. 16+.

Vitalise, 12 City Forum, 250 City Rd., London EC1V 8AF (☎0845 345 1972; www.vitalise.org.uk). Volunteers care for disabled people for 1-2 weeks. Food, accommodations, and travel within Britain provided. 16+.

Worcestershire Lifestyles, Woodside Lodge, Lark Hill Rd., Worcester WR5 2EF (☎01905 350 686; www.worcestershire-lifestyles.org.uk). Work 1-on-1 with disabled adults. 18+.

REFUGEE AND IMMIGRANT ISSUES

Immigration to Britain has been a controversial political issue since the late 1990s. In the spring of 2008, the British immigration minister promised a clampdown on the number of immigrants and asylum-seekers. Human-rights organizations like Amnesty International have argued that detention centers and raids for undocumented workers violate human rights. As immigrants have no legal rights, their pay and living conditions are subject to abrupt changes. The **Association of Visitors to Immigrant Detainees (AVID),** P.O. Box 1496, Oxford OX4 9D4 (☎0188 371 7275) is the national umbrella charity for groups that work to assist immigration detainees. AVID and the other organizations listed below work to provide information, legal assistance, material aid, and national discussion of immigrant and refugee issues in Britain.

Asylum Welcome, 276A Cowley Rd., Oxford OX4 1UR (☎0186 572 2082; www.asylumwelcome.org). Connects volunteers to youth and family work, office reception, fundraising, research, media, and other advocacy projects. Membership £10.

Haslar Visitors Group, All Saints Centre, Commercial Rd., Portsmouth PO1 4BT (☎023 9283 9222; www.haslarvisitors.org.uk). Volunteers visit immigration detainees in a Haslar detention center once a week. Provides some training.

Jesuit Refugee Service (JRS), 6 Melior St., London SE1 3QP (☎020 7357 0974; www.jrsuk.net). Volunteers visit detainees or do administrative work in the London office. JRS provides training, supplies simple meals, and covers local travel expenses.

London Detainee Support Group, Unit 3R, Leroy House, 436 Essex Rd., London N1 3QP (☎020 7226 3114; www.ldsg.org.uk). Gives support and mentorship to detainees in London. 6-month min. commitment. Volunteers work at detention centers in Colnbrook and Harmondsworth.

Refugee Action, The Old Fire Station, 150 Waterloo Rd., London SE1 8SB (☎020 7654 7700; www.refugee-action.org.uk). Fundraising, administration, research, and interpreting positions available for volunteers.

LONDON 2012 OLYMPIC GAMES

The Summer Olympic Games don't officially hit London until July 2012, but the Olympic handover ceremony in Beijing in August 2008 marked the beginning of the "olympiad"—four years of planning and celebration preceding the Summer Games. London 2012 will depend on the help of up to 70,000 volunteers, and those eager to help out with the Games are already signing up online or seeking long-term work with the city's planning and preparation.

Olympic Delivery Authority (ODA), 1 Churchill Pl., Canary Wharf, London E14 5LN (☎020 0201 2000; www.london-2012.co.uk/ODA). ODA has already begun work developing the venues and infrastructure for the Games, including the construction of the Olympic Park. Seeking a wide range of skills, from community relations to transportation planning and operation. Job vacancies on website.

The London Organising Committee of the Olympic Games (LOCOG), 1 Churchill Pl., Canary Wharf, London E14 5LN (☎020 0201 2000; www.london-2012.co.uk/LOCOG). Responsible for preparing and staging the Games, LODOC is hiring for positions in project planning, technology, and cultural curating. Contracts begin in 2009.

The Volunteering Programme, 1 Churchill Pl., Canary Wharf, London E14 5LN (☎020 0201 2000; www.london2012.com/get-involved/volunteering). Volunteer roles available now for community work promoting arts, disability culture, education, and environmental sustainability. Volunteer positions for the Summer Games are of varying length and include translation, transportation, technology services, and help at sporting events. Volunteer registration on website.

STUDYING

VISA INFORMATION. As of November 2003, citizens of Australia, Canada, New Zealand, and the US require a visa if they plan to study in the UK for longer than 6 months. Consult www.ukvisas.gov.uk to determine if you require a visa. Immigration officials will request a letter of acceptance from your UK university and proof of funding for your first year of study, as well as a valid passport, from all people wishing to study in the UK. Student visas cost £99, and application forms can be obtained through the website above.

It's hard to dread the first day of school when London is your campus and exotic restaurants are your meal plan. A growing number of students report that studying abroad is the highlight of their learning careers. If you've never studied abroad, you don't know what you're missing—and if you have studied abroad, you do know what you're missing. Either way, let's go back to school!

Study-abroad programs range from basic language and culture courses to university-level classes, often for college credit (it's legit, Mom and Dad). In

BEYOND TOURISM

order to choose a program that best fits your needs, research as much as you can before making your decision—determine costs and duration, as well as what kind of students participate in the program and what sorts of accommodations are provided. Back-to-school shopping was never this much fun. The **British Council,** Bridgewater House, 58 Whitworth St., Manchester M1 6BB (☎0161 957 7755; www.britishcouncil.org), is an invaluable source of information. The **Council on International Educational Exchange** (☎+1-888-268-6245; www.ciee.org) offers a searchable online database listing study-abroad opportunities according to region. Devoted to international student mobility, the **Council for International Education,** 9-17 St. Albans Pl., London N1 ONX (☎020 7288 4330; www.ukcosa.org.uk), is another important resource.

For accommodations, dorm life provides a better opportunity to mingle with fellow students, but there is less of a chance to experience the local scene while living with other foreigners. If you live with a family, you could potentially build lifelong friendships with natives and experience day-to-day life in more depth, but you might also get stuck sharing a room with their pet iguana. Conditions can vary greatly from family to family.

BEYOND TOURISM

UNIVERSITIES

Tens of thousands of international students study abroad in the UK every year, drawn by the prestige of some of the world's oldest, most renowned universities. Apply early, as larger institutions fill up fast. You can search **www.studyabroad.com** for various semester-abroad programs that meet your criteria, including your desired location and focus of study. If you're a college student, your friendly neighborhood study-abroad office is often the best place to start.

AMERICAN PROGRAMS

American Institute for Foreign Study (AIFS), College Division, River Plaza, 9 W. Broad St., Stamford, CT 06902, USA (☎+1-800-727-2437; www.aifsabroad.com). Organizes programs for high-school and college study in universities in the UK.

Arcadia University for Education Abroad, 450 S. Easton Rd., Glenside, PA 19038, USA (☎+1-866-927-2234; www.arcadia.edu/cea). Operates programs at many universities throughout Britain. Costs and duration vary widely.

Butler University Institute for Study Abroad, 1100 W. 42nd St., Ste. 305, Indianapolis, IN 46208, USA (☎+1-317-940-9336 or 800-858-0229; www.ifsa-butler.org). Organizes term-time and summer study at British universities. Prices vary by location.

Central College Abroad, Office of International Education, 812 University, Pella, IA 50219, USA (☎+1-800-831-3629; www.central.edu/abroad). Offers internships, as well as summer (US$3625-5525), semester (US$13,785-14,875), and year-long (US$27,570-29,750) programs in Britain. Prices vary by location.

Council on International Educational Exchange (CIEE), 300 Fore St., Portland, ME 04101, USA (☎+1-207-553-4000 or 800-40-STUDY/407-8839; www.ciee.org). One of the most comprehensive resources for work, academic, and internship programs around the world, including in Britain.

School for International Training (SIT) Study Abroad, 1 Kipling Rd., P.O. Box 676, Brattleboro, VT 05302, USA (☎+1-888-272-7881 or 802-258-3212; www.sit.edu/studyabroad). Semester-long programs in Northern Ireland cost approximately US$22,000.

UK PROGRAMS

Many universities accommodate international students for summer, single-term, or full-year study. Those listed below are only a few that open their gates to foreign students; the British Council (opposite page) has information on additional universities. Prices listed are an estimate of fees for non-EU citizens. In most cases, room and board are not included.

London School of Economics, Undergraduate Admissions, P.O. Box 13401, Houghton St., London WC2A 2AE (☎020 7955 7125; www.lse.ac.uk). Year-long courses for international students (£11,874).

Queen's University Belfast, International Office, Belfast BT7 1NN (☎028 9097 5088; www.qub.ac.uk/ilo). Study in Belfast for a semester (£3665) or a full year (£7330).

University of Cambridge, Cambridge Admissions Office (CAO), Fitzwilliam House, 32 Trumpington St., Cambridge CB2 1QY (☎01223 333 308; www.cam.ac.uk). Open to overseas applicants for summer (£515-1095) or year-long study (£3070).

University of Edinburgh, The International Office, 57 George Sq., Edinburgh EH8 9JU (☎0131 650 4296; www.ed.ac.uk). Offers summer programs (£950-1335) and year-long courses (£9400) for international students.

University of Glasgow, Student Recruitment and Admissions, 1 The Square, Glasgow G12 8QQ (☎0141 330 4438; www.gla.ac.uk). Offers year-long courses (£9000-16,500).

University of Leeds, Study Abroad Office, Leeds LS2 9JT (☎0113 343 7900; www.leeds.ac.uk/students/study-abroad). One of the largest universities in England, Leeds offers semester (£3800) and full-year (£8600) study-abroad programs.

University College London, Gower St., London WC1E 6BT (☎020 7679 2000; www.ucl.ac.uk). In the center of London. Offers year-long programs (£10,900-14,300).

University of Oxford, College Admissions Office, Wellington Sq., Oxford OX1 2JD (☎01865 288 000; www.ox.ac.uk). Large range of summer programs (£880-3780) and year-long courses (£8880-11,840).

University of St. Andrews, Admissions Application Centre, St. Katharine's W., 16 The Scores, St. Andrews, Fife KY16 9AX (☎01334 462 150; www.st-andrews.ac.uk/services/admissions). Welcomes students for term-time study. Also houses the **Scottish Studies Summer Program** (☎01334 462 238; www.st-andrews.ac.uk/admissions/sssprog.htm). Courses in history, art history, literature, and music of the region for high-school students (£2600 all-inclusive).

University of Ulster, International Office, Shore Rd., Newtownabbey, Co. Antrim BT37 0QB (☎028 7032 4138; www.ulst.ac.uk/international). Semester or year-long programs for visiting international students (£3010-7090).

WORKING

Nowhere does money grow on trees (though *Let's Go*'s researchers aren't done looking), but there are still some pretty good opportunities to earn a living and travel at the same time. As with volunteering, work opportunities tend to fall into two categories. Some travelers want long-term jobs that allow them to integrate into a community, while others seek out short-term jobs to finance the next leg of their travels. In Britain, travelers looking for long-term jobs might be interested in teaching or working as a live-in au pair. Short-term jobs include farming and pub work. **Transitions Abroad** (www.transitionsabroad.com) offers updated online listings for work over any time span. Note that working abroad often requires a special work visa.

LONG-TERM WORK

If you're planning on spending a substantial amount of time (more than 3 months) working in Britain, search for a job well in advance. International placement agencies are often the easiest way to find employment abroad, especially for those interested in teaching. Although they are often only available to college students, **internships** are a good way to ease into working abroad. Many say the interning experience is well worth it, despite low pay (if you're lucky enough to be paid at all). Be wary of advertisements for companies claiming to be able get you a job abroad for a fee—often the same listings are available online or in newspapers. Some reputable organizations include:

Anders Elite, 2nd fl., New London House, 6 London St., London EC3R 7LP (☎020 7680 3100; www.anderselite.com). Large job placement agency with 13 offices in Britain.

Hansard Scholar Programme, 40-43 Chancery Ln., London WC2A 1JA (☎020 7438 1223; www.hansard-society.org.uk). Combines classes at the London School of Economics with internships in British government (£6850).

International Association for the Exchange of Students for Technical Experience (IAESTE), 10 Spring Gardens, London SW1A 2BN (☎020 7389 4771; www.iaeste. org). Chances are that your home country has a local office, too; contact it to apply for hands-on technical internships in Britain. You must be a college student studying science, technology, or engineering. "Cost of living allowance" covers most non-travel expenses. Most programs last 8-12 weeks.

International Cooperative Education, 15 Spiros Way, Menlo Park, CA 94025, USA (☎+1-650-323-4944; www.icemenlo.com). Finds summer jobs for students in Britain. Semester- and year-long commitments also available. Costs include a US$250 application fee and a US$700 fee for placement.

> **MORE VISA INFORMATION. European Economic Area (EEA)** nationals (member countries include EU member states and Iceland, Liechtenstein, and Norway) do not need a work permit to work in the UK. If you live in a Commonwealth country (including Australia, Canada, and New Zealand) and if your parents or grandparents were born in the UK, you can apply for **UK Ancestry Employment** and work without a permit (make sure you have all the relevant birth certificates that can prove your connection to the UK). Commonwealth citizens aged 17-27 can work permit-free under a **working holiday** visa. Foreigners studying at an institution in the UK are able to work within restrictions permit-free. American citizens who are full-time students and are over 18 can apply for a special permit from the **British Universities North America Club (BUNAC),** which allows them to work for up to 6 months in the UK. Contact BUNAC at P.O. Box 430, Southbury, CT 06488, USA (☎+1-203-264-0901) or 16 Bowling Green Ln., London EC1R 0QH (☎020 7251 3472; www.bunac.org.uk). Others will need a work permit to work in the UK. Applications must be made by the employer and can be obtained through the **Home Office,** Work Permits (UK), P.O. Box 3468, Sheffield (☎0114 207 4074; www.workpermits.gov.uk). Applications for work visas must be made through your local consulate. For more information, see www.workpermit.com/uk or **Embassies and Consulates** (p. 11).

BEYOND TOURISM

TEACHING

While some elite private American schools offer competitive salaries, let's just say that teaching jobs abroad pay more in personal satisfaction and emotional fulfillment than in actual cash. Perhaps this is why volunteering as a teacher instead of getting paid is a popular option. Even then, teachers often receive some sort of a daily stipend to help with living expenses.

The British school system comprises **state** (public, government-funded), **public** (independent, privately funded, despite the name), and **international** (both state and public, often for children of expatriates) schools as well as universities. The academic year is divided into **autumn** (September to Christmas), **spring** (early January to Easter), and **summer** (Easter to late July) terms. Applications to teach at state schools must pass through local governments, while public and international schools must be applied to individually.

To obtain a permanent teaching position in state-maintained schools in England and Wales, you must have **Qualified Teacher Status (QTS),** which usually entails a bachelor's degree and some sort of postgraduate teacher training. The government-run **Training and Development Agency for Schools** (☎0845 600 0991; www.tda.gov.uk) manages teacher qualifications. Teachers certified in the European Economic Area (EEA) generally qualify for QTS. The **General Teaching Council for Scotland** (☎0131 314 6000; www.gtcs.org.uk) regulates the teaching profession in Scotland and requires different qualifications for primary- and secondary-school certification. For information on teaching opportunities and certification requirements, see **www.teachinginscotland.com,** a website run by the Scottish government's Education Department. The **British Council** (p. 66) has extensive information for prospective teachers in the UK generally. **Placement agencies** or **university fellowship programs** are the best resources for finding teaching jobs. The alternative is to contact schools directly or to try your luck once you arrive in Britain. In the latter case, the best time to look is several weeks before the start of the school year. The following organizations are extremely helpful in placing teachers in Britain.

Council for International Exchange of Scholars, 3007 Tilden St. NW, Ste 5L, Washington, DC 20008, USA (☎+1-202-686-4000). Administers the Fulbright program for faculty and professionals.

Eteach UK Limited, Academy House, 403 London Rd., Camberley, Surrey GU15 3HL (☎0845 456 4384; www.eteach.com). Online recruitment service for teachers.

European Council of International Schools, 21B Lavant St., Petersfield, Hampshire GU32 3EL (☎01730 268 244; www.ecis.org). Runs recruitment services for international schools in the UK and elsewhere.

International Schools Services (ISS), 15 Roszel Rd., P.O. Box 5910, Princeton, NJ 08543, USA (☎+1-609-452-0990; www.iss.edu). Hires teachers for more than 200 overseas schools, including some in Britain. Candidates should have teaching experience and a bachelor's degree. 2-year commitment is the norm.

The Teacher Recruitment Company, Pennineway Offices (1), 87-89 Saffron Hill, London EC1N 8QU (☎0845 833 1934; www.teachers.eu.com). International recruitment agency that lists positions across the country and provides info on jobs in the UK.

AU PAIR WORK

Au pairs are typically women (although sometimes men) aged 18-27 who work as live-in nannies, caring for children and doing light housework in foreign countries in exchange for room, board, and a small spending allowance or stipend. One perk of the job is that it allows you to get to know Britain without the high expenses of traveling. Drawbacks, however, can include mediocre pay and long hours. Most au pairs receive anywhere between £100 and £300 per month in spending money. Some families will also defray travel expenses to and from Britain. Much of the au pair experience depends on the family with which you are placed. Au pairs from outside the European Economic Area need a letter of invitation from their host family to obtain a visa. The agencies below are a good starting point for looking for employment.

Au Pair UK (☎020 8537 3253; www.aupair.uk.com). Connects host families with prospective au pairs.

Almondbury Au Pair Agency, 4 Napier Rd., Holland Park, London W14 8LQ (☎01803 380 795; www.aupair-agency.com). Lists job openings in the UK and Ireland.

Childcare International, Trafalgar House, Grenville Pl., London NW7 3SA (☎20 8906 3116; www.childint.co.uk).

InterExchange, 161 6th Ave., New York City, NY 10013, USA (☎+1-212-924-0446 or 800-AU-PAIRS/287-2477; www.interexchange.org).

SHORT-TERM WORK

Believe it or not, traveling for long periods of time can be hard on the wallet. Many travelers try their hand at odd jobs for a few weeks at a time to help pay for another month or two of touring around. Although the UK typically does not issue work permits for short-term manual or domestic labor, a popular option is to work several hours a day at a hostel in exchange for free or discounted room and/or board. Most often, these short-term jobs are found by word of mouth or by expressing interest to the owner of a hostel or restaurant. Due to high turnover in the tourism industry, many places are eager for help, even if it is only temporary. *Let's Go* lists temporary jobs of this nature whenever possible; look in the Practical Information sections of larger cities or see below.

British Universities North America Club (BUNAC), 16 Bowling Green Ln., London EC1R 0QH (☎020 7251 3472; www.bunac.org). Lists establishments that have employed short-term workers in the past.

YHA (Youth Hostel Association) and its Scottish counterpart **SYHA** (www.yha.org.uk, www.syha.org.uk). Both list job openings on their websites and hire short-term workers from a pool of globetrotters. Ask at individual hostels as well.

FARMING IN THE UK

Working on a farm offers a chance to get away from the urban sprawl of London and other big cities and to wander among the fluffy sheep. Below are a couple of organizations that can help set up short-term exchange and work programs in the farming industry.

Fruitfuljobs.com (☎0870 727 0050; www.fruitfuljobs.com). Sets up farm work for backpackers and students all over the UK. Online application.

World Wide Opportunities on Organic Farms (WWOOF), P.O. Box 2675, Lewes, East Sussex BN7 1RB (☎01273 476 286; www.wwoof.org.uk). Lists organic farms in the UK that welcome volunteers. In return for 4-6hr. of work, visitors receive a bed and meals.

OTHER OPPORTUNITIES BY REGION

ENGLAND. Most English cities and larger towns have job spaces to fill, especially during the **high season,** mainly in pubs or restaurants. **Brighton** (p. 167) is especially accommodating to people looking for temporary work. Job hunting may be harder in the northern cities, where unemployment is higher. TICs are a good place to start your search (many post listings on their bulletin boards), although you would also be advised to check newspapers or individual establishments. **Job placement organizations** arrange temporary jobs in service or office industries. These include **Manpower** (☎0189 520 5200; www.manpower.com), **Blue Arrow** (☎0800 085 5777; www.bluearrow.co.uk), and **JobCentre Plus** (☎0845 606 0234; www.jobcentreplus.gov.uk), all three of which have offices all over England. **Bournemouth** (p. 204), **Bristol** (p. 193), **Exeter** (p. 220), **Newquay** (p. 243), and **Torquay** (p. 232) are all good places to look for work.

WALES. Many areas of Wales suffer unemployment rates higher than the British average. Picking up short-term work as a traveler may be more of a challenge here than in parts of England. If you are determined to find a job in Wales, first make sure you are not taking away an opportunity from a local who needs it more. **Cardiff** (p. 467), a large, well-touristed city, is perhaps the most feasible option, especially during rugby season when smaller towns may have listings posted at tourist information centers or outside markets.

SCOTLAND. Edinburgh (p. 545) is an excellent place to look for short-term work, especially during the festival in August. The backpacker culture fosters plenty of opportunities, and most of the larger hostels post lists of job openings. **Glasgow** (p. 583) experiences a similar boom during the summer. Try the **Glasgow Central Job Center,** 50-58 Jamaica St. (☎0141 800 3300; www.jobcentreplus.gov.uk). In both cities, low-paying domestic and food service jobs are easy to procure, and computer skills may net you higher-paying office work. Large and

medium-size cities also host offices of major job placement organizations (p. 68). Archaeological digs are commonplace in both **Orkney** and **Shetland,** but the application process is competitive. The fish-processing industry in Shetland (p. 680) provides hard work, good pay, and excellent scenery. Other work in Scotland can be found by visiting **www.s1jobs.com.**

NORTHERN IRELAND. Some of the most common forms of short-term employment in Northern Ireland include **food service, domestic work,** and **farm work. Belfast** is a good place to look for work opportunities and has several placement agencies. As in other regions, word of mouth and postings in hostels are among the best ways to find short-term employment.

FURTHER READING ON BEYOND TOURISM

Alternatives to the Peace Corps: A Guide of Global Volunteer Opportunities, edited by Paul Backhurst. Food First, 2005 (US$12).

The Back Door Guide to Short-Term Job Adventures: Internships, Summer Jobs, Seasonal Work, Volunteer Vacations, and Transitions Abroad, by Michael Landes. Ten Speed Press, 2005 (US$22).

Green Volunteers: The World Guide to Voluntary Work in Nature Conservation, by Fabio Ausenda. Universe, 2007 (US$15).

How to Get a Job in Europe, by Cheryl Matherly and Robert Sanborn. Planning Communications, 2003 (US$23).

How to Live Your Dream of Volunteering Overseas, by Joseph Collins, Stefano DeZerega, and Zahara Heckscher. Penguin Books, 2001 (US$20).

International Job Finder: Where the Jobs Are Worldwide, by Daniel Lauber and Kraig Rice. Planning Communications, 2002 (US$20).

Live and Work Abroad: A Guide for Modern Nomads, by Huw Francis and Michelyne Callan. Vacation Work Publications, 2001 (US$20).

Volunteer Vacations: Short-Term Adventures That Will Benefit You and Others, by Doug Cutchins, Anne Geissinger, and Bill McMillon. Chicago Review Press, 2006 (US$18).

Work Abroad: The Complete Guide to Finding a Job Overseas, edited by Clayton A. Hubbs. Transitions Abroad, 2002 (US$16).

Work Your Way Around the World, by Susan Griffith. Vacation Work Publications, 2007 (US$22).

fringe binge

Where art is concerned at the Edinburgh Fringe Festival, anything goes. It's one of the most supportive artistic environments a performer could want. One could sit in the same seat from 10am to 2am and see everything from a Spanish music tap dance show, a silly romp through the works of Shakespeare for children, a Blues Brothers cover band, and the show I performed *Jihad: The Musical.*

Of course, the sensationalist title of our show led to a blitz of press when we first arrived. "Aren't you worried about offending people? How do you think people will react? Isn't it in poor taste?" Even so, the interviews almost always concluded with, "Well, if there's anywhere in the world a show like yours could succeed, it's at the Edinburgh Fringe Festival."

Before I came, I did my homework on the Fringe Festival: hundreds of venues, thousands of shows, tens of thousands of performers. I wondered how a city with only 500,000 inhabitants could host something so great in size and scope. When I arrived, however, I realized that Edinburgh does not accommodate the festival; it becomes the festival.

Apart from restaurants, hotels, storefronts, and Internet cafes, it seems that every building is a performance venue. The year I performed, there was a gigantic inflatable purple tent that held shows during the day, and, whenever I walked past it, all I could think was, "Yeah, that makes sense."

I did not see a single show for which I booked my ticket in advance. It doesn't seem to be the way things work. Clearly, if a show contains a big star, features a world-famous comedian, or has received an ungodly amount of media attention, it's best to purchase tickets in advance. But it is far more satisfying to stroll the Royal Mile with (or without) a program and enter whatever venue you find yourself near. I have preferred not carrying one of the many comprehensive rosters of the festival's productions—there are too many things here that I would never think I wanted to see until I was standing in front of a church turned theater looking at posters, thinking, "Hmm ... A man standing on his head on top of another man's raised foot. I'll see that!"

Performing is one of the best ways to experience the Fringe. It becomes very easy to make friends at one of Edinburgh's many pubs. ("And why are you four ladies all painted entirely green? Oh, you're doing a show! I'm doing a show too, here's my flyer.") For a mere £5, you get a venue pass that allows you to see all of the shows at your venue for free. For the price of a fish and chips platter, you can see more than 400 productions over the course of a month.

Register your act with the Fringe Festival by early April. A copy of the registration form is available from Performer Services and at www.edfringe.com. It costs £150 to register for a one-night performance, and prices increase for multiple nights.

Not too many shows come here with the intention of making money. Between flight costs, putting up your

"Edinburgh does not accommodate the festival; it becomes the festival."

company in a flat or hotel, and paying the theater overhead, most would rather save their commercially viable ventures for the West End or Broadway. The Fringe is about embracing eccentricities, broadening horizons, and celebrating art.

For more information on the Edinburgh Fringe Festival, see p. 562.

David Ingber *has a degree in English and American Literature and Language from Harvard University. He is an actor and comedian living in New York City.*

ENGLAND

This blessed plot, this earth, this realm, this England...
—William Shakespeare, *Richard II*

The United Kingdom, Great Britain, England—the terms may seem interchangeable, but a slip of the tongue in a pub will provide travelers with a quick education. England, Scotland, and Wales make up the island of Great Britain, the largest of the British Isles. Along with Northern Ireland, the British countries form the United Kingdom of Great Britain and Northern Ireland, commonly called the **UK**. England conquered Ireland in the 12th century, Wales in the 13th, and passed an act of union with Scotland in 1707. Ireland won back its independence in 1921. While Wales and Scotland retain separate cultural identities marked by language and customs, the two remain part of a state administered from London. This chapter focuses on the history, literature, and culture of England. **Wales** (p. 460), **Scotland** (p. 535), and **Northern Ireland** (p. 688) are treated separately, although England's historically dominant position in governing the British countries makes for some inevitable overlap.

LIFE AND TIMES

YE OLDE ENGLAND

2500-2000 BC
An ancient tribe—likely the Druids but likelier a troupe of Martians—constructs the neolithic stone circle at Stonehenge.

AD 23
Emperor Claudius invades Britain and founds Londinium shortly thereafter.

AD 587
St. Augustine begins the conversions of Britons to Christianity, starting with King Æthelbert.

THE ANCIENT ISLE. Britain's residents first developed a distinct culture when the land bridge between the European continent and Britain eroded (c. 6000-5000 BC). Little is known about the island's prehistoric inhabitants, but the massive, astronomically precise stone circles left behind at **Stonehenge** (p. 202) and **Avebury** (p. 203) testify to their scientific and technological prowess. The **Celts** emigrated from the continent in the first millennium BC but were supressed by the invading armies of the Roman emperor Claudius in AD 43. The Roman conquerors established "Britannia" (England and Wales) as the northernmost border of their empire by the end of the first century, building **Londinium** (London; p. 94), **Verulamium** (St. Albans; p. 263), and a resort spa at **Bath** (p. 209). Further expansion proved difficult as the Romans faced marauders and uprisings in the northwest. In defense, Emperor Hadrian constructed his extensive wall (p. 456) in the AD second century. By the fourth century, the Roman Empire had waned and the Angles and the Saxons—tribes from Denmark and northern Germany—established settlements and kingdoms in the south. The name "England" derives from "Anglaland," land of the Angles.

CHRISTIANITY AND CONQUEST. The Britons became Christian when the famed missionary **Augustine** converted King Æthelbert in AD 597 and founded England's first Catholic

74

church at **Canterbury** (p. 151). From the eighth to the 10th centuries, the Norse sacked Scotland and Ireland, and Danish Vikings raided England's eastern coast. The legendary **Alfred the Great** pushed back the Danes in AD 878, but the Anglo-Saxons faced an ultimately graver threat to their dynasty in the Norman invaders from across the English Channel. Led by **William I,** better known as William the Conqueror, the Normans invaded the island in 1066, won the pivotal **Battle of Hastings** (p. 162), slaughtered the last Anglo-Saxon king, Harold II, and founded the **House of Norman.** William then set about cataloguing his new English acquisitions—each peasant, cow, and bale of hay—in the epic **Domesday Book.** He also introduced **feudalism** to England, and, under the "Norman yoke," he doled out vast tracts of land to his barons and subjugated English tenants to French lords.

BLOOD AND DEMOCRACY. The Middle Ages were an era of bloody conquest, bitter wars, and ravenous plague in England. But they also saw real advances in legal rights. In 1154, Henry Plantagenet ascended to the throne as **Henry II,** armed with a healthy inheritance and a dowry from his wife that entitled him to most of France. He quelled internal uprisings, undertook sweeping legal reforms, and spread his influence across the British Isles, claiming Ireland in 1171. Henry's squabbles with the insubordinate archbishop of Canterbury, **St. Thomas Becket,** resulted in Becket's murder at Canterbury Cathedral in 1170 (p. 154). Henry's son, **Richard I** (the Lionheart), was more interested in the Crusades than in domestic intrigues. He spent only six months of his 10-year reign on the island and never even bothered to learn English (the early Norman courts spoke French). Under Richard's hapless younger brother and successor, **King John,** England lost most of its French holdings. John also trampled on the toes of his powerful nobles, who in 1215 forced him to sign the **Magna Carta,** a keystone of modern constitutional law. The first **Parliament** convened 50 years later. Defying this move toward egalitarian rule, **Edward I** absorbed Wales under the English crown in 1284 and came close to conquering Scotland. In the process, he built some of Britain's most impressive castles (see **Caernarfon,** p. 524). While English kings expanded the nation's boundaries, the **Black Death** ravaged its population; between 1348 and 1361, it killed one-third of all Britons. Many more fell in the **Hundred Years' War** (or the 116 Years' War, to be precise), a costly conflict over the French throne.

In 1399, Henry Bolingbroke (later **Henry IV**) brought the House of Lancaster to power when he usurped the throne from his cousin, Richard II. In 1415, Bolingbroke's son, **Henry V,** and his band of brothers defeated the French in the Battle of Agincourt. But his son Henry-VI's failure to stave off the revived French resistance under Joan of Arc resulted in the loss of almost all of England's holdings in France. The **Wars of the Roses** (1455-85)—a crisis of royal succession between the houses of Lancaster and York, whose respective emblems were a red and a white rose—secured the victory of neither

1066
At the epic Battle of Hastings, the Norman William I, the Conqueror, defeats the Anglo-Saxon Harold II.

1170
Followers of King Henry II assassinate the Archbishop of Canterbury, St. Thomas Becket.

1209
Migrant scholars found a university in Cambridge. Learning ensues.

1307
Robert Hood of Wakefield, the real-life Robin Hood, is fined for refusing to invade Scotland.

1327
King Edward II is murdered with a red-hot iron through the bowels at Berkeley Castle.

1348-1361
The Black Death, a pandemic of pneumonic and Bubonic plague, kills one third of all Britons.

ENGLAND

1534
In between wives, Henry VIII founds the Church of England (the Anglican Church).

1599
The Burbage brothers construct Shakespeare's Globe Theatre out of wood and thatch. Flammable.

1603
James I (James VI of Scotland) becomes the first British monarch to rule England, Scotland, and Ireland.

1649
The deposed king Charles I is beheaded, and Oliver Cromwell takes control of the short-lived British Commonwealth. Three years after his death from malaria, he is exhumed, drawn, quartered, and beheaded.

1657
Thomas Garway begins selling tea to the public in London.

house. Instead, the upstart **Henry VII** of the **House of Tudor** defeated Richard III at the Battle of Bosworth Field in 1485, marking the beginning of the Tudor dynasty.

REFORMATION, RENAISSANCE, AND REVOLUTION. England's most infamous Tudor king, **Henry VIII,** solidified England's control over the Irish and struggled with the more intimate concern of producing a male heir. Henry's domestic troubles led him to marry six women (two of whom he executed) and to found the **Anglican Church** when the pope refused his request for a divorce. Henry's only son, Edward VI, was overshadowed by his staunchly Catholic half-sister Mary I, nicknamed **Bloody Mary** for ordering mass burnings of Protestants. Henry's daughter, **Elizabeth I,** inherited the throne after Mary's death. The Protestant Elizabeth reversed the religious persecution enforced by her sister and ensured the triumph of the **Protestant Reformation** in England. Under Elizabeth's remarkable 35-year reign, the English defeated the **Spanish Armada** in 1588, **Sir Francis Drake** circumnavigated the globe, and **William Shakespeare** penned some of the finest literature known to the English language. Henry VII's great-granddaughter, the Catholic **Mary, Queen of Scots,** briefly threatened the stability of the throne, but her involvement in a plot against Queen Elizabeth's life backfired, leading to her 20-year imprisonment and execution in 1587.

The seeds of a formal union between England, Wales, and Scotland were planted in 1603, when the philosopher-prince James VI of Scotland ascended to the English throne as **James I.** But the turbulent reign of James's son **Charles I** threw England into years of political and religious conflict. Charles's Catholic sympathies, extravagant spending, and fixed insistence on the divine right of kings aroused suspicion in the largely Puritan Parliament. After its refusal to fund his wars in Ireland, Charles suspended Parliament for 11 years, provoking the **English Civil War** (1642-51) between Royalists and Parliamentarians. The monarchy came to a violent, if temporary, end with the execution of Charles I and the founding of the first **British Commonwealth** in 1649.

REPUBLICANISM AND RESTORATION. The puritanical **Oliver Cromwell** emerged as the charismatic but despotic leader of the new commonwealth. Cromwell led a bloody conquest of Ireland, ordering the execution of all Catholic priests and every 10th Irish common soldier in some of the towns he captured. Cromwell also enforced oppressive measures in England, outlawing swearing and closing public theaters. The commonwealth collapsed under the lackluster leadership of Cromwell's son Richard, but the subsequent **Restoration** of **Charles II,** son of the beheaded king, did not end the turmoil. Debate raged in Parliament over the succession of Charles's Catholic brother **James II.** Amid the politicking, the two parties that would dominate English politics for the next two centuries emerged: the **Whigs** opposed the kings and supported reform; the **Tories** supported hereditary succession.

LAWS AND LOGIC. James II took the throne in 1685 but was deposed three years later by his son-in-law **William of Orange.** In the **"Glorious Revolution"** of 1688, the Dutch Protestant William and his wife Mary forced James to France and implemented a **Bill of Rights,** ensuring the Protestantism of future monarchs. Supporters of James II (called **Jacobites**) remained a serious threat until 1745, when James II's grandson Charles, commonly known as **Bonnie Prince Charlie,** failed in his attempt to recapture the throne. In 1707, England and Scotland were formally united under the same crown.

By the end of the **Seven Years' War** (1756-63), Britain controlled Canada, 13 unruly colonies to the west, and much of the Caribbean. Parliament prospered thanks to the ineffectual leadership of the Hanoverian kings, **George I, II,** and **III,** and the position of prime minister eclipsed the monarchy as the seat of power. Britain's uppity transatlantic colonial holding declared, fought for, and won its independence between 1776 and 1783, but the crown's overseas empire continued to grow elsewhere. Meanwhile, **Sir Isaac Newton** theorized the laws of gravity and invented calculus on the side, and Enlightenment figures **Thomas Hobbes, John Locke,** and **Jeremy Bentham** made significant contributions to political and philosophical thought. Religious fervor occasionally returned, with Bible-thumping **Methodists** preaching to outdoor crowds in the middle of the century.

MODERN ENGLAND

EMPIRE AND INDUSTRY. During the 18th and 19th centuries, Britain colonized more than one quarter of the world's population and more than two-fifths of its territory, styling itself as "the empire on which the sun never sets." By 1858, Britain controlled India, the "jewel in the imperial crown." Control of the Cape of Good Hope secured shipping routes to the Far East, and plantations in the New World produced staples like sugar and rum. Many British considered imperialism to be not only an economic boon, but also a moral duty to "civilize" the non-Christians in their imperial domain. This paternalistic method of control replaced a more overtly exploitative system of **slavery,** abolished in 1833. In Europe, the **Napoleonic Wars** (1800-15) marked the renewal of Anglo-French rivalry.

The **Industrial Revolution**—spurred by the perfection of the steam engine by James Watt in 1765 and the mechanization of the textile industry—bankrolled Britain's frenzied colonizing. Massive portions of the rural populace migrated to towns like **Manchester** (p. 362) and **Leeds** (p. 413), and a wide economic gap between factory owners and laborers replaced the age-old gap between landowners and tenant farmers. The **gold standard,** fully adopted in 1844, stimulated trade and international investment.

DECADENCE AND DISSENT. The reign of **Queen Victoria** (1837-1901) marked a period of relative stability and peace.

1687
Sir Isaac Newton publishes his *Principia Mathematica.* High school becomes exponentially more difficult.

1688
William of Orange and his wife Mary ascend to the throne, ending the wars of succession.

1776
The colonies in America declare independence and win it seven years later.

1812-1815
The phrase Pax Britannica comes into use, referring to the "civilizing" style of British imperialism.

1832
A reform bill extends the franchise and parliamentary representation to poorer voters.

1833
Parliament passes the Slavery Abolition Act, banning slavery in the British Empire.

1851
Prince Albert opens the Grand Exhibition at the Crystal Palace in London, showcasing marvels of industrial technology.

1856
Thomas Burberry, age 21, opens a small outfitters in Basingstoke.

ENGLAND

1859
Charles Darwin publishes *On the Origin of Species,* proposing a theory of evolution that forms the bedrock of modern biology.

1874
Samuel Bath Thomas leaves England for New York, where he perfects the nooks and crannies of English muffins.

1916
French and British Forces engage the Germans in the Battle of the Somme during WWI. July 1 becomes the bloodiest day in British history, with over 55,000 casualties.

1922
The BBC begins broadcasting live from London.

1940
A month after France's surrender to the Germans during WWII, the Battle of Britain commences. The Germans bomb London and Royal Air Force sites for nearly a year.

1945
WWII ends. Britain, the United States, and the Soviet Union craft a post-war settlement at the Yalta Conference.

1947
India wins independence from British rule.

A series of **Factory** and **Reform Acts** limited child labor, capped the average workday, and made sweeping changes in (male) voting rights. Prince Albert's 1851 **Great Exhibition** in London's newly built **Crystal Palace** displayed over 13,000 consumer goods from Britain's territories. The rich, bohemian upper crust embraced *fin de siècle* decadence with ornate art and clothing and even more ornate social rituals. While commercial self-interest defined much of 19th-century British society, proto-socialists like **John Stuart Mill** and the members of the **Fabian Society**—including **George Bernard Shaw** and **HG Wells**—made the case for reform and against bourgeois values. Trade unions strengthened and found a political voice in the **Labour Party,** founded in 1906. The "Ireland question" became increasingly pressing when Prime Minister **William Gladstone** failed to pass his **Home Rule Bill,** a proposal for partial Irish political autonomy. The **Suffragettes,** led by Emmeline Pankhurst, fought for enfranchisement for women by disrupting Parliament and staging hunger strikes. Women only won the right to vote after **World War I.**

TWO WORLD WARS. The **Great War** (1914-18), as the First World War was known until WWII, left two million Britons injured and one million dead. Technological advances of the 19th century begot powerful weaponry such as the machine gun, poison gas, and the tank. Combined with the European armies' outmoded strategies, these advances contributed to the enormous human cost of the war. WWI destroyed the Victorian dream of a peaceful, progressive society and left continental Europe scarred by millions of deaths and thousands of miles of devestated countryside.

The 1930s brought economic depression and unemployment as well as new tensions with a resurgent and revisionist Germany under Adolf Hitler. When Hitler made demands on regions of Czechoslovakia in 1938, Prime Minister **Neville Chamberlain** concluded a notorious **appeasement** agreement with Hitler in Munich, naïvely promising "peace in our time" to his British compatriots. Following Hitler's invasion of Poland in 1939, however, Britain declared war on Germany. Even the Great War failed to prepare Britain for the utter devastation of **World War II.** During the **Battle of Britain** in the summer of 1940, Royal Air Force pilots did battle with the German Luftwaffe in the skies. In the subsequent **Blitz,** German bombs rained down on London, Coventry, and other industrial cities, leaving scores of British citizens dead or homeless. The fall of France in 1940 precipitated the creation of a war cabinet, led by Prime Minister **Winston Churchill.** In June 1944, Britain and the Allied Forces launched the Battle of Normandy, commonly known as the **D-Day Invasion.** The campaign changed the tide of the war, leading to the liberation of Paris and eventually victory in May 1945.

DECLINE AND RENEWAL. Following the wars, Britain suffered continued economic hardship as its infrastructure and workforce lay in ruins. India declared independence in 1947, signaling the beginning of **decolonization** and the decline of the empire. War rationing did not end until 1954, and the government owed an huge war debt to the United States. As decolonization continued, the flood of immigrants from former colonies put new strains on the economy. In response, the UK adopted socialist economic policies. In 1946, left-wing politicians established the **National Health Service,** which to this day provides free medical care to all British citizens. In the 1960s, the Labour Party relaxed laws against divorce and homosexuality and abolished capital punishment. Despite these new policies, Britain could not replace the economic prosperity generated by its former colonial empire. Unemployment and economic unrest culminated in public service strikes during 1979's **Winter of Discontent.**

In May 1979, conservative Tory **Margaret Thatcher** became Britain's first female prime minister. She espoused an initially unpopular program of reduced government spending, denationalization, and lower taxes. The 1982 **Falkland Islands War** against Argentina elicited a surge of patriotic sentiment and helped to rally Thatcher's political fortunes. She privatized nearly every industry that the Labour government had brought under public control, dismantling vast segments of the welfare state. Her policies brought prosperity to many but sharpened the divide between the rich and the poor. Aggravated by her support of the **poll tax** and resistance to European integration, the Conservative Party presided over a vote of no confidence that led to Thatcher's 1990 resignation and the election of **John Major.**

Under the leadership of the youthful **Tony Blair,** the Labour Party refashioned itself into the alternative for discontented middle-class voters. **"New Labour"** won decisively under Blair in 1997 and garnered a second landslide victory in June 2001. Blair nurtured relations with the European Union and maintained inclusive, moderate economic and social positions.

TODAY

BRITAIN RULES. Britain has become one of the world's most stable constitutional monarchies without the aid of a written constitution. A combination of convention, common law, and parliamentary legislation composes the flexible system of British government. Since the 1700s, the monarch has played a largely symbolic role. Real political power resides with **Parliament,** comprising the **House of Commons,** with its elected **Members of Parliament** (MPs), and the **House of Lords.** Over time, power has shifted from the Lords to the Commons. Reforms in 1999 removed the majority of hereditary peers from the House of Lords, replacing them with Life Peers, appointed by prime ministers to serve for life. Parliament holds supreme legislative power and may change and even directly contradict its previous laws. All members of the executive branch, which includes the **prime minister** and the **cabinet,** are also MPs. This fusing of legislative and executive functions, called the "efficient secret" of the British govern-

1966
England defeats Germany 4-2 in its first and only FIFA World Cup win.

1969
The Beatles record and release their final album, *Abbey Road,* and disband one year later.

1978
The world's first test-tube baby is born in Oldham.

1982
Nationalistic Argentinians invade the British Falkland Islands; Prime Minister Margaret Thatcher rebuffs the attack, boosting morale In the face of an economic downturn.

1997
Diana, Princess of Wales, dies in a Paris car crash.

2001
Reality TV singing competition Pop Idol premiers on ITV1, beginning a franchise of international spinoffs.

2005
Suicide bombings by Islamic terrorists kill 52 communters on the London transportation system.

ENGLAND

ment, ensures the quick passage of the majority party's programs into law. The prime minister is appointed by the sovereign, who typically chooses the leader of the party with the majority in the House of Commons. From an elegant roost on **10 Downing Street,** the prime minister chooses a cabinet, whose members head the government's various ministries and present a cohesive platform to the public. Political parties keep their MPs in line on most votes in Parliament and provide a pool of talent and support for the smooth functioning of the executive. The **Labour** Party is roughly center-left; the **Conservatives,** or Tories, are center-right; and the smaller **Liberal Democrat** Party is left. Labour supported the war in Iraq, which the Conservatives opposed. Gay marriage and abortion are legal in the UK, but the death penalty is not.

CURRENT EVENTS. Terrorist attacks shook the country in July 2005. Four suicide bombs detonated on public transportation in London on the morning of July 7, killing 52. A failed second attack occurred two weeks later. The bombings were the deadliest attack in London since WWII. London received international attention again in August 2006, when government officials thwarted a potential terrorist attack on planes traveling through Heathrow Airport, resulting in a ban on bottled liquids in aircraft cabins.

Blair's popularity dwindled, and in the elections of 2005 his Labour Party only won a narrow victory, which was widely taken as a sign of the British public's lack of confidence in his government. Blair was dogged in particular by his support for the Iraq war and the close alliance he cultivated with the United States. In June 2007, Blair stepped down and was replaced by his former chancellor of the exchequer, **Gordon Brown.** Brown's tenure, after a promising start, was soured by a struggling economy, his own clumsy handling of an early election issue, and several other administrative mishaps. The Tories' impressive performance in the local elections of May 2008 has even caused some Labour MPs to call for Brown's replacement.

A ROYAL MESS? Although largely political figureheads, the royals have long been a juicy subject of gossip among the British public. Interest peaked when the world mourned the untimely death of the "People's Princess," **Diana,** in a Paris car crash in 1997. Matronly **Queen Elizabeth II** won kudos when she began paying income tax in 1993 and threw a year-long Golden Jubilee for the 50th year of her reign in 2002. **Prince Charles** and his paramour Camilla Parker-Bowles married in April 2005 after a clandestine 30-year romance, although the queen did not attend the service. A quick stop at a drug rehab clinic in 2002 heralded the onset of adult celebrity (and tabloid notoriety) for **Prince Harry,** the younger of Charles and Diana's sons. The elder and more popular **Prince William,** "his royal sighness," claimed headlines in 2007 after his public breakup with longtime sweetheart Kate Middleton.

CULTURE AND CUSTOMS

Jane Austen, Sid Vicious, and Winston Churchill all have equally valid claims to quintessentially "English" identity. Stiff-lipped public schoolboys and post-punk Hoxton rockers sit next to Burberry-clad football hooligans on the Tube, belying any notion of a single English" way of life. England, roughly the size of the American state of New York, is home to almost 50 million people from diverse and dynamic local subcultures.

ETIQUETTE

There is little that a traveler can do that will inadvertently cause offense while traveling in England. However, the English do place weight on proper decorum, including politeness ("thanks" comes in many varieties, including "cheers"), queueing (that is, lining up—never disrupt the queue), and keeping a certain respectful distance. You'll find, however, that the English sense of humor—dark, wry, explicit, even raunchy—is somewhat at odds with any notion you may have of English coldness or reserve. Still, no matter how much *Monty Python* may poke fun at the British, they won't appreciate "upstart colonials" doing so—they don't need to be reminded how awful British cuisine is.

FOOD AND DRINK

> English cooking, like the English climate, is a training for life's unavoidable hardships.
> —Historian RP Lister

Historically, England has been derided for its awful fare. But do not fear the bland, boiled, fried, and gravy-laden traditional nosh; Britain's cuisine might leave something to be desired, but food in Britain can be excellent. In the spring of 2008, a panel of chefs, food critics, and restaurateurs cast more than 3000 ballots and voted six British restaurants into the world's top 50; the Fat Duck in Berkshire came in second place for inventive concoctions like "snail porridge" and "sardine on toast sorbet." Popular television chef Jamie Oliver continues to lead a well-publicized campaign to increase the British government's spending on school lunches. Travelers on a budget can eat the benefits, too, of the "naked chef's" campaign for good grub.

The best way to eat in Britain is to avoid British food. Thankfully, ethnic cuisine has rapidly spread from the cities to the smallest of towns, so that most any village with a pub (and you'd be hard-pressed to find one without) will have an Indian takeaway, an Asian noodle shop, or a late-night shawarma stand to feed stumbling patrons late into the night. **Vegetarianism** and organic foods are also popular in Britain. Even the most traditional pubs and local markets, not to mention the trendy cafe-bars, offer at least one meatless option.

All visitors to Britain should try the famed, cholesterol-filled **full English breakfast,** which generally includes fried eggs, bacon, baked beans, sautéed mushrooms, grilled tomato, and black pudding (sausage made with pork blood), smothered in HP sauce (a vinegar base mixed with fruit and spices). The full brekky is served in B&Bs, pubs, and cafes across the country. Toast smothered in jam or Marmite (the most acquired of tastes—a salty, brown spread made from yeast) is a breakfast staple. The best dishes for lunch or dinner are roasts—beef, lamb, and Wiltshire hams—and **Yorkshire pudding,** a type of popover drizzled with meat juices. **Bangers and mash** and **bubble and squeak,** despite their intriguing names, are simply sausages and potatoes and cabbage and potatoes, respectively. Vegetables, often boiled into a flavorless mush, are typically the weakest part of a meal. Beware the British salad, which is often just a plate of lettuce and sweetened mayonnaise called "salad cream." Be careful, too, of sandwiches with hidden mayonnaise (frequently called "club sauce") and butter. Brits make their **desserts** ("puddings" or "afters") exceedingly sweet and gloopy. Sponges, trifles, tarts, and the unfortunately named spotted dick (spongy currant cake) will satiate the sweetest tooth.

ENGLAND

Pub grub is fast, filling, and a fine option for budget travelers. Try savory pies like **Cornish pasties** (PASS-tees), **shepherd's pie,** and **steak and kidney pie.** For those on a serious budget, the **ploughman's lunch** (bread, cheese, and pickles) is a staple in country pubs and can be divine. The local "chippy," or chip shop, sells deep-fried **fish and chips** dripping with grease, salt, and vinegar in a paper cone. Seek out **outdoor markets** for fresh bread and dairy—try **Stilton cheese** with **baps** (bread rolls). Chain stores **Boots, Benjys, Marks & Spencer,** and **Pret A Manger** sell an impressive array of ready-made sandwiches. Crisps, or potato chips, come in astonishing variety, with flavors like prawn cocktail. Try Chinese, Turkish, Lebanese, and especially Indian cuisines—Britain offers some of the best **tandoori** and **curry** outside India. Recently hailed as "a true British national dish" by Britain's foreign secretary, chicken tikka masala was found in a survey by the Food Intelligence Service to be the most popular plate in Britain.

British **"tea"** refers to both a drink and a social custom. The ritual refreshment, accompanying almost every meal, is served strong with milk. The standard tea, colloquially known as a **cuppa,** is PG Tips or Tetley. More refined cups specify particular blends such as **Earl Grey** and **Darjeeling.** Afternoon **high tea** includes cooked meats, salad, sandwiches, and pastries. **Cream tea,** a specialty of Cornwall and Devon, includes toast, shortbread, crumpets, scones, and jam, accompanied by **clotted cream** (a cross between whipped cream and butter). The summer teatime potion **Pimm's** is a sangria-esque punch of fruit juices and gin (the recipe is a well-guarded secret). On the softer side, super-sweet fizzy drinks **Lilt** and **Tango** as well as the popular juice **Ribena** keep whistles wet.

PUBS AND BITTER. Sir William Harcourt believed that English history was made in pubs as much as in the Houses of Parliament. Brits rapidly develop loyalty for neighborhood establishments, which in turn tend to cater to their regulars and develop a particular character. Pubs are everywhere—even the smallest village can support a decent pub crawl. The drinking age is an inconsistently enforced 18, and to enter a pub you need only be 14.

Bitter, named for its sharp, hoppy aftertaste, is a standard pub drink. It should be hand-pumped or pulled from the tap at cellar temperature into government-stamped pint glasses (20 oz.) or the more modest half-pint glass. Real ale retains a diehard cult of connoisseurs in the shadow of giant corporate breweries. Brown, pale, and India pale ales—less common varieties—all have a heavy flavor with noticeable hop. **Stout,** the distinctive subspecies of ale, is rich, dark, and creamy. Try **Irish Guinness,** with its silky foam head. Most draft ales and stouts are served at room temperature, but if you can't stand the heat, try a lager, a precursor of American beer typically served cold. Cider is a fermented apple juice served sweet or dry. Variations on the standard pint include black velvet, which is stout mixed with champagne; black and tan, layers of stout and ale; and snakebite, lager and cider with black currant syrup or Ribena.

Since WWI, government-imposed closing times have restricted pub hours. In England and Wales, drinks are usually served 11am-11pm from Monday to Saturday and noon-3pm and 7-10:30pm Sunday; more flexible hours are in place in Scotland. A bell or the phrase "Last orders!" marks the last call 10min. before closing time. When the bar officially closes, the bar staff traditionally shouts, "Time at the bar!" or (more fun), "Time gentlemen please!" Controversial legislation passed in 2003 allows pubs, clubs, and supermarkets in England and Wales to obtain special licenses and increasingly flexible opening hours—creating the 24hr. pub. Pubs without licenses circumvent closing times by serving food or obtaining an entertainment license.

THE ARTS

LANGUAGE AND LITERATURE

Eclipsed only by Mandarin Chinese in sheer number of speakers, the English language has a history that reflects the diversity of the hundreds of millions who use it today. Once a minor Germanic dialect, English incorporated words and phrases from Danish, French, and Latin, providing even its earliest word-smiths with a vast vocabulary rivaled by few world languages. Throughout centuries of British colonialism, the language continued to borrow from other tongues and supplied a literary and popular voice for people far removed from the British Isles. Welsh (p. 465) and Scottish (p. 541) are treated separately.

BARDS AND BIBLES. Britain is undeniably the birthplace of much of the world's best literature. A strong oral tradition informed most of the earliest poetry in English, little of which survives. The best-known piece of Anglo-Saxon (Old English) poetry is *Beowulf* (c. 700-1000), a tale of an egoistic prince, his heroic deeds, and his ultimate defeat in a battle with a dragon. The unknown author of *Sir Gawain and the Green Knight* (c. 1375) narrates a romance of Arthurian chivalry in which the bedroom becomes a battlefield and a young knight journeys on a mysterious quest. **Geoffrey Chaucer** tapped into the more spirited side of Middle English: his *Canterbury Tales* (c. 1387) remain some of the sauciest, most incisive stories in the English canon and poke fun at all stations of English life. **John Wycliffe** made the Bible accessible to the masses, translating it from Latin to English in the 1380s. **William Tyndale** followed suit in 1525, and his work became the model for the popular **King James** version (completed in 1611).

THE ENGLISH RENAISSANCE. English literature flourished under the reign of Elizabeth I (1559-1603). **Sir Philip Sidney's** sonnet sequences and **Edmund Spenser's** moral allegories like *The Faerie Queene* earned favor at court, while **John Donne** and **George Herbert** crafted metaphysical poetry. Playwright **Christopher Marlowe** lost his life in a pub brawl, but not before he produced popular plays of temptation and damnation such as *Dr. Faustus* (c. 1588). **Ben Jonson,** when he wasn't languishing in jail, redefined satiric comedy in works like *Volpone* (1606). The son of a glove-maker from Stratford-upon-Avon (p. 280), **William Shakespeare** proved to be a writer and linguistic innovator whose influence and brilliance would be impossible to overstate. He coined the words "scuffle," "lonely," "arouse," and "skim milk," among others, leading the world to view him as, in the words of literary critic Harold Bloom, the "inventor of the human." (OK, so maybe his brilliance *is* possible to overstate.)

HOW NOVEL! Britain's civil and religious turmoil in the late 16th and early 17th centuries spurred a huge volume of brilliant literature with theological concerns, like **John Milton's** epic *Paradise Lost* (1667) and **John Bunyan's** allegorical *Pilgrim's Progress* (1678). In the 18th century, **John Dryden** penned neoclassical poetry, **Alexander Pope** satires, and **Dr. Samuel Johnson** his idiosyncratic dictionary. In 1719, **Daniel Defoe** inaugurated the era of the English novel with his swashbuckling *Robinson Crusoe*. Authors like **Samuel Richardson** (*Clarissa*, 1749) and **Fanny Burney** (*Evelina*, 1778) perfected the form, while **Henry Fielding's** wacky *Tom Jones* (1749) and **Laurence Sterne's** experimental *Tristram Shandy* (1759-67) pushed its limits. **Jane Austen's** intricate narratives portrayed the modes and manners of the early 19th century. In the Victorian period, poverty and social change spawned the sentimental novels of **Charles Dickens.** *Oliver Twist* (1837-39) and *David Copperfield* (1849-50) draw on the bleakness of his childhood in Portsmouth (p. 178) and portray the harsh liv-

ENGLAND

ing conditions of working-class Londoners. Secluded in the wild Yorkshire moors (see Haworth, p. 420), the **Brontë sisters** staved off tuberculosis and crafted the tumultuous romances *Wuthering Heights* (Emily; 1847), *Jane Eyre,* and *Villette* (both Charlotte; 1847 and 1853). **George Eliot** (Mary Ann Evans) wrote her intricately detailed *Middlemarch: A Study of Provincial Life* in 1871. *Tess of the d'Urbervilles* (1891) and *Jude the Obscure* (1895) by **Thomas Hardy** mark a somber end to the Victorian age.

ROMANTICISM AND RESPONSE. Partly in reaction to the rationalism of the preceding century, the **Romantic** movement generated turbulent verse that celebrated the transcendent beauty of nature, the power of imagination, and the profound influence of childhood experiences. Reclusive painter-poet **William Blake** printed *The Marriage of Heaven and Hell* using brilliantly painted etched plates in 1790. **William Wordsworth** and **Samuel Taylor Coleridge** wrote the watershed collection *Lyrical Ballads*, which included "Tintern Abbey" (p. 476) and "The Rime of the Ancient Mariner," in the late 1790s. Wordsworth's poetry reflects on a long, full life—he drew inspiration from the Lakes (p. 383) and Snowdonia (p. 516)—but many of his contemporaries died tragically young. The astonishing prodigy **John Keats,** who concocted the Romantic maxim "beauty is truth, truth beauty," succumbed to tuberculosis at 26. Lyric poet and advocate of vegetarianism **Percy Bysshe Shelley** drowned off the Tuscan coast at 29. The pansexual heartthrob **Lord Byron** defined the heroic archetype in *Don Juan* (1819-24) and died fighting in the Greek War of Independence at the age of 36.

The poetry of the Victorian age struggled with the impact of social changes and religious skepticism. **Alfred, Lord Tennyson** spun verse about faith and doubt for over a half-century and inspired a medievalist revival with Arthurian idylls like "The Lady of Shalott" (1842). Celebrating the grotesque, Robert Browning composed piercing dramatic monologues, and his wife Elizabeth Barrett counted the ways she loved him in *Sonnets from the Portuguese* (1850). Meanwhile, fellow female poet **Christina Rossetti** envisioned the fantastical world of "Goblin Market" (1862). **Matthew Arnold** abandoned poetry in 1867 to become the greatest cultural critic of the day, and Jesuit priest **Gerard Manley Hopkins** penned tortuous verse with a unique "sprung rhythm" that makes him the chief forerunner of poetic modernism.

THE MODERN AGE. "On or about December 1910," wrote **Virginia Woolf,** "human nature changed." Woolf, a key member of London's bohemian intellectual **Bloomsbury Group,** captured the spirit of the time and the real life of the mind in her novels. She and Irish expatriate **James Joyce** were among the groundbreaking practitioners of **Modernism** (c. 1910-30). **TS Eliot's** *The Waste Land* (1922), a schizophrenic poem journeying through diverse cultural influences, is one of the 20th century's most important works. Reacting to the Great War, Eliot portrays London as a fragmented and barren desert in his difficult, highly allusive verse. **DH Lawrence** explored tensions in the British working-class family and challenged sexual convention in *Sons and Lovers* (1913). Although he spoke only a few words of English when he arrived in Britain at 21, **Joseph Conrad** demonstrated his mastery of the language in *Heart of Darkness* (1902) and in various novellas. Disillusionment with imperialism surfaces in **EM Forster's** half-Modernist, half-Romantic novels, particularly *A Passage to India* (1924). Authors of the 1930s captured the tumult and depression of the decade: **Evelyn Waugh** turned a ruthlessly satirical eye on society and **Graham Greene** explored moral ambiguity. The sardonic poet **WH Auden,** disturbed by the violence of his age, wrote in 1939, "We must love one another or die."

LATER TWENTIETH-CENTURY. Fascism and the horrors of WWII motivated musings on the nature of evil; **George Orwell's** dystopic *1984* (1949) strove to strip the world of memory and words of meaning. Anthony Burgess's *A Clockwork Orange* (1962) imagines the violence and anarchy of a not-so-distant future. The end of empire, rising affluence, and the growing gap between classes splintered British literature. Nostalgia pervades the poetry of **Philip Larkin** and **John Betjeman,** and an angry working class found voices in **Allan Sillitoe** and **Kingsley Amis.** Postcolonial voices like Indian expatriate **Salman Rushdie** and 2002 Nobel laureate **VS Naipaul** have found a place in British literary tradition. Today, Britain's hip literary circle includes working writers **AS Byatt, Martin Amis, Kazuo Ishiguro, Zadie Smith,** and the masterful neo-realist **Ian McEwan.** British playwrights continue to innovate: **Harold Pinter** infuses living rooms with horrifying silences, **Tom Stoppard** shows off dazzling wordplay and wit in plays like *Rosencrantz and Guildenstern are Dead* (1967), and **Caryl Churchill** provides blistering commentary on the state of Britain in plays like *Cloud Nine* (1988).

OUTSIDE THE CLASSROOM. English literature thrives away from the ivory tower. The mysteries of **Dorothy L. Sayers** and **Agatha Christie** are read worldwide, while the espionage novels of **John le Carré** and **Ian Fleming,** inventor of James Bond, provide more in-your-face thrills. **PG Wodehouse,** creator of Jeeves, the consummate butler, adeptly satirizes the idle aristocrat. **James Herriot** (Alf Wight), beloved author of *All Creatures Great and Small* (1972), chronicled his work as a young veterinarian. **Douglas Adams** parodied sci-fi in his humorous series *Hitchhiker's Guide to the Galaxy*, and **Helen Fielding's** hapless *Bridget Jones's Diary* speaks on behalf of singletons everywhere. British children's literature delights all ages: **Lewis Carroll's** *Alice's Adventures in Wonderland* (1865), **CS Lewis's** *Chronicles of Narnia* (1950-56), **Roald Dahl** stories such as *Charlie and the Chocolate Factory* (1964), *The Witches* (1983), and *Matilda* (1988), and **Brian Jacques's** *Redwall* series (1986-2005) enjoy continued popularity. A linguist named **JRR Tolkien,** Lewis's companion in letters and Oxford pub-readings (p. 279), wrote tales of elves and wizards, including *The Hobbit* (1934) and *Lord of the Rings* (1954-56). **Nick Hornby** writes witty novels like *High Fidelity* and *About a Boy*. Earning herself a fortune greater than that of the queen, **JK Rowling** has enchanted the world with her saga of juvenile wizardry in the *Harry Potter* series.

ART AND ARCHITECTURE

HOUSES OF GODS AND MEN. Early English architects often borrowed styles from mainland Europe, although some are particular to Britain. The Normans introduced **Romanesque** architecture (round arches and thick walls) in the 11th century, and the British adopted the same fashion in the imposing Durham cathedral (p. 439). The **Gothic** style, originating in France (12th-15th centuries), ushered in intricate, haunting buildings like the cathedrals of Wells (p. 217) and Salisbury (p. 200). By the 14th century, the English had developed the unique **perpendicular style** of window tracery, apparent at King's College Chapel in Cambridge (p. 329). Sadly, the **Suppression of Monasteries** in 1536 under Henry VIII spurred the wanton smashing of stained glass and even of entire churches, leaving picturesque ruins scattered along the countryside (like Rievaulx, p. 427, or Glastonbury, p. 215). After the Renaissance, architects used new engineering methods, evident in Christopher Wren's fantastic dome on **Saint Paul's Cathedral** (p. 117), built in 1666.

The architecture of early British homes progressed from the **stone dwellings** of pre-Christian folk (see Skara Brae, p. 676) to the Romans' **forts and villas** (see

Hadrian's Wall, p. 456) to the famed medieval castles. The earliest of these, the hilltop **motte-and-bailey forts,** arrived with William the Conqueror in 1066 (see Round Tower of Windsor, p. 267, or Carisbrooke,p. 185) and progressed into tall, square **Norman keeps** like the **Tower of London** (p. 116). Warmongering Edward I constructed a string of astonishing concentric castles along the Welsh coast (Harlech, p. 521; Caernarfon, p. 524; Beaumaris, p. 530; Caerphilly, p. 474). By the 14th century, the advent of the cannon made castles obsolete, yet they lived on as palaces for the oligarchy (see the breathtaking Warwick, p. 301). During the Renaissance, the wealthy built sumptuous **Tudor homes,** like Henry VIII's Hampton Court (p. 149). In the 18th century, both the heady **Baroque** style of Castle Howard (p. 413) and the severe **Palladian** symmetry of Houghton Hall (p. 338) were in vogue. **Stately homes** like Howard and Houghton were furnished with **Chippendale** furniture and surrounded by equally stately grounds and **gardens** (see Blenheim Palace, p. 280). The Victorians built in the ornate **Neo-Gothic revival** (see the Houses of Parliament, p. 120) and **neoclassical** (see the British Museum, p. 133) styles. Today, hotshots (and colleagues) **Richard Rogers** and **Norman Foster** vie for bragging rights as England's most influential architects, littering London with avant-garde additions like the **Lloyd's Building** (p. 123), City Hall, and a whole host of Millennium constructions.

> **TIP**
> **LEARN A NEW LANGUAGE.** The sheer number of castles and cathedrals in England should be sufficient motivation to learn the words associated with their architecture. A castle's **keep** is the main tower and residence hall. Some early keeps sit atop a steep mound called a **motte.** The slender external wall supports that hold up the tallest castles and the loftiest cathedrals are **buttresses.** A **vault** is a stone ceiling, a ribbed vault is held up by spidery stone arcs or **ribs,** and the **webs** are the spaces in between ribs. Most churches are **cruciform,** or cross-shaped. The head of the cross is the **choir,** the arms are the **transepts,** and support of the cross is the **nave.** Medieval churches usually have a three-tiered nave: the ground level is the **arcade,** the middle level (where monks would walk and ponder scripture) is the **triforium,** and the highest level (where the light comes in) is the **clerestory.** The beautifully detailed stained glass is outlined by **tracery,** the lacy stonework that holds it in place.

ON THE CANVAS. Britain's early religious art, including **illuminated manuscripts,** gave way to secular patronage and the institution of court painters. Renaissance art in England was largely dominated by foreign portraitists such as **Hans Holbein the Younger** (1497-1543) and Flemish masters **Peter Paul Rubens** (1577-1640) and **Anthony van Dyck** (1599-1641). **Nicholas Hilliard** (1547-1619) was the first English-born success of the period. Vanity, and thus portraiture, continued to flourish into the 18th century, with the satirical London scenes of **William Hogarth** (1697-1764), classically inspired poses of **Joshua Reynolds** (1723-92), and provincial backdrops of **Thomas Gainsborough** (1727-1788). Encouraged by a nationwide interest in gardening, **landscape painting** peaked during the 19th century. Beyond the literary realm, Romanticism inspired the vibrant rustic scenes of **John Constable** and the violent sense of the sublime depicted in **JMW Turner's** stunning seascapes. The Victorian fascination with reviving old art forms sparked movements like the Italian-inspired, damsel-laden Pre-Raphaelite school, propagated by **John Everett Millais** (1829-96) and **Dante Gabriel Rossetti** (1828-82). Victorians also dabbled in new art forms like photography and took advantage of early mass media with engravings and cartoons. Modernist trends from the continent such as Cubism and Expressionism were picked up by **Wyndham Lewis** (1882-1957) and sculptor **Henry Moore** (1898-1986). WWII broke art wide open yielding experimental, edgy works by **Francis Bacon** (1909-92) and **Lucian Freud,** whose controversial portrait of the queen was unveiled in 2002. **David Hockney** (b. 1937) and **Bridget Riley** (b. 1931) gave American pop art a dose of British wit. The monolithic, market-controlling collector **Charles Saatchi,** the success of the new Tate Modern (p. 132), the infamy of the Turner Prize, and the rise of the conceptual and sensationalist **Young British Artists (YBAs)** have invigorated Britain's contemporary art scene. The multimedia artists **Damien Hirst** (b. 1965) and **Tracey Emin** (b. 1963) have become the media-savvy *enfants terribles* of modern art. Art galleries in London (see the Tate Britain, p. 133; the British Museum, p. 133; the National Gallery, p. 132; White Cube, p. 137; the Serpentine, p. 124) are among the world's best. Beyond the museums, Bristol-based graffiti artist **Banksy** creates phenomenal and thought-provoking master-pieces for the public with the simple tools of a street artist.

FASHION. First introduced as a trench coat lining, the **Burberry** check, a trade-marked design, has become synonymous with English style. Inspired by the hip street energy of London in the 1960s and movements like op and pop art, England's fashion designers achieved notoriety, although not the fame of continental designers. **Mary Quant** (b. 1934) sparked a fashion revolution by popularizing the miniskirt in 1966. **Vivienne Westwood** (b. 1941) is credited with originating punk fashion in the early 1970s. Young British designers have made their mark at prestigious fashion houses, such as **John Galliano** (b. 1960) at Dior. In recent years, several designers have formed independent houses, as did ex-Givenchy star **Alexander McQueen** (b. 1970) and Sir Paul's daughter, ex-Chloé designer **Stella McCartney** (b. 1972). As British style tends to predict fashions in America, look for euro-mullets and tights to become all the rage across the pond.

MUSIC

CLASSICAL. In the Middle Ages, traveling **minstrels** sang narrative folk ballads and Arthurian romances in the courts of the rich. During the Renaissance, English ears were tuned to cathedral anthems, psalms, and madrigals, along with the occasional lute performance. **Henry Purcell** (1659-95) crafted anthems, instrumental music for Shakespeare's plays, and the opera *Dido and Aeneas.* In the 18th century, regarded as England's musical Dark Age, Britain welcomed visits of the foreign geniuses Mozart, Haydn, and **George Frideric Handel,** a German composer who wrote operas in the Italian style but spent most of his life in Britain. Thanks to Handel's influence, England experienced a wave of **operamania** in the early 1700s. Enthusiasm waned when listeners realized they couldn't understand what the performers were saying; John Gay satirized the opera house in *The Beggar's Opera* (1727), a low-brow comedy in which Italian arias was set to English folk tunes. Today's audiences are familiar with the operettas of **WS Gilbert** (1836-1911) and **Arthur Sullivan** (1842-1900). Although the pair were rumored to hate each other, they managed to produce successes like *The Pirates of Penzance.* A second renaissance of more serious music began under **Edward Elgar** (1857-1934), whose *Pomp and Circumstance* is a staple march of American graduation ceremonies.

Also borrowing from folk melodies, **Ralph Vaughan Williams** (1872-1958) and **John Ireland** (1879-1962) brought musical modernism to the isles. The world wars provided adequate inspiration for this continued musical resurgence, provoking **Benjamin Britten's** (1913-76) heartbreaking *War Requiem* and **Michael Tippett's** (1905-98) humanitarian oratorio, *A Child of Our Time.* The popular

ENGLAND

Proms (short for "promenades") at Royal Albert Hall celebrate classical music with an eight-week festival of whistle-blowing and flag-waving. Commercially lucrative music—like **Oliver Knussen's** one-act opera of Maurice Sendak's *Where the Wild Things Are* and **Andrew Lloyd Webber's** blend of opera, pop, and falling chandeliers—became popular in the 1980s and 90s.

THE BRITISH ARE COMING. Invaded by American blues and rock and roll following WWII, Britain staged a musical offensive unprecedented in history. The **British Invasion** groups of the 60s infiltrated the world with a daring, inventive, and controversial sound. Out of Liverpool, **The Beatles** became gods with their moppy 'dos and maddeningly catchy hooks. The edgier lyrics and grittier sound of the **Rolling Stones** shifted teens' thoughts from "I Wanna Hold Your Hand" to "Let's Spend the Night Together." Over the next 20 years, England exported the hard-driving **Kinks**, the Urban "mod" sound of **The Who**, and guitar gurus Eric Clapton of **Cream** and Jimmy Page of **Led Zeppelin**.

ANARCHY IN THE UK. Despite (or perhaps because of) England's conservative national character, homosexuality became central to the flamboyant musical scene of the mid-70s. British rock split as the theatrical excesses of **glam rock** performers like **Queen, Elton John,** and **David Bowie** contrasted with the conceptual, album-oriented art rock emanating from **Pink Floyd** and **Yes.** Dissonant **punk rock** bands like **Stiff Little Fingers** and **The Clash** emerged from Britain's ailing industrial centers, especially Manchester. London's **The Sex Pistols** stormed the scene with profane and wildly successful antics—their angry 1977 single "God Save the Queen" topped the charts despite being banned. Sharing punk's anti-establishment impulses, the metal music of **Ozzy Osbourne** and **Iron Maiden** still attracts a cult following. Sheffield's **Def Leppard** carried the hard-rock-big-hair ethic through the 80s, while punk offshoots like **The Cure** and **goth** bands rebelled during the era of conservative Thatcherism.

I WANT MY MTV. Buoyed by a booming economy, British bands achieved popularity on both sides of the Atlantic thanks to the advent of MTV. **Dire Straits** introduced the first computer-animated music video, while **Duran Duran,** the **Eurythmics, Tears for Fears,** and the **Police** enjoyed top-10 hits. England also produced some of the giants of the lipstick-and-synthesizer age, including **George Michael,** the **Pet Shop Boys, Bananarama,** and **Boy George.** The music scene splintered along regional and musical lines into countless fragments of electronica, punk, and rock. Modern balladists **The Smiths** developed a cult following. At the end of the decade, a crop of bands from Manchester, spearheaded by **New Order,** galvanized post-punk and the early rave movement. Any clubber can tell you about England's influence on dance music, from the **Chemical Brothers** and Brighton-bred **Fatboy Slim** to the house, trip-hop, and ska sounds of **Basement Jaxx, Massive Attack,** and **Jamiroquai.** Britpop resurged in the 1990s: **Blur** and **Oasis** left trashed hotel rooms and screaming fans in their wake. The tremendous popularity of American grunge rock spread to the UK, where **Radiohead** has become arguably the most influential British rock band since The Beatles. The UK also produced some brilliant, awful pop, including **Robbie Williams** (survivor of the bubblegummy Take That) and the **Spice Girls.**

These days, socially conscious **Coldplay** is one of the UK's bestselling rock exports (thanks in large part to soccer moms and dentist offices). Modern post-punk and New Wave bands like **Bloc Party** and **Franz Ferdinand** enjoy indie cred and impressive fan bases. A product of instant Internet success, **Lily Allen** has established herself as a major player in the world of commercial pop, winning audiences with an upbeat sound and sassy attitude. Meanwhile, **Amy Winehouse** smooths over her rough-and-tumble personality with deep, soulful R&B vocals.

ENGLAND

Formed in 2005, ◪**The Kooks** have exploded out of Brighton to climb the charts with catchy pop rock tunes, and postmodern hipsters **The Rakes** and **The Pigeon Detectives** are drawing attention from young fans of guitar rock revival.

UK GARAGE. Stumble into any nightclub in Britain and feel the two-step sub-bass bypass your ears and get straight to shaking your body. After the mid-90s, a mix of drum and bass and jungle music became **UK Garage (UKG)**—electronica produced in basements and bedrooms around South London and made popular through repeated play on pirate radio stations. Characterized by island rhythms and dark-sounding bass lines that skip every other beat, UKG eventually split into two sub genres: **dubstep** (slow and minimalist) and **grime** (sounding like sped-up reggae instrumentals with rap-like vocals). **Skream** and **Benga** are exemplars of dubstep, and the popularity of **Wiley** and Mike Skinner's ◪**The Streets** stands testament to grime's relative accessibility.

FILM

British film has endured an uneven history, alternating between relative independence from Hollywood and emigration of talent to America. **Charlie Chaplin** and Archibald Alec Leach (a.k.a. **Cary Grant**) were both British-born but made their names in US films. The **Royal Shakespeare Company** has seen heavyweight alumni **Dame Judi Dench, Dame Maggie Smith, Sir Ian McKellen,** and Jeremy Irons make the transition to cinema. Master of suspense **Alfred Hitchcock** snared audiences with films produced on both sides of the Atlantic, terrifying shower-takers everywhere. In a career spanning six decades, Hitchcock saw the transition from silent film to cinema in color. The 60s phenomenon of "swingin' London" created new momentum for the film industry and jump-started international interest in British culture. American Richard Lester made **The Beatles'** *A Hard Day's Night* in 1963, and a year later Scottish **Sean Connery** downed the first of many martinis as **James Bond** in *Dr. No.*

Elaborate costume drama and offbeat independent films characterized British film in the 80s and 90s. The sagas *Chariots of Fire* (1981) and *Gandhi* (1982) swept the Oscars in successive years. Director-producer team **Merchant-Ivory** led the way in adaptations of British novels like Forster's *A Room with a View* (1986). **Kenneth Branagh** focused his talents on adapting Shakespeare for the screen, with glossy, well-received works such as *Hamlet* (1996). **Nick Park** took claymation and British quirkiness to a new level with his *Wallace and Gromit* shorts and the blockbuster feature film *Chicken Run* (2000). The dashing **Guy Ritchie** (former Mr. Madonna) tapped into Tarantino-esque conventions with his dizzying *Lock, Stock and Two Smoking Barrels* (1998), followed by the transatlantic smash *Snatch* (2000), although the film's success may or may not have had something to do with American stud Brad Pitt.

Recent British films have garnered a fair number of international awards; the working-class feel-goods *The Full Monty* (1997) and *Billy Elliot* (2000); Mike Leigh's affecting *Secrets and Lies* (1996) and costume extravaganza *Topsy-Turvy* (1999) as well as the endearing comedies *Bend it Like Beckham* (2002) and *Love, Actually* (2003) have all taken home awards from sources like the Academy, Cannes, and the Golden Globes. Then, of course, there is the *Harry Potter* franchise, which kicked off in 2001 and continues to break box-office records. It has been filmed at gorgeous Alnwick Castle, Christ Church College, Oxford (p. 273), and in Fort William of the Scottish Highlands (p. 645).

ENGLAND

MEDIA

ALL THAT'S FIT TO PRINT. In a culture with a rich print-media history, the influence of newspapers remains enormous. The UK's plethora of national newspapers yields a wide range of political viewpoints. *The Times*, long a model of thoughtful discretion, has turned Tory under the ownership of Rupert Murdoch. *The Daily Telegraph*, dubbed "Torygraph," is fairly conservative and old-fashioned. *The Guardian* (often known as "The Guarniad" after its infamous typos) leans left, while *The Independent* stays true to its name. Of the tabloids, *The Sun*, Murdoch-owned and better known for its Page Three topless pin-up than for its reporting, is the most influential. Among the others, *The Daily Mail*, *The Daily Express*, and *The London Evening Standard* (the only evening paper) make serious attempts at popular journalism, although the first two tend to position themselves as the conservative voice of Middle England. *The Daily Mirror* and *The News of the World* are as shrill and lewd as *The Sun*, laying bare the secrets (and bodies) of showbiz and sports stars. *The Financial Times*, on pleasing pink paper, distributes the news of the City of London. Although closely associated with their sister dailies, Sunday newspapers are actually separate entities. *The Sunday Times*, *The Sunday Telegraph*, *The Independent on Sunday*, and the highly polished *Observer*—the world's oldest paper and now part of *The Guardian*—offer detailed arts, sports, and news coverage, together with more "soft bits" than the dailies.

A quick glance around any High St. newsstand will prove that Britain has no shortage of magazines. World affairs are covered with candor and wit by *The Economist*. *The New Statesman* on the left and *The Spectator* on the right cover politics and the arts with verve. The satirical *Private Eye* is subversive, witty, and overtly political. Some of the best music mags in the world—the highly biased but indispensable *New Musical Express (NME)*, the more intellectual *Q*, and *Gramophone*—are UK-based. Movie and other entertainment news comes in the oversized *Empire*. The indispensable London journal *Time Out* has an exhaustive listings guide to the city; its website (www.timeout.com) also keeps tabs on events in Dublin and Edinburgh. Recent years have seen the explosion of "lads' mags" such as *FHM* and *Loaded*, which feature scantily clad women and articles on beer, "shagging," and "pulling." London-born *Maxim* offers similar content for a marginally more mature crowd. Britain has excellent fashion glossies—there are British versions of *Vogue*, *Mademoiselle*, and *Elle*, which often come in a handy smaller size. *Tatler*, a *W*-made-*Vanity Fair*, is witty, pretty, and snobby. *Hello*, *OK*, and a bevy of imitators feed the insatiable appetites of royal-watchers and B-list aficionados.

ON THE AIRWAVES. The **BBC (British Broadcasting Corporation**, known as "the Beeb") established its reputation with radio services. The World Service provides countries around the world with a glimpse into British life. Within the UK, the BBC has **Radios 1-7,** covering news (4), sports (5), and a spectrum of music from pop (1) to classical and jazz (3) to catch-all (2 and 6)—and, recently, a broadcast for kids (7).

Aside from the daytime suds, British television has brought the world such mighty comic wonders as *Monty Python's Flying Circus*, *Mr. Bean*, *Da Ali G. Show* (booyakasha!), and the across-the-pond hit *The Office*. The BBC has produced some stellar adapted miniseries; 1996's *Pride and Prejudice* sparked an international "Darcy fever" for **Colin Firth** and is widely considered one of the best film versions of Austen's work. Britain currently suffers from an obsession with home-improvement shows, cooking programs, and voyeur TV (they invented *Big Brother* and *Pop Idol*). A commercial-free repository of wit and innovation, the BBC broadcasts on two national channels. **BBC1** carries news and Britcoms, while **BBC2** telecasts cultural programs and fledgling sitcoms (like *AbFab, Blackadder, Coupling,* and *Little Britain*). **ITV,** Britain's first and most established commercial network, carries drama, comedy, and news. **Channel 4** has morning shows, highly respected arts programming, and imported American shows. **Channel 5** features late-night sports shows and action movies. Rupert Murdoch's satellite **Sky TV** shows football, *fútbol*, soccer, and other incarnations of the global game on its Sky Sports channel, while its Sky One channel broadcasts mostly American shows.

SPORTS

There is a great noise in the city caused by hustling over large balls, from which many evils arise which God forbid.
 —King Edward II, banning football in 1314

FOOTBALL. It's the "beautiful game," the world's most popular sport, and a British national obsession. The top 20 English football (soccer) **clubs** (teams) occupy the **Premier League,** populated with world-class players. The powerful Football Association (FA) regulates the British leagues and sponsors the contentious **FA Cup,** held every May in **Wembley,** where a new **National Stadium** opened in March 2007 with the second-largest capacity in Europe. The ultimate achievement for an English football club is to win the treble—the Premier League, the FA Cup, and the Champion's League (a competition between the top teams in several European countries). Clubs like Arsenal, Liverpool, and Everton dominate the Premier League perennially, but **Manchester United** (p. 367) is the red victory machine that many Brits love to hate. Even many Mancunians support the city's other club, Manchester City. Fans and paparazzi alike mourned the team's loss of celebrity star **David Beckham** to Real Madrid in 2003, and Beckham made even more fans weep when he signed with the US-based L.A. Galaxy in January 2007.

Unfortunately, the four British international teams (England, Scotland, Wales, and Northern Ireland compete as separate countries) haven't seen victory in the **World Cup** or in the **European Championships** since England's glorious 1966 World Cup win. The next World Cup will be in South Africa in 2010.

Over half a million fans attend professional matches in Britain every match-day weekend from mid-August to May, and they spend the few barren weeks of summer waiting for the publication of the coming season's **fixtures** (match schedules). It's almost like worship at postmodern cathedrals—grand, storied stadiums full of painted faces and team colors, resounding with rowdy choruses of uncannily synchronized (usually rude) songs. Intracity rivalries (London's Chelsea-Tottenham or Glasgow's "Auld Firm") have been known to divide families. Violence and vandalism used to dog the sport, but matches have become safer now that clubs offer seating-only tickets rather than standing spaces in the terraces, and clubs generally no longer allow drinking in the stands. **Hooligans** ("yobs" or "chavs") are usually on their worst behavior when the England national team plays abroad, while home games are a bit tamer.

OTHER GAMES. According to legend, **rugby** was born one glorious day in 1823 when William Webb Ellis, an inspired (or perhaps slightly confused) Rugby School student, picked up a soccer ball and ran it into the goal. Since then, rugby has evolved into a complex, subtle, and thoroughly lunatic game. The amateur **Rugby Union** and professional **Rugby League,** both 19th-century cre-

ENGLAND

ations, have slightly different rules and different numbers of players (15 and 13). In Britain, the former is associated with Scotland, Wales, and the Midlands, and the latter with northwest England. With little stoppage of play, no non-injury substitutions, and scanty protective gear, rugby is a melee of blood, mud, and drinking songs. An oval-shaped ball is carried or passed backward until the team can touch the ball down past the goal line (a "try" and worth 5 points) or kick it through the uprights (3 points). Club season runs from September to May. The culmination of international rugby is the **Rugby World Cup,** to be hosted by Australia in the fall of 2009.

Although fanatically followed in the Commonwealth, **cricket** remains confusing to the uninitiated. The game is played by two 11-player teams on a green, marked by two **wickets,** which look like three sticks with two bails (dowels) balancing on the top (see www.cricket.org for explanations and diagrams of these mysterious contraptions). In an inning, one team acts as **batsmen** and the other as **fielders.** The batting team sends up two batsmen, and a **bowler** from the fielding side throws the ball so that it bounces toward the wickets. The fielders try to get the batsmen out by **taking** the wickets (hitting the wickets so that the bails fall) or by catching the ball. The batsmen attempt to make as many runs as possible while protecting their wickets, scoring each time they switch places. The teams switch positions once 10 batsmen are out, and both sides usually bat twice. Matches last one to five days. We don't really get it either. International games are known as **Test** matches; the Ashes, named for the remains of a cricket bail, are the prize in England's Test series with Australia. Cricket has its own **World Cup,** set for February and March of 2011. London's **Lords** Cricket Ground is regarded as the spiritual home of the game.

Tennis became the game of the upper class in the 15th century, when Henry VII played in slimming black velvet. As the game developed, white became the traditional color, while today almost any garb goes—that is, except at **Wimbledon,** the uber-traditional grass-court Grand Slam event held in midsummer.

SNITCHED. Sadly, scientists and engineers have not yet developed magical broomsticks to play **Quidditch,** the imaginary sport of flying wizards popularized by the *Harry Potter* series. For now, Chasers and Seekers are stuck firmly on the ground, though this hasn't stopped some from forming Quidditch leagues and playing on college lawns.

HORSES AND COURSES. The Brits have a special affinity for their horses, demonstrated in the (now banned) tallyhooing of fox-killing excursions and Princess Anne's competition in **equestrian events** during the 1976 Olympics. In late June, **polo** devotees flock to the **Royal Windsor Cup.** The Royal Gold Cup Meeting at **Ascot** has occurred in the second half of June every summer since 1711, although some see it as an excuse for Brits of all strata to indulge in drinking and gambling while wearing over-the-top hats. Top hats also distinguish the famed **Derby** (DAR-bee), which has been run since 1780 on Epsom Racecourse, Surrey, on the first Saturday of June.

Britain remains a force in rowing, and the annual **Henley Royal Regatta,** on the Thames in Oxfordshire, is the most famous series of rowing races in the world. The five-day regatta ends on the first Sunday of July. The **Boat Race** (also on the Thames, but in London), between Oxford and Cambridge, enacts the traditional rivalry between the schools. Britain is the center of Formula One racecar design, and the **British Grand Prix** is held every July at Silverstone racecourse in Northamptonshire. Meanwhile, the **TT Races** bring hordes of screeching motorcycles to the Isle of Man (p. 393) during the early days of June.

ENGLAND

HOLIDAYS AND FESTIVALS

It's difficult to travel anywhere in Britain without bumping into some kind of festival. Below is a list of major festivals in England. The local tourist information center for any town can point you toward the nearest scene of revelry and merrymaking, and *Let's Go* lists individual events in the appropriate towns and cities. The chart below also includes some large nationwide festivals and public holidays. See the corresponding sections of Scotland (p. 544) and Wales (p. 466) for more country-specific festivals.

DATE IN 2009	NAME AND LOCATION	DESCRIPTION
January 26	Chinese New Year, London	Fireworks! Lots of fireworks!
April 23	St. George's Day	Honoring England's dragon-slaying patron saint.
May 2-24	Brighton Festival	Largest mixed-arts festival in England.
May 19-23	Chelsea Flower Show	The world's premier garden event.
May 30-June 12	TT Races, Isle of Man	101st anniversary of this annual road-racing celebration.
June 6	The Derby, Surrey	Horses and hats!
June 26-28	Glastonbury Festival	Britain's gigantic three-day homage to rock music.
June 16-20	Royal Ascot, York	Hats and horses!
June 22-July 5	Wimbledon	A lot of racquet and a big silver dish.
July 1-5	Henley Royal Regatta	The world's premier boat race.
August 21-31	Manchester Pride	A wild street party in Manchester's Gay Village.

ENGLAND

LONDON

When a man is tired of London, he is tired of life; for there is in London all that life can afford.
        —Samuel Johnson, 1777

 Those who journey to London expecting friendly, tea-drinking, Royal-loving gardeners may be astounded to find that London is equally the province of black-clad slinky young things who spend their nights lounging around shadowy Soho bars. The stereotypical Londoner is almost impossible to define: both the snooty Kensington resident and the owner of an Indian takeaway in East End hold equal claim to the title. Roman ruins stand next to thatched Shakespearean theaters, which jostle for space with glass skyscrapers and millennial landmarks. It's a dynamic, cosmopolitan city that defies simple categorization—administrative capital of Britain, financial center of Europe, world leader in the arts. While those who come to the city seeking a twee domain of bobbies and Beefeaters will probably be able to find it, you need only look at the array of hip restaurants or the queues in front of clubs to realize why they call it "Swinging London." The London buzz is continually on the move—every few years, a previously disregarded neighborhood explodes into cultural prominence. Most recently, South London has thrived with the rebirth of the South Bank and the thumping nightlife of Brixton, while East London has begun renewal projects to host the 2012 Olympic Games. If you're spending a significant amount of time in London, you'll find more extensive coverage in ▧Let's Go: London.

LONDON HIGHLIGHTS

GO ROYAL in stately Westminster at **Westminster Abbey** (p. 116) and at the **Houses of Parliament** p. 120); take tea with the queen at **Buckingham Palace** (p. 117); gaze up at the dome of **Saint Paul's Cathedral** p. 117) and the pigeons that nest there; and watch your head at the imposing **Tower of London** (p. 116). To cover the highlights of the South Bank, follow our **"Millennium Mile" Walking Tour** (p. 118).

GET LOST in the galleries of London's museums, some of the best in the world; most of the big names are free. The **British Museum** (p. 133) and the **Victoria and Albert Museum** p. 133) recap the glory days of the British Empire, while the **National Portrait Gallery** (p. 133) chronicles the life and times of those who ran it. The **National Gallery** (p. 132) holds the first half of the national collection, and the **Tate Modern** (p. 132) holds, well, everything modern. For a string of up-and-comers, head to galleries in the East End, including **Whitechapel** (p. 136) and **White Cube** (p. 137). The **Courtauld Galleries** (p. 134) at Somerset House are worth the admission fee.

INDULGE in world-renowned drama at **Shakespeare's Globe Theatre** (p. 126), an open-air venue where you can stand right in front of the stage as a "groundling," or take a seat in the **National Theatre** (p. 143) or **Royal Court Theatre** (p. 143). Head to a play in the **West End** (p. 141), which boasts the best of mega-musicals . Fringe theater is alive and well at the **Almeida** (p. 142) and **Donmar Warehouse** (p. 142).

RELAX for an afternoon in one of London's many parks, such as **Hyde Park** and **Kensington Gardens** (p. 124), the perfect escape from the summer heat or urban bustle.

LONDON	❶	❷	❸	❹	❺
ACCOMMODATIONS	under £25	£25-40	£41-55	£56-75	above £75
FOOD	under £6	£6-10	£11-15	£16-24	above £24

◪ INTERCITY TRANSPORTATION

BY PLANE

HEATHROW

Heathrow (☎08700 000 123; www.heathrowairport.com), 15min. by train or 1hr. by bus from central London, is one of the world's busiest international airports and holds four terminals.

Underground: ☎020 7222 1234, toll-free 08453 309 880; www.thetube.com. Heathrow's 2 Tube stations form a loop on the end of the Piccadilly Line—trains stop at **Heathrow Terminal 4** and then at **Heathrow Terminals 1, 2, 3** (both Zone 6) before heading back to central London (from central London 50-75min., every 5-10min., £4-10). Stairs are an integral part of most Tube stations. The Tube can be slow and confusing, especially for 1st-time travelers to London, but it is by far the cheapest route into central London. Don't be shy about asking the airport transportation information desks for help navigating the various lines.

Heathrow Express: ☎08456 001 515; www.heathrowexpress.com. A speedy, expensive train connection from Heathrow to Paddington (15min.; daily every 15min. 5:10am-11:40pm; £15.50, round-trip £29, £2 more if bought on train; AmEx/MC/V). Railpasses and Travelcards not valid. Discounts for day returns, students, and groups. Paddington has check-in facilities. Ticket counters at Heathrow accept foreign currency.

Heathrow Connect: ☎08456 786 975; www.heathrowconnect.com. A cheaper alternative to the Heathrow Express, with direct routes from Paddington, Ealing Broadway, West Ealing, Hanwell, Southall, and Hayes to Terminals 1, 2, and 3 (to Paddington, 20min., daily every 25min. 4:45am-11:30pm; £9.50 to Paddington). Railcards accepted. For Terminal 4, take the 1st Heathrow Express train.

National Express: ☎08705 808 080; www.nationalexpress.com. Runs between Heathrow and Victoria Coach (40-90min.; about every 20min. daily Heathrow-Victoria 5:35am-9:35pm, Victoria-Heathrow 7:15am-11:30pm; from £8; AmEx/MC/V). Railpasses and Travelcards not valid.

Taxis: Licensed (black) cabs cost at least £50 and take 1-1¾hr.

GATWICK

Thirty miles south of the city, Gatwick (☎0870 0002 468; www.gatwickairport.com) seems distant, but train services make transportation a breeze. The **train station** is in the **South Terminal.** Gatwick Express (☎0845 850 1530; www.gatwickexpress.com) services Victoria Station (30-35min.; departs Gatwick every 15min. 5am-11:45pm; £17, round-trip £29). First Capital Connect (☎08457 484 950; www.firstcapitalconnect.co.uk) also heads to King's Cross Station, stopping at London Bridge and Blackfriars (50min., every 30min., £10). Gatwick's distance from London makes **road services** slow and unpredictable. National Express's **Airbus A5** (contact info same as Heathrow) goes to Victoria Coach Station (1½hr., at least every hr. 4:50am-10:15pm; from £6.60). Never take a **taxi** from Gatwick to London; the trip will take over an hour and cost at least £95.

Central London

● SIGHTS

Apsley House, 1 — C4
The Barbican, 2 — E3
Benjamin Franklin House, 3 — D4
British Library, 4 — D2
British Museum, 5 — D3
Buckingham Palace, 6 — C4
Buckingham Palace Gardens, 7 — C4
Cabinet War Rooms, 8 — D4
Chelsea Physic Garden, 9 — C5

Chinatown, 10 — D4
Courtauld Institute Galleries, 11 — D4
Design Museum, 12 — F4
Eversholt Village, 13 — D2
The Gilbert Collection, 14 — D4
Guildhall Art Gallery, 15 — E3
The Houses of Parliament, 16 — D4
ICA, 17 — D4
Imperial War Museum, 18 — E5
Kensington Palace, 19 — B4
London Eye, 20 — D4

Madame Tussaud's, 21 — C3
Marble Arch, 22 — C3
Millennium Bridge, 23 — E4
Monument, 24 — F4
Museum of London, 25 — E3
National Gallery, 26 — D4
National Portrait Gallery, 27 — D4
Natural History Museum, 28 — B5
Royal Academy of Arts, 29 — D4
Royal Albert Hall, 30 — B4
Royal Courts of Justice, 31 — E3

LONDON

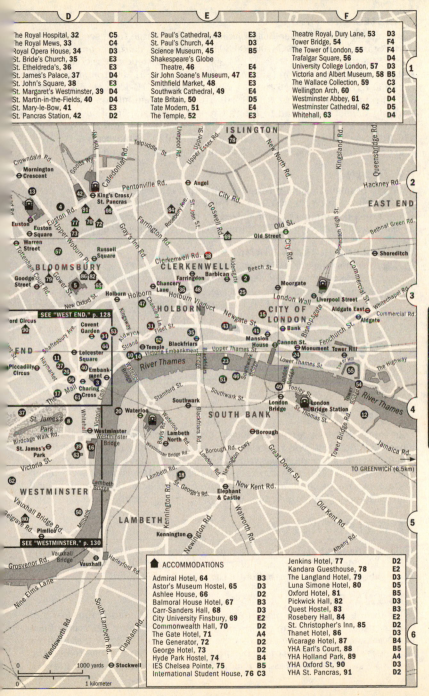

The Royal Hospital, 32 — C5
The Royal Mews, 33 — C4
Royal Opera House, 34 — D3
St. Bride's Church, 35 — E3
St. Etheldreda's, 36 — E3
St. James's Palace, 37 — D4
St. John's Square, 38 — E3
St. Margaret's Westminster, 39 — D4
St. Martin-in-the-Fields, 40 — D4
St. Mary-le-Bow, 41 — E3
St. Pancras Station, 42 — D2

St. Paul's Cathedral, 43 — E3
St. Paul's Church, 44 — D3
Science Museum, 45 — B5
Shakespeare's Globe
  Theatre, 46 — E4
Sir John Soane's Museum, 47 — E3
Smithfield Market, 48 — E3
Southwark Cathedral, 49 — E4
Tate Britain, 50 — D5
Tate Modern, 51 — E4
The Temple, 52 — E3

Theatre Royal, Dury Lane, 53 — D3
Tower Bridge, 54 — F4
The Tower of London, 55 — F4
Trafalgar Square, 56 — D4
University College London, 57 — D3
Victoria and Albert Museum, 58 — B5
The Wallace Collection, 59 — C3
Wellington Arch, 60 — C4
Westminster Abbey, 61 — D4
Westminster Cathedral, 62 — D5
Whitehall, 63 — D4

LONDON

ACCOMMODATIONS

Admiral Hotel, 64 — B3
Astor's Museum Hostel, 65 — D3
Ashlee House, 66 — D2
Balmoral House Hotel, 67 — B3
Carr-Sanders Hall, 68 — D3
City University Finsbury, 69 — E2
Commonwealth Hall, 70 — D2
The Gate Hotel, 71 — A4
The Generator, 72 — D2
George Hotel, 73 — D2
Hyde Park Hostel, 74 — B4
IES Chelsea Pointe, 75 — B5
International Student House, 76 — C3

Jenkins Hotel, 77 — D2
Kandara Guesthouse, 78 — E2
The Langland Hotel, 79 — D3
Luna Simone Hotel, 80 — D5
Oxford Hotel, 81 — B5
Pickwick Hall, 82 — D3
Quest Hostel, 83 — B3
Rosebery Hall, 84 — E2
St. Christopher's Inn, 85 — D2
Thanet Hotel, 86 — D3
Vicarage Hotel, 87 — B4
YHA Earl's Court, 88 — B5
YHA Holland Park, 89 — A4
YHA Oxford St, 90 — D3
YHA St. Pancras, 91 — D2

SEE "WEST END," p. 128

SEE "WESTMINSTER," p. 130

TO GREENWICH (6.5km)

0   1000 yards   Stockwell
0   1 kilometer

STANSTED AND LUTON

Many discount airlines (see **Budget Airlines,** p. 30) operate from secondary airports. Stansted Airport (☎08700 000 303; www.stanstedairport.com) is 30 mi. north. Stansted Express (☎08457 484 950; www.stanstedexpress.co.uk) **trains** run to Liverpool St. Station (45min.; every 15-30min.; £14.50, round-trip £24). National Express's **Airbus A6** runs to Victoria Station (1¼-1¾hr., every 15min., £10). From Luton Airport (☎0158 240 5100; www.londonluton.co.uk), First Capital Connect **trains** head to King's Cross, Blackfriars, and London Bridge (30-40min.; M-Sa every 30min. 3:20am-1am, Su less frequent 6am-11:15pm; £10.40). Green Line (☎08706 087 261; www.greenline.co.uk) **buses** serve West End and Victoria Station (1-1¾hr.; 3 per hr. 8am-6pm; £9, round-trip £12.50).

BY TRAIN

London's train stations date from the Victorian era, when each railway company had its own city terminus; see the box below for service information. Every London terminus is well served by bus and Tube; major stations sell **Railcards,** which offer regular discounts on train travel (see **By Train,** p. 34).

> **LONDON TRAIN STATIONS.**
> **Charing Cross:** Kent (Canterbury, Dover)
> **Euston:** Northwest (Birmingham, Glasgow, Holyhead, Liverpool, Manchester)
> **King's Cross:** Northeast (Cambridge, Edinburgh, Leeds, Newcastle, York)
> **Liverpool Street:** East Anglia (Cambridge, Colchester, Ipswich, Norwich), Stansted Airport
> **Paddington:** West (Bath, Oxford, Windsor), Southwest (Bristol, Cornwall, Exeter), South Wales (Cardiff)
> **Saint Pancras:** Midlands (Nottingham), Northwest (Sheffield)
> **Victoria:** South (Brighton, Canterbury, Dover, Hastings), Gatwick Airport
> **Waterloo:** South and Southwest (Portsmouth, Salisbury)

BY BUS

Long-distance buses arrive at **Victoria Coach Station** (⊖Victoria), Buckingham Palace Rd. National Express is the largest intercity operator. (☎08705 808 080; www.nationalexpress.com.) Eurolines dominates international service. (☎08705 143 219; www.eurolines.co.uk.) **Green Line** coaches serve much of the area around London and leave from the Eccleston Bridge mall behind Victoria station. (⊖Victoria. ☎0870 608 7261; www.greenline.co.uk.)

✦ ORIENTATION

While Greater London consists of 32 boroughs, the City of Westminster, and the City of London, *Let's Go* focuses on central London and divides this area into 12 neighborhoods, plus North, South, East, and West London.

BAYSWATER

Aside from being a cheap place to sleep, Bayswater is nondescript. Rows of Georgian mansions line the quiet streets. The main drags of **Westbourne Grove** and **Queensway** are frequented by teenage mall-hoppers. The longest stretch for walking is along the fringes of the beautiful Kensington Gardens and Hyde Park. Use ⊖Bayswater for the west, ⊖Paddington and ⊖Lancaster Gate for the east.

There are two separate ⊖Paddington stations: the Hammersmith & City line runs from the Paddington train station; the others run from a station underground.

BLOOMSBURY

Bloomsbury is London's intellectual powerhouse, home to the British Museum, near **Russell Square;** the British Library, on **Euston Road;** and University College London, on **Gower Street.** The area was a famous haunt of 20th-century intellectuals, but its squares are some of the best places to throw books aside in the name of picnics and suntans. ⊖King's Cross is the biggest interchange but not the most convenient. ⊖Goodge St. and ⊖Russell Sq. are central; ⊖Euston, ⊖Euston Sq., and ⊖Warren St. hit the north border.

CHELSEA

Chelsea would like to be considered London's artistic bohemia, a desire rooted in the 60s and 70s, when **King's Road** was the birthplace of the miniskirt and punk rock. This makes Chelsea less stuffy than Knightsbridge and Kensington, but today's wealthy neighborhood has little stomach for radicalism. ⊖Sloane Sq. to the east and ⊖South Kensington to the north will put you close to most attractions. Taking a bus is critical during bad weather; most run from ⊖Sloane Sq. down King's Rd. on their way from ⊖Knightsbridge or ⊖Victoria.

THE CITY OF LONDON

The City is where London began—indeed, for most of its history, the City *was* London. Even though urban sprawl has pushed the border of London out, the City remains as tightly knit as ever, with its own mayor, separate jurisdiction, and even sway over the queen, who must ask permission of the lord mayor before entering. **Upper** and **Lower Thames Streets** run along the Thames to the Tower of London; **Aldersgate Street** passes by the Barbican Centre on its way to Clerkenwell; **Ludgate Hill** connects Fleet St. to St. Paul's Cathedral. ⊖Bank and ⊖St. Paul's are close to most sights; use ⊖Tower Hill for eastern stops.

HOLBORN AND CLERKENWELL

London's second-oldest area, Holborn was the first part of the city settled by Saxons—**Aldwych,** on the western edge, is Anglo-Saxon for "old port." **Fleet Street** remains synonymous with the British press even though the newspapers have moved elsewhere. Traveling north to Clerkenwell, **Farringdon Street** intersects **High Holborn** and **Clerkenwell Road** before becoming **King's Cross Road.** A monastic center until Henry VIII closed the Priory of St. John, Clerkenwell became home to London's top artisans. During Victoria's reign, it devolved into slums, as famously described by Dickens. More recently, the area has come storming back onto the London dining and nightlife scene. Holborn is served by ⊖Holborn, ⊖Farringdon, ⊖Chancery Ln., and ⊖Temple. In Clerkenwell, everything is near ⊖Farringdon; southern and eastern parts can be reached from ⊖Barbican, western parts can be reached by ⊖Chancery Ln., and northern parts can be reached by ⊖Angel.

KENSINGTON AND EARL'S COURT

The former stomping ground of Princess Di, Kensington is divided into two distinct areas. To the west is the posh shopper's dream, **Kensington High Street,** while to the east are the museums and colleges of **South Kensington's** "Albertopolis." In the 1960s and 70s, Earl's Court was mainly the destination of Aussie backpackers and home to London's gay population, but today others have caught on to its combination of cheap accommodations and transportation links, while

Soho has taken up the rainbow flag. Since this is one of central London's larger neighborhoods, public transportation is necessary to get around. Tube stations are helpfully named: ⊖High St. Kensington for High St., ⊖South Kensington for the South Kensington museums, and ⊖Earl's Court for Earl's Court.

KNIGHTSBRIDGE AND BELGRAVIA

Knightsbridge and Belgravia are smug and expensive. The primary draw is window-shopping on **Sloane Street** and **Brompton Road** at shopping's biggest names: Harrods and Harvey Nichols. Belgravia lies east of Sloane St., sporting 19th-century mansions occupied by millionaires and embassies. ⊖Knightsbridge is near the shops; most hotels in Belgravia are close to ⊖Victoria, but the north end of the neighborhood is closest to ⊖Hyde Park Corner.

MARYLEBONE AND REGENT'S PARK

Marylebone (MAR-li-bone) is defined by its eclectic borders. Adjacent to academic Bloomsbury in the east, beautiful **Portland Place** stands as an architectural wonder. To the west, **Edgware Road** houses London's largest Lebanese population and boasts many Middle Eastern eateries, shops, and markets. **Marylebone Road** traps tourists with Madame Tussauds wax museum and chain stores but also acts as the gateway to pleasant Regent's Park. ⊖Baker St. is convenient for northern sights; ⊖Bond St. covers the south. There are two separate ⊖Edgware Rd. stations, but they aren't far apart.

NOTTING HILL

Once the stopping point for those traveling between London and Uxbridge, Notting Hill has retained its appeal as an offshoot of central London. Running from Oxford St., **Notting Hill Gate** is not a gate but a main street. Its appeal has much to do with its mix of mansions and artsy hangouts. **Portobello Road** is best known for its market. ⊖Notting Hill Gate serves the south, while ⊖Ladbroke Grove deposits you near Portobello Rd.

THE SOUTH BANK

Just across the river from the City, the South Bank has long been the center of London's entertainment industry. Cross the Thames on **Waterloo Road, Blackfriars Road, Borough High Street,** or **Tower Bridge Road.** Dominated by wharves and warehouses in the 19th and early 20th centuries, the South Bank was rebuilt after its destruction in WWII. Now, the "Millennium Mile" stretches from the London Eye in the west to Butlers Wharf in the east. Use ⊖Waterloo for inland attractions, ⊖Southwark for Bankside, and ⊖London Bridge for Borough and Butlers Wharf. See the **"Millennium Mile" Walking Tour** (p. 118) of the South Bank.

THE WEST END

If Westminster is the heart of historical London, then the West End is at the center of just about everything else. The biggest, brightest, and boldest (although not always best) of London nightlife, theater, shopping, and eating can all be found within this tough-to-define district, wedged between royal regalia to the south and financial powerhouses to the northeast.

See a world-renowned musical at one of over 30 major theaters in the area, head to **Chinatown** for some dim sum, and window-shop on **Oxford Street.** If it's nightlife you're craving, the collection of bars and clubs in **Soho** will keep you busy through the wee hours of morning. Stroll around the gay nightlife nexus of **Old Compton Street** or mingle with street performers in **Covent Garden.**

LONDON

And if none of this sounds like your cup of tea, you can always cruise the posh streets of **Mayfair** and **Saint James's,** which offer a more distinct flavor than the more touristed areas of the West End. Spend a little time in central **Trafalgar Square** to bask in the glory of Britain's days as an imperial power. The Tube is best for getting in and out of the West End. Use ⊖Charing Cross for Trafalgar Sq.; the stops are often only a few blocks apart. Once you've made it, buses are the best way to get around; stops can be found along any major thoroughfare.

WESTMINSTER

Westminster, with its spires and parks, feels like the heart of the old British Empire. It is, after all, home to the Houses of Parliament and the queen—convenient for diehard tourists who want to cram London's biggest sights into one day. Apart from the grandeur of **Westminster Abbey** and the bureaucracy of **Whitehall,** Westminster is a down-to-earth district—thousands of commuting workers make ⊖Victoria the busiest Tube station in the city. South of Victoria, **Pimlico** is residential, with row after row of B&Bs. ⊖Westminster is near most sights; use ⊖St. James's Park for Buckingham Palace and ⊖Pimlico for accommodations and for the Tate Britain.

NORTH LONDON

What *Let's Go* calls North London is actually a group of distinct neighborhoods, all of which lie to the north of central London. Once the centers of London's counter-culture movement, **Camden Town** and **Islington** now offer more posh restaurants and funky pubs than punk rockers. **Hampstead** and **Highgate** still feel like small villages. **Saint John's Wood** and **Maida Vale** are wealthy, residential extensions of Marylebone and Bayswater. Most individual neighborhoods are walkable. Tube stops are ⊖Camden Town for (surprise) Camden Town; ⊖Kentish Town for Camden; ⊖Angel for Islington; and ⊖Kilburn and ⊖Swiss Cottage for St. John's Wood and Maida Vale.

SOUTH LONDON

Historically maligned for being "dodgy," areas of South London are now hot spots for upscale dining and all-night parties. Some areas still feel slightly unsafe; keep an eye on your bag. Once a swanky suburb, **Brixton** has been urbanized, showcasing the charm of its Afro-Caribbean market. **Stockwell** and **Vauxhall** offer pubs, while **Dulwich** and **Forest Hill** have quiet streets and offbeat museums. **Clapham** is experiencing a boom in nightlife and culture. ⊖Stockwell, ⊖Brixton, and the ⊖Claphams serve the area. For access to some areas, overland rail service from ⊖Victoria, ⊖Waterloo, and ⊖London Bridge is necessary. From ⊖Brixton, the P4 bus will take you to all the Dulwich sites.

EAST LONDON

At Aldgate, the wealth of the City of London gives way to the historically impoverished **East End,** the heart of East London. Cheap land and nearby docks made this area a natural gathering point for immigrants, including waves of Huguenots, Jews, and, more recently, Bangladeshis. The East End remains one of the last affordable areas in central London and was the inspiration behind the famous British television series *EastEnders.* Today, it's a site of urban regenerationl towers of steel and glass surge skyward in record time. It's also famous for Spitalfields Market, a funky indoor market bursting with cheap silver jewelry, crafts, food, and antiques. There's no reason to get off the elevated Docklands Light Railway (DLR) trains in **Docklands** until they reach **Greenwich,** home to sights that document its maritime past. Greenwich was also

LONDON

once the favorite residence of Queen Elizabeth. ⊖Old St. and ⊖Liverpool St. are best for the East End. Farther east, Tube lines serve ⊖Canary Wharf and ⊖Wapping. The DLR will take you to ⊖Greenwich.

WEST LONDON

West London stretches for miles along the Thames before petering out in the nearby hills. The river changes course so often and so sharply that it is difficult to distinguish between the north and south banks, and communities have developed almost in isolation from their neighbors. **Shepherd's Bush,** one of these relatively autonomous districts, distinguishes itself with a number of well-known concert and theater venues. **Hammersmith** bridges the gap between the shopping malls around the Tube station and the pleasant parks and pubs along the Thames. To the north, **White City** is home to the world-famous BBC. Historically, the western reaches of the Thames were fashionable spots for country retreats, and the river still winds through the grounds of stately homes and former palaces. The District Line on the Underground goes to most sights.

▐▀ LOCAL TRANSPORTATION

Local gripes aside, London's public transportation system is remarkably efficient. (☎020 7222 1234; www.tfl.gov.uk.) The network is divided into a series of concentric zones; ticket prices depend on the number of zones you cross. There are two different zoning systems. The **Tube, rail,** and **Docklands Light Railway (DLR)** network operates on six zones, with Zone 1 being the most central. **Buses** reduce this to four zones. Bus Zones 1, 2, and 3 are the same as the Tube zones, and bus Zone 4 comprises Tube Zones 4, 5, and 6.

OYSTER CARDS AND TRAVEL PASSES

You'll save money by investing in an Oyster card. Oyster cards work on the zone system and can be purchased at major Tube, DLR, and rail stations. Buying one requires some paperwork and a £3 deposit, renewable upon return, after which all transactions work via a pay-as-you-go scheme. You can add money to your Oyster card at designated kiosks within major Tube stations. Using an Oyster card is extremely convenient: simply touch it on a card reader at the beginning and end of a Tube journey and use it on buses, rails, and trams for a substantial discount off normal fares. Although they are less flexible than Oyster cards, **Travelcards** offer similar discounts. **One-Day Travelcards** are valid for bus, Tube, DLR, and commuter rail services. There are two types of One-Day Travelcards: **Peak** cards (valid all day) and Off-Peak cards (M-F after 9:30am, Sa-Su all day). **Three-Day Travelcards** are also available. **Family Travelcards** and discounts for children are available. **Weekend** or **Weekly Travelcards** are valid two consecutive days on weekends and public holidays or seven consecutive days, respectively. See www.tfl.gov.uk for Travelcard rates. Although they are not a very good deal, you can also buy individual passes for single rides on the Tube. Beware of people trying to sell you secondhand passes—there's no guarantee the ticket will work, and it's illegal (penalties are stiff). Passes expire at 4:30am the morning after the expiration date.

THE UNDERGROUND

The Tube is best suited to longer trips; within Zone 1, adjacent stations are so close that you might as well walk, and buses are cheaper and often get you closer to your destination. The **Docklands Light Railway (DLR)** is a driverless, overland version of the Tube running in East London; the ticketing structure is the same. If you'll be traveling by Tube a lot, you'll save money with an **Oyster card** or a **Travelcard**. The one-week Travelcard grants unlimited Tube and bus rides and some train rides—ideal if you're sightseeing or simply lost. If you choose to buy single-ride paper tickets, you must buy them at the start of your journey; they are valid only for the day of purchase. Keep your ticket for the entire journey, since you'll need it to exit the station. Regular ticket prices depend on two factors: number of zones traveled and whether you traveled through Zone 1. Prices increase if you are traveling in or through zones higher than Zone 4. With an Oyster card, these fares drop significantly. The Tube runs daily from approximately 5:30am to midnight. The time of the first and last train is posted in each station; check if you plan to take the Tube after 11:30pm. Trains run less frequently early in the morning, late at night, and on Sundays.

BUSES

Only tourists use the Tube for short trips in central London—if it's only a couple of stops or if it involves more than one change, a bus will likely get there faster. Excellent signposts make the bus system easy to use; most stops display a map of local routes and nearby stops, along with a key to help you find your bus and stop. Normal buses run from approximately 5:30am to midnight. During the day, double-deckers run every 10-15min.; single-deckers arrive every 5-8min. A reduced network of **Night Buses** fills in the gap. Night Bus route numbers are prefixed with an N; they typically operate the same routes as their daytime equivalents but occasionally start and finish at different points. Buses that run 24hr. have no N Bus and Night Bus fares are the same (£1.20, ages 11-15 40p, under 11 free). All tickets are good for traveling across the network and can be purchased at roadside machines or on the bus. **Keep your ticket** until you get off the bus to avoid a £20 on-the-spot fine.

TAXIS

Taxis in London come in two forms: licensed taxis (**black cabs**) and **minicabs**. Fares for black cabs are regulated by Transport for London. Taxis must take passengers anywhere in central London up to 12 mi., even just one block. Longer journeys are at their discretion—negotiate a fare in advance if you're going outside the city. A **10% tip** is expected. **Taxi One-Number** (☎08718 718 710) connects to six radio taxi circuits, allowing you many booking options.

Anyone with a car and a driver's license can be a minicab company. As a result, competition is fierce and prices are lower than licensed cabs. Minicabs are not always safe for those traveling alone; there have been many reports of sexual assault. Call one of the following reputable companies or take a black cab: **London Radio Cars** (☎020 8905 0000); **Liberty Cars** (☎020 0800 600 006; www.liberty-cars.com); or **Lady Cabs** (☎020 7254 3501).

🔢 PRACTICAL INFORMATION

TOURIST AND FINANCIAL SERVICES

There are 16 Tourist Information Centres spotted around Greater London. Check www.britainexpress.com/TIC/London.htm for a complete list or contact these central offices in the city center.

Tourist Information Centre: Britain Visitor Centres, 1 Regent St. (www.visitbritain.com), ⊖Piccadilly Circus. Open M 9:30am-6:30pm, Tu-F 9am-6:30pm, Sa-Su 10am-4pm.

London Information Centre, 1 Leicester Pl. (☎020 7930 6769; www.londoninforma-tioncentre.com), ⊖Leicester Sq. Open M-F 8am-midnight, Sa-Su 9am-6pm.

Tours: Big Bus Company, 35-37 Grosvenor Gardens (☎020 7233 7797; www.bigbus.co.uk), ⊖Victoria. Multiple routes and buses every 5-15min. 1hr. walking tours and Thames mini-cruise. Buses start at central office and at hubs throughout the city. £20. £2 discount for online purchase. AmEx/MC/V. **Original London Walks** (☎020 7624 3978, recorded info 7624 9255; www.walks.com) runs themed walks, from "Haunted London" to "Slice of India." Most 2hr. £6, concessions £5, under 16 free.

American Express: 84 Kensington High St. (☎020 7795 6703; www.americanexpress.com), ⊖High St. Kensington. Open M-Sa 9am-5:30pm. 30-31 Haymarket (☎020 7484 9610), ⊖Piccadilly Circus. Open M-F 9am-7pm, Sa 9am-6pm, Su 10am-5pm.

LOCAL SERVICES

Transport for London: Access and Mobility (☎020 7222 1234; www.tfl.gov.uk/tfl/ph_accessibility.shtml). Provides info on public transportation accessibility.

GLBT Resources: Gay London (www.gaylondon.co.uk) is an online community for gays and lesbians. A web portal for lesbian and bisexual women, **Gingerbeer** (www.ginger-beer.co.uk), lists clubs, bars, restaurants, and community resources.

EMERGENCY AND COMMUNICATIONS

LONDON CALLING. London's phone code is **020.**

Emergency: ☎999 from any landline or 122 from a mobile phone.

Police: City of London Police (☎020 7601 2222) for the City and the **Metropolitan Police** (☎020 7230 1212) for everywhere else. At least 1 station in each of the 32 boroughs is open 24hr. Call to find the nearest station.

Pharmacies: Open M-Sa 9:30am-5:30pm; a "duty" chemist in each neighborhood opens Su, but hours may be limited. Late-night chemists are rare. A 24hr. option is **Zaf-ash Pharmacy,** 233 Old Brompton Rd. (☎020 7373 2798), ⊖Earl's Court. **Bliss,** 5-6 Marble Arch (☎020 7723 6116), ⊖Marble Arch. Open daily 9am-midnight.

Hospitals: Charing Cross, Fulham Palace Rd. (☎020 8846 1234), entrance on St. Dun-stan's Rd., ⊖Hammersmith. **Royal Free,** Pond St. (☎020 7794 0500), ⊖Belsize Park. **St. Thomas's,** Lambeth Palace Rd. (☎020 7188 7188), ⊖Waterloo. **University College London Hospital,** Grafton Way (☎0845 1555 000), ⊖Warren St.

Internet Access: If you're paying more than £2 per hr., you're paying too much. Try the ubiquitous **easyEverything** (☎020 7241 9000; www.easyeverything.com). Locations include: 9-16 Tottenham Ct. Rd. (⊖Tottenham Court Rd.); 456-459 Strand (⊖Charing Cross); 358 Oxford St. (⊖Bond St.); 160-166 Kensington High St. (⊖High St. Kens-ington). Prices vary with demand, from £1 per 15min. during busy times; usually around £1.60 per hr. Min. 50p-£1. Generally open until 11pm.

Post Office: Post offices are on almost every major road. When sending mail to London, include the full postcode, since London encompasses several. The largest office is the **Trafalgar Square Post Office,** 24-28 William IV St., WC2N 4DL. ⊖Charing Cross. Open M and W-F 8:30am-6:30pm, Tu 9:15am-6:30pm, Sa 9am-5:30pm.

LONDON

▚ ACCOMMODATIONS

Accommodations in London cost more than anywhere else in the UK. The area near **Victoria Station** (Westminster) is convenient for major sights and transportation, but it is expensive. **Bloomsbury** is by far the budget traveler's best option. Competing for second place, **Kensington** and **Earl's Court** have a number of midrange, high-quality digs, while **Bayswater** has less expensive ones that are also a step down in quality. Book well in advance, especially in summer. (Book YHAs online at www.yha.org.) Check out university dorms for good summer deals.

BAYSWATER

Quest Hostel, 45 Queensborough Terr. (☎020 7229 7782; www.astorhostels.com). ◆Queensway. Bus #N15, 94, 148. A chummy staff operates this backpacker hostel with a whiteboard welcoming new guests by name. White pillars evoke elegance mixed with neighborhood friendliness. Board games, TV with DVDs, and a book exchange. Mostly mixed-sex dorms (1 female-only room); nearly all have baths. Otherwise, facilities on every other floor. Kitchen available. Luggage storage. Continental breakfast, lockers, and linen included. Laundry. Free Wi-Fi. 4- to 9-bed dorms £20-24; doubles £32. MC/V. ❶

Hyde Park Hostel, 2-6 Inverness Terr. (☎020 7229 5101; www.astorhostels.com). ◆Queensway. Bus #N15, 94, 148. 260 tightly bunked beds and a veritable theme park of diversions. Jungle-themed basement bar and dance space hosts DJs and parties (open W-Su 8pm-3am). Kitchen, TV lounge, secure luggage room. Continental breakfast and linens included. Laundry. Internet access 50p per 30min. Reception 24hr. Reserve 2 weeks in advance for summer. 24hr. cancellation policy. Online booking with 10% non-refundable deposit. 4- to 18-bed dorms £11-18; twins £25. Weekly rates £81-95 per person. Ages 16-35 only. MC/V. ❶

Admiral Hotel, 143 Sussex Gardens (☎020 7723 7309; www.admiral-hotel.com). ◆Paddington. Bus #N15, 94, 148. Beautifully kept B&B with a sleek bar. Rooms with bath, hair dryers, satellite TV, and kettles. No smoking. English breakfast included. Free Wi-Fi. 4-day cancellation policy. Singles £50-60; doubles £80; triples £90-100; quads £90-120; quints £110-140. Ask about winter and long-stay discounts. MC/V. ❸

Balmoral House Hotel, 156 Sussex Gardens (☎020 7723 7445; www.balmoral-househotel.co.uk). ◆Paddington. Bus #N15, 94, 148. Convenient location close to the Tube station. Well-kept rooms have bathrooms, satellite TV, kettles, and hair dryers. English breakfast included. Singles £55; doubles £85; triples £100; quads £110; quints £125. MC/V with 5% surcharge. ❸

BLOOMSBURY

▨ **The Generator,** Compton Pl. (☎020 7388 7666; www.generatorhostels.com), off 37 Tavistock Pl. ◆Russell Sq. or ◆King's Cross St. Pancras. Bus #N19, N35, N38, N41, N55, N91, N243. Mixed-sex dorms (all-female available), a hopping bar (6pm-2am), cheap pints (6-9pm; £1.50), dinner specials, nightly entertainment, and well-equipped common rooms. You might be greeted with a complimentary beer. All rooms have sinks; private doubles have tables and chairs. Kitchen, ATM, and a shop that sells Tube and train tickets. Continental breakfast included. Lockers (bring your own lock) and laundry. Internet 50p per 7min. Reception 24hr. Credit card required with reservation. 12- to 14-bed dorms M-W and Su £12.50, Th-Sa £17.50; singles £30/35; doubles with 2 twin beds £50/55; triples £60; quads £80. 18+ unless part of a family group. Discounts for long stays. MC/V. ❶

▨ **Jenkins Hotel,** 45 Cartwright Gardens (☎020 7387 2067; www.jenkinshotel.demon. co.uk), entry on Barton Pl. ◆Euston or ◆King's Cross St. Pancras. Bus #N10, N73, N91, 390. A small hotel with plenty of fun. Taller folks should avoid the low-ceilinged basement (although it boasts the nicest bathroom). Rooms have TVs, kettles, phones, fridges, hair dryers, and safes. Access to tennis courts in Cartwright Gardens. English breakfast included. Reserve 1-2 months in advance for summer. Singles £52, with bath £72; doubles with bath (some with tubs) £89; triples with bath £105. MC/V. ❹

Ashlee House, 261-265 Gray's Inn Rd. (☎020 7833 9400; www.ashleehouse.co.uk). ⊖King's Cross St. Pancras. Bus #N10, N63, N73, N91, 390. A "designer" budget accommodation fit for the most discerning of backpackers. Retro-themed rooms and common areas. Mixed-sex (all-female available) dorms are bright and clean, while private rooms include tables, sinks, and kettles. Luggage room, safe, and kitchen. Continental breakfast included. Linen included; towels £1. Laundry. Internet £1 per 30min. 2-week max. stay. Reception 24hr. 16-bed dorms £18; 8- to 10-bed £20; 4- to 6-bed £22. Singles £55; doubles £73. Expect to pay £50 extra on the weekend. MC/V. ❶

George Hotel, 58-60 Cartwright Gardens (☎020 7387 8777; www.georgehotel.com). ⊖Russell Sq. Bus #N10, N73, N91, 390. Rooms with satellite TV, radios, kettles, phones, alarm clocks, and sinks. Hair dryer and iron on request. The forward-facing rooms on the 1st fl. are the best, with high ceilings and tall windows. English breakfast included. Free Internet. Reserve 3 weeks in advance for summer; 48hr. cancellation policy. Singles £50, with showers £75; doubles £68.50/75, with bath £89; triples £79/89/99; basic quad £89. Discount for stays over 4 days. MC/V. ❸

Astor's Museum Hostel, 27 Montague St. (☎020 7580 5360; www.astorhotels.com). ⊖Tottenham Court Rd., Russell Sq., or Goodge St. Bus #N19, N35, N38, N41, N55, N91, N243. This backpackers' hostel is simple but friendly, conveniently located next to the shopping and nightlife of Tottenham Court Rd. Communal kitchen and free DVDs available to watch in downstairs lounge. English breakfast and linen included; towels £2. Reservations recommended. 12-bed dorms £17-19; 10-bed £18-20; 8-bed £21; 6-bed £20-22. Private double £60-70. AmEx/MC/V. ❶

YHA St. Pancras International, 79-81 Euston Rd. (☎0870 770 6044; stpancras@yha. org.uk). ⊖King's Cross St. Pancras. Bus #N10, N73, N91, 390. Opposite the British Library. Caters to families and older adults, but also ideal for students doing research across the street. Historic intellectual flavor of Bloomsbury conversation still colors the air. Family bunk rooms, single-sex dorms, basic doubles, and premium doubles with bath and TVs. Breakfast included. Lockers (bring your own lock). Internet £1 per 15min. 10-day max. stay. Reserve 1 week in advance for Sa-Su or summer, 2 weeks for doubles. Dorms £26.50, under 18 £22.50; doubles £60, with bath £65. MC/V. ❷

Thanet Hotel, 8 Bedford Pl., Russell Sq. (☎020 7636 2869; www.thanethotel.co.uk). ⊖Russell Sq. or ⊖Holborn. Bus #N19, N35, N38, N41, N55, N91, N243. A homey B&B. Some rooms have been recently refurbished with fireplaces and big mirrors, but even the old rooms are bright and comfortable. Request a room with a view of the garden. All rooms with bath, TVs, kettles, and phones. Breakfast included. Reserve 1 month in advance. Singles £78; doubles £104; triples £120; quads £130. AmEx/MC/V. ❹

The Langland Hotel, 29-31 Gower St. (☎020 7636 5801; www.langlandhotel.com). ⊖Goodge St. Bus #N5, N10, N20, 24, N29, N73, 134, N253, N279, 390. A comfortable B&B with low rates. Staff keeps the large rooms spotless. Lounge with satellite TV. Rooms with TVs, kettles, and fans. English breakfast included. 48hr. cancellation policy. Singles £55-65; doubles £70-75; triples £85-90; quads £95-100. Discounts in winter and for longer stays, students, and advance booking. AmEx/MC/V. ❸

Pickwick Hall International Backpackers, 7 Bedford Pl. (☎020 7323 4958; www.pickwickhall.co.uk). ⊖Russell Sq. or Holborn. Night Bus #N7, N91. Namesake of Dickens's first novel, *The Pickwick Papers*. Clean rooms include mini-fridges and microwaves. Kitchen and TV lounge. Continental breakfast included. Lockers (bring your own lock), coin laundry, and Internet available. Reception 8am-10pm. Book 3 weeks in advance for July-Aug. Singles £37; doubles £50, ensuite £60; triples £66; quads £88. MC/V. ❷

Commonwealth Hall, 1-11 Cartwright Gardens (☎020 7121 7000; www.lon.ac.uk/services/students/halls1/halls2/vacrates.asp). ⊖Russell Sq. Bus #N10, N73, N91, 390. Post-WWII block residential hall. 425 recently refurbished student singles. Fridge and microwave on each floor. Elevators and cafeteria. Access to tennis and squash courts for a fee. English breakfast included. Dinner included. Reserve at least 3 months in advance for July-Aug. Walk-ins only accommodated M-F 9am-5:30pm. Open from mid-Mar. to late Apr. and from mid-June to mid-Sept. Singles from £28. AmEx/MC/V. ❷

Carr-Saunders Hall, 18-24 Fitzroy St. (☎020 7955 7575; www.lse.ac.uk/vacations). ⊖Warren St. Bus #N7, N8, N10, 25, N55, N73, N98, 176, N207, 390. Old student residential hall. Rooms are large and include sinks and phones. TV lounge, game room, and elevator to all floors, including roof terrace. English breakfast included. Internet access. Reserve 6-8 weeks in advance for July-Aug., but check for openings any time. Open from late Mar. to late Apr. and from late June to late Sept. 30% deposit required. Singles from £32; doubles from £50, with bath from £52. MC/V. ❷

CLERKENWELL

City University Finsbury Residences, 15 Bastwick St. (☎020 7040 8811; www.city. ac.uk/ems/accomm/fins.html). ⊖Barbican. Buses #N35 and N55 stop at the corner of Old St. and Goswell Rd. A 1970s tower block within walking distance of City sights, Islington restaurants, and Clerkenwell nightlife. Singles in the main building have shared showers, toilets, kitchen access, and a laundry room. Wheelchair-accessible. Open from early June to early Sept. Singles from £32. MC/V. ❷

Rosebery Hall, 90 Rosebery Ave. (☎020 7955 7575; www.lse.ac.uk/collections/vacations). ⊖Angel. Bus #N19, N38, 341. Exit left from the Tube, cross the road, and take the 2nd right on Rosebery Ave. Ring bell to enter. A quick walk from Exmouth Market, the 2 London School of Economics student residence buildings surround a garden. Rooms in the newer block are more spacious, with wheelchair-accessible baths. Pool tables, TV lounge, bar, and laundry. Open from mid-Aug. to Sept. and from mid-Dec. to early Jan. Singles from £32; doubles from £52, with bath £62; triples £64. ❷

KENSINGTON AND EARL'S COURT

YHA Holland House, Holland Walk (☎020 7937 0748; www.yha.org.uk). ⊖High St. Kensington or ⊖Holland Park. Bus #27, 94, 148. One of the loveliest hostels in the city. Half the rooms are in a 17th-century mansion overlooking a large courtyard. Set among the manicured lawns and wild hedges of Holland Park. Peacocks roam the grounds. TV room and kitchen. Full English breakfast included; 3-course set dinners £6.50. Laundry. Internet £1 for 50min. Reception 24hr. Book in advance for summer, although there are frequent last-minute vacancies. Dorms £16.50-24.50, under 18 £12.50-18.50. £3 discount with student ID. AmEx/MC/V. ❶

Vicarage Hotel, 10 Vicarage Gate (☎020 7229 4030; www.londonvicaragehotel.com). ⊖High St. Kensington. Bus #27, N28, N31, N52. Walking on Kensington Church St. from Kensington High St., you'll see 2 streets marked Vicarage Gate; take the 2nd on your right. Victorian house with ornate hallways, TV lounge, and bedrooms; all rooms have solid wood furnishings, kettles, and hair dryers. Ensuite rooms with TVs. Full English breakfast included. Reserve 2 months in advance with 1 night's deposit; personal checks accepted for deposit with at least 2 months notice. Singles £52, with private bath £88; doubles £88/114; triples £109/145; quads £112/160. MC/V. ❸

Oxford Hotel, 24 Penywern Rd. (☎020 7370 1161; www.the-oxford-hotel.com). ⊖Earl's Court. Bus #N31, N74, N97. Sir William Ramsey, the physicist who discovered helium, once lived in this hotel—guests would often hear high-pitched voices coming from his room. Midsize, bright rooms, all with shower and some with full bath. High-quality furnishings: comfortable beds, TVs, kettles, and safes. Continental breakfast included. Reception 24hr. Singles with showers £45, with bath £58; doubles £65/75; triples with bath £83; quads £92/100; quints £120. MC/V. ❸

YHA Earl's Court, 38 Bolton Gardens (☎020 7373 7083; www.yha.org.uk). ⊖Earl's Court. Bus #N31, N74, N97. Victorian townhouse. Single-sex dorms (4-10 people) have wood bunks and sink. Small garden, spacious kitchen, 2 TV lounges, and luggage storage. Serve yourself at the continental breakfast bar, which also offers pure fruit smoothies. Breakfast included only for private rooms; otherwise £4. Lockers (bring your own lock or buy at reception for £3.50). Towels £3.50. Laundry. Internet £1 per hr. 2-week max. stay. £5 cancellation charge. Dorms £19.50, under 18 £17.20; doubles £60; quads £82. Prices subject to change; check online for updates. MC/V. ❶

OTHER NEIGHBORHOODS

▨ **Luna Simone Hotel,** 47-49 Belgrave Rd. (☎020 7834 5897; www.lunasimonehotel. com). ⊖Victoria or ⊖Pimlico. Bus #N2, 24, N36. Sparkling, spacious showers, modern decor, and a staff that takes a kind interest in its guests. Full English breakfast included. Free Internet access. Reserve at least 2 weeks in advance. 48hr. cancellation policy £10; 1 night's charge if less than 48hr. notice. Singles £35-45, with bath £55-65; doubles with bath £75-95; triples with bath £95-115; quads with bath £100-140. 10-20% discount in low season. MC/V. ❸

YHA Oxford Street, 14 Noel St. (☎020 7734 5984; www.yha.org.uk). ⊖Oxford Circus. More than 10 Night Buses run along Oxford St., including #N7, N8, and N207. Clean, sunny rooms and an unbeatable location for nightlife. Some double rooms have bunk beds, sinks, mirrors, and wardrobes; others have single beds and wardrobes. Toilets and showers off the hallways. TV, smoking lounge, and bar. Travelcards sold at reception. Towels £3.50. Internet terminal and Wi-Fi £1 per 15min. May-Sept. 3- to 4-bed dorms £22-25, under 18 £16.50-19.50; 2-bed dorms £54-60. Oct.-Mar. 3- to 4-bed dorms £23.50, under 18 £19; 2-bed dorms £25.50. MC/V. ❶

IES Chelsea Pointe (☎020 7808 9200; www.iesreshall.com), corner of Manresa Rd. and King's Rd.; entrance on Manresa Rd. ⊖Sloane Sq., then Bus #11, 19, 22, 319;, or ⊖South Kensington, then Bus #49. Direct on Bus #N11, N19, N22. Brand-new university residence hall offers clean, spacious dorm rooms year-round. In the heart of trendy Chelsea, these prices are unheard of. 5 TV lounges. All rooms have bath, access to laundry services, and free Internet. Wheelchair-accessible. Reservations recommended. 72hr. cancellation policy. More availability during summer and winter school breaks. Singles £285 per week; doubles £342 per week. AmEx/MC/V. ❸

Morgan House, 120 Ebury St. (☎020 7730 2384; www.morganhouse.co.uk). ⊖Victoria. Midsize, stylish rooms, many with fireplaces, all with TVs, kettles, and phones for incoming calls. English breakfast included. Reserve 2-3 months in advance. 48hr. cancellation policy. Singles with sinks £52; doubles with sinks £72, with bath £92; triples £92/112; quads (1 double bed and 1 set of bunk beds) with bath £132. MC/V. ❸

International Student House, 229 Great Portland St. (☎020 7631 8310; www.ishweb. squarespace.com). ⊖Great Portland St. Bus #N18. As a large dorm, ISH offers the opposite of most other hostels: a good selection of rooms during summer and limited options during the school year. Most rooms have desks, sinks, phones, and fridges; some have ensuite bath. Bar, nightclub, cafeteria, fitness center (£6 per day), and cinema (Su only). Continental breakfast included except for dorms (£2.30); English breakfast £3. Laundry. Internet £2 per hr. £20 key deposit. Wheelchair-accessible. 3-week max. stay. Advance booking recommended. Dorms £12; singles £34; doubles £52; triples £62; quads £76. 10% discount on singles, doubles, and triples with ISIC. MC/V. ❶

The Gate Hotel, 6 Portobello Rd. (☎020 7221 0707; www.gatehotel.co.uk). ⊖Notting Hill Gate. Bus #N52. A great base for Notting Hill and West End excursions. Clean, relatively spacious, and a good deal for the area. Rooms have bath, TVs, DVD players, desks, minifridges, and phones. Continental breakfast included, served in yolur room. 48hr. cancellation policy. Singles £55-70; doubles £75-90; triples £90-120. MC/V. ❹

Kandara Guesthouse, 68 Ockendon Rd. (☎020 7226 5721; www.kandara.co.uk). From ⊖Angel, take Bus #38, 56, 73, 341 to the Ockendon Rd. stop. Direct on Bus #N38, N73, 341. Far from the Tube but with ample access to downtown. Bustling atmosphere and clean rooms with plenty of privacy. 11 rooms with 5 communal baths. Hair dryer and iron on request. Breakfast included. Reserve well in advance; call for family quad. 1-night deposit required with reservation; 1-week cancellation notice or loss of deposit. Singles from £58; doubles from £79; triples £80. MC/V. ❸

St. Christopher's Inn, 48-50 Camden High St. (☎020 7388 1012; www.st-christophers. co.uk). ⊖Mornington Crescent. Bus #N5, N20, N253. Reception in Belushi's Bar downstairs is a fitting entrance to this party-friendly backpacker hostel. Nicknamed the "hostel with attitude," St. Christopher's gets you started right with 10% off all food and drinks at the bar. Near Camden Town bars and Clerkenwell clubs. Most rooms ensuite. Luggage room, safety deposit boxes, and common rooms. Continental breakfast included. Lockers and laundry. Internet access. Reception 24hr. 10-bed dorms from £18-21; 8-bed £19-22; 6-bed £23. Doubles £26-29. Discount with online booking. MC/V. ❶

◘ FOOD

While insiders have known London as a hot spot for internationally influenced cuisine for years, it has taken a little while to spread the word that Britain is more than just bangers and mash. London's food scene is fueled by its growing ethnic communities. Head to Whitechapel for the region's best Baltic food, to Chinatown for traditional dim sum, to South Kensington for French pastries, and to Edgware Rd. for a stunning assortment of Lebanese shawarma. Recently, a flourishing green movement has produced a crop of new vegetarian eateries and restaurants that emphasize local products. Still, it would be a shame to come to the home of afternoon tea and fish and chips and deny yourself these delicious British traditions.

BAYSWATER

Levantine, 26 London St. (☎020 7262 1111; www.levant.co.uk). ⊖Paddington. A Lebanese restaurant with the faint aroma of incense and rose petals. Indulge in *mezze* offerings like falafel and homemade hummus (£4.25). Loads of vegetarian options. Belly-dancing and *shisha* (water pipe) nights. Open daily noon-12:30am. MC/V. ❷

Italian Ice Cream cart, near 122 Bayswater Rd. Luscious piles of creamy gelato are perfect to take on a stroll in the Kensington Gardens across the street. Try the pistachio. 1 scoop £1.50, 2 scoops £2. Open daily 11am-11pm. ❶

Durbar Tandoori, 24 Hereford St. (☎020 7727 1947; www.durbartandoori.co.uk). ⊖Bayswater. One of London's more famous Indian resturants. The large and low-priced menu showcases several regions of India with a wide range of curries, meat and vegetarian, that arrive sizzling at the table (from £5.25). The rich and almost chocolatey dinner special *chicken l'orient* is special indeed (£10). Bargain takeaway lunch box £4. Chef's dinner £23 for 2. Open M-Th and Sa-Su noon-2:30pm and 5:30-11:30pm, F 5:30-11:30pm. Restaurant AmEx/MC/V. Cafe cash only. ❷

Aphrodite Taverna, 15 Hereford Rd. (☎020 7229 2206). ⊖Bayswater. Fabulous menu is a grab bag of polysyllabic treats, like dolmades (stuffed grape leaves; £9.80) or *keftedes* (Greek meatballs; entree £9.50). £1 cover is amply rewarded with baskets of fresh pita bread and other appetizers. Cafe Aphrodite next door offers some of Taverna's specialties at lower prices as well as a full sandwich menu (from £2.60). Restaurant open M-Sa noon-midnight. Cafe open daily 8am-5pm. AmEx/MC/V. Restaurant ❷/Cafe ❶

Khan's Restaurant, 13-15 Westbourne Grove (☎020 7727 5420; www.khanrestaurant. com). ⊖Bayswater. Just around the corner from Durbar Tandoori, this family-run halal restaurant, with landscape murals and faux-palm tree pillars, dishes out hearty portions of Indian favorites. Chicken tikka (£5) and fish curry (£5.55) are favorites from the extensive menu. Special all-you-can-eat lunch deal £8.50. Takeaway available. Open M-Th and Sa-Su noon-3pm and 6pm-midnight, F 6pm-midnight. AmEx/MC/V. ❷

BLOOMSBURY

🖾 **Navarro's Tapas Bar,** 67 Charlotte St. (☎020 7637 7713; www.navarros.co.uk). ⊖Goodge St. Colorful, bustling tapas restaurant with tiled walls and flamenco music. The authenticity carries over to the excellent food—try the spicy *patatas bravas* (fried potatoes; £3.75). Tapas £3.50-11; 2-3 per person is plenty. £7.50 min. purchase. Set-price menu £17. Open M-F noon-3pm and 6-10pm, Sa 6-10pm. AmEx/MC/V. ❸

Newman Arms, 23 Rathbone St. (☎020 7636 1127). ⊖Tottenham Court Rd. or ⊖Goodge St. Squirreled away among Tottenham Court Rd.'s long chains of Carphone Warehouses and Chinese takeaways, this pub with a famous upstairs pie room and restaurant maintains a slice of Olde English charm. Connoisseurs at 10 sought-after tables relish the homemade puff-pastry meat pies with fillings like beef and kidney and lamb with rosemary. Seasonal game fillings are the most popular; vegetarian and fish options available. Pie with potatoes and vegetables on the side £9. Pints start at £3. Book in advance or you'll be faced with a hungry wait. Pub open M-F 11am-11pm. Restaurant open M-Th noon-3pm and 6-9pm, F noon-3pm. ❷

Savoir Faire, 42 New Oxford St. (☎020 7436 0707). ⊖Tottenham Court Rd. or ⊖Holborn. Cherubic murals cover the walls of this bistro. Sit at wood tables and enjoy continental standards like *steak frites* and salad (£12) or swankier fare like honey-roast pork with apple relish. Entrees with vegetables and basket of bread from £16. 2-course vegetarian dinner £9. Also a popular brunch spot serving eggs Benedict and Florentine (£7). Open M-Sa noon-4pm and 5-11:30pm, Su noon-10:30pm. AmEx/MC/V. ❷

Diwana Bhel Poori House, 121-123 Drummond St. (☎020 7387 5556). ⊖Euston or ⊖Euston Sq. No frills here—just great, cheap South Indian vegetarian food and efficient service. Try the all-you-can-eat lunch buffet (served daily noon-2:30pm; £6.50) or enjoy ample portions on the regular menu. Outside buffet hours, *thali* set menu is a good deal (£6-9). Open daily noon-11:30pm, Su noon-10:30pm. AmEx/MC/V. ❷

North Sea Fish Restaurant, 7-8 Leigh St. (☎020 7387 5892). ⊖Russell Sq. or ⊖King's Cross St. Pancras. Fish and chips done right. This classy little restaurant, heavily populated by retired Brits, offers a boatload of fresh seafood dishes (£9-19) in a warm setting. For lower prices, order from the takeaway shop next door (cod fillets £4.30-6). Restaurant open M-Sa noon-2:30pm and 5:30-10:30pm. Takeaway open M-Sa noon-2:30pm and 5-11pm. AmEx/MC/V. Restaurant ❸/Takeaway ❶

CHELSEA

Buona Sera, 289A King's Rd. (☎020 7352 8827), at the Jam. ⊖Sloane Sq., then Bus #19 or 319. With patented "bunk" tables stacked high into the air, the treetop-esque dining experience alone justifies a visit. Waiters climb small wood ladders to deliver sizable pasta plates (£8.20-10.80) along with fish and steak dishes (£11.50-15). Alcohol only served with food. Kids eat at ½-price. Open M 6pm-midnight, Tu-F noon-3pm and 6pm-midnight, Sa-Su noon-midnight. AmEx/MC/V. ❸

Chelsea Bun, 9A Limerston St. (☎020 7352 3635). ⊖Sloane Sq., then Bus #11 or 22. Spirited, casual Anglo-American diner that serves heaping portions of everything from the "Ultimate Breakfast" (eggs, pancakes, sausages, and french toast; £10.30) to "Tijuana Benedict" (eggs with chorizo sausage; £8). Sandwiches, pasta, and burgers

£2.80-8. No need to set the alarm clock: early-bird specials available M-F 7am-noon (£2.20-3.20) and breakfast (from £4) served until 6pm. £3.50 min. per person for lunch, £5.50 for dinner. Open M-Sa 7am-11:30pm, Su 9am-7pm. MC/V. ❸

My Old Dutch, 221 King's Rd. (☎020 7376 5650; www.myolddutch.com). ⊖Sloane Sq., then Bus #11, 19, 319. One of 3 locations in London. Scrumptious Dutch food with offerings like the Amsterdammer (savory pancake with apple, smoked bacon, and maple syrup; £8) and sweet pancakes with fruit and ice cream (£6-7.25), all served on handsome blue Delftware. All pancakes £5 on M. Lunch set menu noon-5pm (2 courses £10, 3 courses £12.50). Open M-Sa 10:30am-11pm, Su 11am-10pm. MC/V. ❷

THE CITY OF LONDON

🏛 **The Place Below** (☎020 7329 0789; www.theplacebelow.co.uk), on Cheapside, in the basement of St. Mary-le-Bow Church. ⊖St. Paul's or ⊖Mansion House. There's nothing like an old stone crypt for atmosphere. Admire the vaulting while waiting in line for sandwiches (from £4.50) and fresh vegetarian quiches (from £6). Desserts are traditional with a twist: try the gooseberry-apple crumble with clotted cream (£3). Be prepared to wait at lunchtime. Watch for the daily health bowl, a concoction of various healthful foods (from £4.50). A cart in the upstairs courtyard sells sandwiches (£3 takeaway, £3.65 stay). Open M-F 7:30am-11am and 11:30am-2:30pm. ❶

🏛 **Cafe Spice Namaste,** 16 Prescot St. (☎020 7488 9242; www.cafespice.co.uk). ⊖Tower Hill or ⊖Tower Gateway. While somewhat out of the way, Spice is well worth the trek. Bright, festive decoration and outdoor courtyard seating bring an exotic feel to this old Victorian warehouse. The extensive menu of Goan and Parsi specialties explains each dish. Meat entrees are on the pricey side (£26-40), but vegetarian dishes (from £6) are affordable. A varied wine list and excellent, expensive desserts. Open M-F noon-3pm and 6:15-10:30pm, Sa 6:30-10:30pm. AmEx/MC/V. ❸

Futures, 8 Botolph Alley (☎020 7623 4529; www.futures-vta.net), between Botolph Ln. and Lovat Ln. ⊖Monument. London's workforce besieges this tiny takeaway joint during lunch; come before noon. A variety of vegetarian soups (from £2.50), salads (from £2.20), and hot dishes (from £5.20) all change weekly. For breakfast, you'll find a nice selection of pastries (from 85p). Open M-F 8-10am and 11:30am-2:30pm. ❶

CLERKENWELL AND HOLBORN

🏛 **Anexo,** 61 Turnmill St. (☎020 7250 3401; www.anexo.co.uk). ⊖Farringdon. This Spanish restaurant and bar serves Iberian dishes in a colorful tiled interior. The large menu has authentic paella (£7.50-9), fajitas (£7.50-11.50), and tapas (from £3.50, most £4-5). 2-course (£6.50) and 3-course (£8.50) lunch specials. Takeaway available. Wheelchair-accessible. Happy hour M-Sa 5-7pm. Open M-F 11am-11pm, Sa 6-11pm, Su 4:30-11pm. Bar open 11am-2am. AmEx/MC/V. ❷

Bleeding Heart Tavern, corner of Greville St. and Bleeding Heart Yard (☎020 7404 0333). ⊖Farringdon. Turn right onto Greville St. from Hatton Gardens. Set squarely in the center of the London gold and diamond district, this restaurant is a jewel of a different flavor. Seasonal menu may feature traditional British favorites like beef and ale sausages with colcannon potatoes (£9) or more sumptuous dishes like roast suckling pig with spiced apple slices (£12). Desserts are equally enticing: steamed treacle sponge cake with butterscotch sauce or chocolate honey pot dessert (both £4.50). Wash everything down with a fine tankard of ale. Open M-F 7-10:30am, noon-2:30pm, 6-10:30pm. Upstairs pub open M-F 11:30am-11pm. AmEx/MC/V. ❸

St. John, 26 St. John St. (☎020 7251 0848; www.stjohnrestaurant.com). ⊖Farringdon. Unusual dishes here reward the adventurous eater. Menu changes daily; meals include veal heart and celeriac (£6.80) and roast bone marrow and parsley salad (£6.60).

Dinner entrees lean toward the pricey side (£13.50-20). Bakery at the back of the bar churns out delicious loaves of bread (£2.50). Drinks £8-12. Open M-F noon-3pm and 6-11pm, Sa 6-11pm. Bar open M-F 11am-11pm, Sa 6-11pm. AmEx/MC/V. ❸

The Greenery, 5 Cowcross St. (☎020 7490 4870). ⊖Farringdon. For the vegetarian or health fanatic, this tiny restaurant is a bit of leafy heaven. Salads fromt £2, savories (lasagna, pizza, quiche) from £2.10, and jacket potatoes from £1.50 are delicious, cheap lunches. Packed sandwiches from £2. Vitamin-enriched smoothies from £2.30. Expect long queues during lunch. There are only a few tables in this busy shop; take your organic goodies with you and head for a nearby park. Open M-F 7am-5pm. ❶

Al's Bar/Cafe, 11-13 Exmouth Market (☎020 7837 4821). ⊖Angel or ⊖Farringdon. A favorite hangout for journalists from the nearby *Guardian, Face,* and *Arena* newspapers. Red-lit with a basement club. With comfortable leather lounge chairs and windows all around, Al's is a prime spot to relax with coffee (£1.70-2.20) and people-watch. Outdoor seating. Sandwiches and salads £7-8. Daily pasta specials £7.50-9.50. All-day breakfast from £8. DJs visit F-Sa 10pm-2am. Open M 8am-midnight, Tu-Sa 8am-2am, Su 9am-10:50pm. AmEx/MC/V. ❶

Aki, 182 Gray's Inn Rd. (☎020 7837 9281). ⊖Chancery Ln. The bambooed warmth of this peaceful Japanese restaurant is an appropriate setting for its traditional menu and dishes. Noodle dishes (from £5), meat dishes (£7-13), and sushi meals (from £5) are bargains. Bento box lunch from £5.20. Wheelchair-accessible. Open M-F noon-2:30pm and 6-11pm, Sa 6-10:30pm. AmEx/MC/V. ❸

MARYLEBONE AND REGENT'S PARK

Mandalay, 444 Edgware Rd. (☎020 7258 3696; www.mandalayway.com). ⊖Edgware Rd. A 5min. walk north from the Tube. Looks ordinary, tastes extraordinary—one of the best deals around. With huge portions of wildly inexpensive food, this Burmese restaurant is justly plastered with awards. Lunch specials offer great value (curry and rice £4; 3 courses £6). Entrees, including sizable vegetarian selection, £4-8. Open M-Sa noon-2:30pm and 6-10:30pm. Dinner reservations recommended. MC/V. ❶

Patogh, 8 Crawford Pl. (☎020 7262 4015). ⊖Edgware Rd. With just 10 tables (5 upstairs and 5 downstairs) and a cave-like interior, this tiny, evocative Persian restaurant gives new meaning to "hole in the wall." Generous portions of sesame-seed flatbread (£2) and freshly prepared starters (£2.50-6) will whet your appetite; flame-grilled entrees like *kabab koobideh* (minced lamb kebab) with bread, rice, or salad (£6-11) will feed you for days. This is mostly a carnivorous enclave, but vegetarians can enjoy the rather unsettingly named "lady fingers stew" filled with okra and fresh tarragon (£8). Takeaway available. Open daily noon-midnight. Cash only. ❷

The Golden Hind, 73 Marylebone Ln. (☎020 7486 3644). ⊖Baker St. or ⊖Bond St. Short of serving its fare on newspaper, this fish and chips joint is as authentic as they come. Open since 1914, the no-nonsense "chippie" serves up fried cod and haddock (£3.40-5.70) to a local clientele and savvy travelers. Takeaway available. Open M-F noon-3pm and 6-10pm, Sa 6-10pm. Reservations recommended. AmEx/MC/V. ❷

Royal China, 24-26 Baker St. (☎020 7487 4688; www.royalchinagroup.co.uk). ⊖Baker St. This upscale branch of the micro-chain straddles the line between faux and real elegance. Large oblong dining room filled with gleaming black marble. Try the 5-course seafood menu (£38) or the standard and vegetarian versions (£30) and keep your eyes open—this restaurant is crawling with minor celebs. Feeling particularly opulent? Spring for a Peking duck (£58; serves 4). Most entrees £12-28. Rice and noodle dishes £8-9.50. Open M-Th noon-11pm, F-Sa noon-11:30pm, Su 11am-10pm. Dim sum served until 5pm. AmEx/MC/V. ❸

THE WEST END

▨ **Masala Zone,** 9 Marshall St. (☎020 7287 9966; www.realindianfood.com). ⊖Oxford Circus. Also in Islington at 80 Upper St. (☎020 7359 3399). Masala Zone oozes hipness with its softly lit interior and sunken dining room. The menu has typical favorites (£7-12) as well as "street food," which is served in small bowls (£4-6). The speciality is *thalis,* or balanced meals, which are platters filled with a variety of contrasting dishes (£7.50-11.50). 2-course meal £8. Open M-F noon-2:45pm and 5:30-11pm, Sa 12:30-11pm, Su 12:30-3:30pm and 6-10:30pm. MC/V. ❷

▨ **Rock and Sole Plaice,** 47 Endell St. (☎020 7836 3785; www.rockandsoleplaice.com). ⊖Covent Garden. One of London's most picturesque fish-and-chips joints, this venerable institution has been operating since 1871. A self-proclaimed "master fryer" (qualifications unclear) turns out haddock, cod, halibut, and sole fillets (all with chips) for £9-11. From the picnic tables outside you can just hear a murmur of nearby Soho. Specialties change daily but range £4-6. Packed during mealtime rushes. Open M-Sa 11:30am-11:30pm, Su 11:30am-10pm. MC/V. ❷

Busaba Eathai, 106-110 Wardour St. (☎020 7255 8686). ⊖Tottenham Court Rd., ⊖Leicester Sq., or ⊖Piccadilly Circus. Large, tightly packed communal tables ensure a wait at this sleek but affordable restaurant. Students and locals line up for pad thai, curries, and wok creations (£7-9). Plenty of vegetarian options. No reservations; come early. Open M-Th noon-11pm, F-Sa noon-11:30pm, Su noon-10pm. AmEx/MC/V. ❷

Golden Dragon, 28-29 Gerrard St. (☎020 7734 2763). ⊖Leicester Sq. The ritziest and best-known dim sum joint in Chinatown. 2 red-and-gold rooms pack them in on weekends. Entrees £6-20. Dim sum £12.50-22.50. £10 per person min. Open M-Th noon-11:30pm, F-Sa noon-midnight, Su 11am-11pm. Dim sum served M-Sa noon-5pm, Su 11am-5pm. AmEx/MC/V. ❸

Cafe in the Crypt, Duncannon St. (☎020 7839 4342). ⊖Embankment or ⊖Charing Cross. In the basement of St. Martin-in-the-Fields Church, this exposed-brick cellar is a monastery gone modern. Hearty food is far from monastic: an excellent fresh salad bar (£7), freshly made sandwiches (£5.25), and traditional English hot dishes (£4.25-8) served cafeteria-style. Linger with a wholesome warm pudding (£3.50) or stay for afternoon tea (£5). Jazz some W nights. Open M-W 8am-8pm, Th-Sa 8am-10pm, Su noon-6:30pm. AmEx/MC/V over £5 min. ❶

Scoop, 40 Shorts Gardens (☎020 7240 7086; www.scoopgelato.com). ⊖Covent Garden. The bright orange storefront attracts passersby, but the creamy gelato and sorbet keeps them coming back. Uses only fresh raw ingredients—many imported from the owner's Tuscan homeland. Flavors range from *pompelmo* (grapefruit) and pineapple to *cioccolato al latte* (milk chocolate) and macaroon. Cups and cones start at £2. Open daily 8am-11:30pm. MC/V. ❶

Carluccio's, St. Christopher's Pl. (☎020 7935 5927; www.carluccios.com). ⊖Bond St. Short menu stocks many variations on pasta as well as a few meat dishes. Choose from shared tables on the ground floor, more formal indoor seating, or the open patio. Antipasti from £4.50. Entrees from £7.60. Carluccio's also has an on-site deli. Branches in Islington and the City and delis all over London. Wheelchair-accessible patio. Open M-F 8am-11pm, Sa 9am-11pm, Su 9am-10:30pm. AmEx/MC/V. ❷

NORTH LONDON

▨ **Gallipoli,** 102 Upper St. (☎020 7359 0630). Gallipoli Again, 120 Upper St. (☎020 7359 1578). Gallipoli Bazaar, 107 Upper St. (☎020 7226 5333). ⊖Angel. Dark walls and patterned blue tiles are the backdrop for Lebanese, North African, and Turkish delights like *iskender kebab* (grilled lamb with yogurt and marinated pita bread in secret sauce; £8.40) and the 2-course lunch (£9). Gallipoli Bazaar sits between the other 2 and serves up food, mixed drinks, and shisha pipes. Open shuttered windows near the tables allow diners to look out on Upper St. and enjoy a breeze. The same windows waft the restaurant's aroma down a block or 2, enticing shoppers from the nearby antique bazaars. Open M-Th and Su 10:30am-11pm, F-Sa 10am-midnight. MC/V. ❷

Le Crêperie de Hampstead, 77 Hampstead High St. (www.hampsteadcreperie.com), the metal stand on the side of the King William IV statue. ⊖Hampstead. Don't let the slow-moving line deter you; these fabulously toothsome crepes are worth the wait. Watching the crepe-maker pouring batter, sautéing bananas, and melting chocolate for 3 different crepes at once is almost as much fun as eating the finished products. Among a bewildering variety try the favorite ham, egg, and cheese (£4), or the maple, walnut, and cream (£3.30). Open M-Th 11:45am-11pm, F-Su 11:45am-11:30pm. ❶

Mango Room, 10-12 Kentish Town Rd. (☎020 7482 5065; www.mangoroom.co.uk). ⊖Camden Town. The small Caribbean menu features fish complemented by a variety of mango, avocado, and coconut sauces. Decor includes funky paintings and orange walls. Entrees from £10. Lunch from £6.50. Wheelchair-accessible. Open daily noon-midnight. Reservations recommended Sa-Su. MC/V. ❷

New Culture Revolution, 42 Duncan St. (☎020 7833 9083; www.newculturerevolution.co.uk). ⊖Angel. The revolution in question is a peaceful one: disestablish greasy Asian takeaway and bring in some leaner, more healthful fare. The menu dishes out huge portions of noodles and soups as well as dumplings (£5), vegetable chow mein (£5.20), and chili and lemongrass seafood lo mein (from £6). Open M-Sa noon-3pm and 5-11pm, Su noon-10pm. AmEx/MC/V. ❶

Bloom's, 130 Golders Green Rd. (☎020 8455 1338). ⊖Golders Green. The takeaway shop in the front serves freshly made offerings like potato salad and sandwich fillers (£4.50), and the sleek restaurant in back has traditional dishes like chopped liver sandwiches (£12.25). Jewish favorites like *gefilte* fish (£5.45) and latkes (£3) served as sides. Kosher. Wheelchair-accessible. Open M-Th and Su noon-11pm, F 11am-3pm. ❷

EAST LONDON

Café 1001, 91 Brick Ln., Dray Walk (☎020 7247 9679; www.cafe1001.co.uk), in an alley just off Brick Ln. ⊖Aldgate East. Bring your sketchpad to this artists' den, wedged among the various Bohemian hangouts of Brick Ln. Spacious upstairs and outdoor seating barely accommodate the large crowds. Freshly baked cakes (£2 per slice), pre-made salads (£3), and sandwiches (£2.50). Nightly DJs 7pm-close. Live jazz W. Open M-W and Su 7am-11:30pm, Th-Sa 6pm-midnight. ❶

Yelo, 8-9 Hoxton Sq. (☎020 7729 4626; www.yelothai.com). ⊖Old St. Pad thai, curry, and stir-fry (from £5.45) make for familiar fare, but the industrial lighting, exposed brick, and house music shake things up. Outdoor seating looks out on grassy Hoxton Sq. For a more formal affair, call to book a "proper" table downstairs. Takeaway and delivery available. Wheelchair-accessible. Open daily 1-3pm and 6-11pm. ❶

Aladin, 132 Brick Ln. (☎020 7247 8210; www.aladinbricklane.co.uk). ⊖Aldgate East. Praised by Prince Charles on his visit through the East End, Aladin serves up Pakistani, Bangladeshi, and Indian food. Inexpensive meals (3-course lunch menu £6.50; 3-course dinner £8) prepared by the veteran chef. A new downstairs lounge can be reserved free of charge. Open M-Th and Su noon-midnight, F-Sa noon-1am. ❷

The Real Greek, 14-15 Hoxton Market (☎020 7739 8212; www.therealgreek.com). ⊖Old St. Hidden except for its cobalt blue doors, this Mediterranean restaurant serves a variety of hot and cold *mezze* dishes such as grilled octopus and stuffed grape leaves (£3.25-5.75). Several dining rooms with large windows facing onto the square accommodate large crowds. Open M-Sa noon-midnight. ❷

The Drunken Monkey, 222 Shoreditch High St. (☎020 7392 9606; www.thedrunken-monkey.co.uk). ⊖Liverpool St. This dim sum restaurant-bar is hipper than most Shanghai nightclubs with its spacious wood tables and large lounge area in the front. Rice and noodle dishes £4-5; small dim sum plates £2.50-4.50. Set menu £15. Free Wi-Fi. Takeaway available. DJs Tu-Su. Happy hour M-F 5-7pm, Sa 6-8pm, Su noon-11pm with drinks from £4.50. Open M-F and Su noon-11pm, Sa 6-11pm. AmEx/MC/V. ❷

OTHER NEIGHBORHOODS

🖼 **George's Portobello Fish Bar,** 329 Portobello Rd. (☎020 8969 7895). ⊖Ladbroke Grove. George opened here in 1961, and, although the space has lived through various incarnations, the fish and chips are still as good as ever: cod, rockfish, plaice, and skate with chips (from £6.30). Open M-F 11am- 11:45pm, Sa 11am-9pm, Su noon-9:30pm. ❷

🖼 **Jenny Lo's Teahouse,** 14 Eccleston St. (☎020 7259 0399). ⊖Victoria. Around the corner from Jenny's father's high-end restaurant (Ken Lo is one of the most famous chefs in the UK). Delicious *cha shao* (pork noodle soup; £6.50) and a broad selection of Asian noodles (£6.50-8) make eating here worth the wait. Finish with honey and stem ginger ice cream (£3.25). Patio lit with Japanese globe lamps. Takeaway available (min. £5 per person). Open M-F noon-3:30pm and 6-10pm, Sa 6-9:30pm. Cash only. ❷

Cantina del Ponte, 36C Shad Thames, Butlers Wharf (☎020 7403 5403; www.cantina.co.uk). ⊖Tower Hill. Right on the Thames, this classy Italian place serves fine pasta (try the pesto, green bean, and potato; £8.50) and bruschetta against the backdrop of Tower Bridge. Fixed-price lunch menu is a bargain at 2 courses for £10, 3 for £13.50. Pizzas from £5. Dinner entrees from £10.50. Wheelchair-accessible. Open M-Sa noon-3pm and 6-10:45pm, Su noon-3pm and 6-9:45pm. AmEx/MC/V. ❸

Tas, 33 The Cut (☎020 7403 7200; www.tasrestaurant.com). ⊖Southwark. Also at 72 Borough High St.; Tas Cafe, 76 Borough High St.; Tas Pide, 20-22 New Globe Walk (☎020 7928 3300). ⊖London Bridge. A group of affordable Turkish restaurants. Soups and baked dishes outshine the respectable kebabs. Entrees from £6, 2-course fixed-price menus from £9. Live music daily from 7:30pm. Open M-Sa noon-11:30pm, Su noon-10:30pm. Dinner reservations recommended at Tas and Tas Pide. AmEx/MC/V. ❷

Goya, 34 Lupus St. (☎020 7976 5309; www.goyarestaurant.co.uk). ⊖Pimlico. Join the local clientele for a post-siesta meal. Mirrors, large windows, and bright wood. Generous, diverse tapas (mostly £4-7), including plenty of vegetarian options; 2-3 per person is more than enough. Alcohol served only with food. Wheelchair-accessible. Open daily 11:30am-11:30pm. AmEx/MC/V over £10. ❸

Newens Maids of Honour, 288 Kew Rd. (☎020 8940 2752). ⊖Kew Gardens. Facing Kew Rd. from the Victoria Gate of Kew Gardens, cross the street and walk left for 5min. Sip tea with an extended pinky finger at this historical teahouse. The specialty is the maid of honor itself; reputedly beloved by King Henry VIII and a tradition in this town for over 300 years, maids of honor are buttery pastries filled with sweetened cheese curds. Take a box of other bakery delectables with you to eat in Kew Gardens or stay for set tea (2:30-5:30pm; £7) served with traditional fixtures. Open M 9:30am-1pm, Tu-F 9:30am-5:30pm, Sa 9am-5:30pm. MC/V. ❶

🔄 SIGHTS

To walk through London is to watch the city unfold through time, a rich slice of England's 2000-year-old history: from the ancient city center, rebuilt by Christopher Wren after the Great Fire of 1666, down to Westminster to hold court with the regents and royals who run this capital, and then to Bloomsbury, heart of early-20th-century intellectual radicalism and still home to students today.

Unlike London's many free museums, the most famous sights tend to cost. From avant-garde architecture in Islington to the urban wilderness of Hampstead Heath, many of London's sights are those seen on foot.

MAJOR SIGHTS

◙**WESTMINSTER ABBEY.** Founded as a Benedictine monastery, Westminster Abbey has become a house of kings and queens living and dead. Almost nothing remains of the original St. Edward's Abbey, built here in the 11th century; Henry III's 13th-century Gothic reworking created most of the current grand structure. Britons buried or commemorated inside the Abbey include **Henry VII, Mary, Queen of Scots, Elizabeth I,** and the scholars and artists honored in the **"Poet's Corner"** (Chaucer, Dylan Thomas, the Brontë sisters, Jane Austen, Handel, and Shakespeare). A door off the east cloister leads to the octagonal **Chapter House,** the original meeting place of the House of Commons with a 13th-century tiled floor. Next to the abbey (through the cloisters), the **Abbey Museum** is housed in the Norman undercroft. The highlights of the collection are medieval royal **funeral effigies,** undergarments and all.

Saint Margaret's Church, just north of the Abbey, enjoys a strange status: as a part of the Royal Peculiar, it is not under the jurisdiction of the diocese of England or the archbishop of Canterbury. It was built for local residents by abbey monks and has been beautifully restored in the past few years. Since 1614, it's been the official worshiping place of the House of Commons—the first few pews are cordoned off for the speaker, black rod (an official of Parliament), and other dignitaries. *(Parliament Sq. Access Old Monastery, Cloister, and Garden from Dean's Yard, behind the Abbey.* ⊖*Westminster Abbey.* ☎*020 7222 5152, Chapter House 7654 4840; www.westminster-abbey.org. No photography. Abbey open M-Tu and Th-F 9:30am-3:45pm, W 9:30am-7pm, Sa 9:30am-1:45pm, Su for services only. Museum open daily 10:30am-4pm. 1hr. tours Apr.-Oct. M-F 10, 10:30, 11am, 2, 2:30pm, Sa 10, 10:30, 11am; Oct.-Mar. M-F 10:30, 11am, 2, 2:30pm, Sa 10:30, 11am. Partially wheelchair-accessible. Abbey and museum £12, students and ages 11-17 £9, families of 4 £28. Services free. Tours £5. Audio tours £4; available M-F 9:30am-3pm, Sa 9:30am-1pm. AmEx/MC/V.)*

TOWER OF LONDON. The turrets of this multi-functional block—which has served as palace, prison, royal mint, and museum over the past 900 years—are impressive not only for their appearance but also for their integral role in England's history. A popular way to get a feel for the Tower is to join one of the theatrical ◙**Yeoman Warders' Tours.** Queen Anne Boleyn passed through **Traitor's Gate** just before her death, but entering the Tower is no longer as perilous as it used to be. St. Thomas's Tower begins the self-guided tour of the **Medieval Palace.** At the end of the **Wall Walk**—a series of eight towers—is **Martin Tower,** which houses an exhibit that traces the history of the British Crown and is now home to a fascinating collection of retired crowns (without the gemstones that have been recycled into the current models); informative plaques are much better here than in the **Jewel House,** where the Crown Jewels are held. With the exception of the Coronation Spoon, everything dates from after 1660, when Oliver Cromwell melted down the original booty. The centerpiece of the fortress is **White Tower,** which begins with the ◙**Chapel of Saint John the Evangelist.** Outside, **Tower Green** is a lovely grassy area—not so lovely, though, for those once executed there. *(Tower Hill, next to Tower Bridge, within easy reach of the South Bank and the East End.* ⊖*Tower Hill or* ⊖*Tower Gateway.* ☎*0870 751 5175, ticket sales 0870 756 6060; www.hrp.org.uk. Open Mar.-Oct. M 10am-6:30pm, Tu-Sa 9am-6:30pm, Su 10am-6:30pm; buildings close at 6pm; Nov.-Feb. all closing times 1hr. earlier. Tower Green open only by Yeoman tours, after 4:30pm, or for daily services. Yeoman Warders' Tours meet near entrance; 1hr., every 30min. M and Su 10am-3:30pm, Tu-Sa 9:30am-3:30pm. £16.50, concessions £14, ages 5-15*

£9.50, under 5 free, families of 5 £46. Tickets also sold at Tube stations; buy them in advance to avoid long queues at the door. Audio tours £3.50, concessions £2.50.)

SAINT PAUL'S CATHEDRAL. Architect Christopher Wren's masterpiece is the fifth cathedral to occupy the site. The original, built in AD 604, burned down in 675, while the fourth St. Paul's, constructed in the 11th century, burned down in the Great Fire of 1666. Construction of the present cathedral commenced two years later. Inside, the **nave** leads to the second-tallest freestanding dome in Europe (after St. Peter's in the Vatican), its height accentuated by the tricky perspective of the paintings on the inner surface. The first stop to scaling the heights yourself is the narrow **Whispering Gallery,** reachable by 259 shallow wood steps. Climbing the stairs is exhausting, but the view from the top of the dome is extraordinary: a panoramic cityscape. Circling the base of the inner dome, the Whispering Gallery is a perfect resounding chamber: whisper into the wall, and your friend on the other side will hear you—or theoretically she could, if everyone else weren't trying the same thing. Far, far below the lofty dome, the crypt is packed wall to wall with plaques and tombs of great Britons and a gift shop. Admiral Lord Nelson commands a prime location, but radiating galleries of gravestones and tributes honor other military heroes as well, from Epstein's bust of TE Lawrence (of Arabia) to a plaque commemorating the casualties of the Gulf War. The carved stone of the exterior is warmed and softened by the cathedral gardens, which curve around the sides in a ramble of roses and clipped grass. *(St. Paul's Churchyard.* ⊖*St. Paul's.* ☎*020 7246 8350; www.stpauls.co.uk. Open M-Sa 8:30am-4pm. Last entry 3:45pm. Dome and galleries open M-Sa 9:30am-4pm. Open for worship daily 7:15am-6pm. "Supertour" M-F 11, 11:30am, 1:30, 2pm. Partially wheelchair-accessible. £10, concessions £8.50, ages 7-16 £2.50, worshippers free. Groups of 10 or more 50p discount per ticket. Supertours £3, concessions £2, ages 7-16 £1. Audio tour available in many languages daily 9am-3:30pm; £4, concessions £3.50.)*

SAINT PAUL'S FOR POCKET CHANGE. To gain access to the cathedral's nave for free, attend an Evensong service (45min., M-Sa 5pm). Arrive at 4:50pm to be admitted to seats in the choir.

BUCKINGHAM PALACE. The palace has been the official residence of the British monarchs since 1837, when a youthful Queen Victoria decamped from nearby Kensington Palace to set up house in this English Taj Mahal. With 755 rooms and a suite of state chambers sumptuously hung with Rembrandt and Vermeer, Buckingham Palace celebrates the splendor and power of the 19th-century English monarchy. The palace is open to visitors from the very end of July to the end of September every year, but don't expect to get any gossip about the lives of royalty—the **State Rooms** are the only ones on view, and they are used only for formal occasions. "God Save the Queen" is the rallying cry at the **Queens Gallery,** dedicated to changing exhibits of ridiculously valuable items from the Royal Collection. Detached from the palace and tour, the Royal Mews acts as a museum, stable, riding school, and working carriage house. The main attraction is the queen's collection of coaches, including the Cinderella-like glass coach used to carry royal brides, including Diana, to their weddings, and the State Coaches of Australia, Ireland, and Scotland. Another highlight is the four-ton Gold State Coach, which can occasionally be seen wheeling around the streets in the early morning on practice runs for major events. To witness the palace for free, attend a session of the Changing of the Guard. Show up well before 11:30am and stand in front of the palace in view of the morning guards or use the steps of the Victoria Memorial as a vantage point. *(At the end of the Mall, between Westminster, Belgravia, and Mayfair.* ⊖*St. James's Park,* ⊖*Victoria,* ⊖*Green Park,*

THE MILLENNIUM MILE

Stark, modern monuments to London's present—the round glass sphere of City Hall, the con verted power station that is the Tate Modern—line one side of the river, while stately relics of rich past—the Tower of London and St. Paul's Cathedral—stand on the opposite bank. Whethe it's a search for Shakespeare and Picasso that brings you to the South Bank, or just a hankerin for a nice walk, you will find yourself rewarded.

1. TOWER OF LONDON. Begin your trek to the Tower early to avoid the crowds. Tours given b the Yeomen Warders meet every 1½hr. near the entrance. Listen as they expertly recount tale of royal conspiracy, treason, and murder. See the **White Tower,** once a fortress and residence c kings. Shiver at the executioner's stone on the tower green and pay your respects at the Chape of St. Peter ad Vinculum, which holds the remains of three queens. First, get the dirt on th gemstones at **Martin Tower,** then wait in line to see the **Crown Jewels.** The jewels include suc glittering lovelies as the largest cut diamond in the world (p. 116). Time: 2hr.

2. TOWER BRIDGE. The Tower Bridge is an engineering wonder that puts its plainer sibling the London Bridge, to shame. Marvel at its beauty, but skip the Tower Bridge Experience. Call i advance to inquire what times the drawbridge is lifted (p. 122). Time: no need to stop walking take in the mechanics as you head to the next sight.

3. DESIGN MUSEUM. On Butler's Wharf, let the Design Museum introduce you to the lates innovations in contemporary design. See what's to come in the forward-looking Review Galler or hone in on individual designers and products in the Temporary Gallery (p. 135). From the museum, walk along the **Queen's Walk.** To your left you will find the *HMS Belfast,* which wa launched in 1938 and led the landing on D-Day in 1944. Time: 1hr.

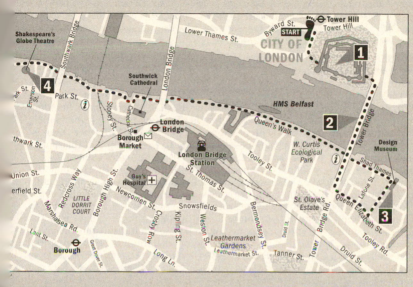

5. SHAKESPEARE'S GLOBE THEATRE. "I hope to see London once ere I die," says Shakespeare's Davy in *Henry IV*. In time, he may see it from the beautiful recreation of the Bard's most famous theater. Excellent exhibits detail the intricacies of costuming and stage effects in Shakespeare's day as well as the more modern process of rebuilding of the theater almost 400 years after the original burned down. You might be able to catch a matinee performance. Call in advance for tour and showtimes (p. 126). Time: 1hr. for tour; 3hr. for performance.

5. TATE MODERN. It's hard to imagine anything casting a shadow over the Globe Theatre, but the massive former Bankside Power Station does just that. One of the world's premier modern art museums, the Tate promises a new spin on well-known favorites and works by emerging British artists. Be sure to catch one of the informative docent tours and don't forget to check out the rotating installation in the Turbine Room (p. 132). Time: 2hr.

6. GABRIEL'S WHARF. Check out the cafes, bars, and boutiques of colorful Gabriel's Wharf. If you missed the top floor of the Tate Modern, go to the public viewing gallery on the eighth floor of the **OXO Tower Wharf.** On your way to the London Eye, stop by the **South Bank Centre.** Established as a primary cultural center in 1951, it now exhibits a range of music from philharmonic extravaganzas to low-key jazz. You may even catch one of the free lunchtime or afternoon events. Call in advance for dates and times. Time: 1½hr.

7. LONDON EYE. The London Eye has firmly established itself as one of London's top attractions, popular with locals and tourists alike. The Eye offers amazing 360° views from its glass pods; you may be able to see all of London lit up at sunset. Book in advance to minimize queue time (p. 127). Time: 1hr.

or ☺Hyde Park Corner. ☎020 7766 7324; www.the-royal-collection.com. Palace open from late July to late Sept. daily 9:30am-6:30pm. Last entry 4:15pm. £15, concessions £13.50, ages 6-17 £8.50, under 6 free, families of 5 £69.50. Advance booking is recommended; required for disabled visitors. Queens Gallery open daily 10am-5:30pm. Last entry 4:30pm. Wheelchair-accessible. £8, concessions £7, families £22. Royal Mews open from late July to late Sept. daily 10am-5pm. Last entry 4:15pm; from late Sept. to late Oct. and Mar.-July. M-Th and Sa-Su 11am-4pm. Last entry 3:15pm. Wheelchair-accessible. £7, under 17 £4.50, seniors £6, families £18.50. Changing of the Guard from Apr. to late July daily; Aug.-Mar. every other day, excepting the queen's absence, inclement weather, or pressing state functions. Free.)

HOUSES OF PARLIAMENT. Soaring spikily against the London skyline, the **Palace of Westminster** is a monument to English Gothic architecture and one of the most recognizable buildings in the city. It has been home to both the **House of Lords** and the **House of Commons** (together known as Parliament) since the 11th century, when Edward the Confessor established his court here. Standing guard on the northern side of the building is the clock tower, nicknamed **Big Ben,** named after the robustly proportioned Benjamin Hall, a former commissioner of works. "Big Ben" actually refers only to the 14-ton bell that hangs inside the tower. **Victoria Tower,** at the south end of the palace building, contains copies of every act of Parliament since 1497. Sir Charles Barry rebuilt the tower in the 1850s after it burned down in 1834; his design won an anonymous competition, and his symbol, the portcullis, remains the official symbol of the Houses of Parliament. A flag flying from the top signals that Parliament is in session. When the queen is in the building, a special royal banner is flown instead. Visitors with enough patience or luck to make it inside the chambers can hear the occasional debates between members of both the House of Lords and the House of Commons. *(Parliament Sq., in Westminster. Queue for both Houses forms at St. Stephen's entrance, between Old and New Palace Yards. ☺Westminster. ☎08709 063 773; www.parliament.uk/visiting/visiting.cfm. Open Aug. M-Tu and F-Sa 9:15am-4:30pm, W-Th 1:15-4:30pm; Sept. M and F-Sa 9:15am-4:30pm, Tu-Th 1:15-4:30pm. 75min. tours depart every few minutes. "Line of Route" tour includes both Houses. UK residents can contact their MPs for tours year-round, generally M-W mornings and F. Foreign visitors may tour Aug.-Sept. Book online, by phone, or in person at Abingdon Green ticket office (open mid-July) across from the Palace of Westminster. £12, students £8, families of 4 £30. MC/V.)*

PARLIAMENTARY PROCEDURE. Arrive early in the afternoon to minimize the wait, which often exceeds 2hr. Keep in mind that the wait for Lords is generally shorter than the wait for Commons. To sit in on Parliament's "question time" (40min.; M-W 2:30pm, Th-F 11am), apply for tickets several weeks in advance through your embassy in London.

BLOOMSBURY

BRITISH LIBRARY. The British Library is a paradox: the sleekest, most modern of buildings (finished in 1998), it contains in its vast and comprehensive holdings some of the oldest and most precious of English literary and historical documents. Most of the library is underground, with 12 million books on 200 mi. of shelving; the aboveground brick building is home to cavernous reading rooms and an engrossing museum. Displayed in a glass cube toward the rear of the building, the 65,000 volumes of the **King's Library,** collected by George III, were bequeathed to the nation in 1823 by his less bookish son, George IV. Among the treasures of the British Library Room are Beethoven's tuning fork, Lewis Carroll's diary, and Shakespeare's signature on various documents. The plaza out front hosts a series of free concerts and events. *(96 Euston Rd. ⊖Euston Sq. or King's Cross St. Pancras. ☎020 7412 7332; www.bl.uk. Open M 9:30am-6pm, Tu 9:30am-8pm, W-F 9:30am-6pm, Sa 9:30am-5pm, Su 11am-5pm. Tours of public areas M, W, F, S 10:30am and 3pm. Tours including one of the reading rooms Su and bank holidays 11:30am and 3pm. Reservations recommended. Wheelchair-accessible. To use reading rooms, bring 2 forms of ID—1 with a signature and 1 with a home address. Free. Tours £8. Audio tours £3.50, concessions £2.50.)*

OTHER SIGHTS. A cofounder and key advisor of **University College London**—the first in Britain to ignore race, creed, and politics in admissions and, later, the first to allow women to sit for degrees—social philosopher Jeremy Bentham still watches over his old haunts; his body has sat on display in the South Cloister since 1850, wax head and all. *(Main entrance on Gower St. South Cloister entrance through the courtyard. ⊖Euston. ☎020 7679 2000; www.ucl.ac.uk/Bentham-Project/info/ jb.htm. Quadrangle gates close at midnight; access to Jeremy Bentham ends at 6pm. Wheelchair-accessible. Free.)* Next to the British Library are the soaring Gothic spires of **Saint Pancras Chambers.** Formerly housing the Midland Grand Hotel, today the gorgeous red-brick building is a hollow shell being developed as apartments and a five-star hotel. *(Euston Rd. just west of ⊖King's Cross St. Pancras.)*

CHELSEA

ROYAL HOSPITAL. The environs—a chapel, a small museum detailing the history of the hospital, and a retirement home—house the Chelsea pensioners, former British soldiers now living in the Royal Hospital. The main draw is the once-ritzy **Ranelagh Gardens.** They're now a quiet oasis for picnicking and frolicking—except during the Chelsea Flower Show in late May, when members of the Royal Horticultural Society descend en masse. *(2 entrance gates on Royal Hospital Rd. ⊖Sloane Sq., then bus #137. ☎020 7881 5200; www.chelsea-pensioners.co.uk. Great Hall and chapel open daily 10am-noon and 2-4pm. Museum open Apr.-Sept. daily 10am-noon and 2-4pm; Oct.-Mar. M-Sa 10am-noon and 2-4pm. Grounds open May-Aug. daily 10am-8:30pm; Sept. daily 10am-7pm; Oct. daily 10am-5pm; Nov.-Mar. M-Sa 10am-4:30pm, Su 2-4:30pm; Apr. daily 10am-7:30pm. Wheelchair-accessible. Free. Flower show www.rhs.org.uk.)*

CHELSEA PHYSIC GARDEN. Founded in 1673 to furnish locals with medicinal herbs, the Physic Garden remains a carefully ordered living repository of useful, rare, and just plain interesting plants. It has also played an important historical role as the staging post from which tea was introduced to India and cotton to America. Today, the garden is a quiet, if expensive, place for picnics, teas, and scenic walks. You can purchase flora on display. *(66 Royal Hospital Rd.; entrance on Swan Walk. ⊖Sloane Sq., then bus #137. ☎020 7352 5646; www.chelseaphysicgarden.co.uk. Open from early Apr. to Oct. W noon-9pm, Th-F and Su noon-6pm; during Chelsea Flower Show in late May and Chelsea Festival in mid-June M-F noon-5pm. Tea served M-Sa from 12:30pm, Su from noon. Call in advance for wheelchair access. £7, students and under 16 £4.)*

THE CITY OF LONDON

GUILDHALL. This used to be the administrative center of the City of London Corporation, but the lord mayor and his associates have since moved to more modern digs in the City and on the South Bank. Before heading into the building itself, take a moment in the open stone **Guildhall Yard.** The towering Gothic building dates from 1440, although after repeated remodeling in the 17th and 18th centuries—not to mention almost complete reconstruction following the Great Fire and the Blitz—little of the original remains. Still, the hall maintains its style and skeleton; statues and gargoyles inside preserve the Gothic image. The quiet staidness of the hall today masks its historical drama: here, Lady Jane Grey was tried for treason in 1553, and Thomas Cranmer, famous victim

LONDON

of Mary I's bloody reign, was sentenced to death for his Protestantism. The stained-glass windows bear the names of all mayors and lord mayors of the Corporation, past and present—the builders must have foreseen the City's longevity, since there is still room for about 700 more. The downstairs crypt is only open by guided tour. Guildhall is more often than not closed for events, but arrive early and you might be able to pop in for a look. The **Guildhall Library,** in the 1970s annex and accessed via Aldermanbury or the Guildhall Yard, specializes in the history of London and owns an unparalleled collection of microfilm and books. It houses the **Guildhall Clockmaker's Museum** as well. *(Off Gresham St. Enter the Guildhall through the low, modern annex; entrance to library on Aldermanbury.* ⊖*St. Paul's,* ⊖*Moorgate, or* ⊖*Bank. Guildhall* ☎*020 7606 3030, for occasional tour information ext. 1463. Open May-Sept. daily 10am-5pm (Sept. weekends are open house); Oct.-Apr. M-Sa 10am-5pm. Last entry 4:30pm. Free. Library* ☎*020 7332 1862. Open M-Sa 9:30am-5pm. Free.)*

MONUMENT. The only non-ecclesiastical Wren building in the City, the Monument was built to commemorate the devastating Great Fire of 1666. Finished in 1677, the 202 ft. column stands 202 ft. from the bakery on Pudding Ln. where the fire first broke out. The colossal monument can only be scaled by climbing the very narrow spiral staircase inside. The climb brings you close to the copper urn of flames that caps the pillar, a mythic reminder of the fire. The enclosed platform at the top, however, offers one of the best views of London, especially of the Tower Bridge. The brave who make the steep climb are rewarded with a certificate of completion on the way out—the best souvenir. *(Monument St.* ⊖*Monument.* ☎*020 7626 2717. Open daily 9:30am-5pm. Last entry 4:40pm. £2.50. The Monument and the Tower Bridge Exhibition (below) offer joint admission for £7.)*

TOWER BRIDGE. Not to be mistaken for its plainer sibling, London Bridge, Tower Bridge is the one you know from all movies set in London. A relatively new construction—built in 1894—its bright blue suspension cables connect the banks of the Thames and rise above the cluster of other bridges in the area. The Victorian steam-powered lifting mechanism remained in use until 1973, when electric motors took over. Although clippers no longer sail into London very often, there's still enough large river traffic for the bridge to be lifted around 1000 times per year and five or six times per day in the summer. Call for the schedule or check the signs posted at each entrance. Historians and technophiles will appreciate the **Tower Bridge Exhibition,** which combines scenic 140 ft. glass-enclosed walkways with videos presenting a history of the bridge. *(Entrance to the Tower Bridge Exhibition is through the west side, upriver of the North Tower.* ⊖*Tower Hill or* ⊖*London Bridge.* ☎*020 7403 3761, for lifting schedule 7940 3984; www.towerbridge.org.uk. Open daily Apr.-Sept. 10am-6:30pm; Oct.-Mar. 9:30am-6pm. Last entry 1hr. before close. Wheelchair-accessible. £6, concessions £4.50, ages 5-16 £3.)*

ALL HALLOWS-BY-THE-TOWER. Nearly hidden by redevelopment projects and nearby office buildings, All Hallows stands quietly and proudly ancient. Just inside the entrance on the left is the oldest part of the church, a Saxon arch dating from AD 675. The main chapel has three parts: the right and left transepts date from the 13th and 14th centuries, respectively, and the central ceiling from the 20th. The undercroft museum is home to a diverse collection of Roman and Saxon artifacts, medieval art, and church record books from the time of the plague, all well worth a look. The spectacular **Lady Chapel** contains a magnificent altarpiece dating from the 15th century and has been restored to look like it did when it was built in 1489. The stark cement arches and barred windows of the nave, rebuilt after the Blitz, give this church a mysterious dignity. *(Byward St.* ⊖*Tower Hill.* ☎*020 7481 2928; www.allhallowsbythetower.org.uk. Church open M-F 8:30am-5:45pm, Su 9:30am-5pm. Crypt and museum open daily 10:30am-4pm. Free.)*

OTHER SIGHTS. The most famous modern structure in the City is **Lloyd's of London.** What looks like a towering postmodern factory is actually home to the world's largest insurance market, built in 1986. With raw metal ducts, lifts, and chutes on the outside, it wears its heart (or at least its internal organs) on its sleeve. *(Leadenhall St. ⊖Bank. Wheelchair-accessible.)* Only the tower and outer walls remain of Wren's **Saint Dunstan-in-the-East.** The Blitzed, mossy ruins have been converted into a quiet garden and peaceful picnic spot. The vine-covered Gothic-style walls and bubbling fountain make it an oasis in the City. *(St. Dunstan's Hill. ⊖Monument or ⊖Tower Hill. Wheelchair-accessible.)*

CLERKENWELL AND HOLBORN

Many Clerkenwell buildings are beautiful from the outside but inaccessible to tourists; walk the **Clerkenwell Historic Trail** to get a fine gander at the exteriors. Free maps are available at the **3 Things Coffee Room,** 53 Clerkenwell Close. (⊖Farringdon. ☎020 7125 37438. Open daily 8am-8pm.)

▓TEMPLE. The curious name derives from the crusading Order of the Knights Templar, which embraced this site as its English seat in 1185. Today this complex of buildings houses legal and parliamentary offices, but it hasn't lost its clerical flavor; instead of frocked priests, silent, suited barristers (lawyers) hurry by at all hours clutching briefcases. The charming network of gardens and the medieval church remain open to the enterprising visitor. Make sure to see the **Inner Temple Gateway,** between 16 and 17 Fleet St., the 1681 fountain of **Fountain Court** (featured in Dickens's *Martin Chuzzlewit*), and **Elm Court,** a tiny yet exquisite garden ringed by massive stone structures. *(Between Essex St. and Temple Ave.; church courtyard off Middle Temple Ln. ⊖Temple or ⊖Blackfriars. Free.)* **Temple Church** is both one of the finest surviving medieval round churches and London's first Gothic church, completed in 1185 on the model of Jerusalem's Church of the Holy Sepulchre. Intricately crafted stained-glass windows, towering ceilings, an original Norman doorway, and 10 armored effigies complete the impressive interior, although much of it was rebuilt after WWII bombings. Adjoining the round church is a rectangular Gothic choir, built in 1240, with a 1682 altar screen by Christopher Wren. The church hosts frequent recitals and musical services, including weekly organ recitals. *(☎020 7353 3470. Hours vary depending on the week's services and are posted outside the door of the church for the coming week. Organ recitals W 1:15-1:45pm; no services Aug.-Sept.)* The **Middle Temple** escaped the destruction of WWII and retains fine examples of 16th- and 17th-century architecture. In Middle Temple Hall (closed to the public), Elizabeth I saw Shakespeare act in the premiere of *Twelfth Night;* his *Henry VI* points to Middle Temple Garden as the origin of the red and white flowers that served as the emblems of Lancaster and York in the War of the Roses. *(Open May-Sept. M-F noon-3pm.)*

ROYAL COURTS OF JUSTICE. This massive Neo-Gothic structure, designed in 1874 by GE Street, holds its own among the many distinguished facades of Fleet St. Inside are 88 courtrooms, chambers for judges and court staff, and cells for defendants. The architecture is dazzling, more akin to a castle than a courthouse. Aside from the Great Hall's mosaic floor—the largest in Europe—the interior is much less impressive. Skip the uninspired display of legal costume at the rear and instead watch the real thing. The back bench of every courtroom is open to the public during trials unless the courtroom door says "In Chambers." The notice boards beside the Enquiry Desk in the Great Hall display a list of cases being tried. *(Where the Strand becomes Fleet St.; rear entrance on Carey St. ⊖Temple or ⊖Chancery Ln. ☎020 7947 6000, tours 7947 7684. Open M-F 9am-4:30pm; cases are heard 10:30am-1pm and 2-4pm. Wheelchair-accessible. Be prepared to go through a security checkpoint with metal detector. Free. Tours £6.)*

OTHER SIGHTS. The mid-13th-century **Church of Saint Etheldreda** is the last remaining vestige of the bishop of Ely's palace and the only pre-Reformation Catholic church in the city. *(In Ely Pl. ☎020 7405 1061. Church open daily 7:30am-7pm. Free.)* The unusual spire of Wren's 1675 **Saint Bride's Church** is one of the most imitated pieces of architecture in the world: a local baker used it as the model for the first-ever multi-tiered wedding cake. *(St. Bride's Ave., just off Fleet St. ✪Blackfriars. ☎020 7427 0133; www.stbrides.com. Open daily 8am-4:45pm. Lunchtime concerts and nighttime classical music; call for details. Free.)* Legend places **Saint Clement Danes Church** over the tomb of Harold Harefoot, a Danish warlord who ruled England in the 11th century. Its fame with Londoners stems from its opening role in the famous nursery rhyme—"'Oranges and lemons,' say the bells of St. Clement's," and they still do, daily, at 9am, noon, 3, and 6pm. *(186A Fleet St.✪Temple or ✪Chancery Ln. ☎020 7405 1929; www.stdunstaninthewest.org. Open Tu 11am-3pm. Free.)*

KENSINGTON AND EARL'S COURT

◪**HYDE PARK AND KENSINGTON GARDENS.** Enclosed by London's wealthiest neighborhoods, Hyde Park has served as the model for city parks around the world, including Central Park in New York City and Paris's Bois de Boulogne. Kensington Gardens, contiguous with Hyde Park and originally part of it, were created in the late 17th century when William and Mary set up house in Kensington Palace. *(Framed by Kensington Rd., Knightsbridge, Park Ln., and Bayswater Rd. ✪Queensway, ✪Lancaster Gate, ✪Marble Arch, ✪Hyde Park Corner, or ✪High St. Kensington. ☎020 7298 2100; www.royalparks.org.uk. Open daily 6am-dusk. "Liberty Drive" rides available Tu-F 10am-5pm for seniors and the disabled; call ☎077 6749 8096. A full program of music, performance, and children's activities takes place during the summer; see park notice boards for details. Free.)* In the middle of the park is the **Serpentine,** officially known as the "Long Water West of the Serpentine Bridge." Dog-paddling tourists and boaters have made it London's busiest swimming hole. Nowhere near the water, the **Serpentine Gallery** showcases contemporary art and is free and open daily 10am-6pm. *(✪Hyde Park Corner. Boating ☎020 7262 1330. Open daily Apr.-Sept. 10am-6:30pm or later in fine weather. £6.50 per hr. for up to 4 people, plus a £5 deposit. Swimming at the Lido, south shore, ☎020 7706 3422. Open daily from June to early Sept. 10am-6pm. Lockers and sun lounges available. £4, after 4pm £3.50; students £3/2.50; children £1/80p; families £9. Gallery open daily 10am-5pm. Free.)* At the northeast corner of the park, near Marble Arch, you can see free speech in action as proselytizers, politicos, and flat-out crazies dispense wisdom to bemused tourists at **Speaker's Corner** on Sundays, the only place in London where demonstrators can assemble without a permit.

KENSINGTON PALACE. In 1689 William and Mary commissioned Christopher Wren to remodel Nottingham House into a palace. Kensington remained the principal royal residence until George III decamped to Kew in 1760, but it is still in use—Princess Diana was the most famous recent inhabitant. It was here that in 1837 the young Victoria was awakened from her canopied bed and told the crown was hers. Royalty fanatics can tour the rather underwhelming Hanoverian **State Apartments,** with *trompe l'œil* paintings by William Kent, or the **Royal Ceremonial Dress Collection,** a magnificent spread of tailored and embroidered garments. *(Western edge of Kensington Gardens; enter through the park. ✪High St. Kensington, ✪Notting Hill Gate, or ✪Queensway. ☎020 7937 9561; www.hrp.org.uk/kensingtonpalace. Open daily 10am-6pm. Last entry 1hr. before close. Wheelchair-accessible. £12.30, concessions £10.75, children free, families of 5 (no more than 2 people over 15) £34. Combo passes with Tower of London or Hampton Court available. MC/V.)*

HOLLAND PARK. Smaller and less touristed than Kensington Gardens, Holland Park is shady with trees and thick with hedges. Hidden among the paths are cricket nets, tennis courts, a golf bunker, and Japanese gardens. *(Bordered by Kensington High St., Holland Walk, and Abbotsbury Rd. Enter at Commonwealth Institute. ☉High St. Kensington. ☎020 7471 9813, police 7441 9811, sport league and recreation info 7602 2226. Open daily 7:30am-dusk. Free.)*

KNIGHTSBRIDGE AND BELGRAVIA

🖼**APSLEY HOUSE.** Named for Baron Apsley, the house later known as "No. 1, London" was bought in 1817 by the duke of Wellington, whose heirs still occupy a modest suite on the top floor. Most visitors come for Wellington's fine art collection, much of which was given to him by the crowned heads of Europe following the Battle of Waterloo. The Old Masters hang in the **Waterloo Gallery,** where the duke held his annual Waterloo banquet around the stupendous silver centerpiece, now displayed in the dining room. *(Hyde Park Corner. ☉Hyde Park Corner. ☎020 7499 5676; www.english-heritage.org.uk/london. Open Apr.-Oct. W-Su 10am-5pm; Nov.-Mar. Tu and W-Su 10am-4pm. Wheelchair-accessible. £5.50, students £4.40, ages 5-18 £2.80. Joint ticket with Wellington Arch £7/5.20/3.50. Audio tour free. MC/V.)*

WELLINGTON ARCH. Standing at the center of Hyde Park Corner, the Wellington Arch was ignored by tourists and Londoners alike until April 2001, when the completion of a restoration project revealed the interior to the public for the first time. Exhibits on the building's history and the changing nature of war memorials play second fiddle to the two observation platforms, which command views of Buckingham Palace gardens, Green Park, and Hyde Park. *(Hyde Park Corner. ☉Hyde Park Corner. ☎020 7930 2726; www.english-heritage.org.uk/london. Open W-Su Apr.-Oct. 10am-5pm, Nov.-Mar. 10am-4pm. Wheelchair-accessible. £3.30, students with ISIC £2.60, ages 5-16 £1.70. Joint tickets with Apsley House available. MC/V.)*

MARYLEBONE AND REGENT'S PARK

🖼**REGENT'S PARK.** When Crown Architect John Nash designed Regent's Park, he envisioned a residential development for the "wealthy and good." Fortunately for us commonfolk, Parliament opened the space to all in 1811, creating London's most handsome and popular recreation area. Most of the park's top attractions and activities lie near the **Inner Circle,** a road that separates the rose-rich, meticulously maintained 🖼**Queen Mary's Gardens** from the rest of the grounds. While the few villas in the park—**The Holme** and **Saint John's Lodge**—are private residences for the unimaginably rich and not available for public viewing, the formal **Gardens of Saint John's Lodge** ("The Secret Garden"), on the northern edge of the Inner Circle, give a peek into the backyard of one such mansion. The climb up **Primrose Hill,** just north of Regent's Park proper, offers a glorious view of central London. The famous **Open Air Theatre,** which began in 1932, is now Britain's premier outdoor Shakespeare theater and stages performances from May to September. *(☉Baker St., ☉Regent's Park, ☉Great Portland St., or ☉Camden Town. ☎020 7486 7905, police 7706 7272; www.royalparks.org. Open daily 5am-dusk. Free. Open Air Theatre ☎020 826 4242; www.opentheatre.org. Tickets £10-35.)*

LONDON ZOO. First opened in 1826, the London Zoo has a range of expansive modern exhibits along with a few less current bars-and-cement enclosures. The very oldest buildings are now considered too small to house animals and instead test parents with an array of stuffed toys at exorbitant prices. Dangerous animals (lions and tigers and bears, oh my) were euthanized during WWII in fear that bombing might set them loose on a beleaguered and defenseless London. The London Zoo was also home to the original Winnie-the-Pooh, who died in 1934. She was an American black bear who reportedly was tame enough to be fed condensed milk and golden syrup by children in her den.

When exactly "she" became a "he" is unclear. **Gorilla Kingdom** and the **Meet the Monkeys Enclosure** allow visitors to view the primates at close quarters. Pick up a *Daily Event Planner* leaflet to catch all the free special displays and keeper talks. *(Main gate on Outer Circle, Regent's Park. ✪ Camden Town, plus a 10-15min. walk guided by signs or a short ride on bus #274. ☎ 020 7722 3333; www.zsl.org. Open daily Apr.-Oct. 10am-5:30pm; Nov.-Mar. 10am-4pm. Last entry 1hr. before close. Wheelchair-accessible. £15.40, concessions £14, ages 3-15 £12, families of 4 £49.10. AmEx/MC/V.)*

MADAME TUSSAUDS. This wax museum may be one of London's top tourist attractions, but it is also the most expensive round-the-block queue in the entire city. For those unwilling to pass up a photo op with wax models of everyone from Pope John Paul II to Tom Cruise, it is at least an indisputably unique 1hr. experience. The Spirit of London ride inside conjures memories of old-fashioned carnivals. *(Marylebone Rd. ✪ Baker St. ☎ 0870 999 0293; www.madame-tussauds.com. Open July-Aug. daily 9am-6pm; Sept.-June M-F 9:30am-5:30pm, Sa-Su 9am-6pm. Wheelchair-accessible. Prices depend on day of the week, entrance time, and season. £14-23, under 16 £7-17. "Chamber Live" exhibit adds £2. Advance booking by phone or online £2 more; groups of 10+ about £1.50 less per person. Call in advance. AmEx/MC/V.)*

THE SOUTH BANK

⌘SHAKESPEARE'S GLOBE THEATRE. This incarnation of the Globe is faithful to the original, thatched roof and all. The original burned down in 1613 after a 14-year run as the Bard's preferred playhouse. Today's reconstruction had its first full season in 1997 and now stands as the cornerstone of the **International Shakespeare Globe Centre.** The informative exhibit inside covers the theater's history and includes displays on costumes and customs of the theater, as well as information on other prominent playwrights of Shakespeare's era. There's also an interactive display where you can trade lines with recorded Globe actors. Try to arrive in time for a tour of the theater itself. Tours that run during a matinee skip the Globe but are the only way to gain admission to the neighboring **Rose Theatre,** where both Shakespeare and Christopher Marlowe performed. For info on performances, see p. 143. *(Bankside, close to Bankside pier. ✪ Southwark or ✪ London Bridge. ☎ 020 7902 1500; www.shakespeares-globe.org. Exhibit open daily Apr.-Sept. 9am-5pm; Oct.-Apr. 10am-5pm. Tours daily Apr.-Sept. 9am-noon; Oct.-Apr. 10am-5pm. Wheelchair-accessible. £10.50, concessions £8.50, ages 5-15 £6.50, families of 5 £20.)*

THRIFT, THRIFT, HORATIO. While a tour of Shakespeare's Globe will cost a pound of flesh, a groundling ticket at one of the shows costs £5 and includes access to the exhibits. Consider attending a live performance and taking a self-guided tour before the curtain opens.

SOUTHWARK CATHEDRAL. A site of worship since AD 606, the cathedral has undergone numerous transformations in the last 1400 years; it was a convent in 606, a priory in 1106, a parish church in 1540, and, finally, a cathedral since 1905. Shakespeare's brother Edmund is buried here. In the retrochoir, many high-profile Protestant martyrs were tried during the reign of Queen Mary. Near the center, the **archaeological gallery** is actually a small excavation by the cathedral wall, revealing a first-century Roman road. Free organ recitals on Mondays from 1:10 to 1:50pm. *(Montague Close. ✪ London Bridge. ☎ 020 7367 6700; www.southwark.anglican.org/cathedral. Open M-F 8am-6pm, Sa-Su 9am-6pm. Wheelchair-accessible. Suggested donation £4. Groups should book in advance; group rates available. Audio tours £5, concessions £4, ages 5-15 £2.50. Camera permit £2; video permit £5.)*

LONDON EYE. Also known as the Millennium Wheel, at 135m (430 ft.) the British Airways London Eye is the biggest observational wheel in the world. The ellipsoidal glass "pods" give uninterrupted views from the top during each 30min. revolution. Try riding the Eye at night to see the city ablaze with lights. *(Jubilee Gardens, between County Hall and the Festival Hall. ⊖Waterloo. ☎087 990 8883; www. ba-londoneye.com. Open daily July-Aug. 10am-9:30pm; Sept. and June 10am-9pm; Oct.-May 10am-8pm. Wheelchair-accessible. Buy tickets from box office at the corner of County Hall. Advance booking recommended, but check the weather. £15.50, concessions £12, under 16 £7.75.)*

> **⚡TIP** **MORE THAN MEETS THE EYE.** While the London Eye does offer magnificent views (particularly at night), the queues are long, and it's expensive. For equally impressive sights in a quieter atmosphere, head to the Monument (p. 122), Primrose Hill (p.126), or Hampstead Heath (p. 130).

THE WEST END

TRAFALGAR SQUARE. John Nash first suggested laying out this square in 1820, but it took almost 50 years for London's largest traffic roundabout to take on its current appearance. The square is named in commemoration of the defeat of Napoleon's fleet at Trafalgar, considered the UK's greatest naval victory. It has traditionally been a site for public rallies and protest movements, but it is now packed daily with tourists, pigeons, and black cabs. Towering over the square is the 170 ft. granite **Nelson's Column,** which until recently was one of the world's tallest displays of decades-old pigeon droppings. Now, thanks to a deep clean sponsored by the mayor, this monument to naval hero Lord Nelson sparkles once again. *(⊖Charing Cross.)*

SAINT MARTIN-IN-THE-FIELDS. The fourth church to stand here, James Gibbs's 1726 creation is instantly recognizable: the rectangular portico building supporting a soaring steeple made it the model for countless Georgian churches in Ireland and America. Handel and Mozart both performed here, and today the church host frequent concerts with some of Europe's premier symphonies and conductors. In order to support the cost of keeping the church open, a delicious cafe (p. 111), bookshop, and art gallery dwell in the crypt. *(St. Martin's Ln., northeast corner of Trafalgar Sq.; crypt entrance on Duncannon St. ⊖Leicester Sq. or ⊖Charing Cross. ☎020 7766 1100; www.smitf.org. Call or visit website for hours and further information.)*

SAINT PAUL'S CHURCH. Not to be confused with St. Paul's Cathedral, this 1633 Inigo Jones church is now one of the last remnants of the original square. It follows a double-cube design, standing 80 ft. long and 40 ft. high. Known as "the actors' church" for its long association with nearby theaters, the interior is festooned with plaques detailing the achievements of Boris Karloff, Vivien Leigh, and Charlie Chaplin. *(On Covent Garden Piazza; enter via the piazza, King St., Henrietta St., or Bedford St. ⊖Covent Garden. ☎020 7836 5221; www.actorschurch.org. Open M-F 8:30am-5:30pm. Morning services Su 11am. Evensong 2nd Su of month 5pm. Free.)*

SAINT JAMES'S PALACE. Built in 1536 over the remains of a leper hospital, St. James's is London's only remaining palace built as such (Buckingham Palace was a rough-and-ready conversion of a duke's house). Upon the death of a monarch, royal proclamations are issued from the balcony in the interior Friary Court. Unless your name starts with "His Royal Highness," the only part you'll get into is the **Chapel Royal,** open for Sunday services from October to Easter at 8:30 and 11:30am. From Easter to July, services are held in Inigo Jones's

LONDON

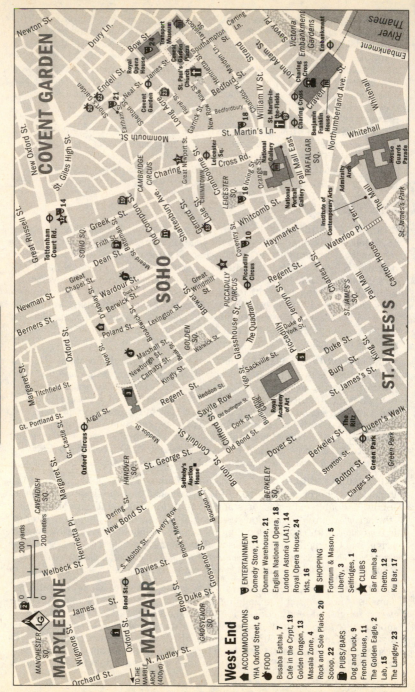

COVENT GARDEN

SOHO

MAYFAIR

MARYLEBONE

ST. JAMES'S

West End

▲ ACCOMMODATIONS
YHA Oxford Street, **6**

🍴 FOOD
Busaba Eathai, **7**
Cafe in the Crypt, **19**
Golden Dragon, **13**
Masala Zone, **4**
Rock and Sole Plaice, **20**
Scoop, **22**

🍺 PUBS/BARS
Dog and Duck, **9**
French House, **11**
The Golden Eagle, **2**
Lab, **15**
The Langley, **23**

🎭 ENTERTAINMENT
Comedy Store, **10**
Donmar Warehouse, **21**
English National Opera, **18**
London Astoria (LA1), **14**
Royal Opera House, **24**
tkts, **16**

🛍 SHOPPING
Fortnum & Mason, **5**
Liberty, **3**
Selfridges, **1**

★ CLUBS
Bar Rumba, **8**
Ghetto, **12**
Ku Bar, **17**

Queen's Chapel, across Marlborough Rd. from the palace, which was built in the 17th century for the marriage of Prince Charles I. (⊖*Green Park.*)

SOHO. A glitteringly eclectic conglomeration of squares, Soho is one of the most diverse areas in central London. **Old Compton Street** is the center of London's GLBT culture. In the 1950s, immigrants from Hong Kong started moving en masse to the few blocks just north of Leicester Sq., around Gerrard St. and grittier Lisle St., which now form **Chinatown.** Gaudy, brash, and world-famous, **Piccadilly Circus** is made up of four of the West End's major arteries (Piccadilly, Regent St., Shaftesbury Ave., and the Haymarket). In the middle of all the glitz and neon stands the Gilbert's famous **Statue of Eros.** (⊖*Piccadilly Circus.*) Lined with tour buses, overpriced clubs, and generic cafes, **Leicester Square** is one destination that Londoners go out of their way to avoid but that attracts sneaker-and-shorts-clad tourists like a magnet. (⊖*Piccadilly Circus or Leicester Sq.*) A calm in the middle of the storm, **Soho Square** is a scruffy patch of green space popular with picnickers. Its removed location makes the square more hospitable and less trafficked than Leicester. (⊖*Tottenham Court Rd. Park open daily 10am-dusk.*)

WESTMINSTER

⊠**SAINT JAMES'S PARK AND GREEN PARK.** The streets leading up to Buckingham Palace are flanked by two expanses of greenery: St. James's Park and Green Park. In the middle of St. James's Park is the placid St. James's Park Lake, where you can catch glimpses of the pelicans that call it home—the lake and the grassy area surrounding it make up an official waterfowl preserve. In the back corner, closest to the palace, is a children's playground in memory of Princess Diana. Across the Mall, the lush Green Park is the creation of Charles II; it connects Westminster and St. James's. "Constitution Hill" refers not to the king's interest in political theory but to his daily exercises. If you sit on one of the lawn chairs scattered enticingly around both parks, an attendant will magically materialize and demand money. Alternatively, bring a blanket for a picnic at no charge. (*The Mall.* ⊖*St. James's Park or* ⊖*Green Park. Open daily 5am-midnight. Lawn chairs available, weather permitting, Apr.-Sept. 10am-10pm or in daylight hours; Oct. and Mar. 10am-6pm. £2 per 2hr., students £30 for the season. Last rental 2hr. before close. Tour behind the Changing of the Guard every Th; £6. Summer walks in the park some M 1-2pm, including tour of Guard's Palace and Victoria Tower Gardens. Book in advance by calling ☎020 7930 1793.*)

WESTMINSTER CATHEDRAL. Following Henry VIII's break from the Catholic Church, London's Catholic community remained without a cathedral until 1884, when the church purchased a derelict prison on what used to be a monastery site. The Neo-Byzantine church looks somewhat like a fortress and is now one of London's great religious landmarks. An elevator, well worth the minimal fee, carries visitors up the striped 273 ft. bell tower for an all-encompassing view of Westminster, the river, and Kensington. (*Cathedral Piazza, off Victoria St.* ⊖*Victoria.* ☎*020 7798 9055; www.westminstercathedral.org.uk. Open daily 8am-7pm. Bell tower open daily 9:30am-12:30pm and 1-5pm. Organ recitals Su 4:45pm. Suggested donation £2.*)

WHITEHALL. Synonymous with the British civil service, Whitehall refers to the stretch of road connecting Trafalgar Sq. with Parliament Sq. From 1532 until a devastating fire in 1698, it was the home of the monarchy and one of the grandest palaces in Europe, although little remains today. Toward the north end of Whitehall, **Great Scotland Yard** marks the former headquarters of the Metropolitan Police. Nearer Parliament Sq., heavily guarded steel gates mark the entrance to **Downing Street.** In 1735, No. 10 was made the official residence of the first lord of the treasury, a position now permanently identified with the prime minister. The chancellor of the exchequer traditionally resides at No. 11

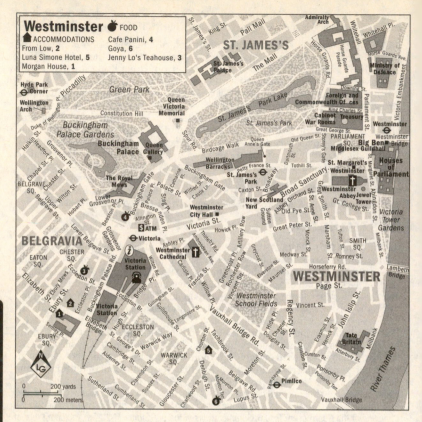

Westminster 🍎 FOOD

🏠 ACCOMMODATIONS
From Low, **2**
Luna Simone Hotel, **5**
Morgan House, **1**

Cafe Panini, **4**
Goya, **6**
Jenny Lo's Teahouse, **3**

and the parliamentary chief whip at No. 12, sandwiching No. 10 between them in a cozy parliamentary trio. When Tony Blair's family was too big for No. 10, he switched with Gordon Brown, a move that proved convenient when Brown was appointed prime minister in 2007. The street is closed to visitors, but, if you wait long enough, you might see one the dignitaries. South of Downing St., in the middle of Whitehall, stands Edward Lutyen's **Cenotaph** (1919), a proud tribute to WWI's dead. Many of the islands in the middle of the road hold statues honoring monarchs and military heroes. *(Between Trafalgar Sq. and Parliament Sq. ⊖Westminster, ⊖Embankment, or ⊖Charing Cross.)*

NORTH LONDON

⬛**HAMPSTEAD HEATH.** Unlike so many other manicured London parks, Hampstead Heath is wild, with unmown meadows and forests cut through by narrow grass paths. Bring a map to avoid getting lost. The **Vale of Health,** an oasis of summer cottage real estate in the center of the grounds, is postcard-picturesque. Doors are draped in rambler roses, and tabby cats, watering pails, and green wellies stand on the doorstep. Even further in is ⬛**Hill Garden**—unless you're specifically on the lookout for this lovely secret garden, you're unlikely to find it. The flower-encrusted walkway passes over the former kitchen gardens of Lord Leverhulme's (founder of Lever Soap) mansion. A necklace of pools across the heath is open to bathers, some women only, others mixed. (⊖ Hampstead or the train to Hampstead Heath. Bus #210. Wheelchair-accessible. Open 24hr. For Hill Garden, take North End Way to Inverforth Close. Open daily 8:30am-1hr. before sunset.)

LORD'S CRICKET GROUND. The most famous cricket ground in England, Lord's is home to the local Marylebone Cricket Club (MCC) and hosts most of London's international matches. To see the **Lord's Museum,** home to the **Ashes Urn** and all the cricket-related memorabilia you could ever want to see, attend a match or take a 1hr. tour led by a senior club member. On game days, tours after 10am skip the Long Room and media center (no tours during major international test matches). Games take place on most summer days. MCC games are around £10, but tickets to the rare international test matches are £45-60 and difficult to come by. Book tickets as far in advance as possible. (10min. walk from ⊖ St. John's Wood. Enter at Grace Gate, on St. John's Wood Rd. ☎ 020 7616 8595; www.lords.org. 1¾hr. tours daily Apr.-Sept. 10am, noon, 2pm; Oct.-Mar. noon, 2pm. Wheelchair-accessible. Tours £12, concessions £7, under 16 £6, families £31.)

ABBEY ROAD. Abbey Rd. is a residential street stretching from St. John's Wood to Kilburn. Most visitors are only interested in the **zebra crossing** at its start, where it merges with Grove End Rd. The best way to stop traffic: a photo op crossing the street a la John, Paul, George, and Ringo. (⊖ St. John's Wood.)

EAST LONDON

ROYAL OBSERVATORY GREENWICH. The climb to the peak of Greenwich Park is not for the lazy, but the view is worth the trek; you can see all of the Docklands and Westminster on a clear day. The peak is home to the Royal Observatory, founded by Charles II in 1675 to accelerate the task of "finding the longitude" after one too many shipwrecks led to public outcry. The **Prime Meridian,** marked by a constantly photographed red LED strip in the courtyard, is the axis along which the astronomers' telescopes swung. Stand with one foot in each hemisphere before ducking into **Flamsteed House,** a Christopher Wren creation originally designed as a living space for Astronomer Royal John Flamsteed and now home to famous clocks and old astronomical equipment. Next to the Meridian Building's telescope display, you can climb the **Observatory Dome,** cunningly disguised as a freakishly large rust-colored onion, to see the cleverly named 28 in. Telescope, constructed in 1893. It's still the seventh-largest refracting lens in the world, and, although it was officially retired in 1971, it is still fully functional. Check the offerings at the **Peter Harrison Planetarium** and shift from Earth time to space time. (To get to Greenwich, take a train from ⊖ London Bridge, platform 4. A few per hr.; £3-4. At the top of Greenwich Park, a short but fairly steep climb from the National Maritime Museum; for an easier walk, take the Avenue from St. Mary's Gate at the top of King William Walk. Tram leaves the back of the Museum every 30min. on the hr. ☎ 020 8858 4422; www.nmm.ac.uk. Open daily 10am-5pm. Last entry 4:30pm. Sometimes closes at 6pm in summer; call to confirm. Free daily tour leaves at 2:30pm in front of the Flamsteed House.)

OTHER SIGHTS. The **Thames Barrier** is the world's largest movable flood barrier. When raised, the main gates stand as high as a five-story building—you can see it from the Thames Barrier Information Centre. Call to verify times. (Information Centre 1 Unity Way. ☎ 020 8305 4188; www.environment-agency.gov.uk. Open daily Apr.-Sept. 10:30am-4:30pm; Oct.-Mar. 11am-3:30pm. £2, concessions £1.50, children £1.) The newly renovated **O2 Dome** is a modern entertainment venue that hosts everything from concerts to museum exhibits. (Drawdock Rd. ⊖ Greenwich. www.millennium-dome.com.)

LONDON

WEST LONDON

WIMBLEDON LAWN TENNIS MUSEUM. The All England Lawn Tennis and Croquet Club—the proper name for the arena that hosts the Wimbledon tennis championships every summer—includes a brand-new museum dedicated to the history of tennis. Visitors can peruse memorabilia displays and interactive video exhibits. Tours (2hr.) of the grounds are led by certified Blue Badge guides and include stops in the Millennium Building and the iconic Centre Court, which will be off view until the spring of 2009. *(Church Rd. ⊖Southfields. From the Tube station, take bus #493 or cross the street and walk south on Wimbledon Park Rd. Visitors to the museum should enter through Gate 3. ☎020 8946 6131; www.wimbledon. org/museum. Museum open daily 10:30am-5pm. Guided tours at noon, 1:30, 2:30pm. Museum £8.50, students £7.50, children £4.75; museum and guided tour £15.50/13.75/11.)*

🏛 MUSEUMS AND GALLERIES

For centuries, rich Londoners have exhibited a penchant for collecting. On top of private collections, London also has a substantial national collection, helped in large part by its position in the 18th and 19th centuries as the capital of an empire. In the 2002 celebration of the Queen's Golden Jubilee, the City made admission to all major collections free indefinitely.

MAJOR COLLECTIONS

TATE MODERN. Sir Giles Gilbert Scott's mammoth building, formerly the Bankside power station, houses the second half of the national collection (the earlier set is held in the National Gallery). The Tate Modern is probably the most popular museum in London and one of the most famous modern art museums in the world. The public galleries on the third and fifth floors are divided into four themes. The collection is enormous, while gallery space is limited—works rotate frequently. If you are dying to see a particular piece, head to the museum's computer station on the fifth floor to browse the entire collection. The seventh floor has unblemished views of the Thames and north and south of London. *(Main entrance on Bankside, on the South Bank; 2nd entrance on Queen's Walk. ⊖Southwark or ⊖Blackfriars. From the Southwark Tube, turn left up Union, then left on Great Suffolk, then left on Holland. ☎020 7887 8888; www.tate.org.uk. Open M-Th and Su 10am-6pm, F-Sa 10am-10pm. Free 45min. tours meet on the gallery concourses: Level 3 at 11am, noon, Level 5 at 2, 3pm. 5 types of audio tours include highlights, collection tour, architecture tour, children's tour, and the visually impaired tour. Wheelchair-accessible on Holland St. Museum free; special exhibits up to £10. Free talks M-F 1pm; meet on the appropriate level. Audio tours £2.)*

NATIONAL GALLERY. The National Gallery was founded by an act of Parliament in 1824 with 38 pictures displayed in a townhouse; over the years it has grown to hold an enormous collection of Western European paintings ranging from the 13th to the 20th centuries. The Sainsbury Wing holds almost all of the museum's large exhibitions as well as restaurants and lecture halls. If pressed for time, head to **Art Start** in the Sainsbury Wing, where you can design and print out a personalized tour of the paintings you want to see. Don't miss the fabulously detailed *Arnolfini Wedding Portrait* by Van Eyck or Van Gogh's iconic *Sunflowers.* Themed audio tours and family routes are also available from the information desk. *(Main Portico entrance on north side of Trafalgar Sq. ⊖Charing Cross or ⊖Leicester Sq. ☎020 7747 2885; www.nationalgallery.org.uk. Open M-Tu and Th-Su 10am-6pm, W 10am-9pm. Special exhibitions in the Sainsbury Wing occasionally open until 10pm. 1hr. tours start at Sainsbury Wing information desk. Tours M-F and Su 11:30am, 2:30pm, Sa 11:30am, 12:30, 2:30, 3:30pm. Wheelchair-accessible at Sainsbury Wing on Pall Mall East, Orange St., and*

Getty Entrance. Free. Some temporary exhibitions £5-10, students and ages 12-18 £2-5, seniors £4-8. Audio tours free, suggested donation £3.50. AmEx/MC/V for ticketed events.)

█NATIONAL PORTRAIT GALLERY. This vast and magnificent tour of who's who in Great Britain begins with priceless portraits of the Tudors and ends with the famous of today. Try to trace family resemblances through the royal families—the Stuarts sported stupendous noses—or admire the centuries of changing costume: velvet, silk, fabulously patterned brocade. Look out for the fine collection of stockinged legs in the 16th- and 17th-century galleries. The famous picture of Shakespeare with an earring hangs near the Queen Elizabeth I portraits in the Tudor wing. New facilities include an IT Gallery, with computers to search for pictures and print out a personalized tour, and a third-floor restaurant with an aerial view of London. To see the paintings in historical order, take the escalator in the Ondaatje Wing to the top floor. *(St. Martin's Pl., at the start of Charing Cross Rd., Trafalgar Sq. ⊖Leicester Sq. or ⊖Charing Cross. ☎020 7312 2463; www. npg.org.uk. Open M-W and Sa-Su 10am-6pm, Th-F 10am-9pm. Wheelchair-accessible on Orange St. Lectures Tu 3pm free, but popular events require tickets, available from the information desk. Some evening talks Th 7pm free, others up to £3. Talks Su 3pm. Live music F 6:30pm free. Museum free. Some special exhibitions free, others up to £6. Audio tours £2.)*

BRITISH MUSEUM. With 50,000 items from all corners of the globe, the magnificent collection is expansive and, although a bit difficult to navigate, definitely worth seeing. Most people don't even make it past the main floor, but they should—the galleries upstairs and downstairs are some of the best. Must-sees include the Rosetta stone, which was the key in deciphering ancient Egyptian hieroglyphs, and the ancient mummies. *(Great Russell St. ⊖Tottenham Court Rd., ⊖Russell Sq., or ⊖Holborn. ☎020 7323 8299; www.britishmuseum.org. Great Court open in summer M-W and Su 9am-6pm, Th-Sa 9am-11pm; in winter M-W and Su 9am-6pm, Th-Su 9am-9pm. Most galleries open daily 10am-5:30pm. Selected galleries open Th-F 10am-8:30pm. Free 30-40min. tours daily starting at 11am from the Enlightenment Desk. "Highlights Tour" daily 10:30am, 1, 3pm; advance booking recommended. Wheelchair-accessible. Suggested donation £3. Temporary exhibitions around £5, concessions £3.50. "Highlights Tour" £8, concessions £5. Audio tours £3.50, family audio tours for 2 adults and up to 3 children £10. MC/V.)*

VICTORIA AND ALBERT MUSEUM. As the largest museum of decorative (and not-so-decorative) art and design in the world, the V and A has over 9 mi. of corridors open to the public and is twice the size of the British Museum. It displays "the fine and applied arts of all countries, all styles, all periods." Highlights include the Glass Gallery, the Japanese and Korean areas with suits of armor and kimonos, and the Indian Gallery. The **Gilbert Collection,** once housed in nearby Somerset House, is set to move into the Victoria and Albert Museum in the fall of 2009. Its 800 pieces fall into three categories: mosaics, gold- and silverwork, and snuffboxes. Themed itineraries (£5) available at the desk can help streamline your visit, and Family Trail cards suggest kid-friendly routes. *(Main entrance on Cromwell Rd., wheelchair-accessible entrance on Exhibition Rd. ⊖South Kensington. ☎020 7942 2000; www.vam.ac.uk. Open M-Th and Sa-Su 10am-5:45pm, F 10am-10pm. Free tours meet at rear of main entrance. Introductory tours M-Th and Th-Su 10:30, 11:30am, 1:30, 3:30pm, W 10:30, 11:30am, 1:30, 3:30, 4:30pm. British gallery tours daily 12:30, 2:30pm. Wheelchair-accessible. Talks and events meet at rear of main entrance. Free gallery talks Th 1pm and Su 3pm; ¾-1hr. Museum free; additional charge for some special exhibits.)*

TATE BRITAIN. Tate Britain is the foremost collection on British art from 1500 to the present, including pieces from foreign artists working in Britain and Brits working abroad. There are four Tate Galleries in England; this is the original Tate, opened in 1897 to house Sir Henry Tate's collection of "modern" British art and later expanded to include a gift from famed British painter JMW Turner.

LONDON

Turner's modest donation of 282 oils and 19,000 watercolors can make the museum feel like one big tribute to the man. The annual and always controversial **Turner Prize** for contemporary visual art is still given here. Four contemporary British artists are nominated for the £40,000 prize; their short-listed works go on show from late October through late January. In 2008, the exhibition moves temporarily to the Liverpool branch of the Tate (p. 358). The Modern British Art Gallery inside, featuring works by Vanessa Bell and Francis Bacon, is also worth a look. *(Millbank, near Vauxhall Bridge, in Westminster. ⊖Pimlico. Information ☎020 7887 8888; www.tate.org.uk. Open daily 10am-5:50pm; 1st F of each month 10am-10pm. Last entry 5pm. Free tours include "Art from 1500-1800" 11am; "1800-1900" M-F noon; "Turner" M-F 2pm; "1900-2005" M-F 3pm; "Collection Highlights" Sa-Su noon, 3pm. Wheelchair-accessible via Clore Wing. Regular events include "Painting of the Month Lectures"; 15min.; M 1:15pm, Sa 2:30pm. Occasional "Friday Lectures" F 1pm. Special exhibitions £7-11. Audio tours free.)*

THE CITY OF LONDON

MUSEUM OF LONDON. Located in the southwest corner of the Barbican complex, the gray and brown Museum of London resembles an industrial fortress from the outside. Inside, the collection traces the history of London from its Roman foundations to the present day, incorporating architectural history. You can view the ruins of the ancient **London Wall** from the museum walkway. Select collections are off display due to renovation and will open again in 2010. *(London Wall. Enter through the Barbican or from Aldersgate. ⊖St. Paul's or ⊖Barbican. ☎08704 444 3851; www.museumoflondon.org.uk. Open M-Sa 10am-5:50pm, Su noon-5:50pm. Last entry 5:30pm. Wheelchair-accessible via the elevator at Aldersgate entrance. Frequent demonstrations, talks, and guided walks; some free, others up to £10. Museum free. Audio tour £2.)*

BANK OF ENGLAND MUSEUM. This museum traces the history of the Bank of England from its foundation (1694) to the present day. Mini-displays showcase items like the bank's official silver and German firebomb casings. The bank itself is open only to those on business; for the museum, you will be shuttled by security. *(Threadneedle St. ⊖Bank. ☎020 7601 5545; www.bankofengland.co.uk. Open M-F 10am-5pm. Wheelchair-accessible. Free. Audio tours £1.)*

GUILDHALL ART GALLERY. Devoted to displaying the City's art collection, the walls are home to portraits of former lord mayors. Downstairs is a fine collection of Victorian and Pre-Raphaelite art that includes works by Stevens, Poynter, Rossetti, and Millais. John Singleton Copley's gigantic *Defeat of the Floating Batteries at Gibraltar* is also on display. *(Guildhall Yard, off Gresham St. ⊖Moorgate or ⊖Bank. ☎020 7332 3700; www.guildhall-art-gallery.org.uk. Open M-Sa 10am-5pm, Su noon-4pm. Last entry 30min. before close. Wheelchair-accessible. £2.50, concessions £1, under 16 free. Free M-Th and Sa-Su 3:30-5pm, F all day.)*

CLERKENWELL AND HOLBORN

COURTAULD INSTITUTE GALLERIES. The Courtauld's small, outstanding collection ranges from 14th-century Italian icons to 20th-century abstractions. Works are arranged by collector, not chronologically, so don't fret if you think you skipped a few hundred years. The undisputed gems of the collection are from the Impressionist and Post-Impressionist periods: Manet's *A Bar at the Follies Bergères*, Van Gogh's *Self-Portrait with Bandaged Ear*, and a room devoted to Degas bronzes. *(In Somerset House. The Strand, just east of Waterloo Bridge. ⊖Charing Cross or ⊖Temple. ☎020 7420 9400; www.courtauld.ac.uk. Open daily 10am-6pm. Last entry 5:30pm. Wheelchair-accessible. £5, concessions £4, under 18 free. Tours £6.50, concessions £6; M 10am-2pm free. Lunchtime talks free.)*

SIR JOHN SOANE'S MUSEUM. Eccentric architect John Soane let his imagination run free when designing this intriguing museum for his own collection of art and antiquities. Framed by narrow hallways and oddly shaped nooks and crannies, its items range from the mummified corpse of his wife's dog to an extraordinary sarcophagus of Seti I, for which Soane personally outbid the British Museum when it wasn't willing to pay £2000 for it. See the museum by candlelight on Tuesdays 6-9pm. *(13 Lincoln's Inn Fields. ⊖Holborn. ☎020 7405 2107; www.soane.org. Open Tu-Sa 10am-5pm; 1st Tu of each month also 6-9pm. Tours Sa 11am; tickets sold from 10:30am. Suggested donation £3. Tours £3, students free.)*

KENSINGTON AND EARL'S COURT

SCIENCE MUSEUM. Dedicated to the Victorian ideal of progress, the Science Museum focuses on the transformative power of technology in all its guises. It is also home to an IMAX theater, which shows 45min. scientific documentaries. Breeze through the entrance hall on your way to the Welcome Wing. Highlights include the "Who Am I?" exhibit, the Flight Lab, and the Science of Art and Medicine. *(Exhibition Rd. ⊖South Kensington. ☎08708 704 868, IMAX 08708 704 771; www. sciencemuseum.org.uk. Open daily 10am-6pm. Closed Dec. 24-26. Wheelchair-accessible. IMAX shows usually every hr. daily 10:45am-5pm; £7.50, concessions £6. Call to confirm showtimes and for bookings. Online booking available. Daily demonstrations and workshops in the basement galleries and theatre. SimEx £4, concessions £3. Museum free. Audio tours £3.50. MC/V.)*

NATURAL HISTORY MUSEUM. Architecturally the most impressive of the South Kensington trio, this cathedral-like museum has been a favorite with Londoners since 1880. Shudder from Creepy Crawlies into the dinosaur galleries, making sure to swing by the blue whale. *(Cromwell Rd. ⊖South Kensington. ☎020 7942 5000; www.nhm.ac.uk. Open daily 10am-5:50pm. Last entry 5:30pm. Closed Dec. 24-30. Wheelchair-accessible. Free; special exhibits usually £5, children £3.50. MC/V.)*

THE SOUTH BANK

IMPERIAL WAR MUSEUM. Naval guns guard the entrance to the building, formerly the infamous asylum known as Bedlam. The best and most publicized display is on the third floor: the **Holocaust Exhibition** gives an honest, poignant look at all the events surrounding the tragedy (not recommended for children). On the fourth floor, Crimes Against Humanity is a sobering interactive display with a 30min. film. *(Lambeth Rd., Lambeth. ⊖Lambeth North or ⊖Elephant & Castle. ☎020 7416 5000; www.iwm.org.uk. Open daily 10am-6pm. Free. Special exhibits may carry an additional fee. Audio tour £3.50, concessions £3.)*

DESIGN MUSEUM. Housed in a white Art Deco riverfront building, this contemporary museum's installations fit right into the cool surroundings. You might find anything from avant-garde furniture to galleries on big-name graphic designers, depending on when you visit; all exhibitions are temporary. *(28 Shad Thames, Butlers Wharf. ⊖Tower Hill or ⊖London Bridge. ☎0870 833 9955; www.designmuseum. org. Open daily 10am-5:45pm. Wheelchair-accessible. £8.50, concessions £6.50, students £5.)*

THE WEST END

▨ROYAL ACADEMY OF ARTS. Founded in 1768 with King George III's patronage, the academy was designed to cultivate sculpture, painting, and architecture. Today, it shares courtyard space with the Royal Societies of Geology, Chemistry, Antiquaries, and Astronomy. The academics in charge are all accomplished artists or architects. The Summer Exhibition (June-Aug.), held every year since 1769, is open to any artist for submissions, providing an unparalleled range of contemporary art in every medium, much of which is available for purchase. On Friday nights, the museum stays open late with free jazz in the Friends Room after 6:30pm and candlelit suppers in the cafe. *(Burlington House, Piccadilly. ⊖Piccadilly Circus or ⊖Green Park. ☎020 7300 8000, tickets 848 8484; www.royalacademy. org.uk. Open M-Th and Sa-Su 10am-6pm, F 10am-10pm. Wheelchair-accessible. Free. Exhibits in the Main Galleries £8, concessions £6, seniors £7.)*

▨**PHOTOGRAPHERS' GALLERY.** This is one of London's only public galleries devoted entirely to photography. A few exhibits run concurrently at the larger location (No. 5), which also boasts a cafe. Displays usually feature a single artist's work, ranging from classic landscape to socially conscious photography. The gallery and small bookshop at No. 8 house an equally exemplary show and also have a good selection of photographic monologues. Frequent gallery talks, book readings, and film screenings are free; occasional photographers' talks may charge admission. In 2010, the Photographers' Gallery will move to new digs on Ramilies St. in Soho. *(5 and 8 Great Newport St. ⊖Leicester Sq. or ⊖Covent Garden. ☎020 7831 1772. Open M-W and F-Sa 11am-6pm, Th 11am-8pm, Su noon-6pm. Free.)*

BENJAMIN FRANKLIN HOUSE. Minutes away from ⊖Charing Cross lies the world's only remaining Franklin residence. Franklin lived in the house from 1757 to 1775, and not much has changed since then; the tilted floors and ceilings are evidence that the original interior has been well preserved. This living museum combines history with theater. Costumed guides lead visitors around the house, conveying a sense of Franklin's life and inventions. *(36 Craven St. ⊖Charing Cross or Embankment. ☎020 7839 2006; www.benjaminfranklinhouse.org. Open W-Su noon-5pm. Tours at noon, 1, 2, 3:15, 4:15pm. £7, under 16 free.)*

INSTITUTE OF CONTEMPORARY ARTS (ICA). A minute's walk out of Trafalgar Sq. through the Admiralty Arch, the ICA is London's center for avant-garde art and contemporary artists. Films, talks, performances, and club nights can all be found here. *(The Mall. ⊖Charing Cross or ⊖Piccadilly Circus. ☎020 7930 0493; www. ica.org.uk. Galleries open daily noon-7pm. Cafe and bar open M noon-11pm, Tu-Sa noon-1am, Su noon-10:30pm. Day membership with access to galleries, cafe, and bar M-F £2, Sa-Su £3; concessions £1.50/2. Cinema £8, M-F before 5pm £7; concessions £7/6.)*

CHRISTIE'S. Like a museum but more crowded and all for sale, Christie's is the best of the auction houses. The public can enter on days before an auction to peruse what's up for grabs. Lots range from busts of Greek gods to Monets to sports memorabilia. *(8 King St. ⊖Green Park. Smaller branch at 85 Old Brompton St. in Kensington. ☎020 7839 9060; www.christies.com. Open M-F 9am-5pm; call in advance for exact timings. Public viewings can close early for evening auctions. Wheelchair-accessible. Free.)*

SOTHEBY'S. Before each auction, the items to be sold here are displayed for viewing in the many interlocking galleries. Aristocratic Sotheby's is a busy place; auctions occur within days of one another. Each sale is accompanied by a glossy £20-30 catalog. *(34-35 New Bond St. ⊖Bond St. ☎020 7293 5000; www.sothebys. com. Open for viewing M-F 9am-4:30pm, Sa and occasionally Su noon-4pm; call in advance for exact hours. Public viewings can close early for evening auctions. Wheelchair-accessible. Free.)*

EAST LONDON

▨**WHITECHAPEL ART GALLERY.** Long the only artistic beacon in a culturally impoverished area, Whitechapel is now at the forefront of a buzzing art scene, featuring international and contemporary artists. Thursday nights bring music, poetry readings, and film screenings in addition to regular events and talks during the week. Because the gallery is expanding into a former library next door, visitors access the museum from a new entrance on Angel Alley. As you face the gallery on Whitechapel High St., Angel Alley is the first passage to the left of the building. *(Whitechapel High St. ⊖Aldgate East. ☎020 7522 7888; www.whitechapel. org. Open W-Su 11am-6pm. Wheelchair-accessible. Th talks until 9pm. F music until 11pm. The expanded Whitechapel is due to open in 2009. Call for opening details. Free.)*

■**WHITE CUBE.** This stark white building has showcased some of the biggest names in contemporary art. White Cube has an impressive list of alums and featured exhibits, including heavyweights Chuck Close and Damien Hirst. *(48 Hoxton Sq. ⊖Old St. ☎020 7930 5373; www.whitecube.com. Open Tu-Sa 10am-6pm. Sometimes closes for exhibit installation; call in advance. Wheelchair-accessible. Free.)*

OTHER NEIGHBORHOODS

■**CABINET WAR ROOMS.** From 1939 to 1945, what started as a government coal storage basement quickly became the bombproof nerve center of a nation at war. Winston Churchill stood in the Cabinet Room and declared, "This is the room from which I will direct the war." The day after WWII ended in August 1945, the Cabinet War Rooms were abandoned, closed off, and left undisturbed for decades until their re-opening in 1984 by Margaret Thatcher. The display includes the ■**Churchill Museum,** with all sorts of WWII artifacts. A giant interactive timeline produces sound effects and visuals in the center of the exhibit. *(Clive Steps, far end of King Charles St. ⊖Westminster. ☎020 7930 6961; www.iwm.org.uk. Open daily 9:30am-6pm. Last entry 5pm. £12, concessions £9.50, under 16 free. MC/V.)*

■**BRITISH LIBRARY GALLERIES.** Housed within the British Library (p. 120) is a display of books, manuscripts, and related artifacts from around the world and throughout the ages. Highlights include the second-century Unknown Gospel, The Beatles' hand-scrawled lyrics, a Gutenberg Bible, Joyce's handwritten draft of *Finnegan's Wake*, and pages from Leonardo da Vinci's notebooks. Grab a free map at the main info desk. *(96 Euston Rd. ⊖King's Cross St. Pancras. ☎020 7412 7332; www.bl.uk. Open M and W-F 9:30am-6pm, Tu 9:30am-8pm, Sa 9:30am-5pm, Su 11am-5pm. Wheelchair-accessible. Free. Audio tours £3.50, concessions £2.50.)*

WALLACE COLLECTION. Housed in palatial **Hertford House,** this stunning array of paintings, porcelain, and armor was bequeathed to the nation by the widow of Sir Richard Wallace in 1897. Excellent daily gallery tours will ensure that you see a good overview of the collection. The Wallace Restaurant, unusually smart for a gallery cafe, has a raw bar with terrines and fine cheeses. *(Hertford House, Manchester Sq. ⊖Bond St. or ⊖Marble Arch. ☎020 7563 9505; www.wallacecollection.org. Open daily 10am-5pm. Free 1hr. tours M-Tu and Th-F 1pm, W and Sa 11:30am, 1, 3pm, Su 1, 3pm. Wheelchair-accessible. Free talks M-F 1pm and occasionally Sa 11:30am. Suggested donation £2. Audio tour £3. Cafe open M-Th and Su 10am-5pm, F-Sa 10am-11pm. Entrees £12.50-18.)*

IVEAGH BEQUEST. The Iveagh collection in **Kenwood House** was given to the nation by the earl of Iveagh, who purchased the estate in 1922. Highlights include *The Guitar Player*—one of 35 Vermeers in the world—and a number of Rembrandt's compelling self-portraits. It also contains the magnificently stocked library of Robert Adam, who extensively remodeled the house from 1764 to 1779. *(Kenwood House. Road access from Hampstead Ln. Walk or take bus #210 from North End Way or Spaniards Rd. or from ⊖Archway or ⊖Golders Green. ☎020 8348 1286. Open daily Apr.-Oct. 11am-5pm; Nov.-Mar. 11am-4pm. Wheelchair-accessible. Free.)*

▣ ENTERTAINMENT

Although West End ticket prices are through the roof and the quality of some shows is highly questionable, the city that brought the world Shakespeare, the

LONDON

Sex Pistols, and Andrew Lloyd Webber still retains its originality and theatrical edge. London is a city of immense talent, full of student up-and-comers, experimental writers, and undergrounders who don't care about the neon lights.

CINEMA

The heart of the celluloid monster is **Leicester Square,** where new releases premiere a day before hitting the city's chains. The dominant cinema chain is **Odeon.** (☎08712 241 999, filmline 08712 244 007; www.odeon.co.uk.) Tickets to **West End cinemas** cost £12-15.50; weekday matinees are cheaper. For less mainstream offerings, try the █**Electric Cinema,** 191 Portobello Rd., for a combination of the big screen and baroque stage splendor. For a special experience, choose a luxury armchair or two-seat sofa. (⊖Ladbroke Grove. ☎020 7908 9696; www. the-electric.co.uk. Wheelchair-accessible. Front 3 rows M £7.50, Tu-Su £10; regular tickets £12.50/14.50; 2-seat sofa £25/30. Double features Su 2pm £5-20. Box office open M-Sa 9am-8:30pm, Su 10am-8:30pm. MC/V.) **Riverside Studios,** Crisp Rd., shows a variety of excellent foreign and classic films. (⊖Hammersmith. ☎020 8237 1111; www.riversidestudios.co.uk. Double features £7.50, concessions £6.50.) The **National Film Theatre (NFT),** in South Bank, under Waterloo Bridge, screens a mind-boggling array of films—six movies hit the three screens every evening, starting around 6pm. (⊖Waterloo, ⊖Embankment, or ⊖Temple. ☎020 7633 0274, booking 0870 787 2525; www.bfi.org.uk. £12.50)

COMEDY

On any given night, you'll find at least 10 comedy clubs in operation: check listings in *Time Out* or in a newspaper. London empties of comedians in August, when most head to Edinburgh to take part in the annual festivals (p. 562). Consequently, July brings plenty of comics trying out material.

- █ **Comedy Store,** 1A Oxendon St. (club inquiries ☎020 7839 6642, tickets 08700 602 340; www.thecomedystore.co.uk), in Soho. ⊖Piccadilly Circus. The UK's top comedy club (founded in a former strip club) that gave rise to *Absolutely Fabulous* and *Whose Line is it Anyway?* All 400 seats have good views of stage. The bar serves hot food with vegetarian options. Tu Cutting Edge (contemporary news-based satire); W and Su London's █**Comedy Store Players improv.** Shows Tu-F 8pm, Sa-Su 8pm, midnight, sometimes M 8pm. 18+. Shows Tu-W £15.25, Th-F £17, Sa £17.50, Su £17.25. Box office open M-Th and Su 6:30-9:30pm, F-Sa 6:30pm-1:15am. AmEx/MC/V.

- █ **Canal Cafe Theatre,** Delamere Terr. (☎020 7289 6056; www.canalcafetheatre.com), above the Bridge House pub, in North London. ⊖Warwick Ave. One of the few comedy venues to specialize in sketch comedy. Cozy red velvet chairs and a raised rear balcony mean that everyone gets a good view. Get dinner below and enjoy your drinks around the small tables. Weekly changing shows W-Sa 7:30, 9:30pm (£5, concessions £4). "Newsrevue," Th-Sa 9:30pm and Su 9pm, is London's longest-running comedy sketch show, a satire of weekly current events (£9, concessions £7). £1.50 membership included in ticket price. Box office opens 30min. before performance. MC/V.

DANCE

Dancing in the Royal Opera House, the **Royal Ballet** is one of the world's premier companies (see **Royal Opera,** opposite page). The **Barbican Theatre** at Barbican Hall (opposite page) hosts contemporary troupes on tour.

Peacock Theatre, Portugal St. (☎0894 412 4322; www.sadlerswells.com). ⊖Holborn. A 5min. walk from Holburn station off Kingsway. A program that leans toward contemporary dance, ballet, popular dance-troupe shows, and family-geared productions. Some wheelchair-accessible seats can be booked in advance. £10-35. Standby concession tickets 1hr. before show £15 (cash only). Box office on Rosebery Ave. open M-Sa 9am-8:30pm. Box office at the Peacock Theatre open M-F 10am-6:30pm, performance days 10am-8:30pm. AmEx/MC/V.

Sadler's Wells, Rosebery Ave. (☎020 7863 8198; www.sadlerswells.com), in Islington (right next to Clerkenwell). ⊖Angel. Exit left from the Tube, cross the road, and take the 2nd right on Rosebery Ave. London's premier dance theater, with many contemporary shows and the occasional ballet. Recent performances have included Matthew Bourne's *Swan Lake,* which premiered at Sadler's Wells in 1995. Sadler's Wells Express (SWX) bus to Waterloo via Farringdon and Victoria leaves 8min. after the end of each mainstage evening show (£1.50, with period Travelcard £1). Wheelchair-accessible. £10-50, students and seniors £15, under-16 standbys 1hr. before curtain £15 (cash only). Box office open M-Sa 9am-8:30pm, Su opening times vary. AmEx/MC/V.

MUSIC

CLASSICAL

▨ **Barbican Hall,** Silk St. (☎020 7638 4141; www.barbican.org.uk), in the City of London. ⊖Barbican or ⊖Moorgate. Recently refurbished, Barbican Hall is one of Europe's leading concert halls, with excellent acoustics and a nightly performance program. The resident **London Symphony Orchestra** plays here frequently. The hall also hosts concerts by international orchestras, jazz artists, and world musicians. Barbican is also the place to go for information on festivals and season-specific events. Call in advance for tickets, especially for popular events. Otherwise, the online and phone box offices sometimes have good last-minute options. £6-35. Also includes the Barbican Centre (below).

Barbican Centre. Famous for the quality of its diverse offerings and its mildly confusing layout, the Barbican is a 1-stop cultural powerhouse including the following 3 venues. The main **Theatre** is a futuristic auditorium that hosts touring companies and short-run shows as well as frequent short-run multicultural and contemporary dance performances. Prices vary considerably by seat, day, and production: £10-35, cheapest M-F evening and Sa matinee; student and senior standbys from 9am on performance days. **The Pit** is a smaller, intimate theatre used primarily for new and experimental productions. £10-15. The 2 screens in the **Cinema** rotate the latest blockbusters, art-house, international, and classic movies. £8.50, students and seniors £6, under 15 £4.50.

English National Opera (ENO), London Coliseum, St. Martin's Ln. (☎020 7632 8300; www.eno.org), in Covent Garden. ⊖Charing Cross or ⊖Leicester Sq. The Coliseum is staggering—huge, ornate, and complete with 500 balcony seats (£15-18) for sale every performance. The ENO has proven it can fill the venue with its innovative, updated productions of classics as well as contemporary work. Purchase best available standby student tickets (£12.50) antd balcony tickets (£10) at box office 3hr. before show. Wheelchair-accessible. Tickets £16-87. Box office open M-Sa 10am-8pm. AmEx/MC/V.

Holland Park Theatre, Holland Park (☎08452 309 769; www.rbkc.gov.uk/holland-park), in Kensington and Earl's Court. ⊖High St. Kensington or Holland Park. Open-air performance space in the ruins of Holland House. Sitting outside is generally the most adventurous part of the program. No need to fear the rain—everything is held under a huge white canopy. Special allocation of tickets for wheelchair users. Performances June-Aug. Tu-Sa 7:30pm, matinees Sa 2:30pm. Tickets £10-52. Free Ticket Scheme gives free tickets to those aged 9-18; call ☎0845 230 9769 to apply. Box office in the Old Stable Block west of the opera, open from late Mar. M-Sa 10am-6pm or 30min. after curtain. AmEx/MC/V.

Royal Opera, Bow St. (☎020 7304 4000; www.royaloperahouse.org), in Covent Garden. ⊖Covent Garden. Productions in this refurbished venue tend to be conservative but lavish, although recent experiments with contemporary works have proven successful as

THE LOCAL STORY
QUEEN'S GUARD

Let's Go got the scoop on a London icon. Corporal of Horse Simon Knowles is a 20-year veteran of the Queen's Guard.

LG: What sort of training did you undergo?
SK: In addition to a year of basic military camp, which involves mainly training on tanks and armored cars, I was also trained as a gunner and radio operator. Then I joined the service regiment at 18 years of age.

LG: So it's not all glamor?
SK: Not at all. That's a common misconception. After armored training, we go through mounted training on horseback in Windsor for six months, where we learn the tools of horseback riding, beginning with bareback training. The final month is spent in London training in full state uniform.

LG: Do the horses ever act up?
SK: Yes, but it's natural. During the Queen's Jubilee Parade, with three million people lining the Mall, to expect any animal to be fully relaxed is absurd. The horses rely on the rider to give them confidence. If the guard is riding the horses confidently and strongly, the horse will settle down.

LG: Your uniforms look pretty heavy. Are they comfortable?
SK: They're not comfortable at all. They were designed way back in Queen Victoria's time, and the leather trousers and boots are

well. Prices for the best seats (orchestra stalls) regularly top £160, but standing room and restricted-view seating in the upper balconies (for those not afraid of heights) runs for as little as £7 for opera and £5 for ballet. For some performances, 100 of the very best seats sell for £10; apply a minimum of 2 weeks in advance at www.esales.roh.org.uk. 67 seats available from 10am on performance days; limit 1 per person. Any unsold tickets are available at ½-price 4 hr. before the performance. Box office open M-Sa 10am-8pm. AmEx/MC/V.

JAZZ

Jazz Café, 5 Parkway (☎020 7534 6955; www.jazzcafe.co.uk), in North London. ♦Camden Town. Famous and popular. Shows can be pricey at this nightspot, but the top roster of jazz, hip hop, funk, and Latin performers (£10-30) explains its popularity. Jazzy DJs spin F-Sa following the show. Partially wheelchair-accessible. Cover £5-10. Open daily 7pm-2am. Box office open M-Sa 10am-1pm and 3-6pm. MC/V.

Ronnie Scott's, 47 Frith St. (☎020 7439 0747; www.ronniescotts.co.uk), in Soho. ♦Tottenham Court Rd. or ♦Leicester Sq. London's oldest, most famous jazz club, having hosted everyone from Dizzy Gillespie to Jimi Hendrix. Support and main acts switch back and forth throughout the night. Table reservations essential for big-name acts, although there's limited unreserved standing room at the bar; if it's sold out, try coming back at the end of the main act's 1st set, around midnight. Chicken, pasta, and traditional English dishes £7-28; mixed drinks £7-9. Live music nightly from 6:30pm. Tickets generally £26, M-Th after 11pm £10. Box office open M-F 11am-6pm, Sa noon-6pm. Club open M-Sa 6pm-3am, Su 6pm-midnight. AmEx/MC/V.

100 Club, 100 Oxford St. (☎020 7636 0933; www.the100club.co.uk), in Soho. ♦Tottenham Court Rd. Stage, audience, and bar are all bathed in sallow orange light in this jazz venue that makes frequent excursions into indie rock. Weekdays offer serious indie and jazz, while weekends tend to become more "date-friendly" and mellow. Punk burst on the scene at a legendary gig here in 1976, when the Sex Pistols, the Clash, and Siouxsie and the Banshees shared the stage. Stompin' (swing and big band) M. Swing Sa. Cover £7-15, students with ID £5-10. Open F-Su 7:30pm, closing time varies; other nights vary. AmEx/MC/V.

606 Club, 90 Lots Rd. (☎020 7352 5953; www.606club.co.uk), in Chelsea. ♦Sloane Sq., then bus #11 or 22. Look for the brick arch labeled "606" opposite the "Fire Access" garage; ring the bell to enter downstairs. The intrepid will be rewarded with live jazz music in a candlelit basement venue, billed as one of the best jazz clubs in Europe. Entrance F-Su is with a meal only.

Entrees £9-18. Cover (added to bill) M-Th £8, F-Sa £12, Su £10. M-W doors open 7:30pm, 1st band 8-10:30pm, 2nd 10:45pm-1am; Th-Sa doors open 8pm, music 9:30pm-1:30am; Su doors open 8pm, music 9pm-midnight. MC/V.

POP AND ROCK

The Water Rats, 328 Gray's Inn Rd. (☎020 7837 4412; www.themonto.com), in Bloomsbury. ⊖King's Cross St. Pancras. A hip pub-cafe by day, a stomping venue for top new talent by night—this is where young indie rock bands come in search of a record deal. Oasis was signed here after its 1st London gig, although the place has been spiffed up since. Cover £6 in advance, £8 at the door. Open for coffee M-F 8:30am-midnight. Excellent, generous gastropub lunches (fish and chips and baguettes £6-9) daily noon-3pm. Music M-Sa 7pm-late (headliner 9:45pm). MC/V.

Carling Academy, Brixton, 211 Stockwell Rd. (☎020 7771 3000; www.brixton-academy.co.uk), in South London. ⊖Brixton. Art Deco ex-cinema with a sloping floor ensures a good view of the band. Named *Time Out*'s "Live Venue of the Year" in 2004 and New Music Express's "Best Live Venue" in 2007. Recent performers include Lenny Kravitz, Pink, and Basement Jaxx. Tickets £20-40, cheaper if booked ahead online. Box office open only on performance evenings; order online, by telephone, or at Carling Academy Islington box office, 16 Parkfield St., Islington (open M-Sa noon-4pm).

London Astoria (LA1), 157 Charing Cross Rd. (☎020 7434 9592; www.festivalrepublic.com), in Soho. ⊖Tottenham Court Rd. The building was a pickle factory, strip club, and music hall before it became a full-time rock venue in the late 1980s. The venue hosts big names (recently, Amy Winehouse and The Shins). The **Astoria 2,** 165 Charing Cross Rd., a venue holding 1000, sits in the underbelly of Astoria 1. Besides hosting fresh, new bands, Astoria 2 also turns into a disco house every Sa 11pm-4am. AmEx/MC/V.

THEATER

LONG-RUNNING SHOWS (WEST END)

London's West End is dominated by musicals and plays that run for years—if not decades. For discounted tickets on the day of a performance, head to the **tkts** booth in Leicester Sq. (⊖Leicester Sq. www.tkts.co.uk. Most musicals around £23; plays £20-22. Up to £2.50 booking fee per ticket. Open M-Sa 10am-7pm, Su noon-3pm. MC/V.) It's nearly always cheaper to go to the theater itself, especially for less popular shows; you are likely to get a better seat and pay less for same-day, rush, or

solid. The uniform weighs about three stone [about 45 lb.].

LG: How do you overcome the itches, sneezes, and bees?
SK: Discipline is instilled in every British soldier during training. We know not to move a muscle while on parade no matter what the provocation or distraction—unless, of course, it is a security matter. But our helmets are akin to wearing a boiling kettle on your head; to relieve the pressure, sometimes we use the back of our sword blade to ease the back of the helmet forward.

LG: How do you make the time pass while on duty?
SK: The days are long. At Whitehall, the shift system is derived upon inspection in Barracks. Smarter men work on horseback from 10am to 4pm; less smart men work on foot from 7am to 8pm. Some guys count the number of buses that drive past. Unofficially, there are lots of pretty girls around here, and we are allowed to move our eyeballs.

LG: What has been your funniest distraction attempt?
SK: One day a taxi pulled up, and out hopped four Playboy bunnies, who then posed for a photo shoot right in front of us. You could call that a distraction if you like.

concession tickets. However, try www.londontheatrebookings.com (☎020 7851 0300) or one of the discount shops that line Leicester Sq. if you are really looking for a cheap deal.

Billy Elliot: The Musical, Victoria Palace Theatre, Victoria St. (☎0870 4248 5000). ⊖Victoria. Based on the 2000 movie with music by Elton John. £17.50-50. Shows M-W and F 7:30pm, Th and Sa 2:30, 7:30pm. Call for student standby tickets. AmEx/MC/V.

The Lion King, Lyceum Theatre, Wellington St. (☎08702 439 000; www.thelionking. co.uk). ⊖Covent Garden. Same old script, gorgeous new puppets. £20-50. Shows Tu and Th-F 7:30pm, W and Sa 2, 7:30pm, Su 3pm. Limited day-of seats and standing-room tickets released at noon. Ask about student discounts. Purchase 2 tickets max. in person at box office. AmEx/MC/V.

Mamma Mia!, Prince of Wales Theatre, Coventry St. (box office ☎0870 950 0902, agents 0870 264 3333; www.mamma-mia.com). ⊖Leicester Sq. One of the best of the "pop's greatest hits"-style megashows—it is so popular that it is nearly always sold out. £25-49. Shows M-Th 7:30pm, F 5, 8:30pm, Sa 3, 7:30pm. AmEx/MC/V.

Mary Poppins, Prince Edward Theatre, Old Compton St. (☎08708 509 191; www.mary-poppinsthemusical.co.uk). ⊖Leicester Sq. Has gotten rave reviews and is ideal for kids and families. £15-55. Shows M-W and F 7:30pm, Th and Sa 2:30, 7:30pm. Same-day tickets released at noon; limit 2 per person. AmEx/MC/V.

"OFF-WEST END"

The Almeida, Almeida St. (☎020 7359 4404; www.almeida.co.uk), in North London. ⊖Angel or ⊖Highbury & Islington. The top fringe theatre in London, if not the world. Always comes up with novel scripts and quality shows, both dramatic and opera; also puts on classics from the likes of Shakespeare and Molière. Hollywood stars, including Kevin Spacey and Nicole Kidman, have performed here. The metallic bar and foyer areas were part of expensive renovations in 2003. Wheelchair-accessible. Tickets from £15, with restricted view £6. Show M-F 7:30pm, Sa 3, 7:30pm. Box office open M-Sa 10am-6pm, performance days 10am-7:30pm. MC/V.

Donmar Warehouse, 41 Earlham St. (☎08700 606 624; www.donmarwarehouse.com), in Covent Garden. ⊖Covent Garden. In the mid-90s, artistic director Sam Mendes (later of *American Beauty* fame) transformed this gritty space into one of the best theaters in the country, featuring highly regarded contemporary shows with an edge. This is the infamous stage where Nicole Kidman bared all in *The Blue Room* in 1998, so it's not surprising that this nondescript warehouse rarely has difficulty filling its 251 seats. Wheelchair-accessible. Tickets £13-29; under 18 and students standby 30min. before curtain £12; £7.50 standing-room tickets available once performance sells out. 10 tickets available on the day of a performance from 10:30am; limit 2 per person. Box office open M-Sa 10am-7:30pm. AmEx/MC/V.

Royal Academy of Dramatic Arts (RADA), 62-64 Gower St. (☎020 7636 7076; www. rada.org), entrance on Malet St., in Bloomsbury. ⊖Goodge St. A cheaper alternative to West End venues, Britain's famous drama school has 3 on-site theaters. Call for event details. Wheelchair-accessible. Tickets £3-11, concessions £2-7.50. Regular Foyer events during the school year include plays, music, and readings, M-Th 7pm (up to £6). Box office open M-F 10am-6pm, performance days 10am-7:30pm. AmEx/MC/V.

Old Vic, Waterloo Rd. (☎020 7369 1722, box office 0060 0628; www.oldvictheatre. com), in the South Bank. ⊖Waterloo. Still in its original 1818 hall (the oldest theater in London), the Old Vic is one of London's most historic theatres. These days, it hosts touring companies like the Royal Shakespeare Company, which set their own prices and schedules. Check website for listings. Box office M-Sa 10am-7pm. MC/V.

REPERTORY

 Shakespeare's Globe Theatre, 21 New Globe Walk (☎020 7401 9919; www.shake-speares-globe.org), in the South Bank. ⊖Southwark or ⊖London Bridge. Innovative, top-notch performances at this faithful reproduction of Shakespeare's original 16th-century playhouse. Choose among 3 covered tiers of hard, backless wood benches (cushions £1 extra) or stand through a performance as a "groundling"; come 30min. before the show to get as close as you can. Should it rain, the show must go on, and umbrellas are prohibited. For tours of the Globe, see p. 126. Wheelchair-accessible. Seats from £12, concessions from £10, yard (i.e., standing) £5. Raingear £2.50. Performances June-Sept. Tu-Sa 2, 7:30pm, Su 1, 6:30pm; late Sept. and late May Tu-Sa 7:30pm, Su 6:30pm. Box office open M-Sa 10am-6pm, performance days 10am-8pm.

 Royal Court Theatre, Sloane Sq. (☎020 7565 5000; www.royalcourttheatre.com), in Chelsea. ⊖Sloane Sq. Recognized by *The New York Times* as a standout theater in Europe, the Royal Court is dedicated to challenging new writing and innovative interpretations of classics. Its 1956 production of John Osborne's *Look Back in Anger* is universally acknowledged as the starting point of modern British drama. Tackles politically thorny issues like AIDS and the Middle East. Wheelchair-accessible. Main auditorium £10-25, concessions £10, standing room 10p 1hr. before curtain. 2nd venue upstairs £15, concessions £10. M all seats £10, with some advance tickets and some released 10am on performance days. Box office open performance weeks M-Sa 10am-7:45pm; otherwise M-Sa 10am-6pm. AmEx/MC/V.

National Theatre, South Bank (info ☎020 7452 3400, box office 7452 3000; www.nationaltheatre.org.uk), in the South Bank. ⊖Waterloo or ⊖Embankment. Founded by Laurence Olivier, the National Theatre opened in 1976 and has been at the forefront of British theater ever since. The schedule often includes Shakespearean classics and hard-hitting new works from Britain's brightest playwrights. Bigger shows are mostly staged on the **Olivier,** seating 1160. The 890-seat **Lyttleton** is a proscenium theater, while the **Cottesloe** offers flexible staging for new works. Wheelchair-accessible. Tickets typically start at £10. Complicated pricing scheme, which is liable to change from show to show; contact box office for details. Box office open M-Sa 9:30am-8pm. MC/V.

> **NATIONAL THEATRE FOR POCKET CHANGE.** Almost every day in the summer, the courtyard at the National Theatre holds a free concert, film, or performance art exhibition. From magic shows to physical comedy, the theater will satisfy anyone looking for live entertainment.

⌐ SHOPPING

London has long been considered one of the fashion capitals of the world. Unfortunately, the city that was at the forefront of the historical development of shopping malls features as many underwhelming chain stores as it does one-of-a-kind boutiques. The truly budget-conscious should forget buying altogether and stick to window-shopping for ideas in **Knightsbridge** and **Regent Street.** Vintage shopping in **Notting Hill** is a viable alternative; however, shoppers generally steer clear of Oxford St., where so-called "vintage" clothing was probably made in 2002 and sells for twice as much as the regular line.

MAJOR CHAINS

As in any large city, London retail is dominated by chains. Fortunately, local shoppers are picky enough that buying from a chain doesn't mean abandoning the style for which Londoners are famed. Most chains have a flagship on or near **Oxford Street,** a second branch in **Covent Garden,** and another on **King's Road** or Kensington High St. Branches keep different hours, but usually stores are open 10am-7pm on weekdays and noon-5pm on weekends. Popular chains include Jigsaw, Karen Millen, Monsoon, Topshop/Topman, and Zara.

Harrods, 87-135 Brompton Rd. (☎020 7730 1234; www.harrods.com). ⊖Knightsbridge. In the Victorian era, this was the place for the wealthy to shop. Over a century later, it is a tourist extravaganza. Given the sky-high prices, it's no wonder that only tourists and oil sheiks actually shop here. Do go, though; it's an iconic bit of London that even the cynical visitor shouldn't miss. If nothing else, ride the Egyptian escalator in the middle, which leads down to the eerie "Diana and Dodi" memorial, which includes Diana's engagement ring and a wine glass she drank out of on her last night alive. Wheelchair-accessible. Open M-Sa 10am-8pm, Su noon-6pm. AmEx/MC/V.

Harvey Nichols, 109-125 Knightsbridge (☎020 7235 5000; www.harveynichols.com). ⊖Knightsbridge. Imagine Bond St., Rue St. Honoré, and 5th Ave. all rolled up into 1 store. 5 of its 7 floors are devoted to the sharpest fashion, from the biggest names to the hippest unknowns. Food hall on the 5th floor has a swanky restaurant, a YO!Sushi, and the chic 5th Floor Cafe; there's a juice bar on the main fl. and a Wagamama in the basement. Sales from late June to late July and from late Dec. to late Jan. Wheelchair-accessible. Open M-F 10am-8pm, Sa 10am-8pm, Su noon-6pm. AmEx/MC/V.

Selfridges, 400 Oxford St. (☎0870 837 7377; www.selfridges.com). ⊖Bond St. Tourists may flock to Harrods, but Londoners head to Selfridges. Fashion departments run the gamut from traditional tweeds to space-age clubwear. They also include small selections from many chain stores, such as Oasis and Topshop. With 18 cafes and restaurants, a hair salon, a bureau de change, and even a hotel, shopaholics need never leave. Massive Jan. and July sales. Wheelchair-accessible. Open M-W and F-Sa 9:30am-8pm, Th 9:30am-9pm, Su noon-6pm. AmEx/MC/V.

Liberty, 210-220 Regent St. (☎020 7734 1234; www.liberty.co.uk), entrance on Marlborough St. ⊖Oxford Circus. Liberty's imitation Tudor chalet (built in 1922) sets the regal tone for this department store. The focus on top-quality designed handcrafts makes the store more like 1 giant boutique. Famous for custom fabric prints—with 10,000 Liberty prints now archived—which appear sewn into everything from shirts to pillows. Wheelchair-accessible. Open M-Sa 10am-9pm, Su noon-6pm. AmEx/MC/V.

Fortnum & Mason, 181 Piccadilly (☎020 7734 8040; www.fortnumandmason.co.uk). ⊖Green Park or ⊖Piccadilly Circus. As the official grocer of the royal family, this gourmet department store provides quality foodstuffs fit for a queen. Don't come here to do your weekly shopping—prices aside, the focus is very much on gifts and luxury items. A complete renovation in 2007 added a basement wine bar to the existing 3 restaurants. The fancy **Saint James Restaurant** serves a lovely formal afternoon tea M-Sa 3-7:30pm. Classic set tea £24, rare set tea £27. The **Fountain Restaurant** is open M-Sa 8:30am-8pm. Wheelchair-accessible. Fortnum & Mason open M-Sa 10am-6:30pm, Su noon-6pm (food hall and patio restaurant only). AmEx/MC/V.

STREET MARKETS

Better for people-watching than hard-core shopping, street markets may not bring you the big goods but are a refreshing alternative to chain stores.

▨ **Spitalfields,** Commercial St., in East London. ⊖Shoreditch (during rush hour), ⊖Liverpool St., or ⊖Aldgate East. Formerly a wholesale vegetable market, now the best of the East End markets. On Su, food shares space with clothing by local designers. Crafts market open M-F 10am-4pm, Su 9am-5pm. Antiques market open Th 9am-5pm.

▨ **Camden Passage Market,** Islington High St., in North London. ⊖Angel. Turn right from the Tube; it's the alleyway that starts behind The Mall antiques gallery on Upper St. A market more for looking than for buying—London's premier antique shops line these charming alleyways. Some stores open daily, others W 7:30am-6pm, Sa 9am-6pm.

Portobello Road Markets, ⊖Notting Hill Gate, ⊖Westbourne Park, or ⊖Ladroke Grove. Includes foods, antiques, secondhand clothing, and jewelry. In order to see it all, come F-Sa when everything is sure to be open. Stalls set their own times. Generally open Th 8am-1pm, F 9am-5pm, Sa 6:30am-5pm.

Camden Markets (☎020 7969 1500). ⊖Camden Town. Make a right out of the Tube station to reach Camden High St., where most of the markets start. Includes cheap clubbing gear and tourist trinkets. The best bet is to stick with the Stables Market, farthest north from the Tube station. Many stores open daily 9:30am-6pm; stables open F-Su.

Brixton Market, along Electric Ave., Pope's Rd., and Brixton Station Rd. and inside markets in Granville Arcade and Market Row, in South London. ⊖Brixton. London's best selection of Afro-Caribbean fruits, vegetables, spices, and fish. It is unforgettably colorful, noisy, and fun. Open M-Sa 10am-sunset.

Petticoat Lane Market, Petticoat Ln., off Commercial St. Spitalfield's little sister market, selling everything from clothes to crafts. Open M-F 10am-2:30pm, Su 9am-2pm.

Sunday (Up) Market (☎020 7770 6100; www.bricklanemarket.com). Housed in a portion of the old Truman Brewery just off Hanbury St., in East London. ⊖Shoreditch or ⊖Aldgate East. Find similar market items and calmer crowds. Open Su 10am-5pm.

◪ NIGHTLIFE

From pubs to taverns to bars to clubs, London has all the nightlife that a person could want. First-time visitors may initially head to the **West End,** drawn by the flashy lights and pumping music of Leicester Sq. For a more authentic experience, head to the **East End** or **Brixton.** Soho's **Old Compton Street** is still the center of GLBT nightlife. Before heading out for the evening, make sure to plan out **Night Bus** travel. Night Buses in the West End run frequently—head to Trafalgar Sq., Oxford St., or Piccadilly Circus to catch buses to all destinations.

PUBS

▨ **Fitzroy Tavern,** 16 Charlotte St. (☎020 7580 3714). ⊖Goodge St. The center of Bloomsbury's "Fitzrovia" neighborhood (guess where the area's name came from). Popular with artists and writers (Dylan Thomas was a known patron), this pub now oozes with students. Outdoor seating in summer. Comedy night (£5) W 8:30pm. Open M-Sa 11:30am-11pm, Su noon-10:30pm. MC/V.

▨ **The Golden Eagle,** 59 Marylebone Ln. (☎020 7935 3228). ⊖Bond St. The quintessence of "olde worlde"—both in clientele and in charm. Sidle up to this local-filled bar and enjoy authentic pub sing-alongs (Tu 8:30-10:30pm, Th-F 8:30-11pm) around the piano in the corner. Open M-Sa 11am-11pm, Su 11am-7pm. MC/V.

▨ **The Jerusalem Tavern,** 55 Britton St. (☎020 7490 4281; www.stpetersbrewery.co.uk). ⊖Farringdon. Showcase pub for St. Peter's Brewery. The availability of brews changes with the seasons and is advertised on a chalkboard outside. Specialty ales (£2.65-3) like grapefruit or cinnamon, several organic ales, Honey Porter, Summer Ale, and Suffolk Gold are available in season. Bring home a case of its speciality beer (£30). Popular with locals. Pub grub £8-10. Open M-F 11am-11pm. Kitchen open M and F-Su noon-3pm, Tu-Th noon-3pm and 5-9:30pm. MC/V.

French House, 49 Dean St. (☎020 7437 2799), in Soho. ⊖Piccadilly Circus. This small Soho landmark used to be frequented by personalities such as Maurice Chevalier, Charlie Chaplin, Salvador Dalí, and Dylan Thomas before it became the unofficial gathering place of the French Resistance during WWII. It's said that Charles de Gaulle wrote his "Appeal of 18 June," a speech to the French people, in this very pub. Enjoy beer or an extensive wine selection (available by the glass) and hobnob with some of the most interesting characters in Soho. Wheelchair-accessible. Open M-Sa noon-11pm, Su noon-10:30pm. Restaurant on 1st fl. open M-Sa noon-midnight. AmEx/MC/V.

Ye Olde Cheshire Cheese, 145 Fleet St. (☎020 7353 6170; www.yeoldecheshirecheese. com). Entrance in alleyway. ⊖Blackfriars. Not to be confused with The Cheshire Cheese on the other side of Fleet St. Dating from 1667, the Cheese was once a haunt of varied figures: Samuel Johnson, Charles Dickens, Mark Twain, and Theodore Roosevelt. Open M-Sa 11am-11pm, Su noon-5pm. Cellar Bar open M-F noon-2:30am. Restaurant open M-F noon-9pm, Sa noon-2:30pm and 5-9pm, Su noon-4pm. AmEx/MC/V.

Ye Olde Mitre Tavern, 1 Ely Court (☎020 7405 4751), off 8 Hatton Garden, in Holborn. ⊖Chancery Ln. Look for the street lamp on Hatton Garden bearing a sign of a miter; the pub is in the nearby alley. Unlike many imitations, this classic pub fully merits the "ye olde"—it was built in 1546 by the bishop of Ely. With oak beams and spun glass, the 2 rooms are perfect for nestling up to a bitter, and the winding courtyard outside is ideal in nice weather. Bar snacks and superior sandwiches (£1.75) served 11:30am-9:30pm. Open M-F 11am-11pm. AmEx/MC/V.

The Troubadour, 265 Old Brompton Rd. (☎020 7370 1434; www.troubadour.co.uk). ⊖Earl's Court. A combination pub/cafe/deli. Once upon a time, the likes of Bob Dylan, Joni Mitchell, and Paul Simon played in the intimate basement club. The quirky decor is equally suited to morning espresso shots as to evening vodka shots. Live music or poetry readings most nights. Breakfast (9am-3pm) £3-9, meals £5.50-10. 2-for-1 mixed drinks in the cafe M-F 5-7pm. Open daily 9am-midnight. MC/V.

Dog and Duck, 18 Bateman St. (☎020 7494 0697). ⊖Tottenham Court Rd. This historic establishment sits on the site of the duke of Monmouth's Soho house and is the oldest pub in Soho. The name refers to Soho's previous role as royal hunting grounds. This was a regular haunt of George Orwell's; the bar on the 1st fl. is named in his honor. Standing room is available near the bar or outside on the sidewalk when the weather is nice. Wheelchair-accessible. Open M-Sa 11am-11pm, Su 11am-10pm. MC/V over £5.

The George Inn, 77 Borough High St. (☎020 7407 2056). ⊖London Bridge. With a mention in Dickens's *Little Dorrit* and the honor of being the only remaining galleried inn in London, the George takes great pride in its tradition. A deceptively tiny interior leads out into a popular patio. The ale (from £2.50) is top-notch. Patio wheelchair-accessible. Open M-Sa 11am-11pm, Su noon-10:30pm. AmEx/MC/V.

BARS

▨ **Absolut Icebar,** 31-33 Heddon St. (☎020 7478 8910; www.belowzerolondon.com). ⊖Oxford Circus. Because it's everyone's dream to get tipsy in the Arctic. Absolut Icebar is kept just below freezing year-round, and guests are escorted in wearing silver capes and hoods for their pre-booked 40min. time slot. The entire bar is constructed completely of Swedish-imported ice and undergoes a complete renovation every 6 months. Cover includes use of cape and hood, an ice mug, and vodka cocktail. M-W and Su £12, Th-Sa £15; open M-W 3:30-11pm, Th 3:30-11:45pm, F 3:30pm-12:30am, Sa 12:30pm-12:30am, Su 3:30-10:15pm.

▨ **Lab,** 12 Old Compton St. (☎020 7437 7820; www.lab-townhouse.com), in the West End. ⊖Leicester Sq. or ⊖Tottenham Court Rd. With restroom signs for "bitches" and "bastards," the only thing this mixed-drink bar takes seriously is its stellar drink menu. Licensed mixologists serve up their own award-winning concoctions (£7). DJs play every night starting at 9pm. Open M-Sa 4pm-midnight, Su 4pm-10:30pm. AmEx/MC/V.

Bar Kick, 127 Shoreditch High St. (☎020 7739 8700), in East London. ⊖Old St. The dozens of flags on the ceiling add international flavor to the European-style food, while football paraphernalia and foosball tables give the bar its sports "kick." Wheelchair-accessible. Open M-W and Su 11am-11pm, Th-Sa 11am-midnight. Kitchen open M-F 12:30-3:30pm and 6:30-10:30pm, Sa noon-11pm, Su noon-10:30pm. AmEx/MC/V.

Filthy MacNasty's Whiskey Café, 68 Amwell St. (☎020 7837 6067; www.filthymacnastys.com), in North London. ⊖Angel or ⊖King's Cross. Bus #N10, 63, 73, 91, 390. Shane MacGowan, U2, and the Libertines have all played in this laid-back semi-Irish pub. Outside, red picnic benches support the rowdy overflow. Live music and occasional literary readings add to the hipster-intellectual atmosphere. 14 varieties of whiskey from £2. Open M-Sa noon-11pm, Su noon-10:30pm. MC/V.

Vibe Bar, 91-95 Brick Ln. (☎020 7247 3479; www.vibe-bar.co.uk), in East London. ⊖Aldgate East or ⊖Liverpool St. Night Bus hub at ⊖Liverpool St. Once the home of the Truman Brewery, this funky bar is heavy on style and light on pretension. Prides itself on promoting new artists. Free Internet access. Dance to hip hop, soul, funk, and jazz. Pints £3. DJs spin daily from 7:30pm. Cover F-Sa after 8pm £4. Open M-Th and Su 10am-11:30pm, F-Sa 10am-1am. AmEx/MC/V.

Big Chill Bar, Dray Walk (☎020 7392 9180; www.bigchill.net), off Brick Ln. ⊖Liverpool St. or ⊖Aldgate East. Despite its lack of address, no one seems to have trouble finding this watering hole off Brick Ln. DJs spin nightly while famously friendly crowds chat it up on big leather couches and on the patio. Mixed drinks from £5. Menu of shareable foods and tapas (£1-6). Stay all day during popular "Big Chill Sundae," with board games, brunch, and prime people-watching amid the surrounding market crowds. Su brunch noon-9pm. Open M-Th noon-midnight, F-Sa noon-1am, Su 11am-midnight. MC/V.

The Langley, 5 Langley St. (☎020 7836 5005). ⊖Covent Garden. This all-purpose basement party bar draws the crowds in early and keeps them there. Head to the Geneva Bar, a cavernous dance floor and bar out back with DJs playing old-school dance and pop music. Exposed brick and piping and chain-link chairs make for a sleek, casual experience. DJs Th-Sa from 9pm. Cover some nights after 10pm £2-7. Happy hour daily 5-8pm; mixed drinks £4. Open M-Sa 4:30pm-1am, Su 4-10:30pm. AmEx/MC/V.

CLUBS

■ **Fabric,** 77A Charterhouse St. (☎020 7336 8898; www.fabriclondon.com), in Clerkenwell. ⊖Farringdon. Night Bus #242. This club, deep underground, has 5 bars, 3 dance floors, and packs in 2000 Londoners and visitors. Home to Europe's first vibrating "bodysonic" dance floor that is actually 1 giant speaker. Arrive before 11pm on Sa to avoid lines. "Polysexual Night" Su once a month. Wheelchair accessible. Cover F £13, Sa after 11pm £16. Open F 10pm-6am, Sa 11pm-8am, Su 10pm-10am. AmEx/MC/V.

■ **Notting Hill Arts Club,** 21 Notting Hill Gate (☎020 7598 5226; www.nottinghillartsclub.com). ⊖Notting Hill Gate. Bus #N94, 148, 207, 390. Unlabeled and unmarked (but right next to the Tex-Mex Tapas Bar). Chill out in this undertouristed space. 1-in, 1-out policy later in the night. No suits or team colors allowed. Cover W-Sa after 8pm £5-7. Open M-F 6pm-2am, Sa 4pm-2am. MC/V.

■ **Ministry of Sound,** 103 Gaunt St. (☎087 0060 0010; www.ministryofsound.com), in the South Bank. ⊖Elephant & Castle; take the exit for South Bank University. Bus #N35, 133, 343. A mecca for serious clubbers worldwide. Massive main room, smaller 2nd dance floor, and perpetually packed overhead balcony bar. Casual dress, but famously unsmiling door staff make it prudent to err on the side of smartness: no sneakers, especially on weekends. Cover F £12, Sa £15. Hours vary; check website. MC/V.

Aquarium, 256 Old St. (☎020 7253 3558; www.clubaquarium.co.uk). ⊖Old St.; Exit 3. The only club in London where bringing your bathing suit is par for the course. A huge pool and hot tub open to revelers. The 4 bars and 2 sofa-laden chill-out rooms keep the dry occupied. "Eastern European Night" (techno and commercial pop; smart casual) F

10pm-4am. "Carwash" (funky/retro-glam-funk fashion fest) Sa 10pm-3:30am—one of the most awe-inspiring clubbing experiences in London; join stiltwalkers and dancers in your finest 70s, 80s, and 90s gear (tickets ☎08702 461 966; www.carwash.co.uk). Cover F men £15, women £10; Sa online £12, at door £15. Open F 10pm-4am, Sa 4:30-11am and 7pm-3:30am, Su 4:30-11am and 10pm-4am. MC/V.

The End, 16A W. Central St. (☎020 7419 9199; www.endclub.com), in the West End. ⊖Tottenham Court Rd. Located just off High Holborn, behind New Oxford St., this is a cutting-edge clubber's Eden. Speaker walls capable of earth-shaking bass, a huge dance floor, and a lounge bar. Theme nights online. Wheelchair-accessible. Stylish casual dress, but no office wear allowed. Cover varies; check website. Open M 10pm-3am, W 10:30pm-3am, Th-F 10pm-4am, Sa 6pm-7am. AmEx/MC/V.

Ghetto, Falconberg Court (☎020 7287 3726; www.ghetto-london.co.uk). ⊖Tottenham Court Rd. Behind the Astoria. Crusading against "lack of originality," Ghetto squeezes alternative nightlife into Soho. Mixed crowd. Frat Party M; "Don't Call Me Babe" (bubblegum pop) Tu; "Calling All Tribes" (mixed music creative night) W; "Miss Shapes" (pop and indie) Th; "The Cock" (gay night, electro) F; "Wig Out" (kitsch, pop) Sa; "Pretty Young Thing" (R&B, hip hop, pop) Su. Cover M £3, with flyer £2; Tu after 11:30pm £3; W after 11:30pm £5; Th with flyer before 11:30pm £3, otherwise £4; F £7; Sa £7, students before 11:30pm £5; Su from £4. Open M-W 10:30pm-3am, Th-F 10:30pm-4am, Sa 9:30pm-5am, Su 9:30pm-2am.

Bar Rumba, 36 Shaftesbury Ave. (☎020 7287 6933; www.barrumba.co.uk), in the West End. ⊖Piccadilly Circus. The Rumba crowd makes good use of the industrial-strength interior for dancing, mostly to R&B. Check website for events and theme nights. Cover £5-10, students £3 on select nights. Open M-W 9pm-3am, Th 8pm-3:30am, F 6pm-3:30am, Sa 9pm-4am, Su 8:30pm-2:30am. MC/V.

GLBT NIGHTLIFE

Many venues have gay and lesbian nights on a rotating basis. Check *Time Out* and look for flyers and magazines floating around Soho. *The Pink Paper* (free from newsstands) and *Boyz* (www.boyz.co.uk; free at gay bars and clubs) are the main gay listings magazines for London. In addition to the listings below, try "The Cock" at Ghetto or "Polysexual Night" at Fabric.

The Edge, 11 Soho Sq. (☎020 7439 1313; www.edgesoho.net), in the West End. ⊖Tottenham Court Rd. A friendly gay and lesbian drinking spot off Soho Sq. offers several venues, complete with ice cream and £14 bottles of wine. 4 floors of brick, silver, and hot-pink interior feature a lounge bar on the 1st fl., a piano bar on the 2nd, and a newly refurbished disco dance bar at the top. Piano bar Tu-Sa. DJs and dancing Th-Sa. Wheelchair-accessible. No cover. Open M-Sa noon-1am, Su noon-midnight. MC/V.

The Black Cap, 171 Camden High St. (☎020 7485 0538; www.theblackcap.com), in North London. ⊖Camden Town. North London's most popular gay bar and cabaret is always buzzing. Mixed crowd. The rooftop patio is the highlight of the place. Live shows and club scene downstairs F-Su nights and some weeknights (times vary; call for details). Cover Th-Su after 10pm £2-4. Club open M-Th 10pm-2am, F-Sa 10pm-3am, Su 9pm-1am. Bar open M-Th noon-2am, F-Sa noon-3am, Su noon-1am. AmEx/MC/V.

G-A-Y, 157 Charing Cross Rd. (☎020 7434 9592; www.g-a-y.co.uk). ⊖Tottenham Court Rd. Madonna previewed 6 songs from her newest album here. G-A-Y (you spell it out when you say it) has become a Soho institution. "Pink Pounder" (90s classics with 70s and 80s faves in the bar) M. "Camp Attack" (attitude-free 70s and 80s cheese with a 2nd room devoted to 90s music) F. "G-A-Y big night out," Sa, rocking the capacity crowd with commercial-dance DJs and live pop performances. Wheelchair-accessible. Cover varies by night and by week; free some nights with a flyer or ad; Sa depending on performer £10-16. Open M and Th-F 11pm-4am, Sa 10:30pm-5am. Cash only.

Comptons of Soho, 53 Old Compton St. (☎020 3238 0163). ⊖Leicester Sq. or ⊖Piccadilly Circus. Soho's oldest gay pub. Fills up early. Horseshoe-shaped bar is open all the time, while upstairs the Soho Club Lounge (opens 6:30pm) has a more mellow scene and a break from the noise. Open M-Sa noon-11pm, Su noon-10:30pm. MC/V.

Ku Bar, 30 Lilse St. (☎020 7600 4353; www.ku-bar.co.uk). ⊖Leicester Sq. Dance space in the basement, a bar on the ground floor, and a lounge on the top floor. Theme nights include "Karaoke" (a live band followed by open mike) M; "Ruby Tuesdays" (for girls and their guy friends) Tu; "Cabaret" W; "Silk" (screenings of gay films from around the world) Th; "Gay Tea Dance" (dance party) Su. Main bar open M-Sa noon-11pm, Su 1-10:30pm. Downstairs Dance Bar open M-Sa 8pm-3am. AmEx/MC/V.

Heaven, The Arches, Craven Terr. (☎020 7930 2020; www.heaven-london.com). ⊖Charing Cross or ⊖Embankment. Intricate interior and fantastically lit main floor, 5 bars, and a coffee bar. "Popcorn" (mixed crowd; chart-toppers, 70s-80s disco hits, and commercial house) M. "Work" (gay night; mix of commercial pop and R&B) W. Music and crowd varies F. "Heaven's Flagship Night" (5 rooms with music from house to pop) Sa. Cover varies by night and time of entrance; £2-12. Bring a flyer for a reduced cover. Open M and F-Sa 11pm-6am, W 11pm-5am.

⚎ DAYTRIPS FROM LONDON

▨**ROYAL BOTANICAL GARDENS, KEW.** In the summer of 2003, UNESCO named the Royal Botanical Gardens a World Heritage site. The 250-year-old Royal Botanical Gardens, about an hour's Tube ride outside of central London, extend in a verdant 300-acre swath along the Thames. The complimentary guide highlights which plants are in season. In the spring, wander through the woodland glades at the back of the park where thick English bluebells bloom knee-high. In early summer the rose gardens and azalea dells are at their peak. Take a tour through the autumn treetops on the new elevated walkway (soon to be wheelchair-accessible) and appreciate the leaves from the vantage of a squirrel. If English rain dampens the scenery, head to one of the three conservatories to steam your clothes with the palms and potted plants. The **Princess of Wales Conservatory** houses 10 different climate zones, from rainforest to desert, including two devoted entirely to orchids. Close to the Thames in the northern part of the gardens, **Kew Palace** is a modest red-brick affair used by royalty on garden visits, now open to the public for the first time in 200 years. On the hill behind and to the right of the palace, 17th-century medicinal plants flourish in the **Queen's Nosegay Garden.** *(Kew, on the south bank. Main entrance and Visitors Centre are at Victoria Gate, nearest the Tube. Climb the white stairs that go above the station tracks and walk straight down the road. ⊖Kew Gardens; Zone 3. ☎020 8332 5000; www.kew.org. Open Apr.-Aug. M-F 9:30am-6:30pm, Sa-Su 9:30am-7:30pm; Sept.-Oct. daily 9:30am-6pm; Nov.-Jan. daily 9:30am-4:15pm. Last entry 30min. before close. Glasshouses close Apr.-Oct. 5:30pm; Nov.-Feb. 3:45pm. Free 1hr. walking tours daily 11am, 2pm; start at Victoria Gate Visitors Center. "Explorer" hop-on, hop-off shuttle makes 40min. rounds of the gardens daily 11am-4pm; £4, under 17 £1. "Discovery Bus" tours for mobility-impaired daily 11am, 2pm; booking required; free. £13, concessions £12, under 17 free; 45min. before close £10.25.)*

▨**HAMPTON COURT PALACE.** A monarch hasn't lived here for 250 years, but Hampton Court still basks in regal splendor. Cardinal Wolsey built the first palace here in 1514, showing the young Henry VIII how to act the part of a powerful ruler. Henry learned the lesson all too well: he confiscated Hampton in 1528 (because Wolsey's palace was nicer than his) and embarked on a major building program. In 1689 William and Mary employed Christopher Wren to bring Hampton Court up to date—you can still see the place where the 15th-

and 17th-century wings join—but less than 50 years later George II abandoned it for good. The palace is divided into six 20-60min. tour routes, all starting at **Clock Court,** where you can pick up a program of the day's events and an informative, well-paced audio tour. In ⬛**Henry VIII's State Apartments,** the grandly carved ceiling and tapestried walls of the massive Great Hall hint at past magnificence. Below, the **Tudor Kitchens** offer insight into how Henry ate himself to a 54 in. waist: food historians estimate that fully three-quarters of the early Tudor diet was meat, most boiled in suet-and-lard pie crusts. Predating Henry's additions, the 16th-century **Wolsey Rooms** glow with Renaissance masterpieces. The **Queen's Apartments** weren't completed until 1734, postponed by Mary II's death. Although she designed them, she never enjoyed the finished work. No less impressive are the gardens, with Mantegna's *Triumphs of Caesar* paintings secreted away in the Lower Orangery. North of the palace, the **Wilderness,** a pseudo-natural area earmarked for picnickers, holds an ever-popular maze, planted in 1714. Its small size belies a devilish design. *(45min. from Waterloo by train; round-trip £5.60. 3-4hr. by boat; daily 10:30, 11am, noon, 2pm; £13.50, round-trip £19.50, concessions £9/13, children £6.75/9.75. Westminster Passenger Cruises ☎ 020 7930 4721; www.thamesriverboats.co.uk. Palace ☎ 08707 527 777; www.hamptoncourtpalace.org.uk. Open daily from late Mar. to late Oct. 10am-6pm; from late Oct. to late Mar. 10am-4:30pm. Palace and gardens £13.30, concessions £11.30, ages 5-15 £6.65. Audio and guided tours included. Admission free for worshippers at Chapel Royal; services Su 11am, 3:30pm.)*

SOUTH ENGLAND

Visitors to South England never seem to want to leave. Early Britons who crossed the English Channel settled the counties of Kent, Sussex, and Hampshire, and William the Conqueror left his mark in the form of castles and cathedrals, many built around former Roman settlements. Today, Victorian mansions balance atop seaside cliffs, and the masts of ships grace the skyline. An easy escape from London, the region offers seaside relaxation, while the cobbled-stone streets of Canterbury still draw pilgrims.

HIGHLIGHTS OF SOUTH ENGLAND

SHIMMY until the break of dawn at the nightclubs in **Brighton** (p. 167).

CAPTURE a photograph of the famous chalk-white cliffs of **Dover** (p. 158)—and look across the water to the French border.

CATCH YOUR BREATH while walking or biking the **South Downs Way** (p. 163), strewn with Bronze Age burial mounds.

KENT

CANTERBURY   ☎(0)1227

In 1170, four knights left Henry II's court in France and traveled to Canterbury to murder Archbishop Thomas Becket beneath the massive columns of his own cathedral. Three centuries of innumerable pilgrims in search of miracles flowed to St. Thomas's shrine, creating a great medieval road between London and Canterbury. Chaucer caricatured the pilgrimage in *The Canterbury Tales*, which have done more to enshrine the cathedral than the saint's now-vanished bones. In summer, swarms of tourists descend upon the cobbled city center, while for the rest of the year Canterbury remains a lively college town.

⬛ TRANSPORTATION

Trains: Canterbury has 2 central stations.

East Station, Station Rd. E., off Castle St. Open M-Sa 6:10am-8:20pm, Su 6:40am-8:20pm. South Eastern trains to **Cambridge** (3hr., 2 per hr., £32.40), **Dover** (20min., 3 per hr., round-trip £6), and **London Victoria** (1hr., 2 per hr., £20.50), .

West Station, Station Rd. W., off St. Dunstan's St. Open M-Sa 6:15am-7:30pm, Su 8:30am-5pm. Trains to **Brighton** (3hr., 3 per hr., £16.30), and **Central London** (1½hr., every hr., £12).

Buses: Station at St. George's Ln. (☎01227 472 082). Open M-Sa 8am-5pm. National Express (☎08705 808 080) to **London** (2hr., 2 per hr., £14). Explorer tickets allow 1-day unlimited bus travel in Kent (£5).

Taxis: Longport Cars Ltd. (☎01227 458 885). 24hr.

Bike Rental: Downland Cycle Hire, Malthouse, St. Stephen's Road (☎01227 479 643; www.downlandcycles.co.uk). £10 per day; bike trailers £12 per day; £25 deposit. Open M-Sa 9:30am-5pm, Su 10am-4:30pm.

✈ 🛈 ORIENTATION AND PRACTICAL INFORMATION

Canterbury's center is roughly circular, defined by the eroding medieval city wall. The main street crosses the city northwest to southeast, changing names from **Saint Peter's Street** to **High Street** to **The Parade** to **Saint George's Street**. Butchery Ln. and Mercery Ln., each only a block long, run north to the **Cathedral Gates**, while numerous other side streets lead to hidden pubs and chocolatiers.

Tourist Information Centre: The Buttermarket, 12-13 Sun St. (☎01227 378 100; www.canterbury.co.uk). Books beds for £2.50 plus a 10% deposit. Open Easter-Christmas M-Sa 9:30am-5pm, Su 10am-4pm; Christmas-Easter M-Sa 10am-4pm.

Tours: 1½hr. tours leave from the TIC. July-Sept. M-Sa 11:30am, 2pm; Oct. and Apr.-June daily 2pm. £4.75, concessions £4.20, under 12 £3.20, families £16.

Currency Exchange: Banks line High St. **Thomas Cook,** 9 High St. (☎01227 772 299). Open M-W and F-Sa 9am-5:30pm, Th 10am-5:30pm, Su 10:30am-4:30pm.

Library: Canterbury Library, High St. (☎01227 463 608), in the Beaney Institute. Open M-W and F 9am-6pm, Th 9am-8pm, Sa 9am-5pm.

Launderette: Canterbury Clothes Care Company, 4 Nunnery Fields (☎01227 452 211). Open M-F 9am-6pm, Sa 9am-4pm, Su 9am-3pm. Last wash 30min. before close.

Police: Old Dover Rd. (☎01227 762 055), outside the eastern city wall.

Pharmacy: Boots, 12 Gravel Walk (☎01227 470 944). Open M-W and F 9am-6pm, Th and Sa 8am-7pm, Su 11am-5pm.

Hospital: Kent and Canterbury Hospital, 28 Ethelbert Rd. (☎01227 766 877).

Internet Access: Dot Cafe (☎01227 478 778; www.ukdotcafe.com), at the corner of St. Dunstan's St. and Station Rd. £3 per hr. Open daily 9am-9pm.

Post Office: 19 St. George St. (☎01227 473 810). **Bureau de change.** Open M-Sa 9am-5:30pm. **Postcode:** CT1 2BA.

🏠 🛏 ACCOMMODATIONS AND CAMPING

Canterbury attracts visitors throughout the year, and single rooms are scarce; reserve ahead. B&Bs cluster around High St. and near West Station. The less expensive options (£18-20) on **New Dover Road,** half a mile from East Station, fill fast; turn right from the station and continue to Upper Bridge St. At the second roundabout, turn right onto St. George's Pl., which becomes New Dover Rd.

Kipps Independent Hostel, 40 Nunnery Fields (☎01227 786 121), 10min. from the city center. Century-old townhouse with modern amenities. Self-catering kitchen and TV lounge. If there are no vacancies, ask to set up a tent in the garden. Laundry £3. Internet £1 per 30min. Free Wi-Fi. Dorms £15; singles £20; doubles £34. MC/V. ❷

YHA Canterbury, 54 New Dover Rd. (☎01227 462 911), located 1 mi. from East Station and town center. The trek through town is rewarded with large, quiet rooms and an all-you-can-eat breakfast buffet. Game room, TV lounge, and self-catering kitchen. Lockers £1. Laundry £2.10. Reception 7:30-10am and 3-11pm. Book ahead in summer. Tents accommodate overflow. Dorms £20, under 18 £15. MC/V. ❷

Camping & Caravanning Club Site, Bekesbourne Ln. (☎01227 463 216), off the A257, 1 mi. east of the city center on a large plot of land near the golf course. Hot showers, laundry (£3), and facilities for the disabled. £6 per person. Electricity £3. MC/V. ❶

🍴 FOOD

Cafe des Amis du Mexique, St. Dunstan's St. (☎01227 464 390; www.cafedez.co.uk), just outside the West Gate. Inspired Mexican dishes in a funky cantina setting. Share a

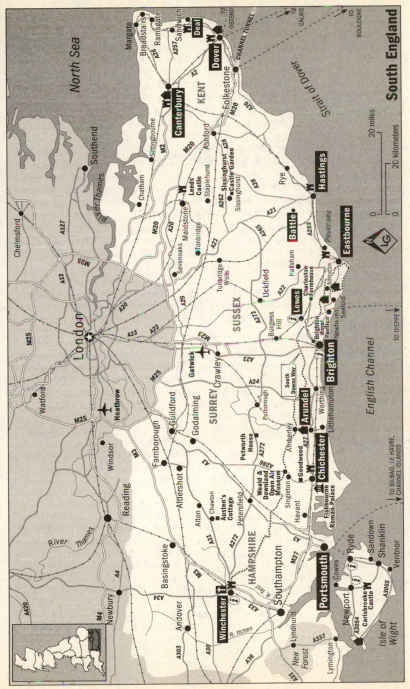

South England

North Sea

Margate
Broadstairs
Ramsgate
Sandwich
Deal
Dover
OSTEND
CALAIS
BOULOGNE
CHANNEL TUNNEL
Folkestone
A2
A20
KENT
Canterbury
Strait of Dover
Sittingbourne
M2
M20
Ashford
A28
Hastings
Sissinghurst
Castle Garden
Staplehurst
A262
Sissinghurst
Rye
A28
Battle
Pevensey
A259
Eastbourne
Chatham
Leeds
Castle
Maidstone
Tonbridge
A21
M20
A265
Hailsham
Charleston
Farmhouse
Alfriston
Sevenoaks
A21
A25
Tunbridge
Wells
Uckfield
A22
SUSSEX
Lewes
Seaford
Newhaven
TO DIEPPE
Southend
River Thames
Chelmsford
A127
A12
M25
A20
London
A23
A22
A24
Burgess
Hill
M23
Crawley
Brighton
Royal
Pavilion
Gatwick
South
Downs Way
English Channel
Watford
M25
Heathrow
M25
M3
Windsor
Reading
River Thames
SURREY
Guildford
Godalming
Farnborough
Aldershot
A3
A3
A31
Alton
Chawton
Austen's
Cottage
Petersfield
A272
Petworth
House
A272
A286
Amberley
Pulborough
Goodwood
Singleton
Weald &
Downland
Open Air
Museum
Chichester
Arundel
A27
Worthing
Littlehampton
Fishbourne
Roman Palace
Havant
A3
HAMPSHIRE
Basingstoke
Andover
A303
A30
A34
A31
A272
Newbury
A4
A4
A34
A303
M3
Southampton
R. Test
M27
A3
Portsmouth
Ryde
Sandown
Shanklin
Ventnor
Cowes
Newport
Carisbrooke
Castle
A3054
A3055
Isle of
Wight
Winchester
R. Itchen
A33
A31
A36
A337
New
Forest
Lymington
Andover
A303
M4
A420
River Thames

20 miles
20 kilometers
0

SOUTH ENGLAND

plate of the sizzling steak fajitas (£27) and grab your own margarita (£6). Open M-Th noon-10pm, F-Sa noon-10:30pm, Su noon-9:30pm. AmEx/MC/V. ❸

Café Belge, 89 St. Dunstan's St. (☎01227 768 222; www.cafebelge.co.uk), outside the West Gate. Read the menu for "50 ways to eat fresh mussels." No cutlery necessary; diners scoop up the meat and sauce with the shells. For dessert, try a sugary Belgian waffle with densely whipped cream and blackberries (£5.50). Open M-F 11am-3pm and 6pm-late; Sa 11am-late, Su 11am-4pm and 6-9pm. ❸

Marlowe's, 55 St. Peter's St. (☎01227 462 194; www.marlowesrestaurant.co.uk). The walls, covered with black-and-white photos from New York City's Broadway, are as busy as the restaurant. Entrees like salmon teriyaki (£11.15) give American standbys an international spin. Choose from 7 toppings for 8 oz. burgers (£7.25). Sit outside to watch shoppers on High St. Open M-Sa 9am-10:30pm, Su 10am-10:30pm. MC/V. ❷

Azouma, 4 Church St. (☎01227 760 076; www.azouma.co.uk). Arabic music, pillow seating, and belly dancers. Morroccan and Lebanese lunch buffet (£9). Dinner brings generous portions of Middle Eastern and Mediterranean cuisine (£11-14). Open M-F noon-2:30pm and 6-11pm, Sa noon-midnight, Su noon-10pm. MC/V. ❸

The Good Shed, Station Rd. W. (☎01227 459 153; www.thegoodsshed.net), right outside of West station. A farmers' market and restaurant. Sandwiches (£3) are stuffed with delicious fillings: try the Italian soft cheese with caramelised onion or roast chicken with tarragon. Open Tu-Sa 9am-7pm, Su 10am-4pm. ❶

C'est la Vie, 17B Burgate (☎01227 457 585). Grab an inventive takeaway sandwich and head to the nearby cathedral. Fill a chicken baguette (£2.80) with any of the 30+ fillings. 10% student discount. Open M-Sa 9:30am-3:30pm. Cash only. ❶

⊙ SIGHTS

⬛**CANTERBURY CATHEDRAL.** For centuries, English pilgrims journeyed to this vast stony edifice to reverence the shrine of **Saint Thomas Becket,** archbishop of Canterbury from 1162 to 1170. After disagreeing with King Henry II over clerical privileges, Becket was murdered by four thuggish knights who may or may not have acted with the king's sanction. Almost overnight, Becket skyrocketed to saintly fame as pilgrims swarmed Canterbury Cathedral. Their contributions funded most of the cathedral's architectural wonders, including the early Gothic **nave,** constructed chiefly during the 14th century on a site allegedly consecrated by St. Augustine 700 years earlier. The shrine to the great saint, destroyed by Henry VIII in 1538, used to fill **Trinity Chapel,** radiant with gold and pilgrim offerings. Today a single candle marks the place where Becket fell—the fatal strike was supposedly so forceful that the blade's tip shattered as it sliced his skull. The beautifully preserved medieval stained glass that surrounds the shrine records St. Thomas's many miracles. Look for the panels about Adam the Forester, a luckless hunter who got an arrow through the throat but survived through the grace of this powerful saint. The steps leading to the nave have been worn shallow by centuries of plodding pilgrim feet. Henry IV, possibly uneasy after having usurped the throne, had his body entombed near Becket's sacred shrine rather than in Westminster Abbey. Across from Henry lies Edward, the Black Prince, and the decorative armor he wore at his 1376 funeral adorns the wall. The **treasury** houses a 1200-year-old pocket sundial among other excavated objects. The **Corona Tower** rises above the eastern apse but is closed to visitors. Stand under the **Bell Harry Tower,** at the crossing of the nave and transepts, to see arches supporting the 15th-century fan vaulting. (*☎01227 762 862; www.canterbury-cathedral.org. Cathedral open Easter-Sept. M-Sa 9am-5:30pm, Su 12:30-2:30pm; Oct.-Easter M-Sa 9am-5pm, Su 12:30-2:30pm. 1hr. tours avail-*

able, M-Sa 3 per day; check nave for times. Evensong M-F 5:30pm, Sa 3:15pm, Su 3:15, 6:15pm. £7, concessions £5.50. Tours £3.50/3. Audio tour £3.50/2.50.)

SAINT AUGUSTINE'S ABBEY. The skeletons of once-magnificent arches and walls are all that remain of one of the most significant abbeys in Europe, built in AD 598 to house Augustine and 40 monks sent to convert England to Christianity. Indoor exhibits and a free audio tour reveal the abbey's history as a burial place, royal palace, and pleasure garden. Don't miss St. Augustine's humble tomb under a pile of rocks. *(Outside the city wall near the cathedral, ☎01227 767 345. Open July-Aug. daily 10am-6pm; Sept.-Dec. Sa-Su 11am-5pm; Jan.-Mar. W-Su 10am-5pm. £4.20, concessions £3.40, children £2.10, families £10.50.)*

CHURCH OF SAINT MARTIN. The oldest parish church in England stands just beyond St. Augustine's Abbey. In AD 562, it witnessed the marriage of pagan King Æthelbert and Princess Bertha, a Christian from Merovingian Gaul, which paved the way for England's conversion to Christianity. The church also holds the mortal remains of author Joseph Conrad. *(North Holmes St. ☎01227 453 469. Open Apr.-Sept. Tu, Th, Sa 11am-4pm; Sept.-Mar. Su 11am-5pm. Free; donations welcome.)*

MUSEUM OF CANTERBURY. Housed in the medieval Poor Priests' Hospital, the museum spans Canterbury's history from St. Thomas to WWII bombings to children's book character Rupert the Bear. Browse through displays to learn about Roman foundations and Becket's unsanitary undergarments. *(20 Stour St. ☎01227 475 202. Open June-Sept. M-Sa 10:30am-5pm, Su 1:30-5pm; Nov.-May M-Sa 10:30am-5pm. Last entry 4pm. £3.50, students £2.25. The Museum Passport grants admission to the Museum of Canterbury, the Westgate Museum, and the nearby Roman Museum; £6, concessions £3.60.)*

CANTERBURY TALES. Interested in literature but not in reading? Chaucer's England is recreated in scenes complete with moving wax characters. The smell isn't the guy standing next you—the facility pipes in the "authentic" stench of sweat, hay, and horses to help bring you back in time. Headphone narrations take you through the scenes in a 45min. abbreviation of Chaucer's bawdy masterpiece. *(St. Margaret's St. ☎01227 479 227; www.canterburytales.org.uk. Open daily July-Aug. 9:30am-5pm; Sept.-Oct. and Mar.-June 10am-5pm; Nov.-Feb. 10am-4:30pm. £7.75.)*

GREYFRIARS. England's first Franciscan friary, Greyfriars was built over the River Stour in 1267. It was used as a prison in the 19th century, and prisoners' etchings still mark the cell walls. Now the building has a museum about the local order and a chapel. For a quiet walk, stroll through the riverside gardens and wildflower meadows. *(6A Stour St. ☎01227 479 364. Gardens open daily 10am-5pm. Chapel open Easter-Sept. M-Sa 2-4pm. Free.)*

WESTGATE TOWERS MUSEUM. The Westgate Towers have guarded the road to London for centuries and are some of the few medieval fortifications to survive waritime Blitzing. Built in 1380 as a defense against France in the Hundred Years' War, the structure served as a town prison before it was converted into a museum for armor and old weapons. Up a steep, winding staircase sits James, the perennially incarcerated wax figure, enjoying a commanding view and plotting his escape from his cell atop the gates. *(☎01227 789 576; www.canterbury-museums.co.uk. Open M-Sa 11am-12:30pm and 1:30-3:30pm. £1.25. Gardens free.)*

OTHER SIGHTS. Canterbury Historic River Tours runs 30min. cruises several times per day. *(1 St. Peter's St. ☎07790 534 744. £7.)* In the city library, the **Royal Museum and Art Gallery** showcases paintings by locally born artists of earlier centuries and recounts the history of the "Buffs," one of the oldest regiments of the British Army. Don't miss the newly acquired Van Dyck and collections by TS Cooper. *(18 High St. ☎01227 452 747. Open M-Sa 10am-5pm. Free.)* Near the city walls

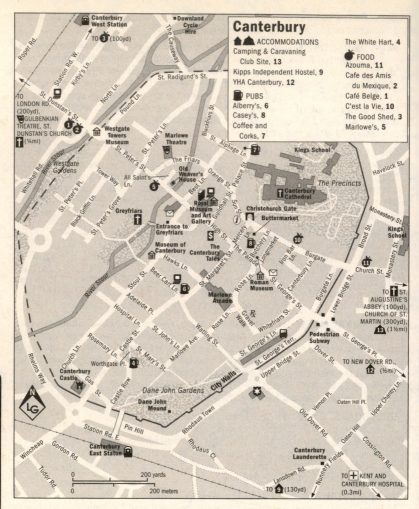

Canterbury

🏠🏠 **ACCOMMODATIONS**
Camping & Caravaning
  Club Site, **13**
Kipps Independent Hostel, **9**
YHA Canterbury, **12**

🍺 **PUBS**
Alberry's, **6**
Casey's, **8**
Coffee and
  Corks, **7**

The White Hart, **4**

🍎 **FOOD**
Azouma, **11**
Cafe des Amis
  du Mexique, **2**
Café Belge, **1**
C'est la Vie, **10**
The Good Shed, **3**
Marlowe's, **5**

to the southwest lie the remnants of **Canterbury Castle.** (☎01227 378 100. *Open daily 8:30am-dusk. Free.*) The vaults of **Saint Dunstan's Church** contain a buried relic said to be the head of Sir Thomas More; legend says that his daughter bribed the executioner for it. (*St. Dunstan's St.* ☎01227 463 654. *Open daily 8am-4pm; call to confirm. Free.*) The **Hospital of Saint Thomas the Martyr** served as a shelter for Canterbury pilgrims in the 12th century. (*25 High St.* ☎01227 471 688. *Open M-Sa 10am-5pm.*)

🎵 🎇 **ENTERTAINMENT AND FESTIVALS**

Buskers (street performers) especially along **Saint Peter's Street** and **High Street,** play street-side Vivaldi while bands of impromptu players ramble from corner to corner, acting out the more absurd of Chaucer's scenes. The TIC distributes brochures on up-to-date entertainment listings in Canterbury.

SOUTH ENGLAND

Marlowe Theatre, The Friars (☎01227 787 787; www.marlowetheatre.com), across from the Pilgrim Hotel. Puts on touring productions in the largest theater in Kent. Wheelchair-accessible. Tickets £10-35, concessions £2 off. £5-10 student standbys 30min. before performances. Box office open M and W-Sa 10am-9pm, Tu 10:30am-9pm, Su 2hr. before performances. MC/V.

The Gulbenkian Theatre, University of Kent, University Rd. (☎01227 769 075; www.gulbenkiantheatre.co.uk), west of town on St. Dunstan's St. Shows films and stages dance, drama, music, and comedy performances. Tickets £7-25; student prices available. Box office open M-F 11am-5pm, Sa 11am-9pm, Su 5:30-9pm.

Canterbury Festival (☎01227 452 853, box office 378 188; www.canterburyfestival.co.uk), in Ashford, 5 mi. southwest of Canterbury. Fills 2 weeks in Oct. with drama, music, dance, walks, and exhibitions.

Stour Music Festival (☎01227 378 188), at All Saint's Boughton Aluph Church, on the A28 and accessible by rail from West Station. Celebrates Renaissance music for seven days in mid-June. Tickets £10-18. Call a month in advance for bookings.

PUBS AND CLUBS

Coffee & Corks, 13 Palace St. (☎01227 457 707). Cafe-bar with a cool, bohemian feel. Mixed drinks (£4), wines by the bottle (£10), and a wide selection of teas (£1.50). Scrabble, occasional live music, and Wi-Fi. Open daily noon-midnight. MC/V.

Alberry's, 38 St. Margaret's St. (☎01227 452 378; www.alberrys.co.uk). Cuddle on leather couches in the corners of this stylish wine bar that pours late into the evenings. Sandwiches and salads £5.50-7. Free Wi-Fi. Live music M. DJs Tu-Th. Smart casual attire required. Happy hour 5:30-7pm. Open M 11am-1am, Tu-Sa 11am-2am.

Casey's, Butchery Ln. (☎01227 463 252). Centrally located near the cathedral, Casey's offers quasi-Irish ambience and traditional food (£6), all in the company of Harry the cat. Schedule of live Irish music (Th-Sa) posted outside. Open M-Th noon-11pm, F-Sa 11am-midnight, Su noon-10:30pm. Kitchen open daily until 3:30pm.

The White Hart, Worthgate Pl. (☎01227 765 091), near East Station. Walk off the train and into this congenial pub with Canterbury's biggest beer garden. Like a good metaphor for life, this pub serves sweets (£3.75) and bitters (£2.30-2.80)—some of Canterbury's best, actually. Lunches £6-9. Open M-Sa noon-11pm, Su noon-6pm. Kitchen open W-F noon-2:30pm, Sa noon-11pm, Su noon-6pm.

DAYTRIPS FROM CANTERBURY

SISSINGHURST CASTLE GARDEN

Trains run from Canterbury West to Staplehurst (50min., round-trip £9.10), where buses #4 and 5 run to Sissinghurst (M-Sa every hr., round-trip £3.50). Shuttle runs from Staplehurst station to Sissinghurst gardens (15min., round-trip £4). The garden is 1 mi. from the bus stop; face away from The Street and walk ¼ mi. before turning left onto the footpath. ☎01580 710 700; www.nationaltrust.org.uk/sissinghurst. Open from mid-Mar. to Oct. M-Tu and F 11am-6:30pm, Sa-Su 10am-6:30pm. Last entry 1hr. before close. £7.80, children £3.50.

A masterpiece of floral design by Bloomsbury Group stalwarts Vita Sackville-West and her husband, Harold Nicolson, Sissinghurst is one of the most popular gardens in a garden-obsessed nation. Eight gardeners maintain the original design, a varied array of carved hedges and flower beds. After touring the **White Garden** or the **Cottage Garden,** visitors may visit the property's **Elizabethan mansion** or stroll along the moat to forested lakes. The library and tower are open to the public and chronicle the garden's development. The staff encourages visitors to come after 4pm, when the afternoon sunlight enhances the garden's beauty.

SOUTH ENGLAND

LEEDS CASTLE

Near Maidstone, 23 mi. west of Canterbury on the A20. Trains run from Canterbury West to Bearsted (every hr., £11.50); a shuttle goes from the station to the castle (£4). Shuttles leave the train station M-Sa every hr. 10:35am-2:35pm, Su every hr. 10:55am-2:55pm; return shuttles leave the castle every hr. M-Sa 2-6pm, Su 2:15-6:15pm. ☎01622 765 400 or 0870 600 8880; www.leeds-castle.com. Castle open daily Apr.-Sept. 10:30am-7pm; Oct.-Mar. 10:30am-5pm. Last entry 1½hr. before close. Grounds open daily Apr.-Sept. 10am-7pm; Oct.-Mar 10am-5pm. Last entry 2hr. before close. Castle and grounds £14, concessions £11. Call for combined transportation and admission tickets, available at train and bus stations.

Sitting amid 500 acres of parkland and 1000 years of history, Leeds Castle was built immediately after the Norman conquest. The Tudor-style ground floor contrasts sharply with the modern second floor, which was impeccably outfitted by the same interior decorator responsible for Jackie Kennedy's White House overhaul. One wing displays a collection of medieval dog collars. The grounds host a jousting tournament at the beginning of June and summer concerts in July (consult TIC for exact dates). Outdoors, wind through a maze of 2400 yew trees, practice your swing on the nine-hole golf course, or take one of the woodland walks, which cross paths with black swans and unusual waterfowl. Come back often—a ticket is good for one year from the purchase date.

DOVER ☎(0)1304

From the days of Celtic invaders to the age of the Chunnel, the white cliffs of Dover have been many a traveler's first glimpse of England. In July, swimmers make the 21 mi. dog-paddle across the English Channel to France. The less adventurous stay on land to see the formidable castle that guards the port.

TRANSPORTATION

Trains: Priory Station, Station Approach Rd. Ticket office open M-Sa 4:15am-11:20pm, Su 6:15am-11:20pm. Trains (☎08457 484 950) to **Canterbury** (20min., 2 per hr., round-trip £6.40) and **London** (2hr., 4 per hr., £24). Eurostar runs a high-speed rail to Paris and other destinations throughout the continent.

Buses: Pencester Road Station between York St. and Maison Dieu Rd. Office open M-Tu and Th-F 8:45am-5:15pm, W 8:45am-4pm, Sa 8:30am-noon. National Express (☎08705 808 080) runs to **London,** continuing to the **Eastern Docks** (2½hr., every hr., £11.80). Stagecoach (☎08702 433 711) runs to **Canterbury** (30min., every hr., £3.80) and **Deal** (45min., every hr., £3). A bus runs to **Folkestone,** a stop for Chunnel trains (30min., every hr., £3.40). A **Day Explorer** ticket (£5) gives 1 day of unlimited travel on Stagecoach buses in East Kent.

Ferries: Eastern Docks sails to **Calais, FRA** and **Ostend, BEL;** the TIC offers a booking service. P&O Stena (☎08705 980 333) sails to **Calais** (40 per day, £18), as does SeaFrance. (☎0870 443 1653. 15 per day, £6.) Speedferries (☎08702 200 570 or 08701 22 7456) takes foot passengers to **Boulogne, FRA** (£7.50). A bus (£1) leaves Priory Station for the docks 45-60min. before sailing. (See **By Ferry, p. 40**.)

Taxis: Central Taxi Service (☎01394 240 0441). 24hr.

PRACTICAL INFORMATION

Tourist Information Centre: The Old Town Gaol (☎01304 205 108, after hours 336 093; www.whitecliffscountry.org.uk), off High St. where it divides into Priory Rd. and Biggin St. Helpful staff sells ferry, bus, and Hoverspeed tickets and books accommoda-

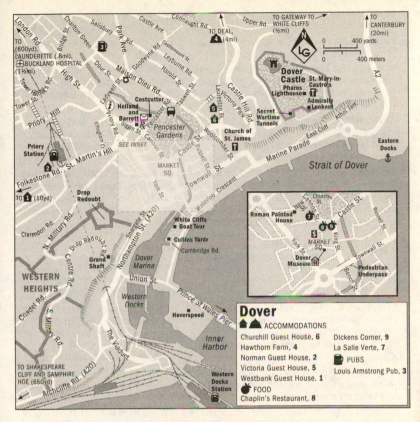

Dover

🏠 ♦ **ACCOMMODATIONS**

Churchill Guest House, **6**   Dickens Corner, **9**
Hawthorn Farm, **4**   La Salle Verte, **7**
Norman Guest House, **2**   🍺 **PUBS**
Victoria Guest House, **5**   Louis Armstrong Pub, **3**
Westbank Guest House, **1**
🍴 **FOOD**
Chaplin's Restaurant, **8**

tions for a 10% deposit. Open June-Aug. daily 9am-5:30pm; Sept. and Apr.-May M-F 9am-5:30pm, Sa-Su 10am-4pm; Oct.-Mar. M-F 9am-5:30pm, Sa 10am-4pm.

Tours: White Cliffs Boat Tours at the Marina (☎01303 271 388). 4 per day. £6.

Banks: Several banks and ATMs are in Market Sq., including **Barclays** in the northwest corner. Open M-F 9:30am-5pm, Sa 9am-noon.

Launderette: Cherry Tree Launderette, 2 Cherry Tree Ave. (☎01304 242 822), off London Rd. Wash and dry £3. Full service available. Open daily 8am-8pm.

Police: Ladywell St. (☎01304 240 055), off High St.

Hospital: Buckland Hospital, Coomb Valley Rd. (☎01304 304 612), northwest of town. Take bus #67 or 67A from the post office.

Post Office: 68-72 Pencester Rd. (☎01304 241 747). Open M-Tu and Th-F 8:30am-5:30pm, W 9am-5:30pm, Sa 8:30am-2pm. **Postcode:** CT16 1PW.

🏠 🏕 ACCOMMODATIONS AND CAMPING

Rooms are scarce in summer; book well ahead. July and August are especially busy due to the influx of distance swimmers eager to try the Channel. Cheaper B&Bs gather on **Folkestone Road,** a hike past the train station.

Churchill Guest House, 6 Castle Hill Rd. (☎01304 208 365). Enormous, ensuite rooms near the castle base. Breakfast included. Singles £35; doubles £55-70. Cash only. ❸

Victoria Guest House, 1 Laureston Pl. (☎01304 205 140). Large mansion with cheerful ensuite rooms, talkative owners, and views of Dover. Doubles £50-58. AmEx/MC/V. ❸

Norman Guest House, 75 Folkestone Rd. (☎01304 207 803; www.thenorman-guest-house.co.uk). Welcoming couple greets guests by name. Clean rooms with TVs and beautiful bedding. English, vegetarian, and continental breakfast included. Singles £30-50, ensuite £35-55; doubles and twins £50-60/55-65. MC/V. ❸

Westbank Guest House, 239 Folkestone Rd. (☎01304 201 061; www.westbankguest-house.co.uk). Jolly and philosophical owner. Lounge decorated in Tudor style with a large fireplace. Charming, homey rooms. Full English breakfast included. Singles £25-40; doubles £45-60; family rooms from £65. MC/V. ❷

Hawthorn Farm (☎01304 852 658), at Martin Mill Station off the A258 between Dover and Deal. 2min. walk from the train station; follow the signs. Set among 28 acres of gardens. Hot showers and laundry facilities available. Open Mar.-Oct. 2-person tent and car June-Aug. £15.50, with electricity £18; Sept.-Oct. and Mar.-May £14.75 with electricity. Hikers and bikers £1 discount. MC/V. ❶

FOOD AND PUBS

Despite Dover's proximity to the continent, its cuisine remains strictly English. Most of the city's restaurants are unimpressive, but diligent travelers will find a few worthwhile options. Chip shops line **London Road** and **Biggin Street.**

La Salle Verte, 14-15 Cannon St. (☎01304 201 547). A relative newcomer to the city center, this modern cafe has old-fashioned charm. Specialty coffees (£1.50-2) and a selection of pastries (£2-4) served on a garden patio or comfy leather loveseats. Open M-Sa 9am-5pm, Su 10am-3pm. Cash only. ❶

Dickens Corner, 7 Market Sq. (☎01304 206 692). The ground floor bustles with channelers downing baguettes and cakes (£2-3.50) or hot lunches (£4-5.50) in a sun-filled room. Upstairs, avoid the wait and have a more leisurely meal. Additional outdoor seating faces the water fountain in Market Sq. Open M-Sa 9am-4:30pm. MC/V. ❶

Chaplins, 2 Church St., off Market Sq. (☎01304 204 870). Huge portions of traditional English food. Sandwiches (£2.75), savory pies (£6), and heavenly apple pie with cinnamon cream (£2.75). Su roast noon-3pm. Open daily 8am-5pm. MC/V. ❷

Louis Armstrong Pub, 58 Maison Dieu Rd. (☎01304 204 759), on the outskirts of town, marked by a picture of Satchmo himself. Excellent selection of ales. Live music with Su jazz nights. Open M-Sa 11am-11pm, Su 4-11pm. Cash only. ❶

SIGHTS

DOVER CASTLE. More fortress than fairy tale, Dover Castle is imposing and magnificent. The safeguard of England since Roman times, the castle was a focus of conflict from the Hundred Years' War to WWII, when its guns were pointed toward German-occupied France. Watch the introductory video in the **keep** before entering simulations of the castle under siege and in preparation for a visit from King Henry VIII. The **Pharos lighthouse**—the only extant Roman lighthouse and the tallest remaining Roman edifice in Britain—towers over **Saint Mary-in-Castro,** a tiled Saxon church. Climb to the platform of the **Admiralty Lookout** for views of the cliffs and harbor. For 20p, you can spy on France through binoculars. The (not so) **Secret Wartime Tunnels,** a 3 mi. labyrinth deep within the white rock, were only recently declassified. Begun in 1803, when Britain was under threat of attack by Napoleon, the underground burrows dou-

SOUTH ENGLAND

bled as the base for the WWII evacuation of Allied troops from Dunkirk and a shelter for Dover citizens during air raids. The lowest of the five levels, not open to the public, was intended to house the government if the Cuban Missile Crisis had gone sour. Tours fill quickly, and there is often a long wait; check in at the tunnels first. Give yourself at least 3hr. to tour the entire castle and grounds. *(Castle Hill Rd., on the east side of town. Buses from the town center run daily Apr.-Sept. every hr., 55p. Otherwise, scale Castle Hill using the pedestrian ramp and stairs to the left of Castle St. ☎01304 211 067. Open Apr., June-July, Sept. daily 10am-6pm; Aug. daily 9:30am-6pm; Oct. daily 10am-5pm; Nov.-Jan. M and Th-Su 10am-4pm; Feb.-Mar. daily 10am-4pm. £10.30, concessions £8.20, children £5.20, families £25.80.)*

WHITE CLIFFS. Lining the most famous strip of England's coastline, the white cliffs make a beautiful backdrop for a stroll along the pebbly beach. A few miles west of Dover, the whitest, steepest, and most famous of them all is **Shakespeare Cliff,** traditionally identified as the site of blind Gloucester's battle with the brink in *King Lear. (25min. by foot along Snargate St. and Archcliffe Rd.)* To the east of Dover, past Dover Castle, the **Gateway to the White Cliffs** overlooks the Strait of Dover and is an informative starting point. *(Buses go from the town center to Langdon Cliff at least once per hr. ☎01304 202 756. Open daily Mar.-Oct. 10am-5pm; Nov.-Feb. 11am-4pm.)* Dozens of **cliff walks** lie a short distance from Dover; consult the TIC or the visitors center at the Gateway to the White Cliffs for trail information. Dover White Cliffs Boat Tours, at the clock tower in Dover Marina, leads 40min. trips around the coastline. *(☎01303 271 388; www.whitecliffsboattours.com. £6, children £3, families £16.)* The **Grand Shaft,** a 140 ft. triple-spiral staircase, was shot through the rock in Napoleonic times to link the army on the Western Heights with the city center. The cliffs to the east and west of Dover can be viewed and photographed at a distance from the tip of Prince of Wales Pier. *(Snargate St. ☎01304 201 066. Open select days throughout year; call for dates.)*

DOVER MUSEUM. This museum depicts Dover's Roman days as the colonial outpost Dubras. The **Bronze Age Boat Gallery** houses the remnants of the oldest ship ever discovered—it's 3550 years old. *(Market Sq. ☎01304 201 066. Open Apr.-Sept. M-Sa 10am-5:30pm, Su noon-5pm; Oct.-Mar. M-Sa 10am-5:30pm. £2.50.)*

OTHER SIGHTS. Recent excavations unearthed a remarkably well-preserved **Roman painted house.** It's the oldest Roman house in Britain, with central heating and indoor plumbing. It also holds the best-preserved Roman wall painting in Britain, more than 1800 years old. *(New St., off York St. and Cannon near Market Sq. ☎01304 203 279. Open Apr.-Sept. Tu-Sa 10am-5pm, Su 1-5pm. Last entry 4:30pm. £2, concessions £1.60.)* For striking views, take the A20 toward Folkestone to **Samphire Hoe,** a park planted in the summer of 1997 with material dug from the Channel Tunnel. The D2 bus to Aycliffe (£1) stops about a 10min. walk from the park, or follow the North Downs Way along the clifftop. *(Open daily 7am-dusk.)* Climb the 73 steps of the **South Foreland Lighthouse** for 360° views of Kent and the Channel. *(2 mi. from the Gateway to the White Cliffs Visitor Centre. ☎01304 852 463. Open in summer M and F-Su 11am-5pm. Visits by guided tours only. £3.60, children £1.80, families £9.)*

▶️ DAYTRIPS FROM DOVER

DEAL. Julius Caesar landed here in 55 BC, and Deal's castles represent Henry VIII's 16th-century attempt to prevent similar invasions. **Deal Castle,** south of town at the corner of Victoria and Deal Castle Rd., is one of Henry's largest Cinque Ports (anti-pirate establishments). The 16th-century fortress is one of the spookiest in England. Its symmetrical maze of coal-black cells and corridors, often puddled from sea seepage, holds a dozen places to conceal some murderous lurking Norman (or to break your neck). With no artificial lighting in

SOUTH ENGLAND

the passageways, the castle constitutes a national hazard as well as a national treasure. (☎01304 372 762. Open Apr.-Sept. M-F and Su 10am-6pm, Sa 10am-5pm. Last entry 5:30pm. £4.20, concessions £3.40, children £2.10, families £10.50.) **Walmer Castle,** half a mile south of Deal via the beachfront pedestrian path or the A258 and 1 mi. from the Walmer train station, is the best-preserved and most elegant of Henry VIII's citadels. Walmer has been transformed into a country estate, which has been the official residence of the lords warden of the Cinque Ports since the 1700s. Notable wardens past include the duke of Wellington, William Pitt, Winston Churchill, and, most recently, the queen mother. The gardens were planted with her favorite flowers for her 95th birthday. (Trains from Dover Priory arrive in Deal Station (15min., every hr., £3.40). Open M-F 10am-4pm, Sa 10am-2pm. Walmer Castle ☎01304 364 288. Open Apr.-Sept. M-F and Su 10am-6pm, Sa 10am-4pm; Oct. W-Su 10am-4pm; Mar. daily 10am-4pm. Last entry 30min. before close. Closed when the lord warden is in residence. £6.50, concessions £5.20, children £3.30, families £16.50. Free 30min. audio tour.)

SUSSEX

HASTINGS   ☎(0)1424

Huddled between sandstone cliffs and the emerald Channel, Hastings has been claimed by Romans, Normans, and Victorians throughout its turbulent history. Having finally surrendered its name and identity to a decisive battle (p. 75), the seaside resort town of Hastings still relishes its 1000-year-old claim to fame. The remains of **Hastings Castle,** built by William the Conqueror, mark the spot where the Norman duke's troops camped before confronting Harold II and the Saxons. Catch the *1066 Story,* a 20min. film on the famous tussle, and visit the castle's dungeons. Take the West Hill Railway (round-trip £1.80) from George St. to the top of the hill. (☎01424 781 111; www.discoverhastings.co.uk. Open daily from mid-Mar to mid-Sept. 10am-5pm; from mid-Sept. to mid-Mar. 11am-4pm. £3.75.) Before heading back to sea level, duck into **Saint Clements Caves** for the **Smugglers Adventure.** Once the center of the Sussex smuggling ring, these miles of caves and tunnels are now more like a theme park, complete with games and smuggling simulations. (☎01424 422 964; www.smugglersadventure.co.uk. Open daily Mar.-Sept. 10am-5:30pm; Oct.-Feb. 11am-4:30pm. £6.40.) Exhibits about the area's nautical past reside in several seafront museums. The **Shipwreck Heritage Centre,** Rock-a-Nore Rd. at the end of Marine Parade, is the largest, showcasing the hull of a Victorian river barge. (☎01424 437 452. Open daily Mar.-Sept. 10am-5pm; Nov.-Feb. 11am-4pm. Free.)

B&Bs crowd around Cambridge Gardens by the train station. A 5min. walk from the town center, **Apollo Guest House ❸,** 25 Cambridge Gardens, is trimmed in pink. (☎01304 444 394. Full breakfast. Singles £23-33; doubles £46-66. Apartment £350 per week.) For groceries, visit **Morrisons,** Supermarkets Pl., behind the train station. (☎01304 720 833. Open M-W and Sa 8am-8pm, Th-F 8am-10pm, Su 10am-4pm.) Restaurants and takeaways are everywhere. Try **Frenz Grill Bar ❶,** 46 Robertson Rd., for its delicious assortment of sandwiches (from £3.50), "wrapz" (£2.75), and £1 pizza slices. (☎01304 426 832. Open M-W and Su 11am-11pm, Th-Sa 11am-3am.) Around the corner, **Bor Thong Thai Restaurant ❷,** 6 Claremont, serves sizzling fish, noodle entrees (£5-10), and abundant vegetarian options. (☎01304 429 629. Open daily noon-3pm and 6-11pm.)

Hastings is a good base for exploring its historic neighbors. **Trains** (☎08457 484 950) go from Hastings Station to Brighton (1hr., every hr., £10.60), Dover (2hr., every hr., £15.30), and London Victoria (2hr., every hr. £22.70). The helpful staff at the **Tourist Information Centre,** Queens Sq., signposted from the train station, books accommodations for £2. (☎08452 741 001; www.hastings.gov.uk. Open M-Sa 10:30am-5pm, Su 10am-4:30pm.) The **post office** is at 10 Cambridge Rd. (Open M and W-Sa 9am-5:30pm, Tu 9:30am-5:30pm.) **Postcode:** TN34 1AA.

BATTLE   ☎(0)1424

The small town of Battle was named after the famous 1066 clash between the Norman William the Conqueror and his Anglo-Saxon rival, King Harold. To commemorate his victory in the Battle of Hastings, William built **Battle Abbey** in 1094, spitefully positioning its altar upon the spot where Harold fell (p. 75). Little remains of the abbey apart from the gate and a series of 13th-century monks' quarters. An excellent free audio tour narrates the story of the action blow by blow as you walk along the meadowed battlefield. Like William after so many hours of heavy fighting, you crest the hill at the end. Battle Abbey is in the center of town; turn left out of the train station and walk to the signposts at the end of the road. (☎01304 331 181. Open daily Apr.-Sept. 10am-6pm; Oct.-Mar. 10am-4pm. £6.50, concessions £5.20, children £3.30.)

Trains run from Hastings (15min., 2 per hr., round-trip £3). The **Battle Abbey TIC** books accommodations for a 10% deposit. (☎01424 773 721; www.battletown. co.uk. Open Apr.-Sept. daily 10am-6pm; Oct.-Mar. M-Sa 10am-4pm.)

SOUTH DOWNS WAY   ☎(0)1323

The South Downs Way stretches 99 mi. from Eastbourne west toward Portsmouth and Winchester. The paths meander through chalk hills and livestock-laden meadows, never far from coastal towns, yet rarely crossing into civilization. The Downs were initially cultivated by prehistoric peoples, whose settlements still mark the countryside. The Way is marked from start to finish, but a detailed guide is available at any local TIC. The walking is moderate, wooing novice hikers and making the South Downs one of the most accessible outdoor experiences in England.

▣ TRANSPORTATION

Trains (☎08457 484 950) run from Eastbourne to London Victoria (1hr., 2 per hr., £19) and from Petersfield to London Waterloo (1hr., 3 per hr., £16.20). Eastbourne's helpful Bus Stop Shop, Arndale Centre, dispenses info on **buses.** From the train station, turn left onto Terminus Rd.; Arndale Centre is on the left. (☎01323 416 416. Open M-Sa 9am-5pm.) Walking the South Downs Way takes about 10 days, but public transportation allows you to take it in segments. Trains connect Lewes to Southease (6min., 2 per hr., £2), County buses #143 and 21 connect Eastbourne to Lewes (20min., 2 per day, £2), and bus #126 connects Eastbourne with Alfriston (40min., 5 per day, round-trip £5). For details, call Eastbourne Buses (☎01323 416 416) or Traveline (☎870 608 2608).

Cycling has long been a popular means of seeing the Downs. DH Lawrence cycled the Way in 1909 to visit his friend Rudyard Kipling. Cyclists and **horses** have access to most of the trail, but in a number of places their routes diverge from those of the walkers. Cycling the Way takes two or three days. The Harvey map (£10 at the TIC or bookstores) shows all of the cycling paths in detail. If you're starting from Eastbourne, try **Nevada Bikes,** 324 Seaside (☎01323 411 549), for bike rental. At the other end of the trail, in Winchester, is **Halford's,** Moorside Rd. (☎01962 853 549). The **Cyclists Touring Club** (☎0870 873 0060; www. ctc.org.uk) answers questions. **Audiburn Riding Stables,** Ashcombe Ln., Kingston, conducts guided 1hr. horseback tours. (☎01273 474 398. £18, under 16 £15.)

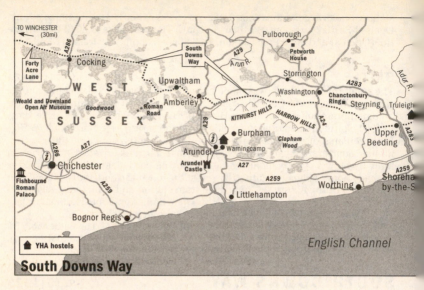

South Downs Way

✦ ORIENTATION

Serious hikers begin their trek in **Eastbourne,** the official start of the Way. East-bourne's **Beachy Head** cliff (p. 166) is accessible by bus #12A to Brighton and is marked from the train station. From **Winchester** town center (p. 185), at the other end of the Way, head east on Bridge St., right on Chesil St., and left on East Hill. When East Hill splits, take the right fork onto Petersfield Rd. and head for the car park, where signs for the Way will appear. From **Amberley,** just north of Arundel (p. 173), the Way runs north, parallel to the B2139.

🛈 PRACTICAL INFORMATION

Eastbourne is the most convenient location to arrange accommodations and find local services. Any of the following TICs can provide information, maps, and accommodations bookings for the Way.

Tourist Information Centres:

Eastbourne: Cornfield Rd. (☎09067 112 212; www.visiteastbourne.com). Gives out basic maps and sells guides. Open Mar.-Oct. M-F 9:30am-5:30pm, Sa 9:30am-5pm; Nov.-Feb. M-F 9:30am-4pm, Sa 9:30am-1pm.

Brighton: Royal Pavilion Shop, 4-5 Pavilion Bldg. See p. 168.

Lewes: 187 High St. (☎01273 483 448). Books rooms and sells maps and guides. Open Apr.-Sept. M-F 9am-5pm, Sa 10am-5pm, Su 10am-2pm; Oct.-Mar. M-F 9am-5pm, Sa 10am-2pm.

Winchester: The Guildhall. See p. 186.

Guidebooks:

In Print: *Harvey's South Downs Way* (£10) is the Bible of the Downs, available at all local TICs. It includes a waterproof map. The Eastbourne and Lewes TICs sell *50 Walks in Sussex* (£8). The South Downs Way accommodation guide (£3.50) is helpful for finding places to stay, as is the free *Caravan and Camping Sites in Sussex* brochure, available at local TICs.

Online: Find more info at the South Downs Way Virtual Information Centre (www.vic.org.uk) and the Rural Walks site (www.ruralways.org.uk). YHA listings are available at www.yha.org.uk.

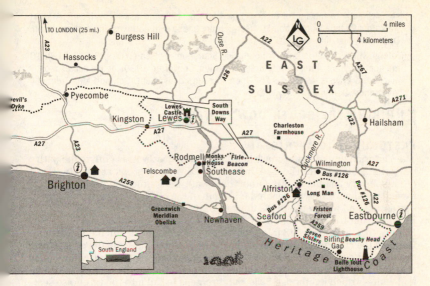

Camping Gear: Millets The Outdoors Store, 146-148 Terminus Rd., Eastbourne (☎01323 728 340). Stocks camping supplies and Ordnance Survey maps. Open M-Sa 9am-5pm, Su 10:30am-4pm. Brighton also has many outdoors shops.

Banks: Throughout the Eastbourne town center and in bigger cities on the Way. Pick up cash before hitting the trail. **Lloyd's TSB,** 104 Terminus Rd. (☎08453 000 000). Open M-Tu and Th-F 9am-5pm, W 10am-5pm, Sa 9am-2pm.

ACCOMMODATIONS

There are few towns along the Way, and B&Bs fill quickly. **Brighton** (p. 167) makes a good base, as do **Lewes** (p. 173), **Arundel** (p. 173), **Alfriston,** and Southcliff Ave. in **Eastbourne.** For a relaxing night on the seafront, take a room at **Alexandra Hotel ❸**, King Edward's Parade, in Eastbourne. (☎01323 720 131. Breakfast included. June-Sept. from £35 per person; Oct.-Dec. and Mar.-May from £30 per person. MC/V.) The **Atlanta Guest House ❸**, 10 Royal Parade, rents comfortable ensuite rooms with seaside views. (☎01323 730 486. Singles £35; doubles £60.) **Camping** on the Way is permitted with the landowner's permission. A guide to camping sites can also be obtained at the Eastbourne TIC.

The following **YHA hostels** lie along the Way, each within a day's walk of the next and each with an 11am-8pm lockout and 11pm curfew. For other hostels, check accommodations in Brighton (p. 167) or Arundel (p. 173).

Alfriston, Frog Firle, Alfriston (☎0870 770 5666). 1 mi. from the Way and Alfriston, 8 mi. from Eastbourne. Bus #126 from Seaford to Eastbourne passes the hostel. By foot from Alfriston, turn left from the market cross and pass the village green, then follow the overgrown riverside trail to Litlington footbridge and turn right along the path; the hostel is at the end in a stone house with bovine neighbors. 16th-century house with spacious rooms. Full breakfast £4. Internet access. Open July-Aug. daily; Sept.-Oct. and Feb.-June. M-Sa; Nov.-Dec. F-Sa. Dorms £14-16. MC/V. ❶

Telscombe, Bank Cottages, Telscombe Village (☎0870 770 6062). 2 mi. south of Rodmell, 2 mi. from the Way, 12 mi. west of Alfriston. From Rodmell (next page), follow signs directly to the hostel or take bus #14A or 123 and ask to be let off. A short walk from Virginia Woolf's house. 18th-century house with cottages and a cheery staff. Open daily Apr.-Aug. Dorms £14. MC/V. ❶

Truleigh Hill, Tottington Barn, Truleigh Hill, Shoreham-by-Sea (☎01903 813 419). 10 mi. from Brighton, 4 mi. from Shoreham station. Converted 1930s house serves mostly hikers and cyclists. Meals £3.75. Open July-Aug. daily; Sept.-Oct. and Mar.-June call in advance. Dorms £14. MC/V. ❶

⬛ HIKING THE SOUTH DOWNS WAY

EASTBOURNE TO ALFRISTON

The Victorian city of **Eastbourne,** sheltered by the **Beachy Head** cliff, is the path's official starting point. The 12A bus toward Brighton stops at Beachy Head (10min., every 20min., £1.50). Otherwise, walk west along the promenade following the signs until you reach the bottom of the cliffs, then make the strenuous ascent and follow the fields upward past wind-bent trees. The entire 4 mi. journey from the town center to the top of Beachy Head takes about 1½hr. Beware that, at a sheer 543 ft. above the sea, Beachy Head can induce vertigo. Because the chalky cliffs are eroding, it is wise to stay far from the edge. From the top you can view the **Seven Sisters,** 4½ mi. away, a series of white chalk ridges carved by centuries of receding waters. Far below, the 19th-century red-and-white-striped lighthouse **Belle Tout** threatens to fall into the turquoise sea.

From Beachy Head, the path winds past a number of **tumuli,** Bronze Age burial mounds dating to 1500 BC. The Way continues west to **Birling Gap,** the last undeveloped stretch of coast in South England. To reach **Alfriston,** a one-road village called "the last of the old towns," follow the Way 4 mi. inland over a path once used by smugglers between the Cinque Ports. Another option is the **bridleway path** to Alfriston (8 mi.), which joins a trail just below East Dean Rd. The path passes through **Wilmington** and its famous **Long Man,** a 260 ft. earth sculpture variously attributed to prehistoric peoples, Romans, monks, and aliens. The Long Man is unmarked by signs and best viewed from a distance.

A great starting point for walks, the **Giant's Rest ❷,** on The Street in Wilmington, serves freshly poached fish and splendid desserts, like the summer pudding with clotted cream (£5). A number of table games keep people amused as they wait for their food. (☎01323 870 207. Entrees £5-14. Open M-F 11am-3pm and 6-11pm, Sa 11:30am-11pm, Su noon-10:30pm. Kitchen open noon-2pm and 7-9pm. MC/V.) Fuel up at **The Singing Kettle ❷,** Waterloo Sq., at the end of High St. in Alfriston. Specials are £4-7, including the leeky Welsh rarebit on walnut bread for £6. (☎01323 870 723. Open daily 10am-5pm. Cash only.) To continue from Wilmington to Alfriston, go back through Long Man's gate and over Windover Hill to the South Downs Way.

ALFRISTON TO FORTY ACRE LANE

From Alfriston, join the Way behind the Star Inn, on High St. (the only street), and continue 7 mi. down gentle slopes to **Southease.** The Way crosses **Firle Beacon,** which has a mound at the top said to contain a giant's silver coffin. From Southease, proceed north three-quarters of a mile to **Rodmell.** Rodmell's single street contains **Monk's House,** home of Virginia Woolf from 1919 until her death. The faithful can retrace the writer's last steps to the River Ouse (1 mi. away), where she committed "the one experience I shall never describe"; her ashes nourish a fig tree in the garden. (☎01892 870 001. Open Apr.-Oct. W and Sa 2-5:30pm. £3.50.) Home cooking awaits at the **Abergavenny Arms ❷,** Newhaven Rd. (☎01273 472 416. Open M-Sa 11am-2:30pm and 6-9pm, Su noon-3:30pm.)

The closest that the Way comes to **Lewes** (LEW-is) is the village of **Kingston,** where hikers from **Brighton** should pick up the trail. Fortifying pub grub (£7-10) is available at **Juggs Inn ❷**, Juggs St. in Kingston. (☎01273 472 523. Open M-Sa 11am-11pm, Su noon-10:30pm. Kitchen open M-Sa noon-2:30pm and 6-9pm, Su noon-4pm. Longer hours in summer.) A stone at the parish boundary, called **Nan Kemp's Corner,** represents a gruesome Downs legend: Nan, jealous of her husband's affection for their newborn, roasted it for him to eat and then killed herself here. Continue from Kingston for 8 mi. to **Pyecombe,** which brings you to **Ditchling Beacon,** the highest point in East Sussex Downs.

The path from Pyecombe to **Upper Beeding** (8 mi.) goes to **Devil's Dyke,** a cliff supposedly built by Lucifer himself in an attempt to let the sea into the Weald and wash away all the churches. Climb through fields of poppies to reach the **YHA Truleigh Hill ❷** (opposite page), 1½ mi. east of Upper Beeding. On the path from Upper Beeding to Washington (6¾ mi.) lies the grove of **Chanctonbury Ring**—trees planted in the 18th century around a third-century Roman template.

The 6½ mi. trek from Washington to **Amberley** brings you to a path leading to **Burpham,** 3 mi. from the **YHA Warningcamp ❷** (p. 174). The 19 mi. of orchids and spiked rampion fields from Amberley to **Buriton,** passing through **Cocking,** complete the Way to the northwest. Southward, across the River Arun to **Littleton Down,** are views of the Weald and the North Downs. The spire of Chichester Cathedral marks the beginning of **Forty Acre Lane,** the Way's final arm.

BRIGHTON ☎(0)1273

Brighton (pop. 250,000) is one of Britain's largest seaside resorts. King George IV came to Brighton in 1783 and enjoyed the anything-goes atmosphere so much that he transformed a farmhouse into his headquarters for debauchery (the Royal Pavilion). A regal rumpus ensued. Since then, Brighton continues to turn a blind eye to some of the more scandalous activities that occur along its shores, as holidaymakers and locals alike peel it off—all off—at England's first bathing beach. Kemp Town (also known as Camp Town), has a thriving gay and lesbian population. The huge student crowd and flocks of foreign youth feed the notorious clubbing scene of this "London-by-the-Sea."

▐ TRANSPORTATION

Trains: Brighton Station, uphill at the northern end of Queen's Rd. Ticket office open 24hr. Travel center open June-Sept. M-F 8am-5pm, Sa 9am-5pm, Su 9:30am-3pm; Oct.-May M-F 8am-5pm, Sa 9am-5pm. Trains (☎08457 484 950) to: **Arundel** (1hr., every hr., £7.70); **London Victoria** (1hr., 2 per hr., £19.50); **Portsmouth** (1hr., 2 per hr., £14.50); **Rye** (1hr., every hr., £14).

Buses: Tickets and info at **One Stop Travel,** 16 Old Steine (☎01273 700 406). Open June-Sept. M-Tu and Th-F 8:30am-5:45pm, W 9am-5:45pm, Sa 9am-5pm, Su 9:30am-3pm; Oct.-May M-Tu and Th-F 8:30am-5:45pm, W 9am-5:45pm, Sa 9am-5pm. National Express (☎08705 808 080) buses leave from Preston Park to **London Victoria** (2-3hr., every hr., £11). Tickets available on board or online.

Public Transportation: Local **buses** operated by Brighton and Hove (☎01273 886 200; www.buses.co.uk) congregate around Old Steine. The TIC can give route and price information for most buses; all carriers charge £1.20 in the central area. Frequent local buses serve Brighton. **Daysaver** tickets before 9am £3.20, after 9am £3.

Taxis: Brighton Taxis (☎01273 202 020). 24hr.

✈ ⓘ ORIENTATION AND PRACTICAL INFORMATION

Brighton is easily explored on foot. **Queen's Road** connects the train station to the English Channel, becoming **West Street** halfway down the slope at the intersection with Western Rd. Funky stores and restaurants cluster around **Trafalgar Street,** which runs east from the train station. From Queen's Rd., head east onto North St. to reach the narrow streets of the **Lanes,** a pedestrian shopping area by day and nightlife center after dark. **Old Steine,** a road and a square, runs in front of the **Royal Pavilion,** while **King's Road** parallels the waterfront.

Tourist Information Centre: Royal Pavilion Shop, 4-5 Pavilion Bldg. (☎09067 112 255; www.visitbrighton.com). Staff sells guides and maps, books National Express tickets, and reserves rooms for £1.50 plus a 10% deposit. Open June-Sept. daily 10am-5pm; Oct.-May M-F 9:30am-5pm, Sa 10am-5pm.

Tours: CitySightseeing (☎01708 886 200; www.city-sightseeing.com). 50min. bus tours leave from Brighton pier every 30min. with stops at Royal Pavilion, the railway station, and Brighton Marina. Apr.-Oct. £7, concessions £6, children £3, families £15.

Banks: All along North St., near Castle Sq. **ATMs** outside **Lloyds** (after hours ☎08453 000 000), at the corner of North St. and East St. Open M-Tu and Th-F 9am-5pm, W 10am-5pm, Sa 9:30am-1:30pm.

Special Concerns: Disability Advice Centre, 6 Hove Manor, Hove St., Hove (☎01273 203 016). Open M-F 10am-4pm.

GLBT Resources: Lesbian and Gay Switchboard (☎01273 204 050). Open daily 5pm-11pm. The TIC also stocks a list of gay-friendly accommodations, clubs, and shops.

Launderette: Preston St. Launderette, 75 Preston St. (☎01273 738 556). Wash and dry £4. Open M-Sa 8am-9pm, Su 9am-7pm. Last wash 1hr. before close.

Police: John St. (☎0845 607 0999).

Hospital: Royal Sussex County, Eastern Rd. (☎01273 696 955).

Internet Access: Internet cafes cluster in the town center, especially along West St. and St. James's St. Try **Starnet,** 94 St. James's St. £1 per hr.

Post Office: 20 St. James's St. **Bureau de change.** Open M-F 8:30am-5:30pm, Sa 9am-2pm. **Postcode:** BN1 1BA.

🏠 ACCOMMODATIONS

On weekdays, accommodations in Brighton go for about half the price of their weekend markups. Brighton's best budget beds are in its hostels; the TIC has a complete list. The city's B&Bs and hotels begin at £25-30 and skyrocket from there. Many midrange (£35-50) B&Bs line **Madeira Place;** cheaper establishments abound west of **West Pier** and east of **Palace Pier.** To the east, perpendicular to the shoreline, **Kemp Town** has a huge number of B&Bs.

🛏 **Baggies Backpackers,** 33 Oriental Pl. (☎01273 733 740). Join in the fun at this supersocial hostel, where spontaneous parties on "Baggies Beach" are common. Racecar sheets and welcoming staff. Co-ed bathrooms. Kitchen with complimentary tea and coffee. Laundry. Free Wi-Fi. Key deposit £5. Dorms £13; doubles £35. Cash only. ❶

Hotel Pelirocco, 10 Regency Sq. (☎01273 327 055; www.hotelpelirocco.co.uk). Wannabe rock stars will revel in the over-the-top, hip-to-be-different atmosphere. Each of 19 individually themed rooms (try the leopard-print "Betty's Boudoir" or Jamie Reid's "Magic Room," decorated by the Sex Pistols artist himself) has video games and a private bath. Singles £50-65; doubles £100-145. AmEx/MC/V. ❹

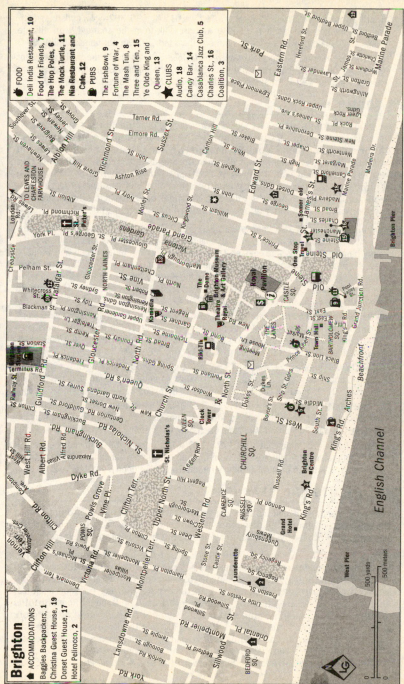

Brighton

♦ ACCOMMODATIONS
Baggies Backpackers, 1
Christina Guest House, 19
Dorset Guest House, 17
Hotel Pelirocco, 2

★ FOOD
Deli India Restaurant, 10
Food for Friends, 7
The Hop Poles, 6
The Mock Turtle, 11
Nia Restaurant and
Cafe, 12

■ PUBS
The FishBowl, 9
Fortune of War, 4
The Mash Tun, 8
Three and Ten, 15
Ye Olde King and
Queen, 13

★ CLUBS
Audio, 18
Candy Bar, 14
Casablanca Jazz Club, 5
Charles St., 16
Coalition, 3

SOUTH ENGLAND

English Channel

Brighton Pier

West Pier

500 yards
500 meters

Christina Guest House, 20 St. George's Terr. (☎01273 690 862; www.christinaguest-housebrighton.co.uk). Family-run house a short walk from the seafront, with ensuite rooms. Full breakfast with vegetarian options included. £25-35 per person. MC/V. ❸

Dorset Guest House, 17 Dorset Gardens (☎01273 571 750). On the lively streets of Kemp Town, this B&B rents pleasant rooms with all the amenities of home. Convenient location near the Lanes. Breakfast included. Singles £30; doubles £40. MC/V. ❸

▸ FOOD

Over 400 restaurants in the city satisfy almost any craving. **Queen's Road** is lined with chains and fast food. Cheap ethnic eateries from Indian to Mediterranean to Moroccan can be found along **Preston Street.** Swanky patisseries and cafes fill the **Lanes,** offering overpriced but memorable meals and people-watching. Get groceries at **Somerfield,** 6 St. James's St. (☎01273 570 363. Open M-Sa 7am-10pm, Su 11am-5pm.) Brighton's history as a health resort has not been forgotten—vegetarian options pervade the city. Satisfy sugar cravings with Brighton rock candy from any of the many shops claiming to have invented it.

Food for Friends, 17A-18A Prince Albert St. (☎01273 202 310). This bright corner restaurant is a paradise of tasty vegetarian cuisine. Omnivores of every stripe will savor the minty beetroot hummus and roasted pear salad with Italian blue cheese and walnuts. Desserts are especially delectable, especially the baked chocolate pudding with home-made Bailey's ice cream (£5.75). Don't miss the Sunday "roast": all the fixings, none of the meat (£9.50). Entrees £10-13. Live jazz Tu. Tea served 3-6pm. Open M-Th and Su noon-10pm, F-Sa noon-10:30pm. AmEx/MC/V. ❷

Nia Restaurant and Cafe, 87 Trafalgar St. (☎01273 671 371), east of the train station. Elegant dishes like duck breast with poached plum (£11-15) in a romantic cafe near the North Laine. International flavors, drawing from Japanese, French, and Mediterranean cuisine. Open M-Sa 9am-11pm, Su 9am-6pm. MC/V. ❸

Deli India, 81 Trafalgar St. (☎01273 699 985). A standout among Brighton's many Indian restaurants. Deli and teashop with mouthwatering vegetarian and meat *thalis* (£6.50-7.50). Open M-Th 10am-7:30pm, F-Sa 10am-10pm, Su noon-3pm. MC/V. ❷

The Mock Turtle, 4 Pool Valley (☎01273 327 380). Half-hidden behind lace curtains, this tucked-away cafe is the perfect stop for a giant jelly doughnut or afternoon tea (£5.50). Open Tu-Su 9:30am-6:30pm. Cash only. ❶

The Hop Poles, 13 Middle St. (☎01273 710 444). Popular bar and hangout with a heated garden. Unique entrees, like ham in plum ginger chili sauce and vegan options. Entrees £7-8. Kitchen open M-Th and Su noon-9pm, F-Sa noon-7pm. MC/V. ❷

◎▸ SIGHTS AND BEACHES

In 1752, Dr. Richard Russell's treatise on the merits of drinking and bathing in seawater to treat glandular disease was published in English. Thus began the transformation of sleepy Brighthelmstone into a free-spirited beach town.

ROYAL PAVILION. A touch of the Far East in the heart of England. Much of Brighton's present extravagance can be traced to the construction of the unabashedly gaudy Royal Pavilion. In 1815, George IV enlisted architect John Nash to turn an ordinary farm villa into an ornate fantasy palace, with Taj Mahal-style architecture offset by Chinese interiors. The **Banquet Room** unfolds beneath a 30 ft. chandelier clutched in the claws of a black and gold dragon. Smaller dragons hold lotus lamps that, when lit, give the impression of breathing. In the music room, an exquisitely restored golden dragon-scale ceiling vaults over the prince regent's prize pipe organ. After your tour, find a seat on the balcony of the **Queen Adelaide Tea Room** for tea and scones. (☎01273 290 900.

Open daily Apr.-Sept. 9:30am-5:45pm; Oct.-Mar. 10am-5:15pm. Last entry 45min. before close. Queen Adelaide Tea Room open daily Apr.-Sept. 10am-5pm; Oct.-Mar. 10:30am-4:30pm. Tours daily 11:30am, 2:30pm. £8.50, concessions £6.50. Tours £2. Free audio tour.)

☒DOWN BY THE SEA. Brighton's original attraction is, of course, the beach, but don't expect silky Southern California sand. Here, bikini-clad beachgoers have to make do with fist-size rocks. Turquoise waters, beach bums, live bands, and umbrella-adorned drinks still make the seaside a must-visit. A debaucherous Brighton weekend would not be complete without a visit to the **nude beach**, 20min. east of Brighton Pier, marked by green signs.

PIERS. The bright lights of the **Brighton Pier** give the oceanfront some kitsch and character. Past the slot machines, video games, and candy-colored condom dispensers is a mini amusement park complete with roller coaster, haunted house, and merry-go-round. Give weary legs a rest on **Volk's Railway**, the oldest electric railway in the world, which shuttles along the waterfront from the pier to the marina. *(☎01273 292 718. Open Apr.-Sept. M-F 11am-5pm, Sa-Su 11am-6pm. Round-trip £2.50.)* The **Grand Hotel** has been rebuilt since a 1984 IRA bombing that killed five but left target Margaret Thatcher unscathed. *(King's Rd.)* A walk along the coast past the ruins of West Pier leads to the residential community of **Hove.**

BRIGHTON MUSEUM AND ART GALLERY. This gallery holds English and international paintings, pottery, Art Deco, and an extensive Brighton historical exhibit that fully explicates the phrase "dirty weekend." The fine **Willett Collection of Pottery** has postmodern porcelains and Neolithic relics. *(Church St., around the corner from the Pavilion. ☎01273 292 882. Open Tu 10am-7pm, W-Sa 10am-5pm, Su 2-5pm. Free.)*

LANES AND LAINES. Small fishermen's cottages once thronged the Lanes, an intricate maze of 17th-century streets (some no wider than 3 ft.) south of North St. in the heart of Old Brighton. Replace those cottages with touristy boutiques and chic restaurants, and you have the Lanes today. For a less commercialized foray into shopping, head to North Laines, off Trafalgar St., where a variety of novelty shops crowd around colorful cafes and impromptu markets.

ENTERTAINMENT AND FESTIVALS

Pick up free *Events Guide* and *Theatre Royal Brighton* brochures at the TIC for the latest info on dates and locations. **Brighton Centre**, King's Rd. (☎0870 606 650; www.brightoncentre.co.uk; box office open M-Sa 10am-5:30pm), and **The Dome**, 29 New Rd. (☎01273 709 709; www.brighton-dome.org.uk; box office open 10am-6pm), host Brighton's biggest events, from Chippendales shows to big-name concerts. Local plays and London productions take the stage at the **Theatre Royal** on New Rd., a Victorian beauty with a plush interior. (☎01273 606 650; www.theatreroyalbrighton.co.uk. Tickets £10-25. Open M-Sa 10am-6pm, performance days 10am-8pm. **Komedia**, on Gardner St., houses a cafe with Wi-Fi, bar, comedy club, and cabaret. (☎01273 647 100; www.komedia.co.uk. Tickets £5-12; discounts available. Box office open Tu-Su noon-4pm, performance days noon-9pm.) The **Brighton Festival** (box office ☎01273 709 709), held each May, is one of the largest arts festivals in England, celebrating music, film, and other art forms. The **Brighton Pride Festival** in early August is the largest gay pride festival in the UK (☎01273 730 562; www.brightonpride.org).

◧ NIGHTLIFE

For info on happening nightspots, check *Latest 7* or *The Source*, free at pubs, newsstands, and record stores, or *What's On*, a poster-size flyer also found at record stores and pubs. GLBT-friendly venues can be found in the free

SOUTH ENGLAND

monthly issues of *G Scene* and *3Sixty*, available at newsstands; *What's On* also highlights gay-friendly events. Night buses N69, 85, and 98-99 run infrequently but reliably in the early morning, picking up at Old Steine, West St., Clock Tower, North St., the train station, and in front of many clubs, usually hitting each spot twice between 1 and 2:30am (£1-4).

PUBS

JB Priestley once noted that Brighton was "a fine place either to restore your health ... or to ruin it again." The waterfront between West Pier and Brighton Pier is a good party spot, and there is a pub or bar on practically every corner of the city center. Many pubs host long happy hours during the week.

- **The Fish Bowl,** 73 East St. (☎01273 777 505). Crowded by hip 20-somethings and students, this bar is a chilled-out hot spot that's cool without trying to be. Free Wi-Fi. Open M-Sa 11am-2am, Su noon-late. Kitchen open noon-7pm.

- **Fortune of War,** 157 King's Rd. Arches (☎01273 205 065), beneath King's Rd. Popular beachfront bar shaped like the hull of a 19th-century ship. Patrons sip their beverage of choice (pints £3.10-3.55) and watch the sun set over the Channel; night owls keep the place packed until it rises again. Open daily from noon until they feel like closing.

- **The Mash Tun,** 1 Church St. (☎01273 684 951). Lounging in plush leather sofas and on wood church pews, a laid-back student crowd parties until the wee hours. Good food, graffiti-adorned walls, and music ranging from hip hop to rock to country. Happy hour M-Th and Su 3-9pm; £4 for a "double spirit and splash." Open M-Th and Su noon-late, F-Sa noon-later. Kitchen open daily noon-5pm.

- **Three and Ten,** 10 Steine St. (☎01273 609 777). Polished floor and gleaming pints. Fills early and stays busy with a mellow crowd of locals and tourists in the know. Cheap beer (£2-3) and mixed drinks (£3). Happy hour M-Sa 4-8pm, Su noon-10pm; all drinks £2.50. Open M-Th and Su 4pm-1am, F-Sa noon-3am.

- **Ye Olde King and Queen,** Marlborough Pl. (☎01273 607 207). This 1779 farmhouse now has a beer garden and multiple bars. With the TV tuned to sports, the place is packed during football matches. Open M-Th noon-11pm, F-Sa noon-late, Su noon-10:30pm. Kitchen open M-Sa 12:30-5pm, Su 12:30-4pm.

CLUBS

The clubbing capital of the south, Brighton is also the hometown of Fatboy Slim and major dance label Skint Records—it's no surprise that Brightonians know their dance music. Most clubs are open Monday through Saturday 10pm-2am; after 2am, the party moves to bonfires and revelry on the waterfront.

- **Audio,** 10 Marine Parade (☎01273 606 906; www.audiobrighton.com). This nightlife fixture is the place to be in Brighton. Mixed music. Cover M-Th £3-4, F £5, Sa £7. Open M-Th 10pm-2:30am, F-Su 10pm-4am. Bar open M-Sa noon-2am, Su 2pm-1am.

- **Coalition,** 171-181 King's Rd. Arches (☎01273 772 842; www.thebrightoncoalition.co.uk). Restaurant by day and wild club scene by night. Big beats right on the shore. Packed with weekenders dancing to an eclectic mix of hits. Salsa Tu 8-10pm. Cover £4-8. Open daily 8am-late. Kitchen open 8am-10pm.

- **Charles Street,** 8-9 Marine Parade (☎01273 624 091). Gay-friendly party with DJs and dance tracks. Cover Th £1, F-Sa £1-5. Open M-W noon-1am, Th-Su noon-3am.

- **Casablanca Jazz Club,** 3 Middle St. (☎01273 321 817). One of few clubs in Brighton that regularly offers live bands. Jazz, funk, disco, and Latin tunes for a mix of students and 20-somethings. Dance floor, DJ, and bar upstairs. Bands in the basement. Cover Th £2, F-Sa £5-7; students £1 less. Open M and Th-Sa 9:30pm-4am, Tu-W 9:30pm-2am.

SOUTH ENGLAND

Candy Bar, 129 St. James's St. (☎01273 622 424; www.candybar.com). Caters mainly to lesbian clubbers with always entertaining, often risqué theme nights. Swirling disco and pink lights. "Big Mama" (drag queen) party nights Th with free entry. 80s Tropicana Night 1st Su of the month. Cover £3-6. Open M-Th 9pm-2am, F-Su 9pm-late.

▶ DAYTRIPS FROM BRIGHTON

LEWES. The hilltop city of Lewes (LEW-is), set in the Sussex chalklands, is a gateway to South Downs Way trails (p. 163). Consult the Lewes TIC (p. 164), right out of the train station and uphill on Station Rd., which becomes Station St. The views of the countryside from the **Lewes Castle** ruins recall the 1264 battle between Simon de Montfort and King Henry III. Much of the site will be closed for refurbishment until March 2009, so call before heading out. *(High St., a 5min. walk uphill from the TIC. ☎01273 486 290. Open M and Su 11am-5:30pm, Tu-Sa 10am-5:30pm or dusk. Last entry 5pm. £5, students £4.35.)* The 15th-century **Anne of Cleves House Museum,** 15min. from the castle, celebrates Henry VIII's fourth wife, the clever woman who managed to keep her head and her house. Today it is home to an eclectic collection of artifacts relating to the history of Lewes, including a dead rat found buried with a stolen spoon. *(Southover High St. ☎01273 474 610. Open Mar.-Oct. M and Su 11am-5pm, Tu-Sa 10am-5pm; Nov.-Feb. Tu-Sa 10am-5pm. £3.65, concessions £3.25. Castle and museum combination ticket £6.40/5.50.)* Past Anne of Cleves's house down Cockshut Rd. lie the ruins of **Lewes Priory,** where Henry III, after his loss at the Battle of Lewes in 1264, signed the treaty that ended the struggle with his barons and to recognize the nation's first representative parliament. *(Trains from Brighton's Queen's Rd. station leave for Lewes every 15min. £3.80.)*

CHARLESTON FARMHOUSE. Artist Vanessa Bell and her husband Duncan Grant moved here in 1916, turning the house into a Bloomsbury Group retreat. Every available space in the house is decorated, and the walls are hung with Duncan Grant's occasionally disturbing paintings. Virginia Woolf was a frequent guest at the house. On Fridays, visitors can take *A Day in the Life of Charleston* tours. *(East of Lewes, off the A27. Take bus #125 from the Lewes station (Sa 6 per day). ☎01323 811 265; www.charleston.org.uk. Open July-Aug. W-Sa 11:30am-6pm, Su 2-6pm; Sept.-Oct. and Apr.-June W and Sa 11:30am-6pm, Th-F and Su 2-6pm. Last entry 5pm. W and Sa entrance by guided tour only. M-Th and Sa-Su £7.50; F £ 9. Garden without house £3.)*

ARUNDEL   ☎(0)1903

Arundel sits in the shadow of towers and spires. The town center is littered with antique shops and other small-town staples, but the magnificent fairy-tale castle and the gently running River Arun give the sleepy town an enchanting quality. Arundel provides an ideal base from which to explore the surrounding countryside and the **South Downs Way** (p. 163).

▣ TRANSPORTATION

Trains (☎08457 484 950) run to: Brighton (1hr., every hr., £7.70); Chichester (20 min., 2 per hr., £3.70); London Victoria (1hr., 2 per hr., £22); Portsmouth (1hr., every hr., £9.20). Routes connect at Littlehampton to the south or Barnham to the west. (Ticket office open M-F 6am-7:25pm, Sa 8:10am-2:45pm, Su 8:10-4:45.) Stagecoach Coastline **buses** (☎0845 121 0170) stop on High St. and on the town's side of the river and leave for Littlehampton (#702, 2 per hr.). South Downs Cycle Hire rents **bikes** just east of Arundel on Blakehurst Farm. (☎01903 889 562. £16 per day.) Call Castle Cars (☎01903 884 444; 24hr.) for a **taxi.**

PRACTICAL INFORMATION

The **Tourist Information Centre,** 1-3 Crown Yard Mews River Rd., dispenses the free *Town Guide* and information on the South Downs Way. (☎01903 882 268. Open M-Sa 10am-5pm, Su 10am-4pm.) Other services include: a **Lloyds Bank** with **ATM,** 14 High St. (☎01903 717 221; open M-Tu and Th-F 9:30am-3:30pm, W 10am-3:30pm); **police,** on the Causeway (☎01903 882 676; open M-F 10am-8pm, Sa 10am-6pm); and the **post office,** 2-4 High St. (☎01903 882 113; open M-F 9am-5:30pm, Sa 9am-12:30pm). **Postcode:** BN18 9AA.

ACCOMMODATIONS AND CAMPING

The elegant B&Bs (£30-40) in the town center can be pricey. Reserve ahead in summer and ask the TIC for an up-to-date list of vacancies.

YHA Warningcamp (☎0870 770 5676), 1½ mi. out of town. Turn right out of the train station, cross the railroad tracks, turn left on the next road, and follow the signs. Family- and group-oriented accommodations near the River Arun. 2 kitchens. Breakfast included. Laundry. Internet. Reception open 8am-11pm. Lockout 10am-5pm. Curfew 11pm. Open July-Aug. daily; Sept.-Oct. Tu-Sa; Nov.-Dec. F-Sa; Apr.-June M-Sa. Camping £10-12.50 per person. Dorms £24, under 18 £18.50. MC/V. ❷

Arden House, 4 Queens Ln. (☎01903 882 544). 8 beautifully kept, centrally located rooms. Look out the windows at the weathered red-slate rooftops of nearby houses. Full breakfast included. Singles £38-45; doubles £56, ensuite £64. Cash only. ❹

Ship and Anchor Marina, Ford Rd. (☎01243 551 262), 2 mi. from Arundel beside the River Arun. 12 acres of countryside with pub and shops nearby. Showers 50p. Apr.-Sept. £7 per person; Oct. and Mar. £5 per person. £1.50 per vehicle. ❶

FOOD

Arundel's pubs and teashops are expensive and unremarkable. For produce, a **farmers' market** meets on the third Saturday morning of each month. The **Co-op,** 17 Queen St., sells groceries. (Open M-Sa 6:30am-10pm, Su 7:30am-10pm.)

Belinda's, 13 Tarrant St. (☎01903 882 977). Once a 16th-century barn, this tearoom is a local favorite for its large selection of traditional English fare. Linger over cream teas (tea and 2 scones £5.36) and famous homemade jam in the cheerful outdoor tea garden. Open daily 9am-5pm. MC/V over £10. ❶

White Hart, 12 Queen St. (☎01903 882 374). Pub grub and local ales in a bridge-side garden. Homemade meals (£7-11) and veggie options. Open M-Sa noon-11pm, Su noon-10:30pm. Kitchen open M-Sa noon-2:30pm and 6-9:30pm, Su noon-4:30. ❷

India Gate, 3 Mill Ln. (☎01903 884 224). Traditional entrees (£7-10) will leave you full and happy. Open daily noon-2:30pm and 5:30-11:30pm. AmEx/MC/V. ❷

SIGHTS AND FESTIVALS

At the end of August, Arundel Castle is the centerpiece of the **Arundel Festival,** 10 days of theatrical performances. The **Festival Fringe** simultaneously offers inexpensive events from concerts to visual art shows. (☎01903 889 821; www. arundelfestival.org.uk. Tickets up to £30.)

ARUNDEL CASTLE. Poised high above the town like an enchanted palace, the castle looks like something conjured out of a fairy tale. A privately owned estate, it has been the seat of the duke of Norfolk for over nine centuries. One hundred thirty one steps lead to the Norman **keep,** which recreates scenes from 12th-century life using models, music, and stories. The keep also offers panoramic views of the surrounding countryside. **The Castle Rooms,** a suite of chambers that combine 16th-century grandeur with Victorian domesticity, are hung with Caneletto and Van Dyck and carpeted with lion skins. Enjoy cream tea (£5) and gaze at the grounds' manicured gardens from the **tea terrace,** near the car park. (☎01903 882 173. *Entrances at the top of High St. or on Mill Rd. Keep open Apr.-Oct. Tu-Su 11am-4:30pm. Castle rooms open Apr.-Oct. Tu-Su noon-5pm. Fitzalan Chapel and grounds open Apr.-Oct. Tu-Su 10am-5pm. Last entry 4pm. £13. Grounds without castle £7.50.)*

RUINS OF BLACKFRIARS. Along the river across from the castle, a placard describes the monks of Blackfriars, the Dominican priory whose ruins are nearby. The ruins were given to the town by the duke of Norfolk in 1935.

CATHEDRAL OF OUR LADY AND SAINT PHILIP HOWARD. Atop the same hill as Arundel Castle, the cathedral is more impressive for its French Gothic exterior than its standard interior. Sixty days after Easter, the cathedral celebrates **Corpus Christi** by laying a carpet of thousands of flowers in a pattern stretching 93 ft. down the aisle. The tradition dates from 1877. (☎*01903 882 297; www.arundelcathedral.org. Open daily in summer 9am-6pm; in winter 9am-dusk. Free.)*

WILDFOWL AND WETLANDS TRUST CENTRE. Paths through over 60 acres of wetlands let visitors watch rare birds in a natural habitat. Many of them will feed right from your hands. (*On Mill Rd.* ☎*01903 883 355. Open daily in summer 9:30am-5:30pm; in winter 9:30am-4:30pm. Last entry 30min. before close. £7.75.)*

🔅 DAYTRIP FROM ARUNDEL

PETWORTH HOUSE. Housing one of the UK's finest art collections, the 17th-century mansion is more like a handsome museum that happens to have bedrooms. JMW Turner often painted the house and landscape, and many of his works hang beside canvases by masters like Van Dyck, Blake, Bosch, Dahl, and Reynolds. The house is also famous for the Petworth Chaucer, an early 15th-century manuscript of *The Canterbury Tales,* and for the intricate carvings in the legendary **Carving Room;** delicate leaves and birds curl out of the wall as if alive. Set among the marble nudes is a beautiful **Molyneux Globe** from 1592, one of the earliest globes made in England. Ask a guide to point out the school medal given to one of the Petworths for saving Winston Churchill from drowning. The house and grounds are a National Trust site, though the Wyndham family still lives in the south wing. (*Take the train 10min. to Pulborough and catch bus #1 to Petworth.* ☎*01798 342*

THE LOCAL STORY

DUKING IT OUT

From the 17th to the 20th centuries, England enjoyed the smallest, wealthiest, and most powerful aristocracy in the world. The dividing line between titled and non-titled has always been fairly clear—e.g., I am a duke, you are a titleless, estateless, repellent clod—but navigating the echelons within the aristocracy can be tricky. For anyone who has ever wondered whether an earl is nobler than a viscount, if a baronet is a clip to wear in your hair, and who on earth is served first at dinner, here is a primer on the peerage.

The orders of the peerage are, from lowest to highest:
Baronet (technically a commoner; addressed as "sir")
Baron (addressed as "lord")
Viscount/Viscountess
Earl/Countess
Marquess/Marquise
Duke/Duchess
Prince/Princess
King/Queen

The word "peerage" refers to the body of hereditary and non-hereditary titles that compose the English aristocracy. The earliest titles were conferred in the 13th century and, until 1958, were exclusively hereditary. Today the monarch can recognize extraordinary merit and achievement by conferring an honorary title that cannot be passed on to children. Peers sit in the House of Lords and are exempt from jury service.

207. House open Apr.-Oct. M-W and Sa-Su 11am-5pm. Last entry 4:30pm. Grounds open daily 8am-dusk. Tours of house 11am-1pm. House and grounds £8.60. Grounds only £3.80/2.)

CHICHESTER ☎(0)1243

Confined for centuries within Roman walls, Chichester remains insular: it thrives off its own markets, and all roads lead to the 16th-century Market Cross. However, Chichester's tourist appeal relies on modern attractions. The town has excellent theater, a summer arts festival, gallery exhibits, and racing spectacles (both motor and horse) in nearby Goodwood. Chichester's cathedral and the Fishbourne Roman Palace are permanent worthwhile sights.

▐ TRANSPORTATION

Trains: Trains (☎08457 484 950) leave Southgate station for **Brighton** (45min., 3 per hr., £9.40), **London Victoria** via **Horsham** (1hr., 2 per hr., £21.40), and **Portsmouth** (30min., 3 per hr., £5.60).

Buses: The bus station (☎01903 237 661) is opposite the train station. National Express (☎08705 808 080) goes to **London Victoria** (3hr., 2 per day, prices vary). Stagecoach Coastline buses connect Chichester with **Brighton** (#700, 3hr., 2 per hr.) and **Portsmouth** (#700, 1hr., 2 per hr.).

Taxis: Central Cars (☎0800 789 432). 24hr.

◀✦ 🛈 ORIENTATION AND PRACTICAL INFORMATION

Four Roman streets named for their compass directions converge at **Market Cross** and divide Chichester into quadrants.

Tourist Information Centre: 29A South St. (☎01243 775 888; www.visitsussex.org). Walk along Southgate from the train station until it becomes South St. Books rooms for £2 plus a 10% deposit. Open Apr.-Sept. M 10:15am-5:15pm, Tu-Sa 9:15am-5:15pm, Su 11am-3:30pm; Oct.-Mar. M 10:30am-5:15pm, Tu-Sa 9:15am-5:15pm.

Tours: Leave from the TIC. May-Sept. Tu 11am, Sa 2:30pm; Oct.-Apr. Sa 2:30pm. £3.50.

Bank: HSBC, Market Cross at the corner of South and East St. Open M and W-F 9am-5pm, Tu 9:30am-5pm, Sa 10am-2pm.

Library: Tower St. (☎01243 777 351). Open M-F 9am-7:30pm, Sa 9am-5pm.

Police: Kingsham Rd. (☎0845 607 0999).

Internet Access: At the **library** (above). Also at **Internet Junction,** 2 Southgate (☎01243 776 644). £2.50 per hr. Open M-F 9am-8pm, Sa-Su 11am-8pm.

Post Office: 10 West St. (☎08457 223 344). **Bureau de change.** Open M and W-F 9am-5:30pm, Tu 9:30am-5:30pm, Sa 9am-3pm. **Postcode:** PO19 1AB.

♠ ♠ ACCOMMODATIONS AND CAMPING

B&Bs abound, but cheap rooms are rare, especially during July's theater festival or on big race weekends in **Goodwood** (p. 178). Plan on paying at least £30 and expect a 15min. walk from the town center.

🏠 **Bayleaf,** 16 Whyke Rd. (☎01243 774 330). Lovely rooms in a house with an antique library upstairs. Full English breakfast. Singles £27; doubles £60. Cash only. ❸

University College Chichester, College Ln. (☎01243 816 070). Rents out singles in student housing as a B&B. Open June-Aug. Singles £27, ensuite £33. ❸

Southern Leisure Centre, Vinnetrow Rd. (☎01243 787 715), 2 mi. southeast of town. Facilities include heated outdoor swimming pool, showers, and laundry. Open Apr.-Oct. £21 per person, with electricity £23. ❷

FOOD

A **market** convenes in the car park at Market Ave. and East St. on Wednesdays. Fresh produce fills the **farmers' market** in Cattle Market car park 8:30am-1:30pm on the first and third Fridays of each month. **Bakeries** line North St. Find groceries at **Iceland,** 55 South St. (Open M-Sa 9am-6pm, Su 10am-4pm.)

- **Maison Blanc Boulangerie and Patisserie,** 56 South St. (☎01243 539 292). The Francophile staff makes sandwiches (£4-5) and an assortment of desserts (£4-6), like the pear and chocolate mousse torte, for dining in the rear cafe or as takeaway. Open M-F 8:45am-5:30pm, Sa 8:45am-6pm, Su 9:30am-4pm. MC/V. ❶

- **The Organic Café,** Cooper St. (☎01243 774 444), off South St. All sandwiches (£2-4), soup (£3.75), and salads (small £3.50, large £4.55) are, you guessed it, organic. A salad bowl allows you to try any or all of the freshly prepared salads with choices ranging from carrot and pumpkin seed to potato to couscous with lemon and red onion. ❶

- **Woodies Wine Bar and Brasserie,** 10 St. Pancras (☎01243 779 895). A hungry pre-theater crowd flocks to the dim interior of the oldest wine bar in Sussex. Innovative meals, like crayfish and avocado salad (£6.50), are served in a sophisticated, informal atmosphere. Entrees £10-18. Open M-Th noon-2pm and 5:45-10:30pm, F-Sa noon-2:30pm and 5:45-11pm, Su noon-4pm and 5:45-11pm. MC/V. ❸

SIGHTS

CHICHESTER CATHEDRAL. Begun in 1076, the cathedral links medieval Christianity to modern Anglicanism. **Norman arches** frame Reformation stained glass, Queen Elizabeth II and Prince Philip peer from the recently renovated **West Front,** and Marc Chagall's **stained-glass window** depicts Psalm 150 with intense colors and detailed symbolism. The two Romanesque sculptures of the raising of Lazarus are widely considered some of the finest of their age. The tomb of Joan de Vere depicts one of the first English examples of "weepers" on its side, while the 14th-century tomb of Earl Fitzalan and his wife scandalously displays a rare image of medieval hand-holding. *(Just west of the Market Cross. ☎01243 782 595; www.chichestercathedral.org.uk. Open daily in summer 7:15am-7pm; in winter 7:15am-6:30pm. Tours Apr.-Oct. M-Sa 11:15am, 2:30pm. Evensong M-Sa 5:30pm, Su 3:30pm. Free.)*

OTHER SIGHTS. The **Pallants** are a quiet area with 18th- and 19th-century houses in the southeast quadrant. The **Pallant House,** 9 N. Pallant, is a restored Queen Anne building attributed to Christopher Wren. Both the cathedral and the Pallant house hold collections of 20th-century British art. *(☎01243 774 557; www. pallant.org.uk. Open Tu-Sa 10am-5pm, Su 12:30-5pm. Last entry 4pm. £7.50, students £4.)*

ENTERTAINMENT AND FESTIVALS

Just north of town, the **Chichester Festival Theatre,** in Oaklands Park, is the cultural center of Chichester. Founded by Sir Laurence Olivier, the venue has attracted such artists as Maggie Smith, Peter Ustinov, and Julie Christie. The theater is complemented by the **Minerva Studio Theatre,** a new addition used for more intimate productions. A guide to each year's program is available at the TIC and online at www.cft.org.uk. Booking in advance reduces regular ticket prices (£10-35) for students. For budget entertainment, attend a Saturday Short at 11am, which has shows for £4. Close by, the **Theatre Restaurant and Cafe** caters to theatergoers from noon on matinee days and from 5:30pm for evening shows. (☎01243 781 312; www.cft.org.uk. Student rush seats £6-8, available 1hr. before the performance. Box office open M-Sa 10am-6pm; until 8pm on performance days.) During the first two weeks in July, artists and musicians collaborate for the **Chichester Festivities.** (Box office in the cathedral bell tower. ☎01243 785 718; www.chifest.co.uk. Talks £2-10; concerts £8-35. Open from June to festival's end M-Sa 10am-8pm.)

DAYTRIPS FROM CHICHESTER

WEALD AND DOWNLAND OPEN AIR MUSEUM. The 45 historical buildings of this museum were saved from destruction when they were transplanted from the southeastern countryside to this parkland in the South Downs. The mostly medieval structures contain exhibits on husbandry, forestry, and culture, but more interesting is the architecture itself and its meticulous, affectionate restoration. A fully functioning Tudor kitchen churns out samples from morning to early afternoon, including frumenty and elderflower fritters. (*7 mi. north of Chichester off the A286; take bus #60 to Singleton Horse and Groom (round-trip £6), then head back up the road and take the 1st left at the brown sign; ask the driver for a combination bus and admission ticket for £8.50. ☎01243 811 363. Open June-Aug. daily 10:30am-6pm; Sept.-Dec. and Mar.-May daily 10:30am-4pm; Jan.-Feb. W and Sa-Su 10:30am-4pm. Last entry 1hr. before close. £8.50, students and children £4.50, seniors £7.50.*)

FISHBOURNE ROMAN PALACE. Built around AD 80, possibly by local ruler Togidubnus, the Fishbourne Palace is the largest extant domestic Roman building in Britain. Today, the most beautiful part of the ruined mansion is the floor, covered in tile mosaics. Don't miss the largely intact mosaic of Cupid on a dolphin from the mid-second century. Outside, a formal garden was replanted according to the original excavated Roman layout. (*About 2 mi. west of the town center; follow the signs from the end of Westgate St. or take bus #700 to Salthill Rd. and follow the brown signs. ☎01243 785 859. Open Aug. daily 10am-6pm; Sept.-Oct. and Mar.-July daily 10am-5pm; Nov.-Dec. and Feb. daily 10am-4pm; Jan. Sa-Su 10am-4pm. £7, students £5.50.*)

GOODWOOD. Three miles northeast of Chichester, works by Canaletto, Reynolds, and Stubbs vie for attention with a world-famous sculpture collection in **Goodwood House,** the seat of the duke of Richmond for over 300 years. (*☎01243 755 040; www.goodwood.co.uk/house. Open Aug. M-Th and Su 1-5pm; Sept.-Oct. and Apr.-July M and Su 1-5pm. Last entry 4pm. 5 tours per day. The schedule is irregular; call ahead. £8.50, students £4.*) Goodwood also has some of England's best horse and motor racing. From May to September, the rich and famous come to watch the "Glorious Goodwood" horse race, a 200-year-old tradition. (*☎01243 755 022. Runs from May-Sept.*) In early July and September, the motor-racing extravaganzas **Festival of Speed** and **Goodwood Revival** take center stage.

HAMPSHIRE

PORTSMOUTH   ☎(0)1023

Sailing enthusiasts and history buffs will wet themselves at this waterfront destination, a famous naval port since Henry V set sail for France in 1415. Portsmouth's Victorian seaside setting and its 900-year history of prostitutes, drunkards, and cursing sailors give the city a compelling, gritty heritage. Despite modern attempts to build up the waterfront, the pride of Portsmouth is still its

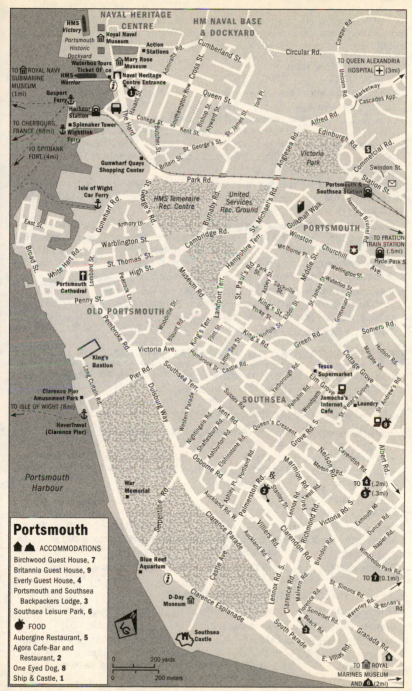

Portsmouth

🏠🏠 ACCOMMODATIONS

Birchwood Guest House, 7
Britannia Guest House, 9
Everly Guest House, 4
Portsmouth and Southsea
   Backpackers Lodge, 3
Southsea Leisure Park, 6

🍎 FOOD

Aubergine Restaurant, 5
Agora Cafe-Bar and
   Restaurant, 2
One Eyed Dog, 8
Ship & Castle, 1

harbor, whose waters teem with ferries, barges, and boats. Unfortunately, the city's naval prominence caused its devastation during WWII, and today many of its buildings are examples of 1950s utilitarian (read: ugly) architecture.

▝ TRANSPORTATION

Trains: Portsmouth and Southsea Station, Commercial Rd., in the city center. Ticket office open M-Sa 5:40am-8:30pm, Su 6:40am-8:40pm. **Portsmouth Harbour Station,** The Hard, is a train station with limited ferry service. Office open M-F 5:50am-7:30pm, Sa 5:55am-7:30pm, Su 6:40am-8:10pm. **Fratton Station,** Selbourne Terr., is closest to **Southsea.** Ticket office open M-Sa 6am-7pm, Su 7am-11pm. Trains (☎08457 484 950) go to **Chichester** (30min., 2 per hr., £5.60), **London Waterloo** (1¾hr., 4 per hr., £26.10), and **Salisbury** (1hr., every hr., £14.40).

Buses: The Hard Interchange, The Hard, next to Harbour Station. National Express (☎08705 808 080) buses go to **London Victoria** (2½hr., every hr., £17.60) and **Salisbury** (1½hr., 1 per day, £9).

Ferries: Portsmouth Harbour Station (above) sends ferries to the **Isle of Wight.** Frequent Wightlink (☎0871 376 4342; www.wightlink.co.uk) ferries run to **Fishbourne** (35min.; round-trip £10.80, children £5.40) and **Ryde** (15min.; round-trip £13.52). Hovertravel (☎01983 811 000; www.hovertravel.co.uk) sails from Clarence Esplanade in **Southsea** to **Ryde** (9min.; 2 per hr.; round-trip £12.50).

Public Transportation: A reliable, comprehensive **bus** system connects the city. Local bus companies First (☎08700 106 022) and Stagecoach (☎01903 237 661) run throughout. Daily pass £4, weekly pass £13.

Taxis: Aqua Cars (☎0800 666 666). 24hr.

✦ ▝ ORIENTATION AND PRACTICAL INFORMATION

Portsmouth sprawls along the coast for miles—**Portsmouth, Old Portsmouth** (near the Portsmouth and Southsea train station and Commercial Rd.), and the resort community of **Southsea** (stretching to the east) can seem like entirely different cities. Sights cluster at Old Portsmouth, **The Hard,** and Southsea's **Esplanade.**

Tourist Information Centre: The Hard (☎01023 826 722; www.visitportsmouth.co.uk), by the historic ships. Bursting with brochures and maps (£1.50). Books accommodations for £2 plus a 10% deposit. Discounts available for museum and attractions. Open daily 9:30am-5:15pm. **Southsea Offices,** in front of the Blue Reef Aquarium, also has info. Open daily 9:30am-5:15pm.

Tours: Waterbus (☎07889 408 137) offers 1hr. guided rides in Portsmouth Harbour, leaving from The Hard. Open daily 10:20am-4:30pm. £5, children £3. Cash only.

Banks: Around the Commercial Rd. shopping precinct, north of Portsmouth and Southsea Station. **Barclays** (☎01023 305 858), at the corner of Commercial and Edinburgh Rd. Open M-F 9am-5pm, Sa 9am-3:30pm.

Launderette: Laundrycare, 121 Elm Grove (☎01023 826 245). Wash £3, dry £2. Open daily 8am-6pm. Last wash 4:45pm.

Police: Winston Churchill Ave. (☎0845 454 545).

Pharmacy: Boots, 31 Palmerston Rd. (☎01023 821 046). Open M-Sa 9am-5:30pm.

Hospital: Queen Alexandra Hospital, Southwick Hill Rd. (☎01023 286 000).

Internet Access: Online Cafe, 163 Elm Grove (☎01023 831 106). 50p per 10min. Open M-Th 9am-10pm, F 9am-9pm, Sa-Su 10am-9pm. **Jamochas,** 99 Elm Grove (☎01023 875 000). Wi-Fi £1.50 per 30 min. Open M-F 9am-8pm, Sa 9am-5:30pm.

Post Office: Swindon St. (☎08457 223 344), opposite the train station. Open M and W-Sa 9am-5:30pm, Tu 9:30am-5:30pm. **Postcode:** PO1 1AA.

ACCOMMODATIONS AND CAMPING

Moderately priced B&Bs (£35-40) can be found in **Southsea**. Many are located along Waverley, Clarendon, Festings, and Granada Rd. as well as on South Parade. If you're arriving via the Portsmouth and Southsea Station, catch one of the frequent buses on Commercial Rd. (#1 and 40). From Portsmouth Harbour, take one of the buses (#5 and 6) that run from The Hard to South Parade.

Britannia Guest House, 48 Granada Rd., Southsea (☎01023 814 234). Colorful, spotless rooms decorated with the owner's modern artwork. Full English breakfast included. Singles £25; doubles £45-50. MC/V. ❸

Everly Guest House, 33 Festings Rd. (☎01023 731 001). Comfortable ensuite rooms on a quiet street near the Southsea Esplanade. Swap tips with world-traveling owners. Full English and vegetarian breakfast included. Singles £25; doubles £35. MC/V. ❸

Portsmouth and Southsea Backpackers Lodge, 4 Florence Rd. (☎01023 832 495). Take #5 or 6 to The Strand and walk back up to the 2nd road on the left. Pan-European crowd and accommodating owners. Clean rooms. Lounge, satellite TV, well-stocked kitchen, and grocery counter. Laundry £2. Internet access £2 per hr. Key deposit £5. Dorms £15; doubles £32. Cash only. ❷

Birchwood Guest House, 44 Waverley Rd. (☎01023 811 337). Bright, spacious rooms have TVs, coffee, hair dryers, and alarm clocks. Personable hosts make sure your stay is comfortable. Flowerbeds outside. Wi-Fi. Singles £28-36; doubles £62-68. MC/V. ❹

Southsea Leisure Park, Melville Rd., Southsea (☎01023 735 070). At the eastern end of the seafront, 5-6 mi. from The Hard. Site has toilets, shop, restaurant-bar, pool, showers, and laundry. Tent sites for 1 £10; tent sites for 2 £18. Electricity £2. ❶

FOOD AND PUBS

Chain restaurants sit along the waterfront, between the shopping districts in Southsea, and on Commercial Rd. There is no shortage of pubs in Portsmouth, especially near The Hard. Ethnic eateries are clustered along Albert Rd. near the University of Portsmouth's student housing. **Tesco** supermarket is at 56-61 Elm Grove. (☎08456 269 090. Open daily 6am-midnight.)

Agora Cafe-Bar and Restaurant, 9 Clarendon Rd. (☎01023 822 617). Turkish and Greek barbecue (£7.50-11) enlivened by belly dancing. Open M-Th 5:30-11pm, F-Sa 5:30pm-midnight, Su 5:30-10:30pm. Student discount. MC/V over £10. ❷

One Eyed Dog (☎01023 827 188), at the corner of Elm Grove and Victoria Rd. Trendy pub draws a steady flow of students in the afternoon and evening. Sate your thirst (mixed drinks £2-3) but not your hunger (bar snacks only). Open M 3pm-midnight, Tu-Th and Su 4pm-midnight, F 3pm-1am, Sa 1pm-1am. MC/V. ❶

Aubergine, 93 Albert Rd. (☎01023 820 116). Among the many options for Indian takeaway, this small eatery is one of the best. Entrees like chicken tikka or eggplant for £5-7. 4-course meal for £8 M. Open M-Th and Su 6pm-1:30am, F-Sa 6pm-3am. MC/V. ❷

Ship & Castle, 1-2 The Hard (☎01023 832 009). The oldest pub and restaurant in Portsmouth. A good stop after a day of sightseeing by the harbor. Stretching down the block, it offers ample space including a play barn for children and a hip bar for adults. Entrees £7-10. Kitchen open daily 11:30am-7:30pm. MC/V. ❷

👁 SIGHTS

Portsmouth is a seafarer's paradise, overflowing with ships and sea-weary relics. Most of the naval attractions are in the historic harbor near The Hard. The sail-shaped **Spinnaker Tower,** with three observation decks high above the harbor, offers panoramic views of the city. To satisfy a less nautical fancy, **Gunwharf Quays** has shopping, while **Clarence Pier** has traditional amusement-park fare.

📜PORTSMOUTH HISTORIC DOCKYARD
In the Naval Yard. Entrance next to the TIC; follow the signs. ☎01023 839 762; www.historic-dockyard.co.uk. Ships open daily Apr.-Oct. 10am-5:30pm; Nov.-Mar. 10am-5pm. Last entry 1hr. before close. Each sight £12. All-inclusive ticket £18.50.

Historians and armchair admirals can plunge headfirst into the **Historic Dockyard,** which brings together a trio of Britain's most storied ships and nautical artifacts. The *Mary Rose, HMS Victory,* and *HMS Warrior* were launched in 1512, 1765, and 1860, respectively. These floating monuments chronicle Britain's mastery of the seas. The five galleries of the **Royal Naval Museum** fill in the temporal gaps between the three ships.

MARY ROSE. Henry VIII's *Mary Rose* is one of England's earliest warships and the only 16th-century ship of its kind on display in the world. Henry was particularly fond of her, but, like many of his women, she died before her time. Sunk by the French after sailing from Portsmouth in July 1545, it wasn't until 1982 that Henry's flagship rose from her watery grave. The hull can be seen behind a glass display. It will be sprayed with a preservative until 2009, a 15-year process that should make *Mary* immortal. The **Mary Rose Museum** displays over 19,000 artifacts discovered with the ship, including a collection of 168 longbows.

HMS VICTORY. Napoleon must be rolling over in his spacious tomb knowing that Admiral Lord Nelson's flagship, which helped bring Napoleon's fleet to brook at Trafalgar, is still afloat. The vessel holds artifacts of British nationalism, from the plaque on the spot where Nelson fell to the flag code display of his statement, "England expects that every man will do his duty." The *Victory* is still a commissioned warship, the oldest in the world, so espionage laws prohibit taking photographs on board. Visitors can take a tour of the ship through five levels of compartments, including the sick berth and the captain's quarters. Don't miss Nelson's own hammock, embarrassingly embroidered with flowers and birds by his longtime mistress, the notorious Emma Hamilton.

HMS WARRIOR. The fast and furious *HMS Warrior* was the pride of Queen Victoria's navy and the first iron-hulled warship in the world. Its revolutionary design, however, also led to its downfall, as even faster, larger, and more powerful warships soon replaced it. After some hard times as an oil jetty and depot ship, the *Warrior* returned once again to the limelight as one of the few surviving Victorian battleships. Visitors can explore the gun decks, living quarters, and engine room of the most expensive ship restoration ever completed.

ACTION STATIONS. After you see the Navy, you can pretend to be the Navy at the Action Stations. High-tech simulations let you pilot a helicopter. Alternatively, you can test your prowess on the climbing wall. The short Omni film shows a typical day aboard a Type 23 frigate: missiles fly as the ship engages in a war with modern-day pirates. *(June-Sept. every 30min.; Oct.-May every hr.)*

THE BEST OF THE REST

SOUTHSEA. The ◾D-Day Museum leads visitors through life-size dioramas of the June 6, 1944, invasion. Recreations of life at home and in the tunnels share perspectives from soldiers and the families they left behind. The museum also houses the **Overlord Embroidery,** a 272 ft. tapestry that details the events surrounding Overlord Operation. *(Clarence Esplanade. ☎01023 827 261. Open daily Apr.-Sept. 10am-5:30pm; Oct.-Mar. 10am-5pm. Last entry 30min. before close. £6, students £4.20. Embroidery audio tour 50p.)* **Southsea Castle,** built by Henry VIII at the point of the Esplanade, was an active fortress until 1960. The underground **Time Tunnels** are not to be missed. *(Clarence Esplanade. Open daily Apr.-Sept. 10am-5:30pm; Oct. 10am-5pm. Last entry 30min. before close. £3.50, students £2.50.)* The **Blue Reef Aquarium** features otters, sharks, anacondas, and poison dart frogs. *(Towan Promenade. ☎01023 9287 5222. Open daily Mar.-Oct. 10am-5pm; Nov.-Feb. 10am-4pm. £8.75, students £8.)*

OTHER NAVAL SIGHTS. The **Royal Navy Submarine Museum** is inside Britain's only walk-on submarine, the *HMS Alliance*. It also displays the Royal Navy's first submarine, *Holland I*. The control room trainer lets visitors play captain. The Gosport ferry crosses from the Harbour train station (£2); follow the signs or take bus #9 to Haslar Hospital. *(☎01023 529 217; www.rnsubmus.co.uk. Open daily Apr.-Oct. 10am-5:30pm; Nov.-Mar. 10am-4:30pm. Last entry 1hr. before close. £6.50, children £5.)* **Spitbank Fort,** a peculiar manmade island, protected Portsmouth through two World Wars. It is a tour site by day and, oddly, a swinging party venue by night. *(25min. crossing from the Dockyard. ☎01329 242 077; www.spitbankfort.co.uk.)* The **Royal Marines Museum** chronicles the British military abroad through its four-century trajectory of triumph and failure. A newly opened £300,000 exhibit on becoming a marine commando demonstrates through interactive displays and games how a raw recruit gains a green beret. Upstairs the medal room exhibits 6500 medals, including every Victoria Cross—given to a member of the British armed forces who demonstrates "conspicuous bravery"—ever presented to a Marine. *(In Southsea down the Esplanade. ☎01023 819 385. Open daily 10am-5pm. £5.25.)*

ISLE OF WIGHT   ☎(0)1983

More tranquil and sun-splashed than its mother island to the north, the Isle of Wight's stunning countryside and sandy beaches are the perfect backdrop to a leisurely weekend or daytrip. Wight has softened the hardest of hearts, from Queen Victoria, who found the island a perfect setting for her lavish country house, to Karl Marx, who proclaimed the island "a little paradise." Follow in the footsteps of these famous fans along the Isle's 67 mi. of romantic coastline.

▣ TRANSPORTATION

Ferries: Wightlink (☎08705 827 744; www.wightlink.co.uk) ferries frequently from Lymington to **Yarmouth** (30min., round-trip £11.10) Portsmouth Harbour to **Fishbourne** (35min., round-trip £15.20), and Portsmouth Harbour to **Ryde** (15min., round-trip £18.20). Red Funnel ferries (☎08704 448 898; www.redfunnel.co.uk) run from Southampton to **East Cowes** (1hr., round-trip £13.20). Hovertravel (☎01983 811 000; www. hovertravel.co.uk) sails from Southsea to **Ryde** (9min., 2 per hr., round-trip £12.50).

Public Transportation: Train service on the Island Line (☎08457 484 950; www.island-line.com) is limited to the eastern end of the island, including Ryde, Brading, Sandown, Shanklin, and a few points between. Southern Vectis buses (☎01983 827 000; www.svoc.co.uk) cover the entire island; TICs and travel centers (☎01983 827 005) in Cowes, Shanklin, Ryde, and Newport sell the complete timetable (50p). Buses meet ferries at Yarmouth and Ryde. Buy tickets on board.

Bike Rental: Tav Cycles, 140 High St. (☎01983 812 989; www.tavcycles.co.uk), in Ryde. £12 per day. Longer rentals available. MC/V.

✦ ▯ ORIENTATION AND PRACTICAL INFORMATION

The Isle of Wight is 23 mi. by 13 mi. and shaped like a diamond. Towns are clustered along the coasts: **Ryde** and **Cowes** are to the north, **Sandown** and **Shanklin** lie along the east coast heading south, and **Yarmouth** is on the west coast. The capital, **Newport,** sits in the center, at the source of the River Medina.

Tourist Information Centres: Located close to the bus station or ferry port in most of the major cities. Each center supplies individual town maps and information along with travel and attraction guides for the entire island. A general inquiry service (☎01983 813 813; www.islandbreaks.co.uk) directs questions to one of the 7 regional offices listed below. In winter, TICs have reduced hours.

Ryde: Western Esplanade, at the corner of Union St., opposite Ryde Pier and the bus station. Open M-Sa 9:30am-5pm, Su 10am-4pm.

Cowes: Fountain Quay, in the alley next to the Red Jet ferry terminal. Open M-Sa 9:30am-5:30pm, Su 10am-4pm; during Cowes Week (1st week in Aug.) daily 8am-8pm.

Newport: The Guildhall, High St. Open M-Sa 9:30am-5pm, Su 10am-4pm.

Sandown: 8 High St., across from Boots pharmacy. Open July-Aug. M-Sa 9:30am-5:30pm, Su 9:30am-4:30pm; Sept.-Oct. and Apr.-June M-Sa 9:30am-5:30pm, Su 10am-4pm.

Shanklin: 67 High St. Open Apr.-Oct. M-Sa 9:30am-5:30pm, Su 10am-4pm.

Yarmouth: The Quay; signposted from ferry. Open Apr.-Oct. M-Sa 9:30am-5:30pm, Su 10am-4pm.

Banks: Found in all major town centers. ATMs are rare in smaller towns.

Libraries and Internet Access: Ryde Library, 101 George St. (☎01983 562 170). Free with membership. **Lord Louis Library,** Orchard St. (☎01983 823 800), behind the bus station in Newport. Free.

Police: Isle of Wight Police (☎0845 454 545).

Hospitals: St. Mary's, Parkhurst Rd. (☎01983 524 081).

Post Office: In every town center. **Postcode:** PO30 0HD.

🏠 🏕 ACCOMMODATIONS AND CAMPING

Accommodation prices on Wight range from economical to exorbitant, often depending on proximity to the shore. Budget travelers should try one of the YHA hostels at either end of the island or look into less visited areas.

YHA Totland Bay, Hurst Hill, Totland Bay (☎01983 752 165), on the west end of Wight. Take Southern Vectis bus #7 or 7A to Totland War Memorial; turn left up Weston Rd. and walk 10min. to the fork in the road. Hostel is on the top of Hurst Hill on the left fork. Brown signs guide you from the bus station. Lodgings near the Needles and Alum Bay. Kitchen. Dorms £16, under 18 £12. AmEx/MC/V. ❷

Claverton House, 12 The Strand, Ryde (☎01983 613 015). Lavish bedrooms and baths tempt even ardent sightseers to spend the day in the tub. Doubles £50. Cash only. ❸

Big Farm Camping Site (☎01983 615 210; www.bigfarm.co.uk), between Ryde and Sandown. Take bus #3. Welcomes guests near the beach. Showers and laundry. Tent sites for 2 £10. Electricity £2. ❶

🍴 FOOD

Wanderers on Wight can find food on High St. or the Esplanade. Local fish is a specialty. Most larger cities have supermarkets, and the island has nearly one pub per square mile. **S. Fowler & Co. ❶,** 41-43 Union St., Ryde, buzzes with hungry tourists and locals. Plenty of pub meals are under £6, including several vegetarian options. (☎01983 812 112. Open M-Th 9am-midnight, F-Sa 9am-1am. Kitchen open daily 9am-10pm. AmEx/MC/V.) In Ryde, **Liberty's Cafe-Bar ❷**, 12 Union St., serves tasty lunch entrees (£7-12) in a stylish atmosphere. (☎01983 811 007. Open M-Th 10am-11pm, F-Sa 10am-midnight, Su 11am-11pm. MC/V.)

SIGHTS

Wight's natural sights are especially beautiful in the west, with hillsides, multi-colored beaches, and the famous **Needles** overlooking the sea. Keep your camera nearby on the ride along cliff roads on buses #7, 7A, and 7B to **Alum Bay.** Sandier beaches next to shopping areas are on the eastern coast in **Ventnor,** Shanklin, Sandown, and Ryde. Ryde is a convenient hub but is less scenic than the western side of the island.

ALUM BAY AND THE NEEDLES. On the western tip of the island lie three white peaks jutting from the water. The Needles are actually made of chalk—break out a sheet of paper to see for yourself. A chairlift runs down the cliffs to the colored beaches. The Needles Pleasure Park on the cliff offers activities and street performers. *(Take bus #7, 7A, 7B, or 42 to Alum Bay. ☎0870 458 0022; www. theneedles.co.uk. Open daily Easter-Oct. 10am-5pm. Free. Chairlift round-trip £4.)*

CARISBROOKE CASTLE. Carisbrooke includes one of England's most complete Norman shell keeps, an interior wall that has been sitting atop its moat for 900 years. A walk along its ramparts offers unbeatable views of the Isle. Visitors can see where Charles I, a prisoner at Carisbrooke in 1647, got stuck in a window during his first attempt to escape from the castle. The museum details the structure's history and includes the **Tennyson Room,** with the Victorian poet laureate's desk, cloak, and funeral pall. *(From Newport, follow Upper St. to James St., turn right on Trafalgar St., and bear left on Castle Rd., which becomes Castle Hill. The 30min. walk from the bus station can be shortened by taking bus #7 to Carisbrooke, at the beginning of Castle Rd. ☎01983 522 107. Open daily Apr.-Sept. 10am-5pm; Oct.-Mar. 10am-4pm. £6.50.)*

OSBORNE HOUSE. Along with halls full of paintings and statues of Victoria, Albert, and family, this former royal residence offers a peek into Queen Victoria's private life. Victoria and Prince Albert commissioned it as a "modest" country home and refuge. After Albert died in 1861, it became Victoria's retreat, decorated with mementos and family photographs. In the **Horn Room,** nearly all of the furniture is made from antlers. *(Take Southern Vectis bus #4 or 5 from Ryde or Newport, respectively. ☎01983 200 022. Open Apr.-Sept. daily 10am-5pm; Oct. M-Th and Su 10am-4pm. House and grounds £10, concessions £8, children £5.)*

FESTIVALS

Walkers and cyclists enjoy 500 mi. of footpaths and 60 mi. of coastal paths stretching from Totland, past lighthouses both modern and medieval at St. Catherine's Point, to St. Lawrence at the southern end of the island. Explore the island footpaths during the **Walking Festival** (☎01983 813 800), the UK's largest, in mid-May and the **Cycling Festival** (☎01983 823 347) in late September. The **Isle of Wight Summer Festival** has hosted bands like REM, Coldplay, The Who, and David Bowie. More information can be obtained at any of the TICs.

WINCHESTER   ☎(0)1962

This ancient capital of medieval England is now a modern hot spot best known for its massive cathedral. Home to Jane Austen and John Keats, Winchester was the center of the kingdoms of both Alfred the Great and William the Conqueror.

During the Great Plague of 1665, the town was also a temporary court for the newly restored King Charles II. Winchester's royal history continues to draw visitors, particularly during the floral summer season.

TRANSPORTATION

North of Southampton, Winchester makes an excellent daytrip from **Salisbury** (p. 198), 25 mi. west, or **Portsmouth** (p. 178), 27 mi. south.

TXT 4 TIMES. Public transportation got you flustered? Bus stands all over England have a bus stop code posted on their flag. Text the code to 84268 (25p), and you'll get a text back with the bus timetable for that stop.

Trains: Winchester Station, Station Hill, northwest of the city center. Ticket counter open M-F 6am-8:30pm, Sa 6am-7:30pm, Su 7am-8:30pm. Trains (☎08457 484 950; www.visitwinchester.co.uk) to: **Brighton** (1½hr., every hr., £21.20); **London Waterloo** (1hr., 3-4 per hr., £25.50); **Portsmouth** (1hr., every hr., £8.60); **Salisbury** (1hr., 2 per hr., £12.20). Be prepared to change trains at Basingstoke or Fareham.

Buses: Stop on Broadway near Alfred's statue or inside the **bus station** on Broadway. Open M-F 8:30am-5:30pm, Sa 8:30am-12:30pm. National Express (☎08705 808 080) runs to **London** via **Heathrow** (1½hr., 7 per day, £14.25) or **Victoria Station** (2hr., 12 per day, £14), **Oxford** (2½hr., 2 per day, £10.20), and **Southampton** (30min., 12 per day, £3.20). Wilts and Dorset (☎01722 336 855) runs bus #68 to **Salisbury** (1¼hr., 6 per day, £5). **Explorer** tickets are available for buses in Hampshire and Wiltshire (£7, children and seniors £5.50, families £13).

Public Transportation: Local **buses** (☎0845 121 0180) stop by the bus and train stations. Day pass £3.10. Ask for a bus timetable at the TIC.

Taxis: Francis Taxis (☎01962 884 343), by the market. **WinTaxi** (☎01962 866 208).

ORIENTATION AND PRACTICAL INFORMATION

Winchester's main commercial axis, **High Street,** stretches from the statue of Alfred the Great at its east end to the arch of **Westgate** opposite. The city's bigger roads stem off High St., which becomes **Broadway** as you approach Alfred.

Tourist Information Centre: The Guildhall, Broadway (☎01962 840 500; www.visitwinchester.co.uk), across from the bus station. Stocks free maps, seasonal *What's On* guides, and other city guides. Books accommodations for £3 plus a 10% deposit. Open May-Sept. M-Sa 9:30am-5:30pm, Su 11am-4pm; Oct.-Apr. M-Sa 10am-5pm.

Tours: Guided walking tours leave the TIC. £3, children free.

Banks: At the junction of Jewry and High St. **Royal Bank of Scotland,** 67-68 High St. (☎01962 863 322). Open M-Tu and Th-F 9:15am-4:45pm, W 9:45am-4:45pm.

Library and Internet Access: Winchester Library, Jewry St. (☎0845 603 5631). Free Internet. Open M-F 9am-7pm, Sa 9am-5pm, Su 10am-4pm.

Launderette: 27 Garbett Rd., Winnall (☎1962 840 658). Climb Magdalen Hill, turn left on Winnall Manor Rd., and follow until Garbett Rd. is on your left. £3.20. Open M-F 8am-8pm, Sa 8am-6pm, Su 10am-4pm. Last wash 1hr. before close.

Police: North Walls (☎08450 454 545), near the intersection with Middle Brook St.

Hospital: Royal Hampshire County, Romsey Rd. (☎01962 863 535), at St. James Ln.

Post Office: 110 High St. Open M and W-Sa 9am-5:30pm, Tu 9:30am-5:30pm. **Postcode:** SO23 8UT.

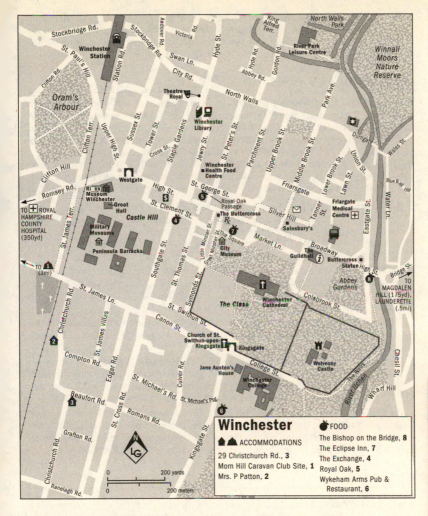

Winchester

🏠🏕 ACCOMMODATIONS

29 Christchurch Rd., **3**
Morn Hill Caravan Club Site, **1**
Mrs. P Patton, **2**

🍴FOOD

The Bishop on the Bridge, **8**
The Eclipse Inn, **7**
The Exchange, **4**
Royal Oak, **5**
Wykeham Arms Pub &
Restaurant, **6**

SOUTH ENGLAND

🏠🏕 ACCOMMODATIONS AND CAMPING

B&Bs are the best option in Winchester but are difficult to find and book. For last-minute bookings, the TIC is your best bet. Buses #29 and 47 (2 per hr.) make the journey from the town center to the corner of **Ranelagh** and **Christchurch Roads,** where many B&Bs are located. Many pubs also rent rooms.

Mrs. P. Patton, 12 Christchurch Rd. (☎01962 854 272), down the road from the train station. Elegant Victorian mansion on beautifully landscaped property. Homemade bread and preserves with breakfast. Singles £30-40; doubles £50. Cash only. ❸

29 Christchurch Road, 29 Christchurch Rd. (☎01962 868 661), 10min. from the city center. Well-kept rooms with TVs and soft beds. 2 blocks from Mrs. P. Patton. Singles from £35; doubles from £75. Cash only. ❸

Morn Hill Caravan Club Site, Morn Hill (☎01962 869 877), 3 mi. east of Winchester off the A31, toward New Forest. Mainly for caravans. Limited facilities for campers. Open Mar.-Oct. £8.50-30 per caravan, depending on occupancy. Tent sites (at warden's discretion) £4-6 plus £5 per person; call ahead. Cash only. ❶

FOOD AND PUBS

High Street and **Saint George's Street** brim with markets, fast-food chains, and teahouses. Restaurants serve more substantial fare on **Jewry Street,** where you'll also find **Winchester Health Food Centre,** 41 Jewry St. (☎01962 851 113. Open M-F 10am-5pm, Sa 9:15am-5pm.) For groceries, go to **Sainsbury's,** Middle Brook St., off High St. (☎01962 861 792. Open M-Sa 7am-8pm, Su 11am-5pm.) For a fresher option, try the open-air **market** (open W-Sa 8am-6pm) or the **farmers' market**—the largest in the UK, with everything from ostrich meat to locally grown watercress (2nd and last Su of every month; open early morning until 3pm).

The Bishop on the Bridge, 1 High St. (☎01962 855 111), on the river. Nearby cathedral and gardens bring some floral elegance to this urban pub. Enjoy a leisurely meal on the heated terrace or lounge inside on leather chairs. Students flock here and stay late. Most entrees £8.50-12. Open M-Th noon-11pm, F-Sa noon-midnight, Su noon-10:30pm. Kitchen open M-Sa noon-9:30pm, Su noon-7pm. MC/V. ❷

The Eclipse Inn, The Square (☎01962 865 676). Winchester's smallest pub is also one of its most popular. Located in a 16th-century rectory. Attracts regulars and, according to legend, ghosts. Entrees £6.75-7.50. Open M-Sa 11am-11pm, Su noon-11pm. Kitchen open daily noon-3pm. MC/V. ❶

Wykeham Arms, 175 Kingsgate St. (☎01962 854 411). A Winchester institution. Draws a crowd day and night. Sit in an old school desk and check the blackboard for traditional daily specials. Try the Wyke cottage pie (£6). Open daily 6:30-9:30pm. MC/V. ❷

Royal Oak, Royal Oak Passage (☎01962 842 701). Squeeze into the alley by God Begot House and descend underground. Yet another pub that claims to be the kingdom's oldest, tracing its origins back to 1390. Enjoy the locally brewed cask ale (£2.35) and pub food (£5-8). Open daily 11am-11pm. Kitchen open daily 11am-9pm. MC/V. ❶

The Exchange, 9 Southgate St. (☎01962 854 718). Sports pub with burgers ("gourmet" has goat cheese and red onion jam), sandwiches, and jacket potatoes (all £2-5). Tables fill with students and locals, but the multi-level beer garden provides additional space. Open M-F noon-2:30pm and 5-8pm, Sa-Su noon-3pm and 5-10:30pm. MC/V. ❷

SIGHTS

WINCHESTER CATHEDRAL. Winchester and Canterbury, housing the respective shrines of St. Swithun and St. Thomas Becket, were the two spiritual capitals of medieval England. Built on a mess of peat bogs, Winchester Cathedral has faced several reconstructions, making it something of a stylistic hybrid. The Norman transept, crypt, and tower are juxtaposed with a Gothic nave—the longest medieval nave in Europe at 556 ft. The oddly proto-Cubist stained glass, replaced after Cromwell's window-shattering soldiers, offsets the older architecture. Jane Austen is entombed beneath a humble stone slab in the northern aisle in the company of several former English kings. *(5 The Close. ☎01962 857 200; www.winchester-cathedral.org.uk. Open daily 9am-5pm. Free tours depart from the west end of the nave daily 10am-3pm on the hr. 1 hr. tower tours also available W 2:15pm, Sa 11:30am, 2:15pm. £5, concessions £4, students £2.50. Photography permit £2. Tower tours £3.)* In the south transept, the illuminated 12th-century Winchester Bible resides in the **library,** and the **Triforium Gallery** contains several relics, including a Saxon bowl

SOUTH ENGLAND

said to have held King Canute's heart. *(Open in summer M 2-4pm, Tu-Sa 11am-4pm; in winter W and Sa 11am-3:30pm. £1.)* Outside, to the south of the cathedral, tiny **Saint Swithun's Chapel** sits above **Kingsgate**. *(Free.)*

GREAT HALL. William the Conqueror built **Winchester Castle** in 1067, but unyielding forces (time and Cromwell) have all but destroyed the fortress. The Great Hall remains, a gloriously intact medieval structure containing an imitation (or, according to locals, legendary) Arthurian Round Table. Henry VIII tried to pass the table off as authentic to Holy Roman Emperor Charles V, but the painted-on "Arthur," resembling Henry himself, fooled no one. Outside is **Queen Eleanor's Garden**, a recreated medieval herb and flower garden, modeled after the gardens painted in medieval manuscripts. *(At the end of High St. atop Castle Hill. ☎01962 846 476. Open daily Mar.-Oct. 10am-5pm; Nov.-Feb. 10am-4pm. Free.)*

MILITARY MUSEUMS. From the Great Hall, cut through Queen Eleanor's Garden to the Peninsula Barracks. Five military museums (the **Royal Hampshire Regiment Museum,** the **Light Infantry Museum,** the **Rifles Museum Winchester,** the **Royal Hussars Museum,** and the **Gurkha Museum**) celebrate the city's military might. The Rifles Museum Winchester is the best of the bunch. The highlight is a 276 sq. ft. diorama of the Battle of Waterloo containing 21,500 tiny soldiers and 9600 tiny steeds. *(Between St. James Terr. and Southgate St. ☎01962 828 549. www.winchestermilitary-museums.co.uk. Open M-Sa 10am-5pm, Su noon-4pm. £3. Hours for the other 4 museums are similar. The Gurkha Museum is the only other to charge entry; £2, concessions £1.)*

CITY MUSEUM. The city's history is displayed through archaeological finds, photographs, and interactive exhibits. The Roman gallery includes a floor mosaic from the local ruins of a Roman villa, and the Anglo-Saxon room holds a 10th-century tomb. *(At Great Minster St. and The Square. ☎01962 863 064. Open Apr.-Oct. M-Sa 10am-5pm, Su noon-5pm; Nov.-Mar. Tu-Sa 10am-4pm, Su noon-4pm. Free. Audio tour £2.)*

WOLVESEY CASTLE. In 1554, this castle was the scene of Philip II's and Mary Tudor's wedding feast, but now its ruins molder in the sunshine. Check out the mansion next door, where the current bishop resides. *(The Close. Walk down The Weir on the river or to the end of College St. ☎01962 252 000. Open Apr.-Sept. daily 9am-5pm. Free.)*

OTHER SIGHTS. The **Buttercross,** 12 High St., is a good starting point for several walking routes through town. This statue, portraying St. John, William of Wykeham, and King Alfred, derives its name from the shadow it cast over the 15th-century market, keeping the butter cool. A beautiful walk runs along the **River Itchen,** the same route taken by poet John Keats. Directions and his "Ode To Autumn" are available at the TIC (£1). For a panoramic view of the city, including the Wolvesey ruins, climb to **Saint Giles's Hill Viewpoint.** Pass the mill and take Bridge St. to the gate marked Magdalen Hill; follow the paths from there.

🎵 🎴 ENTERTAINMENT AND FESTIVALS

Bars along **Broadway** and **High Street** attract weekend revelers. The **Theatre Royal,** Jewry St., hosts regional companies and concerts. *(☎01962 840 440; www.the-atre-royal-winchester.co.uk. Box office open M-F 10am-6pm, Sa 10am-5pm.)* The **Homelands Music Festival** takes place the last weekend of May, drawing big names in rock every year. (Buy tickets from the TIC.) In early July, Winchester plays host to the **Hat Fair** (☎01962 849 841; www.hatfair.co.uk), the longest-running street theater festival in all of Britain. The event fills a weekend with free theater performances and peculiar headgear.

⏩ DAYTRIPS FROM WINCHESTER

AUSTEN'S COTTAGE. From 1809 to 1817, Jane Austen lived in the village of **Chawton.** In this ivy-covered cottage at a tiny wood table in the dining room, Elizabeth Bennet, Emma Woodhouse, and their respective suitors were brought to life. Personal letters, belongings, and a copy of her will fill the house, although visitors should be warned that many of the documents are not originals. *(Take Hampshire bus #X64 (40min., M-Sa 11 per day, round-trip £6) or London and Country bus #65 on Su from Winchester. Ask to be let off at the Chawton roundabout and follow the brown signs.* ☎ *01420 832 62. Open Mar.-Dec. daily 10:30am-4:30pm. £6, students £5, children £2.)*

NEW FOREST. England's newest national park was once William the Conqueror's 145 sq. mi. personal hunting ground. It remains, 1000 years later, a model of rural England. Wild ponies, donkeys, and deer wander freely along winding roads. As you explore the park, stop by the historic villages in the countryside. The **Rufus Stone** (near Brook and Cadnam) marks the spot where William's son was accidentally slain. For the young, pony rides are popular; the young at heart can play cowboy at **Burley Villa Riding School** (☎01425 610 278) in New Milton, which offers 2hr. Western riding tours for £50. The **Museum and Visitor Centre** is at High St. and Gosport Ln. (☎02380 282 269 or 01590 646 600; www.newforestmuseum.org.uk. Open daily 10am-5pm. £3, concessions £2.50, families £9.) It can furnish you with a list of accommodations. *(20 mi. southwest of Winchester. Take bus #46 to Southampton (round-trip £5) and transfer to bus #56 or 56A to Lyndhurst (round-trip £5.40) or catch a train to Southampton and then a bus to Lyndhurst.)*

SOUTHWEST ENGLAND

In a country with an incredibly rich history, no other region is as steeped in legend, mystery, and monument as England's southwest. King Arthur is said to have been born at Tintagel on Cornwall's northern coast. One village purports to be the site of Camelot, another the resting place of the Holy Grail, and no fewer than three small lakes are identified as the grave of Arthur's sword, Excalibur. Cornwall was the last stronghold of the Celts in England, and evidence of even older Neolithic communities remains, most famously at Stonehenge. Other eras have left their monuments as well, from Salisbury's medieval cathedral and Bath's Roman spas to the fossils on Dorset's Jurassic Coast.

HIGHLIGHTS OF SOUTHWEST ENGLAND

COMMUNICATE with Martians at **Stonehenge,** one of history's most mysterious engineering feats (p. 202).

DALLY in the world of 18th-century pleasure-seekers in **Bath,** a Roman spa town with a history of improper behavior (p. 209).

DIG for fossils along the shore of **Lyme Regis** (p. 209).

TRANSPORTATION

It is generally easier to get to Somerset, Avon, and Wiltshire than regions farther southwest. **Trains** (☎08457 484 950) offer service from London and the north. The region's primary east-west line from London passes through Taunton, Exeter, and Plymouth before ending at Penzance. Trains from London Waterloo connect to Bath, Bristol, and Salisbury. Branch lines connect St. Ives, Newquay, Falmouth, and Barnstaple to the network. A variety of Rail Rover passes can be used in the region: the **Freedom of the Southwest Rover** covers Cornwall, Devon, Somerset, and parts of Avon and Dorset (8 days out of 15 £61). The **Devon Rail Rover** includes the Taunton-Exmouth line on the east and the Gunnislake-Plymouth line in the west (3 days out of 7 £24). The **Cornish Rail Rover** runs on the Gunnislake-Plymouth line (£18). The **Cornwall Explorer** pass allows one day of travel on all trains and buses in Cornwall (£12).

Buses are a cheaper option, but mastering the complicated regional companies and schedules can be a pain. National Express (☎08705 808 080) runs to major points along the north coast via Bristol and to points along the south coast (including Penzance) via Exeter and Plymouth. For journeys within the region, local buses are usually less expensive than trains. **First** (☎01752 402 060) is the largest bus company in the area. The comprehensive **Traveline** service (☎0870 608 2608; open daily 7am-10pm) can help plan travel to any destination. **Explorer** and **Day Rambler** tickets (£5-6, concessions £4.25, families £12.50) allow unlimited travel on all buses within one region, while the **DaySouthwest** ticket allows travel on all First buses in the southwest area (£6). Many tourist destinations are only served by trains and buses seasonally. For transportation from October to May, call Traveline to check routes and schedules.

HIKING AND OUTDOORS

Distances between towns in southwest England are so short that you can travel through the region on your own steam. The narrow roads and hilly landscapes

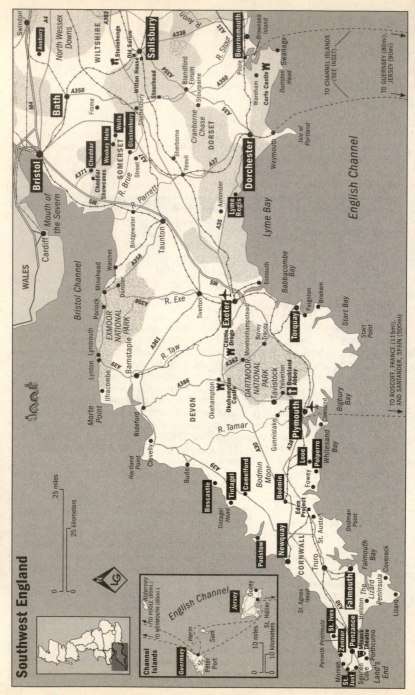

Southwest England

can make biking difficult, but hardy cyclists will find the quiet lanes rewarding. Bring along a large-scale Ordnance Survey map (£7; available at TICs).

The region's most popular walk is the 630 mi. **South West Coast Path,** England's longest coastal path, which originates in Somerset (at Minehead, in Exmoor National Park) and passes through North Devon, Cornwall, and South Devon, ending in Dorset (Poole). It takes several weeks to walk the whole path. However, it is accessible by bus and features B&Bs and hostels at manageable intervals. Many rivers intersect the path, some requiring ferries—check times carefully to avoid being stranded. Most TICs sell guides and Ordnance Survey maps covering sections of the path, which is generally smooth enough to cover by bike; rental shops can often suggest three- to seven-day cycling routes. The path is divided into four parts. The **Somerset and North Devon Coastal Path** extends from Minehead through Exmoor National Park to Bude and features the highest cliffs in southwest England. The **Cornwall Coast Path,** with some of the most rugged stretches, starts in Bude, where Cornish cliffs harbor a vast range of birds and marine life. It then rounds the southwest tip of Britain and continues along the coast to Plymouth. The **South Devon Coast Path** runs from Plymouth to Paignton, tracing cliffs, estuaries, and remote bays set off by wildflowers. The final section, the **Dorset Coast Path,** picks up in Lyme Regis and runs to Poole Harbor. For more information, contact the **South West Coast Path Association** (☎01752 896 237) or any local TIC.

BRISTOL
☎(0)117

Well cultured and hip, Bristol is Britain's latest urban renewal success story. Ten years ago, you'd have been hard-pressed to find someone who wanted to visit Bristol—let alone live there. But today, the southwest's largest city (pop. 410,000) is one of England's fastest-growing communities, with expansive docks and a famed annual hot-air balloon festival. A growing population of students and young professionals has reinvigorated the city and made its nightlife one of Britain's best-kept secrets.

◤ TRANSPORTATION

Trains: Temple Meads Station. Ticket office open M-Sa 5:30am-9:30pm, Su 6:45am-9:30pm. Trains (☎08457 484 950) to: **Bath** (15min., 4 per hr., £5.50-6); **Cardiff** (50min., 2 per hr., £8.80-11.70); **London Paddington** (1¾hr., 2 per hr., £48-68.50); **Manchester** (3hr., 2 per hr., £53). Another station, **Bristol Parkway,** is far, far away—make sure to get off at Temple Meads.

Buses: Marlborough Street Bus Station. Ticket office open M-Sa 7:20am-6pm, Su 9am-6pm. National Express (☎08717 818 181) buses to **London** (2½hr., every hr., £18.40) and **Manchester** (5¾hr., 6 per day, £32.50) via **Birmingham** (2½hr., £17.50). National Express info shop open daily 7am-8:45pm.

Ferries: Bristol Ferry Boat Co. (☎0117 927 3416; www.bristolferry.com). Brings commuters and tourists to various stops along the harbor. £1.60-3.30, round-trip £2.70-4.90; concessions £1.30-2.70/2.10-3.30; day pass £7.

Public Transportation: First (☎08456 020 156) **buses** run in the city. Buses #8 and 9 are the primary routes through the city center, making a circular route through Temple Meads, Broadmead, Redland, and Clifton Downs. Get info at the **Travel Bristol Info Centre,** Colston Ave. (☎08706 082 608). Open M-F 8:30am-5:30pm, Sa 8:30am-1pm. Day pass £3. Explorer ticket, for 1-day unlimited travel in the southwest, £7.

Taxis: Trans Cabs (☎0117 953 8638) or 24hr. **Streamline** (☎0117 926 4001).

Bike Rental: Ferry Station (☎0117 376 3942; www.ferrystation.co.uk). £2 per hr., £7 per ½-day, £12 per day; deposit required.

✈ 🛈 ORIENTATION AND PRACTICAL INFORMATION

Bristol is a sprawling mass of neighborhoods. **Broadmead** is the shopping and commercial center, while restaurants and clubs fill the heart of the city along **Park Street** and **Park Row** in the **West End.** The student population in the northwest makes **Whiteladies Road** (follow Queen's Rd. north) another option for cafes and hip shopping. Upriver, **Clifton Village** offers elegant Georgian architecture, while **Old City,** just to the east of the quay, houses the area's oldest pubs and shops.

Tourist Information Centre: Harbourside (information ☎09067 112 191, accommodations booking 0845 408 0474; www.visitbristol.co.uk), inside @Bristol. From the train station, take bus #8 or 9 to the city center. Follow signs to Millennium Sq. Books beds for £3 plus a 10% deposit. Open M-F 10am-5pm, Sa-Su 10am-6pm.

Tours: Several companies run tours of the city and surrounding sights.

CitySightseeing (☎01934 830 050; www.city-sightseeing.com). Runs bus tours every 15-90min. 10am-4pm. £10, concessions £9, children £5.

Bristol Packet (☎0117 926 8157; www.bristolpacket.co.uk). Begins at Wapping Wharf near the *SS Great Britain.* Also runs boat tours, including daytrips to Avon Gorge and Bath. Sa-Su and during school holidays. £4.75, children £2.75, seniors £4.25.

Guided Walks of Bristol (☎0117 968 4638; www.bristoltours.co.uk). Tours such as "Bristol Merchants and the Slave Trade" and "Historic Wine Merchants." Walks start at the TIC. Mar.-Sept. Sa 11am. £3.50, children free.

Currency Exchange: Banks and **ATMs** on Corn St. and The Centre Promenade.

Library: Bristol Central Library, College Green (☎0117 903 7200). Free Internet in 20min. time slots. Free Wi-Fi. Open M-Tu and Th 9:30am-7:30pm, W 10am-5pm, F-Sa 9:30am-5pm, Su 1-5pm.

Police: Bridewell St. (☎0845 456 7000).

Pharmacy: Boots, 59 Broadmead (☎0117 929 3631). Open M-W and F-Sa 8:15am-6pm, Th 8:15am-7pm, Su 11am-5pm.

Hospital: Bristol Royal Infirmary, Upper Maudlin St. (☎0117 923 0000). **Frenchay** (☎0117 970 1212), in North Bristol near the M32.

Internet Access: Free at the **libary** (above). Also at **Watershed Cafe** (see **Food**).

Post Office: Mall Bristol, Union St. (☎08457 223 344), on the top floor of the shopping center. Open M and W-Sa 9am-5:30pm, Tu 9:30am-5:30pm. **Postcode:** BS1 3XX.

⌂ ACCOMMODATIONS

A few cheap, comfortable B&Bs lie south of the harbor on **Coronation Road.** Walk west along Cumberland Rd. for 15min., cross the red footbridge, turn right on Coronation Rd., and walk a few blocks past Deans Ln.

Bristol Backpackers, 17 St. Stephen's St. (☎0117 925 7900; www.bristolbackpackers. co.uk). This former newspaper office in the heart of Bristol is more like a youth apartment building than a hostel. Great facilities and location mean that many residents stay for months. Well-stocked bar, huge kitchen, and common spaces. Big-screen TV. Laundry £2. Internet £1 per hr. Free Wi-Fi. Reception 9am-11:30pm. Book at least a week in advance for the summer months. Dorms £15. MC/V. ❷

YHA Bristol, Hayman House, 14 Narrow Quay (☎0117 922 1659). From the city center, cross Pero's Bridge. Spacious, clean rooms and cafe-bar in a central location overlook-

Bristol

♠ ACCOMMODATIONS
Bristol Backpackers, 11
Full Moon Hostel, 15
YHA Bristol, 2
Wesley College, 13

🍴 FOOD
M&M, 7
Sergio's, 9
Spyglass, 6
Tequila Max, 14
Thekla Social, 1
Watershed Cafe/Bar, 4

★ NIGHTLIFE
Mr. Wolf's, 8
🍺 PUBS
The Apple, 3
The Hatchet, 10
The Old Duke, 5
The White Harte, 12

ing the water. Breakfast included. Free luggage storage. Laundry. Internet £1 per 30min. Reception 24hr. Dorms £16-24.50, under 18 £12-18.50; singles £19-30. MC/V. ❷

Full Moon Hostel, 1 North St. (☎0117 9245 007; www.fullmoonbristol.co.uk). Brand-new, eco-friendly hostel with organic sheets and tons of room in the courtyard. 2 bars, plasma TVs, and massive parties on full-moon nights. Pool room. Internet available. Free Wi-Fi. Dorms £16; twins £38. MC/V. ❷

Wesley College, College Park Dr. (☎0117 958 1200; www.wesley-college-bristol.ac.uk), 5 mi. outside the city center. Take bus #1 north to Falcondale Rd. and walk up Henbury Rd. The college is signposted at the top of the hill. The area's cheapest single rooms and a self-catering kitchen. Lounge area with TV. Laundry. Internet £2 per night. Reception 9am-5pm. Dorms £15; singles £25; doubles £40. AmEx/MC/V. ❷

■ FOOD

Restaurants line **Park Street,** with trendier options on **Whiteladies Road.** On Wednesdays, a **farmers' market** takes over Corn St. (Open 9:30am- 2:30pm.)

Watershed Cafe/Bar, 1 Canons Rd. (☎0117 927 5101; www.watershed.co.uk). Lovely deck seating overlooks the quay. Filling sandwiches and entrees £6-7. Free Internet and Wi-Fi. Open M 11am-11pm, Tu-Th 9:30am-11pm, F 9:30am-midnight, Sa 10am-midnight, Su 10am-10:30pm. Kitchen open M 10:30am-9pm, Tu 9:30am-9pm, W-F 9:30am-10pm, Sa 10am-10pm, Su 10am-7pm. AmEx/MC/V. ❶

Thekla Social, The Grove, East Mud Dock (☎0117 929 3301), on a boat. Long tables and large booths make this the perfect boat for a bite with friends. Sandwiches (£5), steaks and burgers (£7), and a scrumptious Su roast served inside the boat or on the outdoor deck over the water. Stick around at night for live music. Open daily noon-late. Kitchen open M-F noon-3pm and 5-9pm, Sa noon-9pm, Su noon-5pm. MC/V. ❷

M&M, 1 Marsh St. (☎0117 929 1906). Perfect for late-night munchies and shallow pockets. Burgers and kebabs under £5. Open until 3am. Cash only. ❶

Spyglass, Welsh Back (☎0117 927 2800), in the Old City. Unique food on a classy boat. Heaping portions of Mediterranean food with a large vegetarian selection served on the quay. Entrees from £7. Open daily 11am-11pm. MC/V. ❷

Sergio's, 1-3 Frogmore St. (☎0117 929 1413; www.sergios.co.uk), right before the underpass. This Italian eatery serves up delicious dishes in a cozy atmosphere. Entrees from £9. Open M-F noon-2:30pm and 5:30pm-late, Sa 5:30pm-late. AmEx/MC/V. ❷

Tequila Max, 109 Whiteladies Rd. (☎0117 946 6144; www.tequilamax.co.uk). Mexican restaurant by day, tequila bar by night. Select entrees 2-for-1 for students on W. Open M-Th and Su 5-11pm, Sa 5pm-12:30am. AmEx/MC/V. ❷

◉ SIGHTS

▨@BRISTOL. Get ready for sensory overload at this interactive science center. **Explore** features hands-on exhibits in physics and biology with simulations of space flight and what it's like to be an embryo in the womb (cozy). You can also play memory games and learn how many pints are too many—and how many are just right. (Anchor Rd., Harbourside. ☎0117 915 5000; www.at-bristol.org.uk. Open M-F 10am-5pm, Sa-Su 10am-6pm. Last entry 1hr. before close. £9, concessions £7.)

▨BRITISH EMPIRE AND COMMONWEALTH MUSEUM. Britain may be small, but no other state since Rome has had as expansive an empire. Nation- and time-specific exhibits bring museum-goers back to when "the sun never set on the British Empire," offering even-handed perspectives on the development of imperialism and the effects of colonialism on native populations. "Breaking the Chains," a special exhibit celebrating the 200th anniversary of the abolition of the British slave trade, is an audio-visual display documenting the history of slavery. (Station Approach, Temple Meads, in a former rail station. ☎0117 925 4980; www. empiremuseum.co.uk. Open daily 10am-5pm. £8, concessions £7, children £4, families £20.)

CLIFTON SUSPENSION BRIDGE. The unofficial symbol of Bristol, this sight is a must-see. Isambard Kingdom Brunel, famed engineer of London's Paddington Station, built this masterpiece spanning the Avon Gorge, which looks like a scientific impossibility. The visitors center explains just how Brunel did it. Check it out at night, when the lights over the water add a little something extra. (Take bus #8 or 9. ☎0117 974 4664; www.clifton-suspension-bridge.org.uk. Bridge open 24hr. Visitors center open 10am-5pm. Free guided tours Easter-Sept. Su 3pm. Free.)

SS GREAT BRITAIN. The *Great Britain* was the largest ship in the world when it was launched in 1843. The "world's first great ocean liner" traveled a million miles and now plays host to a display on the realities of 19th-century boating, from the elegant lodging of first-class passengers to the grit of the ship's engine room. (☎ *0117 926 0680; www. ssgreatbritain.org. Open daily June-Aug. 10am-6pm; Sept.-Oct. and Apr.-July 10am-5:30pm; Nov.-Mar. 10am-4:30pm. £11, students and children £6. Audio tour included.*)

BRANDON HILL. Just west of Park St. lies one of the most peaceful and secluded sights in Bristol. Pathways snake through flower beds to **Cabot Tower,** a monument commemorating the 400th anniversary of explorer John Cabot's arrival in North America. Ascend the 108 steps for a stunning panoramic view. (☎ *0117 922 3719. Open daily until dusk. Free.*)

OTHER SIGHTS. The **City Museum and Art Gallery** collects everything from minerals to mummies. The Bristol dinosaur and gypsy car are highlights of the collection. (*Queen's Rd.* ☎ *01772 922 3571; www.bristol. gov.uk/museums. Open daily 10am-5pm. Free.*) From April to October, you can also visit the **Georgian House,** built in 1791, and the **Red Lodge,** an Elizabethan home. (*Georgian House 7 George St.* ☎ *0117 921 1326. Red Lodge Park Row* ☎ *0117 921 1360. Both open M-W and Sa 10am-5pm. Free.*) The **Arnolfini Gallery** houses contemporary works. (*16 Narrow Quay* ☎ *0117 917 2300; www.arnolfini.org.uk. Open Tu-Su 10am-6pm. Free.*) **John Wesley's Chapel** is the world's oldest Methodist building. (*36 The Horsefair, Broadmead.* ☎ *0117 926 4740; www.newroombristol.org.uk. Open M-Sa 10am-4pm. Free.*) Founded in 1140, **Bristol Cathedral** is known as a "hall church" because the nave, quire, and aisles are of equal height. The windows memorialize the 1940 bombing of Bristol and a mark in the floor is spot where Queen Elizabeth II stood. The beautiful **Norman Chapter House** housed the monks' many books. (☎ *0117 926 4879; www.bristol-cathedral.co.uk. Open M-Sa 8am-5:30pm, Su 7:30am-5:30pm. Evensong M-F 5:15pm, Sa 3:30pm. Free tour Sa 11:30am.*)

🎵 🎆 ENTERTAINMENT AND FESTIVALS

Britain's oldest theater, the **Theatre Royal,** King St., was widely rebuked for debauchery until George III approved the actors' antics in the late 18th century. (☎ *0117 987 7877. Box office open M-Sa 10am-6pm. Tickets £7-20, £2 student discount.*) The **Hippodrome,** St. Augustine's Parade, presents the latest touring productions. (☎ *0800 587 5007; www. bristolhippodrome.org.uk. Tickets £12.50-25, concessions up to £5 off M-Th. Box office open M-Sa 10am-6pm, performance days 10am-8pm.*) The

THE LOCAL STORY

BANKSY'S BRISTOL

In most cities, graffiti is an eyesore. In Bristol, pseudo-anonymous street artist Banksy is taking graffiti from vandalism to modern art. His distinctive stenciling techniques have become iconic, and his satirical masterpieces are now cropping up on streets, buildings, and other public places worldwide. In his hometown of Bristol, a high concentration of Banksy creations makes it easy to catch a glimpse of this guerrilla Van Gogh.

On the side of the Sexual Health Clinic on Frogmore St., down the steps from Park St., a naked man dangles from a stenciled window while a couple peers out at him from inside. Bristolians have wisely voted to preserve this piece as public art.

From Cheltenham Rd., opposite the junction with Jamaica St., look for "The Mild, Mild West," which features a white bear tossing a Molotov cocktail at a group of police with the Banksy tag below.

A ghost sailor rows a boat tagged onto the side of the Thekla Social boat, moored in the harbor. For the best view, cross the Prince St. bridge from the city center and turn left along the quayside.

A 25 ft. Banksy mural adorns the side of a house at 21 Mivart St. In order to make sure the work is preserved, the owners have decided to sell the mural with their five-bedroom house included "for free" in the £160,000 price tag.

popular **Watershed,** 1 Canon's Rd. (☎0117 927 5100; www.watershed.co.uk), an art-house cinema on the quay, holds discussions on independent and foreign films and has a lively cafe. (£6, concessions £4.50. Box office open M-F from 9am to 15min. after the final showtime, Sa-Su from 10am.) **Bristol Harbour Festival** (☎0117 903 1484) explodes with fireworks, raft races, live music, boats, and a French market at the end of July. During the **Bristol International Balloon Fiesta** (☎0117 966 8716) in early August, hot-air balloons fill the sky while acrobats and motorcycle teams perform at ground level.

PUBS AND NIGHTLIFE

On weekend nights, the entire city turns out in clubwear. Bars and clubs cluster around Park St. and Park Row in the West End, and Baldwin and St. Nicholas St. in the Old City. A handful of gay clubs line Frogmore St. If you're looking for a late-night dance club, popular chains like Revolution and Walk-A-Bout run up and down Corn and Baldwin St., near St. Nicholas Markets.

The Apple, Welsh Back (☎0117 925 3500; www.applecider.co.uk). This cider bar's signature Old Bristolian cider (strong cider with a sweet sherry finish) is so strong that they're only allowed to serve it in ½-pints (£2). Huge range of ciders on tap. £1 ½-pints of Old Bristolian all day M. Open daily noon-midnight.

The White Harte, 54-58 Park Row (☎0117 929 2490). Collegiate crowd packs in for cheap pints. A good place to start a pub crawl up Park St. Beer and a burger/curry £3 after 3pm. £1 pints M. Open M-Th and Su noon-11pm, F-Sa noon-1:30am.

The Old Duke, King St. (☎0117 929 7137). High energy and crowds spilling outside. It tends to get packed (and loud) inside, so enjoy your cider or ale on the outdoor patio connected with 4 other bars—you can still hear the music, try out other bars, and keep your table. Live jazz, blues, or folk music nightly. Open daily noon-midnight.

Mr. Wolf's, 33 St. Stephen's St. (☎0117 927 3221). A late-night cafe and excellent live music forum make a great place to start or end your night. DJs on nights without live music. Open M-Tu 6pm-2am, W-Sa 6pm-4am, Su 6pm-12:30am.

The Hatchet, 27 Frogmore St. (☎0117 929 4118; www.thehatchet.co.uk). The fact that this is the oldest pub in Bristol is overshadowed by the rumor that the door was originally made of human flesh. Either way, you'll have a great story to tell after you have a pint in this classic pub. Live music F-Sa. Open M-W and Su noon-11pm, Th-Sa noon-2am.

WILTSHIRE

SALISBURY
☎(0)1722

Salisbury's winding alleyways are a step back in time. Despite its popularity among tourists, Salisbury retains a small-town charm. Town life spirals outward from the market, overlooked by the towering cathedral spire. On a windy plain nearby, awe-inspiring Stonehenge stands on a lonely plain.

TRANSPORTATION

Trains: Station on S. Western Rd., west of town across the River Avon. Ticket office open M-Sa 5:30am-8pm, Su 7:30am-8:45pm. Trains (☎08457 484 950) to: **London Water-**

loo (1hr., 2 per hr., £29.50); **Portsmouth** and **Southsea** (1hr., 2 per hr., £14.40); **Southampton** (40min., every hr., £7.20); **Winchester** (1hr., 2 per hr., £12.20).

Buses: Station at 8 Endless St. (☎01722 336 855). Open M-F 9:30am-5pm. National Express (☎08705 808 080) runs to **London** (3hr., 3 per day, £13.70). Buy tickets at the bus station. Wilts and Dorset (☎01722 336 855) runs to **Bath** (#X4, M-Sa every hr. 8am-4pm, £4.50) and **Winchester** (#68, 1hr., 8 per day, £4.65). An **Explorer** ticket is good for 1 day of travel on Wilts and Dorset buses and some Hampshire, Provincial, Solent Blue, and Brighton & Hove buses (£7.50, children £4.50).

Taxis: A queue forms by the train station. **505050 Value Cars** (☎01722 505 050).

Bike Rental: Hayball Cycles Sport, 26-30 Winchester St. (☎07909 883 006), across from Coaches and Horses. £10 per day, £5 overnight, £65 per week; deposit £25. Open M-Sa 9am-5:30pm; bikes due back at 5pm.

🛈 PRACTICAL INFORMATION

Tourist Information Centre: Fish Row (☎01722 334 956, accommodations booking 01271 336 066; www.visitsalisbury.com), the Guildhall, in Market Sq. Free maps and suggested bike routes. Books rooms for a 10% deposit. Open June-Sept. M-Sa 9:30am-6pm, Su 10:30am-4:30pm; Oct.-May M-Sa 9:30am-5pm.

Tours: 1hr. guided walks leave the TIC Apr.-Oct. M-Th and Sa-Su 11am, F 11am, 8pm; Nov.-Mar. Sa-Su 11am. £3.50, children £2.

Banks: Everywhere. **Thomas Cook,** 18-19 Queen St. Open M-W and F-Sa 9am-5:30pm, Th 10am-5:30pm. **HSBC,** corner of Market Pl. and Minster St., has a 24hr. **ATM.**

Library: Salisbury Library, Market Pl. (☎01722 324 145). Open M 10am-7pm, Tu-W and F 9am-7pm, Th and Sa 9am-5pm.

Launderette: Washing Well, 28 Chipper Ln. (☎01722 421 874). Open daily 8am-9pm.

Police: Wilton Rd. (☎01722 411 444).

Pharmacy: Boots, 51 Silver St. (☎01722 333 233). Open M-Tu and Th-Sa 8:30am-5:30pm, W 9am-5:30pm, Su 10:30am-4:30pm.

Hospital: Central Health Clinic, Avon Approach (☎01722 328 595).

Internet Access: Free at the **library** (above) for 30min. with a photo ID.

Post Office: 24 Castle St. (☎08457 223 344), at Chipper Ln. Open M and W 9am-5:30pm, Tu and Th-F 8:30am-5:30pm, Sa 9am-4pm. **Postcode:** SP1 1AB.

🏠 🏕 ACCOMMODATIONS AND CAMPING

Salisbury's proximity to a certain stone circle breeds numerous guesthouses and B&Bs, most of them starting at around £35 per person—ask for an accommodations guide or free booking assistance from the TIC. Be sure to book ahead in the busy summer season.

Farthings B&B, 9 Swaynes Close (☎01722 330 749). Comfortable retreat with large, floral rooms. Smaller rooms share a bath. Continental breakfast included. May-Sept. singles £35; doubles £60. Oct.-Apr. singles £27; doubles £50. Cash only. ❸

YHA Salisbury, Milford Hill House, Milford Hill (☎01722 327 572), on the edge of town. 70 beds. Bathrooms may be less than clean. Kitchen and TV lounge. Breakfast (baked beans and cereal) included. Laundry £3. Internet access £1 per 15min. Book in advance, especially Easter-Oct. Dorms £15-17.50, under 18 £14. MC/V. ❷

Old Rectory Bed and Breakfast, 75 Belle Vue Road (☎01722 502 702; www.theoldrectory-bb.co.uk). Huge rooms with big beds and baths. Ensuite doubles £70. MC/V. ❸

IN RECENT NEWS

A CHIP OFF THE ANCIENT BLOCK

Every year, visitors flock to see Stonehenge, the gigantic ring of stones towering over the Salisbury plain. Most are content with just the sight of the ancient boulders.

But on May 15, 2008, two souvenir hunters took this stone devotion to the next level. Armed with a hammer and screwdriver, the men broke into the site at 10pm and chipped a coin-size piece of rock from the side of the Heel Stone, a single block of eroded stone that stands just 250 ft. from the main circle of Stonehenge.

Ironically enough, vandalism of this sort was once encouraged at Stonehenge. Up until 1900, tourists were given chisels in order to chip pieces from the stones as souvenirs. In 1900, however, landowner Sir Edmund Antrobus decided to protect the monument, and this type of souvenir-collecting is now illegal.

The Wiltshire police emphasize that chipping pieces off the monument is damage to a national site and constitutes vandalism. According to the BBC, the two tourists—not content with sightseeing—were chased away from the monument by security guards, but not before they had scored a Stonehenge souvenir.

Hudson's Field, Castle Rd. (☎01722 320 713). Between Salisbury and Stonehenge, 30min. from city center. Clean, modern facilities. Vehicle curfew 11pm. Open Mar.-Oct. £7.60 per person, children £2.35. Electricity £3. MC/V. ❶

🏠🍴 FOOD AND PUBS

Market Square, in the town center, fills from May to December on Tuesdays and Saturdays for the **market** and on Wednesdays for the **farmers' market** (open 7am-4pm). A **Sainsbury's** supermarket is at The Maltings. (☎01722 332 282. Open M-Sa 7am-10pm, Su 10am-4pm.) Even jaded pub-dwellers can find a pleasant surprise among Salisbury's 60-odd watering holes.

🏠 **Harper's "Upstairs Restaurant",** 6-7 Ox Rd., Market Sq. (☎01722 333 118). Gaze down into the bustling market square while deliberating between turkey tagine with couscous or sweet potato and cashew pancakes (£8-14). 2-course early-bird dinner before 8pm (£11.50) lets you end with *pain au chocolate* bread pudding. Open M-F noon-2pm and 6-9:30pm, Sa noon-2pm and 6-10pm. AmEx/MC/V. ❷

Alchemy @ the Chough, Blue Boar Row (☎01722 330 032; www.thehiddenbrewery.com). Find a couch in one of Alchemy's many nooks and crannies. Original art and signs still hang on the walls. The Alchemy mix (£10) is a platter of finger foods. Entrees £8-10. Open M-Th 11am-11:30pm, F-Sa 11am-12:30am. MC/V. ❷

Coach and Horses, 39 Winchester St. (☎01722 414 319). Generously poured drinks (pints £2.70) flow nonstop in Salisbury's oldest pub, open since 1382. Check out the beer garden in the back. Pub food £9-15. Open M-Sa 11:30am-11pm, Su noon-10:30pm. Kitchen open M-Sa 11:30am-9:30pm, Su noon-9pm. MC/V. ❶

Salisbury Chocolate Bar & Patisserie, 33 High St. (☎01722 327 422). Indulge your sweet tooth with luscious hot chocolates (£2) or pastries (£3-4), like the delectable whipped cream-filled *foret noir*. Open daily 9:30am-5pm. MC/V. ❶

The Old Mill Hotel, Town Path (☎01722 327 517). At the end of a 10min. walk along Town Path through the Harnem Water Meadow, in a 12th-century mill. Entrees £14-18; pub food £7-9. Open M-Sa 11am-11pm, Su noon-10:30pm. Kitchen open M-Sa noon-2pm and 7-9pm, Su noon-10:30pm. AmEx/MC/V. ❸

📷 SIGHTS

🏛 **SALISBURY CATHEDRAL.** Salisbury Cathedral, built between 1220 and 1258, rises to a neck-breaking 404 ft., making it medieval England's

Salisbury

🏠🏠 ACCOMMODATIONS

Farthings B&B, **8**
Hudson's Field, **3**
Old Rectory, **7**
YHA Salisbury, **11**
🍴 FOOD
Alchemy @ the Chough, **6**
Coach and Horses, **9**
Harper's "Upstairs
   Restaurant," **5**
Salisbury Chocolate Bar
   & Patisserie, **4**
The Old Mill Hotel, **1**
⭐ MUSIC AND CLUBS
The Chapel, **10**
MOLOKO, **2**

highest spire and one of Britain's most amazing displays of Gothic architecture. The bases of the marble pillars bend inward under the strain of 6400 tons of limestone. Nearly 700 years have left the building in need of repair, and scaffolding obscuress parts of the outer walls that are under extensive renovation, expected to be completed by 2015. A tiny stone figure rests in the nave—legend has it that either a boy bishop is entombed on the spot or that it covers the heart of the cathedral's founder. The 🔲**Chapter House** holds the best-preserved of the four surviving copies of the Magna Carta. The text is still legible, great for those who can read medieval Latin. Cromwell's soldiers knocked out the stained glass, but the Chapter House still retains most of its medieval sculpture, including an architrave of the seven virtues and vices (the female figures are the virtues, the male figures the vices) over the door and the Old Testament Bible scenes that ring the entire room. (☎01722 555 120. *Cathedral open daily 7:15am-6:15pm. More limited hours in winter. Free tours every 30min. May-Oct. M-Sa 9:30am-4:45pm, Su 4-6:15pm; Nov.-Feb. M-Sa 10am-4pm. 1hr. roof and tower tours June-Aug. M-Sa 11am, 2, 3, 6:30pm, Su 4:30pm; Sept. and May M-Sa 11:15am, 2:15, 3:15, 5pm, Su 4:30pm. Requested donation £5. Roof and tower tour £5.50.)*

SALISBURY AND SOUTH WILTSHIRE MUSEUM. The museum, in the cathedral's close, has a collection ranging from Turner's watercolors to period clothing and

HERE COMES THE SUN

Perhaps no manmade structure evokes more mystical associations than Stonehenge. Ties to Arthurian legend, Celts, druids, aliens, giants, and witches bring tourists to the mysterious stones year-round. For 364 days of the year they are roped off—almost regal in their standoffishness. But every June, the summer solstice arrives, the ropes are pulled back, admission is free, and visitors enter the circle to worship as they like.

In droves they come: druids with staffs waiting for the sun, hippies carrying magical plants and caressing the stones, and curious bystanders unsure of what will happen next. In a matter of hours, the previously vacant field is transformed into a drum-filled festival complete with glow sticks and champagne.

As the crowd swells to an impenetrable mob, the drumming thunders and the sun finally rises, casting a shadow perfectly across the center of the stones. Suddenly, cheering erupts from the milling masses—an unforgettable energy that validates the mystical qualities of Stonehenge.

The 2009 summer solstice occurs on June 21. There is no admission fee the night before or morning of the solstice, but be sure to make plans to get a bus early, as crowds form quickly.

dollhouses. The Stonehenge exhibit gives extensive history and displays the bones of an archer buried at Stonehenge around the time the first stones were raised. *(65 The Close, along the West Walk. ☎ 01722 332 151. Open July-Aug. M-Sa 10am-5pm, Su 2-5pm; Sept.-June M-Sa 10am-5pm. £5, concessions £3.50, families £11.)*

♫ 🎭 ENTERTAINMENT AND NIGHTLIFE

The sign outside **The Chapel,** 30 Milford St., states, in mathematical terms, "no effort = no entry." Loosely translated—dress to impress. This club advertises itself as one of the UK's best. Without much competition in Salisbury, it can surely claim to be the best in town. (☎01722 504 255; www.thechapelnightclub.com. Cover W £2; Th £4, women before 11:30pm free; F £8; Sa £10. Open W-Th 10:30pm-2:30am, F-Sa 10:30pm-3am.) **MOLOKO,** 5 Bridge St., is a chain bar but still one of the most popular hangouts in town. There's an endless list of vodkas (£2.50-4.50) and a stylish crowd. (☎01722 507 050. Special £1 house vodkas Th 7-9pm. Open M-Th 4pm-midnight, F-Sa 4pm-2am, Su 3-10:30pm.)

Salisbury's repertory theater company puts on shows at the **Playhouse,** Malthouse Ln., over the bridge off Fisherton St. (☎01722 320 333; www.salisburyplayhouse.com. Tickets £8.50-17. ½-price tickets available same day. Box office open M-Sa 10am-6pm; until 8pm on performance days.) Enjoy free Sunday concerts in the park; call the TIC for info. The **Salisbury International Arts Festival** features dance exhibitions, music, and wine tasting for two weeks in late May and early June. Contact the Festival Box Office at the Playhouse for a program. (☎01722 320 333; www.salisbury-festival.co.uk. Tickets from £2.50.)

🎭 DAYTRIPS FROM SALISBURY

■**STONEHENGE.** A half-ruined ring of colossal stones amid swaying grass and indifferent sheep has become a world-famous attraction. Tourists visit Stonehenge in droves to see the 22 ft. high stones, pockmarked by the wind that whips across the flat Salisbury plains. The current ring is actually the fifth temple constructed on the site—Stonehenge was already ancient in ancient times. The first arrangement probably consisted of an arch and circular earthwork furrowed in 3050 BC. Its relics are the **Aubrey Holes** (white patches in the earth) and the **Heel Stone** (the rough block standing outside the circle). The present shape, once a complete circle, dates from about 1500 BC. The tremendous workforce—estimated at tens of millions of man-hours—and innovation required to transport and erect the 45-ton stones make Stonehenge an extraordinary monument to human (alien?) effort. Sensationalized religious and scientific explanations for Stonehenge's purpose deepen the intrigue. Some believe the stones are oriented as a calendar, with the position of the sun on the stones indicating the time of year. Celtic druids, whose ceremonies took place in forests, did not actually worship here, but modern druids are permitted to enter Stonehenge on the summer solstice to perform ceremonial exercises. Admission to Stonehenge includes a 30min. audio tour with mystical background music and information about legends and the surrounding landscape. English Heritage also offers free 30min. guided tours. From the roadside or from Amesbury Hill, 1½ mi. up the A303, you can get a free, if distant, view of the stones. There are also many walks and trails that pass by; ask at the Salisbury TIC. *(There are two ways to reach Stonehenge: the Stonehenge Tourbus departs the Salisbury train and bus station and includes an audio tour. Every 30min. from 9:30am. Ride £11, with combined Stonehenge admission £17; students £11/14. Combined ticket allows visitors to bypass the lines at the Stonehenge. Stonehenge Tourbus stops at Old Sarum (this page) but not at Avebury (p. 203).* ☎ *01980 624 715. Open daily June-Aug. 9am-7pm; from Sept. to mid-Oct. and from mid.-Mar. to May 9:30am-6pm; from mid-Oct. to mid-Mar. 9:30am-4pm. £6.50.)*

STOURHEAD. Once the home of a wealthy English banking family, this 18th-century estate is a classic marriage of architecture and landscape. The Palladian mansion is surrounded by endless gardens, lakes, and waterfalls. The miniature reproductions of Greek temples are visited by colorful peacocks. *(Transportation difficult without a car. Trains run to Gillingham from Salisbury. 25min., W and F every hr., £4.20. Bus #58A runs infrequently between Gillingham station and Stourhead. Bus #25 runs from Salisbury Bus Station to Hindon Sq. 45min., Tu-F 11:40am. Then take the Wigglybus from Hindon Sq. to Stourton. £1.20. For the return journey, catch the 4:50pm bus #25 from Hindon Sq. back to Salisbury.* ☎ *01747 841 152. Open from late Mar. to late Oct. M-Tu and F-Su 11:30am-4:30pm. Last entry 30min. before close. Garden and house £10.50, children £5.20. Grounds without house £6.10/3.40. King Alfred's Tower without house £2.20/1.20.)*

WILTON HOUSE. Declared by James I to be "the finest house in the land," the home of the earls of Pembroke is the quintessential aristocratic country estate and the setting for films like *Sense and Sensibility* (1995) and *Pride and Prejudice* (2005). Historically a center of art patronage, Wilton House welcomed the glittering literati of the 16th and 17th centuries, hosting such illustrious writers as John Donne and Sir Philip Sidney. The painting collection includes the largest assortment of Van Dycks in the world. *(3 mi. west of Salisbury on the A30; take bus #60 or 61. M-Sa every 15min., Su every hr.; round-trip £3.20.* ☎ *01722 746 720; www. wiltonhouse.com. Open from late Mar. to Oct. M-Th 10:30am-5:30pm. Last entry 4:30pm. House and grounds £12, concessions £9.75. Grounds only £5, children £3.50.)*

OLD SARUM. This unassuming grassy mound evolved from a Bronze Age gathering place into a Celtic fortress, which was won by the Romans, taken by the Anglo-Saxons, and seized by the Normans before falling into the hands of the British Heritage Society. Civilization left Old Sarum in the 1300s when a new cathedral was built nearby, leaving stone ruins of the earlier castle strewn across the hill. *(Off the A345, 2 mi. north of town. Buses #3 and 6-9 run every 15min. from Salisbury.* ☎ *01722 335 398. Open daily July-Aug. 9am-6pm; Sept.-Oct. and Apr.-June 10am-5pm; Nov.-Feb. 11am-3pm; Mar. 10am-4pm. £3, concessions £2.40, children £1.40.)*

AVEBURY. A quandry for the reader: why is Avebury's stone circle, larger and older than its cousin Stonehenge, often so lonely during the day? Avebury gives an up-close and largely untouristed view of its 98 stones, standing in a circle with a 1000 ft. diameter. Visitors can amble among the megaliths and have

SOUTHWEST
ENGLAND

a beer in the **Red Lion Pub,** which sits in the center of the circle. Dating from 2500 BC, Avebury was built over the course of centuries but has remained steadfast in its original form. Outside the ring, mysterious **Silbury Hill** rises from the ground; its date of origin, 2660 BC, was only determined by the serendipitous excavation of an ant. Due to previous excavations, the top of the hill has collapsed and visitors are no longer allowed to reach the top. The **Alexander Keiller Museum** details the history of the stone circle. (☎ *01722 539 250. Open daily Apr.-Oct. 10am-5pm; Nov.-Mar. 10am-4pm. £4.20, children £2.10, families £7.50.)* Locate the Avebury **Tourist Information Centre,** in the Avebury Chapel Center, next to the bus stop. (☎ *01672 539 425. Open Apr.-Oct. M-Sa 9:30am-5pm; Nov.-Mar. W-Su 9:30am-5pm. Bus #2 from Salisbury departs from Endless St. off of Main St.)*

DORSET COAST

BOURNEMOUTH   ☎ (0)1202

Visitors may be pleasantly surprised by Bournemouth's cosmopolitan seaside manner. The town's Victorian buildings, lavish gardens, and expansive beach are colonized by swimsuit-toting daytrippers in summer. Unpretentious and student-friendly, Bournemouth houses some of England's best nightlife, ensuring that the fun doesn't stop when the sun dips below the gentle waves.

TRANSPORTATION. The **train station** lies on Holdenhurst Rd., 15min. east of the town center. (Travel center open M-F 9am-7pm, Sa 9am-6pm, Su 9am-5pm. Ticket office open M-Sa 5:40am-9pm, Su 6:40am-9pm.) Trains (☎ 08457 484 950) depart to: Birmingham (3hr., every hr., £61); Dorchester (40min., every hr., £9); London Waterloo (2hr., 2 per hr., £40); Poole (10min., 2 per hr., £3). National Express (☎ 08717 818 181) **buses** queue in front of the train station (ticket office open M-Th 8am-5:30pm, F 7:45am-6pm, Sa 7:45am-5:30pm, Su 9:15am-4:45pm) and serve: Birmingham (5-6hr., 3 per day, £40); Bristol (3hr., 1 per day, £16.20); London (3hr., every hr., £19); Poole (20min., 2-3 per hr., £1.60). Tickets are also sold at the TIC. Wilts and Dorset (☎ 01202 673 555) runs local buses, including services to Poole and Southampton. An **Explorer** ticket (£7.50) provides unlimited travel. **United Taxi** (☎ 01202 556 677) runs 24hr.

ORIENTATION AND PRACTICAL INFORMATION. The downtown centers on **The Square,** which is flanked by the **Central Gardens** to the northwest and the **Lower Gardens** toward the beach. The **Tourist Information Centre,** Westover Rd., sells a map (£1.50) and guide (£1) and books rooms for a 10% deposit. From the train station, turn left on Holdenhurst Rd. onto Bath Rd. and follow the signs. (☎ 0845 051 1700; www.bournemouth.co.uk. Open in summer M-Sa 9:30am-6pm, Su 10am-5pm; limited winter hours.) Other services include: **American Express,** 95A Old Christchurch Rd. (☎ 01202 780 752; open M-F 9am-5:30pm, Sa 9am-5pm); **Washeteria** launderette, Southcote Rd., near the train station. (☎ 0700 520 3385; open daily 7am-6:30pm); **police,** Madeira Rd. (☎ 01202 552 099); **Boots** pharmacy, 18-20 Commercial Rd. (☎ 01202 551 713; open M-Sa 9am-6pm, Su 10:30am-4:30pm); **Bournemouth Hospital,** Castle Land East, Littledown (☎ 01202 303 626); **Internet** access at the **library,** 22 The Triangle, uphill from City Sq. (☎ 01202 454 848; 1hr. free; open M 10am-7pm, Tu and Th-F 9:30am-7pm, W 9:30am-5pm, Sa 10am-4pm) and at **Cyber Place,** 25 St. Peter's Rd. (☎ 01202 290 099; 50p per 10min., students £1.50 per hr.; open daily

9:30am-midnight); and the **post office,** 9-13 Old Christchurch Rd. (☎08457 223 344; open M-Sa 9am-5:30pm) inside WHSmith. **Postcode:** BH1 1DY.

🏠🍴 **ACCOMMODATIONS AND FOOD.** The **East Cliff** neighborhood, 5min. from the train station, bristles with B&Bs. Exit left from the station, cross Holdenhurst Rd. to St. Swithuns, and turn left on Frances Rd.; the route is signposted. **Bournemouth Backpackers ❷,** 3 Frances Rd., is a small hostel with a comfy lounge and a barbecue pit. (☎01202 299 491; www.bournemouthback-packers.co.uk. Kitchen. Reception 5:30-6:30pm. Dorms £13-18; doubles £36-44. F and Sa nights only as a package (£34). Cash only.) **Kantara ❸,** 8 Gardens View, has bright rooms close to the train and bus stations. (☎01202 557 260; www.kantaraguesthouse.co.uk. £18-32 per person. MC/V.)

Christchurch Road has diverse eateries; **Charminster Road** is a center of Asian cuisine. Get groceries at **ASDA,** St. Paul's Rd., across from the train station. (☎01202 298 900. Open M 8am-midnight, Tu-F 6am-midnight, Sa 6am-10pm, Su 10am-4pm.) **Eye of the Tiger ❷,** 207 Old Christchurch Rd., serves Bengali curries for £6.50-10 and other tandoori specialties for £8-11. (☎01202 780 900. Vegetarian options available. 10% takeaway discount. Open daily noon-2pm and 6pm-midnight. MC/V.) **Shake Away ❶,** 7 Post Office Rd., provides over 150 flavors of milkshakes (£2.70-3.70), from marshmallow to rhubarb. (☎01202 310 105. Open M-F 9am-5:30pm, Sa 9am-6pm, Su 10:30am-5pm. Cash only.) For coffee and people-watching, stop at **Obscura Cafe ❶,** The Square. (☎01202 314 231. Baguettes £4-5. Open daily 9am-11:30pm. MC/V.)

🏛️🏖️ **SIGHTS AND BEACHES.** The city center holds a few interesting attractions. The **Russell-Cotes Art Gallery and Museum,** Russell-Cotes Rd., East Cliff, houses a collection of Victorian art in a lavish turn-of-the-century seaside house. (☎01202 451 858; www.russell-cotes.bournemouth.gov.uk. Open Tu-Su 10am-5pm. Free.) On the corner of Hilton and St. Peter's Rd., **Saint Peter's** parish church holds the remains of Mary Shelley, author of *Frankenstein.* (☎01202 290 986. Open M-F 9am-5pm, Sa 10am-4pm, Su for services.) You can't miss the **Bournemouth Eye,** a helium-filled balloon that gives visitors a bird's-eye view of the boardwalk. (☎01202 314 539; www.bournemouthballoon.com. Open Apr.-Sept. 7:30am-11pm; hours vary with weather conditions. £10.) Most visitors come for **Bournemouth Beach** (☎01202 451 781), a 7 mi. sliver of shoreline packed with sun worshippers on hot summer days. Amusements and a theater can be found at **Bournemouth Pier.** (Open July-Aug. 9am-11pm; Sept.-Oct. and Apr.-June 9am-5:30pm.) A short walk leads to quieter spots.

A 95 mi. stretch of the Dorset and East Devon coast, dubbed the **Jurassic Coast,** was recently named a World Heritage Site for its famous fossils and unique geology. Beautiful **Studland Beach** sits across the harbor, reachable by Wilts and Dorset bus #150 (50min., every hr.). Take bus #150 or 151 (25min., 2 per hr.) to reach the themed landscapes of **Compton Acres,** featuring an Italian garden with Roman statues and a sensory garden designed for the blind. (☎01202 700 778; www.comptonacres.co.uk. Open daily Apr.-Oct. 9am-6pm; Nov.-Mar. 10am-4pm. Last entry 1hr. before close. £7, concessions £6.45, children £4, families £17.) The 1000-year-old **Corfe Castle** is no gently weathered pile of ruins: Parliamentarian engineers were ordered to destroy the castle during the English Civil War. Travel to Poole (bus #151) or Swanage (#150) to catch bus #142 (every hr.) to the castle. (☎01929 481 294. Open daily Apr.-Sept. 10am-6pm; Oct. and Feb.-Mar. 10am-5pm; Nov.-Jan. 10am-4pm. £5.60, children £2.80. Discount for those arriving by public transportation.)

SOUTHWEST ENGLAND

NIGHTLIFE AND FESTIVALS. Students and vacationers fuel Bournemouth's nightlife. Check www.bournemouthbynight.com to make plans for the evening's festivities. Gay-friendly nightlife options cluster where Commercial St. meets The Triangle. Most partygoers start at the roundabout up the hill from **Fir Vale Road,** working downhill through the numerous bars on **Christchurch Road. Toko,** 33-39 St. Peters Rd., is a sleek, sophisticated bar with fish tanks, flatscreen TVs, and free Wi-Fi. (☎01202 315 821; www.toko-bar.co.uk. "Retox" student night Th with £1.50 drinks. Open M 10pm-3am, Tu 8pm-1am, W-Th 8pm-4am, F-Sa 8pm-6am.) The nearby **Bliss,** 1-15 St. Peter's Rd., offers an upscale night out with mood lighting and a sleek bar. (☎01202 297 149; www.bliss-bar.co.uk. Free Wi-Fi. Open M and Th-F noon-4am, Tu-W and Su noon-2am, Sa 8pm-4am.) The biggest club in Bournemouth, **Elements** attracts hordes of vacationing students from London. (☎01202 311 178; www.elements-nightclub.co.uk. Student night W. Cover £3-8; often free before 10pm. Open W-F 10pm-3am, Sa 10pm-4am.) A mile east of The Square, the **Opera House,** 570 Christchurch Rd., a former theater renovated into two dance floors, is one of the wildest (and cheapest) clubs in town, also hosting frequent concerts and live acts. Take bus #22 from The Square. (☎01202 399 922; www.operahouse. co.uk. Most drinks £1-2. Cover £1-15. Opening hours vary each night; check the website for details.) In a tradition dating from 1896, 15,000 candles light up the Lower Gardens every Wednesday in summer during the **Flowers by Candlelight Festival.** In late June, **Bournemouth's Live! Music Festival** (☎01202 451 702; www. bournemouth.co.uk) hosts free concerts.

DORCHESTER ☎(0)1305

Stratford has Shakespeare, Swansea has Thomas, Haworth has the Brontës, and Dorchester has Thomas Hardy. Locals invoke his spirit to no end, from pub regulars sharing time-worn stories about the author to the somber statue towering over the town's main street. In addition to being the inspiration for the fictional Casterbridge, the sleepy town has a rich history and serves as a convenient base for exploring the fossil-laden Jurassic Coast.

TRANSPORTATION

Trains: Leave from **Dorchester South,** off Weymouth Ave., south of the town center. Ticket office open M-F 5:50am-6:15pm, Sa 7:55am-3:15pm, Su 8:45am-3pm. Trains (☎08457 484 950) run to **Bournemouth** (40min., every hr., £9) and **London Waterloo** (2½hr., every hr., £44.20). Some trains leave the unmanned station, **Dorchester West,** also off Weymouth Ave., including those to **Weymouth** (15min., every hr., £3.20).

Buses: Dorchester has no bus station, but buses stop at **Dorchester South** train station and on **Trinity Street.** National Express (☎08717 818 181) runs buses to **Exeter** (2hr., 1 per day, £11.60) and **London** (5hr., 3 per day, £20.70). Tickets are sold at the TIC. Wilts and Dorset (☎01305 673 555) bus #184 goes to **Salisbury** via **Blandford** (2hr., 6 per day). First bus #212 goes to **Yeovil** (1hr., every hr.), with connections south.

Public Transportation: Coach House Travel (☎01305 267 644) provides local service.

Taxis: Bob's Cars (☎01305 269 500). 24hr. **Dorset Cars** (☎01305 250 666).

Bike Rental: Dorchester Cycles, 31 Great Western Rd. (☎01305 268 787; www. dorchestercycles.co.uk). £12 per day. ID required. Open M-Sa 9am-5:30pm.

◢ 🛈 ORIENTATION AND PRACTICAL INFORMATION

The intersection of **High West Street** and **South Street** (which eventually becomes **Cornhill Street**) is the unofficial center of town. The main **shopping district** extends along South St. and runs parallel to Trinity St.

Tourist Information Centre, 11 Antelope Walk, off Trinity St. (☎01305 267 992; www.westdorset.com). Stocks free town maps and books accommodations for a 10% deposit. Open M-Sa Apr.-Oct. 9am-5pm; Nov.-Mar. 9am-4pm.

Banks: Many banks and ATMs are along South St.

Library and Internet Access: Colliton Park (☎01305 224 448), off The Grove. 1st 30min. free. Open M 10am-7pm, Tu-W and F 9:30am-7pm, Th 9:30am-5pm, Sa 9am-4pm.

Launderette: 16C High E. St. Open daily 8am-8pm.

Police: Weymouth Ave. (☎01305 222 222).

Pharmacy: Boots, 12-13 Cornhill St. (☎01305 264 340). Open M-W 9am-5:30pm, Th-Sa 8:30am-5:30pm.

Hospital: Dorset County Hospital, Williams Ave. (☎01305 255 130).

Post Office: Trinity St. (☎08457 223 344). **Bureau de change.** Open M-Th 8:30am-5:30pm, F 9am-5:30pm, Sa 9am-4pm. **Postcode:** DT1 1DH.

◤ 🏠 ACCOMMODATIONS AND CAMPING

The White House, 9 Queens Ave. (☎01305 266 714), off Weymouth Ave. 2 gorgeous rooms in a residential neighborhood. From the train station, exit left onto Station Approach and turn left onto Weymouth Ave.; Queen's Ave. is a few blocks up, past Lime Close. Breakfast included. Singles £33; doubles £50. Cash only. ❸

YHA Litton Cheney (☎01308 482 340), 10 mi. west of the city. Take bus #31 to White-way and follow the signs for 1 mi. Reception 8-10am and 5-10pm. Lockout 10am-5pm. Curfew 11pm. Open Apr.-Aug. Dorms from £14, under 18 £10.50. MC/V. ❷

YHA Portland (☎0870 770 6000), just outside of Weymouth. From Dorchester, take bus #10 to Weymouth (20min., every 10min.), then bus #1 toward Portland (15min., every 7-8min.). Get off at Victoria Sq. and follow signs up the hill to the hostel. Reception 8-10am and 5-10pm. Open Mar.-Oct. Dorms £19-21, under 18 £14-16. ❷

Giant's Head Caravan and Camping Park, Old Sherborne Rd. (☎01300 341 242; www.giantshead.co.uk), in Cerne Abbas, 8 mi. north of Dorchester. If you're driving, head out of town on The Grove and bear right onto Old Sherborne Rd. For bus travel, take the #216 from Dorchester to Cerne Village and take the road to Buckland Newton. Elecricity, showers, and laundry. Open Apr.-Sept. Tent, car, and 2 adults £7-12. Cash only. ❶

◣ 🍴 FOOD AND PUBS

Get your groceries at the weekly **Dorchester Market,** in the car park near South Station (open W 8am-3pm), or at **Waitrose,** in the Tudor Arcade, off South St. (☎01305 268 420. Open M-W and Sa 8:30am-7pm, Th-F 8:30am-8pm, Su 10am-4pm.) A range of eateries lines **High West Street** and **High East Street.**

No. 6 North Square (☎01305 267 679; www.no6northsquare.co.uk), off High St. near the town hall. Fresh Dorset seafood. Lunch £4.25-8; dinner entrees £10.50-16. Open M-Th 11am-3pm and 6-11pm, F-Sa 11am-3pm and 6pm-midnight. MC/V. ❸

The Celtic Kitchen, 17 Antelope Walk (☎01305 269 377), near the TIC. Delicious Cornish pasties for £1.30-2.30. Open M-Sa 9:30am-5:30pm. Cash only. ❶

THE HIDDEN DEAL

FOSSILS FOR FREE

Antiques can cost a pretty penny, but one British collectible can be obtained absolutely free of charge: fossils. The beaches surrounding Lyme Regis are littered with specimens from 65 to 200 million years ago. How can Wedgwood china compete with a perfectly preserved prehistoric fish?

The best way to make a fossil find is to join an expert-led tour. Steve Davies, owner of Dinosaurland Fossil Museum, has decades of experience, degrees in geology and micropaleontology, and the fossils to prove it. Steve conducts 2hr. fossil-hunting excursions at Black Ven, the mudflow 1 mi. east of Lyme in which Mary Anning discovered her famous *Ichthyosaurus* in 1811. Due to the erosion of the cliffs, a new crop of fossils arises every day, virtually guaranteeing a geological discovery.

The most common fossil finds are belemnites (squid-like mollusks) and ammonites (beautiful spiral-shaped cephalopods). The fossils often striate the soft, sandy rock into interesting shapes. Some fossils are preserved in iron pyrite, or fool's gold, which gives them a lustrous apearance. Other common fossils include oysters, snails, fish, and even Ichthyosauri.

For tour times, contact Dinosaurland Fossil Museum, Coombe St., Lyme Regis (☎01297 443 541) or consult the chalkboard outside the museum doors.

Potters Cafe Bistro, 19 Durngate St. (☎01305 260 312), off South St. Dishes made with local and organic products. Lunch £5.25-7.25. Open M-F 10am-4pm, Sa 9:30am-4pm, Su 11am-3pm. MC/V over £15. ❷

Spice Centre, 37-38 High W. St. (☎01305 267 850). An extensive menu including curries for £4.20-7.50. Takeaway discount 10%. Open M-Th and Su noon-2:30pm and 6-11:30pm, F-Sa noon-2:30pm and 6pm-midnight. MC/V. ❸

The George (☎01305 268 821), at the bottom of Trinity St. DJs and live bands F-Sa. Open M-W 11am-11pm, Th-Sa 11am-2am, Su noon-11pm. ❶

Bar Rouge, 33 Trinity St. (☎01305 263 404). Black and red leather couches. DJs Th and Sa. Happy hour 5-7pm. Open M-W 5-11:30pm, Th-F 5pm-2am, Sa noon-2am. ❶

👁 SIGHTS

Dorchester is quaint, but its attractions can fill a day. East of town, Hardy-related sites hint at the poet-novelist's inspiration for Wessex, a fictional region based on Dorset. West of town, remnants of Iron Age and Roman Britain appear. Hardy designed **Max Gate,** 1 mi. southwest of town off Arlington Rd., and lived there from 1885 until his death in 1928, penning *Tess of the D'Urbervilles* and *Jude the Obscure.* (☎01305 262 538. Open Apr.-Sept. M, W, Su 2-5pm. £3, children £1.50.) He was christened in **Stinsford Church,** 2 mi. northeast of town in Stinsford Village. The yard holds the family plot where his first and second wives are buried, although only his heart is buried here—his ashes lie in Westminster Abbey (p. 116). Take bus #184 from Trinity St. toward Puddletown; ask to be dropped off near the church. (Free.) Finally, he was born in **Hardy's Cottage,** Bockhampton Ln., deep in the woods 3 mi. northeast of Dorchester. Take bus #184 or 185 and ask to be let off at the cottage. (☎01305 262 366. Open Apr.-Oct. M-Th and Su 11am-5pm. £3.50.) Finish your literary tour at the Hardy **memorial statue,** located at the "Top o' Town."

The **Dorset County Museum,** 66 High W. St., has a replica of Hardy's study and relics of the city's other keepers—druids, Romans, and Saxons. (☎01305 262 735; www.dorsetcountymuseum.org. Open July-Sept. daily 10am-5pm; Oct.-June M-Sa 10am-5pm. £6.50, concessions £4.50. Audio tour free.) On the other side of town is **Maiden Castle,** the largest Iron Age fortification in Europe, dating to 3000 BC. Modern visitors can scale what little is left of the ramparts, today patrolled by sheep. Take shuttle #2 (M-Sa 5 per day) to Maiden Castle Rd., three-quarters of a mile from the hill. If weather permits, opt to hike the scenic 2 mi. from the town center down Maiden Castle Rd. Closer to town is the first-century **Roman Town House,** at the back of the County Hall complex. Glass walls complete the remains of the house and allow visitors to view the mosaic floors inside. Just past the South Station entrance sprawls the **Maumbury Rings,** a monument dating from the Bronze Age.

▶ DAYTRIPS FROM DORCHESTER

LYME REGIS. Known as the "Pearl of Dorset," Lyme Regis (pop. 3500) surveys a majestic coastline. In 1811, a resident shopkeeper named Mary Anning discovered the first *Ichthyosaurus* fossil 1 mi. west of Lyme Regis. Since then, the town has thrived on its prehistoric past, even forming the streetlights into a spiral shell shape. Paleontologist Steve Davies has amassed an immense collection of local fossils, artfully displayed in the **Dinosaurland Fossil Museum,** Coombe St. (☎01297 443 541; www.dinosaurland.co.uk. Open daily 10am-5pm. £4.50, students £3.50, families £14.) The museum has 200-million-year-old shells and a 100-million-year-old lobster fossil. Davies leads a 2hr. **dinosaur hunting walk** (£6); contact Dinosaurland for times, which depend on the tides. Lyme Regis is also renowned for the **Cobb,** a 10-20 ft. manmade seawall that cradles the harbor. The **Marine Aquarium** on the Cobb exhibits a small collection of local sea creatures, including a 5 ft. conger eel. (☎01297 444 230; www.lymeregis-marineaquarium.co.uk. Open Mar.-Oct. daily 10am-5pm. £4, children £3.50.) The **Lyme Regis Museum,** Bridge St., chronicles Lyme's history. (☎01297 443 370; www.lymeregismuseum.co.uk. Open Apr.-Oct. M-Sa 10am-5pm, Su 11am-5pm; Nov.-Apr. Sa 10am-5pm, Su 11am-5pm. £3, concessions £2.50.) The TIC, Guildhall Cottage, Church St., downhill from the bus stop, locates lodgings and stocks walking guides. (*☎01297 442 138; www.westdorset.com. Open Apr.-Oct. M-Sa 10am-5pm, Su 10am-4pm; Nov.-Mar. M-Sa 10am-3pm. To get to Lyme Regis from Dorchester, take First (☎01305 783 645) bus #31 from South Station 1hr., every hr., £6.)*

SOMERSET

BATH   ☎(0)1225

The world's original tourist town, Bath has been a must-see since AD 43, when the Romans built an elaborate complex of baths to house the curative waters of the town they called *Aquae Sulis.* In the 18th and 19th centuries, Bath became a social capital second only to London, immortalized by Jane Austen and others. Today, hordes of tourists and backpackers admire the Georgian architecture by day and continue to create scandal by night.

▌ TRANSPORTATION

Trains: Bath Spa Station, Dorchester St., at the south end of Manvers St. Ticket office open M-F 5:30am-8:30pm, Sa 6am-8:30pm, Su 7:30am-8:30pm. Trains (☎08457 484 950) to: **Birmingham** (2hr., 2 per hr., £36); **Bristol** (15min., every 10-15min., £5.50-6); **Exeter** (1½-2hr., 2 per hr., £25); **London Paddington** (1hr., 2 per hr., £47-66.50); **London Waterloo** (2hr., every hr., £28.20); **Plymouth** (2½-3½hr., every hr., £42-48.30); **Salisbury** (1hr., every hr., £13).

Buses: All buses depart from the **Bath Bus Station,** Churchill Bridge. Ticket office open M-Sa 8am-5:30pm. National Express (☎08717 818 181) to **London** (3hr., every hr., £17.50) and **Oxford** (2hr., 1 per day, £9.50). First (☎0871 200 2233) bus #X39 runs

SOUTHWEST ENGLAND

to **Bristol** (M-Sa every 12min. 6am-7pm, £4.25). Badgerline sells a **Day Explorer** ticket, good for 1 day of unlimited bus travel in the region (£6.30-7).

Taxis: Abbey Radio (☎01224 444 444). **V Cars** (☎01225 464 646).

🚹 PRACTICAL INFORMATION

The **Roman Baths**, the **Pump Room**, and **Bath Abbey** cluster in the city center, bounded by York and Cheap St. The River Avon flows just east of them and wraps around the south part of town near the train and bus stations. Uphill to the northwest, historic buildings lie on **Royal Crescent** and **The Circus**.

Tourist Information Centre: Abbey Chambers (☎09067 112 000; www.visitbath.co.uk). Town map and mini-guide £1. Books rooms for £3 plus a 10% deposit. Open June-Sept. M-Sa 9:30am-6pm, Su 10am-4pm; Oct.-May M-Sa 9:30am-5pm, Su 10am-4pm.

Tours: Several companies run tours of the city and surrounding sights.

Bizarre Bath (☎01225 335 124; www.bizarrebath.co.uk). The guides impart few historical facts on this comedic walk, but their tricks (including a bunny escape) prove entertaining. 1hr. tours begin at the Huntsman Inn at N. Parade Passage. Daily tours Apr.-Sept. 8pm. £8, concessions £5.

Ghost Walk (☎01225 350 512; www.ghostwalksofbath.co.uk). Tours leave the Nash Bar of Garrick's Head, near Theatre Royal. 2hr. tours Apr.-Oct. M-Sa 8pm; Nov.-Mar. F 8pm. £6, concessions £5.

Mad Max Tours (☎01225 505 970; www.madmaxtours.com). Tours begin at the abbey and go to Stonehenge, Avebury, Castle Combe in the Cotswolds, and Lacock National Trust Village (where classroom scenes in *Harry Potter* films were shot). Full-day tours depart daily 8:45am, ½-day tours depart daily 1:15pm. ½-day £15, full-day £27.50. Entrance to Stonehenge not included.

Bank: Barclays, Milsom St. (☎08457 555 555). Open M-F 9am-5pm, Sa 9am-3pm.

Library: Central Library, Podium Shopping Centre (☎01225 394 041). Free Internet. Open M 9:30am-6pm, Tu-Th 9:30am-7pm, F-Sa 9:30am-5pm, Su 1-4pm.

Launderette: Spruce Goose, Margaret's Bldg., off Brock St. (☎01225 483 309). Open M-F and Su 8am-9pm, Sa 8am-8pm. Last wash 1hr. before close.

Police: Manvers St. (☎0845 456 7000), near the train and bus stations.

Pharmacy: Boots, 33-35 Westgate St. (☎01225 482 069). Open M-Sa 8:30am-6pm, Su 10:30am-4:30pm. **Internet Access:** Free at the **library** (above). **@ Internet,** 13A Manvers St. (☎01225 443 181). £1 per 20min. Open daily 9am-10pm.

Hospital: Royal United, Coombe Park (☎01225 428 331), in Weston. Take bus #14.

Post Office: 27 Northgate St. (☎08457 223 344), across from the Podium Shopping Centre. Open M and W-Sa 9am-5:30pm, Tu 9:30am-5:30pm. **Postcode:** BA1 1AJ.

🏠 ACCOMMODATIONS

Well-to-do visitors drive up prices in Bath, but the city's location and sights bring in enough backpackers and passing travelers to sustain several budget accommodations. B&Bs cluster on **Pulteney Road** and **Pulteney Gardens. Marlborough Lane** and **Upper Bristol Road,** west of the city center, also have options.

YMCA, International House, Broad St. Pl. (☎01225 325 900; www.bathymca.co.uk). Up the stairs from High and Walcot St. Bright, clean, colorful dorms. Spacious rooms overlooking a courtyard garden. Continental breakfast included. Internet 50p per 15min. Free Wi-Fi. Dorms £14-16; singles £26-30; triples £54-60; quads £64-72. MC/V. ❷

Bath Backpackers, 13 Pierrepont St. (☎01225 446 787; www.hostels.co.uk). Laid-back backpacker's lair with music-themed dorms. Hang out in the lounge with a big-screen TV or have a drink in the "Dungeon." Bathrooms may be less than shining and beds a bit creakier than at home, but still a solid budget option. Self-catering kitchen. Luggage storage £2 per bag. Internet access £2 per hr. Reception 8am-11pm. 10-bed dorms £13-15; 8-bed £14-16; 4-bed £16-18. MC/V. ❷

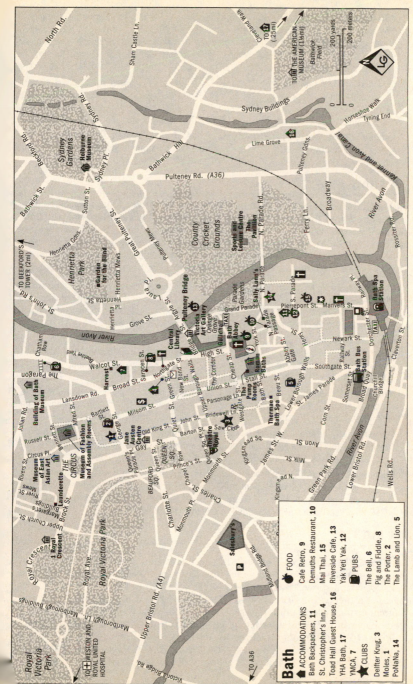

Bath

▲ ACCOMMODATIONS
Bath Backpackers, 11
St. Christopher's Inn, 4
Toad Hall Guest House, 16
YHA Bath, 17
YMCA, 7

★ CLUBS
Deltfer Krug, 3
Moles, 1
PoNaNa, 14

● FOOD
Cafe Retro, 9
Demuths Restaurant, 10
Mai Thai, 15
Riverside Cafe, 13
Yak Yeti Yak, 12

🍺 PUBS
The Bell, 6
Pig and Fiddle, 8
The Porter, 2
The Lamb and Lion, 5

YHA Bath, Bathwick Hill (☎01225 465 674). From N. Parade Rd., turn left on Pulteney Rd., swing right on Bathwick Hill, and climb the hill (40min.) or take bus #18 or 418 (every 20min.). Beautiful secluded Italianate mansion. Spacious facility frequented mostly by families and school groups. Kitchen. Internet £1 per 15min. Reception 7am-11pm. Dorms £12-18, under 18 £10.50; private rooms £21-124. MC/V. ❷

St. Christopher's Inn, 16 Green St. (☎01225 481 444; www.st-christophers.co.uk). Downstairs bar an ideal hangout area for young crowd. Simple and clean bunks, but not a lot of space to do much else but sleep. Free luggage storage. Internet access £1 per 20min. Free Wi-Fi at the bar. Dorms £16-23.50. Online booking discounts. MC/V. ❷

Toad Hall Guest House, 6 Lime Grove (☎01225 423 254). Turn left off Pulteney Rd. after going under the overpass. Peaceful green carpet and pink rooms inspired by *The Wind in the Willows*. Hearty breakfast included. Singles £30; doubles £50. Cash only. ❸

FOOD

Although the restaurants in Bath tend to be expensive, reasonably priced eateries can be found throughout the city. For fruits and vegetables, visit the **Bath Guildhall Market.** (☎01225 477 945. Open M-Sa 9am-5:30pm.) Delicious vegetarian food can be found at **Harvest,** 37 Walcot St., an inexpensive organic grocery with local produce and takeaway food. (☎01225 465 519; www.harvest-bath.coop. Sandwiches £2. Open M-Sa 9am-6pm, Tu 10am-6pm. MC/V.)

Cafe Retro, 18 York St. (☎01225 339 347). Mismatched chairs and wood floors give this cafe-bar a simultaneously hip and Old World feel. 2 floors and plenty of space to enjoy your sandwich (£4.60-6.15) or entree (£5.20-7). Breakfast served all day. Open M-W 9am-5pm, Th-Sa 9am-8pm, Su 10am-5pm. AmEx/MC/V. ❶

Riverside Cafe, below Pulteney Bridge (☎01225 480 532; www.riversidecafebar.co.uk). Light dishes and coffee in a sheltered enclave overlooking the River Avon. If you can't get a table outside, take your food to the nearby park. Sandwiches and soups £5-6.20. Open M-Sa 9am-9pm, Su 9am-5pm. MC/V. ❶

Mai Thai, 6 Pierrepont St. (☎01225 445 557). Huge portions of Thai food at affordable prices. Ornate tables and authentic decorations make the atmosphere as rich as the food. Entrees £5-7.25. Open daily noon-2pm and 6-10:30pm. AmEx/MC/V. ❷

Yak Yeti Yak, Pierrepont St. (☎01225 443 473; www.yakyetiyak.co.uk). Dine on floor cushions at this colorful Nepalese restaurant. Spices ground in-house. Set menu £9.50-11.50. Open M-Sa 10am-10:30pm, Su 11am-10pm. AmEx/MC/V. ❸

Demuths Restaurant, 2 N. Parade Passage (☎01225 446 059; www.demuths.co.uk), off Abbey Green. Exotic vegetarian and vegan dishes (£11-12) served in a small, purple-tinted dining room. Open M-F and Su 10am-5pm and 6-10pm, Sa 9am-5pm and 6-10pm. Reservations recommended in summer. MC/V. ❷

SIGHTS

ROMAN BATHS. In 1880, sewer diggers uncovered an extravagant feat of Roman engineering. For 400 years, the Romans harnessed Bath's bubbling springs, which spew 264,000 gallons of 115°F (47°C) water every day. The city became a mecca for Britain's elite. The **museum** has displays on excavated Roman artifacts and building design. It's also the only way to get up close and personal with the ancient baths. Make sure to see the Roman curses (politely referred to as offerings to Minerva), wishing eternal damnation upon rival neighbors. Audio tours are a must. (*Stall St.* ☎*01225 477 785; www.romanbaths.co.uk. Open daily July-Aug. 9am-10pm; Sept.-Oct. and Mar.-June 9am-6pm; Nov.-Feb. 9am-5:30pm. Last* *entry 1hr. before close. Guided tours every hr. £10.50, concessions £9, children £6.80, families £30. Joint ticket with Museum of Fashion £14/12/8.30/38.)*

BATH ABBEY. Occupying the site where King Edgar was crowned the first king of England in AD 973, the 140 ft. abbey stands in the city center. Bishop Oliver King commissioned the abbey to replace a Norman cathedral, and the crowned olive tree on the ceiling symbolizes the message he heard from God: "let an Olive establish the Crown and a King restore the Church." A stunning stained-glass window contains 56 scenes from the life of Christ. Also note the church's extraordinarily high number of memorial plaques. The underlying **Heritage Vaults** contain an exhibit on the abbey's uses through the ages. *(Next to the Baths. ☎01225 422 462; www.bathabbey.org. Open M-Sa 9am-6pm, Su 1-2:30pm and 4:30-5:30pm. Suggested donation £2.50. Heritage Vaults open daily 10am-4pm.)*

MUSEUM OF FASHION AND ASSEMBLY ROOMS. The museum hosts a dazzling parade of 400 years of catwalk fashions, from 17th-century silver tissue garments to Jennifer Lopez's racy Versace jungle-print ensemble. Thematic displays show how fashion has changed through the years in everything from pockets to gloves, and interactive displays let visitors try on a corset and hoop skirt for a feel of how the Victorians felt. *(Bennett St. ☎01225 477 785; www.fashion-museum.co.uk. Open daily Mar.-Oct. 10:30am-6pm; Nov.-Feb. 10:30am-5pm. Last entry 1hr. before close. £7, concessions £6, children £5, families £20. Joint ticket with baths £14/12/8.30/38.)* The museum is in the basement of the Assembly Rooms, which once held *fin de siècle* balls and concerts. Bombing during WWII ravaged the rooms, but a renovation has duplicated the originals. *(☎01225 477 785. Open daily Mar.-Oct. 10:30am-6pm; Nov.-Feb. 10:30am-5pm. Sometimes closed for private functions. Free.)*

OTHER MUSEUMS AND GALLERIES. Next to Pulteney Bridge, the **Victoria Art Gallery,** Bridge St., holds a collection of paintings from the mid-18th century to today. It houses Thomas Barker's *The Bride of Death*—Victorian melodrama at its sappiest. Rotating exhibits take place on the ground floor. *(☎01225 477 233; www.victoriagal.org.uk. Open Tu-Sa 10am-5pm, Su 1:30-5pm. Free.)* The **Jane Austen Centre** depicts Austen's time in Bath, where she visited her family and lived briefly. Ironically, she disliked living in Bath and wrote nothing while living here, but she frequently wrote about the city in her novels—most notably in *Persuasion* and *Northanger Abbey.* Tours of Bath sights mentioned in Austen's books and her family's homes are also available. *(40 Gay St. ☎01225 443 000; www.janeausten.co.uk. Open July-Aug. M-W 9:45am-5:30pm, Th-Su 9:45am-7:30pm; Nov.-Mar. M-F and Su 11am-4:30pm, Sa 9:45am-5:30pm. Last entry 1hr. before close. Tours Sa-Su 11am. Talks every 30min. £6.50, concessions £5. Tours £5, concessions £4.)* Architecture buffs will enjoy the **Building of Bath Museum,** which explains the extensive planning of Bath as well as the history of the city's famous Gregorian buildings. Check out the model of the city—it took 10,000hr. to perfect its 500:1 scale layout. *(Countess of Huntingdon's Chapel, the Paragon. ☎01225 333 895; www.bath-preservation-trust.org.uk. Open from mid-Feb. to Nov. Tu-Sa 10:30am-5pm. £4, concessions £3.50.)* The **American Museum,** Claverton Manor, has enough colonial relics to make any Yank feel at home. *(☎01225 460 503; www.americanmuseum.org. Open from mid-Mar to Oct. Tu-Su 2-5:30pm. Last entry 5pm. Gardens and tearoom open Tu-Su noon-5:30pm. £7.50, concessions £6.50. Grounds £5/4/3.)*

HISTORIC BUILDINGS. The city's oldest house in Bath is **Sally Lunn's,** 4 N. Parade Passage, built on the sight of an old monastery. You can check out the ancient "faggot" oven used to bake her world-famous buns and buy a giant bun to take home. *(Buns £1.50. Open M-Sa 10am-6pm, Su 11am-6pm. 30p, students and children free.)* In the city's residential northwest corner are the **Georgian row houses,** built by famed architects John Wood the Elder and John Wood the Younger. One of the houses, **The Circus,** which has the same circumference as Stonehenge, has attracted illustrious inhabitants for two centuries; former residents include Thomas Gainsborough and William Pitt. Proceed up Brock St. to the **Royal Crescent,** a half-moon of 18th-century townhouses. The interior of **1 Royal Crescent** has been restored to the way it was in 1770, down to the last butter knife. *(☎01225 428 126. Open from mid-Feb. to Oct. Tu-Su 10:30am-5pm; Nov. Tu-Su 10:30am-4pm. Last entry 30min. before close. £5, concessions £4, children £2.50, families £12.)* For stupendous views, climb the 154 steps of **Beckford's Tower,** Lansdown Rd., 2 mi. north of town. Take bus #2 or 702 to Ensleigh; otherwise, it's a 45min. walk. *(☎01225 460 705. Open Easter-Oct. Sa-Su 10:30am-5pm. £3, concessions £2, children £1.50, families £8.)*

GARDENS AND PARKS. Consult a map or the TIC's *Borders, Beds, and Shrubberies* brochure to find the city's many stretches of cultivated green. High in the hills above above Bath, the 🏞**Bathwick field** offered such stunning views of the city and surrounding area that it was made into National Trust land. Now, it's the perfect place to escape for a picnic, away from the touristy city center. *(15min. walk up Bathwick Hill, across the river.)* Next to the Royal Crescent, **Royal Victoria Park** contains rare trees and an aviary. *(Always open. Free.)* **Henrietta Park,** laid in 1897 to celebrate Queen Victoria's Diamond Jubilee, was redesigned as a garden for the blind—only the most fragrant plants were chosen for its grounds. The **Parade Gardens,** at the base of N. Parade Bridge, won the Britain in Bloom competition so often that they were asked not to enter again. *(☎01225 391 041. Open daily 10am-7pm. Apr.-Sept. £1; Oct.-Mar. free.)*

🎵 🎭 ENTERTAINMENT AND FESTIVALS

In summer, buskers (street musicians) fill the streets with music, and a brass band often graces the Parade Gardens. The magnificent **Theatre Royal,** Saw Close, at the south end of Barton St., showcases opera and theater. *(☎01225 448 844; www.theatreroyal.org.uk. Box office open M-Sa 10am-8pm, Su noon-8pm. Tickets £15-30.)* The **Little Theatre Cinema,** St. Michael's Pl., Bath St., is Bath's local art-house cinema. *(☎0871 704 2061. Tickets £6.20-7, concessions £5-5.70. Box office open daily 1-8pm.)*

Bath hosts several festivals; for information or reservations, call the Bath Festivals Box Office, 2 Church St., Abbey Green. *(☎01225 463 362; www.bathfestivals.org.uk. Open M-Sa 9:30am-5:30pm.)* The **Bath International Music Festival** (typically May-June; check www.bathmusicfest.org.uk for updates) features world-class symphony orchestras, choruses, and jazz bands. The overlapping **Fringe Festival** *(☎01225 480 079; www.bathfringearts.co.uk)* celebrates the arts with over 200 live performances (May-June annually). The **Jane Austen Festival,** at the end of September, features Austen-themed walks, meals, and movies (contact the Jane Austen Centre; see **Sights,** previous page). The **Literature Festival** is held in March, the **Balloon Fiesta** in mid-May, and the **Film Festival** in late October. Pick up the weekly *Venue* (£1.30), available at bookstores.

🍸 🍹 PUBS AND CLUBS

Tourists and two universities keep this small town full of nightlife. Most pubs close around 11pm, and late-night clubs almost always charge a cover.

The Porter, 15 George St. *(☎01225 424 104; www.theporter.co.uk).* This offbeat pub offers a completely vegetarian/vegan menu and free live music M-Th nights in the basement. Pictures of artists who have performed there grace the walls, including such popular bands as The Killers. DJs F-Sa. Comedy Su 7pm (£7, students £5). Open M-Th 11am-midnight, F-Sa 11am-1am, Su 11am-11:30pm. Kitchen open daily until 9pm.

Pig and Fiddle, 2 Saracen St. *(☎01775 460 868),* off Broad St. The 1st stop for many pub crawlers. The cozy interior and huge heated patio are always full of backpackers enjoying cider and local ales. Open-mike nights Tu. Movie nights Su 8pm. Open M-Sa 11am-11:30pm, Su noon-10:30pm. Kitchen open M-F 11am-7pm, Sa-Su noon-6pm.

The Lamb and Lion, 15 Lower Borough Walls (☎01225 334 617). Cheap pints and grub make this a popular pre-club pub with students and locals on the weekends. Beer garden out back is fabulous in the summer, as is the perfectly crafted fruit-filled Pimm's. Open M-W 10am-11pm, Th-Sa 10am-12:30pm, Su noon-10:30pm. Kitchen open M-Sa 11am-8pm, Su noon-8pm. MC/V.

Moles, 14 George St. (☎01225 404 445; www.moles.co.uk). Pounds out soul, funk, and house in an underground setting. Up-and-coming live bands M and Th. Dance club night Tu and F-Sa. Cover £3-8. Open M-Th 9pm-2am, F-Sa 9pm-4am, Su 8pm-12:30am.

The Bell, 103 Walcot St. (☎01225 460 426; www.walcotstreet.com). Challenges its clientele to talk over (or sing along with) the live folk, jazz, blues, funk, salsa, and reggae playing most nights. Pizza served in the garden on weekend evenings. Free Wi-Fi. Live music M and W evenings, Su lunch. Open M-Sa 11:30am-11pm, Su noon-10:30pm.

Delfter Krug, Saw Close (☎01225 443 352; www.delfterkrug.com). Draws a large weekend crowd with its outdoor seating and lively 2-story club. Comfy couches offer a break from the crowded dance floor. Jams hip hop and pop with drink specials almost every night. Drum and bass alternate Th. Cover £2-10. Open M-Sa noon-2am, Su noon-7pm.

PoNaNa, N. Parade and Pierrepont St. (☎01225 424 592; www.ponana.com/bath). Descend the staircase into a subterranean lair to find hot beats and sweaty dancers. Drum and bass W. "Squeeze the Cheese" F. Cover £3-5. Open M and W 9:30pm-2am, Tu and Th 10pm-2am, F-Sa 10:30pm-2:30am.

GLASTONBURY ☎(0)1458

The reputed birthplace of Christianity in England and an Arthurian hot spot, Glastonbury is a quirky intersection of mysticism and pop culture. According to legend, King Arthur, Jesus, Joseph of Arimathea, and St. Augustine all came here. The town's appeal continues today as huge crowds return every year for England's biggest music festival. Glastonbury's shops do their part to perpetuate a mystical vibe, peddling trinkets and "healing" crystals.

TRANSPORTATION. Glastonbury has no train station; **buses** stop at the town hall in the town center. Consult the *Public Transport Timetable for the Mendip Area,* free at TICs, for schedules. First (☎08706 082 608, fare info 08456 064 446) buses run to Bristol (#375 or 376, 1hr., £5.10) via Wells. Travel to Yeovil (#376; 1hr.; M-Sa every hr., Su every 2hr.) to connect to destinations in the south, including Lyme Regis and Dorchester. Travel a full day on all buses with the **Explorer Pass** (£6, concessions £5, families £15).

ORIENTATION AND PRACTICAL INFORMATION. Glastonbury is 6 mi. southwest of Wells on the A39 and 22 mi. northeast of Taunton on the A361. The town is bounded by **High Street** in the north, **Bere Lane** in the south, **Magdalene Street** in the west, and **Wells Road/Chilkwell Street** in the east. Most shops line High St. and Magdelene St. The **Tourist Information Centre,** The Tribunal, 9 High St., books rooms for £3 plus a 10% deposit and has an accommodations book (£1.50); after hours, find the B&B list behind the building in St. John's car park. (☎01458 832 954; www.glastonburytic.co.uk. Open Apr.-Sept. M-Th and Su 10am-5pm, F-Sa 10am-5:30pm; Oct.-Mar. M-Th 10am-4pm, F-Sa 10am-4:30pm.) Other services include: **Barclays** bank, 21-23 High St. (☎08457 555 555; open M-F 9:30am-4:30pm); **Internet** access at the **library,** 1 Orchard Ct., The Archer's Way, left off High St. as you head up the hill (☎01458 832 148; free for 1hr.; photo ID required; open M-F 10am-5pm, Tu and Th 10am-6pm, Sa 10am-4pm);

police, 1 West End (☎01823 337 911); **Boots** pharmacy, 39 High St. (☎01458 831 211; open M-F 9am-6pm, Sa 9am-5:30pm); and the **post office,** 35 High St. (☎08457 223 344; open M-F 9am-5:30pm, Sa 9am-1pm). **Postcode:** BA6 9HG.

⌐ ACCOMMODATIONS. Glastonbury offers expensive, luxurious B&Bs—don't be surprised if your accommodation also offers "healing treatments" and meditation. Buses stop by **Glastonbury Backpackers ❶,** 4 Market Pl., at the corner of Magdalene and High St. The bright blue building houses a popular pub and a small cafe with terrific coffee. (☎01458 833 353; www.glastonburybackpackers.com. Kitchen. Internet access until 6pm £1 per 20min. Free Wi-Fi at the pub downstairs. Reception open until 11pm. Dorms £14-16; twins £35-45; ensuite double £40-50. MC/V.) Off Chickwell on the way to the tor, **Shekinashram ❷,** Dod Ln., is a serene B&B and retreat center. A wide range of rooms, from a secluded yurt to a king-size suite, all include an organic breakfast and morning meditation. (☎01458 832 300; www.shekinashram.org. Kitchen. Use of the sauna £4. Curfew 10pm. Cabin dorms £19; singles £29; doubles £50; triples £75. Single in yurt £27; double in yurt £45. MC/V.) The nearest YHA hostel is the **YHA Street ❶,** Higher Brooks Rd., off the B3151 in the town of Street. On public transportation, take bus #20, 375, or 376 to Street, turn onto Gooselade Rd., and follow the footpath on the right; the hostel will be signposted at the end of the path. The hostel overlooks the tor. (☎01458 442 961. Kitchen. Reception 8:30-10am and 5-9pm. Lockout 10am-5pm. Open July-Aug. daily; Sept.-Apr. call 48hr. in advance; May-June Tu-Su. Dorms £14, under 18 £10.50. MC/V.)

⌐⌐ FOOD AND PUBS. A **farmers' market** takes place behind the TIC on the last Saturday of the month. **Heritage Fine Foods,** 32-34 High St., stocks groceries. (☎01458 831 003. Open M-Th 7am-9pm, F-Sa 7am-10pm, Su 8am-9pm.) Find yummy muffins (80p) and sandwiches (£1.25-3) at **Burns the Bread ❶,** 14 High St. (☎01458 831 532. Open M-Sa 6am-5pm, Su 11am-4pm. Cash only.) The vegetarian menu at **Rainbow's End ❶,** 17A High St., changes with the chef's whims. Soups, salads, and quiches run £3.25-3.65. (☎01458 833 896. Open daily 10am-4pm. Cash only.) Carnivores should head to **Gigi's ❸,** 2-4 Magdalene St., for Italian dishes and sizable portions. (☎01458 834 612. Entrees £6.30-17. Open Tu-Th 6-10:45pm, F 6-11pm, Sa-Su noon-2:30pm and 6-11pm. MC/V.)

◢ SIGHTS. Legend holds that Joseph of Arimathea, the Virgin Mary's uncle, traveled with the young Jesus to do business in modern-day Somerset. Joseph later returned in AD 63 and founded a simple church that would later become the massive **▨Glastonbury Abbey,** on Magdelene St. Although the abbey was destroyed during the English Reformation, the colossal pile of ruins that remains still evokes the grandeur of the original church. After a fire damaged the abbey in 1184, the monks needed to raise some cash. Fortunately, they "found" King Arthur's grave on the south side of Lady Chapel in AD 1191 and reburied the bones here, inviting the king and queen—and the royal treasurer—to attend the ceremony. A metal chain surrounds the anticlimactic **Tomb of Arthur and Guinevere,** in the center of the pillars. Near the entrance to the abbey, the **Holy Glastonbury Thorn** blooms every Christmas and Easter. The original thorn, on **Wearyall Hill** southeast of town, is said to have miraculously sprouted when Joseph of Arimathea drove his staff into the ground. The **Lady Chapel, Abbot's Kitchen,** and **museum** recreate the history of the sacred ground. (☎01458 832 267; www.glastonburyabbey.com. Open daily June-Aug. 9am-6pm; Sept. and Apr.-May 9:30am-6pm; Oct. 9:30am-5pm; Nov. 9:30am-4:30pm; Dec.-Jan. 10am-4:30pm; Feb. 10am-5pm; Mar. 9:30am-5:30pm. £5, concessions £4.50.)

A place of pilgrimmage, **Saint Michael's Tower** stands at the top of the 526 ft. **Glastonbury Tor.** A steep 15min. hike yields 360° views as far as Bristol—a reward worth the climb. To reach the tor, turn right at the top of High St. on Lambrook, which becomes Chilkwell St.; turn left at Wellhouse Ln. and follow the footpath uphill. Excavations have revealed a pre-Christian settlement on the hill, thought to have been an Arthurian fort. The tor's crowning feature is a 14th-century bell tower, guarded by cows who have deftly marked their territory—keep one eye on the ground. In summer, the **Glastonbury Tor Bus** takes weary pilgrims from the city center (St. Dunstan's car park, next to the abbey) to a shorter climb on the far side of the tor, returning to town via Chalice Well and the Rural Life Museum. (Always open. Free. Hop-on, hop-off bus Apr.-Sept. every 30min. 9:30am-7pm; Oct.-Mar. every 30min. 10am-3pm. £2.50.)

At the base of the tor on Chilkwell St., **Chalice Well** is said to be where Joseph of Arimathea washed the Holy Grail, the cup from which Jesus drank at the Last Supper. Legend once held that the well ran with Christ's blood. The red tint actually comes from rust deposits in the stream, but the revelation has not stopped modern-day mystics from making pilgrimages to wade in and drink the waters. Ancient believers interpreted the iron-red water's mingling with clear water from nearby **White Well** (which runs from a tap across the street) as a symbol of balance between the divine feminine and divine masculine. Regardless of whether you think that the well has holy properties, it's well worth a visit for the surrounding healing gardens, the perfect setting for reflection, meditation, or maybe just a picnic. (☎01458 831 154. Open daily Apr.-Oct. 10am-6pm; Nov.-Mar. 10am-4:30pm. Last entry 30min. before close. £3.25, children £1.60, seniors £2.70.)

🎆 **FESTIVALS.** One of Glastonbury's biggest celebrations occurs in early November during the **Guy Fawkes Night Carnival.** The city lights up with elaborate floats and parades for a day of Mardi Gras-like festivities. (1st Sa after November 5.) Glastonbury's greatest attraction is 5 mi. away in Pilton, the site of the annual 🎆**Glastonbury Festival,** undoubtedly the biggest and best of Britain's multitude of summer music festivals. Recent headliners include The Killers, The Who, the White Stripes, Coldplay, and Radiohead. The festival takes place at the end of June for three mud-covered and music-filled days. The festival office is at 28 Northload St. (☎01458 834 596; www.glastonburyfestivals.co.uk.)

WELLS ☎(0)1749

The main feature of Wells (pop. 10,000), named for the natural springs at its center, is undoubtedly its cathedral. Charming and self-consciously classy, this little town is lined with petite Tudor buildings and golden sandstone shops.

📠 TRANSPORTATION

Wells has no train station. **Buses** stop at the Princes Rd. Bus Park. (Ticket office open M-F 9am-5:30pm.) National Express (☎08717 818 181) buses go to London (3½hr., 1 per day, £19). First runs to: Bath (#173; 1¼hr.; M-Sa every hr., Su 7 per day; £5.20); Bridgewater (#375, 1½hr., every hr., £4.25) via Glastonbury (20min., every hr., £2.70); Bristol (#375 or 376, 1½hr., every hr., £5.20); Taunton (#29, 1hr., every hr.). **Day Explorer** passes (£6.20-7) grant unlimited transportation on all First buses. For a **taxi,** call Wookey Taxis (☎01749 678 039; 24hr.).

☀ 🛈 ORIENTATION AND PRACTICAL INFORMATION

Navigation in Wells is easy. The town's spring runs in a paved channel through the main streets. Follow the water upstream to the cathedral and the TIC and downstream to the bus station. The **Tourist Information Centre,** Market Pl., at the end of High St., books rooms for £3 plus a 10% deposit and has bus timetables. Exit left from the bus station and turn left onto Priory Rd., which becomes Broad St. and merges with High St. (☎01749 672 552. Open M-Sa 9:30am-5:30pm, Su 10am-4pm.) Other services include: **Barclays** bank, 9 Market Pl. (☎08457 555 555; open M-F 9:30am-4:30pm); free **Internet** access at the **library** (open M-Th 9:30am-5:30pm, F 9:30am-7pm, Sa 9:30am-4pm); **police,** 18 Glastonbury Rd. (☎0845 456 7000); **Boots** pharmacy, 19-21 High St. (☎01749 673 138; open M-Sa 9am-5:30pm); and the **post office,** Market Pl. (☎08457 223 344; open M and W-F 8:30am-5:30pm, Tu and Sa 9am-5:30pm). **Postcode:** BA5 2RA.

ACCOMMODATIONS AND FOOD

Most B&Bs only offer doubles, so making Wells a daytrip from Bristol or Bath may be a better option for solo travelers. At **17 Priory Road ❸,** across from the bus station, Mrs. Winter offers warm, spacious rooms with books lining the walls. (☎01749 677 300; www.smoothhound.co.uk/hotels/brian.html. Breakfast included. Singles £25-30; doubles £50. Cash only.) **Canon Grange ❹,** Cathedral Green, Sadler St., with the cathedral in its backyard, features rustic decor and a glass of sherry for each guest. Follow the directions to the TIC, but, from High St., turn left on Sadler. (☎01749 671 800. Rooms £52-68. MC/V.)

Wells is not exactly a wellspring of culinary talent. While food options tend more toward takeaway and ice-cream shops, a handful of quality restaurants can be found along Sadler St. near Cathedral Green. Assemble a picnic at the **market** on High St., in front of the Bishop's Palace (open W and Sa), or purchase groceries at **Tesco,** across from the bus station on Tucker St. (☎08456 779 710. Open M 8am-10pm, Tu-Sa 6am-10pm, Su 10am-4pm.) At **Good Earth ❶,** 4 Priory Rd., enjoy vegetarian soups (£2.60-3.60), quiches (£3.50), and homemade pizza (£3.50 per slice) on the backyard patio. (☎01749 678 600. Open M-Sa 9am-5pm. MC/V over £10.) **Goodfellows ❸,** 5 Sadler St., is a delicious patisserie and fish delicatessen. The lunch special (£10) includes any dish on the menu, a glass of wine, and a piece of cake. (☎01749 673 866. Patisserie open M-Tu 8:30am-5pm, W-Sa 8:30am-5pm and 6-10pm; restaurant open Tu-Sa noon-2pm and 6:30-9:30pm. MC/V.) A 16th-century city jail, the **City Arms ❸,** 69 High St., serves delicious meals, including a number of vegetarian options (entrees £7.50-9). At night, this is the town's most popular pub. (☎01749 673 916. Restaurant open M-Th 9am-9:30pm, F-Sa 9am-10pm, Su 9am-9pm. Bar open M-W 9am-11pm, Tu-Sa 9am-midnight, Su 11am-10pm. MC/V over £10.)

SIGHTS

WELLS CATHEDRAL. The 12th-century church at the center of town is also the center of a preserved cathedral complex, with a bishop's palace, vicar's close, and cavernous octagonal chapter house. The facade is one of England's best collections of medieval statues (293 figures). The grandeur and precision of medieval architecture is displayed in the 14th-century **scissor arches,** which prevent the tower from sinking. The church's **astronomical clock** (c. 1390) is the second-oldest working clock in the world. The **Wells Cathedral School Choir,** an institution as old as the building itself, sings services from September to April. (☎01749 674 483. Open daily Apr.-Sept. 7am-7pm; Oct.-Mar. 7am-6pm. Jousting every 15min. Free tours 10, 11am, 1, 2, 3pm. Evensong M-Sa 5:15pm, Su 3pm. Suggested donation £5.50.) Beside the cathedral, **Vicar's Close,** constructed to house the choir members, is Europe's oldest continuously inhabited street. Its houses date to 1363.

BISHOP'S PALACE. This palace has been the residence of the bishop of Bath and Wells for 800 years. Wood sculptures sit on the grounds, including *Adam and Eve*. **Saint Andrew's Well** offers beautiful views of the cathedral and benches for picnicking. On a calm day, you can even see the cathedral reflected in the glassy water. The mute swans in the moat pull a bell rope when they want to be fed—the first swans to learn lived here 150 years ago, and their descendants have continued to teach their young. Visitors can feed them brown bread—white makes them sick. *(Near the cathedral. ☎01749 678 691; www.bishopspalacewells. co.uk. Open Easter-Dec. M-F and Su 10:30am-6pm, Sa 10:30am-2pm. £5, concessions £4.)*

WELLS AND MENDIP MUSEUM. This tiny museum contains archaeological finds of the Mendip area and remnants of the cathedral's decor, including several statues found during renovations. Also on display are the milking pot, crystal ball, and bones of the "Witch of Wookey Hole," a woman who, after mysteriously losing her beauty, retreated to a cave and occasionally spooked the locals. *(8 Cathedral Green. ☎01749 673 477. Open Easter-Oct. M-Sa 11am-5pm, Su 11am-4pm; Nov.-Easter M and W-Su 11am-4pm. £3, children £1, families £6.)*

▶ DAYTRIPS FROM WELLS

CHEDDAR. A short journey from Wells, the town of Cheddar is laden with dairy products, cheesy attractions, and Neolithic goats. **Cheddar Gorge and Caves** is both a miracle of nature as well as a kitsch attraction. Carved by the River Yeo (YO), the gorge is perforated by the **Cheddar Showcaves,** limestone hollows extending deep into the earth. Colored lights and an audio tour guide you through **Gough's Cave,** which also houses a replica of **Cheddar Man,** a 9000-year-old skeleton (the original is now in the British Museum in London). More info on Cheddar Man can be found at the **Museum of Prehistory,** at the base of the gorge across from the TIC. Parental supervision is required for this over-the-top museum that explains everything from theories of evolution and our cannibalistic human ancestors to prehistoric sex and religion. **Caveman kama-sutra** isn't your thing? **Cox's Cave** provides a more subdued experience. Admission to the caves includes a ride on an **open-top bus,** which travels through the gorge and to the cave entrances in summer, and access to ◨**Jacob's Ladder,** a 274-step climb to a lookout. At the top, a 3 mi. **cliff-top gorge walk** has views that outstrip the sights below. No trip to a town called Cheddar would be complete without a taste of the good stuff. The ◨**Cheddar Gorge Cheese Company,** at the hill's base, features cheese-making and tasting. *(From Wells, take bus #126 (25min.; M-Sa every hr. at 40min. past the hr., Su 7 per day; round-trip £6.10). Purchase tickets at the base of the hill near the bus stop or at Gough's Cave. ☎01934 742 343; www.cheddarcaves.co.uk. Open daily July-Aug. 10am-5pm; Sept.-June 10:30am-4:30pm. Caves and Gorge Explorer Ticket grants access to all of the attractions. £15, children £9.50. Discount tickets available from the Wells TIC. Cheddar's TIC is at the base of the hill. ☎01934 744 071. Open daily 10am-5pm. Cheddar Gorge Cheese Company ☎01934 742 810; www.cheddargorgecheese.co.uk. Open daily 10am-5:30pm. Free.)*

WOOKEY HOLE. Two miles west of Cheddar, the **Wookey Hole Caves** are as beautiful as their neighbor's. A 35-40min. tour takes visitors into the caves, which legend holds once contained the Holy Grail. The caves have also inspired Coleridge, Wordsworth, and Alexander Pope, who stole stalactites that are now on display in his London home. The faint smell of cheese is, in fact, local cheddar aging in the caves. After the caves, visitors must slog through a bevy of smaller attractions—including a **dinosaur park,** a working **paper mill,** a **penny arcade,** and a **hall of mirrors**—to get back to the car park. *(From Wells, take bus #670 (15min., M-Sa 8 per day, round-trip £2.45). Caves ☎01749 672 243; www.wookey.co.uk. Caves and paper mill open daily Apr.-Oct. 10am-5pm; Nov.-Mar. 10am-4pm. £15, concessions £10.)*

DEVON

EXETER   ☎(0)1392

Legend holds that in 1068 the inhabitants of Exeter earned the respect of William the Conqueror by holding their defenses against his army for 18 days. When the city's wells ran dry, the Exonians used wine for cooking, bathing, and drinking—which might help to explain the city's eventual fall. Today, restaurants, shops, and wine bars surround the magnificent cathedral, which miraculously avoided bombardment during WWII. The rest of the city was far less fortunate: High St. and the city center were rebuilt in the 1950s. Rapid growth and a desire for a more modern aesthetic led to a massive makeover in 2007.

◪ TRANSPORTATION

Trains: Exeter has 2 stations. Central Station mostly serves local areas, whereas St. David's Station is the main station for long-distance travel.

St. David's Station, St. David's Hill, 1 mi. from town. Ticket office open M-F 5:45am-8:40pm, Sa 6:15am-8pm, Su 7:30am-8:40pm. Trains (☎08457 484 950) to **Bristol** (1hr., every hr., £20.50), **London Paddington** (2½hr., every hr., £58-89.50), and **Salisbury** (2hr., every 2hr., £25.70).

Central Station, Queen St. Ticket office open M-Sa 7:50am-6:15pm, Su 9:05am-4:30pm. To **London Waterloo** (3hr., every 2hr., £53.20).

Buses: Station on Paris St. Ticket office open M-F 8:45am-5:30pm, Sa 8:45am-1pm. National Express (☎08717 818 181) sends buses to **Bristol** (2hr., 4 per day, £13), **Dorchester** (1hr., 1 per day, £11.60), and **London** (4½hr., 8 per day, £23.50). First (☎01752 402 060) handles most travel throughout Devon and Dorset, including to **Bude** (#X9, 1¼hr., every 2hr.) via **Okehampton** (45min., every 2hr.) and **Weymouth** (#X53, 3hr., every 2hr., £6). The #X53 Coast Link runs along the Jurassic Coast between **Exeter** and **Bournemouth.** Bus tickets on this service include discounted entry at sights along the coast. Day pass £6.

Public Transportation: An **Exeter Freedom Ticket** (£4.50 per day, £12 per week) allows unlimited travel on city minibuses. The **Explorer Ticket** (£6 per day, £17 per week) allows unlimited travel on Stagecoach (☎01392 427 711) buses.

Taxis: Capital (☎01392 433 433). **Club Cars** (☎01392 213 030).

◪ PRACTICAL INFORMATION

Tourist Information Centre: Dix's Field (☎01392 665 700). Books accommodations for £3 plus a 10% deposit and sells National Express tickets. Open July-Aug. M-Sa 9am-5pm, Su 10am-4pm; Sept.-June M-Sa 9am-5pm.

Tours: The best way to explore is with the City Council's free 1½hr. themed walking tours (☎01392 265 203), including "Murder and Mayhem," "Ghosts and Legends," and "Medieval Exeter." Most leave from the Royal Clarence Hotel off High St.; some depart from the Quay House Visitor Centre. Apr.-Oct. 4-5 per day; Nov.-Mar. 11am, 2pm.

Banks: Thomas Cook, 7 High St. (☎01392 213 224). Open M-Th and Sa 9am-5:30pm, F 10am-5:30pm, Su 11am-4pm.

Beyond Tourism: JobCentre Plus, Clarendon House, Western Way (☎01392 474 700), on the roundabout near the bus station. Open M-Tu and Th-F 9am-5pm, W 10am-5pm.

Library and Internet Access: Central Library, Castle St. (☎0845 155 1001). 1st 30min. free, £1.50 thereafter. Free Wi-Fi. Open M-Tu and Th-F 9:30am-7pm, W 10am-5pm, Sa 9:30am-4pm, Su 11am-2:30pm.

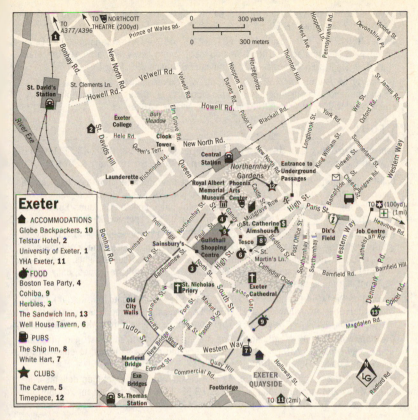

Exeter

🏠 ACCOMMODATIONS
Globe Backpackers, **10**
Telstar Hotel, **2**
University of Exeter, **1**
YHA Exeter, **11**

🍴 FOOD
Boston Tea Party, **4**
Cohiba, **9**
Herbies, **3**
The Sandwich Inn, **13**
Well House Tavern, **6**

🍺 PUBS
The Ship Inn, **8**
White Hart, **7**

⭐ CLUBS
The Cavern, **5**
Timepiece, **12**

Launderette: St. David's Launderette, 24 St. David's Hill. Open daily 8am-8pm.

Police: Heavitree Rd. (☎08452 777 444).

Pharmacy: Boots, 251 High St. (☎01392 432 244). Open M, W, F-Sa 8:15am-6pm, Tu 9am-6pm, Th 8:15am-7pm, Su 10:30am-4pm.

Hospital: Royal Devon and Exeter, Barrack Rd. (☎01392 208 630).

Post Office: 28 Bedford St. (☎08457 223 344). **Bureau de change.** Open M and W-Sa 9am-5:30pm, Tu 9:30am-5:30pm. **Postcode:** EX1 16J.

🏠 ACCOMMODATIONS

There are B&Bs near the **Clock Tower** roundabout just north of Queen St., especially on **Saint David's Hill,** between St. David's Station and the center of town.

🏠 **Globe Backpackers,** 71 Holloway St. (☎01392 215 521; www.exeterbackpackers. co.uk). Spacious common rooms full of social backpackers. Luggage storage £1 per bag. Laundry. Internet 50p per 30min. Key deposit £5. Reception 8am-11pm. Book ahead. Dorms £15; doubles £40. MC/V with 50p surcharge. ❷

YHA Exeter, 47 Countess Wear Rd. (☎01392 873 329), 2 mi. southeast of city center. Take minibus K or T from High St. to the Countess Wear post office; follow signs 10min.

to the spacious, cheery hostel. Internet £1 per 15min. Reception 8-10am and 5-10pm. Dorms £12-20, under 18 £9-15. MC/V. ❷

Telstar Hotel, 75-77 St. David's Hill (☎01392 272 466; www.telstar-hotel.co.uk). Family-run B&B with comfortable, floral-themed rooms, many newly renovated. Full breakfast included. Singles £33, ensuite £38; doubles £58; triples £90. MC/V. ❸

University of Exeter (☎01392 215 566; www.exeter.ac.uk/hospitality). A range of accommodations throughout the city when students are off campus. Open Apr. and July-Sept. Singles £20, ensuite £30; doubles £20, ensuite £46. ❸

🍴 FOOD

A **Sainsbury's** grocery is in the Guildhall Shopping Centre. (☎01392 432 741. Open M-W 8am-6:30pm, Th-F 8am-7pm, Sa 7:30am-6:30pm, Su 10:30am-4:30pm.)

Cohiba, 36 South St. (☎01392 678 445; www.restaurantexeter-cohiba.co.uk). Let the suede couches engulf you at this delicious tapas bar. Latin tunes complement the sexy lighting and flavorful food. 2 tapas and drink lunch special £8. Tapas £5; entrees £12-16. Open M-Th noon-3pm and 6-11pm, F-Su noon-11pm. MC/V. ❸

Well House Tavern, Cathedral Close (☎01392 223 611). Good pub grub with a view of the cathedral in an annex of the beautiful Royal Clarence Hotel. Check out the skeleton in the crypt downstairs. Entrees £5.50-13. Live music some nights. Open M-Th 11am-11pm, F-Sa 11am-midnight, Su 11am-10:30pm. Kitchen open daily noon-2:30pm, bar menu served 2:30-5:30pm. AmEx/MC/V. ❷

Boston Tea Party, 84 Queen St. (☎01392 201 181; www.bostonteaparty.co.uk). Cheap prices and delicious sandwiches (£2.25-4). Enjoy freshly prepared meals on the 2nd fl. cafe overlooking the city. Open M-Sa 7am-6pm, Su 8am-6pm. AmEx/MC/V. ❶

The Sandwich Inn, 36 Magdalen St. The singing chef/owner/sandwich god whips up food to go (from £2.70). The dining area is tiny, but grab a sandwich to enjoy on the quay. Open daily 8:30am-3:30pm. Cash only. ❶

Herbies, 15 North St. (☎01392 258 473). A casual venue for vegetarian delights. Fairtrade wines and local ingredients. Entrees £3.55-8.50. Open M-F 11am-2:30pm and 6-9:30pm, Sa 10:30am-4pm and 6-9:30pm. MC/V. ❷

👁 SIGHTS

EXETER CATHEDRAL. Largely spared from the WWII bombings in Exeter, this cathedral is one of England's finest. Two massive Norman towers preside over the **West Front,** decorated with kings, saints, and a sculpture of St. Peter as a nude fisherman. The 16th-century **astronomical clock** is reputed to be the source of the nursery rhyme "Hickory Dickory Dock" and shows Earth as the center of the universe. The cathedral is home to the 60 ft. **Bishop's Throne** (made without nails), disassembled and taken to the countryside in 1640 and again during WWII. The Bishop's Palace library is home to the **Exeter Book,** the world's richest treasury of early Anglo-Saxon poetry. (☎01392 255 573. Cathedral open daily 9:30am-5pm. Library open M-F 2-5pm. Evensong M-F 5:30pm, Sa-Su 3pm. Free guided tours Apr.-Oct. M-F 11am, 2:30pm, Sa 11am, Su 4pm. £4, concessions £2.)

UNDERGROUND PASSAGES. The ancient underground passages in Exeter are the only of their kind that can be explored in England. Originally built to protect the city's lead water pipes, the tunnels are full of mysterious stories of rogue nuns and priests, buried treasure, and ghosts. The museum and information center contain everything you could ever hope to learn about subterranean history. (Entrance on Paris St., within the Princesshay quarter. Info center next to TIC in Princesshay.

☎ *01392 665 887. Open June-Sept. M-Sa 9:30am-5:30pm, Su 10:30am-4pm; Oct.-May Tu-F 11:30am-5:30pm, Su 11:30am-4pm. Last tour 1hr. before close. £5, concessions £4.)*

SAINT CATHERINE'S ALMSHOUSES. Hidden among the cafes and shops near the cathedral, these sobering red ruins were originally 15th-century housing for the poor. After WWII, they were preserved and dedicated to those who lost their lives in battle. Inscriptions surround the ruins, and a Roman mosaic found after the bombing is in the center. *(Bedford St., near Princesshay. Open daily. Free.)*

♫ 🌴 ENTERTAINMENT AND FESTIVALS

In July and August, the **Northcott** company performs Shakespeare in the park. Tickets can be booked at Exeter Tickets, which supplies monthly listings of cultural events in the city. (☎01392 493 493; www.exetertickets.co.uk.) The **Exeter Festival,** in late June and early July, features concerts, dance lessons, comedy, and theater. For tickets, contact the Festival Box Office, inside the Guildhall Shopping Centre. (☎01392 213 161. Tickets £8-20. Open M-Sa 10am-5pm.)

Northcott Theatre, Stoker Rd. (☎01392 493 493; www.exeternorthcott.co.uk). The Northcott company performs year-round. Tickets £5-24. Concessions available. Box office open M-Sa 10am-6pm, performance days 10am-8pm.

Exeter Phoenix Arts Center, Gandy St. (☎01392 667 080; www.exeterphoenix.org.uk). Dance classes, gallery talks, and summer movie screenings in Northernhay Gardens.

🅜 🅖 PUBS AND NIGHTLIFE

Exeter boasts growing nightlife, with bars and clubs in the alleyways off **High Street,** near **Exeter Cathedral,** and on **Gandy Street.**

Timepiece, Little Castle St. (☎01392 493 096; www.timepiecenightclub.co.uk). Young partygoers enjoy the slightly rustic atmosphere and beer garden. Cover £2-5. Open M-W and Su 7pm-1am, Th 7pm-1:30am, F-Sa 7pm-2am.

The Cavern, 83-84 Queen St. (☎01392 495 370; www.cavernclub.co.uk), just off Gandy St. Hosts live bands several nights a week. Cover after 10pm £2-5. Open M-Th 8pm-1am, F 8pm-2am, Sa 8pm-2:30am, Su 8pm-midnight.

White Hart, 66 South St. A 14th-century house with a "secret garden" outside and a tap room. Car park in the back. Open M-Th noon-11pm, F-Sa noon-11:30pm, Su noon-10:30pm. Kitchen open M-Sa noon-10pm, Su noon-9pm.

The Ship Inn, 1-3 St. Martin's Ln. (☎01392 272 040). Over 700 years old. A favorite of Sir Francis Drake, who wrote, "next to mine own shippe I do love that Shippe in Exon." Open M-W and Su noon-11pm, Th-Sa noon-midnight.

EXMOOR ☎ (0)1643

Once a royal hunting preserve, Exmoor is among the smallest and most picturesque of Britain's national parks, covering 265 sq. mi. on the north coast of the southwestern peninsula. The park's lush woods grow up to the shoreline, offering spectacular hiking ground. Wild ponies still roam the area, and England's last herds of red deer graze in the woodlands. Most of Exmoor is privately owned, but the territory is accommodating to respectful hikers and bikers.

⬛ TRANSPORTATION

Exmoor's western gateway is **Barnstaple;** its eastern gateway is **Minehead.** Most transportation into and within the park runs through one of these towns, often connecting in **Taunton.** Bus service within the park is poor; some small villages are served only once per day, and many services operate only in a 9am-6pm window. Western Exmoor lies in Devon, and bus routes are detailed in *North Devon Bus Times*. Eastern Exmoor occupies the western part of Somerset and is covered by the *Public Transport Timetable for the Exmoor and West Somerset Area*. Both are free at TICs. *Accessible Exmoor*, free from National Park Information Centres (NPICs), provides a guide for disabled visitors. Since single bus fares in the park are £3-4, it's wise to purchase **First Day Explorer** (£7) or **First Week Explorer** (£22) tickets, which allow unlimited travel on all First buses. Call to check times. Traveline (☎0870 608 2608) is the most helpful resource for planning public transportation in the park.

Trains: From Barnstaple, trains travel to **Bristol** (2½hr., 12 per day, £28), **Exeter Central** and **Saint David's** (1¼hr.; M-Sa 12 per day, Su 5 per day; £7-9.40), and **London Paddington** (4hr., 12 per day, £58).

Buses: From Barnstaple, National Express (☎08705 808 080) buses travel to **Bristol** (3hr., 1 per day, £19) and **London Victoria** (5½hr., 3-4 per day, £28). First Devon (☎01752 402 060; open M-F 9am-4pm) buses #86 and X85 to **Plymouth** (3¼hr.; M-Sa 6 per day, Su 2 per day; £4), #337 to **Taunton** (2hr., M-Sa 9am, £5.50), and #319 to **Bude** (2hr., 3 per day, £5.50) via **Hartland**. Minehead serves First #28/X28 to **Taunton** (1¼hr.; M-Sa every 30min., Su 9 per day; £4). Drivers sell combined bus and train tickets (£12). No buses directly connect Minehead to Barnstaple.

Public Transportation: Listed prices are for off-peak hours (purchased after 8:45am). Quantock bus #300 runs along the coast, from **Minehead** to **Lynmouth** (1hr., M-Sa every hr., £3.30). In Lynmouth, the connecting Filers bus #300 runs to **Ilfracombe** (daily 11am, 2, 5pm). **Barnstaple** serves Devon buses (☎01752 402 060) to **Ilfracombe** (#103; 40min.; M-Sa 4 per hr., Su every hr.; £2), **Lynmouth** (#309-310, 1hr., M-Sa 3 per day), and **Lynton** (#309-310, 1hr., M-Sa every hr.). **Minehead** sends Somerset (☎01823 272 033) buses to **Dunster** (#28, 39, 300, and 398; 10min.; 1-2 per hr.; £1.25) and **Porlock** (#38 or 300; 15min.; M-Sa 9 per day, Su 3 per day; £2). West Somerset Railway offers steam and diesel trains (5 per day) from **Minehead** to **Dunster** (6min., £2.60) on its way to **Bishops Lydeard** (45min., £9).

Bike Rental: See **Outdoor Activities**, p. 226.

ORIENTATION AND PRACTICAL INFORMATION

Exmoor lies on 23 mi. of the Bristol Channel coastline, between Barnstaple and Minehead. The park spans Somerset and Devon counties and sits north of Dartmoor National Park. Both TICs and NPICs stock maps (£7-8), transportation timetables, and the invaluable *Exmoor Visitor* newspaper, which lists events, accommodations, and walks and has a useful map and articles on the park. This information can also be found at www.exmoor-nationalpark.gov.uk.

Tourist Information Centres: All TICs book accommodations for a 10% deposit.

Combe Martin: Seacot, 13 Cross St. (☎01271 883 319), 3 mi. east of Ilfracombe. Open daily Easter-Oct. 10am-5pm; Nov.-Easter 10am-4pm.

Ilfracombe: The Landmark, Seafront (☎01271 863 001). Shares a building with the Landmark Theatre. Open Easter-Oct. daily 10am-5pm; Nov.-Easter M-Sa 10am-4pm.

Lynton: Town Hall, Lee Rd. (☎01598 752 225; www.lyntourism.co.uk). Open M-Sa 9:30am-5pm, Su 10am-4pm.

Minehead: Warren Rd., Seafront (☎01643 702 624). Open July-Aug. M-Sa 10am-5pm, Su 10am-2pm; Nov.-Feb. M-Sa 10am-4pm.

Porlock: West End High St. (☎01643 863 150; www.porlock.co.uk). Open Easter-Oct. M-F 10am-1pm and 2-5pm, Sa 10am-5pm, Su 10am-1pm; Nov.-Easter Tu-F 10am-1pm, Sa 10am-2pm.

SOUTHWEST ENGLAND

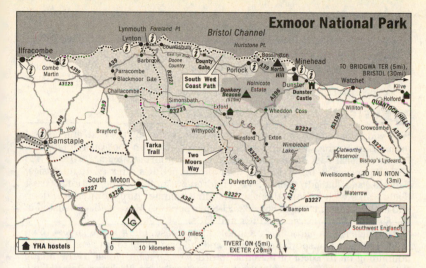

National Park Information Centres: Provide updated trail information. All NPICs are open Apr.-Oct. daily 10am-5pm; Dulverton is open year-round. **Dulverton:** Dulverton Heritage Centre, The Guildhall, Fore St. (☎01398 323 841). **Dunster:** Dunster Steep Car Park (☎01643 821 835). **Lynmouth:** Lyndale Car Park (☎01598 752 509).

Police: Somerset (☎01275 181 181). Devon (☎08705 777 444).

Hospitals: Barnstaple: North Devon District Hospital (☎01271 322 577). **Lynton:** Lynton Distric Cottage Hospital, Lee Rd. (☎01598 753 310). **Minehead:** The Avenue/Blenheim Rd. (☎01643 707 251). **Taunton:** Musgrove Park Hospital (☎01823 333 444).

ACCOMMODATIONS

Hostels and B&Bs (£20-25) fill up quickly; check listings and the *Exmoor Visitor* at the TIC. At busy times, **camping** may be the easiest way to see the park. Most land is private; before pitching a tent, get consent from the owner.

YHA Elmscott (☎01237 441 367). Buses #319 and X19 from Barnstaple go to Hartland; from the west end of Fore St., a footpath leads 2 mi. through the vale to the hostel. Located in a renovated Victorian school, this hostel is just a few minutes' walk from the South West Coastal Path. Kitchen. Laundry £3. Lockout 10am-5pm. Open Easter-Sept. Frequently closed on Su; call ahead. Dorms £15, under 18 £10.50. MC/V. ❶

YHA Exford, Withypoole Rd. (☎01643 831 288), next to the River Exe bridge in the center of the village. Take bus #178 (F), 285 (Su), or Red Bus #295 from Minehead (June-Sept. 1 per day). Victorian house in the middle of Exmoor makes a good base for hiking. Kitchen and laundry. Reception 7:30-10am and 5-10:30pm. Lockout 10am-5pm. Curfew 11pm. Dorms £14, under 18 £10.50. MC/V. ❷

YHA Minehead, Alcombe Combe (☎01643 702 595). Between the town center and Dunster (2 mi. from either). A 35min. walk from town, or take bus #28 toward Dunster and ask the driver to stop at Alcombe (15min. walk from the main road). Beautiful location in the forest with easy access to 2 short walks in the park. Large, comfortable rooms and a cozy lounge area. Organic meals served by request. Buffet breakfast £4.50. Laundry £1.50. Lockout 10am-noon. Dorms £14, under 18 £10.50. MC/V. ❷

Ocean Backpackers, 29 St. James Pl. (☎01271 867 835; www.oceanbackpackers. co.uk). Surfer-centric hostel on Ilfracombe's main drag. Ensuite rooms. Kitchen and lounge with pool table and video games. Dorms £10-14; doubles £17.50. MC/V. ❶

South Leigh Hotel, Runnacleave Rd., Ilfracombe (☎01271 863 976; www.south-leigh. co.uk), next to the Tunnels Beaches. Least expensive B&B in town, with huge ensuite rooms and a bar. Typically full of tour groups, so call ahead. Light continental breakfast included. Full English breakfast £5. £15 per person. MC/V. ❶

🖐 🏔 SIGHTS AND OUTDOOR ACTIVITIES

With wide-open moorland in the west, wooded valleys in the east, and coastal paths, Exmoor has a varied landscape best toured on foot or by bike. The **Exmoor National Park Rangers** lead nature and moorland **tours.** (☎01398 323 665. £3 per person for up to 4hr., over 4hr. £5.) NPICs offer 1½-10 mi. **Exmoor National Parks Authority Walks** (£3-5, children £3; p. 225). The National Trust leads walks with various themes, including summer birds, butterflies, deer, and archaeology. (☎01643 862 452. £1-8 per person.) More walks are listed in the *Exmoor Visitor,* free at NPICs and TICs.

Barnstaple isn't a particularly suitable hiking base, but it is the largest town in the region, a transportation center, and the best place to get gear. Consider continuing on to **Exford** or **Dulverton** in order to be a bit closer to the hiking action. Two good points to start woodland treks are **Blackmoor Gate,** 11 mi. northwest of Barnstaple, and **Parracombe,** 2 mi. farther northwest. Both are on the Barnstaple-Lynton bus route (#309). The **Tarka Trail** starts in Barnstaple and traces a 180 mi. figure-eight, 31 mi. of which are bicycle-friendly. **Tarka Trail Cycle Hire,** at the Barnstaple train station, is located at the trailhead. (☎01271 324 202; www.tarkabikes.co.uk. £7.50 per ½-day, £10 per day; £2 deposit. Open Apr.-Oct. daily 9:15am-5pm.) Only 1 mi. from the park's eastern boundary, **Minehead** is a fantastic place to start hiking. The busy seaside resort provides plenty of lodging and a **nature trail** beginning on Parkhouse Rd. The 630 mi. **South West Coast Path** (p. 193) starts in Minehead and ends in Poole. Contact the South West Coast Path Association for more information (☎01752 896 237; www.swcp. org.uk). The trailhead is on Quay St.—follow signs for "Somerset and North Devon Coastal Path." To the east of Minehead lie the **Quantock Hills,** England's first designated "Area of Outstanding Beauty." Ordnance Survey Map Explorer 140 marks all the walking paths through Quantock (☎01278 732 845).

Set in wooded valleys 9 mi. along the South West Coast Path from Minehead, **Porlock** offers hiking and horseback riding. A 2 mi. walk from the village along a footpath, **Porlock Weir** is a picturesque port with a 6000-year-old shingle ridge. The TIC sells *13 Narrated Walks around Porlock* (£2), which includes a 2 mi. hike to **Culbone Church,** England's smallest church, as well as trail maps of the 8 mi. trek to Exmoor's highest point, **Dunkery Beacon** (1721 ft.). The TIC also has a list of local stables, including **Burrowhayes Farm Riding Stables,** West Luccombe, 1 mi. east of Porlock off the A39. (☎01643 862 463; www.burrowhayes.co.uk. Open Easter-Oct. M-F and Su. Last ride 3:30pm. Pony rides £15 per hr.)

England's "Little Switzerland," the upper village of **Lynton** sits overlooking its twin village, the lower, waterfront **Lynmouth.** The **Cliff Railway,** a Victorian-era water-powered lift, shuttles visitors between the two villages—otherwise it's a steep walk between them. (☎01598 753 486; www.cliffrailwaylynton.co.uk. Open daily from late July to Aug. 10am-9pm; Sept. and June 10am-7pm; Oct.-May call ahead. £2, round-trip £2.85.) **Exmoor Coast Boat Trips,** at the Lynmouth Quay, leads drift-fishing trips and runs sightseeing trips to Lee Bay and the Valley of Rocks. (☎01598 753 207. 1 trip per day; inquire before 11am. Both trips 1hr. £10.) A short walk from the harbor, **Glen Lyn Gorge,** at the Lynmouth

Crossroads, showcases hydroelectric power on its ravine walk. (☎01598 753 207. Open Easter-Oct. 10:30am-5:30pm. Last entry 5pm. £4, children and seniors £3.) A mile and a half along the South West Coast Path from Lynmouth, the **Valley of Rocks** provides stunning coast views, ancient rock formations, and feral goats. Lynmouth is also at one end of the **Two Moors Way,** a 102 mi. trail that cuts across the southwest peninsula from coast to coast, ending in Wembury. **Dunster** is a tiny village of cobblestone sidewalks 2 mi. east of Minehead. Set above the town on a tor, the **Dunster Castle** houses England's only leather tapestries and what's rumored to be the oldest bathroom in Somerset. (☎01643 821 314. Open M-W and F-Su from mid-Mar. to July and Sept.-Oct. 11am-4:30pm; Aug. 11am-5pm. Last entry 30min. before close. Gardens open daily from mid-Mar. to Oct. 10am-5pm. £8.60. Gardens without castle £4.80.)

Whitewashed **Ilfracombe** sits between Lynton and Woolacombe on the coastal path. With sandy beaches, hidden coves, and active surf, the small town makes a great seaside alternative to explore Exmoor. The **Tunnels Beaches** were built by Victorians as saltwater bathing pools in the 1820s. Hand-carved tunnels open onto secluded beaches, with one pool still open and plenty of salty water to dive into. **Kayaking** from the beaches is fun and affordable. (Tunnels Beaches ☎01271 879 882; www.tunnelsbeaches.co.uk. Open daily July-Aug. 9am-9pm; Sept. and June 9am-6pm; Oct. and Easter-May 10am-6pm. £2, concessions £1.75. Kayaking £10 per hr., £30 per ½-day, £40 per day; double kayak, £5 more.)

DARTMOOR   ☎(0)1837

Although it is just a few miles from Plymouth and the crowded streets of Exeter, Dartmoor National Park seems a world away. Hikers fill the park each summer, and small villages greet travelers with local brews and Devon cream tea.

⌫ TRANSPORTATION

Public transportation is scarce in Dartmoor. The bus stations and TICs carry booklets of bus schedules for the four areas of Dartmoor. Disabled visitors should look for the *Access Guide to Dartmoor Towns and Villages,* available at TICs. Travelers planning to use public transportation in Dartmoor should consider purchasing **Explorer** tickets, which allow unlimited travel on services like Stagecoach (1-day £6) and First (1-day £6). **Sunday Rover** tickets allow unlimited travel on buses and local trains in summer on Sundays (£6, children £4, families £16). The Rover Helpline (☎01837 54545) is open from 9am to 6pm on Sundays and bank holidays. For updated timetables, contact Traveline (☎08706 082 608). Only one **train** services the park. The Dartmoor Line (☎01837 556 37) runs from Okehampton to Exeter Central and Exeter St. David's from late May to mid-September (45min., Su 5 per day, £3.50).

Bus service is slightly more extensive. Make sure to pick up a free local bus guide from the TIC for the most up-to-date information. First DevonBus (☎0845 600 1420) bus #82, a.k.a. the "Transmoor Link," connects Plymouth to Exeter (late July and Aug. M-F 2 per day; from late May to mid-July and Sept. Sa 2 per day, Su 5 per day) via Yelverton, Princetown, Postbridge, Moretonhampstead, and Steps Bridge. Bus #359 also connects Exeter to Moretonhampstead (50min., M-Sa 7 per day). For the northwestern parts of the park, take bus #86 from Plymouth to Tavistock and Yelverton in the west (#83, 84, or 86; 1hr.; 3 per hr.) or Okehampton in the north (1-2hr.; M-Sa 9 per day, Su 3 per day). To reach Okehampton from Exeter, take #X9 (1hr.; M-Sa every hr., Su 2 per day). Connect to smaller towns via bus #86 in Tavistock (1hr.; M-Sa every hr., Su 7 per day). To reach the park's southern towns, try Stagecoach Devon (☎01392 427

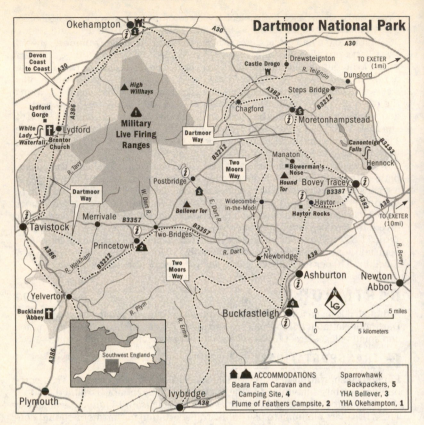

Dartmoor National Park

Okehampton

Devon
Coast
to Coast

A30

Castle Drogo

Drewsteignton

TO EXETER
(1mi)

R. Teignon

Dunsford

High
Willhays

A382

Steps Bridge

B3212

Lydford
Gorge

A386

Chagford

Moretonhampstead

Military
Live Firing
Ranges

Dartmoor
Way

Canonteign
Falls

B3193

White
Lady
Waterfall

Brentor
Church

R. Tavy

Manaton

Hennock

Two
Moors
Way

B3212

Bowerman's
Nose

Bovey Tracey

Postbridge

Hound
Tor

B3387

A382

A38

Dartmoor
Way

3

W. Dart R.

Bellever Tor

E. Dart R.

Widecombe-
in-the-Moor

Haytor

Haytor Rocks

TO EXETER
(10mi)

Merrivale

B3357

B3357

Two-Bridges

R. Bovey

Tavistock

Princetown

2

B3212

R. Walkham

R. Dart

Newbridge

A38

Ashburton

Newton
Abbot

Two
Moors
Way

Yelverton

R. Plym

Buckland
Abbey

Buckfastleigh

4

LG

0   5 miles

0   5 kilometers

Southwest England

Plymouth

Ivybridge

A38

A386

R. Erme

ACCOMMODATIONS
Beara Farm Caravan and
Camping Site, **4**
Plume of Feathers Campsite, **2**

Sparrowhawk
Backpackers, **5**
YHA Bellever, **3**
YHA Okehampton, **1**

711). Bus #X38 runs from Plymouth to Exeter (daily every hr.). First #X80/81 runs to Ivybridge (45min.; M-Sa at least 1 per hr., Su 8 per day) and Torquay (1¼hr.). Some travelers report that hitchhiking is an easier way to get around Dartmoor, but *Let's Go* does not recommend hitchhiking. **Okehampton Cycle Hire** rents bikes. From Fore St., go uphill on North St., then bear left off the main road, continuing downhill to the T junction; follow signs for Garden Centre. (☎01837 532 48. £9.50 per day. Open M-Sa 9am-5pm, Su 10am-4pm.)

⚹ 🛈 ORIENTATION AND PRACTICAL INFORMATION

Dartmoor National Park sits in Dartmoor county, 7 mi. inland from the southern coast. Roughly diamond-shaped, the park lies between the towns of **Okehampton** in the north, **Tavistock** in the west, **Ivybridge** in the south, and **Bovey Tracey** and **Ashburton** in the east. Rivers and hiking paths crisscross the park. A **Range Danger Area** (used by the military) occupies its northwest corner—keep out of this area. The city of **Exeter** (p. 220) is 10 mi. east of the park; **Plymouth** (p. 233) is 5 mi. south. All NPICs and TICs stock the free *Dartmoor Visitor*, which has a map and listings of events, accommodations, and guided walks. As signs in TICs will often tell you, you can "learn moor" at www.dartmoor-npa.gov.uk.

Tourist Information Centres: The following TICs offer in-town and regional advice as well as information about Dartmoor.

Ashburton: Town Hall, North St. (☎01364 653 426; www.ashburton.org/infocentre.htm). Open Easter-Oct. M-Sa 9:30am-4pm; Nov.-Easter M-F 9:30am-4pm, Sa 9:30am-1pm.

Bovey Tracey: Lower Car Park, Station Rd. (☎01626 832 047; www.boveytracey.gov.uk). Open Mar.-Nov. daily 10am-4pm.

Buckfastleigh: The Valiant Soldier (☎01364 644 522). Open Easter-Oct. M-Sa 12:30-4:30pm.

Moretonhampstead: 11 The Square (☎01647 440 043). Books accommodations. Donations requested. Open Apr.-Oct. daily 9:30am-5pm; Nov.-Mar. limited hours.

Okehampton: 3 West St. (☎01837 53020; www.okehamptondevon.co.uk), in the courtyard adjacent to the White Hart Hotel. Books accommodations with a 10% deposit. Open Easter-Oct. M-Sa 10am-5pm; Nov.-Easter M and F-Sa 10am-4:30pm.

Tavistock: Town Hall Bldg., Bedford Sq. (☎01822 612 938). Books accommodations for a 10% deposit. Open Apr.-Oct. M-Sa 9:30am-5pm; Nov.-Mar. M-Tu and F-Sa 10am-4:30pm.

National Park Information Centres: The NPICs are staffed by park officials and often house small park exhibits.

Haytor: On the B3387 (☎01364 661 520), midway between Bovey Tracey and Whitticombe. Open Easter-Oct. daily 10am-5pm; limited hours in winter.

Postbridge: Yelverton Rd., Moretonhampstead (☎01822 880 272), in a car park off the B3212. Open Easter-Oct. daily 10am-5pm; Nov.-Dec. Sa-Su 10am-4pm.

Princetown (High Moorland Visitor Centre): The Square, Tavistock Rd. (☎01822 890 414), in the former Duchy Hotel. The main visitors center for the park. Sells hiking supplies like walking sticks and waterproof map cases. Open daily Easter-Oct. 10am-5pm; Nov.-Easter 10am-4pm.

ACCOMMODATIONS

B&B signs often appear in pubs and farmhouses along the roads. It's wise to stick to those listed at the TIC and to book ahead. Try www.dartmooraccommodation.co.uk for more options. In **Okehampton,** a few B&Bs are on **Station Road** between the train station and the town center. **Tavistock,** the largest town in the area, has more expensive options near the bus station, but single rooms are scarce. Tavistock is best for stocking up on supplies and is a transportation hub for the park. **Moretonhampstead** ("Moreton" to the locals) and **Princetown** are the two largest villages in the park and can serve as good hiking bases.

YHA Bellever (☎01822 880 227), 1 mi. southeast of Postbridge village. Bus #98 from Tavistock stops in front. #82 from Exeter or Plymouth (from late July to Aug. M-F; Oct.-Easter Sa-Su) stops in Postbridge; from there, walk west on the B3212 and turn left on Bellever (20-25min. walk). In the heart of the park. Popular with adventure-bound school groups. Reception 7-10am and 5-10:30pm. Dorms £12-18. MC/V. ❷

YHA Okehampton, Klondyke Rd. (☎01837 539 16), a 15min. walk from the town center. From the TIC, bang a right on George St., turn right onto Station Rd., and continue under the bridge. Converted railroad warehouse. Game room and kitchen. Mountain-bike rental £7.50 per day. Reception 8-10am and 5-10pm. Camping Feb.-Nov. £6 per person. Dorms £14-18, under 18 £10.50-13.80. MC/V. ❷

Sparrowhawk Backpackers, 45 Ford St., Moretonhampstead (☎01647 440 318; www.sparrowhawkbackpackers.co.uk). From the bus car park, turn left toward the town center; take the left fork and turn left onto Ford St. Sky-lit bunkhouse and courtyard. Knowledgeable owner dispenses hiking and biking advice. Vegetarian kitchen and comfortable beds. Dorms £15; doubles £35. Cash only. ❷

CAMPING

Although official campsites and camping barns exist, many camp on the open moor. Most of Dartmoor is privately owned, but permission of the owner is required only in certain areas; consult a park map or NPIC for information on land access. Check www.dartmoor-npa.gov.uk or www.discoverdartmoor.com before heading out or consult *Camping and Backpacking on Dartmoor* (free at NPICs). When using official campsites, call ahead for reservations, especially in summer. **YHA Okehampton ❶** also offers camping (above).

> **Buckfastleigh: Beara Farm Caravan and Camping Site,** Colston Rd. (☎01364 642 234), 1 mi. from the town center. Follow the signs for the Otter Park, continue 600 ft. past the entrance, and walk 1 mi. down Old Totnes Rd. £8 per 2-person tent. ❶

> **Princetown: Plume of Feathers Campsite and Camping Barn** (☎01822 890 240; www.theplumeoffeathers.co.uk), behind the Plume of Feathers Inn, opposite the NPIC. Solid bunks with showers and access to TV. The "new bunk" has an indoor bathroom; the "old bunk" bathroom is outdoors. Sites from £5. Dorms £10. MC/V. ❶

 RULES OF THE WILD. Camping is allowed on non-enclosed moorland more than three-quarter of a mile from the road or out of sight of inhabited areas; camping is prohibited within sight of any paved road, in common areas used for recreation, or on archaeological sites. Campers may stay only two nights in a single spot and must not build fires.

👁 SIGHTS

Bronze Age burial mounds and stone circles are scattered about 368 sq. mi. of moorland. Also prevalent are tors, granite towers that resulted from thousands of years of geological activity.

CASTLE DROGO. The "last castle in England" was built from 1910 to 1930 for tea baron Julius Drewe, who believed he was a descendant of a 10th-century Norman and wanted to live accordingly. Ancient tapestries surround "modern" conveniences and 20th-century furniture, including a pre-WWII foosball table. From the castle, easy 3-4 mi. hikes go to the **River Teign** and its **Fingle Bridge,** where there are croquet lawns open all summer with equipment for rent. *(Take bus #173 from Moretonhampstead or Exeter or 174 or 179 from Okehampton. ☎01647 433 306. Open Mar.-Oct. M and W-Su 11am-5pm; from Nov. to mid-Dec. M-F noon-4pm. Last entry 30min. before close. £7.80. Garden and grounds without castle £5, children £2.75.)*

PRINCETOWN PRISON. Dartmoor's maximum-security prison in Princetown, the highest town in England, is still in use today and has a museum to showcase its history. The surrounding moorland is the setting for Sherlock Holmes's famed escapade, *The Hound of the Baskervilles,* which emerged from a Dartmoor legend of a black dog that stalked a not-so-nice aristocrat. The **Dartmoor Prison Heritage Centre,** a 15min. walk up Tavistock Rd. from the TIC, has a gallery of weapons made by inmates, including a knife made of matchsticks. *(☎01822 892 130; www.dartmoor-prison.co.uk. Open M-Th and Sa 9:30am-12:30pm and 1:30-4:30pm, F and Su 9:30am-12:30pm and 1:30-4pm. £2.50, concessions £1.50, families £7.)*

BUCKLAND ABBEY. A few miles south of Yelverton, the abbey was built by Cistercian monks in 1273 and was later bought by Sir Francis Drake, who was born on a nearby farm. The abbey houses Drake's drum, and it is said that, when England is in grave danger, the drum will sound to defend the mother country. *(Citybus #48 or 55 from Yelverton or 48 from Plymouth to the Milton Combe stop. ☎01822 853 607. Open from mid-Mar. to Oct. M-W and F-Su 10:30am-5:30pm; Nov.-Dec. F-Su noon-4pm; from mid-Feb. to Mar. Sa-Su 2-5pm. Last entry 45min. before close. £7.80, children £4, families £19.50. Grounds without abbey £4, children £2.)*

🔾 🛤 HIKING AND OUTDOOR ACTIVITIES

The Dartmoor Commons Act of 1985 gives visitors free reign to trek the registered common land in Dartmoor, but access may be restricted in other areas; consult the free pamphlet *Walking on Dartmoor* or www.openaccess.gov.uk. Ordnance Survey Explorer Map #28 (₤8) is essential. The **Dartmoor Rescue Group** is on call at ☎999. The Devon Air Ambulance, for medical emergencies only, can be reached directly at ☎01392 466 666 (see **Wilderness Safety, p. 51**).

The rugged terrain of Dartmoor offers unparalleled hiking. The **National Park Authority** conducts guided walks (1-6hr.; ₤3-8, free if arriving at starting point by public transportation), which are listed in the *Dartmoor Visitor* and by the events hotline (☎01822 890 414). The *Dartmoor Walks*, free at TICs, pamphlet compiles eight of the most popular routes. **Dartmoor Way** is a 90 mi. circular route that hits the park's main towns. The 180 mi. **Tarka Trail** runs from Okehampton to Exmoor National Park in the north (p. 223). The trail recently went digital with audio tours marking the way. You can download the audio clips at www.northdevonbiosphere.co.uk, put them on your MP3 player, and listen when you come to markers. The 102 mi. **Two Moors Way** also connects the two parks, running from Lynmouth to Ivybridge.

The area is crowned by several peaks, the highest of which is **High Willhays** (2038 ft.). The peak, a hilly 4 mi. from Okehampton, is accessible only by foot. A mile from Lydford, the 1½ mi. **Lydford Gorge** has a lush forest and a whirlpool known as the **Devil's Cauldron.** Walk along the top of the gorge to reach the 90 ft. **White Lady Waterfall.** A circular walk of the gorge takes about 2hr., but you can also start at one entrance and walk to the other. The latter option lets you see both the cauldron and the waterfall, and buses pick up and drop off at both entrances. (☎01822 820 320. Open from mid-Mar. to Oct. daily 10am-5pm; from Nov. to mid-Mar. F-Su 11am-3:30pm. Last entry 30min. before close. ₤5.40, children ₤2.70, families ₤13.50.) **Wistman's Wood,** a national nature reserve north of Two Bridges, is an ancient oak woodland that offers beautiful hiking.

> ❗ **NATIONAL PARK OR WAR ZONE?** The Ministry of Defense uses parts of the northern moor for target practice and has done so since the 1880s. Consult the *Dartmoor Visitor* or a current Ordnance Survey map for the boundaries of the danger area, which changes yearly. Weekly firing schedules are available in NPICs, post offices, police stations, hostels, campsites, and pubs, from the military hotline (☎0800 458 4868), and online at www.dartmoor-ranges.co.uk. Boundaries are marked by red and white posts, and live firing areas are designated by red flags by day and red lamps by night.

A wealth of Bronze Age structures, the remains of a Neolithic civilization, cluster near **Merrivale.** Merrivale is on the #98 and 172 (summer only) bus routes. **Haytor,** near Bovey Tracey, features numerous tors, including the massive **Haytor Rocks** and the ruins at **Hound Tor,** where excavations unearthed the remains of 13th-century huts and longhouses. Venture 1 mi. north from Manaton to discover the 40 ft. **Bowerman's Nose,** named after the man who first recognized the rock's resemblance to the human organ. Also near Bovey Tracey is the 220 ft. **Canonteign Falls,** England's highest waterfall. (☎01647 252 434; www.canonteignfalls.co.uk. Open from mid-Mar. to Oct. 10am-5pm. Last entry 4pm. ₤5.75, concessions ₤5, children ₤4.50, families ₤19.50.)

Dartmoor's roads are good for **cycling.** Bookended by Ilfracombe and Plymouth, the 102 mi. **Devon Coast to Coast** route winds along rivers and rural countryside. The 11 mi. portion between Okehampton and Lydford is known as the **Granite Way** and offers traffic-free biking along a former railway line. For **horseback riding**, NPICs can refer you to stables (rides £8-16 per hr.). Dartmoor Safaris operates **tours** through the moors in SUVs. Most tours leave from Plymouth Bus Station. Thursday tours leave from The Strand, Torquay. (☎01752 500 567; www.dartmoorsafaris.co.uk. 8hr. tours depart Apr.-Sept. 9-9:30am. £30.)

TORQUAY   ☎(0)1803

The largest city in the Torbay resort region and the self-proclaimed "English Riviera," Torquay (tor-KEY) isn't quite as glamorous as the French original. However, the town Agatha Christie called home and in which the fictional Basil Fawlty ran his madcap hotel does have plenty of beaches, palm trees, and stimulating nightlife. A popular resort area for British city dwellers, Torquay is a good base for exploring the sunnier parts of the southwestern English coast.

TRANSPORTATION AND PRACTICAL INFORMATION. Torquay's **train station** (open M-F 7:10am-5pm, Sa 7am-5pm, Su 9:40am-5:10pm) is off Rathmore Rd., near the Torre Abbey gardens. To get to town, take a left and walk along the shoreline. Trains (☎08457 484 950) go to: Bristol (2hr., every hr., £28); Exeter (45min., every hr., £5); London Paddington (3hr., every hr., £62); London Waterloo (4hr., every hr., £62); Plymouth (1hr., every hr., £5.50). **Buses** depart from The Pavilion, the roundabout where Torbay Rd. meets The Strand. The Stagecoach office, 15 Victoria Parade, has information on its buses. (☎01803 664 500. Open M-F 9am-5pm, Sa 9am-1pm.) Bus #X46 runs to Exeter (1hr.; M-Sa every hr., Su 7 per day; £6). First buses #X80 and X81 run to Plymouth (1hr., every hr., £6). Torbay Cab Co. **taxis** (☎01803 292 292) are on call 24hr.

The **Tourist Information Centre**, Vaughan Parade, past the Pavilion shopping center, arranges theater bookings, sells tickets for the **Eden Project** (p. 249), and books accommodations for a 10% deposit. (☎01803 211 211; www.englishriviera.co.uk. Open May-Sept. M-Sa 9:30am-5:30pm, Su 10am-4pm; Oct.-Apr. M-Sa 9:30am-5pm.) Cruise Tours leads **tours** (1hr., £6) from Princess Pier to Brixham (Western Lady Ferry Service ☎01803 842 424) and Paignton (Paignton Pleasure Cruises ☎01803 529 147). Buy tickets for both at the booth on Victoria Parade (open daily 9am-5pm). Other services include: **banks** on Fleet St.; **Thomas Cook**, 54 Union St. (☎0845 308 9610; open M and W-Sa 9am-5:30pm, Tu 10am-5:30pm); **JobCentre**, Regal House, Castle Circus, across from town hall (☎01803 356 000; open M-Tu and Th-F 9am-5pm, W 10am-5pm); **Sparkle** launderette, 63 Princes Rd., off Market St. (☎01803 293 217; open M-F 9am-7pm, Sa 9am-6pm, Su 10am-4pm); **police**, South St. (☎08452 777 444); a **Superdrug** pharmacy, Fleet St. (☎01803 299 276; open July-Sept. M-Sa 8:30am-9pm, Su 10am-4pm; Oct.-June M-Sa 8:30am-5:30pm, Su 10am-4pm.); **Torbay Hospital**, Newton Rd. (☎01803 614 567); free **Internet** access at the **library**, Lymington Rd., beside the Town Hall (☎01803 208 300; open M, W, F 9:30am-7pm, Tu 9:30am-5pm, Th 9:30am-1pm, Sa 9:30am-4pm) and at **Jon's Internet and Computer Services**, Market Shopping Court, Market St. (☎01803 297 760; £2.50 per hr.; open M-Sa 9am-5pm); and the **post office**, inside WH Smith on Union St, with a **bureau de change** (☎0845 722 3344; open M-Sa 9am-5:30pm). **Postcode:** TQ1 1ES.

ACCOMMODATIONS AND FOOD. Torquay's hotels and B&Bs are busy during summer, especially in August; book rooms in advance. Find less expensive beach hotels on **Babbacombe Road**, including **Torwood Gardens Hotel ❸**, 531 Babbacombe Rd., where rooms provide respite 5min. from the surf. (☎01803 298 408. Breakfast included. £30 per person. MC/V.) Cheaper B&Bs line **Scarborough Road** and **Morgan Avenue**. Walls covered in chalk-scrawled poems foster a warm atmosphere at **Torquay Backpackers ❷**, 119 Abbey Rd. (☎01803 299 924; www.torquaybackpackers.co.uk. Laundry £3.50. Internet £1 per 20min. June-Sept. dorms £14; doubles £30. Oct.-May dorms £12; doubles £28. MC/V.)

Buy groceries at **Tesco**, 25-26 Fleet St. (☎01803 351 400. Open M-Sa 7am-10pm, Su 11am-5pm.) ◪**One World Cafe**, in the middle of Abbey Park, is an elaborately decorated cafe and bistro serving food from all over the world. The cafe also sells the arts and crafts used as its decor, with all proceeds going to the villages where they were made. (☎07737 193 613. Free Wi-Fi. Open Apr.-Oct. daily 9am-9pm; Nov.-Mar. Sa-Su 9am-9pm.) **No. 7 Fish Bistro ❸**, Inner Harbor, Beacon Terr., across from Living Coasts, is the place to splurge for superb seafood (£14-20.50) and views of the harbor. (☎01803 295 055; www.no7-fish.com. Open M and Su 7-9:30pm, Tu 7-9:45pm, W-Sa 12:15-2:15pm and 6-9:45pm. AmEx/MC/V.) Locals flock to **Hanbury's ❷**, Princes St., 2 mi. up Babbacombe Rd., for sit-down fish and chips (£7-11) and takeaway. Take bus #32 or 85 (8min., every 10-30min.) from The Strand to the Babbacombe stop. Hanbury's is up the road on the right. (☎01803 314 616; www.hanburys.net. Open M-Sa 11:45am-1:45pm and 4:30-9:30pm; takeaway only 4:30-9:30pm. MC/V.)

◪◪ **SIGHTS AND BEACHES.** Opened in 2003 with a spectacular view of the bay, **Living Coasts**, Beacon Quay, is an aviary that recreates nearly all of the world's major coastal environments, from Africa to the Antarctic. (☎01803 202 470; www.livingcoasts.org.uk. Open daily Easter-Sept. 10am-6pm; Oct.-Easter 10am-dusk. Last entry 1hr. before close. £8, concessions £6.20, children £6, families £25.) To get out of the sun, head for the **Torquay Museum**, 529 Babbacombe Rd., which features an exhibition of Agatha Christie's time in Torquay. (☎01803 293 975; www.torquaymuseum.org. Open from mid-July to Sept. M-Sa 10am-5pm, Su 1:30-5pm; from Oct. to mid-July M-Sa 10am-5pm. £4.35, concessions £3.25, children £2.75, families £13.50.) Mystery enthusiasts can also walk the **Agatha Christie Mile**, which starts at the Grand Hotel and visits places in Torquay that inspired the author. Pick up a free map from the TIC. **Princess Theatre**, Torbay Rd., offers a weatherproof option, presenting live entertainment throughout the year. (☎0844 087 2315. Tickets £12-25. Box office open M-Sa 10am-6pm, performance days 10am-7:30pm)

The weather in the "English Riviera" is not quite as ideal as in its French cousin, yet on the precious sunny days locals flock to the beaches. **Torre Abbey Sands** draws hordes, but visitors can reach better beaches by bus. Just southeast of Torquay, **Meadfoot** (bus #200) features beach huts and pebbly shores. Take bus #200 north to rockier **Oddicombe**, hidden under a cove (every 10min.) and **Babbacombe**, for watersports. Bus #34 heads farther north to peaceful **Watcombe** (15min., every 30min.) and nearly deserted **Maidencombe** (20min.).

◪◪ **NIGHTLIFE AND FESTIVALS.** When the sun dips and beaches empty, nightlife options come alive. **Mojo**, Palm Court Hotel, Torbay Rd., is a seaside hangout with Torquay's latest bar hours and dancing. Look for the huge murals as you head into town. (☎07831 409 471. Jam night W. DJs F. Live bands Sa. Open daily 11am-1am.) **Mambo**, 7 The Strand, changes from a spicy Thai restaurant to a saucy club at night. Enjoy two-for-one drinks daily 8pm-midnight. (☎01803 291 112. Open M-Sa 9am-3am, Su 9am-2am.) During the last week of August, Torquay lives the high life during its annual **Regatta**; call the TIC.

PLYMOUTH

☎(0)1752

Plymouth is best known not as a destination but as a point of departure—Sir Francis Drake, Captain Cook, Lord Nelson, and the Pilgrims all left from the city's harbor. Heavily bombed during WWII, much of Plymouth was rebuilt in an unfortunate industrial style. Now, modern shopping centers stand alongside the ancient pubs and cobblestone streets of the harborside Barbican district.

⌐ TRANSPORTATION

Plymouth lies on the southern coast between Dartmoor National Park and the Cornwall peninsula along the A38.

Trains: Plymouth Station, North Rd. Ticket office open M-Sa 5am-8:30pm, Su 8am-8:30pm. Buses #5 and 6 run to the city center. Trains (☎08457 484 950) to **Bristol** (2hr., every 30min., £42-48), **London Paddington** (3½hr., every hr., £64-117.50), and **Penzance** (2hr., every 30min., £9.40-13).

Buses: Bretonside Station. Ticket office open M-Sa 9am-5:30pm, Su 9:30am-3:30pm. National Express (☎08717 818 181) to **Bristol** (3hr., 4 per day, £27.50) and **London** (5-6hr., 8 per day, £31). Stagecoach bus #X38 runs to **Exeter** (1¾hr., 13 per day, £6).

Ferries: Brittany Ferries (☎08703 665 333; www.brittanyferries.com), at Millbay Docks. Follow signs to "Continental Ferries," 15min. from the town center. Buy tickets 24hr. ahead, although foot passengers may be able to purchase tickets upon arrival. Check in well before departure. To **Roscoff, FRA** (4-6hr., 12 per week, £93-107) and **Santander, ESP** (18hr., W and Su, £144-232).

Public Transportation: Citybus (☎01752 222 221; line open M-F 8am-5:30pm, Sa 9am-5:30pm) buses run from Royal Parade around the city.

Taxis: Plymouth Taxis (☎01752 606 060). **Taxi Fast** (☎01752 222 222).

◢ ◗ ORIENTATION AND PRACTICAL INFORMATION

The commercial district formed by **Royal Parade, Armada Way,** and **New George Street** is Plymouth's city center. Directly south, the **Hoe** (or "High Place") is a large, seaside park. The **Royal Citadel** is flanked by the Hoe to the west and **The Barbican,** Plymouth's historic harbor, to the east.

Tourist Information Centre: 3-5 The Barbican (☎01752 306 330; www.plymouth.gov. uk). Shares a building with the Mayflower Museum. Books accommodations for 10% deposit and distributes a free map and visitor guide. Open May-Sept. M-Sa 9am-5pm, Su 10am-4pm; Oct.-Apr. M-F 9am-5pm, Sa 10am-4pm.

Tours: Plymouth Boat Cruises (☎01752 822 797; www.soundcruising.com) leave from Phoenix Wharf for short trips around Plymouth Sound (1hr., £6).

Banks: Line Old Town St., Royal Parade, and Armada Way. **American Express,** 139 Armada Way (☎01752 502 701). Open M-F 9am-5:30pm, Sa 9am-5pm.

Library and Internet Access: Northhill (☎01752 305 923). Free Internet. 30min. slots. Open M-F 9am-7pm, Sa 9am-5pm. Computers close 30min. before library.

Launderette: Hoegate Laundromat, 55 Notte St. (☎01752 223 031). Service wash only. £7 per load. Open M-F 9am-6pm, Sa 9am-1pm.

Police: Charles Cross (☎08705 777 444), near the bus station.

Pharmacy: Superdrug, Cornwall St. (☎01752 671 203). Open M-Sa 8am-6pm, Su 10:30am-4:30pm.

Hospital: Derriford Hospital (☎01752 777 111), in Derriford, about 5 mi. north of the city center. Take bus #42 or 50 from Royal Parade.

Post Office: 5 St. Andrew's Cross (☎08457 223 344). **Bureau de change.** Open M and W-Sa 9am-5:30pm, Tu 9:30am-5:30pm. **Postcode:** PL1 1AB.

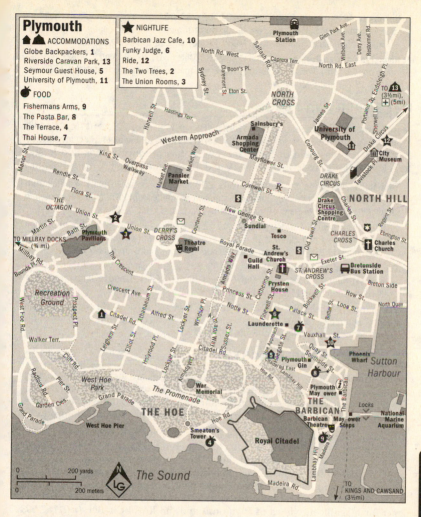

Plymouth

▲▲ ACCOMMODATIONS
Globe Backpackers, 1
Riverside Caravan Park, 13
Seymour Guest House, 5
University of Plymouth, 11

🍴 FOOD
Fishermans Arms, 9
The Pasta Bar, 8
The Terrace, 4
Thai House, 7

★ NIGHTLIFE
Barbican Jazz Cafe, 10
Funky Judge, 6
Ride, 12
The Two Trees, 2
The Union Rooms, 3

SOUTHWEST ENGLAND

🏠 🏠 ACCOMMODATIONS AND CAMPING

B&Bs (£18-35) line **Citadel Road;** rooms tend to be small with a shared bath.

Globe Backpackers, 172 Citadel Rd. (☎01752 225 158; www.exeterbackpackers. co.uk/plymouth). Minutes from the Hoe. Comfortable beds, kitchen, patio, and cozy TV room. Laundry £3. Free Wi-Fi. Reception 8am-11pm. Dorms £13; doubles £35. Weekly dorms £65. MC/V with 50p surcharge. ❶

Seymour Guest House, 211 Citadel Rd. E. (☎01752 667 002; www.seymourguest-house.co.uk), where Hoegate St. meets Lambhay Hill. Rooms have cushions on the beds and soft beige carpets. Great location between The Barbican and the Hoe. Breakfast included. Singles £27, ensuite £35; ensuite doubles £50; triples £65. MC/V. ❸

University of Plymouth, Gibbon St. (☎01752 232 061; www.plymouth.ac.uk/holiday-accommodation). Self-catering university dorm rooms in the city center. Singles £18, ensuite £25; ensuite doubles £45. MC/V. Weekly singles £112, ensuite £160. ❷

Riverside Caravan Park, Longbridge Rd., Marsh Mills (☎01752 344 122; www.riverside-caravanpark.com). Follow Longbridge Rd. 3 mi. toward Plympton or catch the #50 bus. £6.75-12 per night. MC/V. ❶

📷🎵 FOOD AND PUBS

Tesco Metro, on the corner of New George St., sells groceries. (☎01752 617 400. Open M-Tu and Th-Sa 8am-5:30pm, W 8am-4:30pm.) **Pannier Market,** an indoor bazaar at the west end of New George St., has produce stands and knick-knacks. (☎01752 306 551. Open M-Tu and Th-Sa 8am-5:30pm, W 8am-4:30pm.)

Thai House, 63 Notte St. (☎01752 661 600; www.thethaihouse.com). A black-and-white facade hides a brightly colored restaurant at the heart of Plymouth. Delicious pad thai (£6.50). Open M-Sa 6-10:30pm, Su 6-10pm. AmEx/MC/V. ❷

Fishermans Arms, 31 Lambhay St. (☎01752 661 457). Close to the harbor and Plymouth's 2nd-oldest pub. Open M-Th noon-11pm, F-Sa noon-midnight, Su noon-10:30pm. Kitchen open M-Th and Su noon-3pm, F-Sa noon-3pm and 6-9pm. MC/V. ❶

The Pasta Bar, 40 Southside St. (☎01752 671 299), near the intersection with The Barbican. Heaping bowls of creative pasta dishes (£7-10) and a large vegetarian selection. Open daily 11:30am-11pm. MC/V. ❷

The Terrace, Madeira Rd. (☎01752 603 533). A self-service cafe with reasonably priced light meals (salads and sandwiches £6.25-7). Sit on the terrace and watch the ships docking. Open daily 8am-8pm. MC/V. ❶

👁🎵 SIGHTS AND BEACHES

Plymouth's shores are ideal for ships, but the beaches are just OK. Ferry to **Kingsand** and **Cawsand,** villages with pretty slips of sand. Cawsand Ferry leaves from the Mayflower Steps but sometimes cancels trips due to unfavorable winds. (☎07763 110 526; www.cawsandferry.com. 30min.; 4 per day; £4, children £2.)

HOE. Legend has it that Sir Francis Drake was playing bowls on the Hoe in 1588 when he heard that the Armada had entered the English Channel. Finger in the air, he tested the wind and said, "There is time still for me to win this game and defeat the Spanish." He did both. Today, the soft grass, sound of the ocean, and passing ice-cream trucks make the Hoe a perfect place to spend the afternoon. Climb 93 spiral steps and leaning ladders to the balcony of **Smeaton's Tower** for magnificent views of Plymouth and the Royal Citadel. (☎01752 603 300; www.plymouth.gov.uk/museums. Tower open Apr.-Sept. Tu-F 10am-noon and 1-4:30pm, Sa 10am-noon and 1-4pm; Oct.-Mar. Tu-Sa 10am-noon and 1-3pm. £2, children £1.)

PLYMOUTH GIN. The oldest working gin distillery in England, Plymouth has produced gin here since 1793. A tour of the factory includes an introduction to the ingredients specific to Plymouth gin, a tasting, and a free gin and tonic. Keep your eyes open for monk figurines, harking back to the building's days as an abbey. (60 Southside St. ☎01752 665 292; www.plymouthgin.com. Open Mar.-Dec. M-Sa 10:30am-4:30pm, Su 10:30am-3:30pm. 35min. tours run every hr. at 30min. past. £6.)

PLYMOUTH MAYFLOWER. The small museum tells the tale of the *Mayflower* and everything you could possibly want to know about the Pilgrims. (3-5 The Barbican, above the TIC. ☎01752 306 330. Open M-Sa 10am-4pm, Su 11am-3pm. £2.)

SAINT ANDREW'S CHURCH. St. Andrew's has been a site of Christian meetings since 1087. Three days of bombing in 1941 left it gutted. The building's brilliant stained glass and arching rafters are the products of post-war restoration. *(Royal Parade. ☎01752 661 414. Open M-F 9am-4pm, Sa 9am-1pm, Su for services only.)*

NATIONAL MARINE AQUARIUM. The UK's largest and Europe's deepest tank is home to six sharks as well as Britain's only giant squid. The aquarium also has several interactive displays, including one on water energy. *(The Barbican. ☎01752 600 301; www.national-aquarium.co.uk. Open daily Apr.-Oct. 10am-6pm; Nov.-Mar. 10am-5pm. Last entry 1hr. before close. £11, concessions £9, children £6.50, families £30.)*

OTHER SIGHTS. The still-in-use **Royal Citadel,** built 300 years ago by Charles II, may be seen only via a guided tour. *(Tours May-Sept. Tu and Th 2:30pm; £4, children £3.)* At the **Mayflower Steps,** on The Barbican, a balcony monument and American flag mark the spot from which the Pilgrims set off in 1620. The actual steps are across the street, but the marked ones make for better pictures. The blackened shell of **Charles Church,** destroyed by a bomb in 1941, now stands in the middle of the Charles Cross roundabout as a memorial for victims of the Blitz.

🎵 🎦 ENTERTAINMENT AND NIGHTLIFE

Both young and old enjoy the traditional pubs along The Barbican. Farther inland, Union St. offers a string of bars and clubs.

Theatre Royal, on Royal Parade (☎01752 267 222). One of the West Country's best stages, featuring ballet and touring companies, including the Royal National Theatre. Tickets £16-44. Box office open M-Sa 10am-6pm, performance days 10am-8pm.

Barbican Jazz Cafe, 11 The Parade (☎01752 672 127; www.barbicanrhythmand-jazzclub.co.uk). Daily live jazz. Open M-Sa 8pm-2am, Su 8pm-midnight.

Funky Judge, 2 St. Andrews St. (☎01752 295 240). The perfect mix of soul and style. Enjoy drinks in the outdoor garden. Free live music F-Sa. Open daily 11am-11pm.

The Union Rooms, 19 Union St. (☎01752 254 520). A popular early-evening bar; pints and wines are £1.50-2.50. Free Wi-Fi. Open W-Th 9am-1am, F-Sa 9am-3am.

Ride, 2 Sherwell Arcade, North Hill (☎01752 205 5552), beyond the City Museum. Draws a rowdy crowd of University of Plymouth students. £1 pints M with £1 entry fee. "Cheese and Wine" Su; cheese free, bottle of wine £6. Open M-Th 4:30pm-4am, F-Sa 4:30pm-5am, Sa 4:30pm-2am.

Two Trees, 30 Union St. (☎01752 561 189). Late bar hours and a small venue. Karaoke Su 10pm. Open M-Sa 8pm-4am, Su 7pm-2am.

🎇 FESTIVALS

On the August bank holiday in even-numbered years, the public can explore the ships and submarines in the city's maximum-security naval base during **Plymouth Navy Days.** (☎01752 553 941. Tickets go on sale in late June.) The British **National Fireworks Championship** explodes in mid-August, while the **Powerboat Championships** take place in mid-July.

🏞 DAYTRIPS FROM PLYMOUTH

LOOE. Picturesque Looe is split in half by a wide estuary. Far from the sandy shores and into the sea lies mile-wide **Looe Island,** until recently the only privately owned island in the UK, now under the care of the Cornish Wildlife Trust. **Boat tours** run around the coast and the bay; check for information at the quay. For hiking, the **Discovery Centre,** Millpool, on Looe's west side, stocks the free *Looe Valley Line Trails from the Track*. *(Reach Looe by train from Plymouth via Liskeard (1hr.). Discovery Centre ☎01503 262 777. Open daily July-Sept. 10am-6pm; Oct. and Feb.-June 10am-4pm; Nov.-Dec. 10am-3pm.)*

POLPERRO. Polperro was once England's most notorious smuggling bay—its proximity to the Channel Islands made it perfect for illegal alcohol and tobacco transportation. The **Polperro Heritage Museum of Smuggling and Fishing** displays photos of smugglers, a smuggler's sword, and stories about smugglers. This place loves its smugglers. The **Visitor Information Centre,** Talland St., is at end of New St. *(From Looe, take Hamblys Coaches (☎01503 220 660) or First buses #80A and 81A (all 3 per day, £4.80). Heritage Museum ☎01503 273 005. Open daily Easter-Oct. 10am-6pm. Last entry 5:15pm. £1.75. Visitor Centre ☎01503 272 320. Open M-Sa 9:30am-5pm.)*

CLOVELLY. Clovelly's steep main street has 170 treacherous cobbled steps. The Rous family has owned the entire town for 700 years, but time-capsule upkeep isn't cheap—visitors pay a town entry fee, after which most sights are free. Choose between the restored 1930s **Fisherman's Cottage** (open 9am-4:45pm) or making your own pottery at **Clovelly Pottery.** *(☎01237 431 042. £1.50 per pot. Open M-Sa 10:30am-5:30pm, Su 11am-5pm.)* In winter, a short walk east along the shore brings trekkers to a surging waterfall, which slows to a stream in warmer months. **Boat trips** from the harbor run to **Lundy Island,** a nature reserve. *(☎01271 863 636; www.lundyisland.co.uk. 2-4 per week. 1-day round-trip £30; concessions available.)* Visitors pay entry to the village at the **Clovelly Visitor Centre,** in the car park. *(First bus #319 connects Clovelly to Bideford (40min.; M-Sa 6 per day, Su 2 per day) and Barnstaple (1hr.). Town entry £5.50, children £3.50, families £15. Visitors Centre ☎01237 431 781. Open daily July-Aug. 9am-5:30pm, Sept.-June 9am-6:30pm.)*

CORNWALL

A rugged landscape of cliffs and sandy beaches, it's no wonder the Celts chose to flee to Cornwall in the face of Saxon conquest. Today, the westward movement continues with surfers, artists, and vacationers. Ports like Falmouth and Penzance celebrate England's maritime heritage, while beach-laden St. Ives and Newquay fulfill many a surfer's fantasies.

⯐ TRANSPORTATION

Penzance is the southwestern terminus of Britain's **trains** (☎08457 484 950) and the best base from which to explore the region. The main rail line from **Plymouth** to **Penzance** bypasses coastal towns, but connecting rail service reaches **Newquay, Falmouth,** and **St. Ives.**

The **First bus** network is thorough, although the interior of Cornwall is more often served by smaller companies. *The Public Transport Guide,* free at bus stations and TICs, compiles every route in the region. Buses run from **Penzance** to **Land's End** and **St. Ives** and from St. Ives to **Newquay,** stopping in the smaller towns along these routes. Many buses don't run on Sundays, and often operate only from May to September. The cliff paths, with their evenly spaced hostels, make for easy hiking. Serious trekkers can try the famous **Land's End** to **John O'Groats** route, running from the tip of Cornwall to the top of Scotland.

BODMIN MOOR

Bodmin Moor is high country, containing Cornwall's highest points, Rough Tor (1312 ft.) and Brown Willy (1378 ft.). The region is rich with ancient remains, like the stone circles that crowd Rough Tor. Legend has it that Camelford, at the moor's north edge, is the site of King Arthur's Camelot and that Arthur and his illegitimate son Mordred fought each other at Slaughter Bridge. The moor is in central Cornwall, directly west of Dartmoor National Park.

TRANSPORTATION. The town of Bodmin is at the southern edge of Bodmin Moor, which spreads north to coastal (but not beachfront) Tintagel and Camelford. **Trains** (☎08457 484 950) travel from **Bodmin Parkway** (station open M-F 6:10am-8pm, Sa 6:30am-8pm, Su 10:35am-7:40pm) to London Paddington (4hr., every hr., £72), Penzance (1hr., 15 per day, £8-11.60), and Plymouth (40min., every hr., £6.40-8.70). National Express **buses** (☎08705 808 080) go to Plymouth (1hr., 2 per day, £50). Western Greyhound (☎01637 871 871) runs bus #593 to Newquay (1hr., M-Sa 5 per day). Access Camelford by first hopping the #555 to Wadebridge (30min., every hr.); from Wadebridge, take the #594 to Camelford (30min., M-Sa 5 per day). To get to Camelford on weekends or to reach Tintagel and Boscastle, take the #555 to Wadebridge (30min., every hr.) and transfer to #524 (M-Sa 4 per day, Su 3 per day). **Hiking** is convenient from Camelford and is the only way to reach the tors. Rent **bikes** at Bodmin Bikes & Cycle Hire, 3 Hamley Ct., across the street from where the Camel Trail hits Bodmin. (☎01208 731 92; www.bodminbikes.co.uk. £10 per day. Open daily 9am-5pm.) **Hitchhiking** in this area is dangerous and *Let's Go* does not recommend it.

HIKING AND OUTDOOR ACTIVITIES. Most of the moor is privately owned, but as of 2005 hikers can use the areas of the moor that are mapped as "Access Land." Camping and fires are not allowed. The moor was originally used to mine copper and quarry granite; stay aware of your footing, as mineshafts and abandoned buildings remain.

The **River Fowley** divides the moor in half, running from the slopes of **Brown Willy** to end at **Golitha Falls** just outside Common Moor. The 60 mi. **Copper Trail** circumnavigates the moor, while the 17 mi. **Camel Trail** starts in Padstow and passes through Bodmin on the way to Poley's Bridge. A former railway track, the trail is mostly smooth and level, providing excellent biking. Numerous trails lead to the area's curious rock structures, including the **Cheesewring**, a precariously balanced set of rocks near the town of Minions. **Cardinham Woods**, to the east of Bodmin, is a dense forest that was originally planted for timber production but now offers shaded hiking and **cycling** paths. **Colliford Lake**, south of Bolventor, is the region's largest body of water, and nearby **Dozmary Pool** is rumored (among other places) to be the resting place of Excalibur. Ordnance Survey Explorer Map 109 (£7-8) covers Bodmin Moor and is available for purchase at most local TICs. **Guided walks** are offered through the Coast and Countryside Service. A schedule of these walks is available in *Coast Lines and Countryside News*, a guide distributed by the North Cornwall District Council (☎01208 265 644).

BODMIN
☎(0)1208

The town of Bodmin is at the heart of northern Cornwall. The historical capital of the region, Bodmin now caters to hikers, who pass through on their way to the Arthurian stomping grounds of Bodmin Moor. The **Military Museum,** off St. Nicholas St., behind Bodmin General Station, displays several artifacts related to Tommy Atkins, the heroically ordinary soldier, as well as George Washington's Bible and account book, which reveals a missing US$3000. (☎01208 728 10. Open July-Aug. M-F 9am-5pm, Su 10am-5pm; Sept.-June M-F 9am-5pm. £2.50.) The **Bodmin Jail,** Berrycombe Rd., was the safekeep for the Crown Jewels and Domesday Book during WWI. The jail is also near the Camel Trail and offers discounted bike rental with admission price. (☎01208 762 92; www.

bodminjail.org. Open daily 10am-dusk. £5.50.) Hidden in Bodmin's forests, the 17th-century mansion **Lanhydrock** has plaster ceilings portraying scenes from the Old Testament. From Bodmin, take Western Greyhound bus #555 or travel 2 mi. southeast on the A38. (☎01208 265 950. House open from mid-Mar. to Sept. Tu-Su 11am-5:30pm; Oct. Tu-Su 11am-5pm. Gardens open daily 10am-6pm. £9. Garden and grounds £5.) Outside Bodmin, **Camel Valley Vineyards** sit in the moors from which they create their award-winning wine. A full tour and wine tasting is a steal at £7.50 (Apr.-Oct. W at 5pm), while a shorter tour and glass of wine on the terrace is £5 (Apr.-Sept. M-F at 2:30pm). Follow the signs on the A389 toward Wadebridge or follow the Camel Trail out of Bodmin for 3 mi. (☎01208 779 59. Open Easter-Oct. M-Sa 10am-5pm; Nov.-Easter M-F 10am-5pm. MC/V.)

Although the plastic gnomes in the garden of **Elm Grove ❷**, Cardell Rd., are rather kitsch, the rooms are anything but. (☎01208 740 44. Full English breakfast included. £27 per person, £25 if more than one night. Cash only). A mile north of town, camp at the **Camping and Caravanning Club ❶**, Old Callywith Rd., with showers and laundry. Head north of town on Castle St., which becomes Old Callywith Rd. (☎01208 738 34. £7 per person. Electricity available. Cash only.) The **Bodmin General Station,** St. Nicholas St. (☎0845 125 9678), serves Bodmin & Wenford Railway's trains, which run to the area's main railway hub, **Bodmin Parkway Station.** (☎0845 125 9678. Apr.-Sept. 4-7 per day, £10.) To reach town from the Bodmin Parkway Station, 3 mi. away on the A38, take Western Greyhound bus #555 (every hr., £1.40) or call **Parnell's Taxis** (☎01208 750 00; £8 between station and town). The **Tourist Information Centre,** Shire Hall, Mount Folly, sells maps for £7-8. (☎01208 766 16. Open Easter-Oct. M-Sa 10am-5pm; Nov.-Easter M-F 10am-5pm.) Other services include: **banks** on Fore St.; **police** (☎08705 777 444), up Priory Rd.; a **Boots** pharmacy, 34 Fore St. (☎01208 728 36; open M-Sa 9am-5:30pm); and the **post office,** 40 Fore St. (☎08457 223 344; open M-F 9am-5:30pm, Sa 9am-12:30pm), inside Cost Cutters. **Postcode:** PL31 2HL.

TINTAGEL   ☎(0)1840

Tintagel is a tiny seaside village proud of its connection to Arthurian lore. Its star attraction is the sprawling ruin of **▧Tintagel Castle,** rumored to be the site of King Arthur's birth. Even if you don't buy into the lore, the views are worth the admission price. Be sure to see the rocky **Merlin's Cave,** beneath the castle ruins, at low tide, when you can climb through the caves to the other side of the island. (☎01840 770 328. Open daily Apr.-Sept. 10am-6pm; Oct. 10am-5pm; Nov.-Mar. 10am-4pm. £4.60. Merlin's Cave free.)

Inland, **King Arthur's Great Halls of Chivalry,** Fore St., allegedly held the round table of King Arthur. The Great Hall has two rooms: an antechamber with a light show telling the legend of King Arthur and a hall with three round tables. (☎01840 770 526. Open daily Easter-Oct. 10am-5pm; Nov.-Easter 11am-3pm. £3.50, concessions £2.50.) Escape homages to Arthur on a 1½ mi. walk through **Saint Nectan's Glen** to a 60 ft. waterfall, historically a space for spiritual healing. From the Visitor Centre, head toward Bossiney for about 1 mi., then follow signs along the footpath to your right. (☎01840 770 760. Open Easter-Oct. daily 10:30am-6:30pm. £3.50, children £1.75, families £10.)

The **Tintagel Visitor Centre,** Bossiney Rd., has an exhibit separating Arthurian fact from fiction. (☎01840 779 084; www.visitbostcastleandtintagel. com. Internet access £1 per 15min. Open daily Mar.-Oct. 10am-5pm; Nov.-Feb. 10:30am-4pm.) Western Greyhound **buses** #594 (M-Sa) and 524 (Su) go to Wadebridge (40min., M-Sa 5 per day, £5) via Camelford (20min.; M-Sa 5 per day, Su 3 per day). Perched on a cliff, the **YHA Tintagel ❷**, at Dunderhole Point, is three-quarters of a mile from Tintagel and has views of the coast. The facilities are a bit cramped, but eating dinner on the patio overlooking the water more than makes up for it. Basic food is sold on site. Head out of town past St. Materiana's Church, then follow the footpath along the shore. The hostel is set in the side of the cliff and is nearly invisible from this approach; you'll be on top of it after about a quarter-mile. (☎0870 770 6068. Kitchen. Laundry £2.50. Reception 8-10am and 5-10pm. Lockout 10am-noon; no room access 10am-5pm. Open Easter-Oct. Dorms from £12, under 18 from £9. MC/V.)

BOSCASTLE ☎(0)1840

Flanked by two grassy hills, tiny Boscastle is a scenic Cornish village divided by a sparkling river. This enviable valley location proved destructive in August 2004, when a flash flood swept through the village and destroyed the town center. The community recovered quickly and the village's charm remains. The **National Trust Information Centre,** The Old Forge, Boscastle Harbour, offers hiking suggestions and sells maps. (☎01840 250 353. Open Feb.-Oct. 10:30am-5pm.) The new **Boscastle Visitor Centre,** The Harbour, shows a video about the flood and has a small exhibit about the history of the town. Pick up the *Boscastle Village Trail Guide* (£1), which outlines walks through the area and points out the village's quaint sights. (☎01840 250 010; www.visitboscastleandtintagel. com. Internet £1 per 15min. Open daily Easter-Sept. 10am-5pm; Oct.-Easter 10am-4pm.) Before he picked up his pen, Thomas Hardy was an architect and designed the church. In town, the **Museum of Witchcraft** is the largest of its kind. Its quirky collection of artifacts, trinkets, and newspaper articles explain and defend the occult. Look for the weighing chair used by witch hunters as well as audio stations containing spells from modern witches. (☎01840 250 111. Open Easter-Halloween M-Sa 10:30am-6pm, Su 11:30am-6pm. £3, children and seniors £2, "naughty children and little monsters" £10.)

The self-catering **YHA Boscastle Harbour ❶** has an incredible location on the water. Reconstructed after the flood, the former stables now boast spacious rooms. (☎0870 770 5710. Dorms from £14, under 18 from £10.50. MC/V.) Ten minutes from the coast, **The Old Coach House ❸,** on Tintagel Rd. at the top of the village, has ensuite rooms and English breakfast. A dog named Pearl sits in the large, beautiful lounge area. (☎01840 250 398. Wheelchair-accessible. Open Mar.-Oct. £27-32 per person. MC/V.) Western Greyhound **buses** #524 and 594 leave from Boscastle to Wadebridge (1-1hr.; M-Sa 9 per day, Su 3 per day; £3.40) via Tintagel (10min., £1.70) and to Bude (40min.).

PADSTOW ☎(0)1841

Near the more heavily touristed Newquay and St. Ives, Padstow has become a quiet alternative for a seaside holiday. The small town has drawn Rick Stein, the famous British seafood chef, and four of his restaurants to the streets of Padstow. Gourmet food and quaint culture come with a high price tag, so those not intent on blowing their budget on bite-size portions and expensive B&Bs may choose to make this scenic town a daytrip.

◪◪ TRANSPORTATION AND PRACTICAL INFORMATION. Western Greyhound **buses** #555 and 556 go to Bodmin from Padstow (45min., every hr.) via Wadebridge and between Newquay and Padstow (2hr., 4-5 per day). Buses arrive on the far side of the South Quay, a few minutes from the center of town and the TIC. Rent **bikes** at Padstow Cycle Hire, South Quay, in the car park. (☎01841 533 533; www.padstowcyclehire.com. £12 per day. Open daily from mid-July to Aug. 9am-9pm; from Sept. to mid-July 9am-5pm.) The **TIC,** Red Brick Building, North Quay, books rooms for a 10% deposit. (☎01841 533 449; www. padstow.com. Internet £1.20 per 15min. Open Apr.-Oct. M-F 9:30am-5pm, Sa

10am-4pm; Nov.-Mar. M-F 9:30am-4:30pm.) Other services include: **banks** on Market Pl. and Duke St.; **Boots** pharmacy, 8-10 Market St. (☎01841 532 327; open M-F 9am-5:30pm, Sa 9am-5pm); and the **post office** on Duke St. (☎08457 223 344; open M-F 9am-5:30pm, Sa 9am-1pm). **Postcode:** PL28 8AA.

▊▊ ACCOMMODATIONS AND FOOD. Lodgings in Padstow are pleasant but pricey (from £30). **Ms. Anne Humphrey ❸,** 1 Caswarth Terr., offers cozy rooms. (☎01841 532 025. Breakfast included. Singles £25; doubles £45. Cash only.) Find a wealth of local knowledge at the home of **Peter and Jane Cullinan ❷,** 4 Riverside, along the harbor. The top-floor double has a balcony overlooking the bay, but the small room in the back is the cheapest. (☎01841 532 383. Doubles £27-37. Cash only.) The nearest hostel, the **YHA Treyarnon Bay ❷,** is 4½ mi. from Padstow, on Tregonnan in Treyarnon. It's off the B3276; take bus #56. (☎0870 770 6076. Open Apr.-Feb. Dorms from £14, under 18 from £10.50. MC/V.) **Padstow Touring Park ❶,** a mile south of town on the B3274/A389, offers camping and caravanning. (☎01841 532 061; www.padstowtouringpark.co.uk. Camp shop and laundry. Sites £10-15.50. Electricity £3. MC/V.)

With fresh fish and the almost unavoidable influence of Rick Stein, you're pretty much guaranteed quality, expensive food in Padstow. Splurge at **Saint Petrocs Bistro ❹,** New St., a Rick Stein creation, offering mouthwatering seafood for £13-16. (☎01841 532 700; www.rickstein.com. Open daily noon-3pm and 7-10pm. MC/V.) Take afternoon tea on 19th-century china at the intimate **Victorian Tea Room ❷,** 22 Duke St. (☎01841 533 161. All-day breakfast £6. Open daily 9am-5pm. Cash only.) Grab a plate of fish and chips (from £6) at **Stein's Fish & Chips ❷,** South Quay, the most affordable of Rick Stein's many eateries. (☎01841 532 700. Open daily noon-2:30pm and 5-9pm. MC/V.)

▊▊ SIGHTS AND BEACHES. Beyond the ferry point near the TIC, an easy **coastal walk** ascends the cliffs for ocean views—follow the path past the war memorial to reach expansive sands and an island-studded bay. Cyclists converge in Padstow for the start of the **Camel Trail** and the 26 mi. **Saints' Way,** which follows the route of the Celtic saints who landed here from Ireland and Wales. The **National Lobster Hatchery,** South Quay, across from the bus stop, was built to save the ailing lobster industry from overfishing. Expectant lobster moms are brought here to lay their eggs, and visitors can see the insect-like babies in various stages of development. (☎01841 533 877; www.nationallobsterhatchery.com. Open from May to mid-Sept. daily 10am-6pm; from mid-Sept. to Apr. M-Sa 10am-4pm. £3, children £1.50, seniors £2, families £7.) Numerous nearby beaches are perfect for exploring, surfing, and sunbathing. Cave-pocked **Trevone Beach** can be reached via bus #556 (5min.; M-Sa 7 per day, Su 5 per day). Bus #556 continues to remote **Constantine Bay** (15min.), with great surfing, and **Porthcothan Beach** (30min.), a good spot for tanning. The professionals at **Harlyn Surf School,** 23 Grenville Rd. in Padstow, teach to all levels at nearby Harlyn Bay. (☎01841 533 076; www.harlynsurfschool.co.uk. Book in advance and meet at the school's trailer on Harlyn Beach. Open May-Oct. Lessons £35, 4 lessons £110.) **Black Tor** ferries chug from Padstow Harbor across the bay to nearby **Rock,** where visitors will find sailing, water-skiing, windsurfing, and golfing. (☎01841 532 239. 10-15min. Easter-Oct. daily 8am-8pm; Nov.-Easter M-Sa 8am-5pm. £3, children £1.) Fishing and boating trips depart from the harbor. **Sport&Leisure,** North Quay, books and operates fishing trips (2-8hr.) on the *Celtic Warrior;* anything you catch is yours. (☎01841 532 639; www.celticwarrior.me.uk. Also rents surf gear. Trips daily Easter-Oct. 9am-5pm. £13 for 2hr., £30 for 4hr.)

NEWQUAY

☎(0)1637

Known as "the new California" to the hordes of teenage travelers who crowd the streets, Newquay (NEW-key; pop. 20,000) is an incongruous slice of surfer culture in the middle of Cornwall. The town has long attracted riders for its superior waves (by England's standards), and a steady stream of revelers has transformed the once-quiet seaside resort into an English Ibiza, with wet T-shirt contests and dance parties that rage late into the night.

◩ TRANSPORTATION

Trains: Train station on Cliff Rd. Ticket office open M-F 9:30am-3pm, Sa 9:30am-1pm. Trains (☎08457 484 950) to Newquay pass through **Par** (50min.; in summer M-F 8 per day, Sa-Su 5 per day), where they connect to **Bodmin** (1hr.; M-F 8 per day, Sa-Su 5 per day), **Penzance** (1hr., 12 per day), and **Plymouth** (50min., 15 per day).

Buses: National Express (☎08717 818 181) buses leave Manor Rd. for **London** (7hr., 4-7 per day, £38.50). Western Greyhound buses leave Manor Rd. for **Padstow** (#556, 1hr., 1 per hr.), **St. Austell** (#521, 1hr., every hr.), and **St. Ives** (#501, 2hr., 2 per day, £5). Buses #89 and 90 go to **Falmouth** (1hr., M-Sa every hr.).

Taxis: Fleet Cabs (☎01637 875 000). 24hr.

◪ PRACTICAL INFORMATION

Tourist Information Centre, Marcus Hill (☎01637 854 020; www.newquay.co.uk), a few blocks toward the city center from the train station. Gives out free maps, books tours, handles Western Union money transfers, and books accommodations for £2.50 in the office (£4 by phone) plus a 10% deposit (20% by phone). 24hr. computer information system open to the public. Open M-F 9:30am-4:30pm, Su 9:30am-12:30pm.)

Tours: Western Greyhound, 14 East St. (☎01637 871 871). Runs bus tours to the Eden Project (p. 249) and nearby coastal towns. 5-8hr. daily tours. £8-15.

Banks: Most are on Bank St. Open M-Tu and Th-F 9am-4:30pm, W 10am-4:30pm.

Beyond Tourism: JobCentre, 32 East St. (☎01637 894 900). Open M-Tu and Th-F 9am-5pm, W 10am-5pm.

Launderette: 1 Beach Parade (☎01637 875 901). Open M-Sa 10am-4pm.

Police: Tolcarne Rd. (☎08452 777 444).

Pharmacy: Boots, 15 Bank St. (☎01637 872 014). Open M-F 8:30am-8:30pm, Sa 8:30am-7pm, Su 10:30am-4pm.

Hospital: St. Thomas Rd. (☎01637 893 623).

Internet Access: Cyber Surf @ Newquay, 2 Broad St. (☎01637 875 497), across from Somerfield. 5p per min. Open M-Sa 9:30am-8pm, Su noon-6pm.

Post Office: 31-33 East St. (☎08457 223 344). Open M and W-F 9am-5:30pm, Tu 9:30am-5:30pm, Sa 9am-12:30pm. **Postcode:** TR7 1BU.

◪ ◪ ACCOMMODATIONS AND CAMPING

B&Bs (£18-30) are near the TIC; numerous hostels and surf lodges (£12-16) gather on **Headland Road** and **Tower Road,** near Fistral Beach. Accommodations fill up in advance during surfing competitions, so call ahead in summer.

Matt's Surf Lodge, 110 Mt. Wise (☎01637 874 651; www.surflodge.co.uk), between Fistral Beach and the town. You can't get much more laid-back than this. 100s of DVDs and a bar keep visitors happy when they're not hanging 10. Some rooms look out on the sea. Rooms July-Aug. £15-20 per person; Sept.-June £8-10 per person. Cash only. ❷

Newquay International Backpackers, 69-73 Tower Rd. (☎01637 879 366; www.backpackers.co.uk). Friendly and funky, with a dining area that looks like the tube of a wave. Dorms named after world metropolises like Rome and London. Rooms and showers are co-ed; call ahead to request single-sex room. Dorms £10-18; twins £11-19. MC/V. ❷

Original Backpackers, 16 Beachfield Ave. (☎01637 874 668; www.originalbackpackers.co.uk), off Bank St. Smallish dorms are steps from the beach and nightlife. Kitchen. Single-sex dorms. Laundry. Dorms May-Sept. £20; Oct.-Apr. £12. AmEx/MC/V. ❷

Trenance Chalet and Caravan Park, Edgcumbe Ave. (☎01637 873 447; www.trenance-holidaypark.co.uk). A campsite miraculously located in town. From the train station, turn right on Cliff Rd., then right on Edgcumbe Ave., and follow it for 15min. Restaurant, cafe, and laundry. Open Easter-Oct. £6.50-8 per person. Electricity 50p. AmEx/MC/V. ❶

🐱🍴 FOOD AND PUBS

Sit-down restaurants in Newquay tend to be costly. Pizza and kebab shops, catering to late-night stumblers, fill the town center. Most takeaway is relatively cheap. For other options, head to pubs or **Somerfield** supermarket, at the end of Fore St. (☎01637 876 006. Open M-Sa 8am-9pm, Su 10am-4pm.)

Cafe Irie, 38 Fore St. (☎01637 859 200; www.cafeirie.co.uk). Cafe and coffee bar serving creative dishes and all-day breakfast options (full English £5.15, pancakes and bacon £3.75). Waitstaff plops down on sofas next to you to take your order while you groove to the music. Board games and funky art. Open daily 10am-5pm. Cash only. ❶

Ye Olde Dolphin, 39-47 Fore St. (☎01637 874 262). Laden with Old World decor, combining kitsch and class to create a quality seafood restaurant. Meals are expensive (£12-20), but take advantage of specials (6-7pm), including a 3-course meal for £15. Open M-Sa 6-10pm, Su noon-3pm and 6-10pm. MC/V. ❸

The Shack, 52 Bank St. (☎01637 875 675). Sit-down restaurant with a beach theme and tasty dishes (£4-11), from vegetarian and Caribbean plates to the lunchtime sandwiches (£4). Open in summer daily 10am-2am; in winter reduced hours. MC/V. ❶

The Chy Bar and Kitchen, 12 Beach Rd. (☎01637 873 415). Enjoy one of the best views in Newquay in this chic upstairs eatery on the beach. Lunch £4.30-7.75. Dinner entrees £10-18. Open daily 10am-3am. MC/V. ❷

🌙 NIGHTLIFE

Newquay teems with large groups of sun-kissed surfers and visitors ready to drink, dance, and drink some more. Watch out for frequent stag and hen parties, and head toward the shore for more relaxed nightlife venues. The trail of surfer bars begins on **North Quay Hill,** at the corner of Tower Rd. and Fore St.

Central Inn, 11 Central Sq. (☎01637 873 810), in the town center. A great place to grab early drinks. Outdoor seating. Open M-Sa 11am-midnight, Su noon-10:30pm. Kitchen open daily in summer noon-8pm; in winter noon-3:30pm and 5-8pm.

On The Rocks, 14 The Crescent (☎01637 872 897; www.ontherocksbar.co.uk). Eclectic live music, ocean views, pool tables, and big-screen TVs playing surfing footage. A good time for everyone, from the posh to flip-flop devotees. £1 bottles and shots on W. Free live music W and F-Sa. Open daily 8am-2am. Kitchen open 8am-6pm.

Belushi's, 35 Fore St. (☎01637 859 111). Popular bar beneath St. Christophers. A great place to meet fellow travelers. Live music most nights, but, if nothing's on, enjoy the billiards and loyal patrons. Open M-W 10am-midnight, Th-Sa 10am-2am, Su 10am-1am.

Sailors, 15 Fore St. (☎01637 872 838; www.sailorsnightclub.com). Elaborate lighting enhances the vibrant dance scene. Crowded pub next door. Beach party W. Open M 8-11pm, Tu-Th 10:30pm-3am, F-Sa 10pm-4am.

The Koola, 8-10 Beach Rd. (☎01637 873 415). A relaxed crowd, with barefoot surfers fresh from the waves and dolled-up locals out on the town. Less hectic than other clubs in the area. 3 levels of dancing. Sister club to the Chy; at night, the door between them opens up to form 1 big area. Locals night M. Open daily 10pm-3am.

Buzios, Cliff Rd. (☎01637 870 300; www.buziosbar.co.uk). Contemporary decor gives a Miami-like feel to this ultra-chic bar and pool hall. Dance the night away or cavort in the leather booths. The red carpet and outdoor terrace add nice touches. Free Wi-Fi. Open M-Th and Su noon-midnight, F-Sa noon-3am.

FESTIVALS

Several festivals and concerts coincide with local surf competitions. May is a busy month, with the **English Surf Championships** during the first week and the **Red Stripe British Longboard Championships** at the end. Souped-up VWs come to Newquay for May's **Run to the Sun** festival. In early August, the **RipCurl Boardmasters Championships** bring six days of surfing, music, and mayhem to Fistral's shoreline. (☎020 8789 6655. Tickets £29 per day, £50 for the weekend.) Check with the TIC events hotline (☎01637 854 040) for the most up-to-date information, as weather can affect dates, especially of surfing competitions.

BEACHES AND OUTDOOR ACTIVITIES

Atlantic winds descend on **Fistral Beach** with a vengeance, creating what most consider to be the best surfing in Europe. The shores are less cluttered than the sea, where throngs of wetsuited surfers paddle out between the crests. Local surfers say that ominous skies often forecast the liveliest surf, but use caution. Lifeguards roam the sands from May to September from 10am to 6pm.

 SOARING SYMBOLS. Pay close attention to safety flags while spending time in the water. The space between checkered flags is designated for watercraft, while swimming is permissible between red-and-yellow-striped flags. Inflatables are forbidden when an orange flag is flying, and no swimming at all is allowed when the red flag flaps over the beach.

On the bay side, the sands are divided into four beaches: tamer waters at **Towan Beach** and **Great Western Beach,** smack dab in the middle of town, lure throngs of sunbathers and novice surfers. **Tolcarne Beach** and **Lusty Glaze Beach** are privately owned, with spotless sand and dry day facilities. Cross the Trethellan footbridge and head toward the sea to reach **Crantock Beach** and its sandy shores. **Sunset Surf Shop,** 106 Fore St., rents out surf paraphernalia. (☎01637 877 624. Boards £5-10 per day, £25-40 per week; wetsuits or bodyboards £4/20. Open Apr.-Oct. daily 9am-6:30pm.) The professionals at **O'Neill Surf Academy** teach intro, one-day, and two-day courses for both amateur and advanced surfers. (☎01841 520 052. Courses Mar.-Dec. Intro £30, 1-day £40, 2-day £75.)

Everyone knows that there's great surfing and partying in Newquay, but, on the off chance that bad weather or a hangover prevents one or the other, the city also provides other diversions. Head to the Rowing Club at the Harbour for **gig racing,** a traditional form of Cornish rowing. Refreshments follow at the clubhouse. (☎01637 876 810. Races M 7pm.) **Pitch & Putt,** where you hit a golf ball as hard as possible then tap, tap, tap it home, is popular. The most central course is located off Narcliff Rd. between Tolcarne and Lusty Glaze beaches.

Enjoy the coastline on a stallion from the **Newquay Riding Centre,** Trenance Stables, Trenance Ln. ☎01637 872 699; www.newquayridingstables.co.uk. Ride length varies based on experience. (Open M-Sa. Call for tour times. Prices vary depending on horse and length of ride.)

FALMOUTH   ☎(0)1326

The historic port of Falmouth offers five sandy beaches, a busy city center with one-of-a-kind shops, and a harbor full of sailboats from around the world. Get a taste of history at the 450-year-old twin fortresses of Pendennis and St. Mawes, built by Henry VIII to protect England from Spanish and French invasion, or live the local life in the town's thriving restaurant and pub scene.

▶ TRANSPORTATION

Trains: Falmouth has 3 unmanned train stations. **Penmere Halt** is near Melvill Rd. and Killigrew St., **Falmouth Town** is near the town center, and **Falmouth Docks** is near Pendennis Castle. Buy tickets M-F 9am-5pm by calling Lynne at ☎0870 224 9545. Debit or credit card only. Trains (☎08457 484 950) to: **Exeter** (3½hr., 8 per day, £15-30); **London Paddington** (5½hr., 5 per day, £69); **Plymouth** (2hr.; M-Sa 12 per day, Su 7 per day; £13); **Truro** (20min., every hr., £3-6).

Buses: All buses stop at the **Moor station,** directly off the main road next to the large traffic circle. National Express (☎08717 818 181) to **London** (8hr., 2 per day, £38.50) and **Plymouth** (2½hr., 2 per day, £6). Pick up schedules and tickets at the TIC. First bus #2 runs to **Penzance** (2hr., every 1-2hr.) via Helston (50min.), while #89 and 90 go to **Newquay** (1½hr., M-Sa every 2hr.) via Truro (30min.). First #88 runs to Truro more frequently. Truronian (☎01872 273 453) sends buses to the **Lizard Peninsula** (p. 250).

Ferries: Ferries leave from Prince of Wales Pier and Custom House Quay. St. Mawes Ferry Company (☎01326 313 201; www.kingharryscornwall.co.uk/ferries) sails to **St. Mawes** (25min.; 2 per hr.; £4.50, round-trip £7). Runs July-Aug. 8:30am-11pm; Sept.-June 8:30am-5:15pm. Newman's Cruises (☎01872 580 309) runs to **Smuggler's Cottage,** up the River Fal (45min., M-Sa 2 per day, round-trip £6.50). Enterprise (☎01326 374 241; www.enterprise-boats.co.uk) makes the idyllic trip to **Truro** (1hr.; May-Sept. M-Sa 5 per day, Oct.-Apr. call ahead; £7, round-trip £11).

Taxis: Checkers (☎01326 212 127). 24hr. **Radio Taxis** (☎01326 315 194).

✈❓ ORIENTATION AND PRACTICAL INFORMATION

The rail line runs along the highest parts of Falmouth; streets to the sea and to B&Bs are steep in areas. **The Moor** is Falmouth's main square. The main street extends from there, changing names from **High Street** to **Market Street, Church Street, Arwenack Street,** and finally **Grove Place,** which leads to **Discovery Quay,** the dockside area home to the Maritime Museum and to many shops and cafes.

Tourist Information Centre, 11 Market Strand (☎01326 312 300; www.acornishriver. co.uk), Prince of Wales Pier. Open July-Aug. M-Sa 9:30am-5:15pm, Su 10am-2pm; Sept. and Mar.-June M-Sa 9:30am-5:15pm; Oct.-Feb. M-F 9:30am-5:15pm.

Tours: Many companies run cruises (1-2hr., £5-7) on River Fal to the north and Helford River to the southwest. K&S Cruises (☎01326 211 056) offers fishing trips (daily 5-7:15pm, £10); book trips at the yellow kiosk on the Prince of Wales Pier.

Banks: Banks and ATMs line Market St.

Library: Falmouth Library, The Moor (☎01326 314 901). Internet £1 per 15min. Open M-Tu and Th-F 9:30am-6pm, Sa 9:30am-4pm.

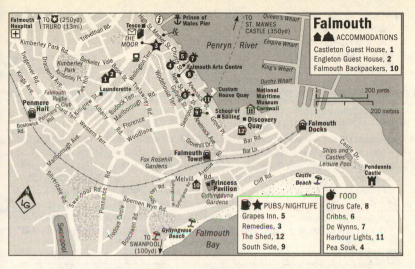

Falmouth

▲▲ ACCOMMODATIONS

Castleton Guest House, **1**
Engleton Guest House, **2**
Falmouth Backpackers, **10**

🍺★ PUBS/NIGHTLIFE
Grapes Inn, **5**
Remedies, **3**
The Shed, **12**
South Side, **9**

🍴 FOOD
Citrus Cafe, **8**
Cribbs, **6**
De Wynns, **7**
Harbour Lights, **11**
Pea Souk, **4**

Launderette: Bubbles, 99 Killigrew St. (☎01326 311 291). Open M-F 8am-7pm, Sa 9am-7pm, Su 10am-3pm.

Police: Dracaena Ave. (☎08452 777 444).

Pharmacy: Boots, 47 Market St. (☎01326 312 373). Open M-Sa 9am-5:30pm, Su 10:30am-4:30pm.

Hospital: Trescobeas Rd. (☎01326 434 700).

Internet Access: At the **Falmouth Library** (above). Also at **Q Bar** (☎01326 210 294), across from where buses stop on The Moor. £2 per 30min. Free Wi-Fi. Open M-Th 10am-1am, F-Sa 10am-2:30am, Su noon-midnight.

Post Office: The Moor (☎08457 223 344). **Bureau de change.** Open M and W-F 8:30am-5:30pm, Tu and Sa 9am-5:30pm. **Postcode:** TR11 3RB.

🛏 ACCOMMODATIONS

Western Terrace, a 15min. walk from town, has a wealth of B&Bs (£25-45 per person). **Avenue** and **Melvill Roads** sport additional lodgings.

▨ **Falmouth Backpackers,** 9 Gyllyngvase Terr. (☎01326 319 996). Run by the knowledge-able Charlotte, who has been around the world to Timbuktu and back. Self-catering kitchen and Internet access. Dorms £17. Cash only. ❷

Castleton Guest House, 68 Killigrew St. (☎01326 372 644; www.falmouth-bandb. co.uk). The proprietors are happy to meet requests, from veggie breakfasts to a spare umbrella. £27.50 per person. MC/V. ❸

Engleton Guest House, 67 Killigrew St. (☎01326 372 644), next door to the Castleton Guest House (and of the same owner). Clean rooms and personalized service for a reasonable price. Breakfast included. £27.50 per person. MC/V. ❸

🍴 FOOD

Pick up groceries at **Tesco,** The Moor. (☎0845 677 9267. Open M-Sa 7am-9pm, Su 10am-4pm.) Falmouth has many options for quality eats, from cheap pasties to outrageously priced (but oh so fresh and tasty) lobsters.

■ **Pea Souk,** 19C Well Ln. (☎01326 317 583), hidden away off Church St. A funky little vegetarian cafe serves homemade soup (£3) and large sandwiches (£3.75). Open M-Sa 9am-5pm, Su 10am-3pm. Cash only. ❶

Citrus Cafe, 6 Arwenack St. (☎01326 318 585). Delicious Indian and Mediterranean fusion dishes, served among bright yellow walls and bamboo seats. Takeaway baguettes and smoothies. Open M-Tu and Th-Sa 10am-5pm, Su 11am-4pm. Cash only. ❷

Cribbs, 33 Arwenack St. (☎01326 210 000). During the day, enjoy sandwiches (£6-7) and coffee on the couches. Late at night, the bar fills up for good drinks and music. Free Wi-Fi. Open daily 9:30-11am, noon-3pm, 6pm-late. AmEx/MC/V. ❷

Harbour Lights, Arwenack St. (☎01326 316 934; www.hlfish.co.uk). Award-winning fish and chips and other battered treats. The price jumps dramatically in the restaurant, so take your fish and chips to the pier and have a picnic—just watch for crazy seagulls dive-bombing for fries. Takeaway open M-Th and Su 11:30am-10pm, F-Sa 11:30am-11pm. Restaurant open M-Th and Su 11:30am-3:30pm and 4:30-9pm, F-Sa 11:30am-3:30pm and 4:30am-9:30pm. Takeaway cash only; restaurant MC/V. ❶

De Wynns, 55 Church St. (☎ 01326 319 259). A tearoom with views of the harbor. Try Granny Nunn's bread pudding—the recipe's a secret. Open M-Sa 10am-5pm. MC/V. ❶

👁 SIGHTS

NATIONAL MARITIME MUSEUM CORNWALL. The museum covers all aspects of the sea, from interactive exhibits on navigation and weather patterns to boat-building to search and rescue. A collection of boats is suspended mid-air in one gallery. (*Discovery Quay.* ☎*01326 313 388; www.nmmc.co.uk. Open daily 10am-5pm. £8, students and children £5.25, seniors £6.25, families £21.*)

PENDENNIS CASTLE. A Tudor castle built by Henry VIII to guard the harbor, the site features a walk-through diorama with wax gunners and battle reenactments in summer. The grounds also contain massive WWII "disappearing" guns and a strategic half-moon battery. Walking to the castle is a bit of a hike from town, but the First bus #41 and Truronian #400 ("Falmouth Explorer") drop you off nearby. (☎*01326 316 594. Open July-Aug. M-Th and Su 10am-6pm, Sa 10am-4pm; Sept. and Apr.-June M-F and Su 10am-5pm, Sa 10am-4pm; Oct.-Mar. daily 10am-4pm. £5.50, concessions £4.40, children £2.80, families £13.80.*)

SAINT MAWES CASTLE. Surrounded by the thatched roofs and tropical gardens of St. Mawes village, the castle is a circular battlement built by Henry VIII—the second line of defense after Pendennis Castle. (*A 25min. ferry across the channel (p. 246). The castle is 10min. uphill from the ferry dropoff point.* ☎*01326 270 526. Open July-Aug. M-F and Su 10am-6pm; Sept. and Apr.-June M-F and Su 10am-5pm; Oct. daily 10am-4pm; Nov.-Mar. M and F-Su 10am-4pm. £4, concessions £3.20, children £2. Free 1hr. audio tour.*)

FALMOUTH ART GALLERY. The museum holds a small but wonderful permanent collection and regular exhibitions. (*Above the library.* ☎*01326 313 863; www.falmouthartgallery.com. Open M-Sa 10am-5pm. Free.*)

🎵 🎭 ENTERTAINMENT AND NIGHTLIFE

For a small town, Falmouth has a surprisingly vibrant social scene. At night, tourists and locals head to the main street, where many of the cafes turn into pubs. **Regatta Week,** the second week of August, is Falmouth's main sailing event, with boat shows and music performances. The mid-October **Oyster Festival** features oyster tasting, craft fairs, and a parade. Contact the TIC for details.

Poly Arts and Science Centre, 24 Church St. (☎01326 212 300; www.thepoly.org). Hosts exhibitions, concerts, theater, and films. Exhibitions free. Theater and concert tickets £5-10. Box office open daily 10am-5pm and 1hr. before any event or screening.

Princess Pavilion, Melvill Rd. (☎01326 211 222). Hosts live music in an outdoor venue. Gardens, patio, and bandstand with free shows £10-20.

Grapes Inn, 64 Church St. (☎01326 314 704). Enjoy a harbor view with your pint. Open M-Th and Su 11am-11pm, F-Sa 11am-midnight. Kitchen open noon-3pm and 6-9pm.

South Side, 35-37 Arwenack St. (☎01326 212 122; www.southside-falmouth.co.uk). Relaxed cafe-bar with colorful artwork on the walls and cushion-covered couches for lounging. Free Wi-Fi. Happy hour 10-11pm. Open daily 11am-midnight.

Remedies, The Moor (☎01326 314 454). The town's hottest club. Best on weekends, when young crowds groove to Top 40 hits on 2 floors. "Bar 150" M has £1.50 cover and £1.50 drinks. Cover M and F-Sa £1.50-5. Open daily noon-2am.

The Shed, Discovery Quay (☎01326 318 502). Start a night with wine, coffee, and hot-pink 50s decor in this cafe-bar. Open M-Sa 10am-midnight, Su 10am-11pm.

◢ BEACHES

Falmouth has five beaches, four of which are within a 15min. walk of the town center. "Falmouth Explorer" bus #400 runs a route along all the beaches. **Castle Beach,** on Pendennis Head, may be too pebbly for sunbathing, but it's great for snorkeling. At low tide, **Tunnel Beach** connects Castle Beach with **Gyllyngvase Beach.** Gyllyngvase, the town's main beach, has pristine sand and a cafe that rents chairs for sunbathing. **Swanpool Beach** also has sandy shores, and both Gyllyngvase and Swanpool offer windsurfing. **Maenporth Beach,** about 2 mi. south of town, makes up for the distance with soft sand and views of Pendennis Castle and the St. Anthony Lighthouse.

◢ DAYTRIPS FROM FALMOUTH

▓**EDEN PROJECT.** A "living theatre of plants and people," the Eden Project is one of England's most unique and fascinating sights. Nestled into hills on the site of a former clay quarry, space-age biomes and awe-inspiring gardens recreate the most beautiful ecosystems on earth. Enter the Mediterranean villas of the **Warm Temperate Biome** and breathe in the scent of olive groves and citrus trees. Keep your eyes open for the steel sculptures that recreate the rites of Bacchus. Brave the heat and humidity to enjoy the palm-tree-laden **Humid Tropics Biome,** the world's largest greenhouse, which houses a rainforest of over 1000 plants. The 30-acre **Roofless Biome** features hemp, sunflowers, tea, and a host of public art displays. The Alchemy Centre shows how to recycle trash into art, while the Plant Takeaway display is a representation of what would befall humans if all plants vanished. The stage acts as a major concert venue, bringing the likes of Amy Winehouse and Rufus Wainwright to the gardens for evening concerts. Check the website for details. Plans are in the works for a fourth biome, dedicated to the world's deserts, which would contain a gigantic oasis. Allow 3hr. to walk through the grounds. *(Bodelva, St. Austell. The St. Austell railway station is located on the Plymouth-Penzance line. From the station, Truronian (☎01872 273 453; www.truronian.com) bus T9 runs daily (20min., 1 per hr.). Bus T10 runs from Newquay in summer (50min., 2 per day); bus T11 runs from Falmouth in summer (1hr., 1 per day). Combined bus and Eden Project ticket (£15, students £10.50) available from any Truronian bus line running to the project. Western Greyhound bus #527 also runs from Newquay year-round via the St. Austell Railway station (2hr., M-Sa every hr.). Signposted from the A390, A30, and A391. ☎01726 811*

972. Open daily from mid-Mar. to Oct. 10am-6pm; from Nov. to mid-Mar. 10am-4:30pm. Last entry 1½hr. before close. £15, students £7; £4 discount for those who arrive on foot or by bicycle.)

THE LIZARD PENINSULA ☎(0)1326

The beautiful, remote Lizard Peninsula is one of England's least touristed corners. Although its name has nothing to do with reptiles—"Lizard" is a corruption of Old Cornish *Lys ardh*, meaning "the high place"—the peninsula does possess a significant outcrop of serpentine rock, so called because of its uncanny resemblance to snake skin. **South West Coastal Path** (p. 193) traces the Lizard around Britain's southernmost point, through dramatic seascapes and lonely fishing villages. The tiny village of **Lizard** receives the most attention thanks to Lizard Point, the southernmost tip of Britain. A short, signposted walk from the village, this outcrop houses a few "most southerly" shops and a **National Trust Information Centre** but is otherwise largely undeveloped. (☎01326 290 604. Sells *Five Walks from the Lizard* for £3.75. Open Easter-Oct. daily 10am-5pm.) ▪**Kynance Cove,** a hard 3 mi. hike northwest along the South West Coast Path from Lizard Point, is a sandy beach studded by masses of rock that create lively surf and ocean spray. Along the South West Coast Path 4 mi. from Lizard in the other direction lies **Cadgwith,** a picturesque fishing village with a sum total of one restaurant and one pub.

Escape the summer crowds by trekking 3hr. farther northwest to rocky **Mullion Cove,** where steep but climbable cliffs await. **Mullion Island,** 750 ft. off the cove, is home to more seabirds than officials can count. The cove is also accessible from Mullion village, 1 mi. inland. Seven miles from Helston in the middle of the peninsula, over 60 satellite dishes make up **Goonhilly Satellite Earth Station Experience,** the world's largest satellite station. The site covers an area equivalent to 160 soccer fields. Visitors can take a 40min. bus tour through the facility and use what might be the fastest Internet connection on earth. (☎0800 679 593; www.goonhilly.bt.com. Open daily July-Aug. 10am-6pm; Sept.-Oct. and Apr.-June 10am-5pm; Nov.-Mar. 11am-4pm. Last entry 1hr. before close. £8, children £5.50, seniors £6.50, families £18.) **The National Seal Sanctuary,** Europe's leading marine mammal rescue center and home to sea lions, otters, and seal pups, is 6 mi. from Helston in the town of Gweek. The animals are most entertaining during the daily feedings at 12:30pm for the otters and 3:30pm for the seals. (☎01326 221 361; www.sealsanctuary.co.uk. Open daily July-Aug. 10am-6pm; Sept.-Oct. and Apr.-June 10am-5pm; Nov.-Mar. 11am-4pm. £8, concessions £7, children £5.50.) Truronian buses run from Helston to Goonhilly (T2, 20min., M-Sa every 2hr.; T3, 20min., Su 2 per day, round-trip £2.50) and Gweek (T2, 30min., 2 per day, round-trip £2.30). The ▪**YHA Lizard ❷,** a refurbished Victorian villa, boasts clean facilities and stunning views of the Lizard Point waters. (☎01326 291 145. Kitchen and laundry. Reception 8:30-10am and 5-10pm. Open Easter-Sept. Dorms £16-18; twins £46; 6-bed family rooms £88. MC/V.)

The easiest way to reach Lizard's coasts is by car. If you're taking the bus, you'll need to connect to Truronian buses in Helston. The T34 runs a direct route between Helston and Lizard, while the T3 "Lizard Rambler" takes the scenic route along the coast. The Truronian day pass (£7) covers both buses.

PENZANCE ☎(0)1736

Although Penzance was formerly an English pirate town, it appears Disney has moved all the pirates to the Caribbean, because you won't find too many here that aren't wax figures or in murals. What Penzance lacks in swashbucklers it makes up for in galleries and stores—the city has a veritable armada of antique

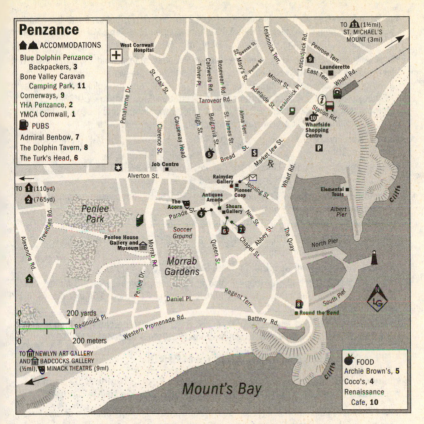

Penzance

⌂ ▲ ACCOMMODATIONS

Blue Dolphin Penzance
  Backpackers, **3**
Bone Valley Caravan
  Camping Park, **11**
Cornerways, **9**
YHA Penzance, **2**
YMCA Cornwall, **1**

🍺 PUBS

Admiral Benbow, **7**
The Dolphin Tavern, **8**
The Turk's Head, **6**

🍅 FOOD
Archie Brown's, **5**
Coco's, **4**
Renaissance
Cafe, **10**

Mount's Bay

shops of flea markets. Sights are few, but, with glorious sunsets and bawdy
pubs, it's difficult not to enjoy such an irreverent town.

TRANSPORTATION

Trains: Station on Wharf Rd. at Albert Pier. Ticket office open M-F 6:05am-8:10pm, Sa
6:15am-8:10pm, Su 8:45am-5:30pm. Trains (☎08457 484 950) to: **Exeter** (3hr.,
every hr., £15-34); **London** (5½hr., 7 per day, £74); **Newquay** (3hr., 4 per day, £7-13);
Plymouth (2hr., every hr., £9.40-13); **St. Ives** via **St. Erth** (1hr., every hr., £3-5).

Buses: Station on Wharf Rd., at the head of Albert Pier. Ticket office open M-F
8:30am-4:45pm, Sa 8:30am-1:30pm. National Express (☎08717 818 181) to **London** (8½hr., 6 per day, £34.50) and **Plymouth** (3hr., 6 per day, £7).

Taxis: Nippy Cabs (☎01736 366 666). **A Cars** (☎01736 350 666).

ORIENTATION AND PRACTICAL INFORMATION

Penzance's train station, bus station, and TIC are all on **Wharf Road.** Pasty shops
and bargain stores line **Market Jew Street** (a corruption of the Cornish *Marghas
Yow,* meaning "Market Thursday"). It becomes **Alverton Street,** then **Alverton Road,**
before turning into the **A30,** the road to Land's End.

Tourist Information Centre: Station Rd. (☎01736 362 207), between the train and bus stations. Books beds for £3 plus 10% deposit. Open May-Sept. M-F 9am-5pm, Sa 10am-4pm, Su 9am-2pm; Oct.-Apr. M-F 9am-5pm, Sa 10am-1pm.

Tours: Anyone interested in riotous jokes about Neolithic man should try **Harry Safari** (☎08456 445 940; www.harrysafari.co.uk), a trip through the Cornish wilds with stops at all of Cornwall's hidden attractions. Call Harry to book, and he'll pick you up on the morning of the tour. 4hr. Leaves from the train station M-F and Su at 9:30am. £20. **Elemental Tours,** Albert Pier (☎01736 811 200; www.elementaltours.co.uk). Provide marine wildlife tours in Cornish waters. Tours held year-round. £25-45.

Banks: Barclays, 8-9 Market Jew St. (☎08457 555 555). Open M-F 9am-4:30pm, Sa 9am-1:30pm.

Library: Penzance Public Library, Morrab Rd. (☎01736 363 954). Internet access £1.80 per 30min. Open M-F 9:30am-6pm, Sa 9:30am-4pm.

Launderette: Polyclean, 4 East Terr. (☎01736 364 815), opposite the train station. Open daily 9am-8pm; last wash 7pm.

Police: Penalverne Dr. (☎08452 777 444), off Alverton St.

Pharmacy: Boots, 100-102 Market Jew St. (☎01736 362 135). Open M-Sa 9am-5:30pm, Su 10am-4pm.

Hospital: West Cornwall Hospital, St. Clare St. (☎01736 874 000).

Internet Access: At the **library** (above). Also at **Penzance Computers,** 36B Market Jew St. (☎01736 333 391), opposite the Wharfside Centre. £1.05 per 15min. Open M-Sa 9am-6pm, Su noon-4pm.

Post Office: 113 Market Jew St. (☎08457 223 344). **Bureau de change.** Open M and W-F 9am-5:30pm, Tu 9:30am-5:30pm, Sa 9am-12:30pm. **Postcode:** TR18 2LB.

ACCOMMODATIONS AND CAMPING

Penzance's B&Bs (£25-35) are mostly on **Alexandra Road,** a 10min. walk from the town center. Buses #1, 1A, 5A, and 6A run from the station to Alexandra Rd.

YHA Penzance, Castle Horneck (☎01736 362 666). Walk 20min. from town or take First bus #5 or 6 to the Pirate Pub and walk up Castle Horneck Rd. Greyhound runs 2 buses per day directly between town and the hostel. 18th-century Georgian manor house with spacious dorms and beautiful gardens. Tickets reserved for Minack Theatre shows (p. 254). Internet access. Lockout 10am-noon. Dorms £12, under 18 from £9. MC/V. ❶

Blue Dolphin Penzance Backpackers, Alexandra Rd. (☎01736 363 836; www.pzbackpack.com), close to town. Relaxed ensuite dorms in a residential neighborhood. Common room is full of plants and board games. Kitchen with free coffee and tea. Free Wi-Fi. Reception 8am-2pm and 5-10pm. Dorms £15; doubles and twins £32. MC/V. ❷

Cornerways, 5 Leskinnick St. (☎01736 364 645; www.penzance.co.uk/cornerways), across Market Jew St. from the train station. Backpacker-friendly owner manages cozy, ensuite rooms in a central location. Veggie breakfasts available. Breakfast included. Singles, doubles, and triples £30 per person. AmEx/MC/V. ❸

YMCA Cornwall, The Orchard, Alverton (☎01736 334 820, ext. 20; www.cornwall.ymca.org.uk). Spacious hostel with a cafe and lounge. Full English breakfast £5.25. Internet £2 per 30min. Reception M-F 10am-8:30pm. Dorms from £15.40; singles £19.75; twins £34.40. 10% discount with student ID. MC/V. ❷

Bone Valley Caravan Camping Park, Heamoor (☎01736 360 313). Take bus #11 or 17, disembark at the Sportsman's Arms pub, and walk ¼ mi. Family-run site, ½ mi. from the city center. Kitchen and laundry. Open Mar.-Dec. From £6.50 per pitch. AmEx/MC/V. ❶

FOOD

Expect to pay around £10-15 to dine at one of Penzance's excellent seafood spots along The Quay. The best buys are in coffee shops and local eateries on smaller streets and alleyways near Market Jew St. Groceries can be purchased at **Cooperative Pioneer,** on Market Jew St. next to the post office. (☎01736 363 759. Open M-F 8:30am-10pm, Sa 8:30am-9pm, Su 10am-4pm.)

Renaissance Cafe, Wharfside Shopping Centre (☎01736 366 277). Ultramodern coffee bar and restaurant overlooking the harbor. Brilliant views are accompanied by an extensive, moderately priced seafood and vegetarian menu. Seafood enthusiasts should try the Renaissance Pizza, with mussels, anchovies, calamari, prawns, and onions (£6.45). Open M-Th and Su 10am-9pm, F-Sa 10am-11pm. MC/V. ❷

Coco's, 12-13 Chapel St. (☎01736 350 222; www.cocos-penzance.co.uk). Relaxed tapas with Matissean decor. Tapas £6-8; entrees £12.30-14. Open M-F 11am-10pm, Sa 10am-10pm. Cash only. ❷

Archie Brown's, Bread St. (☎01736 362 828; www.archiebrowns.co.uk), above Richard's Health Food Store. Sunny and artsy. Features a changing menu of creative vegetarian dishes. Entrees (£4.50-7) come with salad. Open M-Sa 9am-5pm. AmEx/MC/V. ❷

SIGHTS

SAINT MICHAEL'S MOUNT. St. Michael the Archangel is said to have appeared to some fishermen on Marazion, just offshore from Penzance, in AD 495—reason enough to build a Benedictine monastery on the spot. Today, it is still an active church and castle even at its 30-story peak. At low tide, visitors can stroll there via a cobblestone causeway, but at high tide the small ferries (£1.50) are the only way to go. Keep your eyes open for the ghost of the infamous fifth baron of the castle, who had 15 illegitimate children. (*Walk 3 mi. from the TIC to Marazion Sq. or take bus #2, 2A, 2B, 7, 16B, 17B, or 301. ☎01736 710 507, ferry and tide info 710 265. Open July-Aug. M-F and Su 10:30am-5:30pm; Sept.-Nov. and from mid-Mar. to June M-F and Su 10:30am-5pm. Last entry 45min. before close. £6.60. Garden without castle £3.*)

MUSEUMS AND GALLERIES

Penzance features an impressive number of art galleries, which crop up every other block. **Chapel Street** is particularly full of display rooms. The *Cornwall Gallery Guide* booklet (£1), available at galleries and the TIC, lists the best galleries in Penzance and nearby cities.

PENLEE HOUSE GALLERY AND MUSEUM. Internationally known for its impressive collection of Newlyn School art, the museum holds an eclectic collection of historical artifacts upstairs. Look for the 18th-century Scold's Bridle, a menacing warning against loose lips. (*Morrab Rd. ☎01736 363 625; www.penleehouse.org.uk. Open M-Sa Easter-Sept. 10am-5pm; Oct.-Easter 10:30am-4:30pm. £3. Sa free.*)

RAINYDAY GALLERY. The curator compiles the *Cornwall Gallery Guide*. (*22 Market Jew St. ☎01736 366 077; www.rainydaygallery.co.uk. Open M-Sa 10am-5pm.*)

ROUND THE BEND. Far from your ordinary art house, this museum is England's only permanent exhibition of contemporary automata. The quirky machines range from the daring to the droll, and most are for sale. (*The Barbican, Battery Rd. ☎01736 332 211. Open Easter-Sept. daily 11am-5pm. £2.50.*)

🎵 🎭 ENTERTAINMENT AND PUBS

Cornwall's only art center, **The Acorn,** Parade St., hosts theater productions, comedy clubs, and music. On Wednesday and Thursday nights in August, look for open-air theater and jazz in Penlee Park. (☎01736 365 520; www.acornartscentre.co.uk. Tickets £3-20. Box office open Tu-Sa 11am-3pm.) The week of June 26 brings the **Golowan Festival,** featuring the election of the mock mayor of the Quay. The true characters of Penzance emerge in its excellent pubs.

- 🍺 **Admiral Benbow,** 46 Chapel St. (☎01736 363 448). The town's liveliest scene. Once freqented by Cornish smugglers, the pub has tunnels running under it that lead out to the harbor. Live folk music every other W. Open M-Sa 11am-1am, Su noon-midnight. Kitchen open daily 12:30-2:30pm and 5:30-9:30pm.

- 🍺 **The Turk's Head,** 49 Chapel St. (☎01736 363 093; www.turksheadpenzance.co.uk). Penzance's oldest pub. Dating from the 13th century, it was sacked by Spanish pirates in 1595. Open M-Sa 11am-11pm, Su noon-3pm and 5:30-10:30pm. Kitchen open daily 11am-2:30pm and 6-9:30pm.

- **The Dolphin Tavern,** The Quay (☎01736 364 106). Has the dubious distinction of the being the 1st place tobacco was smoked in Britain upon Sir Walter Raleigh's return from Virginia. The pub is said to be haunted by at least 3 ghosts. Open M-Sa 11am-11pm, Su noon-10:30pm. Kitchen open until 10pm.

🎒 DAYTRIPS FROM PENZANCE

🎭**MINACK THEATRE.** In summer, patrons flock to the open-air theater, hacked into a cliffside at Porthcurno, Minack. The venue hosts performances of everything from classic Shakespearean drama to modern comedies to ballet. As legend has it, a woman named Rowena Cade constructed the amphitheater by hand. The theater's 750 stone seats afford views of the surrounding waters, where dolphins frequently put on their own show behind the stage. On a clear day, visitors can see the Lizard Peninsula, 20 mi. to the southeast. *(9 mi. southwest of Penzance, in the town of Porthcurno. Take First bus #1A from the bus station (30min.; M-Sa 6-9 per day, Su 2 per day) or Western Greyhound #345 or 346 from YHA Penzance or the TIC (1hr.; M-F 2 per day, Sa 1 per day). Car access via the B3283. ☎01736 810 181; www.minack.com. Open to visitors Apr.-May daily 9:30am-5:30pm; June daily 9:30am-noon; Sept. M-Tu, Th, Sa-Su 9:30am-5:30pm W and F 9:30am-noon; Oct. daily 10am-5pm; Nov.-Mar. daily 10am-4pm. Performances M-Tu and Th 8pm, W and F 2, 8pm. Admission £3.50. Tickets £7-8.50. MC/V.)*

ST. IVES

☎(0)1736

St. Ives (pop. 11,400), bordered by pastel beaches and azure waters, has attracted visitors for centuries. The cobbled alleyways, colored by flowerpots, drew a colony of painters and sculptors in the 1920s; today, their legacy fills the windows of local art galleries, including a branch of the Tate.

🚌 🎫 **TRANSPORTATION AND PRACTICAL INFORMATION. Trains** (☎08457 484 950) to St. Ives pass through or change at St. Erth Station (15min., every hr.). National Express (☎08717 818 181) **buses** stop in St. Ives (4 per day) between Plymouth (3hr., £7.20) and Penzance (25min., £3.40). First buses also head to Penzance (#17, 17A, 17B; 40min.; 2 per hr.; £2.80). Bus #501 runs in July and August to Newquay (1hr., 4 per day, £5). First **DayRover** tickets allow unlimited travel on First buses for £6.20.

St. Ives is a jumble of alleyways and tiny streets. Wharf St. runs along the harbor to the north, while Fore St. runs parallel to it. The town is roughly triangular, with beaches to the north and south. The **Tourist Information Centre,** in the Guildhall, books accommodations for £3 plus a 10% deposit, sells maps (20p), and stocks the free *A Walk Around the Historic Town of St. Ives.* From the bus or train station, walk to the foot of Tregenna Hill and turn right on Street-an-Pol. (☎01736 796 297; www.visit-westcornwall.com. Open July-Sept. M-F 9am-5pm, Sa 10am-4pm, Su 10am-2pm; Oct.-Easter M-F 9am-5pm, Sa 10am-1pm; May-June M-F 9am-5pm, Sa 10am-4pm.) Other services include: **banks** along High St., including **Barclays** (☎08457 555 555; open M-F 9:30am-4:30pm); **JobCentre,** Royal Sq. (☎01736 575 200; open M 9am-12:30pm and 1:30-4pm, Tu 10am-12:30pm and 1:30-4pm); **Internet** at the **library,** Andrews St., near the TIC (☎01736 795 377; £1.80 per 30min.; open Tu 9:30am-9:30pm, W-F 9:30am-6pm, Sa 9:30am-12:30pm); **Boots** pharmacy, High St. (☎01736 795 072; open M-Sa 8:30am-8:30pm, Su 10:30am-4:30pm); and the **post office,** Tregenna Hill (☎08457 223 344; open M-F 9am-5:30pm, Sa 9am-12:30pm). **Postcode:** TR26 1AA.

ACCOMMODATIONS AND CAMPING. Expensive B&Bs (£25-35) are near the town center on **Parc Avenue** and **Tregenna Terrace.** Walk uphill on West Pl., which becomes **Clodgy View** and **Belmont Terrace** (10min.), where cheaper B&Bs offer fine sea views. **St. Ives International Backpackers ❷,** The Stennack, a few blocks uphill from the library, is covered with bright murals and has a huge lounge area. (☎01736 799 444; www.backpackers.co.uk. Free Wi-Fi. Dorms £12-18; doubles and twins £28-40. MC/V.) For camping or caravanning, **Ayr Holiday Park ❶** is the closest site. Make the 10min. walk to Bullan's Ln. (off The Stennack), then turn right on Bullan Hill and left on Ayr Terr. at the top of the road. (☎01736 795 855. £5.50-13 per person. MC/V.)

FOOD AND PUBS. Get groceries at the **Co-op,** Royal Sq., two blocks uphill from the TIC. (☎01736 796 494. Open M-Sa 8am-11pm, Su 8am-10:30pm.) For local seafood at reasonable prices, the trendy **Seafood Cafe ❸,** 45 Fore St., can't be beat. Choose your fish raw from the display area (£10-15) and select garnishes. (☎01736 794 004; www.seafoodcafe.co.uk. Open daily 10am-3pm and 5:30-11pm. MC/V.) **The Dolphin ❷,** 57 Fore St., has takeaway and views of the sea if you dine in. Bring your own wine or beer and take advantage of dinner specials, like two meals for £7.50. (☎01736 795 701. Open daily 8am-10pm. Takeaway until around 5pm. MC/V.) Perhaps the best view in Cornwall is from the **Tate Cafe ❷,** on the roof of the Tate, overlooking the beach. Enjoy modern cuisine in a postmodern atmosphere. (☎01736 791 122. Sandwiches £4-7.50. Open Mar.-Oct. daily 10am-4:50pm, Nov.-Feb. Tu-Sa 10am-3:50pm.) At **The Yellow Canary,** 12 Fore St., you can find everything from piping hot Cornish pasties (£1.60-3.10) to baked apple cake for £2.25. (☎01736 797 118; www.theyellow-canary.com. Open daily in summer 9am-10pm; in winter 9am-5pm. MC/V.)

MUSEUMS AND GALLERIES. Renowned for its superb light, St. Ives was once an artists' pilgrimage site, and the town's art community is still strong. *Cornwall Galleries Guide* (£1) navigates the dozens of galleries littered throughout St. Ives's maze-like alleys. Like its sister, the Tate Modern in London (p. 132), the **Tate Gallery,** on Porthmeor Beach, focuses on modern and abstract art. The whitewashed building is a piece of art itself, with rounded corridors and gradual lines mimicking the ocean. (☎01736 796 226; www.tate.org.uk/stives. Open Mar.-Oct. daily 10am-5:20pm; Nov.-Feb. Tu-Su 10am-4:20pm. Last entry 20min. before close. Free 1hr. tours M-Sa 11:30am, 2:30pm. £5.75, concessions £3.25, under 18 free.) Associated with the Tate, the **Barbara Hepworth Museum and Sculpture Garden,** on nearby Ayr Ln., allows visitors to view the famed 20th-century sculptor's former home, studio, and garden. (Open

SOUTHWEST ENGLAND

Mar.-Oct. daily 10am-5:20pm; Nov.-Feb. Tu-Su 10am-4:20pm. Last entry 20min. before close. £4.75, concessions £2.75. Same-day admission to the Tate and the Barbara Hepworth Museum £8.75, concessions £4.50.) To view works in the St. Ives School style, try the **Belgrave Gallery,** 22 Fore St., associated with the Belgrave Gallery London (☎01736 794 888; www.belgravegallery.com; open M-Sa 10am-1pm and 2-6pm), or **Wills Lane Gallery,** Wills Ln. (☎01736 795 723; www. willslanegallery.co.uk; open W-Sa 10:30am-5:30pm).

🔲 **NIGHTLIFE.** St. Ives caters to an older crowd than other resort towns do, and the nightlife tends to wrap up at 11pm, when the pubs close. Beer has flowed at **The Sloop,** Fish St. and Wharf Rd., since 1312. (☎01736 796 584; www. sloop-inn.co.uk. Open daily 9am-midnight. Kitchen open daily 9-11am, noon-3pm, 5-10pm.) Nearby, the **Lifeboat Inn,** Wharf Rd., hosts live music on Friday nights (9pm) and Sunday afternoons at 3-5pm. (☎01736 794 123. Free Wi-Fi. Open daily 10am-1pm.) The **Kettle 'n' Wink,** The Stennack, next to the Western Hotel, got its name from the old practice of hiding smuggled brandy in a kettle. Customers placed their order by looking at the kettle and winking. Jazz, blues, and bluegrass play live three times a week. (☎01736 795 277. Open daily noon-1am.) **Isobar,** at the corner of Street-an-Pol and Tregenna Pl., is St. Ives's busiest club. (☎01736 799 199. All drinks £1 W. Cover from £3. Open M-Sa 11:30am-2am, Su 11:30am-10:30pm.)

🔲 **BEACHES.** St. Ives's beaches are among England's finest. Follow the hill down from the train station to **Porthminster Beach,** a magnificent stretch of golden sand and tame waves. To escape the sunbathing crowds, head for **Porthgwidden Beach.** Below the Tate, **Porthmeor Beach** attracts surfers. Farther east, **Carbis Bay,** 1 mi. from Porthminster, is less crowded and easily accessible. Take the train one stop toward St. Erth or bus #17 (M-Sa) or 17B (Su).

Beach activities in St. Ives are numerous. Rent surfboards from shops on Fore St., like **Wind An' Sea Surf Shop,** 25 Fore St. (☎01736 794 830. £5 per day, £25 per week; £5 deposit. Wetsuit £5 per day, £25 per week. Open daily 10am-5:30pm.) Beginners can start with a lesson at **Saint Ives Surf School,** on Porthmeor Beach. (☎0966 498 021. £25 per 2hr., £100 for 5 days. Price includes equipment. Open daily May-Sept. 9am-6pm.) The less athletically inclined may prefer **boat trips,** which leave from the harbor. **Pleasure Boat Trips** travels around the bay and to Seal Island, a permanent seal colony. (☎07821 774 178. 1¼-2hr. £9.) Many boat companies head to **Godrevy Lighthouse** (£7), which is thought to have been the inspiration for Virginia Woolf's novel *To the Lighthouse.* Rent a motorboat from **Mercury Self-Drive** at the harbor. (☎07830 173 878. £8 per 15min., £12 per 30min., £18 per hr. All for 5-6 people. Open daily Easter-Sept. 9am-dusk.)

PENWITH PENINSULA   ☎(0)1736

A region of cliffs and sandy shores, Penwith was once the center of Cornwall's mining industry. Today, the views over the jagged shoreline from green pastures attract mostly beach-goers and hikers. From June to September, the Cornwall Explorer First #300, on a loop from Penzance, passes through Land's End, Sennen, St. Just, Pendeen, Zennor, and St. Ives (5 per day, day pass £6.20)—the open upper deck offers fantastic views of the drive.

ZENNOR. Legend holds that a mermaid drawn by the singing of a young man in this tiny village returned to the sea with the man in tow. On misty evenings, locals claim to see and hear the pair. The immaculate **Old Chapel Backpackers Hostel ❶** is close to gorgeous hiking and 4 mi. from the beaches at St. Ives. (☎01736

798 307; www.backpackers.co.uk/zennor. Cafe. Continental breakfast £3, English £4.50. Showers 20p. Laundry. 2-night max. stay. Camping £4.50 per person. Dorms £15; family rooms £50. MC/V.) In addition to the First #300 (above), Western Greyhound **bus** #508 comes from St. Ives en route to Penzance (20min., M-Sa 6 per day); First bus #300 runs between St. Ives and Land's End, stopping in Zennor (from mid-May to Sept. 5 per day).

LAND'S END. A small complex of tacky tourist attractions capitalizes on England's westernmost point, but none merits the admission fee. Grab some delicious Cornish ice cream and take in the beautiful views. They're free—unless you want your picture taken in front of the famous sign. That will cost you £15 plus shipping. On Tuesdays and Thursdays in August, there are fireworks over the water. First **buses** #1 and 1A go to Land's End from Penzance (1hr., every hr.). The **Visitor Centre** sells tickets to attractions and eagerly dispenses local history. (☎08704 580 044. Open daily July-Aug. 10am-6pm; Sept.-June 10am-5pm.)

ST. JUST. On Cape Cornwall, 4 mi. north of Land's End, the coast of St. Just (pop. 4000) remains relatively untainted by tourism. One mile from the TIC, **Cape Cornwall** was thought to mark the intersection of the Atlantic Ocean and the English Channel. From the cape, Land's End is a tough 6 mi. walk south along the **South West Coastal Path.** Three miles northeast of St. Just in Pendeen, **Geevor Tin Mine** functioned until 1990 and now has a mining museum. (☎01736 788 662; www.geevor.com. Open M-F and Su Easter-Oct. 9am-5pm; Nov.-Easter 10am-4pm. Last entry 1hr. before close. £7.50. 50% discount with bus ticket.)

The **YHA Land's End ②**, Letcha Vean, in Cot Valley, occupies three pristine acres. From the bus station car park, turn left, keeping the primary school on your right, and follow the road as it becomes a footpath leading to the hostel (25min. walk). A map is posted at the St. Just library. The spacious and comfortable rooms have backyard picnic space and ocean views. (☎01736 788 437. Reception 8:30-10am and 5-10pm. Open May-Sept. daily; Oct. and from mid-Feb. to Apr. Tu-Sa. Dorms £10-18, under 18 £10-12; family rooms £39-44. MC/V.) Most routes to Land's End pass through Pendeen and St. Just. Buses #17, 17A, and 17B go to Penzance (45min., every hr.). The **Tourist Information Centre,** at the library opposite the bus park, books rooms and sells *Ancient Sites in West Penwith* and *Around*

THE LOCAL STORY

CHEERS, MATE

In the canon of Briticisms, which includes such interesting words as "mates" (friends), "butty" (sandwich), "pud" (dessert), and "nappy" (diaper), nothing occurs with more frequency than "cheers." Americans say "cheers" only now and then: at New Year's, or when clinking glasses at dinner. On these occasions, it roughly translates as "I wish you good health" or "good wishes."

In England, however, occasions and definitions spiral infinitely. "Cheers" is used for hello and goodbye. It means "thank you," "what's up?" and "all right, fine." Like the American "like," it fills up gaps in conversation—with no meaning at all. A typical conversation between two English people goes something like this:

One: Cheers.
Two: Cheers.
One: What can I get you, luv?
Two: May I have a package of butter, please?
One: Cheers. How many?
Two: Just one. Cheers.
One: Here you are then. Cheers.
Two: Cheers. How much do I owe you?
One: 78 pence. Cheers.
Two: Cheers.

St. Just and St. Ives, both for £4.50. (☎01736 788 165. Internet 90p per 15min. Open M-F 10am-1pm and 2-5pm, Sa 10am-1pm.)

SENNEN COVE. Just 2 mi. from Land's End along the coast, Sennen Cove is a gorgeous mile-long beach, bordered on the north by a small village. A variety of lodgings and restaurants are available in the cove, but most are pricey. First **buses** #1 and 300 and Western Greyhound Coach #504 come from Penzance (45min.; M-Sa 7 per day, Su 5 per day).

ANCIENT MONUMENTS. Inland on the Penwith Peninsula, some of the least spoiled Stone and Iron Age monuments in England lie on the Land's End-St. Ives bus route. Once covered by mounds of dirt, the quoits (also called cromlechs, dolmens, and old rocks in the middle of nowhere) are thought to be burial chambers from 2500 BC. The **Zennor Quoit** is named for the village. The **Lanyon Quoit,** off the Morvah-Penzance road about 3 mi. from each town, is one of the most impressive megaliths. The famous stone near Morvah, on the Land's End-St. Ives bus route, has the Cornish name **Mên-an-Tol,** or "stone with a hole through the middle." The doughnut allegedly has curative powers. The best-preserved Iron Age village in Britain is at **Chysauster,** about 4 mi. from both Penzance and Zennor; there's a 2 mi. footpath off the B3311 near Gulval.

THE CHANNEL ISLANDS

Situated in the waters between England and France, tiny Jersey and Guernsey (and even tinier Alderney, Sark, and Herm) form the Anglo-French holiday spot that is the Channel Islands. Eighty miles south of England and 30 mi. west of France, the islands provide a fusion of cultures and a touch of elegance for those willing to foot the bill. The Channel Islands declared their loyalty to the British Crown in 1204, but Jersey and Guernsey still consider themselves autonomous, as displayed by their high-flying flags and unique currency. A wealth of cafes, shops, and tourists make the islands a perpetual holiday.

I SEE LONDON, I SEE FRANCE. Although part of the UK, Jersey and Guernsey are self-governing—in some senses, you're in foreign territory. ATMs dish out Jersey or Guernsey pounds. They are equal in value to British pounds but are not accepted outside the islands. Change your money as few times as possible to avoid commissions. Toward the end of your stay, ask merchants to give your change in British pounds. Also, your mobile phone may think you're in France, affecting your rate. Some mobiles may not work at all, and pay-as-you-go phones from the mainland usually can't be topped up. Buy a Speedial international phone card from a post office or newsstand.

⚓ GETTING THERE

From England, **ferries** are your best bet for getting to the islands. Condor Ferries (☎01202 207 216; www.condorferries.com) runs one early and one late high-speed ferry per day to St. Helier, Jersey (3-3¾hr.), and St. Peter Port, Guernsey (2½hr.), from the mainland cities of Weymouth and Poole (£43.50-53.50). Departing from the mainland city of Portsmouth is cheapest (£43.50), but the ferries are slower (10½hr. to Jersey, 7hr. to Guernsey). Condor also runs a return daytrip to Jersey or Guernsey for £26.50. The tides and the season affect frequency and ticket prices. Check the website for schedules or call the reservation hotline (☎0845 609 1024). Arrive 1hr. prior to departure. ISIC holders (p. 14) receive a 20% discount.

JERSEY   ☎(0)1534

Jersey, the largest Channel Island, is notorious for both its landscape-altering tides and its budget-altering high prices. You can avoid the latter by breaking free from the pull of trendy shops and eateries in the port of St. Helier and escaping to the island's countryside, where you'll truly experience the region's beguiling blend of British sensibility and French *joie de vivre*.

TRANSPORTATION. An efficient, color-coded system of **buses** makes local travel on the 45 sq. mi. island relatively painless. The public buses, Connex (☎01534 877 772; www.mybus.je), are based at Liberation Station, on the Esplanade next to the TIC in St. Helier, and travel all over the island. Look for the conspicuous "Out of the Blue" signs. (Office open M-Sa 7:30am-8pm, Su 9am-6pm. Many auxiliary routes stop service around 7pm. Tickets £1-1.50, all fares £1 after 7pm. 1-day unlimited travel passes £6, 3-day £15, 5-day £22.) Island Explorer, a part of Connex, offers a hop-on, hop-off **tour** service. **Explorer** tickets are valid on both services. For a **taxi**, call Yellow Cabs (☎01534 888 888). Rent **bicycles** at Zebra Car and Cycle Hire, 9 The Esplanade. (☎01534 736 556; www.zebrahire.com. £11 per day. Open daily 8am-5pm.)

ORIENTATION AND PRACTICAL INFORMATION. The ferry drops travelers at **Elizabeth Harbor,** which lies at the southwest corner of **Saint Helier,** the hub of the island's nightlife and shopping. From the harbor, follow the pedestrian pathway signs along the pier toward Liberation Sq. and the **Tourist Information Centre,** which books accommodations and stocks a variety of maps. (☎01534 448 800; www.jersey.com. Open June-Sept. M-Sa 8:30am-5:30pm, Su 9am-2pm; Oct.-May M-F 8:30am-5:30pm, Sa 9am-1pm.) **Les Petits Trains** runs 40min. **tours** through St. Helier or to St. Aubin village with English or French commentary from the TIC (Train-Hopper pass for both routes £12). Also try **Tantivy Blue Coach Tours,** which takes bookings over the phone. (☎01534 706 706; www.jerseycoaches.com. All-day island tour £19, children £9.) Other services include: **banks** at the intersection of Conway, New, and Broad St.; **Thomas Cook,** 14 Charing Cross (☎08450 772 299; open M-Tu and Th-Sa 9am-5:30pm, W 10am-5:30pm); luggage storage at **Ace Travel,** 5 Esplanade, Liberation Sq. (☎01534 488 488; ½-day £3, full day £5); **Internet** access at **Jersey Library,** Halkett Pl. (☎01534 448 700; £1 per 30min.; open M and W-F 9:30am-5:30pm, Tu 9:30am-7:30pm, Sa 9:30am-4pm); **police,** Rougebouillon St. (☎01534 612 612); **Boots** pharmacy, 23-29 Queen St. (☎01534 730 432; M and W-Sa 8:30am-5:45pm, Tu 9am-5:45pm); **Jersey General Hospital,** Gloucester St. (☎01534 622 000); and the **post office,** Broad St. (☎01534 616 616; open M and W-F 8:30am-5pm, Tu 9am-5pm, Sa 8:30am-1pm) with a **bureau de change. Postcode:** JE1 1AA.

ACCOMMODATIONS AND FOOD. With tourism as its biggest industry, Jersey is teeming with accommodation options. Pick up *Out of the Blue*, an accommodations guide (free at the TIC) or contact the **Jersey Hospitality Association** (☎01534 721 421; www.jerseyhols.com). The only hostel on the island is closed until further notice (call or check the YHA website for updated information). In St. Helier, pretty—and pricey—B&Bs line the Havre des Pas, south of the town center by the beach. Expect to pay at least £30-45 for a single in summer. Travelers looking for a cheaper night's rest should head east to the coastal St. Martin area. Located along the Havre des Pas, the **Havelock Inn ❸** offers a convenient location and an elegant English breakfast. (☎01534 730 663. ₤15-34 per person. MC/V.) **Rozel Camping Park ❶,** St. Martin, offers a view of the French coast. Take bus #3 and ask to be let off at the camping park. (☎01534 855 200; www.rozelcamping.co.uk. Tents only. Pool, toilet access, showers, and laundry. Open from mid-May to early Sept. ₤8-9.40 per person. MC/V.)

Jersey offers a range of excellent restaurants. St. Helier has numerous Chinese and ethnic takeaway eateries that serve filling, low-priced entrees. For fresh fruits and vegetables, meat, and cheese, try **Central Market,** Halkett Pl. (Open M-W and F-Sa 7:30am-5:30pm, Th 7:30am-2pm.) Chic furnishings decorate the **Beach House ❷,** Gorey Pier. Enjoy an extensive menu, from tortilla wraps (₤6) to salmon (₤9). Call ahead to reserve an outdoor table. (☎01534 859 902. Open M 11am-6pm, Tu-Su 12:30-3:30pm and 6:30-9:30pm. MC/V.) Pass through the bright red door of **Rojo ❷,** 10 Bond St., for filling tapas. (☎01534 729 904. Tapas ₤2-7.45. Open daily noon-2pm and 6:45-10pm. MC/V.) **City Bar and Brasserie ❷,** 75-77 Halkett Pl., has sizable portions and free Internet in a sleek coffee shop. (☎01534 510 096. Open M-Sa 10am-11pm. AmEx/MC/V.)

◻ SIGHTS. Jersey's sights celebrate the island's ever-changing role in the world beyond its waters. The **Jersey Heritage Trust** oversees many of the museums; check out www.jerseyheritagetrust.org. **▨Mont Orgueil Castle,** on Gorey Pier, was built in the 13th century to protect the island from the French. Most of the rooms are open for exploring. (☎01534 633 375. Open Apr.-Oct. daily 10am-6pm; Nov.-Mar. M and F-Su 10am-dusk. Last entry 1hr. before close. ₤9.30, students and children ₤5.50, seniors ₤8.50, families ₤26.) Across from Liberation Sq. by the St. Helier marina, the **Maritime Museum and Occupation Tapestry Gallery** contains a nautical hodgepodge. You'll find hands-on exhibits about tides, sailing, and seascape painting. Open the boxes throughout the museum to see ancient weapons and documents, including a letter from George III legalizing piracy in times of war. (☎01534 633 372. Open from mid-Mar. to Nov. daily 9:30am-5pm. ₤7.50, students and children ₤4.50, seniors ₤7, families ₤22.) The **Jersey War Tunnels,** Les Charrieres Malorey, St. Lawrence, provide a somber history lesson about life in Jersey under Nazi occupation. Exhibits are housed in a former German military hospital. (☎01534 860 808; www.jerseywartunnels. com. Open Feb.-Nov. daily 10am-6pm. Last entry 4:30pm. ₤10, students ₤6.75, children ₤5.75, seniors ₤9.) **Durrell Wildlife** (formerly the Jersey Zoo), in Trinity Parish, is run by a conservation trust and features endangered species on its 31 acres of land. The zoo has an organic garden where it grows food for the animals. Take bus #3A, 3B, or 23. (☎01534 860 000; www.durrell.org. Open daily July-Aug. 9:30am-6pm; Sept.-June 9:30am-5pm. ₤12, concessions ₤9.50.)

◻◻ ENTERTAINMENT AND NIGHTLIFE. The **Opera House,** Gloucester St., features both West End hits and local productions. (☎01534 511 115; www. jerseyoperahouse.co.uk. Open M-Sa 10am-6pm, performance days 10am-8pm, Su from 1hr. before performances.) Various pubs and clubs offer nightlife options. At the popular **Liquid and Envy Club,** at the Waterfront Centre, tourists in posh fashions fill the dance floors until the early morning. (☎01534 789 356; www.liquid.je. Dance music F-Sa. Alternative Su. 23+. Open daily 10pm-2am.) Escape the ruckus of St. Helier's pubs and head to the **Golden Buddha Bar,** 10 Wharf St., off Conway St. Patrons curl up with their drinks in lounge chairs or munch on entrees, which often run against the bar's theme and cater to British tastes for meat and gravy. (☎01534 729 111. Free Wi-Fi. Appetizer and entree ₤11 M-Th evenings and Su afternoons. Open daily noon-1am. Kitchen open M-Th noon-2:30pm and 6-9:30pm, F and Su noon-3pm, Sa noon-6pm. MC/V.) In

October, take a bite of **Tennerfest,** which challenges local restaurants to come up with the best £10 menu. Check out www.jersey.com for more on festivals.

GUERNSEY   ☎(0)1481

Guernsey, 25 mi. west of Jersey, is quieter than its sister island but harbors the bustling town of St. Peter Port. With a carefree island spirit and an expansive seascape view that inspired Victor Hugo during his exile from France, the island draws well-heeled travelers seeking both surf and serenity.

☐ TRANSPORTATION. Island Coachways **buses** (☎01481 720 210; www.icw.gg) operate island-wide, with frequent service to tourist favorites. The bus terminal is on the waterfront, where Quay and South Esplanade converge. Buses #7 and 7A (every hr., 60p) circle the coast. "Wave and Save" cards (£4.50 for 10 rides) offer discounts on fares. Island Coachways also offers island **tours.** (Tours leave at 10:30am from the bus terminal and return at 1:30pm. May-Sept. M, W, Sa; £12.50.) For a **taxi,** call Island Taxis. (☎01481 700 500. 24hr.)

■ ☑ ORIENTATION AND PRACTICAL INFORMATION. Ferries land at St. Julian's Pier in St. Peter Port. To reach the **Tourist Information Centre** on North Esplanade, take a left at the end of the pier. The TIC has maps and the helpful *Absolute Guernsey,* which provides information on the attractions of the island as well as nearby Herm, Sark, and Alderney. The center also books accommodations for a £2 charge plus a 10% deposit and maintains a small accommodations info booth at the ferry terminal. (☎01481 723 552; www.visitguernsey.com. Open June-Aug. M-F 9am-6pm, Sa 9am-5pm, Su 9am-1pm; Sept.-May M-Sa 9am-5pm.) Other services include: **banks** on High St.; **Thomas Cook,** 22 Le Pollet (☎01481 724 111; open M-Tu and Th-Sa 9am-5:30pm, W 10am-5:30pm); **Internet** access at the TIC and at **Guille-Alles Library,** The Market, St. Peter Port (☎01481 720 392; £1 per 30min.; open M and Th-Sa 9am-5pm, Tu 10am-5pm, W 9am-8pm); **police,** Hospital Ln. (☎01481 725 111); **Boots** pharmacy, 26-27 High St. (☎01481 723 565; open M-Sa 8:30am-5:30pm); **Princess Elizabeth Hospital,** Le Vauquiedor, St. Martin (☎01481 725 241); and the **post office,** Smith St. (☎01481 711 720; open M-F 8:30am-5pm, Sa 8:30am-noon). **Postcode:** GY1 2JG. St. Martin, southwest of St. Peter's Port, also has a number of necessities.

☐ ☐ ACCOMMODATIONS AND FOOD. With more reasonable prices than Jersey, hotels fill quickly. The TIC posts vacancies in front of the building. For lodgings near town with views of Sark and Herm, try **Saint George's Guest House** ❸, St. George's Esplanade, St. Peter Port. (☎01481 721 027; www.stgeorges-guernsey.com. Breakfast included. Free Wi-Fi. May-Sept. £36 per person; Oct. and Apr. £31 per person; Nov.-Mar. £29.50 per person. £5 charge for single-night stays. MC/V.) A 20min. uphill walk from the pier, the **Grisnoir Guest House** ❸, Les Gravees, at the top of Grange Rd., has friendly hosts and a great price. (☎01481 727 267; www.grisnoir.co.uk. Shared bathrooms. Breakfast included. Reservations recommended. £25-29 per person. MC/V with surcharge.)

Takeaway places line the street behind the TIC and are the best bet for cheap eats. Get fresh fruit and veggies at the **Cooperative Food Market,** on Market St. (open M-Sa 7:30am-7pm). The **Terrace Bar** ❷, on Corner St., serves sandwiches (£2.70-4) and Thai dishes (£4-9) under a vine-laced terrace overlooking the harbor. (☎01481 724 478; www.terracegardencafe.com. Open M and W-Su 8am-10pm, Tu 8am-7pm. MC/V.) **Christie's** ❸, Le Pollet, has a bistro facing the street and a more expensive restaurant overlooking the harbor. (☎01481 726 624. Lunch entrees £4-17.50. Open daily 8am-12:30am. AmEx/MC/V.)

SIGHTS. Pull yourself away from Guernsey's wildflowers and beaches long enough to tour **Hauteville House,** Hauteville St., St. Peter Port. Victor Hugo's home during his exile from France remains virtually unaltered since the days when he wrote *Les Misérables*. The house is full of hidden inscriptions and mantles constructed by Hugo from recycled furniture. (☎01481 721 911. Open M-Sa May-Sept. 10am-4pm; Apr. noon-4pm. Entrance by guided tour only. ₤6, seniors ₤4, ages 14-26 ₤3, under 13 free.) The **Castle Cornet,** on the marina in St. Peter Port, has unbeatable views. Built in 1204, the castle has changed hands often, most recently when Britain gave it back to Guernsey in 1947 in recognition of the island's loyalty during WWII. Time your visit with the noon gun salute. (☎01481 721 657. Open daily Apr.-Oct. 10am-5pm; Nov.-Mar. 10am-4pm. Last entry 45min. before close. ₤6.50, students and children free.) A "Venue" ticket (₤10) may be purchased for entrance into the castle, the **Fort Grey Shipwreck Museum** (☎01481 265 036; open Easter-Oct. daily 10am-5pm), and the **Guernsey Museum and Art Gallery** (☎01481 726 518; open daily 10am-5pm).

Island RIB Voyages takes visitors on a 34 ft. commercial boat to see puffins, seals, and other wildlife in their natural habitats while learning about their environment from the on-board marine zoologist. (☎01481 713 031; www.islandribvoyages.com. Open Apr.-Oct. daily 10am-dusk. 1hr. tour ₤24.50-27.50, children ₤17-19.) Nearby **Herm** (www.herm-island.com) and **Sark** (www.sark.info) are worthwhile daytrips. Pristine beaches await travelers at Herm, and Sark is untouched by cars—transportation on the island is left to foot, bicycle, and horse-drawn carriage. In July, check out the annual **Sheep Racing** competition.

PUBS AND FESTIVALS. Shopping in Guernsey is particularly popular due to the absence of Britain's staggering 17.5% value added tax (VAT; p. 18). After collecting your bargains, plop down for a pint at one of the bars that line the waterfront. **Ship & Crown,** N. Esplanade, is a local favorite with frequent live music (☎01481 721 368; open daily 10:30am-12:15am; kitchen open daily 11am-9pm), and the **Albion House Tavern,** Church Sq., is a historical experience in its own right—it's the closest tavern to a church in the British Isles, thanks to a gargoyle that almost bridges the alleyway (☎01481 723 518; open M-Th and Su 10am-midnight, F-Sa 10am-1am; kitchen open M-Th 11:30am-2:30pm and 6-8:30pm, F-Su 11:30am-2:30pm). Don't miss the **Battle of Flowers** (☎01481 254 473) in August, when locals duke it out for the honor of best floral float.

SOUTHWEST ENGLAND

HEART OF ENGLAND

The pastures and half-timbered houses that characterize the countryside west of London are the stuff of stereotype. Traveling through the Heart of England, however, you'll be hard-pressed to find a field, dale, or town that isn't picturesque. The Heart has England's most famous attractions: Oxford, Britain's oldest university town; Stratford-upon-Avon, Shakespeare's home; and the gorgeous villages of the Cotswolds. The region's touring hordes can be hard to avoid, but resourceful travelers will find an abundance of untrod adventures.

HIGHLIGHTS OF THE HEART OF ENGLAND

ADMIRE the gargoyles in **Oxford,** a stunning university town, rich in architecture and bizarre student traditions (p. 268).

PLAY PRINCESS at **Windsor,** one of the world's most sumptuous royal residences, which has housed 40 reigning monarchs (p. 266).

SHAKE IT UP in **Stratford-upon-Avon,** where tourist trails honor the Bard's footsteps and the Royal Shakespeare Company venerates his every syllable (p. 280).

ST. ALBANS
☎ (0)1727

From the Roman legion to Norman conquerors, each new ruling class has wanted either to set St. Albans on fire or to make it a capital. In the third century, the Roman soldier Alban was beheaded here, making him England's first Christian martyr. Because of the town's traditional architecture, it is frequented by film crews as a substitute for Westminster Abbey and Oxford University.

TRANSPORTATION. St. Albans has two train stations: **City Station,** the main one, and **Abbey Station,** which runs local services. To get to the town center from City Station, turn right out of the station onto Victoria Rd., follow the road back over the train tracks, and continue uphill for 10min. Avoid the hike by riding any "Into Town" bus (75p). **Trains** (☎08457 484 950) leave City Station to London's King's Cross Thameslink (25min., 4 per hr.). Sovereign (☎01727 854 732) **buses** stop at City Station and along St. Peter's St. Bus #724 leaves from St. Peter's St. in front of the post office for London Heathrow (2hr., every hr., £7).

ORIENTATION AND PRACTICAL INFORMATION. Leaving City Station, **Hatfield Road** to the left and **Victoria Street** to the right both lead uphill to town; at the town center, they are intersected by the main drag. To get to the main attractions, turn left onto this street, which changes from **Saint Peter's Street** to **Chequer Street** to **Holywell Hill.**

The **Tourist Information Centre,** at the intersection of Victoria and St. Peter's St., books accommodations for £3 plus a 10% deposit. (☎01727 864 511; www.stalbans.gov.uk. Open Easter-Oct. M-Sa 10am-5pm, every other Su 10am-4pm; Nov.-Easter M-Sa 10am-4pm.) Other services include: **banks** at the beginning of

THE BIG SPLURGE

ELIZABETHAN BANQUET

In the days before she started fighting the Spanish, presiding at Parliament, and manipulating courtiers, Elizabeth I was kept out of treason and trouble at Hatfield House by her sister Queen Mary.

Nowadays, Hatfield House is a more welcoming place, opening its sumptuous doors to paying tourists by day and even higher-paying guests by night. For a little under £48, guests can feast on a four-course banquet in the 15th-century Great Hall of the Old Palace while the Hatfield Players, a troupe of Elizabethan clowns, musicians, and actors, bring to life the best and bawdiest of merry olde England. Queen Elizabeth herself graces the table, as do King Henry VIII (who died 11 years before she even ascended the throne) and gaggles of winsome courtiers.

The fun gets a little more modern as the night wears on: at the stroke of 10pm, the Elizabethans disappear and guests dance at the resident disco.

The Hatfield Banquet occurs on most Friday evenings and on other selected evenings throughout the year. Call ☎01707 262 055 or email banquets@theoldpalace. co.uk for information and to make bookings. Smart casual dress or period costume is requested. The Hatfield House website has a list of costume providers: www.hatfield-house.co.uk/hospitality.

Chequer St.; **Internet** at the **library** in The Maltings Shopping Centre, across from the TIC (☎01438 737 333; £1.25 per 30min.; open M-Th 9am-8pm, F 10am-8pm, Sa 9am-4pm, Su 1-5pm); **police**, on Victoria St. (☎08453 300 222); **Maltings** pharmacy, 6 Victoria St. (☎01727 839 335; open M-F 9am-6:30pm, Sa 9am-5pm); and the **post office**, 2 Beaconsfield Rd. (☎01727 860 110). **Postcode:** AL1 3RA.

🛏️🍴 ACCOMMODATIONS AND FOOD. Reasonably priced B&Bs (£20-40) are scattered and many times unmarked. The best way to secure a room is through the TIC. Near City Station, **Mrs. Murphy ❷**, 478 Hatfield Rd., rents tidy rooms at reasonable prices. (☎01727 842 216. Singles £20-35; doubles, twins, and family rooms £40-60. Cash only.) **Mrs. Norton ❷**, 16 York Rd., has comfortable rooms with shared bath. Breakfast comes with homemade preserves. (☎01727 853 647. Singles £25; doubles £50. Cash only.) **178 London Road ❸** is a beautiful home with satellite TV in all rooms. (☎01727 846 726; www.178londonroad.co.uk. Singles £35; doubles £50; family rooms £50-80. Cash only.)

Buy produce at the **market** (W and Sa by the TIC) and **Iceland** grocery, 144 Victoria St. (☎01727 833 908. Open M-F 9am-8pm, Sa 9am-7pm, Su 11am-5pm.) For lunch, visit 🍺**Ye Olde Fighting Cocks ❶**, Abbey Mill Ln., between the cathedral and Verulamium park. Once a 16th-century public house, this octagonal building may be the oldest pub in England. Tunnels, used by monks to see cockfights and later to flee Henry VIII's cronies, run from the cathedral to the pub. Oliver Cromwell reputedly stabled his horse at one of the bars before setting off to raid the countryside. (☎01727 865 830. Open M-Th 11am-11pm, F-Sa 11am-midnight, Su noon-11pm. Kitchen open daily noon-9:30pm. MC/V.) Ducks waddle from the River Ver near the **Waffle House ❷**, St. Michael's St., toward the Roman quarter. Choose from many toppings (£2.40-7), ranging from bananas to hummus. (☎01727 853 502. Open daily Apr.-Oct. 10am-6pm; Nov.-Mar. 10am-5pm. MC/V.) For a delicious Moroccan meal in a cozy cafe, try **Little Marrakech ❷**, 31 Market St., with spiced couscous and omelettes (£5-8) or a set lunch for £8. (☎01727 853 569. Open daily 9am-4pm and 6:30pm-11pm. MC/V.)

◩ SIGHTS. Dark, gloomy, and splendid in stone, the 🏛️**Cathedral of Saint Alban** was built around the shrine of St. Alban, the first Christian martyr in England. At 227 ft., the medieval nave is the longest in Britain. Painted while the outcome of the Wars of the Roses was uncertain, the ceiling is

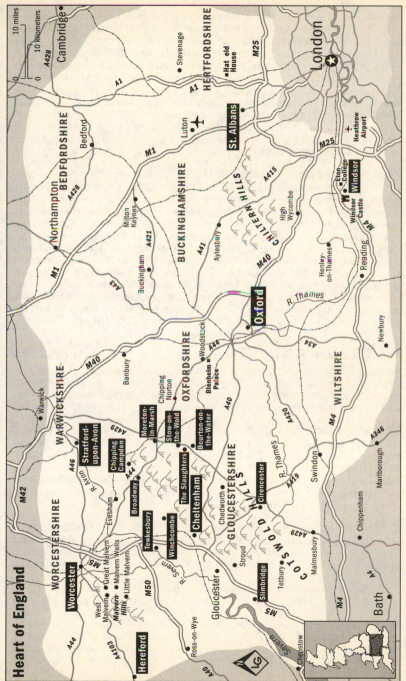

Heart of England

10 miles

10 kilometers

A428 Cambridge

A1

Stevenage

HERTFORDSHIRE

Hat eld House

London

M25

St. Albans

Luton

M25

Heathrow Airport

Windsor

Eton College

Windsor Castle

Henley-on-Thames

Reading

M4

Bedford

BEDFORDSHIRE

A428

Northampton

M1

A428

Buckingham

Milton Keynes

A421

A43

BUCKINGHAMSHIRE

Aylesbury

A41

CHILTERN HILLS

A415

High Wycombe

M40

Oxford

R. Thames

Newbury

A34

WILTSHIRE

M4

A346

Marlborough

Chippenham

Bath

M4

A4

Woodstock

Blenheim Palace

A44

Banbury

M40

WARWICKSHIRE

Warwick

Chipping Norton

OXFORDSHIRE

A40

Moreton-in-Marsh

Stow-on-the-Wold

Bourton-on-the-Water

Stratford-upon-Avon

A46

Chipping Campden

A44

A429

R. Avon

Broadway

The Slaughters

Cheltenham

Winchcombe

Evesham

WORCESTERSHIRE

M42

Worcester

West Malvern

Great Malvern

Malvern Hills

Little Malvern

Malvern Wells

M5

A44

A4103

Hereford

Ross-on-Wye

A40

R. Wye

R. Severn

Tewkesbury

M50

Gloucester

M5

Chedworth

GLOUCESTERSHIRE

Cirencester

A420

R. Thames

Swindon

A419

COTSWOLD HILLS

Stroud

Slimbridge

Tetbury

Malmesbury

A429

Chepstow

R. Severn

N

HEART OF ENGLAND

entwined with the white and red roses of York and Lancaster. (☎01727 860 780. Open daily 8:30am-5:45pm. Suggested donation £2.50. Guided tours £1.) From the cathedral, walk 10min. down Fishpool St., over the river, and uphill as it becomes St. Michael's St. to visit the ▓Verulamium Museum. Homes of the rich and poor of Roman Britain have been recreated with mosaics, painted wall plasters, and artifacts. (☎01727 751 810. Open M-Sa 10am-5:30pm, Su 2-5:30pm. £3.30, concessions £2, families £8.) A block away, the remains of one of five Roman theaters huddle against a backdrop of English countryside. (☎01727 835 035. Open daily 10am-5pm. £2, concessions £1.50, children 50p.) Two miles south of St. Albans, the fragrant **Gardens of the Rose** in Chiswell Green are the "flagship gardens" of the Royal National Rose Society. Over 30,000 roses bloom in summer. (☎01727 334 344. Open June-Sept. W-Su 11am-5pm. £5.)

⚑ DAYTRIP FROM ST. ALBANS: HATFIELD HOUSE. Stately 225-room Hatfield House is best known as Queen Elizabeth I's childhood home. Placed under house arrest here for suspected treason, Elizabeth was sitting under one of the ancestral oaks when the news arrived that her sister Mary had died and she was queen. Hatfield holds two famous portraits of Elizabeth, and, although the stockings attributed to her are fakes, the gloves are real. Keep an eye out for the queen's 22 ft. family tree, tracing her lineage to Adam and Eve via Noah, Julius Caesar, King Arthur, and King Lear. All that remains of her original palace is the Great Hall; the rest was razed to make way for the mansion that dominates the estate today. *(Buses #300 and 301 link St. Albans and Hatfield House (20min., 1-3 per hr., round-trip £4.20). The Hatfield train station, across from the main gate, makes the house easily accessible from other towns. ☎01707 287 010. House open Easter-Sept. W-Su noon-4pm. 1hr. guided tours Th. House, park, and gardens £10. Park and gardens £5.50. Park only £2.50.)*

WINDSOR AND ETON ☎(0)1753

Tourism in the town of Windsor and the attached village of Eton centers entirely on Windsor Castle and Eton College, two famed symbols of the British upper crust. Windsor is thick with specialty shops, teahouses, and pubs, which cater mostly to the throngs of daytrippers from nearby London.

▣ TRANSPORTATION. Two train stations lie near the castle. **Trains** (☎08457 484 950) pull out of Windsor and Eton Royal Station to London Paddington via Slough (40min., 2 per hr., round-trip £7.70). Trains leave Windsor and Eton Riverside to London Waterloo (40min., 4 per hr., round-trip £8.20). Green Line **bus** #702 goes to London Victoria (1hr., every hr., round-trip £5-10) from High St. opposite Parish Church. Bus #77 to London Heathrow (45min., every hr., round-trip £4.50) leaves from St. Leonard Rd.

▣⚑ ORIENTATION AND PRACTICAL INFORMATION. Windsor village slopes from the foot of the castle. **High Street** spans the hilltop to become **Thames Street** at the statue of Queen Victoria and continues to the river, at which point it reverts to High St. as it enters Eton. The main shopping area, **Peascod Street,** meets High St. at the statue.

The **Tourist Information Centre,** Old Booking Hall, Windsor Royal Shopping Centre, has free brochures, great maps, and an accommodations guide. (☎01753 743 900; www.windsor.gov.uk. Open M-Sa 10am-5pm, Su 10am-4pm.) Other services include: **banks** with **ATMs** along Peascod St.; **Internet** at the **library** on Bachelors Acre (☎01753 743 9940; guest pass for 30min. free; open M and Th 9:30am-5pm, Tu 9:30am-8pm, W 2-5pm, F 9:30am-7pm, Sa 9:30am-3pm); **police,** on the corner of St. Mark's Rd. and Alma Rd. (☎08458 505 505; M-Sa 8am-10pm,

Su 9am-5pm); **Boots** pharmacy, 113 Peascod St. (☎01753 863 595; open M-Sa 8:30am-6pm, Su 10:30am-4:30pm); and the **post office,** 38-39 Peascod St. (open M and W-F 9am-5:30pm, Tu 9:30am-5:30pm, Sa 9am-4pm). **Postcode:** SL4 1LH.

🏠 🍴 ACCOMMODATIONS AND FOOD. Windsor lacks budget accommodations. You can avoid the high prices by making it a daytrip from London. For those who decide to stay, the TIC booking service (☎01753 743 907; windsor. accommodation@rbwm.gov.uk) will book B&Bs for £5 plus a 10% deposit. **Rutlands ❸,** 102 St. Leonard's Rd., is a centrally located Victorian guesthouse with two ensuite rooms. (☎01753 859 533. Single £35-40; double £65-70.) **The Clarence Hotel ❹,** 9 Clarence Rd., offers spacious rooms and includes a lounge with cable TV. (☎01753 864 436; www.clarence-hotel.co.uk. Breakfast included. Singles £45-69; doubles £50-79; family rooms £70-92.)

Chain restaurants dominate Thames St. **Waterman's Arms ❶,** Brocas St., is the first left after crossing the bridge to Eton. Founded in 1542, it's still a local favorite, selling pub classics for £6-9. (☎01753 861 001. Kitchen open M-F noon-3pm and 6-9pm, Sa noon-9pm, Su noon-4:30pm.) **Olivia ❶,** 49 Thames St., has sandwiches (£3.50-4.60) and jacket potatoes for £4.50. (☎01753 853 991. Open M-Sa 8am-7pm, Su 8am-6pm. Cash only.)

🏛 SIGHTS. The largest and oldest continuously inhabited castle in the world, **Windsor Castle** features some of the most sumptuous rooms in Europe and some of the rarest artwork in the Western tradition. The castle was built high above the Thames by William the Conqueror as a fortress rather than as a residence, but 40 reigning monarchs have softened the battlements into a series of superbly furnished apartments. In 1992, a fire devastated over 100 rooms, including nine staterooms, but a massive project has restored them to their original glory. Windsor is the official residence of the queen, who spends the month of April and many of her private weekends here. During royal stays, large areas of the castle are unavailable to visitors, and the admission prices are lowered on these occasions. It is wise to call ahead or check out the flag-pole—when the queen is in residence, the castle flies the light blue flag of the monarchy. Visitors can watch the Changing of the Guard in front of the Guard Room at 11am (Apr.-July M-Sa; Aug.-Mar. alternate days M-Sa). The guards can also be seen at 10:50 and 11:30am as they march to and from the ceremony. (☎01753 831 118. Open daily Mar.-Oct. 9:45am-5:15pm; Nov.-Feb. 9:45am-4:15pm. Last entry 1¼hr. before close. £14.80. Audio tours free.)

Reach the upper ward through the Norman tower and gate. Stand in the far left line to enter **🏰Queen Mary's Doll House,** a replica of a home on a one-to-12 scale, with tiny, handwritten classics in its library, miniature crown jewels, and functional plumbing and electrical systems. Velvet ropes lead to the **state apartments,** used for ceremonial events and to entertain international heads of state. The rooms are ornamented with art from the **Royal Collection,** including works by Reubens, Rembrandt, Van Dyck, and Queen Victoria herself. Cabinets are stuffed with imperial curios, jewelled swords, and Jubilee porcelain. The **Waterloo room** memorializes England's vanquishing of Napoleon, while the ceiling of the **Grand Reception Room,** stamped with the shields of the Knights of the Garter, celebrates the oldest continuous chivalric order in Europe.

The **Round Tower** dominates the middle ward. A stroll downhill to the lower ward brings you to **Saint George's Chapel,** a 15th-century structure with a wall of stained glass dedicated to the Order of the Garter. Used for the marriage of Sophie and Prince Edward, the chapel also holds the tombs of the queen mother, George III, and Queen Mary. Ask a guide to explain how the bones of Charles I and Henry VIII were accidentally placed under the same stone.

HEART OF ENGLAND

A 10-15min. walk down Thames St., across Windsor Bridge and along Eton High St., stands **Eton College.** This charming chunk of English upper crust is one of England's most elite public—which is to say, private—schools. Ironically, it was founded by Henry VI in 1440 as a college for paupers. Despite its position at the apex of the British class system, Eton has shaped some notable dissident thinkers, including Aldous Huxley, George Orwell, and former Liberal Party leader Jeremy Thorpe. The male students still stay true to many of the old traditions, including wearing tailcoats to class. The 25 houses that surround the quad act as residences for the approximately 1250 students. The **Museum of Eton Life** displays relics and stories of the school's odd and storied past. (☎01753 671 177. Open daily from late Mar. to mid-Apr. and July-Aug. 10:30am-4:30pm; from Sept. to late Mar. and from mid.-Apr. to June 2-4:30pm; schedule depends on academic calendar. Tours daily 2:15, 3:15pm. £4.20. Tours £5.50.)

OXFORD   ☎(0)1865

Oxford has been home to nearly a millennium of scholarship—25 British prime ministers and numerous other world leaders have been educated here. In 1167, Henry II founded Britain's first university, and its distinguished spires have since captured the imaginations of luminaries such as Lewis Carroll and CS Lewis. The city's legendary scholarship and enthralling architecture also make Oxford a must-see for tourists and a popular place to study abroad. For a true sense of this academic enclave, avoid the hordes choking Broad St. and roam the alleyways to find ancient bookshops, serene college quads, and, of course, history-laden pubs inviting you to sample their brew.

▮ TRANSPORTATION

Trains: Station on Botley Rd., down Park End. Ticket office open M-F 5:45am-8pm, Sa 6:45am-8pm, Su 7:15am-8pm. Trains (☎08457 000 125) to: **Birmingham** (1hr., 2 per hr., £23); **Glasgow** (5-7hr., every hr., £86); **London Paddington** (1hr., 2-4 per hr., £19-22.50); **Manchester** (3hr., every 2hr., £51.50).

Buses: Station on Gloucester Green. Stagecoach (☎01865 772 250; www.stagecoach-bus.com; ticket office open M-F 9am-5pm, Sa 9:30am-1pm) runs to **Cambridge** (3hr., 2 per hr., £9) and operates the Oxford Tube (☎01865 772 250) to **London** (1hr.; 3-4 per hr.; £12, students £9). National Express (☎08717 818 181; ticket office open M-Th 8:30am-5:45pm, F-Sa 8:30am-6pm, Su 9am-4:30pm) runs to **Bath** (1hr., 5 per day, £9.50); **Birmingham** (1hr., 5 per day, £11); **Bristol** (3hr., 2 per hr., £13.80); **Stratford-upon-Avon** (1hr., 2 per day, £8.50). The Oxford Bus Company (☎01865 785 400; www. oxfordbus.co.uk; ticket office in Debenhams Department store, at the corner of George St. and Magdalen St., open M-W 9:30am-6pm, Th 9am-8pm, F-Sa 9am-7pm) runs to **London** (1hr.; 3-5 per hr.; £12, students £9), **Gatwick** (2hr.; every hr. 8am-9pm; £22, concessions £11), and **Heathrow** (1hr.; 3 per hr.; £18, concessions £9).

Public Transportation: The Oxford Bus Company Cityline (☎01865 785 400) and Stagecoach Oxford (☎01865 772 250) offer frequent service to: **Abingdon Road** (Stagecoach #32, 33, Oxford Bus X3, X4); **Banbury Road** (Stagecoach #2, 2A, 2B, 2D); **Cowley Road** (Stagecoach #1, 5A, 5B, 10, Oxford Bus #5); **Iffley Road** (Stagecoach #3, Oxford Bus #4, 4A, 4B, 4C). Fares are low (60p-£1.40). Stagecoach offers a **Day-Rider ticket** (£3.30 day, £15-23 week) and the Oxford Bus Company a **Freedom ticket** (£3.30 day, £17 week), which give unlimited travel on the respective company's local routes. A **Plus Pass** grants unlimited travel on all Oxford Bus Company and Stagecoach buses and can be purchased on board (☎01865 785 410; £5 day, £17 week).

Taxis: Radio Taxis (☎01865 242 424). **ABC** (☎01865 770 077). Both 24hr.

Boat Rental: Magdalen Bridge Boat House, Magdalen Bridge (☎01865 202 643; www.oxfordpunting.co.uk). Rents punts and rowboats (£14 per hr.) or chauffered punts (£20 per 30min.). Open daily 9:30am-9pm or dusk (whichever comes first).

✈ 🛈 ORIENTATION AND PRACTICAL INFORMATION

Oxford's colleges stand around **Saint Mary's Church,** which is the spiritual heart of both the university and the greater city. The city's center is bounded by **George Street** and connecting **Broad Street** to the north and **Cornmarket** and **High Street** in the center. To the northwest, the district of **Jericho** is less touristed and is the unofficial hub of student life.

Tourist Information Centre: 15-16 Broad St. (☎01865 252 200; www.visitoxford.org). The busy staff books rooms for £4 plus a 10% deposit. Distributes free black-and-white maps (nicer colored maps £1.25), restaurants lists, accommodations lists, and monthy *In Oxford* guides. Job listings, long-term accommodations listings, and entertainment news posted daily at the TIC and at www.dailyinfo.co.uk. Open M-Sa 9:30am-5pm.

Tours: The 2hr. official Oxford University and city **walking tour** (☎01865 252 200) leaves from the TIC and provides access to some colleges otherwise closed to visitors. Tours only allow up to 19 people and are booked on a 1st come, 1st served basis, so get tickets early in the day. Daily in summer 10:30, 11am, 1, 2pm; in winter 11am, 2pm. £7, children £3.50. **Blackwell's** (☎01865 333 606) walking tours leave from Canterbury Gate at Christ Church. Literary tour of Oxford Tu 2pm, Th 11am; "Inklings" tours about CS Lewis, JRR Tolkien, and their circle of friends W 11:45am; Town and Gown Tour about the relationship between the university and the city F 2pm. All tours 1hr. £6.50, concessions £6. **Guided Tours** (☎07810 402 757), 1hr., depart from outside Trinity College on Broad St. and offer access to some colleges and other university buildings. Daily noon, 2, 4pm. £7, children £3. Evening 1hr. Ghost Tours in summer daily 8pm. £5, children £3. **City Sightseeing** (☎01865 790 522; www.citysightseeingoxford.com) offers hop-on, hop-off bus tours of the city with 20 stops. Every 15-20min. from bay 14 of the bus station. Pick up tickets from bus drivers or stands around the city. £11.50, concessions £9.50, children £6, families £31.

Banks: Lining Cornmarket St. The TIC (above) has a commission-free **bureau de change,** as does **Marks & Spencer,** 13-18 Queen St. (☎01865 248 075). Open M-W and F-Sa 8am-7pm, Th 8am-8pm, Su 10:30am-5pm.

Beyond Tourism: JobCentre Plus, 7 Worcester St. (☎01865 445 000). Open M-Tu and Th-F 9am-5pm, W 10am-5pm.

Library: Oxford Central Library, Queen St. (☎01865 815 549), near Westgate Shopping Centre. Free Internet. Open M-Th and Su 9am-7pm, F-Sa 9am-5:30pm.

Launderette: 127 Cowley Rd. Open daily 8am-10pm.

Police: St. Aldates and Speedwell St. (☎01865 505 505).

Pharmacy: Boots, Market St. (☎01865 247 461). Open M-W and F-Sa 8:30am-6pm, Th 8:30am-7pm, Su 11am-5pm.

Hospital: John Radcliffe Hospital, Headley Way (☎01865 741 166). Take bus #13.

Internet Access: Free at the **Oxford Central Library** (above). **Link Communications,** 33 High St. (☎01865 204 207). £1 per 45min. Open M-Sa 10am-9pm, Su 11am-9pm.

Post Office: 102-104 St. Aldates (☎08457 223 344). **Bureau de change.** Open M and W-Sa 9am-5:30pm, Tu 9:30am-5:30pm. **Postcode:** OX1 1ZZ.

🏠 🏕 ACCOMMODATIONS AND CAMPING

Book at least a week ahead from June to September, especially for singles. B&Bs (from £30) line the main roads out of town. Try www.stayoxford.com for

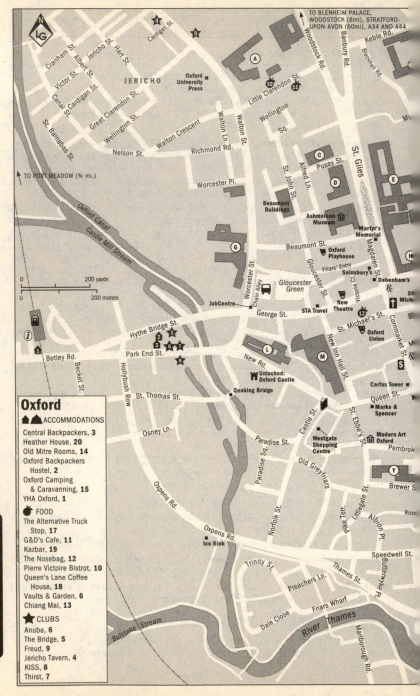

TO BLENHEIM PALACE, WOODSTOCK (8mi), STRATFORD-UPON-AVON (60mi), A34 AND A44

TO PORT MEADOW (¾ mi.)

JERICHO

Oxford University Press

JobCentre

Gloucester Green

Beaumont Buildings

Ashmolean Museum

Martyr's Memorial

Oxford Playhouse

Sainsbury's

Debenham's

New Theatre

STA Travel

Oxford Union

Unlocked: Oxford Castle

Quaking Bridge

Carfax Tower

Marks & Spencer

Westgate Shopping Centre

Modern Art Oxford

Ice Rink

Friars Wharf

River Thames

Bulstake Stream

Oxford

ACCOMMODATIONS
Central Backpackers, **3**
Heather House, **20**
Old Mitre Rooms, **14**
Oxford Backpackers Hostel, **2**
Oxford Camping & Caravanning, **15**
YHA Oxford, **1**

FOOD
The Alternative Truck Stop, **17**
G&D's Cafe, **11**
Kazbar, **19**
The Nosebag, **12**
Pierre Victoire Bistrot, **10**
Queen's Lane Coffee House, **18**
Vaults & Garden, **6**
Chiang Mai, **13**

CLUBS
Anuba, **6**
The Bridge, **5**
Freud, **9**
Jericho Tavern, **4**
KISS, **8**
Thirst, **7**

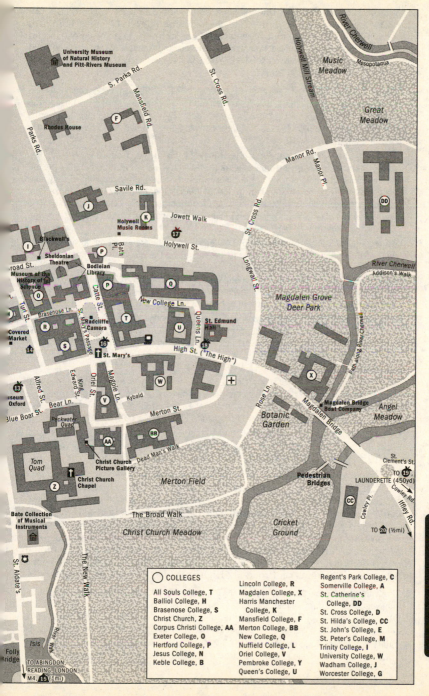

University Museum of Natural History and Pitt-Rivers Museum

River Cherwell

Music Meadow

Mesopotamia

Great Meadow

S. Parks Rd.

St. Cross Rd.

Mansfield Rd.

Rhodes House

Parks Rd.

Manor Rd.

Manor Pl.

F

Savile Rd.

J

K

DD

Holywell Music Rooms

Jowett Walk

St. Cross Rd.

River Cherwell

Addison's Walk

Blackwell's

I

Sheldonian Theatre

P

Bodleian Library

Holywell St.

17

Longwall St.

road St.

Museum of the History of Science

O

P

Brasenose Ln.

Turl St.

Catte St.

New College Ln.

O

Magdalen Grove Deer Park

St. Mary's Passage

Radcliffe Camera

T

Covered Market

R

S

14

16

U

Queen's Ln.

St. Edmund Hall

18

Path along River Cherwell

St. Mary's

High St. ("The High")

X

Magdalen Bridge

Museum Oxford

13

Alfred St.

King Edward St.

Bear Ln.

W

Oriel St.

Kybald

Rose Ln.

Magpie Ln.

Magdalen Bridge Boat Company

Angel Meadow

Blue Boar St.

V

Merton St.

Botanic Garden

St. Clement's St.

Peckwater Quad

Christ Church Picture Gallery

BB

Dead Man's Walk

AA

Pedestrian Bridges

LAUNDERETTE (450yd)

TO 19

Cowley Rd.

Iffley Rd.

Tom Quad

Christ Church Chapel

Z

Merton Field

Cowley Pl.

CC

TO 20 (½mi)

Bate Collection of Musical Instruments

The Broad Walk

Cricket Ground

St. Aldate's

The New Walk

Christ Church Meadow

Isis

River Walk

Folly Bridge

TO ABINGDON, READING, LONDON, M4, 15 (1mi)

HEART OF ENGLAND

○ COLLEGES

All Souls College, **T**
Balliol College, **H**
Brasenose College, **S**
Christ Church, **Z**
Corpus Christi College, **AA**
Exeter College, **O**
Hertford College, **P**
Jesus College, **N**
Keble College, **B**

Lincoln College, **R**
Magdalen College, **X**
Harris Manchester College, **K**
Mansfield College, **F**
Merton College, **BB**
New College, **Q**
Nuffield College, **L**
Oriel College, **V**
Pembroke College, **Y**
Queen's College, **U**

Regent's Park College, **C**
Somerville College, **A**
St. Catherine's College, **DD**
St. Cross College, **D**
St. Hilda's College, **CC**
St. John's College, **E**
St. Peter's College, **M**
Trinity College, **I**
University College, **W**
Wadham College, **J**
Worcester College, **G**

affordable options. The 300s on **Banbury Road** are accessible by buses #2, 2A, 2B, and 2D. Cheaper B&Bs lie in the 200s and 300s on **Iffley Road** (bus #4, 4A, 4B, 4C, and 16B to Rose Hill) and on **Abingdon Road** in South Oxford (bus #16 and 16A). If it's late, call the **Oxford Association of Hotels and Guest Houses** (East Oxford ☎01865 721 561, West Oxford ☎01865 862 138, North Oxford ☎01865 244 691, South Oxford ☎01865 244 268).

▨ **Central Backpackers,** 13 Park End St. (☎01865 242 288; www.centralbackpackers. co.uk). Located above Thirst Bar. Spacious rooms. Have a few drinks on the rooftop terrace—a frequent spot for summertime barbecues. Self-service kitchen. Female dorms available. Continental breakfast included. Free luggage storage and lockers. Laundry. Free Internet and Wi-Fi. 12-bed £16; 8-bed £17; 6-bed £18; 4-bed £19. MC/V. ❷

Oxford Backpackers Hostel, 9A Hythe Bridge St. (☎01865 721 761; www.hostels. co.uk), halfway between the bus and train stations. A self-proclaimed "funky hostel" with murals and music playing in the hallway. The bathrooms may be kind of dirty, and the chairs in the common area may be losing their stuffing, but, after a few drinks from the inexpensive bar, who's going to notice? Clean rooms. Self-catering kitchen. Female dorm available. Continental breakfast included. Luggage storage £2. Laundry. Internet £1 per 30min. Dorms £15-16; quads £68-76. MC/V. ❷

YHA Oxford, 2A Botley Rd. (☎01865 727 275). From the train station, turn right onto Botley Rd. Photos of famous Oxfordians line the walls. The quietest and most spacious of Oxford's 3 hostels. TV room, pool room, library, and ensuite bathrooms. Self-catering kitchen. Full English breakfast included. Lockers £1. Towels 50p. Laundry £3. Internet £1 per 15min. Wi-Fi £5 per hr. Wheelchair-accessible. Reception 24hr. 4- and 6-bed dorms £16-27; twins £40-60. Non-members £3 more. MC/V. ❷

Heather House, 192 Iffley Rd. (☎01865 249 757; www.heatherhouseoxford.com). A 5-10min. walk from Magdalen Bridge, or take the bus marked Rose Hill from the bus or train station or from Carfax Tower. Spotless ensuite rooms complete with small flatscreen TVs. Soft carpet, floral color scheme. Wi-Fi. Singles £35-45; doubles and twins £60-78; triples £81-100; family rooms £81-120. MC/V. ❹

Old Mitre Rooms, 4B Turl St. (☎01865 279 757), between Mahogany Hair Salon and Past Times Stationery. Look for the blue door. Owned by Lincoln College and used as a dorm term-time. Bookings and check-in are at Lincoln College. Continental breakfast. Open July-Sept. Singles £36; twins £65, ensuite £71; triples £83. MC/V. ❸

Oxford Camping and Caravanning, 426 Abingdon Rd. (☎01865 244 088), about 1 mi. from the city center, behind Touchwoods camping store. Toilet and laundry. Reception 9-10:30am and 4-5:30pm. £6-7.60 per person. Electricity £3. MC/V. ❶

◪ FOOD

▨**Gloucester Green Market,** behind the bus station, abounds with tasty treats. (Open W 8am-3:30pm.) The **Covered Market,** between Market St. and Carfax, has produce and deli goods. (Open M-Sa 8am-5:30pm.) Get groceries at the **Sainsbury's** on Magdalen St. (Open M-Sa 7am-11pm, Su 11am-5pm.) Across Magdalen Bridge, you'll find cheap restaurants on **Cowley Road** that serve international food in addition to fish and chips. For an on-the-go meal, try a sandwich from a **kebab van,** usually found on Broad St., High St., Queen St., and St. Aldates.

▨ **The Alternative Tuck Shop,** 24 Holywell St. (☎01865 792 054). Behind an unassuming veneer lies Oxford's most popular sandwich shop. Students and residents alike line up for any number of delicious made-to-order sandwiches (under £3) and panini (£4), along with a sinful assortment of baked goods. Open M-Sa 8:15am-6pm. Cash only. ❶

▨ **Vaults & Garden,** Radcliffe Sq. (☎01865 279 112; www.vaultsandgarden.co.uk), under St. Mary's Church. Follow your nose to the delectable homemade soups and organic entrees (£2-6). Cozy booths in the vaults and outdoor tables in the garden overlooking the iconic Radcliffe Camera. Open daily 9am-6pm. Cash only. ❷

Chiang Mai Kitchen, Kemp Hall Passage (☎01865 202 233; www.chiangmaikitchen. co.uk), in an alley off High St. Tasty Thai cuisine at unbeatable prices. Enjoy the fresh herbs and spices (flown in weekly from Bangkok) while soaking up the peaceful decor. Special vegetarian menu. Open daily noon-2:30pm and 6-10pm. MC/V. ❷

Kazbar, 25-27 Cowley Rd. (☎01865 202 920). Blue and green tiled floor and Moorish cushions. Spanish-style decor and sexy lighting. Tasty tapas (£2.70-4.60) like *patatas con chorizo.* Free tapas with drink M-F 4-7pm, Sa-Su noon-4pm. Open M-Th 4pm-midnight, F 4pm-12:30am, Sa noon-12:30am. AmEx/MC/V. ❶

G&D's Cafe, 55 Little Clarendon St. (☎01865 516 652). Branch on St. Aldates. Superb homemade ice cream (£2), pizza bagels (£3.50-4.20), and a boisterous student atmosphere. The great food and outdoor patio make it a favorite in the Jericho area. Open daily 8am-midnight. Cash only. ❶

The Nosebag, 6-8 St. Michael's St. (☎01865 721 033). Cafeteria-style service on the 2nd fl. of a 15th-century stone building. Eclectic menu includes great vegan and vegetarian options and tasty homemade soups for under £8. Indulge in a scrumptious dessert such as chocolate fudge cake (£3). Open M-Th 9:30am-10pm, F-Sa 9:30am-10:30pm, Su 9:30am-9pm. AmEx/MC/V. ❷

Queen's Lane Coffee House, 40 High St. (☎01865 240 082). Opened in 1654, the Queen's Lane is supposedly the 1st place where coffee was sold in all of Europe. You can still get a good cup of Java here as well as a selection of delicious sandwiches (£2.25-5.25) and desserts (£1.50-3.75). ½-price sandwiches after 5:30pm. Disounts for takeaway. Open M-Sa 7:30am-8pm, Su 9am-8pm. MC/V. ❶

📷 SIGHTS

The TIC sells a map (£1.25) and gives out the *Welcome to Oxford* guide, which lists the visiting hours for all of the college. Hours can also be accessed online at www.ox.ac.uk/visitors/colls.shtml. Note that those hours can be changed without explanation or notice, so confirm in advance. Some colleges charge admission, while others are only accessible through Blue Badge tours, booked at the TIC. Don't bother trying to sneak into Christ Church outside open hours—bouncers, affectionately known as "bulldogs," in bowler hats and stationed 50 ft. apart, will squint their eyes and kick you out.

CHRIST CHURCH

COLLEGE. "The House" has Oxford's grandest quad and its most distinguished students, counting 13 past prime ministers among its alumni. Charles I made Christ Church his headquarters for three and a half years during the Civil Wars and escaped dressed as a servant when the city was besieged. Lewis Carroll first met Alice, the dean's daughter, here. The dining hall and Tom Quad serve as shooting locations for *Harry Potter* films. In June, be respectful of undergrads prepping for exams as you navigate the narrow strip open to tourists.

Through an archway, to your left as you face the cathedral, lie **Peckwater Quad** and the most elegant Palladian building in Oxford. Look for rowing standings chalked on the walls and for the beautiful exterior of Christ Church's library. Spreading east and south from the main entrance, **Christ Church Meadow** compensates for Oxford's lack of "backs" (the riverside gardens in Cambridge). The meadows are beautiful and offer great views of Christ Church College for those who don't want to pay to go inside. *(Down St. Aldates from Carfax. ☎01865 286 573; www.chch.ox.ac.uk. Open M-Sa 9am-5:30pm, Su 1-5:30pm. Last entry 4pm. Dining hall open*

IN RECENT NEWS

TRASHED AT OXFORD

It's summertime, the sun is shining, and you've just completed your final exam at the prestigious Oxford University. The first thing you can look forward to in your newfound freedom? A face-full of raw fish and custard.

Or, at least, a few years ago you could have. The tradition of "trashing," originating in the 1990s, refers to the practice of Oxford students throwing things at their friends upon completion of their final university exams. The items range from champagne to eggs, flour, liver, and dog food.

In 2005, the tradition started to get pretty out of hand. Street cleanups after trashing cost as much as £20,000, and one undergraduate even got an octopus thrown through his open window. Locals complained about food waste and foul-smelling streets.

As a result, the Oxford University Police clamped down on trashing. Knowing it would be impossible to eliminate the custom altogether, they cut back on the kinds of substances that could be thrown. Instead of liver and octopuses, students throw much more harmless substances like confetti and glitter. But if you happen to be hit with a handful of glitter in the cobbled back alleys of Oxford in June—congratulations, you've just been trashed.

10:30am-noon and 2:30-4:30pm. Chapel services M-F 6pm, Su 8, 10, 11:15am, 6pm. £4.70, concessions £3.70.)

CHRIST CHURCH CHAPEL. The only church in England to serve as both a cathedral and college chapel, it was founded in AD 730 by Oxford's patron saint, St. Frideswide, who built a nunnery here in honor of two miracles: the blinding of her persistent suitor and his subsequent recovery. A stained-glass window (c. 1320) contains a rare panel depicting St. Thomas Becket, archbishop of Canterbury, kneeling moments before his death. Look for the floating toilet in the bottom right of a window showing St. Frideswide's death and the White Rabbit fretting in the windows in the hall.

TOM QUAD. The site of undergraduate lily-pond dunking, Tom Quad adjoins the chapel grounds. The quad takes its name from Great Tom, the seven-ton bell, that has rung 101 (the original number of students) times at 9:05pm (the original undergraduate curfew) every evening since 1682. The bell rings at 9:05pm because, technically, Oxford should be 5min. past Greenwich Mean Time. Nearby, the college hall displays portraits of some of Christ Church's famous alums—Sir Philip Sidney, William Penn, John Locke, and a bored-looking WH Auden—in a corner by the kitchen.

CHRIST CHURCH PICTURE GALLERY. Generous alumni gifts have established a small but noteworthy collection of works by Tintoretto, Vermeer, and Leonardo da Vinci, among others. *(In the Canterbury quad. Entrances on Oriel Sq. and at Canterbury Gate; visitors to the gallery should enter through Canterbury Gate. ☎01865 276 172; www.chch.ox.ac.uk/gallery. Open M-Sa 10:30am-5pm, Su 2pm-5pm. Tour M 2:30pm. £2, concessions £1.)*

OTHER COLLEGES

Oxford's extensive college system (totaling 39 official Colleges of the University) means that there are plenty of beautiful grounds to stroll year-round. The following is a selection of the most popular colleges. For information on others, check one of the many guides found at the TIC.

ALL SOULS COLLEGE. Candidates who survive the admission exams to All Souls are invited to a dinner, where the dons confirm that they are "well-born, well-bred, and only moderately learned." All Souls is also reported to have the most heavenly wine cellar in the city. The Great Quad may be Oxford's most serene, as hardly a living soul passes over it. *(Corner of High and Catte St. ☎01865 279 379; www.all-souls.ox.ac.uk. Open Sept.-July M-F 2-4pm. Free.)*

BALLIOL COLLEGE. Students at Balliol preserve tradition by hurling abuse over the wall at their Trinity College rivals. Matthew Arnold, Gerard Manley Hopkins, Aldous Huxley, and Adam Smith were all sons of Balliol's mismatched spires. The interior gates of the college supposedly bear lingering scorch marks from the executions of 16th-century Protestants, and a mulberry tree planted by Elizabeth I still shades slumbering students. *(Broad St. ☎01865 277 777; www. balliol.ox.ac.uk. Open daily 2-5pm. £1, students and children free.)*

MAGDALEN COLLEGE. With extensive grounds and flower-laced quads, Magdalen (MAUD-lin) is considered Oxford's handsomest college. It has a deer park flanked by the River Cherwell and Addison's Walk, a circular path that touches the river's opposite bank. The college's most famous alumnus is wit and playwright Oscar Wilde. *(On High St., near the Cherwell. ☎01865 276 000; www.magd. ox.ac.uk. Open daily June-Oct. noon-6pm; Nov.-May 1-6pm. £4, concessions £3.)*

MERTON COLLEGE. Merton's library houses the first printed Welsh Bible. Tolkien lectured here, inventing the Elven language in his spare time. The college's 14th-century **Mob Quad** is Oxford's oldest and least impressive, but nearby **Saint Alban's Quad** has some of the university's best gargoyles. *(Merton St. ☎01865 276 310; www.merton.ox.ac.uk. Open M-F 2-4pm, Sa-Su 10am-4pm. Free. Library tours £2.)*

NEW COLLEGE. This is the self-proclaimed first real college of Oxford. It was here, in 1379, that William of Wykeham dreamed up an institution that would offer a comprehensive undergraduate education under one roof. The bell tower has gargoyles of the seven deadly sins on one side and the seven heavenly virtues on the other—all equally grotesque. *(New College Ln. Use the Holywell St. Gate. ☎01865 279 555. Open daily from Easter to mid-Oct. 11am-5pm; Nov.-Easter 2-5pm. £2.)*

QUEEN'S COLLEGE. Although the college dates back to 1341, Queen's was rebuilt by Wren and Hawksmoor in the 17th and 18th centuries in the distinctive Queen Anne style. A trumpet call summons students to dinner, where a boar's head graces the table at Christmas. That tradition supposedly commemorates a student who, attacked by a boar on the outskirts of Oxford, choked the beast to death with a volume of Aristotle—probably the nerdiest slaughter ever. *(High St. ☎01865 279 120; www.queens.ox.ac.uk. Open to Blue-Badge tours only.)*

TRINITY COLLEGE. Founded in 1555, Trinity has a Baroque chapel with a lime-wood altarpiece, cedar latticework, and cherub-spotted pediments. The college's series of eccentric presidents includes Ralph Kettell, who would come to dinner with a pair of scissors to chop anyone's hair that he deemed too long. *(Broad St. ☎01865 279 900; www.trinity.ox.ac.uk. Open M-F 10am-noon and 2-4pm, Sa-Su 2-4pm; during vacations daily 10am-noon and 2-4pm. £1.50, concessions 75p.)*

UNIVERSITY COLLEGE. Built in 1249, this soot-blackened college vies with Merton for the title of oldest, claiming Alfred the Great as its founder. Percy Bysshe Shelley was expelled for writing the pamphlet *The Necessity of Atheism* but was later immortalized in a monument, on the right as you enter. Bill Clinton spent his Rhodes days here. *(High St. ☎01865 276 602; www.univ.ox.ac.uk. Entries for individuals at the discretion of the lodge porter.)*

OTHER SIGHTS

ASHMOLEAN MUSEUM. The grand Ashmolean—Britain's finest collection of arts and antiquities outside London and the country's oldest public museum—opened in 1683. The museum is undergoing extensive renovations until 2009 but continues to show an exhibit of "treasures"—more than 200 artifacts from its galleries—including the lantern carried by Guy Fawkes in the Gunpowder

HEART OF ENGLAND

Plot of 1605 and the deerskin mantle of Powhatan, father of Pocahontas. *(Beaumont St. ☎01865 278 000. Open Tu-Sa 10am-5pm, Su noon-5pm. Free. Tours £2.)*

BODLEIAN LIBRARY. Oxford's principal reading and research library has over five million books and 50,000 manuscripts. It receives a copy of every book printed in Great Britain. Sir Thomas Bodley endowed the library's first wing in 1602—the institution has since grown to fill the immense **Old Library** complex, the **Radcliffe Camera** next door, and two newer buildings on Broad St. Admission to the reading rooms is by ticket only. Each case is assessed individually by the Admissions Office—check the library's website for details. No one has ever been permitted to take out a book, not even Cromwell. Well, especially not Cromwell. *(Broad St. ☎01865 277 000; www.bodley.ox.ac.uk. Library open in summer M-F 9am-7pm, Sa 9am-1pm; during term-time M-F 9am-10pm, Sa 9am-1pm. Tours leave the Divinity School in the main quad in summer M-Sa 10:30, 11:30am, 2, 3pm. Tours £6. Audio tour £2.50.)*

BOTANIC GARDEN. Green things have flourished for three centuries in the oldest botanical garden in the British Isles, owned and used by Oxford University. The path connecting the garden to Christ Church Meadow provides a view of the Thames and the cricket grounds on the opposite bank. *(From Carfax, head down High St.; at the intersection of High St. and Rose Ln. ☎01865 286 690; www.botanic-garden.ox.ac. uk. Open daily May-Aug. 9am-6pm, last entry 5:15pm; Sept.-Oct. and Mar.-Apr. 9am-5pm, last entry 4:15pm; Nov.-Feb. 9am-4:30pm, last entry 4:15pm. Glass houses open daily 10am-4pm. Throwing stones in glass houses is not advised. £3, concessions £2, children free.)*

CARFAX TOWER. The tower marks the center of the premodern city. A climb up its 99 (very narrow) spiral stairs affords a superb view from the only remnant of medieval St. Martin's Church. "Carfax" gets its name from the French *carrefour* (crossroads), referring to the intersection of the North, South, East, and West Gates. *(Corner of Queen and Cornmarket St. ☎01865 792 653. Open daily Apr.-Sept. 10am-5:10pm; Oct. and Mar. 10am-4:30pm; Nov.-Feb. 10am-3:30pm. £2.10, children £1.)*

MUSEUM OF OXFORD. From hands-on exhibits to a murderer's skeleton, the museum provides an in-depth look at Oxford's rich 800-year history. *(St. Aldates. Enter at corner of St. Aldates and Blue Boar St. ☎01865 252 761; www.museumoxford.org.uk. Open Tu-F 10am-5pm, Sa-Su noon-5pm. Last entry 30min. before close. £2, concessions £1.50, children 50p, under 5 free, families £4.)*

OXFORD CASTLE. Oxford's newest attraction, the castle has been an Anglo-Saxon church, a Norman castle commissioned by William the Conqueror, a courthouse, and (until 1996) a prison. Now the complex houses restaurants, an open-air theater, and a luxury hotel. Visitors are issued personal video guides outlining life as an inmate and the gory details of 17th-century executions. You can climb to the top of St. George's Tower for a view of the city formerly enjoyed only by prison guards. *(44-46 Oxford Castle on New Rd. ☎01865 260 666. Open daily 10am-5pm. Last entry 4:20pm. £7.50, concessions £6.20, children £5.35.)*

SHELDONIAN THEATRE. This Roman-style auditorium was designed by a teenage Christopher Wren. Graduation ceremonies, conducted in Latin, take place in the Sheldonian, as does everything from student recitals to world-class opera performances. *The Red Violin* and *Quills*, as well as numerous other movies, were filmed here. Climb up to the cupola for views of Oxford's quads. The ivy-crowned stone heads on the fence behind the Sheldonian are a 20th-century study in beards. *(Broad St. ☎01865 277 299. Open in summer M-Sa 10am-12:30pm and 2-4:30pm; in winter M-Sa 10am-12:30pm and 2-3:30pm. £2, concessions £1. Purchase tickets for shows from Oxford Playhouse (☎01865 305 305). Box office open M-Tu and Th-Sa 9:30am-6:30pm or until 30min. before last showing, W 10am-6:30pm. Shows £15.)*

OTHER SIGHTS. Oxford's oldest building, a Saxon tower built in 1040, stands as part of **Saint Michael at the North Gate.** Climb the steps for a brief history of the tower and the church as well as a bird's-eye view of the city. (☎01865 240 940; www.smng.org.uk. Open daily Apr.-Oct. 10:30am-5pm; Nov.-Mar. 10:30am-4pm. £1.80, concessions £1.20, children 90p, families £5.) With 6 mi. of bookshelves, **Blackwell** is by far the largest bookshop in Oxford. (53 Broad St. ☎01865 792 792; www.bookshop. blackwell.co.uk. Open M-Sa 9am-6pm, Su 11am-5pm.)

Behind the **University Museum of Natural History,** the **Pitt-Rivers Museum** has an archaeological and anthropological collection, including shrunken heads and magical amulets. (Parks Rd. Natural History Museum ☎01865 272 950; www.oum.ox.ac.uk. Open daily 9am-5pm. Free. Pitt-Rivers Museum ☎01865 270 927; www.prm.ox.ac.uk. Closed for renovations until spring 2009. Open M noon-4:30pm, Tu-Su 10am-4:30pm. Free.) The **Museum of the History of Science** features clocks, astrolabes, and Einstein's blackboard, preserved as he left it after an Oxford lecture in the 1930s. (Broad St. ☎01865 277 280; www.mhs.ox.ac.uk. Open Tu-F noon-5pm, Sa 10am-5pm, Su 2-5pm. Free. Tours £1.50.) The **Modern Art Oxford** hosts international and community shows. (30 Pembroke St. ☎01865 722 733; www.modernartoxford.org.uk. Open Tu-Sa 10am-5pm, Su noon-5pm. Free.)

🎵 ENTERTAINMENT

Centuries of tradition give Oxford a solid music scene. Colleges offer concerts and evensong services; **New College** has an excellent boys' choir, and performances at the **Holywell Music Rooms,** on Holywell St., are worth checking out. Theater groups stage plays in gardens or cloisters. Pick up *This Month in Oxford,* free at the TIC, or *Daily Information,* posted all over town and online (www.dailyinfo.co.uk), for event listings.

Oxford Coffee Concerts (☎07976 740 024; www.coffeeconcerts.com). Feature famous musicians and ensembles every Su at 11:15am. Tickets £9, concessions £8.

City of Oxford Orchestra (☎01865 744 457; www.cityofoxfordorchestra.co.uk). A professional symphony orchestra. Plays a subscription series at the Sheldonian and in college chapels during the summer. Tickets £14-25, concessions £2 less.

New Theatre, George St. (☎01865 320 760; www.newtheatreoxford.org.uk). Features performances from jazz to musicals to the Welsh National Opera. Tickets £10-50. Box office open M-Sa 10am-6pm, performance days 10am-8pm.

Oxford Playhouse, 11-12 Beaumont St. (☎01865 305 305; www.oxfordplayhouse.com, www.ticketsoxford.com). Hosts amateur and professional musicians and dance performances. The playhouse also sells discounted tickets for venues citywide. Box office open M-Tu and Th-F 9:30am-6:30pm, W 10am-6:30pm.

🍺 PUBS

In Oxford, pubs far outnumber colleges—some even consider them the city's prime attraction. Most open by noon, begin to fill around 5pm, and close at 11pm (10:30pm on Su). Recent legislation has allowed pubs to stay open later, but there may be conditions, including an earlier door-closing time or a small cover charge. Be ready to pub crawl—many pubs are so small that a single band of celebrating students will squeeze out other patrons, while just around the corner others will have several spacious rooms.

The Turf Tavern, 4 Bath Pl. (☎01865 243 235; www.theturftavern.co.uk), hidden off Holywell St. Arguably the most popular student bar in Oxford, this 13th-century pub is tucked in an alley off an alley, but that doesn't stop just about everybody in Oxford from partaking in its 11 different ales. Bob Hawke, future prime minister of Australia, downed

Oxford Pub Crawl

PUBS

All Bar One, **7**
The Bear, **9**
Chequers Inn, **5**
The Eagle and Child, **2**
The Grapes, **3**
The Head of the River, **8**
The Jolly Farmers, **1**
The King's Arms, **10**
St. Aldates Tavern, **4**
Turf's Tavern, **11**
The White Horse, **6**

a yard of ale (over 2 pints) in a record 11 seconds here while at the university. Open M-Sa 11am-11pm, Su noon-10:30pm. Kitchen open noon-7:30pm.

The King's Arms, 40 Holywell St. (☎01865 242 369). Oxford's unofficial student union. Until 1973, the bar was the last male-only pub in the UK. Now, the "KA," as it's called locally, has plenty of large tables for all patrons even when it's busy. Open daily 10:30am-midnight. Kitchen open 11:30am-9pm. MC/V.

The Bear, 6 Alfred St. (☎01865 728 164). Patrons once exchanged their club neckties for a pint at this oldest and tiniest of Oxford's many pubs. Over 4500 adorn the walls and ceiling of the pub, established in 1242. Unfortunately, the deal no longer applies. Open M-Th 11:30am-11pm, F-Sa 11:30am-midnight, Su noon-10:30pm.

The White Horse, 52 Broad St. (☎01865 722 393; www.whitehorseoxford.co.uk), between the 2 entrances of Blackwell's. Step back in time in this tiny, historic pub favored by locals. Supposedly haunted by a witch whose broomstick was found in the living room upstairs (where it remains untouched, for fear of provoking her ghost). Open daily 11am-11pm. Kitchen open until 9pm. MC/V.

The Jolly Farmers, 20 Paradise St. (☎07771 561 848; www.jollyfarmers.com). Oxford's 1st gay and lesbian pub. Popular with students and 20-somethings, especially on weekends. The landlord's standard poodle, Benson, is a regular and a main attraction. Get there early for a seat in the garden. Open daily noon-midnight.

The Eagle and Child, 49 St. Giles (☎01865 302 925). A historic pub. The dark-paneled back (now middle) room hosted "The Inklings," a group of 20th-century writers including CS Lewis and JRR Tolkien, who referred to it as the "Bird and Baby." *The Chronicles of Narnia* and *The Hobbit* were first read aloud here. Open M-Th 10am-11pm, F-Sa 10am-11:30pm, Su 10am-10:30pm. Kitchen open noon-9pm. AmEx/MC/V.

The Head of the River, Folly Bridge, St. Aldates (☎01865 721 600). This aptly named pub has the best location in all of Oxford to view the Thames, known locally as the Isis. Much bigger than the pubs closer to the town center, so you can be sure you'll find a seat. The large beer garden fills up quickly in the early evening. Open M-Sa 11am-11pm, Su 11:30am-10:30pm. Kitchen open daily noon-2:30pm and 5-9pm. AmEx/MC/V.

St. Aldates Tavern, 108 St. Aldates (☎01865 250 201). Local charm and regional ales. Formerly called "the Hobgoblin," the pub is rumored to be haunted. The ceiling is plastered with over 1200 ale labels, all of which went through the pub in 1 year. Student discount 10%. Open M-Sa noon-11:30pm, Su noon-10:30pm.

Chequers Inn, 131 High St. (☎01865 727 463). Leather couches, brick fireplaces, and a heated beer garden make this a great place to kick off a pub crawl. Rustic decor and energetic atmosphere. Open M-Th and Su 11am-11:30pm, F-Sa 11am-midnight.

The Grapes, 7 George St. (☎01865 793 380). This Victorian pub hasn't changed much since the 19th century. A veritable Oxford institution frequented by professors and students alike. Open M-W and Su 11am-11pm, Th-Sa 11am-midnight.

CLUBS

After hitting the pubs, head up **Walton Street** or down **Cowley Road** for clubs.

Jericho Tavern, 56 Walton St. (☎01865 311 775). An upstairs venue where Radiohead had its debut gig in 1984. Downstairs, patrons enjoy the sleek decor, specialty draft beer, and heated beer garden. Live music F-Sa, and some weeknights with £5-8 cover. Open M-F noon-midnight, Sa-Su 10am-midnight.

Thirst, 7-8 Park End St. (☎01865 242 044; www.thirstbar.com). Lounge bar with a DJ and backdoor garden. Popular student hangout during the week. Cheap mixed drinks (from £2.25) with a student ID M-Th and Su. Budget drinks served during "twilight hour" (1am-close). Open M-W and Su 7:30pm-2am, Th-Sa 7:30-3am.

Freud, 119 Walton St. (☎01865 311 171; www.freudliving.com). Formerly St. Paul's Church. Bizarre decoration: part cathedral, part circus, part modern-art installation gone wrong. Occasional art exhibitions, live music, and DJs. Cafe by day, mixed-drink bar by night. Open M and Su 10:30am-midnight, Tu-Th 10:30am-1am, F-Sa 10am-2am.

The Bridge, 6-9 Hythe Bridge St. (☎01865 242 526; www.bridgeoxford.co.uk). Dance to R&B, hip hop, dance, and pop on 2 floors. Erratically frequented by big student crowds. Cover £3-7. Open M-W 9pm-2am, Th 9pm-3am, F-Sa 10pm-3am.

Anuba, 11-13 Park End St. (☎01865 242 526; www.bridgeoxford.co.uk/anuba). Sister club to The Bridge. Intimate pre-club atmosphere. Small dance floor is a nice alternative to the huge clubs throughout the city. Live music F. Salsa night W (cover £3). Happy hour M-Sa 8:30-10:30pm. Open M-Sa 8pm-1am, F 8pm-2am, Sa 8pm-3am.

FESTIVALS

The university celebrates **Eights Week** at the end of May, when the colleges enter crews in bumping races and beautiful people sip Pimm's on the banks. In early September, **Saint Giles Fair** invades one of Oxford's main streets with an old-fashioned English fun fair. Daybreak on **May Day** (May 1) cues one of Oxford's most inspiring moments: the Magdalen College Choir sings madrigals from the top of the tower beginning at 6am, and the town indulges in Morris dancing, beating the bounds, and other age-old rituals of merry men. Pubs open at 7am.

▶ DAYTRIPS FROM OXFORD

BLENHEIM PALACE. The largest private home in England, Blenheim Palace (BLEN-em) was built in honor of the duke of Marlborough's victory over Louis XIV at the 1704 Battle of Blenheim. The 11th duke of Marlborough now calls the palace home. His rent is a flag from the estate, payable each year to the Crown—not a bad deal for 187 furnished rooms. Archways and marble floors accentuate the artwork inside, including wall-size tapestries of 17th- and 18th-century battle scenes. Winston Churchill, a member of the Marlborough family, spent some years here before he was shipped off to boarding school (the palace still houses his baby clothes). He proposed to his wife here and now rests with her in a nearby churchyard. The vast grounds consist of 2100 acres, all designed by that most reliable of landscape architects, Lancelot "Capability" Brown. *(In the town of Woodstock, 8 mi. north of Oxford. Stagecoach (☎01865 772 250) bus #20 runs to Blenheim Palace from Gloucester Green bus station (30-40min., every hr. 8am-5pm, round-trip £4.50). ☎01993 811 091 or 08700 602 080; www.blenheimpalace.com. House open daily from mid-Feb. to mid-Dec. 10:30am-5:30pm. Last entry 4:45pm. Grounds open daily 9am-5:30pm. Tours every 20min. £16.50, concessions £13.50, children £10, families £44. Grounds without house £9.50/7.30/4.80/24. Tours free.)*

STRATFORD-UPON-AVON   ☎(0)1789

Shakespeare was born here. This fluke of fate has made Stratford-upon-Avon a major stop on the tourist superhighway. Proprietors tout the dozen-odd properties linked, however remotely, to the Bard and his extended family: shops and restaurants devotedly stencil his prose and poetry on their windows and walls. Beyond the sound and fury of rumbling tour buses and chaotic swarms of daytrippers, there lies a town worth seeing for the beauty of the River Avon and riveting performances in the Royal Shakespeare Theatre.

◀ HENCE, AWAY!

Trains: Station Rd., off Alcester Rd. Office open M-Sa 6am-8:15pm, Su 9am-8pm. Trains (☎08457 484 950) to **Birmingham** (50min., 2 per hr., £6), **London Marylebone** (2¼hr., 2 per hr., £17-45), and **Warwick** (25min., 9 per day, £4.50).

Buses: Depart from **Riverside Coach Park,** off Bridgeway Rd. near the Leisure Centre. National Express (☎08717 818 181) to **London** (3-4hr., 4 per day, £15.80) and **Oxford** (1hr., 1 per day, £8). Stagecoach (☎08456 001 314) to **Birmingham** (1hr., 1 per hr., £3.60), **Chipping Norton** (45min., 3 per day, £4.50), and **Oxford** (1½hr., 3 per day, £6). Stagecoach #1618 services **Coventry** (2hr., every hr., £3.50) via **Warwick** (20-40min., every hr., £3). Buy bus tickets at the TIC.

Taxis: 007 Taxis (☎01789 414 007). **Shakespeare Taxis** (☎01789 266 100).

Bike Rental: Stratford Bike Hire, Guild St. (☎07711 776 340; www.stratfordbikehire. com). Mountain bikes £13 per day, £7 per ½-day. Delivers and picks up bikes within a 6 mi. radius of Stratford-upon-Avon; call in advance.

Boat Rental: Avon Boating, Swan's Nest Ln. (☎01789 267 073; www.avon-boating. co.uk), by Clopton Bridge. Rents rowboats (£4 per hr.) and motorboats (£25 per hr.). 30min. river trips £4, concessions £3. Open daily Apr.-Oct. 9am-dusk.

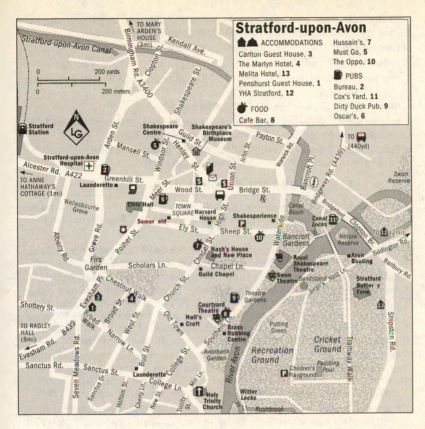

Stratford-upon-Avon

▲▲ ACCOMMODATIONS
Carlton Guest House, **3**
The Marlyn Hotel, **4**
Melita Hotel, **13**
Penshurst Guest House, **1**
YHA Stratford, **12**

Hussain's, **7**
Must Go, **5**
The Oppo, **10**

◆ FOOD
Cafe Bar, **8**

▮ PUBS
Bureau, **2**
Cox's Yard, **11**
Dirty Duck Pub, **9**
Oscar's, **6**

▮ WHO IS'T THAT CAN INFORM ME?

Tourist Information Centre: Bridgefoot (☎0870 160 7930; www.shakespeare-coun-
try.co.uk). Provides maps (£0.80-1.20), guidebooks, tickets, and accommodations
lists. Books rooms for £3 and a 10% deposit. Open Apr.-Oct. M-Sa 9am-5:30pm, Su
10am-4pm; Nov.-Mar. M-Sa 9am-5pm, Su 10am-3:30pm.

Tours: City Sightseeing Bus Tours, Civic Hall, 14 Rother St. (☎01789 412 680; www.
citysightseeing-stratford.com), heads to Bard-related houses every 20-30min. from the
front of the Pen and Parchment next to the TIC. £11, concessions £9, children £5.50.
Office open daily 9am-5pm. **Stratford Town Walk** (☎01789 292 478; www.stratford-
townwalk.com) arranges various walking tours throughout the city, including the popular
Ghost Walks. All walks depart from Waterside St. opposite Sheep St., near the Royal
Shakespeare Theatre. Regular town walk M-W 9am-5pm, Sa 9am-noon; Ghost Walk Th
7:30pm. Advanced booking required for Ghost Walk. £5, children £2, concessions £4.

Banks: Barclays (☎08457 555 555), at the intersection of Henley and Wood St. Open
M-F 9am-5pm, Sa 9am-noon. **Thomas Cook,** 37 Wood St. (☎01789 293 582). Open
M and W-Sa 9am-5:30pm, Tu 10am-5:30pm.

Library: Central Library, 12 Henley St. (☎01789 292 209). Internet £3 per hr. Open M and W-F 9am-5:30pm, Tu 10am-5:30pm, Sa 9:30am-5pm, Su noon-4pm.

Launderette: 34 Greenhill St. (☎07870 425 043). Open daily 8am-10pm.

Police: Rother St. (☎01789 414 111).

Pharmacy: Boots, 11 Bridge St. (☎01789 292 173). Open M-Sa 8:45am-5:30pm, Su 10:30am-4:30pm.

Hospital: Arden St. (☎01789 205 831), off Alcester Rd.

Internet Access: At **Central Library** (above). **Cyber Junction,** 28 Greenhill St. (☎01789 263 400). £4 per hr. Open M-F 10am-6pm, Sa 10:30am-5:30pm.

Post Office: 2-3 Henley St. (☎08457 223 vt344). **Bureau de change.** Open M and W-Sa 8:30am-6pm, Tu 9:30am-6pm. **Postcode:** CV37 6PU.

⌂ TO SLEEP, PERCHANCE TO DREAM

B&Bs are common, but singles are rare. Accommodations in the £25-35 range line **Evesham Place, Evesham Road,** and **Grove Road.** Also try **Shipston Road** across the river, a 15-20min. walk from the station.

▨ **Carlton Guest House,** 22 Evesham Pl. (☎01789 293 548). Spacious rooms and spectacular service. Singles £24-30; doubles and twins £52; triples £60-78. Cash only. ❸

YHA Stratford, Wellesbourne Rd., Alveston (☎01789 297 093; www.stratfordyha.org. uk), a little less than 2 mi. from Clopton Bridge. Follow the B4086 from town center (35min.) or take bus #X18 or 15 from Bridge St. (10min., every hr., £2). Isolated hostel catering mostly to school groups and families. A solid, inexpensive option for longer stays. Full English breakfast included. Laundry. Internet £1 per 15min. Dorms £20-24.50; doubles from £54; triples from £82. £3 more for non-YHA members. MC/V. ❷

Melita Hotel, 37 Shipston Rd. (☎01789 292 432; www.melitaguesthouse.co.uk). Upscale B&B with gorgeous garden, retreat-like atmosphere, and great breakfast. Guests relax on the patio with less-than-intimidating guard dog Harvey and his accomplice, Daisy. Singles £42; doubles £72; triples £98; family rooms £120. AmEx/MC/V. ❹

Penshurst Guest House, 34 Evesham Pl. (☎01789 205 259; www.penshurst.net). 4 distinctly decorated rooms. Self-catering kitchen. Ensuite doubles and triples £39; ensuite family rooms £45-52. Prices can vary; call ahead. Cash only. ❸

◖ IN THE CAULDRON BOIL AND BAKE

Baguette stores and bakeries are scattered throughout the town center; a **Somerfield** supermarket is in Town Sq. (☎01789 292 604. Open M-Sa 8am-7pm, Su 10am-4pm.) A traditional town **market** is held every Friday on Rother St. in Market Pl. The first and third Saturdays of every month, the River Avon's banks welcome a bustling **farmers' market.**

The Oppo, 13 Sheep St. (☎01789 269 980; www.theoppo.co.uk). Low 16th-century-style ceilings and candles. Try the grilled goat cheese and tomato salad (£9). Open M-Th noon-2pm and 5-9:30pm, F-Sa noon-2pm and 5-11pm, Su 6-9:30pm. MC/V. ❸

Hussain's, 6A Chapel St. (☎01789 267 506; www.hussainsindiancuisine.co.uk). Stratford's best Indian menu and a favorite of actor Ben Kingsley. Tandoori with homemade spices served in a red dining room. Entrees from £6. 10% discount for takeaway and pre-theater dining. Open daily 12:30-2:30pm and 5pm-midnight. AmEx/MC/V. ❷

Cafe Bar, inside the Courtyard Theatre (☎01789 403 415). Serves homemade sandwiches and pastries by the river. A perfect spot for a drink during matinee intermission, but be prepared to wait in line. Sandwiches £3.75. Open M-Sa 10:30am-8:30pm. ❷

Must Go, 21 Windsor St. (☎01789 293 679). This Asian restaurant is unabashedly straightforward. After inspecting the 4 ft. long menu outside, enter the "Out" doorway for takeaway or the "In" door for a meal in surprisingly comfortable quarters. "Meal deals" £5-7. Open Apr.-Oct. M-Th and Su noon-midnight, F-Sa noon-12:30am; Sept.-Mar. M-Th and Su noon-2pm and 5pm-midnight, F-Sa noon-12:30am. AmEx/MC/V. ❷

👁 THE GILDED MONUMENTS

TO BARD...

Stratford's Will-centered sights are best seen before 11am, when the daytrippers arrive, or after 4pm, when the crowds disperse. The five official **Shakespeare properties** are Shakespeare's Birthplace, Mary Arden's House, Nash's House and New Place, Hall's Croft, and Anne Hathaway's Cottage. Diehards should get the **All Five Houses** ticket, which also includes entrance to Harvard House. (☎01789 204 016. £14.50, concessions £12.50, children £7.20, families £37.70.) Those who don't want to visit every shrine can get a **Three In-Town Houses** pass, covering the Birthplace, Hall's Croft, and Nash's House and New Place (£10.60/9.30/5.30/27.80).

SHAKESPEARE'S BIRTHPLACE. The only in-town sight directly associated with him includes an exhibit on his father's glove-making business, a peaceful garden, and the requisite walkthrough on the Bard's documented life, including a First Folio and records of his father's illegal refuse dumping. Join such distinguished pilgrims as Charles Dickens in signing the guestbook. *(Henley St. ☎01789 201 806. Open in summer M-Sa 9am-5pm, Su 9:30am-5pm; in fall and spring daily 10am-5pm; in winter M-Sa 10am-4pm, Su 10:30am-4pm. £8, concessions £7, children £4.*

SHAKESPEARE'S GRAVE. The least crowded and most authentic way to pay homage to the Bard is to visit his grave inside the quiet **Holy Trinity Church**—although here, too, groups pack the arched door at peak hours. Rumor has it that Shakespeare was buried 17 ft. underground by request, so that he would sleep undisturbed. To the left is a large bust of Shakespeare and his birth and death records. The church also harbors the graves of wife Anne and daughter Susanna. *(Trinity St. ☎01789 290 128; www.shakespearechurch.org.uk. Entrance to church free; required donation to see grave £1.50, students and children 50p. Open daily 8:30am-6pm.)*

NASH'S HOUSE AND NEW PLACE. Tourists flock to the home of the first husband of Shakespeare's granddaughter Elizabeth, his last descendant.

TOP TEN LIST

SHAKESPEAREAN DISSES

In Stratford-upon-Avon, you can see where Shakespeare is buried, walk through the house where he grew up, and sit on a bench where he kissed his sweetheart. But what no tour guide will tell you is how Will slung out insults. Any of the following might come in handy, in Stratford and beyond:

1. Wipe thy ugly face, thou loggerheaded toad-spotted barnacle! I'm sorry, but you're just not that attractive.

2. Bathe thyself, thou rank reeling-ripe boar-pig! One way to tell that guy in your hostel that he could use a shower.

3. Thou puny milk-livered measel! You're a coward!

4. Thou dost intrude, thou infectious fat-kidneyed woldwarp! Sometimes, you just need some personal space.

5. Thou vain idle-headed strumpet! You spend too much time in front of that mirror.

6. Clean thine ears, thou lumpish boil-brained lout! What? You didn't hear me the first time?

7. Thy breath stinks with eating toasted cheese. That one's pretty self-explanatory.

8. Remove thine ass hence, thou beslubbering beetle-headed clotpole! For that drunkard in the club who just won't leave you alone.

9. Thou droning boil-brained harpy! To let your tour guide know that you're not that interested.

10. I'll see thee hang'd, thou villainous ill-breeding ratsbane! Only to be used when you're truly furious at someone.

Nash's House has been restored to its Elizabethan grandeur and holds temporary exhibits on the Bard, but most want to see New Place, Shakespeare's retirement home and, at the time, Stratford's finest house. Today, only the foundations and a garden remain due to a disgruntled 19th-century owner named Gastrell who razed the building and cut down Shakespeare's mulberry tree in order to spite Bard tourists (jealous much?). Gastrell was run out of town, and to this day Gastrells are not allowed in Stratford. *(Chapel St.* ☎ *01789 292 325. Open in summer M-Sa 9:30am-5pm, Su 10am-5pm; in fall and spring daily 11am-5pm; in winter M-Sa 11am-4pm. £3.75, concessions £3, children £1.75.)* Down Chapel St. from Nash's House, the hedges and abundant flowers of the **Great Garden of New Place** offer a respite from the mobbed streets and hold a mulberry tree said to be grown from the one Gastrell chopped down. *(Open M-Sa 9am-dusk, Su 10am-5pm. Free.)*

MARY ARDEN'S HOUSE. This farmhouse in Wilmcote, a village 3 mi. from Stratford, was only recently determined to be the childhood home of Mary Arden (Shakespeare's mother). Historians thought she grew up in the stately building next door. She didn't. Cattle roam the farm, and a history recounts how Mary fell in love with the elder Shakespeare. *(Connected by footpath to Anne Hathaway's Cottage, or take the train from Stratford 1 stop north.* ☎ *01789 293 455. Open daily in summer 9:30am-5pm; in fall and spring 10am-5pm; in winter 10am-4pm. £7, concessions £6.)*

ANNE HATHAWAY'S COTTAGE. The birthplace of Shakespeare's wife, about a mile away in Shottery, is a fairy-tale, thatched-roof cottage. It boasts original Hathaway furniture and a hedge maze. Entrance entitles you to sit on a bench Will may or may not also have sat on. *(Take the hop-on, hop-off Guide Friday tour bus or head west out of town on Alcester Rd. and look for the sign on the left to the cottage.* ☎ *01789 292 100. Open in summer M-Sa 9am-5pm, Su 9:30am-5pm; in fall and spring M-Sa 9:30am-5pm, Su 10am-5pm; in winter daily 10am-4pm. £6, concessions £5, children £3, families £15.50.)*

SHAKESPEARIENCE. A Shakespearian extravaganza, if you will, and the most unique exhibit in town. A two-act show starting with a visual tour of Shakespeare's life and times and featuring a holographic summary of his most famous works. The blasting winds and surround sound may seem a bit over the top, but it's definitely a fun way to chill with Will. *(Waterside, across from the Bancroft gardens and carousel.* ☎ *01789 290 111. Shows daily every hr. 10am-5pm. £8, concessions £7.)*

...OR NOT TO BARD

Believe it or not, non-Shakespearean sights do exist in Stratford.

STRATFORD BUTTERFLY FARM. Europe's largest collection of butterflies flutters through tropical surroundings. Less beautiful creepy-crawlies—like the salmon pink bird-eating spider—dwell in glass boxes nearby. *(Off Swan's Nest Ln. at Tramway Walk, across the river from the TIC.* ☎ *01789 299 288; www.butterflyfarm.co.uk. Open daily in summer 10am-6pm; in winter 10am-5pm. £5.50, concessions £5, children £4.50.)*

HARVARD HOUSE. Once inhabited by the mother of the founder of that university in Cambridge (across the pond), the house is now owned by the Shakespeare Birthright Trust. It houses more pewter than crimson, but Johnny Harvard gets a small exhibit on the second floor. *(High St.* ☎ *01789 204 507. Open May-July and Sept.-Oct. F-Su noon-5pm; July-Sept. W-Su noon-5pm. £3.50, children free.)*

RAGLEY HALL. Eight miles from Stratford on Evesham Rd. (A435), Ragley Hall houses the earl and countess of Yarmouth. Set in a stunning 400-acre park, the estate has an art collection and a sculpture park. *(Bus #246 (M-Sa 5 per day) runs to Alcester Police Station. Walk 1 mi. to the gates, then ½ mi. up the drive.* ☎ *01789 762 090; www.ragleyhall.com. Park open Mar.-Nov. F-Su and holidays 10am-6pm. House and state rooms open Mar.-Nov. F, Su, holidays noon-4pm. £8.50, concessions £7, children £5, families £27.)*

♫ ALL THE WORLD'S A STAGE

One of the world's most acclaimed repertories, the **Royal Shakespeare Company (RSC)** sells well over one million tickets each year. The **Royal Shakespeare Theatre** is currently undergoing a £100 million renovation and will re-open in 2010 with a 1000-seat thrust stage, bringing the whole audience within 50 ft. of the action. The construction has also closed the **Swan Theatre,** the RSC's more intimate neighbor, until 2010. The company continues to perform shows down the road at **The Courtyard Theatre.** Visitors can get backstage tours and a glimpse at the high-tech stage to be installed at the Royal Shakespeare Theatre. The box office in the Courtyard Theatre handles the ticketing for all theaters. (Ticket hotline ☎0844 800 1110; www.rsc.org.uk. Tickets £10-48, ages 16-25 £5. Standing room £5. Standby tickets in summer £15; in winter £12. Open M and W-Sa 9:30am-8pm, Tu 10am-8pm. AmEx/MC/V.)

🍺 DRINK DEEP ERE YOU DEPART

Dirty Duck Pub, 66 Waterside (☎01789 297 312; www.dirtyduck.co.uk). Originally called "The Black Swan" and rechristened by alliterative Americans during WWII. Huge bust of Shakespeare inside. Actors make entrances almost nightly. Dame Judy Dench got engaged here and has her own table in the backroom. Open daily 10am-midnight.

Cox's Yard, Bridgefoot (☎01789 404 600; www.coxsyard.co.uk), next to Bancroft Gardens. Have an outdoor pint in this massive complex on the banks of the Avon. Upstairs bar with tribute bands. Call for performance times and tickets. Pub and beer garden open in summer M-Tu and Su noon-11pm, W-Th noon-12:30am, F-Sa noon-1:30am.

Oscar's, 14 Meer St. (☎01789 292 202). Cafe by day, bar by night. Feels like a tree house for adults. Red walls, bubble machine, and seats by upstairs windows. Themed nights every day of the week, including live music and DJs. Open daily 7pm-7am.

Bureau, 1 Arden St. (☎01789 297 641). Silver staircase leads to a huge dance area. Cover £2-5. Open M and Th-F 5pm-2am, Tu-W 5pm-midnight, Sa noon-4pm.

🎉 OUR RUSTIC REVELRY

Stratford's biggest festival begins on the weekend nearest April 23, **Shakespeare's birthday.** The modern, well-respected Shakespeare Birthplace Trust, Henley St., hosts a **Poetry Festival** every Sunday evening in July and August. Past participants include poet bigwigs Seamus Heaney, Ted Hughes, and Derek Walcott. (☎01789 292 176. Tickets £7-15.)

WORCESTER ☎(0)1905

Worcester (WUH-ster) sits between Cheltenham and Birmingham, along the Severn. A small city, Worcester has certain quirky claims to fame—Edward Elgar, Worcestershire sauce, and Royal Worcester Porcelain among them. Visitors might find the city's cathedral vaguely familiar: it's on the £20 note.

🚆 TRANSPORTATION. Foregate Street Station, at the edge of the town center on Foregate St., is the main train station. (Ticket window open M-F 6:10am-6:30pm, Su 8:45am-3:45pm.) **Shrub Hill Station,** just outside of town, serves Cheltenham and has service to London and Birmingham. (Ticket window open M-Sa 5:10am-9pm, Su 7:10am-9:30pm.) Trains (☎08457 484 950) travel to Birmingham (1hr., every hr., £6), Cheltenham (30min., every 2hr., £6.40), and London Paddington (2½hr., every hr., £32.30-34.10). The **bus station** is at Angel Pl., near the Crowngate Shopping Centre. National Express buses (☎08717 818 181) run to:

Birmingham (1½hr., 2 per day, £4); Bristol (1½-2hr., 6 per day, £13.80); Cheltenham (1½hr., 2 per day, £4.70); London Victoria (5-7hr., 3 per day, £19.50). First (☎01905 359 393) is the regional bus company, and its **FirstWorcester City** ticket allows for one day of travel within Worcester (£3.20). **Brookside Taxis** (☎01905 748 473) runs 24hr. Rent **bikes** at Peddlers, 46-48 Barbourne Rd. (☎01905 24 238. Open M-F 9:30am-5:30pm, Sa 9:30am-5pm. £8 per day; £50 deposit.)

◢⌷ ORIENTATION AND PRACTICAL INFORMATION. The city center is bounded by Foregate St. Station to the north and the cathedral to the south. The main street runs between the two, switching names from Barbourne Rd. to The Tything to Foregate St. to The Foregate to The Cross to High St.

The **Tourist Information Centre**, High St., distributes the *Worcester Visitor Guide*, books beds for a 10% deposit, and sells National Express tickets. From Foregate St. Station, turn left on Foregate St. and walk 15min. The TIC is on the ground floor of The Guildhall, on High St. (☎01905 726 311; www.visitworcester.com. Open M-Sa 9:30am-5pm.) "Worcester Walks" **tours** leave from the TIC. (☎01905 222 117; www.worcesterwalks.co.uk. 1½hr. tours M-F 11am. Ghost tours also available. £4.) Other services include: a **Barclays** bank, 54 High St. (☎08457 555 555; open M-F 9am-5pm, Sa 9am-3pm); the **Worcester Volunteer Centre** (☎01905 24 741; www.worcestervolunteercentre.org.uk; open M-F 10am-4pm); **Severn Laun-Dri** launderette, 22 Barbourne Rd. (open daily 9am-7pm); **police,** Castle St. (☎0845 113 5000), off Foregate St.; a **Boots** pharmacy, 72-74 High St. (☎01905 726 868; open M and W-F 8:30am-5:30pm, Tu 9am-5:30pm, Sa 8:30am-6pm, Su 10:30am-4:30pm); **Worcestershire Royal Hospital,** Newtown Rd., Charles Hastings Way (☎01905 763 333; bus #31); free **Internet** access at the **library,** in the City Museum (☎01905 765 312; open M, W, F 9:30am-8pm, Tu, Th, Sa 9:30am-5:30pm), and at **Coffee Republic,** 31 High St. (£3 per hr.; free Wi-Fi; open M-Sa 7:30am-6pm, Su 8:30am-5pm); and the **post office,** 8 Foregate St. (☎08457 223 344; open M-Sa 10am-4pm). **Postcode:** WR1 1XX.

⌷⌷ ACCOMMODATIONS AND CAMPING. B&B prices in Worcester are high—proprietors cater to businesspeople and Londoners weekending in the country. Surrounding suburbs offer lower rates, as do the row houses on **Barbourne Road,** a 15-20min. walk north on Foregate St. from the city center or a short ride on buses #144 and 303. The comfortable **Osborne House ❸,** 17 Chestnut Walk, has TVs and showers in every well-decorated room.The owner's experience as a chef is apparent in the tasty included breakfast. (☎01905 22 296; www.osborne-house.co.uk. Singles £30; doubles £50-55; triples £60-68. MC/V.) At **The Barbourne ❸,** 42 Barbourne Rd., many of the pink rooms are ensuite, and some have bathtubs. (☎01905 27 507. Hot, buffet-style breakfast included. Singles £30-40; twins and doubles £50-55. MC/V.) Its blue counterpart, the nearby **City Guest House ❸,** 36 Barbourne Rd., is owned by the same woman as The Barbourne and features comfy beds and great service. (☎01905 24 695. Singles £30; doubles £50-55; triples £60-68. MC/V.) **Riverside Ketch Caravan Park ❶,** Bath Rd., has camping with toilets and showers. Take the A38 2 mi. south of Worcester or take local bus #32, which stops across the road. (☎01905 820 430. Showers 20p. Open Apr.-Oct. £9 per tent. Electricity £1.75. Cash only.)

⌷⌷ FOOD AND PUBS. Look for Indian restaurants and cheap sandwich shops near **The Tything,** at the north end of the city center. At **Chesters ❷,** 51 New St., you'll find outstanding service and quality food to match. An eclectic menu of mainly Mexican-style food features several vegetarian and vegan specialties. (☎01905 611 638; www.chestersrestaurant.co.uk. Lunch £3.45-6. Open M-Tu noon-3pm and 5-10pm, W-Th noon-3pm and 5-10:30pm, F noon-3pm and

5-11pm, Sa noon-11pm. MC/V.) **Monsoon ❷,** 35 Foregate St., delivers well-priced Indian entrees (£6-10) and excellent service. (☎01905 726 333; www.monsoon-indian.co.uk. Takeaway discount 20%. Open M-Th and Su 6pm-midnight, F-Sa 6pm-1am. AmEx/MC/V.) For pint-size entertainment, the pub scene on **Friar Street** is popular. **The Conservatory,** 34 Friar St., has bright decor and ales from £2. (☎01905 26 929. Open M-Sa 11am-11pm. Kitchen open M-Sa 11:30am-3pm.)

SIGHTS. **Worcester Cathedral,** founded in AD 680, towers over the River Severn at the south end of High St. The **choir** contains intricate 14th-century misericords and King John's tomb. To the right of the choir lie the remains of Henry VIII's older brother Arthur, Prince of Wales. **Wulston's Crypt** is the oldest part of the cathedral, an underground chapel dating back to the 11th century with a display of the boot remnants from a skeleton found during construction. Ask about free performances by musicians and choirs. (☎01905 28 854; www.worcestercathedral.org.uk. Open daily 7:30am-6pm. Evensong M-Th and Sa 5:30pm, Su 4pm. Tours late July M-F and Sa; Aug.-Dec. and from Jan. to mid-July Sa. Suggested donation £3. Guided tours £5; book ahead.)

The **Commandery Museum,** Sidbury Rd., offers a one-of-a-kind trip through history. An audio tour takes you through the six "layers" of time, describing the various uses of the house from the 16th century, which include a monastery, a hospital, Civil War headquarters, and a school for the blind. (☎01905 361 821; www.worcestercitymuseums.org.uk. Open M-Sa 10am-5pm, Su 1:30-5pm. £5.25, concessions £4, children £2.25.) The **Royal Worcester Porcelain Company,** Severn St., makes the bone china on which the royal family has been served since the reign of George III. Factory tours show how the dishware goes from the workroom to the dining room. (☎01905 21 247. Book ahead. £5, concessions £4.25.) Crockery junkies can visit the adjacent **Worcester Porcelain Museum,** which holds England's largest collection. (☎01905 746 000. Open M-Sa 9am-5:30pm, Su 11am-5pm. £5, concessions £4.25, families £10.) The highlight of the **Worcester City Museum and Art Gallery,** Foregate St., near the post office, is Hitler's clock, found in his office in 1945 by the Worcester Regiment. (☎01905 25 371. Open M-F 9:30am-5:30pm, Sa 9:30am-5pm. Free.)

HEREFORD ☎(0)1432

Near the Welsh border and the scenic River Wye, Hereford (HAIR-eh-fuhd; pop. 55,000) was for centuries the agricultural hub of the Wye Valley. Once known for its "whiteface" cattle and still known for its cathedral, Hereford now attracts shoppers to the upscale stores of High Town, a pedestrian area that hosts farmers' markets and local entertainment. Good bus and rail connections provide a springboard for travel to the Wye Valley.

TRANSPORTATION. The **train station** is northeast of the city center, on Station Approach, just off Commercial Rd. Trains (☎08457 484 950) depart to: Abergavenny (25min., 1-2 per hr., £6.80); Cardiff (1hr., 1-3 per hr., £14.40); Chepstow via Newport or Worcester Foregate and Gloucester (1½-2½hr., 18 per day, £16.20); London Paddington via Evesham (3hr., 1-2 per hr., £37.20); Shrewsbury (1hr., 1-2 per hr., £13.90). The **bus station** is close to the train station, off Union Walk and Commercial Rd. National Express (☎08705 808 080) runs buses to Birmingham (2hr., 1 per day, £8.10) and London (4½hr., 3 per day, £20.40). A bus stop is on Broad St., past the TIC. Stagecoach Red and White buses go to Cardiff via Abergavenny (#X3 or X4, 2½hr., 7 per day) and Brecon via Hay-on-Wye (#39, 2hr., M-Sa 8 per day). On Sundays, Yeoman's bus #40 takes over the Brecon route (3 per day). For bus info, pick up the free *Herefordshire Public*

Transport Map and bus timetables (50p) or the free *Monmouthshire County Council Local Transport Guide* at the TIC.

◪ PRACTICAL INFORMATION. The **Tourist Information Centre,** 1 King St., books beds for £2 plus a 10% deposit. (☎01432 268 430. Open July-Aug. M-Sa 9am-5pm, Su 10am-4pm; Sept.-June M-Sa 9am-5pm.) **Walking tours** leave from the TIC. (1hr. From mid-May to Sept. M-Sa 11am, Su 2:30pm. £3, children free.) Other services include: **banks** with **ATMs** along Broad St.; free **Internet** at the **library,** Broad St. (open Tu-W and F 9am-7:30pm, Th 9am-5:30pm, Sa 9:30am-4pm); **Coin-Op Launder Centre,** 136 Eign St. (☎01432 269 610; wash £2.50, dry 20p per 5min.; soap 30p; open M-Sa 8am-5:30pm, Su 8:30am-3pm; last wash 1hr. before close); **police** on Bath St. (☎08457 444 888); and the **post office,** St. Peter's Sq. (☎01432 275 221; open M-Sa 9am-5:30pm). **Postcode:** HR1 2LE.

◪ ◪ ACCOMMODATIONS AND FOOD. Cheap lodgings in the center of Hereford are scarce; your best bet is to walk to the B&Bs (£25-45) near the end of Bodenham Rd. or along Whitecross Rd., near the outskirts of town. The **Holly Tree Guest House ❸,** 19-21 Barton Rd., has rooms near the town center. (☎01432 357 845. Singles £25, ensuite £30; doubles £50/55. Cash only.) Recently renovated **Somerville House ❹,** 12 Bodenham Rd, is a stately Victorian villa with understated, modern furnishings. Guests are free to relax in the terraced gardens in back. (☎01432 273 991; www.somervillehouse.net. Free Wi-Fi. From £35 per person. AmEx/MC/V.) **Westfield House ❷,** 235 Whitecross Rd., has low prices a 15min. walk from town. Rooms are clean and bathrooms are spacious (☎01432 267 712. £20-25 per person. Cash only.)

Have breakfast at Tiffany's amid posters of Audrey Hepburn at **Tiffany's Cafe ❶,** High Town, a friendly cafe next to the Market Hall Buttermarket. The large menu has classic dishes like Yorkshire pudding (£7) or corned beef pie (£6) as well as traditional afternoon tea. (☎01432 272 305. Open M-Sa 9am-5pm. Cash only.) **Cafe@All Saints ❶,** in All Saints Church on High St., is a quiet retreat from the bustle of the shopping district. Try the cheddar and chutney sandwich (£5.10) and gaze out of stained-glass windows. (☎01432 370 415. Open M-Sa 8:30am-5:30pm. MC/V.) Fisherman's pie (£6) complements sweet and sudsy ale at the **Black Lion Inn ❷,** 31 Bridge St. (☎01432 343 535. Open M-Tu noon-11pm, W-Th and Su noon-midnight, F-Sa noon-2am. Kitchen open daily noon-3pm. Cash only.) Quiche with salad, takeaway lunch specials (each £3), await at **Andy's Kitchen ❶,** 12 King St., down the road from the TIC. (☎01432 272 001. Open M-Sa 8:30am-4pm. Cash only.) **Tesco** supermarket, Bewell St., has your picnic needs covered. (☎08456 779 365. Open M from 8pm, Tu-F 24hr., Sa until 10pm, Su 10am-4pm.) Stop by the **Market Hall Buttermarket,** High Town, for produce, deli meats, and cheap market wares. (Open M-Sa 8am-5:30pm.)

◪ ◪ SIGHTS AND SHOPPING. The massive **Hereford Cathedral** may surprise visitors—there are few Romanesque basilicas in Britain, and Hereford's is particularly monumental. The cathedral hosts monthly organ concerts in the summer (£6) and offers garden tours (£4), which include tea and cake at the Cloister Cafe. (☎01432 374 200; www.herefordcathedral.org. Open daily 7:30am-5:30pm. Garden tours June-Aug. W and Sa 3pm. Free.) The cathedral holds the 13th-century **Mappa Mundi** ("cloth of the world"), a map that dates from back when the earth was flat and shows little-known regions of the world full of unicorns and headless men. In the **Chained Library,** 1500 volumes are linked to the shelf by slender chains; the practice was common in the 17th century, when books were as valuable as small parcels of land. (☎01432 375 225. Open Easter-Oct. M-Sa 10am-5pm, Su 10am-4pm; Nov.-Easter M-Sa 10am-4pm. Last entry 30min. before close. £4.50, concessions £3.50.) A slew of cider facts and vats are inside the **Cider Museum,** 21 Ryelands St., off Pomona Pl. Don't let their "What Went Wrong with the Brew" display deter you from the free brandy tasting at the on-site King Offa's Distillery. (☎01432 354 207; www.cidermuseum. co.uk. Open Tu-Sa Apr.-Sept. 10am-5pm; Oct.-Mar. 11am-3pm. £3.50.)

Hereford's **High Town** is a network of shop-lined walkways featuring a generic parade of chain stores. Thrifty shoppers might prefer ◪**The Dinosaw Market,** 16-17 Bastion Mews, off Union St., which promises "things that are not normal" and delivers. An array of vintage garb, wood turtles, pink boas, and assorted bric-a-brac fills the store. (☎01432 353 655. Open M-Sa 10am-5:30pm.) **Chapters,** 17 Union St., sells used books. (☎01432 352 149. Open M-Sa 9:30am-4:30pm.)

◪ **NIGHTLIFE.** Old and young come out to play on weekends in Hereford, but options are few and crowded. **Play,** 51-55 Blueschool St., is a fabric-draped haunt of avid clubbers. Ladies drink free on Monday nights until midnight. (☎01432 270 009. Cover £3-5. Open M and Su 9:30pm-2am, Th-Sa 9:30pm-3am.) **Booth Hall,** East St., is a popular pub that cranks up its music during evening hours, although in summer most patrons crowd in the courtyard beer garden. (☎01432 344 487. Open M-F and Su 11am-11pm, Sa 11am-midnight. Kitchen open daily noon-3pm. Cash only.)

CHELTENHAM   ☎(0)1242

Cheltenham (pop. 110,000), also known as Cheltenham Spa, is a small but well-to-do city. Ever since George III sampled its waters in 1788, the town has flourished. Cheltenham's reputation as a fashionable place of leisure is evident in its upscale restaurants, spacious gardens, and trendy boutiques. On weekends, students from the University of Gloucestershire pack the pubs and clubs, energizing the city center. Although it has few important sights, Cheltenham continues to draw visitors as the most convenient base for exploring the Cotswolds.

▥ TRANSPORTATION

Getting There (free from the TIC) details bus services.

Trains: Cheltenham Spa Station, Queen's Rd., at Gloucester Rd. Ticket office open M-F 5:45am-8:15pm, Sa 5:45am-7:15pm, Su 8:15am-8:15pm. Trains (☎08457 484 950) to: **Bath** (1½hr., 2 per hr., £11-14.30); **Birmingham** (45min., 2 per hr., £16); **London** (2½hr., every hr., £49-62.50); **Worcester** (25min., every 2hr., £6.40).

Buses: Royal Well Coach Station, Royal Well Rd. National Express office, 27A Clarence Parade, open M-Sa 9am-4:45pm. National Express (☎08705 808 080) to: **Birmingham** (1½hr., 3 per day, £9); **Bristol** (1¼hr., 3 per day, £6.50); **London** (3hr., every hr., £18); **Manchester** (4hr., 3 per day, £21). Stagecoach (☎0871 200 2233) serves **Gloucester** (40min., every 10min., £1.70). Swanbrook Coaches (☎01452 712 386) runs to **Oxford** (1½hr., 3 per day, £7).

Taxis: Taxi stands by the Royal Well Coach Station and on the Promenade. Free phone in train station. **Handycars** (☎01242 262 611). **A to B** (☎01242 580 580). Both 24hr.

◪ ▮ ORIENTATION AND PRACTICAL INFORMATION

The heart of Cheltenham is the intersection of **High Street** and the **Promenade.** The train station is at the western edge of town; to get there, walk 30min. on a signposted path or catch local bus D or E (5min., every 10min., £1.25).

Tourist Information Centre: Municipal Offices, 77 Promenade (☎01242 522 878, accommodations booking 517 110; www.visitcheltenham.info). Books accommodations with a

THE BIG CHEESE

For nearly 200 years, people have been throwing themselves at full speed down Cooper's Hill, near Gloucester and Cheltenham. The reason? The annual May cheese-rolling competition.

At its heart, the sport is quite simple. A round wheel of double Gloucester cheese is rolled from the top of the hill, and the competitors chase down after it. The first person to reach the bottom of the hill wins. Technically, the objective is to catch the cheese, but, since it has a one-second start and can reach speeds of 70 mph, this is a rare occurrence. Instead, the event turns into a mad flip and tumble down a very steep and uneven hill.

This is no friendly roll in the grass, either; every year, many people sustain sprains and injuries. A team of paramedics waits at the bottom of the hill, ready to treat injuries. In 2008, the BBC reported that 19 people were injured during the cheese-rolling event; the winner of the first race was carried away from the bottom of the hill on a spinal board.

And the prize? The winner of the competition is presented with (what else?) a block of cheese.

For more information or to enter in the event, visit the official cheese-rolling website at www.cheese-rolling.co.uk.

10% deposit. Open M-Tu and Th-Sa 9:30am-5:15pm, W 10am-5:15am.

Banks: Many sit along High St. **Barclays,** intersection of Rodney St. and High St. (☎0845 755 5555). Open M-F 9am-5pm, Sa 9am-3pm.

Library: Central Library, Clarence St. (☎01242 532 685). Internet access in 15min. time slots. Free Wi-Fi. Open M, W, F 9am-7pm, Tu and Th 9am-5:30pm, Sa 9am-4pm.

Launderette: 312 High St. (☎01242 513 632). Open daily 7am-7:30pm.

Police: Holland House, 840 Lansdown Rd. (☎01242 521 321).

Pharmacy: Boots, 1-4 Broad St. (☎01242 241 244). Open M-F 9:30am-6pm, Sa 9am-6pm, Su 11am-5pm.

Hospital: Cheltenham General, Sandford Rd. (☎01242 222 222). Follow Bath Rd. southwest from town and turn left onto Sandford Rd.

Internet Access: Free at the **library** (above). **Smart Space,** Regent St. (☎01242 063 7177), upstairs from the Everyman Theatre. 50p for 45min. with purchase from the cafe. Free Wi-Fi. Open M-W, F, Su 10am-4pm and 6-9:30pm, Th and Sa 10am-9:30pm.

Post Office: 192-194 High St. (☎08457 223 344). **Bureau de change.** Open M-Sa 9am-5:30pm. **Postcode:** GL50 1.

⌂ ACCOMMODATIONS

Most establishments in Cheltenham cluster in the **Montpellier** area and along **Bath Road,** a 5min. walk from the town center. Prices tend to be high (£30-40), but then again so is quality.

Benton's Guest House, 71 Bath Rd. (☎01242 517 417). English countryside decor with hair dryers and towel warmers. Floral bedspreads matched by the lovely gardens out front. Breakfast included. £35 per person. Cash only. ❸

YMCA, 6 Vittoria Walk (☎01242 524 024; www.cheltenhamymca.com). Large facilities frequented by a mix of travelers and locals. 1 4-bed male bunkroom, 1 4-bed female bunkroom. If the bunks are full, inquire about single rooms, which cannot be booked in advance. Self-catering kitchen. Breakfast included. Showers feel slightly spartan, but the water is always warm. Laundry £2. Wi-Fi. Reception M-F 7am-10pm, Sa-Su 9am-10pm. Dorms £18.50; singles £27.50. MC/V. ❷

Lonsdale House, 16 Montpellier Dr. (☎01242 232 379). Elegant dining room and halls. Singles £32, ensuite £42; doubles £55/62. AmEx/MC/V. ❸

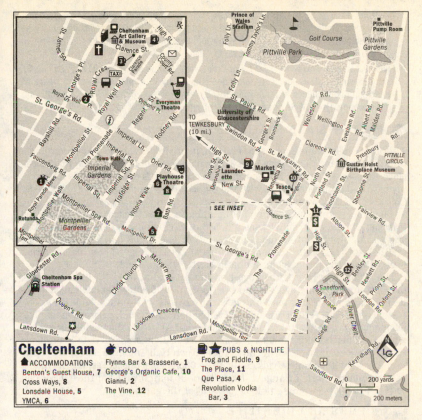

Cheltenham

♠ **ACCOMMODATIONS**
Benton's Guest House, **7**
Cross Ways, **8**
Lonsdale House, **5**
YMCA, **6**

🍎 **FOOD**
Flynns Bar & Brasserie, **1**
George's Organic Cafe, **10**
Gianni, **2**
The Vine, **12**

📖★ **PUBS & NIGHTLIFE**
Frog and Fiddle, **9**
The Place, **11**
Que Pasa, **4**
Revolution Vodka Bar, **3**

Cross Ways, 57 Bath Rd. (☎01242 527 683; www.crosswaysguesthouse.com). The proprietor's experience as an interior designer is apparent in this Regency home's furnishings. Rooms as comfortable as they are lavish, with lush green carpets and soft bedspreads. Singles £45; doubles £85, ensuite £95; triples £120. AmEx/MC/V. ❹

🍴 FOOD

Fruit stands, butchers, and bakeries dot **High Street,** while posh restaurants and cafe-bars line **Montpellier Street** across from Montpellier Gardens. A **Tesco Metro** supermarket is at 233 High St. (☎01242 847 400. Open M-F 7am-11pm, Sa 7am-10pm, Su 11am-5pm.) A **farmers' market** is held the second and last Friday of the month outside the TIC (9am-3pm). A Thursday morning market, in the car park near Henrietta St., sells fruits, meats, and other wares.

Gianni, 1 Royal Well Pl. (☎01242 221 101), just south of the bus stop on Royal Well Rd. Italian food in a homey dining room with red and yellow tablecloths. Enthusiastic waiters (some who sing while serving). Pastas £7-9. Open M-Th and Su noon-2pm and 6:30-10:30pm, F-Sa noon-2pm and 6:30-11pm. AmEx/MC/V. ❸

George's Organic Cafe, 10 Bennington St. (☎01242 238 733). Fresh flowers and checkered floor create a classic diner feel. Huge sandwiches on fresh bread (from £2.45). Daily specials with organic salad (from £4.50). Open M-F 10am-3pm. Cash only. ❶

The Vine, 47 High St. (☎01242 220 170). Rich colors and Old World wax-covered candle holders. Thai-inspired meals are cheap and filling (£3-8). The bar fills up quickly, so get in early for dinner. Open M-Th 4:30pm-midnight, F-Su noon-midnight. Kitchen open M-Th 5-10pm, F-Su noon-10pm. MC/V. ❶

Flynn's Bar and Brasserie, 16-17 The Courtyard, Montpellier St. (☎01242 252 752). Walk down the stairs and look left. Locals swear by it. Appetizers, like the delicious deep-fried goat cheese in phyllo dough (£5), are small—entrees (£9-13) are not. Outdoor seating. Open M-Sa noon-3pm and 6-9pm. AmEx/MC/V. ❷

👁 🌸 SIGHTS AND FESTIVALS

Although Cheltenham is pleasant enough, its main draw is its convenient location for exploring the nearby Cotswold villages. Stop by the **Gustav Holst Birthplace Museum,** 4 Clarence Rd., to relive the composer's early life in his impeccably restored home, complete with the piano where he composed *The Planets.* (☎01242 524 846; www.holstmuseum.org.uk. Open Feb.-Dec. Tu-Sa 10am-4pm. £3.50, concessions and children £3, families £8.) The **Cheltenham Art Gallery and Museum,** Clarence St., showcases a hoard of English miscellany from the Arts and Crafts Movement. Items include stuffed pheasants and Victorian tiaras. (☎01242 237 431; www.artsandcraftsmuseum.org.uk. Open M-Sa 10am-5:20pm. Free.) Down the Promenade, sunbathe at the **Imperial Gardens.**

The *What's On* poster, displayed on kiosks and at the TIC, lists concerts, plays, tours, sporting events, and hot spots. The **Cheltenham International Festival of Music** celebrates modern classical works for three weeks in July. The concurrent **Fringe Festival** organizes jazz, big band, and rock performances. The **International Jazz Festival** takes place at the end of April and the beginning of May, while October heralds the **Cheltenham Festival of Literature.** Full details on these festivals are available from the box office, Town Hall, Imperial Sq. (☎01242 227 979; www.cheltenhamfestivals.co.uk.) The **Cheltenham Cricket Festival,** the oldest in the country, starts in August. Inquire about match times at the TIC or call ☎0117 910 8000. Purchase tickets (£12-15) at the gate.

🍺 🎷 PUBS AND NIGHTLIFE

Nightlife is dead during the week, but Cheltenham springs to life on the weekends as students and 20-somethings invade. Numerous pubs, bars, and clubs line **High Street** east of the Promenade. Popular venues also cluster around **Clarence Street** and at the top of **Bath Road.**

Frog and Fiddle, 315 High St. (☎01242 701 156; www.frogandfiddle.co.uk). Leather couches and outdoor seating. Upstairs billiards. Students and locals mix for a laid-back scene. Deal with the pizza place across the road for pizza and a pint for £5. Live music Sa-Su. Free Wi-Fi. Open M-Th noon-11pm, F-Sa noon-midnight, Su noon-10:30pm.

Que Pasa, 15-21 Clarence St. (☎01242 230 099; www.quepasa.co.uk). Animal-print chairs and glittery disco balls fill this huge tapas bar. £1.50 pints and 2-for-1 mixed drinks for students W. Open M-Th 10:30am-11pm, F-Sa 10:30-1am.

Revolution Vodka Bar, Clarence Parade (☎01242 234 045; www.revolution-bars.co.uk). Huge converted church turned sinful: 2 floors and over 60 types of vodka. Fills with a younger crowd on weekends and has a lounge feel during the day. Hidden booths in the back. Open M-Th 11:30am-midnight, F-Sa 11:30-1am, Su noon-midnight.

The Place, 33-35 Albion St. (☎01242 570 583; www.clubmoda.co.uk). Enter from High St. A stylish place full of equally stylish students. 3 floors of house, R&B, and 80s music. Cover £3-5, Sa before 11pm free. Open M and W-Th 10pm-4am, F-Sa 10pm-5am.

▶ DAYTRIPS FROM CHELTENHAM

TEWKESBURY. Ten miles northwest of Cheltenham, Tewkesbury (TOOKS-bury) is a quiet medieval town with a trove of half-timbered houses. Its most celebrated structure is **Tewkesbury Abbey,** whose Norman tower is the largest such structure in all of England. First consecrated in 1121, the abbey was reconsecrated after the 1471 Battle of Tewkesbury, when Yorks killed the abbey's monks for attempting to protect refuge-seeking Lancastrians in the Wars of the Roses. The townspeople later bought the cathedral from Henry VIII. The cathedral houses three organs, including the Milton Organ, rumored to have been played by John Milton himself. (☎01684 850 959; www.tewkesburyabbey.org.uk. Open Apr.-Oct. M-Sa 7:30am-6pm, Su 7:30am-7pm; Nov.-Mar. M-Sa 7:30am-5:30pm, Su 7:30am-7pm. Services Su 8, 9:15, 11am, 6pm. Suggested donation £3.) Beside the abbey, the **John Moore Countryside Museum,** 45 Church St., is housed in a merchant's cottage built in 1450. The museum displays exhibits of native 15th-century wildlife and has occasional live animal shows. (☎01684 297 174; www.gloster.demon.co.uk/jmcm. Open Apr.-Oct. Tu-Sa 10am-1pm and 2-5pm; Nov.-Mar. Sa and bank holidays 10am-1pm and 2-5pm. £1.50, concessions £1.25.) The small **Tewkesbury Borough Museum,** 64 Barton St., contains an exhibit on the 1471 battle that ended the Wars of the Roses. (☎01684 292 901; www.tewkesburymuseum.org. Open Mar.-Aug. Tu-F 1-4:30pm, Su 11am-4pm; Sept.-Oct. Tu-F noon-3pm, Sa 11am-3pm; Nov.-Mar. Sa 11am-3pm. Free.) The battle is recreated at the annual **Tewkesbury Medieval Festival** in the first weekend of July. *(Stagecoach (☎01242 575 606) bus #41 departs from High St., across from the Tesco Metro, in Cheltenham (25min.; M-Sa every 20-30min., Su every 2hr.; round-trip £4.10). The Tourist Information Centre, 100 Church St. (☎01684 855 040), gives out a map and pamphlet highlighting the town's rich history. Open M-Sa 9:30am-5pm, Su 10am-4pm.)*

THE COTSWOLDS

The Cotswolds have deviated little from their etymological roots: "Cotswolds" means "sheep enclosures in rolling hillsides." Despite the rather sleepy moniker, the Cotswolds are filled with rich history and traditions (like cheese-rolling) that date back to Roman and Saxon times. While it may seem that classic English hedgerows outnumber people, more urban towns like Gloucester, Cirencester, and Cheltenham supply shoppers and hikers in the Cotswolds.

▶ TRANSPORTATION

Public transportation to and within the Cotswolds is scarce; plan ahead. The villages of the "Northern" Cotswolds (Stow-on-the-Wold, Bourton-on-the-Water, Moreton-in-Marsh) are accessed via Cheltenham, while Gloucester serves the remote "Southern" Cotswolds (Slimbridge, Stroud, and Painswick).

Train stations in the Cotswolds are few and far between. **Trains** go to London (1hr., every 1-2hr., £30) via Oxford (30min., £9.50) from **Moreton-in-Marsh Station.** (Open M-Sa 5:45am-7:15pm, Su 5:45am-12:30pm.) In the Southern Cotswolds, trains run from **Cam and Dursley Station** (3 mi. from Slimbridge, unstaffed) to Gloucester (15min., every hr., £4) and London Paddington (2hr., every hr., £20). It's easier to reach the Cotswolds by **bus.** The Cheltenham TIC's free *Getting There* details service between the town and 27 destinations. The free *Explore the Cotswolds by Public Transport* lists routes for major services between villages. Consult the TIC for departure times; schedules vary depending on the day. Pulham's Coaches #801 (☎01451 820 369) runs from Cheltenham to

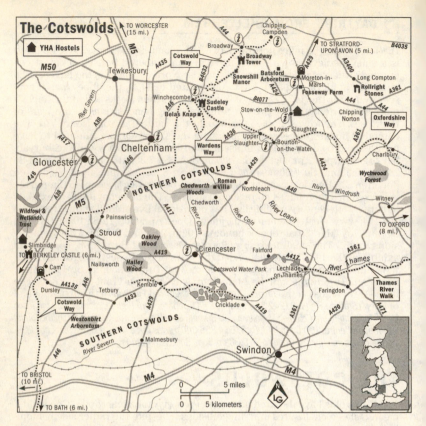

The Cotswolds

TO WORCESTER (15 mi.)

YHA Hostels

M50

M5

A44

Chipping Campden

TO STRATFORD-UPON-AVON (5 mi.)

B4035

Broadway

A435

Tewkesbury

Cotswold Way

B4632

Broadway Tower

Snowshill Manor

Batsford Arboretum

A429

A3400

Long Compton

Moreton-in-Marsh

A424

Fosseway Farm

Rollright Stones

A361

A48

River Severn

Winchecombe

A46

Sudeley Castle

Belas Knap

Stow-on-the-Wold

B4077

Chipping Norton

A44

A46

A38

Cheltenham

Wardens Way

A436

Upper Slaughter

Lower Slaughter

Bourton-on-the-Water

A361

Oxfordshire Way

A417

Gloucester

A46

A429

A424

A361

Charlbury

NORTHERN COTSWOLDS

Wychwood Forest

A48

A38

M5

Chedworth Woods

Roman Villa

Northleach

A40

River Windrush

Witney

Chedworth

River Leach

TO OXFORD (8 mi.)

Wildfowl & Wetlands Trust

Painswick

River Churn

River Coln

Slimbridge

Oakley Wood

TO BERKELEY CASTLE (6 mi.)

A419

Cirencester

Fairford

A417

A361

Stroud

Cam

Nailsworth

Halley Wood

Cotswold Water Park

Lechlade-on-Thames

River Thames

Thames River Walk

B4471

Dursley

A4135

Tetbury

Kemble

A429

A433

A419

A361

Faringdon

A420

Cotswold Way

Westonbirt Arboretum

Cricklade

SOUTHERN COTSWOLDS

River Severn

Malmesbury

Swindon

A46

M4

M4

TO BRISTOL (10 mi.)

TO BATH (6 mi.)

0 — 5 miles

0 — 5 kilometers

N LG

Moreton-in-Marsh (1hr., M-Sa 7 per day, £2) via Bourton-on-the-Water (35min.) and Stow-on-the-Wold (50min.). For Lower and Upper Slaughter, ask to stop at Slaughter Pike, between Bourton-on-the-Water and Stow-on-the-Wold; the villages are half a mile from the road. Castleways Ltd. #606 (☎01242 602 949) goes from Cheltenham to Broadway (50min., M-Sa 4 per day, £2.40) via Winch-combe (20min., £2.20). Johnsons buses #21 and 22 (☎01564 797 000) run to Chipping Campden from Moreton-in-Marsh (20min., M-Sa 9 per day) via Broad-way (5min., M-Sa 5 per day) before ending in Stratford (1hr., M-Sa 8 per day).

TIP

GOOD MORNING SUNSHINE. It is possible to see three or even four small villages in one day by public transportation, but travelers should be mindful that many buses run 9am-6pm. To avoid getting stuck, make the first morning bus out to your destination (typically between 8:45 and 9:30am).

In the Southern Cotswolds, Stagecoach bus #51 runs from Cheltenham to Cirencester (40min., M-Sa every hr., £2.70). Beaumont Travel (☎01452 309 770) bus #855 Fosse Link runs to Cirencester from Moreton-in-Marsh (1hr., M-Sa 8 per day, £2) via Stow-on-the-Wold (40min.) and Bourton-on-the-Water (20min.). Both buses are covered by a **Cotswold Rover** ticket, which may be purchased from the driver (£5, children £3.50). Service from Cheltenham to Gloucester is frequent on Stagecoach bus #94 (30min.; M-F every 10min., Su every 20min.). From Gloucester bus station, Stagecoach bus #91 runs to Slimbridge Crossroads (Su 4 per day). Traveline (☎0870 608 2608) is a lifesaver for those traveling by public transportation, especially in the Cotswolds, where a journey from one small village to another may require a few transfers.

The easiest way to explore is by car, but the best way to experience the Cotswolds is on foot or by bike. The Toy Shop, on High St. in Moreton-in-Marsh, offers **bike** rentals with a lock, map, and route suggestions. (☎01608 650 756. £12 per ½-day, £14 per day. Open M and W-Sa 9am-1pm and 2-5pm.) The YHA in Stow-on-the-Wold (p. 297) also rents bikes with a lock and helmet. (☎01451 830 497. Open daily 8-10am and 5-10pm. £6 per ½-day, £9.50 per day.) **Taxis** are a convenient, if expensive, way of getting to areas inaccessible by public transportation. TICs have lists of companies serving their area: "K" Cars (☎01451 822 578 or 07929 360 712) is based in Bourton-on-the-Water, and Cotswold Taxis (☎07710 117 471) operates from Moreton-in-Marsh. **Coach tours** cover the Cotswolds from Cheltenham, Gloucester, Oxford, Stratford-upon-Avon, Tewkesbury, and other cities. Try the **Cotswold Discovery Tour**, a full-day bus tour that starts in Bath and visits five of the most scenic villages. (☎09067 112 000; www.madmax.abel.co.uk. Tours Apr.-Oct. Tu, Th, Su 9am-5:15pm. £30.)

PRACTICAL INFORMATION

The Cotswolds lie mostly in Gloucestershire, bounded by Stratford-upon-Avon in the north, Oxford in the east, Cheltenham in the west, and Bath in the south. The northern Cotswolds house more postcard-worthy villages and hills, hence more visitors and higher B&B prices. The range hardly towers—the average hill reaches only 600 ft.—but the rolling hills make hiking and biking tough. The best bases from which to explore are Cheltenham, Cirencester, Gloucester, Moreton-in-Marsh, and Stow-on-the-Wold.

Tourist Information Centres: All provide maps, bus schedules, and pamphlets on area walks. They also book beds, usually for a £2 charge plus a 10% deposit.

Bath: See p. 209.

Bourton-on-the-Water: Victoria St. (☎01451 820 211). Open Apr.-Oct. M-F 9:30am-5pm, Sa 9:30am-5:30pm; Nov.-Mar. M-F 9:30am-4pm, Sa 9:30am-4:30pm.

FROM THE ROAD

LOST IN THE COTSWOLDS

The best way to get a good sense of the English countryside? Getting hopelessly lost in it. Or so I discovered on my journey through the Cotswolds, picturesque England at its best.

It started out a normal day. I, the intrepid researcher, on realizing that there was no good way to get between the towns of Broadway and Chipping Campden, decided that I would hike. An elderly local assured me that the Cotswold Way was clearly marked between the two villages. Why, she and her husband did it just last weekend! If a geriatric couple could handle it, surely I'd have no problem.

My hike started out uneventfully—lots of cutting across fields of sheep, hopping wood fences, and walking through fields of grain. But at the top of a hill, surrounded by bleating animals and mud, I finally admitted to myself that I was lost. Retracing my steps, my heart sank. In every direction, all I could see were sheep. No trails, no people, just England in all its green finery. I wondered if this would be the year *Let's Go* reported it had tragically lost a researcher in the English countryside.

Luckily, my guardian angel appeared—in the form of a rather disgruntled farmer. Seeing me standing bewildered in the middle of his very own fields, he pulled up next to me in a pickup truck and pointed me back to the Cotswold Way. Bidding the sheep a hasty goodbye, I went as fast as I could.

—*Shoshanna Fine*

Broadway: 1 Cotswold Ct. (☎01386 852 937). Open M-Sa 10am-5pm, Su 2-5pm.

Cheltenham: See p. 289.

Chipping Campden: Old Police Station, High St. (☎01386 841 206). Open daily 10am-5:30pm.

Cirencester: Corinium Museum, Park St. (☎01285 654 180). Open M-Sa 10am-5pm, Su 2-5pm.

Gloucester: 28 Southgate St. (☎01452 396 572). Open July-Aug. M-Sa 10am-5pm, Su 11am-3pm; Sept.-June M-Sa 10am-5pm.

Moreton-in-Marsh: District Council Bldg, High St. (☎01608 650 881). Open M 8:45am-4pm, Tu-Th 8:45am-5:15pm, F 8:45am-4:45pm, Sa 10am-1pm.

Stow-on-the-Wold: Hollis House, The Square (☎01451 831 082). Open Easter-Oct. M-Sa 9:30am-5:30pm; Nov.-Easter M-Sa 9:30am-4:30pm.

Winchcombe: High St. (☎01242 602 925). Open M-Sa 10am-1pm and 2-5pm, Su noon-4pm.

🏠🏕 ACCOMMODATIONS AND CAMPING

The *Cotswold Way Handbook and Accommodation List* (£2) details B&Bs, which usually lie on roads a short walk from small villages. The *Cotswolds Accommodation Guide* (50p) lists B&Bs in larger towns. There are several campsites close to Cheltenham, but there are also places to rough it within the Cotswolds. Try **Fosseway Farm ❶** (p. 298). *Camping and Caravanning in Gloucestershire and the Cotswolds*, free at TICs, lists more options.

YHA Stow-on-the-Wold, The Square (☎01451 830 497). A 16th-century building beside the TIC. Ensuite rooms with wood bunks and village views. Laundry. Internet £1 per 15min. Reception daily 8-10am and 5-10:30pm. Lockout 10am-5pm. Curfew 11pm. Dorms £14-20. Nonmembers £3 more. MC/V. ❷

YHA Slimbridge, Shepherd's Patch (☎08707 706 036), off the A38 and the M5. The nearest train station (Cam and Dursley) is 3 mi. away. It's easier to take bus #91 from Gloucester to the Slimbridge Crossroads roundabout and walk 2 mi. A large duck pond behind the building. Laundry £2.60. Reception daily 8-10am and 5-10:30pm. Curfew 11pm. Open from mid-Feb. to late Oct. Dorms £14, under 18 £10.50. MC/V. ❶

🥾🚲 HIKING AND BIKING

For centuries, travelers have walked the well-worn Cotswolds footpaths from village to village. Tranquil hillsides and the allure of pubs with local brews make moving at a pace beyond three or four villages per day inadvisable.

The TIC stocks a variety of **walking** and **cycling guides.** The *Cotswold Map and Guidebook in One* (£5) is good for planning bike routes and short hikes. Hikers planning more than a short stroll should use the Ordnance Survey Outdoor Leisure Map #45 (£7), which provides topographic information and highlights nearly all public footpaths. The Cotswolds Voluntary Warden Service (☎01451 862 000) leads free **guided walks** (1½-7½hr.), some with themes. All walks are listed on its website (www.cotswoldsaonb.com) and in the "Programme Guide" section of the biannual *Cotswold LION* (free at the TIC).

Long-distance hikers can choose from a handful of trails. The extensive **Cotswold Way** spans just over 100 mi. from Bath to Chipping Campden, has few steep climbs, and can be done in a week. The trail passes through pastures and the remains of ancient settlements. Pockmarks and gravel make certain sections unsuitable for biking or horseback riding. Consult the **Cotswold Way National Trail Office** (☎01453 827 004) for details. The **Oxfordshire Way** (65 mi.) runs between the popular hyphen havens Bourton-on-the-Water and Henley-on-Thames, site of the famed regatta. Amble through pastures on your way from Bourton-on-the-Water to Lower and Upper Slaughter along the **Warden's Way,** a half-day hike. Adventurous souls can continue to Winchcombe. The **Thames Path Walk** starts on the western edge of the Cotswolds in Lechlade and follows the Thames 184 mi. to Kingston, near London. The section from the Cotswolds to Oxford is low-impact and particularly peaceful. The **Severn Way** runs for 210 mi. from Plynlimon in Wales to Bristol along the River Severn and runs along the western border of the Cotswolds. Contact the **National Trails Office** (☎01865 810 224) for details. Local roads are perfect for biking—rolling hills welcome both casual and hardy cyclers. Parts of the Oxfordshire Way are hospitable to cyclists, if slightly rut-riddled. TICs in all towns have a Cotswolds cycling route packet (£3) that outlines five different routes between villages. They also have free cycling guides detailing trails of 16-30 mi.

WINCHECOMBE   ☎(0)1242

A tiny village 7 mi. north of Cheltenham, Winchcombe is home to the secluded **Sudeley Castle,** a 10min. walk from the town center. Lord and Lady Ashcombe have filled the castle with Tudor memorabilia. 4 acres of prize-winning gardens also have stunning views of the surrounding hills. The chapel contains the tomb of Henry VIII's queen number six, Katherine Parr. In summer, Sudeley holds jousting tournaments and Shakespeare under the stars. (☎01242 602 308; www.sudeleycastle.co.uk. Castle open Mar.-Oct. daily 11am-5pm. Gardens open Mar.-Oct. daily 10:30am-5:30pm. Castle and gardens £7.20. Su May-Aug. £1 more.) **Belas Knap,** a 4000-year-old burial mound, is 1 mi. southwest of Sudeley Castle, accessible from the Cotswold Way or via a scenic 2hr. walk from Winchcombe. The Winchcombe TIC sells a pamphlet (30p) with directions.

BOURTON-ON-THE-WATER   ☎(0)1451

Known as the most beautiful village in the Cotswolds, Bourton-on-the-Water feels like an old-fashioned town. The footbridge-straddled River Windrush runs along the main street, giving Bourton the moniker "Venice of the Cotswolds." The beauty and location of Bourton has made it a popular destination, so expect more tourist traps here than in other villages. The Oxford Way trailhead is here, as is a confluence of other trails, including the Warden's, Heart of England, Windrush, and Gloucestershire Ways. For a taste of life as a giant, follow signs to **The Model Village,** a scale model of Bourton built in 1937. (☎01451 820 467. Open daily in summer 10am-5:45pm; in winter 10am-4pm. £2.75.) **Birdland,** on Rissington Rd., has a motley crew of winged creatures from neon-pink flamingos to penguins. (☎01451 820 480. Open daily Apr.-Oct. 10am-6pm; Nov.-Mar. 10am-4pm. Last entry 1hr. before close. £5.50.) Next door, the **Dragonfly** maze is the best place to get lost in the Cotswolds. An intricate hedge maze contains a hidden chamber where you must solve a puzzle. *Let's Go* could tell you the answer, but then we'd have to kill you. (☎01451 821 794. Open daily 10am-5:30pm, weather permitting. £2.50.) Between rose-laden gates and cobbled streets, the **Cotswold Perfumery,** on Victoria St., offers a factory tour, but a mere visit to the shop is an olfactory adventure. You can purchase one of the nine fragrances made in the shop or splurge and make your own in a daylong perfumery course. (☎01451 820 698. Open M-Sa 9:30am-5pm, Su 10:30am-5pm. Call to book a tour in advance; usually 1-2 per day. £5, concessions £3.50.)

STOW-ON-THE-WOLD   ☎(0)1451

Inns and taverns crowd the Market Sq. of this self-proclaimed "Heart of the Cotswolds." Despite chain stores, like the **Tesco** supermarket on Fosse Way (☎01451 807 400; open M-F 6am-midnight, Sa 6am-10pm, Su 10am-4pm), Stow still exudes Cotswold quaintness. A traditional **farmers' market** takes place on the second Thursday of every month in Market Sq. (☎01453 758 060. Open 9am-1:30pm.) Three miles downhill, off the A424, **Donnington Trout Farm** lets visitors fish, feed, and eat the trout. (☎01451 830 873. Open Apr.-Oct. daily

10am-5:30pm; Nov.-Mar. Tu-Su 10am-5pm.) The **YHA hostel** ❷ (p. 296) is in the center of town. (☎0870 770 6050. Dorms £14-20; family rooms £45-98.)

THE SLAUGHTERS ☎(0)1451

No need to fear—the Slaughters got their names from the Old English word *slough*, meaning "stream." The towns, complete with bubbling brooks, are a few miles southwest of Stow. The less touristed and more charming Lower Slaughter is connected to its sister village, Upper Slaughter, by the Warden's Way. In Lower Slaughter, the **Old Mill**, Mill Ln., scoops water from the river that flows past. A mill has stood on this spot for 1000 years. (☎01451 820 052; www. oldmill-lowerslaughter.com. Open in summer daily 10am-6pm. £1.25.)

MORETON-IN-MARSH ☎(0)1608

With a train station, frequent bus service, and a bike shop, Moreton is a convenient base from which to explore the north. The village has typical Cotswolds charm but holds few attractions. Two miles west on the A44 is **Batsford Arboretum**, with 56 acres of waterfalls, a Japanese rest house, and more than 1600 species of trees. (☎01386 701 441. Open Feb.-Nov. daily 10am-6pm; Dec.-Jan. M-Tu and Th-Su 10am-4pm. £6, concessions £5, children £2.) **Warwick House B&B** ❸, London Rd., has an energetic owner and a friendly cat, Claude. Perks include four-poster beds, access to the leisure center next door, an ample breakfast, and Wi-Fi. Follow the A44 east out of town toward Oxford for 10min.; the hotel is on the left. (☎01608 650 773. Free pickup from station. £27-37 per person. Cash only.) For camping, try **Fosseway Farm** ❶, Stow Rd., 5min. out of Moreton-in-Marsh toward Stow-on-the-Wold. (☎01608 650 503. Campers' breakfast £4. Tents £5.50 per person; caravans £10. Electricity £2.50. MC/V.) A **Tesco Express** market is on High St. in the center of town, next to the bus stop. (☎01608 652 287. Open M-F 6am-11pm, Sa-Su 7am-11pm.) Every Tuesday, High St. plays host to the largest open-air **market** in the region. Enjoy tea and lunch at **Tilly's Tea Room** ❶, 18-19 High St., which has a host of homemade cakes and jams to enjoy in the garden. (☎01608 650 000. Tea and scone £4.35. Cash only.)

BROADWAY ☎(0)1386

Broadway lives up to its name, with a long, wide High St. bordered by pubs and specialty shops. **Broadway Tower**, a 30-40min. uphill hike, inspired the likes of poet Dante Gabriel Rossetti and affords an excellent view of 12 counties. Follow the Cotswold Way from High St. uphill out of town or take Johnson bus #21/22 (10min., M-Sa 4 per day) from High St. to Broadway Tower Park. (☎01386 852 390; www.broadwaytower.co.uk. Open Apr.-Oct. daily 10:30am-5pm; Nov.-Mar. Sa-Su 11am-3pm; weather permitting. £4, concessions £3.50, children £2.50, families £11.) **Snowshill Manor**, 2¼ mi. southwest of Broadway, was once home to a collector of everything and anything. It now houses about 20,000 knick-knacks, including a collection of bicycles. (☎01386 852 410. Open May-Oct. M-W and Su noon-5pm; from late Mar. to Apr. M-Th and Su noon-5pm. £8.10.) Past Snowshill Manor, **Snowshill Lavender Farm**, called the "Provence of the Cotswolds," lets you wander through the sweet-smelling lavender fields. It is best in July, although visiting later also lets you watch the distillation process. (☎01386 854 821. Open May-Aug. daily 10am-5pm. £2.50, children £1.50.)

CHIPPING CAMPDEN ☎(0)1386

Years ago, quiet Chipping Campden was the capital of the Cotswolds' wool trade ("chipping" means "market"). Market Hall, in the middle of the main street, attests to 400 years of commerce. The Gothic **Saint James Church**, a 5min. walk from High St., houses England's only full set of 15th-century altar hangings. From the TIC (p. 296) entrance, turn right onto High St. and take the right fork up the hill to the church. (☎01386 841 927; www.stjameschurch-campden.co.uk. Open Mar.-Oct. M-Sa 10am-5pm, Su 2-6pm; Nov. and Feb. M-Sa 11am-4pm, Su 2-4pm; Dec.-Jan. M-Sa 11am-5pm, Su 2-3pm. Suggested donation £1.) Currently, the town is famous for its **Cotswold Olympic Games,** in the first week of June. The games take place on Dovers Hill and feature traditional sports like "shin-kicking." From St. Catherine's on High St., turn right onto West End Terr., take the first left, and follow the footpath 1 mi. uphill. The 2012 Olympic Games in London will coincide with the 400th anniversary of the Cotswold Games, and the town has scheduled a massive celebration.

CIRENCESTER ☎(0)1285

One of the larger towns in the Cotswolds and regarded as the capital of the region, Cirencester (SI-ruhn-ses-ter) is the site of Corinium, a Roman town founded in AD 49. Although only scraps of the amphitheater remain, the **Corinium Museum,** Park St., has a formidable collection of Roman mosaics as well as exhibits on the region's Anglo-Saxon and wool-producing history. (☎01285 655 611. Open M-Sa 10am-5pm, Su 2-5pm. £4, concessions £2.50.) Cirencester's **Parish Church of Saint John the Baptist** is Gloucestershire's largest "wool church." Although the church is undergoing extensive refurbishments until Easter 2010, it remains open. (☎01285 659 317; www.cirenparish.co.uk. Open in summer M-Sa 10am-5pm, Su noon-5pm; in winter M-Sa 10am-4pm, Su noon-5pm. Grounds close 9pm. 3 services per day. Donation suggested.) The world's highest yew hedge bounds Lord Bathurst's mansion at the top of Park St. Bear right and make a left on Cecily Hill to enter the 3000-acre **Cirencester Park,** whose stately central aisle was designed by Alexander Pope. (Open daily 8am-5pm.) An **antique market** takes place on Fridays in Corn Hall, near the TIC. (☎0171 263 6010. Open 10am-4:30pm.) A short walk south of town center, **Apsley Villa Guest House ❸,** 16 Victoria Rd., rents affordable elegant ensuite rooms. (☎01285 653 489. Breakfast included. Singles £35; doubles and twins £50. Cash only.)

SLIMBRIDGE ☎(0)1453

Slimbridge, 12 mi. southwest of Gloucester off the A38, is a dull village with two draws: a pleasant hostel (**YHA Slimbridge, p. 296**) and the largest of seven **Wildfowl & Wetlands Trust** centers in Britain. Sir Peter Scott has developed the world's biggest collection of wildfowl here, with over 180 different species, including all six varieties of flamingos. To avoid a 3 mi. walk from Slimbridge Crossroads, take the Stagecoach #91A service from Gloucester on Sundays, which goes directly there. (☎01453 891 900; www.wwt.org.uk. Open daily Apr.-Oct. 9:30am-5:30pm; Nov.-Mar. 9:30am-5pm. £8, concessions £6.15.) Six miles southwest of Slimbridge, off the A38 between Bristol and Gloucester, lies massive **Berkeley Castle** (BARK-lay). The stone fortress boasts impressive towers, a dungeon, the cell where King Edward II was murdered, Queen Elizabeth I's bowling green, and the Great Hall, where West Country barons met before forcing King John to sign the Magna Carta. (☎01453 810 332; www.berkeley-castle.com. Open July-Aug. daily 11am-5:30pm; Sept.-Oct. and Mar.-June Su and bank holidays 11am-5:30pm. £7.50, students £6. Gardens only £4. Tours free.)

THE MIDLANDS

Mention "the Midlands," and you'll evoke grim, urban, and decidedly sunless images. But go to the Midlands, and you'll be surprised by the quiet grandeur of the smokestacked center of England. Warwick's castle and Lincoln's cathedral are two of Britain's standout attractions, Shrewsbury and Stamford are architectural wonders, and even Birmingham, the region's oft-maligned center, has its saving graces, among them lively nightlife and the Cadbury chocolate empire. Deep in the Severn Valley, Ironbridge is a World Heritage Site.

HIGHLIGHTS OF THE MIDLANDS

ADMIRE the world's first cast-iron bridge in **Ironbridge** and explore museums at this monument to Britain's Industrial Revolution (p. 308).

CLIMB your way to **Lincoln Cathedral,** once Europe's tallest building and now the stunning centerpiece of this city on a hill (p. 322).

STROLL past the stone buildings of Stamford on your way to **Burghley House,** one of Britain's most lavish homes (p. 314).

WARWICK   ☎(0)1926

Otherwise modest Warwick (WAR-ick) takes fierce pride in its famous castle. Reputedly the UK's biggest attraction, the turreted fortification has brought the town more than its fair share of teashops and bewildered tourists.

⬛🔁 TRANSPORTATION AND PRACTICAL INFORMATION. The Warwick **train station** is off Coventry Rd. To reach town from the station, take a right and follow Coventry Rd. south to Smith Rd. **Trains** (☎08457 484 950) run to Birmingham (40min., 2 per hr., £5.20), London Marylebone (2hr., 3 per hr., £15-41), and Stratford-upon-Avon (25min., every hr., £4.50). National Express (☎08717 818 181) **buses** depart from Puckerings Ln. to Birmingham (2hr., 5 per day, £7), London (3hr., 4 per day, £16), and Heathrow Airport (4hr., 4 per day, £16). Buy tickets at **Co-op Travel,** 15 Market St. (☎01926 410 709. Open M and W-Sa 9am-5pm, Tu 9:45am-5pm.) Local buses #17 and 18 (3-4 per hr., £2.55-4) leave Market Pl. and stop at Coventry (55min.) and Stratford (20min.). Warwickshire Traveline (☎01926 414 140) has local bus info. B&R Cars (☎01926 771 771) runs **taxis.**

The **Tourist Information Centre,** Court House, Jury St., books rooms for £1 plus a 10% deposit. (☎01926 492 212; www.warwick-uk.co.uk. Open daily 9:30am-4:30pm.) **Tours** leave from the TIC (Apr.-Oct. Su 11am, £3). Other services include: **Barclays** bank, 5 High St. (☎0845 755 5555; open M-F 9am-4:30pm); the **police,** Priory Rd. (☎01926 410 111); a **Boots** pharmacy, 6-8 Cornmarket St. (☎01926 247 461; open M-Th and Sa 8:45am-5:30pm, F 9am-5:30pm); **Warwick Hospital,** Lakin Rd. (☎01926 495 321); and the **post office,** Shire Hall, Market Pl. (open M-F 9am-5:30pm, Sa 9am-4pm). **Postcode:** CV34 45A.

🔳🔲 ACCOMMODATIONS AND FOOD. A stay near the castle can be pricey, but **Emscote Road** has quality, affordable options. From the train station, turn right on Coventry Rd. and left at the Crown and Castle Inn on Coten End, which becomes Emscote Rd. (Bus #X17 runs from Market St. to Emscote frequently.)

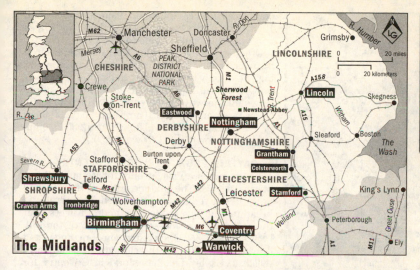

The Midlands

MIDLANDS

A nice young couple runs the bright **Avon Guest House ❸**, 7 Emscote Rd. Guests can stay in the elegant, well-decorated main house or the coach house, which caters to backpackers and long-term guests. (☎01926 491 367; www.avonguesthouse.co.uk. Singles £25-42; doubles and twins £60. MC/V.) Find **Chesterfields ❸**, 84 Emscote Rd., by looking for the sign with the pajama-clad elephant. Cozy floral rooms make this a great place to doze. (☎01926 774 864. Singles from £27; ensuite doubles from £55; family rooms from £60. Cash only.) **Park House ❸**, 17 Emscote Rd., has a castle-like facade. (☎01926 494 359. All rooms ensuite. Full English breakfast. Singles £30; doubles £50. Cash only.)

Find traditional pub fare at the **Tilted Wig ❷**, 11 Market Pl. On warm days, most patrons forgo the dark wood interior and dine alfresco on the square. (☎01926 411 534; www.thetiltedwig.co.uk. Entrees £4-12. Open M-Sa 11am-11pm, Su 11am-10:30pm. Kitchen open daily noon-3pm and 6-8:45pm. MC/V.) Behind the castle, **Catalan ❷**, 6 Jury St., takes you off the streets of medieval England and into a Spanish villa. (☎01926 498 930; www.cafecatalan.com. Tapas £1.55-4. Open M-F noon-3pm and 6-9:30pm, Sa noon-10pm. MC/V.)

INVADING THE CASTLE. Consistently crowded in summer, Warwick Castle is best enjoyed with a little advance planning. If you can, arrive early (expect a queue to form by 9:45am) and head straight to the dungeon and torture chamber on the left as you enter the castle.

🅖 SIGHTS. Many medievalists and architects regard 14th-century ▧**Warwick Castle** as England's finest. The dungeons are manned by life-size wax soldiers preparing for battle, and the castle's main chambers contain rooms with Tudor and Victorian trimmings, complete with royal residents posed in amusing vignettes. The grounds host archery demonstrations and carnival games (£2.50 per play). Highlights include the launching of a massive trebuchet and summertime jousting. Climb to the top of the towers and see the countryside unfold like a fairy-tale kingdom or stroll through one of the many gardens planned by Lancelot "Capability" Brown. (☎0870 442 2000; www.warwick-castle.

LOCAL LEGEND

WAITING FOR GODIVA

Lady Godiva's infamous ride *en déshabillé* through the streets of Coventry has inspired legends, ballads, and a line of gourmet chocolates. But what prompted this display of nudity? Was it lascivious or sensible, heroic or merely bizarre?

The earliest record of the story, dating from the early 13th century, was written a full 200 years after Lady Godiva doffed her dress and mounted her horse, so facts remain thin. According to legend, she was wife to the oppressive Earl Leofric, who burdened the Coventry townsmen with heavy taxes. Kindhearted Lady Godiva pleaded with her husband to relieve them until he, pestered to distraction, agreed to revoke them on the condition that she ride completely naked through the town. Without another word, Lady Godiva undressed, loosened her long blonde hair so that it veiled everything but her beautiful white legs, and cantered modestly through the streets, seen by no one. The earl lifted the taxes, and the townsmen ever after celebrated Lady Godiva for her great deed of mercy.

Lady Godiva's nude ride through town is celebrated in Coventry in the first weekend of June in the Lady Godiva Festival. A statue of the lady stands near Coventry's twin cathedrals.

co.uk. Open daily Apr.-Sept. 10am-6pm; Oct.-Mar. 10am-5pm. ₤18, children ₤11, seniors ₤13; prices may vary seasonally. Audio tours ₤3.)

Other sights include **Saint Mary's Church,** Church St., which has a 12th-century Norman crypt containing one of only two surviving ducking stools (used on witches) in England. The church tower offers views all the way to Coventry. (☎01926 403 940. Open in summer M-Sa 10am-6pm, Su 12:30-6pm; in winter M-Sa 10am-4:30pm, Su 12:30-4:30pm. Requested donation ₤2. Tower ₤2.50.)

⚑ **DAYTRIP FROM WARWICK: COVENTRY.** Coventry deserves a visit, if only for its magnificent **twin cathedrals.** The juxtaposition of the old and new, destroyed and resurrected cathedrals, is breathtaking. The modern cathedral towers over the stained-glass and stone skeleton of the old. (☎024 7652 1200. Open daily 9am-5pm. Suggested donation ₤3.) Behind the cathedrals, **Saint Mary's Guildhall,** Bayley Ln., has stood in Coventry for over 650 years. Surviving election riots and the Blitz, the guildhall displays stained glass and the 16th-century Tournai tapestry. The room where Mary, Queen of Scots, was imprisoned is on the top floor. (☎024 7683 2381. Open in summer daily 10am-4pm; in winter M-Th and Su 10am-4pm. Free.) The underground ruins of the 11th-century **Priory Cathedral** were recently opened for display after a massive archaeological project. Henry VIII destroyed the monastery, but today you can view what's left: a garden and an underground museum complete with wax monks. (☎024 7655 2242. Open M-Sa 10am-5pm, Su noon-4pm. Tours daily at 12:30pm. Gardens free, priory tour ₤1.) The tourist season commences the first weekend of July during the **Lady Godiva Festival,** which honors Countess Godgifu (but who would buy chocolates with that name?) of Coventry. Lady Godiva's renowned nude ride through the town on horseback is celebrated in an annual parade. A statue of the lady lies near the cathedrals. (www.godivafestival.com.) For less scandalous modes of travel, try the **Coventry Transport Museum,** Hales St. The museum displays the largest collection of British cars in the world. (☎024 7683 4270; www.transport-museum.com. Open daily 10am-5pm. Last entry 4:30pm. Free.) The **Tourist Information Centre,** 1 Hill Top, is inside the ruins of the old cathedral. *(Coventry is 12 mi. northeast of Warwick. Take Stagecoach bus X17 from Market St. and Elmscote Rd. (1hr., 4 per hr., £4) to the train station on Trinity St. in Coventry.* ☎*024 7622 7264. Open M-F 9:30am-5pm, Sa 10am-4:30pm, Su 10am-12:30pm and 1:30-4:30pm.)*

BIRMINGHAM

☎ (0)121

Birmingham, second in Britain only to London in population, has a long-standing reputation as a grim, industrial metropolis. To counter this bleak stereotype, the city has revitalized itself with a sure-fire visitor magnet: shopping—and lots of it. The massive Bullring, Europe's largest retail establishment, is the foundation of Birmingham's material-world makeover. The new construction creates a disconnected feeling throughout the city: Gothic churches stand next to ultramodern buildings, and beautiful gardens border nightclubs. Awkward design aside, the city is the hub of Midlands nightlife. It is steadfastly defended by fun-loving "Brummies" as one of the UK's most lively cities.

▐ TRANSPORTATION

Birmingham is situated along train and bus lines running between London, central Wales, and southwest England.

Flights: Birmingham International Airport (☎08707 335 511). Free transfer to the Birmingham International railway station for connections to New St. Station and London.

Trains: New Street Station sends trains (☎08457 484 950) to: **Liverpool Lime Street** (1½hr., every hr., £23.60); **London Euston** (1½hr., every 30min., £61.50); **Manchester Picoadilly** (2hr., 2 per hr., £25.50); **Oxford** (1¼hr., at least 1 per hr., £23); **Sheffield** (1¼hr., 2 per hr., £27). Others pull out of **Moor Street, Jewellery Quarter,** and **Snow Hill** stations. Follow signs to get from New St. to Moor St. Station (10min. walk). The Birmingham Stationlink bus provides connections between train stations.

Buses: Digbeth Station, High St., Digbeth. National Express (☎08717 818 181; office open daily 7am-7pm) to: **Cardiff** (1½hr., 4 per day, £21.50); **Liverpool** (1hr., 5 per day, £10.80); **London Heathrow** (2½hr., every hr., £28); **Manchester** (2½hr., every 2hr., £12); **Oxford** (2¼hr., 5 per day, £11).

Public Transportation: Information at Centro (☎0871 200 2233; www.travelinemidlands.co.uk), in New St. Station. Stocks transit maps and bus schedules. Call ahead. Bus £1.50 to most places; bus and train day pass £5. Open M-F 8:30am-5:30pm, Sa 9am-5pm. Most buses can be caught from Corporation St. just behind the station.

Taxis: TOA (☎0121 427 8888), **Blue Arrow** (☎0833 396 9614).

▐ PRACTICAL INFORMATION

Tourist Information Centre: The Rotunda, 150 New St. (☎0844 888 3883; www.visitbirmingham.com). Distributes the free *Explore Birmingham* pocket guide. Books rooms for free and sells theater and National Express tickets. Open M and W-Sa 9:30am-5:30pm, Tu 10am-5:30pm, Su 10:30am-4:30pm. Also a small information center at the junction of New and Corporation St. Open M-Sa 9am-5pm, Su 10am-4pm.

Tours: Birmingham Heritage Walks (☎0121 427 2555; www.birmingham-tours.co.uk). Offers tours along the canals, through the Bullring, and through the city center to view the Victorian and modern architecture. Public tours £4-5, private tours vary.

Currency Exchange: American Express, 34 Union St. (☎0121 644 5555). Open M-F 9am-5:30pm, Sa 9am-5pm. **Barclays,** 86 High St. (☎0845 755 5555). Open M-Tu and Th-F 9:30am-5pm, W 10am-5pm.

Luggage Storage: At the train station (above). £6 for 24hr.

Library: Central Library, Chamberlain Sq. (☎0121 303 4511; www.birmingham.gov.uk/library). Free Internet access on its 100 computers, but there's usually a wait. Call ahead to book a 1hr. slot. Open M-F 9am-8pm, Sa 9am-5pm.

Police: Steelhouse Ln. (☎0845 113 5000).

Birmingham

ACCOMMODATIONS
Bailey Hotel, **3**
Birmingham Central
  Backpackers, **13**
Nitenite, **7**

FOOD
Cafe Villaggio, **2**
Canalside Cafe, **5**
Mr. Egg, **9**

Thai Edge, **1**
Warehouse Cafe, **11**

NIGHTLIFE
Barfly, **12**
Nightingale, **10**
Sunflower Lounge, **8**
Rococo Lounge, **4**
The Yardbird, **6**

Pharmacy: Boots, Bullring (☎0121 632 6418), across from New St. station. Open M-F 8am-8pm, Sa 9am-8pm, Su 11am-5pm.

Internet Access: Free at **Central Library** (above). **Omega Sektor,** 98 Corporation St., at the intersection with Bull St. (☎0121 200 8383; www.omega-sektor.com). £1.50 per hr. Open M-F 8am-10pm, Sa-Su 10am-6pm.

Post Office: At the intersection of New St. and Victoria Sq. **Bureau de change.** Open M and W-Sa 9am-5:30pm, Tu 9:30am-5:30pm. **Postcode:** B2 4AA.

ACCOMMODATIONS

The TIC holds listings and flyers for budget accommodations in the city. **Hagley Road** houses several B&B budget options—the farther away from the city center you travel, the lower the price (and the standard). Take bus #9, 109, 126, or 139 from Colomore Row to Hagley Rd.

Birmingham Central Backpackers, 58 Coventry St. (☎0121 643 0033; www.birmingham-centralbackpackers.com). Tidy ensuite rooms and large comfortable common area with cotton-candy-colored walls. Full bar stocks plenty of snacks and simple items for dinner. Self-catering kitchen and built-in cinema with vast DVD collection. Free X Box and Wii games at the desk. Garden, library, board games, and pool table. Light breakfast included. Free Wi-Fi; Internet £1 per hr. Dorms from £16. MC/V. ❷

Bailey Hotel, 21 Sandon Rd. (☎0121 434 5700; www.baileyhotel.org), in the Hagley Rd. area. Take any bus that goes along Hagley Rd., get off at Meadow St., and follow it right to the hotel. Clean, bright, and recently renovated rooms. Singles £26, ensuite £36; double £38/45; twin £40/45. MC/V. ❸

Nitenite, 18 Holliday St. (☎0845 890 9099). A 5min. walk from New St. Station. Like something from another planet—seriously. 104 "city boutique" (read: tiny, spaceship-like) rooms with comfy double beds and ensuite showers. In place of windows, a flatscreen TV loops live video of the city. From £45 per person. MC/V. ❹

FOOD

Birmingham is most proud of **balti**, a Kashmiri-Pakistani cuisine invented by immigrants and cooked in a special pan. Brochures at the TIC map outline the city's balti restaurants; the best are southeast of the city center in the "Balti Triangle." The historic **Rag Market** on Edgbaston St. (☎0121 464 8349; www.ragmarket.com) is made up of three sites: the indoor market, which is known for its meat and fish (open M-Sa 9am-5:30pm), the open market, which sells fresh produce (open Tu-Sa 9am-5pm), and the St. Martin's market, which is famous for its fabrics (open Tu and Th-F 9am-5pm, Sa 9am-5:30pm).

Canalside Cafe, 35 Worcester Bar (☎0785 441 9862), by the canal, off Gas St. Baguettes and hearty specials like homemade chili served in a cozy 18th-century canalside house. Outdoor seating along the canal and in the comfortable courtyard. Sandwiches £4-5. Open M-F and Sa noon-11pm, Su noon-10pm. Cash only. ❶

Warehouse Cafe, 54-57 Allison St. (☎0121 633 0261; www.thewarehousecafe.com), off Digbeth. Look for the brick building with the mural on the side. Vegetarian restaurant with plants in the windows, candles on every table, and an organic menu. Entrees £7-8. Open M-Sa 11am-10pm, Su 11am-6pm. MC/V. ❷

Mr. Egg, 22 Hurst St. (☎0121 622 4344), on the corner of Ladywell. Favorite student spot for late-night (or early-morning) grub. Interior features a giant inflatable egg on the ceiling. Food is quick, cheap, and filling. Eggs and sausage £2. Open M-F 10am-4am, Sa 10am-6am, Su 9am-4pm. Cash only. ❶

Thai Edge, 7 Oozells Sq. (☎0121 643 3993; www.thaiedge.co.uk), off Broad St., next to Ikon Gallery. Bamboo poles and stark white walls. Enjoy the £8 lunch special on the patio. Entrees £6-12. Open

CHICKEN TIKKA MASALA

Yorkshire pudding, roast beef, fish and chips—all of these are quintessentially English dishes. But it is chicken tikka masala, a curry concoction whose shadowy origins lie somewhere between India and the UK, that a recent survey identifies as Britain's most popular. With over 23 million portions sold per year, the stuff can be spotted not just at Indian takeaway stands, but also in sandwiches, on pizzas, and even flavoring potato chips.

Some say the creamy, red-and-orange mixture was invented by a chef in a fit of spontaneous creativity, when a dissatisfied customer demanded gravy on his chicken tandoori, the chef poured tomato soup and some spices over it. Several chefs have claimed to be the inspired originators, but one fact is known for sure: the innovation occurred somewhere in Britain, sometime in the mid-20th century. The recipe for the dish itself is uncertain. It is made of tikka (bite-size pieces of tandoori chicken) and masala ("spices," usually in a tomato-based sauce). But a survey of 48 different recipes found that chicken was the only common ingredient.

As a fusion of Asian and European elements, the meal has even taken on wider significance. The late Foreign Secretary Robin Cook called chicken tikka masala "a true British national dish, not only because it is the most popular, but because it is a perfect illustration of the way Britain absorbs and adapts external influences."

M-Th noon-2pm and 5:30-11pm, F-Sa noon-2pm and 5:30-11:30pm, Su noon-3pm and 6-10:30pm. AmEx/MC/V. ❸

Cafe Villaggio, 245 Broad St. (☎0121 643 4224). Budget sibling to adjacent Del Villaggio. Italian cafe serving hearty portions of pizza and pasta. Music and photos pay homage to Italy and famous Italians. Heavenly gelato. Takeaway available. Open M-Th noon-11pm, F-Sa noon-11:30pm. AmEx/MC/V. ❷

👁 SIGHTS

🍫**CADBURY WORLD.** Sniff your way through the story of chocolate's birth in the Mayan rainforests, watch the factory at work, indulge in free samples, and take a trippy train ride through a land of animatronic cacao beans. (☎0121 451 4159; www.cadburyworld.co.uk. Get there by train from New St. to Bournville (every 10min.) or by bus #84 from the city center. Open Mar.-Oct. daily 10am-3pm; Nov.-Feb. Tu-Th and Sa-Su 10am-3pm. Pre-booking highly recommended. Pre-booking ☎0845 450 3599. £13, concessions and children £10, Oompa-Loompas free.)

SAINT MARTIN'S IN THE BULLRING. The site of Birmingham's first parish church has assumed its role as a place of peace in a sea of commercialism. The church, a Gothic building, is also the city's unofficial icon and worth a visit. (☎0121 600 6020; www.stmartininthebullring.com. Open M-Sa 10am-5pm, Su 9am-7pm.)

NATIONAL SEA LIFE CENTRE. Home to over 3000 creatures, the aquarium has the world's first fully transparent 360° underwater tunnel. The Atlantis Hall of Mirrors is a blast to get lost in. (The Water's Edge, Brindleyplace. ☎0847 423 2110. Open M-F 9am-4pm, Sa-Su 9am-5pm. £17, concessions £15, children £11.50, families £52.)

THINKTANK AT MILLENNIUM POINT. The Thinktank offers an interactive science experience geared primarily toward the 12-and-under set. (Curzon St., Digbeth. ☎0121 202 2222; www.thinktank.ac. Open daily 10am-5pm. £9.25, concessions and children £7.25, families £28. Special exhibits add £3-4.)

🏛 MUSEUMS

IKON GALLERY. The Neo-Gothic 1877 building hides a post-postmodern white cube interior where it shows cutting-edge multimedia art and Turner Prize-winning exhibitions. (1 Oozells Sq., in Brindleyplace. ☎0121 248 0708; www.ikon-gallery.co.uk. Open in summer Tu and Th-Su 11am-6pm, W 11am-8pm; in winter Tu-Su 11am-6pm. Free.)

BIRMINGHAM MUSEUM AND ART GALLERY. The beautiful building beneath the clock tower holds costumes, William Blake's illustrations of Dante's *Inferno*, and a new gallery for modern art. It boasts the largest collection of Pre-Raphaelite paintings in the world. (Chamberlain Sq., off Colmore Row. ☎0121 303 2834; www.bmag.org.uk. Open M-Th and Sa 10am-5pm, F 10:30am-5pm, Su 12:30-5pm. Free.)

BARBER INSTITUTE OF FINE ARTS. This museum in the University of Birmingham displays works by Degas, Gauguin, Matisse, Renoir, and Rubens. The institute also organizes related lectures. (Edgbaston Park Rd. Take bus #61, 62, or 63 from the city center. ☎0121 414 7333. Open M-Sa 10am-5pm, Su noon-5pm. Free.)

🎵 🌿 ENTERTAINMENT AND FESTIVALS

Birmingham Academy (officially **Carling Academy Birmingham**), 52-54 Dale End (☎0121 262 3000; www.birmingham-academy.co.uk). Birmingham offshoot of monolithic Brixton music venue. Most popular live venue in Birmingham. Previous performers include Dave Matthews and the Goo Goo Dolls. Hours and ticket prices vary; in summer events nearly every night. Box office open M-F 11am-5pm, Sa 11am-3:30pm.

City of Birmingham Symphony Orchestra, CBSO Centre, Berkley St. (☎0121 616 6500, box office 780 3333; www.cbso.co.uk, box office www.thsh.co.uk). Plays in the glass Symphony Hall, opened by the queen in 1991. Tickets £8-24, student standby tickets 1hr. before concerts £4. Box office open M-Sa 10am-6pm, Su noon-4pm; on performance days M-Sa 10am-8pm, Su noon-8pm.

Birmingham Hippodrome, Hurst St. (☎0870 730 1234; www.birminghamhippodrome. com). Once featuring vaudeville artists, the large stage now hosts West End musicals, ballet, pantomime, and opera. Box office open M-Sa and performance days 10am-8pm. Tickets £10-46, concessions available.

Birmingham Repertory Theatre, Centenary Sq. (☎0121 236 4455; www.birmingham-rep.co.uk), on Broad St. Houses dramas, comedies, Shakespeare, and new plays. Tickets £10-32, student and senior standby tickets available after 1pm on the day of the performance. Box office open M-Sa 10am-6pm; on performance days 10am-8pm.

Birmingham International Jazz Festival (☎0121 454 7020; www.birminghamjazzfestival.com). The first 2 weeks of July bring over 200 jazz bands, singers, and instrumentalists to town. Most events are free; check the website or TIC for specific listings.

🛍 SHOPPING

Birmingham's most significant attraction may be its regenerated shopping districts. The sprawling **Bullring,** in the heart of the city, recognizable by the wavy, scaled Selfridges department store, has over 140 retail shops plus restaurants and cafes. Look for the giant bull made entirely of candy in Selfridges, an exact sugar replica of its metal partner outside. (☎0121 632 1500; www. bullring.co.uk. Open M-F 9:30am-8pm, Sa 9am-8pm, Su 11am-5pm.) **The Mailbox,** Wharfside St., located in a former mail-sorting factory, is home to upscale designers and has three floors of terraced cafe-bars overlooking the city's canals. (☎0121 632 1000; www.mailboxlife.com. Open M-W 10am-6pm, Th-Sa 10am-7pm, Su noon-6pm.) **Brindleyplace,** 2 Brunswick St., along the canals, has more restaurants than shops, but it's still worth a look. (☎0121 643 6866; www. brindleyplace.com.) The **Custard Factory,** Digbeth and Heath Mill Ln., houses small vintage shops and cafes. (☎0121 224 7777. Most open M-Sa 10am-5pm, Su noon-4pm.) Signs point northwest to over 100 shops lining the **Jewellery Quarter,** which hammers out almost all the jewelry in Britain.

🎶 NIGHTLIFE

Birmingham's student population fuels its excellent nightlife venues. **Broad Street** teems with trendy cafe-bars and clubs. A thriving gay-friendly scene centers on **Lower Essex** and **Hurst Streets** southwest of Bullring. Pick up the bimonthly *What's On* for the latest hot spots. Grab a guide to public transportation's Night Network from the Centro office in New St. Station; night buses generally run every hour until 3:30am on Friday and Saturday.

🎷 **The Yardbird,** Paradise Pl. (☎0121 212 2524). This chill jazz club might be the coolest place in Birmingham. No dress code, no cover, no pretense. Arrive early for a spot on the patio. DJs spin drum and bass F, prompting street dancers to break it down in the middle of the bar. Live music Sa. Open M-W and Su noon-midnight, Th-Sa noon-2am.

Sunflower Lounge, 76 Smallbrook Queensway (☎0121 632 6756). Nice alternative to the Broad St. scene. Indie bar and live music venue; check postings at the door for dates. Cover £1-4. Open M-Th noon-11:30pm, F noon-1am, Sa 1pm-1am, Su 5-11:30pm.

Rococo Lounge, 260 Broad St. (☎0121 633 4260; www.rococolounge.com). Popular bar at the heart of Brum nightlife. Classic example of student clubbing. Near similar venues if you get bored with or kicked out of another one. Outdoor patio and retro-modern furnishings. ½-price mixed drinks F. Open M-W and Su 9am-1am, Th-Sa 9am-2am.

Barfly, 78 Digbeth High St. (☎0121 633 8311; www.barflyclub.com), hidden behind an unassuming pub. One of the liveliest spots in Birmingham. Live music nightly, with club nights after the music. Indie and alternative bands F until 4am. 90s night Tu, with your favorite middle-school hits until 3am. Cover £3-14.

Nightingale, Essex House, Kent St. (☎0121 622 1718; www.nightingaleclub.co.uk). 2 frenzied dance floors, 5 bars, jazz lounge, and billiard room attract a mostly gay and lesbian crowd from all over. Karaoke Tu. Dress smart casual. Cover F -Sa after 10pm £3-10. Open Tu-W 9pm-2am, Th 9pm-3am, F 7pm-4am, Sa 7pm-6am, Su 8pm-1am.

IRONBRIDGE ☎(0)1952

Despite its unwieldy moniker, Ironbridge is a quiet, charming town set in thick and hilly woodland. Red-brick homes and warehouses—relics of its rich past as an iron manufacturing hub during the early Industrial Revolution—line the graceful River Severn, now overtaken by sprawling greenery. Most prominently, an 18th-century cast-iron bridge (surprise!) sits in the center of town and arches over the vast gorge containing the Severn. Designated a UNESCO World Heritage Site, the Ironbridge gorge charms visitors with its combination of natural beauty and engaging history.

TRANSPORTATION. The nearest **train** station is at Telford, 15min. from Ironbridge by bus on #39 or 96 (M-Sa 10 per day). The only way to reach Ironbridge directly is by **bus**. Call ahead, as the timetables given at the TIC may not be totally comprehensive. For bus information, call the TIC, Telford Travelink (☎01952 200 005; www.telford.gov.uk) or use Traveline (☎0870 608 2608; www.traveline.org.uk). Arriva Midlands North #96 goes to Telford (15min., M-Sa 6 per day) and Shrewsbury (40min., M-Sa 6 per day). Most buses to and from Ironbridge do not run past 5 or 6pm and don't run at all on Sunday. Arriva (☎0844 800 4411) runs #99 on the Wellington-Bridgnorth route, stopping at Ironbridge and sometimes Coalbrookdale from Telford (20min., M-Sa 10 per day). Arriva #76 and 77 (20min., 6 per day) provide service between Coalbrookdale and Coalport (both home to YHA hostels), stopping at the Ironbridge Museum of the Gorge en route. On weekends and bank holidays, two Gorge Connect services (WH1 and WH2; both 1-2 per hr.) shuttle between the Ironbridge museums (50p per ride; free for Ironbridge Gorge Museum Passport holders), continuing on to Telford before noon and after 3pm. **DayRover** (£2.50, children £1.50) tickets are good for all-day travel. **Bike** rental is also available from **The Bicycle Hub**, the New Building, Jackfield Tile Museum. (☎01952 883 249; www.thebicyclehub.co.uk. Bikes £5 per hr., £15 per day. Credit- or debit-card deposit. Open Tu-Sa 10am-5pm, Su noon-5pm.)

ORIENTATION AND PRACTICAL INFORMATION. Ironbridge is the name of both the river gorge and the village at the gorge's center. The 10 **Ironbridge Gorge Museums** huddle on the banks of the Severn Valley in an area of 6 sq. mi. Some are difficult to reach without a car—buses run infrequently and stop only at selected points. Scenic foot paths also connect most of the sites.

The **Tourist Information Centre,** on the ground floor of the Tollhouse across the Iron Bridge, gives out the free *Ironbridge Gorge Visitor Guide* and books rooms for a £1.60 fee and a deposit of 10% of the first night's stay. (☎01952 884 391; www.ironbridge.org.uk. Open M-F 9am-5pm, Sa-Su 10am-5pm.) The only **ATM** in town is in Chrisalis NewsAgents, Tontine Hill. (£2 surcharge; open daily 7am-6pm), although the post office also offers cash back. **Lloyd's** pharmacy is located on The Square (open M-F 9am-6pm, Sa 9am-1pm) near the **post office.** (☎01952 433 201. Open M-Tu and Th-F 9am-1pm and 2-5:30pm, W 9am-1pm, Sa 9am-12:30pm.) **Postcode:** TF8 7AQ.

📷 📞 ACCOMMODATIONS AND FOOD. A 35min. walk from town, the **YHA Coalport ❷** resides in a renovated china factory next to the Coalport China Museum. Bright hallways have views of the surrounding woods. The hostel hosts children's camps and is rarely available in July and August. Take Arriva bus #76, which stops at the hostel, or #96 from Shrewsbury or Telford, which stops within half a mile. (☎0870 770 5882. Breakfast £4.50. Laundry. Reception closes 10:30pm. Dorms £18, under 18 £13.50; ensuite doubles £45. MC/V.) Built in the center of Ironbridge village in 1784, **The Tontine Hotel ❸,** The Square, was used as a meeting place for local industrialists and is possibly the nicest hotel ever to be named after an investment plan. Rooms have TVs, telephones, and views of the bridge. (☎01952 432 127; www.tontine-hotel.com. Singles £25, ensuite £40; doubles £40/56. MC/V.) Area B&Bs charge from £25 per person; expect to pay at least £35 for a single. Local art and rustic whitewashed walls make the **White Hart ❸,** The Wharfage, a stylish choice. (☎01952 432 901; www.thewhitehartironbridge.com. Breakfast included. Doubles in summer from £55; in winter from £45. AmEx/MC/V.) Facing the Tontine Hotel, turn left from the bridge and walk 5-10min. The nearest campground to Ironbridge is the **Severn Gorge Caravan Park ❶,** Bridgnorth Rd., in Tweedale, roughly 3 mi. from Ironbridge and 1 mi. north of Blists Hill. (☎01952 684 789. Electricity and showers included. £18.75 per person. Adults only. MC/V.)

Walk 10min. uphill on Madeley Rd. for the famed steak and kidney pie (£7.15) at the **Horse and Jockey ❷,** 15 Jockey Bank. (☎01952 433 798. Several vegetarian options. Open daily noon-2pm and 6:30-9:30pm. AmEx/MC/V.) **Tea Emporium Ltd. ❶,** The Square, right next to the post office, has a long tea list (£1.50 per pot) and pretty china to match. The emporium also sells sandwiches (£3-5) on its patio overlooking the bridge. (☎01952 433 302. Open daily 10am-5pm. MC/V.) Try the warm sausage rolls (£1.30) or the world-famous pork pies at **Eley's ❶,** on Tontine Hill. (☎01952 432 030; www.eleys-ironbridge.co.uk. Open M-F 8am-5:15pm, Sa-Su 8am-5:45pm. Cash only.)

🏛 MUSEUMS. The **Ironbridge Gorge Museums** are the area's pride and joy, and with good reason; you'd be hard-pressed to find a better portrayal of Britain's unique industrial heritage. You'll need at least two days to cover them well. If visiting all 10 (or even a significant fraction), buy an **Ironbridge Passport** from any of them. It allows you unlimited visits to all museums for a year. (£15, students and children £10, seniors £13, families £48.) All of the museums are open daily 10am-5pm, except the Broseley Pipeworks (open from mid-May to Sept. daily 1-5pm). The Tar Tunnel is closed from November to March, and other museums may reduce their hours during these months; call the TIC for details. The museums, though scattered, tend to cluster in several areas near town. The smallest museum is in the **Ironbridge Tollhouse** at the southern end of the bridge, upstairs from the TIC. It contains an exhibit about the bridge's history and includes a brief biography of one of its more eccentric funders, John "Iron Mad" Wilkinson, who minted iron coins stamped with his own image. The bulk of the bridge's funding, however, came frome Abraham Darby III, who in 1779 went into debt to create a monument to the new iron industry. The result of his efforts spans the River Severn with eye-catching black trusses. A small sign posted on the side of the Tollhouse at its southern end lists the fares for every carriage, mule, or child that crosses—even royalty isn't exempt. (☎01952 884 391. Open M-F 9am-5pm, Sa-Su 10am-5pm. Free.) Also near the town center, a 5min. walk from the bridge, the **Museum of the Gorge** gives a useful introduction to the area's history. With a model of the river valley region as it looked in 1796 and explanations of the volatile Severn's crucial role in manufacturing, the museum is a good place to begin a day's exploration. (☎01952 884 391. £3, students £2, seniors £2.50.)

To the northwest, another group of museums cluster in the small valley of Coalbrookdale. The **Coalbrookdale Museum of Iron** traces the history of the Darby family iron saga from Abraham Darby's discovery of a new way to mass-produce iron to the the Great Exhibition in London in 1851, where his Coalbrookdale Company displayed a series of intricate cast-iron gates and garden furniture. The massive furnace where Darby first smelted iron with coke (a type of coal, not cola) is also on-site. (☎01952 435 960. £7.25, students and children £5.25, seniors £5.45.) Just up the hill, the **Darby Houses** model the quarters of the multiple generations of ironmasters who lived there. (☎01952 432 551. Free with admission to Museum of Iron.) **Enginuity,** across the courtyard from the Museum of Iron, translates the region's industrial spirit into child-friendly, hands-on displays with interactive machinery and water-powered gears. (☎01952 435 905. £6.25, concessions £5.25.)

To the west, four museums lie near Coalport. As you walk from the bridge, the first is the recently re-opened **Jackfield Tile Museum,** which displays the decorative Victorian tiles that put the village of Jackfield on the map. At the **Coalport China Museum,** across the river from the Tile Museum, climb inside the huge kilns that were used to create the factory's intricate ware. (Both museums ☎01952 580 650. £6, students and children £4.25, seniors £5.45.) Up the road, don a hardhat in the eerie **Tar Tunnel,** where workers first discovered smudgy natural bitumen dripping from the walls and at one time collected 1000 gal. per week. (☎01952 580 827. £2, students and children £1.50, seniors £1.75.) At the **Blists Hill Victorian Town,** half a mile uphill from Coalport, over 40 recreated buildings deliver kitschy antiquity through local craft. (☎01952 582 050. £9.50, students and children £6.50, seniors £8.50.) A 30min. walk across the river and to the south of town, the **Broseley Pipeworks** are the farthest of the museums from Ironbridge. Here, clay-pipe-making workrooms have been preserved in a state of decrepit authenticity. (☎01952 884 391. Open June-Sept. daily 1-5pm. £4, students and children £2.50, seniors £3.)

SHREWSBURY ☎(0)1743

Bright hatters' windows, hole-in-the-wall boutiques, and a crooked network of ancient roads endear Shrewsbury to those with a weakness for stereotypically English streetscapes. Roger de Montegomerie, second in command to William the Conqueror, claimed the area during the 11th century. Shrewsbury's favorite son, however, is Charles Darwin—he and his (r)evolutionary ideas are memorialized all over town in the names of streets and shopping centers.

▐ TRANSPORTATION

Trains: Station at the end of Castle St. Ticket office open M-F 5:20am-8:40pm, Sa 5:20am-7:30pm, Su 7:30am-7:30pm. To: **Aberystwyth** (2hr.; M-Sa 7 per day, Su 6 per day; £13.10); **London** (3hr., 2-4 per hr., £44); **Swansea** (3-4hr.; M-Sa 1-2 per hr., Su 1 per hr.; £18-30); **Wolverhampton** (40min., 2-3 per hr., £7-8); most of North Wales via **Wrexham General** and **Chester** (1hr.; M-Sa every hr., Su 9 per day; £5.50).

Buses: Station on Raven Meadows, which runs parallel to Castle St. National Express (☎08705 808 080) to **Birmingham** (1hr., 2 per day, £5.70), **Llangollen** (1hr., 1 per day, £4), and **London** (4hr., 2 per day, £17.50). Arriva Midlands #96 to **Telford** via **Ironbridge** (1hr., M-Sa 6 per day).

Taxis: Queue in front of the train station. **Access Taxis** (☎01743 360 606). 24hr.

◼ 🛈 ORIENTATION AND PRACTICAL INFORMATION

The **River Severn,** Britain's longest river, circles Shrewsbury's town center in a horseshoe shape, with the curve dipping southward. The town's central axis runs from the train station in the northeast to **Quarry Park** in the southwest. Beginning as **Castle Gates,** the main road becomes **Castle Street,** then pedestrian-only **Pride Hill,** then **Shoplatch, Mardol Head,** and **Saint John's Hill.** From either end of Pride Hill, **Saint Mary's Street** and **High Street** branch off and converge to become **Wyle Cop.** This road turns into the **English Bridge,** crosses the river, and leads to the abbey. Pick up a map at the TIC; the signs claiming to direct tourists around town can be misleading. The accessible A5 nearly circles the city at a distance of 10 mi.

Tourist Information Centre: Music Hall, The Square (☎01743 281 200; www.visit-shrewsbury.com), across from the Market Bldg. Books accommodations for £2 (£3 over the phone) plus a 10% deposit. Open May-Sept. M-Sa 10am-5pm, Su 10am-4pm; Oct.-Apr. M-Sa 10am-5pm. The TIC may be moving in 2009; call for details.

Tours: Historic 1½hr. walking tours (☎01743 281 200) from the TIC pass through Shrewsbury's medieval "shutts" (closeable alleys). Special W summer tours feature tea with the mayor at no extra cost. May-Sept. M-Sa 2:30pm, Su 11am; Oct. M-Sa 2:30pm; Nov.-Apr. Sa 2:30pm. £3.50, children £2.

Banks: Barclays, 44-46 Castle St., off St. Mary's St. Open M-F 9am-5pm, Sa 9:30pm-3:30pm. **ATMs** all around The Square and along High St.

Library: Castle Gates (☎01743 255 380). Photo ID required. Open M, W, F 9:30am-5pm; Tu and Th 9:30am-8pm, Sa 9am-5pm, Su 1-4pm.

Launderette: Stidger's Wishy Washy, 55 Monkmoor Rd. (☎01743 355 151), off Abbey Foregate. Wash £3, dry £2. Service £9 per load. Open M-F 9am-5pm, Sa 10am-4pm.

Police: Clive Rd. (☎08457 444 888) in Monkmoor.

Pharmacy: Boots, 7-9 Pride Hill (☎01743 351 311). Open M-Th 8:30am-6pm, F-Sa 8:30am-5:30pm, Su 10:30am-4:30pm.

Hospital: Royal Shrewsbury, Mytton Oak Rd. (☎01743 261 000).

Internet Access: Free Internet and Wi-Fi at the reference library, 1A Castle Gates, just downhill from the main library (above).

Post Office: In WHSmith (☎08457 223 344), where Castle St. turns into Pride Hill, with a **bureau de change.** Open M-Sa 9am-5:30pm. **Postcode:** SY1 1D.

🛏 ACCOMMODATIONS

Singles are hard to find, so reserve several weeks ahead in summer. Several B&Bs (£20-30) lie along **Abbey Foregate** and **Monkmoor Road.**

Castlecote, 77 Monkmoor Rd. (☎01743 245 473). High ceilings, large windows, and airy rooms ensure a comfortable stay. £25 per person. Cash only. ❷

Trevellion House, 1 Bradford St. (☎01743 249 582), off Monkmoor Rd. Ensuite rooms with wrought-iron beds. The host fosters a quirky atmosphere and keeps a tidy garden out back. Singles £30; doubles £55. Cash only. ❸

Allandale (☎01743 240 173), behind the abbey on Abbey Foregate. From the bridge, follow the road that veers to the left of the abbey. A charming brick townhouse with hanging flower baskets on its porch. Most rooms ensuite. £27.50 per person, without breakfast £20. Cash or check only. ❸

POTATO, POTAHTO. Shrewsbury has two pronunciations, even among locals. "SHROWS-bree" is posher and is usually spoken by people living inside the river's horseshoe. This pronunciation is closer to the town's name in Old and Middle English. "SHREWS-bree" is more working-class, used mostly by residents on the outskirts of town. The choice is yours.

🍴 FOOD

Shrewsbury hosts an indoor **"Market under the Clock"** at the corner of Shoplatch and Bellstone. (☎01743 351 067. Open Tu-W and F-Sa roughly 7:30am-4pm.) A **Somerfield** market is at the Riverside Mall, on Raven Meadows near the bus station. (Open M-W and Sa 8am-6pm, Th-F 8am-7pm, Su 10:30am-4:30pm.)

The Peach Tree, 18-21 Abbey Foregate (☎01743 355 055; www.thepeachtree.co.uk). A stylish grill with Tudor architecture and decidedly modern accents. Excellent fare at good prices and a colossal drinks list. Try one of the huge starter platters or lavish sandwich offerings (£4-7). Open daily 9am-10pm. Lunch and sandwiches served M-Th noon-3pm, F-Sa noon-6pm. AmEx/MC/V. ❷

The Good Life Wholefood Restaurant, Barracks Passage (☎01743 350 455), off Wyle Cop. Serves cheap vegetarian cuisine, including nut loaves (£3) and quiches (£2.75). Open M-Sa 9:30am-4pm. ❶

Bear Steps Coffee House, St. Alkmund's Sq. (☎01743 244 355), by Butcher Row. Patio seating next to a shaded park. Taller guests should watch their heads when dining indoors, as timbers are lower than 6 ft. The delicious quiche goes for £5. Open in summer daily 10am-4pm; in winter M-Sa 10am-4pm. Cash only. ❶

👁 SIGHTS

Aside from its annual flower show, Shrewsbury's biggest attraction is its architecture. Tudoresque houses dot the shopping district but to see the distinct black timbers and white walls in full force, try climbing the **Bear Steps**. They start in the alley on Fish St. across from The Square and emerge in a lovely little park. Churches, many on Saxon foundations, cluster in the town center. Don't miss the circular design of **Saint Chad's** near the park, where Charles Darwin was christened in 1809. At the end of Castle St., the riverside acres of **Quarry Park** are filled with expansive grassy lawns along the oft-flooded Severn. At the center of the park, **Dingle Garden** explodes with bright flowers. A statue of Darwin presides opposite the castle. The colossal **Lord Hill Column** at the end of Abbey Foregate is the tallest Doric column in Europe. A stone likeness of MP Robert Clive of India stands stoically outside Market Sq.

SHREWSBURY CASTLE. Vivid red sandstone makes Shrewsbury Castle truly stand out. Originally built out of wood in AD 1083 and more recently repaired after an IRA bombing, the castle now consists of the Great Hall, which holds the **Shropshire Regimental Museum** and displays arms from as early as the 18th century. The Shropshire regiment guarded Napoleon on the island of St. Helena and saw massive losses in WWI's Battle of the Somme. The exhibit features a roll of actual footage from the battle. For great views, climb to nearby **Laura's Tower,** a summer garden house built in the 1780s. *(Near the train station. ☎01743 358 516; www.shrewsburymuseums.com. Museum and tower open from June to mid-Sept. M-Sa 10am-5pm, Su 10am-4pm; from mid-Sept. to Dec. and from mid-Feb. to May Tu-Sa 10am-4pm. Grounds open June-Sept. M-Sa 9am-5pm, Su 10am-4pm; Oct.-Easter M-Sa 9am-5pm. Museum £2.50, concessions and children free, seniors £1.50. Grounds and tower free.)*

SHREWSBURY MUSEUM AND ART GALLERY. This slightly jumbled but interesting museum displays items from Shrewsbury's extensive history in a timber-framed building that was the 16th-century home of a prominent local business-man. *(In Rowley's House, off Barker St. ☎01743 361 196. Open M-Sa 10am-5pm, Su 10am-4pm. Free. The museum may be moving in 2009; call the TIC for details.)*

SHREWSBURY ABBEY. Beyond the English Bridge stands Shrewsbury Abbey, a Benedictine abbey founded in 1083, dissolved by Henry VIII in 1540, and later reformulated as part of the Church of England. The abbey holds the remains of a shrine to St. Winefride, a seventh-century princess who was decapitated and then miraculously re-capitated to become an abbess and patron of North Wales and Shrewsbury. A memorial to local WWI poet Wilfred Owen stands in the garden. *(☎01743 232 723. Open Easter-Oct. M-Sa 10am-4:30pm, Su between services, about 11am-2:30pm; Nov.-Easter M-Sa 10:30am-3pm. Free.)*

❄ FESTIVALS

Shrewsbury hosts an annual **Art Festival** with events running from May to September. Ask for the *Shrewsbury Summer Season* guide at the TIC. Tickets for many events are available from the Music Hall, in The Square (☎01743 281 281) The mid-August **Flower Show** sees Shrewsbury's population blossom to 100,000 over two days for the world's longest-running horticultural show. (☎01743 234 050; www.shrewsburyflowershow.org.uk. £16 in advance, £18 at the door.)

⚐ DAYTRIP FROM SHREWSBURY

CRAVEN ARMS

Craven Arms is located 20 mi. south of Shrewsbury on the A49. Easiest access is by bus #435 from Shrewsbury (1hr., 7 per day).

Twenty miles south of Shrewsbury in Craven Arms, the ▨**Land of Lost Content,** at the corner of Dale and Market St., offers a fascinating collection of nostal-gic Britpop cultural relics and an entertaining walk down memory lane. The museum holds over 30 displays organized into themes like "pop style" (from beatnik sweaters and Dave Brubeck records up through leather skirts and Johnny Rotten posters), "tobacco" (filled with old Camel packs and cigars), and "toys" (from now-extinct board games to old rocking horses). The items in this one-of-a-kind museum took the owner 35 years to collect. (☎01588 676 176; www.lolc.org.uk. Open Feb.-Nov. M-Tu and W-Su 11am-5pm; Dec.-Jan. by appointment. Last entry 4:15pm. £5, children £2.50.) A few blocks away at the **Secret Hills Shropshire Discovery Centre,** on the corner of School Rd. and the A49, visitors explore exhibits on local history, including a replica of the local mam-moth skeleton. (☎01588 676 000; www.shropshire.gov.uk/discover.nsf. Open daily Apr.-Oct. 10am-5:30pm; Nov.-Mar. 10am-4:30pm. £4.50.)

STAMFORD ☎(0)1780

Limestone architecture holds centuries of history in the city of Stamford, a longtime playground for royalty en route from London to Scotland. Although William the Conqueror's castle was long ago destroyed and is now the site of a bus station, the city continues to lure visitors with its high spires and crooked alleyways. Hollywood and the BBC regularly exploit its "ye olde England" aura to film the 19th-century English novels by Jane Austen and George Eliot.

▐ ▌ TRANSPORTATION AND PRACTICAL INFORMATION. Stamford sits at the edge of Lincolnshire, with Cambridgeshire to the south. **Trains** (☎08457 484 950) leave Stamford Station, south of town, to: Cambridge (1hr., every hr., £15); Lincoln (2hr., 2 per hr., £20.70); Nottingham (1hr., every hr., £17); London King's Cross (1hr., every hr., £28.50). **Buses** are less frequent but pass through Sheepmarket, off All Saints' St. National Express (☎08705 808 080) makes trips to London (3hr., 1 per day, £12.80) and Nottingham (1hr., 9:30am, £15).

To reach the **Tourist Information Centre,** in the Stamford Arts Centre on St. Mary's St., walk straight out of the train station and follow the road as it curves to the right. Take a left on High St. St. Martin's, cross the River Welland, and take a right on St. Mary's St. The TIC gives away a town map, sells the *Town Trail* guide (£1), and books beds for free. (☎01780 755 611. Open Apr.-Sept. M-Sa 9:30am-5pm, Su 10am-4pm; Oct.-Mar. M-Sa 9:30am-5pm.) Other services include: **banks** with **ATMs** along High St.; free **Internet** at the **library,** on High St. (☎01780 782 010; book in advance; open M andW-Th 9am-7pm, Tu and F 9am-6pm, Sa 9am-4pm); **police,** North St. (☎01780 752 222; open daily 8:30am-6:15pm); and the **post office,** 9 All Saints' Pl. (☎08457 223 344; open M and W-F 9am-5:30pm, Tu 9:30am-5:30pm, Sa 9am-12:30pm). **Postcode:** PE9 2EY.

▐ ▐ ACCOMMODATIONS AND FOOD. The limited budget accommodations in town fill quickly; book well in advance during the summer or consider daytripping from Cambridge, Lincoln, or Nottingham. B&Bs are located mostly on the outskirts. Call ahead to get a lift or check for frequent local buses. Try **Gwynne House** ❹, 13 King's Rd., a large Victorian townhouse with a pool and three large ensuite rooms conveniently located a 5min. walk from the town center. (☎01780 615 675; www.gwynnehouse.co.uk. Full English breakfast included. Doubles and twins £65; family room £85. Cash only.)

For groceries, stop at **Tesco,** 46-51 High St. (☎01780 683 000. Open M-Sa 7:30am-7:30pm, Su 10am-4pm.) Don't leave England without trying a treacle tart—scrumptious desserts (from £1.50), hot lunches (£6.75-7.25), and a wide array of sandwiches (£4.50-5.50) await at **Central Kitchen** ❶, 7 Red Lion Sq. (☎01780 763 217. Open M-Th 9am-4:45pm, F-Sa 8am-4:45pm. AmEx/MC/V over £5.) Many small takeaway joints are tucked under the limestone eaves of Stamford, offering the usual selection of jacket potatoes and sandwiches. For an alternative, try **Cloisters Italian Bistro** ❷, 9 St. Mary's St., serving a selection of salads (£7-8), pizzas (£6-9), and pastas (£6-8), including the whimsically translated "angry pasta," which comes with tomato, chili, garlic, and basil. (☎01780 755 162; www.cloistersbistro.com. Open Tu-Sa noon-2pm and 6pm-late.)

▐ ▐ SIGHTS AND ENTERTAINMENT. England's largest Elizabethan mansion, **Burghley House** broods over the Stamford countryside like a turreted fortress, hidden among its ancient oaks and herds of ancestral deer. It was built by William Cecil, Queen Elizabeth's trusted minister and high treasurer from 1555 to 1587, but he would hardly recognize the house today. Subsequent Cecils extensively remodeled the original building, stuffing its rooms with Renaissance paintings and treasures culled from years of profligate travels on the continent. The famous **Heaven Room** and infamous **Hell Staircase** display ceiling-to-floor murals by Antonio Verrio—disporting Olympian gods in Heaven and damned souls in Hell, here figured as a monstrous cat's mouth. From the windows, admire the tree supposedly planted by Queen Elizabeth I herself, now trunkless due to a 19th-century storm. Entrance tickets also include admission to the 12-acre **Sculpture Garden** and the **Garden of Surprises,** a garden of various horticultural whimsies. (☎01780 752 451; www.burghley.co.uk. House open Apr.-Oct. M-Th and Sa-Su 11am-5pm. Last entry 4:30pm. £11, concessions £9.50, children £5.40, families £28. Gardens open Apr.-Oct. £6.30, concessions £5.30, children £3, families £16. Ask about the daily guided tour. Park open daily 10am-8pm or dusk. Free.) The **Stamford Arts Centre,** 27 St. Mary's St., hosts local productions and national tours. (☎01780 763 203; www.stamfordartscentre.com. Box office open M-Sa 9:30am-8pm.) Begun in 1968, the **Stamford Shakespeare Festival** is based at Elizabethan Tolethorpe Hall and attracts over 35,000 visitors each year. The open-air amphitheater lies on gentle slopes—pack a sunset picnic before the performance. (☎01780 756 133; www.stamfordshakespeare.co.uk. June-Aug. Tickets M-Tu £11, W-Th £12, F £14, Sa £16, matinees £9; concessions £1 less except on Sa.)

◪ **DAYTRIP FROM STAMFORD: GRANTHAM.** Some of England's finest attended school in Grantham at the **King's School,** including young Sir Isaac Newton and William Cecil, the first Lord Burghley. Newton carved his name into a windowsill. **Grantham Museum** has exhibits on Newton and Grantham's own, Margaret Thatcher. *(Kimes Coaches #4; 50min., 1 per hr. School on Brook St.* ☎01476 563 180. School library open to visitors M-F 9am-3:30pm. Free; donations accepted. Museum on St. Peter's Hill, by the TIC. ☎01476 568 783. Open M-Sa 10am-4pm. Last entry 3:30pm. Free.)

◪ **DAYTRIP FROM STAMFORD: WOOLSTHORPE-ON-COLSTERWORTH.** Seven miles from Grantham stands Woolsthorpe Manor, Newton's birthplace. A young Isaac scribbled his early musings on the farmhouse wall. Find the apple tree that bonked his famous "what goes up must come down" ideas into existence. The barn holds the **Sir Isaac Newton Science Discovery Centre,** 23 Newton Way, a hands-on exhibit especially for children (or the mathematically disinclined) that clarifies Newtonian ideas. *(Lincolnshire Roadcar (*☎01780 522 255*) runs from Grantham (20min., every 2-3hr., round-trip £3).* ☎01476 860 338. Open Apr.-June W-Su 1-5pm; July-Aug. W-F 1-5pm, Sa-Su 11am-5pm; Sept. W-Su 1-5pm; Oct. and Mar. Sa-Su 1-5pm. Last entry 4:30pm. Manor £5, children £2.45, families £12. Discovery Centre free.)

NOTTINGHAM   ☎(0)115

Nottingham uses its favorite rogue to lure tourists to the city: everything, from streets to buses to Indian restaurants, manages to exploit Robin Hood's legendary name. Designer boutiques and huge malls perpetuate the town's tradition of robbing from the rich. Despite all this, Nottingham is a center of commerce and non-fictional history. Victorian architecture mingles with modern shopping centers, while streets crowd with merry men and women at tiny bar-cafes.

◪ TRANSPORTATION

Trains: Nottingham Station, Carrington St., south of the city, across the canal. Trains (☎08457 484 950) to **Lincoln** (1hr., 1 per hr., £8), **London St. Pancras** (1¾hr., 2 per hr., £49.70), and **Sheffield** (1hr., 2 per hr., £9).

Buses: Broad Marsh Bus Station (☎0115 950 3665), between Collin and Canal St. Ticket and info booth open M-F 9am-5:30pm. National Express (☎08705 808 080) to

London (3hr., 12 per day, £16.80) and **Sheffield** (1½hr., 12 per day, £6.60). **Victoria Bus Station** is at the corner of York and Cairn St. and provides more local services. Nottinghamshire County Council Buses link points throughout Nottinghamshire.

Public Transportation: The best way to see the main attractions in Nottingham is on foot. For short urban journeys, hop on a Nottingham City Transport bus (50p-£1.30). All-day local bus pass £2.50. For public transit info, call the **Nottinghamshire Buses Hotline** (☎0870 608 2608; www.nctx.co.uk). Open daily 7am-9pm. The city also has a **tram** system (☎0115 942 7777; www.thetram.net) that connects Nottingham to points in Nottinghamshire. Peak £2.50, off-peak £1.50, day pass £2.70, week pass £12

◀▪▪ ▶ ORIENTATION AND PRACTICAL INFORMATION

Nottingham is a busy city with confusing and often poorly labeled streets. Its hub is **Old Market Square,** the plaza that spreads before the domed **Council House. Nottingham Canal** cuts across the south of the city.

Tourist Information Centre: 1-4 Smithy Row (☎0115 477 5678; www.visitnotts.com), off Old Market Sq. Many reference guides, tour and job listings, a free city map, and free entertainment listings. Books rooms (before 4:30pm) for a 10% deposit. Open M-F 9am-5:30pm, Sa 9am-5pm, Su 10am-4pm.

Currency Exchange: Banks and ATMs line Long Row and Old Market Sq. **American Express,** 2 Victoria St. (☎0115 924 7701). Open M-F 9am-5:30pm, Sa 9am-5pm, Su 9am-3pm.

Library: Nottingham Central Library, Angel Row (☎0115 915 2841). Open M-F 9am-7pm, Sa 9am-1pm.

Launderette: Brights, 150 Mansfield Rd. (☎0115 948 3670), near the Igloo hostel. Wash £2.60, dry £2. Open M-F 9:30am-6:30pm, Sa 9am-6pm, Su 9:30am-5pm.

Police: North Church St. (☎0115 948 2999).

Hospital: Queen's Medical Centre, Derby Rd. (☎0115 924 9924).

Internet: Free at the **library** (above). £3 per hr. at the **TIC** (above).

Post Office: Queen St. Open M and W-F 9am-5:30pm, Tu 9:30am-5:30pm, Sa 9am-4:30pm. **Postcode:** NG1 2BN.

▐▛ ACCOMMODATIONS

Moderately priced guesthouses (£30-35) cluster on **Goldsmith Street,** near Nottingham Trent University north of the city center.

Lindum House, 1 Burns St. (☎0115 847 1089). Take the tram to the High School station, near the Arboretum, to this Victorian guesthouse. Handsome exterior opens to a clean interior; wood stairs lead to 3 well-kept rooms with TVs. Breakfast included. Singles £35-40; doubles and twins £50-60. Cash only. ❹

Igloo, 110 Mansfield Rd. (☎0115 947 5250), on the north side of town, across from Golden Fleece. Affordable hostel with 36 bunk beds, recently renovated with new TV lounge, game room, and kitchen. Helpful receptionists always on hand. Free maps. Single-sex dorms available. Padlocks and lockers available for a £5 refundable deposit. Free towels. Internet available at 2 computer terminals. Free Wi-Fi. Curfew 3am. Dorms £14.50. Weekly dorms £58 per week. MC/V with 5% surcharge. ❷

Midtown Hostel, 5A Thurland St. (☎0115 941 0150; www.midtownhostel.co.uk). Budget option near Pelham St. nightlife and bus stations. Comfortable and clean bunk beds in co-ed rooms. Lounge with TV and videos. Luggage storage £1. Laundry £3. Free Internet. Dorms £16. MC/V with 50p surcharge. ❷

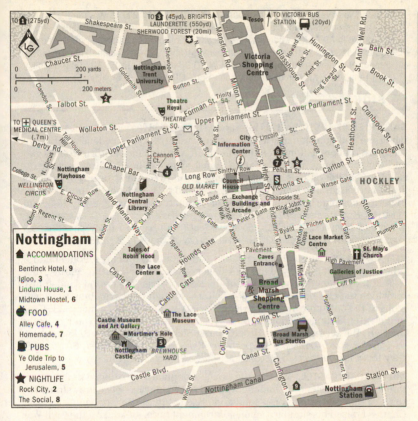

Nottingham

🏠 ACCOMMODATIONS

Bentinck Hotel, 9
Igloo, 3
Lindum House, 1
Midtown Hostel, 6

🍴 FOOD
Alley Cafe, 4
Homemade, 7

🍺 PUBS
Ye Olde Trip to
    Jerusalem, 5

★ NIGHTLIFE
Rock City, 2
The Social, 8

Bentinck Hotel, Station St. (☎0115 958 0285), across from the train station. Convenient location also means some traffic noise. Rooms are clean but hallways have water damage. Downstairs bar open until 11:30pm. Singles £24, ensuite £29.50. MC/V. ❸

🔪🍴 FOOD AND PUBS

Quick, cheap bites are easy to find on **Milton Street** and **Mansfield Road**. Gaggles of sandwich shops and ethnic eateries line **Goosegate**. There is a **Tesco** supermarket in the Victoria Shopping Centre. (☎0115 677 9506. Open M-F 7am-11pm, Sa 7am-8pm, Su 11am-5pm.)

The Alley Cafe, 1A Cannon Ct. (☎0115 955 1013; www.alleycafe.co.uk), off Long Row W. across from the library. Seating is limited, but the vibe is cool and the music is mellow. In the relaxed bohemian atmosphere, service might be erratic. Refreshing smoothies and vegetarian sandwiches are affordable (everything under £6). Try the smoked tofu with roasted peppers or, for something sweeter, the brie with blueberry conserve and grapes (£4.35). The bar is a hot spot after 9pm. Schedule for live DJs Th-Sa nights posted downstairs. Open M-Tu 11am-6pm, W-Sa 11am-late. MC/V. ❶

Homemade, 20 Pelham St. (☎0115 924 3030). Tiny cafe serving tasty sandwiches for even more appetizing prices (all selections under £4). Open M-F 8:30am-4:30pm, Sa 9am-5:30pm, Su 10:30am-3pm. MC/V. ❶

Ye Olde Trip to Jerusalem, 1 Brewhouse Yard (☎0115 947 3171; www.triptojerusalem. com). This popular pub, claiming the title of "Oldest Inn in England," served its 1st pot of ale in AD 1189, when it was a staging point for soldiers setting off on the Crusades. Nowadays the fare—steak and burgers (from £7)—is decidedly un-Crusaderly. Interior of whitewashed timber. Open M-W 10:30am-11pm, Th-Sa 10:30am-midnight, Su 11am-11pm. Kitchen open daily noon-8pm. MC/V over £5. ❷

◉ SIGHTS

GALLERIES OF JUSTICE. This interactive museum gives visitors a taste of British crime and punishment through actors and artifacts. Five levels below the old Shire Hall present information on life in Nottingham's historic county gaol and the sometimes absurd array of punishments. Other features include the repellent exhibit of tools and instruments swallowed (and passed) by inmates. To be herded around by a Victorian gaoler and prison inspector, both dressed in period costume, catch one of the 1hr. group tours, running every 15-30min. *(Shire Hall, High Pavement. ☎0115 952 0555; www.galleriesofjustice.org.uk. Open from mid-July to Sept. Tu-F 10am-4pm, Sa-Su 11am-5pm; from Sept. to mid-July Tu-Su 10am-3pm. £8, concessions and children £6, families £23. Joint ticket with City of Caves £10.50/8.25/32.50.)*

CITY OF CAVES. Nottingham is packed with hundreds of caves, some natural, others painstakingly carved out by villagers. As early as the 10th century, Anglo-Saxon dwellers dug homes out of the soft, porous "Sherwood sandstones" on which the city rests. Tours take visitors through the cave complexes with stops at the only known underground tannery in Britain and a mock WWII air-raid shelter. Strangely enough, the caves are situated beneath (and accessed through) the second floor of Broad Marsh Shopping Centre. *(☎0115 988 1995; www.cityofcaves.com. Open daily 10:30am-4pm. 40min. guided tours M-F every 30min., Sa-Su every 15min. Last tour 4pm. £5.50. Joint ticket with Galleries of Justice £10.50.)*

NOTTINGHAM CASTLE. William the Conqueror put up the original timber structure in 1068, and Henry III had the whole thing redone in stylish gray stone. The ruins of the castle now top a sandstone rise south of the city center. In 1642, Charles I raised his standard against Parliament here, kicking off the Civil War. In retaliation, the Parliamentarians destroyed the castle several years later. What's left now houses the **Castle Museum and Art Gallery,** a collection of exhibits on Nottinghamshire's past, Victorian art, and regimental memorabilia of the Sherwood Foresters, the regional militia. *(Friar Ln. ☎0115 915 3700. Open daily Mar.-Sept. 10am-5pm; Oct.-Feb. 10am-4pm. Last entry 30min. before close. £3.50, concessions £2, families £8.)* While you're there, take a gander at **Mortimer's Hole,** the underground passageway leading from the base of the cliff to the castle. *(☎0115 915 3700. 50min. tours leave the museum entrance M-Sa 11am, 2, 3pm. £2.50, concessions £1.50.)*

TALES OF ROBIN HOOD. Cable cars and audio tours transport visitors through an amusement-park version of Sherwood Forest. Robin Hood and his merry men await you after the child-friendly 45min. ride, and evenings bring the medieval banquet: for £40 per person you get a costume, four courses, and lots of beer. *(30-38 Maid Marian Way. ☎0115 948 3284. Open daily 10am-5pm. £9.)*

🎵 🎭 ENTERTAINMENT AND NIGHTLIFE

Students crowd the city's over thirty clubs and pubs. For weekend festivities, try **Pelham Street** or the outdoor patios along **Forman Street.** Pick up a *Late Night Public Transport Guide* available at the TIC and bus stations for a complete schedule of trams running until midnight and buses running until 4am.

The Social Bodega, 23 Pelham St. (☎0115 950 5078; www.thesocial.com). The name has alternated regularly between Bodega and the Social, finally settling on both. Indie and alternative fans will appreciate the live bands (recent acts include Coldplay and the White Stripes) that play to a young crowd. Club nights W-Sa with free admission downstairs, £2-3 cover upstairs. Open M-Sa noon-3am, Su 5pm-3am.

Rock City, 8 Talbot St. (☎0115 822 1314; www.rock-city.co.uk). Has hosted 25 years of hip hop, heavy metal, and everything in between. Past performers include Nirvana, Marilyn Manson, a naked Robbie Wiiliams, and Guns N' Roses—Axl Rose was almost refused entry because of his bath-towel garb. "Loveshack" F bops to 3 decades of pop, while Sa features alternative music. Cover £5-25. Open F-Sa 10pm-3am. Upstairs room, **Stealth,** is open until 5am. Check online for booking.

Theatre Royal, Theatre Sq. (☎0115 989 5555; www.royalcentre-nottingham.co.uk). Traditional theater, musicals, and the largest pantomime show in the Midlands. Tickets £8-25, up to £53 for ballets. Box office open M-Sa 8:30am-8:30pm.

The Nottingham Playhouse, Wellington Circus (☎0115 941 9419; www.nottinghamplayhouse.co.uk). Features offbeat productions, although it offers its share of Shakespeare as well. Cast restaurant inside serves pre-theater dinner. Tickets £7-35. Discounts for students aged 16-24. Box office open M-Sa 10am-8pm.

▶ DAYTRIPS FROM NOTTINGHAM

NEWSTEAD ABBEY. The ancestral estate of poet **Lord Byron** stands in the village of Linby north of Nottingham. The sprawling, stately home encompasses the remnants of the 1274 Newstead Priory church. Many personal effects remain, including Byron's original writing table and a replica of his "skull cup"—an ancient human cranium the poet coated with silver, inscribed with verse, and filled with wine. The original was reinterred in 1863. As mad, bad, and dangerous to know as Lord Byron was once remembered, his ancestors may have been even wilder. The two nearby lakes were constructed by a rakish progenitor who wished to stage sea battles in his backyard. While servants manned the mock-galleys, he fired cannons from the shore. Frisky peacocks hold court in the gardens and cafe—signs ask patrons to keep their crumbs to themselves and warn that shiny cars are vulnerable in mating season. *(Prontobuses run from Nottingham Victoria Station to the gates. 25min., 3 per hr., round-trip £4. 1 mi. from the grounds. ☎01623 455 900; www.newsteadabbey.org.uk. House open Apr.-Sept. daily noon-5pm. Last entry 4pm. Grounds open 9am-6pm. Last entry 5pm. House and grounds £7, concessions £4.50. Grounds only £3.50, concessions £3.)*

SHERWOOD FOREST. For the "real" Robin Hood experience, travel to the famed 450-acre Sherwood Forest, north of Nottingham. To escape the crowds, take the signposted 15min. walk to the 800-year-old "Major Oak," now supported, like an aging giant, on various wood stakes. At 33 ft. in girth, it allegedly served as Robin Hood's hideout. The **Sherwood Forest Visitor Centre,** near the entrance, has a small museum. Beware of children armed with mini-archery sets. In early August, the medieval **Robin Hood Festival** includes a jousting tournament. Check with the TIC for exact dates. *(Bus #33 leaves Nottingham Victoria Station. 1hr., M-Sa 4 per day, Su every hr. Sherwood Dart Rover Ticket gives unlimited travel for a day; £6, students £3. Visitor Centre ☎01623 823 202. Forest and Visitor Centre open daily 10:30am-5pm. Free.)*

EASTWOOD. Eastwood native and author of *Lady Chatterley's Lover* DH Lawrence (1885-1930) wrote novels that were banned from bookstores. Now, he rests honorably in Westminster Abbey. The **DH Lawrence Birthplace Museum** is in the house where he spent his first two years—look for his original watercolors. Ask the staff about walking brochures for Eastwood. The **Blue Line Trail** is a self-guided tour that links the museum with other Lawrence heritage sites, including three more homes in Eastwood where the family lived. *(Eastwood is 6 mi. west of Nottingham. Rainbow bus #1 leaves often from Nottingham Victoria Station (40min., 6 per hr., £4.20). Museum 8A Victoria St., near Mansfield Rd. ☎01773 717 353. Open daily Apr.-Oct. 10am-5pm; Nov.-Mar. 10am-4pm. M-F free; Sa-Su £2, concessions £1.20, families £5.80.)*

SOUTHWELL MINSTER. The great Norman builders reconstructed the fallen cathedral in 1108. Nine centuries later, the innate Romanesque building hosts weekly organ recitals and an annual August flower festival. *(Southwell is 14 mi. from Nottingham. Dunn Line bus #61 (3 per day) runs from Nottingham to Southwell. www.south-wellminster.org.uk. Open in summer 8am-7pm; in winter 8am to dusk. Wheelchair-accessible.)*

LINCOLN   ☎(0)1522

Cobbled streets climb past half-timbered homes to Lincoln's 12th-century cathedral, a relative newcomer in a town built for retired Roman legionnaires in the AD first century. The city is home to a bustling marketplace selling local produce and famous Lincoln sausage. A steep uphill climb to the city's peak rewards with sweeping views of the dusky Lincolnshire Wolds.

▐ TRANSPORTATION

Trains: Lincoln's **Central Station** is on St. Mary's St. Office open M-F 5:15am-7:30pm, Sa 5:35am-7:30pm, Su 10:30am-9:15pm. Travel center open M-Sa 9am-5pm. Trains to: **Sheffield** (50min., every hr., £11.50); **Leeds** (2hr., 2 per hr., £27); **London King's Cross** (2hr., every hr., £64); and **Nottingham** (1hr.; M-Sa 1 per hr., Su 7 per day; £8).

Buses: Opposite Central Station is **City Bus Station,** Melville St. (Open M-F 8:30am-5pm, Sa 9am-noon.) National Express buses go to **London** (4hr., 1 per day, £20) and **Birmingham** (3hr., 1 per day, £13.80). There is no National Express office in Lincoln; buy tickets online or on the bus. For info on Lincolnshire bus services, contact the station on Deacon Rd. (☎01522 522 255; www.roadcar.co.uk). Open M-F 8:30am-5pm.

▐ ▟ ORIENTATION AND PRACTICAL INFORMATION

Lincoln has an affluent acropolis on **Castle Hill** and a cottage-filled lower town near the tracks. The TIC and major sights lie at the junction of **Steep Hill** and Castle Hill near the cathedral.

Tourist Information Centre: 9 Castle Hill (☎01522 873 800; www.lincoln.gov.uk). Books rooms for £3 plus a 10% deposit. Pick up a mini-guide with map (50p). Open M-F 9:30am-5pm, Sa 10am-5pm, Su 11am-4pm. Branch at The Cornhill (☎01522 873 256). Open M-F 9:30am-5pm, Sa 10am-5pm, Su 11am-4pm.

Tours: 1hr. Cathedral Quarter walking tours depart from the Castle Hill TIC July-Aug. daily 11am, 2pm; Sept.-Oct. and Apr.-June Sa-Su 11am, 2pm. £4, concessions £3. Original Ghost Walks (☎01522 874 056) leave from Castle Sq. W-Sa 7pm and last 1¼hr. Arrive 10min. early. £3, concessions £2, children £2.

Currency Exchange: Lining High St. and Cornhill Pavement. **Thomas Cook,** 4 Cornhill Pavement (☎01522 772 299). Open M-Tu and Th-Sa 9am-5:30pm, W 10am-5:30pm.

Library: Central Library, Free School Ln. (☎01522 782 010). Free Internet. Open M-F 9:30am-7pm, Sa 9am-4pm.

Police: West Parade (☎01522 882 222), near the town hall.

Pharmacy: Boots, 311-312 High St. (☎01522 524 303). Open M-Sa 8:30am-6pm, Su 10:30am-4:30pm.

Hospital: Lincoln County Hospital, Greetwell Rd. (☎01522 512 512).

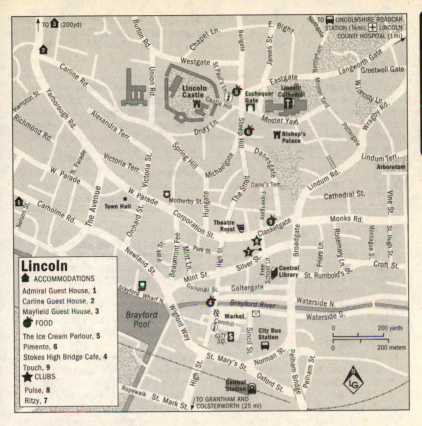

MIDLANDS

Lincoln

⌂ ACCOMMODATIONS

Admiral Guest House, **1**
Carline Guest House, **2**
Mayfield Guest House, **3**

🍎 FOOD

The Ice Cream Parlour, **5**
Pimento, **6**
Stokes High Bridge Cafe, **4**
Touch, **9**

★ CLUBS

Pulse, **8**
Ritzy, **7**

Internet Access: Sun Cafe, 36 Portland St. (☎01522 569 292). Wi-Fi £1 per hr. Open daily 11am-9pm. Also free at **Central Library** (above).

Post Office: City Sq. Centre, Sincil St. (☎01522 513 004). Open M-Tu and Th 8:30am-5:30pm, W and F 9am-5:30pm, Sa 9am-5pm. **Postcode:** LN5 7XX.

🏠 ACCOMMODATIONS

B&Bs (most £25-35) dot **Carline** and **Yarborough Roads,** west of the castle. Consult the accommodations list at the TIC on Cornhill.

Carline Guest House, 1-3 Carline Rd. (☎01522 530 422; www.carlineguesthouse. co.uk). A 15min. walk northwest of the train station, or take bus #7 or 8 to Yarborough Rd. Immaculate house with big beds, big rooms, and a big breakfast in the historic heart of Lincoln. Book ahead in summer. Singles £35-40; doubles £55. AmEx/MC/V. ❸

Mayfield Guest House, 213 Yarborough Rd. (☎01522 533 732). Entrance behind house on Mill Rd., off Long Leys Rd., a 20min. walk northwest from the station (or take bus #7 or 8 to Yarborough Rd.). Victorian mansion near a windmill offering bright, mostly ensuite rooms. Mind the enthusiastic cockatiel. No smoking. Book ahead in summer. Singles £36; doubles £58; twins £60. AmEx/MC/V. ❸

Admiral Guest House, Nelson Yard (☎01552 544 467). Take Bayford Wharf N. to Nelson St. A 10min. walk from the station. Small, clean rooms. Wharfside location gives a nautical feel. Full English breakfast included. Singles £30; doubles from £50. MC/V. ❸

 ## FOOD

The Cornhill **market,** on Sincil St., sells local food and oddities such as household appliances, women's underwear, and infants' clothing. (Open M-F 9am-4pm, Sa 9am-4:30pm.) Farmers' markets crowd City Sq. (1st F of the month), High St. (2nd W of the month), Castle Hill (3rd Sa of the month), and St. Benedict's Sq. (every Sa). Restaurants, tearooms, and takeaways dot **High Street** and **Steep Hill,** while pubs line **Bailgate Street,** on the other side of the hill.

> **TIP** **A POUND FOR £1.** At the farmers' market in Lincoln, load up on 1 lb. of fresh fruit for only £1. Many other British towns offer the same or similar deals, which makes market shopping more cost-effective that grocers.

The Ice Cream Parlour, 3 Bailgate. Tiny shop at the tippy-top of Steep St. with homemade ice cream, frozen yogurt, and sorbet. A single scoop (£1.20) of ginger chocolate chip or passion fruit sorbet may only whet the appetite for a double (£2.30). Downstairs, lunch on Lincolnshire plum loaf with Wensleydale cheese and butter and enjoy affordable afternoon high tea (everything under £2). Open M, W, F-Su 10am-dusk, Tu 10am-5:30pm, Th 11am-dusk. Cash only. ❶

The Cathedral Imp Tea Rooms, 18 Steep Hill (☎01522 537 909). Reward yourself with cream tea after the climb up Steep Hill. Tiny cafe with 3 tea and coffee menus and a delicious selection of sandwiches (£2.50) and pastries (£2-3). Open daily 11am-5pm. Lunch served noon-3pm. Cash only. ❶

Touch, 43-47 Clasketgate (☎01522 522 221; www.touchrestaurantbar.com). The European cuisine is as sleek as the interior. Bargain buffet lunch noon-2pm (£5.25). For dinner, try entrees like lime-scented tuna (£12.50). £1 theater discounts 5-7pm and 10-11pm. Open M-Sa noon-5pm and 5:30-10:30pm. Bar open until 2am. MC/V. ❸

Stokes High Bridge Cafe, 207 High St. (☎01522 513 825; www.stokes-coffee.co.uk). Watch swans float on the canal while you nibble on cheap sandwiches and snacks in this century-old, Tudor-style house on High Bridge. Alternatively, watch people shop on High St. while you relish a spot of afternoon tea. Hot lunches like quiche and Welsh rarebit (£5-6) served 11:45am-2pm. Tea 2-5pm. Open M-Sa 9am-5pm, Su 11am-4pm. Kitchen open until 30min. before close. MC/V over £10. ❶

SIGHTS

For the traveler interested in Lincoln's rich history, a **Time Travel Pass,** available at the TIC, grants entry at Lincoln Cathedral, Lincoln Castle, Museum of Lincolnshire Life, Medieval Bishop's Palace, and Ellis Mill. (£10, valid for 3 days.)

LINCOLN CATHEDRAL. Begun in 1072 but not completed for three centuries, magnificent Lincoln Cathedral was Europe's tallest building until the spire toppled. The creamy Lincolnshire limestone of the facade nests gargoyles and peregrine falcons. Inside, admire the lavishly carved choir screen, where smirking devils are intertwined with the apostles. In the transept, the resplendent medieval stained glass in the Bishop's Eye is currently being restored. The cathedral's most endearing feature is the Lincoln imp in the **Angel Choir,** who supposedly turned to stone while trying to chat with a seraphim. Pay 20p to see him lit up from below—or wait around for another tourist silly enough to pay 20p to light him up and then look. A treasury room displays sacred silver and a shrine to child martyr Sir Hugh. Rotating exhibits reside in the first library designed by Christopher Wren. (☎ *01522 561 600; www.lincolncathedral. com. Open May-Aug. M-F 7:15am-8pm, Sa-Su 7:15am-6pm; Sept.-May M-Sa 7:15am-6pm, Su 7:15am-5pm. Evensong M-Sa 5:30pm, Su 3:45pm. Tours M-Sa 11am, 1, 3pm. Free roof tours M, W, F 2pm. Tu, Th, Sa 11am, 2pm. Tour required to enter tower. Library open Apr-Oct. M-F 1-3pm, Sa 11am-3pm. Cathedral £4, concessions £3, ages 5-16 £1. Audio tour £1.)*

LINCOLN CASTLE. Home to one of four surviving copies of the Magna Carta, this castle, built by William the Conqueror in 1068, later served as a prison. A wall walk and visit to the observatory tower offer panoramic views of Lincolnshire and the Trent Valley. In the dungeon in Cobb Hall, shackles still protrude from the stone walls. (☎ *01522 511 068. Open daily May-Aug. 10am-6pm; Sept. and Apr. 10am-5pm; Oct.-Mar. 10am-4pm. Last entry 1hr. before close. Guided tours daily Sa-Su 11am, 2pm. £4, concessions £2.65, families £10.65.)*

BISHOP'S PALACE. Resting in the shadow of the cathedral, the Bishop's Palace has a vaulted undercroft and a formidable entrance tower. It was the seat of England's largest diocese in the 12th century and is now peacefully ruined, surrounded by vineyards and views. (☎ *01522 527 468. Open July-Aug. daily 10am-6pm; Sept.-Oct. and Apr.-June daily 10am-5pm; Nov.-Mar. M and Th-Su 10am-4pm. £4, concessions £3, children £2, families £10. Audio tour free, guide £3.)*

NIGHTLIFE AND FESTIVALS

In early December, Europe's largest **Christmas Market** takes over Cathedral Quarter when 150,000 people come to peruse 300 stalls. Late July brings the **Waterfront Festival,** with street theater, acrobats, and jet-ski displays. The **Lincoln Early Music Festival,** with workshops and street-dancing lessons, is in August. The monthly *What's On,* at the TIC, has the latest nightlife listings.

Ritzy, Silver St. (☎01522 522 314), on the corner of Silver St. and Flaxengate. Young crowd. Upstairs, **Pulse** (☎01522 522 314; www.pulselincoln.co.uk) has 3 rooms blaring chart-topping hits and a range of theme nights, including weekly student nights. Casual on weekdays, smart dress on weekends. Cover M-Th and Su £4, F-Sa £5; F-Sa "fast track" ticket to Ritzy for £2. Both clubs open M-W 10pm-2am, Th 10pm-2:30am, F-Sa 10pm-3am, Su 9:30pm-2am. Last entry 1hr. before close.

The Theatre Royal, Clasketgate (☎01522 525 555; www.theatreroyallincoln.com), near the corner of High St. Stages concerts and musicals. Tickets £7-22. Box office open M-F 10am-2pm and 3-6pm, Sa 10am-2pm and 5-6pm, Su 2hr. before the performance.

Lincoln Drill Hall, Free School Ln. (☎01522 873 894; www.lincolndrillhall.com), next to the library. An eclectic slate of events including mini film festivals, stand-up comedy, and classical music by the Lincoln Symphony Orchestra. Tickets £3-10.

EAST ANGLIA

The swampy fens in East Anglia were drained in the 1820s, yielding fertile farmland. The water that drenched enormous medieval peat bogs was channeled into a maze of waterways known as the Norfolk Broads, now a popular national park. Norman invaders brought stone over the flooded fens to build the Ely Cathedral. In a village to the south, renegade scholars from Oxford set up a rival institution along the River Cam in the 15th century.

EAST ANGLIA

HIGHLIGHTS OF EAST ANGLIA

PUNT along the River Cam in the university town of **Cambridge,** one of the world's oldest centers of scholarship (opposite page).

GAZE at **Ely Cathedral,** a medieval masterwork towering over fenland (p. 335).

CELEBRATE in **Norwich,** once the largest town in Anglo-Saxon England, where wool markets and festivals have endured for centuries (p. 339).

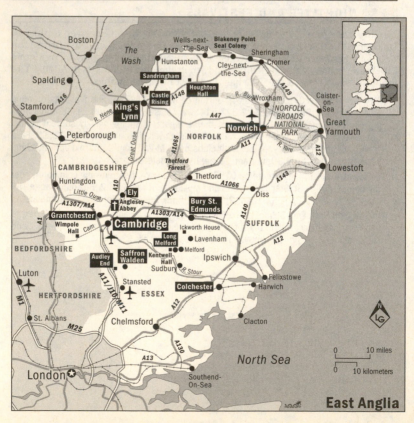

East Anglia

TRANSPORTATION

The major **rail** operator is **National Express East Anglia** (☎0845 600 7245; www. nationalexpresseastanglia.com). An **Anglia Plus** pass (£13), available at stations within East Anglia, grants you a day's unlimited travel on all train and local bus routes in the region. An **Anglia Plus Three Day** pass allows three days (£26).

Cyclists and hikers appreciate East Anglia's flat terrain and relatively dry climate, although **bike**-rental shops are rare outside of Cambridge and Norwich. The area's most popular walking trail is **Peddar's Way,** which runs from Knettishall Heath to Holme and includes the Norfolk Coast Path and **Weaver's Way.** TICs in Norwich, Bury St. Edmunds, and several Suffolk villages issue the guide *Peddar's Way and Norfolk Coast Path.*

Harwich (HAR-idge) is a **ferry** depot for the Netherlands, Germany, and Scandinavia. **Felixstowe** has ferries to Belgium (see **By Ferry, p. 40**). Call the Harwich Tourist Information Centre, Iconfield Park, Parkeston, for details. (☎01255 506 139. Open Apr.-Sept. M-F 9am-5pm, Sa-Su 9am-4pm.) The Felixstowe TIC is on the seafront. (☎01394 276 770. Open daily 9am-5:30pm.)

CAMBRIDGESHIRE

CAMBRIDGE   ☎(0)1223

Unlike museum-oriented, metropolitan Oxford, Cambridge is a town for students before tourists. It was here that Newton's gravity, Watson and Crick's model of DNA, Byron and Milton's poetry, and Winnie the Pooh were born. No longer the exclusive academy of upper-class sons, the university feeds the minds of women, international, and state-school pupils alike. At exams' end, Cambridge explodes in Pimm's-soaked glee, and May Week is a swirl of parties and celebration on the River Cam.

⌐ TRANSPORTATION

Bicycles are the primary mode of transportation in Cambridge, a city that claims more bikes per person than any other place in Britain. If you are prepared to face the maze of one-way streets by driving to Cambridge, take advantage of its efficient park-and-ride system.

Trains: Station (obviously) on Station Rd. Ticket office open daily 5am-11pm. Trains (☎08457 484 950) run to **London King's Cross** (45min., 3 per hr., £18) and **Ely** (20min., 3 per hr., round-trip £3.30).

Buses: Station on Drummer St. Ticket booth open M-Sa 8:45am-5:30pm; tickets often available onboard. National Express (☎08705 808 080) buses and airport shuttles pick up at stands on Parkside St. along Parker's Piece park. Buses to: **London Victoria** (3hr., every hr., £11); **Gatwick** (4hr., every hr., £30.50); **Heathrow** (2½hr., 2 per hr., £26); **Stansted** (1hr., every hr., £10). Stagecoach Express (☎01604 676 060) runs to **Oxford** (3hr., every hr., from £6.50).

Public Transportation: Stagecoach (☎01223 423 578) runs CitiBus from the train station to the city center and around town (£5 for all-day ticket).

Taxis: Cabco (☎01223 312 444) and **Camtax** (☎01223 313 131). Both 24hr.

Bike Rental: Mike's Bikes, 28 Mill Rd. (☎01223 312 591). £10 per day; £35 deposit. Lock included. Open M and F 9am-6pm, Sa 9am-5pm, Su 10am-4pm. MC/V.

⚔ 🔁 ORIENTATION AND PRACTICAL INFORMATION

Cambridge has two central avenues; the main shopping street starts at **Magdalene Bridge** and becomes **Bridge Street, Sidney Street, Saint Andrew's Street, Regent Street,** and **Hills Road.** The other main thoroughfare starts as **Saint John's Street,** becoming **Trinity Street, King's Parade,** and **Trumpington Street.** From the Drummer St. bus station, **Emmanuel Street** leads to the shopping district near the TIC. To get to the TIC from the train station, turn right onto Hills Rd. and follow it three quarters of a mile.

Tourist Information Centre: Wheeler St. (☎09065 268 006; www.visitcambridge.org), 1 block south of Market Sq. Books rooms for £3. Cambridge Visitors Card gives city-wide discounts. Sells National Express tickets. Open Easter-Oct. M-F 10am-5:30pm, Sa 10am-5pm, Su 11am-3pm; Nov.-Easter M-F 10am-5:30pm, Sa 10am-5pm.

Tours: 2hr. walking tours leave from the TIC daily (July-Aug. 4 per day). Tours including King's College £10, concessions £8.50, children £5; St. John's College £8.50, concessions £8, children £5. Call for times and tickets (☎01223 457 574). **City Sightseeing** (☎01353 663 659) runs 1hr. hop-on, hop-off bus tours Apr.-Oct. every 15-30min. £10, concessions £7, children £5, families £25.

Budget Travel: STA Travel, 38 Sidney St. (☎01223 366 966; www.statravel.co.uk). Open M-Th 10am-7pm, F-Sa 10am-6pm, Su 11am-5pm.

Currency Exchange: Banks and **ATMs** on Market Sq. **Thomas Cook,** 8 St. Andrew's St. (☎01223 772 299). Open M-Tu and Th-Sa 9am-5pm, W 10am-5pm.

Beyond Tourism: Blue Arrow, 40 St. Andrews St. (☎01223 323 272 or 324 433; www.bluearrow.co.uk). Year-round temp work. Open M-F 8am-6pm.

Luggage Storage: Cambridge Station Cycles (☎01223 307 125), outside the train station. Open M-Tu and Th-F 8am-6pm, W 8am-7pm, Sa 9am-5pm, Su 10am-5pm.

Police: Parkside (☎01223 358 966).

Pharmacy: Boots, 65-67 Sidney St. (☎01223 350 213). Open M 9am-6pm, Tu 8:30am-6pm, W 8:30am-7pm, Th-Sa 8:30am-6pm, Su 11am-5pm.

Hospital: Addenbrookes Hospital, Long Rd. (☎01223 245 151). Take Cambus C1 or C2 from Emmanuel St. (£1) and get off where Hills Rd. intersects Long Rd.

Internet Access: Jaffa Net Cafe, 22 Mill Rd. (☎01223 308 380). From £1 per hr. 10% student discount. Open daily noon-11pm. **Budget Internet Cafe,** 30 Hills Rd. (☎01223 362 214). 3p per min. Open daily 9am-11pm. AmEx/MC/V. **Web and Eat,** 32 Hills Rd. (☎01223 314 168). 60p per 30min. Open daily 8am-11pm.

Post Office: 9-11 St. Andrew's St. (☎08457 223 344). **Bureau de change.** Open M and W-Sa 9am-5:30pm, Tu 9:30am-5:30pm. **Postcode:** CB2 3AA.

🏠 🏫 ACCOMMODATIONS AND CAMPING

Demand for accommodations in Cambridge is always high, and rooms are scarce. John Maynard Keynes, who studied and taught at Cambridge, tells us that low supply and high demand usually mean one thing: high prices. B&Bs gather around **Portugal Street** and **Tenison Road** outside the city center.

Tenison Towers Guest House, 148 Tenison Rd. (☎01223 363 924; www.cambridgecitytenisontowers.com), 2 blocks from train station. Sunny rooms and freshly baked muffins in a Victorian house. Singles £35-40; doubles £60. Cash only. ❹

YHA Cambridge, 97 Tenison Rd. (☎01223 354 601), close to the train station. Relaxed, welcoming atmosphere draws a diverse clientele. 2 TV lounges and kitchen. English breakfast included; other meals available. Lockers (£1) and luggage storage (£1-2). Laundry. Internet £1 per 30 min. Reception 24hr. Dorms £20. MC/V. ❷

EAST ANGLIA

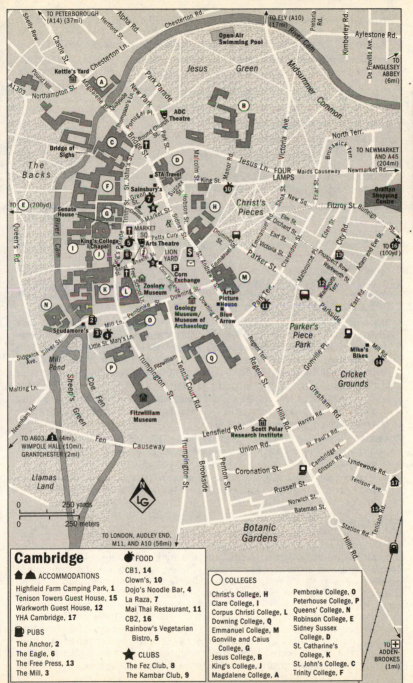

TO PETERBOROUGH (A14) (37mi)
TO ELY (A10) (17mi)
TO ANGLESEY ABBEY (6mi)
TO NEWMARKET AND A45 (204mi)
Newmarket Rd.
Grafton Shopping Centre
TO 16 (100yd)
Fitzroy St.
Four Lamps
Christ's Pieces
Jesus Green
Open Air Swimming Pool
Jesus Lane
Midsummer Common
River Cam
The Backs
Kettle's Yard
Bridge of Sighs
ADC Theatre
STA Travel
Sainsbury's
Senate House
King's College Chapel
Market Sq.
Arts Theatre
Lion Yard
Corn Exchange
Zoology Museum
Geology Museum/Museum of Archaeology
Arts Picture House
Blue Arrow
Scudamore's
Mike's Bikes
Cricket Grounds
Parker's Piece Park
Mill Pond
Fitzwilliam Museum
Scott Polar Research Institute
Llamas Land
Botanic Gardens
TO A603, WIMPOLE HALL (10mi), GRANTCHESTER (2mi)
TO LONDON, AUDLEY END, M11, AND A10 (56mi)
TO ADDENBROOKES (1mi)

0 250 yards
0 250 meters

Cambridge

🏠 ACCOMMODATIONS
Highfield Farm Camping Park, 1
Tenison Towers Guest House, 15
Warkworth Guest House, 12
YHA Cambridge, 17

🍺 PUBS
The Anchor, 2
The Eagle, 6
The Free Press, 13
The Mill, 3

🍴 FOOD
CB1, 14
Clown's, 10
Dojo's Noodle Bar, 4
La Raza, 7
Mai Thai Restaurant, 11
CB2, 16
Rainbow's Vegetarian Bistro, 5

★ CLUBS
The Fez Club, 8
The Kambar Club, 9

○ COLLEGES
Christ's College, H
Clare College, I
Corpus Christi College, L
Downing College, Q
Emmanuel College, M
Gonville and Caius College, G
Jesus College, B
King's College, J
Magdalene College, A

Pembroke College, O
Peterhouse College, P
Queens' College, N
Robinson College, E
Sidney Sussex College, D
St. Catharine's College, K
St. John's College, C
Trinity College, F

Warkworth Guest House, Warkworth Terr. (☎01223 363 682). Spacious ensuite rooms near the bus station in a Victorian mansion. Breakfast included. Free Wi-Fi in lounge. Singles £55; twins and doubles £75; ensuite triples £90; families £95. MC/V. ❹

Highfield Farm Camping Park, Long Rd., Comberton (☎01223 262 308; www.highfield-farmtouringpark.co.uk). Take Cambus #18 to Comberton (every 45min.) from Drummer St. Showers and laundry. July-Aug. £12.50-13.50; Sept. and May-June £11.50 per person; Oct. and Apr. £10 per person. Electricity £3. Cash only. ❶

◪ FOOD

Market Square has bright pyramids of cheap fruit and vegetables. (Open M-Sa 9:30am-5pm.) Get groceries at **Sainsbury's,** 44 Sidney St. (☎01223 366 891. Open M-Sa 8am-10pm, Su 11am-5pm.) Cheap Indian and Mediterranean fare on the edges of the city center satisfies hearty appetites. South of town, **Hills Road** and **Mill Road** are full of budget restaurants popular with the college crowd.

CB2, 5-7 Norfolks St. (☎01223 508 503). Try the salmon niçoise or goat cheese parcels. Entrees are classy but a little pricey (£15). Open daily 10am-midnight. Cash only. ❸

CB1, 32 Mill Rd. (☎01223 576 306). A student hangout coffee shop with piping hot drinks (£1-2) and walls crammed with books. Enjoy free Wi-Fi while lounging on couches. Open M-Th 9am-8pm, F 9am-9pm, Sa-Su 10am-8pm. ❶

Clown's, 54 King St. (☎01223 355 711). The staff at this cozy Italian eatery will remember your name if you come more than once. Children's artwork plasters the orange walls. Huge portions of pasta and dessert (£2.50-7). Set menu includes a drink, salad, small pasta, and cake (£6.50). Open M-Sa 8am-midnight, Su 8am-11pm. Cash only. ❶

Dojo's Noodle Bar, 1-2 Mill Ln. (☎01223 363 471; www.dojonoodlebar.co.uk). Rave reviews bring long lines, but the enormous plates of wok-fried, soup-based, and sauce-based noodles are served quickly from the counter. Wide selection of vegetarian options and rice dishes. Everything under £7. Open M-Th noon-2:30pm and 5:30-11pm, F noon-4pm and 5:30-11pm, Sa-Su noon-11pm. MC/V. ❶

Mai Thai Restaurant, Park Terr. (☎01223 367 480; www.mai-thai-restaurant.com). This stylish, colorful restaurant with great views across Parker's Piece serves authentic Thai food with fresh ingredients. Entrees £7-16. Popular set lunch menu £10. Open daily noon-3pm and 6-11pm. AmEx/MC/V. ❸

Rainbow's Vegetarian Bistro, 9A King's Parade (☎01223 321 551; www.rainbowcafe.co.uk). Even carnivores enjoy this basement bistro. Serves Asian-inspired vegetarian fare, all for £8.40. Open Tu-Sa 10am-10pm. Kitchen open until 9:30pm. Cash only. ❷

La Raza, 4 Rose Crescent (☎01223 464 550; www.laraza.co.uk). Throbbing with live music every night. Affordable tapas menu (£3-14). Long glittering bar gilded with blue light. Open M-Th 9am-1am, F-Sa 9am-2am, Su 9am-midnight. MC/V. ❷

◎ SIGHTS

Cambridge is an architect's utopia, packing some of England's most amazing monuments into less than 1 sq. mi. The soaring King's College Chapel and St. John's Bridge of Sighs are sightseeing staples, while more obscure college quads open onto ornate courtyards and gardens. Most historic buildings are on the east bank of the Cam between Magdalene Bridge and Silver St. On the west bank, the meadowed Backs border the elegant Fellows' Gardens, giving the university a unique juxtaposition of cow and college. The **University of Cambridge** has three eight-week terms: Michaelmas (Oct.-Dec.), Lent (Jan.-Mar.), and Easter (Apr.-June). Visitors can access most of the 31 colleges daily, although times vary; call the TIC for hours. Many are closed to sightseers during Easter term, virtually all are closed during exams (from mid-May to mid-June), and visiting hours are limited during May Week festivities. A visit to King's, Trinity, and Saint John's Colleges should top your to-do list, as should a stroll or punt along the Cam. Porters (bowler-wearing ex-servicemen) maintain security. The fastest way to blow your tourist cover is to trample the grass of the courtyards, a privilege reserved for the elite. In July and August, most undergrads skip town, leaving it to PhD candidates, international students, and mobs of tourists.

COLLEGES

KING'S COLLEGE. King's College was founded by Henry VI in 1441 as a partner school to Eton: it was not until 1873 that students from schools other than Eton were admitted. Today, however, King's is the most socially liberal of the Cambridge colleges, drawing more of its students from state schools than any other. Its most stunning attraction is the Gothic **King's College Chapel.** From the southwest corner of the courtyard, you can see where Henry's master mason left off and the Tudors began work—the earlier stone is off-white. Inside, painted angels hover against the world's largest fan-vaulted ceiling. The nave is decorated with all the symbols of the triumphant Tudor family: wide-petaled roses, snarling dragons, and unicorns. Behind the altar hangs Peter Paul Rubens's painting *Adoration of the Magi* (1639). John Maynard Keynes, EM Forster, and Salman Rushdie all lived in King's College. In mid-June, university degree ceremonies are held in the Georgian Senate House. (*King's Parade.* ☎ 01223 331 100. *Chapel and grounds open M-Sa 9:30am-5pm, Su 10am-5pm. Last entry 4:30pm. Contact TIC for tours. Listing of services and musical events available at porter's lodge. Choral services 10:30am, often 5:30pm. £5, students £3.50. Audio tour £2.50.*)

TRINITY COLLEGE. Henry VIII intended the College of the Holy and Undivided Trinity (founded 1546) to be the largest and richest in Cambridge. Currently Britain's third-largest landowner (after the queen and the Church of England), the college has amply fulfilled his wish. The alma mater of Sir Isaac Newton, who lived in E staircase for 30 years, the college has many other equally illustrious alumni: literati Dryden, Byron, Tennyson, and Nabokov; atom-splitter Ernest Rutherford; philosopher Ludwig Wittgenstein; and Indian statesman Jawaharlal Nehru. The **Great Court,** the world's largest enclosed courtyard, is reached from Trinity St. through **Great Gate.** The castle-like gateway is fronted by a statue of Henry VIII grasping a wood chair leg—the original scepter was stolen so frequently that the college administration removed it. The apple tree near the gate supposedly descended from the tree that inspired Newton's theory of gravity; in the north cloister of **Nevile's Court,** Newton calculated the speed of sound by stamping his foot and timing the echo. On the west side of the court stand the dour **chapel** and the **King's Gate tower.** Lord Byron used to bathe nude in the **fountain,** the only one in Cambridge. The poet also kept a bear as a pet (college rules only forbade cats and dogs). The south side of the court is home to the **Master's Lodge** and the **Great Hall.** The **Wren Library** houses alumnus AA Milne's handwritten copies of *Winnie the Pooh* and Newton's personal copy of his *Principia*. Pass through the drab **New Court** (Prince Charles's former residence) to get to the **Backs,** where you can enjoy the view from **Trinity Bridge.** (*Trinity St.* ☎ 01223 338 400. *Chapel and courtyard open daily 10am-5pm. Easter-Oct. £2.50, concessions £1.30, children £1, families £4.40; Nov.-Easter free for all.*)

SAINT JOHN'S COLLEGE. Established in 1511 by Lady Margaret Beaufort, mother of Henry VIII, St. John's centers on a paved plaza rather than a grassy courtyard. The **Bridge of Sighs,** named after the Venetian original, connects the older part of the college with the towering Neo-Gothic extravagance of **New Court.** The **School of Pythagoras,** a 12th-century pile of wood and stone thought to be the oldest complete building in Cambridge, hides in St. John's Gardens. The college also boasts the longest room in the city—the **Fellows' Room** in Second Court spans 93 ft. and was the site of D-Day planning. *(St. John's St. ☎01223 338 600. Open M-F 10am-5:30pm, Sa-Su 9:30am-5:30pm. Evensong Tu-Su 6:30pm. £2.80.)*

QUEENS' COLLEGE. Aptly named Queens' College was founded by two queens: Queen Margaret of Anjou in 1448 and Elizabeth Woodville (queen consort of Edward VI) in 1465. Queens' College has the only unaltered Tudor courtyard in Cambridge, but the main attraction is the **Mathematical Bridge.** *(Silver St. ☎01223 335 511. Open Mar.-Oct. M-F 10am-4:30pm, Sa-Su 9:30am-5pm. £2.)*

CLARE COLLEGE. Clare's coat of arms—golden teardrops ringing a black border—recalls the college's founding in 1326 by thrice-widowed, 29-year-old Lady Elizabeth de Clare. The college has some of the most cheerful **gardens** in Cambridge, and elegant **Clare Bridge,** dating from 1638, is the oldest surviving college bridge. Walk through Christopher Wren's **Old Court** for a view of the **University Library,** where 82 mi. of shelves hold books arranged by size rather than subject. *(Trinity Ln. ☎01223 333 200. Open daily 10:45am-4:30pm. £3, under 10 free.)*

CHRIST'S COLLEGE. Founded as "God's house" in 1448 and renamed in 1505, Christ's has since won fame for its **gardens** and its association with John Milton and Charles Darwin. Darwin's rooms (unmarked and closed to visitors) were in G staircase in First Court. **New Court,** on King St., is one of Cambridge's most modern structures, with symmetrical concrete walls and dark windows. Bowing to pressure from aesthetically offended Cantabrigians, the college built a wall to block the view of the building from all sides except the inner courtyard. *(St. Andrews St. ☎01223 334 900. Gardens open daily term time 9am-4:30pm; summer 9:30am-noon. Fellows' Garden open M-F 9:30am-noon. Free.)*

JESUS COLLEGE. Beyond the walk called the "Chimney" lies a courtyard fringed with flowers. Through the arch on the right sit the remains of a gloomy medieval nunnery. *(Jesus Ln. ☎01223 339 339. Courtyard open daily 9am-8pm.)*

MAGDALENE COLLEGE. Located within a 15th-century Benedictine hostel, Magdalene (MAUD-lin) was the occasional home of Christian allegorist and Oxford man CS Lewis. **Pepys Library,** in the second court, displays the famous diarist's collections, including the five journals written in his private shorthand code. *(Magdalene St. ☎01223 332 100. Library open M-Sa Easter-Aug. 11:30am-12:30pm and 2:30-3:30pm; Sept.-Easter 2:30-3:30pm. Courtyard open daily until 6pm. Free.)*

SMALLER COLLEGES. Thomas Gray wrote his "Elegy Written in a Country Churchyard" while staying in **Peterhouse College,** the smallest college, founded in 1294. *(Trumpington St. ☎01223 338 200.)* The modern brick pastiche of **Robinson College** is the newest. In 1977, local self-made man David Robinson founded it for the bargain price of £17 million, the largest single gift ever received by the university. *(Across the river on Grange Rd. ☎01223 339 100.)* **Corpus Christi College,** founded in 1352 by the townspeople, contains the oldest courtyard in Cambridge, aptly named Old Court and unaltered since its enclosure. The library has a huge collection of Anglo-Saxon manuscripts. Alums include Sir Francis Drake and Christopher Marlowe. *(Trumpington St. ☎01223 338 000.)* The 1347 **Pembroke College** holds the earliest work of Sir Christopher Wren and counts Edmund Spenser among its grads. *(Next to Corpus Christi. ☎01223 338 100.)* A chapel designed by Wren dominates the front court of **Emmanuel College,** known as "Emma." John Harvard, benefactor of a different university in a different Cambridge, studied here and is commemorated in a stained-glass window in the chapel. *(St. Andrews St. ☎01223 334 200.)* **Gonville and Caius College** (KEYS) was founded twice, once in 1348 by Edmund Gonville and again in 1557 by John Keys, who chose to use the Latin form of his name. *(Trinity St. ☎01223 332 400.)*

MUSEUMS AND CHURCHES

⬛FITZWILLIAM MUSEUM. The museum fills an immense Neoclassical building, built in 1875 to house Viscount Fitzwilliam's collections. Egyptian, Chinese, Japanese, Middle Eastern, and Greek antiquities downstairs are joined by 16th-century German armor. Upstairs, galleries feature works by Rubens, Monet, Van Gogh, and Picasso. *(Trumpington St. ☎01223 332 900. Open Tu-Sa 10am-5pm, Su noon-5pm. Call about lunchtime and evening concerts. Suggested donation £3.)*

OTHER SIGHTS. For those with a green thumb, the **Botanic Garden** displays over 8000 plant species and was opened in 1846 by John Henslow, Darwin's mentor. *(☎01223 336 265. Open daily Apr.-Sept. 10am-6pm; Oct. and Feb.-Mar. 10am-5pm, Nov.-Jan. 10am-4pm. £4, concessions £3.50.)* **Kettle's Yard,** at the corner of Castle and Northampton St., was founded by former Tate curator Jim Ede and displays extensive early-20th-century art. *(☎01223 352 124; www.kettlesyard.org.uk. House open Apr.-Sept. Tu-Su 1:30-4:30pm; Oct.-Mar. Tu-Su 2-4pm. Gallery open Tu-Su 11:30am-5pm. Free.)* The **Scott Polar Research Institute** commemorates Arctic expeditions with photos and memorabilia. *(Lensfield Rd. ☎01223 336 540; www.spri.cam.ac.uk. Open Tu-F 11am-1pm and 2-4pm, Sa noon-4pm. Free.)* The **Round Church (Holy Sepulchre),** where Bridge St. meets St. John's St., is one of five surviving circular churches in England and the second-oldest building in Cambridge, predating even the university. Built in 1130, it is based on the pattern of the Holy Sepulchre in Jerusalem. *(☎01223 311 602. Open M and Su 1-5pm, Tu-Sa 10am-5pm. £2, students and children free. Tours W 11am, Su 2:30pm. £3.50.)* The only older building is **Saint Benet's,** a Saxon church on Benet St., built in 1025. *(☎01223 353 903. Open daily 8am-6pm. Free.)* The tower of **Great Saint Mary's Church,** off King's Parade, gives views of the colleges. Pray that the 12 bells don't ring while you're ascending the 123 tightly packed spiral steps. *(Tower open M-Sa 9:30am-4:30pm, Su 12:30-4pm. £2.50, children £1.25. Church free.)*

🎵 ENTERTAINMENT

CINEMA AND THEATER

The **Arts Box Office** (☎01223 503 333; open M-Sa noon-8pm), around the corner from the TIC on Pea's Hill, handles ticket sales for the **Arts Theatre,** which shows musicals, dramas, and pantomime. The **ADC Theatre** (Amateur Dramatic Club), Park St. (☎01223 359 547), puts up student-produced plays, term-time movies, and a folk festival during the summer months. The **Corn Exchange,** at the corner of Wheeler St. and Corn Exchange St. across from the TIC, is a popular venue for concerts. (☎01223 357 851. £10-30, concessions available. Box office open M-Sa 10am-6pm, until 9pm on performance days; Su 6-9pm on performance days only.) Independent and foreign-language films play at the **Arts Picture House,** 38-39 St. Andrews St. (☎01223 042 050; www.picturehouses. co.uk. M-F £6.40, Sa-Su £7.40, students £5.50.)

⬛PUNTING

Punting on the Cam is as traditional and obligatory as afternoon tea. Touristy and overrated? Maybe, but it's still a blast. Punters take two routes—from Magdalene Bridge to Silver St. or from Silver St. to Grantchester. The shorter, busier, and more interesting first route passes the colleges and the Backs. To propel your boat, thrust the pole behind the boat into the riverbed and rotate the pole in your hands as you push forward. Punt-bombing—jumping from bridges into the river alongside a punt to tip it—is an art form. Some more ambitious punters climb out midstream, scale a bridge while their boat passes underneath, and jump back down from the other side. Be wary of bridge-top pole-stealers. You can rent at **Scudamore's,** Silver St. Bridge. (☎01223 359 750;

TOP TEN LIST

RULES OF THE PUB

British pubs are governed by a set of complex and often unwritten rules. Here's a primer to help you avoid some common mistakes:

1. If you expect someone to come around to your seat, you might be waiting for some time. At most British pubs, you order at the bar.
2. So you've gotten up to go to the bar. But, before you go, check your table number so that the server knows where to bring your food.
3. Get your wallet out right away, as most pubs require payment when you place your order.
4. In groups, it's common to buy drinks in rounds. One person goes to the bar and buys drinks for the whole table, someone else buys the next round, and so on.
5. Put away that pack of cigarettes—as of 2007, it's illegal to smoke in enclosed public spaces.
6. Don't jump the invisible queue. Even if patrons aren't physically lining up to buy drinks, the bartender usually serves them in the order they come to the bar.
7. Don't tip as you leave. If you're impressed by the service, offer to buy the bartender a drink.
8. Pubs don't open before 11am, before which time you probably shouldn't be drinking anyway.
9. You may have seen a pub called the "Red Lion" or the "White Horse" in several towns, but they're not related to one another.
10. Keep your eyes on the clock. Licencing laws require most pubs to close by 11pm, so be sure to heed the call for "last orders" (sometimes indicated by a bell).

www.scudamores.com. M-F £18 per hr., Sa-Su £20 per hr. £70 deposit. MC/V.) Student-punted tours (£12, students £10) are another option.

PUBS AND NIGHTLIFE

King Street has a diverse collection of pubs. Most stay open 11am-11pm (Su noon-10:30pm). The local brewery, **Greene King,** supplies many of them. Pubs are the core of Cambridge nightlife, but clubs are also in the curriculum. The city is small enough that a quick stroll will reveal popular venues.

The Anchor, Silver St. (☎01223 353 554). This jolly-looking pub, overflowing with beer and good cheer, is anchored right on the Cam. Savor a pint in the same spot that Pink Floyd's Syd Barrett drew his inspiration or scoff at amateur punters colliding under Silver St. Bridge. Open M-W and Su 11am-11pm, Th-Sa 11am-midnight. Kitchen open M-Sa noon-10pm, Su noon-9pm.

The Mill, 14 Mill Ln. (☎01223 357 026), off Silver St. Bridge. Low ceilings, wood interior, and great beer. Patrons relax outside for punt- and people-watching. Features a rotating selection of ales. Open M-Th noon-11pm, F noon-midnight, Sa 11am-midnight, Su 11am-11pm. Kitchen open M-F noon-2:30pm and 6-8:30pm, Sa-Su noon-4pm.

The Free Press, Prospect Row (☎01223 368 337). Named after an abolitionist rag and popular with locals. No pool table, no cell phones, no overwhelming music—just good beer and entertaining conversation. Open M-F noon-2:30pm and 6-11pm, Sa noon-3pm and 6-11pm, Su noon-3pm and 7-10:30pm.

The Eagle, 8 Benet St. (☎01223 505 020). Cambridge's oldest pub (in business since 1525) is located in the heart of town and packed with boisterous tourists. When Watson and Crick rushed in to announce their discovery of DNA, the barmaid insisted they settle their 4-shilling tab before she'd serve them. Check out the RAF room, where WWII pilots stood on each other's shoulders to burn their initials into the ceiling. Open M-Sa 11am-11pm, Su noon-10:30pm.

The Fez Club, 15 Market Passage (☎01223 519 224; www.cambridgefez.com). Moroccan setting complete with floor cushions. Dance to everything from Latin to trance. Cover M-Th £2-5, F-Sa £5-7; students free W before 11pm. Open M-Sa 10pm-3am.

The Kambar Club, 1 Wheeler St. (☎01223 842 725), opposite the Corn Exchange box office. A mix of indie and electronica tunes. Drinks can be expensive sometimes, but the club's energy is great on weekends. Cover £5, students £3. Open M-Sa 10pm-2:30am.

❋ FESTIVALS

May Week is actually in June—you would think that all those bright Cambridge students would understand a calendar. A celebration of the end of the term, the week is crammed with concerts, plays, and balls followed by recuperative riverside breakfasts and 5am punting. The boat clubs compete in races known as the **bumps.** Crews attempt to ram the boat in front before being bumped from behind. The celebration includes **Footlights Revue,** a series of skits by current undergrads. Past performers have included future *Monty Python* stars John Cleese and Eric Idle. Guests can partake in the festivities for a mere £250.

Midsummer Fair, dating from the 16th century, fills the Midsummer Common with carnival rides and wholesome fun for five days during the third week of June. (☎01223 457 555; www.cambridge-summer.co.uk.) The free **Strawberry Fair** (www.strawberry-fair.org), on the first Saturday in June, attracts a crowd with food, music, and body piercing. **Summer in the City** (www.cambridge-summer.co.uk) keeps Cambridge buzzing with a series of concerts and special exhibits culminating in a huge weekend celebration, the **Cambridge Folk Festival** (☎01223 357 851; www.cambridgefolkfestival.co.uk) on the last weekend of July. World-renowned musicians—with past performers such as James Taylor and Elvis Costello—gather for folk, jazz, and blues in Cherry Hinton Hall. Book tickets (about £43) well in advance; camping on the grounds is an additional £10-30. The **Cambridge Shakespeare Festival** (www.cambridgeshakespeare.com), in association with the festival at Oxford, features plays throughout July and August. Tickets (£12, concessions £9) are available at the door and from the City Centre Box Office at the Corn Exchange.

▶ DAYTRIPS FROM CAMBRIDGE

GRANTCHESTER

Take the marked path to Grantchester Meadows following the river. Grantchester village lies 1 mi. from the meadows; ask the way or follow the blue bike path signs (1½hr. by foot from Cambridge). If you have the energy to paddle your way, rent a punt or canoe. You can also hop on Stagecoach #18 or 18A (9-11 per day, round-trip £3).

"Grantchester! Ah Grantchester! There's peace and holy quiet there," wrote poet Rupert Brooke in 1912, and his words hold true today. This sweet, unsullied piece of bucolic England is still a mecca for Cambridge literary types. The golden meadows banking the Cam are a refuge from the university's intensity. The 14th-century **Parish Church of Saint Andrew and Saint Mary,** on Millway, is weathered and intimate. (☎01223 840 460. Free.) Have tea among the apple trees at lovely ▓**Orchard Tea Gardens ❶,** 45 Millway, once a haunt of the "neo-pagans," a Grantchester offshoot of the famous Bloomsbury Group. Start your morning with scones (£2) and end your day with one of the occasional summer plays put on there. (☎01223 845 788; www.orchard-grantchester.com. Open daily 9:30am-7pm.) The main village pub, the **Rupert Brooke ❷,** 2 Broadway, is striving to improve the reputation of British cuisine. Its large beer garden overlooks Grantchester meadows. (☎01223 840 295; www.therupertbrooke.com. Open M-Sa noon-9:30pm, Su noon-8pm.)

ANGLESEY ABBEY

6 mi. northeast of Cambridge on the B1102 (signposted from A14). Bus #10 runs from Drummer St. (30min., 2 per hr.); ask to be let off at Lode Crossroads. ☎01223 810 080. House open Mar.-Nov. W-Su and bank holidays 1-5pm. Gardens open Apr.-Oct. W-Su and bank holidays 10:30am-5:30pm. £9.25, children £4.65. Garden and mill without house £5.50, children £2.75. Winter Garden Jan.-Mar. £4.40/£2.20; Nov.-Dec. £4.75/£2.40.

Northeast of Cambridge, 12th-century Anglesey Abbey has been remodeled to house the priceless exotica of the first Lord Fairhaven. The abbey has a collection of over 50 clocks, including the mesmerizing Congreve rolling ball clock in the library. If you have the time (get it?), make your own scavenger hunt and try to find all 50. After contemplating the 7000 volumes on the bookshelves, stroll through the 98 acres of gardens, where trees and statues punctuate lines of clipped hedges and manicured lawns.

AUDLEY END AND SAFFRON WALDEN

Trains leave Cambridge for Audley End (15min., 3 per hr., round-trip £5). ☎01799 522 399. House open Apr.-Sept. W-F and Su 11am-5pm, Sa 11am-3pm. Grounds open W-Su Apr.- Sept. 10am-5pm; Oct. and Mar. 10am-4pm. Last entry 1hr. before close. House can only be viewed as part of a 1hr. guided tour, 10 per day. £10.50, concessions £8.

The magnificent Jacobean hall is only a quarter of Audley End's former size—it once extended down to the river, where part of the Cam was rerouted into an artificial lake. The grand halls display cases of stuffed critters, including some extinct species, amid paintings by Canaletto and Han Holbein the Younger. One mile east of Audley End is the town of **Saffron Walden,** best known for the pargeting (plaster molding) of its Tudor buildings. The town holds a Victorian hedge maze as well as England's largest turf maze, located on the town common. The **Tourist Information Centre** is on Market Sq. (☎01799 510 444. Open Easter-Aug. M-Sa 9:30am-5:30pm, Su 10:30am-1pm; Sept.-Oct. M-Sa 9:30am-5:30pm; Nov.- Mar. M-Sa 10am-5pm.) If you stay for the night, rest at the **YHA hostel ❶**, 1 Myddylton Pl. (☎0870 770 6014. Lockout 10am-5pm. Curfew 11pm. Open July-Aug. daily; Sept.-Oct. and Apr.-June Tu-Sa; Mar. F-Sa. Dorms £14. MC/V.)

ELY ☎(0)1353

The prosperous town of Ely (EEL-ee) was an island until steam power drained the surrounding fenlands in the early 1800s, creating a flat, reed-covered region of rich farmland. Legend has it that the city got its name when St. Dunstan transformed local monks into eels for their lack of piety. A more likely story is that "Elig" (Isle of Eels) was named for the bountiful slitherers that infested the surrounding waters—they were once so numerous that taxes were payable in eels. Today, Ely remains proud of its eel-inspired heritage. The local market sells them fresh from the Great River Ouse, Eel Day celebrates the city's history, and the Eel Heritage Walk snakes through all of the city's major sights.

█ TRANSPORTATION. Ely is the junction for **trains** (☎08457 484 950) between London (1¼hr., 2 per hr., £21) and various points in East Anglia, including Cambridge (15min., 3 per hr., round-trip £3.30) and Norwich (1hr., 2 per hr., £13.50). Cambus **buses** (☎01223 423 554) #9, X9, and 12 leave from Market St. to Cambridge (50min., 1 per hr., £3.70). **Walking** from Cambridge to Ely is also possible, a 17 mi. trek through the flat fens. Ask at the TIC in Cambridge or Ely for a copy of the helpful guide *The Fen Rivers Way* (£2).

█ █ ORIENTATION AND PRACTICAL INFORMATION. Ely's two major streets—**High Street** and **Market Street**—run parallel to the length of the cathedral. To reach the cathedral from the train station, walk up Station Rd., which changes to Back Hill and then to The Gallery. Oliver Cromwell's house is the current home of the **Tourist Information Centre,** 29 St. Mary's St., which books rooms for £2 plus a 10% deposit; call at least two days ahead. (☎01353 662 062. Open Apr.-Oct. daily 10am-5pm; Nov.-Mar. M-F and Su 11am-4pm, Sa 10am-5pm.) Other services include: **Internet** access at the **library,** 6 The Cloisters, just off Market Pl. (☎01353 616 158; Internet 50p per 10min.; open Tu-W and F 10am-5pm, Th 9:30am-8pm, Sa 9:30am-4pm, Su noon-4pm); **police,** Nutholt Ln. (☎0845 456 4564); **Prince of Wales Hospital,** Lynn Rd. (☎01353 652 000); and the **post office,** 19-21 High St. (☎01353 669 946; open M and Th-F 9am-5:30pm, W 9:30am-5:30pm, Sa 9am-1pm). **Postcode:** CB7 4LQ.

⬛⬛ ACCOMMODATIONS AND FOOD. Ely has few single rooms—your best bet is the TIC accommodations booking service. **The Post House ❸,** 12A Egremont St., is a family home close to the city center. (☎01353 667 184. Singles £27; doubles £54, ensuite £60. Cash only.) Find spacious, ensuite rooms in an Edwardian house at **57 Lynn Road ❸,** just steps away from the cathedral. (☎01353 744 662. Doubles and twins from £57.)

Many shops close on Tuesday afternoons, as they have for centuries. Stock up on provisions at the **market** in Market Pl. (Open Th and Sa 8am-3pm.) **Tesco** supermarket, Angel Drove, is next to the train station and has ATMs outside. (☎08456 779 256. Open 24hr. except Sa 10pm-10am, Su 4pm-8am. AmEx/ MC/V.) Don't miss the Tea Guild's "Top Tearoom of 2007," ⬛**Peacocks Tearoom ❶,** 65 Waterside, near the Babylon Gallery on the River Ouse. The teacup-size shop has over 50 varieties of teas (£2.25) and sweet and savory snacks for £4-7. (☎01353 661 100; www.peacockstearoom.co.uk. Open W-Su 10:30am-5pm.) Although the river no longer oozes eels, the **Old Fire Engine House ❸,** 25 St. Mary's St., often features the delicacy on its constantly changing menu. Appropriate to the fire station setting, no smoking is allowed. The handwritten menu of the day is posted in the window. (☎01353 662 582. Entrees £16. Lighter fare £6-10. Open M-Sa 10:30-11:30am, 12:15-2pm, 3:45-5:30pm, 7:15-9pm; Su 12:15-2pm and 4-5:30pm. MC/V.) Affordable Indian restaurants line **Backhill Street.**

◨ SIGHTS. Let the tower of ⬛**Ely Cathedral** guide you to the city center. When lit, it can be seen for miles. The Saxon princess St. Etheldreda founded a monastery on the site in AD 673. Norman masons took a century to construct the nave, and Victorian artists painted the ceiling and completed the stained glass. The **Octagon** replaced the original tower, which collapsed in 1322. Don't overlook the 215 ft. tiled **floor maze** or the movingly spare **Lady Chapel,** shorn of its original statuary. (☎01353 667 735. Open Apr.-Sept. daily 7am-7pm; Oct.-Mar. M-F 7:30am-6pm, Su 7:30am-5pm. Octagon tours Apr.-Oct. 3 per day; Nov.-Mar. call ahead. West Tower tours Apr.-Oct. subject to guide availability. Evensong M-Sa 5:30pm, Su 3:45pm. Cathedral £5.50, concessions £4.70. Octagon tours £5, with cathedral entry £4.50. West Tower tours £5, with cathedral entry £4.50.) In the brilliant ⬛**Stained Glass Museum,** in the cathedral, visitors look at eight centuries of kaleidoscopic glass art. One hundred exquisite pieces detail the history of the art form from yellow-toned medieval peasants to Victorian portraits. (☎01353 660 347; www.stainedglassmuseum.com. Open Easter-Oct. M-F 10:30am-5pm, Sa 10:30am-5:30pm, Su noon-6pm; Nov.-Easter M-Sa 10:30am-5pm, Su noon-4:30pm. Last entry 30min. before close. £3.50, concessions £2.50, families £7. Museum and cathedral £8.30, concessions £6.70.) At the **brass rubbing center** in the cathedral, visitors can use chalk and paper to rub copies of engravings. (☎01353 660 345. Open M-Sa 10:30am-4pm, Su noon-3pm. Materials £2-7.)

For an architectural tour of Ely, follow the path outlined in the TIC's free *Eel Trail* pamphlet, which also notes artwork related to the eel. **Oliver Cromwell's House,** 29 St. Mary's St., where the TIC is housed, still retains its 17th-century decor. The moving wax figures portraying Cromwellian domestic life and the distinctly un-creepy "haunted" bedrooms are not as much fun as the dress-up corner, where you can don plumed hats and military helmets. Fish and chips will look positively gourmet after a perusal of Lady Cromwell's recipe for eel pie with oysters. (☎01353 662 062. Open Apr.-Oct. daily 10am-5pm; Nov.-Mar. M-Sa 10am-5pm, Su 11am-4pm. £4.30, concessions £4, children £3, families £12.50. Free audio guide. MC/V for over £10.) **Ely Museum,** at the Bishop's Gaol on the corner of Market St. and Lynn Rd., gives the history of the Fenland city. (☎01353 666 655; www.elymuseum.org.uk. Open in summer M-Sa 10:30am-5pm, Su 1-5pm; in winter M and W-Sa 10:30am-4pm, Su 1-4pm. £3.)

NORFOLK

KING'S LYNN   ☎(0)1553

King's Lynn was one of England's foremost 16th-century ports. Five hundred years later, the once-mighty current of the River Great Ouse has slowed to an ooze, reflecting the pace of the sleepy town. The dockside city's Germanic look was inspired by former trading partners like Hamburg and Bremen. Although the sights are a little insipid, the town makes a perfect stopover for hikers and tourists exploring the region.

TRANSPORTATION. The bus and train stations are near High St. **Trains** (☎08457 484 950) leave from the station on Blackfriars Rd. to: Norwich via Ely (2hr., every hr., £17.80); Cambridge (50min., every hr., £8.30); London King's Cross (1½hr., every hr., from £26); Peterborough (1½hr., every hr., £9.70). **Buses** arrive at the Vancouver Centre in front of Pedlar's Hall. (Office open M-F 9am-5pm.) First Eastern Counties (☎01603 660 553) bus X1 travels from Vancouver Centre to Norwich (1½hr., 2 per hr., £4.50) and Peterborough (1¼hr., 2 per hr., round-trip £7). National Express (☎08705 808 080) runs to London (4hr., 1 per day, £14.20). Buy National Express tickets at the station or from **West Norfolk Travel,** 2 King St. (☎01553 772 910. Open M-F 8am-5:30pm, Sa 8am-4pm. AmEx/MC/V.) For daytrips from King's Lynn to Hunstanton, Sandringham, or Castle Rising, take local buses #40, 41, or 41A from Vancouver Station.

ORIENTATION AND PRACTICAL INFORMATION. King's Lynn's two main streets are **High Street** and **Broad Street** (which becomes Tower St.). These two roads are parallel, intersected perpendicularly by **New Conduit Street,** and pedestrian-only, as is much of the city center. The **Tourist Information Centre,** in the Custom House on the corner of King St. and Purfleet Quay, 10min. from the train station, books rooms for a 10% deposit and supplies bus timetables and free maps. Take a left out of the station and a right onto Blackfriars St., which becomes New Conduit St. and then Purfleet St. (☎01553 763 044. Open Apr.-Sept. M-Sa 10am-5pm, Su noon-5pm; Oct.-Mar. M-Sa 10:30am-4pm, Su noon-4pm.) Other services include: **banks** on High St., with 24hr. **ATMs** outside (☎0845 300 0000; open M-Tu and Th-F 9am-5pm, W 10am-5pm, Sa 9am-3pm); free **Internet** access at the **library,** London Rd. across from The Walks (☎01553 772 568; open M, W, F 9am-8pm, Tu, Th, Sa 9am-5pm); a **launderette,** 20 St. James St. (☎01553 767 164; wash £2, dry £1.80; open daily 7am-9:30pm); **police,** at the corner of St. James and London Rd. (☎01553 691 211); a Boots **pharmacy** on High St. (open M-Sa 8:30am-5:30pm, Su 10am-4pm); the **hospital,** on Gayton Rd. (☎01553 613 613); and the **post office** at the intersection of Norfolk St. and Broad St. (☎08457 223 344; open M-Sa 9am-5:30pm). **Postcode:** PE30HB.

ACCOMMODATIONS AND FOOD. Budget accommodations in King's Lynn are scarce. The quayside **YHA King's Lynn ❶,** College Ln., a 10min. walk from the train and bus stations, occupies part of 16th-century Thoresby College. Exposed wood beams make the rooms feel cabin-esque, but this is the best budget option in town. (☎0870 770 5902. Well-stocked kitchen. Breakfast buffet £4.20. Reception open from 5pm. Open July-Aug. daily; Sept. M-Tu and Su; Easter-June M-Tu and F-Su. Call ahead for availability. Dorms and singles £13, under 18 £9. MC/V.) Most B&Bs are a 10min. walk east of the train station, away from the River Ouse. Several options line Gaywood Rd. and Tennyson Ave. Eight dainty rooms stocked with homemade biscuits await at the **Victorian Fairlight Lodge ❸**, 79 Goodwins Rd. (☎01553 762 234; www.fairlightlodge-online. co.uk. Full breakfast included. Singles £35; doubles and twins £52. Discount for 3 nights or more. Cash only.) The **Maranatha Guest House ❸**, 115-117 Gaywood Rd. has clean rooms with full English breakfast included. (☎01553 774 596. Most rooms ensuite. Singles £30; twins £44, ensuite £46. MC/V.)

Supermarkets congregate around Vancouver Centre. For fresh fruit, visit the large **Tuesday Market Place,** on the north end of High St., or try the **Saturday Market Place** on the south end. Many King's Lynn restaurants close in the middle of the day; even more take Sundays off. For sandwiches (£4.25) and organic juices (from £1.60), try **Norbury's Deli and Cafe ❶**, 21 Tower St. (☎01553 762 804. Open M-Sa 9:30am-5pm. MC/V.) Creamy risottos await at **Antonio's Wine Bar ❷**, an inexpensive Italian bistro at Baxter's Plain, on the corner of Tower and Blackfriars St. (☎01553 772 324. 2-course lunch £6. Entrees £6.50-10.50. Open Tu-Sa noon-3pm and 6:30-11pm. MC/V.) **The Thai Orchid ❷**, 33-39 St. James St., serves authentic Thai dishes for £6-9. Try a three-course lunch for £7 Tuesdays through Thursdays or the bottomless lunch buffets on Saturday and Sunday, also £7. (☎01553 777 662; www.thethaiorchid.com. Open Tu-Th noon-2pm and 6-11pm, F-Sa noon-2pm and 6-11pm, Su noon-2pm and 6-10:30pm. MC/V.)

🔲 🔳 **SIGHTS AND ENTERTAINMENT.** A leisurely walk through the streets lets you see all of King Lynn's main attractions in a day. Take the *King's Lynn Town Walk* booklet (50p at the TIC) with you or head to the **Old Gaol House,** the starting point for 1½hr. guided tours of the town. (June-Sept. Tu and F-Sa 2pm; Oct. Sa 2pm. £3, concessions £2.50, children £1.) Start your walk at the **Tales of the Old Gaol House,** Saturday Market Pl., the former King's Lynn police station. The 200-year-old cells hold role-playing "criminals," while the **Regalia Room** displays treasures in the undercroft. Take home souvenir fingerprints or try out the stocks for a taste of 17th-century justice. (☎01553 774 297. Open Apr.-Oct. M-Sa 10am-5pm; Nov.-Mar. Tu-Sa 10am-4pm. Last entry 1hr. before close. £3, concessions £2.55, children £2.10; Regalia Room free.) Steps away is historic **Saint Margaret's Church,** also on Saturday Market Pl., built in 1101. (☎01553 772 858; www.stmargaretkingslynn.org.uk. Free.) **Greyfriars Tower** sits in the center of town, surrounded by the **Tower Gardens.** Walk up Market St. to the recently re-opened **Lynn Museum,** which displays all you'd ever want to know (and more) about King's Lynn history. (☎01553 775 001. Open Tu-Sa 10am-5pm. Apr.-Sept. £3, concessions £2.50, children £1.65; Oct.-Mar. free.) The **Town House Museum of Lynn Life,** 46 Queen St., showcases doll-size reconstructions of rooms from medieval kitchens to 1950s living rooms. (☎01553 773 450. Open M-Sa May-Sept. 10am-5pm; Oct.-Apr. 10am-4pm. £3, concessions £2.50, children £1.65.)

The **Corn Exchange** at Tuesday Market Pl. sells tickets for music, dance, and theater events. (☎01553 764 864. Open M-Sa 10am-6pm, Su and performance nights 1hr. prior to show. Shows usually 7:30 or 8pm.) Near Tuesday Market Pl., the 15th-century **Guildhall of Saint George,** 27-29 King St., is said to be the last surviving building where Shakespeare appeared in one of his own plays. Inside, find the auditorium and the **King's Lynn Arts Centre.** (☎01553 764 864. Open M-F 10am-2pm. Free.) King's Lynn comes alive during the last two weeks of July, when the Guildhall brings the **King's Lynn Festival** to town. The festival presents international talent from musicians, operas, ballets, puppet shows, and films. Get schedules at the TIC or the Festival Office, 5 Thoresby College, Queen St. (Info ☎01553 767 557, tickets 764 864; www.kingslynnfestival.org.uk. Box office open M-Sa 10am-6pm. Tickets £3-32. Standby tickets available 30min. prior to performance for £5. MC/V with £1 surcharge.) During the second week of July, the streets of Tuesday Market Pl. are overtaken by live entertainment and fireworks during the free **Festival Too.** (☎01553 817 358; www.festivaltoo. co.uk.) Find further information at the TIC or the Corn Exchange.

▶ **DAYTRIP FROM KING'S LYNN: SANDRINGHAM.** Get a taste of royal living at the 60-acre Sandringham estate. The house has been a royal country retreat since 1862; the final version was built in 1870 by the prince and princess of Wales. Today it serves as the wintering grounds for the royal family, who congregates here every year to celebrate Christmas. The main rooms feature delicate tapestries, King Edward II's collection of weaponry, and Queen Victoria's expensive porcelain tea service, painted with the faces of the family dogs. The nearby museum houses an enormously eclectic collection of gifts presented to Queen Elizabeth II by members of the British Commonwealth. Take time to examine a whale's tooth from Fiji, the wood chain carved from a single piece of Australian honeysuckle root, and the award of honor presented to an RAF flying pigeon. In the garages you can see King Edward VII's 1900 car and the cunningly designed "toy" cars made for toddler Prince Charles to drive. Sandringham closes for one week in July; ask the King's Lynn TIC or call for exact dates. *(10 mi. north of King's Lynn. First Eastern Counties bus #411 arrives from King's Lynn. 25 min.; M-Sa 9 per day, Su every hr.; round-trip £3.50. ☎01553 612 908; www.sandringhamestate. co.uk. Open daily Apr.-Sept. 11am-4:45pm; Oct. 11am-3pm. Museum and gardens open daily Apr.-Sept. 11am-5pm; Oct. 11am-4pm. £9, concessions £7, children £5, families £23. Museum and gardens only £6/ 5/3.50/15.50. Guided garden tours F-Sa 11am, 2pm; £2.)*

▶ **DAYTRIP FROM KING'S LYNN: CASTLE RISING.** Queen Isabella, the "She-Wolf of France," was imprisoned here after she conspired with her lover to murder her husband, Edward II of England, in 1326. Stand in the remains of the castle chapel where she spent hours with her priest, confessing her scheme. It remains one of the largest, most intact castles in the country, with several levels of steep, narrow passageways, now green with moss. The free audio tour details tidbits of history along the way, and the castle's defensive earthworks (up to 120 ft. high) provide beautiful views. *(First Eastern Counties buses #41 and 41A run from King's Lynn. 15min.; M-Sa 17 per day, Su 8 per day; round-trip £3.50. ☎01553 631 330; www.castlerising.com. Open Apr.-Sept. daily 10am-6pm; Oct. daily 10am-6pm or dusk; Nov.-Mar. W-Su 10am-4pm. £4; includes audio tour. Ask about night tours, offered every 2 weeks.)*

▶ **DAYTRIP FROM KING'S LYNN: HOUGHTON HALL.** Built in the 1720s for Robert Walpole, England's first prime minister, Houghton Hall is a magnificent example of Palladian architecture. A museum displaying 20,000 model soldiers in battle formations will delight any war hawks. Five acres of gardens are only the beginning—the hall rests on 4500 acres of estate with over 600 deer. *(13 mi. northeast of King's Lynn and 10 mi. southwest of Fakenham, off the A148 toward Cromer. Easily reached by car; otherwise, take the X8 bus (40min., 6 per day, round-trip £3.80) and ask the driver to stop at Houghton Hall, then follow signs for 1 mi. ☎01485 528 569; www.houghtonhall.com. Grounds and museum open Easter-Sept. W-Th and Su 11am-5:30pm. House open Easter-Sept. W-Th and Su 1:30-5pm. Last entry 4:30pm. £8, children £3, families £20. Grounds only £5.)*

THE NORTHERN NORFOLK COAST

The northern Norfolk Coast is a tranquil expanse of British shoreline full of untamed beaches, salt marshes, and boggy bays punctuated only by the occasional windmill or mansion. Those with a week to spare can traverse the linked 93 mi. of the **Norfolk Coast Path** and **Peddar's Way** (p. 325), two relatively easy treks. The Peddar's Way, an old Roman road to the coast, begins in **Knettishall Heath Country Park,** extending through **Little Cressingham, North Peckenham,** and the medieval ruins of **Castle Acre,** meeting the Norfolk Coast Path between Hunstanton and Brancaster. The Norfolk Coast Path begins 16 mi. north of King's Lynn at Hunstanton, stretches east to **Wells-next-the-Sea, Sheringham,** and the **Norfolk Broads** (p. 344) before finishing in **Cromer.** The trail and its villages are also fine daytrips from both Norwich and King's Lynn. The **Norfolk Coast Hopper** (☎0870 608 2608) follows the coastline and makes numerous stops between Hunstanton and Sheringham (1½hr.; in summer every 2hr., in winter less frequent; all-day ticket £5). **Searles** runs sea tours from Hunstanton Central Promenade. (☎01485 534 444, www.seatours.co.uk. £7-12, children £3.50-6. Book in advance.) The highlight of the coast is ◼**Blakeney Point Seal Colony.** Although the colony is accessible by a 4 mi. footpath from Cley-next-the-Sea, the seals would rather their admirers visit by boat. **Bishop's Boats** runs trips from March to October from Blakeney Quay. (☎01263 740 753; www.bishopsboats.com. Book in advance at ☎08000 740 754. 1-3 trips per day. £8, children £4.) More boat trips to Blakeney run from Morston Quay. In Hunstanton, on the Southern Promenade, the **Hunstanton Sea Life Sanctuary and Aquarium** rehabilitates injured and abandoned seals. (☎01485 533 576 or 0871 423 2110; www.sealsanctuary.co.uk. Open daily July-Aug. 10am-5pm; Sept.-Oct. and Apr.-June 10am-4pm; Nov.-Mar. 10am-3pm. £12.50, concessions £9.50.) For a taste of luxury, visit 18th-century **Holkham Hall,** 2 mi. west of Wells-next-the-Sea, the present-day home of the Earl of Leicester. The **Bygones Museum** has over 4000 knick-knacks from the family's past. Two grass-green, oxidized lions guard the entrance. (☎01328 710 227; www.holkham.co.uk. Open June-Sept. M and Th-Su 1-5pm. Hall and museum £10, children £5. Hall only £7, children £3.50. Museum only £5/2.50.)

On the coast, Hunstanton's **YHA hostel ❷,** 15 Avenue Rd., is a 5min. walk from the bus station. Take Sandringham Rd. uphill, then turn right on Avenue Rd. (☎01485 532 061. TV lounge. Breakfast £4.50. Open Apr.-Oct. W-Sa. Dorms £16, under 18 £12. MC/V.) For a picnic by the beach, grab takeaway toasties (£3) at **Tina's Sandwich Bar,** Le Strange Ct., Unit 2, The Green. (☎01485 535 298. Open M-F 9am-4:30pm, Sa-Su 10am-5:30pm. Cash only.)

The Norfolk Coast is an easy daytrip from King's Lynn and Norwich. **Hunstanton,** at the western edge, is the best base. **Buses** #40, 41, and 41A run from Vancouver Centre in King's Lynn to Hunstanton (45min.; M-Sa 2-4 per hr., Su every hr.; round-trip £5). For details on the Northern Norfolk Coast, maps, and bus schedules, consult the Hunstanton **Tourist Information Centre,** Town Hall, The Green. (☎01485 532 610. Open daily Apr.-Sept. 10am-5pm; Oct.-Mar. 10:30am-3pm.) *Walking the Peddar's Way and Norfolk Coast Path with Weavers Way* (£2.70) are available at the TIC and include accommodations listings.

NORWICH   ☎(0)1603

The dizzying streets of Norwich wind outward from the Norman castle, past the cathedral, to the scattered fragments of the 14th-century city wall. Although Norwich retains the hallmarks of an ancient city, a university and active art community give it a modern feel. The hum of "England's city in the country" is still going strong, with a daily market almost a millennium old thriving alongside busy art galleries, roadside cafes, and nightlife.

▐ TRANSPORTATION

Easily accessible by bus, coach, or train, Norwich makes a logical base for touring both urban and rural East Anglia, particularly the Norfolk Broads.

Trains: Station at the corner of Riverside and Thorpe Rd. Ticket window open M-Sa 4:45am-8:45pm, Su 6:45am-8:45pm. Trains to: **Bury St. Edmunds** (2hr., every hr., £10.70); **Great Yarmouth** (30min., every hr., £5.20); **London Liverpool Street** (2½hr., 2 per hr., £40); **Peterborough** (1½hr., every hr., £19.50).

Buses: Station (☎01603 660 553) on Surrey St., off St. Stephens St. Open M-F 8am-6pm, Sa 8:30am-4:30pm, Su 10am-2pm. National Express (☎08705 808 080) runs to **London** (3hr., 5 per day, round-trip £17). First Eastern Counties (☎08456 020 121) X1 travels to **King's Lynn** (2hr., every 30min., £4.50) and **Peterborough** (3hr., £10). Network tickets give 1 day of unlimited travel on First Eastern Counties (£10, children £6.50, seniors £5, families £20).

Taxis: Bestway (☎0800 666 666). 24hr.

▄ ▐ ORIENTATION AND PRACTICAL INFORMATION

Although the sights are fairly close together, Norwich's twisting streets can cause confusion. Keep a map handy and be wary of deceptive side alleyways that are often hard to spot.

Tourist Information Centre: The Forum, Millennium Plain, Bethel St. (☎01603 727 927; www.visitnorwich.co.uk). Sells mini-guides (50p), gives away the Norwich visitor map, and books rooms for a 10% deposit. Open Apr.-Oct. M-Sa 9:30am-6pm, Su 10am-2pm; Nov.-Mar. M-Sa 10am-5:30pm. Offers 1½hr. **tours** Apr.-Oct. £4, children £1.50.

Currency Exchange: Thomas Cook, 14 London St. (☎01603 772 299). Open M, W, Sa 9am-5:30pm, Tu 10am-5:30pm.

Library: Norwich Library (☎01603 774 774), next to Origins in the Forum. Register for a simple "Internet only" user card and get free access on 20+ computers upstairs or at 6 "Express Terminals" downstairs. Express hours M-F 9am-9:30pm, Sa 9am-8:30pm, Su 10:30am-4:30pm; during express hours, only stand-up 30min. Internet sessions. Library open M-F 9am-8pm, Sa 9am-5pm.

Launderette: Wash-In, 31B Thorpe Rd. (☎01603 762 602), just after Stracey Rd. Wash £3.40, dry £2-4. Detergent 20p. Open daily 7am-9pm. Last wash 8pm.

Police: Bethel St. (☎0845 456 4567). Open daily 8am-midnight.

Pharmacy: Boots, Riverside Retail Park (☎01603 662 894). Open M-F 8:30am-8:30pm, Sa 8:30am-6pm, Su 10:30am-4:30pm.

Hospital: Norfolk and Norwich University Hospital, Colney Ln. (☎01603 286 286), at the corner of Brunswick Rd. and St. Stephens Rd.

Internet Access: The city center has free Wi-Fi, with signal in most of the area surrounding the Forum. Check www.norfolkopenlink.com for a map. **No. 33 Cafe,** 33 Exchange St. (☎01603 626 097). Free Wi-Fi. Open M-F 8:30am-5:30pm, Sa-Su 9am-4:30pm. Free at the **library** (above).

Post Office: Castle Mall (☎08457 223 344). **Bureau de change.** Open M and W-Sa 9am-5:30pm, Tu 9:30am-5:30pm. **Postcode:** NR1 3DD.

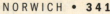

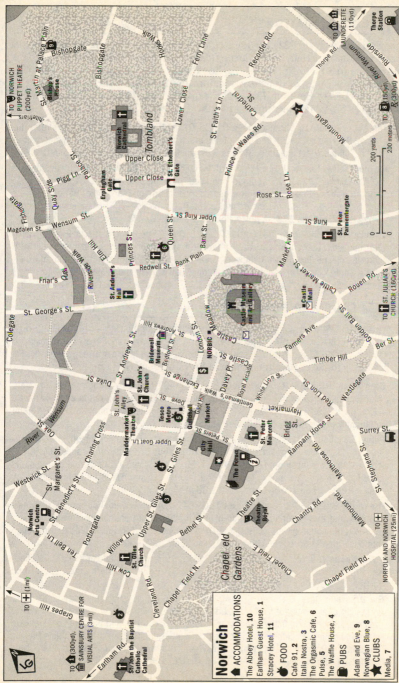

EAST ANGLIA

TO NORWICH
PUPPET THEATRE
(200yd)

Bishopgate **9**

St. Martin at Palace Plain

Bishop's
House

Bishopgate

Whitefriars

Hobart Walk

Ferry Lane

Lower Close

Recorder Rd.

Thorpe Station

LAUNDERETTE
(110yd)

Thorpe Rd.

River Wensum

Riverside

TO **8** (150yd)
R (300yd)

Mountergate

St. Faith's Ln.

Cathedral St.

Quay Side

Pigg Ln.

Fishergate

Magdalen St.

Wensum St.

Elm Hill

Riverside Walk

Friar's Quay

St. George's St.

Colegate

River Wensum

Oak St.

Duke St.

Charing Cross

St. Andrew's St.

St. John's
Maddermarket Alley
St. John's Church

St. John's
Church

Dove St.

St. Andrew's
Hall

Princes St.

Queen St.

Upper King St.

Bank St.

Redwell St. Bank Plain

Bridewell
Museum

Bedford St.

St. Andrews Hill

London St.

Exchange St.

Bank Plain

Erpingham
Gate

Upper Close

Upper Close

St. Ethelbert's
Gate

Norwich
Cathedral

Tombland

Prince of Wales Rd.

Rose St.

Rose St.

Rose Ln.

King St.

St. Peter
Parmentergate

Market Ave.

Cattle Market St.

Rouen Rd.

Castle
Mall

Castle Museum
and Art Gallery

NORBIC

Castle Meadow

Castle St.

Davey Pl.

Royal Arcade

Gentleman's Walk

Farmers Ave.

Timber Hill

White Lion St.

Red Lion St.

Ber St.

Golden Ball St.

TO ST. JULIAN'S
CHURCH (160yd)

Westlegate

Maddermarket
Theatre

Tesco
Metro

Guildhall

Gaol Hill

City
Hall

The Forum

Market

St. Peter's St.

Upper Goat Ln.

St. Giles St.

St. Giles St.

3

4

St. Giles
Church

Upper St. Giles St.

Willow Ln.

Cow Hill

Ten Bell Ln.

Pottergate

St. Benedict's St.

St. Margaret's St.

Westwick St.

Norwich
Arts Centre

TO SAINSBURY CENTRE FOR
VISUAL ARTS (3mi)

Grapes Hill

TO (1mi)

Earlham Rd.

TO (300yd)

St. John the Baptist
Catholic
Cathedral

Cleveland Rd.

Bethel St.

Chapel Field N.

Chapel Field
Gardens

Theatre St.

Theatre
Royal

Chantry Rd.

Chapel Field E.

Chapel Field Rd.

Malthouse Rd.

St. Stephens St.

Haymarket

Brigg St.

Rampant Horse St.

St. Peter
Mancroft

Surrey St.

TO
NORFOLK AND NORWICH
HOSPITAL (25mi)

2

5

0   200 yards

0   200 meters

Norwich

▲ **ACCOMMODATIONS**
The Abbey Hotel, **10**
Earlham Guest House, **1**
Stracey Hotel, **11**

🍴 **FOOD**
Cafe 91, **2**
Italia Nostra, **3**
The Orgasmic Cafe, **6**
Pulse, **5**
The Waffle House, **4**

🍺 **PUBS**
Adam and Eve, **9**
Norwegian Blue, **8**

★ **CLUBS**
Media, **7**

ACCOMMODATIONS

Several B&Bs (from £22) are located on Stracey Rd., a 5min. walk from the train station. Turn right onto Thorpe Rd., walk two blocks from the bridge, and go right onto Stracey Rd. B&Bs also line Earlham and Unthank Rd., but they're at least 20min. west of downtown and farther from the train station (take the #26 or 27 bus to Earlham Rd.). Also worth a try is Dereham Rd.; follow St. Benedict's St., which becomes Dereham.

The Abbey Hotel, 16 Stracey Rd. (☎01603 612 915), 5min. from the train station up Thorpe Rd. Free hot cocoa and chocolates in floral rooms. Owners make you feel right at home. Full breakfast included. Singles £29; ensuite doubles and twins £65. MC/V. ❸

Earlham Guest House, 147 Earlham Rd. (☎01603 454 169; www.earlhamguesthouse. co.uk). Take bus #26 or 27 from city center to The Mitre bus stop or walk 15min. across town to a residential neighborhood near the University of East Anglia. Beautifully kept with roses outside. Rooms clean and comfortably furnished. Full breakfast included. Singles £27, ensuite £29; doubles £50/58. AmEx/MC/V. ❸

Stracey Hotel, 2 Stracey Rd. (☎01603 628 093). Super-soft beds in a large Victorian mansion. Conveniently located near the train station. Rooms show their age with cracking plaster, inconsistent showers, and old-timey TVs, but the hotel is still an excellent deal. Bar, snooker room, and TV lounge. Full English breakfast (cooked to order) included. Singles £22, ensuite £28; twins £40/44; doubles £50. Cash only. ❷

FOOD AND PUBS

In the heart of the city, just a stone's throw from the castle, is one of England's largest and oldest open-air markets, with a wide variety of fresh and organic produce. (Open M-Sa roughly 8:30am-4:30pm.) **Tesco Metro** supermarket, on St. Giles St., is in the city center. (Open M-Sa 7am-10pm, Su 11am-5pm.)

Cafe 91, 91 Upper St. Giles St. (☎01603 627 4229). A cozy French bistro with delicious, homey fare like stewed lamb shank with olives (£8) and butternut and brie risotto (£7). Cakes (£2.50) displayed in the window. Dinner entrees affordable (£7-8) and beautifully presented. Open daily 8am-10pm. MC/V. ❷

Pulse, Guildhall (☎01603 765 562), in the old fire station stables. Fresh, creative vegetarian dishes like pumpkin spring rolls with peanut butter dipping sauce (£4.50) or smoked tofu and mushroom stroganoff (£7.50). Speedy service. Courtyard and upstairs seating. Live acoustic music 1st W of the month 7:30pm. Open M 10am-6pm, Tu-W 10am-10pm, Th-Sa 10am-11pm, Su 11:30am-4pm. MC/V. ❷

The Waffle House, 39 St. Giles St. (☎01603 612 790; www.wafflehouse.co.uk). Waffles, waffles, and more waffles, smothered in everything from chocolate mousse to hummus and avocado. Sweets (£2.50-5.50) and savories (£3-9) are available, with vegan options. Open M-Sa 10am-10pm, Su 11am-10pm. MC/V. ❷

Italia Nostra, 52 St. Giles St. (☎01603 617 199; www.italianostra.co.uk). Sicilian-owned eatery with authentic entrees (£8-18). Save room for the tiramisu (£5). Open M-Th 5:30-9:30pm, F-Sa 5:30-10pm. MC/V. ❷

The Orgasmic Cafe, 6 Queen St. (☎01603 760 650; www.orgasmic-cafe.com). Gasp in delight after a meal of freshly baked bread stuffed with salmon, spinach, and *crème fraiche* (£8) or one of many inventive pizzas (£6-9), risottos, and pastas (£5-7). ½-size pizza and a pint £6. Lounge in the oversized leather chairs when the crowd gets busy in the evening. Open M-Tu 10:30am-11pm, W-Th 10:30am-midnight, F-Sa 10:30am-2am, Su noon-11pm. Kitchen open until 10:30pm. MC/V. ❷

👁 SIGHTS

🖼NORWICH CATHEDRAL. Built by an 11th-century bishop as penance for having bought his position, Norwich Cathedral's buttressed exterior spikes against the sky with the second-tallest spire in the country (315 ft.; Salisbury Cathedral is the highest). Use the magnifying mirror in the **nave** to examine the magnificent medieval ceiling carvings of Old and New Testament scenes. **Saint Luke's Chapel** holds the *Despenser Reredos*, a magnificent 14th-century medieval painting that only escaped the Puritan iconoclasts of the Civil War by being used as a plumber's worktable. It was rediscovered in the late 19th century. In the summer, the cathedral hosts orchestral concerts on the **Close,** 44 acres of land sloping down to the River Wensum. (☎*01603 218 300. Open daily from mid-May to mid-Sept. 7am-7pm; from mid-Sept. to mid-May 7am-6pm. Evensong M-F 5:15pm, Sa-Su 3:30pm. Suggested donation £4. Tours M-Sa 10:45am, noon, and 2:15pm; £1.50.)*

BRIDEWELL MUSEUM. This museum has variously served as a merchant's house, mayor's mansion, factory, and prison for women and beggars. Now, it displays the history of local industry. Linger over mysterious bottles in the recreated 19th-century pharmacy or check out the exhibit on the Canaries, Norwich's favored football team. *(Bridewell Alley, off St. Andrew's St. ☎01603 615 975. Open July-Aug. M-Sa 10am-5pm; Sept.-Oct. and Apr.-June Tu-F 10am-4:30pm, Sa 10am-5pm. £3.20, concessions £2.65, children £1.75, families £9.)*

SAINT JULIAN'S CHURCH. Julian of Norwich, a 14th-century nun, walled herself into a cell behind the altar during a mass for the dead. For years she prayed and meditated there, sometimes dispensing spiritual advice from a window. *Revelations of Divine Love*, the first known book written by an Englishwoman, records her intense visions. The church, first erected in Saxon times, was bombed during WWII and later rebuilt. *(St. Julian's Alley off Rouen Rd. ☎01603 767 380; www.julianofnorwich.org. Open daily May-Sept. 7:30am-4:30pm; Oct.-Apr. 7:30am-4pm. Free.)*

SAINSBURY CENTRE FOR VISUAL ARTS. Located at the University of East Anglia, 3 mi. west of town on Earlham Rd., this center was destroyed during the English Reformation and restored after WWII. Sir Sainsbury, of supermarket fame, donated his small, world-class modern art collection, including works by Picasso and Bacon, to the university in 1973. The building, designed by Sir Norman Foster, is itself a work of art. *(Take bus #22, 25, 26, or 27 and ask for the Sainsbury Centre stop. ☎01603 593 199; www.scva.org.uk. Open Tu and Th-Su 10am-5pm, W 10am-8pm. Free, with separate charges for special exhibitions.)*

NORWICH CASTLE MUSEUM AND ART GALLERY. The original castle was built in the early 12th century by the Norman monarch Henry I, who was intent on subduing the Saxon city. Its exterior dates from an 1830s restoration, although a more recent £12 million facelift—the largest restoration in castle history—has also left its mark. The **Norman Keep** has multimedia displays about the lives of medieval nobility, and the archaeology gallery displays relics of Celtic Queen Boudicca. The art gallery showcases watercolors and the world's largest collection of ceramic teapots. Designed to educate youngsters, some parts of the museum may seem juvenile to older audiences, but the £1 closing-time admission is a great way to see the museum's highlights. *(☎01603 493 645. Open July-Aug. M-Sa 10am-5:30pm, Su 1-5pm; Sept.-June M-F 10am-4:30pm, Sa 10am-5pm, Su 1-5pm. Last entry 30min. before close. £5.80, concessions £5, children £4.25; 1hr. before close £1.)*

EAST ANGLIA

🎵 🎆 ENTERTAINMENT AND FESTIVALS

The TIC, cafes, and B&Bs have information on all things entertaining. Ask the TIC about free summer **Theatre in the Park** (☎01603 212 137). The **Norfolk and Norwich Festival** explodes with music and theater for 10 days every May. **Open Studios,** held in late May, offers two weeks of open artists' studios around the county. July welcomes the **Lord Mayor's Celebration** with a raucous parade. Check the TIC and the free *Norwich City Council Events 2009* for festival details.

Theatre Royal, Theatre St. (☎01603 630 000; www.theatreroyalnorwich.co.uk), next to the Assembly House. Hosts opera, ballet companies, and London-based theater troupes such as the Royal Shakespeare Company and Royal National Theatre. Box office open M-Sa 9:30am-8pm; non-performance days 9:30am-6pm. Tickets £4-45.

Maddermarket Theatre, St. John's Alley (☎01603 620 917; www.maddermarket.co.uk). Home of the Norwich Players. Drama in an Elizabethan-style theater. All actors remain anonymous, as per tradition. Box office open M-F 10am-5pm, Sa 10am-1pm; later on performance days. Tickets £10 for Norwich Players shows, £15 for other shows.

Norwich Arts Centre, St. Benedicts St. (☎01603 660 352; www.norwichartscentre. co.uk), Reeves Yard. Hosts international music, ballet, and comedy. Monday Night Alternative showcases poetry reading by current UK poets. Box office open M-Sa 10am-10pm; non-performance days 10am-7pm. Tickets £3-18, concessions available.

Norwich Puppet Theatre, St. James (☎01603 629 921; www.puppettheatre.co.uk) Whitefriars. 1 of 2 in the country, presenting shows for all ages. Box office open M-F 9:30am-5pm, Sa 1hr. prior to show. Tickets £6.50, concessions £5, children £4.50.

🍸 NIGHTLIFE

Many Norwich pubs and clubs offer live music. On **Prince of Wales Road,** near the city center, five clubs within two blocks jockey for social position. **Tombland,** the area just below the cathedral near the cemetery, serves as a somewhat macabre nightlife center. **Riverside** also has several popular clubs and bars. As always, use caution and common sense when going out at night.

Media, Rose Ln. (☎01603 623 559; www.medianightclub.co.uk). A relaxed club with live music and 2 dance floors. R&B and techno beats Th and Sa. Local radio DJs F. Frequent theme nights include wild foam parties. 18+. Cover usually £1 before 11pm, £3 after. Open F 10pm-3am, Sa 10pm-6am, Su 10pm-2:30am.

Norwegian Blue (☎01603 618 082), in the Riverside Leisure complex. Trendy decor inspired by fjords and IKEA minimalists. A 30 ft. waterfall behind the bar splashes over 27 different vodkas. Theme nights and drink deals reflect the chill atmosphere: Aura on Th, Deep Blue on F, Big Chill on Sa, and Sundaze on Su. 25% off food menu W-Sa. Open M-Sa noon-midnight, Su noon-10:30pm. Kitchen open until 10pm.

Adam and Eve, Bishopgate (☎01603 667 423), behind the cathedral. Beautiful pub built of stone and hung with potted geraniums. Pints of dark ale and walls of dark wood. Norwich's first pub (est. 1249) is now its most tranquil, hugging the wall around the cathedral yard. Open M-Sa 11am-11pm, Su noon-10:30pm.

⛴ DAYTRIPS FROM NORWICH

NORFOLK BROADS NATIONAL PARK

Trains from Norwich, Lowestoft, or Great Yarmouth to Beccles, Cantley, Lingwood, Oulton Broad, Salhouse, or Wroxham. From Norwich, First Eastern Counties buses go to: Brundell (#17, 17A; 30min.; 2 per hr.; round-trip £3.40); Horning (#54, 30min., every hr., round-

trip £5); Strumpshaw (#17A, 30min., every hr., round-trip £3.50); Wroxham (#54, 40min., every hr., round-trip £4); other Broads towns (#705, M-F every hr.).

Birds and birdwatchers flock to the Norfolk Broads, a soggy maze of marsh-lands. The landscape was formed in medieval times when peat was dug out to use for fuel. Over the centuries, water levels rose, and the shallow lakes, or "broads," were born. Boat traffic in hidden waterways conjures the sur-real image of sailboats floating through fields. Travel with care, as floods are frequent. Among the many **nature trails** that pass through the Broads, **Cockshoot Broad** lets you birdwatch, a circular walk around **Ranworth** passes various flora, and **Upton Fen** is, amazingly enough, popular for its bugs. Hikers can challenge themselves with the 56 mi. **Weaver's Way** between Cromer and Great Yarmouth. The village of **Strumpshaw** has a popular bird reserve. (☎01603 715 191. Open daily dawn-dusk. £2.50, concessions £1.50, families £5, children 50p.) The best way to see the Broads is by boat—the 200km of navigable waters are perfect for a nautical jaunt. Many companies in Wroxham rent day launches (£10-17 per hr.) while others offer **cruises** around the Broads. **Broads Tours** of Wroxham, on the right before the town bridge, runs river trips and rents day boats. (☎01603 782 207. Boat rentals £13-15 per hr. Open daily 9am-5pm. 1-2½hr. tours July-Aug. 7 per day; Sept. and June 4-5 per day, less frequent on weekends; Oct. and Apr.-May 11:30am, 2pm. £6.50-8.50, children £5-7.) Certain areas of the Broads are accessible only by car or bike; the pamphlet *Broads Bike Hire,* available at the Wroxham TIC, lists rental shops. A convenient place to rent **bikes** is Broadland Cycle Hire in Wroxham. Follow Station Rd. to the river and take a left onto The Rhond. (☎01603 480 331 www.broadlandcyclehire.co.uk. Book in advance. £7 per ½-day, £10 per day. Open daily 10am-5pm.)

Wroxham, 15min. from Norwich by train (every hr., £3.10), is the best base for information-gathering and preliminary exploration of some of the area's wetlands. To reach the **Wroxham and Hoveton Broads Information Centre** from the train station and bus stop, turn right on Station Rd. and walk about 300 ft. Knowledgeable Broads rangers supply guides and maps for walking and cycling routes. The office also lists boat-rental companies and campgrounds throughout the area and books rooms around the park. (☎01603 782 281. Open Easter-Oct. M-Sa 9am-1pm and 1:30-5pm.)

SUFFOLK AND ESSEX

BURY ST. EDMUNDS   ☎(0)1284

In AD 869, Viking invaders tied the Saxon monarch King Edmund to a tree, used him for target practice, and then beheaded him. Approximately 350 years later, 25 barons met in the Abbey of St. Edmund to swear to force King John to sign the Magna Carta, inaugurating the idea of limited kingship in England. From these two defining moments comes Bury's motto: *sacrarium regis, cunabula legis* ("shrine of the king, cradle of the law"). Bury St. Edmunds is now a vigorous market town. November promises fireworks, December hosts the Christmas Fayre, and May brings in the Bury Festival.

◪ TRANSPORTATION. Bury makes a good daytrip from Norwich or Cambridge, especially if you include a jaunt to Lavenham, Sudbury, or Long Melford. **Trains** (☎08457 484 950) run from Bury to Cambridge (40min., every hr., £7.60) and London (2¼hr., 2 per hr., prices vary). A National Express **bus** (☎08705 808 080) comes from London (2¼hr., 3 per day, £10.30) and continues to Cambridge

(1hr., frequent, £3.30). Cambus #11 (☎0870 608 2608) runs to Drummer St. in Cambridge frequently and cheaply (1hr., M-Sa every hr., round-trip £4.50).

⁊ PRACTICAL INFORMATION. The **Tourist Information Centre** is on 6 Angel Hill opposite Abbey Gate. (☎01284 764 667. Open Easter-Oct. M-Sa 9:30am-5:30pm, Su 10am-3pm; Nov.-Easter M-Sa 10am-4pm.) Other services include: **banks** with **ATMs** on Abbeygate St.; free **Internet** access at the **library** on St. Andrews St.; **police,** Raingate St. (☎01284 774 100); **Boots Pharmacy,** 11-13 Cornhill (☎01284 701 516; open M and W-Sa 8:30am-5:30pm, Tu 9am-5:30pm, Su 10am-4pm); **West Suffolk Hospital** (☎01284 713 000); and the **post office,** 17-18 Cornhill St., with a **bureau de change** (☎08457 223 344; open M and W-F 9am-5:30pm, Tu 9:30am-5:30pm, Sa 9am-12:30pm). **Postcode:** IP33 1AA.

⁊⁊ ACCOMMODATIONS AND FOOD. Most budget accommodations are in the residential outskirts of the historic town center. The TIC books B&Bs in town or on nearby farms (£20-30). For spotless rooms, try **Westland Park ❷,** 116A Westley Rd., a 20min. walk from the train station. (☎01284 753 874; www.west-bank-house.co.uk. Singles £28; twins £45, ensuite £55.) **Dunston Guest House ❷,** 8 Springfield Rd., has 17 bedrooms in a Victorian mansion only 10min. from the town center. (☎01284 767 981; www.dunstonguesthouse.co.uk. Full breakfast included. Singles £30-40; doubles and twins £65.) Pamper yourself at the luxurious **Clarice House ❸,** Horringer Ct., Horringer Rd., a mansion with a health club and 20 acres of parkland. (☎01284 705 550; www.claricehouse.co.uk. Ensuite singles from £27.50; ensuite doubles from £55.)

Bury bustles on **market** days (W and Sa 9am-4pm), when the town center fills with fresh food and flowers. For sandwiches and salads (£5-7), visit the always busy **Wilcroft's Home-Cooked Food House,** Brentgovel St. (☎01284 763 293. MC/V over £10.) The pint-size **Nutshell,** Abbeygate at the Traverse, claims to be Britain's smallest pub—ask about its entry in the *Guinness Book of World Records.* (☎01284 764 867. Open M-Sa 11am-11pm, Su noon-10:30pm. Cash only.)

⦿⌘ SIGHTS AND FESTIVALS. Along Crown St. lie the ▣**Abbey Gardens,** a peaceful park with award-winning flower beds. The gardens also contain the ruins of the 11th-century **Abbey of Saint Edmund,** where the barons met in 1214 to put a check on royal power. Next door, the 16th-century **Saint Edmundsbury Cathedral** stands out with its Millennium Tower and strikingly colorful interior. Painted wood ceilings and the shields of the Magna Carta barons hang above the high altar. (☎01284 754 933; www.stedscathedral.co.uk. Open daily June-Aug. 8:30am-8pm; Sept.-May 8:30am-6pm. Evensong M-Th 5:30pm, F 7pm, Su 3:30pm. 1hr. guided tours M-Sa 11:30am. Suggested donation £3.) **Moyse's Hall Museum,** Corn Hill in the marketplace, is rumored to be one of the oldest townhouses in East Anglia. Since 1899, however, it has been devoted to town history, from mantraps to mummified cats. (☎01284 706 183. Open daily 10am-5pm. £2.60.) In late May, the two-week **Bury Festival** (www.buryfestival.co.uk) brings music, street entertainment, and fireworks to the town center.

⁊ DAYTRIP FROM BURY ST. EDMUNDS: LONG MELFORD. Two Tudor mansions, complete with turrets and moats, grace the village of Long Melford. **Melford Hall,** in its rough red brick, has retained much of its original Elizabethan exterior and its paneled banquet hall. Still the home of the Hyde Parker family, the mansion displays exquisite vases, china, and ivory figures from a Spanish treasure ship captured by Captain Hyde Parker I. (*☎01787 379 228. Open May-Sept. M, W-Su, bank holidays 1:30-5pm; Oct. and Apr. Sa-Su 1:30-5pm. Last entry 4:30pm. £5.80, children £3, family £14.50.)* More entertaining than stately, 500-year-old **Kentwell Hall** is filled with authentically costumed guides who explain the daily ins and outs of Tudor domestic life. The mansion also hosts the occasional WWII recreation and open-air theater in the summer, featuring opera, Shakespeare, and bands. (☎01787 310 207; www.kentwell.co.uk. Open July-Aug. daily noon-5pm; Sept.-Oct. and Mar.-May Su noon-5pm. £8.50, children £5.50. Gardens and farm without mansion £6/4.) Stop by the **Long Melford Church**, built in 1484 with funding from rich wool merchants. Near the back of the church is the tomb of William Compton, longtime lord of Melford Hall. In 1436 he granted the nearby village of Hadleigh a guildhall and space for a marketplace in return for one red rose to be paid per year. Still today, every year, the mayor of Hadleigh presents one red rose to the Compton family descendants, making this rose the longest continually paid rent in England. (☎01787 310 845; www.longmelfordchurch.com. Open daily Apr.-Sept. 10am-6pm; Oct. and Mar. 10am-4:30pm, Nov.-Feb. 11am-3pm. Free. To get to Long Melford, 14 mi. from Bury St. Edmunds, take HC Chambers bus #753. 50min., M-Sa 11 per day, round-trip £4.70.)

COLCHESTER ☎(0)1284

As Britain's oldest town on record, Colchester has seen its share of violence. The first Roman capital in Britain, it was burned to a crisp during Celtic Queen Boudicca's revolt in AD 60. Romans recaptured the place and built what is now the oldest surviving city wall in Britain. It is also the site of one of William the Conqueror's first castles. Colchester's half-timber buildings now make a nicely walkable town center. Completed in 1125, **Colchester Castle** houses the **Castle Museum,** with extensive hands-on displays of Roman artifacts found in the area, including skeletons, coffins, and weapons from the period of the Boudiccan revolt. A tour takes you from the depths of the Roman foundations to the heights of the Norman towers. (☎01284 282 939. Open M-Sa 10am-5pm, Su 11am-5pm. Guided tours of the Roman vaults and castle roof every hr. noon-4pm. Castle £5.10, concessions £3.30. Tours £2, children £3.30.) View the fine collection of 18th-century Colchester grandfather clocks in **Tymperleys Clock Museum,** off Trinity St. (☎01284 282 939. Open Apr.-Oct. Tu-Sa 10am-1pm and 2-5pm. Free.) Colchester has several free museums devoted to tea, jam, and art; visit www.colchestermuseums.org.uk.

If planning to stay overnight, budget travelers can reserve in advance one of the few rooms in **Apple Blossom House ❸,** 8 Guildford Rd., close to the town center. (☎01284 512 303. TVs in all rooms. Full English breakfast included. Singles £26-36; doubles £46-52. Cash only.) At the **Thai Dragon ❷,** 35 East Hill, costumed waitresses serve a three-course lunch for £8. (☎01284 863 414. Open M-Sa noon-2:30pm and 6-11pm, Su noon-2:30pm and 6-10:30pm. MC/V.)

Trains (☎08457 484 950) pull into North Station from Bury St. Edmunds (1hr., every hr., £17.80) and London Liverpool St. (1hr., 12 per hr., £19.50). Regional trains arrive at North Station; take a connecting train to Colchester Town Station or follow the signs 1½ mi. into town. The **Tourist Information Centre,** 1 Queen St., across from the castle, leads 2hr. city tours. (☎01284 282 920. Open Easter-Oct. M-Tu and Th-Sa 9:30am-6pm, W 10am-8pm, Su 11am-4pm; Oct.-Easter M-Sa 10am-5pm. Tours Mar.-Oct.; call ahead for dates.)

NORTHWEST ENGLAND

Once upon a time, Northwest England was a land of sleepy villages and lots of sheep. Then the Industrial Revolution came along and turned the once quiet cities into some of the richest and most cosmopolitan in the world. The decline of industry hit the region hard, but the cities of the Northwest bounced back by embracing their quirky history and avant-garde hipness. Today, their innovative music and art scenes are world-famous—Liverpool and Manchester alone produced four of Q magazine's 10 biggest rock stars of the century—and a large student population feeds through-the-roof nightlife. Travelers can find respite from the frenetic urbanity in the rolling hills and pastures of the Peak District to the east or Cumbria to the north, where the crags and waters of the Lake District have sent poets into pensive meditation for centuries.

HIGHLIGHTS OF NORTHWEST ENGLAND

WORSHIP the Beatles: virtually every pub, restaurant, and corner in **Liverpool** claims some connection to the Fab Four (p. 354).

REVEL in **Manchester's** nightlife, where trendy cafe-bars morph into late-night venues for dancing and drinking (p. 362).

ROAM the hills, caverns, and moors of the **Peak District** (p. 373), then explore the mountains and sparkling waters of the **Lake District** (p. 383).

NORTHWEST CITIES

CHESTER   ☎(0)1244

With fashionable stores behind mock-medieval facades, tour guides in Roman armor, and a town crier, Chester is a proud purveyor—and reenactor—of English history. The city was a base for Plantagenet campaigns against the Welsh in the 15th century—old town law stated that Welshmen in the streets after sunset could be beheaded. Thankfully, today the city is less bloodthirsty. Its Roman ruins and quiet location on the River Dee make Chester a relaxing, historic entry point to the Northwest.

◰ TRANSPORTATION

Chester serves as a rail gateway to Wales. The **train station** lies 10min. northeast of the city proper, off Hoole Rd., but showing your ticket gets a free bus ride downtown. Buses converge between Northgate St. and Inner Ring Rd.

> **Trains:** Station on City Rd. (☎08457 484 950; www.nationalrail.co.uk). Ticket office open M-F 5:45am-11pm, Sa 6:30am-10:30pm, Su 7:30-10pm. Trains to: **Birmingham** (1½hr., 2-3 per hr., £9-20); **Holyhead** (2hr., 1-2 per hr., £18); **London Euston** (2-3hr.,

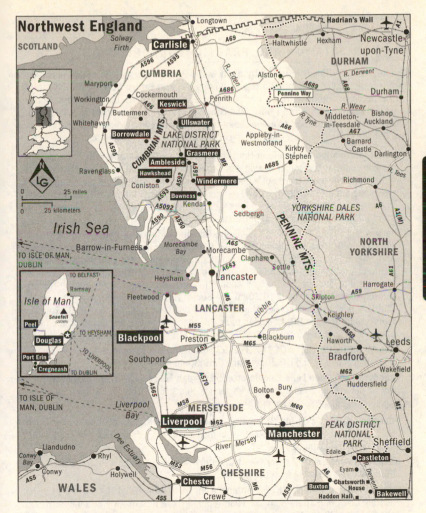

Northwest England

1-2 per hr., £61.60); **Manchester Piccadilly** (1hr., 3 per hr., £11.20). The **Wirral Line,** operated by Merseyrail, runs frequently to Liverpool (45min., 2 per hr., £4.45).

Buses: Station on Princess St., off Northgate St. and near Town Hall. National Express (☎08705 808 080; www.nationalexpress.co.uk) to: **Birmingham** (2-3hr., 4 per day, £11); **Blackpool** (3-5hr., 4 per day, £9.50); **London** (5-6hr., 7 per day, £22); **Manchester** (1½-2hr., 6 per day, £6.10). Huxley Travel (☎01948 770 661; www.huxley-coachholidays.co.uk) bus C56 runs from Foregate St. to **Wrexham** (45min., M-F 9 per day, Sa 6 per day). Buses #1, 401, and X11 connect to **Liverpool** (1½hr., 5-6 per hr.). #1 and X94 also run to **Wrexham** (40min., every 10min.), with X94 continuing to **Llangollen** (70min., M-Sa 6 per day, Su 5 per day).

Public Transportation: Call for local bus info (☎0870 608 2608; line open daily 8am-8pm). Routes can be found in the 15 *Bus Times* booklets, free at the TIC.

Taxis: Radio Taxis (☎01244 372 372). **Abbey Taxis** (☎01244 318 318). **King Cabs** (☎01244 311 551). All 24hr.

⚡ 🛈 ORIENTATION AND PRACTICAL INFORMATION

Chester's center is surrounded by a **city wall** with seven gates. **Chester Cross** is at the intersection of **Eastgate, Northgate, Watergate,** and **Bridge Streets,** which make up the heart of the downtown commercial and pedestrian district. Outside the southern walls, a tree-lined path, **The Groves,** runs along a mile of the **River Dee.** North of the walled city, **Liverpool Road** heads toward the hospital and the zoo. The **Roodee** (Chester Racecourse) is on the city's southwest edge.

Tourist Information Centre: Town Hall, Northgate St. (☎01244 351 609; www.chester-tourism.com), at the corner of Princess St. Books accommodations, National Express tickets, and city tours. Gives out a free visitors guide with accommodations listings. Free city maps are also available as well as more detailed ones for £1. Pick up *What's On in Chester and Cheshire* (free) for information on upcoming events. Open M and W-Sa 9am-5:30pm, Tu 10:30am-5:30pm, Su 10am-5pm.

Tours: A legionnaire in full armor leads the **Roman Soldier Wall Patrol.** Feb., May, and July-Aug. Th-Sa 2pm. Ghouls lurk along the **Ghost Hunter Trail.** Same-night tickets available after 5:30pm at the Shropshire Arms pub. June-Oct. Th-Sa 7:30pm; Nov.-May Sa 7:30pm. A similar self-guided tour is detailed in *Haunted Chester*, a £1 pamphlet sold in bookstores and the TIC. To learn about Chester's 2000-year history, try the **History Hunter,** which departs daily 10:30am. The **Secret Treasures** tour reveals the secrets of Chester's past by granting special access to historic buildings. May-Oct. Th-Su 2pm. All tours depart from the TIC. All guided tours £5, concessions £4. Buy tickets at the TIC or book online. Inquiries for all tours ☎01244 351 609; www.chestertourism.com.

Library: Northgate St. (☎01244 312 935), beside the Town Hall. Open M and Th 9:30am-7pm, Tu-W and F 9:30am-5pm, Sa 9:30am-4pm.

Launderette: Garden Lane Launderette, 56 Garden Ln. (☎01244 380 014). Wash £3, dry £1 per 20min. Soap 50p, required service charge 50p. Open Tu-Sa 9am-5pm.

Police: In the Town Hall (☎01244 350 000).

Pharmacy: Boots (☎01244 342 852), adjacent to the TIC in the Forum Center. Open M-F 8am-6pm, Sa 9am-6pm. Another branch on 47-55 Foregate St. (☎01244 328 421). Open Su 11am-5pm.

Hospital: Countess of Chester (West Chester) Hospital, Liverpool Rd. (☎01244 365 000). Take bus #3 or 3A from the Bus Exchange.

Internet Access: CafenetUK, 63 Watergate St. (☎01244 401 116). £3 per hr., £10 per day. Open M-F 10am-8pm, Sa 10am-7pm, Su 11am-5pm. Free at the library (see above) with a 30min. time limit.

Post Office: 2 St. John St. (☎0845 722 3344), off Foregate St. **Bureau de change.** Open M and W-Sa 9am-5:30pm, Tu 9:30am-5:30pm. Also at 122 Upper Northgate St. (☎01244 326 754). Open M-F 9am-5:30pm, Sa 9am-12:30pm. **Postcode:** CH1 2HT.

🏠 ACCOMMODATIONS

B&Bs (from £30-35) are concentrated on **Hoole Road,** a 5min. walk from the train station. Turn right from the exit, climb the steps to Hoole Rd., and turn right over the train tracks. **Hough Green Street** is also lined with B&Bs. Cross the river on Grosvenor Rd. and turn right off the roundabout. **Brook Street** has budget options. Turn right from the train station, then take the first left. Bus #53 (6 per hr.) runs to the area from the city center.

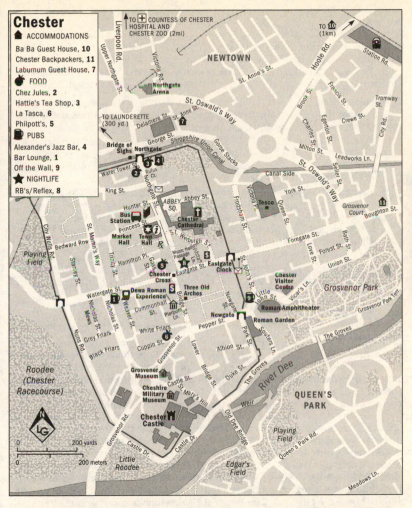

Chester

ACCOMMODATIONS

Ba Ba Guest House, 10
Chester Backpackers, 11
Laburnum Guest House, 7

FOOD

Chez Jules, 2
Hattie's Tea Shop, 3
La Tasca, 6
Philpott's, 5

PUBS

Alexander's Jazz Bar, 4
Bar Lounge, 1
Off the Wall, 9

NIGHTLIFE

RB's/Reflex, 8

NORTHWEST ENGLAND

Chester Backpackers, 67 Boughton St. (☎01244 400 185; www.chesterbackpackers.co.uk). A Tudor-style building with ensuite rooms and a convenient location within a 5-10min. walk from both the train station and the city center. The laid-back TV lounge is decked out with posters of famous musicians and holds a video collection and book exchange. The patio on the 2nd fl. is perfect for an afternoon chat. Kitchen, free luggage storage, laundry, and free Wi-Fi access. M-Th and Su dorms £15, F-Sa £17; singles £22/25; doubles £40/45. AmEx/MC/V. ❷

Laburnum Guest House, 2 St. Anne St. (☎01244 380 313; www.laburnumhousechester.co.uk). 6 large ensuite rooms in a Victorian house close to town. Generous breakfast included. Singles £28; doubles £55. MC/V. ❸

Ba Ba Guest House, 65 Hoole Rd. (☎01244 315 047; www.babaguesthouse.co.uk). Spacious, elegant ensuite rooms in a brick townhouse, 10min. from the city center. Full English breakfast included. Free Wi-Fi. Singles £37.50; doubles £70. AmEx/MC/V.

🏠 FOOD

A **Tesco** supermarket is at the end of an alley off Frodsham St. (Open M-Sa 7am-9pm, Su 11am-5pm.) The **market,** 6 Princess St., in Market Hall, has cheap fruits and vegetables. (☎01244 402 340. Open M-Sa 9am-5:30pm, Su 11am-5pm.) On Sundays the town hosts an outdoor **farmers' market.** (Open 9am-4:30pm.)

🍴 **Philpott's,** 2 Goss St. (☎01244 345 123), off Watergate St. Fabulous made-to-order sandwiches (from £2.30) and fresh ingredients fill the pristine glass case in this take-away shop. Open M-Sa 8am-2:30pm. Cash only. ❶

La Tasca, 6/12 Cuppin St. (☎01244 400 887; www.latasca.co.uk). Soft flamenco drifts through the colorful walls of this lively restaurant as diners sample tapas by candlelight. A variety of meat and vegetarian tapas available—as well as plenty of sangria. Tapas £3-5.50. Open M-Sa 11am-11pm, Su noon-10pm. AmEx/MC/V. ❷

Chez Jules, 71 Northgate St. (☎01244 400 014; www.chezjules.com). Popular gourmet French bistro. Holds splurge-worthy "Gastronomique" evenings every month with 5 award-winning courses of French cuisine (£22). 2-course lunches £8. Every M features a student special (2 courses and a bottle of wine; £15); Tu is the same deal for everyone. Also hosts occasional French movie nights; call or check the website for dates. Open M-Sa noon-3pm and 6-10:30pm, Su noon-4pm. AmEx/MC/V. ❸

Hattie's Tea Shop, 5 Rufus Ct. (☎01244 345 173), off Northgate St. A bustling teashop with great fresh-baked cakes (£2.50), sandwiches (£4-7), and a homey feel. Open M-Sa 9am-5pm, Su 11am-4pm. Cash only. ❶

👁 SIGHTS

CITY CENTER. Chester's architecture is the most prominent feature of its city center. Although many of the buildings are faux historic, housing chain stores and fast-food cafes, some actually do date from medieval times. The 13th-century **Three Old Arches** on Bridge St. are believed to make up the oldest storefront in England. Black-and-white painted facades usually signify Victorian imitations of traditional Tudor style—most of the originals were destroyed by fire or invasion. Occasional street performers grace this much-trafficked area, and the costumed town crier delivers the shocking news of the American colonies' secession. The crier will also announce birthdays and other special occasions; inquire at the TIC to embarrass a friend. *(Crier performs May-Aug. Tu-Sa at noon.)* Climb the famous city walls or the 13th-century **Rows** of Bridge, Watergate, and Eastgate St., where walkways afford access to a second tier of storefronts. **Northgate,** which commands a fine view of the Welsh hills, was rebuilt in 1808 to house the city's jail. The **Bridge of Sighs,** which carried doomed convicts from jail to chapel for their last mass, is outside the gate. Shutterbugs flock to **Eastgate Clock,** atop one of the Roman city gates, whose intricate wrought iron spirals have made it the second-most-photographed timepiece in the world behind London's Big Ben. **Chester Castle,** completed in 1237, is inaccessible to visitors except on the TIC's Secret Chester tour (p. 350).

CHESTER CATHEDRAL. Begun in the 11th century, the construction of Chester Cathedral continued for more than 500 years. Traces of this history of additions and renovations appear in the current building's mix of Norman arches, Gothic carvings, and an 11th-century shrine to St. Werburgh; the cathedral contains materials from every century since the 10th. One-of-a-kind intersecting stone arches known as **"the crown of stone"** support its main tower, and a choir at the front showcases intricate and magnificently preserved woodwork full of strange beasts and battle scenes. More elaborate carvings can be found on the

misericords ("mercy seats") where monks would rest during lengthy worship sessions. A northern niche holds a 19th-century **cobweb painting,** a short-lived art form that used silk instead of canvas. Construction hasn't stopped yet—the most recent addition is the colorful, stained-glass "Creation Window," installed in the refectory in 2001. *(Off Northgate St. ☎01244 324 756. Open M-Sa 9am-5pm, Su 12:30-4pm. £4, concessions £3, children £1.50. Audio tour included.)*

ROMAN SIGHTS. When the Romans conquered Britannia in AD 43, they made Dewa (modern-day Chester) an important strategic outpost. The walled city housed the soldiers' barracks and military headquarters, while the *canabae* (civilian towns) outside were set up for wicked indulgences like prostitutes and gambling. The **Grosvenor Museum** hosts a display of artifacts and models that illustrate a day in the life of a Roman soldier in residence. The rest of the museum is devoted to Chester's later history, with rooms and figures in period adornment and a display of silver from the 17th-20th centuries. *(27 Grosvenor St. ☎01244 402 008; www.grosvenormuseum.co.uk. Open M-Sa 10:30am-5pm, Su 1-4pm. Free.)* At the edge of Grosvenor Park, just outside the city wall, specialists are unearthing the largest **Roman amphitheater** in Britain. In its heyday, it featured animal fights, executions, and bloody gladiatorial bouts. *(Open 24hr. Free.)* Nearby, the **Roman Garden** provides picnic space on shaded grass lined with the remains of Roman columns. Off Bridge St., the **Dewa Roman Experience** is a full-immersion encounter with Chester's classical past. Visitors board a galley vessel bound for a recreated version of old Britannia. The museum chronicles the archaeological exploration of the town with a walk through an actual dig. *(Pierpoint Ln. ☎01244 343 407. Open Feb.-Nov. M-Sa 9am-5pm, Su 10am-5pm; Dec.-Jan. daily 10am-4pm. £4.75, concessions £4.50, children £3.)*

OTHER SIGHTS. Chester Zoo, one of Europe's largest, houses everything from elephants to lions as well as human-size prairie-dog tunnels and a "monkey kitchen." Watch out for the free-roaming peacocks as you make your way to the Twilight Zone, Europe's largest free-flight bat cave. Check the posted signs to witness action-packed animal feedings. *(Take First bus #1 from the Bus Exchange. 2 per hr., round-trip £2. On Su, catch Arriva #41 or 41A. ☎01244 380 280; www.chesterzoo. org. Open in summer M-F 10am-5pm, Sa-Su 10am-6pm; in winter, 10am-4:30pm. Last entry 1hr. before close. £15, concessions £13.50, families £45.)* The **Cheshire Military Museum,** in the castle complex, traces Chester's armed forces from medieval archers to contemporary special forces. Learn how 18th-century recruiting sergeants "enlisted" unsuspecting beer-guzzlers with a well-placed shilling. *(☎01244 327 617; www.chester.ac.uk/militarymuseum. Open daily 10am-5pm. Last entry 4pm. £3.)*

🎵 🎭 ENTERTAINMENT AND NIGHTLIFE

Many of the city's 30-odd pubs mimic Olde English decor, and most are open Monday through Saturday noon-11pm and Sunday noon-10:30pm. Watering holes cluster on **Eastgate** and **Foregate Streets** and the town center. Dusky lighting and exposed brick give **Alexander's Jazz Bar,** Rufus Ct., the feel of a truly hip jazz club. *(☎01244 340 005; www.alexandersjazz.com. Live music daily. Open mike Tu; soul and funk F; live comedy Sa; free jazz Su 2-5pm. Cover after 7pm £2-10. Open M-Sa 11am-2am, Su noon-midnight.)* On weekend nights, the **Juice Bar** next door dishes up champagne and mixed drinks instead of the usual smoothies. (Open M-Th and Su 11am-5pm, F-Sa 7pm-midnight.) Winner of the Best Bar Award in Chester for the past few years, **Bar Lounge,** 75 Watergate St., has something for everyone. The bar caters to a champagne-mixed drink crowd, while the spacious beer garden is more low-key. *(☎01244 327 394. Open in summer M-F 11am-midnight, Sa-Su 11am-1am; in winter daily 11am-midnight.)* Put on your dancing shoes and head to **RB's/Reflex,** 12-16 Northgate St., Chester's only traditional nightclub. Booty shakers come here to explore the club's three floors, each with different music. (☎01244 327 141. Cover £2-8. Open M-Tu and Su 10pm-3am, W-Th 9pm-3am, F 9pm-4am, Sa 8pm-4am.) On a former Roman defense ditch, **Off the Wall,** 12 St. John's St., is a spacious, multi-floored bar. (☎01244 348 964. M and W Beer £1.35. Bottles and pints Tu ½-price. Adjoining coffee bar open M-Sa 7am-7pm, Su 9am-6pm. Kitchen open daily noon-3pm, snacks until 11pm. Bar open daily noon-1am.)

On some spring and summer weekends, England's oldest horse races are held on the Roodee, attracting huge, boisterous crowds. If you plan to visit over a race weekend, book far in advance. (☎01244 304 600. Tickets start at £7 but average £26.) The **Chester Summer Music Festival** draws classical musicians in July. (☎01244 304 618; www.chesterfestivals.co.uk. Ticket prices vary; from £7.) Check the TIC's free *What's On in Chester* for other events.

LIVERPOOL ☎(0)151

Once belittled by southerners as a decaying industrial port town, Liverpool is now an energetic city in the middle of a major cultural facelift. Modern architecture, world-class theaters and museums, and a glimmering art-house cinema and digital media gallery draw culture-lovers from around the world. Last year, Liverpool was named the European Commision's Capital of Culture. Offbeat cafes and vinyl shops crowd the Ropewalks district, while the city's more than 65,000 students fuel a vibrant music scene. This home of the distinct "Scouse" accent, two near-deified football squads, and, of course, The Beatles also boasts some serious nightlife: swank lounges set up shop in the city's aging red- brick warehouses and, come evening, pubbers and clubbers pack the streets.

◪ TICKET TO RIDE

Trains: Lime Street Station, Lime St. and St. John's Ln. Ticket office open M-Sa 5:30am-11:30pm, Su 7:15am-11pm. Trains (☎0845 600 7245) to **Birmingham** (1½hr., 2-3 per hr., £9-22.80), **London Euston** (3hr., 2 per hr., £13-64), and **Manchester** (45min., 2-4 per hr., £8.80). **The Moorfields, James Street,** and **Central** stations serve mainly as transfer points to local Merseyrail trains and to **Chester** (45min., 2 per hr., £4.45).

Buses: Norton Street Station sends National Express (☎08705 808 080) to **Birmingham** (3hr., 4 per day, £10.20), **London** (5-6hr., 8 per day, £23), and **Manchester** (1-2hr., 2-3 per hr., £6). Other buses stop at **Queen Square** and **Paradise Street** stations. The 1-day **Mersey Saveaway** (£3.20-4.30, children £1.80-2.20) works on area buses and is unrestricted during off-peak hours. Also valid on ferry and rail.

Ferries: Ferries arrive at and depart from Pier Head, north of Albert Dock. The Isle of Man Steam Packet Company (☎08705 523 523; www.steam-packet.com) runs ferries from Princes Dock to the **Isle of Man** (p. 393). The P&O Irish Ferry service (☎0871 66 44 999; www.poirishsea.com) runs to **Dublin** from North Quay (see **By Ferry,** p. 40).

Public Transportation: Private buses cover the city and the Merseyside area. Call **Traveline** (☎0871 200 22 33) for information about bus routes or consult the experts at **Mersey Travel** (☎0151 330 1066; www.merseytravel.gov.uk) in the information center in Queen Sq. Open M-Sa 9am-5:30pm, Su 10:30am-4:30pm; 1st Tu of every month 10am-5:30pm. From Princes Dock, #S2 goes to City Centre, stopping at Queen Sq. (20min.; M-Sa every 15-20min., Su every 30min.)

Taxis: Mersey Cabs (☎0151 207 2222). 24hr.

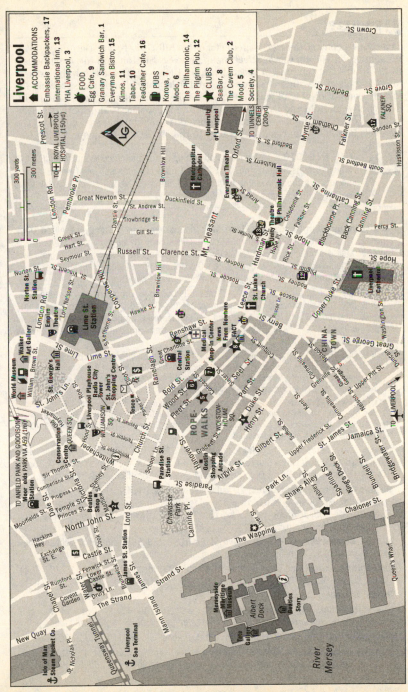

Liverpool

♦ ACCOMMODATIONS
Embassie Backpackers, 17
International Inn, 13
YHA Liverpool, 3

♦ FOOD
Egg Cafe, 9
Granary Sandwich Bar, 1
Everyman Bistro, 15
Kimos, 11
Tabac, 10
TeaGather Cafe, 16

♦ PUBS
Korova, 7
Modo, 6
The Philharmonic, 14
The Pilgrim Pub, 12

★ CLUBS
BaaBar, 8
The Cavern Club, 2
Mood, 5
Society, 4

HELP!

Liverpool's central district is pedestrian-friendly. There are two clusters of museums: on **William Brown Street,** near Lime St. Station and the urban oasis of St. John's Garden, and at **Albert Dock,** on the river. These flank the central shopping district, which is located around **Bold, Church,** and **Lord Streets** and is largely composed of walkways and plazas. The area of shops, cafes, and nightclubs between Bold and Duke St. is called the **Ropewalks.** To the south, a glittering arch over Nelson St.—recently imported from Shanghai as a gift from the People's Republic—marks the entrance to the oldest Chinatown in Europe.

> **TIP**
>
> **THE BIG DIG.** Liverpool is undergoing a structural facelift that will fill the city with construction until 2010. Most road closures still offer pedestrian access, but those traveling by car should check out www.liverpol.gov.uk/big-dig for updated maps of closures and projects.

Tourist Information Centre: 08 Place, Whitechapel and Anchor Courtyard, Albert Dock (☎0151 233 2008; www.visitliverpool.com). Gives away the handy *Visitor Guide to Liverpool, Merseyside, and England's Northwest* as well as a huge stock of pamphlets and local events schedules. Books beds for a 10% deposit. Email kiosks available for 5min. use. Open M and W-Sa 9am-6pm, Tu 10am-6pm, Su 11am-4pm.

Tours: In addition to those listed below, numerous bus tours (from £5) and walking tours (some free, others from £3) run in summer; ask the TIC. The TIC also offers guided 2hr. expeditions around and inside **John and Paul's Liverpool homes** through the National Trust (☎0151 427 7231). Sales office open M-F 9am-5pm. Tours given Mar.-Nov. W and Su. Book in advance. £15, children £3.

  Phil Hughes (☎0151 228 4565, mobile 07961 511 223). Phil will treat you to the most comprehensive Beatles tour in Liverpool. This trained tour guide runs personalized 3-4hr. tours with Liverpool highlights, including Strawberry Fields and Eleanor Rigby's grave. Book in advance. Refreshments included. £70 for groups of 5 or fewer, £14 per person for groups of 5-8.

  Magical Mystery Tour (☎0151 709 3285; www.cavernclub.org/mystery_tour.php). A yellow-and-blue bus takes 40 fans to Fab Four sights, leaving from the TIC on Whitechapel. Purchase tickets in advance at either of the TICs or at the Beatles Story. Tours M-F 2:10pm, Sa-Su 11:40am, 2:10pm. £13, small souvenir included.

Banks: Everywhere in the shopping districts, and **ATMs** seem to sprout from every alleyway. **Lloyd's TSB,** 53 Great Charlotte St. Open M-Tu 9:15am-4:30pm, W 10am-4:30pm, Th-F 9:15am-5pm. **HSBC,** 4 Dale St. Open M and W-F 9am-5pm, Tu 9:30am-5pm.

Beyond Tourism: JobCentrePlus, 20 Williamson Sq. (☎0151 801 5700; www.jobcentreplus.gov.uk). Open M-Tu and Th-F 9am-5pm, W 10am-5pm. **The Volunteer Centre,** Goston Bldg., 32-36 Hanover St. (☎0151 707 1113; www.volunteercentreliverpool.org.uk). Open M-F 9am-5pm.

Library: Central Library, William Brown St. (☎0151 233 5835). Internet access. Open M-F 9am-6pm, Sa 9am-5pm, Su noon-4pm.

Launderette: Associated Liver Launderettes Ltd., 98 North Hill St (☎0151 2807 091). Wash £3, dry 50p per 10min. Open M-F 9am-7pm, Sa 9am-6pm.

Police: St. Anne's St. (☎0151 709 6010).

Pharmacy: Boots, 18 Great Charlotte St. (☎0151 709 4711). Open M-W and F 7am-6:15pm, Th 7am-8pm, Sa 8:15am-6:15pm, Su 10:30am-4:30pm.

Hospital: Royal Liverpool University Hospital, Prescot St. (☎0151 706 2000).

Internet Access: At the **Central Library** (above). Free access for 11- to 25-year-olds at the **Door Cafe** in the Merseyside Youth Association Ltd., 65-67 Hanover St.

(☎0151 702 0700). Open M 10am-5pm, Tu-Th 9:30am-5pm, F 9:30am-4pm. Many cafes around Bold St. also offer Wi-Fi.

Post Office: 42-44 Houghton Way (☎08457 223 344), in St. John's Shopping Centre below the Radio City Tower. **ATM** and **bureau de change.** Open M and W-Sa 9am-5:30pm, Tu 9:30am-5:30pm. **Postcode:** L1 1AA.

A HARD DAY'S NIGHT

Cheap accommodations lie east of the city center. **Lord Nelson Street** is lined with modest hotels, as is **Mount Pleasant,** one block from Brownlow Hill and Central Station. Stay only at places approved by the TIC and, if you need a good night's sleep, consider springing for a single—some hostels host herds of clubbing teens on weekend nights. Demand for beds is highest in early April for the Grand National Race and during the Beatles Convention at the end of August.

International Inn, 4 S. Hunter St. (☎0151 709 8135; www.internationalinn.co.uk), off Hardman St. Clean and modern, this hostel welcomes visitors from all over the world with style and brightly painted ensuite rooms. Pool table, huge lounge, and kitchen. Bedding is provided as well as coffee, tea, and toast. The inn's newer, adjacent "budget boutique pod hotel" component features king-size beds, minimalist design, and chic walnut furnishings. Free Wi-Fi in the rooms and Internet £1.50 per 30min. in the adjoining **Cafe Latténet,** which doubles as a live music venue in the evenings. Cafe open M-F 8am-7pm, Sa-Su 9am-5:30pm. Dorms M-Th and Su £15, F-Sa £20; twins £36/45. Adjacent budget hotel's doubles £43/53. MC/V. ❷

Embassie Backpackers, 1 Falkner Sq. (☎0151 707 1089; www.embassie.com). A comfy remodeled Georgian house with an enjoyable family atmosphere. Evenings often bring free barbecues or karaoke. Embassie has a couple of connections to The Beatles: one of the owners faced (and beat) John Lennon's band in a 1957 competition, and the hostel now arranges for the Phil Hughes tour to pick up from its door. Laundry. Free Wi-Fi. Reception 24hr. Dorms M-Th and Su £15, F £17.50, Sa £20. Cash only. ❷

YHA Liverpool, 25 Tabley St. (☎0870 770 5924). Pristine digs on 3 Beatles-themed floors (hallways are called "Penny Lane" and "Mathew Street") near Albert Dock. Suitable rooms for families and 2 wheelchair-accessible rooms. Kitchen, game room, and Big Apple Diner. Breakfast included. Laundry. Internet £1 per 15min. Dorms £18, under 18 £16. £3 fee for non-YHA members. MC/V. ❷

SAVOY TRUFFLE

Cafes and kebab stands line **Bold, Hardman,** and **Leece Streets,** while takeaways crowd near late-night venues and around **Berry Street.** Cheap all-you-can-eat deals can be found in both posh and dodgy neighborhoods. **Chinatown** abounds with inexpensive buffets. Upscale restaurants cluster around **Queen Square** and downtown. A **Tesco Metro** supermarket is in Clayton Sq., across from St. John's Shopping Centre. (Open M-F 6am-midnight, Sa 6am-10pm, Su 11am-5pm.)

Everyman Bistro, 5-9 Hope St. (☎0151 708 9545). Tucked in a low-beamed basement below the Everyman Theatre, this bistro serves generous portions of tasty dishes. But you won't find the same meal twice—the menu changes twice a day, though it always features several vegetarian and gluten-free options from about £6. Leave room for the famed desserts. Open M-Th noon-midnight, F noon-2am, Sa 11am-2am. MC/V. ❷

Egg Cafe, 16-18 Newington (☎0151 707 2755). Just off the bustling Bold St., Liverpool's self-styled "premier vegetarian and vegan cafe" offers a menu of snacks like fresh hummus (£4) and meals like tandoori mushrooms (£5). Sip your own wine (£1 corkage fee) in this casual upstairs cafe, which also serves as a gallery for local artists. Open M-F 9am-10:30pm, Sa-Su 10am-10:30pm. Cash only. ❶

Kimos, 38-44 Mt. Pleasant (☎0151 707 8288). A large menu of Mediterranean and North African cuisine with lots of vegetarian options. All tapas, salads, burgers, pizzas, soups, and sandwiches are under £5, and specials like Moroccan *harira* (£6.50) are delicious. Breakfast (£3.50) served until 5pm. Open daily 10am-11pm. Cash only. ❷

Tabac, 126 Bold St. (☎0151 709 9502). Sleek, trendy decor and an aquarium in the counter. Sandwiches on freshly baked focaccia bread (melted brie and bacon £4.50) are served until 9pm. Dinner specials £4.50-7.50. Breakfast from £2. Wine bar opens early. Open M-F 9am-11pm, Sa 9am-midnight, Su 10am-11pm. MC/V. ❷

The Granary Sandwich Bar, 7 Drury Ln. (☎0151 236 0509), between Brunswick and Water St. Breakfast, lunch, and snack foods line the walls. Low prices (sandwiches from £2) advertised on brightly colored posters. Open M-F 7:30am-3:30pm. Cash only. ❶

TeaGather Cafe, 12 Myrtle St. (☎0151 703 0222). A spread of English and Chinese cuisine, plus kebabs, sandwiches, pizza, and burgers. 12 varieties of Chinese teas like refreshing honey ginger (£1.30). Squeaky-clean premises. Open M-F 8am-10pm, Sa 10am-10pm, Su noon-6pm. Cash only. ❶

🎧 MAGICAL MYSTERY TOUR

With first-rate museums, two dazzling cathedrals, and the twin religions of football and The Beatles, Liverpool's attractions are filled with spirited heritage and modern vitality. The city center is packed with theaters and cultural centers, while **Hope Street** to the southeast connects Liverpool's two 20th-century cathedrals. Most other sights are located on or near **Albert Dock,** an open rectangle of Victorian warehouses now stocked with offices, restaurants, and museums. In 2010, the **Museum of Liverpool** will become the waterfront's newest landmark.

▧BEATLES STORY. Recreations of the Cavern Club, Abbey Road Studios, and a shiny yellow submarine trace the rise and fall of the Fab Four from their humble beginnings to Beatlemania to shag haircuts to solo careers. The audio tour (included with admission) is narrated by Paul McCartney, Alan Williams (the band's first manager), and numerous family members and friends. Audio-taped screeches of fans and recordings of the band's number-one hits accompany the tour. *(Albert Dock. ☎0151 709 1963; www.beatlesstory.com. Open daily 9am-7pm. Last entry 1hr. before close. £12.50, concessions £8.50, children £6.50, families £32.)*

MERSEYSIDE MARITIME AND INTERNATIONAL SLAVERY MUSEUMS. Liverpool's heyday as a major port has passed, but the six floors of this museum allow you to explore the nautical side of Scouser history, including Liverpool's role as a key port in the slave trade. In the basement, an exhibit on smuggling holds an intriguing array of confiscated goods from smugglers including a mandolin made from a tortoise, a cane that hides a knife, and a teddy bear full of cocaine. Just around the corner, the Immigrant Story exhibit details Liverpool's history as an embarkation port and allows visitors to board a recreated ship, complete with wood bunks, departing for America. The International Slavery Museum, on the third floor, describes more tragic Atlantic crossings, teaching visitors how many of Liverpool's street names, estates, and even charities are connected to the slave trade (answer: a lot). *(Albert Dock. ☎0151 478 4499; www.liverpoolmuseums.org.uk/maritime. Open daily 10am-5pm. Free.)*

TATE GALLERY. The Liverpool branch of this legendary institution boasts a collection of favorites (Warhol, Pollock, Picasso) and more obscure names from the 19th and 20th centuries. Contemporary international art dominates the ground floor, the next level shows a rotating collection, and the top floor is reserved for special exhibitions. *(Albert Dock. ☎ 0151 702 7400; www.tate.org.uk/liverpool. Open Tu-Su 10am-5:50pm. Suggested donation £2. Special exhibits £8, concessions £6.)*

WALKER ART GALLERY. The massive collection in this stately gallery centers on British art from the 18th and 19th centuries, including a particularly impressive set of Victorian narrative paintings. It also features a collection of British art from the last several decades, much of it culled from Liverpool's own biennial painting competition. *(William Brown St. ☎ 0151 478 4199; www.liverpoolmuseums.org.uk/walker. Lecture schedule posted online. Open daily 10am-5pm. Free.)*

LIVERPOOL CATHEDRAL. Begun in 1904 and completed in 1978, this Anglican cathedral makes up for what it lacks in age with sheer size. It claims a number of superlatives: the highest Gothic-style arches ever built (107 ft.), the highest and heaviest (31 tons) bells in existence, and an organ with 10,268 pipes that is the largest in the UK. Take two elevators and climb 108 stairs for awe-inspiring views from the tower. *(St. James's Mount, off Upper Duke St. ☎ 0151 709 6271; www.liverpoolcathedral.org.uk. Cathedral open daily 8am-6pm. Tower open M-Sa Mar.-Oct. 10am-5pm; Nov.-Feb. 10am-4pm. Limited Su openings due to services. Cathedral free. Tower £4.25, concessions £3. Film and audio tour £4.75, concessions £3.50.)*

FACT. Housed in a shimmering metallic building, FACT stands for Film, Art, and Creative Technology. Built to showcase the digital arts, most of the exhibits revolve around film and video—some in the free galleries and some in more traditional theaters. Films shown are a mix of standard Hollywood, experimental, and foreign films. *(88 Wood St. ☎ 0151 707 4450; www.fact.co.uk. Open M-Sa 11am-11pm, Su 11am-10:30pm. Galleries open Tu-Su 11am-6pm. Suggested donation £2. Film screenings about £6.70, W all day and M-Tu and Th-F before 5pm £5.70.)*

METROPOLITAN CATHEDRAL OF CHRIST THE KING. Built in 1967 and controversially "modern," some would sooner call this oddity of the skyline "ugly." A crown of crosses tops its reinforced-concrete **Lantern Tower,** which resembles an upside-down funnel. The payoff is inside: the cavernous main chapel is stunning, with slivers of stained glass sending jewel-toned light glittering across the floor. Dramatic bronze **Stations of the Cross** by sculptor Sean Rice circle the edge, and the several smaller chapels are also worth a look. Ask one of the stewards to see the Edwardian-era **Lutyen's Crypt** that lurks underneath. The cathedral faces its Anglican sister church on

THE LOCAL STORY

SPEAKING SCOUSE

The distinct Liverpudlian lilt has confounded and intrigued visitors for decades. In "Scouse," as the accent is called, "cut" rhymes with "foot," "nurse" has the same vowel as "square," and T is often dropped from the end of words. The accent has a uniquely nasal quality, which some linguists have blamed on air pollution from coal burning that thickened city residents' vocal cords. More likely, it came about because of Liverpool's history as a port city: an inflection imported from Ireland, an idiom from Welsh, the cadences of hundreds of global dialects passing through the docks and mixing with the native Lancashire sounds.

In the 1960s, the accent acquired a counter-cultural coolness with the rise of The Beatles. Some Scousers today, however, say that it invites less-than-favorable perceptions and even discrimination. A recent survey of business directors found that the Liverpool accent was ranked lowest on the list of British accents in terms of appeal and associations with positive qualities like honesty.

But as television (specifically the BBC) moves away from the strict inflections of traditionally upper-class "Received Pronunciation," the stigma seems to be on the decline. Liverpudlians, for their part, haven't tried to adapt to the more dominant southern pronunciations—according to language trackers, the Liverpool accent is still going strong and is even getting thicker and more varied.

aptly named Hope St. *(Mt. Pleasant.* ☎ *0151 709 9222. Open in summer daily 8am-6pm; in winter M-Sa 8am-6pm, Su 8am-5pm. Free.)*

LIVERPOOL AND EVERTON FOOTBALL CLUBS. If you're not here for The Beatles, you're probably here for football. The rivalry between the city's two main teams, Liverpool and Everton, is deep and passionate. Both offer tours of their grounds, Anfield and Goodison Park, respectively. *(Bus #26 from the city center to Anfield. Bus #19 from the city center to Goodison Park. Liverpool* ☎ *0151 260 6677; www.liverpoolfc.tv. Everton* ☎ *0151 330 2212; www.evertonfc.com. Liverpool tour, including entrance to museum, £10, concessions £6. Museum open daily 10am-5pm. Everton tour £8.50/5. Tours M, W, F, Su 11am, 1pm. Match tickets, usually £28-33, sell out well in advance.)*

WILLIAMSON TUNNELS HERITAGE CENTRE. Called "The King of Edge Hill" by some (and "The Mole of Edge Hill" by skeptics), William Josephson kept hundreds of local laborers employed during a 19th-century depression by building huge, multilevel tunnels to nowhere. What little has been excavated can now be explored by visitors in a 40min. guided tour. *(The Old Stableyard, Smithdown Ln.* ☎ *0151 709 6868; www.williamsontunnels.co.uk. Open Tu-Su in summer 10am-6pm; in winter 10am-5pm. Last entry 1hr. before close. £4, concessions £3.50.)*

MORE (BEATLES) SIGHTS. For other Beatles-themed locales, get the *Beatles Map* ($3) at the TIC or the free but less detailed *How to Get to The Beatles Attractions in Merseyside* map from Merseytravel. To reach **Penny Lane,** take bus #86A, 76, or 77 from Paradise St.; for **Strawberry Fields,** take #76 or 77 from Paradise St. Souvenir hunters can raid **The Beatles Shop,** 31 Mathew St., canopied with shirts and the best Beatles posters in town. Doors are open "8 Days a Week." *(*☎ *0151 236 8066. Open M-Sa 9:30am-5:30pm, Su 10:30am-4:30pm.)*

♪ ❀ AND YOUR BIRD CAN SING

Though its reign as the 2008 European Capital of Culture has ended, Liverpool is host to countless festivals, exhibitions, and performances. Pick up the free *What's On* guide at the TIC or check www.visitliverpool.com/site/whats-on for details of events. The **International Street Theatre Festival** (☎ 0151 709 3334; www.brouhaha.uk.com) brings international performances to the city annually from late June to early August. At the end of August, a weeklong **Beatles Convention** draws Fab Four devotees. (☎ 0151 236 9091; www.cavernclub.org/beatle_week.php.) The TIC stocks a comprehensive festival list to add to its year-round entertainment venues.

Philharmonic Hall, Hope St. (☎ 0151 709 3789; www.liverpoolphil.com). Home of the Royal Liverpool Philharmonic, one of England's best orchestras. The hall also hosts jazz and funk bands. Tickets £10-60, same-day concessions £5. Classic film nights £5-6. Open for telephone bookings M-Sa 9:30am-5:30pm, Su noon-5pm; on concert nights, box office open from 7:30pm until 15min. after the performance begins.

Liverpool Empire Theatre, Lime St. (☎ 0844 847 2525; www.liverpoolempire.org.uk). Focuses primarily on touring musicals as well as comedy and music shows. Tickets £6-50; student standby tickets sometimes available. Box office open M-Sa 10am-6pm, performance nights 10am-8pm, Su from 2hr. prior to performances.

Liverpool Playhouse, Williamson Sq. (☎ 0151 709 4776; www.everymanplayhouse. com). Presents classic works, literary adaptations, and productions from other regional theaters. Tickets £9-20; concessions and £5 student standby tickets available. Box office open M-Sa 10am-6pm, performance nights 10am-7:30pm.

Everyman Theatre, 13 Hope St. (☎ 0151 709 4776; www.everymanplayhouse.com). The non-traditional counterpart to Liverpool Playhouse. Focuses on new and experimental works. Tickets £8-12.50; student standby tickets available. Box office open M-Sa 10am-6pm, performance nights 10am-8pm.

Unity Theatre, 1 Hope Pl. (☎0151 709 4988; www.unitytheatreliverpool.co.uk). Founded in the 1930s to use theater as a political instrument to bring "new strength to the progressive struggle." Today it produces work by new and little-known playwrights. Tickets £8-12.50; concessions available. Box office open M 1-6pm, Tu-Sa 10:30am-6pm; closes at 8:30pm on performance nights.

◪ COME TOGETHER

Two of Liverpool's most notable creations—football fans and rock musicians—were bred in pub culture, and the city continues to incorporate both traditions into its nightlife. There's not a spot in Liverpool that's far from a good selection of watering holes. The younger set clusters between **Slater** and **Berry Streets**, where cheap drink specials are in plentiful supply. Several pubs and clubs have a 21+ policy posted, but travelers over 18 often find this loosely enforced.

The Philharmonic, 36 Hope St. (☎0151 707 2837). John Lennon once said the worst thing about being famous was "not being able to get a quiet pint at the Phil." Non-celebrities can still enjoy a beer in this gorgeous turn-of-the-century lounge, where wood-paneled rooms have names like "Liszt" and "Brahms." Don't miss the famous mosaic tiling in the men's bathroom (women should ask at the bar before barging in). Food served daily noon-9pm upstairs, noon-5pm at the bar. Open daily 10am-midnight. MC/V.

Korova, 39-41 Fleet St. (☎0151 706 7770; www.korova-liverpool.com). Co-owned by electroclash band Ladytron, this sleek bar and club hosts daily live music in its intimate basement venue. In the upstairs bar, students and scenesters lounge in retro red leather couches and listen to the likes of Joy Division or The Velvet Underground. Cover can reach up to £10 for better-known groups while some nights feature local groups with no cover. Most nights fall somewhere in between—call or check posters. Open M-Th and Su noon-1am, F-Sa noon-4am. Kitchen open until 8pm. AmEx/MC/V.

Modo, 23-25 Fleet St. (☎0151 709 8832). Bubbling with eager young professionals. Lounge blasts techno nightly. Couches hidden in candlelit nooks provide ample space to hang out. The expansive urban beer garden fills quickly and makes Modo exceedingly popular. Open M-Th noon-2am, F-Sa noon-3am, Su noon-1am. Cash only.

The Pilgrim Pub, 34 Pilgrim St. (☎0151 709 2302), tucked behind an archway under the "Welcome to the Pilgrim" sign. Low-key and unpretentious, the Pilgrim draws a student crowd into its 2 bars and beer garden with cheap drinks and occasional live music. Open daily 10am-11pm. Kitchen open 10am-4pm.

Slaters Bar, 26 Slater St. (☎0151 708 6990). Well known for its cheap drinks. Pints from £1.20. A friendly place to chat in the daytime, that bar gets busy later in the evening. Open M-Th and Su 11am-midnight, F-Sa 11am-1am. Cash only.

▣ TWIST AND SHOUT

The *Liverpool Echo* (35p), sold daily by street vendors, has up-to-date information, especially in the *What's On* section of Friday editions. *Itchy Liverpool* (£3 at TICs or www.itchyliverpool.co.uk) is another useful guide to the nightlife scene. Generally, however, you need only wander near the Ropewalks to find something that suits your style. For information on gay and lesbian events, check out posted bills and pick up the free *Out Northwest* magazine at **News From Nowhere,** 96 Bold St., a "radical and community bookstore" run by a women's cooperative. (☎0151 708 7270; www.newsfromnowhere.org.uk. Open Jan.-Nov. M-Sa 10am-5:45pm; Dec. daily 10am-5:45pm.) Gay nightlife tends to center on Eberle St., off Dale St.

On weekend nights, the downtown area overflows with young pubbers and clubbers, especially **Mathew Street** (www.mathew.st), **Church Street,** and the area known as the **Ropewalks,** bounded by Hanover, Bold, Duke, and Berry St. Dress smartly (no sneakers) to avoid provoking bouncers. The pricier bars and clubs clustered around **Albert Dock** draw well-groomed 20-somethings.

Mood, 18-20 Fleet St. (☎0151 709 8181; www.moodbars.com). The crowds are stylish and the dancing is serious in this 3-tiered nightclub, which plays chart hits, hip hop, and house. Velvet sofas in the hallway lounge provide welcome respite from the busy dance floors. Cover after 11:30pm £2-5. Open M-F and Su 10pm-3am, Sa 9pm-3am.

BaaBar, 43-45 Fleet St. (☎0151 708 8673). Admire the scrolling marquee advertising drink specials behind the bar while deciding among 35 varieties of shooters (£1). Student-oriented and, as its slogan proclaims, "late, cheap, unisex." No cover unless there's live music. Open M-Th 5pm-2am, F-Sa 2pm-3am, Su 3pm-1am.

Society, 64 Duke St. (☎0151 707 3575; www.societyuk.com). With a plush Temple Room and VIP lounge above a steamy dance floor, this club is among Liverpool's sexiest. Open F 10:30pm-2am, Sa 10:30pm-4am, Su 10:30pm-1am.

The Cavern Club, 10 Mathew St. (☎0151 236 1965, tickets 236 4041; www.cavern-club.org). The restored incarnation of this legendary underground Beatles venue still has many of the original brick archways in place. Talented up-and-comers play here, hoping that history will repeat itself. To buy tickets in advance, head across the street to the Cavern Pub. Th features 1st-rate Beatles tribute bands. Live music Th-Su; DJ all other nights. Cover Sa-Su after 6pm £1, varies for concerts. Pub open M-Sa from 11am, Su noon-11:30pm. Club open M-Tu 11am-7pm, W 11am-midnight, Th 11am-2am, F-Sa 11am-2:30am, Su 11am-12:30am. MC/V.

MANCHESTER ☎(0)161

The Industrial Revolution transformed the unremarkable village of Manchester into Britain's second-largest urban area. A center of manufacturing in the 19th century, the city became a hotbed of deplorable working-class conditions and liberal politics. For years it was thought of as just another dirty post-industrial city, but an IRA bomb in 1996 injured over 200 people and sparked a wave of urban renewal, which has given the city a sleek, modern look.

▐ TRANSPORTATION

Flights: Manchester International Airport (☎0161 489 3000, arrival information 090 1010 1000, 50p per call). Trains (15-20min., 4-6 per hr., £3) and buses #44 and 105 run from the airport to Manchester Piccadilly Station.

Trains: 2 main stations, connected by Metrolink, serve Manchester. Additional service to local areas is available at the **Deansgate** and **Oxford Road** stations. Ticket prices are higher for travel during peak hours (7am-9:30am and 4-7pm); try to travel at off-peak times for lower prices.

Manchester Piccadilly, London Rd. Station reception open M-Sa 4:30am-10:30pm, Su 7am-10:30pm. Trains (☎08457 484 950) to: **Birmingham** (1hr., every hr., £25.50); **Chester** (1hr., every hr., £11.20);

Manchester	Trof, 9
	The Ox Pub, 2
♠ ACCOMMODATIONS	Bella Roma, 6
Hilton Chambers, 21	★ NIGHTLIFE
New Union Hotel, 11	Cord, 12
The Hatters Hostel, 22	Cruz 101, 7
The Millstone Hotel, 13	Dry Bar, 19
University of Manchester, 23	Essential, 14
YHA Manchester, 1	The New Union Showbar, 8
❦ FOOD	Night and Day Cafe, 18
Barburrito, 10	Queer, 15
Eden, 16	Simple Bar & Restaurant, 17
Soup Kitchen, 20	Thirsty Scholar, 5
Tampopo Noodle House, 3	The Temple, 4

NORTHWEST ENGLAND

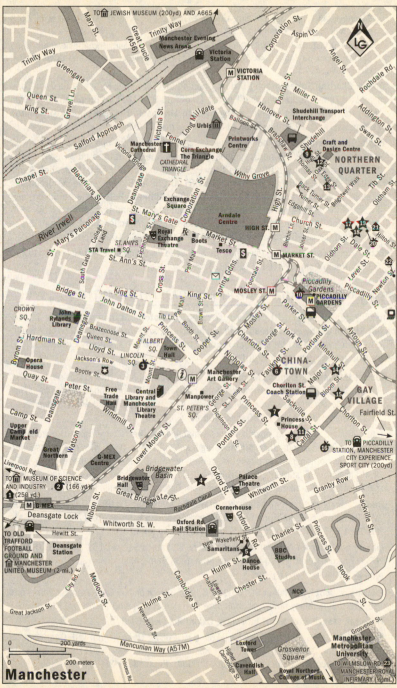

NORTHWEST ENGLAND

TO JEWISH MUSEUM (200yd) AND A665

Trinity Way

Mary St.

Trinity Way

Greengate

Queen St.

King St.

Great Ducie (A56)

Grave Ln.

Gravel Ln.

Manchester Evening
News Arena

Victoria
Station

VICTORIA
STATION

Corporation St.

Aspin Ln.

Angel St.

Rochdale Rd.

Addington St.

Swan St.

Dantzic St.

Miller St.

Hanover St.

Shudehill Transport
Interchange

Shudehill

Craft and
Design Centre

NORTHERN
QUARTER

Salford Approach

Chapel St.

Blackfriars St.

River Irwell

Victoria St.

Fennel

Long Millgate

Urbis

Balloon St.

Bradshaw St.

Manchester
Cathedral

Corn Exchange/
The Triangle

Printworks
Centre

CATHEDRAL
TRIANGLE

Withy Grove

Thomas St.

Tib St.

Oldham St.

Oldham St.

Back Turner St.

Turner St.

Edgehill St.

Church St.

Hilton St.

Newton St.

Piccadilly
Gardens

PICCADILLY
GARDENS

St. Mary's Parsonage

College
Land

Deansgate

Victoria Bridge

St. Mary's Gate

Exchange
Square

Arndale
Centre

HIGH ST.

High St.

Market St.

MARKET ST.

Dale St.

Lever St.

St. Ann's

Royal
Exchange
Theatre

Boots

Tesco

Fountain St.

MOSLEY ST.

STA Travel

St. Ann's St.

Cross St.

Pall Mall

King St.

Spring Gdns.

Parker St.

Piccadilly St.

Bridge St.

King St.

CROWN
SQ.

John Dalton St.

John Rylands
Library

Brazennose St.

Queen St.

Lloyd St.

Hardman St.

Byrom St.

Opera
House

Quay St.

Peter St.

Deansgate

Mount St.

ALBERT
SQ.

LINCOLN
SQ.

Jackson's Row

Bootle St.

Town
Hall

Mosley St.

Charlotte St.

George St.

York St.

Portland St.

Minshull St.

Aytoun St.

CHINA-
TOWN

GAY
VILLAGE

Fairfield St.

Manchester
Art Gallery

Manpower

Nicholas St.

Faulkner St.

Major St.

Bloom St.

Chorlton St.
Coach Station

Sackville St.

Free
Trade
Hall

Central
Library and
Manchester
Library
Theatre

ST. PETER'S
SQ.

St. James's St.

Princess St.

Princess
House

Canal

Camp St.

Upper
Campfield
Market

Windmill St.

St. George's St.

Dickinson St.

Portland St.

TO PICCADILLY
STATION, MANCHESTER
CITY EXPERIENCE,
SPORT CITY (200yd)

Great
Northern

G-MEX
Centre

Lower Mosley St.

Chorlton St.

Granby Row

Liverpool Rd.

TO MUSEUM OF SCIENCE
AND INDUSTRY (166 yd.)

(250 yd.)

M G-MEX

Deansgate Lock

Hewitt St.

Albion St.

Watson St.

Bridgewater
Hall

Bridgewater
Basin

Great Bridgewater St.

Rochdale Canal

Oxford St.

Palace
Theatre

Whitworth St.

Sackville St.

Whitworth St. W.

Oxford Rd
Rail Station

Oxford Rd.

Charles St.

Princess St.

Brook St.

TO OLD
TRAFFORD
FOOTBALL
GROUND AND
MANCHESTER
UNITED MUSEUM (2 mi.)

Deansgate
Station

Cornerhouse

Samaritans

New Wakefield St.

Dance
House

BBC
Studios

City Rd. E.

Medlock St.

Hulme St.

Cambridge St.

Lower Chatham St.

Chester St.

NCC

Great Jackson St.

Newcastle St.

Hulme St.

Princess Rd.

0 200 yards

0 200 meters

Mancunian Way (A57M)

Higher Cambridge St.

Loxford
Tower

Cavendish
Hall

Grosvenor
Square

Royal Northern
College of Music

Manchester
Metropolitan
University

TO WILMSLOW RD.,
MANCHESTER ROYAL
INFIRMARY (½ mi.)

Grosvenor St.

Manchester

Edinburgh (4hr., 5 per day, £46.50); **London Euston** (2-3hr.; every hr.; £61.40 off-peak, £115 peak); **York** (40min., 2 per hr., £19.50).

Manchester Victoria, Victoria St. Serves trains mostly from the north. Ticket office open M-Sa 6:30am-10pm, Su 8am-10pm. Trains to **Liverpool** (1hr., every hr., £8.80) and **Leeds** (1½hr., every 30min., £14.10).

Buses: Chorlton Street Coach Station, Chorlton St. Office open M-Th and Sa 7am-7pm, F and Su 7am-7:30pm. National Express (☎08705 818 181) to: **Birmingham** (2-3hr., every hr., £12); **Leeds** (1¼hr., every hr., £8); **Liverpool** (1hr., every hr., £6); **London** (5-6hr., every hr., £22); **Sheffield** (1-2hr., 3 per day, £7.20).

Public Transportation: Piccadilly Gardens is home to about 50 bus stops, and the new Shudehill station to the north houses even more, making transportation easy. Get a free route map from the TIC. Fares 80p-£2.20. All-day ticket £4.30. **Metrolink** trams (☎0161 205 2000, service information 08706 082 608; www.gmpte.com) connect 8 stops in the city center with Altrincham in the southwest, Bury in the northeast, and Eccles in the west (4 per hr., 60p-£4.60). Combined bus and tram ticket £4.60. Metroshuttle bus service runs from the city center to main attractions and shopping areas throughout the city. Buses every 10min. M-Sa 7am-7pm, Su 10am-6pm. Free.

Taxis: Hail taxis in front of town hall or at Piccadilly Gardens. **Mantax** (☎0161 230 3333). **Radio Cars** (☎0161 236 8033).

✦ 🛈 ORIENTATION AND PRACTICAL INFORMATION

The city center is an odd polygon formed by **Victoria Station** to the north, **Piccadilly Station** to the east, the canals to the south, and the **River Irwell** to the west. The many byways can be tricky to navigate, but the area is fairly compact, and Mancunians are generally helpful.

Tourist Information Centre: Manchester Visitor Centre, Town Hall Extension, Lloyd St. (☎0871 222 8223; www.visitmanchester.com). Books accommodations for free. Distributes the *Manchester Pocket Map, Where To Stay,* and *All About Manchester.* Open M-Sa 10am-5:30pm, Su 10:30am-5:30pm.

Tours: Guided walks and private tours available from the TIC, including the free Discover Manchester tour. **City Sightseeing** (☎01523 473 011; www.city-sightseeing. com). Runs hop-on, hop-off bus tours, departing from St. Peter's Sq. Tours every hr. daily 9:45am-4pm; £7, students £6. **Urbis** (☎0161 605 8200; www.urbis.org.uk). Runs a series of themed walking tours departing from Cathedral Gardens. Tu, F, Su 11am; £3.

Banks: Throughout the city center. **Barclays,** 23 Market St. (☎0870 241 2381). Open M-F 9am-7pm, Sa 9am-5pm, Su 11am-4pm. **American Express,** 10-12 St. Mary's Gate (☎0161 833 7303). Open M-Sa 9am-5pm, Su noon-4pm.

Library and Internet Access: Central Library, St. Peter's Sq. (☎0161 234 1900). Free. Library card required. Open M-Th 9am-8pm, F-Sa 9am-5pm.

Police: Bootle St. (☎0161 872 5050).

Pharmacy: Boots, 32 Market St. (☎0161 832 6533). Open M-F 8am-7pm, Sa 9am-7pm, Su 11am-5pm. Many branches, including 116 Portland St. and 20 St. Ann St.

Hospital: Manchester Royal Infirmary, Oxford Rd. (☎0161 276 1234).

Post Office: 26 Spring Gardens (☎0161 839 0687). Open M and W-F 9am-6pm, Tu 9:30am-6pm, Sa 9am-5:30pm. Poste Restante (☎0161 834 8605) has a separate entrance. Open M-F 6am-1pm, Sa 6am-8:50am. **Postcode:** M2 1BB.

ACCOMMODATIONS

Hostels fill up quickly in the summer, but decently priced student housing can be available when school lets out. Browse the free *Where to Stay* (at the TIC) for listings. Book ahead to be safe.

Hilton Chambers, 15 Hilton St. (☎0161 236 4414 or 0800 083 3848; www.hattersgroup.com). Conveniently located in the Northern Quarter. Spacious and spotless ensuite rooms. Upper roof deck with grill. Self-catering kitchen with coffee and tea. Laundry. Free Wi-Fi. Dorms from £15; singles from £45. AmEx/MC/V. ❷

The Hatters Hostel, 50 Newton St. (☎0161 236 9500; www.hattersgroup.com). Manchester's most popular hostel is a renovated hat factory near the Northern Quarter. Young attendants with the inside scoop on the city. Single-sex dorms available. Light breakfast included. Laundry. Internet £1 per 30min. 18-bed dorm £14.50; 8- or 10-bed £15.50; 4- or 6-bed £17.50. Singles £27.50; twins £50; triples £61.50. MC/V. ❷

YHA Manchester, Potato Wharf, Castlefield (☎08707 705 950; www.yhamanchester.org.uk). Take the Metrolink to G-Mex or bus #33 from Piccadilly Gardens toward Wigan to Deansgate and follow the signs to the youth hostel. Beautiful canal surroundings. Continental breakfast included. Lockers £1-2; free lockable cupboards in rooms. Laundry £1.50. Internet 7p per min. Dorms £25; doubles £62. MC/V. ❸

University of Manchester (☎0161 275 2888; www.accommodation.manchester.ac.uk). Call to find out which dorms are open for lodging during summer (from mid-June to mid-Sept.). 3- to 7-day min. stay. Weekly dorms from £60. MC/V. ❶

New Union Hotel, 111 Princess St. (☎0161 228 1492). This hotel's location within the heart of the glitzy, club-filled Gay Village compensates for its smallish rooms and stained rugs. Breakfast in bed £3. Free Wi-Fi. Doubles £40; twins £50; triples £60. MC/V. ❹

The Millstone Hotel, 67 Thomas St. (☎0161 839 0213). Simple but comfortable ensuite rooms conveniently located near Northern Quarter nightlife. Be sure to say hello to the colorful bar regulars at the pub downstairs. Book ahead on weekdays. Singles £30; doubles and twins £45; triples £65. Cash only. ❹

FOOD

Eat cheap in the pricey **Chinatown** restaurants by eating the multi-course "Businessman's Lunch" offered by most (M-F noon-2pm; £4-8). Better yet, visit **Curry Mile,** a stretch of Asian restaurants on Wilmslow Rd., for quality cuisine. Come evening, hip youths wine and dine in the cafe-bars. A **Tesco** is at 58-66 Market St. (☎0161 911 9400. Open M-F 6am-midnight, Sa 6am-10pm, Su 11am-5pm.)

Soup Kitchen, 31-33 Spear St. (☎0161 236 5100; www.soup-kitchen.co.uk). Communal tables and zesty homemade soups, salads, and sandwiches make this hidden treasure a perfect place for a stop while exploring the Northern Quarter. Soup £2.50-3. Open M-F 10am-3pm, Sa-Su 10am-5pm. AmEx/MC/V. ❶

Trof, 8 Thomas St. (☎0161 833 3197; www.trofnq.co.uk). A 3-story bohemian cafe/bar/restaurant. Wash down Trof's "world-famous" beef burger (£7) with 1 of the more than 40 international beers. Check out the *Trof Times* on the table for upcoming live shows. Open M-W 10am-midnight, Th-Sa 10am-1am, Su 9am-midnight. MC/V. ❷

Tampopo Noodle House, 16 Albert Sq. (☎0161 819 1966; www.tampopo.co.uk). This basement noodle house is one of Manchester's favorites. Noodles (£6.50-8.50) with ingredients from Indonesia, Japan, Malaysia, Thailand, and Vietnam. Plenty of vegetarian and vegan options. Open M-Sa noon-11pm, Su noon-10pm. AmEx/MC/V. ❷

Bella Roma, 42 Portland St. (☎0161 236 6631; www.bellaroma.org.uk). Step into this picturesque basement and step into Italy. Serves authentic southern Italian cuisine. The fake grapes on the walls, candles on every table, and old-school Italian music only add to the charm. Pizza £6-9. Pasta and wine lunch special £5. Takeaway available. Open M-F noon-3:15pm and 5:30pm-midnight, Sa-Su noon-late. MC/V.

The Ox Pub, 71 Liverpool Rd., Castlefield (☎0161 839 7740; www.theox.co.uk). Gourmet pub food may seem like an oxymoron, but that's exactly what you get at this cozy, traditional pub on the canal. 5 cask ales. Light meals from £4. Entrees £7-14. Kitchen open M-Sa noon-1am, Su noon-10pm. MC/V. ❸

Barburrito, 1 Piccadilly Gardens (☎0161 228 6479; www.barburrito.co.uk). Mexican dishes with fresh ingredients. Even more delicious? Just about everything on the menu is under £5. Open M-W 11am-9pm, Th-Sa 11am-10pm, Su noon-7pm. MC/V. ❶

⊙ SIGHTS

For a stunning panoramic view of the city, head to the top of the Shudehill Interchange parking garage, a little-known spot with views of the whole city.

▨MANCHESTER ART GALLERY. Famous for its Pre-Raphaelite paintings, the museum also features an extensive collection of 19th-century British art. Visit the gallery of recently restored paintings or the interactive exhibit, where you try to make one of the paintings burp. *(Nicholas St. ☎0161 235 8888; www.manchester-galleries.org. Open Tu-Su 10am-5pm. Guided tours Sa-Su 2pm. Free.)*

MUSEUM OF SCIENCE AND INDUSTRY. A large complex of buildings shows working looms and steam engines in a dramatic illustration of Britain's industrialization. *(Liverpool Rd., Castlefield. ☎0161 832 2244. Open daily 10am-5pm. Free.)*

URBIS. The awe-inspiring museum is a sculpture itself, clad in 2200 handmade plates of glass with a "ski-slope" copper roof. High-tech interactive exhibits provide insights into city life and culture in Manchester and beyond. *(☎0161 605 8200; www.urbis.org.uk. Open daily 10am-6pm. Free.)*

MANCHESTER CRAFT AND DESIGN CENTRE. Once a Victorian fish market, this glass-roofed atrium now displays crafts from specialty stationary to handmade jewelry. *(17 Oak St. Cathedral Gardens, between Victoria Station and Exchange Sq. ☎0161 832 4274. Open M-Sa 10am-5:30pm. Free.)*

OTHER SIGHTS. Tucked behind the town hall, the **Central Library** is the city's masterpiece. One of the largest municipal libraries in Europe, the domed building has a music and theater library, a literature library, and a library devoted only to the history of the library itself. *(☎0161 234 1900.)* The **John Rylands Library** is a working academic library with a collection of rare books and manuscripts, all housed in a Neo-Gothic building. Its most famous holding is the St. John Fragment, a piece of New Testament writing from the second century. *(150 Deansgate. ☎0161 306 0555. Open M and W-Sa 10am-5pm, Tu and Su noon-5pm. Free.)*

♫ ▩ ENTERTAINMENT AND FESTIVALS

Manchester's many entertainment venues accommodate diverse interests. The **Manchester Evening News (MEN) Arena** (☎0844 847 8000; www.men-arena.com), behind Victoria Station, hosts concerts and sporting events. The **Manchester Festival** (☎0161 234 3157; www.the-manchester-festival.org.uk) runs dramatic and musical events all summer. The Gay Village hosts a number of festivals, most notably late August's **Mardi Gras** (☎0161 238 4548), which raises money for AIDS relief. **Manchester Pride** (☎0161 236 7474; www.manchesterpride.com), held on the August bank holiday weekend (see **Holidays and Festivals,** p. 93), has live entertainment, sporting events, and a parade.

Royal Exchange Theatre, St. Ann's Sq. (☎0161 833 9833; www.royalexchange.co.uk). Originally the Manchester cotton-trading exchange, the Royal Exchange Theatre stages traditional and Shakespearean plays and premieres original works. Although the building was badly damaged by a 1996 IRA bomb and the theater was forced to move, it was restored to its original state by 1998. Tickets £8.50-29. Concessions available. Box office open M-Sa 9:30am-7:30pm. AmEx/MC/V.

Bridgewater Hall, Lower Mosley St. (☎0161 907 9000; www.bridgewater-hall.co.uk). Manchester's foremost venue for orchestral concerts and home of Manchester's own Hallé Orchestra. Tickets £8-35. Open M-Sa 10am-8pm, Su noon-6pm. AmEx/MC/V.

Palace Theatre, Oxford St. (☎0161 245 6600; www.palaceandoperahouse.org.uk). 2000-seat venue caters to classical tastes in theater, opera, and ballet. Tickets £10-75. Box office open M-Sa 10am-6pm and from 2hr. before performances. MC/V.

Cornerhouse, Oxford St. (☎0161 200 1500; www.cornerhouse.org). Screens indie films and hosts art events. Bar and cafe on-site. "Reel Deal" M includes ticket, pizza, and a pint for £11.20. DJ Th-Sa from 8pm. Box office open daily noon-8pm. MC/V.

Library Theatre Company (☎0161 236 7110; www.librarytheatre.com), located in the basement of Central Library. Puts on top-shelf productions of modern plays.

🏈 FOOTBALL

Loved, reviled, and always sung about in the streets, Manchester United is England's reigning football team. The **Manchester United Museum and Tour Centre,** at the Old Trafford football stadium, displays memorabilia dating from the club's inception in 1878 to its recent successes. Follow signs from the Old Trafford Metrolink stop. (☎0870 441 1994; www.manutd.com. Open daily 9:30am-5pm. Tours every 10min. 9:40am-4:30pm. Pre-booking encouraged. No tours on match days. £6.50, concessions £3.75. Tours £10, concessions £6.) For tickets to a match (£10-25), visit www.manutd.com or call the ticket order line at ☎0870 442 1999. Manchester's less infamous team, Manchester City, offers the **Manchester City Experience,** with a tour of the new museum and stadium. A consortium of sporting venues, **Sport City,** in the ReeBok City Building, is a 20min. walk from Piccadilly Station to Ashton New Rd. (☎0161 438 7824. Open M 11am-4:30pm, Tu-Sa 9:30am-4:30pm, Su 11am-3pm. £8.75, concessions £4.75.)

🎷 NIGHTLIFE

CAFE-BARS AND CLUBS

Many of Manchester's excellent lunchtime spots morph into pre-club drinking venues or become clubs themselves. Manchester's clubbing and live music scenes remain national trendsetters. Centered on **Oldham Street,** the **Northern Quarter** is the city's youthful outlet for live music, with its alternative vibe and underground shops attracting a hip crowd. Partiers flock to **Oxford Street** for late-night clubbing and reveling. Don't forget to collect fliers—they'll often score you a discount. **Afflecks Palace,** 52 Church St., supplies paraphernalia from punk to funk—the walls of the stairway are postered with event notices. (Open M-F 10:30am-6pm, Sa 10am-6pm.) **Fat City,** 20 Oldham St., sells hip hop, reggae, funk, and jazz records. (☎0161 237 1181; www.fatcity.co.uk. Open M-Sa 10am-6pm, Su noon-5pm.) If you're feeling unsafe crossing from Piccadilly to Swan St. or Great Ancoats St., use **Oldham Street,** where the neon-lit clubs (and their super-sized bouncers) provide reassurance.

Cord, 8 Dorsey St. (☎0161 832 9494; www.cordbar.co.uk). Where corduroy meets chic. No, really. Cozy home to bohemian intellectuals playing mellow tunes. Giant booths for gathering with friends. "Shoot Speed Social" (disco and funk) F 9pm-late. Open M-Th noon-11pm, F-Sa noon-1am, Su 3-10:30pm.

Dry Bar, 28-30 Oldham St. (☎0161 236 9840). Used to be called Dry 201, in reference to the Factory Records catalogue system. Cavorting clubbers fill this sultry spot, known as the oldest bar in Manchester. Live bands in the front room and DJs in the back. "Out of the Gloom" (funk, hip hop, and soul) Su 4pm-12:30am. Cover F-Sa £4-5.Open M-Th noon-11pm, F-Sa noon-2:30am, Su 4pm-12:30am.

The Temple, 100 Great Bridgewater (☎0161 278 1817). Literally a hole-in-the-street bar, this tiny pub was built in an old Victorian public toilet. Frequented by local artists and students. The German beer selection and intimate setting make it a great place for a relaxed night out. Open M-Th and Su noon-midnight, Sa-Su noon-1am.

Simple Bar and Restaurant, 44 Tib St. (☎0161 835 2526). Fuel up before heading out to the clubs at this pre-party bar with rocking music and great mixed drinks. Free Wi-Fi. Open M-Th 11am-11pm, F 11am-midnight, Sa 11am-1am, Su 11am-10:30pm. MC/V.

Thirsty Scholar (☎0161 236 6071; www.thirstyscholar.co.uk), off Oxford St. Students and young professionals pack into this small bar underneath a railroad bridge. At night, the rumble of overhead trains is drowned out by the thudding beats of local DJs. Acoustic nights Tu-Th. DJs F-Su. Free live music many nights. Happy hour M-F 4-8pm with selected pints for £2.20-2.50. Open M-Th and Su noon-midnight, F-Sa noon-2am.

THE GAY VILLAGE

The Gay Village developed along **Canal Street,** once a run-down part of the city, in the 1990s and has since become one of the premier "going-out" neighborhoods. Northeast of Princess St., the Gay Village fills with mixed crowds that dance by night and mingle by day. When the weather cooperates, patrons can be found flooding the many sidewalk tables lining the canal.

Essential, Bloom St. (☎0161 236 0077; www.essentialmanchester.com), at the corner of Bloom St., off Portland St. One of the Gay Village's more popular gay clubs. Catch the Morning Glory after-party at the bar Sa 4am-10:30pm. Dress smart casual. Cover £3-10. Open F 11pm-5am, Sa 11pm-6am, Su 11am-4am. MC/V.

Queer, 4 Canal St. (☎0161 228 1360; www.queer-manchester.com), midway down Canal St. Huge booths, red leather sofas, and flatscreen TVs create a great atmosphere at this classy gay bar. DJs spin excellent music that will keep you cutting rugs all night long. "Trannyoke" theme night Tu 9pm. Open M-Th 11am-late, F-Sa 11am-4am. MC/V.

New Union Showbar, 111 Princess St. (☎0161 228 1492; www.newunionhotel.com/hotel.asp). Lively show bar and club featuring live entertainment and music. Mixed crowd. Karaoke Tu night. Cabaret and drag show Su 9:30pm. Cover F-Sa after 10pm £1. Open M-Sa 11am-midnight, Su noon-12:30am. Cash only.

BLACKPOOL ☎(0)1253

Blackpool has something for everybody—except, perhaps, lovers of peace and quiet. Arcade games jostle for space with slot machines, liquor stores are outnumbered only by stalls selling "Blackpool Rock" hard candy, ferris wheel lights cast their neon glow on entrances to strip clubs, and a bustling Promenade stands over the crowded beach. Its posh 19th-century resort status has long been lost, but Blackpool's spirit of gaudy hedonism still attracts children, stag parties, grandparents, and everyone in between.

JESMOND DENE HOTEL

27 Argyle Street, Kings Cross London, WC1H 8EP UK
Tel: +44 (0) 207 837 4654   Fax: +44 (0) 207 833 1633

- Given three stars by the London Tourist Board
- One of the Top 10 rated Bed & Breakfasts in London
- Located in the heart of London near the Kings Cross St. Pancras Eurostar terminal
- A walk away from the British Museum and British Library
- Warm family atmosphere • Free Wi-Fi in all rooms

TRANSPORTATION

Buses and trains are regular, but drivers be warned: it's not uncommon to see two or more traffic cops on a single street dispensing fines.

Trains: Blackpool North Station (☎01253 620 385), 4 blocks down Talbot Rd. from North Pier. Booking office open M-Sa 5:30am-9pm, Su 7:30am-9pm. Trains (☎08457 484 950) to: **Birmingham** via **Preston** (2½hr., 1-2 per hr., £34); **Leeds** (2hr., every hr., £15.50); **Liverpool** (1½hr., every 2hr., £12.35); **London Euston** via **Preston** (3hr., every hr., £94); **Manchester** (1¼hr., 2 per hr., £12.40).

Buses: Station on Talbot Rd. Ticket office open M-Sa 5:30am-9pm. National Express (☎08705 808 080) buses to **Birmingham** (3-5hr., 6 per day, £20), **London** (6-8hr., 6 per day, £25), and **Manchester** (2hr., 5 per day, £7).

Public Transportation: Local trains use Blackpool South and Pleasure Beach stations. Local bus info is available from Blackpool Transportation Services, Metro Coastlines, on Rigby Rd. (☎01253 473 000). Bus #1 runs from North Pier to Pleasure Beach every 20min.; on weekends, vintage trams run this route more frequently. A 1-day **Travelcard** (£5.75, concessions £5.25) buys unlimited travel on trams and local buses; otherwise, 1 ride costs about £1.30, a 3-day pass £14.

Taxi: C Cabs (☎01253 292 929)

PRACTICAL INFORMATION

Tourist Information Centre: Central Promenade (☎01253 478 222). Arranges accommodations for a 10% deposit, books local shows for £1.50, and sells maps (50p) that are extremely useful for navigating Blackpool's maze of truncated streets. Open M-Sa 9am-5pm, Su 10am-4:30pm.

Banks: Easy to find, especially along Corporation and Birley St. Most are open M-F 9am-4:30pm. **ATMs** are often share space with phone booths or sit just inside arcades.

Library: Blackpool Public Library, Queen St. (☎01253 478 111). Free Internet limited to 1 hr. slots, 30min. during busy times. Open M and F 9am-5pm, Tu and Th 9am-7pm, W and Sa 10am-5pm, Su 11am-2pm.

Launderette: Albert Road Launderette, Regent Rd. Open M-F 9am-6pm, Sa 9am-4pm, Su 10am-2pm. Last wash 1hr. before close. Wash £2.80, dry £1.20-1.40.

Police: Bonny St. (☎01253 293 933).

Pharmacy: Boots, 23-38 Bank Hey (☎01253 622 276). Open M-F 9am-5:30pm, Sa 8:30am-6pm, Su 10am-4pm.

Hospital: Victoria Hospitals, Whinney Heys Rd. (☎01253 300 000).

Internet Access: Cafe@Claremont, Dickson Rd. (☎01253 299 306). 50p per 10min. Open M-F 9am-4:30pm. **Barista Coffee,** 24 Birley St. (☎01253 626 857). Wi-Fi all day £1.50, kiosks 50p per 10min. Free at the **library** (above).

Post Office: 12 Bank Hey (☎08457 223 344). **Bureau de change.** Open M-Sa 9am-5:30pm. **Postcode:** FY1 1AA.

ACCOMMODATIONS

With over 2600 guesthouses holding 96,000 beds, you won't have trouble finding a room, except on weekends during the Illuminations (p. 371), when prices skyrocket. Budget-friendly B&Bs dominate the blocks behind the Promenade between the North and Central Piers (£15-30 per person). Pick up the free *Visit Blackpool* guide at the TIC for an impressive list.

CITY OF LIGHT

The resort town of Blackpool already sparkles with neon, but every autumn the lights get even brighter. The annual Blackpool Illuminations are the world's largest temporary (and free) light show. Over 500 spotlights and floodlights, 100 mi. of lamps, and one million bulbs shine throughout the city in various interactive exhibits and artistic displays. Visitors walk, drive, or ride in one of the city's horse-drawn carriages to marvel at the stretches of lights strung across buildings, 3D animated scenes, roaming lasers, and tableaux dotted with bulbs. The 66-day festival commences with the Big Switch On, when performances by stars culminate with the flipping of the switch.

The spectacle began in 1879 with a simple installation of eight arc lamps on the Promenade. But this "artificial sunshine," as contemporary observers called it, did not become a tradition until 33 years later, when the lights were switched on again to mark Blackpool's first royal visit. Over the years, as the installations have gotten bigger and more elaborate, engineers have found ways to cut down on electricity consumption using new technology and, for the first time in 2004, the use of power from wind turbines.

The Illuminations run from late August to early November. Visit www.visitblackpool.com to learn more details. Accommodations fill up early, so book ahead.

Summerville Guest House, 132 Albert Rd. (☎01253 621 300; www.summervilleguesthouse.co.uk), corner of S. King St. and Albert Rd. From the train or bus station, head toward the ocean along Talbot Rd., turn left on Topping St., continue straight onto Alfred St., and turn left onto Albert Rd. The radiantly colored rooms all have TVs. Breakfast included. Wi-Fi £5. £16-20 per person. MC/V. ❷

Manor Grove Hotel, 24 Leopold Grove (☎01253 625 577; www.themanorgrove.co.uk). From the train or bus station, head toward the ocean along Talbot Rd., turn left on Topping St., right at Church St., and left onto Leopold Grove, and walk 1 block. Ensuite rooms with TVs and phones. Sumptuous lounge open to guests until midnight. English breakfast included. From £22 per person (except during the Illuminations). MC/V. ❷

Raffles Hotel, 73-77 Hornby Rd. (☎01253 294 713; www.raffleshotelblackpool.co.uk). From the train or bus station, head toward the ocean along Talbot Rd. and turn left on Topping St., left on Church St., right on Regent Rd., and right onto Hornby Rd. Large, comfortable rooms with modern decor. Breakfast included. Free Wi-Fi. Twins and doubles £32-72; family rooms £31-36 per person. MC/V. ❸

🍴 FOOD

Cheap kebab and fish-and-chips stands line the waterfront, but heading off the Promenade usually yields more varied alternatives. The **Iceland** supermarket, 8-10 Topping St., is on the same block as the bus station. (☎01253 751 575. Open M-Sa 8:30am-8pm, Su 10am-4pm.) The award-winning **Kwizeen** ❷, 47-49 King St., uses fresh, local produce in its diverse menu. Try the Catalan chicken breast with chorizo, pimento, and sherry for £13.50. (☎01253 290 045; www.kwizeenrestaurant.co.uk. Open M-F noon-1:30am and 6pm-last customer, Sa 6pm-last customer.) **Mandarin** ❷, 27 Clifton St., serves affordable Cantonese food (dinner from £7.50) with vegetarian options. (☎01253 622 687. Open M-Th noon-2pm and 6-11pm, F-Su noon-2pm and 6pm-midnight. AmEx/MC/V.)

👁 🎵 SIGHTS AND ENTERTAINMENT

Thirty-six nightclubs, 38,000 theater seats, several circuses, and a tangle of roller coasters line the Promenade, which is traversed by Britain's first electric tram line. Even the three 19th-century piers are stacked with Ferris wheels and chip shops. Blackpool quiets down during the week, but, when the town packs with crowds of weekenders from the south, attractions run in full force.

BLACKPOOL TOWER. A Blackpool town councilor and hotel owner returned from the 1890 Paris World Exposition convinced that an Eiffel Tower imitation was just what his hometown needed, and by 1894 the 518 ft. tower graced the city's skyline. It never quite reached international icon status, but the tower retains a kitschy charm all its own. **Towerworld,** the entertainment center surrounding its base, features exhibits on the tower, an elevator to the top, a 3D cinema, a casino, and an aquarium. An ornate Victorian-revival ballroom hosts senior citizens dancing sedately to the sounds of an electric organ by day and live swing band performances by night (8pm). Towerworld's **circus,** named the UK's best, runs up to four shows per day and features mesmerizing dance, tightrope, and stunt acts in a performance arena that converts to a pool in the show's perplexing grand finale. Mooky the Clown was voted Britain's best. Admission covers all activities. (*☎01253 622 242; www.blackpooltower.co.uk. Open daily, generally from 10am; hours vary by season. Check the website or call for details. £14-17, concessions £10-13, children £11-14. Tickets are all-day.*)

PLEASURE BEACH. Around 6,800,000 million people visit this sprawling amusement park each year, second in Europe only to Disneyland Resort Paris (EuroDisney). Modeled after an American amusement park, Pleasure Beach is known for its wood roller coasters—the twin-track **Grand National** (c. 1935) is a mecca for coaster enthusiasts. Thrill-seekers line up for the aptly named **Big One** and aren't disappointed as the 235 ft. steel behemoth—the tallest in Europe—sends them down a heartstopping 65° slope at 74 mph. Admission to the park is free, and the pay-as-you-ride system keeps queues fairly short. By night, Pleasure Beach features illusion shows. (*Across from South Pier. ☎0870 444 5566; www.blackpoolpleasurebeach.com. Opening times vary—call to verify—but are generally in summer daily 10:30am-9:30pm. £1-7 per ride. 1-day pass varies depending on season, but starts at £15-25, children £14.50-17; 2-day £45.*)

ILLUMINATIONS. Blackpool, the first town in Britain with electricity, consummates its love affair with bright lights in the **Illuminations.** The annual display takes place over 6 mi. of the Promenade from August to early November, running from dusk until about midnight. In a colossal waste of electricity, 74 mi. of cables light up the tower, the Promenade, star-encased faces of Hollywood actors, and LED displays. (*More information at www.visitblackpool.com.*)

GRUNDY ART GALLERY. If you've had enough of the dizzying Promenade, head to the Grundy, which showcases up-and-coming artists and displays the original collection of its 19th-century founder. The special galleries on the first floor rotate exhibits, while the second floor has Viking artifacts from around Blackpool's beaches. The Grundy shop specializes in artist made jewelry. (*Queen St. ☎01253 478 170; www.blackpool.gov.uk/grundyartgallery. Open M-Sa 10am-5pm. Free.*)

NIGHTLIFE

Between North and South Piers, Blackpool's famous **Golden Mile** shines with more neon than gold, hosting scores of sultry theaters, cabaret bars, and bingo halls. Clubs fall into two categories: the cool modern and the cheerfully cheesy. Most clubs have a £2-5 cover and are open 10pm-3am. Check out www.blackpoolnightlife.co.uk for more nightlife listings.

> **Syndicate,** Church St. (*☎01253 753 222; www.thesyndicate.com*). Droves of clubbers flock to this enormous club, self-advertised as the biggest in the UK. Cover Th £3; F before 11:30pm £3, after 11:30pm £5; Sa £10. Open Th-Sa 10pm-4am.

NORTHWEST ENGLAND

Sanuk, 168-170 Promenade (☎01253 292 900; www.sanukblackpool.co.uk), at the corner of Springfield Rd. Get on the guest list online and enter for free before 11:30pm. Smart casual. Cover £4-8. Open Tu, F, Su 11pm-4am, Sa 10:30pm-4am.

Rumours, Talbot Sq. (☎01253 293 204; www.rumoursandhush.co.uk), just off the Promenade. Locals hang out at this hip bar and its nightclub, called **Hush,** which plays a mix of hip hop, UK garage, and reggae. Cover £2-5. Open F 10pm-4am, Sa 9pm-4am.

CARLISLE   ☎(0)1228

Carlisle was once nicknamed "The Key of England" for its strategic position in the Borderlands between England and Scotland. Roman Emperor Hadrian, Mary, Queen of Scots, Robert the Bruce, and Bonnie Prince Charlie have all played lord of the land here. However, for many years the city's true rulers were the Border Reiver families, whose gruesome infighting shaped everything from laws to architecture. Today, Carlisle is a stopover for more peaceful border crossings and a good base for exploring Hadrian's Wall (p. 456).

NORTHWEST ENGLAND

▐▊ TRANSPORTATION. Carlisle's **train station** is on Botchergate. (Ticket office open M-Sa 4:45am-11:30pm, Su 9am-11:30pm.) Trains from Carlisle are frequent and can be significantly cheaper if you buy your tickets the day before. Trains leave to: Edinburgh (1½hr.; every hr.; £32, £10.30-13.50 with advance booking for any journey leaving after 9:30am); Glasgow (1½hr.; every hr.; £30.50, £10.50-13.50 with advance booking); London (4hr.; every hr.; £82.10, £16.50-31.50 with advance booking); Newcastle (1½hr.; M-Sa every hr., Su 9 per day; £11.10). The **bus station** is on Lonsdale St. (Open M-F 8:30am-6:30pm.) National Express (☎08705 808 080) goes to London (6½hr., 2 per day, £32). Stagecoach in Cumbria bus #555 provides access to the Lake District via Keswick (1¼hr., 3 per day, £5). Hadrian's Wall Bus AD122 affords easy summertime access to Hexham and Newcastle (M-Sa 13 per day, Su 7 per day; DayRover ticket £7.80). **Bike rental** is available at Scotby Cycles, Church St., on the roundabout. (☎01228 546 931. From £15 per day; £20 deposit. Open M-Sa 9am-5:30pm. MC/V.)

▐▊ ORIENTATION AND PRACTICAL INFORMATION. Carlisle's city center is a pedestrian zone formed (fittingly) by the intersection of **English** and **Scotch Streets.** The **Tourist Information Centre** is in the town center at the Old Town Hall. From the train station, turn left between the large gatehouses and walk three blocks across Old Town Sq. From the bus station, turn right on Lonsdale St. behind the station, cross Lowther St., and continue straight through to English St. (☎01228 625 600. Open May-June M-Sa 9:30am-5pm, Su 10:30am-4pm; July-Aug. M-Sa 9:30am-5:30pm, Su 10:30am-4pm; Sept.-Oct. and Mar.-Apr. M-Sa 9:30am-5pm; Nov.-Feb. M-Sa 10am-4pm.) Other services include: **banks** on English St.; **police** (☎01228 528 191); **Internet** access at @CyberCafe, 8-10 Devonshire St. (☎01228 512 308; £3 per hr.; open M-Sa 10am-10pm, Su 1-10pm) and the **library,** in the Lanes shopping center, across from the TIC (☎01228 607 310; £1 per 30min.; open M-F 9:30am-7pm, Sa 9:30am-4pm, Su noon-4pm); and the **post office,** 20-34 Warwick Rd., with a **bureau de change** (☎01228 512 410; open M-Sa 9am-5:30pm). **Postcode:** CA1 1AB.

▐▊ ACCOMMODATIONS AND FOOD. Carlisle has no hostels, but **Old Brewery Residences ❷,** Bridge Ln., rents YHA-affiliated accommodations in the university's student housing during its summer vacation in July and August. (☎01228 597 352. Breakfast included. Free Wi-Fi. Singles £21. MC/V.) Running east out of the city, Warwick Rd. and its side streets are scattered with B&Bs. The relaxing **Howard Lodge Guest House ❸,** 90 Warwick Rd., delivers privacy and proximity to the city center. (☎01228 529 842. All rooms ensuite. Breakfast included. Singles £35; doubles £60. Cash only.) The welcoming **Cornerways Guest House** ❸, 107 Warwick Rd., is another great option, also close to town. (☎01228 521 733; www.cornerwaysbandb.co.uk. Singles £35; doubles £60-65. MC/V.)

The fairground interior of **The Market Hall**, off Scotch St., peddles fresh fruit, veggies, and baked goods. (Open M-Sa 8am-5pm.) **Teza** ❷, Botchergate, puts a contemporary spin on Indian cuisine, with inexpensive lunch specials like "Naanwiches" (£5) and dinners ranging £7-12.50. (☎01228 525 111; www. teza.co.uk. Open Tu-Su noon-2:30pm and 5:30-10pm. AmEx/MC/V.) Jovial **Casa Romana** ❷, 44 Warwick Rd., has happy-hour specials on pizza, pasta, and risotto (£5.25-7.50) and larger meat and fish dishes around £14. (☎01228 591 969. Happy hour daily until 7pm. Open M-Sa noon-2pm and 5:30-10pm. MC/V.)

◙ SIGHTS. The **Tullie House** museum and gallery on Castle St. traces Carlisle's history from Roman times to the modern day with exhibits ranging from art and archaeology to ecology and fashion. (☎01228 618 718; www.tulliehouse. co.uk. Open July-Aug. M-Sa 10am-5pm, Su 11am-5pm; Sept.-Oct. and Apr.-June M-Sa 10am-5pm, Su noon-5pm; Nov.-Mar. M-Sa 10am-4pm, Su noon-4pm. £5.20, concessions £3.60.) Built by William II with stones from Hadrian's Wall, **Carlisle Castle** looms in the northwest corner of the city. Sucking water from grooves in the dark stone walls kept Scottish prisoners alive after the 1745 Jacobite rebellion failed. Discover these "licking stones" as you learn about forms of torture used on the Scots and the bloody history of the castle. Admission grants access to Cumbria's **Regimental Museum,** which pays tribute to more modern warriors. (☎01228 591 922. Open daily Mar.-Sept. 9:30am-5pm; Oct.-Mar. 10am-4pm. £4.50, concessions £3.60, children £2.30.) Despite centuries of warfare, daily services have been held in the **Carlisle Cathedral,** on Castle St., for nearly 900 years. The cathedral is home to exquisite 14th-century stained-glass windows and the **Brougham Triptych,** a beautifully carved Flemish altarpiece. Also noteworthy are the carved wood **misericords**—seats used by the clergymen so they could rest while standing at prayer. Sir Walter Scott married his sweetheart on Christmas Eve, 1797, in what is now called the **Border Regiment Chapel.** (☎01228 548 151; www.carlislecathedral.org.uk. Open M-Sa 7:40am-6:15pm, Su 7:40am-5pm. Evensong M-F 5:30pm. Suggested donation £2.)

THE PEAK DISTRICT

Despite its lack of any actual mountains or peaks, the Peak District offers dramatic panoramic vistas, miles of stone walls lining grassy hills, and a network of meandering rivers traversing the countryside. The more touristed southern region, known as the White Peak, encompasses miles of gentle walks through meadows and idyllic country villages constructed from the region's native limestone. The more rugged northern region, the Dark Peak, is a playground for hikers seeking moors, cliffs, and peat bottoms. Located between industrial leviathans Manchester, Nottingham, and Sheffield, the Peak District was fenced off as a royal hunting ground before 1951, when it was made Britain's first national park. With over 20 million visitors every year, the Peak District is now one of the most visited national parks in the world.

▐ TRANSPORTATION

Trains (☎08457 484 950) are scarce in the Peak District. Three lines enter its boundaries, but only one crosses the park itself. On the park's southeastern edge, one line travels from Derby to Matlock (30min.; M-Sa 11-12 per day, Su 8 per day; £4.30). In the northwest, another line runs from Manchester to Buxton (55min., at least every hr., £7.30). The third line (M-F 12 per day, Sa 18 per day, Su 12 per day) crosses the park from Manchester to Sheffield (1¼hr., £6.50), stopping at Edale (45min., £8.40), Hope (45min., £8.50), and Hathersage (1hr., £8.50) along the way. Both lines from Manchester enter the park at New Mills—the Buxton line at Newtown Station and the Sheffield line at Central Station. A 25min. signposted walk separates the stations.

Inter-village travel is possible with determination and a sturdy pair of legs. For the less hiking-inclined, the Derbyshire County Council's *Peak District Timetables* (80p) is invaluable. The booklet includes all bus routes as well as a map and info on daylong bus tickets, cycle hire, hostels, TICs, campgrounds, market days, and hospitals. The website www.derbyshire.go.uk/buses is a helpful resource for planning regional travel.

Buses make a noble effort to connect the scattered Peak towns, and Traveline (☎0870 608 2608) is a comprehensive and centralized resource. Coverage to many tourist destinations improves on Sundays, especially in summer. The Transpeak bus makes the journey between Manchester and Nottingham (3½hr., 15 per day), stopping at Buxton, Bakewell, Matlock, Derby, and other towns in between, although some buses only cover part of the route—pick up a free timetable at any TIC. Bus #218 (M-Sa 4 per day, Su 3 per day) runs from Sheffield to Bakewell (45min.) and Buxton (1¾hr.), connecting with #218 to Leek (1¼hr.) en route to Hanley (2¼hr.). Buses #272, 273, and 274 reach Castleton from Sheffield (1hr.; M-F 20 per day, Sa 16 per day, Su 14 per day). Bus #65 runs between Sheffield and Buxton via Eyam (50min., M-Sa 6 per day, Su 3 per day), and bus #173 runs from Bakewell to Castleton (50min., 4 per day). Bus #218 (M-Sa 4 per day, Su 3 per day) runs from Buxton to Bakewell (30min.) and on to Sheffield (1hr.). Bus #200 runs from Castleton to Edale (20min., M-F 3 per day), sometimes continuing to Chapel-en-le-Frith. On Sundays it runs as bus #260 and stops at the Castleton caverns (6 per day). Ride is free with proof of railway transportation. National Express buses run once per day to London from Buxton (5hr., £21.30), Bakewell (4¾hr., £20.80), and Matlock (4½hr., £20.30) with changes in Nottingham, Leicester, and Derby.

Pick up one of the half-dozen bargain day tickets outlined in the *Timetables* booklet—several have their own brochures at the TIC. For short-term visitors, the best deal is the **Derbyshire Wayfarer** (£8.30, concessions £4.15, families £13.10), which allows one day of train and bus travel throughout the Peak District and surrounding area north to Sheffield and south to Derby. It also provides a variety of discounts at local attractions and shops. Day passes are sold at the Manchester train stations, National Park Information Centres (NPICs), local rail stations, and on most buses.

The park authority offers **bike rentals** at four Cycle Hire Centres, all of which are listed in the *Peak District Timetables*. They can be found in Ashbourne (☎01335 343 156), on Mapleton Ln.; Derwent (☎01433 651 261), near the Fairholmes NPIC; Middleton Top (☎01629 823 204), at the visitors center; and Parsley Hay (☎0129 884 493), near Buxton. (Bikes £11 per 4hr., £14 per day; children £8/10; £20 deposit.) Privately run bike rentals are at Waterhouses (☎01538 308 609), in the Old Station Car Park between Ashbourne and Leek on the A523, and Carsington Water (☎01629 540 478), near Matlock off Ashbourne-Wirksworth Rd. (Bikes £5 per hr., £15 per day. Requires deposit of driver's license, passport, credit card, or similar document. Open daily-10am-5:30pm; in winter 10am-4:30pm.) *Cycle Derbyshire*, available at NPICs, includes opening hours, locations, and trail info.

Peak District National Park

○ SIGHTS

Axe Edge Moor, **28**
Birchinlee Pasture, **14**
Black Ashop Moor, **13**
Black Hill (1910 ft.), **5**
Blue John Cavern, **21**
Broomhead Moor, **10**

Derwent Moors, **18**
Dick Hill, **2**
Edale Head, **16**
Edale Moor, **17**
Hartington Upper Quarter, **26**
Middle Moss, **11**
Hope Woodlands, **12**

Jacob's Ladder, **19**
Kinder Low (2087 ft.), **15**
Longsett Moors, **7**
Mam Tor, **20**
Margery Hill (1793 ft.), **9**
Middle Hills, **29**
Peak Cavern, **24**
Raven's Low, **27**
Saddleworth Moor, **3**

Shining Clough Mass, **8**
Shining Tor (1854 ft.), **25**
Speedwell Cavern, **23**
Thor's Cave, **30**
Thurlstone Moor, **6**
Treak Cliff Cavern, **22**
Wessenden Head Moor, **4**
Wessenden Moor, **1**

▲ YHA Hostels

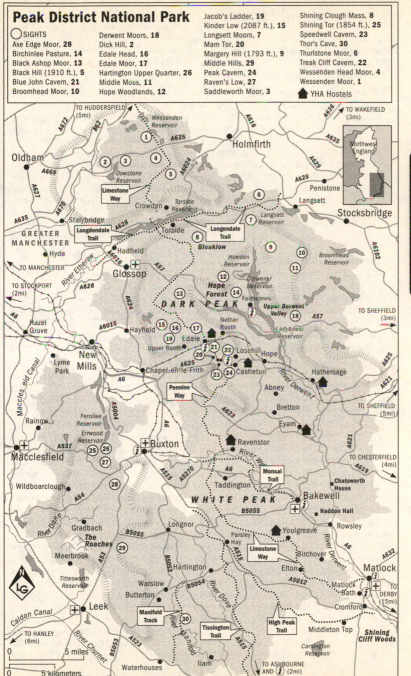

NORTHWEST ENGLAND

PRACTICAL INFORMATION

Daytime facilities in the Peak District generally stay open all winter. The **Peak District National Park Authority**, Aldern House, Baslow Rd., Bakewell, Derbyshire (☎01629 816 200; www.peakdistrict-npa.gov.uk) furnishes travelers with useful information and fun facts about the park.

National Park Information Centres: All NPICs carry town and regional maps (many town maps free, regional maps £8) and detailed walking guides (from £2).

Bakewell: Old Market Hall (☎01629 813 227), at Bridge St. From the bus stop, walk a block down Bridge St. with Bath Gardens on your left. Also a TIC, with accommodations booking. Upstairs exhibit on the town's history. Open daily Mar.-Oct. 9:30am-5:30pm; Nov.-Mar. 10am-5pm.

Castleton: Buxton Rd. (☎01629 816 572). From the bus stop, follow the road past the post office into town and head right; the NPIC is along the road that leads to the caverns. Small geological and historical display in annex. Open daily Easter-Oct. 9:30am-5:30pm; Nov.-Easter 10am-5pm.

Edale: Moorland Center, Fieldhead (☎01433 670 207), between the rail station and village; signs point the way from both directions. Open Easter-Oct. M-F 9:30am-5pm, Sa-Su 9am-5:30pm; Nov.-Easter M-F 10:30am-3:30pm, Sa-Su 9:30am-4:30pm.

Fairholmes: Upper Derwent Valley (☎01433 650 953), near Derwent Dam. Open Easter-Oct. daily 9:30am-5pm; Nov.-Dec. M-F 10am-3:30pm, Sa-Su 9:30am-4:30pm; Jan.-Easter Sa-Su 9:30am-4:30pm.

Tourist Information Centers:

Ashbourne: 13 Market Pl. (☎01335 343 666). Open Mar.-Oct. daily 10am-5pm; Nov.-Feb. M-Sa 10am-4pm.

Bakewell: See NPIC above.

Buxton: Pavilion Gardens, St. Johns Rd. (☎0129 825 106; www.visitbuxton.com). Open daily 9:30am-5pm.

Matlock: Crown Sq. (☎01629 583 388), in the town center. Open daily Mar.-Oct. 9:30am-5pm; Nov.-Feb. 10:30am-4pm.

ACCOMMODATIONS AND CAMPING

NPICs and TICs both distribute the free, park-wide *Peak District Camping and Caravanning Guide*, which lists all campsites and caravan (RV) sites. The *Peak District Visitor Guide* lists accommodations and attractions and is free from TICs and NPICs. Some B&Bs and hostels welcome travelers until December. YHA Eyam is open year-round, although it hosts camps in July and August. Most TICs book accommodations for a 10% deposit or £3. **B&Bs** are plentiful and moderately priced in the countryside (£20-30 per person) and more expensive in towns (£30-40 per person), although single rooms can be in short supply. Check the Visitor Guide for room information. YHA hostels (£13-15) usually fill several weeks in advance, especially on the weekends and in the summer. Note that many hostels are not open every day—many close on Sunday nights. Expect to pay higher rates in more tourist-oriented towns. **Buxton, Bakewell,** and **Matlock Bath** are well stocked with B&Bs.

The nine YHA-operated, farmer-owned **camping barns ❶** are simple shelters, providing a sleeping platform, water tap, and toilet. Visitors should bring a sleeping bag and camping equipment. Lucky travelers will find a shower and/or hot water. Book and pay ahead through the **YHA Camping Barns Department**, Trevelyan House, Dimple Rd., Matlock, Derbyshire, DE4 3YH (☎0870 770 8868). You can pay over the phone with a credit card, or they'll hold your reservation for five days while you mail a booking form, available in camping barn booklets and distributed at NPICs and TICs. Barns can be found in **Abney,** between Eyam and Castleton; **Alstonefield,** between Dovedale and Manifold Valley; **Birchover,** near Matlock off the B5056; **Butterton,** near the southern end of the park, along the Manifold track; **Edale** village; **Middleton-by-Youlgreave; Nab End,** in Hollinsclough; **Taddington,** Main Rd.; and **Underbank,** in Wildboarclough.

The Peak District has about a dozen **YHA hostels,** some of which are listed below. The hostels generally lie within a day's hike of one another and sell maps detailing routes to neighboring hostels. Alternatively, *Peak District Timetables* (80p at TICs) lists both YHAs and the bus services to them. Most hostels serve meals and are phasing out 10am-5pm lockouts, but 11pm curfews are still generally in place. Two of the smaller hostels (Bretton and Langsett) book through the central **YHA Diary** office (☎0870 770 8868).

BOOK A BED, BEAT THE BRATS. Though the Peak District is packed with hostels, most are used to host school groups during the summer. Call from one to three weeks ahead to reserve a space.

Castleton: Castleton Hall (☎0870 770 5758). Pretty country house and attached vicarage in the heart of town. The vicarage has nicer rooms with baths and no curfew or lockout. Spacious self-catering kitchen, several lounges, and small bar with good selection of beer. Book at least 1 week ahead during the week and 2-3 weeks ahead for weekend stays. Curfew in country house 11pm. Dorms £16, under 18 £12. MC/V. ❷

Edale: Rowland Cote (☎0870 770 5808), Nether Booth, 1½ mi. east of Edale railway station. From the train station, turn right and then left onto the main road; follow it to Nether Booth, where a sign points the way. Buses also stop within ½ mi. of the hostel. Closed from mid-July to the end of Aug. for children's camps. Doors locked at 11pm, but keypad allows 24hr. access. Dorms £16, under 18 £12. MC/V. ❷

Eyam: Hawkhill Rd. (☎0870 770 5830). Walk down the main road from the square, pass the church, and look right for the sign. With a turret and an oak door, it's more castle than hostel. Lockout 10am-3pm. Curfew 11pm. Dorms £15, under 18 £11. MC/V. ❶

Hathersage: Castleton Rd. (☎0870 770 5852). Stone building with white-framed windows and creeping ivy. Lockout noon-5pm. Curfew 11pm. Dorms £12. MC/V. ❶

Ravenstor: ½ mi. from Millers Dale (☎0870 770 6008). Buses #65 and 66 will stop here (both M-Sa 10 per day, Su 4 per day). Bar, TV, and game room. 24hr. access. Dorms £12, under 18 £9. MC/V. ❶

Youlgreave: Fountain Sq. (☎0870 770 6104). Take bus #171 or 172 from the nearby Bakewell stop. The building was once used as a village cooperative department store, and the windows still advertise "Groceries and Provisions." Reception closed 10am-5pm, but key allows 24hr. access. Curfew 11pm. Dorms £14, under 18 £10. MC/V. ❶

🥾 HIKING

With over 5000 mi. of public footpaths, the central Peak District is marvelous territory for hiking. Settlement is sparser and buses are fewer north of Edale near the **Kinder Scout Plateau,** the great **Derwent Reservoirs,** and the gritty cliffs and peat moorlands. From Edale, the **Pennine Way** (p. 402) runs north to Kirk Yetholm in Scotland. Local hikers prefer the trails near the Derwent Reservoirs, the paths to Kinder Scout from Edale, and the route from Dovedale to Tissington. Ask at NPICs for details and further recommendations. Be advised that hikers should bring warm clothing and the customary supplies (see **Wilderness Safety,** p. 51). Be respectful of the many acres of private land close to (and sometimes on) the trails. Guidebooks and a variety of walking and hiking maps (some free, others from £2) are available at TICs and NPICs. The park authority offers guided walks most weekends and some weekdays. Inquire at any NPIC for a schedule or check www.peakdistrict.org.

CASTLETON   ☎(0)1433

The small town of Castleton (pop. 1200) lies within easy reach of both the flat woodlands and easy hills of the White Peak and the starker, valley-filled landscape of the Dark Peak. Trekkers of all ages pass through town to explore the various trails and nearby caves, full of the colorful mineral Blue John (from the French "bleu et jaune," or "blue and yellow"), found only in the local bedrock and in gift shops. With its postcard-perfect streets lined with ivy-covered stone buildings and hedged gardens, Castleton is a lovely base from which to explore the rest of the Peak District.

TRANSPORTATION AND PRACTICAL INFORMATION. Castleton lies 2 mi. west of the **Hope** train station (avoid Castleton Station or you'll end up in a suburb of Manchester). From Hope, **trains** run to Manchester (45min., 4 per day, £8), London (3½hr., 10 per day, £16), and Liverpool (2½hr., 3 per day, £15). Bus #272 runs from Hope to Castleton (M-Sa 18 per day, Su 12 per day; £1.70), continuing on to Sheffield (70min.; M-Sa 14 per day, Su 12 per day). **Buses** run to Sheffield, Buxton, and Bakewell (p. 381). Hikers looking for a challenge can set off southward on the 46 mi. **Limestone Way Trail,** which crosses the White Peak and ends at Rocester in Staffordshire.

Castleton's **NPIC** (p. 376) stocks maps and brochures (many under £1) on local walks. Hikers can visit the **SafariQ UIP,** The Stones, in the center of town off the marketplace by the hostel, for supplies and information. (☎01433 620 320; www.safariquip.co.uk. Open M-F 9:30am-5pm, Sa-Su 9:30am-5:30pm. MC/V.) The nearest **bank** is 6 mi. east in Hathersage; on How Ln., the Cheshire Cheese Inn (below) offers cash back for a £1.50-1.80 fee. The **post office,** also on How Ln., is in a convenience store near the bus stop. (☎01433 620 241. Open M-Tu and Th-F 9am-1pm and 2-5pm, W and Sa 9am-12:30pm.) **Postcode:** S33 8WJ.

ACCOMMODATIONS AND FOOD. Castleton is home to several B&Bs, but expect to pay at least £35 for a single and £40-50 for a double. The **YHA Castleton ❶,** Castle St., feels like home, with a friendly staff and cluster of old stone buildings around a quiet courtyard. It sits in the center of town, next to the entrance to Peveril Castle (opposite page). **Ye Olde Cheshire Cheese Inn ❸,** How Ln., above a pub, has one of the few single rooms in town. (☎01433 620 330. Full English breakfast included. Singles £35; doubles £65-70. AmEx/MC/V.) **Ye Olde Nags Head ❸,** also above a pub, has individually decorated rooms with rustic touches. (☎01433 620 248. All rooms ensuite. Doubles M-Th £60, F-Su £75. MC/V.)

Attractive patios and traditional pubs line Castle St. The warm staff at **The George ❷,** Castlve St., whips up excellent pub fare and bedecks the beer garden with flowers. (☎01433 620 238. Open daily noon-11pm. Kitchen open M-Th noon-2pm and 5:30-8pm, Sa noon-9pm, Su noon-3pm. MC/V.)

SIGHTS. Buses don't serve the caves on weekdays, but on weekends #260 makes a loop between Edale and Castleton (Sa-Su and bank holidays 6 per day), stopping at Blue John, Speedwell, and Treak Cliff caverns. The lack of weekday buses should not discourage visitors, since all caves are within walking distance of town. Peak Cavern is 5min. from town, both Speedwell and Treak Cliff caverns are about 20min. outside the city, and Blue John Cavern is within a 45min. walk. All caves are in the same direction; as you leave Castleton on Cross St. (which becomes Buxton Rd.), formerly the A625, pass a large sign for Peak Cavern. Road signs for the other caves appear within 10min. Peak Cavern is also accessible by a footpath starting in the middle of town near

Peveril Castle. Follow the posted signs. Some of the caves are cold and slippery inside; be sure to wear good walking shoes.

Although it's not the first cave on the road out of Castleton, ☙**Treak Cliff Cavern** is the one most worth visiting. The engaging 40min. tours accentuate the amazing natural features of its interiors—deep purple seams of Blue John, frozen cascades of rigid flowstone, and "sculpted" mineral stalactites and stalagmites. Highlights include a view of the huge Dream Cave by candlelight, as miners from a century ago would have seen it. (☎01433 620 571; www.bluejohnstone.com. Open daily Mar.-Oct. 10am-4:20pm; Nov.-Feb. 10am-3:20pm. Tours every 20-30min. £7, concessions or YHA members £6, children £3.60, families £19. MC/V over £10.) Just outside Castleton, in the gorge beneath the castle ruins, **Peak Cavern** features the largest natural cave mouth in Britain. Known in the 18th century as the "Devil's Arse" for the flatulence-like sounds caused by the running waters within, the cavern is known more for its history—highlighted on high-spirited 1hr. tours—than for its natural features. Christmastime brings mincemeat pies and live brass bands for subterranean merrymaking. (☎01433 620 285; www.devilsarse.com. Open Apr.-Oct. daily 10am-5pm; Nov.-Mar. Sa-Su 10am-5pm. 2-3 tours per weekday; call for times. Last tour 4pm. £7.25, concessions £6.75.) A joint pass (£12, concessions £10.25, children £8.50) is sold for Peak Cavern and **Speedwell Cavern.** The latter has boat tours through the underground canals of an old lead mine that end at "The Bottomless Pit," a huge subterranean lake. (☎01433 620 512; www.speedwellcavern.co.uk. Tours daily 10am-5pm. £7.75, concessions £6.75, children £5.75.) **Blue John Cavern** is the only cave besides Treak Cliff Cavern to offer views of the mineral veins from which it takes its name. (☎01433 620 638. Open daily, weather permitting. £8, concessions £6, children £4, families £22.) The caverns are all cold, so dress warmly. Screeching school groups often convene at midday—arrive early.

William Peveril, a baron of William the Conqueror, built 11th-century **Peveril Castle** atop a hill with far-reaching views so that he could survey possible threats to his lead mines. After changing hands several times, it was used as a jail before falling into disrepair in the 1500s. The climb may be daunting, but the view of Hope Valley is worth the effort. (☎01433 620 613; www.english-heritage.co.uk. Open May-Sept. daily 10am-6pm; Oct. daily 10am-5pm; from Nov. to late Mar. M and

FROM THE ROAD

HOW I LEARNED TO LOVE THE FRY-UP

Staying in British B&Bs opened up a new vocabulary to me of phrases like "ensuite doubles," "unrivaled views," "charming oak beams," and "riverside cottage by a quiet cul-de-sac." But perhaps most novel was the staple of these guesthouses, the traditional full English breakfast. I have never been much of a breakfast person. My first morning in Britain, my lovely hostess asked if I would be having "the full cooked," and I declined, deciding to stick with the more familiar yogurt and toast. She seemed a bit let down, and rightly so—it's called a bed and *breakfast* for a reason.

I was more adventurous the next time; I opted for the works. What I got surprised and alarmed me somewhat: cereal, half a grapefruit, toast with jam, thick slices of bacon, shiny sausage, a fried egg, fried bread, black pudding (pork fat and blood), grilled tomatoes, and mushrooms, with a runny serving of baked beans spreading into the empty spaces. No wonder it's also called the fry-up. There are even variations on the full English, I would later learn: some places serve kippers (smoked herring), potato waffles, or porridge with honey, if you're lucky. I cleaned my plate, in any case, and felt, if not completely well, at least initiated into this great British institution.

—*Alanna Windsor*

Th-Su 10am-4pm; from late Mar. to Apr. M and Th-Su 10am-5pm. £3.70, concessions £3, children £2. Guidebooks £3.50.)

BUXTON   ☎(0)1298

Popular since the AD first century, when the Romans discovered its supposedly healing thermal waters, Buxton emerged from a recent cleanup as a picture of Georgian elegance. Conveniently, it is also a transportation hub.

☐ ☑ TRANSPORTATION AND PRACTICAL INFORMATION. Trains run from Buxton to London (3hr., 1 per hr., £14-62), Liverpool (2hr., 1-2 per hr., £16), and Manchester (1-1½hr., 1-2 per hr.). National Express **buses** depart for London (5¾-6½hr., 7 per day, £21.50) and Manchester (1hr., 1 per day).

The well-stocked **Tourist Information Centre** (p. 376) is in the Pavilion Gardens on St. Johns Rd. Other services include: **HSBC Bank,** 1 The Quadrant (☎01298 0845 7404404) with a 24hr. ATM; **camping supplies** at Yeoman's, 41 Spring Gardens (☎01298 743 30; open in summer M-Sa 9am-5:30pm, Su 10am-5pm, in winter M-Sa 9am-5:30pm); a **launderette** at 5-Ways Launderette, at the junction of Dale Rd., London Rd., Green Ln., High St., and West Rd. (☎01298 720 18); **police,** Silverlands (☎0845 123 3333); a **hospital,** London Rd. (☎02198 22 923); free **Internet** at **Buxton Public Library,** Kents Bank Rd. (☎01298 253 31; open M and W-F 9am-7pm, Tu 9am-5:30pm, Sa 9am-4pm) and the Buxton Museum and Art Gallery; and a **post office,** in the Co-op on Spring Gardens (☎01298 230 01; open M-F 8:30am-6pm, Sa 8:30am-3pm). **Postcode:** SK17 6AA.

☐ ☐ ACCOMMODATIONS AND FOOD. The best deal in town is the **Roseleigh Hotel ❸,** 19 Broad Walk, a Victorian-style guesthouse furnished with period decor. The hotel sits along the promenade facing the Pavilion Gardens. The hosts are former adventure guides and give guests free run of their large reading parlor, which is stocked with travel books. (☎01298 249 04; www.roseleigh-hotel.co.uk. Breakfast included. Free Wi-Fi and Internet. Singles with private baths £33-38; ensuite doubles £70, more for lake view. MC/V.) **The Grove Hotel ❷,** 10 Grove Parade, rents basic rooms in a central location. (☎02198 238 04. All rooms ensuite. Singles £25; doubles £40; family rooms £55. MC/V.)

Simply Thai ❷, 2-3 Cavendish Circus, serves tasty Thai food and a large selection of vegetarian entrees from £6 (☎01298 244 71; open daily noon-2:30pm and 5-11pm) while **The Slopes Bar ❶,** 10 Grove Parade, in the Grove Hotel, sells light sandwiches (£2.25-3) and cafe fare in a swank bistro setting. **Waitrose,** 33 Spring Gardens Centre (☎01298 767 469; open M-Tu 8:30am-4pm, W-F 8:30am-8pm, Sa 8am-7pm) and a **Co-op,** 97-103 Spring Gardens (☎01298 278 44; open M-Sa 8am-11pm, Su 8am-10:30pm) sell groceries.

☐ SIGHTS. Visitors lounge on the steep lawns of **The Slopes,** whose curved pathways mirror the arc of **The Crescent** across the street. At the foot of The Slopes, **St. Anne's Well** is a source of Buxton's famous spa mineral water, which is bottled and sold by entrepreneurs. The shady **Broad Walk,** a Victorian-style promenade, runs alongside Pavilion Gardens, St. John's Rd. The meticulously manicured gardens include a calming stream, expanses of grass, and several manmade pools that are a welcome treat for weary hikers. Up the hill on Terrace Rd., the **Buxton Museum and Art Gallery** showcases and sells work by local artists in its two rotating exhibits and chronicles the geology and human history of the Peaks District in a permanent one. (☎01298 246 58. Open Easter-Sept. Tu-F 9:30am-5:30pm, Sa 9:30am-5pm, Su 10:30am-5pm; Oct.-Easter Tu-F 9:30am-5:30pm, Sa 9:30am-5pm. Free.) Just outside of town is the spectacular

Poole's Cavern, Green Ln., within Buxton Country Park. Visitors to the cavern in the 1700s would be met by locals who lured them into the then-unlit caves and mugged them, but today's guides are not so unscrupulous, instead giving informative 45min. tours. The rock formations inside resemble everything from a cauliflower to a man's head to a slab of bacon. Legend has it that Mary, Queen of Scots, visited the caves in 1580, and a large stalactite inside is named in her honor. (☎01298 269 78; www.poolescavern.co.uk. Open Mar.-Dec. daily 10am-5pm. 45min. tours leave every 30min.; last tour departs at 4:30pm. £7, concessions £5.50, children £4.) The surrounding park is a destination in its own right, with scenic **walking trails,** a **zip lining** adventure course (☎0845 643 2039; www.goape.uk; open Mar.-Oct.; book ahead; £25, under 18 £20; MC/V) and **Solomon's Temple,** a 19th-century folly (faux castle).

BAKEWELL ☎(0)1629

Cottages made of burnt-brown gritstone, dusty antique shops, and a gentle river make Bakewell ideal for a day of peaceful strolling and window-shopping. Located near several scenic walks through the White Peaks, the town's claim to fame is Bakewell pudding, a rich, sweet, jelly-like dessert invented there.

TRANSPORTATION AND PRACTICAL INFORMATION. From Bakewell, **buses** depart to Manchester (2 hr., 6 per day), Sheffield (45min.; M-Sa 14 per day, Su 12 per day), and Matlock (Transpeak #172, 20-50min., about 2 per hr.).

Bakewell's stone buildings line a network of crooked streets and hidden courtyards that converge on a park at central **Rutland Square.** Spanned by the five graceful arches of the 14th-century **Town Bridge,** the River Wye curls around the town. Bakewell's **NPIC,** at the intersection of Bridge and Market St., doubles as a **TIC** (p. 376). Other services include: an HSBC **bank,** Rutland Sq. (open M-F 9:30am-4:30pm); **camping supplies** at Yeoman's, 1 Royal Oak Pl., off Matlock St. (☎01629 815 371; open M-Sa 9am-5pm, Su 10am-5pm); **police,** Granby Rd. (☎01629 812 504); free **Internet** access at **Bakewell Public Library,** Orme Ct. (☎01629 812 267; open M-Tu and Th 9:30am-5pm, W and F 9:30am-7pm, Sa 9:30am-4pm); and a **post office,** in the Spar on Granby Rd. (☎01629 815 112; open M 8:30am-5:30pm, Tu-F 9am-5:30pm, Sa 9am-1pm). **Postcode:** DE45 1ET.

ACCOMMODATIONS AND FOOD. Accommodations in Bakewell are expensive. The *Peak District Visitor Guide,* free at the TIC, lists B&Bs in the area, but expect to pay at least £40 for a single and £50 for a double. Truly elegant stays await at the **Rutland Arms Hotel ❹,** The Square, which has lodged famous Peak-country pilgrims like Byron, Coleridge, Wordsworth, and Turner. Individually decorated rooms feature luxurious beds and satellite TVs. (☎01629 812 812; www.bakewell.demon.co.uk. Full breakfast included. Apr.-Oct. singles £59-65; doubles £99-115. Nov.-May singles £55-65; doubles £89-101. 20% discount during the week. AmEx/MC/V.) **The Haven ❸,** Haddon Rd., rents airy rooms in a traditional Victorian house. (☎01629 812 113; www.visitbakewell. com. Breakfast included. Doubles M-F £55, Sa-Su £60. Cash or check only.) **Castle Inn ❸,** Castle St., has tidy rooms near the center of town. (☎01629 812 103. Doubles £60; family rooms £80. MC/V.)

Locals pour into Bakewell's **market,** held since 1330, off Bridge St. (Open M 9am-4pm.) The Midlands **Co-op** sells groceries at the corner of Granby Rd. and Market St. (Open M-Sa 8am-10pm, Su 10am-4pm.) **JR's Brasserie ❷,** Kings Ct., delivers light bistro fare and homemade cakes (£2.65 per slice) in its cozy upstairs dining room and adjoining courtyard. Complete "The Challenge" by eating a 2½ lb. burger in under an hour, and you get the burger free and your name posted on the wall. (☎01629 810 022. Open M-Th and Su 10:30am-4:30pm, F-Sa 10:30am-11pm. MC/V.) **The Wheatsheaf ❷**, Bridge St., serves hearty meals ($5.50-11.25) in a homey setting. (☎01629 8129 85. Open daily 11am-11pm.) The **Old Original Bakewell Pudding Shop ❶**, The Square, claims to have the original 150-year-old pudding recipe and ships the stuff around the world. (☎01629 812 193; www.bakewellpuddingshot.co.uk. Puddings $5.)

◪ SIGHTS. On the hill above town, **All Saints Church** (open to visitors daily) is surrounded by weathered gravestones. Edging the Wye, the tiny **Bakewell Sensory Gardens** (open 24hr.) are worth a look. Nearby on Cunningham Pl., a 16th-century timber-frame house shelters the **Old House Museum,** which displays regional heritage in the form of a Tudor lavatory, blueprints for a house made of cow dung, and other less excrementitious items. (☎01629 813 642; www.old-housemuseum.org.uk. Open Apr.-Oct. daily 11am-4pm. $3. Guidebooks $1.50.)

◪ DAYTRIP FROM BAKEWELL: CHATSWORTH HOUSE. When the sixth Duke of Devonshire ordered a new set of marble carvings for the fireplaces of his (third) dining room at Chatsworth, he was a bit disappointed with the results; he had wanted "more abandon and joyous expression." Only in a house as magnificent as Chatsworth could his complaint seem anything but ridiculous. Once hailed as "the National Gallery of the North," the manor house is a jumble of architectural and artistic treasures ranging from antiquity to the present day: a 2006 Frank Gehry vase sits alongside delicate 18th-century porcelain dishes. Scenes from the 2005 adaptation of *Pride and Prejudice* were filmed on the impressive grounds, which feature several elaborate fountains, a dizzying hedge maze, and an unstructured rock garden that contrasts with the neatly groomed lawns. Explore the elaborate gardens or roam the surrounding acres of grounds for free. A short walk from the back of the house stands **Queen Mary's Bower,** a prospect tower that Mary, Queen of Scots, supposedly used as an outdoor exercise area when she was being held prisoner under the guard of Lord Shrewsbury at Chatsworth. *(Buses #213-214 from Matlock (M-F 7 per day, Sa 6 per day) and #58 from Bakewell (Su 2 per day) go directly to the house. Or take bus #170 from Bakewell to Baslow (M-Sa 12 per day, Su 10 per day) and a scenic 30min. walk through Chatsworth's park to the house. ☎01246 565 300; www.chatsworth.org. House open daily from mid-Mar. to late Dec. 11am-5:30pm. Last entry 4:30pm. Gardens open daily June-Aug. 10:30-5pm; Sept.-May 11am-5pm. House from mid-Mar. to Oct. £11.25, concessions £9.25, children £6, families £28; Nov.-Dec. £12.50/10.50/6.50.33. Gardens £7, concessions £6, children £4.50, families £21. 1hr. audio tour £2.50. House guidebook £4. Gardens guidebook £3.50.)*

◪ DAYTRIP FROM BAKEWELL: HADDON HALL. One of the best-preserved English houses from the Middle Ages, Haddon was spared from the Victorian renovations that altered so many other estates. The house isn't as opulent as Chatsworth, but it retains an Elizabethan ambience and authenticity that make it worth a visit. Its stone walls, covered with climbing roses, seem perfectly at home in the sheep-studded countryside. Visitors can also admire the Wye from Haddon's award-winning gardens. Many filmmakers have been charmed by the building. Visitors may recognize it as the setting for *The Princess Bride,* Franco Zefferelli's *Jane Eyre,* and, most recently, *The Other Boleyn Girl.* The house museum includes numerous artifacts, some dating back to the 16th century, found during a renovation of the house in the 1920s. Have a look at the Long Gallery, a 110 ft. long room lined with oak, painted to resemble marble, and built so that women could get exercise by walking without exposing their fair and delicate complexions to the sun. *(Haddon Hall is 2 mi. from Bakewell. From town, walk down Matlock St. as it becomes Haddon Rd. and then the A6. Several buses, including*

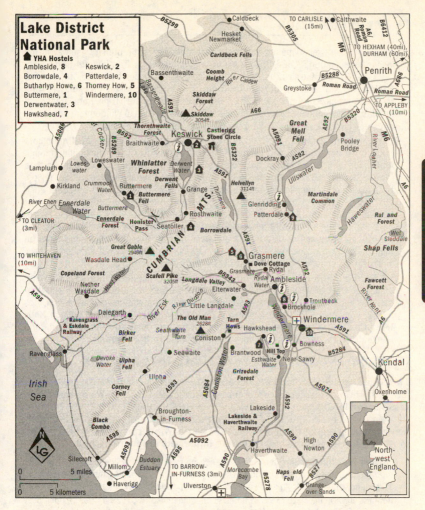

Lake District National Park

⛺ **YHA Hostels**

Ambleside, 8
Borrowdale, 4
Butharlyp Howe, 6
Buttermere, 1
Derwentwater, 3
Hawkshead, 7

Keswick, 2
Patterdale, 9
Thorney How, 5
Windermere, 10

NORTHWEST ENGLAND

#171-172 and the Transpeak, stop outside the gate. ☎01629 812 855; www.haddonhall.co.uk. Open May-Sept. daily noon-5pm; Oct. and Apr. M and Sa-Su noon-5pm. £8.50, concessions £7.50, children £4.50, families £22. Guidebook £5.)

THE LAKE DISTRICT

Blessed with some of the most stunning scenery in England, the Lake District owes its beauty to a thorough glacier-gouging during the Ice Age. The district's jagged peaks and glassy lakes are paradise for countless hikers, bikers, and boaters, who almost outnumber sheep in the summer (almost). However, visitors needn't be hardened explorers to enjoy the region—tranquil valleys and coves are within a short walk of even the busiest towns and roads.

☐ TRANSPORTATION

Trains: By train, Oxenholme, on the West Coast Mainline, is the primary gateway to the lakes. Trains (☎08457 484 950) leave from Oxenholme to: **Birmingham** (2hr., every hr., £48.50); **Edinburgh** (2hr.; M-F 10 per day, Sa-Su 5 per day; £35.50); **London Euston** (3hr.; M-Sa 9 per day, Su 7 per day; £121); **Manchester Piccadilly** (1¾hr.; M-Sa 10 per day, Su 4 per day; £22). A branch line covers the 10 mi. from Oxenholme to **Windermere** (20min., every hr., £3.50). Direct service runs to Windermere from **Manchester Piccadilly** (1-2hr..; M-Sa 5 per day, Su 1 per day; £25.50).

Buses: National Express (☎08705 808 080) goes from Windermere to **Birmingham** (5hr., 1 per day, £34.50) and **London** (8½hr., 1 per day, £32.50), continuing through **Ambleside** and **Grasmere** to **Keswick.** Stagecoach connects Keswick with **Carlisle** (1hr., 3 per day £6.65). Stagecoach in Cumbria is the primary operator in the region. The *Lakesrider,* a complete timetable, is available free from TICs and on board each bus. Major routes include: Lakeslink bus #555 from **Lancaster** to **Carlisle,** stopping at **Kendal, Windermere, Ambleside, Grasmere,** and **Keswick** (M-Sa 14 per day, Su 10 per day), and the open-top #599 between **Bowness** and **Grasmere** (50min., Apr.-Aug. 2-3 per hr.). An **Explorer Ticket,** available on buses and at TICs, offers unlimited travel on area Stagecoach buses. The 4- and 7-day passes save money, even for shorter stays. 1-day £9.50, children £6.25; 4-day £21/14.50; 7-day £30/20.50.

YHA Shuttle: The YHA Ambleside provides a minibus service (☎01539 432 304) that meets the train at Windermere station and ferries hikers (or just their packs) to Windermere and Ambleside hostels (7 per day; 1st trip from station free, additional trips £2.50; bags only £2). It also completes a circular route of hostels in **Coniston Holly How, Coniston Coppermines, Elterwater, Grasmere, Helvellyn, Hawkshead,** and **Langdale** (2 per day, £5), plus a daily service by request to **Patterdale.**

✈ ☑ ORIENTATION AND PRACTICAL INFORMATION

The Lake District National Park occupies the heart of Cumbria. The A591 runs along the north-south axis of the park, joining the towns of **Windermere, Bowness, Ambleside, Grasmere,** and **Keswick.** From these towns, paths snake out into the rest of the park. The major lakes surround Grasmere, at the park's center. **Derwentwater** is one of the most beautiful lakes, Windermere is the largest and most developed, and western lakes like **Buttermere** are more natural.

National Park Information Centres: Dispense maps and fishing licenses, book accommodations (local accommodations 10% deposit; non-local accommodations £4 plus 10% deposit), and offer guided walks. More information at www.lake-district.gov.uk.

Bowness Bay: On the steamer pier in Bowness-on-Windermere (☎01539 442 895). Open daily Apr.-Oct. 9:30am-5:30pm; Nov.-Mar. 10am-4pm.

Brockhole: Between Windermere and Ambleside (☎01539 446 601). Most buses stop here. Exhibits, talks, films, and special events. Open Apr.-Oct. daily 10am-5pm.

Keswick: In the Moot Hall in Market Pl. (☎017687 72645). Open daily Apr.-Oct. 9:30am-5:30pm; Nov.-Mar. 10am-4pm.

Ullswater: Main Car Park (☎01768 482 414). Open daily Easter-Oct. 9:30am-5:30pm; Nov.-Easter 9:30am-3:30pm.

☐ ACCOMMODATIONS

Despite B&Bs lining every street in many towns and hostels around nearly every bend, lodgings in the Lake District fill up quickly in summer. Reserve well in advance, especially for weekend stays. Many B&Bs will refuse to take reservations for fewer than two nights in summer. The Lake District is home to the widest selection of youth hostels in Britain: 24 **YHA hostels** provide accommodations in the park but can differ substantially in facilities and style. *Let's Go* lists only YHA hostels that are located in or near the major Lake District towns. Information regarding YHA hostels in more remote areas of the Lake District is available at www.yha.org.uk or by calling the Lake District Reservations Service (☎01539 431 117). At all YHA hostels, reception is often closed 10am-5pm, although public areas and restrooms are usually accessible throughout the day; larger hostels often open check-in at 2pm. Many of the larger hostels rent mountain bikes (£2 per hr., £7 per ½-day, £10 per day), which can be ridden from hostel to hostel by arrangement. The YHA shuttle (above) travels between the bigger hostels. YHA also operates 14 wilderness **camping barns** in the Lakes; for information or reservations, call the Keswick NPIC (☎01768 772 645). **Campgrounds** are scattered throughout the park; use the convenient YHA reservation service (☎01539 431 117).

Ambleside: Waterhead, Ambleside (☎01539 432 304), 1 mi. south of Ambleside on Windermere Rd. (A591), 3 mi. north of Windermere. Buses #505, 554, 555-599, and 618 stop in front of this mother of all hostels. 257 beds right on the lake. Books tours, rents canoes, and serves great meals. Bar available. Breakfast included. Internet £1 per 15min. Wi-Fi £5 per hr., £12 for 24hr. Dorms £16-21. MC/V. ❷

Borrowdale: Longthwaite, Borrowdale (☎01768 777 257). Take bus #79 from Keswick and follow signs from Rosthwaite Village. Riverside hostel with 88 beds and a laid-back atmosphere. Internet £2.50 per 30min. Reception 7:30am-noon and 1-11pm. Curfew 11pm. Open Mar.-Dec. Dorms £13.50-15.50, under 18 £11. MC/V. ❶

Buttermere: Buttermere, Cockermouth (☎0870 770 5736). Quiet hostel near Crummock Water is a respite from the hustle of larger, more touristed Lake District hostels. Views of Red Pike from the lounge. Ask reception about great walks that start right from the hostel. Reception 8:30-10am and 5-10:30pm. Curfew 11am. Open Mar.-Oct. daily; Nov.-Feb. Sa-Su. Dorms £12-20. ❷

Coniston Holly How: Far End, Coniston (☎01539 441 323), just north of the village at the junction of Hawkshead and Ambleside Rd. Modernized country house with many walks that leave right from the hostel's doorstep. 61 beds. Breakfast £4; packed lunch £3.50-4.50. Laundry available. Curfew 11pm. Open Jan.-Sept.; call ahead. Dorms £16-18, under 18 £12. MC/V. ❷

Derwentwater: Barrow House, Borrowdale (☎01768 777 246), 2 mi. south of Keswick on the B5289. Take bus #79, also a Keswick Launch stop. 88-bed, 200-year-old house with its own waterfall and playground. Self-catering kitchen. Breakfast £4; packed lunch £3.40-4.30; dinner from £7.50. Internet £2.50 per 30min. Curfew 11:30pm. Open Mar.-Oct. daily; Nov.-Feb. F-Sa. Dorms £16-20, under 18 £12-16. MC/V. ❷

Grasmere (☎01539 435 316) has 2 YHA hostels.

Butharlyp Howe: Easedale Rd., 450 ft. from town center. The more modern, conveniently located Grasmere hostel. 81-bed Victorian house with 2- to 9-bed dorms. Breakfast £4; packed lunch £3.40-4.30; dinner from £6.50. Laundry. Internet £1 per 15min. Reception 5-11pm. Curfew 11pm. Open Mar.-Oct. daily; Nov.-Feb. F-Sa. Dorms £16-19.50. MC/V. ❷

Thorney How: Easedale Rd. From Butharlyp Howe, walk another ½ mi. and turn right at the fork; the hostel is ¼ mi. down on the left. 51-bed, 350-year-old farmhouse whose lounge still makes use of the original open fire, although all the rest of the facilities have been updated and modernized. A popular stop for Coast to Coast Walkers. Dorms £16, under 18 £12. MC/V. ❷

Hawkshead: Esthwaite Lodge (☎01539 436 293), 1 mi. south of Hawkshead on a posted route. Bus #505 from Ambleside stops at the village center. Follow Newby Bridge Rd. to this mansion overlooking Esthwaite Water. 109 beds. Self-catering kitchen. Breakfast £4; packed lunch £3.40-4.30; 3-course dinner £7.50. Laundry. Internet £2.50 per

30min. Reception 7:30-10am and 1-11pm. Curfew 11:30pm. Open Feb.-Oct. daily; Nov.-Dec. F-Sa. Dorms £14-22, under 18 £10. MC/V. ❷

Keswick: Station Rd. (☎0870 770 5894). From the TIC, bear left down Station Rd.; YHA sign on the left. Newly renovated with modern facilities in a riverside location near Keswick's bustling town center. 85 beds. Breakfast included. Packed meals and Internet access available. Curfew 11:30pm. Dorms £20, under 18 £14.50. MC/V. ❷

Patterdale: On the A592 to Kirkstone Pass (☎01768 482 394), ¼ mi. south of Patterdale village. Scandinavian-style, grass-roofed building with great access to Ullswater. 82 beds. Remedial massage clinic. Reception 7:30-10am and 5-11:30pm. Curfew 11pm. Open Apr.-Aug. daily; Sept.-Oct. and Feb.-Mar. M and Th-Su; from Nov. to mid-Feb. F-Sa. Dorms £15-20, under 18 £10; doubles £32/20-26. MC/V. ❷

Windermere: Bridge Ln. (☎01539 443 543), 2 mi. north of Windermere off the A591. Catch the YHA shuttle from the train station. Small rooms in 70-bed house with panoramic views of the lake. Breakfast £4; packed lunch £3.50-4.50; 3-course dinner £7.50. Laundry available. Internet £2.50 per 30min. Rents bikes. Open Feb.-Nov. daily; early Dec. F-Sa. Dorms £14-16, under 18 £9-10.50. MC/V. ❷

HIKING AND OTHER OUTDOOR ACTIVITIES

Outdoor enthusiasts run (and walk and climb) rampant in the Lakes. NPICs have guidebooks and advice for mountain-bike trails, pleasant family walks, tough climbs, and hikes ending at pubs. Most also offer guided walks throughout the summer. Hostels are another excellent source of information, with large maps on the walls and free advice from experienced staff.

HIKE NAME	LENGTH	LEVEL	HIKE NAME	LENGTH	LEVEL
Stockghyll Force (p. 390)	1 mi. one-way	Easy	Helm Cragg (p. 391)	4 mi. round-trip	Difficult
Castlerigg Stone Circle (p. 389)	4 mi. loop	Easy	Helvellyn (p. 391)	4 mi. one-way	Difficult
Wordsworth Walk (p. 391)	6 mi. loop	Easy	Catbells/Newlands p. 389)	8½ mi. loop	Difficult
Orrest Head (p. 388)	1½ mi. round-trip	Moderate	Scafell/Great Gable (p. 391)	5 mi. one-way	Difficult

The Lake District has some of the best **hiking** in Britain. While there are many trails, be aware that they can be hard to follow at times—even on popular routes. If you plan to go on a long or difficult outing, check with the Park Service, call **weather information** (☎0870 055 0575; 24hr.; YHAs and TICs also post daily forecasts), and leave a plan of your route with your B&B proprietor or hostel warden before setting out. Steep slopes and unreliable weather can quickly reduce visibility to only a few feet. A good map and compass are necessities. The Ordnance Survey Explorer Maps #4-7 (£8.25) detail the four quadrants of the Lake District, while Landranger Maps #89-91 and 96-98 (£12) chart every hill and bend in the road for those planning especially difficult routes.

The Lakes are also fine **cycling** country. Several long-distance routes (part of the National Cycling Network; ☎01179 290 888) traverse the park. For short routes, pick up *Ordnance Survey One-Day Cycle Rides in Cumbria* (£10). Bike rental is available in many towns. Any cyclist planning an extensive stay should grab the *Ordnance Survey Cycle Tours* (£9), which provides maps of on- and off-trail routes. The circular **Cumbria Cycle Way** tours some of Cumbria's less traveled areas via a 259 mi. route from Carlisle around the park's outskirts. Pick up *The Cumbria Way Cycle Route* (£4) for details. Cycling is not permitted on all footpaths in the Lake District. Accessible paths are designated "bridleways" and are marked on any cycle route map. For a comprehensive map of all cycle routes in the Lake District, pick up *Cycling Cumbria Map & Guide*

(£2). For all travelers in the Lakes, beware of the narrow, stone-walled roads off the A591—cars and large buses careen around on the winding lanes.

The Lake District is popular for **rock climbing.** Shepherd's Crag in Borrowdale is a popular spot offering routes of varying difficulty, including the highly photographed Little Chamonix route. Two good sources for climbing information are Rock and Run, 3-4 Cheapside, Ambleside (☎01539 433 660; open M-Sa 9am-5:30pm, Su 10am-5pm) and the Keswick Indoor Climbing Wall (p. 390).

WINDERMERE AND BOWNESS ☎(0)1539

The largest tourist center in the Lake District, Windermere and its lakeside sidekick, Bowness-on-Windermere (combined pop. 11,000), are packed with vacationers in July and August, when boats swarm England's largest lake. Together, they form transportation hubs and gateways to the rest of the park, while the small streets leading down to the lake retain their own charm.

TRANSPORTATION AND PRACTICAL INFORMATION. The train station and bus depot are in Windermere; Bowness is an easy 1 mi. walk south. From the station, turn left onto Victoria Rd. and stay to the left, following Crescent Rd. through town to New Rd., which becomes Lake Rd. and leads to the pier. **Bus** #599 runs from the station to Bowness (3 per hr., £1.60). For information on getting to Windermere, see p. 384. Try **Lakes Taxis** (☎01539 446 777 or 444 055) for a cab or rent **bikes** from Country Lanes Cycle Hire at the station. (☎01539 444 544. £12-14 per ½-day, £17-20 per day. Open Easter-Oct. daily 9am-5pm; Nov.-Easter hours depend on weather.)

The Windermere **Tourist Information Centre,** near the train station, stocks walking guides (from 40p) and books accommodations for free. (☎01539 446 499. Internet £1 for 15min. Open Easter-Aug. M-Sa 9:30am-5pm, Su 10am-5pm.) The Bowness Bay **NPIC** has a display on the Lake District's topology. Book a **tour** through Mountain Goat, downhill from the TIC. (☎01539 445 161. £33.50, children £23.50). Across the street, **Lakes Supertours,** 1 High St., in the Lakes Hotel, runs similar half- and full-day tours (£19-30). Both Windermere and Bowness have **banks** with **ATMs.** Windermere services include: **luggage storage** at Darryl's Cafe, 14 Church St., just past the TIC (☎01539 442 894; £2.50 per item; open M and Th-Su 8am-6pm); **police,** Lake Rd. (☎0845 330 0247 for the main Cumbria line; ask for Windermere Police Station); **Internet** access at **TriArom,** Birch St. (☎01539 444 639; www.triarom.co.uk; £1 per 10min., £5 per hr.; open M-F 9:30am-5:30pm, Sa 9:30am-5pm); and the **post office,** 21 Crescent Rd. (☎01539 443 245; open M-F 9am-5:30pm, Sa 9am-12:30pm). **Postcode:** LA23 1AA.

ACCOMMODATIONS AND FOOD. Windermere and Bowness have a number of B&Bs, but booking ahead is advisable during the high season. The **YHA hostel ❷** is 2 mi. north of town (opposite page). In town, **Lake District Backpackers ❶** is well suited to independent travelers. (☎01539 446 374; www. lakedistrictbackpackers.co.uk. Internet access. Dorms £10-12.50. MC/V.) The best values among Windermere's B&Bs include the the homey **Greenriggs ❷,** 8 Upper Oak St. (☎01539 442 265; singles £25; doubles £44-50; cash only) and the motorcyclist- and family-friendly **Brendan Chase B&B ❸,** 1-3 College Rd., with a laid-back atmosphere and large rooms. (☎01539 445 638. Singles £25; doubles from £40. Cash only.) In Bowness, quiet **Laurel Cottage ❸,** St. Martins Pl., is a 400-year-old building off the main road. (☎01539 445 594; www.laurelcottage-bnb.co.uk. Singles £27-48; doubles from £52. MC/V.) Find camping at **Park Cliffe ❷,** Birks Rd., 4 mi. south of Bowness. Take bus #618 heading south to Broad

Leys from Windermere station. (☎01539 531 344. Open from early Mar. to early Nov.£9.50-11.50 per tent. Dorms £23-25. MC/V.)

Stock up on supplies in Windermere at **Booth's** grocery, next to the station. (☎01539 446 114. Open M-F 8:30am-8pm, Sa 8:30am-7pm, Su 10am-4pm.) **The Light House ❷,** at the top of Main Rd., sells light fare throughout the day (sandwiches £4-5), and the three floors stay open late as a trendy bar and bistro. (☎01539 488 260. Open Apr.-Oct. M-Sa 8:30am-11pm, Su 8:30am-10:30pm; kitchen open until 10pm; Nov.-Mar. daily 8:30am-9pm. MC/V.) **Jackson's ❸,** St. Martins Pl., serves huge portions of modern British cuisine. (☎01539 446 264. 3-course meal £14. Open M-F 6-11pm, Sa-Su 5:30-11pm. MC/V.)

SIGHTS AND OUTDOOR ACTIVITIES. Sample the natural beauty of Windermere's surroundings on a **lake cruise.** A number of sightseeing boats depart from Bowness Pier. **Windermere Lake Cruises** (☎01539 443 360) is the main operator, with trips north to Waterhead Pier in Ambleside (30min., round-trip £7) and south to Lakeside (40min., £7.50). Nonstop sightseeing cruises are also available (45min.; £6.20, children £3.10, families £17). On all routes, departures are frequent from April to October and reduced for the rest of the year. The **Freedom of the Lake** pass allows unlimited travel for 24hr. from time of purchase (£14.50). A cruise to **Lakeside,** at Windermere's southern tip, lets you visit the freshwater **Aquarium of the Lake** (☎01539 530 153; www.aquariumofthelakes. co.uk; open daily 9am-6pm; last entry 5pm; £7.20, concessions £6.20) or take a ride on the 3 mi. steam-powered **Lakeside and Haverthwaite Railway** (☎01539 531 594; Easter-Oct.; £5.40, children £2.70). Booths at the Bowness and Ambleside piers sell tickets that combine the lake cruise with one or both of these attractions. **Motorboat** and **rowboat** rentals are available at Bowness Pier. (☎01539 440 347. Motorboats for 2 people £14 per hr. Rowboats £5 per person per hr.)

Town sights are less remarkable than the lake's offerings, but Jemima Puddleduck fans both young and old will delight in **The World of Beatrix Potter,** a recreation of scenes from the author's stories. (☎015394 88 444; www.hop-skip-jump.com. Open daily Apr.-Oct. 10am-5:30pm; Nov.-Mar. 10am-4:30pm. £6.) If Peter Rabbit irritates you as much as he did Mr. McGregor, you're better off sticking to the lake. The short climb to **Orrest Head** (1 mi. round-trip) gives 360° views of the Lake District. It begins on the A591 near the TIC.

KESWICK ☎(0)1768

Sandwiched between towering Skiddaw peak and the northern edge of Derwentwater, Keswick (KEZ-ick) rivals Windermere as the Lake District's tourist capital. With tranquil charms and a delightful town center, Keswick is a great place to have a pint after a long day's hike.

TRANSPORTATION AND PRACTICAL INFORMATION. For information on how to get to Keswick, see p. 384. Keswick Mountain Bikes, off Main St., in the Southey Hill Industrial Estate, rents **bikes.** (☎01768 775 202; www.keswickbike.co.uk. £17 per day. Open M-Sa 9am-5:30pm, Su 10am-5:30pm.) The **NPIC** (p. 384) is in the back entrance of Moot Hall (the clock tower in Market Pl.). Other services include: **banks** with **ATMs** on Main St.; a **launderette,** Main St., at the mini-roundabout (open daily 7:30am-7pm); **police,** 8 Bank St. (☎01900 602 422 for the Cumbria line; ask for Keswick Police Station); **Internet** at **Java Cafe,** next to the TIC (☎0168 772 568; £1 per 15min., £3 per hr.; open daily 10am-5pm); and the **post office,** 48 Main St. (☎0168 772 269; open M-F 9am-5:30pm, Sa 9am-1pm). **Postcode:** CA12 5JJ.

▐▌ ACCOMMODATIONS AND FOOD. The YHA hostels ▣**Keswick ❷** and ▣**Derwentwater ❷** are in Keswick (p. 386). The area between Station and St. John St. (Ambleside Rd.) and Penrith Rd. abounds with B&Bs. The **Whitehouse Guesthouse ❸**, Ambleside Rd., is romantic and peaceful, with huge guest rooms. (☎01768 773 176; www.whitehousekeswick.co.uk. £32 per person. Cash only.) Reside in lakeside splendor at **Berkeley Guest House ❸**, The Heads, whose spacious rooms and modern decor are a wonderful welcome after a long hike. (☎01768 774 222; www.berkeley-keswick.com. Singles £36; doubles £50-72.)

Buy groceries at the enormous **Co-op** on Main St., next to the launderette. (☎01768 772 688. Open M-Sa 7:30am-7pm, Su 10am-5pm.) For some meatless treats, grab sandwiches and wraps (£3-5) at the all-vegetarian **Lakeland Pedlar ❶**, off Market Pl., down the narrow passageway next to the pink-painted Johnson's Ice Cream store. (☎01768 774 492. Open July-Sept. M-Th 9am-5pm, F-Sa 9am-9pm; Oct.-Apr. daily 10am-4pm; May-June M-F 10am-4pm, Sa-Su 9am-5pm. MC/V.) **Good Taste ❶**, 19 Lake Rd., whips up great sandwiches and salads (£3-3.75) for takeaway or to enjoy in the sunny upstairs lounge. (☎01768 775 973; www.simplygoodtaste.co.uk. Open M-Sa 8:30am-4:30pm. Cash only.)

◉▐ SIGHTS AND ENTERTAINMENT. The lapping waves of Derwentwater are only a 10min. walk south of the town center along Lake Rd. From here, the **Keswick Launch** sends **cruises** to other points on the lake, rents boats at the marina, and lands at the start of a handful of trails around the shore. (☎01768 772 263. 2-person rowboats £10 per hr. 2-person motorboats £25 per hr. Cruises from mid-Mar. to Nov. 6-11 per day; from Dec. to mid-Mar. Sa-Su 5 per day. £8.50, children £4.25, families £20.) Answer all those burning questions about pencils at the **Cumberland Pencil Museum**, home to the world's longest colored pencil (26 ft.) and right next door to the original factory. The museum lies just out of the town center along Main St. (☎01768 773 626; www.pencilmuseum.co.uk. Open daily 9:30am-5pm. Last entry 4pm. Cafe open 9:30am-5pm. £3, students £2.) A self-described "cabinet of curiosities," the **Keswick Museum and Art Gallery**, in Fitz Park on Station Rd., has an array of Victorian artifacts, including a 666-year-old mummified cat, Napoleon's teacup, and a 14 ft. stone xylophone. (☎01768 773 263. Open Easter-Oct. Tu-Sa 10am-4pm. Free.) For a dose of culture in the evening, the **Theatre by the Lake**, by the, um, lake, features a year-round program of repertory theater, music, and dance. (☎01768 774 411. Concessions available. Box office open daily 9:30am-8pm.)

Compared to the rest of the Lake District, Keswick has thriving nightlife. Many traditional pubs line Market Pl. The **Oddfellows Arms**, Market Sq., hosts nightly live music starting at 9:30pm and has a massive beer garden out back. (☎01768 773 809. Open M-Sa 11am-11pm, Su noon-10:30pm.) **Trendy Bar 26**, Lake Rd., also has live music and creative mixed drinks. (☎01768 780 863. Open daily 11am-11pm.) Most bars close around 11pm, when those looking to dance head to **Loft**, Market Pl., a nightclub that feels like a little slice of London in the Lakes. (☎01768 780 834. Cover F-Sa £5. Open daily 10pm-2am.)

▐ HIKING. A standout 4 mi. amble from Keswick crosses slopeside pastures and visits the **Castlerigg Stone Circle**, a Neolithic henge dating back nearly 5000 years. Archaeologists believe it may have been used as a place of worship, astronomical observatory, or trading center. Another short walk hits the beautiful **Friar's Crag**, on the shore of Derwentwater, and **Castlehead**, a viewpoint encompassing the town, lakes, and peaks beyond. Both of these walks have only a few moderately tough moments. The more strenuous **Catbells and Newlands** hike runs 8½ mi. and includes a short passage on the Keswick Launch. Maps and information on these and other walks are available at the NPIC (guides 60p). Climbing enthusiasts can get in a bit of practice before hitting the hills at the **Keswick Indoor Climbing Wall,** a 5min. walk from town along Main St. The staff also leads outdoor tours for groups of five or more, spanning such pursuits as cycling, climbing, and ghyll scrambling. (☎01768 772 000; www.keswickclimbingwall.co.uk. Instruction available. Climbing wall £6.50, children £4.25. Open daily 10am-9pm.)

AMBLESIDE   ☎(0)1539

Set in a valley 1 mi. north of Windermere's waters, Ambleside is an attractive village with convenient access to the southern lakes. It's popular with hikers, who are drawn by its location and absurd number of outdoor gear shops. Walking trails extend in all directions. Panoramic views of the southern Lakes can be had from the top of **Loughrigg** (moderately difficult, 7 mi. round-trip). The **Stockghyll Force** waterfall is concealed in a wooded area an easy mile from town. Area TICs have guides to these and other walks (most guides 60p).

Ambleside's ⬛**YHA hostel ❷** (p. 385) is near the steamer pier at Waterhead, a pleasant 1 mi. walk from the town center. **Ambleside Backpackers ❷,** Old Lake Rd., rents 72 bunks in a comfortable, clean house. (☎01539 432 340. Self-catering kitchen. Breakfast included. Internet £1 per 30min. Dorms £15. Discount for stays over 3 nights. MC/V.) Several B&Bs cluster on **Church Street** and **Compston Road,** while others line the busier **Lake Road** leading in from Windermere. **Linda's B&B and Bunkhouse ❷,** Compston Rd., is a combination hostel-B&B, renting out four private rooms as well as dorm accommodations with optional breakfast. (☎01539 432 999. Dorms £12; singles £20, with breakfast £25. Cash only.) ⬛**Lucy's ❸,** on Church St., will pack hikers a picnic lunch. Its conservatory restaurant has a large selection of tempting dishes for special diets and allergies, and its wine bar across the street sells tasty tapas. (☎01539 431 191; www.lucysofambleside.co.uk. Entrees £13-15; sandwiches £6.50-8.50. Open daily 10am-9pm. Wine bar open 5-11pm. AmEx/MC/V.) **The Golden Rule ❷,** Smithy Brow, taps local beers in a friendly atmosphere. (☎01539 432 257. Open M-Sa 11am-midnight, Su noon-midnight. Cash only.)

Buses stop on Kelsick Rd. Bus #555 runs within the park to Grasmere, Windermere, and Keswick (every hr.). Bus #505 joins at Hawkshead and Coniston (Apr.-Oct. M-Sa every hr., Su 6 per day). Rent **bikes** at Bike Treks, next door to the Glass House on Rydal Rd. (£15 per ½-day, £18 per day. Open M-Tu 10am-5:30pm, W-Su 9am-5:30pm.) The **Tourist Information Centre** is in the Central Building on Market Cross and doubles as an NPIC. (☎01539 432 582. Open daily 9am-5pm.) Other services include: **Internet** at the **library** on Kelsick Rd. (☎01539 432 507; 50p per 15min.; open M and W 10am-5pm, Tu and F 10am-7pm, Sa 10am-1pm); the **police** (☎0845 330 0247 for the Cumbria line; ask for Ambleside Police); and the **post office,** Market Pl. (☎01539 432 267; open M-F 9am-5:30pm, Sa 9am-12:30pm). **Postcode:** LA22 9BU.

GRASMERE   ☎(0)1539

With a lake and a canonized poet all to itself, the ivy-covered village of Grasmere receives more than its fair share of camera-clicking tourists. Sightseers pour in at midday to visit all things William Wordsworth, but mornings and evenings are peaceful. Guides provide 30min. tours of the early-17th-century **Dove Cottage,** where Wordsworth lived with his wife Mary and his sister Dorothy from 1799 to 1808, almost exactly as he left it. Next door, the outstanding **Wordsworth Museum** includes pages of his handwritten poetry and opinions on his contemporaries. The cottage and museum are 10min. from the center of Grasmere down Stock Ln. (☎01539 435 544; www.wordsworth.org.uk. Open from mid-Feb. to mid-Jan. daily 9:30am-5pm. Museum £5. Cottage and museum £7.50, concessions

£6.10.) Wordsworth's grave is in town at St. Oswald's churchyard. Walks starting from Grasmere range from a steep, strenuous scramble (4 mi. round-trip) to the top of **Helm Cragg** to the gentle 6 mi. **Wordsworth Walk** that circles the two lakes of the Rothay River, passing the poet's grave.

There are two Grasmere YHA hostel buildings within a 15min. walk: **Butharlyp Howe ❷** and **Thorney How ❷** (p. 385). **Beck Allans Guest House ❸** is an ivy-covered house centrally located off College St. (☎01539 435 563; www.beckallens.com. £33-40 per person.) Campsites are available on the grounds of **Rydal Hall ❶**, just off the A591 between Ambleside and Grasmere, across the road from Rydal Mount. (☎01539 320 050; www.rydalhall.org. £6.50 per person.)

The bohemian **Jumble Room ❸**, Langdale Rd., serves a number of organic vegetarian and seafood plates. (☎01539 435 188. Open Easter-Oct. W-Su noon-3pm and from 6pm until food runs out; Nov.-Easter F-Su noon-3pm and from 6pm until food runs out. MC/V.) As if the buttery aroma wafting into the street weren't enough to entice you into ☒**Sarah Nelson's Grasmere Gingerbread Shop ❶**, in the Church Cottage, outside St. Oswald's Church, the world-famous gingerbread is a bargain snack at 35p per piece. (☎01539 435 428; www.grasmeregingerbread.co.uk. Open Easter-Sept. M-Sa 9:15am-5:30pm, Su 12:30-5:30pm; Oct.-Easter M-Sa 9:30am-4:30pm, Su 12:30-5:30pm. Cash only.)

A small, helpful **tourist information point** is in the lobby of the Dale Lodge Hotel on Red Bank Rd. (☎01539 435 300. Open daily 10am-5pm.)

BORROWDALE   ☎(0)1768

One of the Lake District's most beautiful spots, the valley of Borrowdale winds its way south from the tip of Derwentwater. **Ashness Bridge**, in the north, is worth a look but far from the main road. Pick up a guide map at any of the area's hostels or at the TIC for 20p. The tiny village of **Rosthwaite** has a few hotels and B&Bs. Towering over all is **Scafell Pike** (3210 ft.), the highest mountain in England, which, along with nearby and similarly lofty **Scafell** and **Great Gable,** forms an imposing triumvirate with some of the toughest and most rewarding hiking in the lakes. Treks up these peaks begin from **Seatoller,** at the head of the valley. Walks to the summits should not be taken lightly: Scafell Pike is 4 mi. to the top and a 3100 ft. climb; Great Gable is also 4 mi., although not as steep.

Accommodations are scattered throughout the valley. **YHA Borrowdale ❷** (p. 385) is in the valley itself. Follow Prince Charles's example by taking an incognito weekend at the **Yew Tree Farm ❸**, along a small lane opposite the general store in Rosthwaite. (☎01768 777 675. Breakfast included. Ensuite rooms from £32 per person. Cash only.) The **Flock-In Tea Room ❶** is a good bet for a bite to eat. (☎01768 777 675. Open M-Tu and Th-Su 10am-5pm.) **Bus** #79 runs from Keswick to Seatoller via Rosthwaite (30min., 10-20 per day).

ULLSWATER   ☎(0)1768

In Ullswater, a new corner of the lake is visible around each rocky outcrop and grassy bank. The main settlements, **Glenridding** and **Patterdale,** are on the southern tip of the water, and either one can be a departure point for the popular climb up **Helvellyn** (3118 ft.). One vertigo-inducing ascent begins in Glenridding and follows four steep miles to the peak. Departing from the Glenridding Pier, **Ullswater Steamers** cut across the lake with stops at Howtown and Pooley Bridge. (☎01768 482 229; www.ullswater-steamers.co.uk. In summer 19 per day, in winter 4 per day. Round-trip £7.60-11.30, children £3.80-5.65.) A less strenuous route runs along the lake's eastern shore from Glenridding to Howtown, where you can then catch the steamer for a pleasant ride back. Another

Ullswater attraction is **Aira Force,** one of the most accessible waterfalls in the Lakes, a 20min. walk off the A5091 toward Keswick.

Good B&Bs include **Beech House ❷,** on the main road in Glenridding (☎01768 482 037; £30-35 per person; MC/V), and **Elm House ❸,** in Pooley Bridge. (☎01768 486 334; www.stayullswater.co.uk. £30-36 per person. Cash only.) **YHA Patterdale ❷** is a basic hostel (p. 386), and Patterdale village has several guesthouses.

Public transportation to Ullswater is limited. The only year-round **bus** is #108 from Penrith, which runs along the lake and connects to Keswick. Sit on the left side for the best views (40min., 5 per day, £3.80). Two more services operate seasonal schedules: #517 from Bowness/Windermere to Glenridding (55min.; Apr.-July Sa-Su 3 per day, Aug. daily) and #208 from Keswick to Patterdale via Aira Force and Glenridding (35min.; June-July Sa-Su 5 per day, Aug. daily). The **YHA shuttle** (p. 384) goes once daily from the southern lakes to Patterdale.

HAWKSHEAD   ☎(0)1539

In the village of Hawkshead, 4 mi. east of Coniston, you can imagine yourself pulling little Willy Wordsworth's hair and passing him notes at the ◙**Hawkshead Grammar School,** Main St., where the poet studied from 1779 to 1787. See the original desks with inscriptions carved by students dating back as far as the 1500s. (☎01539 436 735. Open Apr.-Oct. M-Sa 10am-1pm and 2-5pm, Su 1-5pm. £2.50.) Also on Hawkshead's main street is the **Beatrix Potter Gallery.** Housed in offices once used by her husband, the gallery displays sketches and water-colors from her beloved children's stories. (☎01539 436 355. Open Apr.-Oct. M-W and Sa-Su 10:30am-4:30pm. Last entry 4pm. £4, concessions £2.) Potter lived 2 mi. from Hawkshead on her farm at **Hill Top.** The house, featured in many of her stories, remains exactly as she left it. (☎01539 436 269. Open Apr.-July and Sept.-Oct. M-W and Sa-Su 10:30am-4:30pm; Aug. M-Th and Sa-Su 10:30am-4:30pm. Last entry 4pm. £5.80, children £3, families £14.50.) **Tarn Hows,** a pond near a pine grove, is a popular picnic spot. Walk uphill past Hawkshead Grammar School through the gate into the churchyard. Go through the church-yard, head through two more gates, and turn right at the fork in the path. The trail to Tarn Hows is signposted from that point.

The nearest accommodation is the ◙**YHA Hawkshead ❷,** 1 mi. south of the village down Newby Bridge Rd. In summer, **bus** #505 stops in Hawkshead on its way between Ambleside and Coniston (M-Sa 12 per day, Su 6 per day). Mountain Goat offers a combined boat and bus shuttle running from Bowness to Hill Top. A Goat bus also runs to Hill Top from Hawkshead. (☎01539 445 164. Apr.-Sept. 8 per day. Round-trip £6, children £4.)

◪ **NIGHTLIFE.** The rowdy Botchergate area is lined with pubs and clubs, including the hugely popular **Terminal 1,** just off the main drag behind the Litten Tree and Walkabout. Patrons choose between an ice bar, sports bar, retro club, and Parisian cabaret bar, with packed theme nights every week-end. On the other side of the town center, **The Brickyard,** 14 Fisher St., is Carlisle's only alternative music venue, keeping the live music scene alive with gigs every weekend and often throughout the week; a mix of genres and a laid-back atmosphere make this place a good hangout spot for all sorts. (☎01228 512 220; www.thebrickyardonline.com. Some gigs 18+. Cover varies. Usually open 5 nights per week 8pm-2am. Tickets usually cheaper if bought ahead of time.) Available free in many bars and restaurants, the monthly *By Night* magazine lists upcoming live music and club events (www.bynightmagazine.co.uk).

ISLE OF MAN

Wherever you go on this small islet in the Irish Sea, you're likely to come across an emblem: three legs joined together like the spokes of a wheel. It's emblazoned on flags flown from buildings, on the carpet of the ferry terminal, and even on shopping bags from local grocery stores. The Three Legs of Man, as the symbol is called, represent Manx pride and independence. Its accompanying motto translates to, "Whichever way you throw me, I stand." This speaks aptly to the predicament of the island over the last few millennia, during which it has been thrown around quite a bit. Vikings conquered the island in the ninth century, and the English and Scottish began to struggle for control in 1266. The English monarchy prevailed and granted dominion over the island to Lord John Stanley in 1405 for a whopping tribute of two falcons per year. Self-government was not restored until 1828.

Today, Man controls its own internal affairs while remaining a crown possession, although it is technically not part of the United Kingdom or the European Union. However limited its version of independence may be, the Tynwald Court, established by the Vikings, is the longest-running parliament in the world. It is still called to session each year on July 5, in a ceremony held completely in Manx (a cousin of Irish and Scottish Gaelic) on Tynwald Hill, site of the original Norse governmental structure. Man takes pride in its unique tailless Manx cats and multi-horned Manx Loghtan sheep, its Celtic and Viking heritage, and its famed local delicacy—kipper (herring smoked over oak chips). The island's beauty—with its jutting reefs, seaside promenades, carpets of wildflowers, and countryside crisscrossed by Victorian-era railways—has made it popular with tourists. The island might be best known, however, for its TT Races, which draw motorcyclists for a fortnight of adrenaline-pumping festivities.

TRANSPORTATION

GETTING THERE

By Plane: Ronaldsway Airport (☎01624 821 600; www.gov.im/airport), 10 mi. southwest of Douglas on the coast road. Buses #1, 1C, 2A, and 2 connect daily to Douglas (25min., 1-2 per hr.), Ballasalla (2min.), Castletown (7min.), and Port Erin (25min.). Bus #8 also stops outside the airport terminal and runs between Peel (30min., M-Sa 4 per day), Foxdale (20min.) and Port Erin (20min.). Several airlines—**Manx2** (☎0871

200 0440; www.manx2.com), **Euromanx** (☎0870 787 7879; www.euromanx.com), **Flybe** (☎0871 522 6100; www.flybe.com), **Eastern Airways** (☎01652 680 600; www. easternairways.com), **Aer Arann** (☎0800 587 2324), and **Loganair** (☎0870 850 9850)—serve the Isle. Flights leave for Birmingham, Glasgow, London Gatwick, Manchester, Liverpool, Dublin, and other locations.

By Ferry: Ferries dock at the **Douglas Sea Terminal.** Ferry shop open M-Sa 9am-6pm. The Isle of Man Steam Packet Company (☎01624 661 661 or 08705 523 523; www.steampacket.com) runs the only ferries to and from the Isle: **Belfast** (3hr.; Mar.-Oct. up to 2 per week); **Heysham** (3hr., 2 per day); **Dublin** (3hr.; June-Aug. 2 per week, Sept.-May 1-2 per month); and **Liverpool** (2½hr.; from mid-Mar. to Sept. 2 per day, Oct. 1 per day, from Nov. to mid-Mar. 2 per week). Fares are highest in summer and on weekends (£15-36, children from £13, round-trip £20-59). Book online and in advance for cheaper fares.

GETTING AROUND

Despite its profusion of cars, the Isle of Man has an extensive system of public transportation, run by **Isle of Man Transport** (☎01624 662 525; www.iombusandrail.info) in Douglas. The Douglas TIC has useful train and bus maps and schedules for free. The TIC and all main tram and train stations sell Island Explorer Tickets, which provide unlimited travel on most Isle of Man Transport buses and trains (1-day £13, children £6.50; 3-day £26/13; 7-day £40/20).

NO, MAN IS AN ISLE. Despite its small size and close ties to the mainland, the Isle of Man is not a part of the UK. Be careful not to provoke Manx nationalism by implying otherwise.

Trains: The Isle of Man's railway system, built to accommodate Victorian vacationers, still operates today using much of the original equipment. 3 lines run along the east coast from Port Erin to Snaefell (Apr.-Sept. daily; limited service in winter). The 1874 Steam Railway runs from **Douglas** to **Port Erin** via **Castletown** (£5.60, round-trip £9.40). The 1893 Electric Railway runs from **Douglas** to **Snaefell** (£5.60, round-trip £9.40). Groudle Glen Railway is a 2 ft. narrow-gauge railway carrying passengers out to Sea Lion Rocks. The Snaefell Mountain Railway runs from the town of Laxey to **Snaefell,** the island's highest peak at 2036 ft. (£5, round-trip £8).

Buses: Frequent buses connect every village. **Douglas** is the hub, with a main station on Lord St. Buses #1 and 2 go from Douglas to **Castletown** (30min.; M-Sa every 30min., Su every hr.) and **Port Erin** (40min.), with #1 sometimes continuing to **Creagneash** (1hr., 2 per day). #3 connects Douglas to **Laxey** (25min., 1-2 per hr.) and **Ramsey** (50min.). #4, 5, and 6 go from Douglas to **Peel** (50min., M-Sa 1-3 per hr., Su 11 per day), stopping at **St. John's** (30min.) along the way. #8 leaves Peel for **Castletown** (40min., M-Sa 4 per day) and **Port Erin** (50min.).

Bike Rental: The island's small size makes it easy to navigate by bike. A path along the eastern side of the island near Laxey is marked by challenging hills—manageable, but worthy of Man's reputation as professional terrain. An easier path near Port Erin gives riders the chance to see wild seals at the island's southernmost point. TICs provide a free map of 6 1-day cycle trails throughout the island. See **Eurocycles** (p. 397) in Douglas and **Pedal Power Cycles** in Peel (p. 399) for rental options.

ESSENTIALS

The **Manx pound** is equivalent in value to the British pound, but it's not accepted outside the Isle of Man. If you use an ATM on the island, it will probably give you all of your bills in Manx currency. Notes and coins from England,

Scotland, and Northern Ireland can be used in Man. Some Manx shops accept euro—look for signs. Manx coins are reissued each year with different and often bizarre designs, which can be viewed at the **Treasury office** on Bucks Rd. in Douglas. In general, you won't have problem exchanging your money for UK tender when preparing to leave the island. **Manx stamps** are also unusual: the eagle-eyed will notice that the queen's head bears no crown. Post offices and newsstands sell Manx Telecom **phonecards,** and mobile-phone users on plans from elsewhere in Britain will likely incur surcharges. The Isle shares Britain's **international dialing code,** ☎44. In an emergency, dial ☎999. It's wise to rely on phone cards and landlines for a short stay, although more long-term visitors should probably invest in a **Manx prepay SIM card,** available at the Manx Telecom shop, 41-43 Victoria St., Douglas. (£10-20. Open M-W and F 8:30am-5pm, Th 9:30am-5pm, Sa 9am-5pm.) These allow access to the only official service, **Manx Pronto.**

THE GREAT OUTDOORS (AND OTHER SIGHTS)

The island-wide **Story of Mann** is a collection of museums and exhibits focused on the island's heritage, including sites in Castletown, Peel, Ballasalla, and Ramsey. The town of Laxey celebrates the **Laxey Wheel,** nicknamed Lady Isabella, a 72 ft. water wheel (the largest in the world), while Castletown, once the island's capital, is the site of Castle Rushen, a medieval fortress that was once the seat of the former kings of Mann. A Heritage Pass (£11, children £5.50), available from any of the museums, gives admission to any four of the nine fee-charging sites, which otherwise cost £3.30-5.50 each. (☎01624 648 000; www.storyofmann.com).

In 2004, the first-ever **Isle of Man Walking Festival** (☎01624 644 644) brought a five-day walking extravaganza to the island, and it has taken place every June and October since. Diehards trek 31 mi. and climb 8000 ft. between Ramsey and Port Erin in the **Manx Mountain Marathon,** Britain's longest one-day race, in early April. **Raad ny Foillan** (Road of the Gull) is a 95 mi. path around the island marked with blue seagull signs. The spectacular ◪**Port Erin to Castletown Route** (12 mi.) offers the best of the south island's beaches, cliffs, nesting birds, and bathing seals; a short detour toward Cregneash leads to Cronk Karran, a Neolithic-era stone burial circle. **Bayr ny Skeddan** (The Herring Road), once used by Manx fishermen, covers the 14 mi. land route between Peel in the west and Castletown

LOCAL LEGEND

MANX TALES

The Isle of Man is best known for its rocky cliffs, dramatic seascapes, and miles of walks through rolling greenery, but it also boasts its own unique breed of tailless cat. These peculiar "rumpies" have intrigued visitors and natives of the island ever since their appearance—so much so that a number of theories seek to explain their origins. These include:

The biblical. One story has it that, when Noah was calling all of the animals to the ark, the Manx cat hesitated in the rain before hopping aboard. The cat ran onto the ship just in time, but its tail was cut off as Noah closed the doors of the ark.

The pseudo-scientific. A more naturalistic explanation has it that the Manx cat is the product of an interesting cross-breed. In 1844, the observer Joseph Train wrote in his history of the Isle: "My observations on the structure and habits of the specimen ... leave little doubt on my mind of its being a mule, or crosses between the female cat and the buck rabbit."

The macabre. Two stories allege that invading Viking or Irish soldiers used to kill the cats to chop off their tails, which they believed would bring them luck. Quick-witted mother cats began biting off the tails of their offspring to protect them from humans.

And, of course, **the mundane reality**—a spontaneous mutation that altered the cat vertebrae combined with centuries of reproductive isolation.

in the east and is marked by signs with pictures of herring. It overlaps with the **Millennium Way,** which covers the more difficult and hilly 28 mi. route from Castletown to Ramsey along the 14th-century Royal Highway, ending 1 mi. from Ramsey's Parliament Sq. *Walks on the Isle of Man,* available free at the TIC, gives a cursory description of 11 walks. Free pamphlets also list dozens of routes. Eleven campsites, listed at the TIC, dot the isle.

HOLIDAYS AND FESTIVALS

The island's economy relies heavily on tourism, so frequent festivals celebrate everything from jazz to angling. TICs stock a calendar of events; ask for the free *What's On the Isle of Man* or check out www.isleofman.com or www. visitisleofman.com. During the two weeks at the end of May and beginning of June, Man turns into a mecca for motorcyclists for the **TT (Tourist Trophy) Races** (www.iomtt.com). The population doubles, 10,000 bikes flood the island, the Steam Packet Co. schedules extra ferries at special rates, and Manx Radio is replaced by "Radio TT." The races were first held on Man in 1907 because restrictions on vehicle speed were less severe (read: nonexistent) on the island than on mainland Britain. The circuit consists of 38 mi. of hairpin turns through towns and countryside that top racers navigate at speeds over 120 mph.

Southern "100" Motorcycle Races (☎01624 822 546; www.southern100.com) run over three days in mid-July, bringing more bikers to the Isle and giving amateurs a chance to race, in contrast to the professional-only TT. July also sees the annual **Manx National Week,** when new legislation is proclaimed on Tynwald Day (☎01624 685 500). Although this ritual relies on fiercely honored traditions (representatives don wigs and traditional robes), other summer activities are a bit looser in execution. The **World Tin Bath Championships** is a race across the harbor in tin tubs in August. A 24hr., 85 mi. **parish walk** to the Isle's 17 churches takes place in June. An **International Chess Tournament** in September, and a **Darts Festival** in March invite Manx natives and visitors to revel in the isle's indiosyncratic traditions.

DOUGLAS
☎(0)1624

Douglas's broad promenade is bordered with pastel-colored row houses, giving it the feel of a Victorian resort town. This belies its checkered past as a smuggling hub for nearby England and Scotland. Sprawling along a bay on the eastern side of the island, the town is a useful gateway from which to explore the Isle's more scenic corners. Most travelers tend to return to Douglas each evening to enjoy its energetic nightlife.

TRANSPORTATION

Ferries arrive at the Sea Terminal, at the southern end of town, where North Quay and the Promenade converge near the bus station. Isle of Man Transport, Banks Circus (☎01624 662 525), runs local trains and buses (p. 394). During the summer, slow but inexpensive horse-drawn **trams** clip-clop down the Promenade between the bus and Electric Railway stations. Stops are posted every 600 ft. (☎01624 662 525. Open Apr.-Sept. daily 9am-6pm. £2, children £1.) Motorized **buses** (70p) also run along the Promenade, connecting the bus and Steam Railway stations with the Electric Railway. For **taxis,** call 24hr. A-1 Radio Cabs (☎01624 663 344) or Telecabs (☎01624 629 191). Several **car-rental** companies are based in Douglas, including Athol, Peel Rd. (☎01624 822 481), or Mylchreests (☎08000 190 335), which operates at Ronaldsway Airport. Eurocycles, 8A Victoria Rd., off Broadway, rents **bikes.** (☎01624 624 909. Call ahead in summer. £15 per day; ID deposit. Open M-Sa 9am-5pm.)

✈ 🛈 ORIENTATION AND PRACTICAL INFORMATION

Douglas stretches for 2 mi. along the shore, from **Douglas Head** to the **Electric Railway terminal.** Douglas Head is separated from town by the **River Douglas.** Ferry and bus terminals lie just north of the river. The **Promenade** curves along the beach from the ferry terminal to the Electric Railway terminal, dividing the coastline from the shopping district with a line of Victorian row houses. Shops and cafes line **the Strand,** a pedestrian thoroughfare that begins near the bus station and runs parallel to the Promenade, turning into Castle St. and ending near the Gaiety Theatre.

Tourist Information Centre: In the Sea Terminal Bldg. just outside the ferry departure lounge (☎01624 686 766; www.visitisleofman.com). Gives out free transportation timetables, city and Isle maps, and the worthwhile *What's On* guide. Open Apr.-Aug. M-Sa 8am-7pm, Su 9am-3pm, Sept.-Mar. M-Sa 8am-6pm.

Banks: Lloyds TSB, 78 Strand St. (☎08457 301 280). Open M-Th 9:30am-4:30pm, F 9am-5pm.

Travel: Thomas Cook, 7/8A Strand St. (☎01624 626 288). Open M-W and F-Sa 9am-5:30pm, Th 10am-5:30pm.

Library: 10-12 Victoria St. (☎01624 696 461). Internet 75p per 15min; free for students after 4pm. Open M-Tu and Th-Sa 9:15am-5:30pm, W 10am-5:30pm.

Launderette: Broadway Launderette, 24 Broadway (☎01624 621 511). Open M, W, F-Sa 8:30am-5pm, Tu 8:30am-4:30pm, Su 11am-4pm.

Police: Glencrutchery Rd. (☎01624 631 212).

Pharmacy: Boots, 14-22 Strand St. (☎01624 616 120). Open M-Sa 8:30am-5:30pm, Su 1-4:30pm

Hospital: Noble's Isle of Man Hospital (☎01624 650 000; www.gov.im/dhss/health/nobles), in Braddan.

Internet Access: At the **library** (above). **Feegan's Lounge,** 8 Victoria St. (☎01624 679 407; www.feegan.com). £1 per 20min. Open M-Sa 8:30am-6pm. Free Wi-Fi in Ronaldsway Airport and the departure lounge of the Sea Terminal.

Post Office: At the corner of Regent and Strand St. (☎01624 686 141). Open M and W-F 9am-5:30pm, Tu 9:30am-5:30pm, Sa 9am-12:30pm. **Postcode:** IM1 2EA.

🏠 🏕 ACCOMMODATIONS AND CAMPING

Douglas is awash with **B&Bs** and **hotels.** For TT weeks, they fill a year in advance and raise their rates. During the TT fortnight, seven makeshift **campsites** open in football fields and public parks in addition to the 11 permanent sites.

The Devonian Hotel, 4 Sherwood Terr. (☎01624 674 676; www.thedevonian.co.uk), on Broadway. A Victorian-style townhouse conveniently located just off the Promenade. Proprietors accommodate ferry schedules by serving a continental breakfast for early departures and holding luggage for late ones. All rooms have TVs. Singles £25-32; doubles from £55. Cash or check only. ❷

Norley House, 4 Mona Drive (☎01624 623 301). Simple but spacious non-ensuite rooms, a game room and bar, and friendly proprietors. Laundry available. Singles £24, without breakfast £20; doubles £48/40; family rooms £24/20 per person. MC/V. ❷

Grandstand Campsite (☎01624 696 330), behind the TT Races' start and finish lines. Showers included. Laundry £1. Reception daily 8-11am and 4-7pm. ❶

◖ FOOD

Lining **Duke, Strand,** and **Castle Streets** are a number of grill and chip shops, many of which sell the distinctively Manx delicacy kipper (smoked herring). Several hotels along the **Promenade** feature more elegant restaurants. The dining rooms in **Copperfield's Olde Tea Shoppe and Restaurant ❸,** 24 Castle St., strive for historical ambience, dividing the menu into sections named after characters from Dickens. The food is classically British, with dishes like roast beef (£7.50) and jacket potatoes from £6.25. (☎01624 613 650. Open in summer M-Th and Sa 11am-6pm, F 11am-9pm; in winter M-Sa 11am-4pm. MC/V with a 50p charge.) At the **Bay Room Restaurant ❶,** in the Manx Museum, diners enjoy hot lunches amid sculptures from the gallery collection. (☎01624 612 211. Open M-Sa 10am-4:30pm. Cash only.) The **Food For Less** grocery is on Chester St., behind the Strand. (Open M-W and Sa 8am-8pm, Th-F 8am-9pm, Su 9am-6pm.)

◖ SIGHTS

From the shopping district, signs point to the Chester St. parking garage next to Food For Less; an elevator ride to the eighth-floor roof grants visitors access to a footbridge and the entrance of the **Manx Museum.** The museum covers Man from all angles, from the geological to the historical to—in the **Manx National Gallery of Art**—the artistic. Particularly lively are sections about the island's days as a Victorian holiday getaway, when it was unofficially known as the Isle of Woman due to its attractive seasonal population. The museum also traces some of the less savory aspects of the island's history, such as the story of Jewish refugees interned on the island during WWII and Man's involvement in the slave trade. Archaeological displays include Celtic artifacts from the Isle's early years. (☎01624 648 000. Open M-Sa 10am-5pm. Free.) At Douglas Head, visitors can enter the **Great Union Camera Obscura** for panoramic views of Douglas Bay. This camera, built in 1892 and restored 100 years later, uses 11 lenses and mirrors to produce the spectacular image. (Open May-Sept. Sa 1pm-4pm, Su 11am-4pm. £2, concessions £1, children free.) Past the Villa Marina Gardens on Harris Promenade sits the **Gaiety Theatre,** designed in 1900 and recently restored to something like its former glory. (☎01624 694 555. The box office, open daily 9:30am-8:30pm, is located in Villa Marina reception. Tickets can also be purchased at the TIC. The box office inside the theater opens 1hr. before curtain. Tickets £5-20, concessions available.)

◖ NIGHTLIFE

Pubs in Douglas are numerous and boisterous, especially during the TT Races. "Cheap beer started here," proclaims a sign outside of **Quids Inn,** 56 Loch Promenade. Once you insert £1 into the subway-like turnstyle at the door, almost all of your drinks will cost £1-1.50. If you go on weekends, prepare to drink standing up. (☎01624 611 769. Open M-F 5pm-midnight, Sa-Su 3pm-midnight.) Some of the **clubs** in Douglas are 21+, and some have free entrance until 10 or 11pm with a £2-5 cover thereafter. Relax at **Colours,** on Central Promenade, in the Hilton. A spacious sports bar gives way to live cover bands and dance music as the night goes on. (☎01624 662 662. £5 cover after 10pm. Open M-W noon-2am, Th-Su noon-3:30am.) At **Brendan O'Donnell's,** 16-18 Strand St., Guinness posters and painted four-leafed clovers remind patrons of the Isle's proximity to Ireland. (☎01624 621 566. Open M-Th and Su noon-11pm, F-Sa noon-midnight. Cash only.) **Paramount City,** Queen's Promenade, has two nightclubs: the first-floor **Director's Bar** pumps chart-toppers while the downstairs **Dark Room** hosts live music sets. (Paramount City ☎01624 622 447. Open F-Sa 10pm-3:15am.)

CREGNEASH
☎ (0)1624

The oldest village on the island, Cregneash is 2.5 mi. from Port Erin. It is known for the open-air **Cregneash Village Folk Museum,** which has preserved (and partially recreated) a Manx crofting town from the late 19th century, complete with thatched-roof cottages and demonstrations of blacksmithing and wool dyeing. Visitors pick their way among roosters as they wander between buildings that include the Karran Farm, where women in period costume work on silk patchwork and show visitors points of interest in the various buildings. (☎01624 648 000. Open daily Apr.-Oct. 10am-5pm. £3.30, children £1.70. MC/V.) **Bus** #1 runs to Cregneash from Douglas (1hr.; M-Sa 2 per day, 5 per day return) and Port Erin (20min.; M-Sa 6 per day, 6 per day return).

PEEL
☎ (0)1624

Long ago, this "cradle of Manx heritage" played host to the Vikings, whose Nordic pedigree still lives on in Manx blood. The Quayside maintains a rough-and-tumble sailor's edge (and holds a miniature Viking longhouse), while ruins across the harbor loom against western sunsets.

🖪🛈 TRANSPORTATION AND PRACTICAL INFORMATION. Buses (☎01624 662 525) arrive and depart across from the Town Hall on Derby Rd., going to Douglas (#4, 4B, 5A, 6, 6B, X5; 50min.; M-Sa 1-3 per hr., Su 11 per day; £2) and Port Erin (#8; 55min., M-Sa 4 per day, £2). Rent **bikes** at Pedal Power Cycles, 19 Michael St. (☎01624 842 472. £8 per day; £50 deposit per bike.) The **TIC** is a window in the Town Hall, Derby Rd. (☎01624 842 341. Open M-Th 8:45am-4:45pm, F 8:45am-4:30pm.) The **post office** is on Douglas St. (☎01624 842 282. Open M-F 9am-12:30pm and 1:30-5pm, Sa 9am-12:30pm.) **Postcode:** IM5 1AA.

🛏🍴 ACCOMMODATIONS AND FOOD. The **Peel Camping Park ❶**, Derby Rd., has laundry facilities and showers. (☎01624 842 341; www.peelonline.net. TV lounge. Open from mid-April to Sept. £5 per person, children £2.50. Electricity £2.) **Shoprite** grocery, 13 Michael St., is in the center of town. (Open M-Sa 8:30am-8pm, Su 10am-6pm.) The 🖪**Harbour Lights Cafe and Tearoom ❷**, Shore Rd., on the Promenade, serves Manx kipper teas—tea, kippers, bread, and teacakes. (☎01624 843 543. Kipper tea £8; 3-course dinner £28. Open Tu-Th 10am-5pm, F 10am-5pm and from 6pm, Sa 10am-5pm and from 7pm. MC/V.) "Often licked but never beaten," 🖪**Davison's Manx Dairy Ice Cream ❶**, on Shore Rd., boasts flavors like Turkish delight and butterscotch. (☎01624 844 761. 1 scoop £1.50. Open daily 9am-8pm. Cash only.)

🗐 SIGHTS. The most prominent relics in town are the stone towers of 🖪**Peel Castle,** which share the skyline of St. Patrick's Isle with the stone arches of **Saint German's Cathedral** and the excavated tomb of a well-to-do Viking woman nicknamed "The Pagan Lady." The audio tour, included in the admission price, informs visitors about the history and significance of the various ruins. The site is located on a cliff overlooking the village of Peel and can be reached by a pedestrian causeway from the Quay. (☎01624 843 232. Open Easter-Oct. daily 10am-5pm. Last entry 1hr. before close. £3.30, children £1.70. Guidebook £2.50. Cash only.) Across the harbor on the Quay, the comprehensive **House of Manannan,** Mill Rd., showcases a panorama of audio-visual displays that usher visitors from a fire-lit Celtic roundhouse to fog-machine-enhanced stone crosses, culminating at a 30 ft. Viking warship shored on a recreated indoor beach. (☎01624 648 091. Open daily 10am-5pm. £5.50, children £2.90. Guidebook £2.50. MC/V.) **Moore's Traditional Curers,** Mill Rd., is supposedly the only remaining kipper factory in the world uses the traditional 19th-century oak-smoking technique to prepare the stuff. Informal tours let visitors watch kippering in action and even climb up the interior of one of the smoking chimneys. You can also sample a fresh kipper sandwich in the shop. (☎01624 843 622; www.manxkippers.com. Shop open in summer daily 8am-5:30pm; in winter M-Sa 8am-5:30pm. Tours M-Sa 3:30pm. £2. Times may vary in the winter, so call ahead.) Just down the Quay, the **Leece Museum** exhibits a jumble of relics from Peel's past. Downstairs is the "Black Hole" prison cell, which now only locks up unfortunate wax figures. (☎01624 845 366. Open Tu-Sa 10am-4pm. Free.) Outside of Peel at Ballacraine Farm, **Ballacraine Quad Bike Trails** leads 1½hr. trail rides, including training and refreshments. (☎01624 801 219. £40 per person.)

PORT ERIN ☎(0)1624

Situated within a bay flanked by imposing cliffs, the quiet city of Port Erin charms trekkers and sea-lovers alike with its modest Victorian buildings, steep coastal pathways, and glimmering beach. A number of hikes start from the town, including the 30min. trail out to **Bradda Head,** which begins at the Bradda Glen gates off the Promenade or from the car park 300 ft. down the road. The trail hugs the bay before giving way to a rocky uphill scramble. At the top of the hill, climbers arrive at **Milner's Tower,** a curious structure built in honor of a Liverpool safemaker and, appropriately, designed to look like a key. Views of the sea and nearby **Calf of Man,** a tiny islet that serves as a nature preserve, compensate for the climb up the spiral staircase. The **Coronation Footpath,** which begins from the same spots, offers a gentler ascent. Trips to the Calf of Man depart daily from Port Erin pier. (☎01624 832 339. Trips depart daily from mid-Apr. to Sept. daily 10:15, 11:30am, 1:45pm; weather permitting. £20. Book ahead.) Railway enthusiasts will enjoy Port Erin's small **Railway Museum,** Station Rd., which traces the life of the train on the Isle since its introduction in 1873 and houses a train car from 1875. (Open Mar.-Oct. daily 9:30am-5:30pm. £1.)

    Anchorage Guest House ❸, Athol Park, has superb views of the town. (☎01624 832 355; www.anchorageguesthouse.com. Open Mar.-Nov. Singles £26; ensuite doubles £60. AmEx/MC/V.) Overlooking the bay, **Falcon's Nest Hotel ❸,** Station Rd., furnishes guests with ensuite rooms, a full Manx breakfast, and an adjoining restaurant that serves local seafood specialties. (☎01624 834 077. From June to mid-Sept. singles £42; doubles £84; family rooms £42 per person. From mid-Sept. to May singles £35; doubles £70; family rooms £35 per person. AmEx/MC/V.) For a quick meal in town, stop by **Shore Cafe ❶,** Shore Rd., which sells sandwiches featuring local ingredients (from £2.50) and freshly baked sweets. An ice-cream bar also sits next door.

    Port Erin is easily accessible as a daytrip from Douglas or a bit more of an expedition from Peel. **Buses** #1, 2, and X2 run to Port Erin from Douglas (50min., 2 per hr.), and two per day continue all the way to Cregneash. Bus #8 runs from Peel to Port Erin less frequently (50min., 4 per day). Hiking pamphlets are available from the **Tourist Information Centre,** on Bridson St., down the road from the bus station. (☎01624 832 298. Open M-F 9am-12:30pm and 1:30-5:30pm, Sa 9am-12:30pm.) The **post office** is at 8 Church Rd. (Open M-F 9:30am-12:30pm and 1:30-5:30pm, Sa 9am-12:30pm.)

A Ruinous State

The British thrive on ruin. The delight in the physical remnants of the past, shared by all classes and passed from generation to generation, is one of those cultural tics that makes Britain singular among nations. This desire to commune with times long gone, to wax wistful about the ambitions of ages past brought low by history's pratfalls, is as British as milky tea and cow parsley in country lanes.

It's possible to experience the great British romance of ruins at many of the most celebrated piles of stones. The shell of **Tintern Abbey** (p. 476), near the River Avon, marks the spot where Wordsworth made introspection a national poetic pastime. But the danger of sampling the obvious sites is, of course, the buzzing business of the present—so many tourist coaches, so much bad ice cream, so many postcards. Better to head to the lesser known and commune with bumblebees and the occasional wandering fellow pilgrim.

Go, for instance, to Northamptonshire to see what's left of **Lyveden New Bield**, the late-16th-century oratory of the Anglo-Catholic Thomas Tresham and a ruin almost as soon as it was constructed. The oratory was supposed to be a place where the Elizabethan gentleman, who tried to be loyal to both his queen and his church, could practice his devotions safe from the prying eyes of Protestant authorities. The entire building was left exposed to the elements, and visitors now wade through knee-high meadowland to see the delicate frieze of the stations of the cross that adorns its exte-rior walls.

Most of the ruins in Britain, however, are the work of sudden disaster rather than the slow crumblings of time. **Corfe Castle** (p. 205) in Dorset bears the charred scars of Oliver Cromwell's besieging army during the Second Civil War of 1647-48. And some of the imposing Iron Age brochs of **Orkney** (p. 671) and **Shetland** (p. 680) look as brutal as they do because at some point they failed to hold back the oncoming waves of invaders and local rivals. Sandstone-red **Lindisfarne**, on the Northumbrian shore, was twice ravaged, first by Vikings who sacked the place and slaughtered the monks. The monastery was hit again during the Protestant Reformation, when it was emptied of its treasures and its community. Equally sudden was the end of the spectacular **Binham Priory** in southern Norfolk. The enforcers of the Reformation under Henry VIII and Edward VI turned what had been one of the most palatial Benedictine foundations into a sparse parish church. Miraculously, the Reformation's erasure of the painted screen separating the nave from the choir has itself become a ruin, peeling away to reveal some of the most astonishing church paintings that survived from the world of Roman Catholic England.

Some of the most commanding ruins are also the most modern. A little way from the center of Dublin

"Head to the lesser known and commune with bumble-bees and fellow pilgrims."

stands Kilmainham Gaol, a working prison until 1924. Now a museum, the Gaol reveals the complications of crime and punishment in nationalist Ireland. The exterior is just standard-issue prison. But the interior is a cathedral of incarceration, shocking and operatically grand, with its iron staircase and rat-hole cells where ancient pallets and fragments of anonymous rags gather grime. The effect is as powerful as it is challenging, but this is how ruins are supposed to get you. Not with a cheap rush of sentiment—much less a pang of nostalgia—but with the tender inspection of ancient scars, which linger to remind us of the resilience and redeeming vulnerability of the human condition.

Simon Schama *is University Professor of Art History at Columbia University. He has written for* The New Yorker *and was the writer and host of the BBC's* History of Britain.

NORTHEAST ENGLAND

Framed by Scotland and the North Sea, the northeast is England's best-kept secret. Although less traveled, this corner of the country has something for everyone, from the notorious nightlife of Newcastle to the idyllic wildlife of Northumberland. Hadrian's Wall marks a history of skirmishes with fierce northern neighbors, and the area's national parks hold some of the most rugged, remote countryside in England. While the principal urban areas of Yorkshire and Tyne and Wear grew out of the wool and coal industries, today the refurbished city centers welcome visitors with a wealth of art and culture.

HIGHLIGHTS OF NORTHEAST ENGLAND

ADMIRE York and its colossal **Gothic cathedral** (p. 411), which contains the largest medieval glass window in the world.

PARTY in the famed nightclubs of **Newcastle** (p. 441), home to crowded dance floors, lively locals, and legendary brown ale.

INVESTIGATE the remains of **Hadrian's Wall** (p. 456), which once delineated the northernmost border of the Roman Empire.

PENNINE WAY

The Pennine Way is Britain's first long-distance trail and still challenges die-hard hikers. The 268 mi. path begins in Edale, crosses the plateau of Kinder Scout, passes into the Yorkshire Dales at Malham, and reemerges at the peak of Pen-y-ghent. The "Long Green Trail" dreamed up by 20th-century writer Tom Stephenson is now one of Britain's most popular routes. Hikers can find solitude among rock-strewn moors as well as lodgings filled with fellow walkers.

ACCOMMODATIONS AND CAMPING

YHA hostels are spaced within a day's hike (7-29 mi.) of one other. Book online at www.yha.org.uk. Any NPIC or TIC can supply details on trails and alternative accommodations; pick up the free *Yorkshire Dales Official Guide*.

YHA HOSTELS

The following hostels are arranged from south to north, with the distance from the nearest southerly hostel listed. Unless otherwise noted, reception is open from 5pm and breakfast and evening meals are served. YHA also books rooms through its Northern Region Offices, P.O. Box 11, Matlock, Derbyshire DE4.

Edale: In the Peak District (☎0870 7705 808). See p. 373. Dorms £16. MC/V. ❷

Mankinholes: 2 mi. outside Todmorden (☎0870 770 5952). 2-, 4-, and 6-person rooms. A 16th-century manor house converted into a self-catering hostel. Dorms £10, under 18 £7.50. MC/V. ❷

Haworth: 18 mi. from Mankinholes (☎0870 7705 858). See p. 420. Dorms £16. ❷

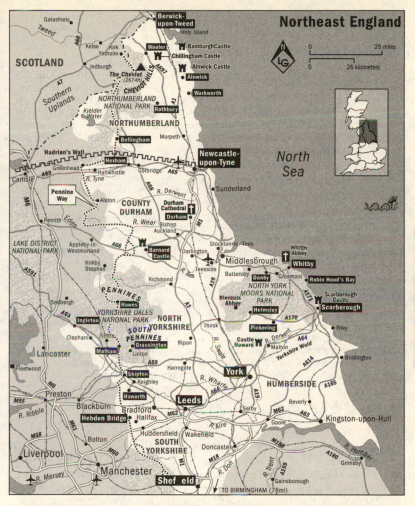

Earby: 9-11 Birch Hall Ln. (☎0870 770 5802), 12 mi. from Haworth. Self-catering. Cottage hostel with garden and waterfall. Open Apr.-Oct. Dorms £12. MC/V. ❷

Malham: 15 mi. from Earby (☎0870 7705 946), in the Yorkshire Dales. See p. 422. Dorms £14, under 18 £10.50. ❷

Hawes: 19 mi. from Stainforth (☎0870 770 5854), in the Yorkshire Dales. See p. 422. Dorms £14, under 18 £10. ❷

Langdon Beck: Forest-in-Teesdale (☎0870 770 5910), 15 mi. from Baldersdale. Great views of the North Pennines. Dorms £14, under 18 £10.50. MC/V. ❶

Dufton: Redstones, Dufton, Appleby (☎0870 770 5800), 12 mi. from Langdon Beck. Access to Pennine and Cumbria Circle Ways. Open Apr.-Oct. Dorms £12. MC/V. ❷

Greenhead: 17 mi. from Alston (☎0870 7747 411). See p. 456. Good base for Hadrian's Wall heritage site. Dorms £15. ❷

Once Brewed: Military Rd. (☎0870 770 5980), 7 mi. east of Greenhead. See p. 456. Dorms £15, under 18 £10. ❷

CAMPING BARNS

In the High Pennines, the YHA operates six camping barns. Amenities—electricity, hot water, heating, showers, and so on—vary from farm to farm. To book, call ☎0870 770 8868 or email campingbarns@yha.org.uk. More information is available on the YHA website (www.yha.org.uk) and in the free *Camping Barns in England*, available at some TICs. The **Holwick Barn ❶**, Low Way Farm, Holwick, is 3 mi. north of Middleton-in-Teesdale. Heaters, gas cooking facilities, showers, and hot water are included. (☎0870 7708 868. £6.50 per person. Electricity on meter. MC/V.)

🏔 HIKING

Hikers have completed the Way in as few as ten days (the record is a two-day relay), but most spend three weeks on the trail. Brief but rewarding forays on well-traveled walkways leave from major towns. The unusual limestone formations in the Yorkshire Dales and the lonely moor of Kinder Scout are Way-cool highlights. The Pennines do not, however, coddle hikers. Sudden storms can reduce visibility, leave paths swampy, and sink you knee-deep in peat. Even the most hard-core hikers stay away in the winter. Bring a map and compass. Rain gear, warm clothing, and food are also essential (see **Wilderness Safety,** p. 51). A. Wainwright's *Pennine Way Companion* (£10), available from bookstores, is a good supplement to Ordnance Survey maps (£6-8), all available at NPICs and TICs. Coverage of the route comes in two National Trail Guides, *Pennine Way North* and *Pennine Way South* (each £12). Information on hikes is also available from *Walk this Way: Pennine Way* (£5). Those wishing to see some of the Way without hoofing the whole thing should pick up bus timetables, available free at NPICs. For £5-10 per bag, the Pennine Way/Dales Way Baggage Courier (☎01729 830 463 or 07713 118 862) will cart your pack as you hike.

YORKSHIRE

SHEFFIELD   ☎(0)114

While Manchester was clothing the world, Sheffield (pop. 550,000) was setting its table with handcrafted flatware and stainless steel (invented here). When the 20th-century steel industry moved elsewhere, economic depression set in. Today, Sheffield is attempting an ambitious scheme of urban renewal, billing itself as a revitalized artistic, cultural, and commercial center. The industrial metropolis has used a green thumb and a keen eye to fill its streets with trendy bar-cafes, popular nightlife, and bountiful gardens.

📇 **TRANSPORTATION AND PRACTICAL INFORMATION.** Sheffield lies on the M1 motorway, about 30 mi. east of Manchester and 25 mi. south of Leeds. Midland Station is on Sheaf St., near Sheaf Sq. **Trains** (☎08457 484 950) leave from Sheffield to: Leeds (45min., 4 per hr., £8.20); Lincoln (1 hr., every hr., £11.50); London St. Pancras (2hr., 4 per hr., £57.80); Manchester (1hr., 3 per hr., £13.80); York (1hr., 3 per hr., £14.50). The major **bus** station in town is the Interchange, between Pond St. and Sheaf St. across from the train station. (☎0114 275 4905.) National Express (☎08705 808 080) buses travel to: Birmingham

Sheffield

🏠 **ACCOMMODATIONS**
York Villa, 6
Gulliver's Guesthouse, 2
Parland's Guesthouse, 1

🍴 **FOOD**
Blue Moon Cafe, 3
Showroom Cafe-Bar, 4

⭐ **CLUBS**
The Leadmill, 5

(2hr., 5 per day, £16); Leeds (55min., every hr., £5); London (4hr., 6 per day, £15.50); Nottingham (1-2hr., 10 per day, £6.60). The **Supertram** covers the city. (☎0114 272 8282; www.supertram.com. Daily pass £2.70.)

Sheffield's **Tourist Information Centre**, 12-14 Norfolk Row, distributes free detailed maps of the city as well as the handy *Sheffield Visitor Guide*. (☎0114 221 1900; www.sheffieldtourism.co.uk. Open M-F 10am-5pm, Sa 10am-4pm.) The TIC does not book accommodations for travelers in town, but a booking service is available for £3 by calling ☎0871 7000 121. Other services in Sheffield include: **banks** and **ATMs** on Pinstone St. and Church St.; **luggage storage** at the train station (£2.50 per 24hr.); **Internet** at the **Central Library**, Surrey St. (☎0114 273 4712; open M 10am-8pm, Tu and Th-Sa 9:30am-5:30pm, W 9:30am-8pm);**police**, West Bar Green (☎0114 220 2020); **Northern General Hospital**, Herries Rd. (☎0114 243 4343); **post office**, 9 Norfolk Row (☎0114 281 4713; open M-Tu and Th-F 8:30am-5:30pm, W 9am-5:30pm, Sa 8:30am-3pm). **Postcode:** S1 2PA.

🛏️🍴 **ACCOMMODATIONS AND FOOD.** Budget accommodations are scarce, and most are a long walk west of the center. The one exception is **York Villa ❷**, 63 Norfolk Rd., which has small rooms with shared bath. Its location 5min. from the train station can't be beat. (☎0114 272 4566. Singles £17; doubles £28. Cash only.) If you don't mind the 30min. commute by train, try the **Hathersage**

YHA Hostel ❶ (p. 377). Most B&B options are converted homes 2-3 mi. outside Sheffield near Ecclesall Rd. S. Local buses #30, 82, and 84 run regularly from the city center to Ecclesall Rd. For spacious rooms with shared baths, try **Gulliver's Guest House ❸**, 167 Ecclesall Rd. S. The matron of the house cooks a delicious breakfast of your choice. (☎0114 262 0729. Singles £25-27; doubles £45-48. Cash only.) **Parklands Guest House ❷**, 113 Rustlings Rd., near Endcliffe Park, has rooms with balconies, shared bath and kitchen. (☎0114 267 0692. Breakfast included. Singles from £20; doubles from £38. Cash only.)

Sheffield's revitalized city center is full of hip (read: pricey) restaurants and cafes. For cheaper options, take a walk west of the city. Wine bars are sandwiched between Indian and Italian restaurants on **Ecclesall Road,** where students from the local universities hang out. Smart eateries with mid-priced menus are located on **Division** and **Devonshire Streets.** The **Spar** supermarket is at the intersection of Division St. and Backfields Alley. (☎0114 275 2900. Open 24hr.) The **Showroom Cafe-Bar ❷**, 7 Paternoster Row, draws a local crowd. Lounge on the couch over butternut squash risotto and bangers and mash (£6.75-12) before watching films next door. (☎0114 249 5479; www.showroom.org.uk. Student tickets £3. Open M-Sa 10am-11pm, Su 10am-midnight. Kitchen open M-Sa until 9pm, Su until 5pm. MC/V.) **Blue Moon Cafe ❶**, 2 St. James St., three blocks up the hill from Castle Sq., after the Cathedral Church of St. Peter and St. Paul, serves a selection of vegetarian entrees under £6, like the sweet potato and green pepper bake, as well as snacks and gluten-free cakes under £3. The bohemian atmosphere includes jazz music and a wall hung with four clocks, all set to the same time. (☎0114 276 3443. Open M-Sa 8am-8pm. AmEx/MC/V.)

◎ SIGHTS. Although it has an industrial shell, Sheffield is also a garden city with over 200 parks, woodlands, and gardens. The indoor **Winter Garden** shelters 2500 varieties of plants from around the world. Sheffield's vibrant art scene centers upon the **Millennium Galleries,** Arundel Gate, linked to Tudor Sq. The galleries host national and international touring exhibitions. (☎0114 278 2600. Open M-Sa 10am-5pm, Su 11am-5pm. Free. Special exhibits £6, concessions £4.) The excellent **Ruskin Gallery** was established in 1875 by Victorian critic John Ruskin, who intended to show that "life without industry is guilt, and industry without art is brutality." Today, rotating pieces—most of them highly skillful copies of Renaissance masterpieces—uphold Ruskin's goal of inspiring the craftsmen (and now visitors) of Sheffield. (☎0114 278 2600; www.sheffieldgalleries.org.uk. Open M-Sa 10am-5pm, Su 11am-5pm. Free. Special exhibits occasionally have an additional charge.) Find works by Picasso and Cézanne in **Graves Gallery,** on Surrey St. above the public library, which also displays post-war British art, Romantic and Impressionist paintings, and modern photography. (☎0114 278 2600. Open M-Sa 10am-5pm. Free.) The **Site Gallery,** 1 Brown St., showcases contemporary art and photography. (☎0114 281 2077. Open W-Sa 11am-5:30pm. Free.)

▣ ▣ ENTERTAINMENT AND NIGHTLIFE. Most clubs are in the southeastern section of the city, around Matilda St. *The Sheffield Guide* has current nightlife listings. For info on Sheffield's gay scene, pick up *Qkultcha* magazine. **The Leadmill,** 6 Leadmill Rd., is a casual hangout with a popular Monday student night and a fine industrial vibe. Live music as well as indie, pop, and R&B tracks play to packed dance floors. (☎0114 221 2828; www.leadmill.co.uk. Cover £3-4. Open M-F 10pm-2:30am, Sa 10pm-3am.) For nightlife without a hangover, visit the **Crucible** and **Lyceum Theatres** for musicals, plays, and dance shows. Both are in Tudor Sq. The complex is the largest center for theater in England outside London. Backstage tours run once a week, usually on the weekends; call for details. (☎0114 249 6000; www.sheffieldtheatres.co.uk. Tickets £10-36, same-day £8.) Events from classical music to comedy liven up the **Sheffield City Hall,** Barkers Pool. (☎0114 2789 789. Box office open 9:30am-5:30pm)

YORK   ☎(0)1904

With its narrow cobblestone streets and pre-1066 churches, York is known as "the most haunted city in the world"—thronged with the ghosts of Romans, Anglo-Saxons, Vikings, and Normans, the last of whom maintained the city as a military stronghold and built Yorkminster Cathedral. With so much ambience and so much violence, York remains one of England's most popular destinations. Tourists come to walk the city walls, tour the Minster, take tea in one of the many cafes, or drink away the evening at a riverside pub. It may be haunted by the dead, but York is still as alive as ever.

◰ TRANSPORTATION

Trains: York Station, Station Rd. Travel center open M-Sa 8am-7:30pm, Su 9am-7:30pm. Ticket office open M-F 5:30am-10:15pm, Sa 5:45am-10:10pm, Su 7:30am-10:10pm. Trains (☎08457 484 950) to: **Edinburgh** (2½hr., 2 per hr., £67); **London King's Cross** (2hr., 2 per hr., £74); **Newcastle** (1hr., 4 per hr., £21); **Scarborough** (45min., every hr., £11). Trains run more sporadically outside of peak hours.

Buses: Stations at 20 Rougier St., Exhibition Sq., the train station, and on Piccadilly. Major bus stop on The Stonebow (information ☎01904 551 400). National Express (☎08705 808 080) to **Edinburgh** (6hr., 1 per day, £31), **London** (5½hr., 15 per day, £23), and **Manchester** (3hr., 15 per day, £12).

Public Transportation: First York (☎01904 622 992, timetables 551 400) has a ticket office at 20 Rougier St. Open M-F 9am-5pm. Yorkshire Coastliner (☎0113 244 8976 or 01653 692 556; www.coastliner.co.uk) runs buses from the train station to **Castle Howard** (p. 413) and other towns toward the coast. Timetables available at TICs.

Taxis: Station Taxis (☎01904 623 332). Wheelchair-accessible service available with advance booking. 24hr.

Bike Rental: Bob Trotter, 13-15 Lord Mayor's Walk (☎01904 622 868; www.bobtrottercycles.com). From £12 per day; £75 deposit. Open M-W and F-Sa 9am-5:30pm, Th 9:30am-5:30pm, Su 10am-4pm.

WHAT'S APUB, DOC? If someone says "apub" to you as you roam the streets of Yorkshire, they're not necessarily directing you to the nearest pint. "Apub" can mean "hello," "what's up?" or even "bloody hell!"

◰ ◰ ORIENTATION AND PRACTICAL INFORMATION

York's streets are winding, short, rarely labeled, and prone to name changes. Fortunately, most attractions lie within the city walls, and the towers of the **Minster,** visible from nearly everywhere, provide easy orientation. The **River Ouse** (rhymes with "muse") cuts through the city, curving west to south. The city center lies between the Ouse and the Minster. **Coney Street, Parliament Street,** and **Stonegate** are the main thoroughfares. **The Shambles,** York's quasi-medieval shopping district, lies between Parliament St. and Colliergate.

Tourist Information Centre: Exhibition Sq. (☎01904 550 099; www.visityork.org). Books rooms for £4 plus a 10% deposit. Gives out a free mini-guide with a detailed map and sells *Snickelways of York* (£6), a handwritten booklet of walks through York's alleyways.

Also sells the **York Pass,** which covers entry into 32 top attractions for 1 (£24), 2 (£32), or 3 (£36) days. Open Apr.-Oct. M-Sa 9am-6pm, Su 10am-5pm; Nov.-May M-Sa 9am-5pm, Su 10am-4pm. Branch in the train station open Easter-Oct. M-Sa 9am-6pm, Su 10am-5pm; Nov.-Easter M-Sa 9am-4pm, Su 10am-4pm.

Tours: Yorkwalk (☎01904 622 303; www.yorkwalk.co.uk) leads 1½-2hr. guided tours from the Museum Gardens Gate on Museum St. Feb.-Nov. daily 10:30am, 2:15pm; Dec.-Jan. Sa-Su 10:30am, 2:15pm. £5. The 1hr. **Ghost Hunt of York** (☎01904 608 700; www.ghosthunt.co.uk) meets at The Shambles daily at 7:30pm. £5. **City Sightseeing** (☎01904 655 585; www.city-sightseeing.com) leads hop-on, hop-off bus tours daily with 22 stops around the city. £9, concessions £7. Several companies along the **River Ouse** near Lendal, Ouse, and Skeldergate Bridges offer 1hr. **boat cruises.** Try **YorkBoat** at Lendal Bridge and Kings Staith Landing (☎01904 628 324; www.yorkboat. co.uk). Office open M-F 9am-5pm. From £7; call ahead for exact times and prices.

Banks: Thomas Cook, 4 Nessgate (☎01904 772 299). Open M-Sa 9am-5:30pm. **Barclays,** 1-3 Parliament St. (☎01904 882 305 or 555 555). Open M-Sa 9am-5pm. Other banks and **ATMs** spot Parliament St. and Coney St.

Luggage Storage: At York Station (previous page). £4 per item. Open daily 8am-8:30pm.

Library: York Central Library, Museum St. (☎01904 655 631). Open M-W and F 9am-8pm, Th 9am-5:30pm, Sa 9am-4pm.

Police: Fulford Rd. (☎01904 631 321).

Pharmacy: Boots, 48 Coney St. (☎01904 653 657). Open M-W and F-Sa 8:30am-6pm, Th 8:30am-7pm. **Oliver's,** 59 Blossom St. (☎01904 622 761). Open M-F 9am-5:30pm, Sa 9am-1pm.

Hospital: York District Hospital (☎01904 631 313), off Wigginton Rd. Take bus #1 or 18 from Exhibition Sq. and ask for the hospital stop. **NIH Walk-in Clinic,** 31 Monkgate St. (☎01904 725 401). Open daily 8am-6pm.

Internet Access: Cafe of the Evil Eye, 42 Stonegate (☎01904 640 002). £2 per hr. Wi-Fi £1 per day. Open M-Th 10am-11pm, F-Sa 10am-late, Su 11am-10:30pm. **City Screen Cimena,** 12-17 Coney St. (☎01904 612 940). £3 per hr. Wi-Fi £1 per day. Open daily 11am-6pm. **York Central Library** (above) has 25 Internet terminals.

Post Office: 22 Lendal St. (☎0845 722 3344), with a **bureau de change.** Open M and W-Sa 9am-5:30pm, Tu 9:30am-5:30pm. Branch at 4 Colliergate (☎01904 651 398). Open M-F 9am-5:30pm and Sa 9am-12:30pm. **Postcode:** YO1 8BP.

ACCOMMODATIONS AND CAMPING

B&Bs (from £30) are mostly located outside the city walls and scattered along **Bootham** and **Clifton Streets, Monkgate** and **Huntington Streets, Bishopthorpe Road,** and in the Mount area down **Blossom Street.**

Foss Bank Guest House, 16 Huntington Rd. (☎01904 635 548). Walk 20min. or take bus #12 from the train station and get off on the 1st stop on Huntington Rd. Sunlit rooms with shower and sink. Wi-Fi. Singles £30; doubles £62. Cash only. ❸

YHA York International, Water End (☎01904 653 147), Clifton, 2 mi. from train station. The long walk from the train station follows the river path, "Dame Judi Dench," which connects to Water End. Caters to school groups but attracts guests of all ages. TV lounge, bar, restaurant, game room, and kitchen. Breakfast included. Internet £1.50 per 15min. Bike rental £1.50 per hr., £9.60 per day. Dorms £20, under 18 £14.50; singles £27.50; doubles £52. £3 charge for non-YHA members. MC/V. ❷

Bar Convent Guest House, 17 Blossom St. (☎01904 464 902; www.bar-convent.org. uk). 18-bedroom guesthouse located in the oldest operational convent in England. Spotless rooms, game room, and kitchen. Continental breakfast is filling and delicious.

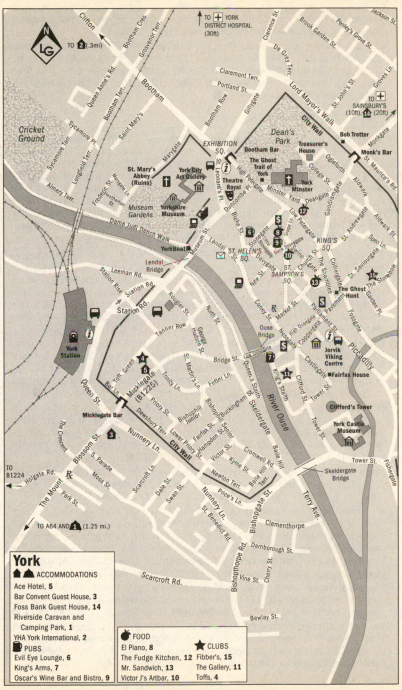

York

ACCOMMODATIONS

Ace Hotel, **5**
Bar Convent Guest House, **3**
Foss Bank Guest House, **14**
Riverside Caravan and
  Camping Park, **1**
YHA York International, **2**

PUBS

Evil Eye Lounge, **6**
King's Arms, **7**
Oscar's Wine Bar and Bistro, **9**

FOOD

El Piano, **8**
The Fudge Kitchen, **12**
Mr. Sandwich, **13**
Victor J's Artbar, **10**

CLUBS

Fibber's, **15**
The Gallery, **11**
Toffs, **4**

Laundry. Wi-Fi £1 per hr., £3.50 per day. Laundry, game room, and kitchen. Reception 8am-10pm. Singles £30; doubles £57, ensuite from £70. MC/V. ❸

Riverside Caravan and Camping Park, Ferry Ln. (☎01904 705 812), Bishopthorpe, 2 mi. south of York off the A64. Take bus #11A to Bishopthorpe's Main St. (2 per hr.) or ask to be let off at the campground. Popular campground close to the river. Open Easter-Oct. Peak-season from July to early Sept. £10 per tent. From mid-Sept. to Oct. and Apr.-June £8 per tent. Cash only. ❶

🄲🄼 FOOD AND PUBS

Greengrocers have peddled at **Newgate Market** for centuries, between Parliament St. and The Shambles. (Open Apr.-Dec. M-Sa 9am-5pm, Su 9am-4:30pm; Jan.-Mar. M-Sa 9am-5pm.) You can also opt to eat street-side and fill up on sausages (£1.65, with cheese £1.80), burgers (£2), and fresh lemonade (£2) from stands parked in St. Sampson's Sq. There are more pubs in the center of York than gargoyles on the Minster's east wall. Feast medievally on pies and ale or find cheap eats at the many Indian restaurants just outside the city gates. Groceries are available at **Sainsbury's,** at the intersection of Foss Bank and Heworth Green. (☎01904 643 801. Open M-Sa 8am-8pm, Su 11am-5pm.)

🄼 **El Piano,** 15 Grape Ln. (☎01904 610 676). Mexican flavors infuse the heart-healthy dishes served up in this laid-back and brightly painted establishment at the corner of the city center. Dishes served in 3 sizes: *chica* (£3), tapas (£4.25), and *ración* (£6) are great for nibblers and cheap dates. All food is vegan and gluten-free. Catch "cheap chow" M-W 10am-7pm (£7). Smaller dining rooms upstairs are aptly named the "Moroccan Room," adorned with floor pillows, and the bright "Sunshine Room." Open M-Sa 10am-midnight, Su noon-5pm. MC/V. ❷

🄼 **Oscar's Wine Bar and Bistro,** 8 Little Stonegate (☎01904 652 002), off Stonegate. Order at the bar and find a seat on the patio (if you can part the crowds) at this local favorite. Huge portions of food like Oscar's special burger (£7.50), lasagna (£7.50), and a spicy bean burger (£7). Sandwiches and starters £4-6. Happy hour M 4-11pm, Tu-F 5-7pm, Su 4-10:30pm. Open M-Sa 11:30am-11pm, Su noon-10:30pm. MC/V. ❷

Evil Eye Lounge, 42 Stonegate (☎01904 464 002). Everything from mixed drinks to computers at this 3-story restaurant and lounge. Thai and Indonesian dishes are affordable and varied. Over 100 mixed-drink selections (£5 each). Internet £2 per hr. Wi-Fi £1 per day. Noodles £5. Entrees £6-10. Kitchen open M-F noon-9pm, Sa noon-7pm. Bar open M-Th 10am-11:30pm, F-Sa 10pm-12:30am. MC/V. ❷

King's Arms, King's Staith (☎01904 659 435). Outdoor seating and cheap drinks (bitters £1.50 per pint). Be wary in the winter, when the riverside spot earns the nickname "the Pub that Floods." Open M-Sa 11am-11pm, Su noon-10:30pm. Cash only. ❶

Mr. Sandwich, 37 The Shambles (☎01904 643 500). Think of all you can buy in England for £1—yup, not a lot. Thank goodness for Mr. Sandwich, who will make you any 1 of 47 kinds of sandwiches for £1. Fillings include chicken, roast pork, mozzarella, and fig. Can't pick? Pay 50p extra and get a Greedy Pig—all the fillings Mr. Sandwich can squeeze into 1 roll. Takeaway. Open M-Sa 8am-5pm, Su 10am-5:30pm. Cash only. ❶

Victor J's Artbar, 1 Finkle St. (☎01904 541 771), hidden down an alley off Stonegate. This Art Deco bar and bistro serves huge portions of tasty sandwiches (brie, roasted veggies, and pesto ciabatta £6) and burgers (£5-6) that will please your belly and your budget. Open M-W and Sa 10am-midnight, Th-Fri 10am-1am, Su 11am-6pm. MC/V. ❷

The Fudge Kitchen, 58 Low Petergate (☎01904 645 596; www.fudgekitchen.co.uk). Over 20 flavors of gooey fudge, from Vintage Vanilla to Banoffee to Strawberries 'n' Cream (£3-4.50 per slice) are made in the shop by energetic chefs. Free samples available all day. Open M-Sa 10am-6pm, Su 10am-5:30pm. MC/V. ❶

SIGHTS

The best introduction to York is a walk along its **medieval walls** (2½ mi.), especially the northeast section and behind the cathedral. The walls are accessible up stairways by the gates. Beware the tourist stampede, which only subsides in the early morning and just before the walls close at dusk.

YORK MINSTER

THE CATHEDRAL. Looming over the shops and crooked streets, the Minster dominates York today just as it did 600 years ago. Step into its vast vaulted stillness, and you sense the scale and grandeur of medieval religion. Tourists and pilgrims alike have visited the Minster—the largest Gothic cathedral outside of Italy—for centuries. Steadily constructed over two centuries, the Norman-built cathedral displays an estimated half of all the medieval stained glass in England. The 15th-century **Great East Window,** which depicts the beginning and end of the world in more than 100 small scenes, is the world's largest medieval stained-glass window. The main chamber of the church is generally mobbed with tourists, but the tombs and stonework are less appreciated and equally impressive. Look for the statue of Archbishop Lamplugn toward the East Window—he has two right feet. The creamy, gargoyle-encrusted exterior looks magnificent at sunset. (*Deangate.* ☎01904 557 216; www.yorkminster.org. Open daily 7am-6:30pm. Evensong M-Sa 5:15pm, Su 4pm. Free 1hr. guided tours from the entrance when volunteers are available Apr.-Sept. daily 9:30am-3:30pm; Oct.-Mar. 10am-2pm. £5.50, concessions £4.50. Combined ticket with Undercroft £7.50, concessions £5.)

TIP SIGHT AND SOUND. See the Minster for free by attending the 5:15pm Evensong (the Anglican Liturgy of Evening Prayer) sung by the Minster Choir.

CHAPTER HOUSE. For something a little less holy, check out the Chapter House's grotesque medieval carvings. Every figure is unique, from mischievous demons to a three-faced woman. Keep an eye out for the tiny Virgin Mary to the right upon entering—so small she went unnoticed by Cromwell's idol-smashing thugs. (*Chapter House open daily 9am-6pm. Free.*)

CENTRAL TOWER. Two-hundred and seventy-five steps lead to the top of the tower. Go early—ascents are only allowed during a 5min. period every 30min. because the staircase is too narrow for passing traffic. (*Open daily Apr.-Sept. 9:30am-6pm; Oct.-Mar. 10am-5pm. £4.*)

UNDERCROFT, TREASURY, AND CRYPT. Deep in the belly of the Minster you can tour the building's huge concrete and steel foundations and learn the story of its founding and construction from Roman legionary headquarters to towering Norman Gothic cathedral. The **Roman level** still includes the site where Constantine was proclaimed emperor. The **crypt**—not a crypt at all but the altar of the Norman-Saxon church—houses a shrine to **Saint William of York** and the 12th-century **Doomstone** upon which the cathedral was built. The **treasury** displays the wealth of the old archbishops, including Yorkshire silver vessels and the Horn of Ulph. Some visitors who haven't paid the entrance fee find they can sneak a quick peek into the crypt through the gate in the East Wing. (*Open daily Apr.-Sept. 9:30am-5:30pm; Oct.-Mar. 10am-5pm. £4, concessions £3. 45min. audio tour included.*)

OTHER SIGHTS

▓YORK CASTLE MUSEUM. Who says time travel is impossible? Billed as Britain's premier museum of everyday life, the York Castle Museum transports visitors back to the days of yore. The comprehensive exhibits are the brainchild of the eccentric Dr. John Kirk, who began collecting household items—Victorian wedding dresses, old-fashioned hard candies, antique vacuum cleaners—during his house calls from the 1890s to the 1920s. The exhibitions include **Kirkgate,** an intricately reconstructed Victorian shopping street, and **Half Moon Court,** its Edwardian counterpart. On both streets, visitors can enter the candy store, bar, police station, and other buildings to view period items close up. *(Between Tower St. and Piccadilly. ☎01904 687 687. Open daily 9:30am-5pm. £7.50, concessions £6.50.)*

JORVIK VIKING CENTRE. Visitors ride through the York of the 10th century in floating "time cars" past artifacts, painfully accurate smells, and animatronic mannequins. Built atop a major archaeological site, the museum contains unusually well-preserved Viking artifacts. Much of the information presented is based on archaeological evidence from the site. As one of the busiest attractions in the city, the center usually has unavoidable lines and hordes of school groups; arrive early or book at least a day ahead in summer. *(Coppergate. ☎01904 615 555 for advance bookings; www.jorvik-viking-centre.co.uk. Open daily 10am-5pm. Last entry 1hr. before close. £7.75, concessions £6.60. Pre-booking charge £1 per person.)*

CLIFFORD'S TOWER. Clifford's Tower is one of the last remaining pieces of York Castle and a chilling reminder of one of the worst outbreaks of anti-Semitic violence in English history. In 1190, Christian merchants tried to erase their debts to Jewish bankers by annihilating York's Jewish community. On the last Sabbath before Passover, 150 Jews sought refuge in the wood tower and, faced with the prospect of starvation or butchery, committed suicide by setting the tower on fire. The tower was rebuilt in 1250. *(Tower St. ☎01904 646 940. Open daily Apr.-Sept. 10am-6pm; Oct. 10am-5pm; Nov.-Mar. 10am-4pm. £3, concessions £2.40.)*

YORKSHIRE MUSEUM AND GARDENS. Hidden in 10 gorgeous acres of gardens, the Yorkshire Museum presents Roman, Anglo-Saxon, and Viking artifacts. The highlight is the priceless **Middleham Jewel** (c. 1450), an enormous sapphire set in a gold amulet engraved with the Trinity and the Nativity. After amassing enough donations, the museum dropped $2.5 million to purchase it from a private seller. Its companion, the **Middleham Ring,** went for $46,000. Also on exhibit are a 2000-year-old boiled egg—some ancient Roman's packed lunch—and various Yorkshire fossils and fauna. In the gardens, children chase pigeons among the ruins of **Saint Mary's Abbey,** once the most influential Benedictine monastery in northern England. *(Enter from Museum St. or Marygate. ☎01904 687 687. Open daily 10am-5pm. £5, concessions £4, families £14. Gardens and ruins free.)*

BEST OF THE REST. See more than six centuries of British and European art at the **York City Art Gallery.** The gallery shows special exhibitions throughout the year and permanently displays the work of William Etty, York native and pioneer of the English painted nude. *(In Exhibition Sq. across from the TIC. ☎01904 687 687; www.yorkartgallery.org.uk. Open daily 10am-5pm. Last entry 4:30pm. Free.)* The **Treasurer's House** holds the collection of antique furnishings amassed by Edwardian connoisseur Frank Green. *(Chapter House St. next to the Minster. ☎01904 624 427. Open Apr.-Oct. M-Th and Sa-Su 11am-4:30pm; Nov. M-Sa 11am-3pm for tours only. £5, children £2.80. Gardens free. Tours of the haunted cellar £2.20.)*

🎵 📻 ENTERTAINMENT AND NIGHTLIFE

To discover the best of after-hours York, consult *What's On* and *The Talk*, available at the TIC, for listings of live music, theater, cinema, and exhibitions. Twilight activities take place in **King's Square** and on **Stonegate**, where barbershop quartets share the pavement with jugglers, magicians, and soapboxers. The Minster and local churches host a series of **summer concerts**, including July's **York Early Music Festival.** (☎01904 658 338; www.ncem.co.uk. Tickets £8-25.)

Theatre Royal, St. Leonards Pl. (☎01904 623 568; www.yorktheatreroyal.co.uk), next to the TIC. The 250-year-old theater offers stage fare. Box office open M 10am-6pm, Tu-Sa 10am-8pm. £10-19, concessions and under 25 £6, all matinees £10.)

The Gallery, 12 Clifford St. (☎01904 647 947). One of the only places in York to get your groove on. 2 hot dance floors and 6 bars. Be prepared to queue up on popular theme nights. Dress smart casual; no sneakers or sportswear on weekends. Cover £3.50-10. Open M-Th and Su 10pm-2am, F-Sa 10pm-3am.

Tru, 3-5 Toft Green (☎01904 620 203). Break out the glow sticks. 3 rooms blast house and chart-toppers. Weekly student nights; discount with student ID. No sneakers or sportswear on weekends. Cover £2-7. Open M-Sa 10pm-3am.

Fibber's, Stonebow House, the Stonebow (☎01904 651 250; www.fibbers.co.uk). York's main music venue has live music nightly. F and Sa become club nights, featuring indie and rock spun by a DJ after live music ends. Live music 8-10:30pm. Club cover £5, students before 11:30pm £3.

🎭 DAYTRIP FROM YORK

CASTLE HOWARD. The tagline in the pamphlets is "there's no house like this house," and you can see why. Still inhabited by the Howard family but open to visitors, domed Castle Howard, with its magnificent Baroque fountain and suites of decorated rooms, is a stunning reminder that from 1700 to 1940 Great Britain possessed the smallest, wealthiest, and most powerful aristocracy in the world. The castle inspired Evelyn Waugh to write *Brideshead Revisited* and was the setting for the BBC's film adaptation. Roman busts and portraits of Howard ancestors in full regalia clutter the halls. Head to the **chapel** for kaleidoscopic Pre-Raphaelite stained glass. The 1000 acres of gardens, perhaps even more stunning than the house itself, are thick with fountains, lakes, and roaming peacocks. The **Temple of the Four Winds** offers views of the rolling hills. (*15 mi. northeast of York off the A64. Yorkshire Coastliner bus #840 runs to the castle, 842 runs from the castle. 40min.; May-Sept. M-Sa 2 per day in each direction, Su 1 per day; round-trip £7-10. 15% off admission with bus ticket (ask for a heritage voucher). Take the morning bus from York to catch the bus back in the afternoon. Bring small bills for the bus. ☎01653 648 444; www.castlehoward. co.uk. Castle open Mar.-Oct. daily 11am-4:30pm. Gardens open Mar.-Oct. daily 10am-6:30pm. Last entry to house 4pm, to gardens 4:30pm. £10.50. Gardens without house £8/7.50).*)

LEEDS ☎(0)113

Once the center of England's textile industry, Leeds and its fortunes declined when the world lost its burning desire for fine wool coats. Changing times have turned Leeds from fabric producer to fashion consumer, and now designer shops and chains fill its grand Victorian buildings. Must-see sights are few, but the city that gave us Marks & Spencer still draws crowds for its theatre venues, restaurants, and pedestrian-friendly shopping streets.

▐ TRANSPORTATION

INTERCITY TRANSPORTATION

Trains: City Train Station, City Sq. Ticket office open 24hr. Trains (☎0845 748 4950; www.nationalrail.co.uk) from Leeds to most major cities, including **London King's Cross** (2hr., every hr., £23-208; book in advance for less expensive fares), **Manchester** (1hr., 4 per hr., £10-20), and **York** (30min., 3-4 per hr., £12.30).

Buses: City Bus Station on New York St., next to Kirkgate Market. Office open M and W-F 8:30am-5:30pm, Tu 9am-5:30pm, Sa 9am-4:30pm. **National Express** (☎0871 781 8181; www.nationalexpress.com) operates from Leeds to most major cities, including: **Birmingham** (3hr., every hr., £22.50); **Edinburgh** (7hr., 4 per day, £38); **Glasgow** (6hr., 4 per day, £38); **Liverpool** (2hr., every hour, £10.80); **London** (5hr., every hr., £19); **Manchester** (1hr., every hour, £8); **York** (45min., 3 per day, £4.70). Metroline (☎0113 245 7676; www.wymetro.com) runs local buses to **Bradford** (1hr., every 30min., £2.10) and **Hull** (1hr., 7 per day, £5.50).

LOCAL TRANSPORTATION

Public Transportation: City Bus Station on New York St., next to Kirkgate Market. Office open M and W-F 8:30am-5:30pm, Tu 9am-5:30pm, Sa 9am-4:30pm. Free bus maps at the City Bus Station or the TIC. Buses also stop in front of the train station on Infirmary St. Bus fares vary with the distance traveled but generally hover around £1.50. All-day ticket £2.70-3.70. The city also runs a **free bus service** that circles downtown; pick up a map from the bus station.

Taxis: City Cabs (☎0113 246 9999). **Streamline Taxis** (☎0113 244 3322). **Telecabs** (☎0113 263 7777). All 24hr.

✦ 🛈 ORIENTATION AND PRACTICAL INFORMATION

Cutting the city through its center, the **Headrow**—Leeds's main thoroughfare—connects the west and east ends. The suburb of **Headingley,** known for its sports venues and student life, lies just 2 mi. outside of the city center.

Tourist Information Centre: Gateway Yorkshire (☎0113 242 5242, bookings 080 080 8050), in the train station. Open M 10am-5:30pm, Tu-Sa 9am-5:30pm, Su 10am-4pm.

Budget Travel: STA Travel, 88 Vicar Ln. (☎0871 230 8569). Open M-W and Sa 9am-6pm, Th 9am-8pm, Su 11am-5pm.

Banks: Many line Park Row. Most open roughly M-F 9am-5:30pm, Sa 9am-1:30pm.

Beyond Tourism: JobCentre, 12-14 Briggate (☎0113 215 5382). Open M-Tu and Th-F 9am-4pm, W 10am-4pm.

Luggage Storage: £2-5 at the bus station; £6 at the train station.

Police: Millgarth St. (☎0113 241 3059), north of the bus station.

Pharmacy: Boots (☎0113 242 1713), in Leeds City Station. Open M-Sa 8am-midnight, Su 9am-midnight. Other locations throughout the city with varying hours.

Hospital: Leeds General Infirmary, Great George St. (☎0113 243 2799).

Internet Access: Art's Cafe (see **Food,** p. 416). **The Internet Cafe** (☎01133 242 615), in Merrion Market Centre. £2 for 30min. and milky coffee.

Library: Leeds Central Library, the Headrow (☎0113 247 8911), across the street from Town Hall. Free. ID required. Often full. Open M-W 9am-8pm, Th-F 9am-5pm, Sa 10am-5pm, Su 1-4pm. Last session 30min. before close.

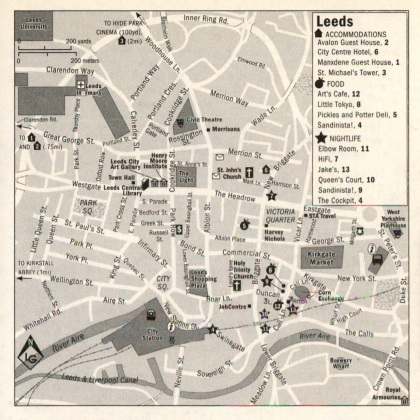

Leeds

🏠 ACCOMMODATIONS
Avalon Guest House, **2**
City Centre Hotel, **6**
Manxdene Guest House, **1**
St. Michael's Tower, **3**

🍎 FOOD
Art's Cafe, **12**
Little Tokyo, **8**
Pickles and Potter Deli, **5**
Sandinista!, **4**

⭐ NIGHTLIFE
Elbow Room, **11**
HiFi, **7**
Jake's, **13**
Queen's Court, **10**
Sandinista!, **9**
The Cockpit, **4**

Post Office: 116 Albion St. (☎0845 722 3344). Bureau de change. Open M-Sa 9am-5:30pm. **Postcode:** LS2 8LP.

🏠 ACCOMMODATIONS

There are no hostels in Leeds, but some low-cost guest houses serve a full English breakfast, saving you money for an extra pint. To get to Headingley's B&B-rich Cardigan Rd., walk 20min. through Hyde Park or take any bus toward Headingley from Infirmary St., get off at St. Michael's Church (20min.), and walk 5min. down St. Michael's Ln.

The Manxdene Hotel, 154 Woodsley Rd. (☎0113 243 2586; www.manxdeneguest-house.com), a 15min. walk from the city center. Head east on Great George St., which becomes Clarendon Rd., and turn left on Woodsley Rd. The free bus stops around the corner at Clarendon and Hyde. Beautiful Victorian B&B within walking distance of the university campus. Wood floors complement red leather chairs and patterned rugs in rich colors. TV and coffeepot in each of the recently renovated, spacious rooms. Breakfast included. Singles £30, ensuite £40; twins and doubles £40, ensuite double £50. Last night free with weeklong stay. AmEx/MC/V. ❸

St. Michael's Tower Hotel, 5-6 St. Michael's Villa, Cardigan Rd. (☎0113 275 5557; www.st-michaels-guesthouse.co.uk). Rooms are small but clean, well kept, and close to

Headingley's cricket ground and student hangouts. Breakfast included and worth waking up for. Singles £27, ensuite £35; twins and doubles £40, ensuite double £48; family rooms £60-80. Book in advance. MC/V. ❸

Avalon Guest House, 132 Woodsley Rd. (☎0113 243 2545; www.avalonguesthouseleeds.co.uk). Near Manxdene Hotel. Bright blue walls adorn this B&B, just minutes from the Leeds University campus. Singles £35, ensuite £40; doubles and twins £40 / ensuite £50; family rooms £75. Call ahead. MC/V. ❸

City Centre Hotel, 51A New Briggate (☎0113 429 019; www.leedscitycentrehotel.com). Entrance on side street. With its cheerful red and yellow color scheme, City Centre offers a lot to be happy about: clean rooms, a central location, and the cheapest in-town rates north of the shopping district. Additional charge for breakfast. Singles £30, ensuite £45; ensuite doubles £50; ensuite triples £69. MC/V. ❸

FOOD

For butcher shops, bakeries, and a taste of local life, head to **Kirkgate Market (Leeds Market),** off New York St. Europe's largest indoor market, Kirkgate hosts 400 indoor stalls and 200 outside as well as a farmers' market the first and third Sunday of every month. (☎0113 214 5162. Indoor stalls open M-Tu 8am-5:30pm, W 8am-2pm, Th-Sa 7:30am-5:30pm; outdoor stalls close 30min. earlier.) For stylish dining, walk along **Greek Street** between East Parade and Park Row. **Vicar Lane,** north of the Headrow, offers less expensive restaurants. Get groceries at **Morrisons** in Merrion Centre. (☎0113 242 2575. Open M-Tu and Sa 8am-7pm, W-F 8am-8pm, Su 11am-5pm.)

Pickles and Potter Deli, 22 Queens Arcade, Victoria Quarter (☎0113 242 7702). Sandwiches, pastas, soups, and salads. Build your own sandwich with fresh, organic ingredients from local farmers. Sit inside the funky restaurant to peruse the cookbook collection lining the walls (£2). Sandwiches from £3.40. Takeaway available. Open M-Sa 9am-5pm, Su 11am-4:30pm. MC/V. ❶

Sandinista!, 5/5A Cross Belgrave St. (☎0113 305 0372; www.sandinistaleeds.co.uk). Namesake of the Nicaraguan revolutionaries (and of the Manchester punk-rock album by The Clash), this warm, inviting Cuban oasis features fantastic tapas and a la carte meals from £3.50. Board games and a special Su "recovery" brunch on the patio. Postcards and pictures line the walls above the bar, where an energetic waitstaff serves from a menu full of vegetarian and vegan options. Open M-Tu noon-1am, W-Th and Su noon-2am, F-Sa noon-3am. MC/V. ❷

Art's Cafe, 42 Calls Ln. (☎0113 243 8243; www.artscafebar.co.uk). Small, trendy restaurant with local artwork on the walls and creative dishes on your plate. Cafe serves coffee, desserts, and a wide selection of wine and beers. Free Wi-Fi; ask for the password at the counter. Lunch £5-8; dinner £10-14. Open M-F noon-11pm, Sa noon-2am, Su 10:30am-11pm. AmEx/MC/V. ❷

Little Tokyo, 24 Central Rd. (☎0113 439 090). Leeds's favorite Japanese joint makes fresh sushi as well as curries, salads, sandwiches, and noodle dishes. The restaurant's promise—"natural, healthy, organic"—matches its zen-inspired interior: wood chairs, bamboo-painted walls, and a stream flowing through the restaurant's center. Takeaway available. Open M-Th 11:30am-10pm, F-Sa 11:30am-11pm. MC/V. ❷

SIGHTS

ROYAL ARMOURIES. Built as an armory in the time of Henry VIII, the museum now holds one of the world's best collections of arms and armor. A war buff's Graceland, the museum features every kind of defense imaginable, from Henry VIII's "horned helmut" (complete with metal beard stubble) to Mughal elephant armor. Galleries also feature exhibits of civilian weaponry and modern-day handguns as well as a "Farewell to Arms" exhibit promoting peace and disarmament. Don't miss the side building, where horses and birds of prey share company with hard-working craftsmen. Demonstrations, including swordplay and an outdoor joust, are held regularly. Call ahead for information on the day's events. *(Armouries Dr. Cross the Millennium footbridge from The Calls and follow the River Aire east until you reach the back of the museum, which is a massive gray stone building. ☎ 1870 0344 344; www.royalarmouries.org. Open daily 10am-5pm. Free. Special exhibits and joust £2-3.)*

LEEDS CITY ART GALLERY. Recently renovated, the Leeds City Art Gallery features one of the best collections of 20th and contemporary British art outside London. *(Headrow. ☎ 0113 247 8248. Open W noon-8pm, Th-Sa 10am-5pm, Su 1-5pm. Free.)*

HENRY MOORE INSTITUTE. The Henry Moore Institute is a center for the study of sculpture that holds exhibitions in a few small galleries. *(Headrow, adjacent to the Leeds City Art Gallery. ☎ 0113 234 3158; www.henry-moore-fdn.co.uk. Open M-Tu and Th-Su 10am-5:30pm, W 10am-9pm. Free.)*

KIRKSTALL ABBEY. Built by Cisterian monks in the 12th century and left to decay, the ruins of Kirkstall Abbey inspired JMW Turner and other artists of the Romantic movement. The lush greens, wildflowers, and river surrounding the abbey make the perfect setting for a bottle of wine and a picnic. *(3 mi. west of the city center on Kirkstall Rd. Take bus #33 or 33A and get off when you see the abbey on your left. ☎ 0113 395 7400. Park open daily dawn to dusk. Abbey open in summer Tu-Su 11am-4pm; in winter Tu-Th and Sa-Su 11am-3pm. Free.)*

SAINT JOHN'S CHURCH. Built in 1632, St. John's Church is the oldest church in Leeds. The chapel is surrounded by a small, gorgeous garden, a great place to meet for lunch and coffee. *(In town. Open Tu-Sa 11am-3pm.)*

OTHER SIGHTS. Leeds's massive **library** and two **art museums,** clustered adjacent to the Victorian **Town Hall,** form the city's small artistic center. The life-size chessboard and Victorian gardens out front seem straight out of *Alice in Wonderland*. **Marks & Spencer** started its empire selling goods for a penny in Leeds in 1884, and today the city is widely known for its shopping. Housed in old sewing houses, the malls and stores are sights in their own right. The **Victoria Quarter,** a series of arcades off Briggate, is a marvel of colored glass and steel. It houses the first **Harvey Nichols** department store outside London.

♪ ENTERTAINMENT

Hyde Park Picture House, Brudenell Rd. (☎0113 275 2045; www.hydeparkpicture-house.co.uk), near the Headingley campus. Bus #56 stops directly outside the theater. 1-room arthouse cinema famous for its frequent use in television programs. Daily showings of international and independent films as well as lesser-known mainstream pictures. Su children's film matinee. £5.50, balcony £6, concessions £4.50. Times vary; check the website or pick up a monthly guide for details.

West Yorkshire Playhouse, Playhouse Sq., Quarry Hill (☎0113 213 7700; www.wyp.org.uk), across from the bus station. Professional productions on 2 stages. Tickets £11-26. Cafe, bar, and restaurant upstairs. Open M-Sa 9am-8pm.

The Cockpit, Swinegate (☎0113 244 1573; www.thecockpit.co.uk), under the railroad bridge. Leeds's premier venue for live bands and hot performers. The stage has been graced by such bands as Coldplay, The White Stripes, and local heroes The Cribs. Doors open at 7pm unless otherwise stated. Buy tickets online.

NIGHTLIFE

With two universities, Leeds wakes up when the sun goes down. Recent grads and young professionals congregate near the city center while eager freshmen shake their jeans and trainers off at New Briggate clubs. Clubbers flock to Leeds to partake in neon nights of dance, house, indierock, and hip hop. Find up-to-date club listings in *Essential Leeds* (free), available at the TIC.

Sandinista!, 5/5A Cross Belgrave (☎0113 305 0372). This tapas bar turns into an energetic live-music venue at night. With creative mixed drinks and an eager, young staff, it's no wonder the small bar is always packed. Try the popular mojito or the manager's own Jamaican Sucker Punch (Appleton VX, Creole Shrubb, fresh lime and strawberries) before dancing. Open M-Tu noon-1am, W-Th and Su noon-2am, F-Sa noon-3am.

HiFi, 2 Central Rd. (☎0113 242 7353; www.thehificlub.co.uk). Basement venue pumps out live jazz, funk, and soul. Popular comedy nights Sa 7-10pm. Cover varies £3.50-11; free Su. Club nights on weekdays. Pick up a coupon for free entry when you eat at Art's Cafe (p. 416). Open M-Th 10pm-3am, F-Sa 7pm-3am, Su noon-3am. AmEx/MC/V.

Elbow Room, 64 Call Ln., 3rd and 4th fl. (☎0113 245 7011; www.theelbowroom.co.uk). Styled after a club by the same name in New York City, Elbow Room is a chill dance club with a neon-lit bar and American-style pool (£5-8 per hr.). Large plush couches and wood tables. Features different live bands every Sa 9pm-4am. Cover Sa £3-7; free before 9pm. Open M-Th and Su noon-midnight, F noon-3am, Sa noon-4am. MC/V.

Queen's Court, 167-168 Lower Briggate (☎0113 245 9449). Leeds's premier gay club, housed in a narrow space with an adjoining courtyard. Both fill up quickly for dancing and cheap drinks. 2 DJs and £1 drinks M 8pm-2:30am. Cover varies, usually around £3. Bar open M-W noon-2:30am, Th noon-midnight, F-Sa noon-3am, Su noon-11pm. Club open M 9:30pm-2:30am, F-Sa 10:30pm-3am. Kitchen open daily noon-6pm. MC/V.

Jakes, 29 Call Ln. (☎0113 243 1110). This laid-back bar, best known for its mixed drinks, feels more like your best friend's house party than a club. Dancers pack the floor when eclectic DJs spin on the weekends. Open M-Sa 5pm-2am. MC/V.

SOUTH PENNINES

Visitors to the South Pennines enjoy brisk country hikes along the dramatic, dandelion-dotted hills known as "the moors." Walks among the abandoned cotton and wool mills always prove breathtaking, especially during long summer days. The picturesque villages of Hebden Bridge and Haworth offer an eyeful of green, a host of fluffy sheep, and the refreshing feel of domestic country life.

TRANSPORTATION

Trains: The proximity of the South Pennines to Leeds and Bradford makes train transportation (☎08457 484 950) fairly easy. From **Hebden Bridge,** Arriva's Transpennine Express (☎08706 023 322) runs to **Blackpool, Leeds** (both M-Sa 7am-9pm several per hr., Su every hr.; £3.50), and **Manchester** (M-Sa 7am-9pm several per hr., Su every hr.; £8). Get to **Haworth** by taking Metro's Airedale line from Leeds to Keighley (KEETH-lee), 5 mi. north of the town (several per hr., £5.50). From there, travel to Haworth via the Keighley & Worth Valley Railway's steam trains (☎01535 645 214; July-Aug. daily 5-10 per day, Sept.-May Sa-Su at least 6 per day; £9, rover ticket £12).

Buses: For an alternative to train travel, take Metroline (☎0113 245 7676) buses #663-665 and 720 (15min., every 15-30min., £1.20-1.40). Metroline bus #500 runs between **Haworth** and **Hebden Bridge** (30min., 4-5 per day, £1.50). Bus travel will take you through smaller cities. Travel to **Halifax** to get to Hebden Bridge and to **Keighley** to get to Haworth—both cities are convenient destinations from **Leeds** and **Manchester.** Local buses make the 30min. journey from these cities to Hebden Bridge and Haworth. For more information, see below or call Metroline.

Trails: The Worth Way traces a 5 mi. route from **Keighley** to **Oxenhope**—ride the steam train or Metroline bus back to your starting point. From Haworth to Hebden Bridge, choose a trail from the TIC's *Two Walks Linking Haworth and Hebden Bridge* (50p), which guides visitors along the paths that inspired the Brontë sisters.

NO ROAMING CHARGES. For a day of exploration throughout West Yorkshire, buy a DayRover bus and train ticket for £5.50. Purchased from most post offices, TICs, or staffed stations, a DayRover ticket gives you a day of unlimited travel on all Metroline buses and trains in West Yorkshire.

HEBDEN BRIDGE   ☎ (0)1422

A historic stone village between two hills, Hebden Bridge lies close to the **Pennine Way** and the 50 mi. **Calderdale Way.** The small medieval village stitched its way to modest expansion in the booming textile years of the 18th and 19th centuries, and many of the trademark "double-decker" stone houses of this period are still standing. Today, there are still more cobblestones than paved streets, and the canals and mountain forests make for excellent walks and hiking.

ORIENTATION AND PRACTICAL INFORMATION. Hebden Bridge lies halfway along the Manchester-Leeds rail line (see **Transportation,** above). The town's train station is half a mile east of town on Station Rd.; follow the signs to town. Buses stop at the train station and on New Rd. The **Hebden Bridge Visitor & Canal Centre** (TIC) sells the popular *Walks Around Hebden Bridge* (50p) and other walking guides. (☎01422 843 831; www.hebdenbridge.co.uk. Open M-F 9:30am-5pm, Sa 10:15am-5pm, Su 10:30am-5pm.) NatWest **bank** is near the town center off Crown St. The **post office** is on Holme St., off New Rd. (☎01422 842 366. Open M-F 9am-5:30pm, Sa 9am-12:30pm.) **Postcode:** HX7 8AA.

ACCOMMODATIONS AND FOOD. Conveniently located 30min. from Leeds and Manchester, Hebden Bridge makes for a great daytrip. For those staying the night, however, **Angeldale Guest House** ❹, a large Victorian house at the north end of Hangingroyd Ln. (not Hangingroyd Rd. or Grove) near the center of town, has beautifully decorated, spacious rooms and a garden-lined path to its doorfront. (☎01422 847 321; www.angeldale.co.uk. Singles £35-64; doubles and twins £25-32. MC/V.)

Purchase groceries at **The Co-Op,** Market St. (Open M-Sa 8am-9pm, Su 11am-5pm.) For scones (£1.50-1.90), crumpets (£1), and a lovely view of the river, visit the **Watergate Tearooms** ❶, 9 Bridge Gate. (☎01422 842 978; www. tandcakes.com. Open daily 10am-4:30pm. MC/V.) Satisfying pizzas and pastas (£5-8) are served at **Pinnochio's Italian Ristorante Pizzeria** ❶, Hangingroyd Ln., just across the bridge from St. George Sq. (☎01422 843 745. Takeaway also available. Open W-Th 4:30-10pm, F-Sa 5:30-10:30pm, Su 4:30-9:30pm. AmEx/MC/V.) Delicious organic smoothies (£3.50) and sandwiches (£5) are on the menu at the all-vegetarian **Organic House** ❶, 2 Market St., which doubles as a specialty organic grocery store with fresh fruits and vegetables, cheese, and chocolate. (☎01422 842 249; www.organic-house.co.uk. Takeaway or sit down. Open M-Sa 9am-5:30pm, Su 10am-5pm. MC/V.) On Wednesday and Thursday, locals congregate at the **Hebden Bridge Market,** in St. George Sq.; buy a picnic lunch on Thursday or shop for secondhand goods on Wednesday.

◪ **SIGHTS.** One of the most popular destinations is National Trust's **Hardcastle Crags** (☎01422 844 518). The ravine-crossed wooded valley is 1 mi. northwest along the A6033; pick up a free guide from the TIC. Day hikes lead to the villages of **Blackshaw Head, Cragg Vale,** or **Hepstonstall.** Hepstonstall holds the remains of Sylvia Plath and the ruins of the oldest Methodist church in the world. **Stubbing Wharf Cruises** gives boat trips along the Rochdale Canal. (☎07966 808 717; www.stubbingwharf.com/cruises. 30min cruises every 30min. daily 2-4pm. £5. Look for special themed cruises in their brochure, available at the TIC.)

HAWORTH   ☎(0)1535

Haworth's (HAH-wuth) *raison d'être* stands at the top of its hill: the parsonage that overlooks Brontëland. A cobbled main street milks all association with the ill-fated literary siblings; tearooms and shops line the climb to the Brontë home. The village currently wants for wandering heroines, but the moors remain.

◪◪ **ORIENTATION AND PRACTICAL INFORMATION.** The train station (☎01535 645 214) only serves the Keighley and Worth Valley Railway's private steam trains (see **Transportation,** p. 419). The **Tourist Information Centre,** 2-4 West Ln., at Main St.'s summit, provides the useful *Four Walks from the Centre of Haworth* (40p) and the town's mini-guide (free) and books beds for the same or following day. (☎01535 642 329. Open daily May-Aug. 9:30am-5:30pm; Sept.-Apr. 9:30am-5pm.) **Tours,** including an evening lantern-light graveyard tour, are available from **Heart of Haworth Village Walks.** Tickets are sold at the TIC. (☎01535 642 329; www.bronteguide.com. Tours daily; call ahead. £3.50-6, concessions available.) The **post office,** 98 Main St., is the place to **exchange currency.** (☎01535 644 589. Open M-F 9am-5:30pm, Sa 9am-12:30pm.) **Postcode:** BD22 8DP.

◪◪ **ACCOMMODATIONS AND FOOD.** Housed in a Victorian mansion, the elegant **YHA Haworth ❶** (also known as Haworth Youth Hostel) is a 15min. hike from the train station; turn left out of the train station up Lees Ln. and then left on Longlands Dr. Guests enjoy the hostel's TV lounge, outdoor garden, and a grand staircase with stained glass. (☎01535 642 234. Meals £2.25-4.50. 12-bed dorms £16. MC/V.) **Ye Sleeping House ❸,** 8 Main St., has affordable standard rooms, a guest library, and free, ample breakfasts. (☎01535 645 992. Rates £25 per person. 2-night min. stay on weekends. Cash only.)

For groceries, try **Spar** on Station Rd. (☎01535 647 662. Open daily 7:30am-10:30pm.) Inexpensive restaurants line **Mill Hey,** just east of the train station. **Haworth Tandoori ❷,** 14 Mill Hey, a neighborhood favorite, serves a wide selection of curries, biryanis, and vegetarian dishes. (☎01535 644 726. 15% takeaway discount. Open M-Sa 5:30pm-midnight, Su 6-11:30pm. MC/V.) **Wharenui ❷,** 27 Main St., sells sandwiches and light fare during the day and cooks up gourmet dishes in the evening in a relaxed, sophisticated atmosphere. (☎01535 644 511; www.wharenui.co.uk. Most entrees £6-12, sandwiches under £5. Open M and Th-Su noon-10pm. MC/V.) One of Haworth's most popular pubs, **The Fleece Inn ❶,** 67 Main St., has a classic pub atmosphere that draws crowds of locals. (☎01535 642 172; www.timothytaylor.co.uk/fleeceinn. Most entrees £8-11, sandwiches under £5. Open M-F 1-9pm. Sa-Su 10am-4pm. MC/V.)

◪ **SIGHTS.** Down a tiny lane behind the village church lies the home where England's most famous literary siblings spent their isolated childhoods. The

Brontë Parsonage details the lives of Charlotte, Emily, Anne, Branwell, and their grumpy father. The quiet rooms, including the dining room where the sisters penned *Wuthering Heights* and *Jane Eyre*, contain original furnishings and momentos. Displays include the sofa on which Emily died, Charlotte's wedding bonnet, locks of the sisters' hair, and the toy figures that inspired their early stories. (☎01535 642 323; www.bronte.info. Open daily Apr.-Sept. 10am-5:30pm, Oct.-Mar. 11am-5pm. ₤6.) A footpath behind the church leads uphill toward the pleasant (if not-so-wuthering) **Brontë Falls,** a 2 mi. hike.

YORKSHIRE DALES

Yorkshire Dales National Park welcomes hikers with scattered pastures and one-pub villages. Its valleys, formed by swift rivers and lazy glacial flows, are filled with evidence of earlier inhabitants—just about everybody left something behind. The Romans abandoned forts. The Bronze and Iron Age tribes blazed "green lanes" and footpaths that remain on the high moorlands. Medieval royalty built castles, and 18th-century workers crafted stone walls.

▐ TRANSPORTATION

Skipton (p. 424) is the most convenient gateway to the park. **Trains** (☎08457 484 950) run to Bradford (35min., 4 per hr., ₤5.70), Carlisle (3hr., every hr., ₤17.50), and Leeds (40min., 5 per hr., ₤7.10). The Settle-Carlisle Railway (www.settle-carlisle.co.uk), run by Northern Rail, meanders through Skipton, Garsdale, and Kirkby Stephen (1hr.; 6-7 per day; Day Ranger ticket ₤21, discount for groups of 10 or more). There is no National Express (☎08705 808 080) office in Skipton, but **buses** run to Leeds (1hr., 4 per day, ₤5) and London (6hr., 3 per day, ₤20) from Skipton's bus station on Keighley St.

Getting around the Dales without a car can be a challenge. Most local bus and train stations have easy-to-use timetables with reliable schedules, but buses between towns often run only a few times per day, and many only run on Sundays and bank holidays. Pride of the Dales (☎01756 753 123) connects Skipton to Grassington (#72, 30min., every hr., round-trip ₤5.60), sometimes continuing to Kettlewell (#72, 1hr., every 2hr., ₤3). Pennine Bus (☎01756 795 515) connects Skipton to Malham (#210; 45min.; 2 per day, more frequently on weekends; return ₤7) and Settle (#580, 40min., every hr., ₤4). Other villages are served less regularly. Although **postbuses** run once per day to scheduled towns, they depart very early and stop frequently.

▋ ▐ ORIENTATION AND PRACTICAL INFORMATION

Sampling the Dales requires several days, a pair of sturdy hiking boots, and careful planning. In the south of the park, **Skipton** (p. 424) serves as a transportation hub and provides services not available in the smaller villages. **Grassington** (p. 425) and **Linton,** just north, are scenic bases for exploring southern Wharfedale. **Malham** (p. 426) is a sensible starting point for forays into western Wharfedale and eastern Ribblesdale. To explore Wensleydale and Swaledale in the north, begin from **Hawes** (p. 426). In addition to the National Park Information Centres listed below, most towns have TICs.

National Park Information Centres: Pick up the invaluable annual park guides, *The Visitor* and *The Yorkshire Dales Official Guide* (both free), along with maps, walking guides, and the weather forecast. All NPICs book accommodations for a 10% deposit and are open Apr.-Oct. daily 10am-5pm; Nov.-Mar. F-Su 10am-4pm.

Aysgarth Falls: in Wensleydale (☎01969 662 910), 1 mi. east of Asygarth off the A684.

Grassington: Hebden Rd., Wharfedale (☎01756 751 690), in the car park near the village center. 24hr. info terminal outside.

Hawes: Station Yard, Wensleydale (☎01969 666 210), in the Dales Countryside Museum. 24hr. info terminal outside.

Malham: Malhamdale (☎01969 652 380), at the southern end of the village.

Reeth: In Hudson House on top of Reeth's village green (☎01748 884 059).

Sedbergh: 72 Main St. (☎01539 620 125).

Tours: Cumbria Classic Coaches (☎01539 623 254; www.cumbriaclassiccoaches. co.uk). Runs trips from Kirkby Stephen to Hawes in 1950s-era double-decker buses. £10 per person.

🏠 🏠 ACCOMMODATIONS AND CAMPING

The free *Yorkshire Dales Accommodation Guide* (also called *Yorkshire Dales: Official Holiday Guide*) is available at most NPICs and TICs. As in all of England, park officials discourage "wild" (unofficial) camping. The NPICs have more complete lists of camping sites and accommodations around the Dales for a nominal photocopying charge.

YHA HOSTELS

The Yorkshire Dales area hosts seven **YHA hostels.** Hard-core hikers on the Pennine Way will cross Hawes, Keld, and Malham. Stainforth, Kettlewell, Dentdale, and Grinton Lodge sit a few miles off the trail. Ingleton, on the western edge of the park, is a good starting point for exploring the Lake District. Those who want to give their feet a rest can get to Kirkby Stephen, north of Hawes, by rail. All YHA facilities fill up weeks ahead, especially in summer, but hostel employees will call other YHAs in search of an empty room.

Grinton: Grinton Lodge (☎08707 705 844), ¾ mi. south on the Reeth-Leyburn road in a former shooting lodge. Kitchen and laundry. Curfew 11:30pm. Open Apr.-Oct. daily; Nov.-Dec. F-Sa; Feb.-Mar. M-Sa. Dorms £16-18, under 18 £12-13. MC/V. ❷

Hawes: Lancaster Terr. (☎0870 770 5854), west of Hawes on Ingleton Rd., uphill from town. 54 beds. Curfew 11pm. Open Apr.-Sept. daily; Sept.-Oct. and Mar. Tu-Sa; Nov.-Dec. and from late Jan. to Feb. F-Sa. Dorms £14, under 18 £10. MC/V. ❷

Ingleton: Greta Tower (☎0870 770 5880), Sammy Ln., near Market Sq. A renovated Victorian house with 58 beds. Convenient to the main street. Kitchen, swimming pool, and laundry. Curfew 11pm. Open Mar.-Sept. and late Dec. daily; Sept.-Oct. M-Sa; from Nov. to mid-Dec. F-Su; Feb. Tu-Sa. Dorms £16, under 18 £12. MC/V. ❷

Kettlewell: Whernside House (☎0870 770 5896), in the village center. Easy access to Boton Abbey. 43 beds. Curfew 11pm. Dorms £16, under 18 £12. MC/V. ❷

Kirkby Stephen: Market St. (☎0870 770 5904), on the Coast-to-Coast walk. In a former Methodist chapel, complete with pews and stained glass. 44 beds. Kitchen and laundry. Lockout 10am-5pm. Curfew 11pm. Dorms £17, under 18 £13. MC/V. ❷

Malham: John Dower Memorial Hostel (☎0870 770 5946). Well equipped and hiker-friendly. 82 beds. Kitchen and laundry. Reception 7-10am and 5-10:30pm. Lockout 11am-5pm. Curfew 11pm. Dorms £14, under 18 £10.50. MC/V. ❶

DALES BARNS AND CAMPING

Numerous **Dales Barns** dot the Yorkshire Dales National Park and cost £5-12 per night. Most have showers, kitchens, and central heating. Book weeks ahead and get specific directions along the trails. **Campgrounds** are difficult to reach on foot. Ask TICs for a full list of both barns and campgrounds.

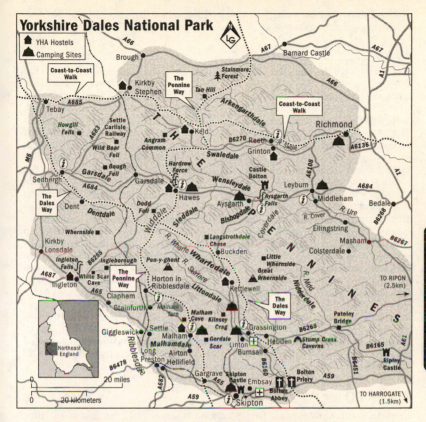

Skirfare Bridge Dales Barn (☎01756 752 465; www.skirfaredalesbarn.co.uk), 1 mi. from Dales Way between Grassington and Kettlewell. £14 per person. Cash only. ❶

Grange Farm Barn (☎01756 760 259), 20 mi. from Skipton. Weekends for parties of 18 only; smaller groups welcome mid-week. Sleeps 18. £8 per person. Cash only. ❶

Hill Top Farm, Malham (☎01729 830 320). A converted 17th-century farmhouse just steps away from the Pennine Way and the limestone formations of Malham Tarn. Sleeps 32. £10 per person. Cash only. ❶

Craken House Farm, Leyburn (☎01969 622 204), ½ mi. south of town center. £5 per person; £12 per RV. Cash only. ❶

Howarth Farm, Appletreewick, Skipton (☎01756 720 226). Basic sites on a working farm. Discounts for extended stays. £6 per person. Cash only. ❶

Wood Nook, Grassington (☎01756 752 412), off the B6265 from Skipton. £3 per person, children £1.50; £7.50 per tent, with electricity £8. ❶

Bainbridge Ings Caravan and Camping Site (☎01969 667 354; www.bainbridgeings. co.uk), ½ mi. from Hawes on Old Gale Rd. off the A684. Open Apr.-Oct. £3.50-10.50 per tent; £11-12.50 per RV. Electricity £1.50. Cash only. ❶

Brompton-on-Swale Caravan and Camping Park (☎01748 824 629), 2 mi. from Richmond. Open Apr.-Oct. Sleeps 12. £4.50 per person. MC/V. ❶

Street Head Caravan Park, Aysgarth (☎01969 663 472). £20 per 2-person tent. Electricity £2.50. Cash only. ❶

HIKING AND CYCLING

Since buses are infrequent and the scenery is breathtaking, hiking remains the best way to see the Dales. The park's six NPICs can help you prepare for a trek along one of three long-distance footpaths. The challenging 268 mi. **Pennine Way** (p. 402) curls from Gargrave in the south to Tan Hill in the north, passing Malham, Pen-y-ghent, Hawes, Keld, and most of the major attractions of the Dales. The more manageable 80 mi. **Dales Way** runs from Bradford and Leeds past Ilkley, through Wharfedale via Grassington and Whernside, and by Sedbergh on its way to the Lake District; it crosses the Pennine Way near Dodd Fell. The 190 mi. **Coast to Coast Walk** stretches from Richmond to Kirkby Stephen.

Stone walls and hills start to look similar after a few hours on the path—arm yourself with a **map and trail guide.** Prevent runaway cows by leaving gates as you found them. Ordnance Survey maps (£7.50) are available for most paths and can be purchased at any NPIC or outdoors supply store. Outdoor Leisure #2 and 30 and Landranger #91 and 98 are good for specific regions; Touring Map and Guide #6 (£5) covers the Dales in general. NPICs sell leaflets (£1-3) covering over 30 short routes. YHA produces its own leaflets (50p) on hikes between hostels. Cyclists can ask at NPICs about rental stores and buy route cards plotting the **Yorkshire Dales Cycleway,** six interconnected 20 mi. routes through the Dales (£2.25). Popular cycle guides include *Harvey's Yorkshire Dales Cycle Way* (£6). Harvey also produces a general Yorkshire Dales guide (£4) with more specific coverage of the East, North, South, and West Dales (£7 each). Bicycles are forbidden on footpaths but not on bridleways (trails for horses). Out of breath just thinking about the trek? The **Pennine Way/Dales Way Baggage Courier** will cart your pack for you and deliver it to each night's resting point. (☎01729 830 463; www.brigantesenglishwalks.com. £5-10 per bag.)

SKIPTON ☎(0)1756

Skipton is most useful as a transportation transfer point or rest stop. Once you've gathered your gear, skip town and strike out for the Dales. Vacant Skipton Castle, at the top of High St., is the main attraction and one of the most complete medieval castles in England.

TRANSPORTATION AND PRACTICAL INFORMATION. Skipton's **train station** is located a quarter-mile west of the city center on Broughton Rd. **Buses** stop at the bus station between Swadford St. and Keighley Rd., behind Westland Department Store. For **taxis,** try Station Taxis, 27 Keighley Rd. (☎01756 796 6666 or 700 777; 24hr.). You can rent **cars** from Skipton Self Drive, Otley Rd. Garage. (☎01756 792 911; www.skiptonselfdriveltd.co.uk. From £30 per day; discounts for longer rentals.) Admire the Dales from the water on a 90min. boat cruise (£3) with Pennine Cruisers of Skipton, The Boat Shop, 19 Coach St. They also rent **day boats** on the Leeds and Liverpool Canals. (☎01756 795 478; www. penninecruisers.com. £75-195 per day, from £430 per week.) For an aerial view, Airborne Adventures sends **hot-air balloons** over the Dales from Skipton and Settle twice per day. (☎01756 730 166. £150 per person; 2-person min.)

The **Tourist Information Centre,** 35 Coach St., books rooms for a 10% deposit. (☎01756 792 809. Open Apr.-Oct. M-Sa 10am-5pm, Su 11am-3pm; Nov.-Mar. M-Sa 10am-4pm.) Other services include: HSBC **bank,** 61 High St. (☎0845 740 4404; open M-F 9:30am-4:30pm); **Internet** at **Skipton Public Library,** High St.

(☎01756 792 926; £2.50 per hr.; open M and W-Th 9:30am-7pm, F 9:30am-5pm, Sa 9:30am-4pm); and the **post office**, Westland Department Store, 8 Swadford St. (☎01756 792 724; open M-F 9am-5:30pm, Sa 9am-1pm). **Postcode:** BD23 1UR.

▐ ▌ ACCOMMODATIONS AND FOOD. B&Bs are the best bet for decently priced accommodations in Skipton. Many line **Keighley Road** and **Gargrave Road** and are generally £25-35 per person per night. Although they are plentiful, rooms fill quickly in summer, so plan ahead or prepare to camp. Sleep comfortably in Victorian-themed rooms with canopy beds at **Carlton House ❸**, 46 Keighley Rd. (☎01756 700 921. Hearty Yorkshire breakfast included. Doubles £55. MC/V.) The **Dalesgate Lodge ❸**, 69 Gargrave Rd., is a comfortable, convenient option whose full English breakfast will energize you for a long day of hiking. (☎01756 790 672; www.dalesgatelodge.co.uk. Singles £30-35; doubles £50. Cash only.) **Westfield Guest House ❷**, 50 Keighley Rd., has huge beds for low prices. (☎01756 790 849. Singles from £30; doubles £48-50. Cash only.)

Load up on fresh gooseberries and cheese at the **market** on High St. (open M, W, F-Sa) or duck inside **✉Bean Loved ❶**, 17 Otley St., for a cup of coffee on an inevitably rainy day. This father-and-son cafe has free Wi-Fi and is worth a stop even in sunny weather. (☎01756 791 534. Open daily 8am-6pm. Cash only.) A downtown favorite, **Bizzie Lizzies ❷**, 36 Swadford St., serves exceptional fish and chips for £7-9. Takeaway from the downstairs window is cheaper than eating in the restaurant. (☎01756 701 131. Open M-Sa 11:30am-9pm, Su noon-9pm. Cash only.) **Nosh ❷**, 1 Devonshire Pl., behind Woolworth's, serves tapas (£3-6) to trendy patrons. (☎01756 700 060. Open M and W-Su noon-midnight. MC/V.) Give your arteries a break from heavy English breakfasts at **Healthy Life ❶**, 10 High St., near the church, which stocks soy haggis and all manner of herbal and vegetable favorites. Upstairs, **Wild Oats Cafe ❶** serves daily vegan and vegetarian specials (£6 with 2 prepared salads). The carrot and feta lasagna is, unbelievably, gluten-free. (☎01756 790 619. Store open M-Sa 9am-5:30pm, Su 11am-4pm. Cafe open M-Sa 9:30am-4:30pm, Su 11am-4:30pm. MC/V.)

◪ SIGHTS. Built in 1090 as a Norman fortress (notice the "Désormais," or "Henceforth," carved over the entrance gate), **Skipton Castle,** off High St., also served as the strongest and last surviving Royalist bastion in the north during the Civil War. You can still see the squints in the thick stone walls from which inmates could pick off advancing Roundheads with a crossbow. The castle finally surrendered to Cromwell's army in 1645. (☎01756 792 442; www.skiptoncastle.co.uk. Open Mar.-Sept. M-Sa 10am-6pm, Su noon-6pm; Oct.-Feb. M-Sa 10am-4pm, Su noon-4pm. £5.80, concessions £5.20.)

WHARFEDALE AND GRASSINGTON   ☎(0)1756

The valley of Wharfedale, along the River Wharfe, is best explored using cobbled Grassington as a base. Spectacular **Kilnsey Crag** lies three-quarters of a mile. from Grassington toward Kettlewell. The **Stump Cross Caverns,** 5 mi. east of Grassington, glisten with stalagmites and rock curtains. (☎01756 752 780. Dress warmly. Open Mar.-Oct. daily 10am-6pm; Nov.-Feb. Sa-Su 10am-4pm. Last entry 1hr. before close. £5-7. Hours and prices may vary.)

Close to the center of Grassington, **Raines Close ❸**, 13 Station Rd., rents spacious rooms with patios or bay windows and panoramic views of the English countryside. (☎01756 752 678; www.rainesclose.co.uk. Doubles £58-64. MC/V.) Across the street, **Springroyd House ❸**, 8A Station Rd., has three lovely clean rooms and generous breakfasts. (☎01756 752 473. Doubles £58. Cash only.) Pubs and cafes pack Main St. Stop by **Cobblestones Cafe ❶**, 3 The Square, for a bowl of homemade sticky toffee pudding with lots of warm custard for £2.75. (☎01756 752 303. Open M-W and F-Su 10am-5pm. Cash only).

Pride of the Dales **bus** #72 leaves Grassington for Skipton at 10min. to the hour (£2.80). To get to Kilnsey, take bus #72 from Grassington to Kilnsey (10min., 8 per day, £1.30). The **NPIC** (p. 422), in the car park on Hebden Rd., stocks the useful *Grassington Footpath Map* (£1.60) and standard park trail guides (£1) and leads occasional guided walks from March to October (£2, free with public transport ticket stub). Other services include: **outdoor gear** at The Mountaineer, Pletts Barn Centre, Main St. (☎01756 752 266; open daily 9am-5pm); **Barclays** bank, at the corner of Main St. and Hebden Rd. (☎01756 656 253; open M-F 9:30am-3:30pm); and the **post office,** 15 Main St. (☎01756 752 226; open M-F 9am-5:30pm, Sa 9am-12:30pm). **Postcode:** BD23 5AD.

MALHAMDALE AND INGLETON ☎(0)1524

Limestone cliffs and gorges slice the pastoral valley of Malhamdale, creating spectacular natural landscapes within easy walking distance of one another. A 3hr. hike from the **Malham NPIC** (p. 422) passes the stunning, stony swath of **Malham Cove,** a massive limestone cliff, and the placid waters of **Malham Tarn.** Two miles from Malham village is the equally imposing **Gordale Scar,** cut by a glacier during the last Ice Age. The **YHA Malham ❶** (p. 422) is a popular hostel with Pennine Way hikers.

Just north of Malham are the high peaks and cliffs of Ingleborough, Pen-y-ghent, and Whernside that form the **Alpes Penninae.** The 24 mi. **Three Peaks Walk,** which connects the Alpes, begins and ends in **Horton in Ribblesdale** at the **Pen-y-ghent Cafe,** a hiker's haunt that also serves as the local TIC. (☎01729 860 333. Open Apr.-Oct. M-F 9am-5:30pm, Sa-Su 9:30am-5pm; Nov.-Mar. M-F 9:30am-4:30pm, Sa-Su 9:30am-5pm.) Ingleton is near the middle of the trek. The village's TIC, in the community center car park, books rooms for a 10% deposit. (☎01524 241 049. Open Apr.-Oct. daily 10am-4:30pm.) The 4½ mi., 2½-4hr. walk through the **Ingleton Waterfalls** is one of the most popular routes in the area. (☎01524 241 930; www.ingletonwaterfallstrail.co.uk. Open 9am-dusk. £4.50.) Pick up a leaflet from the TIC or read the Ingleton town trail sign in the town center. **The YHA Ingleton ❷** (p. 422) and several **B&Bs** on Main St. are good budget options. A 1 mi. walk from Ingleton's town center brings you to **Stacksteads Farm ❶,** Tatterthorne Rd., which offers views of the limestone countryside from its 28 bunks. (☎01524 241 386; www.stacksteadfarm.co.uk. £10. Cash only.)

WENSLEYDALE AND HAWES ☎(0)1969

That familiar smell in northern Wensleydale is fertile dairyland. Base your forays into the Dales from Hawes, which has an **NPIC** (p. 422) in the Dales Countryside Museum that books accommodations for a 10% deposit. Pay 40p at the **Green Dragon Pub** to access the trail to the **Hardrow Force** waterfall, 1 mi. north on the Pennine Way. **B&Bs** (£20-25) line Main St., and the **YHA Hawes ❷** (p. 422) is uphill from town. Pubs, takeaways, and a **Barclays** bank (open M-F 9:30am-3:30pm; 24hr. ATM) are also along Main St. On Gayle Ln., **Wensleydale Creamery** offers tours of its cheese-making facilities with samples. The Cistercian monks who founded the monastery in which the creamery is now housed would be aghast to see the creamy goodness today. (☎01524 667 664; www.wensleydale.co.uk. Open M-Sa 9:30am-5pm, Su 10am-4:30pm.) Farther north, **Swaledale** is known for picturesque barns and meadows. Don't miss **Aysgarth Falls** to the east and the natural terrace of the **Shawl of Leyburn.** Aysgarth and Leyburn are served by Pride of the Dales **buses** #156 and 157 from Hawes to Northallerton (2hr., every hr., £1.40). Aysgarth's **NPIC** is in the car park above the falls (p. 422), and Leyburn has a **TIC** in its city center. (☎01969 623 069. Open Easter-Sept. daily 9:30am-5:30pm; Oct.-Easter M-Sa 9:30am-4:30pm.)

NORTH YORK MOORS

The heather-clad expanses and cliff-lined coast of the North York Moors have changed little since they inspired the gothic imaginations of Emily Brontë and Bram Stoker. The region's landscape, from pastoral towns to dramatic coast-line, makes the Moors one of Britain's most captivating national parks.

TRANSPORTATION

Getting around the North York Moors using public transportation is possible but confusing. The primary gateways are York to the south and Middlesbrough to the north. Middlesbrough is a short train ride from Darlington (30min., 2 per hr., £3.40) on the London-Edinburgh rail line. The Moors Explorer pamphlet, free at TICs and NPICs, covers the unholy mess that is the park's bus and rail service in a clear, color-coded format and glorious detail. Service varies by season and is significantly reduced in winter. **Traveline** also publishes timetables (☎08706 082 608; www.yorkshiretravel.net).

Trains: 3 train lines serve the park. Frequent service between **York** and **Scarborough** (45min., 1-2 per hr., £10.30). The scenic Esk Valley Line runs from **Middlesbrough** to **Whitby** via **Danby** and **Grosmont** (1hr., 4 per day, £9.55). North Yorkshire Moors Railway (reservations ☎01751 472 508, timetables 473 535) links north and south, from **Pickering** to **Grosmont,** with connections to **Whitby** (1hr., 4-9 per day). No service during some low-season times.

Buses: More frequent than trains. Day or week passes are more economical than single rides. Yorkshire Coastliner #840 (☎01653 692 5560) runs between **Leeds, York, Pickering,** and **Whitby** (every hr.). #843 between **Leeds, York,** and **Scarborough** (every hr.). Arriva #93, #93X, and #X56 between **Middlesbrough, Whitby,** and **Scarborough** (every hr.). #93 and #X56 also stop in **Robin Hood's Bay,** but #X56 only runs M-Sa. Scarborough District bus #128 covers **Scarborough, Pickering,** and **Helmsley** (every hr.). The national park operates the Moorsbus (www.visitnorthyorkshiremoors.co.uk), with seasonal routes through the park. Schedules available at TICs. Runs irregularly; plan ahead. From late July to early Sept. daily; Oct.-Apr. Su and holidays only. All-day pass £4.

Bike Rental: Trailways, Old Railway Station (☎01947 820 207; www.trailways.info), in Hawsker, 2 mi. south of Whitby. £8.50-25 per day. Open Easter-Nov. daily 10am-6pm; Dec.-Easter call ahead. TICs and NPICs list other bike-rental stores in the region.

ORIENTATION

North York Moors National Park is 30 mi. north of York. Centrally located Pickering is the starting point for the scenic **North Yorkshire Moors Railway**—a relaxing way to take in the views and take on the park's excellent hikes. Just a short 20min. bus ride toward the park's southwest corner, the tiny market town of **Helmsley** lies near the ruins of **Rievaulx Abbey** and affords convenient access to hiking, particularly when the Moorsbus shuttle is operating. The **Esk Valley,** another popular terrain for hikers, cuts across the north of the park and is served by the **Esk Valley Line** railway (this page). The seaside resort town of **Scarborough** is often flooded with summer vacationers looking for boardwalk amusements, while to the north the fishing village of **Whitby** greets tourists with a rich history and a host of local legends. Tucked along the coast between Whitby and Scarborough, the small town of **Robin Hood's Bay** is a picturesque maze of teashops and pubs. The first part of this section provides an overview of transportation, practical information, and general accommodations (such as YHA hostels) for the entire park. Local services, B&Bs, and activities are listed within the coverage for the individual towns.

⁊ PRACTICAL INFORMATION

The Moors & Coast visitor guide (50p), available at any TIC or NPIC, is particularly useful, highlighting the region's events and attractions.

National Park Information Centres:

Danby: The Moors Centre (☎01439 772 737; www.moors.uk.net). From the Danby train station, turn left after you pass the gate and right at the crossroads before the Duke of Wellington Inn; the center is ½ mi. ahead on the right. Open Apr.-Oct. daily 10am-5pm; Nov.-Mar. Sa-Su 11am-4pm.

Sutton Bank: (☎01845 597 426), 6 mi. east of Thirsk on the A170. Open Apr.-Oct. daily 10am-5pm; Nov.-Feb. Sa-Su 11am-4pm; Mar. daily 11am-4pm.

Tourist Information Centres:

Goathland: The Village Store and Outdoor Centre (☎01947 896 207). Open Apr.-Sept. daily 10am-6pm; Oct.-Apr. M-W and F-Su 10am-4pm.

Great Ayton: High Green Car Park (☎01642 722 835). Open Easter-Oct. M-Sa 10am-4pm, Su 1-4pm.

Guisborough: Priory Grounds, Church St. (☎01287 633 801). Open Apr.-Sept. Tu-Su 9am-5pm; Oct.-Mar. W-Sa 9am-5pm, Su 9am-4:30pm.

Helmsley: (☎01439 770 173), at the entrance to Helmsley Castle. Open Mar.-Oct. daily 9:30am-5pm; Nov.-Feb. F-Su 10am-4pm.

Pickering: The Ropery (☎01751 473 791; pickering@btconnect.com), down the road from the train station, beside the library. Open Mar.-Oct. M-Sa 9:30am-5pm, Su 9:30am-4pm; Nov.-Feb. M-Sa 9:30am-4pm.

Scarborough: Brunswick Shopping Centre, Westborough (☎01723 383 636). Open M-Sa 9:30am-5:30pm, Su 11am-5pm. Alternate branch at Sandside by South Bay (☎01723 383 636). Open daily Easter-Oct. 9:20am-5:30pm; Nov.-Easter 10am-4:30pm.

Whitby: Station Sq. (☎01723 383 636), across Langborne Rd. Open daily July-Aug. 9:30am-6pm; May-June and Sept. 9:30am-5pm; Oct.-Apr. 10am-12:30pm and 1-4:30pm. Some visitors find that the TIC does not close for lunch as the hours claim.

⌂ ⁊ ACCOMMODATIONS AND CAMPING

Local TICs book beds for £2 plus a 10% deposit. B&Bs, hotels, and caravan parks in or near the national park are listed under the appropriate towns.

YHA HOSTELS

The following YHA hostels rent beds in the Moors. Reservations are highly recommended throughout the year, especially in summer when accommodations fill early. Clearly named bus stops are rare; tell drivers where you're headed. Online bookings can be made at www.yha.org.uk.

Lockton: (☎0870 770 5938), Old School, off Pickering-Whitby Rd. 2 mi. from the North Yorkshire Moors Railway Station at Levisham. 4 mi. north of Pickering. Take Coastliner bus #840 toward Whitby. Self-catering kitchen. Awarded "Green Beacon" for eco-friendly renovations. Reception 8-10am and 5-10pm. Curfew 11pm. Dorms £14. MC/V. ❷

Whitby: (☎01947 602 878), next to Whitby Abbey in the newly restored Abbey House. Immaculate hostel with ensuite family rooms and over 100 beds. Spectacular view. Prices for dorms vary week to week (around £20 in the summer). MC/V. ❶

Boggle Hole: (☎0870 770 5704), Fylingthorpe. Follow the posted signs on Cleveland Way 1 mi. south from Robin Hood's Bay, either along the cliffs or on the beach at low tide. Large rooms with comfortable mattresses. Breakfast £4; packed lunch £4; 3-course dinner £8.50. Reception 7:30-10am and 1-11pm. Dorms £16-17. MC/V. ❷

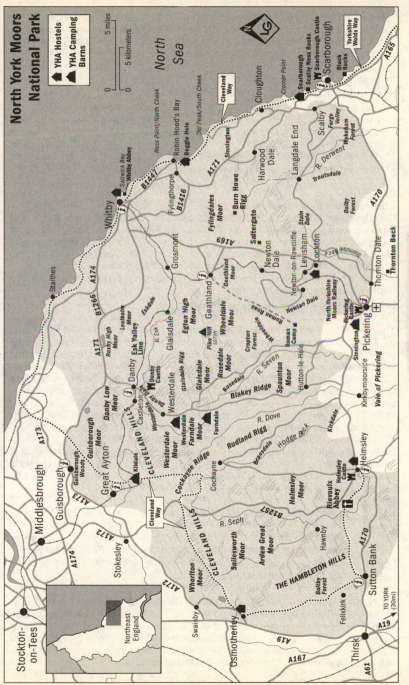

North York Moors
National Park

YHA Hostels
YHA Camping
Barns

5 miles
5 kilometers

North
Sea

Scarborough
Scarborough Castle
Scalby Ness Rocks
Black
Rocks

Yorkshire
Wolds Way

A165

Cromer Point

Cloughton

Scalby
Forge
Valley
Wykeham
Forest

Ness Point/North Cheek
Robin Hood's Bay
Boggle Hole

Old Peak/South Cheek

Cleveland
Way

Saltwick Bay
Whitby Abbey

Langdale End

Troutsdale

Harwood
Dale

A170

B1447

Sinnington

Fylingthorpe

A171

Fylingdales
Moor

Burn Howe
Rigg

Dalby
Forest

B1416

Whitby

Saltergate

Stain
Dale

Thornton Dale

Thornton Beck

A174

Staithes

Grosmont

A169

Newton
Dale

Leysham
Lockton

Standale Beck

A170

Goathland
Moor

Newton-on-Rawcliffe

Eskdale

Lealholm
Moor

Egton High
Moor

Goathland

Newton Dale

Pickering
Castle

North Yorkshire
Moors Railway

R. Esk

Roxby High
Moor

Esk Valley
Line

Wheeldale
Moor

Pike Hill
107m

Roman Road

Cropton
Forest

Roman
Camp

Pickering

Sinnington

Danby
Castle

Danby

Glaisdale

Glaisdale Rigg

Rosedale
Moor

R. Seven

Spaunton
Moor

Hutton-le-Hole

Kirkbymoorside

Vale of Pickering

B1266

A171

Westerdale

Glaisdale
Moor

Rosedale

Blakey Ridge

Guisborough
Moor

Danby Low
Moor

CLEVELAND HILLS

Castleton

Westerdale
Moor

Farndale

R. Dove

Kirkdale

Helmsley

Helmsley
Castle

Guisborough
Woods

Kildale

Westerdale
Moor

Farndale
Moor

Rudland Rigg

Hodge Beck

Rievaulx
Abbey

Helmsley
Moor

Middlesbrough

A173

Guisborough

Great Ayton

Cleveland
Way

Cockayne Ridge

Cockayne

Bransdale

Kirkdale

A172

A174

Stokesley

CLEVELAND HILLS

Whorlton
Moor

Spilsworth
Moor

R. Seph

Arden Great
Moor

Helmsley
Moor

B1257

Hawnby

A170

Sutton
Bank

Boltby
Forest

Felixkirk

TO YORK
(30mi)

Swainby

Osmotherley

A19

Thirsk

A167

A61

A172

Stockton-
on-Tees

Stokesley

Northeast
England

Helmsley: (☎0870 770 5860). Take Bondgate Rd. from Market Pl. Turn left on Carlton Rd. and left again at Carlton Ln.; hostel is on the left. Breakfast £4; packed lunch from £4.50; dinner £7. Reception 8-10am and 5-10pm. Lockout 10am-5pm. Curfew 11pm. Open from Apr. to late Aug. Dorms £16, under 18 £12, under 5 free. MC/V. ❷

Osmotherley: (☎0870 770 5982), Cote Ghyll, Northallerton. Between Stockton and Thirsk, northeast of Osmotherley. Reception 7-11am and 5-10:30pm. Curfew 11:30pm. Open daily from early Mar. to late Oct. Dorms £14, under 18 £10.50. MC/V. ❷

Scarborough: Burniston Rd. (☎0870 770 6022), 2 mi. from Scarborough. Take bus #3 from York Pl., just down the road from the train station, to Scalby Mills Rd. Follow Burniston Rd. away from town. Turn a sharp left immediately after crossing a small river into an unmarked drive at the end of the bridge. In a former mill on a river, 15min. from the sea. 48 beds in 4- to 6-bed dorms. Self-catering kitchen. Lockout 10am-5pm for 1-night stays. Curfew 11:30pm. Open Mar.-Aug. daily; Sept.-Nov. Tu-Sa. Dorms £16. MC/V. ❷

CAMPING

YHA operates four **camping barns** (p. 404) in the Moors. Ambitious hikers on the Cleveland Way should consider the barn in **Kildale,** right along the trail (also accessible by the #27 bus). The barn in **Farndale** lies on the Oakhouse farmyard about 2 mi. westward of Lion Inn (take the M1 or M3 bus). The #26 and #27 buses run to **Westerdale,** on the Broadgate Farm, and the #128 goes to **Sinnington,** on the edge of the park between Pickering and Helmsley. (Reservations ☎0870 770 8868. Barns from £6.50 per person; families with children under 5 must book the entire barn.)

 HIKING AND CYCLING

The vast tracts of the North York Moors make for excellent hiking. The 93 mi. **Cleveland Way** wraps all the way around the national park and can be easily accessed from many youth hostels and campsites. A particularly well-marked and beautiful portion of the Way is the 20 mi. stretch between Whitby and Scarborough. Those who lack the steam to make it all the way to Scarborough may prefer to stop short in Robin Hood's Bay, 5 mi. from Whitby, where scenic hills and views of the North Sea lie to either side of the path, and miles of shoreline cliffs loom ahead. Hard-core hikers might consider tackling the 79 mi. **Wolds Way,** an idyllic coastal hike that extends from the Humber Estuary at Hessle to the sandstone cliffs of Filey. The popular **Coast to Coast Walk** (192 mi.) begins in St. Bees and ends in Robin Hood's Bay (at a pub, of course). Day hikes begin at stations on the park's two scenic **railways,** the **Esk Valley Line** (p. 427) and the **North Yorkshire Moors Railway** (p. 427). Trails are not always marked or even visible; hikers should carry a map and compass (see **Wilderness Safety,** p. 51).

> **TIP** **A WEIGHT OFF YOUR SHOULDERS.** For hikers tackling the massive Coast to Coast Walk, carrying a heavy pack can be exhausting. If your backpack is more pain than gain, head to www.cumbria.com/packhorse and book its baggage transfer service (£6 for a single day, £82 for the full trail). Packhorse will pick up your bag in the morning and deliver it safely to your next night's accommodations.

Cycling around the Moors is a challenge because of their steepness, but the paths along the plateaus are less strenuous. The **Whitby to Scarborough Coastal Railtrail,** with sea views, refreshment stops, and sections for all skill levels, is especially popular. There are also many well-marked sections of the National Cycle Network that pass through the area. (For more info see www.sustrans.org.uk.) For bike-rental options, see **Transportation,** p. 427.

The Moors can be either horribly hot or bitterly cold in the summer. Call the Danby NPIC (☎01439 772 737; p. 428) for the weather forecast before setting out. Be aware that conditions can vary dramatically even within the park, and it is England—bring rain gear. The National Park Authority produces a number of guides on the Moors such as the *Walks Around* booklet (£1.90), which details short walks. The Ordnance Survey Explorer Maps (£7.50) include guides to the east and west sides of the park. **Disabled travelers** should pick up the *Easy Going North York Moors Guide* (£4.50) or call ☎01439 770 657 for guidance.

SCARBOROUGH   ☎(0)1723

Situated on a hilly peninsula separating two long beaches and dominated by a castle-topped crag, Scarborough combines the flashy glitz of a carnival with the charm of a traditional seaside town. Frequented by vacationers since the mid-17th century, Scarborough continues to be a favorite destination for English families. Its seafront amusements walk the line between tacky and delightful. Young and old flock here to enjoy the boardwalk attractions and traditional fish and chips, all under the watchful gaze of the seagulls circling the coastline.

ORIENTATION AND PRACTICAL INFORMATION. A cliff crowned by Scarborough Castle divides the town into two main areas, **North Bay** and **South Bay**, both fronted by a long stretch of beach. The **train station** is on Westborough, the main shopping street. There are three bus stops in front of the train station. The first two service **regional buses**, while the last services **local buses** only. For transportation info inside North York Moors National Park, see p. 427.

Scarborough is home to two helpful **TICs** (p. 428). Other services include: **banks** with ATMs, along Westborough; **Internet** at the public **library** on Vernon Rd. (£1.25 per 30min.); a **launderette**, 48 North Marine Rd. (☎01723 375 763; wash £2-3, dry 20p per 3min.); **police**, on the corner of Northway and Victoria Rd.; and the **post office**, 11-15 Aberdeen Walk (open M and W-F 9am-5:30pm, Tu 9:30am-5:30pm, Sa 9am-12:30pm). **Postcode:** YO11 1AB.

ACCOMMODATIONS AND FOOD. YHA Scarborough ② is 2 mi. from town (opposite page). The cheapest B&Bs (£17-20) can be found across from the railway station on West Sq. or along Blenheim Terr., Rutland Terr., and Trafalgar Sq. near North Bay. **The Whiteley ③,** 99-101 Queen's Parade, offers attentive service and well-kept ensuite rooms, some overlooking the North Bay. (☎01723 373 514. £32 per person. MC/V.) The family-oriented **Clarence Gardens Hotel ④,** 45 Blenheim Terr., takes pride in weekly theme nights like Boogie Nights 70s Disco Fridays and is ideal for families and groups. (☎01723 374 884; www.clarencegardenshotel.net. Rooms from £40. MC/V.) Old-fashioned **Parmelia Hotel ②,** 17 West St., has conveniently located accommodations just south of the town center. (☎01723 361 914. Singles £21.50; doubles £23.50. Cash only.)

You haven't experienced the true Scarborough until you've sampled its fish and chips. Many locals swear by **Mother Hubbards ②,** 43 Westborough, where generous portions of haddock with chips, bread, and tea or coffee are £6. (☎01723 376 109; www.mother-hubbards.co.uk. Open M-Sa 11:30am-6:30pm.) The harbor is lined with dozens of waterside fish-and-chip stands offering the traditional dish for dirt-cheap prices (£1.15-3.50). Try family-owned **Ruby's Coffee House ①,** 23 Foreshore Rd., for the self-advertised "best view in Scarborough" as well as warm panini and coffee for under £5. (☎01723 363 734. Open 10am-late.) **Alonzi's Harbour Bar ①,** 1-3 Sandside, serves fantastic ice cream from a seaside location. Challenge yourself with The Mega (£3), an ice-cream cone measuring well over a foot tall. (☎01723 373 662. Open 7:45am-6pm, ice cream served at the bar outside until 9pm.)

◘ ♫ **SIGHTS AND ENTERTAINMENT.** Dominating the horizon atop the city's headland, ▓**Scarborough Castle** was built by Henry II in 1158. A longtime strategic stronghold, the site also served as a home to Bronze Age warriors, a Roman signal station, and a Viking fort. History buffs will enjoy the free 1hr. audio tour. (☎01723 372 451. Open daily Apr.-Sept. 10am-6pm; Oct. M and Th-Su 10am-5pm; Nov.-Mar. M and Th-Su 10am-4pm. ₤4, concessions ₤3.20.) Just down the hill across Church Ln., the cemetery of the 12th-century **Saint Mary's Parish Church** holds the grave of Anne Brontë. (☎01723 500 541. Open May-Sept. M-F 10am-4pm, Su 1-4pm.) The **Stephen Joseph Theatre,** at the corner of Westborough and Northway across from the train station, stages plays and shows films. (☎01723 370 541; www.sjt.uk.com. Box office open M-Sa 10am-8pm, Su and performance days 6-7pm)

WHITBY   ☎(0)1947

The breathtaking ruins of Whitby Abbey loom above this small fishing village of cobblestone streets and steep hills. Once known for having the highest number of practicing witches in all of England, Whitby is swimming in legend and lore, thanks in part to Bram Stoker, who set part of his novel *Dracula* here. Wander amid the twisting narrow streets to sample fish and chips or while away an afternoon over a pint in one of the many traditional seaside pubs.

◼▟ **ORIENTATION AND PRACTICAL INFORMATION.** Whitby populates the west and east banks of the River Esk, with the North Sea bordering the town to the north. The remnants of Whitby Abbey stand atop 199 steps on the east bank of the river. **Trains** and most **buses** stop at **Station Square,** Endeavour Wharf, on the west side of the river. Whitby's **TIC** (p. 428) books rooms for ₤2 plus a 10% deposit. Other services include: **banks** with ATMS on Baxtergate near the bridge; a **launderette,** 71 Church St. (☎01947 603 957; wash ₤3-4, dry 20p per 5min.; open M-Tu and Th-Sa 8:30am-5pm); **police,** Spring Hill (☎01947 603 443); **Internet** access at the Coliseum, Victoria Pl., next to the bus station (☎01947 825 000; ₤2 per hr.; open M-Th 9am-5pm); and the **post office,** Langborne Rd., inside the North Eastern Co-op next to the train station (☎01947 600 710; open M-F 8:30am-5:30pm, Sa 9am-3pm). **Postcode:** YO21 1DN.

▛▟ **ACCOMMODATIONS AND FOOD.** Don't be fooled by the haunting exterior of the ▓**YHA Whitby ❶** (p. 428), on a hill next to the abbey—the spotless hostel has sensational views. For those not so keen on climbing the hill's 199 steps to their bed, the **Whitby Backpackers Harbour Grange ❶**, Spital Bridge on the harbor, rents basic but comfortable rooms, including a self-catering kitchen and a porch with views of the sea. Walk south on Church St. and turn right just after Green Ln. (☎01947 600 817. Linens ₤1. Curfew 11:30pm. Dorms ₤15-16. Cash only.) Many B&Bs are on West Cliff, along Royal Crescent, Crescent Ave., Abbey Terr., and nearby streets. **Chiltern Guest House ❸**, 13 Normanby Terr., is a clean, well-priced option. (☎01947 604 981. ₤25 per person. Cash only.)

Whitby plays host to an outdoor **market** on Church St. on Tuesdays and Saturdays and a farmers' market on Thursdays from May to September. A giant co-op **grocery** sits next to the train station. (☎01947 600 710. Open M-F 8am-10pm, Sa 8am-8pm, Su 10:30am-4:30pm.) Be prepared to queue at ▓**The Magpie Cafe ❷**, 14 Pier Rd., where the fish and chips are renowned throughout England and well worth the wait. (☎01947 602 058. Entrees ₤8-15. Open daily 11:30am-9pm.

MC/V.) The "Fast Track Menu" at the **White Horse and Griffin Restaurant ❷**, Church St., offers elegant cuisine for budget prices, with selections such as homemade soup, fisherman's pie, and even chargrilled steak from £4-10, all served in an old-fashioned, rustic interior. (☎01947 604 857. Fast Track Menu daily noon-3pm and 5-7pm. Reservations recommended for dinner. MC/V.)

⬛🅼 SIGHTS AND NIGHTLIFE. With marvelous views of the bay below, the splendid ruins of ⬛**Whitby Abbey** sit atop a wind-blown hill. Bram Stoker was a frequent visitor to Whitby, and the abbey and graveyard are believed to have inspired *Dracula*. The site's non-fictional history began in AD 657 when it was founded by St. Hilda, and the present structure dates to the 14th century. The textured stone walls, grass-filled nave, and views of the sea and the town below make this spot a must-see. (☎01947 603 568. Open Apr.-Sept. daily 10am-6pm; Oct.-Mar. M and Th-Su 10am-4pm. £5, students £4. Free audio tour.) Next to the Abbey, the medieval **Saint Mary's Church** has a unique, three-tiered pulpit and a maze of box pews. (☎01947 603 421. Open daily June-Sept. 10am-4pm; Oct. 10am-3:30pm; Nov.-May 10am-3pm. Donation suggested.) The **Captain Cook Memorial Museum** is at Grape Ln., on the east side of the river. In a house where James Cook once lived and worked, the museum contains original letters, drawings, navigational instruments, Captain Cook wax figures, and special exhibits. (☎01947 601 900; www.cookmuseumwhitby.co.uk. Open Apr.-Oct. daily 9:45am-5pm; Mar. Sa-Su 11am-3pm. Wheelchair-accessible. £3, students £2, seniors £2.50.) If seafaring stories don't pique your interest, visit the **Whitby Museum,** located in Pannett Park. The museum houses England's second largest collection of fossils, most found locally. (☎01947 602 908. Open Tu-Su 9:30am-4:30pm. £3, under 16 £1.)

While Whitby is generally quiet after dark, a few of its bars fill to capacity on Friday and Saturday nights. The retro-modern **Bar 7**, Pier Rd., serves up mixed drinks (£5-6.50) to a trendy, young crowd. (☎01947 605 777. Open daily 11am-11pm.) For a more traditional seaside pub experience, numerous pubs line Church St. on the east side of the river, home to many ghostly legends. The **Black Horse,** Church St., is supposedly the haunt of the spooky Whitby puppeteer, although it is perhaps better known for selling some of the best cask ales in town (☎01947 602 536. Open M-Sa 11am-11pm, Su noon-10pm.) The town takes particular pride in its **Folk Festival** (☎01947 708 424; www.folk-whitby.co.uk), which features dance, concerts, and workshops during the last full week in August. The *What's On* brochure at the TIC and the *Whitby Gazette* (published Tu and F) list events around town.

ROBIN HOOD'S BAY ☎(0)1947

Despite the name, the village of Robin Hood's Bay has little to do with the famous outlaw. When the smugglers who once dominated the isolated town stole from the rich, they only gave to themselves. Robin's Hood Bay is divided into the older Baytown, where alleys snake between stone cottages, and the Upper Bay. The Bolts, a small street leading out of town, earned its name as the easiest escape route for smugglers trying to avoid excise officers.

Many of the 19th-century sea captains' villas have been converted into B&Bs with sea views. **YHA Boggle Hole ❶** (p. 428), popular with families and walkers on the Cleveland Way, is 1 mi. from town. The cozy B&B accommodations of **The Old School House ❷**, Fisherhead, fill up quickly; book far in advance. (☎01947 880 723; www.old-school-house.co.uk. M-F £30 per person, Sa-Su £25 per person. Call ahead.) At the upper edge of town on the main road, **Candy's Coffee Bar ❶**, Bank Top Rd., is a popular lunch destination known for its homemade cakes

($5), sandwiches ($3-5), and breathtaking view of the bay below. (☎01947 880 716. Open daily Mar.-Oct. 9:30am-5pm; Nov.-Feb. 9:30am-4:30pm.)

A small **information center** on King St. has free **Internet** access and a dryer (20p). There are no ATMs in the bay, so plan ahead. Robin Hood's Bay is an easy daytrip from either Whitby (20min.) or Scarborough (40min.). Arriva **bus** #X56 stops here en route between the two towns (M-Sa every hr.), as does the #93 between Scarborough and Middlesbrough (M-Sa every hr., less on Sunday). Travelers making connections should aim to catch an early bus.

PICKERING   ☎(0)1751

The attractive market town of Pickering is best known as an endpoint of the popular **North Yorkshire Moors Railway (NYMR)**, although it can also serve as a central base for exploring the national park.

◼️🔃 ORIENTATION AND PRACTICAL INFORMATION. Pickering lies just outside the southern perimeter of the North York Moors National Park, at the intersection between the A170 and the A169. Pickering's **Tourist Information Centre** is at The Ropery (p. 428). Other services include: **banks** with ATMs on Market Pl.; **Internet** access at the **library,** next to the TIC (open M-Tu and Th 9:30am-5pm, W 1:30-5pm, F 9:30am-7:30pm, Sa 9:30am-4:30pm); and the **post office,** 7 Market Pl., inside Morland's News Agents, with a **bureau de change** (☎01751 472 256; open M-F 9am-5:30pm, Sa 9am-1pm). **Postcode:** YO18 7AA.

🔃🗂 ACCOMMODATIONS AND FOOD. Budget accommodations are scarce in Pickering. The nearest hostel is the ◼️**YHA Old School ❶** in Lockton, the first eco-friendly "green" hostel in Britain (p. 428). Among B&Bs, **Bridge House ❸,** 8 Bridge St., is a pleasant choice close to the train station, with a relaxing garden in the back beside a stream. (☎01751 477 234. Singles $35; doubles $56. Extra people $28 each. Discounts for 2+ nights.)

Country Crust ❶, 16A Market Pl. across from the train station, is a basic but convenient place to grab a quick sandwich ($1.80) for your travels. (☎01751 477 322. Open M-Sa 10:30am-7pm, Su 11am-6pm.) Across the square, **Tutti ❷,** 3 Market Pl., is a solid choice for Italian dishes. (☎01751 470 121. Entrees $4-10. Open M and Th-Su noon-10pm. MC/V.)

◼️ SIGHTS. Originally built by William the Conqueror to defend against northern invasions, **Pickering Castle** is a classic example of a Norman "motte-and-bailey" castle, originally surrounded by a moat with a keep built on top of a mound. Ruins of this 12th-century keep command expansive views of the countryside. (☎01751 474 989. Open Apr.-Sept. daily 10am-6pm; Oct. M and Th-Su 10am-4pm. $3, concessions $2.30.) The **Parish Church of Saint Peter and Saint Paul** is a small Norman building with a 15th-century Gothic spire. Its medieval frescoes are in surprisingly good condition. (Open daily dawn to dusk. Suggested donation $1.) Around the corner from the train station, the **Beck Isle Museum,** on Bridge St., recreates rural village life over the past two centuries and includes a unique and extensive collection of early local photographs. (☎01751 473 653; www.beckislemuseum.co.uk. Open Mar.-Oct. daily 10am-5pm. Last entry 4:30pm. $4, students $3, children $2.50, families $9.)

🔃 DAYTRIP FROM PICKERING: NORTH YORKSHIRE MOORS RAILWAY. The North Yorkshire Moors Railway (NYMR) is an easy way to access some of the most beautiful terrain in the Moors. The route itself offers spectacular views, and stations along the way offer some good hiking and a closer look. Pick up *Twelve Scenic Walks from the North York Moors Railway* (£2.50) at any TIC.

Although mainly geared toward tourists, the steam-pulled train is the only railway available in Pickering. Traveling north, the train stops at Levisham, from which you can access the nearby Lockton YHA, and Newton-Dale, the starting point of many backcountry walks (Newton-Dale stop by request only). Goathland has become a popular stop in recent years—the village is featured in the British TV series *Heartbeat*, and aficionados of the *Harry Potter* films will recognize the rail station as the setting for Hogsmeade. *(NYMR information ☎01751 472 508, timetable 01751 473 535; www.nymr.co.uk. Apr.-Oct. 4-9 round-trips per day, with some trains offering additional service to Whitby; Nov.-Dec. most weekends; Jan.-Feb. select holidays. Grosmont to Pickering and all-day rover tickets £14.50, concessions £12.)*

HELMSLEY   ☎(0)1439

A medieval castle looms over the scenic and charming Helmsley, one of York-shire's most popular market towns. Life in Helmsley centers on its cobbled **Market Place**, site of a Friday market since the 14th century.

█▐ ORIENTATION AND PRACTICAL INFORMATION. Helmsley sits on the southern end of the North York Moors National Park, along the A170 and about 14 mi. west of Pickering. The **Tourist Information Centre** (p. 428), is in Helmsley Castle. Buses stop on Market Pl., where you'll find most of Helmsley's **banks** with ATMs. The **library,** in the Town Hall, has free **Internet** access. (Open M 2-5pm and 5:30-7pm, W and F 10am-12:30pm and 2-5pm; Sa 10am-12:30pm.) Other services include the **police,** Ashdale Rd. (☎01439 1606 0247; open daily 9-10am and 6-7pm; North Yorkshire Police ☎0845 606 0247) and the **post office,** Bridge St., just off Market Pl. (open M-Tu and Th-F 9am-12:30pm and 1:30-5:30pm, W and Sa 9am-12:30pm). **Postcode:** YO62 5AB.

▐▐ ACCOMMODATIONS AND FOOD. Helmsley has a comfortable **YHA hostel** (p. 430) and B&Bs. **Carlton Lodge ❸**, Bondgate, offers cheerful service and a hearty Yorkshire breakfast in an ivy-covered cottage. (☎01439 770 623; www.carlton-lodge.com. £37.50 per person.) **No 54 ❸**, Bondgate, is a cheery B&B where rooms come with little perks such as bathrobes, tea service, and a garden out back. (☎01439 771 533; www.no54.co.uk. From £35 per person.)

Nice Things Cafe ❶, 10 Market Pl., serves up toasted sandwiches for £4.20-4.75. (☎01439 771 997. Open M-F 9am-5pm, Sa-Su 9am-5:30pm. Hot food served until 3:30pm.) After lunch, treat yourself at **Chocolaterie ❶**, Market Sq. The Belgian hot chocolate (£2.65) is heavenly, and the artistically dipped strawberries are only £2.40 for a box of seven. (☎01439 787 378; www.chocolaterie.co.uk. Open daily 10am-4pm. MC/V.) Numerous pubs and cafes line Market Pl.; stop in at **The Feathers** for a friendly chat and a pint (from £2.20) or fill up on hearty servings of pub grub at the **Jessa Rose** next door. Outside of town, the **█Rievaulx Cafe,** at the entrance to Rievaulx Abbey (p. 427), sells Brother Anthony's Rievaulx Ale (£3.35) to quench historic thirsts along with more contemporary refreshments such as soft drinks (from £2) and caramel shortbread (£1.35).

◨ SIGHTS. Built in 1120 to strengthen the Scottish border, **Helmsley Castle** acquired its shattered profile during the Civil War, when Cromwell blew the place in half. (☎01439 770 442. Open daily Apr.-Sept. 10am-6pm; Oct. and Mar. 10am-5pm; Nov.-Feb. 10am-4pm. £4, concessions £3.20.) *Secret Garden* readers will appreciate the **walled garden** behind the castle, a hidden floral escape containing over 70 varieties of Heritage apples and showcasing orchids in winter.

(☎01439 771 427; www.helmsley-walledgarden.co.uk. Open Apr.-Oct. daily 10:30am-5pm. Last entry 4:30pm. ₤4, concessions ₤3.) **Duncombe Park,** three quarters of a mile south of Market Pl. on Buckingham Sq., is a large park and nature reserve, home to the palatial 18th-century villa of Lord and Lady Feversham. (☎01439 770 213; www.duncombepark.com. Gardens open May-Oct. M-Th and Su 11am-5:30pm. Last admission 4:30pm. House open by tour only every hr., 12:30-3:30pm. Gardens ₤4, concessions ₤3.50. Tours ₤7.25, concessions ₤5.50.) An idyllic 3 mi. walk out of town along the beginning of the Cleveland Way leads to the stunning 12th-century **Rievaulx Abbey** (REE-vo). Founded by monks from Burgundy, the abbey was an aesthetic masterpiece until Thomas Mannus, first Earl of Rutland, stripped it of its valuables—including the roof. It is now one of the most spectacular ruins in England, with graceful arches of gray stone set amid pastures and wooded valleys. (Open Apr.-Sept. daily 10am-6pm; Oct. M and Th-Su 10am-5pm; Nov.-Mar. M and Th-Su 10am-4pm. ₤5, concessions ₤4. Audio tour free.) A steep half-mile uphill, the **Rievaulx Terrace & Temples** is a small park above the abbey with 17th-century faux-classical temples at either end. (☎01439 798 340. Open daily Apr.-Sept. 10:30am-6pm; Oct.-Nov. 10:30am-5pm. Last entry 1hr. before close. ₤4.)

DANBY AND THE ESK VALLEY   ☎(0)1287

The gorgeous Esk Valley cuts across the northern reaches of North York Moors. Panoramic views can be had without leaving the railcars of the **Esk Valley Line** (p. 427) as they travel between Whitby and Middlesbrough. It's well worth stopping off, however—this is a splendid spot for **hiking,** and marked trails leave from almost every station along the rail route. TICs and NPICs provide further details and literature, such as *Walks in the Esk Valley* (₤1.90). At the small town of **Grosmont,** the Esk Valley Line connects with the **North Yorkshire Moors Railway** (p. 427). Farther west in the valley, rolling hills give way to some of the national park's finest moorland. **The Moors Centre** NPIC (p. 428) is the best place to research possible routes. The *Walks from the Moors Centre* brochure (₤2) lists excellent nearby walks, among them an easy 30min. jaunt to **Danby Castle,** a roofless jumble of 14th-century stones attached to a working farm. In good weather, the peak of the 981 ft. **Danby Beacon** affords views stretching to the coastline. The village of **Castleton** is one stop beyond Danby, and from here the **Esk Valley Walk** (35 mi.) begins winding its way back to the coast. A lovely walk follows its first 2 mi. and ends in Danby.

Two hundred yards from the train station, the luxurious **Duke of Wellington Inn** ❹ and pub is the only accommodation in the town of Danby. (☎01287 660 351; www. dukeofwellingtondanby.co.uk. Breakfast and dinner included. Check-in before 2pm or after 4pm. Singles from ₤45; doubles and twins from ₤70.)

COUNTY DURHAM

DURHAM   ☎(0)191

The commanding presence of England's greatest Norman Romanesque cathedral lends grandeur to the small city of Durham (pop. 90,000). From 1071 until 1836, the prince bishops of Durham exercised an outsize influence over the surrounding county, with their own currency, army, and courts. After the Great Reform Act of 1832 abolished the bishop's powers, Durham University students became the dominating force in the hilltop city. Today, hordes of tourists and revelers flow through the narrow cobblestone streets, artists and artisans from

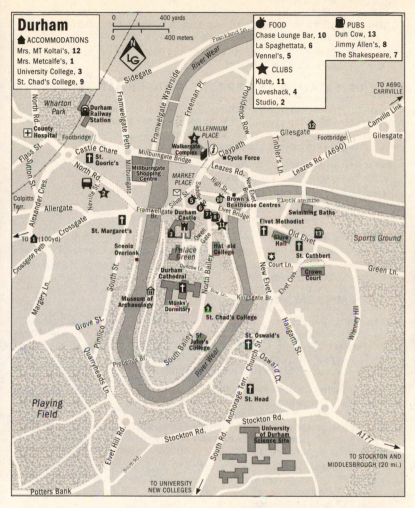

Durham

ACCOMMODATIONS
Mrs. MT Koltai's, **12**
Mrs. Metcalfe's, **1**
University College, **3**
St. Chad's College, **9**

FOOD
Chase Lounge Bar, **10**
La Spaghettata, **6**
Vennel's, **5**

CLUBS
Klute, **11**
Loveshack, **4**
Studio, **2**

PUBS
Dun Cow, **13**
Jimmy Allen's, **8**
The Shakespeare, **7**

NORTHEAST ENGLAND

across Europe vend their wares in the bustling outdoor market, and street musicians serenade dining couples on the banks of the winding River Wear.

TRANSPORTATION

Trains: The train station (☎08457 225 225) is on a steep hill west of town. Ticket office open M-F 6am-9pm, Sa 6am-8pm, Su 7:30am-9pm. Trains (☎08712 004 950) depart to: **Edinburgh** (2hr., every hr., £46); **London King's Cross** (3hr., 2 per hr., £94.30); **Newcastle** (20min., 4 per hr., £4.80); **York** (45min., 4 per hr., £19.70).

Buses: The bus station is on North Rd., across Framwellgate Bridge from the city center. National Express (☎08705 808 080) runs to **Edinburgh** (4hr., 2 per day, £26), **Leeds** (2hr., 4 per day, £14.20), and **London** (6-7hr., 6 per day, £27.50). Arriva (www.arrivabus.co.uk) buses X1, X21, and X41 run to Eldon Sq. station in nearby **Newcastle** (1hr., 2 per hr., £5) and serve most local routes. The Cathedral Bus runs from the cathedral green to the Durham train station for 50p.

Bike Rental: Cycle Force, 29 Claypath (☎0191 384 0319). £15 per day; £35 deposit. Open M-F 9am-5:30pm, Sa 9am-5pm.

⚒🎇 ORIENTATION AND PRACTICAL INFORMATION

Durham is 20 mi. south of Newcastle on the A167 and 20 mi. north of Darlington. The **River Wear** curls around Durham, crossed by a handful of footbridges. With its cobbled medieval streets, Durham is pedestrian-friendly, although travelers burdened with heavy packs may curse its many steep hills.

Tourist Information Centre: 2 Millennium Pl. (☎0191 384 3720), on the eastern side of the Millburngate Bridge. Open M-Sa 9:30am-5:30pm, Su 11am-4pm.

Banks: Market Pl. Most have ATMs.

Library: Millennium Pl. (☎0191 386 4003), right across from the TIC. Free Internet. Open M-F 9:30am-7pm, Sa 9am-5pm, Su 10:30am-4:30pm.

Police: New Elvet (☎0191 386 4222).

Internet Access: Free at the library and the **Chase Lounge Bar** (see **Food,** below).

Post Office: 33 Silver St. (☎0191 386 0839). Open M and W-Sa 9am-5:30pm, Tu 9:30am-5:30pm. **Postcode:** DH1 3RE.

🏠 ACCOMMODATIONS

Durham's accommodations can fill quickly. Reserve ahead (especially during university graduation in late June) or take advantage of the TIC's free in-office booking service (£3 charge if booking by phone). Durham lacks hostels, but the availability of centrally located **dormitory rooms** is a boon for summer travelers. A handful of budget B&B options are also available.

- 🏰 **University College** (☎0191 334 4106 or 334 4108; www.durhamcastle.com). Others merely tour it, but you can pretend to be lord or lady of Durham Castle in the dorms of Durham's University College, known to students as "Castle." Has a small number of luxurious ensuite rooms, including the fabulous Bishop's Suite, a massive 2-room affair with 17th-century tapestries on the walls and views of the river. Breakfast in the Great Hall included. Singles from £28.50; doubles £51; Bishop's Suite £95. MC/V. ❸

- **St. Chad's College,** 18 North Bailey (☎0191 334 3358; www.dur.ac.uk/stchads.conference/bb), behind Durham Cathedral. Rents YHA-affiliated rooms during university vacations. Parking available. Reception 9am-6pm. Dorms £25, members £21; ensuite singles £32; twins £40; doubles £50. ❸

- **Mrs. Metcalfe's,** 12 The Avenue, (☎0191 384 1020), near the bus and train stations. Only 2 rooms, so book ahead. £20 per person. ❷

- **Mrs. M.T. Koltai's,** 10 Gilesgate (☎0191 386 2026), a short 10min. walk up the hill from the city's center. Singles £25; doubles £35. ❸

🍴 FOOD

A Tesco's grocery store sits one block from the bus station toward the city center. Durham's other eats are friendly and cheap.

- **Vennel's,** Saddler St., up a narrow passage from the street. Students congregate over sandwiches and sweet treats (£1-3) in the 16th-century courtyard of this cool bohemian alcove. Open daily 9:30am-5pm. ❶

Chase Lounge Bar, Elvet Bridge (☎0191 386 62100), at the boathouse. The upstairs terrace of this riverside beer garden overlooks the Wear and is the perfect place for a drink and a late lunch. Sandwiches and wraps £3. Pizzas £5. Free Wi-Fi. Kitchen open daily noon-6pm. Bar open daily noon-1am. ❶

La Spaghettata, 66 Saddler St. (☎0191 383 9290). This upbeat restaurant is a good representative of the many Italian places that dot the central city, a number of which offer happy-hour deals before 7pm. Cheap pizza and pasta from £4.50. Always filled with a raucous and cheerful crowd, possibly due to their specials on 2L bottles of wine. Open M-F 5:30-10:30pm, Sa-Su 11:30am-2pm and 5:30-10:30pm. ❶

👁 SIGHTS

🏛**DURHAM CATHEDRAL.** Built between 1093 and 1133 and still largely intact, the extraordinary Durham Cathedral stands, in the words of Sir Walter Scott, as "half church of God, half castle 'gainst the Scot." It is considered the finest Norman cathedral in the world. Explanatory panels guide visitors through the cathedral, although a more detailed pamphlet (£1) is available. The stunning nave was the first in England to incorporate pointed arches, and the beautiful **Galilee Chapel** at the end features 12th-century wall paintings. To the left of the information desk is the simple tomb of the Venerable Bede, author of the 8th-century *Ecclesiastical History of the English People*, the first history of England. Behind the choir is the **tomb of Saint Cuthbert,** who died in AD 687 and was buried on Holy Island until his monks moved his body while fleeing from Viking raiders in the ninth century. After 120 years of wandering, a vision led the monks to build what would eventually become Durham Cathedral. The **bishop's throne,** next to the choir, has been controversial since its construction in the 14th century; it stands nearly 3 in. higher than the pope's throne at the Vatican. *(Crowning the hill in the middle of the city. ☎0191 386 4266; www.durhamcathedral.co.uk. Open June-Aug. M-Sa 9:30am-8pm, Su 12:30-8pm; Sept.-May M-Sa 9:30am-6pm, Su 12:30-5pm. Tours July-Sept. Suggested donation £4.)* The cathedral's 218 ft. central **tower** is supported by intricately carved stone pillars. The spectacular view from the top is well worth the dizzying 325-step climb. *(Open from mid-Apr. to Sept. M-Sa 10am-4pm; from Oct. to mid-Apr. M-Sa 10am-3pm; weather permitting. £3, families £8.)* The **Monks' Dormitory** houses pre-Conquest stones and casts of crosses under an enormous 600-year-old timber roof made from 21 trees. *(Open Apr.-Sept. M-Sa 10am-4pm, Su 12:45-4pm. £1.)* Off the cloister lie the 🏛**Treasures of Saint Cuthbert,** which include saintly relics, holy manuscripts dating back 1300 years, and rings and seals of the bishops. *(Open M-Sa 10am-4:30pm, Su 2-4:30pm. £2.50, concessions £2.)*

DURHAM CASTLE. Begun in 1072, this fortress was for centuries a key bastion of the county's prince bishops. Today, it's a splendid residence for university students and summer travelers. *(Across the green from the Cathedral. ☎0191 334 3800. Admission by guided tour only. Open Mar.-Sept. daily; Oct.-Feb. M, W, Sa-Su. Schedule changes daily; call for tour times. £5.)*

OTHER SIGHTS. Wandering the horseshoe bend of the River Wear is a pleasant way to spend an afternoon. A scenic walk along the bank between Framwellgate Bridge and Prebends Bridge leads to the **Museum of Archaeology,** which showcases an extensive collection of Roman stone altars alongside finds from prehistory to the present. *(☎0191 334 1823. Open Apr.-Oct. daily 11am-4pm; Nov.-Mar. M and F-Su 11:30am-3:30pm. £1, students free, concessions 50p.)* **Brown's Boathouse Centres** rents rowboats. *(Elvet Bridge. ☎0191 386 3779. £3 per hr. per person; £10 deposit.)* For a less arduous journey, the center runs a 1hr. cruise on the **Prince Bishop River Cruiser.** *(☎0191 386 9525. Easter-June Sa-Su, July-Sept. daily; times depend on weather and university boating events. £4.50, concessions £4. Departs next door from the Chase Lounge Bar.)*

NORTHEAST ENGLAND

🌸 🔆 FESTIVALS AND NIGHTLIFE

The TIC stocks the free pamphlet *What's On*, a great source of information on festivals and local events. Durham holds its **Summer Festival** during the first weekend of July, showcasing folk music, craftsmaking, and other amusements, including a town-crier competition. Other major events include the June **Durham Regatta**, England's foremost amateur rowing competition since 1834.

Don't let Durham's stuffy history fool you: come evening, a rollicking crowd of students and locals enlivens the scene. Most students start the night at a local pub like **The Dun Cow,** Old Elvet St. (☎0191 386 9219; open M-Sa 11am-11pm, Su noon-10:30pm) or **The Shakespeare,** Saddler St. (☎0191 384 3261; open M-Sa 11am-midnight, Su noon-11pm) to sample some of the area's famous cask ale. A little later, hit up a few trendy riverside bars.

Jimmy Allen's, 19-21 Elvet Bridge (☎0191 357 7574). Draws students on weeknights with £2 mixed drinks, while an older crowd of locals fills its three floors and stylish bar on weekends. Open daily 7pm-1am.

Studio, 15-17 North Rd. (☎0191 384 3900). Spins house music on the top floor and R&B below. Monday through Wednesday require a Durham University student ID for entrance, although non-Durham students sometimes find that their IDs are accepted. Open daily if university is in session; Th-Su during university holidays. Cover £0.50-£3.)

Loveshack, Walkergate Complex (☎0191 386 4789). Nightly themes, elaborate 70s decor, and specialty drinks such as the Toffee Orgasm and the Brain Hemorrhage draw a libidinous crowd every night. Open daily 8pm-2am. Cover M-Th £1-3, no cover F-Sa.

Klute Nightclub beneath Elvet Bridge (☎0191 386 9589). So bad that it's good. Ranked the second-worst nightclub in Europe by *FHM* in 1996. When the winning Belgian club later burned down, Klute was catapulted into the number-one spot. Clubbers form long lines in a filthy alleyway to get inside, where 1980s taped rugby championships play on loop and Barry Manilow croons overhead. Open daily 8pm-2am. Cover £1-3.)

🔲 DAYTRIP FROM DURHAM

BEAMISH OPEN AIR MUSEUM. Perhaps the area's most famous attraction outside of Durham, Beamish is a detailed recreation of 19th- and early-20th-century life in North England, featuring an 1825 replica railway, a manor house, villages with costumed actors, and a tour of a former drift mine. There's a lot to see; plan on spending about 3hr. *(12 mi. northwest of Durham on the A693. Take Arriva bus X1 or X21 to Chester-le-Street (2 per hr.), then change to Go North East bus X8 or #28, which stop at Beamish Museum Main Gates (2 per hr.). ☎0191 370 4000. Open Apr.-Oct. daily 10am-5pm; from Nov. to mid-Dec. and Mar. Tu-Th and Sa-Su 10am-4pm. Last entry 3pm. High-season £16, students £12.50; low-season £6.)*

BARNARD CASTLE   ☎(0)1833

Twenty miles southwest of Durham along the River Tees, Barnard Castle—the name of both a peaceful market town and its Norman ruins—is the best base for exploring the castles of Teesdale and the peaks of the North Pennine Hills in addition to being a worthwhile destination in its own right.

🔲 🔆 TRANSPORTATION AND PRACTICAL INFORMATION. Arriva **buses** #75 and 76 (both 40min., every hr.) run from Barnard Castle to Darlington, where you can change to #723 to Durham (1hr., 2 per hr.). A day pass (£5) is valid on both services. Buses start and end on Galgate, at the end of which is the

well-stocked **Tourist Information Centre,** Woodleigh, Flatts Rd., which also has **Internet** access. (☎01833 690 909. Internet £1.50 per 30min. Open Apr.-Oct. M-Sa 9:30am-5pm, Su 11am-5pm; Nov.-Mar. M-Sa 11am-4pm.) Other services include: **banks** with ATMs on Market Pl.; **police,** Harmire Rd. (☎01833 637 328); and the **post office,** 2 Galgate, with a **bureau de change** (☎01833 638 247; open M-Sa 9am-5:30pm). **Postcode:** DL12 8BE.

⚏⚏ ACCOMMODATIONS AND FOOD. Barnard Castle has no hostels but is blessed with excellent B&Bs, most of which can be found on tree-lined Galgate. One option is the **Homelands Guest House ❸,** 85 Galgate, which offers airy rooms, bathrobes, and a garden. (☎01833 638 757; www.homelandsguesthouse.co.uk. Singles £35, ensuite £45; doubles £65-70. MC/V.) Numerous cafes and small restaurants line the streets of Galgate and Horsemarket. **The Hayloft,** 27 Horsemarket, is an eclectic indoor market jammed with antiques, bric-a-brac, and produce. (Open W and F-Sa 10am-5pm.)

◙ SIGHTS. Perched above the River Tees, the remains of **Barnard Castle,** including a well-preserved inner keep, sprawl across six acres. (☎01833 638 212. Entrance beside the TIC at the end of Galgate. Open Apr.-Sept. daily 10am-6pm; Oct. daily 10am-4pm; Nov.-Mar. M and Th-Su 10am-4pm. £4, concessions £3.20.) In the 19th century, John and Josephine Bowes built the remarkable ◪**Bowes Museum** along Newgate. It houses the couple's extensive private collection of European decorative arts. Among its many treasures is the largest gathering of Spanish paintings in Britain—El Greco's magnificent *Tears of St. Peter,* among others—as well as a mechanized silver swan (activated every day at noon and 3pm) so impressive that, when Mark Twain saw it in 1867, he claimed the swan "had a living grace about his movement and a living intelligence in his eyes." The museum also hosts a regular program of plays and concerts. (☎01833 690 606; www.thebowesmuseum.org.uk. Open daily 11am-5pm. Grounds open 24hr. Tours June-Sept. £7, concessions £6, under 16 free.) For those traveling by car, the **Dickens Drive** is a 25 mi. route that traces the path the author took in 1838 while researching for his novel *Nicholas Nickleby.* Pick up *In the Footsteps of Charles Dickens,* free from the TIC. Overlooking the River Tees, the ruins of 12th-century **Egglestone Abbey** are a pleasant 3 mi. circular walk along the river to the southeast of town. Dales and District Bus #79 from Barnard Castle will also drop you there. (Open daily 10am-6pm. Free.) Northeast of Barnard Castle on the A688, 14th-century **Raby Castle** (RAY-bee) is set in a deer park. If some of the stonework looks familiar, it's probably because Barnard Castle was partially dismantled in the 16th century to provide materials for Raby's completion. Take Arriva bus #75 (20min., every hr.) toward Darlington. (☎0191 660 202; www.rabycastle.com. Castle open July-Aug. M-F and Su 12:30-5pm; Sept. and May-June W-Su 12:30-5pm. Park and gardens open M-F and Su 11am-5:30pm. Last entry 4:30pm. £9.50, students £8.50; park and gardens without castle admission £5/4.)

TYNE AND WEAR

NEWCASTLE-UPON-TYNE   ☎(0)191

The largest city in the northeast, Newcastle (pop. 278,000) is notorious as one of Britain's nightlife capitals. Beyond the nightly party, Newcastle's varied past has produced a city combining medieval history, beautiful 19th-century

NORTHEAST ENGLAND

architecture, and a lively contemporary art scene. The one constant in this rapidly changing city is its spirit: Newcastle Geordies are proud of their accent, very proud of their football club, and very, very proud of their brown ale.

⌐ TRANSPORTATION

Newcastle lies 1½hr. north of York on the A19 and 1hr. east of Carlisle on the A69. Edinburgh is 2½hr. north of Newcastle on the A1, which follows the North Sea coast, or on the A68, which cuts inland.

Trains: Central Station, Neville St. Sells same-day tickets M-Sa 4:30am-9:20pm, Su 7:10am-10pm; advance tickets M-F 7am-8pm, Sa 7am-7pm, Su 8:40am-8pm. Trains (☎08457 484 950) to: **Carlisle** (1½hr., every hr., £11.80); **Durham** (15min., 4 per hr., £4.80); **Edinburgh** (1½hr., £39); **London King's Cross** (3hr.; every 30min.; Saver Pass available M-F for trains leaving after 8:30am, all day Sa-Su £95 with some restrictions; book ahead online for further deals); **York** (1hr.; several per hr.; Saver Pass available M-F for trains leaving after 9am, all day Sa-Su £20.40; trains M-F before 9am £23).

Buses: Newcastle has 3 main bus stations.

St. James Station, St. James Blvd. National Express (☎08705 808 080) buses to **Edinburgh** (3hr., 4 per day, £15) and **London** (7hr., 4 per day, £26.50).

Haymarket Station, by the Metro stop, and adjunct **Eldon Square Station,** Percy St., are the gateways for local and regional service by Arriva (☎0191 261 1779) and Go Northeast (☎0845 606 0260). Ticket office open M-F 7am-5pm, Sa 9am-4pm.

Central Station, Neville St., is a stop on the Megabus line (☎0900 160 0900; www.megabus.com), which offers £1 fares to **Edinburgh, London, Leeds,** and other cities throughout Great Britain. No ticket office; call in advance or book ahead online.

Ferries: International Ferry Terminal, Royal Quays, 7 mi. east of Newcastle. DFDS Seaways (☎08705 333 000; www.dfdsseaways.co.uk) offers ferry service to **Norway** and the **Netherlands** (see **By Ferry,** p. 40). Bus #327 serves all ferry departures, leaving from Central Station. From the Percy Main Metro stop, the quay is a 20min. walk.

Public Transportation: Call Traveline (☎08706 082 608) for complete details. The Metro **subway** system runs from the city center to the coast, the airport, and to neighboring towns like Gateshead and Sunderland. Tickets (£1.30-2.60) must be purchased ahead and are checked on board. Many stations don't have change machines; bring enough coins. The **DaySaver** allows 1 day of unlimited travel (£3.40). Trains run 6am-12:15am; pick up subway maps at most stations or TICs. Local **buses** stop throughout the city, with main terminals at the Haymarket Metro and the Eldon Sq. Shopping Centre. The bright yellow Quaylink buses follow 2 routes that connect many of the central city's key attractions (80p, HourRider £1, Day Pass £1.50). A **DayRover,** available at Metro and bus offices, offers unlimited travel on all Tyne and Wear public transportation (£5, under 18 £2.50). Pick up a bus route map at either TIC.

Taxis: Taxis are easy to find in the city center, although you must pick one up from a taxi rank (found on most main streets and in front of Central Station as well as at both bus stations). They won't stop if you try to flag one down; your best bet is to call ahead. One company is **Noda Taxi** (☎0191 222 1888).

Bike Rental: Tyne Bridge Bike Hire (☎0191 277 2441; www.tynebridgebikehire.co.uk), in the Guildhall TIC. £5 per hr., £10 per ½ day, £15 per full day.

◢✳ 🛈 ORIENTATION AND PRACTICAL INFORMATION

Most of Newcastle's attractions are within easy walking distance of one another in the city's center. **Grey's Monument** is a useful orientation point. Dedicated to Charles, Earl of Grey, author of the 1832 Reform Bill and namesake of the tea, this 80 ft. pillar was erected as the keystone of the famed **Grey Street,** whose ornate 19th-century architecture has earned it the reputation as the

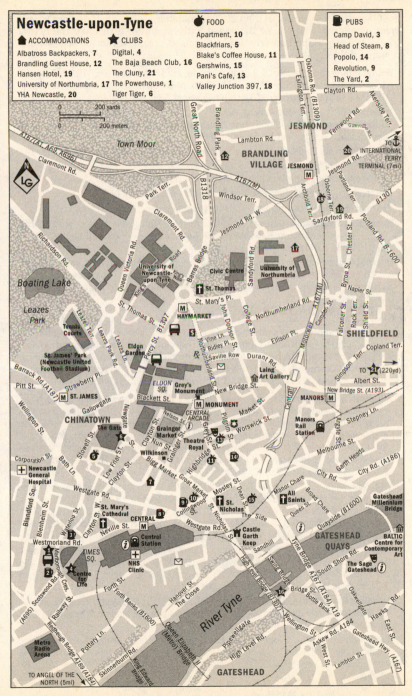

Newcastle-upon-Tyne

ACCOMMODATIONS
Albatross Backpackers, **7**
Brandling Guest House, **12**
Hansen Hotel, **19**
University of Northumbria, **17**
YHA Newcastle, **20**

CLUBS
Digital, **4**
The Baja Beach Club, **16**
The Cluny, **21**
The Powerhouse, **1**
Tiger Tiger, **6**

FOOD
Apartment, **10**
Blackfriars, **5**
Blake's Coffee House, **11**
Gershwins, **15**
Pani's Cafe, **13**
Valley Junction 397, **18**

PUBS
Camp David, **3**
Head of Steam, **8**
Popolo, **14**
Revolution, **9**
The Yard, **2**

NORTHEAST ENGLAND

most beautiful city street in the UK. The main shopping drag, **Northumberland Street,** is nearby. The city of **Gateshead,** only a 10min. walk over the Swing Bridge, sits across the Tyne (rhymes with "mine") from Newcastle and is home to many of the area's newer attractions.

Tourist Information Centres: 8-9 Central Arcade, 26-30 Market St. (☎0191 277 8000). Book rooms for a 10% deposit. Open M-F 9:30am-5:30pm, Sa 9am-5:30pm. Branch at Guildhall, Quayside open M-F 10am-5pm, Sa 9am-5pm, Su 9am-4pm.

Tours: The TIC gives various walking tours June-Sept. for £3. **Citysightseeing Newcastle Gateshead** (☎08716 660 000; www.city-sightseeing.com) operates a popular hop-on, hop-off tour. Departures every hr. from Central Station (£8, concessions £6).

Banks: There are banks with ATMs on most main streets, including **Barclay's Bank,** 141 Northumberland St. (☎0845 755 5555).

Luggage Storage: At the Central Train Station. £4 per bag.

Police: At the corner of Market St. and Pilgrim St. (☎0191 214 6555).

Pharmacies: Numerous pharmacies along Northumberland St. and Grainger St.

Hospital: Emergencies: General Hospital, Westgate Rd. (24hr. hotline ☎0191 233 6161). **Non-emergencies: National Health Services,** walk-in clinic at Central Station (☎0191 233 3760). Open M-F 7am-7pm.

Internet Access: Free for 15min. at both **TICs** (above). **Starbucks Coffee Shop,** Grainger St. Wi-Fi £5 for 1st hr. Also available free at all Newcastle branch **libraries.**

Post Office: Inside WHSmith behind Central Station. **Postcode:** NE2 4RP.

ACCOMMODATIONS

Inexpensive lodgings are scarce in Newcastle, and weekends in particular fill up well in advance; call ahead. Pickings are slim in the city center, but the city's few B&Bs, the local YHA hostel, and numerous overpriced small hotels cluster in residential Jesmond, 1 mi. from the city center and serviced by the Metro (last service from city center around 12:15am, depending on the stop).

Albatross Backpackers, 51 Grainger St. (☎0191 233 1330; www.albatrossnewcastle. com). This new addition to Newcastle's budget scene has everything you could want in a city hostel: secure, modern facilities; excellent location 2min. from the train station and adjacent to major nightlife areas; self-catering kitchen with free tea, coffee, and toast; and a lounge with TVs and a pool table. Don't count on a full night's sleep on weekends, when partiers fill its 171 beds. Internet £1 per 30min. Free Wi-Fi. Reception 24hr. Dorms £16.50-22.50. MC/V. ❷

YHA Newcastle, 107 Jesmond Rd. (☎08707 705 972). Metro: Jesmond. A 20min. walk from the city center. 52 beds in a comfortable townhouse. Often full; call well in advance. Self-catering kitchen. Internet £2.50 per 30min. Reception 7am-11pm. Curfew 11pm. Open mid-Jan. to mid-Dec. Dorms £18, under 18 £13.50. AmEx/MC/V. ❷

University of Northumbria, Sandyford Rd. (☎0191 227 3215; www.unn.ac.uk). Metro: Haymarket. Check in at Claude Gibb Hall. Standard dorm bed-basin-desk combos in close proximity to the city center. Breakfast included. Reception M-Th and Su 7am-midnight, F-Sa 24hr. Open from mid-June to Aug. Singles M-Th and Su from £24.50, F-Sa from £29. MC/V. ❸

Brandling Guest House, 4 Brandling Park (☎0191 281 3175). Metro: Jesmond. Family-run B&B 5min. from the Metro station with spacious and quiet rooms. Singles from £32; doubles from £56. MC/V. ❸

Hansen Hotel, 131 Sandyford Rd. (☎0191 281 0289). Metro: Jesmond. Even the basic rooms of this small hotel, a 15min. walk from the city center, are fully booked on weekends. Singles on weekends £25, on weeknights £28; doubles £46-50. AmEx/MC/V. ❸

◨ FOOD

Newcastle has plenty of inexpensive curry, fish and chips, pasta, pizza, and tandoori spots. Chinese eateries form a small Chinatown along **Stowell Street** near St. James Blvd.; all-you-can-eat specials for £6 are common. Many of the restaurants lining Dean St. serve cheap lunch and happy-hour specials until 7 or 7:30pm. The **Grainger Indoor Market** is on Grainger St., near the monument. (Open M and W 8am-5pm, Tu and Th-Su 8am-5:30pm.)

Apartment, 28 Collingwood St. (☎0191 230 4114; www.apartment-luxebar.com). Newcastle's most stylish club offers reasonable set-price menus (2 courses £11, 3 courses £14) in its dining room designed to feel like a New York City loft apartment, with exposed brick, gleaming wood floors, and trendy decorator touches. Open M-Sa noon-2:30pm and 6-11pm, Su noon-4pm and 6-11pm. ❸

Pani's Cafe, 61 High Bridge St. (☎0191 232 4366; www.paniscafe.com). Italian eatery with a bustling vibe just steps from Grey St. A great place to unwind after a long day of shopping or sightseeing. Entrees £5-12. Open M-Sa 10am-10pm. MC/V. ❷

Gershwins, 54 Dean St. (☎0191 261 8100; www.gershwinsrestaurant.co.uk). Swanky underground restaurant with overhead star lighting. Serves special theater menus and continental cuisine (with a few notable exceptions like seared ostrich) for £10-15. Excellent lunch and early-bird (until 7pm) specials—2 courses for £6, with wine £7. Live jazz in the summer F-Sa 8pm, Su 2pm. Open M-F 11:30am-2:30pm and 5:30-11pm, Sa 11:30am-11pm. Reservations recommended on theater nights. MC/V. ❸

Valley Junction 397, Archbold Terr. (☎0191 281 6397), in an old train station near the Jesmond Metro terminal. Delicious Bengali-influenced cuisine served in an antique railway car. The Indian lager Kingfisher (£3.25) blends well with *saag paneer* (£6-7). Voted the most original Indian restaurant in the UK by the Curry Club of Great Britain. Vegan fare available. Open Tu-Sa noon-2pm and 6-11:30pm, Su 6-11:30pm. MC/V. ❷

Blake's Coffee House, 53 Grey St. (☎0191 261 5463). A popular and jazzy central hangout with a range of lunch fare (£4-5) and sandwiches (£2-3). Open M-Sa 7am-6pm, Su 10am-4pm. Cash only. ❶

Blackfriars Restaurant, Friar St. (☎0191 261 5945; www.blackfriarsrestaurant.co.uk). Originally built as a refectory (dining hall) for 13th-century monks, Blackfriars still feels like a medieval monastary, with stonework fireplaces and beautiful wall tapestries. But the fare today is probably tastier (and less ascetic) than it was for the original patrons: try the seared kingfish or wild mushroom and chestnut pie. Entrees £15-20. Early set menu available for lunch daily or for dinners M-F 6-7pm (2 courses £12.50). Open Tu-Sa noon-2:30 and 6pm-late. ❹

◉ SIGHTS

BALTIC CENTRE FOR CONTEMPORARY ART. Newcastle is home to one of the largest public art collections in Europe—statues, sculptures, bridge lightings, and even short films can be enjoyed free any time simply by walking down the street. Housed in a renovated warehouse on the Gateshead side of the Tyne, the BALTIC Centre for Contemporary Art is the largest center for contemporary visual art outside London. Its rotating exhibits keep it on the cutting edge of the art scene. (☎0191 478 1810; www.balticmill.com. Open M and W-Su 10am-8pm, Tu 10:30am-8pm. Last entry 15min before closing. Free.)

CASTLE GARTH KEEP. The motte-and-bailey "New Castle" for which the city is named was built in 1080 by Robert Curthose, William the Conqueror's illegitimate son. The largely intact keep is all that remains of the 12th-century stone

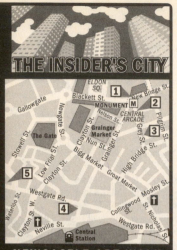

THE INSIDER'S CITY

NEWCASTLE ART WALK

Newcastle is home to one of the largest collections of public art in Europe. Nearly everywhere you look in the city—on the walls of buildings, in sculpture gardens, sometimes even on the sidewalk itself—artwork lends individuality to the city's bustling streets. Here are a few highlights of Grainger Town, the historic heart of the city.

1. The 80 ft. pillar of **Grey's Monument** is hard to miss. Modeled after a Romanesque icon column, this statue commemorates Charles Earl Grey (the tea man himself), who wrote the Great Reform Bill of 1832 and was a prominent voice in the British antislavery movement. A spiral staircase leads to the top of the monument, which is occasionally open to viewers.

2. After craning your neck up to see Grey's Monument, take a look down at your feet. Four **head cubes**, each containing a cast of Charles Grey's noggin at different angles, are set into the monument's plinth. Artist Simon

castle that replaced the original structure. Excellent views of the city are the reward for the dizzying climb up the keep's narrow stairs. *(St. Nicholas St.* ☎ *0191 232 7938. Open daily Apr.-Sept. 9:30am-5:30pm; Oct.-Mar. 9:30am-4:30pm. £1.50.)*

THE CATHEDRAL CHURCH OF SAINT NICHOLAS. This remarkable cathedral tells the story of Newcastle's medieval history in wood, glass, and stone. *(At the corner of Mosley St. Open M-F 7am-6pm, Sa 8am-4pm, Su 7am-noon and 4-7pm. Free.)*

RIVER TYNE. A walk along the Quayside is most beautiful in the evening, when the city's stunning riverside architecture and bridges, like the **Gateshead Millennium Bridge,** are illuminated by colored lights. Also impressive is the **Swing Bridge,** built in 1876, which swivels once or twice a day to allow ships to pass. *(Usually morning or midday; check signs at the bridge's end for the week's time.)*

CENTRE FOR LIFE. Recently, Newcastle has spearheaded urban renewal projects showcasing science, technology, and the arts. The Centre for Life is a family-friendly, hands-on science museum with a motion simulator, 3D movies, and an ice-skating rink from September to January. *(Times Sq., on Scotswood Rd. by the train station.* ☎ *0191 243 8208; www. life.org.uk. Open M-Sa 10am-6pm, Su 11am-6pm. Last entry 3:30pm. Prices vary based on exhibitions but generally are around £8, concessions £6.)*

SAGE GATESHEAD CONCERT HALL. This giant expanse of steel and glass dominates the riverbank and looks spectacular at night. Completed in 2004, the world-class complex of performance halls is home to **Northern Sinfonia,** the orchestra of the Northeast, and **Folkworks,** an agency dedicated to promoting traditional music. *(*☎ *0191 443 4661; www.thesagegateshead.org. Box office open M-Sa 10am-8pm, Su 10am-6pm. Tours available for groups of 10 or more Sa-Su noon, 5:30pm. Tours £6. Tickets for shows from £7. MC/V.)*

OTHER SIGHTS. Another host of Newcastle's vibrant art scene, the **Laing Art Gallery** displays an array of watercolors, sculptures, and pieces by pre-Raphaelite masters. *(New Bridge St.* ☎ *0191 232 7734; www.twmuseums.org.uk/laing. Open M-Sa 10am-5pm, Su 2-5pm. Free.)* Heading south from Newcastle by rail or road, you can't miss the **Angel of the North.** Built in 1994 by Antony Gormley and admired by about 33 million people per year, the striking 200-ton steel sculpture is 66 ft. tall and wider than a jumbo jet. *(4 mi. from the city at the junction of the A1 and A167.)*

🎭 ENTERTAINMENT

The lush, gilt-and-velvet **Theatre Royal,** 100 Grey St., shows over 380 performances per year as the regional home to the **National Theatre, Opera North,** and the **Rambert Dance Company.** (☎08448 112 121; www.theatreroyal.co.uk. Booking office open M-Tu and Th-Sa 9am-8pm, W 10am-8pm.) Concession tickets are half-price on the day of the performance when not sold out. The **Royal Shakespeare Company** also makes a month-long stop at the theater, complementing the top-notch program of operas and musicals with Shakespeare and contemporary plays (usually in the fall; check the box office or TIC for exact dates).

Saint James's Park, home of the **Newcastle United Football Club,** is a prominent feature of the city skyline and a testament to how seriously the Geordies take their football. Tickets can be hard to come by and are only available for sale up to two weeks in advance. (☎0191 201 8400, ticket office 261 1571; www.nufc.co.uk. Open M-F 8am-8pm, Sa 9am-6pm, Su 11am-5pm.) The **Newcastle Racecourse,** in the enormous High Gosforth Park, holds a number of top horse-racing events each year and makes for a great day at the track. (☎0191 236 2020.) **Kingston Park Stadium,** a 5min. walk from the Kingston Park Metro station, is home to one of Britain's top rugby teams, the **Newcastle Falcons.** (☎0871 226 6060; www.newcastle-falcons.co.uk. Call ahead for tickets.)

🍸 NIGHTLIFE

Newcastle's streets are home to a seemingly insupportable number of bars and clubs. But support them the locals do, with considerable help from a massive influx of weekend partiers from across Britain and Northern Europe. Rowdy Geordies line **Bigg Market.** Be cautious in this area—it is notoriously rough. Close by is the classier **Diamond Mile,** along Collingwood and Mosley St. These streets are lined with opulent clubs and lounges, most with their own exclusive members' areas. Beside the river, **Quayside** (KEY-side) and Gateshead (across the Tyne) attract a slightly younger crowd, while **The Gate** complex on Newgate has a bit of something for everybody. Newcastle's underground music venues are scattered throughout the city and churn out a countless number of successful bands. For a less heart-stopping, bass-thumping night out, **Osborne Road,** in Jesmond, 1 mi. north of the city center, is increasingly popular with students and locals for traditional barhopping. *The Crack* (monthly; free at record stores) is the best source

Watkinson created the cubes after hearing a legend of the earl's head being knocked off the monument by a bolt of lightning. The cubes are lit by neon-colored lights.

3. At night, a canopy under the portico of the **Theatre Royale** is lit with a variety of colors. The lights can be seen from up and down Grey St. and were meant to provide a modern contrast to the classical facade of the theater.

4. From the theater, a 5min. walk leads to **Man with Potential Selves.** The lifelike bronze sculptures stand, walk, and float along Grainger St. Artist Sean Henry intended the figures to be three alter egos of the same man, representing different concepts and experiences of reality.

5. At the end of Grainger St., turn right on Westgate Rd. to reach **Ever Changing,** an inverted cone of polished stainless steel standing at the bottom of Bath Ln. The cone acts as a warped mirror that reflects the continual changes in the surrounding pedestrians, traffic, and sky. It was designed by modern artist Eilis O'Connell.

For more information on the public art in Grainger Town, check out www.newcastle.gov.uk/core. nsf/a/pubartgraingertown.

for music and club listings in Newcastle. Newcastle's "Pink Triangle" of gay bars and clubs lies just west of the Centre for Life, along Westmorland Rd., St. James Blvd., and Marlborough Crescent. Check out www.newcastlegayscene. co.uk for upcoming events and new openings.

PUBS AND BARS

Pubs and bars in Newcastle are generally open from Monday to Saturday 11am-11pm and Sunday noon-10:30pm; some are only open in the evenings. Most offer happy hours until 8pm.

- **Revolution,** Collingwood St. (☎0191 261 5774). A modern mecca of mixed drinks in a sizzling atmosphere. Treat your friends to the specialty raspberry mojito (£6). Impressive decor melds the city's 19th-century architecture with massive Roman pillars, flashing lights and pumping bass. Open daily 11am-1am.

- **The Head of Steam,** 2 Neville St. (☎0191 230 4236), across from Central Station. This venue features a chill upstairs bar and up-and-coming bands in the basement. DJs F-Sa 9pm. Live bands M-Th and Su 8pm. Open M-Sa noon-1am, Su noon-midnight.

- **Popolo,** 82 Pilgrim St. (☎0191 232 8923). This stylish hangout has some of the best mixed drinks (£6-8) in Newcastle; try the Tea Green Martini (£6) for a twist on the traditional English drink. Open M-W 11am-midnight, Th-Sa 11am-1am, Su noon-midnight.

- **The Yard,** 2 Scotswood Rd. (☎0191 232 2037). Laid-back GLBT-friendly pub that gets slightly clubbier late at night; the music volume increases, as does the likelihood of sporadic dancing. Uproarious drag shows M and Su. Karaoke Su 5-11pm. Open M-Th 1pm-1am, F-Sa noon-1am, Su 1pm-12:30am.

- **Camp David,** 8-10 Westmorland Rd. (☎0191 232 0860). Casual bar that hosts a free BBQ on its rooftop terrace each evening, with talented DJs spinning nightly. Open M-W 5pm-12:30am, Th-Sa 5pm-1:30am, Su 1pm-12:30am.

CLUBS

Opening hours and special events vary by season. Most clubs expect sharp street wear; leave the sneakers at home.

- **The Cluny,** 36 Lime St. (☎0191 230 4474). Housed in a converted warehouse, this hidden indie hot spot is well worth the 20min. walk from the city center. Catch live bands any night of the week in an intimate gig space and make sure you keep track of that £4 LP you pick up at the merch table—the band you see here tonight will be big tomorrow. Cover changes nightly. Open daily 11am-late.

- **Digital,** Times Sq. (☎0191 261 9755; www.yourfutureisdigital.com). A state-of-the-art sound system keeps things pumping through dawn. Sa night "Shindig" attracts the area's top DJs. Cover £3-12. Open M-Tu and Th 10:30pm-2:30am, F-Sa 10:30pm-4am.

- **The Powerhouse,** Westmorland Rd. (☎0191 261 6824). This large, über-popular gay club is always packed, and with good reason (good music, good drinks, good location). Cover £5-10. Open M-Tu and Su 11pm-3am, F-Sa 11pm-4am.

- **The Baja Beach Club,** Pipewellgate, Gateshead (☎0191 477 6205). Churning out hip-hop hits and pop anthems, this club maintains a huge following thanks in large part to its bikini-clad staff. Stag (bachelor) parties constitute a large chunk of the crowd, especially on weekends. Cover £2-6. Open M and Th-Su 10pm-2am.

- **Tiger Tiger,** The Gate (☎0191 235 7065; www.tigertiger.co.uk). There is always a party to be found at this giant club's 7 bars; you can even time travel through 90s-, 80s-, and 70s-themed rooms. Phone ahead on weekends to be added to the guest list and cruise past the queues, which can be daunting otherwise. M student night. Tu popular salsa night. Cover £4-11. Open M-Sa noon-2am, Su noon-12:30am.

NORTHEAST ENGLAND

NORTHUMBERLAND

While often forgone by tourists in favor of more famed or central destinations, Northumberland National Park is a beautiful area with landscapes varying from the rocky hills of the Cheviots to the heathered moors and green valleys of Tyne and Rede. This corner of England has not always been so tranquil; Hadrian's Wall (p. 456) and the intensely fortified border towns hint at the violence that once dominated the region's history. Today, the park is every outdoorsman's dream, with thrilling hiking, horseback riding, and cycling.

TRANSPORTATION

Renting a car is the easiest way to access the park. Public transportation is limited and requires advance planning. **Buses** offer the most extensive services, and, although getting to the area by bus is tricky (and getting around by bus is even trickier), it is definitely doable with proper planning. The best transportation hubs are Newcastle, Hexham, Alnwick, and Berwick. **Hexham** is best for accessing Hadrian's Wall, and the AD122 bus connects Hexham with Carlisle, Haltwhistle, Corbridge, and Newcastle (in summer M-Sa 12 per day; in spring and fall Su only. Does not run Oct.-Apr.). During the winter, your best bet is to take the train. Hexham also has reliable bus service to many towns with great hiking in the southern region: take bus #880 to Bellingham (M-Sa 10 per day, Su 3 per day). **Alnwick** is a good hub for transportation to the middle of the park, with service to Chillingham and Wooler on buses #470 and 473 (M-Sa 5 per day) and to Warkworth on bus #518 (daily every hr.). In the north, travel from **Berwick** to Wooler on bus #464 (M-Th 6 per day, F-Sa 8 per day), to Bamburgh on bus #411 (M-F 10 per day, Sa 8 per day, Su 4 per day), and to Holy Island on bus #477 (July-Aug. W and Sa 7 per day; Sept.-June M-Sa 7 per day, Su 5 per day). **Newcastle** links all of these hubs, with service to Hexham, Haltwhistle, and Carlisle on bus #685 (M-Sa every hr., Su 4 per day) and service to Morpeth, Alnwick, and Berwick on buses #505, 515, and 525 (M-Sa 14 per day, Su 8 per day). If you're stranded on the west side of the park, don't panic: make your way back to **Carlisle,** where frequent buses and trains run back to Hexham or Newcastle. **Post buses** run varying routes between most towns; contact local TICs for information. Although transportation is complicated, don't give up on your travel plans: the *Experience Northumberland by Bus* brochure is free at any bus station, TIC, or NPIC. This handy little booklet demystifies the entire Northumberland bus system with clear maps and organized timetables.

ORIENTATION AND PRACTICAL INFORMATION

The park runs from **Hadrian's Wall** (p. 456) in the south up along the Scottish border as far north as the Cheviot foothills. **Bellingham, Rothbury,** and **Wooler** are small towns near the park's eastern edge that offer accommodations and access to walking routes. In the southwest just outside the park, Europe's largest manmade lake, **Kielder Water,** surrounded by England's largest manmade forest, **Kielder Forest,** is a popular destination for hikers and cyclists. The A69 marks the park's southern border while the A68 cuts through the center. The Ministry of Defense operates a live firing range in the middle of the park south of the Cheviot Hills. While its well-kept paths make for scenic walking and cycling, they are only open to the public for a month or so each year, usually from mid-April to mid-May. At all times, walkers should heed the warning signs.

Northumberland National Park operates three **National Park Information Centres (NPICs),** which can recommend hikes and activities and book accommodations.

During the warmer months, they offer ranger-led talks and walks. There are also several **Tourist Information Centres** in the area.

National Park Information Centres:

Ingram: Visitor Centre (☎01665 578 890). Open Mar.-Oct. daily 10am-5pm.

Once Brewed: For Hadrian's Wall, see p. 456.

Rothbury: Coquetdale Centre, Church St. (☎01669 620 887). Open May-Oct. daily 10am-5pm; Nov.-Apr. Sa-Su 10am-5pm.

Tourist Information Centres:

Bellingham: Station Yard (☎01434 220 616). Open from mid-May to Sept. M-Sa 9:30am-1pm and 2-5:30pm, Su 1-5pm; Oct and from Easter to mid-May M-Sa 9:30am-1pm and 1:30-5pm, Su 10am-1pm and 1:30-5pm; Nov.-Easter M-F 1-4pm.

Kielder Forest: Visitor Centre (☎01434 250 209), off the C200 in Kielder Castle. Open Apr.-Oct. daily 10am-5pm; Nov.-Dec. Sa-Su 11am-4pm.

Tower Knowe (Kielder): Visitor Centre (☎01434 240 436), off the C200. Open daily July-Aug. 10am-6pm; Sept.-Oct. and Apr.-May 10am-5pm.

Wooler: Cheviot Centre, 12 Padgepool Pl. (☎01668 282 123). Open Easter-Oct. daily 10am-4:30pm; Nov.-Easter. Sa-Su 10am-4:30pm.

CYCLING AND HIKING

Northumberland offers some of the best cycling in England, with miles of traffic-less roads, bridleways, and unused railways. A spectacular section of the mammoth 355 mi. **Pennine Cycleway** runs through Northumberland, as do 92 mi. of the **Tynemouth-Edinburgh Coast and Castles Cycle Route.** The **Reivers Cycle Route** crosses Britain and passes through Kielder Water on its way to the border. The National Cycle Network (☎0845 113 0065; www.nationalcyclenetwork.org.uk) has complete information on all long-touring routes, while TICs and NPICs can give information on short daytrips from most of the towns in the park. Get the free *Cycle Northumbria* brochure at any TIC or check out www.cyclenorthumbria.org.uk to get details on bike-rental shops in the area.

There are also plenty of options for those without wheels. The 268 mi. **Pennine Way** (p. 402) traverses the park, entering at Hadrian's Wall, passing through Bellingham and the Cheviot Hills, and terminating at Kirk Yetholm, Scotland. The slightly shorter, but still ambitious, 80 mi. **Saint Cuthbert's Way** runs through the Cheviot Hills and Wooler on its way between Melrose, Scotland, and Holy Island. Shorter options include walks in the **Simonside Hills,** based out of Rothbury, and the **Cheviot foothills,** based out of Wooler. Ordnance Survey publishes two Explorer maps that together cover the entire park and are available at local NPICs and TICs (£8 each). Many books, including *Walking the Cheviots* (£8), describe walks in depth. The area's isolation makes for beautiful walks, but maps and proper equipment are essential (see **Wilderness Safety,** p. 51). NPICs and TICs can provide hiking tips and suggestions. There are also a number of camping and caravan sites near each town; call the TIC for details. Be prepared to share your tent with swarms of gnats in the warmer months.

BELLINGHAM   ☎(0)1434

With an attractive rural backdrop, modest Bellingham (BELL-in-jum) sits right along the Pennine Way near Hadrian's Wall. Beginning hikers will enjoy the easy 3 mi. round-trip walk to **Hareshaw Linn,** a beautiful waterfall in a rocky gorge that has attracted picnickers since Victorian times. A free guide is available at the TIC at Station Yard (p. 451). A longer 18 mi. hike goes south to Once Brewed. In town, the 12th-century **Church of Saint Cuthbert** was built with a rare stone-vaulted roof so that raiding Border Reivers couldn't burn it down.

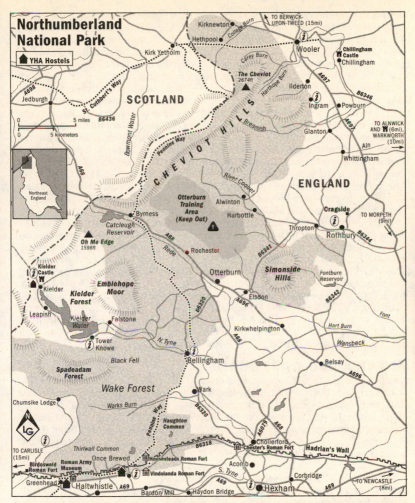

About 10 mi. beyond Bellingham and just outside the park lies **Kielder Water**, the largest artificial lake in the United Kingdom, where travelers can partake in a number of outdoor amusements, from canoeing to stargazing. Buses run only on Sundays, however, so plan your trip carefully. Back in Bellingham, the YHA-affiliated **Demesne Farm** ❶ has a campsite and a small but comfortable bunkhouse. (☎01434 220 258. Self-catering kitchen. Dorms £15, under 18 £12. MC/V.) The all-ensuite **Lyndale Guest House** ❸, West View, has pleasant decor and a hot tub. (☎01434 220 361. Singles £30; doubles £60. MC/V.)

ROTHBURY ☎(0)1669

Rothbury, a market town along the River Coquet, is a popular starting point for excursions into the nearby **Simonside Hills.** Rothbury's NPIC (p. 451) gives advice on local trails. Among them, the **Sacred Mountain Walk** (9 mi.) is a great choice for intermediate hikers, rewarding those who complete its 3-hr. climb with some of the finest views in the park. Another popular choice, **the Rothbury Terraces** (2 mi.), is a good walk for beginning hikers, following an old carriage path and crossing the old Cragside Estate. For detailed information on walks, pick up the free *Rothbury and Coquetdale: Northumberland National Park* at the NPIC or check out www.visit-rothbury.co.uk. One mile north of Rothbury on the B6341 sits ▨**Cragside,** one of the most technologically advanced houses of the 19th century. Built by Lord Armstrong, the house was the first in the world to be lit by hydroelectricity, and today it is home to Lord Armstong's eclectic collection of gadgets. The extensive grounds contain formal gardens, a rhododendron forest, one of the largest rock gardens in Europe, and 1000 acres of woodlands with hiking trails. Bus #508 (5min., June-Sept. Su 2 per day, 70p) connects Newcastle and Cragside via Rothbury. (☎01669 620 333. House open from mid-Mar. to Sept. Tu-Su 1-5:30pm; Oct.-Nov. Tu-Su 1-4:30pm. Last entry 1hr. before close. Gardens open from mid-Mar. to Oct. Tu-Su 10:30am-5:30pm; from Nov. to mid-Dec. W-Su 11am-4pm. £12, children £6, families £29.20; gardens without house £7.70/3.30/18.70.)

Rothbury is home to a host of cozy, if expensive, B&Bs. Charming **Katerina's Guest House** ❹ offers four-post, quilt-covered beds, home-baked scones, and knowledgeable, friendly hosts. (☎01669 620 691; www.katerinasguesthouse. co.uk. Singles from £40; doubles £62-68. Cash only.) Just around the corner from the bus stop, **The Railway Hotel** ❷, on Bridge St., has rooms overlooking the river. (☎01669 620 669; www.railwayhotelrothbury.co.uk. £25 per person. Cash only.) The **Co-op,** High St., sells groceries. (☎01669 620 456. Open daily 8am-10pm.) The **Turk's Head** ❷, on High St., serves pub fare (£6-7) in a cozy indoor room or large garden out back. (Open M-Th and Su noon-2:30pm, F noon-2:30pm and 6:30-9:30pm, Sa 6:30-9:30pm. AmEx/MC/V.) Bus #516 connects Newcastle and Thropton via Rothbury (M-Sa, 7 per day).

ALNWICK AND WARKWORTH   ☎(0)1665

About 31 mi. north of Newcastle off the A1, the small town of Alnwick (AHN-ick) surrounds the magnificent ▨**Alnwick Castle,** home to the Percy family since 1309 (including the current duke and duchess of Northumberland). The castle's memorable profile may look familiar: its manicured grounds and stately home appeared most recently as Hogwarts in the *Harry Potter* films. Don't miss the ornamented state rooms, which display the family's heirlooms and an impressive art collection. (☎01665 510 777. Open from mid-Mar. to Oct. daily 10am-6pm. State rooms open from mid-Mar. to Oct. daily 11am-5pm. Last entry 4:30pm. £10.50, concessions £9, children £4.50, families £27.50.) A short walk from the castle leads to the 40-acre ▨**Alnwick Garden.** Far more than your typical English ornamental rose garden (although it has one of those, too), Alnwick has a bamboo maze, a giant tree house, a carefully gated poison garden, and a cascading fountain. (☎01665 511 350; www.alnwickgarden.com. Open daily Apr.-Sept. 10am-6pm; Oct.-Mar. 10am-4pm. Last entry 45min. before close. £9, concessions £6.50, children 1p.) Although Shakespeare described it as a "worm-eaten hold of ragged stone," today the ruins of 12th-century **Warkworth Castle** make a great stop 7 mi. outside Alnwick. Guarding the mouth of the River Coquet, this Percy fortress was the setting for many scenes of the Bard's *Henry IV.* (☎01665 711 423. Open Apr.-Sept. daily 10am-5pm; Oct. daily 10am-4pm; Nov.-Mar. M and Sa-Su 10am-4pm. £4, concessions £3.20, children £2, families £10. Free audio tour.) A short walk down the river lies the 14th-century **hermitage,** artfully carved right into the Coquet cliffs. Walk down the river from the castle, and the staff will ferry you to the opposite bank. (Open Apr.-Sept. W and Su 11am-5pm. £3, concessions £2.40, children £1.50.)

Many **B&Bs** line Alnwick's Bondgate St. The **Georgian Guest House ❸** has hotel-like rooms just outside the town walls. (☎01665 602 398. Singles from £25; doubles £59.) The **Eating Room ❶**, 39 Market St., is a great place to design your own gourmet sandwich for takeaway or eat-in. (☎01665 606 601. Sandwiches £2-3.50. Open M-Sa 8am-4pm. MC/V.)

The **bus station** is at 10 Clayport St. Buses #505, 515, and 525 connect Alnwick with Berwick (1hr.; M-Sa 8 per day, Su 5 per day) and Newcastle (1hr.; M-Sa 14 per day, Su 5 per day). Buses #420, 422, and 518 make hourly trips between Alnwick and Warkworth (25min.). The **Tourist Information Centre** is located at 2 The Shambles, Market Pl. (☎01665 511 333. Open July-Aug. M-Sa 9am-6pm, Su 10am-4pm; Sept.-June M-Sa 9am-5pm, Su 10am-4pm.) Along Bondgate Without (yes, that's a street name), **Barter Books,** housed in a disused Victorian railway station, provides **Internet** access. The secondhand bookshop also has one of the largest used-book selections in Britain, including shelves upon shelves of rare first editions. (☎01665 604 888. Internet £2 per 30min. Open daily Easter-Oct. 9am-7pm; Nov.-Easter 9am-5pm.) The **post office** is at 19 Market St. (☎01665 602 141. Open M-F 8:45am-5:30pm, Sa 8:45am-12:30pm.) **Postcode:** NE66 1SS.

WOOLER   ☎(0)1668

The town of Wooler makes a good base for exploring the northern part of the park and the nearby **Cheviot Hills** (CHEE-vee-it). A number of short walks include the popular routes to **Humbleton Hill** and a self-guided trail to the Iron Age **Yeavering Bell hill fort,** where evidence of prehistoric civilization is still visible. The long-distance **Saint Cuthbert's Way** also pays Wooler a visit (p. 450). Numerous other hikes leave from Wooler; call the Wooler TIC (p. 450) for suggestions on the walk best suited to your needs. Six miles southeast of Wooler, **Chillingham Castle** is proud of its reputation as "the most haunted castle in England." English eccentricity is on full display here—the castle is crammed with a variety of bizarre objects collected by current owner Sir Humphry Wakefield. Every room holds something different, from tapestries to taxidermy, sculptures to scepters, and gadgets to ghosts; displays have entertaining letters of explanation from Sir Humphry himself. The gloomy dungeon is so dark that some torture devices are only visible using flash photography. The castle also offers a few self-catering **apartments ❹**. Call for rates. (☎01668 215 359. Grounds and garden open May-Sept. M-F and Su noon-5pm. Castle rooms open May-Sept. M-F and Su from 1pm. £6.) In a park beside the castle graze 60-odd **Wild Cattle,** the only entirely purebred cattle in the world. Originally enclosed in 1235, the cattle have been inbred for over seven centuries. They resemble other cattle but cannot be herded, are potentially dangerous, and even kill one of their own if he or she is touched by human hands. (☎01668 215 250. Open Apr.-Oct. M and W-Sa 10am-noon and 2-5pm, Su 2-5pm; by warden-led 1hr. tours only. Tours begin on the hour from the entrance to the cattle park; from the parking lot, follow the signs for "Forest Walk" for two-thirds of a mile and cross the field. £5, concessions £3.) The **Co-op,** 14-18 High St., sells groceries. (☎01668 281 528. Open M-Sa 8am-6pm.) **Internet** access is in the Cheviot Centre, below the TIC. (£1.50 per session. Open M-F 9am-5pm, Sa-Su 10am-4:30pm.)

BERWICK-UPON-TWEED   ☎(0)1289

Just south of the Scottish border, Berwick-upon-Tweed (BARE-ick) has changed hands more often than any town in Britain—13 times between 1296 and 1482 alone. The town's history has helped propagate the local legend that Berwick is still at war with Russia (see **A Really Cold War,** p. 455).

NORTHEAST ENGLAND

⊑ TRANSPORTATION. Berwick is a useful transportation hub for both the Northeastern coast and crossings into Scotland. The **train station** has rail service to Edinburgh (45min., 1-2 per hr., £15.30), London King's Cross (4hr., 1-2 per hour, £116), and Newcastle (50min., 1-2 per hr., £16.30). From the train station, it's a 5min. walk down Castlegate to the town center. Most buses stop at the train station and on Golden Sq. Bus #505/515/525 travels to and from Newcastle (2hr.; M-Sa 7 per day, Su 5 per day; £12.20) via Alnwick (1hr.). Tweed Cycles, 17A Bridge St., provides **bike rental** and good trail advice. (☎01289 331 476. £15 per day. Open M-Sa 9am-5:30pm.)

🔌🔢 ORIENTATION AND PRACTICAL INFORMATION. Berwick straddles the River Tweed via three bridges, including a striking Victorian viaduct that supports the railway. The **Tourist Information Centre,** 106 Marygate, books rooms for a 10% deposit. (☎01289 330 733. Open June-Sept. M-Sa 10am-6pm, Su 11am-4pm; Oct.-May M-Sa 10am-3pm, Su 11am-3pm.) Get free **Internet** access at the **Berwick Library,** Walkergate. (☎01289 334 051. Open M-Tu 10am-5:30pm, W and F 10am-7pm, Sa 9:30am-12:30pm.) The **post office** is on West St. (☎01289 307 596. Open M-F 9am-5:30pm, Sa 9am-12:30pm.) **Postcode:** TD15 1BH.

🔢🔢 ACCOMMODATIONS AND FOOD. Church St. and Castlegate St. are both lined with B&Bs. ◼**Berwick Backpackers ❷,** 56-58 Bridge St., proves that hostels can feel like homes. A jumble of rooms with 20 beds around a central courtyard connects to a bright kitchen and common room. Rooms fill up fast, so book ahead. (☎01289 331 481; www.berwickbackpackers.co.uk. Laundry £5. Free Wi-Fi. Reception M-Sa 9am-noon and 4-8pm. Dorms £17; doubles £60. Cash only.) Warm hospitality greets visitors on the other bank of the Tweed at **Maggie's Guest House ❸,** Main Rd. (☎01289 307 215. Singles £30; doubles £60, ensuite £70. Cash only.) Stock up on groceries at **Somerfield,** Castlegate. (☎01289 308 911. Open M-Sa 8am-8pm, Su 10am-4pm. MC/V.)

Just because Berwick lacks hopping nightlife doesn't mean you can't have a hot night. ◼**Magna Tandoori ❷,** Bridge St., boasts some of the spiciest curry in Northern England. (☎01289 302 736. Entrees £7-12.50; 20% off takeaway. Open daily noon-2pm and 5-11:30pm. MC/V.) At **Foxton's ❸,** 26 Hide Hill, diners can survey exhibitions of local art while they eat. (☎01289 308 448. Entrees £9-12. Open June-Aug. M-Sa 9am-11pm, Su 11am-2pm; Sept.-May M-Sa 9am-11pm. MC/V.) Castlegate is lined with fish-and-chips shops and sandwich places.

◎ SIGHTS. Most of the original **Berwick Castle** is buried beneath the train station, although some of the 13th-century fortress still stands beside the river. The best way to see the town is via a walk around the town wall, including the **Elizabethan Berwick Ramparts,** which replaced the northern and eastern sections of the original medieval wall. Besides affording dramatic views of the coastline and back over the town itself, the walk will take you past the **Berwick Barracks,** at the corner of Parade and Ravensdowne, England's first purpose-built infantry barracks. Before the barracks, soldiers were housed in local taverns or private homes. The barracks also hold the regimental museum of the King's Own Scottish Borderers. (☎01289 307 426. Open Apr.-Sept. W-Su 10am-5pm. £3.40, concessions £2.60, children £1.70.)

🔢 DAYTRIP FROM BERWICK-UPON-TWEED: BAMBURGH CASTLE. Perched high on a rocky outcropping above the shore, **Bamburgh Castle,** a Northumbrian landmark, commands stirring views of the coastline 25 mi. south of Berwick. The public rooms offer a look at one of the largest armories outside London, while the ornate, vaulted ceilings of **King's Hall** house beautiful works of art. Visitors can also watch archaeologists dig in the castle's northern trenches, where workers have unearthed evidence of thousands of years of continuous human occupation. Beyond the dunes, the beaches are better suited for brisk walks than tanning, but they provide great views of the castle. *(Take the 45min. bus #411 from Berwick; the #501 bus between Berwick and Newcastle also offers occasional service to Bamburgh. ☎01668 214 515; www.bamburghcastle.com. Open Apr.-Oct. daily 11am-5pm. Last entry 4:30pm. £7, concessions £6.)*

HOLY ISLAND ☎(0)1289

Ten miles from Berwick-upon-Tweed, windswept Holy Island rises just off the coast. At low tide, it is connected to the mainland by a 5 mi. seaweed-strewn causeway, allowing access to the island via bus, car, or adventurous walk. In AD 627, the missionary Aidan arrived from the Scottish island of Iona to found England's first monastery; while his original wood structure is long gone, the red sandstone ruins of the later **Lindisfarne Priory** offer haunting views from the edge of the island's tiny village. (☎01289 389 200. Open Apr.-Sept. daily 9:30am-5pm; Oct. daily 9:30am-4pm; Nov.-Jan. M and Sa-Su 10am-2pm; Feb.-Mar. M and Sa-Su 10am-4pm. £4, concessions £3.20, children £2.) A free view is available from the low hill behind the ruins. **Saint Cuthbert's Isle,** marked by a wooden cross 660 ft. off the coast of the priory, is where the hermit saint took refuge when even the monastery proved too distracting. A mile's walk from the priory, **Lindisfarne Castle** is a dramatic 16th-century fort that sits atop a hill beside the beach, with a crowded and less inspiring interior of 19th-century furnishings. (☎01289 389 244. Open Mar.-Oct. Tu-Su 4 hr. per day, always including noon-3pm; opening times vary with the tide, so call for exact times the day before. Last entry 30min. before close. £5.40, concessions £2.70.) After returning to the village, try the blend of fermented honey and white wine known as **Lindisfarne Mead,** a syrupy-sweet concoction brewed since ancient times. Free samples are available at **Lindisfarne Limited,** across from the priory. (☎01289 389 230. Opens 30min. before low tide, closes 30min. after.) If the waves trap you, the island does have a few beds, but they fill up quickly despite their staggering rates. The comfortable rooms of **The Bungalow ❹,** Chaire Ends, have views across the fields to the castle. (☎01289 389 308; www.holy-island.info/bungalow. No smoking. 2-night min. stay. Book in advance. Doubles £70. MC/V.) Bus #477 runs from Berwick to Holy Island; times change depending on the tide

THE LOCAL STORY

A REALLY COLD WAR

Since the end of WWII, Europe has embarked on a process of political and economic integration that has only accelerated since the fall of the Soviet Union. For many Europeans, the future holds a promise of cooperation and peace. Not, however, for the citizens of Russia and the small English village of Berwick-upon-Tweed.

Due to an unfortunate accident of semantics, Berwick-upon-Tweed may have been at war with Russia for 153 years. In a 1502 treaty, Berwick was described as being "of" the Kingdom of England rather than "in" it; Berwick received special mention in every ensuing royal proclamation. Nothing came of this inconvenience until 1853, when Queen Victoria signed a declaration of war on Russia, in the name of "Victoria, Queen of Great Britain, Ireland, Berwick-upon-Tweed, and the British Dominions beyond the sea." In the peace treaty ending the war, no mention of Berwick appeared.

Sources vary on what happened next. Some say the matter was cleared up by tsarist Russia in 1914. Others assert a Soviet official signed a peace treaty in 1966 with the mayor of Berwick, who then said, "please tell the Russian people that they can sleep peacefully in their beds." Either way, no official documents have surfaced that can resolve the debate. Berwick, for its part, appears to have no intention of backing down.

(Aug. daily; Sept.-July W and Sa). **Border Cabs** can drive you over the causeway before the tide sweeps in. (☎07769 515 915. £23 to Berwick.)

TIP

TIDAL TROUBLES. Pay close attention to the tide schedules on Holy Island and remember that during high tide the island's causeway becomes completely submerged. Each season, dozens of visitors must be rescued from the water because they try to cross during unsafe times. Even if the causeway looks safe, the tide can rise in a matter of minutes, leaving you in a pretty soggy predicament.

HADRIAN'S WALL   ☎(0)1434

In AD 122, the Roman Emperor Hadrian ordered the construction of a wall to guard Rome's farthest borders, hoping to prevent those uncouth blue-tattooed barbarians to the north from infiltrating his civilized empire. Hadrian's order created the most important Roman monument in Britain, stretching 73 mi. from Bowness on the Solway Firth to Wallsend on the River Tyne. The years have not been kind to the emperor's massive undertaking. Most of the stones have been carted off and reused in surrounding structures, and the portions of wall that do remain either stand at half their original height or are buried under a modern highway. However, the wall and the surrounding Roman ruins give travelers a rare insight into the daily lives of Roman soldiers and citizens. The best-preserved ruins are along the midsection of the wall, at the southern edge of Northumberland National Park (p. 449).

TRANSPORTATION. Although traveling by **car** is the easiest way to see the wall, the **Hadrian's Wall Bus AD122** (who knew public transportation had a sense of humor?) provides daily reliable service to the ruins. Twice a day, the bus has a guide on board who gives an overview of different sights along the wall and their place in Roman England's history. Service runs from Carlisle to Newcastle, stopping at every historical sight, including ruins and museums. Buy the **Hadrian's Wall Bus DayRover Ticket,** available from TICs or bus drivers, to get the most out of your AD122 experience. (2hr.; Apr.-Oct. M-Sa 7 per day, Su 8 per day; 2 per day with guides; DayRover ticket £7.80.) Bus #685 runs year-round between Newcastle and Carlisle via Hexham, Haltwhistle, Greenhead, and other wall towns (2hr.; M-Sa every hr., Su 4 per day). **Trains** (☎08457 484 950) run frequently between Carlisle and Newcastle (1hr., every hr., £10.60), but stations lie at least 1 mi. from the wall; be prepared to hike to the nearest stones. Trains stop at: Brampton, 2 mi. from Lanercost and 5 mi from Birdoswald; Haltwhistle, 2 mi. from Cawfields; Bardon Mill, 2 mi. from Vindolanda and 4 mi. from Housesteads; and Hexham. Make sure to pick up *Hadrian's Wall Bus AD122 Bus & Rail Timetables*, free at any area TIC or bus station.

ORIENTATION AND PRACTICAL INFORMATION. Hadrian's Wall runs 73 mi. between Carlisle in the west and Newcastle in the east, spanning Cumbria, Northumberland, and Tyne and Wear. The towns of **Greenhead, Haltwhistle, Once Brewed, Bardon Mill, Haydon Bridge, Hexham** (the hub of Wall transportation), **Corbridge,** and **Prudhoe** lie parallel to the wall from west to east. For general information, call the **Hadrian's Wall Information Line** (☎01434 322 002; www.hadrians-wall.org). The **National Park Information Centre** in Once Brewed, on Military Rd. (☎01434 344 396; open Apr.-Oct. daily 9:30am-5pm; Nov.-Mar. Sa-Su 10am-3pm), dispenses useful information on outdoor activities around the wall, as does the **Hexham Tourist Information Centre,** at the bottom of the hill from the abbey on Hallgate Rd. (next page), which also books accommodations.

⛺ ACCOMMODATIONS. A number of towns along the wall, such as Carlisle, Hexham, Corbridge, and Haltwhistle, all have many **B&Bs** and make good bases for daytrips. Two hostels lie along the Hadrian's Wall Bus route. **YHA Greenhead ❷,** 16 mi. east of Carlisle near the Greenhead bus stop, is in a converted chapel a short walk from the wall. (☎08707 705 842. Self-catering kitchen. Reception 8-10am and 5-10pm. Curfew 11pm. Dorms £15. MC/V.) **YHA Once Brewed ❷,** Military Rd., Bardon Mill, is centrally located—the AD122 stops right at its front door half a mile from the wall. (☎08707 705 980. Breakfast £4. Packed lunch £3.50-4.50. Dinner from £7. Laundry £1. Internet £2.50 per 30min. at the Twice Brewed pub next door. Reception 8-10am and 4-10pm. Open Feb.-Nov. Dorms £15, under 18 £10. MC/V.) The isolated **Hadrian Lodge ❸** makes a good base for serious walkers. Take a train to Haydon Bridge, then follow the main road uphill 2 mi. Relax in the spacious rooms and have a pint at the bar and lounge. (☎01434 684 867. Singles £39.50; doubles £59.50. AmEx/MC/V.)

🏛🚶 SIGHTS AND OUTDOOR ACTIVITIES. As you head west from Newcastle or north from Hexham, the cavalry fort of **Chesters** lies beside the wall a quarter-mile walk west of Chollerford. The well-preserved remains of a bathhouse show just how seriously the Romans took their hygiene—hot saunas and cooling rooms sit alongside a still-intact latrine. (☎01434 681 379. Open daily Apr.-Sept. 10am-6pm; Oct. 10am-5pm; Nov.-Mar. 10am-4pm. £4.50, concessions £4.) Even farther to the west, **Housesteads** is a popular site because of its size and location. Set half a mile from the road on a ridge overlooking the Northumbrian countryside, the extensive ruins adjoin one of the best-preserved sections of the wall. (☎01434 344 363. Open daily Apr.-Sept. 10am-6pm; Oct. 10am-5pm; Nov.-Mar. 10am-4pm. £4.50, concessions £3.80, children £2.60.) Just 1 mi. southeast of Once Brewed, archaeologists find artifacts daily at the ongoing excavation of the 🏛**Vindolanda** fort and settlement; watch them at work any day of the week. Wander around the ruins of a fort, bath, temples, and reconstructed turf and stone walls. The on-site museum houses their previous finds, including the oldest writing in Britain. (☎01434 344 277; www.vindolanda.com. Open daily Apr.-Sept. 10am-6pm; from Oct. to mid-Nov. and from mid-Feb. to Mar. 10am-5pm; from mid-Nov. to mid-Feb. 10am-4pm. Last entry 45min. before close. £5.20, concessions £4.30; Joint Saver tickets with Roman Army Museum £8/6.80.) In Carvoran, 1 mi. northeast of Greenhead, the **Roman Army Museum,** five stops from Vindolanda on the AD122, houses an impressive array of Roman artifacts. A short film (every 30min.) and interactive displays help recreate the daily lives of the soldiers on the wall and give a feel for how impressive the wall was in its heyday—which is helpful, because now there isn't much left of it to see. (☎01697 747 485. Open daily Apr.-Sept. 10am-6pm; Oct.-Nov. and Feb.-Mar. 10am-5pm. Last entry 30min. before close. £4.20, concessions £3.70; Joint Saver tickets with Vindolanda £8/6.80.)

Known to the Romans as "Banna," **Birdoswald Roman Fort,** 15 mi. east of Carlisle, affords views of the surrounding walls, turrets, and milecastles. The interactive **Visitor's Centre** traces Birdoswald's 2000-year-old history with an audiovisual exhibit. (☎01697 747 602. Open daily Apr.-Sept. 10am-5:30pm; Oct. and Mar. 10am-4pm. Last entry 30min. before closing. Museum and wall £4.50, concessions £3.60, child £3.30.) To the west of Carlisle, on the cliffs of Maryport, the **Senhouse Museum** houses Britain's oldest antiquarian collection, with exhibits on Roman religion and warfare. (☎01900 816 168; www.senhousemuseum.co.uk. Open July-Oct. daily 10am-5pm; Nov.-Mar. F-Su 10:30am-4pm; Apr.-June

Tu and Th-Su 10am-5pm. £2.50.) Follow the footsteps of the legions on the **Hadrian's Wall National Trail,** an 84 mi., six-day route from coast to coast. The trail also links to over 80 short walks around the wall. Guides and information are available at TICs. Alternatively, the recently opened **Hadrian's Cycleway** gives access to all the wall's main attractions following minor roads and traffic-free cycle paths. *The English Heritage Guidebook of Hadrian's Wall* (£5 from TICs, some hostels, and entrances to some sights) describes tours through each attraction, pointing out highlights and detailing history.

HEXHAM   ☎(0)4134

The small market town of Hexham is one of the best bases for exploring Hadrian's Wall. The cobbled town center encircles the impressive **Hexham Abbey,** a site of Christian worship since AD 674. The abbey's main building dates mostly to the 12th century, although the seventh-century crypts are largely intact. (☎04134 602 031; www.hexhamabbey.org.uk. Open daily 9:30am-5pm. Suggested donation £3.) Facing the abbey, the well-fortified 14th-century **Moot Hall** bears the marks of Hexham's turbulent struggle against Scottish Border Reivers. More of the area's dark history can be found in the 14th-century dungeon of the **Hexham Old Gaol,** England's first purpose-built prison (before then, most prisons were converted castles or abbeys with dungeons), behind Market Pl. on Hallgate. Even prisons have a sense of humor: a sign above the entrance reads, "Welcoming guests for 600 years..." (☎04134 652 351. Open daily Mar.-Oct. 10am-4:30pm; Nov. and Feb. M-Tu and Sa 10am-4:30pm. £3.80.)

Budget accommodations are scarce in Hexham; call the TIC for availability. A path lined with flowers leads to the front door of the ◪**West Close House** ❸, which treats you like family and boasts beautiful, gleaming wood floors and a garden. Walk along Priestpopple Rd. away from town for 10min. and take a left at the stoplight onto Allendale Rd.; the next left is Hextol Terr. Follow this all the way to the end, and the house will be on your left. (☎04134 603 307. From £27.50 per person. Cash or check only.) Hungry in Hexham? Right across from the abbey, ◪**Not Simply Capuchin** ❶, 17 Market Pl., is a tiny hole in the wall that whips up mouthwatering takeaway meals in minutes. Try its huge sandwiches made on freshly baked bread with fillings like chicken tikka for just £2.50. (☎04134 600 165. Food from £2-4.50. Open M-Sa 9am-5pm. MC/V.)

The **train station** is a 10min. walk from the abbey and the town center. The **Tourist Information Centre** stands between the train station and town center, on the edge of a large car park and down Hallgate from the marketplace. (☎04134 652 220. Open May-Sept. M-Sa 9am-6pm, Su 10am-5pm; Oct.-Apr. M-Sa 9am-5pm.) Other services include: **banks** with **ATMs,** along Priestpopple Rd.; **Internet** access at the **library,** Beaumont St., inside Queens Hall (☎04134 652 488; open M and F 9:30am-7pm, Tu-W 9:30am-5pm, Sa 9:30am-12:30pm; Internet £1 per session); and the **post office,** Priestpopple Rd., in Robbs (☎04134 602 001; open M-F 9am-5:30pm, Sa 9am-3pm). **Postcode:** NE46 1NA.

WALES (CYMRU)

Known to early Anglo-Saxon settlers as *waleas* (foreigners), but self-identified as *cymry* (compatriots), the people of Wales (pop. 3,000,000) have always had a fraught relationship with their neighbors to the east. Although they share an island with the English, the Welsh assert their national independence with pride; if many had their choice, they would be floating miles away. The Welsh language endures in conversation, commerce, and literature. When heavy industry became unprofitable after a technology boom in the 1970s, Wales turned its attention to tourism. Travelers today are lured by peaceful towns and imposing castles nestled among miles of beaches, cliffs, and mountains.

TRANSPORTATION

GETTING THERE

Most travelers reach Wales through London. **Flights** to Cardiff International Airport originate within the UK and from a few European destinations. **Aer Arann** flies to Cardiff from Dublin for about £20-40. **Ferries** cross the Irish Sea, shuttling travelers between Ireland and Holyhead, Pembroke, Fishguard, and Swansea (see **By Ferry**, p. 40). Frequent trains leave London for Cardiff (2hr., from £11); call **National Rail Enquiries** (☎08457 484 950; www.nationalrail.co.uk) or **Arriva Wales** (☎08456 061 660; www.arrivatrainswales.co.uk) for schedules and prices. National Express **buses** (☎08717 818 181; www.nationalexpress.com) are a slower, cheaper way to get to Wales: a trip from London to Cardiff takes about 3hr. and costs £5-25.

GETTING AROUND

BY TRAIN. BritRail (☎+1-866-BRIT-RAIL; www.britrail.com) passes are accepted on all trains, except narrow-gauge railways, throughout Wales; check their website for more information about a variety of combination passes. Call Arriva Trains (☎08456 061 660) for information. **Narrow-gauge railways** tend to be tourist attractions rather than actual means of transportation, but train-spotters can purchase a **Great Little Trains of Wales Discount Card** (£10; www.greatlittletrainsofwales.co.uk), which gives a 20% discount on a round-trip journey on each of the nine member rail lines.

BY BUS. The overlapping routes of Wales's numerous bus operators are difficult to navigate. Most are local services; most regions are dominated by one or two companies. **Traveline** has updated bus information for all services (☎08712 002 233; www.traveline-cymru.org.uk); regional carriers, unless noted, use Traveline for ticket booking and customer service. **Cardiff Bus** (☎02920 666 444; www.cardiffbus.com) blankets the area around the capital. **TrawsCambria** runs the main north-south bus routes from Cardiff and Swansea to Aberystwyth, Machynlleth, and Bangor. **Stagecoach** (www.stagecoachbus.com) buses serve routes from Cambridge and Hereford in England; the routes cover the Wye

WALES

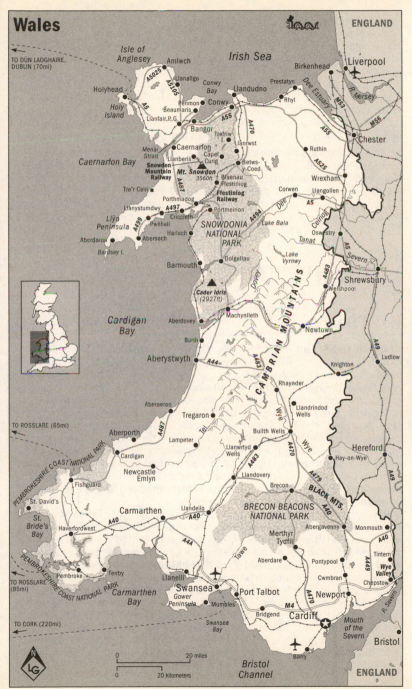

Wales

Isle of Anglesey

TO DÚN LAOGHAIRE, DUBLIN (70mi)

Irish Sea

ENGLAND

Amlwch
Llanallgo
Holyhead
A5025
A5105
Llanddwyn
Conwy Bay
Llandudno
Prestatyn
Rhyl
Birkenhead
Liverpool
R. Mersey

Holy Island
Penmon
Beaumaris
Conwy
A55

Llanfair P.G.
Bangor
Trefriw
Llanrwst
Ruthin
Chester
A55

Caernarfon Bay
Caernarfon
Capel Curig
Betws-y-Coed
Corwen
Wrexham
A525

Menai Strait
Llanberis
Snowdon Mountain Railway
Mt. Snowdon
3560ft
Blaenau Ffestiniog
Llangollen
A5

Tre'r Ceiri
Porthmadog
Ffestiniog Railway
Lake Bala
Oswestry
Dee
Ceiriog

Llanystumdwy
A497
Criccieth
Portmeirion
A494
Tanat

Llŷn Peninsula
A499
Pwllheli
Harlech
SNOWDONIA NATIONAL PARK
Lake Vyrnwy
Severn
A5

Aberdaron
Abersoch
Barmouth
Dolgellau
Dovey
Welshpool
Shrewsbury
A483

Bardsey I.

Cader Idris (2927ft)

Cardigan Bay
Aberdovey
Machynlleth
Newtown
A49

Borth
CAMBRIAN MOUNTAINS
Ludlow

Aberystwyth
A44
A483
Knighton

Rhayader
Wye

Aberaeron
Llandrindod Wells

Tregaron
Teifi
Builth Wells
Hereford

Aberporth
A487
Lampeter
Llanwrtyd Wells
Hay-on-Wye
A49

TO ROSSLARE (65mi)
Cardigan
Llandovery
A483
A470
A479

PEMBROKESHIRE COAST NATIONAL PARK
Newcastle Emlyn
Llandeilo
Brecon
BLACK MTS.
A40

Fishguard
Carmarthen
A40
BRECON BEACONS NATIONAL PARK
Abergavenny
Monmouth
A40

St. David's
Haverfordwest
A40
A4A
Merthyr Tydfil
Pontypool
Tintern
A449

St. Bride's Bay
Tawe
Aberdare
Cwmbran
Wye Valley
Chepstow

Pembroke
Tenby
Llanelli
Port Talbot
Newport
A470

TO ROSSLARE (85mi)
PEMBROKESHIRE COAST NATIONAL PARK
Carmarthen Bay
Gower Peninsula
Swansea
Mumbles
M4
R. Severn

TO CORK (220mi)
Swansea Bay
Bridgend
Cardiff
Mouth of the Severn
Bristol

Barry
Bristol Channel
ENGLAND

0   20 miles
0   20 kilometers

Valley, Abergavenny, and Brecon. **First Cymru** (☎01792 582 233; www.firstgroup. com/ukbus/wales/swwales/home) covers the Gower peninsula and southwest Wales, including Pembrokeshire Coast National Park. **Arriva Cymru** (☎08448 004 411; www.arriva.co.uk) provides service in North Wales. Regional public transportation guides, available free at Tourist Information Centres (TICs), exist for many areas, but for some you'll have to consult an array of small brochures. The very useful *Wales Bus, Rail, and Tourist Map and Guide* gives information on routes but not timetables. Local buses often don't run on Sunday. Some special tourist buses, however, run only on Sundays in summer. Bus schedules and prices change often; check them often and in advance.

BY FOOT, BICYCLE, AND THUMB. Wales has numerous beautiful, well-marked footpaths and cycling trails; the **Offa's Dyke Path** (p. 475) and the **Pembrokeshire Coast Path** (p. 491) are particularly popular. The **Wales Tourist Board** (☎08708 300 306; www.visitwales.com) maintains the websites Walking Wales (www.walking.visitwales.com) and Cycling Wales (www.cycling.visitwales.com) and publishes print guides of the same names. The **Countryside Council for Wales** (☎0845 1306 229; www.ccw.gov.uk) may also be helpful.

LIFE AND TIMES

HISTORY

CELTS, ROMANS, AND NORMANS. Thanks to widespread emigration and invasion by its neighbors, Wales has been influenced by an eclectic mix of peoples and cultures since prehistoric times. Stone, Bronze, and Iron Age inhabitants dotted the Welsh landscape with stone villages, earth-covered forts, and *cromlechs* (stone-chambered tombs also known as dolmens). Ruins of these settlements still stand as reminders of Wales's earliest residents. It was the **Celts,** however, who became the area's most influential settlers and resident rabble-rousers. Celts from northern Europe and the Iberian peninsula immigrated to Wales during the fourth and third centuries BC and established a lively warrior culture. In AD 59, when Romans had invaded much of Britain, the wily Celts resisted occupation and fought the Romans at the fortress at Segontium (present-day Caernarfon, p. 524), beginning a long Welsh tradition of conflict and struggle for independence.

When the Romans departed from Britannia in the early 5th century, they left behind not only towns, amphitheaters, and roads but also the Latin language and Christianity—both of which became central to the development of Welsh society. For the next 700 years, the Celts (supposedly once ruled by **King Arthur** and his wizard friend Myrddin, or **Merlin**) did their best to hold back invasions from Saxons, the Irish, and Vikings. Their best wasn't quite enough in the eighth century, when the Anglo-Saxon **King Offa** and his troops pushed what Celts remained in England into Wales and other corners of the island. To make sure they stayed put, Offa built **Offa's Dyke** (p. 475), a 150-mile dirt wall that marked the first official border between England and Wales. Although connected by language and law, the Celtic kingdoms of Wales did not unify until the 13th century, when **Llywelyn ap Gruffydd** became the only Welsh ruler recognized by the English as the Prince of Wales.

THE ENGLISH CONQUEST. Within 50 years of William the Conqueror's invasion of England in 1066, the **Normans** had taken over a quarter of Wales. They built a series of castles and market towns, established the feudal system, and introduced a variety of continental monastic orders. The English **Plantagenet** kings invaded Wales throughout the 13th century. After killing Prince Llywelyn Ein Llyw Olaf (or "Llywelyn the Last") in 1282, **Edward I** of England dubbed his son the new "Prince of Wales." Two years later, he dubbed the Welsh "English subjects." To keep these perennially unruly subjects in check, Edward constructed a ring of castles at strategic spots throughout Wales. These include magnificent surviving fortresses at **Conwy** (p. 510), **Caernarfon** (p. 524), **Caerphilly** (p. 474), **Harlech** (p. 521), and **Beaumaris** (p. 530).

In the early 15th century, the bold insurgent warfare of **Owain Glyndŵr** temporarily freed Wales from English rule. Reigniting Welsh nationalism, Glyndŵr and his followers captured the castles at Conwy and Harlech, threatened the stronghold of Caernarfon, and convened a national parliament at **Machynlleth.** Despite support from abroad the rebellion soon waned due to poverty, war, plague, and Glyndŵr's mysterious disappearance. With one leader gone, Wales placed its hope in Welsh-born **Henry VII**, who emerged victorious from the Wars of the Roses and ascended to the English throne in 1485.

The 1536 **Act of Union** granted the Welsh the same rights as English citizens and returned the administration of Wales to the local gentry. The act officially "united and annexed" the country and gave Wales parliamentary representation. The **Court of Great Session** was established in 1543 and remained the law of the land until 1830. Legal equality came at the price of assimilation, and English quickly became the language of the Welsh courts, government, and gentry.

Throughout the 17th century, the consolidation of land into large **gentry estates** stratified Welsh society and demonstrated the difficulty of sustaining the booming population. Though certain prominent noblemen supported the parliamentary cause, many Welsh harbored sympathy for the monarchy at the onset of the Civil War. Pockets of religious resistance also proliferated as the result of the efforts of Puritan missionaries; Baptists, nonconformists, and Quakers all gained footholds during this period.

CHURCH AND CHARTISTS. Profound religious shifts changed Welsh society in the 18th and 19th centuries. As the church became more Anglicized and tithes grew more burdensome, the Welsh grew receptive to new Protestant sects. The **Methodist revolution** attracted 80% of the population by 1851. Life centered on the chapel, which housed tight local communities of shared religion, heritage, and language. **Chapel life** remains one of the most distinctive features of today's Welsh society, and many businesses still close on Sunday.

As the **Industrial Revolution** swept the isles in the 19th century, industrialists exploited Wales's rich deposits of coal, slate, and iron. New roads, canals, and, most importantly, **steam railways** were built to transport these raw materials, and the Welsh population grew from 450,000 to 1,200,000 between 1750 and 1851. Especially in the south, pastoral landscapes were transformed into grim mining wastelands. Those who labored in these dismal mines also endured dangerous working conditions and low pay. When early attempts at unionism failed, the workers turned to violence. The **Chartist Movement,** which demanded political representation for all men, culminated in a deadly uprising in Newport in 1839 and won small victories for organized labor. Welsh society became characterized by two forces: emigration and a leftist political consciousness. Welsh tenant farmers led the **Rebecca Riots** against the government and wealthy landowners from 1839 to 1843. Attempts to secure autonomy reached a peak in the **Home Rule** movement of 1886-96 but fizzled due to internal dissent.

WALES

The strength of the Liberal Party bolstered the career of Welshman **David Lloyd George,** who rose from homegrown rabble-rouser to be Britain's prime minister from 1916 to 22. **World War I** hit Wales hard; over 35,000 Welsh soldiers never returned from battle. This loss was compounded by continued emigration and the **economic depression** of the 1930s.

THE LANGUAGE BARRIER. Issues of national language came to the forefront in the latter half of the 20th century. Renewed nationalism and nonviolent protest led to the **1967 Welsh Language Act,** which established the legitimacy of both Welsh and English in legal courts. The 1988 **Education Reform Act** ensured that all Welsh children would be introduced to English. Welsh publications, radio stations, and even a Welsh television channel (Sianel Pedwar Cymru, "Channel 4 Wales") have emerged and thrived, and the **1993 Welsh Language Act** stipulated that Welsh and English should be regarded as equal in public business.

Nationalist movements emerged in other political arenas as well. The efforts of **Plaid Cymru,** the Welsh Nationalist Party, were rewarded on September 18, 1997, when the Welsh voted in favor of **devolution** to make Wales a sovereign nation. The referendum squeaked by with only 50.3% support, but Wales has finally gotten a taste of its long-sought self-governance with the 60-seat **Welsh Assembly.** Still, Wales retains strong bonds with Westminster. Unlike Scotland, it shares its educational and legal system with England.

WALES TODAY

Long home to a distinct culture and people, Wales is beginning to grow into its new role as a more independent political entity. The road has been rocky: poverty and unemployment, caused by the decline of the coal and steel industries, have proven stubborn despite efforts at **economic rebuilding.** A recent surge in **tourism** is promising, however, and visitors are discovering a Wales that outshines its conflict-ridden, industrial past. **Cardiff** (p. 467), the Welsh capital since 1955, has reinvented itself as a center of art and culture, and much of the rest of the country is following suit.

CULTURE AND CUSTOMS

Cardiff's cosmopolitan bustle rivals that of other European cities, but the real Wales lies in rural towns and villages, where pleasantries are exchanged across hedges, locals swap gossip at the post office, and a visitor can expect to remain anonymous for about three minutes. Welsh friendliness and hospitality seem unfailing: conversations and cheerful attention abound. The Welsh language is an important part of everyday life, and travelers can expect to find road signs, pamphlets, and timetables written both in English and Welsh. **Nationalism** runs deep, and the Welsh are fiercely proud of their history and heritage.

Wales has long been a country defined by a tradition of **folk culture.** The country's unique traditions—witnessing an **eisteddfod** (p. 466), listening to a harmonic male choir, or tasting homemade baked goods—are as enlightening as they are enjoyable. Welsh national symbols include the **red dragon,** the **leek,** and the **daffodil.** The red dragon, a battle emblem throughout Welsh history, also appears on the Welsh flag. In honor of Wales's patron saint, **Saint David's Day** is celebrated on March 1 and is a perfect opportunity to see the Welsh **national costume**—a long red cloak and tall black hat. **All Hallow's Eve** (Oct. 31) has traditional significance for the Welsh as the Celtic New Year.

LANGUAGE

Let me not understand you, then; speak it in Welsh.
—William Shakespeare, *Henry IV, Part 1*

Although modern *Cymraeg* (Welsh) borrows from English, as a member of the **Celtic family** of languages, it is based on an entirely different grammar. Today, one fifth of the country speaks Welsh, one eighth as a first language. Welsh-speaking communities are particularly common in the rural north and west.

Although English suffices nearly everywhere in Wales, some familiarity with the language will help to avoid garbling the names of destinations. Welsh shares with German the deep, guttural **ch** heard in "Bach" or "loch." **Ll**—the unfortunately common and confounding Welsh consonant—is produced by placing your tongue against the top of your mouth as if you were going to say "l" and blowing. If this technique proves baffling, try saying "hl" (hlan-GO-hlen for "Llangollen"). **Dd** is pronounced "th" as in "there" (hence the county of Gwynedd is pronounced "Gwyneth"). **C** and **g** are always hard, as in "cat" and "Gosh, this language is complicated." **W** is generally used as a vowel and sounds like the "oo" in either "drool" or "good." **U** is pronounced like the "e" in "he." Tricky **y** changes its sound with its placement in the word, sounding either like the "u" in "ugly" or the "i" in "ignoramus." **F** is spoken as a "v," as in "vertigo," and **ff** sounds exactly like the English "f." Emphasis nearly always falls on the penultimate syllable, and there are (happily) no silent letters.

Most Welsh place names are derived from prominent features of the landscape. *Afon* means "river," *betws* or *llan* "church" or "enclosure," *caer* "fort," *llyn* "lake," *mynydd* "mountain," and *ynys* "island." The Welsh call their land *Cymru* (KUM-ree) and themselves *Cymry* (KUM-ruh). Because of the Welsh system of letter mutation, many words appear with different initial consonants. For example, *cath* (meaning "it"), pronounced "cat," may be seen as "gath," "chath," or "nghath." For more Welsh words, see the **Appendix**, p. 719.

THE ARTS

LITERATURE

In Wales, as in other Celtic countries, much of the national literature stems from a vibrant **bardic tradition.** The earliest poetry in Welsh comes from sixth century northern England, where the **cynfeirdd** (early poets), including the influential poet **Taliesin,** composed oral verse for their patron lords. The ninth through 11th centuries brought sagas focusing on pseudo-historical figures, most notably the legend of **King Arthur.** In the 14th century, **Dafydd ap Gwilym** developed the flexible poetic form *cywydd*. Often called the greatest Welsh poet, he turned to nature, love, and sexual ribaldry as subjects and influenced the work of later poets such as **Dafydd Nanmor** and **Iolo Goch.** The Anglicization of the Welsh gentry in the 18th century led to a decline in the tradition of courtly bards.

In 1588, Bishop William Morgan wrote the **Welsh translation of the Bible,** which helped standardize the language and provided the foundation for literacy throughout Wales. A circle of popular romantic Welsh poets, **Y Beirdd Newydd** (the New Poets), including **T. Gwynn Jones** and **WJ Gruffydd,** were active in the early 20th century, but the horrors of the First World War caused an anti-Romantic backlash typified by the poetry of **Hedd Wyn.** Subsequent authors wrote about Welsh identity and national ideals in both Welsh and English. One of the best-known Welsh writers is Swansea's **Dylan Thomas,** whose emotionally powerful poetry, as well as popular works like *A Child's Christmas in Wales* and the radio play *Under Milk Wood*, describe his homeland with nostalgia, humor, and occasional bitterness. Wales's literary heritage is preserved in the **National Library of Wales** in Aberystwyth (p. 501), which receives a copy of every Welsh-language book published in the UK.

MUSIC

The Welsh word **canu** means both "to sing" and "to recite poetry," and indeed music and literature are closely linked in Welsh culture. Although little Welsh music from before the 17th century has survived, traditional medieval music was likely played on instruments like the **harp**, the **pipe** (hornpipe or bagpipe), and the **crwth**, a six-stringed bowed instrument. The indigenous musical tradition began to disappear in the 16th century, and traditional playing died out by the 17th century. The rise of chapels in the 18th century led to a lasting tradition of church music. Composers adapted Welsh folk tunes into sacred songs, and the hymns of composers such as **Ann Griffiths** became popular. Wales developed its famed harmonic **choral singing** in the 19th and 20th centuries. Although many associate the all-male choir with Welsh culture, both single-sex and mixed choirs are still an integral part of traditional life, and choral festivals like the **cymanfa ganu** (singing meeting) occur throughout Wales.

Cardiff's **Saint David's Hall** regularly hosts both Welsh and international orchestras. The **Welsh National Opera,** featuring renowned tenor **Bryn Terfel,** has established a worldwide reputation. The most famous classical export is soprano **Charlotte Church,** who earned international attention with her 1998 debut, *Voice of an Angel.* Pop stars **Tom Jones** and **Shirley Bassey** topped charts in the 70s, but **rock music** is the voice of today's youth, expressing satirical but often fiercely nationalist sentiment about life in Wales. Current popular Welsh bands, like the **Lostprophets, Super Furry Animals,** and **Funeral for a Friend,** range from Britpop to hardcore and are gaining recognition on an international scale.

FOOD

Traditional Welsh cooking relies on leeks, potatoes, onions, dairy products, lamb (considered the best in the world), pork, fish, and seaweed. Rich soups and stews like **cawl** are usually accompanied by bread. Wales produces a wide range of dairy products, including **Caerphilly,** a soft white cheese. **Welsh rarebit** (also called "Welsh rabbit") is buttered toast topped with a thick, cheesy, mustard-beer sauce. Most visitors are drawn to the distinctive, tasty **breads and cakes**—buttery, scone-like treats studded with currants and golden raisins and traditionally cooked on a bakestone or griddle. The adventurous may want to sample **laverbread** (a cake-like slab made of seaweed), while the sweet-toothed will love **bara brith** (a fruit and nut bread served with butter) and **teisennau hufen** (fluffy, doughnut-like cakes filled with whipped cream). **Cwrw** (beer) is another Welsh staple; **Brains SA** is the major brewer in Wales.

FESTIVALS

The most significant of Welsh festivals is the **eisteddfod** (ice-TETH-vod), a celebration of Welsh literature (chiefly poetry), music, and arts and crafts that dates back to the 12th century. Hundreds of local *eisteddfodau* are held each year, generally lasting from one to three days. The most important of these is the **Eisteddfod Genedlaethol Cymru** (National Eisteddfod), which takes place annually in the first week of August and usually alternates between North and South Wales (www.eisteddfod.org.uk). The **International Musical Eisteddfod,** held in Llangollen (p. 507) in July and August, draws folk dancers, singers, and choirs from around the world for performances and competitions.

SOUTH WALES

The coasts and crags of South Wales have witnessed countless episodes of invasion and oppression, from 12th-century English kings to 1980s mining shutdowns. Once reliant upon the coal and shipping industries, South Wales has reinvented itself with cultural centers and peaceful wilderness trails. The scarred mining fields of its central hills, pastoral scenes of its river valleys, and grit and hum of its major ports draw tourists in rapidly increasing numbers. Today, the land manages to maintain both its rural charms and growing urban savvy, drawing from the best of its English influences and Welsh heritage.

HIGHLIGHTS OF SOUTH WALES

HIKE the Wye Valley for views of **Tintern Abbey** (p. 476) and proceed north to the stark peaks of **Brecon Beacons National Park** (p. 477).

BROWSE the shelves of **Hay-on-Wye's** literary wonderland, which boasts the largest secondhand bookstore in the world (p. 484).

EXPLORE the rugged coastline of **Pembrokeshire National Park** (p. 491), home to the holiday town of **Tenby** (p. 494) and the majestic St. David's Cathedral (p. 498).

CARDIFF (CAERDYDD) ☎ (0)2920

Cardiff calls itself "Europe's Youngest Capital" and seems eager to meet the demands of the title, presenting rich history alongside its metropolitan renaissance. Standing next to traditional monuments are landmarks of a different tenor: a towering new stadium by the River Taff and an array of cosmopolitan dining and entertainment venues. At the same time, local pride, shown in the red dragons on flags and in windows, remains as strong as ever.

▣ TRANSPORTATION

Trains: Central Station, Central Sq., south of the city center, behind the bus station. Ticket office open M-Sa 5:40am-9:30pm, Su 8am-9:30pm. Trains (☎08457 484 950; www.nationalrail.com) to: **Bath** (1-1½hr., 1-3 per hr., £15); **Birmingham** (2hr., 3 per hr., £35); **Bristol** (35min., 4 per hr., £8.80); **Edinburgh** via **Bristol Parkway** or **Crewe** (6½-8hr., 2 per hr., £110.50); **London Paddington** (2hr., 2 per hr., £56); **Swansea** (1hr., 2-3 per hr., £5.20).

Buses: Central Station, on Wood St. National Express booking office and travel center. Open M-Sa 7am-6pm, Su 9am-5:45pm. National Express (☎08705 808 080; www. nationalexpress.com) to: **Birmingham** (2½hr., 4 per day, £22.50); **London** (3hr., 17 per day, £21.30); **London Gatwick** (5hr., 17 per day, £42.50); **London Heathrow** (3hr., 17 per day, £38.50); **Manchester** (5-8hr., 6 per day, £35.10). Pick up timetables at the bus station and a free *Wales Bus, Rail, and Tourist Map and Guide* at the TIC.

Local Transportation: Cardiff Bus (Bws Caerdydd), St. David's House, Wood St. (☎02920 666 444). Office open M-F 8:30am-5:30pm, Sa 9am-4:30pm. Runs a 4-zone network of green and orange buses in Cardiff and surrounding areas. Stops are often shared with Stagecoach and other carriers. Schedules can be unreliable, especially on Su. Service ends M-Sa 11:20pm, Su 11pm. Fares start at £1.20, reduced for seniors and children. Week-long **Multiride Passes** available (£14, children £8.50). **Day to Go** tickets allow

1 day of unlimited travel in the greater Cardiff area and can be purchased from drivers (£3, children £2, families £7). Pick up the free *Pocket Guide to Bus Services and Bus, Rail and Tourist Map* from the bus station or TIC.

Taxis: Delta (☎02920 202 020). **Dragon** (☎02920 333 333). Both 24hr.

◼ ☐ ORIENTATION AND PRACTICAL INFORMATION

Cardiff Castle is the historical center of the city, although the shops lining **Queen Street** and **The Hayes** see much of Cardiff's foot traffic. Farther west, the **River Taff** bounds **Bute Park Arboretum,** separating residential neighborhoods from downtown and flowing into **Cardiff Bay.** The Civic Centre, university, and National Gallery are north of the castle. Cardiff's signature **arcades,** covered pedestrian shopping lanes south of the castle, provide much of the city's cultural fare.

Tourist Information Centre: The Hayes (☎0870 1211 258; www.visitcardiff.com), in the newly renovated Old Library. Books rooms for £2 plus a 10% deposit. Luggage storage available. Internet £1 per 30min. Open M-Sa 9:30am-6pm, Su 10am-4pm.

Tours: City Sightseeing Cardiff (☎02920 473 432; www.city-sightseeing.com). Hop-on, hop-off bus tour that departs from Cardiff Castle. From mid-Mar. to Sept. daily every 30min.; Sept.-Nov. Sa-Su every hr.; from Feb. to mid-Mar. daily every hr. Purchase tickets on board or online. £8, concessions £6, children £4, families £20. **Cardiff Waterbus** (☎07940 142 409; www.cardiffcats.com) vehicles tour Cardiff Bay, starting in Penarth and passing Mermaid Quay. In summer every hr. £5, children £3.

Banks: Banks with **ATMs** line Queen St. and St. Mary St. **American Express,** 3 Queen St. (☎02920 649 305). Open M-F 9am-5:30pm, Sa 9am-5pm. **Thomas Cook,** 16 Queen St. (☎08453 089 192). Commission-free **bureau de change.** Open M-Th and Sa 9am-5:30pm, F 10am-5:30pm, Su 11am-4pm.

Beyond Tourism: Signs advertising work appear in many windows during the tourist and rugby seasons. **The Volunteer Centre,** 109 St. Mary St. (☎02920 227 625; www.volunteering-wales.net), on the 3rd fl. Listings for volunteer possibilities in and around Cardiff. Open M-F 10am-4pm. **Job Centre Plus,** 64 Charles St. (☎02920 428 400). Open M-Tu and Th-F 9am-5pm, W 10am-5pm.

Luggage Storage: At the TIC. £3-5 per item; £3 deposit.

Library: Bute St. (☎02920 382 116), just past the rail bridge. Free Internet in 30min. slots. Sign up in advance. Open M-W and F 9am-6pm, Th 9am-7pm, Sa 9am-5:30pm. In March 2009, the library will relocate to The Hayes.

Launderette: Drift In, 104 Salisbury Rd. (☎02920 239 257), northeast of Cardiff Castle. Open M-Th and Sa 9am-6pm, F 9am-9pm, Su 10am-9pm.

Police: King Edward VIII Ave. (☎02920 222 111).

Pharmacy: Boots, 36 Queens St. (☎02920 231 291). Open M-F 8am-9pm, Sa 8am-6pm, Su 11am-5pm.

Hospital: University Hospital of Wales, Heath Park, North Cardiff (☎02920 747 747), 3 mi. from the city center.

Internet Access: At the TIC and library (both above). BT public telephones are sometimes accompanied by Internet booths, starting at 10p per min. **Talk and Surf,** 62 Tudor St. (☎02920 226 820). £1 per hr. Open M-Sa 9am-10pm, Su 10am-10pm. Many cafes and bars in the main shopping districts have free Wi-Fi.

Post Office: In the St. David's Centre, on the 1st fl. of Queen's Arcade. **Bureau de change.** Open M and W-Sa 9am-5:30pm, Tu 9:30am-5:30pm. **Postcode:** CF10 2SJ.

SOUTH WALES

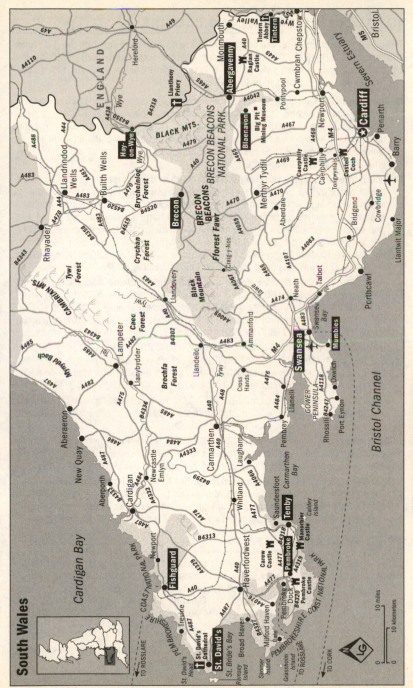

South Wales

SOUTH WALES

ACCOMMODATIONS AND CAMPING

Budget accommodations are tough to find in the city center, but the TIC lists reasonable B&Bs (£18-20) on the outskirts. More expensive B&Bs (£25-40) lie on **Cathedral Road,** a short ride on bus #32 or a 15min. walk from the town center; better bargains await on side streets.

River House Backpackers, 59 Fitzhamon Embankment (☎02920 399 810; www.riverhousebackpackers.com), facing Millenium Stadium. Cardiff's newest hostel, in a riverside Victorian villa with stylish, modern amenities. Run by a friendly brother and sister team eager to offer advice about the city's attractions. Spotless bathrooms, kitchen, TV lounge, and barbecue terrace. Breakfast included. Laundry. Internet £1 per 30min. Free Wi-Fi. Dorms £17.50-20; twins £40. MC/V.

Cardiff International Backpacker (to be called **Urban Bunkhouse** in Feb. 2009), 96-98 Neville St. (☎02920 345 577; www.cardiffbackpacker.com). From Central Station, go west on Wood St., turn right onto Fitzhamon Embankment just across the river, and take a left onto Despenser St. (not Pl.). Centrally located hostel with a distinctive purple and yellow exterior. Backpackers swing in hammocks on the rooftop terrace. Lounge, kitchen, and bar with colorful art splashed on the walls. Happy hour M-Th and Su 7-9pm. Lockers free with £5 deposit. Internet £1 per hr. Curfew M-Th and Su 2:30am. Open F-Sa to all; M-Th and Su only groups of 20 or more. Dorms £17. MC/V. ❷

Nos Da (to be called **Nos Da Hotel** and **Cardiff International Backpacker** in Feb. 2009), 53-59 Despenser St. (☎02920 378 866; www.nosda.co.uk). Combined hostel and budget hotel set to undergo a massive refurbishment in early 2009. Central location on the banks of the river. Lounge, kitchen, restaurant, and nightclub. Free Internet and Wi-Fi. Dorms M-Th £18, F-Sa £20; doubles £55/65. MC/V. ❷

YHA Cardiff, 2 Wedal Rd., Roath Park (☎02920 462 303). Take bus #28 or 29 from Central Station (10min., 2 per hr., £1.40) and get off at Wedal Rd. No-frills hostel perfect for escaping the downtown bustle. Nearby public gardens offer streamside walks. Breakfast included. Internet. Dorms £12-24.50, under 18 £9-18.50. MC/V. ❷

Austin's, 11 Coldstream Terr. (☎02920 377 148; www.hotelcardiff.com). On the River Taff opposite Millennium Stadium, 3min. from the castle. An affordable B&B option with basic rooms. Singles £32; doubles £49. MC/V. ❸

Annedd Lon, 157 Cathedral Rd. (☎02920 223 349; www.anneddlon.co.uk). Beautifully decorated rooms in a tree-shaded stone mansion, 20min. from the city center. All rooms ensuite. Breakfast included. Reserve ahead. Singles £45; doubles £55. MC/V. ❹

Acorn Camping and Caravanning (☎01446 794 024; www.acorncamping.com), near Rosedew Farm, Ham Ln. S., Llantwit Major. 1hr. by bus #X91 from Central Station; 15min. walk from the Ham Ln. stop. In high season £8.50 per person; in low season £10.75 per 2 people, £4.25 per person thereafter. Electricity £3.25. AmEx/MC/V. ❶

FOOD AND PUBS

Pubs, chains, and British fare dominate popular locations like **Mill Lane.** The **Old Brewery Quarter,** at the corner of St. Mary St. and Caroline St., offers midrange and higher-end restaurants. Eclectic, midrange cafes await in the Victorian arcades off High St. and St. Mary's St. **Caroline Street** shops are post-club hot spots, selling fish and chips and kebabs past clubs' closing hours (most open M-W until 3am, Th-Sa until 4am). Greek, Indian, and kebab takeaways cluster near the university on **Salisbury Street.** The **Cardiff Bay** area has tons of restaurants—most of which are sleek and expensive. On Sundays, a **farmers' market** takes over the southern half of Fitzhamon Embankment (10am-2pm).

SOUTH WALES

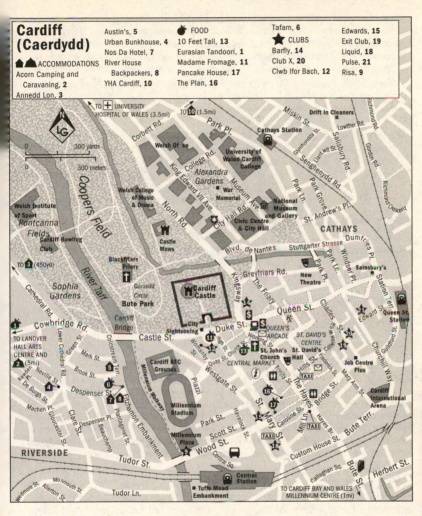

Cardiff (Caerdydd)

♠▲ACCOMMODATIONS
Acorn Camping and Caravaning, 2
Annedd Lon, 3
Austin's, 5
Urban Bunkhouse, 4
Nos Da Hotel, 7
River House Backpackers, 8
YHA Cardiff, 10

🍎 FOOD
10 Feet Tall, 13
Eurasian Tandoori, 1
Madame Fromage, 11
Pancake House, 17
The Plan, 16

Tafarn, 6
★ CLUBS
Barfly, 14
Club X, 20
Clwb Ifor Bach, 12

Edwards, 15
Exit Club, 19
Liquid, 18
Pulse, 21
Risa, 9

Madame Fromage, 21-25 Castle Arcade (☎02920 644 888). This modest cafe and deli is a Francophile's dream, selling an array of cheeses, meats, olives, and jams. Wash down the famous homemade lamb cawl (£6) or an overflowing grilled French goat cheese salad (£7.50) with a glass of wine. Daily specials and baguettes made from fresh ingredients. Open M-F 10am-5:30pm, Sa 9:30am-6pm, Su 11am-5pm. MC/V. ❷

10 Feet Tall, 11A-12 Church St. (☎02920 228 883), near the Queen's Arcade. North African and Mediterranean-inspired dishes in a rich, wood-paneled lounge. Savor tapas like stuffed chili peppers or *patatas bravas* (£2.50), light lunches (£4-7), or hearty dishes like venison haunch (£12.50). Turns into a popular nighttime hangout, with live music every night and a house jazz band on F. Free Wi-Fi. Open M-Th and Su 11am-3am, F-Sa 11am-4am. Kitchen open daily 11am-11pm. MC/V. ❷

Pancake House, 18 Old Brewery Quarter (☎02920 644 954). A glass cube in the middle of the quarter. Specialty crepes at reasonable prices. Try the bacon, avocado, and sour cream (£4) or the pear and chocolate (£3.80). The decadent might try the chocolate fondue with fruit and marshmallows (£4.50). Newspapers and magazines provided. Open M-Th 10am-10pm, F 10am-11pm, Sa 9am-11pm, Su 9am-10pm. Cash only. ❶

Tafarn, 53-59 Despenser St. (☎02920 378 866), in Nos Da. Bright-walled, spacious bar serving snacks (£4.25-9) and Welsh favorites such as hearty cawl (£6). Cozy patio overlooking the Taff. Wi-Fi. Open M-Th and Su 11am-11:30pm, F-Sa 11am-12:30am. Kitchen open 11am-10pm. MC/V. ❶

Eurasian Tandoori, 66 Cowbridge Rd. E. (☎02920 398 748). Indian and Indonesian cuisine a cut above standard. Entrees £4.25-10. Free delivery for orders over £10.50. Open M-Th and Su 6pm-12:30am, F-Sa 6pm-2am. AmEx/MC/V. ❷

The Plan, 28-29 Morgan Arcade (☎02920 398 764). Watch shoppers as you eat organic breakfasts and lunches, including filled baguettes (£4.70-5.20), elaborate salads (£6.20-7.50), and specialty coffees. Open M-Sa 9am-5pm, Su 11am-4pm. MC/V. ❶

SIGHTS AND SHOPPING

CARDIFF CASTLE. First a Roman legionary outpost, then a Norman keep, then a medieval stronghold, and finally a Victorian Neo-Gothic curiosity, Cardiff Castle has seen some drastic changes in its nearly 2000-year existence. The central keep, or "White Tower," was built in 1120 on the ruins of the Roman fort. The newer great halls were only completed in the late 1800s at the request of the third marquess of Bute, who hired the medieval enthusiast William Burges to recreate his vision of the castle's past. Watch for owls during falconry shows and peacocks wandering the grounds. (*Castle St. ☎02920 878 100; www.cardiffcastle. com. Open daily Mar.-Oct. 9am-6pm; Nov.-Feb. 9:30am-5pm. Last entry 1hr. before close. Audio and guided tours every 20min. £9, concessions £7.50, children £6.35. Tours free.*)

NATIONAL MUSEUM AND GALLERY. The gallery holds fine collections of priceless Impressionist works as well as several newer galleries featuring 18th-century Welsh artists and Welsh landscape painting. The local history displays are also extensive and intriguing. See a room full of Celtic stone crosses, the "world's largest turtle," a stuffed basking shark, and a walk-through "evolution of Wales" exhibit on Wales's turbulent environmental history. (*Cathays Park, next to City Hall. ☎02920 397 951. Open Tu-Su 10am-5pm. Donation requested.*)

LLANDAFF CATHEDRAL. A Celtic cross, one of the oldest Christian relics in Britain, stands outside this 12th-century cathedral. Inside, the ancient arch over the altar contrasts with a controversial 1950s aluminum-plated installation over the nave. St. Dyfrig and St. Teilo are entombed here, and Dante Gabriel Rossetti's triptych *Seed of David* stands in one corner. The ivy-covered ruins of the **Castle of the Bishops of Llandaff** lie nearby. Although its luster has somewhat faded—800 years have seen the cathedral used as a tavern and hog trough by Cromwell and gutted by a German bomb—Llandaff's grounds still emanate grace and history. (*Take bus #25, 60 or 62 from Central Station to the Black Lion Pub to walk up High St. or walk down Cathedral Rd., through Llandaff Fields, and straight on the small path behind the rugby club. ☎02920 564 554. Open daily 7am-7pm, staffed by helpful volunteers 10am-4pm. Evensong M-Tu and Th-Su 6pm, W 5:30, 6pm. Free.*)

ARCADES. Cardiff is a shopper's haven, but the city center is dominated by chain stores and restaurants. The famous Victorian arcades, however, house offbeat stores and eclectic cafes. Everything from vintage clothing shops, music stores, and upscale jewelers can be found in Castle Arcade, High St.

Arcade, and Duke Arcade, all at the northern end of High St. Morgan Arcade has a number of interesting and alternative dining options. *(South of the castle.)*

CIVIC CENTRE. Carved from Portland stone in English Renaissance style, the Civic Centre comprises the City Hall, the National Museum, the courts, and the police building. The majestic Edwardian-era structures overlook Alexandra Gardens among statues and quiet fountains. *(Cathays Park. Free.)*

CARDIFF BAY. The 21st century's answer to the 19th-century Civic Centre, Cardiff Bay has been the target of a massive regeneration project over the last two decades. Today, a Ferris wheel and merry-go-round appear as relics from an older era, next to the glass and steel Millennium Centre, the National Assembly Building, and a crop of ultramodern, glass-fronted restaurants and stores. Backstage tours of the Millennium Centre are available. *(Walk ¾ mi. down Lloyd George Ave. or take a bus (every 10min.) from the city center. Millennium Centre ☎ 08700 402 000. 1hr. tours £5.50, concessions £4.50.)*

🎵 NIGHTLIFE

After 11pm, most of Cardiff's downtown pubs stop serving alcohol, and the action migrates to nearby clubs—most located around **Saint Mary Street.** Cardiff's dress code is trendy but not strict. Hail a cab after dark. For nightlife listings, pick up the *Itchy Cardiff* guide ($3.50) or *Buzz* (free) from the TIC. Cardiff's gay scene revolves around **Charles Street,** where black lights and multi-leveled neon walls give clubbers a thrill.

- **Clwb Ifor Bach** (The Welsh Club), 11 Womanby St. (☎02920 232 199; www.clwb.net). 3 worlds collide in the eclectic Clwb: the ground floor plays cheesy pop; the middle-floor bar has softer music; the top rocks out to live bands or trance. Drink specials every night. Student night W. Cover £3-5, higher (up to £10) when popular bands play. Open W until 2am, Th-Sa until 3am. Call ahead or check the website for opening hours.

- **Liquid,** St. Mary St. (☎02920 645 464; www.liquidnightclub.co.uk). 2-tiered dance floor with flashing screens and lighting effects make this Cardiff's trendiest new venue. Cover £5-10. Open F-Sa 9:30pm-5am.

- **Pulse,** 3 Churchill Way (☎02920 398 030; www.pulsecardiff.com). "Gay, but straight-friendly." The newest, most popular entry to the city's gay scene. Features an extensive ground-floor bar and basement dance club. The stage sees live shows 3 times per week. Cover W £3, F £4, Sa £5. Open M-Tu and Th 11am-midnight, W 11am-3am, F-Sa 11am-4am. Club open W and F-Sa from 10pm.

- **Risa,** Millennium Plaza (☎02920 377 184; www.cardiff.risa.uk.com), via Wood St. New, chic venue with huge crowds in its 3-floor complex. Entry level has a bar and lounge area; below is a dance floor. On the top floor is the comedy club **Jongleurs,** which offers live entertainment, a bar, and a moonbounce. Student night W during term time. Salsa lessons Th 8pm-1am. Comedy shows F-Sa. Dress smartly. F-Sa 21+. Cover £5-7, comedy shows £10-12. Open W 7:30pm-3am, Th 8pm-1am, F-Sa 7pm-2am.

- **Barfly,** The Kingsway (☎02920 396 590; www.barflyclub.com/cardiff), across from Cardiff Castle. At the center of Cardiff's alternative rock scene, Barfly hosts indie bands most nights in a basement venue with low brick arches and bright red walls. "Hammertime" 90s night Tu. "Skinny Jean" indie night W. "Discord" rock night Th. Club nights Tu and F-Sa. Cover £5-6 most nights, up to £15 for popular bands. Open M and Su 7:30-11pm, Tu-Th 7:30pm-2am, F-Sa 7:30pm-3am.

- **Club X,** 35-37 Charles St. (www.clubxcardiff.com). Mixed gay and straight crowd in Wales's largest gay venue, with a capacity of over 900. Front room with commercial chart, a backroom with funk and electronic, and a lower-level bar and beer garden. Cover £2-10. Keeps the latest hours in Cardiff: open W 10pm-4am, F-Sa 10pm-6am.

SOUTH WALES

Exit Club, 48 Charles St. (☎02920 640 102; www.exitclubcardiff.com). GLBT-oriented bar located across the street from Club X. A relaxed setting on the lower entrance level and a dance floor with chart-topping hits above. Live entertainment or drag shows Su night. Cover £2-3. Open M-Th and Su 9:30pm-2am, F-Sa 9:30pm-4am.

Edwards, 84-86 St. Mary St. (☎02920 371 315). 20-somethings lounge in the swank, chandelier-hung bar area or party away on an industrial-style dance floor. Student night and drink specials W. Smart casual. Open M-Th and Su noon-1am, F-Sa noon-2am.

♫ ENTERTAINMENT

ARTS

Cardiff is experiencing a renewed interest in Welsh vocal, theatrical, and artistic traditions. The TIC offers free brochures for local events.

Wales Millennium Centre, in Cardiff Bay (☎08700 402 000; www.wmc.org.uk). Built in 2004, the center is the crown jewel of the Cardiff arts scene. It hosts a variety of Broadway-style shows, ballets, and traditional music events. Backstage tours 5-6 times daily. £5.50, concessions £4.50. Tickets £5-35. Box office open M-F 10am-6pm, Sa-Su 11am-5pm, performance nights until 30min. after curtain.

New Theatre, Park Pl. (☎02920 878 889; www.newtheatrecardiff.co.uk), north of Queen St. The former home of the Welsh National Opera. Now hosts musicals, ballets, and comedies. Tickets £8-50; student standby tickets (£5) available M-F after 6pm. Box office open M-Sa 10am-6pm, performance days 10am-8pm.

St. David's Hall, The Hayes (☎02920 878 444; www.stdavidshallcardiff.co.uk), opposite the TIC. One of Britain's best-known concert halls. The venue hosts the **BBC National Orchestra of Wales** as well as various bands and comedians throughout the year. Tickets £5.50-60, concessions available. Box office open M-Sa 9:30am-5:30pm, performance days 9:30am-8pm, Su from 9:30am until 1hr. before performances.

SPORTS

Rugby matches are played at the **Millennium Stadium,** a 74,000-seater with a retractable roof. (☎02920 822 228; www.millenniumstadium.com. Open M-Sa 10am-5pm, Su 10am-4pm. Book tours in advance. £6.50.) Tours leave from the **Millennium Stadium Shop,** at Entrance 3, Westgate St. (Open M-Sa 9:30am-5pm, Su 10am-4pm.) During the fall rugby season, tickets are available at the shop or from the **Welsh Rugby Union** (☎08705 582 582; www.wru.co.uk).

☒ DAYTRIPS FROM CARDIFF

▨CAERPHILLY CASTLE. Visitors might find this 30-acre castle easy to navigate, but 13th-century attackers had to contend with a "Chinese Box" system of concentric walls, double parapets, and moats. It is small wonder the castle withstood every assault it faced, although parts of the castle were eventually defeated by the marshy ground—one tower leans 10° from the vertical. The castle was built by an English baron around 1270 to defend against the Welsh and remains the largest castle in Wales. *(Take the train (20min., M-Sa 2 per hr., round-trip £5) or bus #26. ☎02920 883 143. Open Apr.-Oct. daily 9am-5pm; Nov.-Mar. M-Sa 9:30am-4pm, Su 11am-4pm. Last entry 30min. before close. £3.70, concessions £3.30.)*

MUSEUM OF WELSH LIFE (AMGUEDDFA WERIN CYMRU). Four miles west of Cardiff in St. Fagan's Park, this open-air museum occupies more than 100 acres with over 40 buildings from different historical periods rebuilt on-site—some nearly 500 years old. The Celtic Village and Welsh peasant cottage are full of authentic touches—buy treats from an old-fashioned bakery or walk around one of the few surviving circular pigsties in Wales. A highlight is St. Teilo's church, a 15th-century structure undergoing restoration using traditional techniques. Horse-and-cart rides are available (£1, children 50p), as are crafts workshops. *(Buses #32 and 320 run to the museum from Central Station (20min., 1-2 per hr., round-trip £2.80).* ☎*02920 573 500. Open daily 10am-5pm. Free. Guidebook £2, map 30p.)*

CASTELL COCH. Lord Bute and architect William Burges rebuilt the ruins of this 13th-century castle in the late 19th century. Their attempt to resurrect a medieval style ultimately looks like something from a fairy tale, with spires, latticed gables, and ornate decorative murals. Unlike other castles near Cardiff, Castell Coch occupies a secluded forest hillside and offers hikers connections to the **Taff Trail,** which winds toward Brecon Beacons National Park (p. 477) through the Taff Valley. *(Take bus #26 or 26A (25min., 1-2 per hr.) from Central Station to Tongwynlais. Get off across from the post office and walk 15min. up Mill St.* ☎*02920 810 101. Open Apr.-Oct. daily 9am-5pm; Nov.-Mar. M-Sa 9:30am-4pm, Su 11am-4pm. £3.70.)*

WYE VALLEY

The occasional 12th-century fortress marks this once turbulent Welsh-English border territory, but today it's hard to imagine a more peaceful area. Its landscape of thick oak forests and "hanging" beech hugging the sides of the Wye gorge has charmed poets and painters from Wordsworth to Turner. Few towns interrupt the flow of the meandering River Wye, but those that do have varied histories as outposts, sheep farms, and trading centers.

TRANSPORTATION

Chepstow provides the easiest entrance to the valley. **Trains** (☎08457 484 950; www.nationalrail.com) run from Chepstow to Cardiff (40min., 15 per day, £6.30) and Newport (25min., every 2hr., £5). National Express (☎08705 808 080; www.nationalexpress.com) **buses** go to Cardiff (1hr., 7 per day, £5), London (3hr., 5 per day, £20.80), and Newport (30min., 7 per day, £3.40). Stagecoach Red and White buses #65 and 69 loop between Chepstow and Monmouth (15 per day); bus #69 stops in Tintern (15min., 9 per day). Stagecoach sells one-day **Network Rider** passes (£6.50, children £4.30, families £14) for travel on all Stagecoach Red and White, Phil Anslow, and Cardiff buses. Few buses run on Sunday in the valley. TICs offer the free *Monmouthshire Local Transport Guide* for timetables and *Discover the Wye Valley by Foot and by Bus* for hikes. **Bike** rental is available in Monmouth from Pedalbikeaway, Hadnock Rd. (£8 per 2hr., £14 per day. Open July-Aug. daily 9am-5pm; Sept.-Oct. and Apr.-June Tu-Sa 9am-6pm; Nov.-Mar. Tu-Su 9am-5pm. £50 or car-key deposit. MC/V.) Hitchhikers wait on the A466 in the summer; some stand near Tintern Abbey or the Wye Bridge in Monmouth. *Let's Go* does not recommend hitchhiking.

HIKING

The hills near the Wye offer wooded trails, open meadows, and valley views. Two main trails, the Wye Valley Walk and Offa's Dyke Path, follow the river on either side and are accessible from many different points. TICs disperse pamphlets and sell Ordnance Survey maps (£6.50-8). Campsites are scattered throughout the area; ask at the Chepstow, Tintern, Hereford, and Powys TICs.

Wye Valley Walk (136 mi.), west of the river. Marked by a leaping salmon logo. This walk heads north from Chepstow via Hay-on-Wye to Prestatyn along forested cliffs and farmland, eventually ending in Rhayader. From **Eagle's Nest Lookout,** 3 mi. north of Chepstow, 365 steps descend to the riverbank. At **Symond's Yat Rock,** 15 mi. north of

Chepstow, the hills drop away to a panorama of the Wye's horseshoe bends. The Chepstow TIC sells a guide to this 12 mi. hike for 80p. Consult www.wyevalleywalk.org.

Offa's Dyke Path (177 mi.), east of the river. Starts in Sedbury's Cliffs and winds along Offa's Dyke on the Welsh-English border, ending at Prestatyn on the northern coast. Built by Saxon King Offa to keep the Welsh at bay, it is Britain's longest archaeological monument, and some of the earthwork (25 ft. high) still stands. Join at Chepstow, Monmouth, Bisweir, or Redbrook and follow the yellow arrows and acorn signs. Check trail maps (available at TICs); some paths change grade suddenly. Consult the **Offa's Dyke Association** (☎01547 528 753), halfway up the trail in Knighton.

Royal Forest of Dean. This 27,000-acre forest lies across the English border. Once the hunting ground of Edward the Confessor and Williams I and II. Contact the **Tourist Information Centre,** High St. (☎01594 812 388), in Coleford, England, across the river from Monmouth. Open July-Aug. M-Sa 10am-5pm, Su 10am-2pm; Sept. and Apr.-June M-Sa 10am-5pm; Oct. and Feb.-Mar. M-F 10am-4pm, Sa 10am-2pm; Nov.-Jan. M-F 10am-4pm. For more info, visit www.visitforestofdean.co.uk.

TINTERN   ☎(0)1291

The village of Tintern, 5 mi. north of Chepstow on the A466, is a small grouping of stone houses, shops, and inns on the banks of the Wye. It thrives on the tourism brought by ◙**Tintern Abbey,** the center of a 12th-century society of Cistercian monks. Doves now roost in the abbey's ancient walls, and visitors crowd the site daily. (☎01291 689 251. Open Apr.-Oct. daily 9am-5pm; Nov.-Mar. M-Sa 9:30am-4pm, Su 11am-4pm. £3.70, concessions £3.30, families £10.70. Last entry 30min. before close.) William Wordsworth reflected on the beauty and tranquility of the Wye banks in one of his most famous poems—those interested in his view from "a few miles above" should ask for directions to **Monk's Trail,** a wooded path that winds through the hills across the river. An uphill hike (2 mi.) leads to **Devil's Pulpit,** a huge stone from which Satan is said to have tempted the monks as they worked in the fields. The Tintern TIC sells a guide (£3) that includes both walks.

Several sights lie between the abbey and the Old Station (below) on the A466. **Stella Books,** on Monmouth Rd., in the middle of the village proper, stores over 50,000 volumes behind its unassuming storefront. (☎01291 689 755; Open daily 9:30am-5:30pm.) **Parva Farm Vineyard,** next to the Wye Valley Hotel on the A466, produces nearly 4000 bottles of wine and honey mead per year. The owners let visitors tour the hillside for £1.50, lead guided group tours for £3, and give wine tastings for free. (☎01291 689 636. Open daily 11:30am-6:30pm.)

A few B&Bs lie along the A466 in the village. Enjoy panoramic views of swans on the Wye at the **Old Rectory ❸,** Monmouth Rd., the only B&B in the town of Tintern itself. Soft colors and delicate decorative touches in this graceful Tudor-style home suit the peaceful natural surroundings. (☎01291 689 920; www.tintern-oldrectory.co.uk. Free Wi-Fi. Ensuite doubles and twins £65. MC/V.) **Moon and Sixpence ❶,** Monmouth Rd., serves country foods (£5-15) with glorious views of the Wye. (☎01291 689 284. Live music F. Open daily noon-midnight. Kitchen open M-Th noon-3pm and 6-9pm, F noon-3:30pm and 6-9:30pm, Sa-Su noon-midnight. MC/V.)

Bus #69 shuttles between Chepstow, Tintern, and Monmouth (M-Sa 8 per day, Su 4 per day). Tintern's **Old Station** lies a mile north of the abbey on the A466, but the Wye Valley Path provides a more scenic route. The out-of-service train station holds old railway carriages, one of which houses the **Tourist Information Centre.** The TIC books accommodations for a £1 fee and 10% deposit. (☎01291 689 566. Open Apr.-Oct. daily 10:30am-5:30pm.)

SOUTH WALES

BRECON BEACONS

Brecon Beacons National Park (Parc Cenedlaethol Bannau Brycheiniog) encompasses 520 sq. mi. of varied landscape. The park divides into four regions: the mist-cloaked farms and peaks of Brecon Beacons; the lush woods of Fforest Fawr, with the waterfalls of Ystradfellte; the rocky, desolate Black Mountains to the east; and the remote western ridges of Black Mountain (singular), above Upper Swansea Valley. The park, founded in 1957, is almost entirely owned by farmers. Fringe towns make pleasant touring bases, but hostels allow easier access to the inner parts of the park.

TRANSPORTATION

Getting to the more remote hostels and trails not serviced by public transportation proves a challenge. The **train** line (☎08457 484 950) from London Paddington to South Wales runs via Cardiff to Abergavenny at the park's southeastern corner and to Merthyr Tydfil on the southern edge (1 per hr.). The Heart of Wales rail line begins in Shrewsbury and passes through Llandeilo and Llandovery in the Black Mountain region, eventually terminating in Swansea (4 per day). National Express (☎08705 808 080) **bus** #509 runs once per day from Brecon, on the northern side of the park, to London (5 hr., £23.50) and Cardiff (1hr., £4). Stagecoach Red and White (☎01685 388 216) buses cross the park en route to Brecon from Abergavenny (#X43, 1hr., 8 per day), Hay-on-Wye (#39; 45min.; M-Sa 8 per day, Su 2 per day), and Swansea (#X63, 1½hr., M-Sa 4 per day). CardiffBus (☎08712 002 233) #B4 runs between Brecon and Abergavenny on Sundays (1hr., 4 per day). Many buses reduce their services on Sundays and bank holidays; the tourist-oriented Beacons Buses (☎01873 853 254; www.visitbreconbeacons.com) sends buses to all major towns in the park on Sundays from June to September. The free *Powys County* timetables, *Monmouthshire* timetables, and a park supplement aimed at tourists detail all bus and rail services. Bipedcycles (p. 483), among others, rents **mountain bikes**.

PRACTICAL INFORMATION

Stop at a **National Park Information Centre (NPIC)** before venturing forth. Free maps are available, but Ordnance Survey Outdoor Leisure Maps #12 and 13 (£14) are indispensable for serious exploring and for reaching safety in bad weather. The park staff conducts guided walks between April and November; call ahead.

National Park Information Centres:

Mountain Centre (National Park Visitor Centre in Libanus): ☎01874 623 366; www.breconbeacons.org. Walk or take bus #X43 to Libanus (10min., M-Sa 9 per day), 5 mi. from Brecon, then walk 2 mi. uphill. Or take Beacons Bus #B11 to the door (15min., June-Sept. Su 4 per day) from Brecon. Open daily Mar.-Oct. 9:30am-5pm; Nov.-Feb. 9:30am-4:30pm.

Abergavenny: See p. 480.

Craig-y-nos: At the Craig-y-nos Country Park (☎01639 730 395). Take Stagecoach bus #63 (from Brecon 30min., M-Sa 6 per day); ask to be dropped at Craig-y-nos. Open Easter-Sept. daily 10am-5pm; Oct.-Easter Sa-Su 10am-4:30pm.

Llandovery: Kings Rd. (☎01550 720 693), near Black Mountain. Take Heart of Wales train or bus #280 from Carmarthen. Open Easter-Oct. daily 10am-1pm and 1:45-5pm; Nov.-Easter M-Sa 10am-1pm and 1:45-4pm, Su 10am-noon.

ACCOMMODATIONS

The most comprehensive accommodations listing is at www.brecon-beacons.com, which lists guesthouses, hostels, cottages, caravans, farms, and campsites.

Campgrounds (£4-10 per tent) are plentiful but often difficult to reach without a car. Many offer laundry and grocery facilities, and all have parking and showers. Farmers may let you camp on their land if you ask first and leave the site as you found it. Be prepared to make a donation. The *Stay on a Farm* guide, available at TICs, lists over 100 such farms across Wales. NPICs in the region also give out *Camping on Farms*, which lists options in the park.

Scattered across the park are five YHA hostels, including Ty'n-y-Caeau, near Brecon (p. 483), and YHA Abergavenny (p. 481). The other three are:

Danywenallt (DAN-you-eh-nahlt; ☎0870 770 6136; danywenallt@yha.org.uk), in the Brecon Beacons near Talybont-on-Usk. Take the X43 bus from Brecon or Abergavenny and ask to be let off at the post office in Talybont-on-Usk (35min. from both, M-Sa 6 per day). From the post office, cross the canal bridge and follow signs for the Talybont Reservoir. Turn left onto the dam wall and left again onto the track to Danywenallt. Breakfast included. Reception 8am-noon and 5-10:30pm. Dorms £12-24.50. MC/V. ❷

Llanddeusant (HLAN-thew-sont; ☎0870 770 5930; llanddeusant@yha.org.uk), at the foot of Black Mountain near Llangadog village. Take the Trecastle-Llangadog road for 9 mi. off the A40. The nearest bus stop is in Llangadog. Reception 8-10am and 5-10pm. Curfew 11pm. Dorms £12, under 18 £9. MC/V. ❶

Llwyn-y-Celyn (HLEWN-uh-kel-in; ☎0870 770 5936; llwynycelyn@yha.org.uk), 7 mi. south of Brecon, 2 mi. north from Storey Arms car park on the A470. Take Sixty Sixty Bus #X43 from Brecon or Merthyr Tydfil (M-Sa every 2hr., Su 3 per day). Reception 8-10am and 5-10:30pm. Curfew 11pm. Dorms £10-16, under 18 £7.50-12. MC/V. ❷

📷 HIKING

THE BRECON BEACONS

Llangorse Lake, 8 mi. from Brecon, is the largest natural lake in South Wales and is home to several unusual bird species and a crannog (Iron Age dwelling) on a manmade island. To the south, the Mountain Centre NPIC, outside Libanus (previous page), houses an exhibit on the lake's history and wildlife. Paths weave through fields of sheep and occasionally stop at sights. The most popular path to the top of **Pen-y-Fan** (pen-uh-VAN; 2907 ft.), the highest mountain in South Wales, begins at Storey Arms (a car park and bus stop 5 mi. south of Libanus on the A470) and offers views of **Llyn Cwm Llwch** (HLIN koom hlooch), a 2000 ft. glacial pool in the shadow of **Corn Du** (CORN dee) peak. The easiest route begins behind a car park and public toilets called Pont ar Daf, just past Storey Arms on the A470 coming from Brecon. Most other paths are unmarked—consult NPICs for recommendations and directions. Pen-y-Fan has a reputation as the most dangerous mountain in Wales. An arduous ridge path leads from Pen-y-Fan to other peaks in the Beacons.

> **WARNING.** Even in summer, winds over 20 mph and sudden mists can cause summit temperatures to plummet below freezing. In violent weather, do not take shelter in caves or under isolated trees, which tend to draw lightning. Move to lower altitude and avoid exposed ridges and open areas. A compass is essential; landmarks get lost in mists. In an emergency, call ☎999 and ask for Mountain Rescue. Keep in mind that mobiles do not work in some areas of the park. For more information, see **Wilderness Safety**, p. 51.

The touristy **Brecon Mountain Railway,** which departs from Pant Station in Merthyr Tydfil, allows a glimpse of the south side of the Beacons and vast limestone quarries as the narrow-gauge train runs along the Taf Fechan Reservoir

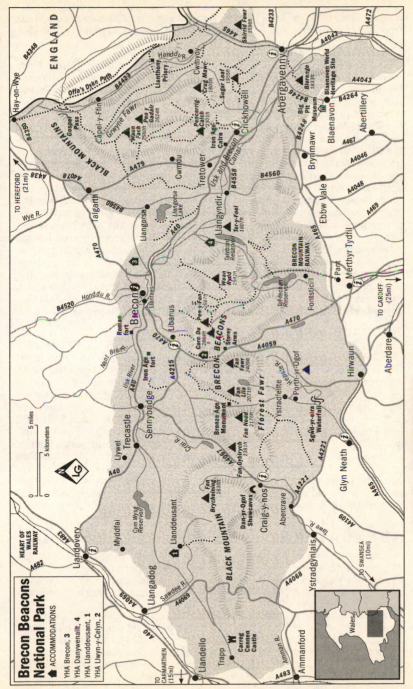

Brecon Beacons National Park

▲ ACCOMMODATIONS

YHA Brecon, 3
YHA Danywenallt, 4
YHA Llanddeusant, 1
YHA Llwyn-y-Celyn, 2

SOUTH WALES

north to Pontsticill. (☎01685 722 988; www.breconmountainrailway.com. Runs from late Mar. to early Nov. 5 per day 11am-4pm. £9.50, children £4.75. MC/V.)

THE WATERFALL DISTRICT (FFOREST FAWR)

Near the southern edge of the park on a limestone outcrop, Fforest Fawr erupts with mosses and ferns. The triangle defined by the towns of **Hirwaun, Ystradfellte,** and **Pontneeddfechan** marks the boundaries of the 300 sq. mi. forest. Rivers tumble through rapids, gorges, and spectacular falls near Ystradfellte, 7 mi. southwest of the Beacons. Various circular walks pass waterfalls along the Rivers Mellte, Hepste, Pyrddin, and Nedd Fechan; consult the *Waterside Places* booklet, available for £1 at TICs. At **Porth-yr-Ogof** ("Mouth of the Cave"), the River Mellte ducks into a cave at the base of the cliff and emerges as an icy pool. Swimming is ill-advised—the stones are slippery and the pool deepens suddenly. Erosion makes the paths narrow and hard to navigate. Remote but worth the sweat is the **Sgwd yr Eira** ("Fall of Snow") waterfall, where the River Hepste drops more than 50 ft., half a mile from its intersection with the Mellte. You can stand behind thundering water in the hollow of a cliff face and remain dry as a bone. Follow the marked paths to the falls from Gwaun Hepste. Hikers reach the waterfall district from the Beacons by crossing the A470 near the YHA Llwyn-y-Celyn, climbing Craig Cerrig-gleisiad cliff and Fan Frynych peak and descending along a rocky Roman road. The route crosses a nature reserve and trackless heath. Just west of the waterfall district loom the limestone ridges of the **Black Mountain Range** (not to be confused with the Black Mountains on the park's eastern border), containing two elevated glacial lakes (**Llyn y Fan Fach** and **Llyn y Fan Fawr**) and the summit of **Fan Brycheiniog** (2631 ft.).

THE BLACK MOUNTAINS

Located in the easternmost section of the park, the Black Mountains are a group of ridges offering 80 sq. mi. of solitude. Summits like **Waun Fach** (2660 ft.), the highest point, may seem dull and boggy, but ridge walks offer views unsurpassed in Wales. Ordnance Survey Outdoor Leisure Map #13 (£13) is essential. **Crickhowell,** on the A40, is one of the best starting points for forays into the area, although hikers staying overnight might want to base themselves in Abergavenny. You can also explore by bus: Stagecoach Red and White #39 between Brecon and Hay-on-Wye descends the north side of the Black Mountains (30min.; M-Sa 7-8 per day, Su 2 per day). **Gospel Pass,** the park's highest mountain pass, often sees sun above the cloud cover. Nearby, **Offa's Dyke Path** (p. 475) traces the park's eastern boundary. On Sundays and bank holidays from May to September, Beacons Bus #B17 runs from Hay-on-Wye to Llanfihangel Crucorney and stops at access points to the Black Mountains on the way. (☎01873 853 254; www.breconbeacons.org. 3 per day.)

ABERGAVENNY (Y FENNI)   ☎(0)1873

On the eastern edge of Brecon Beacons National Park, Abergavenny trumpets itself as the "Gateway to Wales." While shop-lined pedestrian areas offer all the charms of Welsh village life, the region's real draw lies outside city limits: Abergavenny is the starting point of countless hikes through the Black Mountains.

▣ **TRANSPORTATION. Trains** (☎08457 484 950; www.nationalrail.com) run to: Bristol (1hr., 1-2 per hr., £9.70); Cardiff (40min., 1-2 per hr., £9); Hereford (25min., 1-2 per hr., £6.80); London (2½hr., 1-2 per hr., £24-53); Newport (25min., 1-2 per hr., £6). To get to town, turn right at the end of Station Rd. and walk 5min. along Monmouth Rd. The **bus station** is on Monmouth Rd., by the TIC.

Stagecoach Red and White (☎01633 838 856) buses roll out to Brecon (#X43, 1hr., M-Sa 6 per day), Cardiff (#X3, 1hr., every hr.), and Hereford (#X4, 1hr., 7 per day). The *Monmouthshire Bus Guide* details all bus routes in the area.

🛈 PRACTICAL INFORMATION. The well-stocked **Tourist Information Centre,** Monmouth Rd., across from the bus station, reserves beds for £2 and a 10% deposit. It doubles as the **National Park Information Centre,** with helpful maps and trail guides (£1-13) for hikers. (☎01873 857 588. Open daily Easter-Oct. 9:30am-5:30pm; Nov.-Easter 10am-4pm.) Other services include: **banks** with **ATMs** along Cross St. and High St.; free **Internet** access at the **library,** Library Sq., Baker St. (☎01873 735 980; open Tu 10am-7pm, W and F 9am-5:30pm, Th 9am-7pm, Sa 9am-1pm); **police,** Tudor St. (☎01873 852 273), between Nevill and Baker St.; the **hospital** (☎01873 732 732), Nevill Hall, on the A40; and the **post office,** 1 St. John's Sq., where Tudor St. turns into Castle St. (☎08457 223 344; open M and W-F 9am-5:30pm, Tu 9:30am-5:30pm, Sa 9am-12:30pm). **Postcode:** NP7 5EB.

🛏🍴 ACCOMMODATIONS AND FOOD. B&Bs (£23-27.50) lie on **Monmouth Road,** past the TIC, and **Hereford Road,** 15min. from town. Two hostels lie closer to the city center. In a former Georgian convent surrounded by apple trees, **Abergavenny YHA ❷** (also called Mulberry House), Pen-y-pound, doubles as an environmental study center; guests can browse through the library's extensive collection of books on ecology. (☎01873 855 959; www.mulberrycentre.com. Breakfast included. £24 per person, under 18 £14.50. MC/V.) **Black Sheep Backpackers ❷,** 24 Station Rd., across from the train station, has basic dorms above a lively pub. (☎01873 859 125; www.blacksheepbackpackers.com. Large basement dorms £13.50; nicer upper dorms £15; twins £30. Cash only.)

The market in **Market Hall** on Cross St. has fresh produce and baked goods (open Tu and F-Sa 9am-5pm; largest on Tu) and a weekly flea market (W 9am-5pm). Enjoy a soup, sandwich, and specialty coffee (£1.45) in the large dining room of **The Trading Post ❶,** 14 Nevill St. (☎01873 855 448. Open M-F 9am-5pm. Cash only.) **Harry's Carvery ❶,** 3 St. John's St., off High St., has lunch treats and just-sliced meats (£2-3). The overstuffed breakfast baguette (£3) draws long lines. (☎01873 852 766. Open M-Sa 7:30am-4pm. Cash only.) The sunlit dining room at **The Angel Hotel ❹,** 15 Cross St., delivers inventive dishes using local ingredients as well as afternoon tea with a selection of freshly baked cakes and pastries. (☎01873 857 121. Entrees £7.80-19.80. Afternoon tea 3-5:30pm £9.80. Open daily noon-2:30pm, 3-5:30pm, 7-10pm. AmEx/MC/V.)

📷🥾 SIGHTS AND HIKING. In 1175, the Norman lord of Abergavenny, William de Braose, invited his Welsh rival and his men to a Christmas feast at **Abergavenny Castle** and had them all massacred. Today, the castle's crumbling stone gatehouses stand peacefully among weeping willows and a small flower garden. A 19th-century hunting lodge on the grounds houses the **Abergavenny Museum,** which displays artifacts from the Iron Age to the 19th century. (☎01873 854 282. Open Mar.-Oct. M-Sa 11am-1pm and 2-5pm, Su 2-5pm; Nov.-Feb. M-Sa 11am-1pm and 2-4pm. Grounds open daily dawn-5pm. Free.) In late September, the **Abergavenny Food Festival** draws foodies from around the world for a weekend of master classes, cookery demonstrations, competitions, and over 160 market stalls. (☎01873 850 805. Weekend ticket £9, children £2.50.)

Abergavenny's real attractions are the surrounding hills. Because almost all of the Black Mountains' trails are unmarked, it's crucial to get detailed directions and an Ordnance Survey Map (£6-13) from the NPIC. Three major summits are accessible from Abergavenny by foot, although all require fairly long hikes. **Blorenge** (1833 ft.) is 2 mi. southwest of town. A path begins off the B4246 or from the TIC, traversing woodlands to the uplands, and ascends the remaining 1500 ft. in 4½ mi. (12 mi., 6hr. round-trip). The trail to the top of **Sugar Loaf** (1955 ft.), 2½ mi. northwest, starts half a mile west of town on the A40. The path to **Skirrid Fawr** ("Holy Mountain"; 1595 ft.) lies northeast of town and starts 2 mi. down the B4521. **Pony trekking** is an enjoyable way to see the hills. Try Grange Trekking Centre. (☎01873 890 215. £26 per ½-day, £43 per day.)

 NETWORKING. When traveling to the sights near Abergavenny by bus, a **Network Rider** pass (p. 475) is usually cheaper than round-trip tickets.

▶ DAYTRIP FROM ABERGAVENNY: BIG PIT NATIONAL COAL MUSEUM AND BLAENAVON IRONWORKS. Recently named a World Heritage Site, the quarry-filled hillsides of Blaenavon, 9 mi. southwest of Abergavenny, were a center of the coal-mining and iron-production industries of South Wales. Visitors descend a 300 ft. shaft to experience the cramped conditions under which miners labored, where ex-miners share stories in the subterranean workshops. Aboveground exhibits explain all aspects of coal mining, including the role of children, who regularly worked in mines as doorkeepers until well into the 19th century. Up the street, the Blaenavon Ironworks were the second-largest ironworks in Wales. They hold the remains of six giant 18th-century blast furnaces, a towering water balance tower used for materials transport, and exhibits on the process of iron production and the lives of workers. *(Take bus #X3 to Pontypool (20min., 13 per day) or bus #X4 to Brynmawr (30min., every 30min.). Transfer to bus #30 to Blaenavon (15min. from both, every hr.). Coal Museum ☎01495 790 311. Open daily Feb-Nov. 9:30am-5pm; Dec.-Jan. 9:30am-4:30pm. Underground tours Jan.-Nov. 10am-3:30pm; Dec. 10am-3pm. Those under 3 ft. 3 in. not admitted underground. Under 16 not admitted without a guardian. Free. Ironworks ☎01495 792 615. Open Apr.-Oct. M-F 9:30am-4:30pm, Sa 10am-5pm, Su 10am-4:30pm. £2.50, concessions £2.)*

▶ DAYTRIP FROM ABERGAVENNY: LLANTHONY PRIORY. All the megaliths in the Black Mountains are said to point toward the majestic ruins of Llanthony Priory. In the 12th century, founder William de Lacy rebuilt ancient ruins left at this site so that he could live a hermetic life. *(The priory is 6 mi. from the nearest bus stop, in Llanfihangel Crucorney. Take Stagecoach Red and White bus #X3 (20min., M-Sa 7 per day) or follow the A465 to Llanfihangel Crucorney. Offa's Dyke Flyer stops directly at the priory from Hay-on-Wye (45min., June-Sept. Su 3 per day). Open daily 10am-4pm. Free.)*

▶ DAYTRIP FROM ABERGAVENNY: RAGLAN CASTLE. Warm sandstone towers and French-influenced decorative details set Raglan castle, the last medieval castle built in Wales, apart from older, more austere fortresses. A mere 570 years old, it was constructed by Sir William Thomas as an extravagant display of wealth, and the castle played the part of a palace in addition to a military defense. Still, it withstood an English Civil War siege before finally falling to Cromwell's troops in 1646. The remaining ruins constitute a network of open-air towers and crumbling staircases. *(Take bus #83 from Abergavenny or Monmouth. 25min.; M-Sa 6 per day, Su 4 per day; £5.25. Bus #60 runs from Monmouth or Newport. From Newport 40min., from Monmouth 15min.; every 2hr. From the bus stop in Raglan, follow Castle Rd. to the highway and cross over the pedestrian path to the road up to the castle. ☎01291 690 228. Open June-Sept. daily 9:30am-6pm; Oct. and Apr.-May daily 9:30am-5pm; Nov.-Mar. M-Sa 9:30am-4pm, Su 11am-4pm. Last entry 30min. before close. £3, concessions £2.50.)*

BRECON (ABERHONDDU)   ☎ (0)1874

Just north of the mountains, Brecon is the best base for exploring the dramatic northern region of Brecon Beacons National Park. Georgian architecture looms over tiny side streets where residents and backpackers sip tea and plan hikes through neighboring forests. A motley crew comes to Brecon in August, when the exceptional Jazz Festival fills every bed and street corner.

TRANSPORTATION. Buses arrive regularly at the Bulwark in the central square. Ask for schedules at the TIC. National Express (☎08705 808 080) bus #509 runs to London (5hr., 1 per day, £32.50) via Cardiff (1hr., £3.90). Stagecoach Red and White (☎01633 838 856) buses run to Abergavenny (#X43, 1hr., 8 per day) and Swansea (#X63, 1½hr., M-Sa 4 per day, £4-5). Bus #39 goes to Hereford via Hay-on-Wye (M-Sa 8 per day, Su 2 per day); on Sundays, Yeomans (☎01432 356 202) follows the same route (#40, 2 per day). Bipedcycles, 10 Ship St., rents **mountain bikes.** (☎07970 972 186 or 622 296. £20 per day. Open M-Tu and Th-F 9am-5:30pm, W and Sa 9am-5pm; ID deposit. MC/V.)

PRACTICAL INFORMATION. The **TIC** is located in the Cattle Market car park; walk through Bethel Sq. off Lion St. (☎01874 622 485. Open May-Sept. M-F 9:30am-5:30pm, Sa 9:30am-5pm, Su 9:30am-4pm; Oct.-Apr. M-F 9:30am-5pm, Sa-Su 9:30am-4pm.) Other services include: **Barclays** bank, 9 The Bulwark (☎08457 555 555; open M-F 9am-5pm); **police,** Cambrian Way (☎01874 622 331); **Boots** pharmacy, 8 Bethel Sq. (☎01874 622 917; open M-Sa 9am-5:30pm); **Internet** access at **Brecon Branch Library,** Ship St. (☎01874 623 346; free; open M and W-F 9:30am-5pm, Tu 9:30am-7pm, Sa 9:30am-1pm); and **Brecon Cyber Cafe,** 10 Lion St. (☎01874 624 942; £1 per 12min., students 60p; £10 max.; open M-Sa 10am-5pm); and the **post office,** in the Cooperative Pioneer, on Lion St. (☎01874 623 735; open M-F 8:30am-5:30pm, Sa 8:30am-4pm). **Postcode:** LD3 7HY.

ACCOMMODATIONS AND CAMPING. In mid-August, Jazz Festival-goers claim every pillow in town up to a year in advance. In a stone cottage near the town center, **The Grange Guest House ❸,** 22 The Watton, feels more like a countryside retreat. Rooms are large, and the owners give guests free rein of the large flower garden in back, complete with fancy wrought-iron tables. (☎01874 624 038; www.thegrange-brecon.co.uk. Free Wi-Fi. Singles £30, ensuite £35; doubles £40/50. MC/V.) Nearby **Paris Guest House ❸,** 28 The Watton, has clean ensuite rooms with satellite TV. (☎01874 624 205; www.parisguesthouse.co.uk. Free Wi-Fi. Singles £35; doubles £60. Cash only.) The nearest YHA hostel is **Brecon (Ty'n-y-Caeau) ❶** (tin-uh-KAY-uh), 3 mi. out of town. From the town center, walk 20-25min. down The Watton to the A40-A470 roundabout, follow the Abergavenny branch of the A40, take the path to the left of Groesffordd, and turn left on the main road. Continue 10-15min., bearing left at the fork; the hostel is on the right. Bus #X43 stops in Groesffordd (7 per day), a three-quarter-mile walk away. The Victorian house has a TV room and kitchen. (☎01874 665 270. Dorms £12-20, under 18 £9-15. MC/V.) Camp at **Pencelli Castle Caravan and Camping Park ❶,** 2 mi from Brecon on the Taff Trail. (☎01874 665 451; www.pencelli-castle. com. £8-9.50 per person.) During the Jazz Festival, campsites open on farms.

FOOD. Morrisons, Free St., near the TIC, sells groceries. (☎01874 620 063. Open M-W and Sa 8am-8pm, Th-F 8am-9pm, Su 10am-4pm.) Lush floor plants and bay windows give **The Red Dragon ❶,** 1 The Bulwark, an upscale feel, but the prices are budget—most entrees on the huge menu are under £7. (☎01874 611 611. Open daily 5pm-midnight. MC/V.) **Pilgrim's Tea Rooms and Restaurant ❶,** attached to the cathedral's Heritage Centre, is a small, peaceful cafe run by parishioners. (☎01874 610 610. Open daily 10am-5pm. MC/V.) Enjoy traditional pub fare at **The Wellington ❶**, a family-friendly inn across from the bus stop in the town center. (☎01874 625 225. Most entrees under £8. Open M-W and Su noon-11pm, Th-Sa noon-midnight. MC/V.)

◙ ✿ SIGHTS AND FESTIVALS. History is literally carved into the stone columns of **Brecon Cathedral**—see the "mason's marks" that illiterate stoneworkers used to label their work. The **Heritage Centre**, in the cathedral enclave, describes the art of bell ringing and tells the story of the cathedral. (Cathedral ☎01874 623 857, Heritage Centre 625 222. Cathedral open daily 9am-5:30pm. Centre open Apr.-Oct. M-Sa 10:30am-4:30pm, Su 12:15-4:15pm; Nov.-Mar. M-Sa 10:30am-4:30pm. Free.) The **Brecknock Museum and Art Gallery,** in the Assize Courthouse near the Bulwark, holds artifacts from rural Wales such as walking sticks and milk churns. From an upstairs balcony, visitors can peer down at a tableau recreating the 19th-century courtroom dramas that took place regularly in the old courthouse. (☎01874 624 121. Open Apr.-Sept. M-F 10am-5pm, Sa 10am-1pm and 2-5pm, Su noon-5pm; Oct.-Mar. M-F 10am-5pm, Sa 10am-1pm and 2-5pm. £1, concessions 50p.) At the **Regimental Museum Brecon,** The Barracks, on The Watton, 300 years' worth of military paraphernalia commands all available space. (☎01874 613 310; www.rrw.org.uk. Open Easter-Sept. M-F 10am-5pm, Sa 10am-4pm; Oct.-Easter M-F 10am-5pm. Last entry 4:30pm. £3.) For the August **Brecon Jazz Festival** (☎0870 990 1299; www.breconjazz.co.uk), the streets are blocked as thousands converge to enjoy jazz and local brews.

▷ DAYTRIP FROM BRECON: DAN-UR-OGOF SHOWCAVES. Between Swansea and Brecon, off the A4067, the Dan-yr-Ogof Showcaves are the park's most highly promoted attractions. Although their stalagmites and eerie rock formations are impressive, their "showcave" status has left them commercial and heavily trafficked. One of the biggest draws is the award-winning **Dinosaur Park,** complete with a *T. rex*. Ten miles of trails pass Fforest Fawr on their way to the caves. *(Stagecoach bus #X63 from Brecon (30min., 6 per day) stops at the caves. ☎01639 730 284, 24hr. info 730 801. Open daily from mid-Mar. to Oct. 10am-3pm. £11.50.)*

HAY-ON-WYE (Y GELLI) ☎(0)1497

Hay-on-Wye is a town defined by its more than 30 bookstores. The little village owes its reputation as the world's foremost "Town of Books" mainly to Richard Booth, founder of Booth's Books, the largest secondhand bookstore in the world. But Hay's natural attractions are also a draw, surrounded as it is by gentle hills, edged by the winding River Wye, and a short drive from the 2227 ft. Hay Bluff and the Black Mountains.

◧ ▷ TRANSPORTATION AND PRACTICAL INFORMATION. The closest train station is in Hereford, England (p. 287). Stagecoach Red and White (☎01633 838 856) **bus** #39 stops at Hay between Hereford and Brecon (to Hereford 1hr., to Brecon 45min.; M-Sa 7 per day). Yeoman's (☎01432 356 202) bus #40 runs the same route (Su 4 per day). The **TIC**, Oxford Rd., in the shopping center, has Internet (75p per 15min.) and books beds for £2. (☎01497 820 144; www.hay-on-wye.co.uk. Open daily Apr.-Oct. 10am-1pm and 2-5pm; Nov.-Mar. 11am-1pm and 2-4pm.) Other services include: **Barclays** bank, on Broad St. (open M-F 10am-4pm); free **Internet** at the **library,** Chancery Ln. (☎01497 820 847; open M 10am-1pm, 2-4:30pm, 5-7pm; Th-F 10am-1pm and 2-5pm, Sa 9:30am-1pm); and the **post office,** 3 High Town (☎01497 820 536; open M, W, F 9am-1pm and 2-5:30pm, Tu 9am-1pm, Th 9am-5:30pm, Sa 9am-12:30pm). **Postcode:** HR3 5AE.

SOUTH WALES

ACCOMMODATIONS AND FOOD. B&Bs occupy the center of town. Delightful stays await at **The Bear ❸**, 2 Bear St., a 16th-century coaching inn with low-timbered ceilings and fireplaces, several of which are filled with books. (☎01497 821 302; www.thebear-hay-on-wye.com. Singles from £31; twins from £56; ensuite doubles from £68. MC/V.) Expect lots of personal attention and bedside chocolates at **Aldemiro ❷**, Forest Rd. The hosts have a wealth of knowledge about the town—one is the town crier. (☎01497 820 488; www.haye-on-wye.co.uk/aldemiro. £25 per person. Cash only.) Camp along the Wye Valley Walk or Offa's Dyke (p. 475); inquire at the TIC.

Get groceries at **Spar,** 26 Castle St. (Open M-F 7:30am-10pm, Sa-Su 8am-10pm.) **The Granary ❷**, Broad St., has extravagant salads (£8-9), free Wi-Fi, and patio seating. (☎01497 820 790. Open M-Sa 9am-9pm, Su 9am-5:30pm. AmEx/MC/V.) **Three Tuns ❷**, Broad St., is the oldest pub in town and is said to have been a hangout for the fugitive Great Train Robbers, who committed Britain's then-largest act of theft in 1963. Recently damaged in a fire, it's been beautifully restored with a light, Mediterranean feel and a menu that goes far beyond the typical pub fare. (☎01497 821 855. Entrees £7-15. Open M-Th 11am-3pm and 6-11pm, F 11am-3pm and 5pm-midnight, Sa 11am-midnight, Su noon-10:30pm.) Cheaper eats await at **Xtreme Organix ❶**, 10 Castle St., a burger joint that uses local organic meat. (☎01497 821 921. Open daily 9:30am-11pm. Cash only.) **Shepherd's Ice Cream Parlour and Coffee Bar ❶**, 9 High Town, sells its signature sheep's-milk ice cream for £1.50. (☎01497 821 898. Open M-Sa 9:30am-6pm, Su 10am-5pm. Cash only.)

SIGHTS AND FESTIVALS. Hay's 13th-century **Norman castle,** scarred by wars, fires, and neglect, no longer houses traditional royalty. Rather, Richard Booth, the "King of Hay," stores just a fraction of his unfathomable number of secondhand books on the first floor. The castle is part of Booth's huge network of stores (many of them **honesty bookshops,** where a paybox sits near outdoor shelves of 30-50p books), which shaped Hay into a bibliophile's dream. Other independent stores offer equally delightful selections; some shops have specialties, like the Poetry Bookshop, the Children's Bookshop, or Murder and Mayhem, dedicated to mysteries. To browse Hay's offerings, pick up the TIC's free *Secondhand & Antiquarian Booksellers & Printsellers* map and brochure or search over a million titles at www.haybooks.com. The world-renowned annual 10-day **literary festival,** in late May

HAY DAY

It's the "Woodstock of the mind," according to Bill Clinton. The Guardian Hay Festival, held in late May and early June in Hay-on-Wye, is a celebration of all things literary, packing the town with over 100,000 bibliophiles and hundreds of speakers and performers. Street banners all over the city proclaim, "People say that life is the thing, but I prefer reading."

It all began rather modestly in 1988 with a festival that was not so much a monumental meeting of the minds as a dinner party with some friends and authors. Two decades later, it pulls in Nobel laureates, academics, and political, theatrical, and literary dignitaries by the hundreds for 392 events over the course of just 10 days. It has spawned sister festivals in Colombia and Spain. The concurrent Hay Fringe Festival has more informal readings and musical performances ranging from folk to punk rock.

Book accommodations months in advance of the festival and expect queues at restaurants and events. If you don't mind working a bit, sign up as a volunteer. Workers get to see some events for free in exchange for working as many 3-4hr. shifts as they wish.

For more information or to sign up to be a steward, visit the festival website at www.hayfestival.com.

and early June, brings international luminaries (recently Seamus Heaney, Bill Clinton, and Al Gore) to give readings. (www.hayfestival.com. Book accommodations far in advance. Tickets £5-19.)

GLAMORGAN

SWANSEA (ABERTAWE)   ☎(0)1792

Native son Dylan Thomas got it right when he called Swansea (pop. 230,000) an "ugly, lovely town." The ugly bit is obvious: concrete buildings line urban roads, industrial equipment borders the coast, and box houses cover the hillsides in well-defined grids. Yet Swansea is an active city, with a university, colorful cafes, thriving nightlife, and excellent museums. To the west, a beautiful expanse of sandy beaches extends onto the nearby Gower Peninsula.

TRANSPORTATION. At the train station, 35 High St., **trains** (☎08457 484 950; www.nationalrail.com) depart to Birmingham (3hr., 2 per hr., £39), Cardiff (1hr., 2-3 per hr., £5.20), and London (3hr., 1-2 per hr., £61). The Quadrant Bus Station (☎0870 608 2608) is near the Quadrant Shopping Centre and the TIC. National Express (☎08705 808 080; www.nationalexpress.com) runs **buses** to Birmingham (3½-6½hr., 6 per day, £29.50), Cardiff (1hr., 16 per day, £7), and London (5-6hr., 12 per day, £24.50). First Cymru (☎08706 082 608) and Veolia (☎01443 215 105) buses cover the Gower Peninsula and southwest Wales. First Cymru #100 runs to Cardiff (1hr., M-Sa 1-4 per hr.). A First Cymru **FirstDay ticket** (£3.35-4, concessions £2.20, families £8) allows unlimited travel on First buses for a day in Swansea. The **Swansea Bay FirstWeek** ticket, purchased on the bus, covers a week of travel on First buses on the peninsula (£16.50, concessions £12). **Gower Day Explorer** tickets are valid for a day's travel on all Veolia buses in the Gower Explorer network (£4). Veolia buses also run to smaller towns, including Brecon (1½hr., 4 per day). Data Cabs (☎01792 474 747 and 545 454) and Yellow Cab (☎01792 644 446) offer 24hr. **taxi** services.

ORIENTATION AND PRACTICAL INFORMATION. Swansea is bordered by **Swansea Bay** to the south and the **River Tawe** to the east. **Oystermouth Road** stretches along the bay, with museums clustering at its eastern end, by the marina. The city center is dominated by the giant **Quadrant Shopping Centre,** which is surrounded by pedestrian-only streets. **The Kingsway** is the the main avenue just north of the shopping area; it runs southwest, turning into **Saint Helen's Road** and then **South Road,** eventually connecting with Oystermouth Rd.

On the north side of the bus station, the **Tourist Information Centre** books rooms for £2 plus a 10% deposit. (☎01792 468 321; www.visitswanseabay.com. Open in summer M-Sa 9:30am-5:30pm, Su 10am-4pm; in winter M-Sa 9:30am-5:30pm.) Other services include: **Barclays** bank, 70 The Kingsway (☎01633 205 000; open M-F 9am-5pm, Sa 9:30am-3pm); free **Internet** access at the **Swansea Central Library,** in the Civic Centre, Oystermouth Rd. (☎01792 636 464; photo ID required; open Tu-F 8:30am-8pm, Sa-Su 10am-4pm); **police,** Grove Pl. (☎01792 456 999), at the bottom of Mt. Pleasant Hill; **Co-op** pharmacy, 13 Orchard St. (☎01792 643 527; open M-F 9am-5:30pm, Sa 9am-1pm); **Singleton Hospital,** Sketty Park Ln. (☎01792 205 666); and the **post office,** on the second floor of WHSmith in the Quadrant Shopping Centre (open M-Sa 9am-5:30pm). **Postcode:** SA1 5LF.

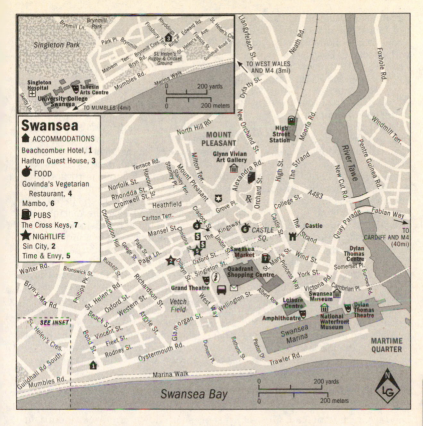

Swansea

🏠 ACCOMMODATIONS
Beachcomber Hotel, 1
Harlton Guest House, 3

🍎 FOOD
Govinda's Vegetarian
   Restaurant, 4
Mambo, 6

🍺 PUBS
The Cross Keys, 7

⭐ NIGHTLIFE
Sin City, 2
Time & Envy, 5

SOUTH WALES

🏠🏛 **ACCOMMODATIONS AND FOOD.** The closest hostel is the popular
YHA Port Eynon ❶, an hour out of town by bus (p. 490). Inexpensive B&Bs and
guesthouses (£15-30) line Oystermouth Rd., along the bay. Buses on their way
to and from Quadrant Station stop at various points around the city, making
downtown access easy. **The Beachcomber Hotel ❸,** 364 Oystermouth Rd., is a nice
option, with clean, pastel-colored rooms overlooking the bay. (☎01792 651
380; www.beachcomberhotel.co.uk. Breakfast included. Singles £25, ensuite
doubles £60. MC/V.) **Harlton Guest House ❶,** 89 King Edward Rd., offers small,
inexpensive rooms with TVs and Wi-Fi. (☎01792 466 938; www.harltonguest-
house.co.uk. £15 per person. MC/V.) In summer, many travelers camp at sites
along the Gower Peninsula, many of which are accessible by bus.

Indian and Chinese takeaways line St. Helen's Rd. Small cafes, bistros, and
trendy restaurants dominate Oxford and Wind St. Shoppers convene at the
Swansea Market, the largest indoor market in Wales, on the side of the Quadrant
Shopping Centre opposite the bus station. (Open M-Sa 8:30am-5:30pm.) **Govinda's Vegetarian Restaurant ❶,** 8 Cradock St., is a small, quiet spot just off The Kingsway specializing in Indian-inspired dishes. (☎01792 468 469. Open M-Th and Su
noon-3pm, F noon-4pm, Sa noon-6pm. MC/V.) Brightly colored **Mambo ❶,** 46 The
Kingsway, serves tasty Caribbean and Mediterranean fare (tapas £3; fajitas and

panini £4-4.50) and becomes a trendy watering hole in the evening. (☎01792 456 620. Mixed drinks £3. Open M and W-Th 5pm-2am, Tu 5pm-1am, F noon-2am, Sa noon-3am. AmEx/MC/V.) **The Cross Keys ❶**, 12 St. Mary's St., is a sprawling pub with a menu as large as its beer garden and flashy games to occupy the bar-shy. (☎01792 630 921; www.oxkeys.com. Open M-Sa 11am-11pm, Su noon-10:30pm. Kitchen open M-Sa 11am-8pm, Su noon-8pm. MC/V.)

◙ SIGHTS. The bronze, hollowed eyes of **Dylan Thomas's** statue gaze seaward at the end of Swansea's marina. The late poet, a demigod of local culture and national literature, inspires many tours, which shepherd tourists along the **Dylan Thomas Uplands Trail** and **City Centre Trail** past the poet's favorite haunts. Detailed guidebooks to the trails (£1.50) are available at the **Dylan Thomas Centre,** Somerset Pl., which venerates Thomas and his "craft of sullen art." Visitors can listen to Thomas breathlessly recite five of his poems. Famous portraits hang alongside his notoriously sizable bar tabs (£8 in 1953). The center also presents dramatic, cinematic, and literary performances. (☎01792 463 980. Open daily 10am-4:30pm. Free.) In a shiny, modern building near the marina, the **◪National Waterfront Museum** illustrates the social and industrial history of Swansea through a series of interactive displays. Highlights include a virtual tour of Swansea at the time of the 1851 census and a gallery of industrial artifacts ranging from a rolling mill to a giant brick press. (☎01792 638 950; www.waterfrontmuseum.co.uk. Open daily 10am-5pm. Free.) The collection of paintings, porcelain, glassware, and even ceramic cow-shaped cream dispensers at the **Glynn Vivian Art Gallery,** Alexandra Rd., reflects the eclectic tastes of its largest donor, Richard Glynn Vivian. (☎01792 516 900; www.glynnviviangallery.org. Open Tu-Su 10am-5pm. Free.) The **Swansea Museum,** Victoria Rd., is the oldest in Wales and features an extensive collection of cycling memorabilia, the Egypt Centre, and the Cabinet of Curiosities, a celebration of randomness in the style of Victorian-era museums. (☎01792 653 763; www.swanseaheritage.net. Open Tu-Su 10am-5pm. Last entry 4pm. Free.)

◪◪ ENTERTAINMENT AND NIGHTLIFE. The students of Swansea do not go gentle into weekend nights. Festivities begin at pre-club bars as early as 7pm and rage, rage until 3am. Most clubs see a sharp downturn or close outright during summer vacation. Nightlife centers on The Kingsway, where swarms of students club-hop on weekend nights. **Time & Envy,** 72 The Kingsway, is the most popular club simply because it can squeeze in the biggest crowd. (☎01792 653 142. Cover F £10 including 6 drinks, Sa £5 including 4 drinks. Open F-Sa 10pm-3:30am.) A couple blocks away, the two floors of **Sin City** blast metal, indie, and pop tunes, with occasional live music. (☎07976 136 194; www.alternativeswansea.com. Cover £3-15. Open F-Sa 10pm-4am.)

The bimonthly *What's On*, free at the TIC, lists events around town. The **Dylan Thomas Theatre,** located along the marina, stages dramas and musicals. (☎01792 473 238; www.dylanthomastheatre.org.uk. Tickets £8, concessions £6. Box office open M-F 10am-2pm.) **The Grand Theatre,** on Singleton St., puts on operas, ballets, concerts, and comedies. (☎01792 475 715; www.swanseagrand.co.uk. Tickets £7-35; same-day concessions often available. Box office open M-Sa 9:30am-6pm, until 8pm on performance days, Su 1hr. before show.) The **Taliesin Arts Centre,** on the Swansea University campus, Singleton Park, hosts films, art shows, and dance performances and also has a bookstore and cafe on site. (☎01792 602 060; www.taliesinartscentre.co.uk. Box office open M-F 10am-6pm, Sa 10am-1pm and 1:30-4pm, performance days 10am-8pm.)

In mid-August, the village of Pontardawe, located 8 mi. north of Swansea, is flooded with folk and rock musicians from all over the world, in town for the annual **Pontardawe International Music Festival** (☎01792 830 200; www.pontardawefestival.com; weekend ticket £58). The **Swansea Festival,** held in October of every year, features classical, dance, opera, and jazz performances, art exhibitions, and family activities. (☎01792 411 570, bookings 475 715; www.swanseafestival.com. Tickets £11-30.) The revelry continues with the **Dylan Thomas Celebration** (☎01792 463 980; www.dylanthomasfestival.com), which includes a variety of readings, shows, and lectures that run from Thomas's birthday all the way through to the date of his death (Oct. 27-Nov. 9).

MUMBLES AND
THE GOWER PENINSULA ☎(0)1792

The 19 mi. Gower Peninsula is full of unexpected sights. Ancient burial mounds, castles, and churches dot the land, and expansive white beaches border flower-covered limestone cliffs. Mumbles, its largest city, has beaches, bistros, and a seaside as unassuming as its name.

▤ TRANSPORTATION. Buses to the peninsula leave primarily from Swansea's Quadrant Station. The two main bus companies are First Cymru (☎08706 082 608), which mostly services Mumbles, and Veolia (☎01443 215 105), which shuttles around the smaller towns. Unfortunately, schedules are not very well integrated, and passes are not transferable. First Cymru buses #1, 2, 2A, 2B, 3A, and 37 travel between Oystermouth Sq. in Mumbles and Swansea (20min., 4 per hr.). Buses #1, 2, 2A and 2B continue to Langland Corner (30min.) and Caswell Bay (35min.). Bus #14 shuttles to Swansea from Pennard (35min., every hr.). Veolia runs Gower Explorer buses #117 and 118 between Swansea, Oxwich (40min., 5 per day, £3.65), and Rhossili via Port Eynon (1hr., every hr., £3.65). The First Cymru FirstDay ticket is valid on First buses through Gower and Swansea (£3.35-4), while the Gower & City Rider allows a week's unlimited travel around the peninsula (£8). Gower Day Explorer tickets are valid for a day's travel on all buses in Veolia's Gower Explorer network (£4). AA Taxis (☎01792 360 600) provides 24hr. **taxis.** The Swansea Bikepath and Promenade traces the coast from Swansea Bay to Mumbles pier; rent **bikes** in Swansea at Action Bikes, St. David's Sq. (☎01792 464 640. Open M-Sa 9am-5:30pm, Su 11am-4pm. £15 per day. ID required.)

⁊ PRACTICAL INFORMATION. Mumbles, the largest city on Gower, has the most helpful services. The **Tourist Information Centre** shares space with Mumbles Methodist Church on Mumbles Rd. (☎01792 361 302. Open Aug. M-Sa 10am-4:30pm, Su noon-4pm; Sept.-July M-Sa 10am-4:30pm.) Other services include: **Barclays** bank, 16 Newton Rd. (☎0870 241 281; open M-F 9am-4:30pm); free **Internet** at **Oystermouth Library,** Dunns Ln., a block from the TIC (☎01792 368 380; photo ID required; open M-Th 9am-6pm, F 9am-8pm, Sa 9am-5pm, Su noon-4pm); **police** on Newton Rd., near Castle St.; **Boots** pharmacy, 133 Mumbles Rd., across from the TIC (☎01792 366 195; open M-F 9am-6pm, Sa 8:30am-6pm); **Singleton Hospital,** Sketty Park Ln. (☎01792 205 666); and the **post office,** 522 Mumbles Rd. (☎01792 366 821; open M-Sa 9am-5:30pm). **Postcode:** SA3 4DH.

▐▣ ACCOMMODATIONS AND FOOD. West Gower, including Oxwich, Port Eynon, and Rhossili, has cheaper accommodations than Mumbles does. Your best bet is probably to stay in nearby Swansea (p. 486). B&Bs in Mumbles charge £25-35 for singles and cluster on **Mumbles Road** and in the South End area (a 10min. walk from the TIC); singles are hard to find. With large bay windows, the gabled **Coast House ❸,** 708 Mumbles Rd., has views of schooners in the quiet harbor. (☎01792 368 702. All rooms are ensuite and have TVs. Singles £35; doubles £60. MC/V.) To camp at **Three Cliffs Bay Caravan Park ❶**, North Hills Farm, Penmaen, take bus #118 (40min., 1 per hr.) from Swansea. (☎01792 371 218; www.threecliffsbay.com. Tent site with electricity £17. MC/V.) Bus #118 runs from Swansea to Port Eynon, west of Mumbles, home to the **YHA Port Eynon ❷**. You won't find a better location than this former lifeboat house, situated right on the beach. Book ahead in summer—with its clean kitchen, comfortable common area, and wall-spanning windows, the hostel fills early with families. (☎08707 705 998. Laundry £2 per load. Reception 8-10am and 5-10pm. Check-in 5pm. Open Easter-Nov. Dorms £18, under 18 £12; doubles £45-55. MC/V.) **Tan-y-Bryn ❸** provides B&B accommodations in Port Eynon. (☎01792 391 182. £30 per person, £25 for multiple-night stays. Cash only.) Beachside camping is also possible in Port Eynon at **Carreglwyd Camping and Leisure ❶**. (☎01792 390 795; www.porteynon.com. High-season sites for 2 £18. Electricity £2.)

In Mumbles, the **Somerfield** supermarket is at 512 Mumbles Rd. (☎01792 361 859. Open daily 8am-9pm.) Both locations of **The Choice is Yours,** at 7 Newton Rd. and 508 Mumbles Rd. near the TIC, sell fresh produce. (☎01792 367 255. Open M-F 8:30am-5:30pm. MC/V.) Summer crowds flock to **Verdi's ❶**, at the southern end of Mumbles Rd., for pizzas, pasta, sandwiches (£4-9.70), and bay views on all sides. It also has an ice-cream bar, scooping out 32 flavors in summer, including honeycomb and apple crumb. (☎01792 369 135. 1 scoop £1.80. Open June-Sept. daily 10am-9:30pm; Oct. and Apr.-May daily 10am-9pm; Nov.-Mar. M-Th 10am-6pm, F-Su 10am-9pm. MC/V.) **Madisons ❶**, 620 Mumbles Rd., is a small cafe with a big view of the bay. (☎01792 368 484. Open daily 8:45am-4pm. Cash only.) In Rhossili, **Bar Helvetia ❷** is a bright, airy pub. Diners gaze out at the rocky peaks of Worm's Head while relaxing after a day at the beach. (☎01792 390 512. Entrees £5-14. Open daily noon-9pm. MC/V.)

SIGHTS AND OUTDOOR ACTIVITIES. High above Mumbles, the ramparts of 13th-century **Oystermouth Castle**, on Castle Ave. off Newton Rd., offer a bird's-eye view of the labyrinthine streets. (☎01792 368 732. Open Apr.-Sept. daily 11am-5pm. £1, concessions and children 80p.) **Clyne Gardens and Country Park,** at Blackpill between Mumbles and Swansea, is a riot of color in spring. Woodland walking and cycle paths and a mid-1800s castle draw visitors year-round. First Cymru buses #1, 2A, 2B, 3A, 3B (and 37 buses from Swansea and Mumbles) stop at Blackpill. (☎01792 205 327; www.swansea.gov.uk/clyneinbloom. Open daily dawn-dusk. Free. Weekly guided walks £1.) The small collection at the **Lovespoon Gallery,** 492 Mumbles Rd., displays and sells traditional Welsh love tokens. (☎01792 360 132; www.welsh-lovespoons.co.uk. Spoons from £3.75; engravings £10. Open M-Sa 10am-5:30pm. AmEx/MC/V.) The **Gower Festival** fills the peninsula's churches with string quartets and Bach chorales during the last two weeks of July (booking ☎01792 475 715; tickets average £12). The *What's On* guide, free at the Mumbles TIC, has details.

The Gower Peninsula is strewn with gorgeous beaches, some more swimming-friendly than others. From Southgate and Pennard, a 30min. walk along the Coast Path brings you to **Three Cliffs**, a cave-ridden area largely submerged at high tide. **Langland Bay, Caswell Bay, Oxwich Bay,** and **Port Eynon Bay** are all popular and clean, with superb views. To reach Langland, walk 45min. along the Bays Footpath that begins around the point of Mumbles Head. Caswell is another 45min., and Oxwich and Port Eynon are several miles beyond; buses #117 and 118 from Swansea will stop there. On the peninsula's western tip, cliffs hug the sweeping curve of **Rhossili Beach,** whose wide expanse and seclusion make overcrowding unlikely (take bus #118 from Swansea). Within about 2hr. of low tide, a causeway of jagged black rocks provides access to the seabird haven **Worm's Head**, crags that look like a *wurm* (the Old English word for "dragon") lumbering out to sea. A National Trust visitors center (☎01792 390 707) near the head posts safe crossing times and information on tides. **Llangennith Beach**, north of Rhossili, draws surfers from all over Wales. Gower's expansive beaches are ideal for **watersports**. Euphoria Sailing rents boats and organizes activity days ranging from wakeboarding to kayaking. (☎01792 234 502; www.euphoriasailing.com. Activities from £10 per hr., up to £95 per day.) Surfgsd gives **surfing** lessons in Caswell Bay and Rhossili Beach. (☎01792 360 370; www.surfgsd.com. £35 per ½-day session, £50 per full day.)

PEMBROKESHIRE COAST

The 225 sq. mi. of Pembrokeshire Coast National Park (Parc Cenedlaethol Arfordir Penfro) spread across oceanside stretches of sand and limestone, wildlife sanctuaries for rare seabirds, and inland pockets with historic towns. The park spans the Gwaun Valley and Celtic ruins in the Preseli Hills, but the coastline remains its biggest draw. Coves and sea cliffs lure hikers along 186 mi. of coastal trail, while beaches attract sunbathers, kayakers, and surfers.

▐ TRANSPORTATION

Public transportation in Pembrokeshire leaves much to be desired; many routes run sporadically and not at all on Sundays. The region's best base is **Haverfordwest**. Buses travel from this hub to most towns on the Pembrokeshire coast. Some hitchers frequent the area, but *Let's Go* does not recommend hitchhiking. Bikes are a good means of transportation on one-lane roads, but do not ride on the coastal path—it is illegal and dangerous.

Trains: ☎08457 484 950. From Haverfordwest to **Cardiff** (2½hr., 8-10 per day, £17.10) and **London Paddington** (4-7hr., 5-9 per day, £31.50). Also to **Fishguard** on the north coast and **Tenby** and **Pembroke Dock** on the south (change at **Whitland**).

Buses: Richards Brothers (☎02139 613 756) #412 runs from Haverfordwest to **Fishguard** (45min.; M-Sa 1 per hr., Su 3 per day) and #411 to **St. David's** (45min.; M-Sa 12 per day, Su 4 per day). First Cymru (☎01792 580 580) runs from Haverfordwest to **Tenby** via **Pembroke** (#349; 1½hr.; M-Sa every hr., Su 2-4 per day). Silcox Coaches (☎01646 683 143) and Acorn Travel (☎01348 874 728) run from Haverfordwest to **Broad Haven** (#311, 20min., M-Sa 5-7 per day). The Puffin Shuttle #400 runs between **St. David's** and **Milford Haven** (2hr.; May-Sept. daily 3 per day, Oct.-Apr. M, Th, Sa 3 per day), and the Strumble Shuttle #404 connects **St. David's** and **Fishguard** (1¼hr.; May-Sept. 3 per day, Oct.-Apr. M, Th, Sa 2 per day). First Cymru's FirstDay Pass (£5) gives unlimited bus transportation within Pembrokeshire on its buses, while the more useful **West Wales Rover Ticket** (£6.60, children £4.40) works all day on any bus. The free *Pembrokeshire Bus Timetables* and *Pembrokeshire Coastal Bus Services Timetables* are available at local TICs.

Bike Rental: Re-Cycles Bike Hire, Simpson Cross, about 12 mi. from St. David's (☎07816 140 616). Helmets and maps included. £10 per day, children £6. Free delivery; call ahead. **Mike's Bikes,** 17 Prendergast, Haverfordwest (☎01437 760 068; www.mikes-bikes.co.uk). £10 per day; delivery available. MC/V.

Outdoor Equipment Rental: You can find everything from canoes to ponies for rental or guided lessons and trips. Check *Explore Pembrokeshire* or *Coast to Coast,* available free at NPICs, for outdoor shop locations. Among the most popular outdoor activity centers is the excellent **TYF Adventure** (see **Crazy or Coasteering?,** p. 498), 1 High St. in St. David's (☎01437 721 611; www.tyf.com).

PRACTICAL INFORMATION

The **National Park Information Centers (NPICs)** below sell annotated maps (50p) of the coastal path. Guides for the entire trail are pricey (£10-13) but detailed and include color maps. Ask about guided walks offered by the park. For weather information, call any NPIC. All Tourist Information Centres book accommodations for a £2 fee and 10% deposit of the first night's stay.

National Park Information Centres:

Newport: 2 Bank Cottages, Long St. (☎01239 820 912). Open June-Aug. M-Sa 10am-5:30pm, Su 10am-1:15pm; Sept.-Oct. and Apr.-May M-Sa 10am-5:30pm.

St. David's: The Grove (☎01437 720 392; www.stdavids.co.uk). From Cross Sq., walk up High St. 5-10min. Also a TIC. Open Easter-Oct. daily 9:30am-5:30pm; Nov.-Easter M-Sa 10am-4pm.

Tourist Information Centres:

Fishguard: See p. 499.

Haverfordwest: 19 Old Bridge (☎01437 763 110), adjacent to the bus stop. Open M-Sa Easter-Oct. 9:30am-5pm; Nov.-Easter 10am-5pm.

Milford Haven: 94 Charles St. (☎01646 690 866). Open Easter-Oct. M-Sa 9:45am-4:15pm.

Saundersfoot: The Barbecue, Harbour Car Park (☎01834 813 672). Open Mar.-Oct. M-Sa 9:30am-5pm, Su 10am-4pm; Nov.-Feb. F-Su 10am-4pm.

Tenby: See p. 494.

ACCOMMODATIONS

Many farmers convert fallow fields into summer **campgrounds** (about £6 per person); inquire before pitching. Roads between Tenby, Pembroke, and St. David's are home to plenty of B&Bs (£15-30), but they fill quickly in summer and buses are infrequent. Along the coastal path, the park's **YHA hostels,** listed below, are all within a day's walk of one another. If you plan at least two weeks ahead, you can book these by calling ☎01629 592 700 or visiting www.yha.org.uk.

Broad Haven (☎01437 781 688), on St. Bride's Bay off the B4341. Take bus #311 from Haverfordwest to Broad Haven (20min., 5 per day) or #400 from St. David's (35min., 3 per day) or Milford Haven (1hr., 3 per day). 78 beds near the beach. Kitchen and laundry. Curfew 11pm. Book in advance. Dorms £14-20, under 18 £10.50-15. MC/V. ❷

Manorbier, Skrinkle Haven (☎08707 705 954; manorbier@yha.org.uk). First Cymru (☎01792 580 580) bus #349 runs from Tenby and Pembroke to Skrinkle Haven (20min. from both; M-Sa 1 per hr., Su 2-5 per day). Follow the signs from the stop to the hostel. Modern building a 25-30min. walk from Manorbier Castle (p. 496). Meals available. Access to kitchen, laundry, and computer lab with free Internet. Open Apr.-Oct., Nov.-Apr. for group rentals only. Dorms £13-19, under 18 £10-14.50. MC/V. ❷

Marloes Sands (☎01646 636 667), near the Dale Peninsula. Take Puffin bus #400 (1hr., 3 per day) from St. David's or Milford Haven; ask to be let off at the hostel. Farm buildings with access to a huge beach. Good site for watersports. Book through Broad Haven. Open Apr.-Oct. Dorms £14, under 18 £10.50. MC/V. ❶

St. David's (☎01437 720 345), near St. David's Head. From the A487 (Fishguard Rd.), turn onto the B4583 and follow signs from the golf club. Celtic Coaster bus runs every hr. in summer and drops off 1 mi. from St. David's. Converted farm buildings. Reception 9-10am and 5-10pm. Open Easter-Oct. Dorms £14, under 18 £10.50. MC/V. ❶

HIKING AND OUTDOOR ACTIVITIES

For short hikes, stick to accessible **Saint David's Peninsula** in the northwest. Otherwise, set out on the 186 mi. **Pembrokeshire Coast Path,** marked with acorn symbols. For general information on the path, call the **Pembrokeshire Coast National Park Authority** at ☎0845 345 7275. Leaflets, available at NPICs and TICs for 50p, describe points of interest and transportation along individual sections of the path. Larger booklets describe four circular walks near towns (£1.50). The coast path begins in the southeast at Amroth and continues west across sandstone through Tenby. **Bosherton's Lily Ponds,** manmade inlets that bloom in early summer, circle around to St. Govan's Head, where steps lead to **Saint Govan's Chapel.** The waters of the well are said to heal ills and grant wishes, and supposedly no mortal can count the steps. From here to **Elegug Stacks**—offshore rocks with the largest seabird colonies of the coastline—the path passes natural sea arches and limestone stacks. The famous 80 ft. **Green Bridge** is particularly striking. The stretch from St. Govan's Head to the Stacks (6 mi.) is sometimes used as an artillery range and closed to hikers. Call the **Castlemartin Range Office** (☎01646 662 367) or the **Pembroke National Visitor Centre** (☎01646 622 388) for openings or check at the Tenby TIC. For 10 mi. west of the Stacks, the coast is permanently off-limits, and the path veers inland to **Freshwater West,** passing **Stack Fort,** built to defend against the French.

From Freshwater West to **Angle Bay,** the coastline walk covers mild terrain. At **Milford Haven,** the path is cut by a large channel. From the **Dale Peninsula,** the path passes by the long beaches of **Saint Bride's Bay, Marloes Sands,** and the **Three Chimneys,** columns of stone shaped by erosion. The path curves to **St. David's Head,** the site of many Iron Age hill settlements. Past St. David's at Abereiddi, the sea has refilled an old slate quarry to create the **Blue Lagoon.** The final stretch of the Coastal Path, between Newport and St. Dogmaels, is strenuous—its total ascent is equal to that of Mt. Snowdon (p. 519). The free *Explore Pembrokeshire,* available at TICs, gives trail tips and bus information. To explore Pembrokeshire by horseback, contact **Maesgwynne Riding Stables,** near Fishguard. (☎01348 872 659; david-llewhelin1@virgin.net. £12 per hr.)

🏝 ISLANDS OFF THE PEMBROKESHIRE COAST

RAMSEY ISLAND

Once used as a retreat for monks, then as farmland, today Ramsey is operated as a nature reserve by the Royal Society for the Protection of Birds. The island's dark cliffs and quiet caves host many rare sea birds and the largest gray-seal colony in Wales off St. David's Peninsula. On the east side of the island lurk **The Bitches,** a rock chain ostensibly named for its resemblance to a dog with her pups but more likely because its jagged edges have brought countless sailors to their doom. Brave sea kayakers test their fate in the surrounding rapids. Several companies based in St. David's operate tours to or around the island, most departing from St. Justinian's lifeboat station. Celtic Coaster bus #403 runs between St. David's and St. Justinian's from late March to September (15min., 2 per hr., £1). Landing tours allow visitors to birdwatch along the trails of the nature reserve, but tours around the island afford better views of coastal wildlife hiding near the caves. **Thousand Islands Expeditions,** Cross Sq., operates landing cruises to Ramsey (£15, children £7.50) and organizes walking tours of the island. (☎01437 721 686; www.thousandislands.co.uk. Boat trips run from late Mar. to Oct. Trips depart from 9am. Book ahead.) **Voyages of Discovery,** 1 High St., runs 1-1½hr. bird-, seal-, and porpoise-watching cruises on specially designed rubber craft. (☎0800 854 367. Tours £24-55, children £12-30.)

TIP

NATURE STALK. The coastal islands hold a wealth of interesting creatures, but the chances of seeing certain wildlife vary by the time of day and the tides. Inquire about sea conditions at one of the tour companies ahead of time to avoid being disappointed.

SKOMER, SKOKHOLM, AND GRASSHOLM

Pembrokeshire's smaller offshore islands hold some of the largest sea-bird populations in Britain. Minke whales, dolphins, porpoises, and orcas are also regularly seen off their coasts. Skomer is a marine reserve for auks, seals, and puffins. By night, tens of thousands of Manx shearwaters fill the air as they return to their burrows, possibly the largest colony of such birds in the world. The smaller Skokholm holds up to 20% of the European Union's population of breeding storm petrols as well as rare grasslands and cliff lichens. On Grassholm, the most distant island, 35,000 pairs of gannets raise their young each year. **Dale Sailing** (☎01646 603 123; www.dale-sailing.co.uk) makes landing cruises and guided daytrips to Skomer and Skokholm and runs 3hr. tours around Grassholm. Boats leave from Martin's Haven, accessible by the #400 bus from St. David's (1½hr., 3 per day).

TENBY (DINBYCH-Y-PYSGOD)   ☎(0)1834

Called "the Welsh Riviera," Tenby is a mix between a traditional walled Welsh town and a polished seaside resort. The colorful rows of beachfront guesthouses, boutiques, and cafes are popular year-round, but it is only during July and August that Tenby sees big crowds, when multitudes of English holidaymakers pour onto its beaches.

TRANSPORTATION. Trains (☎08457 484 950; www.nationalrail.co.uk) depart to: Cardiff (2¾hr., 9 per day, £17.10); Carmarthen (45min., 9 per day, £6.30); Pembroke (20min.; M-Sa 9 per day, Su 5 per day; £3.60); Swansea (1¾hr., 9 per day, £10.10). **Buses** leave from the bulwark in front of the car park on Upper Park Rd. First Cymru (☎01792 580 580) #349 goes to Haverfordwest via Pembroke (M-Sa every hr. until 6:05pm, Su 4 per day). From Swansea, take #X11 to Carmarthen (M-Sa 2 per hr.) and transfer to Silcox Coaches (☎01834 842 189; www.silcoxcoaches.co.uk) bus #333 (1hr., M-Sa 1 per day). A Silcox Coaches office is in the Town Hall Arcade between South Parade and Upper Frog St. (Open M-F 9am-12:30pm and 1:30-5pm.) National Express (☎08705 808 080) also runs to Swansea (#508, 1½hr., 3 per day, £7.60). **First Cymru FirstDay Ticket** (£6.25) and **FirstWeek Ticket** (£22) allow unlimited weekly travel within Pembrokeshire on First buses, while the **West Wales Rover Ticket** (£6.60) works on all bus lines. **Taxis** congregate near pubs on Friday and Saturday nights; call Tenby's Taxis (☎01834 843 678).

PRACTICAL INFORMATION. The Tourist Information Centre, 2 Upper Park Rd. by the bus station and Somerfield, gives out free accommodations listings. (☎01834 842 404. Open Apr.-Oct. daily 9:30am-5pm; Nov.-Mar. M-Sa 10am-4pm.) Other services include: **Barclays** bank, 18 High St. (**ATM** on Frog St.; open M-F 9am-5pm); **Internet** access at **Tenby County Library,** Greenhill Ave. (☎01834 843 934; free; open M and W-F 9:30am-5pm, Tu 9:30am-6pm, Sa 9:30am-12:30pm); **Washeteria** launderette, Lower Frog St. (☎01834 842 484); **police,** Warren St. (☎0845 330 2000), near the church off White Lion St.; **Boots** pharmacy, High St.

(☎01834 842 120; open M-Sa 9am-5:30pm); and **Tenby Cottage Hospital,** Narbeth Rd. (☎01834 845 400), near Trafalgar Rd. **Postcode:** SA70 7JR.

🄵🄲 **ACCOMMODATIONS AND FOOD.** The streets just behind the Esplanade along **South Beach** are lined with B&Bs, as is **Warren Street,** outside the town wall near the train station. Overlooking North Beach, bright rooms await in the **Blue Dolphin Hotel ❷,** St. Mary's St. (☎01834 842 590. £21 per person, ensuite with breakfast £27-30. MC/V.) **The Hildebrand Hotel ❸,** Victoria St., has large cream-colored rooms and a lively hostess who makes guests feel at home. (☎01834 842 403. £25-33 per person. MC/V.)

Although many of Tenby's restaurants cater to vacationers and charge accordingly, the variety of eateries will accommodate most budgets. The streets just inside the town walls, including **Upper Frog, Lower Frog,** and **Saint George's Street,** have several cheap takeaways. Cafes, from the contemporary to the quaint, are ubiquitous. One of the nicest is 🄲**Caffe Vista ❷,** 3 Crackwell St., a continental-style cafe with beautiful sea views and Greek dishes like traditional butter-bean stew for £6.75. (☎01834 849 636. Free Wi-Fi. Open daily 9am-11pm. MC/V.) In an alleyway connecting Bridge St. and St. Julian's St., a jungle of flowers marks **Plantagenet House ❹,** Quay Hill. Diners feast by candlelight on organic venison from the Brecon Beacons (£21) or local sea bass (£22) in the hearth of the oldest (10th century) and tallest (39 ft.) medieval Flemish chimney in Wales. (☎01834 842 350. Entrees £15-24. Open Easter-Oct. daily 10am-2:30pm and 5pm-late; Nov.-Easter F-Su 5pm-late. MC/V.) **The Coach and Horses ❸,** Upper Frog St., is the oldest continuously operating pub in town and serves Thai cuisine alongside traditional pub fare. (☎01834 842 704. Entrees £8-13. Live music Su. Open daily noon-11pm. Kitchen open noon-3pm and 6-9pm. Cash only.)

🄶🄰 **SIGHTS AND BEACHES.** The three floors of the **Tudor Merchant's House,** on Quay Hill off Bridge St., reveal much about life in a 16th-century Welsh household, with staff in each room to point out highlights. (☎01834 842 279. Open daily from mid-Mar. to Oct. M-F and Su 11am-5pm. £2.70.) A sun-bleached statue of **Prince Albert the Good** stands atop Castle Hill, overlooking the ruins of the castle and colorful Tenby. On clear days, the views reach across Carmarthen Bay, Rhossili Beach's Worm's Head, and the Devon coast. In a renovated section of the castle, the **Tenby Museum and Art Gallery** has a small archaeological display and an exhibit on Tenby's maritime history, including a wax recreation of the Tenby pirate Leekie Porridge. (☎01834 842 809. Open Apr.-Oct. daily 10am-5pm; Nov.-Mar. M-F 10am-5pm. £4, concessions £3.) At night, Tenby's ghouls share the streets with resort revelers. The guided 1hr. **Walk of Tenby** and **Ghost Walk of Tenby** depart from the Lifeboat Tavern in Tudor Sq. at 8pm. (☎01834 845 841. From mid-July to mid-Sept. daily; from mid-Sept. to mid-July M-Sa. Advance booking required. £4, concessions £3.75, children £3, families £13.)

On sunny days, **North Beach,** below the Croft, and **South Beach,** beyond the Esplanade, swarm with pensioners and toddlers. A small, flower-filled garden surrounds a pathway leading down to South Beach from the town walls and makes a nice picnic spot (open until dusk). At the eastern tip of Tenby, **Castle Beach** reaches into caves that lure curious explorers, but more remote beaches offer escape from the oceanside throng. A variety of **boat excursions** leaves from the harbor; check the kiosks at Castle Beach (Apr.-Sept. ☎07980 864 509, Oct.-Mar. 07973 280 651) for the Seal Safari, a 1hr. boat ride to St. Margaret's Island and Cathedral Caves (£15, children £8), or the Sunset Cruise, a 1½hr. excursion held only in July and August (£9, children £5).

⚡ DAYTRIP FROM TENBY: CALDEY ISLAND. Three miles south of Tenby, this largely unspoiled island hosts a diverse community of sea birds, seals, and 20 Cistercian monks, who produce perfume from indigenous lavender in their Italianate monastery. The chocolate factory, inspired by the monks' Belgian roots, turns out over 12 tons of sweets per year (bars from £1.10), sold on the island and in a shop in Tenby. *(Caldey Boats sails from Tenby Harbor. ☎01834 844 453; www.caldey-island.co.uk. Cruises 20min. Easter-Oct. 3 per hr. M-Sa 10am-3pm; last round-trip 5pm, weather permitting. Round-trip £10, children £5, seniors £9.)*

⚡ DAYTRIP FROM TENBY: MANORBIER CASTLE. Gerald of Wales, a noted 12th-century historian of rural life, called Manorbier "the pleasantest spot in Wales." He may have been a little biased (he was born here), but the castle is certainly a contender for that title. It affords stunning views of Manorbier beach and gardens. Life-size wax figures inside the castle recreate scenes of medieval life and Welsh legend. Manorbier has a **YHA hostel ❷** (p. 492) as well as numerous B&Bs. *(First Cymru bus #349 shuttles between Tenby, Manorbier, Pembroke, and Haverfordwest. In summer M-Sa every hr., Su 4 per day; in winter M-Sa every hr. Castle ☎01834 871 394. Open daily Easter-Sept. 10am-5:30pm. £3.50, concessions £2.50, children £1.50.)*

⚡ DAYTRIP FROM TENBY: CAREW CASTLE. Handsome Carew Castle, 5 mi. northwest of Tenby, is an odd mixture of Norman fortress and Elizabethan manor. Strong defensive towers give way to large, delicate windows. Check *Coast to Coast*, free at most TICs, for events at the castle. *(Take Silcox bus #361 from Tenby to the castle. 45min., M-Sa 3 per day. ☎01646 651 782. Open daily from late Mar. to Oct. 10am-5pm; Nov.-Easter 11am-3pm. Free guided tours at 2:30pm. Castle and mill £3.50, concessions £2.50, children £1.50, families £9.50.)*

PEMBROKE (PENFRO)   ☎(0)1646

In a county known as "Little England beyond Wales," Pembroke no longer feels like the military stronghold its Norman occupants designed. Battlements that once formed anti-Cromwell resistance now shade hungry picnickers, and the waters that once served to protect the castle now harbor swans.

▣ TRANSPORTATION. Pembroke's unstaffed **train station** is on Station Rd. at the opposite end of Main St. from the castle. Trains (☎08457 484 950) run from Pembroke and Pembroke Dock to Tenby (20min., 9 per day, £3.60), Swansea (2hr.; M-Sa 9-10 per day, Su 5 per day; £10.10), and points farther east. **Buses** going east from Pembroke stop outside the Somerfield supermarket; those going north stop at the castle. National Express (☎08705 808 080) runs to Cardiff via Swansea (3½hr., 3 per day, £15.10) and London (7hr., 3 per day, £28). First Cymru (☎01792 580 580) #349 stops in Pembroke and at Pembroke Dock on its route between Tenby (40-50min.; M-Sa every hr., Su 5 per day; £2-3) and Haverfordwest (35-40min.; M-Sa every hr., Su 5 per day).

◪ ⚡ ORIENTATION AND PRACTICAL INFORMATION. Pembroke Castle lies up the hill on the western end of **Main Street;** the street's other end fans into five roads from a roundabout. Across the river and to the north is **Pembroke Docks.**

Downhill from Pembroke's town center, the **Tourist Information Centre,** Commons Rd., has displays on the Pembrokeshire Coastal Path. The staff books accommodations for £2 plus a 10% deposit. (☎01437 776 499. Open Easter-Oct. M-Sa 9:30am-5pm, Su 10am-4pm; winter hours are irregular, call ahead.) Other services include: **Barclays** bank, 35 Main St. (open M-F 9am-5pm); **police,** 4 Water St. (☎08003 302 000); **Internet** at the **Pembroke Library,** 38 Main St. (☎01646

682 973; free; open Tu and F 10am-1pm and 2-5pm, W and Sa 10am-1pm, Th 10am-1pm and 2-7pm; book ahead) and at **Dragon Alley**, 63 Main St. (☎01646 621 456; £1 per 15min., £3 per hr.; open Tu-Sa 10am-5pm); and the **post office**, 49 Main St. (open M-F 9am-5:30pm, Sa 9am-1pm). **Postcode:** SA71 4JT.

ACCOMMODATIONS AND FOOD. The nearest YHA hostel is in Manorbier between Tenby and Pembroke (p. 492). The few B&Bs in Pembroke are scattered, although some options are on Main St. Mrs. Willis fosters an elegant atmosphere at her bright blue **Beech House ❷**, 78 Main St. With sweet-smelling rooms and crystal chandeliers, you'll be amazed that you aren't spending more. (☎01646 683 740; www.beechhousepembroke.com. £17.50 per person. Cash only.) **Woodbine ❸**, 84 Main St., pampers guests with grand, ensuite rooms with TV and flowers. (☎01646 686 338. Singles £35; doubles £50. Cash only.)

Stock up at **Somerfield** supermarket, 6-10 Main St. (Open M-Sa 8am-9pm, Su 10am-4pm.) **Browns Restaurant ❶**, 51 Main St., a delightful fish-and-chips diner, harks back to the 1950s with brown leather booths, mirrored walls, and a neon sign over the door. (☎01646 682 419. Entrees £3.45-6.20. Open M-Sa 9am-5pm. Cash only.) **The Lemon Tree ❶**, Main St., is more modern, serving sandwiches (£3.25) and baguettes (£3.75) in a room full of brightly colored art. (☎01646 689 867. Open daily 10am-4pm. Cash only). Across the Northgate St. bridge is **Watermans Arms ❷**, 2 The Green, where locals and tourists alike enjoy quality pub fare on the waterfront patio. (☎01646 682 718. Open daily noon-11pm. Kitchen open noon-2:30pm and 6-8:30pm; hours longer in summer.)

SIGHTS. Austere **Pembroke Castle** shadows Pembroke's Main St. Henry VII, founder of the Tudor dynasty, was born in one of the seven massive towers. Today, the castle's stone chambers provide hours of exploration. The **Great Keep** rises 75 ft., and visitors ascend more than 100 slippery steps to reach its domed top. The underground gloom of **Wogan's Cavern**, a natural limestone cave beneath the castle, gave shelter to Stone Age cave dwellers. (☎01646 684 585; www.pembrokecastle.co.uk. Open daily Apr.-Sept. 9:30am-6pm; Oct. and Mar. 10am-5pm; Nov.-Feb. 10am-4pm. Last entry 45min. before close. Tours May-Aug. M-F and Su 4 per day. Castle £3.50, concessions £2.50. Tours £1.)

ST. DAVID'S (TYDDEWI) ☎(0)1437

St. David's is little more than a few streets curled around a central village green, but its towering, dark-stone cathedral has been a favored destination among pilgrims (and Viking raiders) for almost a millennium. Since the burg was the birthplace of Wales's patron saint, two pilgrimages to St. David's were considered equivalent to one trip to Rome in the Middle Ages.

TRANSPORTATION AND PRACTICAL INFORMATION. Pick up the *Pembrokeshire Bus Timetables*, free at any Pembrokeshire TIC. Richards Brothers (☎01239 613 756) **bus** #411 leaves for Haverfordwest (40min.; M-Sa 11-12 per day, Su 4 per day), while #413 hugs the coastline on its way to Fishguard (40min.; M-Sa 5-6 per day, Su 1 per day). #400 goes to Milford Haven (2hr., 3 per day in summer), stopping in Marloes (1¼hr.) and Dale (1½hr.) along the way. Other buses terminate at St. David's during the week. For a **cab**, call Tony's Taxis. (☎01437 720 931. Last taxi midnight. Book ahead for Sa trips.)

The **National Park Information Centre** is a 5min. walk up High St. (☎01437 720 392. Open Easter-Oct. daily 9:30am-5:30pm; Nov.-Easter M-Sa 10am-4pm.) Other services include: **Barclays** bank, 3 High St. (open M-F 9:30am-4pm); **police**, High St. (☎0845 330 2000); free **Internet** at the **library** on High St. (open Tu and F

THE BIG SPLURGE

CRAZY, OR COASTEERING?

St. David's may be the birthplace of the Welsh patron saint, but in recent years it has witnessed a different kind of *naissance*: the rise of a unique adventure sport (or insanity) called coasteering.

Picture it—you swim through churning waves to a rocky outcropping at the base of a cliff. You clamber out of the sea, then scale the rock face until you reach a ledge 30 ft. above. You pause and peer into the water far below. The crashing surf obscures the surface, but you know what to do: you draw in a deep breath, brace yourself, and take the plunge.

Inspired by Pembrokeshire's dramatic shoreline, coasteering is a thrilling combination of rock scrambling, cliff jumping, and open-water swimming. You'll spend at least 3hr. navigating up and down the coast, so some level of fitness is required. Still, the beginner-level trips are far from grueling, so coasteering is a surprisingly accessible sport.

TYF Adventure in St. David's specializes in coasteering. A half-day of coasteering is £54. TYF also offers weekend packages, including meals, two nights' stay in the TYF-run B&B, and multiple sessions of coasteering.

Booking office on High St. in St. David's. ☎01347 721 611; www.tyf.com. Open daily 9am-5:30pm; longer in summer.

10am-1pm and 2-5:30pm); and the **post office,** 13-15 New St. (☎01437 720 283; open M-F 9am-5:30pm, Sa 9am-1pm). **Postcode:** SA62 6SW.

⚑⬚ ACCOMMODATIONS AND FOOD. The **YHA Saint David's ❶** (p. 492) lies 2 mi. northwest of town at the foot of a rocky outcrop near St. David's Head. **Pen Albro ❷,** 18 Goat St., offers simple, cheap rooms with a shared bathroom in the center of St. David's. (☎01437 721 865; www.stdavids.co.uk/guesthouse/alandale.htm. £20 per person; £5 fee for single-night stays. Cash only.) **Beautiful Alandale ❸,** 43 Nun St., has lovely ensuite rooms, some with balconies overlooking the rugged hills and sea. (☎01437 720 404. £36 per person. Cash only.) In the center of town, **The Coach House ❷,** 15 High St., has clean lodgings, all with TVs and most ensuite. A comfortable cottage in back sleeps four. (☎01437 720 632. Cottage £35 per person; singles £45; doubles £60. Cash only.)

At **Pebbles Yard Gallery and Espresso Bar ❶,** Cross Sq., a cafe serves generous portions of stuffed pitas, salads, and coffee in a trendy loft. (☎01437 720 122. Open daily Apr.-Oct. 9:30am-5:30pm; Nov.-Mar. 10am-5pm. Cash only.) Across the street is **⬚Chapel Chocolates ❶,** The Pebbles, whose ice cream became so popular that the cathedral had to prohibit its consumption inside. (☎01437 720 023; www.chapelchocolates.com. £1.70 per scoop. Open daily July to mid-Sept. 10am-8pm; mid-Sept. to June 10am-5pm. AmEx/MC/V.) **The Bishops ❸,** 22-23 Cross Sq., serves a variety of entrees ranging from Thai green chicken curry (£9) to the more traditional Welsh lamb shank (£16) in its cavernous dining room. (☎01437 720 422. Open daily 11am-9:30pm. AmEx/MC/V.)

⬚ SIGHTS. ⬚Saint David's Cathedral, perhaps the finest in Wales, stands below the village. It was built in the late 1100s on the site of a monastery founded by St. David in the sixth century. Modern-day pilgrims file past the **reliquary** reputed to hold the bones of St. David, patron saint of Wales, and his comrade St. Justinian. The latter was killed on nearby Ramsey Island and, with saintly conscientiousness, carried his own head back to the mainland. In the **Saint Thomas Becket Chapel,** a stained-glass window portrays three surly knights jabbing swords at the martyr. (☎01437 720 199; www.stdavidscathedral.org.uk. Open M-Sa 9am-5:30pm, Su 12:30-5:30pm. Suggested donation £3, concessions £2.) Those with a love for pealing bells are welcome to sit in on a ringer's practice session in the tower. (W and F 7:45-9pm. Suggested donation £1.)

The **Bishop's Palace,** a collection of ruins across a stream from the cathedral, was built largely by Bishop Henry Gower in the 14th century. Arcaded parapets and intricate stone carvings hint at the luxury enjoyed by resident bishops of this truly palatial estate. (☎01443 336 000. Open Apr.-Oct. daily 9am-5pm; Nov.-Mar. M-Sa 9:40am-4pm, Su 11am-4pm. £3.10, concessions £2.70.) A mile south of town, overlooking a bay, the ruins of **Saint Non's Chapel** mark St. David's birthplace. Today, worshippers gather at the altar of a neighboring chapel, built in 1937 in the same style as the original. Water from a nearby well, said to have sprung up during a thunderstorm when St. David was born, supposedly cures all ills; take Goat St. downhill and follow the signs.

FISHGUARD   ☎(0)1348

Fishguard's rows of low, candy-colored cottages and tiny harbor give it the appeal of a picturesque fishing village. Buses run to smaller villages on the Pembrokeshire Coast, making the town a convenient hub for the region. The area offers many scenic walks and short hikes, while longer coastal paths hug the cliffs. Proud of their maritime history, Fishguard's pubs play host to numerous local legends of smugglers' caves and pirate attacks.

TRANSPORTATION. Trains (☎08457 484 950) leave Fishguard Harbour for London via Bristol, Newport, Cardiff, Swansea, and Whitland (5hr., 2 per day, £70). **Buses** stop at Fishguard Sq. Ask at the TIC for a free bus and train timetable. To travel north, take Richards Brothers (☎01239 613 756) bus #412 to Cardigan (45min.; M-Sa 11 per day, Su 3 per day; £3-4), which then connects with #550/X50 to Aberystwyth (2hr., M-Sa 5 per day). Take Richards Brothers bus #412 to Haverfordwest (45min., every hr.) and change to #349 for Tenby (1½hr.; M-Sa every hr., Su 4 per day) or Pembroke (50min.; M-Sa every hr., Su 5 per day; £2.40). Richards Brothers #413 goes to St. David's (40min.; M-F 5 per day, Sa 6 per day). Town bus #410 shuttles between Fishguard Harbour and Fishguard Sq. (5min., 1-2 per hr., 45p).

PRACTICAL INFORMATION. The **Tourist Information Centre,** in the Town Hall in Market Sq., books rooms for £2 plus a 10% deposit. (☎01437 776 636. Open Easter-Oct. M-Sa 9:30am-5pm, Su 10am-4pm; Nov.-Easter M-Sa 10am-4pm.) Other services include: **Barclays** bank, across from the TIC in Market Sq. (open M-F 9am-5pm); free **Internet** at the **library** in the Town Hall, upstairs from the TIC (☎01437 776 638; open Apr.-Sept. M-W and F-Sa 9:30am-5pm, Th 9:30am-6:30pm; Oct.-Mar. M-W and F 9:30am-5pm, Th 9:30am-6:30pm, Sa 9:30am-1pm); a **laun-derette,** Brodog Terr. (☎01348 872 140; open M-Sa 8:30am-5:30pm); **police,** Brodog Terr. (☎0845 330 2000); **Boots** pharmacy, Market Sq. (☎01348 872 856; open M-Sa 9am-5:30pm); and the **post office,** 57 West St. (☎01348 873 863; open M-F 9am-5:30pm, Sa 9am-12:30pm). **Postcode:** SA65 9NG.

ACCOMMODATIONS AND FOOD. B&Bs (£20) are on High St. in Upper Fishguard. In a small stone cottage, ⚑**Hamilton Guest House and Backpackers Lodge ❷,** 21-23 Hamilton St., has a book-lined TV lounge, toast-and-tea breakfasts, and a sauna. (☎01348 874 797. Free Wi-Fi. Dorms £16; doubles £36. Cash only.) **Avon House ❷,** 76 High St., rents rooms 5min. from the town center. (☎01348 874 476; www.avon-house.co.uk. £22.50 per person, ensuite £25. Cash only.) You won't find a cheaper place for a quick bite than **Y Pantri ❶,** 31 West St., which makes filled baguettes (£2) and pasties (£1) for sit-down or takeaway. (☎01348 872 637. Open M-Sa 9am-5pm. Cash only.) Lounge in a huge bay window overlooking the sea at **Bar Five ❸,** 5 Main St. The dinner menu specializes in local shellfish, though entrees (£12-15) can be pricey. (☎01348 875 050. Open Tu-Sa 11am-3pm and 6pm-midnight, Su noon-4pm. AmEx/MC/V.)

◙ 🎝 SIGHTS AND NIGHTLIFE. Fishguard was, notoriously, the site of the last invasion of Britain when a squadron of French soldiers disembarked at a nearby harbor in 1797 and began raiding the town's farms and cottages. In a **gallery** above the TIC, visitors can gaze at a 100 ft. long **tapestry,** commissioned as part of the 1997 bicentennial celebrations, which tells the story of the French attack and surrender in imaginative and dramatic fashion. Don't miss the account of Jemima Nicholas, a local cobbler who single-handedly captured a dozen French soldiers by pitchfork and locked them in nearby St. Mary's Church. (Open Apr.-Sept. M-W and F-Sa 9:30am-5pm, Th 9:30am-6:30pm; Oct.-Mar. M-W and F 9:30am-5pm, Th 9:30am-6:30pm, Sa 9:30am-1pm. Free.) The **Marine Walk** is a paved path that follows the coastline through woods and along grassy cliffs. Ramblers can also see **Goodwick Harbor,** where the flagship *Lusitania* stopped on its ill-fated voyage from Liverpool to New York in 1915. **Preseli Venture,** based in nearby Mathry, offers half- and full-day adventures that include sea kayaking, surfing, and coasteering. (☎01348 837 709; www.preseliventure.co.uk. £89 per day. 18+.) During the day, sunbathers dot pebbly **Goodwick Beach.** Inquire at the TIC about hikes into the **Preseli Hills,** ancient grounds full of stone circles and a mysterious standing stone.

Weekend nightlife erupts into a lively pub scene, with all the pubs along **High Street** seeing some action until 11pm. With cheap pub food (£6-9) and live music on Fridays, **The Old Coach House,** 10 High St., is the place to be. (☎01348 875 429. Open M-F and Su 11am-midnight, Sa 11am-1am. Kitchen open 11am-7pm. AmEx/MC/V.) **The Royal Oak,** Market Sq., is proud of its history—the "last invasion" surrender treaty was signed here in 1797. The pub keeps the original table on display and serves pub food starting at £9. (☎01348 872 514. Live music Tu and Sa. Open daily 10:30am-11pm. Kitchen open noon-2pm and 6-9pm. MC/V.)

NORTH WALES

North Wales is a land of impressive fortresses. Edward I built an "iron ring" of castles in the 12th century to aid in his campaigns against the Welsh kings, who defended their land in the natural strongholds of Snowdonia. Their patriotism is still evident in signs printed only in Welsh and devotion to local traditions. To escape the crowds swarming the coastal castles, head to Snowdonia National Park, which spans most of northwest Wales. To the west, the Llŷn Peninsula's sandy beaches beckon; to the northwest, the Isle of Anglesey is rich in prehistoric remains; and to the east, quiet villages sit in the Vale of Conwy.

HIGHLIGHTS OF NORTH WALES

SCALE one of many craggy peaks at **Snowdonia National Park** (p. 516), land of high moors, dark pine forests, and deep glacial lakes.

FROLIC in the refreshing streams and unspoiled surroundings of villages like **Betws-y-Coed** (p. 514) in the Vale of Conwy.

ADMIRE Edward I's castles at **Beaumaris** (p. 530), **Caernarfon** (p. 524), **Conwy** (p. 510), and **Harlech** (p. 521).

ABERYSTWYTH   ☎(0)1970

Home of the largest university in Wales, Aberystwyth (ah-ber-RIST-with) thrives on youthful vigor. Where 19th-century vacationers once enjoyed the frivolities of resort living, bars now buzz with spirited academics during the school year. In the summer months, the Georgian boardwalk is awash with activity as locals thread through shopping districts and take in bayside breezes.

▐ TRANSPORTATION

A transport hub for all of Wales, Aberystwyth sits at the end of a rail line running from Birmingham, England.

Trains: Station on Alexandra Rd. Office open M-F 7:10am-5:40pm, Sa 7:15am-5:40pm. Trains (☎08457 484 950) to **Machynlleth** (30min.; M-Sa 10 per day, Su 7 per day; £4.20) and **Shrewsbury** (2hr.; M-Sa 8 per day, Su 6 per day; £13.10). Aberystwyth is the southern terminus of 1 branch of the Cambrian Coast line, which runs from Pwllheli. The **Day Ranger** ticket covers travel on the line (£7.70, children £4, families £15).

Buses: Station on Alexandra Rd., beside the train station. National Express (☎08705 808 080) to **London** (7hr., 1 per day, £30.50) via **Birmingham** (4hr., £24). TrawsCambria bus #X40 to **Cardiff** via **Swansea** (4hr.; M-Sa 2 per day, Su 1 per day). Arriva Cymru (☎08706 082 608) #X32 to **Bangor** via **Porthmadog** (4hr.; M-Sa 5 per day, Su 2 per day) and **Machynlleth** (45min.; M-Sa 7 per day, Su 2 per day). Richard Brothers (☎01239 613 756) to **Cardigan** via **Synod Inn** (#550/X50, 2hr., M-Sa 5 per day). West Wales **Day Rover** tickets (£6.30, children £4.20) are valid on most buses in the Ceredigion, Carmarthenshire, and Pembrokeshire areas. The **North and Mid-Wales Rover** is valid on buses and trains on the North Wales main line, the Conwy Valley, and the Cambrian Line (1-day £22, 4-day train and 8-day bus £47).

Taxis: Express (☎01970 612 319). Last taxi M-Th and Su 2am, F-Sa 4am.

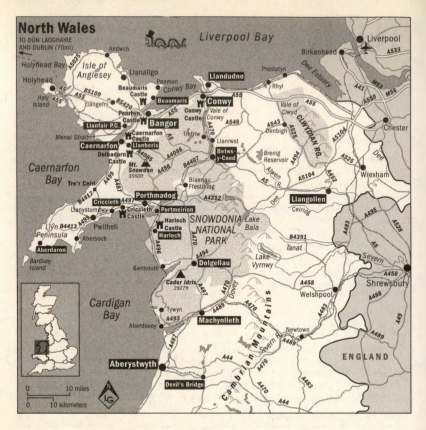

North Wales

⊞ 🔢 ORIENTATION AND PRACTICAL INFORMATION

Aberystwyth is bounded by the **Cardigan Bay** on its western side and the university to the east. **Marine Terrace** stretches alongside the promenade, connecting the city's **North** and **South Beaches**. The **castle** sits at the southern end of Marine Terr., while the **National Library of Wales** lies just east of the city center. **Queen's Road, Terrace Road,** and **Great Darkgate Street** make up the city's main pedestrian zone and hold most of the city's shops, restaurants, and pubs.

Tourist Information Centre: Lisburne House, Terrace Rd. (☎01970 612 125). Open July-Aug. daily 10am-5pm; Sept.-June M-Sa 10am-5pm.

Bank: Barclays, 26 Terrace Rd. (☎08457 555 555). Open M-F 9am-5pm.

Library and Internet Access: Corporation St. (☎01970 633 703), at the corner of Baker St. Open M-F 9:30am-6pm, Sa 9:30am-5pm.

Police: Park Ave. (☎0845 330 2000).

Pharmacy: Boots, 53-55 Terrace Rd. (☎01970 612 292). Open M-F 9am-6pm, Sa 9am-5:30pm, Su 10am-4pm.

Hospital: Bronglais General, Caradog Rd. (☎01970 623 131), off Penglais Rd.

Post Office: 8 Great Darkgate St. (☎01970 632 630). **Bureau de change.** Open M and W-F 9am-5:30pm, Tu 9:30am-5:30pm, Sa 9am-12:30pm. **Postcode:** SY23 1DE.

ACCOMMODATIONS AND CAMPING

Aberystwyth's streets overflow with B&Bs (£20-30) and more upscale seaside hotels, especially near the beachfront.

Maes-y-Môr, 25 Bath St. (☎01970 639 270). With boldly patterned bedspreads and multi-toned walls, proves that budget accommodations need not sacrifice style. 1 block from the sea. Kitchen. Launderette on ground floor wash £2.20, dry 20p per 4min. Singles £22; doubles £38. Cash only. ❷

The Cambria, Marine Terr. (☎01970 626 350; www.thecambria.co.uk). Right across from the pier, with views of the sea. Student housing with rooms available July-Aug. Singles £19; twins £33. Cash only. ❷

Sunnymead B&B, 34 Bridge St. (☎01970 617 273). Cheerful, yellow-trimmed home with hospitality to match. Bright, cozy rooms with TV. £27.50 per person. MC/V. ❷

YHA Borth (☎01970 871 498; borth@yha.co.uk), 8 mi. north of Aberystwyth, overlooking the ocean. Take the train to Borth or ride Crosville bus #511 or 512 and ask to stop at the hostel. From the train station, turn right onto the main road and walk 5min. Kitchen and laundry. Dorms £9-18, under 18 £7-13.50. MC/V. ❶

Midfield Caravan Park (☎01970 612 542; www.midfieldcaravanpark.co.uk), 1½ mi. from town on the A4120, uphill from the A487 junction. From Alexandra Rd., take any bus to Southgate. Turn left for Devil's Bridge and walk 600 ft. uphill. Lovely site with views of town. £8-12 per person. Electricity included. AmEx/MC/V. ❶

FOOD

Pier Street takeaways are cheap, as are beachside shacks and some sit-down restaurants. **Spar** market, 32 Terrace Rd., is open 24hr. A picnic at the castle will save you some money and gives great views.

The Treehouse Cafe, 14 Baker St. (☎01970 615 791; www.treehousewales.co.uk). Feel wholesome when eating your veggie burger (£6) or any one of the daily specials (£6.40-8.50)—they're all organic, as are the various fruits and vegetables sold on the ground floor. Open M-Sa 9am-5pm. Kitchen open M-Sa noon-3:30pm. Food store open M-Th 9am-6pm, F 9am-6:30pm, Sa 9am-5pm. MC/V. ❷

Fresh Ground Cafe, Cambrian Pl. (☎01970 611 472), off Terrace Rd. Trendy but comfortable vibe, with globe lanterns in bright dining rooms. Grab a leather couch and sip a steaming mocha (£1.50). Guests can bring their own wine in the evenings. Dinner entrees £7-10.50. Live music Th. Open daily July-Sept. and Dec. 8:30am-7pm; Oct.-Nov. and Jan.-Apr. 8:30am-9:30pm. Cash only. ❶

The Olive Branch, 35 Pier St. (☎01970 630 572). Casual, lively seaside restaurant serving Greek specialties like hummus *kavurma* (with diced lamb and pine kernels; £5) and vegetarian moussaka (£10). Save room for the baklava (£3.50). Open M-Th and Su 10:30am-10pm, F-Sa 10:30am-11pm. MC/V. ❷

SIGHTS

NATIONAL LIBRARY OF WALES. Occupying a grand Classical building overlooking the sea, town, and surrounding cliffs, this library houses almost every Welsh book or manuscript ever printed. First-rate galleries feature work by local artists, clips from the film and sound archive, and displays ranging from designer bookbinding to traditional Welsh costume. *(Signposted off Penglais Rd.,*

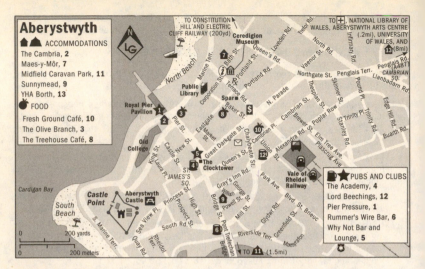

Aberystwyth

▲▲ ACCOMMODATIONS

The Cambria, **2**
Maes-y-Môr, **7**
Midfield Caravan Park, **11**
Sunnymead, **9**
YHA Borth, **13**

🍴 FOOD

Fresh Ground Café, **10**
The Olive Branch, **3**
The Treehouse Café, **8**

Cardigan Bay

South Beach

Castle Point

Aberystwyth Castle

Old College

Royal Pier Pavilion

Public Library

North Beach

Ceredigion Museum

Spar

0   200 yards
0   200 meters

TO CONSTITUTION HILL AND ELECTRIC CLIFF RAILWAY (200yd)

TO ✚, NATIONAL LIBRARY OF WALES, ABERYSTWYTH ARTS CENTRE (.2mi), UNIVERSITY OF WALES, AND (8mi)

★ PUBS AND CLUBS

The Academy, **4**
Lord Beechings, **12**
Pier Pressure, **1**
Rummer's Wire Bar, **6**
Why Not Bar and Lounge, **5**

past the hospital. ☎ 01970 632 800; www.llgc.org.uk. Reading room open M-F 9:30am-6pm, Sa 9:30am-5pm; free ticket required. Exhibitions open M-Sa 10am-5pm. Free.)

CONSTITUTION HILL AND ELECTRIC CLIFF RAILWAY. At the northern end of the promenade, an electric railcar has been creaking up the steep 430 ft. slope of Constitution Hill since 1896. At the top are shops, a cafe, a Frisbee golf course, and the world's largest camera obscura. The camera's crisp magnification led some locals to protest on grounds that viewers could peer into their windows. (☎ 01970 617 642. Runs daily July-Aug. M-W 10am-6pm, Th-Su 10am-9:30pm; Sept.-Oct. and from mid-Mar. to June 10am-5:30pm. 6 per hr. Round-trip £3, concessions £2.)

ABERYSTWYTH CASTLE. Castle Point, the site of one of Edward I's many ruined castles, is an ideal picnic site, with benches and tables scattered around the surrounding park. Though the castle was once a mighty seat of government during Owain Glyndŵr's brief 15th-century occupation, it fell to ruin in later centuries as townspeople snatched its stones for other buildings; all that remains are a few crumbling towers and rough foundations. (Open 24hr. Free.)

OTHER SIGHTS. Located directly above the TIC, the **Ceredigion Museum** fills a grand Edwardian theater and houses three floors on local history. Exhibits are varied, ranging from a recreation of an 1850s cottage to displays of 19th- and 20th-century undergarments. (☎ 01970 633 088. Open M-Sa 10am-4:45pm. Free.) Up Penglais Rd., at the University of Wales, the **Aberystwyth Arts Centre** sponsors drama and films in Welsh and English and has a bookstore, gallery, and cafe. (☎ 01970 623 232; www.aberystwythartscentre.co.uk. Box office open M-Sa 10am-8pm, Su 1:30-5:30pm. Films M-F. Tickets from £4; concessions available.)

🎭📻 PUBS AND NIGHTLIFE

Rummer's Wine Bar, Pont Trefechan Bridge, Bridge St. (☎ 01970 625 177). A vine-covered riverside beer garden packed with students. Views of the nearby bridge and hills. Live music Th. Open M-Th and Su 7pm-1am, F-Sa 7pm-2am.

The Academy, Upper Great Darkgate St. (☎ 01970 636 852). This converted chapel piles bottles of absinthe (£3.40 per shot) on the organ. Barflies flank the pulpit, watching the 16 ft. screen. Drink specials M-Th and Su. Open M-W and Su noon-11pm, Th noon-midnight, F noon-1am, Sa noon-2am. Kitchen open noon-3pm and 6-8:30pm. MC/V.

Pier Pressure, The Royal Pier, Marine Terr. (☎01970 636 100). Mirrors quake and clubbers shake. "Cheese Factory" pulls a young crowd for pop tunes Sa. Popular drinks £1 Tu and Th-F. Cover £3-5. Open Tu and Th-Sa 10:30pm-3:30am.

Why Not Bar and Lounge, 2 Pier St. (☎01970 623 963). Young clubbers crowd comfy couches and a steamy dance floor. Crowd thins in summer. Cover in summer free; during term time F £3-4, Sa £5. Open in summer M-W and Su 9pm-3am, Th-Sa 9pm-4am; during term time M-Th and Su 9pm-3am, F-Sa 9pm-4am.

Lord Beechings, Alexandra Rd. (☎01970 625 069). Dark wood interior and an enormous array of comfort foods (most under £6). Open M-Th 11am-midnight, F-Sa 11am-1am, Su noon-midnight. Kitchen open daily 11am-9pm. MC/V.

◪ DAYTRIP FROM ABERYSTWYTH

DEVIL'S BRIDGE

The scenic narrow-rail Vale of Rheidol train runs from Aberystwyth. The area is not accessible by other forms of public transportation. From mid-July to Aug. M-Th 4 per day, F-Su 2 per day; Sept.-Oct. and from Easter to mid-July 2 per day. £13.50, children £3.

Originally built to serve lead mines, the **Vale of Rheidol Railway** (☎01970 625 819) winds through farmland and gorgeous hills. An hour's ride leads to Devil's Bridge (reputedly built by the Evil One himself), which is actually three bridges of varying ages built atop one another. The lowest bridge was probably constructed in the 11th century by monks from the nearby **Strata Florida Abbey,** whose ruined arches make it worth a visit of its own. (☎01143 336 000. Abbey open Apr.-Sept. W-Su 10am-5pm. Last entry 30min. before close. Grounds open daily Apr.-Sept. 10am-5pm; Oct.-Mar. 10am-4pm. £3.10, concessions £2.70, families £8.90. Oct.-Apr. grounds free, but exhibits and museum closed.) Catch great views of the bridge with a 10min. walk down the turnstile-accessible path to **Jacob's Ladder** and the **Devil's Punchbowl** in the stream. (☎01970 890 233. Jacob's Ladder £3.50, concessions £2.50, children £1.50. Punchbowl £1.) From there, an easy 30min. walk through the hills affords views of the 300 ft. **Mynach Falls** waterfall and more of the bridge.

MACHYNLLETH   ☎(0)1654

The bustling, medieval market town of Machynlleth (mach-HUN-hleth) is best known for its brief stint as the capital of Wales. Freedom-fighter Owain Glyndŵr set up a parliament here in the 15th century, summoning delegates from across Wales and even signing an alliance with France against the British. Although the rebellion unraveled, the Celtic pride behind it lives on in the museums and street signs of Machynlleth's city center.

⌸ TRANSPORTATION. The **train station** (☎0845 6061 660), Doll St., sends trains (☎08457 484 950) to Aberystwyth (30min., 11 per day, £4.20), Birmingham (2¼hr.; M-Sa 8 per day, Su 6 per day; £10-12), and Shrewsbury (1¼hr.; M-Sa 8 per day, Su 6 per day; £11). The **Cambrian Coaster Day Ranger** covers routes from Aberystwyth (£7.70, children £3.85, families £15, after 6:30pm £4.50). **Buses** stop by the clock tower. Arriva Cymru (☎08706 082 608) buses #32 and X32 pass through Machynlleth as they shuttle between Aberystwyth and Dolgellau (30min. to both; M-Sa 8 per day to Aberystwyth, 9 per day to Dolgellau, both Su 2 per day). Buses #28 and 33 provide east-west transportation to and from smaller towns. Rent **bikes** at The Holey Trail Cycle Hire, 31 Maengwyn St.

(☎01654 700 411; www.theholeytrail.co.uk. £22 per day. Open M-Sa 10am-6pm; sometimes closes early on Th. Call ahead.)

■▪ ▣ ORIENTATION AND PRACTICAL INFORMATION. Pentrehedyn, Penrallt, and **Maengwyn Streets** converge at the clock tower. From the train station, turn left onto Doll St., veer right at the church onto Penrallt St., and continue until you see the tower. The **Tourist Information Centre,** located in the Royal House, Penrallt St., near the clock tower, books rooms for £2 plus a 10% deposit. (☎01654 702 401. Open Apr.-Oct. M-Sa 9:30am-5pm, Su 9:30am-4pm; Nov.-Mar. M-Sa 9:30am-5pm, Su 10am-4pm.) Other services include: **Barclays** bank, 4 Pentrerhedyn St., beneath the clock tower (open M-F 9am-5pm); free **Internet** access at the **library,** Maengwyn St. (☎01654 702 322; open M and F 9:30am-1pm and 2-7pm, Tu-W 9:30am-1pm and 2-5pm, Sa 9:30am-1pm); a **launderette,** New St., around the corner from Spar (open M-Sa 8:30am-8pm, Su 9am-8pm; last wash 7:15pm); **police,** Doll St. (☎0845 330 2000); **Rowland's** pharmacy, 8 Pen-trerhedyn St., near the tower (☎01654 702 237; open M and F 9am-6pm, Tu-W 9am-5:30pm, Th 9am-12:30pm, Sa 9am-4:30pm); the **hospital,** off Maengwn St. (☎01654 702 266); and the **post office,** 51 Maengwyn St., inside Spar (☎01654 702 323; open M-F 8:30am-6pm, Sa 8:30am-3pm). **Postcode:** SY20 8AF.

▛▐ ACCOMMODATIONS AND FOOD. Machynlleth has few budget accom-modations, one of the few exceptions being the simple, clean, and comfort-able **Reditreks Bunkhouse ❷,** Graig Fach, Heol Powys. Turn left off the Spar on Maengwyn St., then left again onto Graig Fach. The bunkhouse is a red house surrounded by a small stone wall. (☎01654 702 184; www.reditreks.co.uk. TV lounge, kitchen, and 16 beds. Showers and lockers. Sheets and pillows pro-vided; duvets and covers £3.50 extra. Dorms £15, groups of 8 or more £12.50 per person. Cash only.) Nearby Corris has a bunkhouse and a hostel with sce-nic views. Take bus #32 or X32 bus to Corris Braich Goch (10min.; M-F 10 per day, Sa 9 per day, Su 2 per day). **Braich Goch Bunkhouse ❷,** across from the bus stop, has a climbing wall, kitchen, and laundry. Bring a sleeping bag or rent one for £2.50. (☎01654 761 229; www.braichgoch.co.uk. Dorms £16. MC/V.) **Corris Youth Hostel ❷,** on Corris Rd., is housed in an old schoolhouse 10min. from the bus stop by foot. Go into town and turn left up the hill after the creek and walk 600 ft. (☎01654 761 686. Laundry available. Dorms £15, under 18 £12; singles from £16. Cash only.) B&Bs in Machynlleth are expensive and scarce; ask the TIC for a free accommodations guide. **Maenllwyd Guest House ❸,** Newtown Rd., has bright, ensuite rooms with TV. (☎01654 702 928. Singles £35, with breakfast £40; doubles £50/60. Campers can seek out riverside **Llwyngwern Farm ❶,** off the A487 next to the Centre for Alternative Technology. (☎01654 702 492. Open Easter-Oct. Sites for 2 £10. Cash only.)

A **Spar** supermarket is at 51-53 Maengwyn St. (Open M-Sa 7am-11pm, Su 7am-10:30pm.) An impressive **market,** which dates from 1291, runs along Maengwyn St., Pentrerhedyn St., and Penrallt St. (Open W 9:30am-4pm.) The **▨Quarry Cafe and Shop ❶,** 13 Maengwyn St., part of the Centre for Alterna-tive Technology, serves delicious vegan soups and salads (under £3) as well as a rotating list of daily entrees (£5-6.15). The poster-plastered wall of the cafe publicizes festivals and concerts. (☎01654 702 624. Open M-W and F 9am-5pm, Th 9am-2pm and 5:30-9pm, Su 10am-4pm. Cash only.) Typical pub fare is served beside a massive hearth at the **Skinners Arms ❷,** Penrallt St., near the clock tower. Entrees in the lounge are £5.45-11.45; lighter meals are £5.45-7 at the bar. (☎01654 702 354. Open M-Tu noon-11pm, W-Sa 11am-11pm, Su noon-10:30pm. Kitchen open daily noon-2pm and 6-8pm. Cash only.)

◼ ▓ SIGHTS AND FESTIVALS. On a former slate quarry 3 mi. north of town along the A487 is the ▓**Centre for Alternative Technology.** The staff here has been developing and promoting environmentally sound lifestyles since 1974. Chug up the 200 ft. cliff via a funicular (inclined railway) powered by water imbalances. Fascinating outdoor displays teach about wave, wind, and solar power sources, like a wind seat turbine, which lifts visitors from the ground using wind power. Don't miss the child favorite "Mole Hole," featuring models of various tiny critters, or the "Compost Sampler," which encourages you to touch and smell different types of natural fertilizer. Take Arriva bus #34 (5min., M-Sa 11 per day) to the entrance or bus #32 (5min.; M-Sa 10 per day, Su 2 per day) to Pantperthog and walk 600 ft. north across the bridge. (☎01654 705 950; www.cat.org.uk. Open daily from Easter to early Nov. 10am-5:30pm; from early Nov. to Easter 10am-dusk. Last entry 1hr. before close. Funicular open from mid-Mar. to early Nov. Jan-Oct. £8.40, concessions £7.40, children £4.20; Nov.-Dec. £6.40, concessions £5.40, children £4.20. Arrive by foot, bus, or bike and get £1 off admission price. ½-price with valid train ticket. Free audio tour.) Farther up the A487, the passages of another old slate mine lure tourists to **King Arthur's Labyrinth,** a surreal celebration of the Arthurian legend on a subterranean boat tour. After riding past waterfalls and a smoke-breathing dragon, a guide in medieval robes leads groups through eerily lit chambers with visual displays as recordings narrate tales of Arthur. To get there from Machynlleth, take bus #32 or 35 toward Dolgellau and ask to get off at the Corris Craft Centre. (☎01654 761 584; www.kingarthurslabyrinth.com. Open Apr.-Oct. daily 10am-5pm. Trips 45min. Dress warmly. £6.50, concessions £6, children £4.65.) Next to Y Tabernacl on Penrallt St., the **Museum of Modern Art, Wales,** has rotating exhibits of contemporary Welsh art. Don't miss the Taliesin mosaics, created by villagers under the guidance of a local artist. On some evenings, the neighboring performance hall fills with music. (☎01654 703 355; www.momawales. org.uk. Open M-Sa 10am-4pm. Free.) The museum and theater are central to the late-August **Machynlleth Festival,** which features musical performances and lectures. (☎01654 703 355; www.momawales.org.uk. Tickets free-£15.)

LLANGOLLEN ☎(0)1978

Set in a hollow in the hills near the English border, Llangollen (hlan-GOTH-hlen) is best known for its annual International Musical Eisteddfod, a festival that has drawn over 400,000 performers and competitors since it began in 1947. The town is also close to several natural attractions; hikers head to Horseshoe Pass, and whitewater enthusiasts tackle the Dee and its tributaries.

◻ TRANSPORTATION. Despite being a tourist town, Llangollen can be difficult to reach by public transportation. **Trains** (☎08457 484 950; www.national-rail.co.uk) leave from Wrexham, 30min. away, for Chester (20min., every hr., £3.50), London (3-4hr., 2 per hr., £24-61.60), and Shrewsbury (40min., 1-2 per hr., £5.50). A closer station is Ruabon, from which B&B owners occasionally fetch travelers. To get to Llangollen from Wrexham, take Bryn Melyn (☎01978 860 701) bus #X5 or 555 (30min., M-Sa every 15-20min., £2.60). Direct service from Llangollen is possible on some **buses;** Arriva Cymru (☎0870 608 2608) bus #94 goes to Barmouth (2hr.; M-Sa 8 per day, Su 4 per day; £5.20) and Dolgellau (1½hr.; M-Sa 9 per day, Su 6 per day; £3.50). Arriva Cymru's buses #X5 and 555 go to Chester (1-1¼hr., 3 per hr.) while #X19 runs to Llandudno via Conwy and Betws-y-Coed (2¼hr., M-Sa 3 per day). Lloyd's Coaches (☎01654 702 100) runs #694, which stops at Llangollen on the first and third Saturdays of the month.

⏸ PRACTICAL INFORMATION. The **Tourist Information Centre**, on Castle St. in The Chapel, displays art and books rooms for £2 plus a 10% deposit. (☎01978 860 828. Open daily Easter-Oct. 9:30am-5:30pm; Nov.-Easter 9:30am-5pm.) Activity weekends are available from **Pro Adventure**, 23 Castle St. (☎01978 861 912; www.proadventure.co.uk. Open M-Sa 9am-5pm. Kayaking lessons £44 per ½-day. Bike rental £18 per day.) Other services include: **Barclays** bank, with an **ATM**, 9 Castle St., opposite the TIC (☎01978 202 700; open M-F 10am-4pm); free **Internet** at the **library**, upstairs from the TIC (☎01978 869 600; open M 9:30am-7pm, Tu-W and F 9:30am-5:30pm, Sa 9:30am-12:30pm); **Blue Bay** launderette, 3 Regent St. (open M-Sa 9am-6pm); **police**, Parade St. (☎01492 517 171, ext. 54940); and the **post office**, 41 Castle St., with a **bureau de change** (☎01978 862 812; open M-F 9am-5:30pm, Sa 9am-12:30pm). **Postcode:** LL20 8RU.

⏸⏸ ACCOMMODATIONS AND FOOD. B&Bs are numerous, especially along **Berwyn Street,** which turns into **Regent Street.** Find pleasant rooms in an old coaching inn near the center of town at **Cambrian House ❸**, Berwyn St. (☎01978 861 418. Breakfast included. Free Wi-Fi. From £25 per person. MC/V.) **Glasgwm ❸**, Abbey Rd., features thoughtfully furnished rooms and huge breakfasts in a sunlit front room. (☎01978 861 975. Breakfast included. Singles £32.50-42.50, doubles £50-60. Cash only.) Campsites abound; ask at the TIC or try **Abbey Farm Caravan Park ❶**, at the Valle Crucis Abbey. (☎01978 861 297. £4.50 per person, children £3.50; £2.50 per car. Electricity £3. AmEx/MC/V.)

Spar, 26-30 Castle St., in the center of town, sells groceries. (☎01978 860 275. Open M-Sa 7am-11pm, Su 8am-11pm.) Classy cuisine has found a home in the rustic quarters of **⯐The Corn Mill ❸**, Dee Ln., where the patio hangs low over the River Dee. If the entrees are too expensive (£9-16), spend a few pounds on a pint or a sizable starter (£4.50-6.50) and watch the water wheel spinning outside. (☎01978 869 555. Open M-Sa noon-11pm, Su noon-10:30pm. Kitchen open M-Sa noon-9:30pm, Su noon-9pm. AmEx/MC/V.) At **Maxine's Cafe and Books ❶**, 17 Castle St., thumb through thousands of volumes in the warehouse upstairs and grab a meal in the dining room below. (☎01978 861 963. All-day breakfast £4.55. Sandwiches and salads £2.25-2.45. Open daily 9am-5pm. AmEx/MC/V.) **Ecclestons Bakers and Confectioners ❶**, Castle St., serves cheap and freshly prepared takeaway pasties, sandwiches, and salads including local specialties like Welsh minted lamb oggies and fruit loaves, both £2. (☎01978 861 005. Open M-Sa 8:30am-4:30pm, Su 10am-3pm. Cash only.)

◐ SIGHTS. The ruins of **⯐Castell Dinas Brân** (Crow Castle) lie on a hilltop above town, "to the winds abandoned and the prying stars," as Wordsworth once mused. On a clear day, the view spans from Snowdonia to the English Midlands, and the grassy mounds of the summit are scattered with crumbling archways and walls. Two main paths lead to the castle: a 40min. gravel trail zigzags up the side facing Llangollen, while a 1hr. walk from the other side follows a pastoral road. To get to both, cross the River Dee, turn right on Mill St., and take an immediate left at the next street. When the road splits, turn left and cross the canal. The paths begin via an unmarked trail originating where Wharf Hill and Dinbren Rd. meet, uphill from the canal bridge. Up Hill St. from the town center, **Plas Newydd** is the former *ferme ornée* (estate in miniature) of two noblewomen who fled their families in Ireland in 1778, forsaking marriage to live together in an unconventional—and perhaps more than platonic—arrangement. Famous among the era's intellectuals and a curiosity among locals, the women were known alternately as "the ladies of Llangollen" and "two of the most celebrated virgins in Europe." Wellington and Sir Walter Scott visited, as did Wordsworth, who penned a poem in their honor. Today, the women are remembered by the modest cottage they left behind, which they renovated with "Gothic revival" oak carvings and stained-glass windows. (☎01978 861 314. Open Easter-Oct. daily 10am-5pm. Last entry 4:15pm. Guided tours of the servants' quarters by request. £3.50, concessions £2.50, families £10. Includes audio tour. Gardens open 24hr. Free.) The ruins of 13th-century **Valle Crucis Abbey** grace a valley 30-45min. from Llangollen along Abbey Rd. Its empty arches frame trees, sky, and a cluster of caravans from the campground next door. (☎01978 860 326. Open Apr.-Sept. daily 10am-5pm; Oct.-Mar. the abbey is open but unstaffed. £2.50, concessions £2, families £7.) Both the abbey and Castell Dinas Brân have been considered as possible locations of the Holy Grail. Other sights in the area include **Croes Gwenhwyfar** (Guinevere's Cross) and **Eliseg's Pillar**, both ancient stone monuments.

Views of the gently sloping Dee Valley greet passengers on the **Llangollen Railway**, which stops at a convenient station where Castle St. hits highway A593/A452. (☎01978 860 951; www.llangollen-railway.co.uk. Runs May-Sept. daily 3-8 per day; Oct.-Apr. generally only on weekends. Times vary; call ahead.)

🎭 **FESTIVALS.** Every summer, Llangollen's population of 3000 swells to 80,000 for the **International Musical Eisteddfod** (ice-TETH-vod). In early July, the hills are alive with the singing and dancing of competitors from 50 countries. Book tickets and rooms far in advance through the TIC or the Eisteddfod Box Office, Royal International Pavilion, Abbey Rd. (☎01978 862 000, bookings 862 001; www.international-eisteddfod.co.uk. Open from mid-Mar. through the festival M-F 10am-4pm. Tickets £9-45. Unreserved seats and admission to grounds sold on performance days. £8, children £5.)

VALE OF CONWY

Much of the Vale of Conwy lies within Snowdonia National Park, but its lush swales, tall conifers, and streams suggest an ecosystem far gentler than Snowdon's desolate peaks. Biking is popular here, and the excellent *Gwydyr Forest Guide* (£2) details 14 walks through the mossy glens and waterfalls.

TRANSPORTATION

The single-track, 27 mi. Conwy Valley line (☎08457 484 950; www.conwyvalleyrailway.co.uk) offers unparalleled views. **Trains** run between Llandudno and Blaenau Ffestiniog, stopping at Llandudno Junction (15min.; M-Sa 4 per day, Su 3 per day) via Llanrwst (40min.) and Betws-y-Coed (45min.). The **North and Mid-Wales Rover** ticket is good for nearly unlimited bus and train travel as far south as Aberystwyth (4-day train and 8-day bus £47). Most area **buses** stop at Llandudno Junction and Llanrwst; some also stop at Betws-y-Coed. Arriva's **Day Ticket** allows unlimited travel for one day on all Arriva buses in northwest England and Wales (£5, children £3.50), while the **Weekly Ticket** allows the same for one week (£15/7.50). The main bus operator along the Conwy River is Arriva Cymru (☎0871 200 2233) #19/X19, which runs from Llandudno and Conwy to Llanrwst (55min.; M-Sa 1-2 per hr., Su 11 per day). Sherpa bus S2 runs from Llanrwst to Betws-y-Coed (10min.; M-Sa 11 per day, Su 6 per day), sometimes continuing to Pen-y-Pass (30min.; M-Sa 3 per day, Su 1 per day). Buses #S6 and S97 also shuttle between Betws-y-Coed to Llanrwst (20min., 1-2 per hr.). Bus #97A connects Betws-y-Coed with Porthmadog (1½hr., M-Sa 4 per day, Su 3 per day). Routes often change; consult the invaluable (and free) *Gwynedd* or *Conwy County* transportation booklets, available at local TICs.

NORTH WALES

CONWY
☎(0)1492

Conwy's distinctive town walls, remnants of Edward I's attempt to keep the Welsh out of his 13th-century castle, now enclose a town that is more willing to share its narrow streets and quayside.

⬅ TRANSPORTATION

Trains: Conwy Station, off Rosehill St. Trains (☎08457 484 950) stop only by request—ask the conductor in advance. The station lies on the North Wales line, between **Holyhead** and **Chester.** Trains stop at nearby **Llandudno Junction,** which connects to the Conwy Valley line. Ticket office open M-F 5:25am-6:25pm, Sa 6am-7pm, Su 11am-6:30pm. Not to be confused with Llandudno proper (a resort town 1 mi. north; p. 512), Llandudno Junction is a 20min. walk from Conwy. Turn left after exiting the station, walk under a bridge, and climb the stairs to another bridge across the estuary.

Buses: Buses are the best way to get directly to Conwy, with 2 main stops on Lancaster Sq. and on Castle St. before the corner of Rosehill St. Arriva Cymru (☎0871 200 2233) buses #5 and 5X stop in Conwy as they climb the northern coast from **Caernarfon** via **Bangor** to **Llandudno** (1¼hr.; M-Sa every 15min., Su every hr.). Bus #9 leaves Conwy for **Llangefni,** on the Isle of Anglesey, in one direction (1hr., M-Sa every hr.) and **Llandudno** in the other (15min., M-Sa every hr.). Buses #19 and X19 cross Conwy on the Llandudno-Llanrwst journey down the Vale of Conwy (to Llandudno 15min., to Llanrwst 30min.; M-Sa 1-2 per hr., Su 12 per day, continuing on to **Llangollen** 3 times per day, Su twice per day). The TIC gives out the *Conwy Public Transport Information* booklet.

Taxis: Rogers Taxis (☎01492 572 224). 24hr.

✦ ⓘ ORIENTATION AND PRACTICAL INFORMATION

Old Conwy is roughly triangular in shape. The castle is in one corner; **Castle Street,** which becomes **Berry Street,** runs from the castle parallel to the **Quay** and the river beyond it. **High Street** stretches from the Quay's edge to **Lancaster Square,** from which **Rosehill Street** circles back to the castle. In the opposite direction, **Bangor Road** heads north past the wall.

Tourist Information Centre: In the same building as the castle entrance (☎01492 592 248). Stocks street maps and books beds for £2 plus 10% deposit. Open daily Apr.-Oct. 9am-5pm; Nov.-Mar. M-Sa 9:30am-4pm, Su 11am-4pm.

Bank: Barclays, 23 High St. (☎01492 616 616), with an ATM. Open M-F 10am-4pm.

Library: Town Hall, Castle St., at the end of High St. (☎01492 596 242). Free Internet. Open M and Th-F 10am-5:30pm, Tu 10am-7pm, Sa 10am-1pm.

Pharmacy: Numark, 24 High St. (☎01492 592 418). Open daily 9am-5:30pm.

Internet Access: Free at the **library** (above).

Post Office: 7 Lancaster Sq. (☎01492 573 990). Open M-Tu 8:30am-5:30pm, W-F 9am-5:30pm, Sa 9am-1:30pm. **Postcode:** LL32 8HT.

🏠 🏕 ACCOMMODATIONS AND CAMPING

Accommodations within the town walls are scarce, though a few B&Bs can be found along the main roads of **Castle Street** and **Rosehill Street.** Outside of town, **Llanrwst Road** and **Synchnant Pass** also hold a few scattered guesthouses. Call the TIC or pick up the free visitor's guide for listings.

🛏 **YHA Conwy,** Larkhill, Sychnant Pass (☎01492 593 571), a 10min. uphill hike from the town walls. From Lancaster Sq., head down Bangor Rd., turn left on Mt. Pleasant, and go right at the top of the hill. The hostel is up a signposted driveway on the left. Tidy rooms with the feel of a camping lodge, floor-to-ceiling windows, and views of the surrounding wooded hills. Self-catering kitchen, observation deck, and TV room. Full breakfast £4.50. Free lockers. Laundry. Internet access 50p per 7min. Bike rental £7 per ½-day. Dorms M-Th and Su £12, F-Sa £22; under 18 £9/16.50. MC/V. ❷

Swan Cottage, 18 Berry St. (☎01492 596 840; www.swancottage.net). This cozy B&B may reside in a simple 16th-century timbered building, but the interior is pure Victorian-era frills and florals. One of few B&Bs within the town walls. All rooms ensuite. Singles £25; doubles £50. Cash only. ❷

Glan Heulog, Llanrwst Rd., Woodlands (☎01492 593 845), a 5-10min. walk from the castle. Go under the arch near the visitors center on Rosehill St., down the steps, and across the car park. Turn right and walk 5min. down Llanrwst Rd. Huge manor house with sloping lawns and a trellised flower garden. Ensuite rooms with TVs and fresh fruit at breakfast. Free Wi-Fi. Singles £33-40; doubles £54-64. AmEx/MC/V. ❸

Bryn B&B (☎01492 592 449; www.bryn.org.uk), outside the gates at St. Agnes Rd. and Synchant Pass. Flanked by a colorful garden and the city wall. Ensuite rooms with views of the valley and castle. Singles £45; doubles £65. £5 single-night fee. Cash only. ❹

Conwy Touring Park, Trefriw Rd. (☎01492 592 856; www.conwytouringpark.com). Follow Trefriw Rd. (B5106) out of town for 1½ mi. and turn left at the sign. Open Easter-Sept. £9-21 per tent, depending on season. Electricity £3.30. MC/V. ❶

🍴 FOOD

While the usual assortment of tearooms and pubs grace Conwy's town center, **High Street** is lined with a number of classier (and pricier) restaurants. **Spar,** on High St., sells inexpensive groceries. (Open daily 7am-10pm.)

Pen-y-Bryn Tea Rooms, High St. (☎01492 596 445). Great tea (full Welsh tea £7, including sandwiches) and rich 16th-century timbered nooks. Assortment of sandwiches (£4.50). Open daily 10am-5pm. Cash only. ❶

Edward's Butchery, 18 High St. (☎01492 592 443; www.edwardsofconwy.co.uk). Well-deserved accolades adorn the huge meat counter. Hearty pies (£1.25-3.25) are the specialty. Takeaway available. Open M-Sa 7am-5:30pm. MC/V. ❶

Shakespeare Restaurant, High St. (☎01492 582 800), in the Castle Hotel. This award-winning venue uses local foods in daily specials. Decorated with panels of Shakespeare-inspired scenes by Victorian artist John Dawson-Watson, who supposedly used the paintings to pay rent. Entrees are pricey (£10.50-16), but the starter menu (£2.50-6.75) offers fairly large portions. Open noon-9:30pm. AmEx/MC/V. ❸

Bridge Inn Conwy, Rosehill St. (☎01492 573 482). Enjoy hearty, meat-heavy dishes like cottage pie (beef, potatoes, and cheese) by the fireplace in this homey pub. Entrees £7-10. Kitchen open noon-2:30pm and 6-8:30pm. MC/V. ❷

👁 SIGHTS

CONWY CASTLE. Conwy is possibly the most imposing and magnificent of Edward I's 13th-century fortresses. Parapets joining eight rugged towers sit atop craggy rocks to form a natural defense. An untold number of Normans wasted away in the prison, and Richard II was betrayed in the chapel in 1399, imprisoned after being promised safe passage by an earl acting on behalf of Richard's rival to the throne, Henry IV. The castle is a UNESCO World Heritage Site. (☎01492 592 358. Open Apr.-Oct. daily 9am-5pm; Nov.-Mar. M-Sa 9:30am-4pm, Su 11am-4pm. £4.70, concessions £4.20, families £14. Guided tours £1; book ahead.)

PLAS MAWR. The National Trust has lovingly restored this 16th-century mansion to its days as the home of merchant Robert Wynn, right down to the exquisite furnishings, plasterwork, and sweet-smelling herbs hanging in the pantry. Don't miss the display on Tudor-era hygiene and its discussion of so-called "pisse prophets," who would diagnose patients solely by analyzing their urine. The entrance price includes a free 1hr. audio tour that surmises how the rooms may have been used in their heyday. (☎01492 580 167. Open Apr.-Sept. Tu-Su 9am-5pm; Oct. Tu-Su 9:30am-5pm. £5.10, concessions £4.70.)

SMALLEST HOUSE. When this nearly 400-year-old house was condemned in 1900, its owner (a strapping 6 ft., 3 in. fisherman) spent years measuring other tiny homes to prove that this one was the smallest in Britain. You can question his taste in housing all you like, but with a frontage measuring 6 ft., you can't question the legitimacy of his claim. There's (obviously) not much to see here beyond the house's two floors and understandably minimal period furnishings. (Head down High St. and onto the Quay. ☎01492 593 484. Open daily Easter-July and Sept.-Oct. 10am-6pm; Aug. 10am-9pm. Closing times are approximate. £1, children 50p.)

LLANDUDNO ☎(0)1492

Around 1850, the Mostyn family envisioned the farming village of Llandudno (hlan-DID-no) as a resort town. They constructed a city with wide avenues open to sea and sky, and, sure enough, the tourists arrived. Today, though its brightly painted Victorian facades have somewhat faded, the town's shores packed with sunbathers prove the family's foresight. The Great Orme, a massive craggy hill on a peninsula, lures many to its slopes for hiking in the summer and tobogganing in the winter.

▐▀ TRANSPORTATION. Llandudno is the northern end of several transportation lines. The **train station** is at the end of Augusta Rd. (Ticket office open July-Aug. M-Sa 8:40am-3:30pm, Su 10:15am-5:45pm; Sept.-June M-Sa 8:40am-3:30pm.) Trains (☎08457 484 950) run to Blaenau Ffestiniog via Llanrwst and Betws-y-Coed (1¼hr.; M-Sa 4 per day, Su 3 per day; £5.30-6). Trains leave Llandudno Junction, 1 mi. south of town, to Bangor (20min., 1-3 per hr., £4.60), Chester (45min., 1-4 per hr., £10.30-12.80), and Holyhead (1hr., 1-3 per hr., £12.80). Trains sometimes stop at Llandudno by request—ask the conductor beforehand. National Express (☎08705 808 080) **buses** stop at Mostyn Broadway daily and go to Chester (1¾hr., £10), London (8hr., £3 per day, £28.50), and Manchester (4¼hr., 4 per day, £13). Arriva Cymru (☎0871 200 2233) buses #5, 5A, and 5X run to Conwy (10-20min., 2-4 per hr.), Bangor (1hr., 1-4 per hr.), and Caernarfon (1½hr., 1-4 per hr.). Bus #19 goes to Llanrwst, passing through Conwy (1hr., M-Sa 2 per hr., Su 11 per day). Snowdon Sherpa S2 runs to Betws-y-Coed (1hr., 1 per day) and Pen-y-Pass (80min.). Kings Cabs (☎01492 878 156; last cab M-Tu and Su 1am, W-Th 2am, F-Sa 3-4am) runs **taxis.** Rent **bikes** at Snowdonia Cycle Hire and Training, 34 Tan-y-Bryn Rd. (☎01492 878 771. £11-12 per ½-day, £15-17 per full day; £30 deposit. Open daily 9am-5pm.)

▅▐ ORIENTATION AND PRACTICAL INFORMATION. Llandudno is flanked by two beaches with pretty boardwalks; the **West Shore** is less built up than the **North Shore,** which has Victorian promenades and a long pier. **Mostyn Street,** which follows the shore a block inland from the promenade, is the main drag. To find the **Tourist Information Centre,** turn left from the train station onto Augusta St. and right on Trinity Sq. until you hit Mostyn St. The TIC is in the library building on Mostyn St. It books rooms for £2 plus a 10% deposit. (☎01492 876 413. Open June-Sept. M-Sa 9am-5pm, Su 9:30am-4:30pm; Oct.-May M-Sa 9am-5pm.) Other services include: **Barclays** bank, at the corner of Mostyn St. and Market St.

(open M-F 9am-5pm, Sa 10am-3pm); **ATMs,** all along Mostyn St.; **police,** Oxford Rd. (☎01492 517 171); **General Hospital,** near the Maesdu Golf Course on the West Shore (☎01492 860 066); **Internet** access at the **library** upstairs from the TIC (☎01492 876 826; free; open M-Tu and F 9am-6pm, W 10am-5pm, Th 9am-7pm, Sa 9:30am-1pm) and at **Le Moulin Rouge** (see **Food**); and the **post office,** 14 Vaughn St., with a **bureau de change** (☎01492 876 125; open M and W-F 9am-5:30pm, Tu 9:30am-5:30pm, Sa 9am-12:30pm). **Postcode:** LL30 1AA.

▐▌ ◻ ACCOMMODATIONS AND FOOD. Lodging is easy to find in Llandudno, although the town becomes crowded in summer. The ▨**Llandudno Hostel ❷,** 14 Charlton St., near the Alice in Wonderland Centre, offers bright, clean dorms and sturdy bunks near the city center and train station. School groups usually rent the building out Monday through Thursday from September to July, so call ahead. (☎01492 877 430. Dorms £17; twins £40, ensuite £44. Cash only.) Budget travelers can also seek out B&Bs (£20-25) on **Chapel Street, Deganwy Avenue,** and **Saint David's Road.** Modern style meets Belle Epoque elegance at **Burleigh House ❸,** 74 Church Walks, which rents large ensuite rooms close to the beach. (☎01492 875 946. Breakfast included. Free Wi-Fi. Singles £25; doubles £52-60. MC/V.) Like its name suggests, **Beach Cove ❷,** 8 Church Walks, is a waterside retreat, with soothing rooms in neutral tones and a location just off the Promenade. (☎01492 879 638. Singles £22.50; doubles £45, ensuite £50-54. MC/V.) Nearby **Glascoed ❷,** 5 Chapel St., has ensuite rooms and a large DVD collection. (☎01492 877 340. Free Wi-Fi. From £24 per person. AmEx/MC/V.)

Dozens of dining options line main streets, including an enormous **ASDA** supermarket on Conway Rd. (☎01492 864 300. Open M-Sa 8am-10pm, Su 10am-4pm.) To get away from the many quaint sidewalk cafes, head to the modern, sea-blue rooms of **The Fat Cat Cafe-Bar ❷,** 149 Mostyn St., which serves non-traditional dishes and two-for-one meals weekdays 3-5pm. (☎01492 871 844; www.fatcatcafebar.co.uk. Open M-Th and Su 10am-11pm, F-Sa 10am-midnight. Kitchen open until 10pm. AmEx/MC/V.) Down a set of stairs off an alleyway, **The Cocoa House ❷,** 2 George St., used to provide the social atmosphere of a pub while serving cocoa instead of alcohol during the temperance movement. These days, it is fully licensed and sells creative lunch specials for £8.30. (☎01492 876 601. Open Tu-F 11am-4pm and 6-9pm, Sa 11am-9pm, Su 11am-4pm. MC/V.) With red checkered tablecloths and paintings of the Eiffel Tower, **Le Moulin Rouge ❶,** 104 Mostyn St., brings continental Europe to coastal Wales, serving crisp panini with fillings like bacon, tomatoes, Stilton, and chicken tikka. (☎01492 874 111. Panini £5-5.45. Free Internet for 20min. with £3 purchase. Open daily 8:30am-5:30pm. Downstairs bistro open F-Sa 6-9:30pm. MC/V.) **Bonjour Café ❷,** on Madoc St., specializes in crepes (most £5) and hot drinks in huge mugs. Sip a "cho-rum," a cream-topped hot chocolate infused with rum (£3), as you listen to accordion music. (☎01492 878 930. Open daily 10:30am-4pm.) **The Cottage Loaf ❷,** Market St., makes good pub grub in a tavern-like atmosphere with a beer garden. (☎01492 870 762. Entrees £6.50-8.50. Open daily 11am-11pm. Kitchen open noon-2:30pm. MC/V.)

◨ SIGHTS. Llandudno's pleasant beaches—the Victorian **North Shore** and the quieter **West Shore**—are both outdone by the looming **Great Orme,** a huge nature reserve full of caves, pastures, and some 200 Kashmir goats. At the 679 ft. summit, even gift shops and arcades cannot entirely distract from the flowered hillside. Pick up the free *Walks to the Summit* brochure from the TIC. The **Great Orme Tramway,** which departs from Church Walks, allows a quicker trip. (☎01492 879 306; www.greatormetramway.co.uk. 20min. Trams leave every 20min. daily Apr.-Sept. 10am-6pm; Oct. and Mar. 10am-5pm. Last return trip

NORTH WALES

1hr. before close. Round-trip £5.20, children £3.60.) Perhaps the most exciting way to reach the summit, however, is on one of the **Llandudno Cable Cars,** which depart from the Happy Valley Gardens. (☎01492 877 205. 20min. round-trip. Open daily 10am-4pm, weather permitting. Round-trip £6.50, children £4.50.) Halfway up the side of the Great Orme, stop for a tour of the **Bronze Age Copper Mines** and explore narrow underground passages where miners exposed ore veins with rocks and animal bones 4000 years ago. (☎01492 870 447. Open Mar.-Oct. daily 10am-5pm. £6, children £4, families £16.)

Near the TIC, the **War Museum's** "Homefront Experience," New St., off Chapel St., has torch-lit corridors and a bomb shelter, introducing visitors to the black-out and Blitz of the British home front. (☎01492 871 032. Open from mid-Mar. to mid-Nov. M-Sa 10am-4:30pm, Su 11am-3pm. £3.25, children £2, seniors £2.75, families £9.) Alice Liddell, muse to Lewis Carroll, spent her childhood summers in Llandudno, and enterprising citizens have used this connection to justify a fantasy recreation at the **Alice in Wonderland Centre,** 3-4 Trinity Sq. Walk through "The Rabbit Hole" and other scenes from the famous story accompanied by mannequins and dramatic readings. (☎01492 860 082; www.wonderland.co.uk. Open Easter-Oct. M-Sa 10am-5pm, Su 10am-4pm; Nov.-Easter M-Sa 10am-5pm. £3.25, children £2.50. Audio tour free with admission.)

Eight miles south of Llandudno, twisting pathways cross the lawns and carp-filled ponds of **Bodnant Gardens.** The upper terraces give way to a river glen down the hill. From Llandudno, take Arriva bus #25 (45min., M-Sa 11 per day) to the gates or the Conwy Valley train (M-Sa 6 per day, Su 3 per day) to the Tal-y-Cafn stop, 2 mi. away. (☎01492 650 460; www.bodnantgarden.co.uk. Open daily from Mar. to early Nov. 10am-5pm. Last entry 4:30pm. £7.20.)

ENTERTAINMENT AND NIGHTLIFE. Llandudno's two clubs are a 10min. walk from the town center down Mostyn St. **Broadway Boulevard,** Mostyn Broadway next to the North Wales Theatre, is a student-friendly venue with cheap drinks and a solid mix of chart favorites. (☎01492 879 614. No sneakers. Cover £3-6. Open W and F-Sa 10pm-3am. Last entry 1am.) A bit farther down Mostyn Broadway and left on Clarence Rd., **Washington,** East Parade St., has an upscale wine bar on the ground floor and a two-tiered dance club upstairs. (☎01492 877 974. "Upfront" (gay night) Th. No sneakers. Cover £3-4. Open W-Sa 10pm-2am; wine bar open daily 4pm-12:30am.)

Venue Cymru, the large theater between Mostyn Broadway and the Promenade, hosts plays and concerts. (☎01492 872 000; www.venuecymru.co.uk. Tickets £10-45, concessions available. Box office open M-Sa 9:30am-8:30pm, Su noon-4pm, performance days noon-8pm.)

BETWS-Y-COED ☎(0)1690

At the southern tip of the Vale of Conwy and the eastern edge of the Snowdonia mountains, picturesque Betws-y-Coed (BET-oos-uh-COYD) has evolved from an artist colony in the 1840s into a haven for lovers of the outdoors. Its main street is crammed with novelty shops, hotels, and outdoor supply stores, and visitors arrive on coach tours in droves—not so much for the town itself as for cycling, hiking, camping, climbing, and kayaking in the surrounding areas. There's little to see within Betws-y-Coed, but its Victorian stone buildings overlooking thick pine forests make it a relaxing retreat after a long day of activity.

TRANSPORTATION. Trains (☎08457 484 950) stop in Betws-y-Coed on the Conwy Valley line (p. 516). Sherpa **buses** #S2 and S97, operated by Arriva Cymru, connect Betws-y-Coed with Pen-y-Pass, stopping at some area hostels

(20min., M-Sa 1 per hr.). Buses #S2, S3, X1, X19, and 64 also stop at Llanrwst (10min., 4 per hr.). Bus #S97 continues on to Porthmadog (1hr., 3 per day). Bus #19 runs to Llandudno (50min., 2 per hr.), and X19 goes to Llangollen (1hr., 3 per day). Rent **bicycles** from **Beics Betws,** behind the post office. (☎01690 710 766; www.bikewales.co.uk. From £16 per day. Open daily 9:30am-5pm.)

⚡🖪 ORIENTATION AND PRACTICAL INFORMATION. The main street is **Holyhead Road** (A5). It runs northwest from the River Conwy, slants past the park at the town center where Station Rd. branches toward the train station, and turns west toward Swallow Falls. Possibly the busiest **Tourist Information Centre** in North Wales (also a Snowdonia NPIC), the Betws TIC is at the Old Stables, between the train station and Holyhead Rd. An energetic staff books rooms for £2 plus a 10% deposit. (☎01690 710 426; www.eryri-npa.gov.uk. Open daily Easter-Oct. 9:30am-5:30pm; Nov.-Easter 9:30am-4:30pm.) A number of **outdoor stores** line Holyhead Rd. Two Cotswold outlets (see **The Great Outdoors,** p. 49) are among them, one (☎01244 710 710) next to the Royal Oak Hotel, the other (☎01244 710 234) south of town. Other services include: an **HSBC** bank at the southern edge of Holyhead Rd. near the train station (open M 9:15am-2:30pm, Tu 9:30am-1pm, W-F 9:15am-1pm); **police** (☎01690 710 222); an **Internet** kiosk and **Wi-Fi** at Vagabond Bunkhouse during reception hours (daily 7:30-10:30am and 4:30-7:30pm; £1 per session); and the **post office,** inside the Londis, at the T junction of Holyhead and Station Rd. (☎01690 710 565; open M-F 9am-5:30pm, Sa 9am-12:30pm). **Postcode:** LL24 0AA.

🖪🗘 ACCOMMODATIONS AND FOOD. The best deal among Betws's expensive, centrally located accommodations is **Vagabond Bunkhouse ❶,** Craiglan Rd., right off the southern end of Holyhead Rd. It has clean bunks and beautiful views the the forests. (☎01690 710 850; www.vagabondbunkhouse.co.uk. Breakfast £4; evening meals £7. Linen provided. Reception 7:30-10:30am and 4:30-7:30pm. Dorms £14, MC/V.) Another cheap option is the **Glan Aber Hotel Bunkhouse ❶,** Holyhead Rd. The price and location make up for the spartan amenities—don't expect anything more than a bed and a bathroom down the hall. (☎01690 710 325; www.glanaberhotel.com. Bring your own sleeping bag. Duvets and towels available to rent. Dorms £13, with breakfast £18. MC/V.) Two hostels are located somewhat near town: **YHA Capel Curig ❷** (p. 517) and **YHA Betws-y-Coed ❷,** at the Swallow Falls Complex 2 mi. west of town on the A5. (☎01690 710 796; www.swallowfallshotel.co.uk. Kitchen and restaurant. Laundry. Reception 8am-9pm. £15, under 18 £10.50. MC/V.) Most B&Bs (from £25) cluster along **Holyhead Road.** For views of lambs grazing along the riverside, head to **Glan Llugwy ❸,** on the western edge of town, about 5min. from the railway station. Walk along Holyhead Rd. toward Swallow Falls or call the owners for a lift. They provide packed lunches (£4.50) and laundry service (£6 per load) on request. (☎01690 710 592. Singles £25-28; doubles £50-56, ensuite £60-66. MC/V.) **Bryn Llewelyn ❸** is a bit closer to the town center on Holyhead Rd. (☎01690 710 601; www.bryn-llewelyn.co.uk. Free Wi-Fi. Singles £28.50; doubles £57. MC/V.) For camping, **Riverside Caravan Park ❶** sits behind the train station. (☎01690 710 310. Open from mid-Mar. to Jan. £6.40 per person. MC/V.)

Spar market, at the northern bend of Holyhead Rd., houses a large bakery and sandwich bar. (☎01690 710 324. Open daily 8am-10pm.) A sign over the counter at 🏴**Caban-y-Pair ❷,** Holyhead Rd., reads, "Ring bell for service and comfort," and the colorful cafe's hot soups (£3-5) and specialty coffees (£2.20) do the trick. (☎01960 710 505. Open daily 9am-5pm. Cash only.) Dinner on a budget can be tough to find in Betws-y-Coed; the town center is lined with pricy bistros and daytime cafes. Apart from fish and chips, the Chinese diner **Dragon ❷,**

at the northern end of Holyhead Rd., is one of the cheapest options. (☎01690 710 334. Entrees £8.50-12.50. Open daily 5pm-late.)

◎ ⚠ SIGHTS AND OUTDOOR ACTIVITIES. Betws is well connected with eight **bridges,** the first of which was built in 1475. Renaissance architect Inigo Jones may have played a role in building the second, which consists of 11 stone arches vaulting from rock to rock. Of particular note is Telford's 1815 cast-iron **Waterloo Bridge,** situated at the village's southern end and named for the battle that cut Napoleon down to size. A miniature suspension bridge spans the Conwy, while **Pont-y-Pair Bridge,** "the bridge of the cauldron," crosses the Llugwy to the north. Behind the train station, weathered gravestones surround the humble 14th-century **Saint Michael's Church.** Two miles west, signposted off the A5, the waters of the Llugwy froth at **Swallow Falls.** Local lore claims that the soul of an evil 17th-century sheriff is trapped below. (Open 24hr. £1.50.) Bus #S2 between Betws and Snowdon stops at the falls, as do most #97A buses to Porthmadog (4min., 1-3 per hr.). A half-mile farther along the A5, "the Ugly House," **Ty Hyll** (tih-hih), lives up to its name, with a rough facade of randomly stacked boulders. Now the house serves as the Snowdonia Society headquarters and has a display and shop area. (☎01690 720 287. Open daily 9am-5pm. £1 admission gets you into the gardens out back.) Outdoor stores on Holyhead Rd. can arrange excursions into the stunning surroundings. The **National Whitewater Centre,** in nearby Bala, offers river expeditions. (☎01678 521 083; www.ukrafting.co.uk. Expeditions £31-310. Wetsuit rental £5.)

SNOWDONIA

Surrounded by Edward I's 13th-century "iron ring" of castles, Snowdonia is a huge (823 sq. mi.) natural fortress. Known in Welsh as Eryri ("Place of Eagles"), Snowdonia has diverse terrain—green slopes rise above mountain lakes, and the cliff faces of abandoned slate quarries sit among wooded hills. Rock climbing attracts many to Snowdonia; Sir Edmund Hillary trained here before conquering Everest. Although Snowdonia is largely private—only 0.3% belongs to the National Park Authority—public footpaths accommodate visitors.

⌐ TRANSPORTATION

Trains (☎08457 484 950) stop at larger towns, including Bangor and Conwy. The Cambrian Coast Railway travels along the Gwynedd coastline, beginning in Pwllheli and stopping in Criccieth, Porthmadog, Harlech, and Barmouth before ending in Aberystwyth. The **Conwy Valley Line** runs across the park from Llandudno through Betws-y-Coed to Blaenau Ffestiniog (1¼hr.; M-Sa 5 per day, 6 per day from Llandudno Junction, Su 3 per day). **Buses** serve the interior. The *Gwynedd Public Transport Maps and Timetables* and *Conwy Public Transport Information* booklets, indispensable for travel in the two counties that constitute the park, are both available for free in the region's TICs. Snowdon Sherpa buses maneuver between the park's towns and trailheads with irregular service and will stop at any safe point in the park on request. A **Gwynedd Red Rover** ticket (£5, children £2.45) buys a day's unlimited travel on all buses in Gwynedd and Anglesey; a **Snowdon Sherpa Day Ticket** (£4, children £2) secures a day's worth of rides on Sherpa buses (most routes run every 1-2hr.)

Narrow-gauge railway lines let you enjoy the countryside without a hike, although they tend to be pricey. The **Ffestiniog Railway** (p. 526) weaves from Porthmadog to Blaenau Ffestiniog, where mountain views give way to the

raw cliffs of slate quarries. You can travel part of its route to Minffordd, Pen-rhyndeudraeth, or Tan-y-Bwlch. At Porthmadog, the rail meets the Cambrian Coaster service from Pwllheli to Aberystwyth; at Blaenau Ffestiniog, it connects with the Conwy Valley Line. (☎01766 516 000. 3hr.; 4-8 per day; £17.50, concessions £15.75, one-way £10.80/9.75.) The **Snowdon Mountain Railway** and the **Llanberis Lake Railway** make trips from Llanberis (p. 522).

🛈 PRACTICAL INFORMATION

TICs and **National Park Information Centres (NPICs)** stock leaflets on walks, drives, and accommodations as well as Ordnance Survey maps (£7-13). For details, contact the **Snowdonia National Park Information Headquarters** (☎01766 770 274). A booklet published by the Snowdonia National Park Authority, free at TICs across North Wales, is a good source of information on paths, attractons, and safety information for the park. You can also check out www.eryri-npa.gov. uk or www.gwynedd.gov.uk. Snowdonia has six NPICs. The busiest and best stocked is in Betws-y-Coed (p. 514). Other large offices are in **Dolgellau** (p. 520) and **Harlech** (p. 521). There are also offices in **Aberdyfi** (☎01654 767 321; open Apr.-Oct. daily 9:30am-5:30pm), **Beddgelert** (☎01766 890 615; open Easter-Oct. daily 9:30am-5:30pm; Nov.-Easter F-Su 9:30am-4:30pm) and **Blaenau Ffestiniog** (☎01766 830 360; open Apr.-Oct. daily 9:30am-12:30pm and 1:30-5:30pm).

🛏 ACCOMMODATIONS

The National Park Authority permits **camping** only on recognized campsites or private land with the landowner's consent. Public campsites line the roads in summer; check listings below and inquire at NPICs. This section lists **YHA hostels** in Snowdonia; B&Bs are listed under individual towns. The seven hostels in the mountain area offer some of the best scenery and access to outdoor activities in Wales. All have kitchens, and most offer meals and laundry. Some have an 11pm curfew. YHA strongly advises booking hostels 48hr. in advance, as many have unpredictable opening dates in winter and fill with groups in the summers. Book online at www.yha.org.uk.

Bryn Gwynant (☎08707 705 732), above Llyn Gwynant and along Penygwryd-Beddgelert Rd. In summer, Sherpa bus #97A comes from Porthmadog or Betws-y-Coed (30min., 3 per day). Victorian house in the heart of the park. Reception 8-10am and 5-11pm. Curfew 11pm. Dorms from £16, under 18 £12. MC/V. ❷

Capel Curig (☎08707 705 746). 5 mi. from Betws-y-Coed on the A5. Sherpa bus 97A from Porthmadog and Betws-y-Coed, S6 from Bethesda, and S2 from Betws-y-Coed and Pen-y-Pass all pass the hostel. At the crossroads of many mountain paths. Spectacular view of Mt. Snowdon across the lake. Kitchen. Breakfast included; evening meals available. Laundry. Reception 7:30-10am and 5-10:30pm. 24hr. access. Open in summer daily; in winter F-Su. Dorms from £14, under 18 £10.50. MC/V. ❶

Kings (☎08707 705 900), 1 mi. west of Penmaenpool, 4 mi. from Dolgellau. Take Arriva bus #28 from Dolgellau (5min., M-Sa 9 per day). The hostel is 1 mi. uphill from the Abergwynant stop. Country house in the Vale Ffestiniog. Kitchen. Reception 8am-10am and 5pm-10:30pm. Curfew 11pm. Open from mid-Apr. to Aug. daily; Sept.-Oct. Tu-Sa; Nov.-Mar. for rent only. Dorms from £10, under 18 £7.50. MC/V. ❶

Llanberis (☎08707 705 928), ½ mi. up Capel Goch Rd., Follow signs from High St. Views of Llyn Peris, Llyn Padam, and Mt. Snowdon. Kitchen and game room. Fills up with school groups during much of July and Aug. Reception 5-10pm. 24hr. access. Dorms from £15, under 18 £11.50. MC/V. ❷

Pen-y-Pass, Nant Gwynant (☎08707 705 990), 6 mi. from Llanberis and 4 mi. from Nant Peris. Take Sherpa bus S1 from Llanberis (15min.; Easter-Oct. 2 per hr., Nov.-Easter 1 per hr.) or S2 from Betws-y-Coed (20min.; Easter-Oct. 1-2 per hr., Nov.-Easter 1 per hr.). At the head of Llanberis Pass, 1170 ft. above sea level. Doors open onto a track to the Snowdon summit. Outdoors shop sells supplies and rents hiking gear. Kitchen. Reception 8am-11pm. 24hr. access. Dorms from £16, under 18 £12. MC/V. ❷

 WHAT'S IN A NAME? Snowdonia's place names are often combinations of descriptive and poetic terms in Welsh. Some common terms you'll come across are Aber (mouth of a river), Afon (river), Bryn (hill), Dyffryn (valley), Llan (church), Llys (court, palace), Mawr (large), and Pont (bridge).

⚡ OUTDOOR ACTIVITIES

Weather on Snowdonia's mountains shifts quickly, unpredictably, and with a vengeance. No matter how beautiful the weather is below, it will be cold and wet on the high mountains. The free *How to Enjoy Wales Safely* is available at NPICs and offers advice and information on hiking and climbing. (See **Wilderness Safety,** p. 51.) Pick up the Ordnance Survey Landranger Map #115 (£7), Outdoor Leisure Map #17 (£8), and path guides (30-40p) at TICs and NPICs. Call **Mountaincall Snowdonia** (☎09068 500 449) for the forecast. For outdoor adventures, check the listings below or pick up the *Snowdon Peninsula: North Wales Activities* brochure, available at TICs and NPICs. The YHA Pen-y-Pass (p. 517) puts groups in touch with guides for outdoor sports.

Snowdonia National Park Study Centre, Plâs Tan-y-Bwlch, Maentwrog, Blaenau Ffestiniog (☎01766 590 324). Conducts 2- to 7-day courses on naturalist topics such as botanical painting. Courses £150-500; includes accommodations.

Beics Eryri Cycle Tours, 44 Tyddyn Llwydyn (☎01286 676 637). Forays from Caernarfon into the park. Supplies maps, bikes, and accommodations. From £40 per night.

Snowdon Gliders (☎01248 600 330; www.snowdongliders.co.uk). Paragliding equipment and instruction. 3-day elementary course £500. Call ahead. MC/V.

Beacon Climbing Centre (☎01286 650 045; www.beaconclimbing.com). Indoor climbing. 1½hr. session £50, groups of 4-7 £60; equipment included. Open M-F 11am-10pm, Sa-Su 10am-10pm.

Boulder Adventures, Brym Du Mountain Center, Ty Du Rd., Llanberis (☎01286 870 556; www.boulderadventures.co.uk). From ½-day to weeklong activity breaks, including rock climbing, bouldering, canoeing, kayaking, coasteering, gorge scrambling, and more. Supplies instruction, equipment, and optional accommodation. ½-day £35, full-day £55.

MOUNT SNOWDON AND VICINITY ☎(0)1286

By far the most popular destination in the park, Mt. Snowdon (3560 ft.) is the highest peak in both England and Wales. The Welsh name for the peak, Yr Wyddfa (ur-WITH-va; "burial place"), comes from a legend that Rhita Gawr, a giant cloaked with the beards of the kings he slaughtered, is buried here. Over half a million hikers tread the mountain each year. In fair weather (ha), the steep green slopes and shimmering lakes tucked beneath the mountain's ragged cliffs are stunning. In 1998, a plot of land that included Snowdon's summit was put up for sale, imperiling public access, but celebrated Welsh actor Sir Anthony Hopkins contributed a vast sum to the National Trust to save the pristine peak. Park officers request that hikers stick to the six well-marked trails to avoid damaging Snowdon's ecosystem. The most popular route is the **Llanberis Path** (5 mi.), which begins right outside of Llanberis. It is the longest and easiest of the trails, but other paths, like the Miner's Track (3.3 mi.), offer superior views and cross numerous valleys. Like the **Miners Track,** the more challenging **Pyg Track** (4 mi.) begins in nearby Pen-y-Pass, 5 mi. southeast of Llanberis on the A4086. The most difficult path is the 4 mi. **Watkin Path,** where erosion can make finding the route difficult; in harsh weather conditions, only the most experienced mountain walkers with proper equipment should attempt this route. Start climbing early in the day to avoid crowds. Trains run up to the summit on the **Snowdon Mountain Railway** (p. 523); a mailbox at the top allows you to send postcards with a special stamp.

Although Mt. Snowdon is the main attraction in the northern part of the park, experienced climbers cart pickaxes and ropes to **Ogwen Valley.** Climbs to **Devil's Kitchen** (Twll Du), the **Glyders** (Glyder Fawr and Glyder Fach), and **Tryfan** all begin from Llyn Ogwen. The elevation of Tryfan's peak has been set at 3010 ft., but nobody's quite sure which of two adjacent rocks (nicknamed Adam and Eve) is the summit. For the complete experience, some travelers jump through the crags at the top (about 3 ft.), a feat performed at their own risk. Pick up an Ordnance Survey map and get advice on equipment at **Joe Brown** (p. 523).

CADER IDRIS

The dark mountain of Cader Idris (2930 ft.) has woodland terrain and scenic walks that are less crowded than those of Mt. Snowdon. All paths cross privately owned farmland; be courteous and leave all gates as you found them. The 5 mi. pony track from **Llanfihangel-y-Pennant** is the longest but easiest path to the summit. After a level section, the path climbs through wind-sculpted rocks overlooking the Mawddach estuary and continues over the mountain. The 3 mi. trail from Ty Nant is moderately strenuous and begins at **Ty Nant Farm,** 3 mi. from Dolgellau. Avoid **Fox's Path,** which ascends Idris from the same place: many accidents occur on its steep slope. The **Minffordd Path** (about 3 mi.) is the shortest and steepest ascent. On its way to the summit, the path crosses through an 8000-year-old oak wood and rises above the lake of **Llyn Cau.** Watch out for the mythical Cwn Annwn (Hounds of the Underworld), said to fly around the range's peaks. Allow 5hr. for any of these walks. Booklets (40p) charting each are available at the NPIC, and detailed desciptions of the walks are available on the Snowdonia National Park Authority website (www. eryri-npa.gov.uk). For longer treks, pick up the the Ordnance Survey Outdoor Leisure #23 or Landranger #124 maps (£7-8).

The 9000-acre **Coed-y-Brenin Forest Park** covers the area around the Rivers Mawddach and Eden and is known for its world-class mountain biking trails.

The **Temptiwr Cycling Trail** covers 5.6 mi. and is suitable for intermediate cyclists. The aptly named **Beast Trail** covers nearly 24 mi. of hills that total nearly one vertical kilometer. Difficult hills channel the Addams Family with names like "Morticia" and "Gomez." The forest also has trails reserved for hikers and is best entered 7 mi. north of Dolgellau off the A470, near the Coed-Y-Brenin Visitor Centre. (☎01341 440 747. Open daily 9:30am-4:30pm.) Mountaineers and sportsmen will find the town of Dolgellau this page) and the **Corris Youth Hostel ❷** (p. 506) convenient spots to rest. Arriva bus #35 stops at the park from Dolgellau (15min., M-Sa 4 per day). Rent mountain bikes in the park from **Beics Brenin** for £22 per day. (☎01341 440 728. Open June-Sept. daily 10am-5pm; Oct.-Nov. and Mar.-May M and Th-Su 10am-5pm; Dec.-Feb. F-Su 10am-5pm.)

DOLGELLAU   ☎(0)1341

Set in a deep river valley, Dolgellau (dohl-GECTH-hlai) is a refuge from the formidable mountains above. Low clouds drift overhead, often shrouding the nearby peaks. The majestic views and extensive paths attract hikers of all skill levels to the town, whose stone and slate houses are hewn from local rock.

⌨ TRANSPORTATION. Buses stop in Eldon Sq. near the TIC, which details all local services in *Gwynedd Public Transport Maps and Timetables.* Arriva (☎0870 608 2608) bus #X94 (M-Sa 1-2 per hr., Su 5 per day) heads to Llangollen (1½hr.) and Wrexham (2hr.). Buses #32 and X32 pass through Dolgellau on their way to Porthmadog, Caernarfon, and Bangor in one direction (M-Sa 6 per day, Su 2 per day) and Machynlleth (40min.; M-Sa 10 per day, Su 2 per day; £2.80) and Aberystwyth (1¼hr.; M-Sa 8 per day, Su 2 per day) in the other. Bus #28 goes to Machynlleth (1½hr., M-Sa 5 per day).

◪ PRACTICAL INFORMATION. The **Tourist Information Centre,** Eldon Sq., by the bus stop, books rooms for £2 plus a 10% deposit. It doubles as a **Snowdonia National Park Information Centre,** with an exhibit on local mountains and trails. (☎01341 422 888. Open Easter-Oct. daily 9:30am-5:30pm, Nov.-Easter M and Th-Su 10am-5pm.) Equip yourself with camping and hiking gear and Ordnance Survey maps (£7-13) at **Cader Idris Outdoor Gear,** Eldon Sq., across from the bus stop. (☎01341 422 195; www.cader-idris.co.uk. Open June-Sept. M-Sa 9am-5:30pm, Su 10am-4pm; Oct.-May M-Sa 9am-5:30pm.) Other services include: **HSBC** bank, Eldon Sq. (☎08457 404 404; open M-F 9:30am-4:30pm); free **Internet** access at the **library,** Bala Rd. (☎01341 422 771; open M and F 9:30am-7pm, Tu and Th 9:30am-5pm, W 9:30am-1pm, Sa 9:30am-noon); a **launderette,** Smithfield St., across from Aber Cottage Gallery (wash £2.60, dry £1 per 15min.; open M and W-Su 9am-7pm; last wash 6:30pm); **police,** Old Barmouth Rd. (☎0845 607 1002); **Boots** pharmacy, Queen's Sq. (☎01341 422 471; open M-Sa 9am-5:30pm); **Dolgellau/Barmouth District Hospital,** off Penbrynglas (☎01341 422 479); and the **post office,** inside Spar at Plas yn Dre St. (☎01341 422 466; open M-F 9am-5:30pm, Sa 9am-12:30pm). **Postcode:** LL40 1AD.

⌨⌂ ACCOMMODATIONS AND FOOD. The **YHA Kings ❶** (p. 518) is a cheap option 4 mi. away. In Dolgellau itself, lodging is scarce and expensive, starting around £25-30. The refurbished 350-year-old **Aber Cottage Gallery B&B ❸,** on Smithfield St. near the bridge, has pristine bedrooms and houses the owner's art gallery in the stone-walled dining room. (☎01341 422 460. Breakfast included. Laundry upon request. Singles £40; doubles £60. 20% discount for stays of more than 2 nights. Cash only.) **Torrent Walk Campsite ❶,** 1½ mi. from Dolgellau off the A470, has clean, basic bunkhouses and campsites with a detached toilet and shower block. (☎01341 422 269. Breakfast £5. Duvets £2 per stay. Camping £6 per person, children £3. Electricity £3. Dorms £12 per person, £10 for multiple nights.) The deluxe **Tanyfron Caravan and Camping Park ❶** is a 10min. walk south on Arron Rd. on the A470. (☎01341 422 638. Free showers. £14 per tent; £2 more for a car. Electricity £2. Cash only.) Linger over afternoon wine, pastries, and tapas (£4.60-6) at **Bwyty Dylanwad Da ❸**, Ffos-y-Felin, a casual cafe and bistro that serves innovative dinner entrees like sesame-crumbed pecan and vegetable cake (£12) in the evenings. (☎01341 422 870. Open Tu-Sa 10am-3pm and 7-9pm. MC/V.) Duck under the low portal at **Y Sospan ❷**, Queen's Sq., behind the TIC, for sandwiches (£2.65-4) and Welsh lamb mince with gravy (£6.50). The venue turns into an upscale bistro and wine bar after 6pm. (☎01341 423 174. Open M and W-Su 9am-5:30pm and 6-9pm, Tu 9am-5:30pm. MC/V.)

🔲 **HIKING.** The famous **Precipice Walk** (3 mi., 2hr.) follows an easy path revealing views of Mawddach Estuary and the huge Idris range. Once restricted to the well-to-do guests of the nearby Caeynwch estate, the **Torrent Walk** (2½ mi., 1½hr.) circles along an ancient Roman path through woods and past waterfalls. Walks after heavy rains are deluged with gushing torrents. The **Llyn Cau, Cader Idris,** and **Tal-y-Llyn Walk** (7 mi., 5½hr.) is a strenuous excursion that should only be attempted in good weather. The hard work pays off with views of a glacial lake from 2617 ft. Mynydd Pencoed. Pick up pamphlets (30-40p) for individual walks or *Local Walks Around Dolgellau* (£4) at the TIC. The entrances to most footpaths are a few miles from the town itself; ask for directions at the TIC.

HARLECH ☎(0)1766

From the Welsh *harddlech*, meaning "beautiful slope," Harlech's name says it all. The steep ascent from the coast rises above sand dunes and passes tearooms and inns before leading to Harlech's castle above the sea. From the castle, clear days allow views of mountainous skyline and town lights.

🔲 **TRANSPORTATION.** Harlech lies midway along the **Cambrian Coast** line. The uphill walk to town from the unstaffed train station is a challenge; facing the castle, turn left and walk up the first road on your right until you reach town. **Trains** (☎08457 484 950) leave for Machynlleth (1¼-1½hr.; M-Sa 8 per day, Su 2 per day; £7.70), Porthmadog (20min.; M-Sa 7 per day, Su 3 per day; £2.50), Pwllheli (45min.; M-Sa 8 per day, Su 3 per day; £5.60), and other towns on the Llŷn Peninsula. The **Cambrian Coaster Day Ranger** (£7.70, children £4, families £15) allows an unlimited day of travel on the Cambrian Coast line. Arriva Cymru (☎0870 608 2608) **bus** #38 stops at the train station, linking Harlech to southern Barmouth (M-Sa 12 per day, Su 3 per day; £2-3) and northern Blaenau Ffestiniog (M-Sa 10 per day, Su 2 per day).

🔲🔲 **ORIENTATION AND PRACTICAL INFORMATION.** The castle opens out onto **Twtill.** Slightly uphill is the town's major street, **High Street.** Near the castle, the **Tourist Information Centre,** Llys y Graig, High St., doubles as a **National Park Information Centre.** The staff stocks Ordnance Survey maps (£7-13) and books accommodations for £2 plus a 10% deposit. (☎01766 780 658. Open Easter-Oct. daily 9:30am-12:30pm and 1:30-5:30pm.) Other services include: **HSBC** bank with an **ATM,** High St. (open M-F 9:30-11:30am); free **Internet** access at the **library,** up the hill on High St. past the Spar (☎01766 780 565; open M and F 3:30-6pm, W 10am-1pm); **police** (☎01341 422 222); and the **post office,** High St. (open M-Tu and Th-F 9:30am-5:30pm, W and Sa 9am-12:30pm). **Postcode:** LL46 2YA.

ACCOMMODATIONS AND FOOD. Relax in spacious rooms at ◪**Arundel** ❷, High St., where breakfast is served in a conservatory with views of the ocean and castle. Walk past the TIC and take a right before the Yr Ogof Bistro. The proprietor, Mary Stein, will pick you up from the train station. (☎01766 780 637. Singles £16. Cash only.) The **Byrdir Guest House** ❷, on High St. near the bus stop, has a ground-floor bar and rooms with TVs. (☎01766 780 316; www. byrdir.com. Singles £55; doubles £69. Cash only.)

Spar market is near the edge of High St.'s main drag, right before the road curves. (☎01766 780 592. Open daily 8am-8pm.) The charming ◪**Cemlyn Tea Shop** ❶, High St., serves delicious sandwiches on homemade bread (£4.80-5.60). Gaze at the castle from the sun terrace in back and choose from over 30 different teas. (☎01766 780 425; www.cemlynrestaurant.co.uk. Open W-Su 10am-5pm. MC/V.) **The Weary Walker's Cafe** ❶, on High St. near the bus stop, has sandwich options for £2.50-4.65. (☎01766 780 751. Open in summer M-W and Sa-Su 9:30am-5pm. Cash only.) The bar at the **Lion Hotel** ❷, off High St. above the castle, provides pints in this nearly publess town. Bar snacks are 50p-£5.60; meals run £6.75-9.50. (☎01766 780 731. Open M-F and Su noon-11pm, Sa 11am-11pm. Kitchen open noon-2:30pm and 6-9pm. AmEx/MC/V.)

SIGHTS AND ENTERTAINMENT. Harlech Castle's walls, once touched by the now-receded oceans, seem to spring naturally from the craggy 200 ft. cliff. It was one of the "iron ring" fortresses built by Edward I to watch over spirited Welsh troublemakers. Though its symmetrical plan of concentric walls is confined by the Irish Sea, its strategic location provided a natural defense and a crucial route for supplies and reinforcements during battle. Welsh rebel Owain Glyndŵr had a brief occupancy and parliament here in 1404. (☎01766 780 552. Open Apr.-Oct. daily 9am-5pm; Nov.-Mar. M-Sa 9:30am-4pm, Su 11am-4pm. Last entry 30min. before close. £3.70, concessions £3.30, families £10.70. Audio tours £1.) Public **footpaths,** signposted from the main roads, run from Harlech's grassy dunes to the forested hilltops above the town; get recommendations and directions at the TIC. The 4 mi. white sand **beach,** 20min. from town on foot, is an especially worthy jaunt. Walk down the road by the castle, turn right on the A496, and turn left through the golf course, following the signs. **Theatr Harlech** (☎01766 780 667; www.theatrardudwy.co.uk), on the A496, hosts a variety of operas, comedies, concerts, and the occasional band of dancing Buddhist monks. (Tickets £5-20. Box office open M-F 9:30am-5:30pm; also 6:30-9:30pm on performance nights.)

LLANBERIS   ☎(0)1286

Beneath its quiet facade, Llanberis brims with youthful energy, local pride, and rugged outdoorsmanship. The town's shifting community of climbers, cyclists, and hikers keeps it lively seven days a week (and most nights as well), while its lake and mountains provide numerous forays for outdoor adventurers.

TRANSPORTATION AND PRACTICAL INFORMATION. Situated on the western edge of the park, Llanberis is a short ride from Caernarfon on the A4086. Catch KMP (☎01286 870 880) **bus** #88 to Caernarfon (25min.; M-Sa every 30min., Su 8 per day; £2, round-trip £2.40). KMP #85 and 86 run frequently to Bangor (35-50min.; M-Sa 1-2 per hr., Su 6 per day).

The **Tourist Information Centre,** 41B High St., gives hiking tips and books beds for £2 plus a 10% deposit. It stocks a number of brochures on hikes in Snowdonia, including pamphlets (40p) on the six routes up Mt. Snowdon. (☎01286 870 765. Open Easter-Oct. daily 9:30am-4:30pm; Nov.-Easter M and F-Su

10:30am-3:30pm.) Pick up hiking gear, maps, and trail advice at **Joe Brown,** Menai Hall, High St. (☎01286 870 327. Open M-Sa 9am-5:30pm, Su 9am-5pm.) Other services include: **HSBC** bank, 29 High St. (open M and W 9:30am-11:30pm, Tu and Th-F 1:30-3:30pm) and the **Barclays ATM,** at the entrance to Electric Mountain on the A4086; **Rowlands** pharmacy, High St. (☎01286 870 264; open M-F 9am-1pm and 2-5:30pm, Sa 9am-1pm); **Internet** access at **Pete's Eats** (below); and the **post office,** 36 High St. (☎01286 870 201; open M-Tu and Th-F 9am-1pm and 1:30-5:30pm, W and Sa 9am-1pm and 1:30-7:30pm). **Postcode:** LL55 4EU.

▮▯ ACCOMMODATIONS AND FOOD. During summer weekends, the town fills fast; plan ahead. The outskirts of town hold idyllic ◪**Snowdon Cottage ❸**. From the bus station, walk up the hill past the railway station. The cottage is about 600 ft. past the Victoria Hotel, around the bend and on your left. With a castle-view garden, sweet-smelling rooms, an Egyptian-inspired bathroom, and a gracious host, guests may be tempted to ditch the mountains and stay indoors. (☎01286 872 015. Packed lunches available upon request. Laundry £5. £27 per person. Cash only.) Plenty of sheep keep hostelers company at the **YHA Llanberis ❷** (p. 518). **Pete's Eats ❶** (below) has basic dorm-style rooms. (Linen and towels included. Dorms £13.) **The Heights Hotel ❷,** 74 High St., provides bunk beds as well as ensuite singles and doubles. On weekends, locals flock to its two ground-floor bars, glass-walled "conservatory" (smoking lounge), and pool room. (☎01286 871 179. Dorms £12.50; singles £35; doubles £55. MC/V.)

Spar is at the corner of High St. and Capel Goch Rd. (Open M-Sa 7am-11pm, Su 7am-10:30pm.) Lively ◪**Pete's Eats ❶,** 40 High St., opposite the TIC, is the place to refuel with a vegetarian walnut cheeseburger (£5.60) or chili (£6.10) with a mug of tea (90p) among an eclectic crowd of highchair-bound tots and grungy hikers. Opened in 1978 to cater to climbers visiting the area, the cafe has an upstairs map library with climbing routes and magazines. (☎01286 870 117. Internet 5p per min. Open daily July-Aug. 8am-9pm; Nov.-June 8am-8pm. MC/V.) **Snowdon Honey Farm ❶,** High St., sells a huge selection of its own meads, Celtic wines, and honey as well as sandwiches, cakes, and ice cream. The owners dish out samples—try the parsnip wine. (☎01286 870 218. Open daily 7am-5pm; closing times can vary. Cash only.) **Georgio's ❶,** 49 High St., scoops out ice cream in seasonal flavors like chocolate honeycomb and toffee fudge. (☎01286 871 211. Open Easter-Oct. daily 11am-5:30pm. 1 scoop £1.50.)

◪ SIGHTS. Most attractions lie near the fork where the A4086 meets High St. Part self-promotion, part journey to the center of the earth, **Electric Mountain** takes visitors on an underground tour of the Dinorwig power station. Located deep in a mountain formerly quarried for slate, the station occupies the largest manmade cavern in Europe—St. Paul's Cathedral could fit inside. (☎01286 870 636. Open daily June-Aug. 9:30am-5:30pm; Sept.-May 10am-4:30pm. Advance bookings recommended. £7, concessions £3.50, families £19.50.) The immensely popular but pricey **Snowdon Mountain Railway** has been letting visitors "climb" Snowdon's summit since 1896, winding along tracks from its base station on the A4086. The 2½hr. round-trip loop allows 30min. at the peak, but one-way tickets are available. (☎08704 580 033; www.snowdonrailway.co.uk. Runs daily from Easter to early Nov. 9am-5pm. Trains may stop partway up, depending on the weather. £15, concessions £12; round-trip £22/19.)

In nearby **Parc Padarn,** accessed by a footpath next to the bus stop on the A4086, the excellent ◪**Welsh Slate Museum** explores Wales's industrial past with a 3D film, displays of old machinery in dusty workshops, and live demonstrations of slate splitting and finishing. In the back, don't miss the largest water wheel in mainland Britain. (☎01286 870 630; www.museumwales.ac.uk/en/

slate. Open Easter-Oct. daily 10am-5pm; Nov.-Easter M-F and Su 10am-4pm. Last entry 1hr. before close. Free.) A short walk takes you to the **Quarry Hospital Visitor Centre.** This old hospital, built by the owner of the mines to deal with health issues "privately," now houses morbid artifacts from the days before anti-germ procedures, including sinister medical instruments and a morgue with slate tables. (☎01286 870 892. Temporarily closed for renovations and set to re-open in 2009. Call for hours.) The park is also home to the **Llanberis Lake Railway,** which runs from Gilfach Ddu station at Llanberis through the woods along the lake. (☎01286 870 549; www.lake-railway.co.uk. 40min. round-trip. Open June-Aug. daily; Sept.-Oct. and Apr.-May M-F and Su; Nov-Mar. intermittently; call ahead. £6.50, children £4.50.) On the return journey, the train stops at **Cei Llydan** station, a nice picnic spot. From the main road into the park, a footbridge to the right leads to **Dolbadarn Castle,** where Prince Llywelyn of North Wales is said to have imprisoned his traitorous brother for 23 years. Only a single ragged tower remains, framed by rocky hills. The area affords views of the **Lady of Snowdon,** a rock formation that supposedly resembles Elizabeth II. For views of the waterfall **Ceunant Mawr,** follow the marked footpath (¾ mi.)from Victoria Terr. by the Victoria Hotel.

CAERNARFON ☎(0)1286

Standing on a site occupied since pre-Roman times and once the center of English government in northern Wales, Caernarfon has witnessed countless struggles for regional political control. The walled town was built for English settlers, but during a 1294 tax revolt the Welsh managed to break in, sack the town, and massacre its English inhabitants. Caernarfon is now the traditional place for the crowning of Princes of Wales, most recently Charles in 1969. Although its streets are lined with modern shops and cafes, Caernarfon embraces its traditional Welsh character; visitors can hear the town's own dialect used in its streets and pubs.

▇ TRANSPORTATION. The nearest **train** station is in Bangor (p. 526), but numerous **buses** pass through Caernarfon on their way north. The central stop is on Penllyn in the city center. Arriva Cymru (☎0871 200 2233) buses #5 and 5X run to Conwy and Llandudno via Bangor (to Llandudno 1½hr.; M-Sa 4 per hr., Su every hr.). Express Motors (☎01286 881 108) bus #1 goes to Porthmadog (50min., M-Sa every hr., £4), as does Arriva bus #32 (M-Sa 7 per day, Su 2 per day). Clynnog & Trefor (☎01286 660 208) and Berwyn (☎01286 660 315) run bus #12 to Pwllheli (45min.; M-Sa every hr., Su 3 per day). KMP (☎01286 870 880) bus #88 goes to Llanberis (25min., M-Sa every 30min., Su 9 per day). National Express (☎08705 808 080) bus #545 runs to London via Chester (9hr., daily, £28.50) or with a change in Liverpool (11¾hr., daily, £28.50). National Express buses also go daily to Cardiff (9hr., £47.50). A **Gwynedd Red Rover** ticket provides unlimited bus travel in the county for one day (£5, children £2.45). *Gwynedd Public Transport Maps and Timetables* gives info on bus and train routes. Castle Sq. shelters a **taxi** stand. **Bike rental** is available at Beics Menai Cycles, 1 Slate Quay. (☎01286 676 804; www.beicsmenai.co.uk. £12 per 2hr., children £8; ID deposit. Open daily 9:30am-5pm.)

▇▇ ORIENTATION AND PRACTICAL INFORMATION. The heart of Caernarfon lies within and just outside the town walls. From the castle entrance, the TIC is across **Castle Ditch Road,** which runs past **Castle Square** in one direction and down to the **Promenade** in the other. **Castle Street** intersects Castle Ditch Rd.

at the castle entrance and leads to **High Street.** Running north from Castle Sq. is **Bridge Street,** which turns into the busy **Bangor Street.**

The **Tourist Information Centre,** Castle St., facing the castle entrance, stocks the free *Visitor's Guide to Caernarfon* and books accommodations for £2 plus a 10% deposit. (☎01286 672 232. Open Easter-Oct. daily 9:30am-4:30pm; Nov.-Easter M-Sa 10am-4pm.) Other services include: **banks** with **ATMs** in Castle Sq. and down Bridge St.; free **Internet** at the **library,** at the corner of Bangor St. and Lon Pafiliwn (☎01286 675 944; open M-Tu and Th-F 9:30am-7pm, W and Sa 9:30am-1pm); **Pete's Launderette,** 10 Skinner St., off Bridge St. (☎01286 678 395; open M-Sa 9am-6pm, Su 11am-4pm); **police,** Maesincla Ln. (☎01286 673 333); **Castle Pharmacy,** 1A Castle Sq. (☎01286 672 352; open M-Sa 8:30am-6:30pm, Su 11am-2pm); and the **post office,** Castle Sq. (☎08457 223 344; open M and W-F 9am-5:30pm, Tu 9:30am-5:30pm, Sa 9am-12:30pm). **Postcode:** LL55 2ND.

🛏 🍴 ACCOMMODATIONS AND FOOD. Rooms abound, but not cheap ones. B&Bs ($25-35) line **Church Street** inside the old town wall. Cheaper options can be found on **Saint David's Road,** a 10min. walk from the castle and uphill off the Bangor St. roundabout. 🏠**Totter's Hostel ❷,** 2 High St., mixes the modern with the medieval: bright, spacious dorms lead to a 14th-century basement with a kitchen, a handcrafted banquet table, and stone arches. Across the street, the owners let out apartment-style doubles with a self-catering kitchen. (☎01286 672 963; www.totters.co.uk. Dorms £15; doubles $36-45. Cash only.) **Tegfan ❸,** 4 Church St., offers an excellent location one block from the castle. (☎01286 673 703. Singles £27; doubles £50-55. Cash only.) Camp at **Cadnant Valley ❶,** Llanberis Rd. (☎01286 673 196; www.cwmcadnantvalley.co.uk. Showers and laundry. £2.25 per person, children £1.74; $4-9 per tent. MC/V.)

A **Morrison's** supermarket sits on North Rd. (A487), just to the left of the roundabout on Bangor St. (Open M-W and Sa 8am-8pm, Th-F 8am-9pm, Su 8am-4pm.) **Spar,** 29-31 Castle Sq., stocks a much smaller selection closer to the center of town. (☎01286 676 805. Open M-Sa 7am-11pm, Su 7am-10:30pm.) On Saturdays and Mondays in the summer, an open-air **market** takes over Castle Sq. (Open 9am-5pm.) **Hole-in-the-Wall Street** is a narrow alleyway known for its dense collection of eateries. **Stones Bistro ❸,** 4 Hole-in-the-Wall St., near Eastgate, has candlelit tables and local art adorning its walls. Welsh lamb (£14.50) is served with your choice of mint, honey, yogurt, pepper, or tomato-garlic sauce. (☎01286 671 152. Open Tu-Sa 6-10pm. Reservations strongly recommended. MC/V.) Relax within the stone walls of **Bwyty Ogof Y Ddraig's (The Dragon's Cave) ❸,** 26 Hole-in-the-Wall St., which serves innovative Welsh fare. A variety of meat, vegetarian, and fish options, such as salmon and spinach in a pastry (£12), await in the cozy dining room. (☎01286 677 322. Open M-Tu and Su 6:30pm-late, W-Sa noon-3pm and 6:30pm-late. MC/V.) The stout wood doors of the **Anglesey Arms ❶** open onto the Promenade just below the castle. Relax outdoors with a pint as the sun dips into the shimmering Menai. (☎01286 672 158. Live entertainment F. Open M-Th and Su noon-midnight, F-Sa noon-12:30am. Kitchen open daily noon-3pm and 4-8pm. MC/V.)

🏰 SIGHTS. Built by Edward I to resemble Roman battlements, 🏰**Caernarfon Castle** has been called by one resentful Welshman a "magnificent badge of our subjection." Its eagle-crowned turrets, colorful stones, and polygonal towers cost Edward the equivalent of the Crown's annual budget and nearly 17% of his skilled labor force. Its walls withstood a rebel siege in 1404 with only 28 defenders. Wisecracking docents run tours every hour for £2, and a free 20min. video recounts the castle's history. Inside the castle is the huge and worthwhile **regimental museum** of the Royal Welsh Fusiliers, Wales's oldest infantry regiment, formed in 1689. Medals, uniforms, and helmets accompany rich historical exhibits. (☎01286 677 617. Open Apr.-Oct. daily 9am-5pm; Nov.-Mar. M-Sa 9:30am-4pm, Su 11am-4pm. £5.10, concessions £4.70, families £15.) Most of Caernarfon's 13th-century **town wall** survives, and a stretch between Church St. and Northgate St. is open for climbing during the same hours as the castle. The remains of a Celtic settlement scatter atop **Twt Hill,** alongside the Bangor St. roundabout. The jutting peak offers an excellent overlook above the town and castle. Six miles south of Caernarfon, Parc Glynllifon is bordered by the remains of a log fence built to "keep the peasants out and the pheasants in," but visitors are now welcome to wander through some 6 mi. of footpaths through exotic woodland forests. Take bus #12 (15min., every hr., round-trip £2.80) south from Caernarfon to the Parc Glynllifon stop. (☎01286 830 222. Open daily 10am-5pm. £4, seniors £2, children £1.50, families £10.) From St. Helen's Rd., the **Welsh Highland Railway** runs to the foot of Snowdon at Rhyd Ddu. In Easter 2009, it will extend through Beddgelert and Aberglaslyn Pass to connect to the Blaenau Ffestiniog Railway in Porthmadog. (☎01286 677 018; www.festrail. co.uk. 2hr. round-trip to Rhyd Ddu. Timetables available at the TIC; call the station for exact schedules. Easter-Sept. 2-6 per day; Oct.-Easter call railway for running times. All-day rover £10; round-trip £17.50.)

BANGOR   ☎(0)1248

Once a stronghold of Welsh princes, Bangor is now a lively university town and the most convenient base from which to explore the coast and nearby Isle of Anglesey. Dozens of shops line Bangor's town center, and term-time students cram its pubs at all hours.

⊑ TRANSPORTATION. Bangor is the transportation hub for the Isle of Anglesey to the west and Snowdonia to the southeast. The **train station** is on Station Rd., where Deiniol Rd. and Holyhead Rd. meet. (Ticket office open M-Sa 5:45am-6:15pm, Su 8am-6:30pm.) Trains (☎08457 484 950) go to Chester (1¼hr., 1-2 per hr., £14.20), Holyhead (30min.; M-Sa 1-3 per hr., Su 12 per day; £6.60), and Llandudno Junction (20min.; M-Sa 1-2 per hr., Su 10 per day; £4.60). The **bus station** is on Garth Rd., downhill from the town clock. Arriva Cymru (☎0871 200 2233) bus #4 runs to Holyhead via Llangefni and Llanfair PG (1-1½hr., M-Sa every 30min.). On Sunday, #44 makes the trip six times. Buses #53, 57, and 58 go to Beaumaris (30min.; M-Sa 1-3 per hr., Su 8 per day). Arriva buses #5 and 5X journey to Conwy (40min.; M-Sa 2-4 per hr., Su every hr.) and Llandudno (1hr.). Transfer at Caernarfon for the Llŷn Peninsula, including Porthmadog. National Express (☎08705 808 080) buses come from London (8½hr., 1 per day). For **taxis,** call Ace Taxi (☎01248 351 324; 24hr.).

⊡ 🖈 ORIENTATION AND PRACTICAL INFORMATION. As with many small Welsh towns, Bangor's age-old street plan and unmarked roads can be confusing. The central corridor is bounded by **Deiniol Road** (Fford Deiniol) and **High Street** (Stryd Fawr), which run parallel to each other. **Garth Road** (Fford Garth) starts from the town clock on High St. and goes past the bus station, merging with Deiniol Rd. **Holyhead Road** begins its ascent at the train station. The **University of Wales** at Bangor straddles both sides of **College Road.** The free map from the TIC lists most streets in Welsh.

The **Tourist Information Centre,** Town Hall, Deiniol Rd., by the bus station, books rooms for £2 plus a 10% deposit. (☎01248 352 786. Open Mar.-Sept. M-F 9:30am-4pm.) Other services include: **banks** with **ATMs** on High St. near the clock tower; free **Internet** access at the **library,** across from the TIC (☎01248 353 479; open M-Tu and Th-F 9:30am-7pm, W and Sa 9:30am-1pm); **police** (☎01248 370 333), behind the Town Hall on Deiniol Rd.; the **hospital** (☎01248 384 384), Penthosgarnedd; and the **post office,** 264 High St., inside WHSmith, with a **bureau de change** (☎08457 468 469; open M-Sa 9am-5:35pm). **Postcode:** LL57 1PB.

⚑❒ ACCOMMODATIONS AND FOOD. Finding a room in Bangor during graduation festivities (the 2nd week of July) is difficult; book months ahead. The nearest YHA is **Idwal Cottage ❷,** 10 mi. from Bangor at the west end of Llyn Ogwen, 5 mi. south of Bethesda. (☎0870 770 5874. Self-catering kitchen, game room, lounge, and laundry. Reception 8am-10am and 5-10pm. Dorms £16, under 18 £12.) The Snowdon Sherpa S6 runs to Llyn Ogwen from Bangor (20min.; M-Sa 1 per day, Su 2 per day) and Bethesda (10min., 5 per day). The best B&B options (£20-30) in Bangor occupy the townhouses on **Garth Road** and its extensions. **Mrs. S. Roberts ❷,** 32 Glynne Rd., between Garth Rd. and High St., has a colorful garden, an affectionate cat, and a breakfast menu with 16 options. (☎01248 352 113. Singles £20. Cash only.) Comfortable **Dilfan ❸** is a 5min. walk from the TIC, across from the swimming pool on Garth Rd. (☎01248 353 030. Singles £30; doubles £50. Cash only.) The **University of Wales at Bangor ❷,** Victoria Dr., offers dorm accommodations from June to mid-September. (☎01248 382 558. Ensuite rooms. Advance booking only. Singles £20, with breakfast £26. No children under 11. MC/V.) Camp at **Dinas Farm Touring Farm ❶,** 3 mi. from Bangor on the banks of the River Ogwen. Follow the A5 past Penrhyn Castle and turn left off the A5122 or take the #7 bus from Bangor. (☎01248 364 227. Open Easter-Oct. £5 per person. Electricity £3. Cash only.)

High Street has a surprisingly varied selection of bakeries, pubs, and eateries. The closest supermarket is **Aldi,** on Garth Rd. by the bus station. (Open M-F 9am-8pm, Sa 8:30am-8pm, Su 10am-4pm.) Vegetarian-friendly **Herbs ❷,** 162 High St., has salads (£6.75-8), cheap lunches (£4.50-8.75), and a multicultural menu in a dining room decorated with mosaics and potted plants. (☎01248 351 249; www.herbsrestaurant.co.uk. Open M-Th 9am-3pm, F-Sa 9am-9pm. AmEx/MC/V.) **Noodle One ❷,** 166 High St., is a no-frills noodle bar where diners sit at long wood tables and slurp ramen (£6-7.50) from large bowls. (☎01248 354 418. Open M-Sa noon-2:30pm and 6-10pm.) **Gerrards ❶,** 251 High St., near the clock tower, has bakery fare and specials like steak pie with chips (£4.05) in a spacious, old-fashioned venue. Don't miss the caramel fudge—only 80p! (☎01638 371 341. Open M-Sa 9am-5pm. Sandwiches served until 4pm. Cash only.)

◗ SIGHTS. The stone towers and medieval arches of ▧**Penrhyn Castle** may recall Edward I's "iron ring" of fortresses around North Wales, but they're really 19th-century recreations, the result of sugar plantation owner and slate baron George Hay Dawkins-Pennant's foray into Neo-Norman architecture. Inside, the intricate main staircase is full of carved faces that took over 10 years to complete; whimsical figures stick out their tongues at passersby. The house is also home to the second-largest art collection in Wales, after the National Gallery, including a Rembrandt over the dining room fireplace. This otherwise tasteful room was often put to less-than-classy use in the 19th century—the ornate screen in the corner hides a shelf of chamber pots where drunken guests would relieve themselves when they couldn't make it all the way to the bathroom. The house's owner was on a mission to prove that the slate that made him wealthy had numerous uses—elaborate slate dressers, a slate billiard table, and even a slate canopy bed can be found inside. Walk up High St. toward the bay, then turn right on the A5122 and go north 1 mi.—or catch bus #5 or 5X from town to the grounds entrance (10min.; M-Sa 2 per hr., Su every hr.; 80p). The castle is another mile farther. (☎01248 353 084. Castle open M and W-Su from late Mar. to June and Sept.-Oct. M noon-5pm; July-Aug. 11am-5pm. Grounds open M and W-Su from late Mar. to June and Sept.-Oct. 11am-5pm; July-Aug. 10am-5pm. Last entry 30min. before close. ₤9, children ₤4.50, families ₤22.50. Audio tours ₤1.)

The site of **Saint Deiniol's Cathedral,** Gwynedd Rd., off High St., has been the ecclesiastical center of this corner of Wales for 1400 years, and the building has been there for over 700. Today, it sits humbly amid the commercial district. (☎01248 353 983. Open M-Sa 8am-6pm, Su for services.) The **Bangor Museum and Art Gallery,** Gwynedd Rd., houses an authentic mantrap—a leg-breaking contraption used as an anti-poaching device by unscrupulous landowners—and a collection of regional crafts and artifacts, with local art on the first floor. (☎01248 353 368. Open Tu-F 12:30-4:30pm, Sa 10:30am-4:30pm. Free.) Watch tides ebb and flow at the long, onion-domed Victorian **pier** at the end of Garth Rd. (Open M-F 8:30am-9pm, Sa-Su 10am-9pm. 25p, children 10p.)

ISLE OF ANGLESEY (YNYS MÔN)

Anglesey's old name, Môn mam Cymru (Anglesey, mother of Wales), indicates roots embedded deep in old Celtic culture. Although you won't find spectacular castles or cathedrals, druidic burial sites and tiny chapels dot farmlands whose granaries have long fed northern Wales. Anglesey's Welsh heritage is hardly confined to history: three out of five islanders speak Welsh as a first language.

▐ TRANSPORTATION

Apart from its major towns, Anglesey can be difficult to explore without a car—buses connect much of the island, but routes are sporadic. Bangor, on the mainland, is the best hub. **Trains** (☎08457 484 950) run from Holyhead to Bangor (30min.; M-F 1-2 per hr., Su 13 per day; ₤6.60); some stop at Llanfair PG (30min.). The main **bus** company is Arriva Cymru (☎0870 608 2608), whose **buses** make the trip out to most of the island's major towns from the Menai and Britannia bridges. Smaller bus companies fill the gaps. These buses are reliable, albeit bumpy. Arriva bus #4 travels north from Bangor to Holyhead via Llanfair PG and Llangefni (1½hr., M-Sa every 30min.). On Sundays, #44 follows a similar route (6 per day). Buses #53, 57, and 58 hug the southeast coast from Bangor to Beaumaris (30min.; M-Sa 2 per hr., Su 8 per day); some continue to Penmon (40min.; M-Sa 11 per day, Su 4 per day). Bus #62 goes to Amlwch, on the northern coast, from Bangor (1hr.; M-Sa 1-2 per hr., Su 5 per day). Bus #42 from Bangor curves along the southwest coast to Aberffraw before continuing north to Llangefni (to Aberffraw 50min., to Llangefni 1¼hr.; M-Sa 10 per day, Su 4 per day). Lewis y Llan (☎01407 832 181) bus #61 travels from Amlwch to Holyhead (50min., M-Sa 7 per day). Bus #32 shuttles north from Llangefni to Amlwch (40min.; M-Sa 8 per day). The Gwynedd **Red Rover** ticket (₤5, children ₤2.45) covers a day's travel in Anglesey and Gwynedd. Pick up the free *Isle of Anglesey Public Transport Timetable* at TICs.

◉ SIGHTS

Burial chambers, cairns, and other prehistoric remains are scattered in Holyhead and along the eastern and western coasts. Most ancient monuments now lie on farmers' fields, so a map detailing exactly how to reach them is helpful. TICs sell Ordnance Survey Landranger Map #114 (₤7) and the more detailed

Explorer #262 and 263 (£8), each of which covers half of the island. The *Guide to Ancient Monuments* (£3) details the history of various prehistoric relics, while the free pamphlet *Rural Cycling on Anglesey* is a must for bikers. Bus drivers will drop you off as close to sights as possible if you ask.

PLAS NEWYDD. The 19th-century country home of the Marquess of Anglesey, 2 mi. south of Llanfair PG, is filled with ornate decor. The 58 ft. Rex Whistler *trompe l'oeil* mural in the dining room is a whimsical Mediterranean cityscape (with images of Wales, the painter, and the Marquess's family sneakily slipped in) and the largest painted canvas in Britain. Don't miss the painter's trick: the mountains and footprints seem to move as you walk across the dining room. *(Take bus #42 from Bangor to the house. 30min.; M-Sa 11 per day, Su 4 per day. House ☎01248 714 795. Open Mar.-Oct. M-W and Sa-Su noon-5pm. Garden open M-W and Sa-Su 11am-5:30pm. Last entry 4:30pm. £7, children £3.50. Garden without house £5/2.50.)*

BRYN CELLI DDU. The most famous of Anglesey's remains, Bryn Celli Ddu (brin kay-HLEE thee; "The Mound in the Dark Grove") is a burial chamber dating from the Neolithic period. It's actually two monuments built into one—a henge, with upright stones enclosing a ditch, and a large communal burial mound, built over the henge by adherents to a rival religion. Excavators reconstructed most of the chamber and mound in 1928. The original 5000-year-old construction was at least three times larger. Bring a flashlight to view the wall etchings inside. The spiral rock outside the chamber is a reproduction—the original is at the National Gallery in Cardiff. *(Bangor-Holyhead bus #4 stops at Llandaniel (M-Sa 15 per day); continue walking for 600 ft. toward Holyhead until a sign directs you left, down the A4080. Site is signposted 1 mi. down the sidewalk-less road. Bus #42 will stop close by; tell the driver you're going to Bryn Celli Ddu. Free.)*

PENMON PRIORY. The late medieval priory of Penmon houses two ruined buildings and Europe's largest dovecote (a cylinder of nesting holes for pigeons). From the parking lot, a path leads to sixth-century **Saint Seiriol's Well,** reputed to have healing qualities. *(Take Arriva Cymru bus #57 or 58 from Bangor or Beaumaris to Penmon (from Bangor 40min., from Beaumaris 20min.; M-Sa 11 per day, Su 4 per day) and follow the sign to Penmon Point. The priory is a 25min. walk on the same road. Free.)*

LLANFAIRPWLL...   ☎(0)1248

Llanfairpwllgwyngyllgogerychwyrndrobwllllantysiliogogogoch (don't try to impress the locals with this: HLAN-vair-poohl-gwin-gihl-go-ger-uch-wern-drobwihl-hlan-tu-sil-eyo-go-go-goch) prides itself on having the longest name of any village in the world (58 letters). Mercifully, the town is known locally as "Llanfairpwll" or "Llanfair PG." The full name is on any sign that will fit it, and a pronunciation guide hangs in the train station. Give or take a controversial adjective, the name translates to "St. Mary's Church in the hollow of white hazel near the rapid whirlpool and the Church of St. Tysillio near the red cave." Sights in both New Zealand and Thailand claim longer titles—at 92 and 163 letters, respectively—although these names (one of them packed with extensive reference to "the man with the big knees ... known as land eater") bear signs of publicity-seeking embellishment. For more information on this otherwise nondescript village's claim to fame, visit the **Tourist Information Centre,** Holyhead Rd., which conveniently adjoins a network of shops selling heaps of commemorative trinkets. (☎01248 713 177. Books accommodations for £2 plus a 10% deposit. Open Mar.-Oct. M-Sa 9:30am-5:30pm, Su 10am-5pm; Nov.-Apr. M-Sa 9:30am-5pm, Su 10am-5pm.) The #4 bus comes through Llanfair PG on its route between Bangor and Holyhead (M-Sa 1-2 per hr., Su every hr.).

NORTH WALES

BEAUMARIS   ☎(0)1248

Four miles northeast of the Menai Bridge lies the tiny town of Beaumaris. It's a lively, colorful, tourist-fueled place, mostly built alongside the last and largest of Edward I's famous "iron ring" of castles.

⊟ 📶 TRANSPORTATION AND PRACTICAL INFORMATION. Buses stop on Castle St. (see **Transportation, p. 528**). The **Tourist Information Centre** is in the lobby of the Town Hall, on Castle St. It contains a collection of free brochures but is rarely staffed. An **HSBC** bank is also on Castle St. (Open M-F 1-3:30pm.) The **post office** is at 10 Church St. (☎01248 810 320. Open M-Tu and Th-F 9am-5:30pm, W and Sa 9am-12:30pm.) **Postcode:** LL58 8AB.

📠 🛏 ACCOMMODATIONS AND FOOD. Few of the town's B&Bs have singles; consider sleeping in Bangor (p. 526) or Caernarfon (p. 524). Summers are extremely busy. Camping is best at **Kingsbridge Caravan Park ❶**, 1½ mi. from town, toward Llangoed. At the end of Beaumaris's main street, follow the road past the castle to the crossroads, turn left toward Llanfaes, and continue 1200 ft. Arriva buses #57 and 58 from Bangor will stop nearby if you ask. (☎01248 490 636. £3.50-4 per person, children £1.50-2. Electricity £2.50. Cash only.) Buy groceries at **Spar**, 11 Castle St. (Open M-Su 7am-11pm.) Teashops cluster around the castle. **The Coffee House ❶**, 11 Church St., is a pleasant street-side cafe with bright tables and a large dessert list. Its delicatessen next door sells gourmet fare and local cheeses. (☎01248 811 534. Open daily Apr.-Sept. 9am-5:30pm; Oct.-Mar. 9am-5pm. MC/V.) At the quaint **Beau's Tea Shop ❶**, 30 Castle St., stained-glass lamps cast an amber glow on dark timbers and floral tablecloths. (☎01248 811 010. Open M-Sa 10am-4:30pm, Su 11am-4:30pm. Cash only.)

◨ SIGHTS. 🖾Beaumaris Castle sits in marshland just off the Menai's shore. With a moat, drawbridge, and inner and outer circles of walls containing over 300 shooting positions at multiple heights, it was to be the finest of Edward I's iron ring castles. Building began in 1295 in response to a Welsh uprising, employing over 2000 laborers at one point. But resources dwindled by 1298, and the castle stands unfinished today. Nonetheless, its symmetrical, concentric design is still regarded as one of the best in Britain. (☎01248 810 361. Open Apr.-Oct. daily 9:30am-5pm, from late Oct. to Mar. M-Sa 9:30am-4pm, Su 11am-4pm. Last entry 30min. before close. £3.70, concessions £3.30, families £10.) **Beaumaris Gaol**, on Bunkers Hill, presents a fascinating and chilling view of incarceration in Victorian Anglesey. Individual cells feature histories of past occupants and hold grim relics like whips, shackles, and nooses. Out back, visitors can see one of Britain's only remaining human treadwheels, which demanded hours of grueling labor from inmates to supply the prison with water. (☎01248 810 921. Open Easter-Sept. daily 10:30am-5pm. Last entry 4:30pm. £3.50, concessions £2.75, families £12.) Its sister museum is the **Old Courthouse**, which lacks the morbid fascination of the gaol but provides insight into the workings of the courts over the last several centuries, including the days when juries were locked in a room with no toilet to encourage a speedy verdict. (Open Easter-Sept. daily 10:30am-5pm. £3, concessions £2.25.) Inexpensive **catamaran cruises** (1¼hr.) down the **Menai Strait** and around **Puffin Island** leave from the Cerismar Two booth on the pier. (☎07860 811 988. Weather permitting. £7, children £5.)

LLŶN PENINSULA

The pastoral scenes and cliffs of the Llŷn Peninsula are the stuff of fairy tales. They have humbled visitors since the Middle Ages, when pilgrims crossed the peninsula on their way to Bardsey Island, the site where St. Cadfan is believed to have built a monastery in the sixth century. Though some locals decry the influx of English vacationers, it's easy to understand why the Llŷn has become a holiday haven. The golden beaches fill with weekenders—Hell's Mouth is famous for surfing, and the wide Black Rock Sands, 2 mi. from Porthmadog, is a favorite for everything from windsurfing to kite buggying.

TRANSPORTATION

The northern end of the Cambrian Coast **train** line (☎08457 489 450) runs through Porthmadog to Pwllheli. Trains from Porthmadog and Pwllheli to Aberystwyth or Birmingham require a change at Machynlleth (M-Sa 8 per day, Su 3 per day). The **Cambrian Coaster Day Ranger** offers unlimited travel along the line (£7.70 per day, children £3.85, after 6:30pm £4.50).

National Express (☎08705 808 080) **bus** #545 runs from Pwllheli to London via Chester, Bangor, Birmingham, Caernarfon, and Porthmadog (10½hr., 1 per day, £28.50.) Bus #380 goes to Newcastle via Manchester, Liverpool, and Bangor (12½hr., 1 per day, £54). Express Motors (☎01286 881 108) buses #1 and 1B stop in Porthmadog on its route to Blaenau Ffestiniog (30min.; in summer M-Sa every hr., Su 5 per day) while #1 goes to Caernarfon (50min.), continuing to Bangor (1-1¼hr.; M-Sa 6 per day, Su 4 per day). Berwyn (☎01286 660 315) and Clynnog & Trefor (☎01286 660 208) run bus #12 between Pwllheli and Caernarfon (45min.; M-Sa every hr., Su 3 per day).

Several bus companies, primarily Arriva Cymru (☎0870 608 2608), serve most spots on the peninsula for about £2-3. Check schedules in *Gwynedd Public Transport Maps and Timetables*, available from TICs and on buses. Arriva and Caelloi (☎01758 612 719) run bus #3 from Porthmadog to Pwllheli (30-40min.; M-Sa 1-3 per hr., Su 6 per day). Leaving from Pwllheli, buses #8, 17, 17B, and 18 weave around the western tip of the peninsula. A **Gwynedd Red Rover** ticket (£5) secures a day of bus travel throughout the peninsula.

PORTHMADOG ☎(0)1766

In the late 19th century, the coastal town of Porthmadog (port-MA-dock) was a conduit for slate as the stuff was shipped from Wales to around the world. Now that the slate industry has dried up, the town has become a hub for tourists instead, most of them bound for other destinations in North Wales.

⊡ ⊓ TRANSPORTATION AND PRACTICAL INFORMATION. From the train station, a right turn on High St. leads to town. **Buses** stop on High St. and outside the park. **Dukes Taxis** (☎01766 514 799) is reliable (last taxi about 2am; book ahead for late nights). The **Tourist Information Centre**, High St., by the harbor, books rooms for £2 plus a 10% deposit. (☎01766 512 981. Open daily Easter-Oct. 9:30am-5pm; Nov.-Easter M-Sa 10am-4pm.) Other services include: **Barclays** bank, 79 High St. (☎0845 600 0651; open M-F 9:30am-5pm); free **Internet** access at the **library**, Chapel St. (☎01766 514 091; open M-W and F 10am-12:30pm and 2-6pm, Th and Sa 10am-12:30pm); a **launderette**, 34 Snowdon St. (☎01766 512 121; wash £3, dry £1.20; open daily 8am-7pm; last wash 6pm); **Rowland** pharmacy, 68 High St. (☎01766 513 921; open M-F 9am-5:30pm, Sa 9am-12:30pm); and the **post office**, at the corner of High St. and Bank Pl.

LOCAL LEGEND

CHANGING TIDES

Cardigan Bay is a 40 mi. sweep of beaches, cliffs, seaside resorts, and campsites, but an ancient legend has it that a giant kingdom used to jut out into its waters. The story of Cantre'r Gwaelod, the Lost Land of Wales, is one of the most famous legends in a land full of fantastic myths of fairies, giants, and everything in between.

According to the tale, the Lost Land was a lowland kingdom in the seventh century that relied upon a set of walls and dams to protect it from the sea. One day, a visiting king named Seithennin became infatuated with a maiden, Mererid, who was responsible for controlling the gates to the kingdom's seawalls. Seithennin was so successful in winning her attentions that she forgot to shut the gates. A storm came and caused the sea to flood all of the villages in the kingdom. Various versions of the legend, passed down orally through the centuries, have made their way into medieval Welsh poetry and even pub songs.

But the story may be based on more than just imagination—scientists believe that the land beneath Cardigan Bay was, in fact, forested and likely inhabited by humans up to 7000 years ago, the end of the last ice age. Although the tale of Cantre'r Gwaelod postdates this period, like other global myths of floods and sunken cities, it may simply reflect a remote memory of the rising sea levels that accompanied the melting of glaciers.

(☎01766 512 010; open M-F 9am-5:30pm, Sa 9am-12:30pm). **Postcode:** LL49 9AD.

🛏🍴 ACCOMMODATIONS AND FOOD. The best places to stay in town are a scenic 10-15min. walk down High St. (past the railway station, where it becomes Church St.) in neighboring **Tremadog.** National Express #545 and 380 and local bus Arriva #3 stop in Tremadog. The first house on the right on Church St., best known as the birthplace of TE Lawrence (Lawrence of Arabia), now houses the colorful **Snowdon Lodge ❷,** with a TV, fireplace, and kitchen. The owners offer expert hiking advice. (☎01766 515 354; www.snowdonlodge. co.uk. Continental breakfast included. Laundry £2. Dorms £16.50; twins and doubles £40; family rooms £70. Cash only.) At the popular **Jessie's ❶,** 75 High St., choose from a huge range of cheap sandwiches and baked goods. (☎01766 512 814. Open M-Sa 9am-5pm. Cash only.) **Yr Hen Fecws ❸,** 16 Lombard St., serves traditional Welsh fare in a candlelit dining room with exposed stone walls. (☎01766 514 625. Entrees £10-16.75. Open M-Sa 6-10pm. AmEx/MC/V.) Settle into wood booths at the trendy **Big Rock Cafe ❶,** 71 High St., to enjoy sandwiches and wraps for £2.65-3.50. (☎01766 512 098. Open M-Sa 9:30am-5pm. Cash only.)

◻ SIGHTS. Porthmadog's principal attraction is the **Ffestiniog Railway,** a narrow-gauge line that departs from Harbour Station on High St. The train is only three seats wide, but it offers spectacular views and a bumpy 13½ mi. ride into Snowdonia. (☎01766 516 000; www.festrail.co.uk. 3hr. roundtrip. May-Aug. 2-8 per day; Sept.-Oct. and Mar.-Apr. 2-6 per day; Nov.-Feb. call for timetables. All-day rover ticket £17.50, concessions £15.75.) At the **Llechwedd Slate Caverns,** outside of Blaenau Ffestiniog, visitors can venture into the leftovers of the Welsh slate-mining industry. The **Deep Mine Tour,** Britain's steepest passenger railway, offers a Victorian ghost for a guide and views of an underground lake. The **Miner's Tramway Tour** guides visitors through cathedral-like caves and mining demonstrations. Bus #142 connects the slate mines to the Blaenau Ffestiniog station (5min.) and coordinates with trains (5 per day)—it runs irregularly, so call ahead for the schedule. By Easter 2009, the Welsh Highland Railway will connect to the Ffestiniog railway in Porthmadog, allowing passengers to travel the 40+ mi. scenic route between Caernarfon and Blaenau Ffestiniog by narrow-gauge steam rail. The mines are just off the A470, 1 mi. north of Blaenau Ffestiniog and 10 mi. south of Betws-y-

Coed. (☎01766 830 306; www.llechwedd-slate-caverns.co.uk. Open daily from 10am. Last tours leave Mar.-Sept. 5:15pm; Oct.-Feb. 4:15pm. Book ahead. Tours £9.25, concessions £7.75, children £7. Both tours £14.75/12.50/11.25.)

⚑ DAYTRIP FROM PORTHMADOG: PORTMEIRION. The pet project of conservationist architect Clough Williams-Ellis, the fantasy town of Portmeirion recreates a Mediterranean seaside village in the hilly North Wales coastline. Built with the intention of showing how development could complement rather than sully natural surroundings, the town is a hodgepodge of architectural styles: Neoclassical pillars, a 17th-century Jacobean ceiling, and a domed pantheon are crowded by stucco cottages in warm hues of turquoise and peach. Framed by Cardigan Bay, Portmeirion seems designed for taking pictures; it's a popular place for weddings. There is little to do in town besides window-shopping, admiring the quirky architecture, and eating in cafes, but visitors can wander through the more than 70 acres of subtropical woodland gardens. *(Buses #1 and 2 run from Porthmadog to Minfford (5min.; M-Sa every hr., Su 9 per day). From the bus stop, follow the sign and walk 20min. to the village entrance. A gravel footpath through the woods runs parallel to the street. ☎01766 770 000. Open daily 9:30am-5:30pm. £7.)*

CRICCIETH ☎(0)1766

Colorful High St. shops and seaside charm make coastal Criccieth (KRIK-key-ith), 5 mi. west of Porthmadog, ideal for a pleasant, if quiet, afternoon daytrip. Above town, the remains of **Criccieth Castle** stand on a windy hilltop tucked into Tremadog Bay. Repeatedly attacked and conquered by both Welsh and English, its walls still bear the scars of Owain Glyndŵr's attempt to scorch them in the 15th century in what was the last major Welsh rebellion against the English. Little remains after the repeated ransackings, but the site itself is beautiful enough, flanked by two sandy beaches and with views over the peninsula and across to Snowdonia. (☎01766 522 227. Open Apr.-Oct. daily 10am-5pm; Nov.-Mar. M-Th 10am-4pm, F-Sa 9:30am-4pm, Su 11am-4pm. Unstaffed Nov.-Mar. M-Th; use side gate. Apr.-Oct. and Nov.-Mar. F-Su £3.10, concessions £2.70, families £9; Nov.-Mar. free.) **B&Bs** (£23-34) are scattered on **Marine Terrace** and **Marine Crescent,** by the beach near the castle, but Criccieth is best as a daytrip. **Cadwalader's ❶** ice-cream store, Castle St., has expanded across the Llŷn since this flagship store gained fame for its creamy vanilla. Now, a multitude of flavors greets long lines of customers. (☎01766 523 665. Open M-F 11am-8pm, Sa-Su 11am-9pm. £1.35 per scoop. MC/V.)

Trains go to Pwllheli (15min.; M-Sa 7 per day, Su 3 per day) and Machynlleth via Porthmadog (10min.), Harlech (30min.), and Barmouth (1hr.). From the station, turn right on High St. for the town center. Arriva **bus** #3 runs to Porthmadog and Pwllheli (15min.; M-Sa 2-3 per hr., Su 6 per day). The closest **TIC** is in Porthmadog (p. 531). **HSBC** bank is at 51 High St. (Open M-F 9:15-11:30am.) Find **Internet** access at **Roots Bookshop,** 46 High St. (☎01766 523 564. 5p per min. Open M-Sa 10am-5pm.) The **post office,** with a **bureau de change,** is around the corner from the station on High St. (☎01766 522 764. Open M-F 9:30am-5:30pm, Sa 9:30am-noon.) **Postcode:** LL52 OBU.

ABERDARON AND BARDSEY ISLAND ☎(0)1758

Once the penultimate stop on the holy Ynys Enlli (Bardsey Island) pilgrimage, the tiny village of Aberdaron sits on the tip of Llŷn Peninsula. In a quiet inlet bounded by steep green hills, Aberdaron has retained some of the small-town serenity that other Llŷn towns have lost. Right next to the ocean, the **Church of Saint Hywyn** has held fast against the tides and winds since medieval times, when pilgrims used the church as a resting place on their way to Bardsey

Island. (Open daily in summer 10am-6pm; in winter 10am-4pm. Free.) Long a religious site for the Celtic Christian Church—its first monastery was allegedly built here in the sixth century—Bardsey, the "Island of 20,000 Saints," was once so holy that three pilgrimages there equaled one to Rome. Because so many holy men made the pilgrimage late in life, the "20,000" in its name refers to the number of pilgrims buried there. Visitors can admire the ruins of the old abbey and observe hundreds of migratory birds. **Enlli Charter** runs ferries to and from the island from nearby Porth Meudwy. The trip takes 20min., allowing 3½hr. visits. Call or stop by **Y Gegin Fawr** cafe (below) for bookings. (☎07836 293 146; www.enllicharter.co.uk. Trips depart daily at 10, 11am, noon; subject to weather and demand. ₤30, children ₤15.)

For accommodations in Aberdaron, head up the hill following the sign pointing toward Whistling Sands to **Bryn Mor** ❷, where rooms have sea views and TVs. (☎01758 760 344. ₤28 per person. Cash only.) For views of Bardsey, camp at **Mynydd Mawr** ❶, Llanllawen Fawr, near the very tip of the peninsula. (☎01758 760 223; www.aberdaroncaravanandcampingsite.co.uk. ₤6 per tent.) Food has been served since 1300 in the small building now occupied by **Y Gegin Fawr (The Big Kitchen)** ❶. Enjoy a "Pilgrim's Lunch" of cheese, fruit, and bread (₤6) on the creekside patio or in the tea room. (☎01758 760 359. Open daily July-Aug. 10am-6pm; Sept.-Oct. and Easter-June 10am-5:30pm. Cash only.)

Buses #17 and 17B run from Pwllheli (40min., M-Sa 11 per day). The **post office** is inside the Spar market. (Open M-Tu and Th-F 9am-12:30pm and 1:30-5:30pm, W and Sa 9am-noon.) **Postcode:** LL53 8BE.

NORTH WALES

SCOTLAND

Half the size of England with only a tenth the population, Scotland possesses open spaces and natural splendor unrivaled by its neighbor to the south. The craggy Highlands, beaches of the western coast, and mists of the Hebrides are awe-inspiring, while the farmland to the south and tiny fishing villages to the east convey a more subtle beauty. The Scots revel in a distinct culture ranging from the fevered nightlife of Glasgow and the festival atmosphere of Edinburgh to the tight-knit communities of the Orkney and Shetland Islands. The Scots defended their independence for hundreds of years before joining England to create Great Britain in 1707, and they only regained a separate parliament in 1999. The mock kilts and bagpipes of the big cities can grow tiresome: discover Scotland's true colors by venturing off the beaten path to find Gaelic-speaking B&B owners, peat-cutting crofters, and fishermen setting out in skiffs at dawn.

TRANSPORTATION

GETTING THERE

Reaching Scotland from outside Britain is often easiest and cheapest through London, where the **Scottish Tourist Board,** 19 Cockspur St., London SW1 Y5BL (☎020 7930 2812; www.visitscotland.com), gives out brochures and reserves train, bus, and plane tickets.

BY PLANE. The cheapest fares between England and Scotland are available from no-frills airlines. **EasyJet** (☎0871 244 2366; www.easyjet.com) flies to Edinburgh and Glasgow from London Gatwick, Luton, and Stansted. The fares are web-only; book in advance and fly for as little as £5. **Ryanair** (☎08712 460 000; www.ryanair.com) flies to Edinburgh and to Glasgow Prestwick (1hr. from the city) from Dublin and London. **British Airways** (☎0844 493 0787; www.britishairways.com) sells round-trip tickets between England and Scotland from £85. **British Midland** (☎08706 070 555; www.flybmi.com) offers round-trip fares from London to Glasgow and Edinburgh from £85. Book as far in advance as possible to guarantee a reservation and the cheapest available fare.

BY TRAIN AND BUS. From London, National Express runs **trains** (☎08457 225 333; www.nationalexpress.com) to Edinburgh and Glasgow, which take 4-6hr. Fares vary depending on when you buy (£27-100). A pricier option is the **Caledonian Sleeper,** run by First Scotrail (☎08456 015 929; www.firstgroup.com/scotrail), which leaves London Euston near midnight and gets to Edinburgh at 7am (fares range £20-140). Although **buses** from London to Glasgow and Edinburgh can take 8-12hr., it may be much cheaper than rail travel.

GETTING AROUND

BY TRAIN AND BUS. In the Lowlands (south of Stirling and north of the Borders), trains and buses run many routes frequently. In the Highlands, Scotrail and National Express **trains** run a few routes. Many stations are unstaffed—buy tickets on board. **Buses** tend to be the best and cheapest way to travel. **Scottish**

Citylink (☎08705 505 050; www.citylink.co.uk) runs most intercity routes; **Traveline Scotland** has the best information on all routes and services (☎0871 200 2233; www.travelinescotland.com). Bus service is infrequent in the northwest Highlands. **Postbuses** (Royal Mail customer service ☎08457 740 740) pick up passengers and mail once or twice per day in the most remote parts of the country, typically charging £2-5 (and sometimes nothing). Many travelers find that they can be a reliable way to get around the Highlands.

The **Freedom of Scotland Travelpass** allows unlimited train travel and transportation on most Caledonian MacBrayne ("CalMac") ferries. Purchase the pass before traveling to Britain at any BritRail distributor (see **By Train**, p. 34).

BY BUS TOUR. A thriving industry of tour companies is eager to whisk travelers into the Highlands. **HAGGiS** (☎0131 557 9393; www.haggisadventures.com) and **MacBackpackers** (☎01315 589 900; www.macbackpackers.com) cater to the young and adventurous, with a number of tours departing from Edinburgh. Both run hop-on, hop-off excursions that let you travel Scotland at your own pace (usually under 3 months). HAGGiS is geared toward set tours with specific itineraries and run by witty local guides; the company guarantees accommodation at a few favorite stopping points. MacBackpackers guarantees accommodation at any of the social Scotland's Top Hostels in Edinburgh, Fort William, Skye, Oban, and Inverness (see **Tours**, p. 553). **Celtic Adventures** (☎01312 253 330; http://celticadventures.com) covers Scotland and Ireland in a variety of four- to 12-day tours, with one-way, round-trip, and hop-on, hop-off options.

BY CAR. Driving affords travelers access to Scotland's remote corners without the fear of being stranded by complicated bus services. As in the rest of Britain, driving in Scotland is on the left, seat belts are required at all times, the minimum age to drive with a foreign license is 17, and the legal minimum age to rent is 21. In rural areas, roads are often single-track, and vehicles may have to slow to a crawl to negotiate oncoming traffic. Often one car must pull into a passing place (shoulder turnoff) to enable another to pass. Drivers should also use caution on rural roads, which are often traversed by livestock. Sure, Highland cattle are cute, but not once they've gone through your windshield.

BY BICYCLE. Scotland's biking terrain is scenic and challenging. You can usually rent bikes, even in very small towns, and transport them by ferry for little or no charge. Fife and regions south of Edinburgh and Glasgow offer gentle country lanes. Orkney, Shetland, and the Western Isles are negotiable by bicycle, although cyclists should be aware of strong winds and wet roads. In the Highlands, touring by bike is more difficult. Most major roads have only one lane, and locals drive at high speeds. Transporting a bike by public transportation in the Highlands can be challenging. Many trains can carry four or fewer bikes, so reservations are essential.

BY THUMB. Hitchhikers report that drivers tend to be most receptive (and often downright friendly) in the least traveled areas. Far to the northwest and in the Western Isles, the Sabbath is strictly observed, making it difficult to get a ride on Sundays. *Let's Go* does not recommend hitchhiking.

BY FOOT. Two long-distance footpaths, established under the Countryside Act of 1967, traverse Scotland. The **West Highland Way** begins just north of Glasgow in Milngavie and continues 95 mi. north along Loch Lomond, through Glen Coe to Fort William and Ben Nevis. The **Southern Upland Way** runs 212 mi. from Portpatrick on the southwest coast to Cockburnspath on the east coast, snaking through Galloway Forest Park and the Borders. Most Tourist Information Centres (TICs) distribute simple maps of the ways and a list of

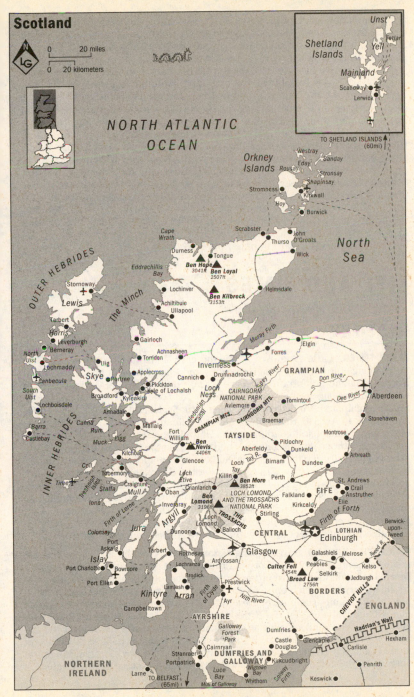

Scotland

N LG

| 0 | 20 miles |
| 0 | 20 kilometers |

Unst

Shetland Islands

Fetlar

Yell

Mainland

Scalloway

Lerwick

TO SHETLAND ISLANDS
(60mi)

NORTH ATLANTIC OCEAN

Orkney Islands

Westray
Eday   Sanday
Rousay   Stronsay
Shapinsay
Stromness   Kirkwall
Hoy   Burwick

Scrabster

North Sea

John O'Groats
Thurso
Wick

Cape Wrath

Durness   Tongue
Ben Hope   **Ben Loyal**
3041ft   2507ft

Eddrachillis Bay

Lochinver
Achiltibuie   **Ben Kilbreck**   Helmsdale
Ullapool   3153ft

OUTER HEBRIDES

Stornoway

Lewis

The Minch

Tarbert

Harris
Leverburgh
Berneray
North Uist   Gairloch   Moray Firth
Lochmaddy   Achnasheen   Forres   Elgin
Uig   Torridon   **GRAMPIAN**
Benbecula   Applecross   **Inverness**   Don River
South Uist   Skye   Cannich   Drumnadrochit   Aberdeen
Lochboisdale   Portree   Plockton   Spey River   Dee River
Barra   Broadford   Kyle of Lochalsh Loch   CAIRNGORM   Stonehaven
Castlebay   Kyleakin   Ness   NATIONAL PARK
                Armadale   Aviemore Tomintoul
Canna   Fort   **GRAMPIAN MTS.**
Rum   Eigg   Mallaig   William   **CAIRNGORM MTS.** Braemar
Muck   Montrose
        Kilchoan   **Ben Nevis** **TAYSIDE**   Arbreath
Coll   4406ft   Aberfeldy Pitlochry
INNER HEBRIDES Tobermory Glencoe   Loch   Dunkeld Dundee
Tiree   Treshnish Isles   Loch   Tay   Killin Birnam St. Andrews
Staffa Mull   Craignure   Etive   **Ben More** Perth   Anstruther
Iona   Oban Crianlarich 3852ft   Crail
        Firth of Lorne   **Ben** **LOCH LOMOND** **FIFE** Elie
Colonsay   Inveraray   **Lomond** AND THE TROSSACHS Falkland Firth of Forth
Jura   **Argyll**   3196ft NATIONAL PARK Kirkcaldy
Port   Dunoon   Loch **THE** Stirling   Berwick-
Askaig   Lomond **TROSSACHS**   upon-Tweed
Islay   Balloch **CENTRAL** **Edinburgh** **LOTHIAN**
Port Charlotte Lochranza Ardrossan **Glasgow**   Galashiels Melrose
Bowmore   Rothesay   Peebles   Teed R. Kelso
Port Ellen   Brodick   Prestwick **Culter Fell** Selkirk Jedburgh
        Lamlash   2454ft   **Broad Law**
Kintyre **Arran**   Ayr Nith River 2756ft **BORDERS** **ENGLAND**
        Campbeltown   **CHEVIOT HILLS**

AYRSHIRE

Galloway Forest Park

Dumfries
Cairnryan   Castle   Glencaple Hadrian's Wall
Stranraer   Douglas   Carlisle   Hexham
Portpatrick **DUMFRIES AND** Kirkcudbright
NORTHERN **GALLOWAY**   Penrith
IRELAND Larne   Luce   Wigtown
        TO BELFAST Bay Bay Solway   Keswick
        (65mi) Mull of Galloway Whithorn Firth

SCOTLAND

accommodations along the routes. For information on these paths, write or call the **Scottish Tourist Board,** 23 Ravelston Terr., Edinburgh EH4 3EU (☎0845 225 5121; www.visitscotland.com) or visit www.walkscotland.com. Detailed guidebooks are available at most bookstores.

Mountain ranges, like the Cuillins, the Cairngorms, and Glen Coe, have hostels that are bases for hillwalking or biking. Walk along mainland Britain's highest cliffs at Cape Wrath or ramble across the windswept isles of the Outer Hebrides. One of the most attractive aspects of hiking in Scotland is that you can often pick your own route. The wilds do pose certain dangers: stone markers can be unreliable, and expanses of open heather can be disorienting. Heavy mists are always a possibility, and blizzards occur even in July. Never go up into the mountains without proper equipment (see **Wilderness Safety**, p. 51). Many trails cross privately owned land. Be respectful and ask permission from the landowner. Leave a copy of your route and timetable at a hostel or rescue station, and, if you're out between mid-August and mid-October, be sure to ask about areas in which deer hunters might be at work. For info on walking and mountaineering in Scotland, consult Poucher's *The Scottish Peaks* (£13), the Scottish Mountaineering Club's *The Munros* (£20), or the introductory Tourist Board booklet, *Walk Scotland.*

LIFE AND TIMES

HISTORY

EARLY TIMES. Little is known about the early inhabitants of Scotland, but they managed to repel Roman incursions and forced **Emperor Hadrian** to shield Roman England behind an immense 73 mi. long wall (p. 456). Later invaders were more successful, however, and by AD 600 four groups inhabited the Scottish mainland: the native **Picts,** the Celtic **Scots,** and the Germanic **Angles** and **Saxons.** In AD 843, the Scots decisively defeated the Picts and formed the beginnings of a consolidated kingdom. United against the threat of encroaching **Vikings,** various groups gathered under **King Duncan** (later killed by a certain Macbeth in 1040), and the House of Dunkeld or Canmore reigned over Scotland for 200 years. In the early 12th century, Scotland prospered under the popular and pious **King David I** (1124-53), who built castles, abbeys, and cathedrals all over the Lowlands. Subsequent Scottish monarchs found their independence threatened by an increasingly powerful England. During the 13th century, Scotland maintained a tenuous peace punctuated with occasional fighting as Scottish kings struggled to contend with civil revolts and Scandinavian attacks.

WAR WITH ENGLAND. In 1286, **King Alexander III** died without an heir, and the resulting contest over the Scottish crown fueled the territorial ambitions of **Edward I** of England. Edward promptly seized most of Scotland and commenced a long history of English oppression. His not-so-gentle governing hand earned him the nickname "Hammer of the Scots." The **Wars of Independence** bred figures like William Wallace (yes, the *Braveheart* guy), but it was **Robert the Bruce** who emerged as Scotland's leader after a spate of assassinations. Robert led the Scots to victory over Edward II's forces at **Bannockburn** (p. 599) in 1314, and won Scotland its independence. In the next centuries the Scottish kings frequently capitalized on an **"Auld Alliance"** with France to stave off the English.

SCOTLAND

The reigns of **James IV** (1488-1513) and **James V** (1513-42) saw the arrival of both the **Renaissance** and the **Reformation** (p. 76). Following the death of James V, the infant **Mary, Queen of Scots** (1542-67), ascended the throne and was promptly shipped off to France. Lacking a strong ruler during her absence, Scotland was vulnerable to the revolts of the Reformation as the iconoclastic preacher **John Knox** spread his austere brand of Protestantism, called **Presbyterianism,** among the nobility. In 1560, the **Scottish Parliament** denied the pope's authority in Scotland and established the Presbyterian Church as Scotland's official church.

In 1561, after the death of her husband, the staunchly Catholic Mary returned to Scotland. Unpopular with Scottish nobles and Protestants, Mary's rule fanned the flames of discontent, and civil war resulted in her forced abdication and imprisonment in 1567. She escaped her Scottish captors only to find another set of shackles accross the border in England, where her cousin Elizabeth I ruled. As Mary languished in an English prison, her son **James VI** was crowned king of Scotland. Nine years later, with Catholic Spain becoming a rising threat, Queen Elizabeth forged a tentative alliance with the nominally Protestant James, which didn't stop her from executing his mother in 1587.

UNION WITH ENGLAND. When Elizabeth died without an heir in 1603, James VI was crowned **James I,** for the first time uniting Scotland and England under the same monarch. James ruled from London, and his halfhearted attempts to reconcile the Scots to British rule were tartly resisted. Scottish Presbyterians supported Parliamentary forces against James's successor **Charles I** during the English Civil War (p. 76), but, when the Parliamentarians under **Oliver Cromwell** executed Charles, the Scots shifted alliances and named the deceased king's son **King Charles II.** In response, Cromwell invaded Scotland and integrated it into the Commonwealth. Charles's restoration in 1660 returned some measure of autonomy, but conflict simmered between the high-handed Stuart kings and their proud subjects in Scotland. The victory of the Protestant William of Orange over James II in the **Glorious Revolution** (p. 77) convinced many of Scotland's Presbyterian leaders that its interests were safer with the Anglicans than with longtime Catholic ally France. Scotland was formally unified with England in the 1707 Act of Union.

THE JACOBITE REBELLION. Scottish supporters of James II (called Jacobites) attempted a series of unsuccessful anti-union uprisings, after which they launched the **"Forty-Five"**—the 1745 rebellion that captured the imaginations of Scots and Romantics everywhere. James's grandson Charles (or **Bonnie Prince Charlie**) landed in Scotland, where he succeeded in mustering unseasoned troops from various Scottish clans. He rallied the troops in Glenfinnan (p. 651) and marched to Edinburgh, where he prepared a rebellion. Despite the Jacobite victories at Stirling and Falkirk in 1746, desertions and the uncertainty of French aid undermined the rebellion. While Charles, disguised as a serving maid, eventually escaped back to France, his Highland army fell heroically on the battlefield of **Culloden** (p. 644). The English subsequently enacted a new round of oppressive measures: they forbade hereditary **tartans** and the playing of **bagpipes,** discouraged the speaking of **Gaelic,** and forcibly eradicated much of traditional Scottish culture.

ENLIGHTENMENT AND THE CLEARANCES. Despite Jacobite agitation and reactionary English countermeasures, the 18th century proved to be one of the most prosperous in Scotland's history. As agriculture, industry, and trade boomed, a vibrant intellectual environment and close links to continental **Enlightenment** thought produced such luminaries as **Adam Smith, David Hume,** and **James Mill.**

SCOTLAND

Although political reforms did much to improve social conditions in the 19th century, economic problems proved disastrous. The Highlands in particular were affected by a rapidly growing population, limited arable land, archaic farming methods, and the demands of rapacious landlords. The resulting poverty led to mass **emigration** and the infamous **Highland Clearances.** Between 1810 and 1820, the Sutherland Clearances, undertaken by the Marquis of Stafford, forcibly relocated thousands of poor farmers to small landholdings called **crofts** to make way for expanded sheep ranching. Resistance to the relocations was met with violence—homes were burned and countless people were killed. Other clearances occurred throughout the Highlands, in some cases evicting entire villages and shipping their people overseas. The **Industrial Revolution** led to growth in Glasgow and the rest of southern Scotland and contributed to increasingly poor living conditions for new industrial laborers. The situation worsened in the mid-19th century, when the **Highland Potato Famine** caused widespread starvation, death, and continuing emigration from the Highlands.

THE 20TH CENTURY. Scotland, like the rest of Britain, lost countless young men in WWI and suffered the ensuing economic downturn. In the 1930s, the **Depression** hit Scotland hard. The **Home Rule** (or **Devolution**) movement, begun in 1886 and put on hold during WWI, continued the push for a separate parliament in Edinburgh. The **Scottish National Party** (SNP) was founded in 1934 on the strength of nationalist sentiments. On Christmas of 1950, young agitators broke into Westminster Abbey and stole (or liberated, depending on your political persuasion) the **Stone of Scone**—a block of sandstone historically used as a seat in the coronation of the Scottish monarchy that had been removed from Scotland by Edward I. The discovery of North Sea oil gave Scotland an economic boost and incited a new breed of nationalism embodied by the SNP's 1974 political slogan, "It's Scotland's Oil!" Polls in the 70s indicated that Scotland's population favored devolution, but the crucial **1979 referendum** failed to garner the required 40% approval of the entire electorate.

SCOTLAND TODAY

Stands Scotland where it did?
—William Shakespeare, *Macbeth*

CURRENT POLITICS. September 1997 brought a victory for nationalists when Scottish voters supported **devolution** by an overwhelming three-to-one margin. The first elections for the new **Scottish Parliament** in 1999 inaugurated a Labour-Liberal Democrat coalition and the SNP in the position of primary opposition. Although Scotland has a new Parliament house at **Holyrood,** Edinburgh (p. 545), it is still represented in the United Kingdom's House of Commons. The precise nature of Scotland's constitutional relationship with England remains disputed, as Scottish politicians debate whether to seek incremental or immediate independence from Parliament. On the one hand, the mention of Bannockburn still stirs nationalist feeling among Scots, and the main unionist party languishes in obscurity in the Scottish Parliament. On the other, many Scottish politicians remain more closely tied to London than to their own constituents.

WHAT'S HAPPENIN'. Out of its post-industrial ruins, **Glasgow** (p. 583) began a cultural revitalization in the late 80s that continues today. **Edinburgh** (p. 545), long a magnet for cultural events, has recently seen its 61-year-old **International Festival** (and attendant events like the **Fringe Festival,** p. 562) make headlines around the world. Edinburgh's festivals peak during August but fuel the economy year-round, generating millions of pounds and thousands of jobs.

Cultural tourism draws droves of heritage-seekers and Celtic devotees to the country each summer. Although industrial trades still constitute Scotland's largest workforce, tourism employs more people than any other field in holiday spots like the Highlands and islands. On July 5, 1996, **Dolly** the sheep—the first mammal to be cloned from an adult cell—was "born" in the labs of the Roslin Institute. Scotland also produces a large portion of the superconductors in the UK, earning central Scotland the nickname "Silicon Glen." In March 2006, the Scottish government implemented a smoking ban in enclosed public places, despite substantial opposition from Scottish citizens. The rest of Britain followed Scotland's lead in July 2007.

CULTURE AND CUSTOMS

Scotland's cold, drizzling skies loom over some of the warmest people on earth. Life is generally slower outside the densely populated belt running between Glasgow and Edinburgh, and etiquette is somewhat less important here than in London's urban sprawl. But this is no reason to forget your manners. **Hospitality** and **conversation** are highly valued, and most Scots will welcome you with geniality (unless you call them English). In parts of the Highlands, **nationalism** runs deep and strong. Here, using the technically correct "British" will win you no friends. **Religion** and **football,** and the religion of football, are topics best left untouched if you're not prepared to defend yourself—verbally and otherwise.

A WORD ABOUT KILTS. Although it's unlikely you'll see very many during your travels, the kilt is not a purely romanticized concept. Criminalized as Highland garb after the Jacobite rebellion, kilts were revived during the mid-19th-century nostalgia for Highland culture. **Tartan** plaids originally denoted the geographic base of the weaver. Today, few Scots still wear their family tartan, although many do own one for use at formal gatherings and sporting events.

> **KILT IT UP.** You don't have to be Scottish to wear a kilt. Renting a kilt costs upward of £45, or £50 for the whole traditional getup, including kilt, **hose** (socks), **flashes** for the hose (worn facing outward), **Ghillie Brogues** (shoes), **sgian dubh** (ceremonial dagger, usually fake, that tucks into the right sock), **Bonnie Prince Charlie jacket** (a tuxedo-like top), **waistcoat** (vest), and the important **sporran,** worn across the front and serving as your only pocket. What goes underneath is up to you.

LANGUAGE

The early Picts left behind almost no record of their language, but settlers in southern Scotland transported their native tongues—Gaelic from Ireland, Norse from Scandinavia, and an early form of English (Inglis) from northern England. By the 11th century, **Scottish Gaelic** (pronounced GAL-ick; Irish Gaelic is GAYL-ick) had become the official language of Scottish law. As southern Scotland expanded and spread its political influence, Gaelic speakers migrated to the Highlands. Inglis, a dialect of English now called **Scots,** became the language of the Lowlands and the monarchy.

While a number of post-1700 Scottish literati, most notably Robert Burns and the 20th-century poet Hugh MacDiarmid, have written in Scots, union with England led to the rise of the English language in Scotland. Today, standard English is spoken throughout Scotland, but with a strong Scots influence.

In the Highlands, for example, "ch" often becomes a soft "h." Modern Scottish Gaelic, a linguistic cousin of modern Irish, is spoken by approximately 60,000 people in Scotland, particularly in the western islands. Recent attempts to revive Gaelic have led to its introduction in the classroom and even on street signs in the Hebrides. (For a glossary of Scottish Gaelic and Scots words and phrases, see the **Appendix,** p. 719.)

THE ARTS

LITERATURE

In a nation where stories have long been recounted by fireside, **oral literature** is as much a part of the literary tradition as novels. Unfortunately, most medieval Scottish manuscripts were lost in raids on monastic centers of learning, effectively erasing pre-14th-century records. **John Barbour** is the best-known writer in Early Scots. His epic poem, *The Brus* (c. 1375), preceded Chaucer and favorably chronicled the life of Robert I in an attempt to strengthen national unity.

In 1760, **James Macpherson** published the works of **"Ossian,"** supposedly an ancient Scottish bard who rivaled Homer. Macpherson was widely discredited, however, when he refused to produce the original manuscripts. **James Boswell** (1740-95), the biographer of **Samuel Johnson**, composed Scots verse as well as journals detailing his travels with the good doctor. "Scotland's National Bard," **Robert Burns** (1759-96), ignored pressure from the south to write in English, instead composing in his native Scots. New Year's Eve revelers owe their anthem to him, although most mouth "Auld Lang Syne" (Old Long Time) without knowing what it means. **Sir Walter Scott** (1771-1832) was among the first Scottish authors to win international accolades for his work. The chvalric *Ivanhoe* is one of the best-known, if sappiest, novels of all time. Scott was also quite nostalgic, and his historic novels (such as *Waverley*) helped to spark the 19th-century revival of Highlands culture. **Robert Louis Stevenson** (1850-94) is most famous for his tales of high adventure, including *Treasure Island*, which still fuel children's imaginations. His *Strange Case of Dr. Jekyll and Mr. Hyde* is nominally set in London, but some recognize Edinburgh's streets in Stevenson's Gothic descriptions. Scotland's authorial sons also include **Sir Arthur Conan Doyle** (1859-1930), whose *Sherlock Holmes* series is beloved by would-be gumshoes across the world, and **JM Barrie** (1860-1937), inventor of Peter Pan.

Scotland's literary present is as vibrant as its past. A series of 20th-century poets—most notably **Hugh MacDiarmid** and **Edwin Morgan**—have returned to the language of Burns, fueling a renaissance of Scottish Gaelic, particularly the Lowlands ("Lallands") dialect. **Neil Gunn** (1891-1973) wrote short stories and novels about Highland history and culture. More recent novelists include **Alasdair Gray, Tom Leonard, James Kelman,** and **Irvine Welsh.**

ART

Scotland has produced fewer famous visual artists than it has writers, but the extrordinary galleries and museums of Glasgow and Edinburgh display a rich aesthetic history. Eighteenth- and 19th-century portraitists like **Allan Ramsay** and **Sir Henry Raeburn** and genre painter **David Wilkie** have international reputations, while **James Guthrie** and others from the **Glasgow School** reveal the influence of Impressionism in their works. As a participant in both the Arts and Crafts Movement and the Art Nouveau scene, Glaswegian artist and architect **Charles Rennie Mackintosh** (1868-1928) boosted Scotland's artistic prestige with his elegant designs, many of which can be found around Glasgow (p. 583).

MUSIC

The Gaelic music of western Scotland has its roots in the traditional music of Irish settlers. As in Ireland, **ceilidhs** (KAY-lees)—spirited gatherings of music and dance—bring jigs, reels, and Gaelic songs to halls and pubs. The *clarsach*, a Celtic harp, was the primary medium for musical expression until the 16th century, when Highlander **bagpipes** and the violin introduced new creative possibilities. **Ballads**—narrative songs often performed unaccompanied—are a significant Scottish musical heritage. The folk tradition is evident in Scottish pop music, including **The Proclaimers**, folk rockers **Belle and Sebastian,** and Britpop entries **Texas** and **Travis.** Glasgow has been an exporter of talent since the 80s, generating bands like **Simple Minds** and **Tears for Fears.** Today, Glaswegians are proud of their stylish guitar rock revival band **Franz Ferdinand.**

FOOD AND DRINK

B&B regulars will encounter many a **Scottish breakfast,** consisting of beans, fried eggs, potato cakes, fried tomato, and a rasher of bacon. In general, Scottish cuisine greatly resembles English food. Although buttery shortbread will please everyone, only adventurous travelers are likely to sample more traditional dishes, which include **Scotch eggs** (boiled eggs wrapped in a sausage meat mixture, breaded, and fried) and **haggis,** the infamous national dish made from sheep stomach. Those courageous enough to try it will be rewarded with a zesty, if mushy, delicacy. Scotland's most deliciously foul specialty is the **fried Mars bar.** While the fad may have peaked in the 1990s, many chip shops will still make you the crispy, gooey treat.

If many visitors are disappointed by the fare, few can find fault with Scotland's **whisky** (spelled without the "e"). Remember: all Scotch is whiskey, but not all whiskey is whisky. Scotch whisky is either "single malt" (from a single distillery) or "blended" (a mixture of several brands). The malts are excellent and distinctive, with flavors and strengths varied enough to accommodate novices and lifelong devotees alike. Raise a glass yourself at the **distilleries** in Pitlochry (p. p. 612), the Speyside area (p. 638), or on the Isle of Islay (p. 622). Due to heavy taxes on alcohol sold in Britain, Scotch may be cheaper at home or from duty-free stores than it is in Scotland. The Scots know how to party: they have the highest alcohol consumption rate in Britain and, no surprise, are more generous with their

ON THE MENU

DEEP-FRIED MARS BAR

Welcome to Scotland, home of everything fried. In the myriad chip shops that fill the country's cities and small fishing towns, there can be found a delicacy that sounds like a little kid's dream: the deep-fried Mars Bar.

Not just an urban legend, this mind-blowing and artery-clogging treat was supposedly invented in Stonehaven in 1995. And it's exactly what it sounds like—a Mars Bar (the sweeter cousin of the American Milky Way candy bar), battered and fried. The same batter that is used for fish and chips coats the candy bar to prevent the chocolate from dissolving in the hot oil. The batter also soaks up all that tasty grease, providing a salty and crispy coating.

After a few minutes bobbing around in the oil (along with the chips and anything else that might be in the deep fryer), the chocolate is gooey and warm inside the crunchy shell. Sprinkle your fried Mars Bar liberally with salt and vinegar to ensure you cover all of the major food groups: sweet, salty, and sour.

The crazy confection is worth a try, although, if you fancy seeing old age, a deep-fried Mars Bar should definitely not be a staple of your regular diet. One bite of this tasty junk food indulgence will make your heart skip a beat—a preview of a more serious condition that too many of these treats might bring on.

licensing laws than England and Wales—drinks are served later and pubs are open longer (often until midnight or later).

SPORTING AND MERRYMAKING

The Scottish are as passionate about **football** as their English neighbors. Glasgow is particularly devoted to its two main clubs, **Celtic FC** and **Rangers FC**. Scottish **rugby** takes a close second to football, with three professional teams drawing crowds in the thousands. Golf, the "tyrannizing game" that continues to dominate St. Andrews (p. 603), was first invented in 14th-century Scotland. The over 400 golf courses in Scotland testify to the persistent influence of this sport. Traditional Scottish or **Highland games** originated from competitions under English military oppression, when participants could use only common objects such as hammers, rounded stones, and tree trunks to compete. Although "tossing the caber" may look easy, it actually requires a good deal of talent and practice to chuck an 18 ft., 150 lb. pine trunk. Weekend clan gatherings, bagpipe competitions, and Highland games occur frequently in Scotland, especially in summer; check for events at TICs and in local newspapers.

Each year, a spate of festivals celebrate Scotland's distinctive history and culture. June and July's **Common Ridings** in the Borders (p. 564) and the raucous **Up Helly Aa** in Shetland on the last Tuesday in January (p. 682) are among the best known. Scotland is also famous for its New Year's Eve celebration, known as **Hogmanay** (p. 563). The party goes on all over the country, taking over the streets in Edinburgh and Glasgow. The granddaddy of all events is the **Edinburgh International Festival** (p. 562), one of the largest in the world. The concentration of musical and theatrical events in the space of three weeks is dizzying, and Edinburgh's cafes and shops stay open all hours as pipers roam the streets. Be sure to catch the **Fringe Festival** (p. 562), the much less costly sibling of the International Festival. There are literally hundreds of performances every day, including drama, comedy acts, and jazz concerts.

SOUTHERN SCOTLAND

Southern Scotland has a rich past and a vibrant present. Nearly 80% of Scots cluster in the metropolitan areas of Edinburgh and Glasgow. Scotland's capital and the fountainhead of the Enlightenment, Edinburgh is a exceptionally beautiful city that draws enormous crowds each summer and during its festivals. Glasgow hosts formidable art collections as well as kinetic, student-fed nightlife. In the Borders region, castles and ruined abbeys chronicle Scotland's struggles with England—and paradoxically provide some peace and quiet.

HIGHLIGHTS OF SOUTHERN SCOTLAND

CATCH a play (or 19) at the world's biggest arts festival—the simultaneous **Edinburgh International** and **Fringe**—held every August (p. 562).

PONDER the past at the four **Border Abbeys** (p. 564), a ring of medieval ruins with a bloody history set among quiet villages and hills.

INDULGE at **Gourmet Glasgow,** a two-week festival in August when over 50 restaurants and bars offer free tastings (p. 593).

EDINBURGH ☎(0)131

A city of elegant stone set between rolling hills and ancient volcanoes, Edinburgh (ED-in-bur-ra; pop. 500,000) is the pride of Scotland. Since King David I granted it "burgh" (town) status in 1130, Edinburgh has been a haven for forward-thinking intellectuals and innovative artists. Today, world-class universities craft the next generation of Edinburgh's thinkers. Businessmen, students, and lots of backpackers mix amid the city's medieval architecture and mingle in lively pubs and cutting-edge clubs. In August, Edinburgh becomes a mecca for the arts, drawing talent and crowds from around the globe to its International and Fringe Festivals.

✈ INTERCITY TRANSPORTATION

Edinburgh lies 45 mi. east of Glasgow and 405 mi. northwest of London on Scotland's east coast, on the southern bank of the Firth of Forth.

Flights: Edinburgh International Airport (☎0870 040 0007), 7 mi. west of the city. Lothian Airlink (☎0131 555 6363) shuttles between the airport and Waverley Bridge (25min.; every 10-15min.; £3, children £2, round-trip £5/3). Flights to major international cities, including **New York City** (9hr.), as well as UK destinations such as **Birmingham, London Gatwick, London Heathrow** (90min.), and **Manchester.**

Trains: Waverley Station, between Princes St., Market St., and Waverley Bridge. Free bike storage beside platforms 1 and 11. Ticket office open M-Sa 4:45am-12:30am, Su 7am-12:30am. Trains (☎08457 484 950) to: **Aberdeen** (2½hr.; M-Sa every hr., Su 8 per day; £33.20); **Glasgow** (1hr., 4 per hr., £9.70); **Inverness** (3½hr., every 2hr., £32); **London King's Cross** (4¾hr., every hr., £103); **Stirling** (50min., 2 per hr., £6.10).

Buses: The modern **Edinburgh Bus Station** is on the eastern side of St. Andrew Sq. Open daily 6am-midnight. Ticket office open daily 8am-8pm. National Express (☎08705 808 080) to **London** (10hr., 4 per day, £30). Scottish Citylink (☎08705 505 050) to **Aberdeen** (4hr., every hr., £17.20), **Glasgow** (1hr.; M-Sa 4 per hr., Su 2 per hr.; £4.10), and **Inverness** (4½hr., 8-10 per day, £17.20). A bus-ferry route via Stranraer goes to **Belfast** (2 per day, £20) and **Dublin, IRE** (1 per day, £26.50). Edinburgh is also serviced by Megabus; for cheapest fares, book ahead online at www.megabus.com or call ☎0900 160 0900 7am-10pm.

✴ ORIENTATION

The city center is divided into two halves, **Old Town** and **New Town,** connected by three bridges: **North Bridge, Waverly Bridge,** and **The Mound.** The bridges cross over **Waverley Station,** which lies directly between Old Town and New Town. The **Royal Mile** and **Edinburgh Castle** are in Old Town and are the center of most tourist activities, while New Town plays host to upscale shopping. When reading maps, remember that Edinburgh is a multidimensional city—many streets that appear to intersect are actually on different levels. Two miles northeast of New Town, **Leith** is the city's seaport on the Firth of Forth.

▝ LOCAL TRANSPORTATION

Public Transportation: Although walking is usually the fastest and easiest way around the city center, Edinburgh has a comprehensive bus system. Lothian (☎0131 555 6363; www.lothianbuses.com) operates most buses. Exact change required (£1.10, children 70p). Buy a 1-day **Daysaver** ticket (£2.50, children £2.20) from any driver or in the Lothian Travelshops (☎0131 555 6363) on Waverley Bridge, Hanover St., and Shandwick Pl. Open M-Sa 8:15am-6pm. **Night buses** cover selected routes after midnight (£2). First Edinburgh (☎0870 872 7271) also operates local buses. Traveline (☎0870 608 2608; www.traveline.co.uk) has more information.

Taxis: Stands located at all stations and on almost every corner on Princes St. **City Cabs** (☎0131 228 1211). **Central Radio Taxis** (☎0131 229 2468). **Central Taxis Edinburgh** (☎0131 229 2468; www.taxis-edinburgh.co.uk).

Car Rental: The TIC has a list of rental agencies, most from £25 per day. **Thrifty,** 42 Haymarket Terr. (☎0131 337 1319). **Avis,** 100 Dalry Rd. (☎0131 337 6363).

Bike Rental: Biketrax, 11 Lochrin Pl. (☎0131 228 6633; www.biketrax.co.uk). Mountain bikes £12 per ½-day, £16 per day. Open M-Sa 9:30am-5:30pm, Su noon-5pm. **Edinburgh Cycle Hire,** 29 Blackfriars St. (☎0131 556 5560), off High St. Organizes cycle tours. Mountain bikes £10-15 per day, £50-70 per week. Open daily 10am-6pm.

🔢 PRACTICAL INFORMATION

TOURIST AND FINANCIAL SERVICES

Tourist Information Centre: Waverley Market, 3 Princes St. (☎0845 22 55 121), north of Waverley Station. Helpful and often mobbed, the mother of all Scottish TICs books rooms for £4 plus a 10% deposit; sells bus, museum, tour, and theater tickets; and has free maps and pamphlets. **Bureau de change.** Open July-Aug. M-Sa 9am-8pm, Su

SOUTHERN SCOTLAND

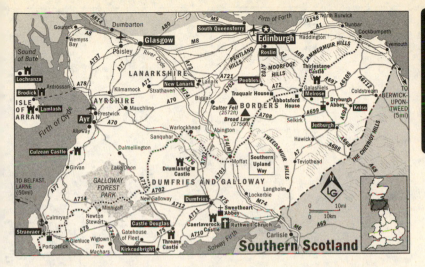

Southern Scotland

10am-8pm; Sept. and May-June M-Sa 9am-7pm, Su 10am-7pm; Oct. and Apr. M-Sa 9am-6pm, Su 10am-6pm; Nov.-Mar. M-Sa 9am-5pm, Su 10am-5pm.

Budget Travel: STA Travel, 27 Forrest Rd. and 72 Nicholson St. (both ☎0131 230 8569). Open M-W and F 10am-6pm, Th 10am-7pm, Sa 10am-5pm.

Beyond Tourism: In summer, young travelers are employed by festival organizers to help manage offices, set up, etc. Hostel notice boards often help employment agencies seeking temporary workers. **Temp Agency** (☎0131 478 5151). **Wesser and Partner** (☎01438 356 222, www.wesser.co.uk). **Kelly Services** (☎0131 220 2626).

LOCAL SERVICES

Luggage Storage: At the Waverley train station or the bus station. £5 per item per day.

Camping Gear: Millets the Outdoor Store, 12 Frederick St. (☎0131 220 1551). All the essentials, but no rentals. Open M-Sa 9am-7pm, Su 11am-6pm.

Library: Central Library (☎0131 242 8000), on George IV Bridge. Free Internet. Open M-Th 10am-8pm, F 10am-5pm, Sa 9am-1pm.

GLBT Resources: Edinburgh Lesbian, Gay, and Bisexual Centre, 58A-60 Broughton St. (☎0131 478 7069). **Gay Edinburgh** (www.visitscotland.com).

Disabled Services: Contact the TIC prior to traveling for a free *Accessible Scotland* guide or check www.edinburgh.org and www.capability-scotland.org.uk for info on access to restaurants and sights. **Shopmobility,** The Mound (☎0131 225 9559), by the National Gallery, lends motorized wheelchairs for free. Open Tu-Sa 10am-3:45pm.

Public Toilets and Showers: In the "Superloo" at the train station. Shower, toilet, and towel £3. Toilet 20p. Open daily 4am-12:45am.

EMERGENCY AND COMMUNICATIONS

Police: Headquarters at Fettes Ave. (☎0131 311 3131; www.lbp.police.uk). Other stations at 14 St. Leonard's St. (☎0131 662 5000) and 188 High St. (☎0131 226 6966). Blue **police information boxes** are scattered throughout the city center, with tourist information and an emergency assistance button.

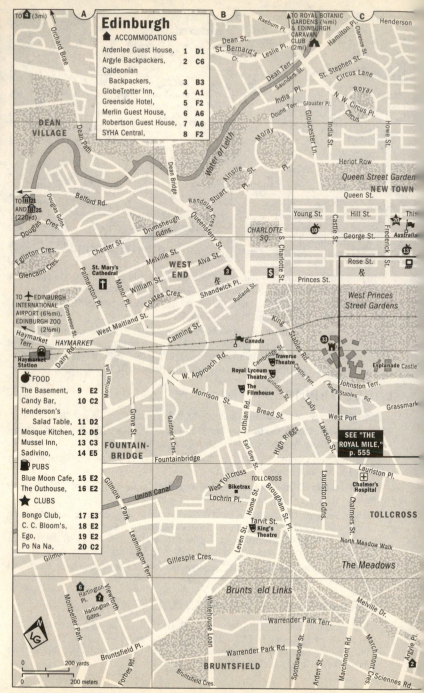

Edinburgh

ACCOMMODATIONS

Ardenlee Guest House,	**1** D1
Argyle Backpackers,	**2** C6
Caldeonian	
Backpackers,	**3** B3
GlobeTrotter Inn,	**4** A1
Greenside Hotel,	**5** F2
Merlin Guest House,	**6** A6
Robertson Guest House,	**7** A6
SYHA Central,	**8** F2

FOOD

The Basement,	**9** E2
Candy Bar,	**10** C2
Henderson's	
Salad Table,	**11** D2
Mosque Kitchen,	**12** D5
Mussel Inn,	**13** C3
Sadivino,	**14** E5

PUBS

Blue Moon Cafe,	**15** E2
The Outhouse,	**16** E2

CLUBS

Bongo Club,	**17** E3
C. C. Bloom's,	**18** E2
Ego,	**19** E2
Po Na Na,	**20** C2

SEE "THE ROYAL MILE," p. 555

0   200 yards

0   200 meters

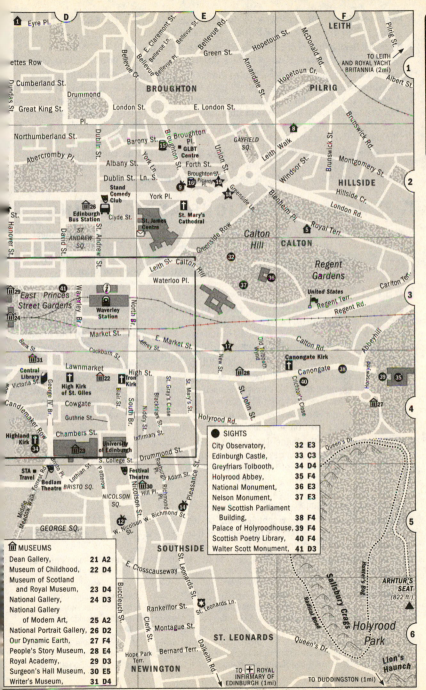

● SIGHTS

City Observatory,	32 E3
Edinburgh Castle,	33 C3
Greyfriars Tolbooth,	34 D4
Holyrood Abbey,	35 F4
National Monument,	36 E3
Nelson Monument,	37 E3
New Scottish Parliament	
Building,	38 F4
Palace of Holyroodhouse,	39 F4
Scottish Poetry Library,	40 F4
Walter Scott Monument,	41 D3

🏛 MUSEUMS

Dean Gallery,	21 A2
Museum of Childhood,	22 D4
Museum of Scotland	
and Royal Museum,	23 D4
National Gallery,	24 D3
National Gallery	
of Modern Art,	25 A2
National Portrait Gallery,	26 D2
Our Dynamic Earth,	27 F4
People's Story Museum,	28 E4
Royal Academy,	29 D3
Surgeon's Hall Museum,	30 E5
Writer's Museum,	31 D4

Pharmacy: Boots, 48 Shandwick Pl. (☎0131 225 6757) and 101-103 Princes St. (☎0131 225 8331). Open M-F 8:30am-6pm, Sa 9am-6pm.

Hospitals: Royal Infirmary of Edinburgh, 51 Little France Crescent. (☎0131 536 1000, emergencies 536 6000). **Royal Hospital for Sick Children,** 9 Sciennes Rd. (☎0131 536 0000).

Internet Access: Signs to Internet cafes are on every 2nd corner along the Royal Mile. **EasyInternetcafé,** 58 Rose St. (☎0131 220 3577), inside Caffe Nero, has 100s of terminals in the New Town. £1 per 30min. Open M-Sa 7am-10pm, Su 9am-10pm. A few free terminals are in the **Bongo Club Cafe,** 6 New St. (☎0131 558 7604). Open M-F 11am-late, Sa 12:30pm-late. Free at the **Central Library** (above). Many cafes throughout Old Town offer Internet access.

Post Office: St. James Centre (☎0131 556 9546). **Bureau de change.** Open M-Sa 9am-5:30pm. Branch at 46 St. Mary's St. (☎0131 556 6351). Open M-Tu and Th-F 9am-12:30pm and 1:30-5:30pm, Sa 9am-noon. **Postcode:** EH1 3SR.

⌂ ⚲ ACCOMMODATIONS AND CAMPING

Hostels and **hotels** are the only options in the city center, while **B&Bs** and **guesthouses** appear on the edges of town. Book ahead in summer. During the Festival (from late July to early Sept.) and New Year's, prices often rise significantly. Many locals let their apartments; the TIC's booking service works magic.

HOSTELS

This backpacker's paradise offers a bevy of convenient hostels, many of them smack-dab in the middle of town. New hostels open all the time—check with the TIC for the latest listings. Hostels range from the small and cozy to the huge and party-oriented. Expect cliques of long-term residents. Several also offer more expensive private rooms with varying amenities.

▦ **Budget Backpackers,** 37-39 Cowgate (☎0131 226 2351; www.budgetbackpackers. co.uk). The most modern of the inner-city hostels. Spacious 2- to 12-bed rooms; female dorms available. Free city tour daily; pub crawl M-Sa starting at 9pm. Key-card access. Breakfast £2. Lockers free (bring your own padlock). Laundry £1 each for washer and dryer. Internet £1 per 30min. Reception 24hr. Rooms £9-24. 18+. MC/V. ❶

▦ **Globetrotter Inn,** 46 Marine Dr. (☎0131 336 1030; www.globetrotterinns.com), a 15min. bus ride from Waverley train station and Edinburgh International Airport. Large grounds next to the Firth of Forth. An hourly shuttle service runs to and from the city, although a shop, TV room, gym, hot tub, and 24hr. bar make it tempting to stay put. Curtained bunks offer privacy. Key-card access. Light breakfast included. Lockers free. Dorms £15-19; ensuite doubles and twins £46. MC/V. ❷

Scotland's Top Hostels (www.scotlands-top-hostels.com). This chain's 3 Edinburgh hostels all have a fun, relaxed environment and nice facilities. Also runs MacBackpacker tours in the city and around Scotland.

Royal Mile Backpackers, 105 High St. (☎0131 557 6120). The smallest of the chain's hostels. Well-kept and cozy, with a community feel (and free tea and coffee). Shared laundry facilities. Free Wi-Fi. 8-bed dorms £13-15. AmEx/MC/V. ❶

Castle Rock Hostel, 15 Johnston Terr. (☎0131 225 9666, www.castlerockedinburgh.com). Just steps from the castle, with a party atmosphere and a top-notch cinema room that shows nightly movies. Ask about their haircut offer: £10 with a complimentary shot of vodka. Breakfast £2. Free Wi-Fi. Dorms £13-15; doubles £30-34; triples £45-51. AmEx/MC/V. ❷

High St. Hostel, 8 Blackfriars St. (☎0131 557 3984). Ideally located just off the Royal Mile. Laid-back party environment and 16th-century architecture. Pub crawls, movie nights, and pool competitions. 4- to 18-bed rooms; co-ed available. Free Wi-Fi. Dorms £13-15. AmEx/MC/V. ❶

Edinburgh Backpackers, 65 Cockburn (CO-burn) St. (☎0131 220 2200; www.hoppo. com). Energetic hostel with common areas, pool table, jukebox, and TV. 15% discount at the downstairs cafe. 96 beds in 8- to 16-bed co-ed dorms. Laundry and Internet access. Check-out 10am. Dorms £14-18.50; private rooms £45-52. MC/V. ❷

SYHA Hostels (www.syha.org.uk). Not the most popular with the young and the restless, but clean, safe, and some of the few child-friendly hostel options in the city's center.

Central, 9 Haddington Pl. (☎0131 524 2090), off Leith Walk. Brand-new, with modern ensuite rooms, bar, and bistro. Singles, doubles, and family rooms in addition to 4- to 8-bed dorms. Laundry and Internet access £1 each. Dorms £10-25, under 18 £10-22.50. MC/V. ❷

International and Metro. SYHA turns 2 University of Edinburgh dorms into hostels during the university's summer vacation in July and Aug. **International,** Kincard's Ct., Guthrie St. (☎0871 330 8519) and **Metro,** Robertson's Close, Cowgate (☎0131 556 8718). Plain, spacious single rooms. Self-catering kitchens on each floor. Laundry. Rooms £20.50-26. MC/V. ❷

Argyle Backpackers, 14 Argyle Pl. (☎0131 667 9991; www.argyle-backpackers.co.uk). Take bus #41 from The Mound to Warrender Park Rd. 3 renovated townhouses with a backyard and free coffee. A B&B-like alternative to louder city hostels. Private rooms, many with TVs, along with 4- to 10-bed dorms. Lockable dorms. Laundry facilities available. Internet access £1.50 per hr. Reception 9am-10pm. Check-in 2-10pm. Dorms £12-23; doubles and twins £40-60; triples £45-75. MC/V. ❶

Caledonian Backpackers, 3 Queensferry St. (☎0131 476 7224; www.caledonianback-packers.com), at the west end of Princes St. Make friends from around the world and join in the cacophony of snoring in the 38-bed dorm. Backpackers' bar stays open late with Tu open mike and live music F-Sa. 284 beds. 2 kitchens. Lockers, laundry, and Internet access. Dorms £16-22; private rooms £50-72. MC/V. ❷

CAMPING

Edinburgh Caravan Club Site, Marine Dr. (☎0131 312 6874), by the Firth. Take bus #8A from North Bridge. Clean and family-friendly. Electricity, shop, hot water, showers, and laundry. £4.60-6 per person; £4.80-7.60 per pitch. Cash only. ❶

HOTELS

Most of the independent city center hotels have stratospheric prices. At the affordable end are budget **chain hotels**—lacking in character but comfortable.

Greenside Hotel, 9 Royal Terr. (☎0131 557 0121). A refurbished Georgian building with views of the Firth from its top floors. Free Wi-Fi. Singles £40-90. AmEx/MC/V. ❹

Grassmarket Hotel, 94 Grassmarket (☎0131 220 2299). Formerly Premier Lodge. In the heart of Old Town. Singles £46-72. MC/V. ❹

B&BS AND GUESTHOUSES

B&Bs cluster in three colonies, all of which you can walk to or reach by bus from the city center. Try Gilmore Pl., Viewforth Terr., or Huntington Gardens in the **Bruntsfield** district, south from the west end of Princes St. (bus #11, 16, or 17 west/southbound); Dalkeith Rd. and Minto St. in **Newington,** south from the east end of Princes St. (bus #7, 31, or 37, among others); or **Pilrig,** northeast from the east end of Princes St. (bus #11 east/northbound). See www.visitscotland.com/listings/edinburgh-guest-houses.html for a thorough list or call the TIC.

▨ Ardenlee Guest House, 9 Eyre Pl. (☎0131 556 2838; www.ardenlee.co.uk). Take bus #23 or 27 from Hanover St. northbound to the corner of Dundas St. and Eyre Pl. Near the beautiful Royal Botanic Gardens. Comfortable beds complete with teddy bears. £25-45 per person; prices vary with season. MC/V. ❸

Merlin Guest House, 14 Hartington Pl. (☎0131 229 3864), just over 1 mi. southwest of the Royal Mile. An easy walk to the castle and other attractions—or you can take bus #10 or 27 from Princes St. Clean, well-priced rooms. £18-24 per person. Cash only. ❷

Robertson Guest House, 5 Hartington Gardens (☎0131 229 2652; www.robertson-guesthouse.com). Bus #10 or 27 from Princes St. Quiet and welcoming, with a relaxing garden patio. £29-60 per person. MC/V. ❸

🗋 FOOD

Edinburgh features a wide range of cuisines and restaurants. If it's traditional fare you're after, find everything from pub haggis to creative "modern Scottish" at the city's top restaurants. For food on the cheap, many **pubs** offer student and hosteler discounts in the early evening, while fast-food joints are scattered across New Town. Takeaway shops on **South Clerk** and **Leith Streets** and **Lothian Road** have affordable Chinese and Indian fare. For groceries, try **Sainsbury's,** 9-10 St. Andrew Sq. (☎0131 225 8400; open M-Sa 7am-10pm, Su 10am-8pm) or the **Tesco** on South Bridge (open M-Sa 7am-10pm, Su 9am-9pm).

OLD TOWN

🏴 **The City Cafe,** 19 Blair St. (☎0131 220 0125), right off the Royal Mile behind Tron Kirk. This perennially popular Edinburgh institution is a cafe by day and a flashy pre-club spot by night. Sip a milkshake and people-watch from the cafe's street-side seating. Happy hour daily 5-8pm. Open daily during the festival 11am-3am; otherwise 11am-1am. Kitchen open M-Th until 11pm, F-Su until 10pm. MC/V. ❷

🏴 **The Mosque Kitchen,** 50 Potterrow. Tucked away in the courtyard of Edinburgh's modern central mosque, a jumble of mismatched chairs and long tables make up an outdoor cafeteria. Popular with students. Heaping plates of curry (£4) are hard to beat. Open M-Th and Sa-Su 11:30am-7pm, F noon-1:20pm and 1:45-7pm. Cash only. ❶

The Elephant House, 21 George IV Bridge (☎0131 220 5355). Harry Potter and Dumbledore were born here on scribbled napkins. A perfect place to chill, chat, and read a newspaper. Exotic teas and coffees and the best shortbread in the universe. Great views of the castle. 1hr. of Internet and a coffee just £2.50. Live music Th 8pm. Happy hour daily 8-9pm. Open daily 8am-11pm. MC/V. ❶

Sadivino, 52 W. Richmond St. (☎0131 667 7719). A friendly sidewalk cafe that fills up quickly at lunchtime. Best of all, everything from panini to more substantial Italian fare is under £4. Open M-F 9am-6pm, Sa 10am-6pm. Cash only. ❶

The Outsider, George IV Bridge (☎0131 226 3131). A stylish restaurant without the usual high price tag or attitude. Chunky kebabs (£9) are great for sharing, or look down the menu to the excellent seafood section (£9-15). Su brunch is a laid-back affair with live DJ sets. Reservations recommended; request a window table for a view of the castle lit up at night. Open daily noon-11pm. MC/V. ❷

NEW TOWN

The Basement, 10A-12A Broughton St. (☎0131 557 0097; www.thebasement.org. uk). Menu changes daily, with plenty of vegetarian options. Energetic vibe draws students, artists, performers, and other creative types. Entrees £6-9.50, set 2-course lunch £7.50. Mexican night Sa-Su, Thai night W. Reservations recommended. Kitchen open daily noon-10:30pm. Bar open until 1am. AmEx/MC/V. ❷

Henderson's Salad Table, 94 Hanover St. (☎0131 225 2131). The founding member of Edinburgh's vegetarian scene, Henderson's has been dishing up seriously good salads (£2.10-7.30) for as long as anyone can remember. At night the wine bar gets going, offering a range of organic wines, beers, and spirits. Wi-Fi. Open M-F 7:30am-10:30pm, Sa 8:30am-10:30pm, Su 10am-4pm; hot food daily 11:30am-10pm. MC/V. ❶

Mussel Inn, 61-65 Rose St. (☎0131 225 5979; www. mussel-inn.com). Muscle in for superior local shellfish. Gourmet entrees £10.75-18. Open M-Th noon-3pm and 5:30-10pm, F-Sa noon-10pm, Su 5-10pm. MC/V. ❷

Candy Bar, 113-115 George St. (☎0131 225 9179). A world away from the tartan plaid of the Royal Mile, this popular bar serves up a great value menu of burgers, noodles, and salads (most around £6.50-8). Excellent sharing platters (£7.50-9.50). Steer clear of the tempting 14-page drink menu outside of happy hour (5-8pm) if you want to leave with your wallet intact. Open daily noon-9pm. Bar open until 1am. AmEx/MC/V. ❷

👁 SIGHTS

TOURS

Edinburgh is best explored by foot, but Lothian buses run several hop-on, hop-off open-top bus tours around the major sights, beginning at Waverley Bridge. **City Sightseeing Edinburgh** is popular; others include the **Majestic Tour** to New Haven and the Royal Yacht Britannia, vintage **MacTours,** and **Edinburgh Tours.** (General tour bus information ☎0131 220 0770; www.edinburghtour.com. All tours run Apr.-Oct. every 20-30min. £10, concessions £9. Tickets can be used for reduced admission at many attractions.) A 24hr. Edinburgh **Grand Tour** ticket (£13, concessions £11) combines all four.

While a great array of tour companies in Edinburgh tout themselves as "the original" or "the scariest," the most worthwhile of the bunch is 🔖**McEwan's Edinburgh Literary Pub Tour.** Led by professional actors, this 2hr., booze-filled crash course in Scottish literature meets outside the Beehive Inn on Grassmarket. (☎0800 169 7410; www. edinburghliterarypubtour.co.uk. May-Sept. daily 7:30pm; Oct. and Mar.-Apr. Th-Su 7:30pm; Nov.-Feb. F 7:30pm. £8, concessions £7. £1 discount for online booking.) The popular **City of the Dead Tour,** convening nightly outside St. Giles's Cathedral, promises a one-on-one encounter with the MacKenzie poltergeist. (☎0131 225 9044; www. blackhart.uk.com. Daily Easter-Halloween 8:30, 9:15, 10pm; Halloween-Easter 7:30, 8:30pm. £8.50, concessions £6.50.) **Mercat Tours,** leaving from Mercat Cross, enters Edinburgh's spooky underground vaults, relying upon long ghost stories rather than staged frights. (☎0131 225 5445; www.mercat-tours.com. £7.50-8.50, families £20-23.)

THE LOCAL STORY

STONE OF DESTINY

Traveling from the Holy Land to Egypt, Sicily, and Spain before arriving in Ireland in AD 700, the Stone of Scone (sometimes called the "Stone of Destiny") covered a lot of ground before it began its more recent commute between England and Scotland. The stone gained prominence because of its use in the coronation ceremonies of Scottish kings, but its recent shuttling between the two lands has created a contemporary folklore almost as legendary as the origins of the stone.

On Christmas Day, 1950, Scottish patriot Ian Hamilton hid in Westminster Abbey, where the stone had resided since 1296. He intended to steal the 440 lb. stone and return it to Scotland, but he was detected before the heist was completed. Hamilton (later a prominent Scottish MP) convinced the watchman that he had been locked in accidentally.

That same night, Hamilton and accomplices pulled the stone from its stand, breaking it into two pieces in the process. The stone was sent to a Glasgow workyard for repairs. While in Scotland, it was displayed at the altar in Arbroath Abbey before returning to Westminster. But the stone never made it back. Glasgow councilor Bertie Gray later revealed that the stone was copied and a fake returned. The real deal is now on display at Edinburgh Castle, where it stays under heavy guard.

OLD TOWN

Edinburgh's medieval center, the **Royal Mile,** is the heart of Old Town and home to many attractions—it's an energetic traveler's playground. The Mile gets its name from the royal edifices on either end: **Edinburgh Castle** on top of the hill and the **Palace of Holyrood** anchoring the bottom of the hill. The top of the Mile is known as **Castle Hill.** Continuing east downhill from the castle, the street becomes **Lawnmarket,** then **High Street,** then **Canongate,** and finally ends at **Holyrood.** Each segment is packed with attractions and souvenir shops.

CASTLE HILL AND LAWNMARKET

EDINBURGH CASTLE. Looming over the city center atop a dormant volcano, Edinburgh Castle dominates the skyline. Its oldest surviving building is tiny, 12th-century **Saint Margaret's Chapel,** built by King David I of Scotland in memory of his mother. The castle compound developed over the course of centuries; the most recent additions date to the 1920s. The central **Palace,** begun in the 1430s, was home to Stuart kings and queens and contains the room where Mary, Queen of Scots, gave birth to James VI. It also houses the **Scottish Crown Jewels,** which are older than those in London. The storied (although visually unspectacular) **Stone of Scone,** more commonly known as the Stone of Destiny, is also on permanent display. Other sections of the sprawling compound, like the Scottish National War Memorial, the National War Museum of Scotland, and the 15th-century monster cannon Mons Meg, definitely merit a visit, despite the uphill climb. The **One O'Clock Gun** fires from Monday to Saturday—you can guess the time. Buy tickets online to skip the queues. (☎0131 225 9846; www.edinburghcastle.gov.uk. Open daily Apr.-Oct. 9:30am-6pm; Nov.-Mar. 9:30am-5pm. Last entry 45min. before close. Free guided tours of the castle depart regularly from the entrance. £12, concessions £9.50, children £6. Excellent audio tour £3, concessions £2, children £1.)

CAMERA OBSCURA AND WORLD OF ILLUSIONS. Climb **Outlook Tower** to see the 150-year-old camera obscura, which captures moving color images of the street below. The museum's dazzling exhibits use lights, mirrors, lenses, and other 19th-century technology to create illusions that still manage to amaze and confound visitors; displays with more modern technology are equally astonishing and amusing, including a photographic face-morphing booth and a hall of holograms. (☎0131 226 3709. Open daily July-Aug. 9:30am-7pm; Sept.-Oct. and Apr.-June 9:30am-6pm; Nov.-Mar. 10am-5pm. Presentations every 20min., last presentation 1hr. before close. £8, concessions £6.50, children £5.50.)

THE SCOTCH WHISKY EXPERIENCE. Learn about the "history and mystery" of Scotland's most famous export at the Scotch Whisky Heritage Centre, located right next to the castle. The 1hr. tour takes you on a barrel ride through animatronic displays and lots of free samples—it's like Disney, but drunk. (350 Castle Hill. ☎0131 220 0441; www.scotchwhiskyexperience.co.uk. Open daily June-Sept. 9:45am-5:30pm; Oct.-May 10am-5pm. Tours every 15min. £9.50, concessions £7.25.)

MARY KING'S CLOSE. Under the souvenir shops and cafes of the Royal Mile lies a long-abandoned underground neighborhood. Accessed just off the Mile via Warriston's Close, the narrow alley of Mary King's Close was sealed off when the Royal Exchange was built in 1753. Today, tours of the street and its dark dwellings allow a fascinating glimpse into the lives of its 16th- and 19th-century residents. (☎08702 430 160. Open Apr.-Oct. daily 10am-9pm; Nov.-Mar. M-F and Su 10am-4pm, Sa 10am-9pm. 1hr. tours every 20min. Book ahead. £9.50, concessions £8.50.)

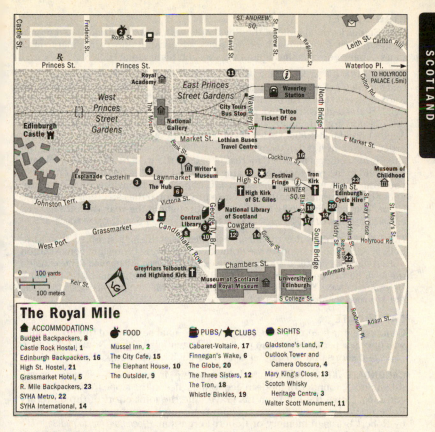

The Royal Mile

🏠 ACCOMMODATIONS
Budget Backpackers, 8
Castle Rock Hostel, 1
Edinburgh Backpackers, 16
High St. Hostel, 21
Grassmarket Hotel, 5
R. Mile Backpackers, 23
SYHA Metro, 22
SYHA International, 14

🍴 FOOD
Mussel Inn, 2
The City Cafe, 15
The Elephant House, 10
The Outsider, 9

🍺 PUBS/⭐CLUBS
Cabaret-Voltaire, 17
Finnegan's Wake, 6
The Globe, 20
The Three Sisters, 12
The Tron, 18
Whistle Binkies, 19

🔵 SIGHTS
Gladstone's Land, 7
Outlook Tower and
 Camera Obscura, 4
Mary King's Close, 13
Scotch Whisky
 Heritage Centre, 3
Walter Scott Monument, 11

GLADSTONE'S LAND. Staffed with knowledgeable guides, the oldest surviving house on the Royal Mile (completed in 1620) has been carefully preserved, with hand-painted ceilings and period furniture. *(477B Lawnmarket ☎0844 493 2120. Open daily July-Aug. 10am-7pm; Sept.-Oct. and Apr.-June 10am-5pm. Last entry 30min. before close. £5, concessions £4, families £14. Braille guidebook available.)*

WRITER'S MUSEUM. Inspirational quotations are etched in the pavement of this tribute to literary greats, just off the Royal Mile down Lady Stair's Close. The museum contains memorabilia and manuscripts from three of Scotland's greatest wordsmiths: Robert Burns, Sir Walter Scott, and Robert Louis Stevenson. *(Lawnmarket. ☎0131 529 4901. Open during the Festival M-Sa 10am-5pm, Su 2-5pm; otherwise M-Sa 10am-5pm. Free.)*

PRINCES STREET GARDENS. The gardens are in the city center, with fantastic views of Old Town and the castle. The lush park stands on the site of now-drained Nor'Loch, where Edinburghers used to drown accused witches. The loch has been replaced with an impeccably manicured lawn, stone fountains, winding avenues with benches, and enough trees to provide shade from the Scottish "sun." *(Open daily. Hours vary; usually closes at dusk.)*

HIGH STREET

High St. marks the middle of the Royal Mile with *kirks* (churches) and monuments. Watch for sandwich board signs advertising ghost or underground tours—many convene throughout the day and night along High St.

HIGH KIRK OF SAINT GILES. This *kirk* is Scotland's principal church, sometimes known as **Saint Giles's Cathedral.** From its pulpit, Protestant reformer John Knox delivered the sermons that drove the Catholic Mary, Queen of Scots, into exile. Stained-glass windows illuminate the structure, whose crown spire is one of Edinburgh's hallmarks. The 20th-century **Thistle Chapel** honors the Most Ancient and Most Noble Order of the Thistle, Scotland's prestigious chivalric order. The church is flanked on the east by the stone **Mercat Cross,** marking the site of the medieval market ("mercat"), and on the west by the **Heart of Midlothian,** inlaid in the pavement. According to legend, spitting on the Heart protects you from being hanged in the square. It appears as though many visitors are under the impression that they get extra protection if they spit their gum on the Heart. The cathedral hosts free concerts throughout the year. *(Where Lawnmarket becomes High St. ☎0131 225 9442. Open M-Sa 9am-5pm, Su 1-5pm. Suggested donation £1.)*

TRON KIRK. A block downhill from St. Giles rises the high-steepled Tron Kirk, built in part to accommodate the dramatically growing Protestant congregation during the 16th century. Today, it houses the **Old Town Information Centre,** inside the *kirk* beside an open archaeological dig, and is the focus of Edinburgh's Hogmanay (New Year's) festival. *(☎0131 225 8408. Open daily Apr.-Oct. 11am-7pm; Nov.-Mar. noon-5pm; extended festival hours. Free.)*

CANONGATE

Canongate, the steep hill that constitutes the final segment of the Royal Mile, was once a separate burgh and part of an Augustinian abbey. Now it is home to cafes and shops that are quieter than their High St. counterparts.

CANONGATE KIRK. Royals used to worship in this 17th-century chapel. Adam Smith, founder of modern economics, lies in the slope to the left of the entrance. Down the hill from his grave, find the joint effort of three literary Roberts: Robert Louis Stevenson commemorated a monument erected by Robert Burns in memory of Robert Fergusson. *(Open from Apr. to mid-Sept. M-F 9am-7pm, Sa 9am-5pm, Su 1-5pm; from mid-Sept. to Mar. M-Sa 9am-5pm, Su 1-5pm. Free.)*

SCOTTISH POETRY LIBRARY. In an award-winning piece of modern architecture, the library has a fine collection of Scottish and international poetry. *(5 Crichton's Close. ☎0131 557 2876; www.spl.org.uk. Open M-F 11am-6pm, Sa 1-5pm. Free.)*

HOLYROOD

Holyrood, at the lower end of the Royal Mile, is mostly occupied by the huge palace, park, and parliament.

PALACE OF HOLYROODHOUSE. This Stuart palace at the base of the Royal Mile remains Queen Elizabeth II's official Scottish residence. As a result, only parts of the ornate interior are open to the public. Once home to Mary, Queen of Scots, whose bedchamber is on display, the palace is every bit a royal residence. Dozens of portraits inside the **Great Gallery** chronicle its proud history. On the palace grounds lie the ruins of **Holyrood Abbey,** built by King David I in 1128 and ransacked during the Reformation. Most of the ruins date from the 13th century, but only a single doorway remains from the original construction. Located in a recently renovated 17th-century schoolhouse near the palace entrance is the **Queen's Gallery,** which displays exhibits from the royal art collection. *(At the bottom of the Royal Mile. ☎0131 556 5100. Open Apr.-Sept. daily 9:30am-6pm;*

Nov.-Mar. M-Sa 9:30am-4:30pm. Last admission 1hr. before close. No admission while royals are in residence (often June-July). Palace £9.80, concessions £8.80, children £5.80, under 5 free, families £25.40. With admission to Queen's Gallery £13/11.50/7.50/free/33.50. Audio tour free.)

HOLYROOD SCOTTISH PARLIAMENT BUILDING. After years of controversy and massive budget overdraws, the new Scottish Parliament Building is functional and open to visitors. A winner of numerous architectural awards, the building is a complex design of steel, glass, oak and stone fanning out every which way. Architect Enric Miralles was influenced by the surrounding landscapes, the paintings of Charles Rennie Mackintosh, and boats on the seashore. (☎0131 348 5200; www.scottish.parliament.uk. Open Apr.-Oct. M and F 10am-6pm, Tu-Th 9am-7pm, Sa-Su 10am-4pm; Nov.-Mar. M and F-Su 10am-4pm, Tu-Th 9am-7pm. Hours may vary; call ahead. Guided tours on non-business days £6, concessions and children £3.60, under 5 free. Free tickets to the parliamentary sessions; book in advance.)*

HOLYROOD PARK. A true city oasis, Holyrood Park is filled with hills, moorland, and lochs. At 823 ft., ⧉**Arthur's Seat,** the park's highest point, affords views of the city and Highlands. Considered a holy place by the Picts, the name "Arthur's Seat" is derived from *"Ard-na-Saigheid,"* Gaelic for "the height of the flight of arrows." Traces of forts and Bronze Age terraces dot the surrounding hillside. From the Palace of Holyroodhouse, the walk to the summit takes about 45min. **Queen's Drive** circles the park and intersects with Holyrood Rd. by the palace.

ELSEWHERE IN THE OLD TOWN

Believe it or not, there is more to Old Town than the Royal Mile.

GREYFRIARS TOLBOOTH AND HIGHLAND KIRK. Off George IV Bridge, the 17th-century *kirk* rests in a churchyard that, while lovely, is estimated to contain 250,000 bodies and has long been considered haunted. A few centuries ago, the infamous body snatchers Burke and Hare dug up corpses here before resorting to murder in order to keep the Edinburgh Medical School's anatomy laboratories well supplied. A more endearing claim to fame is the loyal pooch Greyfriars Bobby, whose much-photographed statue sits at the southwestern corner of George IV Bridge in front of the churchyard's gates. (Beyond the gates, atop Candlemakers Row. ☎0131 225 1900. Open for touring Apr.-Oct. M-F 10:30am-4:30pm, Sa 10:30am-2:30pm; Nov.-Mar. Th 1:30-3:30pm. Free.)*

NATIONAL LIBRARY OF SCOTLAND. The library rotates exhibitions from its archives, which include a Gutenberg Bible, the last letter of Mary, Queen of Scots, and the original copy of *The Wallace,* an epic poem. (George IV Bridge. ☎0131 226 4531. Open M-Tu and Th-F 9:30am-8:30pm, W 10am-8:30pm, Sa 9:30am-1pm. Free.)*

THE NEW TOWN

Don't be fooled by the name—Edinburgh's New Town, a masterpiece of Georgian design, has very few buildings newer than 1900. James Craig, an unknown 23-year-old architect, won the city-planning contest in 1767. His rectangular grid of three parallel streets (**Queen, George,** and **Princes**) linking two large squares (**Charlotte** and **Saint Andrew**) reflects the Scottish Enlightenment belief in order. Queen and Princes St., the outer streets, were built up on only one side to allow views of the Firth of Forth and Old Town. Princes St., Edinburgh's main shopping drag, is also home to the venerable **Jenners,** the Harrods of Scotland. (☎0131 225 2442. Open M-Sa 9am-6pm, Su 11am-5pm. AmEx/MC/V.)

⧉**WALTER SCOTT MONUMENT.** Statues of Sir Walter and his dog preside inside the spire of this Gothic "steeple without a church." Climb 287 narrow, winding steps past carved figures of Scott's most famous characters to reach the top. An eagle's-eye view of Princes St., the castle, and the surrounding city awaits. The journey to the top is not recommended for those who suffer from claustrophobia or vertigo. *(Princes St. between The Mound and Waverley Bridge. ☎ 0131 529 4098. Open Apr.-Sept. M-Sa 9am-6pm, Su 10am-6pm; Oct.-Mar. M-Sa 9am-3pm, Su 10am-3pm. £3.)*

CALTON HILL. This hill at the eastern end of New Town commands views of the city and the Firth of Forth. Climb 143 steps inside the **Nelson Monument,** built in 1807 in memory of the admiral and the Battle of Trafalgar. *(☎ 0131 556 2716. Open Apr.-Mar. M 1-6pm, Tu-Sa 10am-6pm; Oct.-Mar. M-Sa 10am-3pm. £3.)* The hilltop is also home to two 19th-century landmarks: the old **City Observatory** and the **National Monument,** affectionately known as "Edinburgh's Disgrace." The structure, a poor man's Parthenon designed to commemorate those killed in the Napoleonic Wars, was scrapped when civic coffers ran dry after a mere 12 columns were built. For all its faults, the monument does offer beautiful views of the sunrise between its columns from Waverley Bridge.

BEYOND THE CITY CENTER

LEITH. Two miles northeast of the city center, the neighborhood of **Leith** has undergone a dramatic revival. Its abandoned warehouses have been replaced (or at least supplemented) by upscale flats, restaurants, and bars. The ⬛**Royal Yacht Britannia,** used by the royal family from 1953 to 1997 (when the government decided it was too expensive and decommissioned it), sailed around the world on state visits and royal holidays. Visitors can listen to a free audio tour of the entire flagship, which remains exactly as it was when decommissioned, and visit the royal apartments. Even the queen's bedroom, off-limits at every other royal residence, is open to visitors. Other highlights include the officers' mess and the engine room. *(Entrance on the Ocean Terminal's 3rd fl. Take bus #22 from Princes St. or #35 from the Royal Mile to Ocean Terminal. £1.10. ☎ 0131 555 5566; www.royalyachtbritannia.co.uk. Open daily Apr.-Oct. 9:30am-4:30pm; Nov.-Mar. 10am-3:30pm. £9.75.)*

CRAIGMILLAR CASTLE. This 15th-century castle stands 3½ mi. southeast of central Edinburgh. Mary, Queen of Scots, fled here after the murder of her secretary at Holyroodhouse. While she was here, plans emerged for the murder of her second husband, Lord Darnley. *(Take bus #2, 14, or 32 from Princes St. to the corner of Old Dalkeith Rd. and Craigmillar Castle Rd., then walk 10min. up the castle road. ☎ 0131 661 4445. Open daily Apr.-Sept. 9:30am-5:30pm; Oct.-Mar. 9:30am-4:30pm. £4.20.)*

EDINBURGH ZOO. At long last, your search for the world's largest penguin pool has come to an end. You'll find it 2 mi. west of the city center along with exhibits featuring some 1000 other animals. *(Take bus #12, 26, or 31 westbound from Princes St. ☎ 0131 334 9171. Open daily Apr.-Sept. 9am-6pm; Oct. and Mar. 9am-5pm; Nov.-Feb. 9am-4:30pm. £10.35, concessions £9, children £7.20; various family packages available.)*

ROYAL BOTANIC GARDENS. Edinburgh's herbaceous oasis has plants from around the world. Guided tours wander across lush grounds and greenhouses crammed with orchids, tree ferns, and towering palms. *(Inverleith Row. Take bus #23 or 27 from Hanover St. ☎ 0131 552 7171. Open daily Apr.-Sept. 10am-7pm; Oct. and Mar. 10am-6pm; Nov.-Feb. 10am-4pm. Free. Greenhouses £4, concessions £3, children £1.)*

🏛 MUSEUMS

NATIONAL GALLERIES OF SCOTLAND

Edinburgh's four major galleries are an elite group, all connected by a free shuttle that runs every 45min. *(☎ 0131 624 6200; www.nationalgalleries.org. All open daily during the festivals 10am-6pm; otherwise 10am-5pm. All free.)*

NATIONAL GALLERY OF SCOTLAND. Housed in a grand 19th-century building designed by William Playfair, this gallery has a superb collection of works by Renaissance, Romantic, and Impressionist masters, including Raphael, Titian, El Greco, Turner, Gauguin, and Monet. Don't miss the octagonal room, which displays Poussin's entire *Seven Sacraments*. The basement houses a selection of Scottish art. *(On The Mound between the halves of the Princes St. Gardens.)* The next-door **Royal Academy** hosts exhibits from the National Gallery and runs a high-profile show each summer. *(At the corner of The Mound and Princes St. Special late night Th until 7pm. Exhibit prices vary; visit www.royalscottishacademy.org for information.)*

SCOTTISH NATIONAL PORTRAIT GALLERY. The gallery displays the stern faces of the famous men and women who have shaped Scotland's history. Military, political, and intellectual figures are all represented, including definitive portraits of renegade Bonnie Prince Charlie, royal troublemaker Mary, Queen of Scots, and wordsmith Robert Louis Stevenson. *(1 Queen St., north of St. Andrew Sq.)*

SCOTTISH NATIONAL GALLERY OF MODERN ART. In the west end of town, this permanent collection includes works by Braque, Matisse, and Picasso as well as a post-war collection with works by Andy Warhol and Damien Hirst. The landscaping in front of the museum, a bizarre spiral of grass set into a pond, represents the concept of chaos theory with dirt and greenery. *(75 Belford Rd. Take the free shuttle, ride bus #13 from George St., or walk along the Water of Leith Walkway.)*

DEAN GALLERY. The newest addition to the National Galleries is dedicated to Surrealist and Dada art. The gallery owes much of its fine collection to the sculptor Eduardo Paolozzi, whose towering three-story statue, *Vulcan*, stands at the main entrance. *(73 Belford Rd. Special exhibits £3.50.)*

OTHER MUSEUMS AND GALLERIES

MUSEUM OF SCOTLAND AND ROYAL MUSEUM. The superbly designed Museum of Scotland traces the whole of Scottish history through an impressive collection of treasured objects and decorative art. Highlights include the working Corliss Steam Engine and the Maiden, Edinburgh's guillotine, used on High St. around 1565. The rooftop terrace provides a 360° view. Gallery and audio tours in various languages are free. The Royal Museum has rotating exhibits on natural history, European art, and ancient Egypt, to name a few. The **Millennium Clock,** a towering, ghoulish display of figures representing human suffering in the 20th century, chimes three times per day. Free tours, from useful intros to 1hr. circuits of the highlights, leave from the Main Hall's totem pole in the Royal Museum and the Museum of Scotland's Hawthornden Court. *(Chambers St. ☎0131 247 4422; www.nms.ac.uk. Both open daily 10am-5pm. Free.)*

OUR DYNAMIC EARTH. This glitzy, high-tech lesson in geology is part amusement park, part science experiment, appealing mainly to children. Look for the white, tent-like structure next to Holyroodhouse. *(Holyrood Rd. ☎0131 550 7800; www.dynamicearth.co.uk. Open daily July-Aug. 10am-6pm; Sept.-June 10am-5pm. Last entry 70min. before close. £9.50, concessions £7.50, children £6.)*

OTHER MUSEUMS. The **Museum of Childhood** displays an array of antique and contemporary childhood toys, from 19th-century dollhouses to 1990s Teletubbies. *(42 High St. ☎0131 529 4142. Open M-Sa 10am-5pm, Su noon-5pm. Free.)* **Canongate Tolbooth** (c. 1591), with a beautiful clock face above the Royal Mile, once served as a prison and gallows for "elite" criminals. Now it houses the **People's Story Museum,** an eye-opening look at the life of Edinburgh's working classes. *(163 Canongate. ☎0131 529 4057. Open during the Festival daily 10am-5pm; otherwise M-Sa 10am-5pm. Free.)* The **Surgeon's Hall Museum,** in the majestic Royal College of

Surgeons, has displays on the history of surgery and dentistry. *(Nicholson St. ☎0131 527 1649; www.edinburgh.surgeonshall.museum. Open from mid-July to mid-Sept. daily 10am-4pm; from mid-Sept. to mid-July M-F noon-4pm. £5, concessions £3.)*

🎵 ENTERTAINMENT

For all the latest listings and local events in Edinburgh, check out *The List* (£2.25), available at newsstands or watch for ads in clubs and pubs.

COMEDY, FILM, AND THEATER

For mainstream cinema, try **Odeon,** 7 Clerk St. (☎0131 667 0971) or **UGC Fountainpark,** Dundee St., Fountainbridge (bus #1, 28, 34, or 35; ☎0870 902 0417).

- 🎭 **The Stand Comedy Club,** 5 York Pl. (☎0131 558 7272; www.thestand.co.uk). Hilariously unhinged acts every night. Free improv Su 1:30pm. Special program with 17 shows per day for the Fringe Festival. Call ahead. Tickets £1-10.

- **Festival Theatre,** 13-29 Nicholson St. (☎0131 529 6000; www.eft.co.uk). Stages predominantly ballet and opera, turning entirely to the Festival in August. Box office open M-Sa 10am-6pm and before performances. Tickets £5-55.

- **King's Theatre,** 2 Leven St. (☎0131 529 6000; www.eft.co.uk). Promotes musicals, opera, and the occasional pantomime. Box office open 1hr. before show and between matinee and evening performances. Tickets also available through the Festival Theatre.

- **Royal Lyceum Theatre,** 30 Grindlay St. (☎0131 248 4848; www.lyceum.org.uk). The finest in Scottish and English theater, with many international productions. Box office open M-Sa 10am-6pm, performance nights 10am-8pm. Tickets £8-20, students ½-price.

- **Traverse Theatre,** 10 Cambridge St. (☎0131 228 1404; www.traverse.co.uk). Presents almost exclusively new drama and experimental theater with lots of local Scottish work. Box office open daily 10am-6pm. Ticket prices vary, usually around £7-12.

- **Bedlam Theatre,** 11B Bristo Pl. (☎0131 225 9893). A university theater with student productions, ranging from comedy and drama to F night improv, all in a converted church. A Fringe Festival hot spot. Box office open M-Sa 10am-6pm. Tickets £4-5.

- **The Filmhouse,** 88 Lothian Rd. (☎0131 228 2688). European and arthouse films, though Hollywood fare appears as well. Tickets £3.50-5.50.

LIVE MUSIC

Thanks to an abundance of university students who never let books get in the way of a good night out, Edinburgh's live music scene is vibrant and diverse. Excellent impromptu and professional folk sessions take place at pubs (opposite page), and many university houses sponsor live shows—look for flyers near Bristol Sq. *The List* (£2.25) has comprehensive listings. **Ripping Records,** 91 South Bridge (☎0131 226 7010), sells tickets to rock and pop performances.

- 🎭 **Whistle Binkie's,** 4-6 South Bridge (☎0131 557 5114). A subterranean pub with 2 live shows every night, open to bands of any genre. Gets busy late. Open daily until 3am.

- **Henry's Cellar,** 8A Morrison St. (☎0131 467 5200), downstairs off Lothian Rd. Hosts both local and international jazz and alternative musicians in a laid-back atmosphere. Cover varies, usually around £5. Open daily 8pm-3am.

- **The Royal Oak,** 1 Infirmary St. (☎0131 557 2976). Classic pub setting with live traditional and folk music every night. Live music from 9:30pm. Tickets £1-3. Open M-F 10am-2am, Sa 11am-2am, Su 12:30pm-2am.

NIGHTLIFE

PUBS

Pubs on the **Royal Mile** tend to attract a mixed crowd of old and young, tourists and locals. Students and backpackers gather in force each night in the Old Town. Casual pub-goers groove to live music on **Grassmarket, Candlemaker Row,** and **Victoria Street.** The New Town also has its share of worthy watering holes, some historical and most strung along **Rose Street,** parallel to Princes St. Wherever you are, you'll usually hear last call sometime between 11pm and 1am, or 3am during the Festival.

The **Broughton Street** area of the New Town (better known as the Broughton Triangle) is also the center of Edinburgh's gay community. Lesbian club nights, such as the long-running Velvet and the younger Fur Burger, are held monthly—check *The List* (£2.25) for venues and times.

> **TIP**
>
> **TOURIST TO PURIST.** Don't order your Scotch on the rocks if you want to avoid looking like a tourist. Scotch whisky should be drunk neat, with no ice. Locals may mix with a splash of water—real pros ask for mineral water from the region in which the whisky was distilled.

The Tron, 9 Hunter Sq. (☎0131 226 0931), behind Tron Kirk. Friendly student bar. Downstairs is a mix of alcoves and pool tables. Frequent live music. Burger and a pint £3.50 after 3pm, or get 2 meals for just £7. Open during the Festival daily 8:30am-3am; otherwise M-Sa noon-1am, Su 12:30pm-1am. Kitchen open until 9pm.

The Outhouse, 12A Broughton St. (☎0131 557 6668). Hidden up an alleyway off Broughton St. and well worth the hunt. More stylish than your average pub but just as cheap, with one of the best beer gardens in the city. Open daily 11am-1am.

Finnegan's Wake, 9B Victoria St. (☎0131 226 3816). Drink the Irish way at this traditional pub. Several stouts on tap, road signs from Cork, and live music nightly at 10pm. Gaelic football and hurling on a big screen during the summer. Open daily 1pm-1am.

The Three Sisters, 139 Cowgate (☎0131 622 6801). Loads of space for dancing, drinking, and lounging. Attracts a young crowd to its 3 bars (Irish, Gothic, and American). Beer garden sees close to 1000 people pass through on Sa nights. Open daily 9am-1am. Kitchen open M-F 9am-9pm, Sa-Su 9am-8pm.

Blue Moon Cafe, 36 Broughton St. (☎0131 557 0911), entrance around the corner on Barony St. A popular GLBT pub serving food to a mixed gay and straight crowd in a chic setting. Kitchen open M-F 11am-10pm, Sa-Su 10am-10pm. Bar open M-F 11am-11pm, Sa 10am-11pm, Su noon-11pm.

The Globe, 13 Niddry St. (☎0131 557 4670). This hole in the wall is recommended up and down the Royal Mile by sports fans and karaoke enthusiasts. DJs and quiz nights. Occasional live entertainment. Open during the Festival M-F 4pm-3am, Sa noon-3am, Su 12:30pm-3am; otherwise M-F 4pm-1am, Sa noon-1am, Su 12:30pm-1am.

Jolly Judge, 7 James Ct. (☎0131 225 2669). Hidden just off the Royal Mile, with a cozy atmosphere. 17th-century painted ceiling. Free Wi-Fi with any purchase. Quiz night M 9pm. Live music Th 9pm. Open M and Th-Sa noon-midnight, Tu-W noon-11pm, Su 12:30-11pm. Kitchen open noon-2pm.

CLUBS

Edinburgh may be best known for its pubs, but the club scene is none too shabby. It is, however, in constant flux, with club nights switching between venues and drawing a very different clientele from one night to the next. Consult *The List* (£2.25), a comprehensive guide to events, available from any local newsstand, for the night's hot spot. Clubs cluster around the city's historically disreputable **Cowgate**, just downhill from and parallel to the Royal Mile; most close at 3am (5am during the Festival). Smart street wear is a must.

Cabaret-Voltaire, 36-38 Blair St. (☎0131 220 6176, www.thecabaretvoltaire.com). Playing everything from jazz to breakbeat, this innovative club knows how to throw a party. Cavernous interior packs a loyal crowd. Cover up to £12. Open daily 7pm-3am.

Bongo Club, 37 Holyrood Rd. (☎0131 558 7604), off Canongate. Particularly noted for its hip hop and the immensely popular "Messenger" (reggae; 1 Sa per month) and "Headspin" (funk and dance; 1 Sa per month) nights. Cafe with free Internet access during the day. Cover up to £9. Open M-W and Su 10am-noon, Th-Sa 10am-3am.

CC Bloom's, 23-24 Greenside Pl. (☎0131 556 9331), on Leith St. No cover and a new up-and-coming DJ each night at this gay club. Su cabaret from 3pm, karaoke from 10pm. Open M-W and F-Su 3pm-3am, Th 8pm-3am.

Po Na Na, 43B Frederick St. (☎0131 226 2224), beneath Cafe Rouge. Go down the steps to a yellow cartoon image of a man in a fez. Moroccan-themed, with parachute ceilings, red velvet couches, and an eclectic blend of R&B, hip hop, disco, and funk. Cover £3-6.50. Open during the Festival, M, Th, Su 11pm-5am, F-Sa 10:30pm-5am; otherwise M, Th, Su 11pm-3am, F-Sa 10:30pm-3am.

Ego, 14 Picardy Pl. (☎0131 478 7434; www.clubego.co.uk). Not strictly a gay club, but hosts gay nights, including Vibe (Tu) and Blaze (4th Sa of the month). Cover £3-10. Open M-W and Su 10pm-1am, Th-Sa 11pm-3am.

FESTIVALS

Edinburgh has special events year-round, but the real show is in August. Prices rise, pubs and restaurants stay open later than late (some simply don't close), and street performers have the run of the place. What's commonly referred to as "the Festival" actually includes a number of independently organized events. For more information, check out www.edinburghfestivals.co.uk.

Edinburgh International Festival (☎0131 473 2000; www.eif.co.uk), Aug. 14-Sept. 6, 2009. Begun in 1947, the International Festival attracts the top performers from all over the globe, mainly in the realms of classical music, ballet, opera, and drama. The most popular single event is the festival's grand finale: a spectacular **Fireworks Concert** with pyrotechnics choreographed to orchestral music. Most tickets go on sale in early Apr., and a full program is published by then. Tickets to the biggest events sell out well in advance, but at least 50 tickets for major events are held and sold on the day of the performance at the venue. Throughout the festival, visitors can buy tickets at **The Hub** or at the door 1hr. prior to showtime. Selected shows are ½-price on the day of performance. Bookings can be made by post, phone, web, or in person at The Hub, Edinburgh's Festival Centre, Castlehill, Edinburgh EH1 2NE. Tickets £7-60, students and children ½-price. Open M-Sa from early Apr.; from late July daily.

Edinburgh Festival Fringe (☎0131 226 0000; www.edfringe.com), generally in Aug. Longer and more informal than the International Festival, the Fringe is the world's biggest arts festival, showcasing everything from Shakespeare to coconut-juggling dwarfs. It began in 1947, when 8 theater companies arrived to Edinburgh uninvited and had to book "fringe" venues to perform. Today, the Fringe draws more visitors to Edinburgh than any other event. Anyone who can afford the small registration fee can perform; this orgy of eccentricity attracts a multitude of good and not-so-good acts and guarantees a wild month. Head to the **Half Price Hut** bright and early to grab tickets for that day's shows at 50% off. *The Fringe* editorial, published in late spring, has a full listing of festivities (available free in just about every doorway of the city). Tickets available online, by phone, in person, or by post at The Fringe Office, 180 High St., Edinburgh EH1 1QS. Tickets up to £25. Open M-F 10am-5pm; during Festival daily 10am-9pm.

Hogmanay (☎0131 529 3914; www.edinburghshogmanay.org), New Year's Eve. The long, dark winter can't stop the party. Having long marked the turn of the calendar and the return of the sun, Hogmanay is Scotland's traditional New Year's Eve celebration, a nationwide party with pagan roots. Official events in Edinburgh include concerts, torchlight processions, and a street party that packs the Royal Mile and bursts into a rousing rendition of "Auld Lang Syne" at midnight. New Year's Day sees a number of options to shake that hangover, from a triathlon to a mid-winter dip in the Forth. Many events are free, though some require tickets to limit numbers. The Hub also provides ticket information. Tickets and program available from Oct.

Military Tattoo (☎08707 555 118; www.edintattoo.co.uk), Aug. 1-29, 2009. A magnificent spectacle of military bands, bagpipes, and drums performed at the gates of the castle. Buy tickets from the **Tattoo Ticket Sale Office,** 33-34 Market St.. Book well in advance—they sell out as early as Feb. Tickets £13-36.

Jazz and Blues Festival (☎0131 467 5200; www.edinburghjazzfestival.co.uk), from late July to early Aug. Britain's biggest jazz festival, drawing local and international talent. The highlight is the free **Jazz on a Summer's Day** in Ross Theatre. Program available in June. Bookings by phone or at The Hub. Tickets £5-25.50.

International Book Festival (☎0131 718 5666; www.edbookfest.co.uk), in Aug. at Charlotte Sq. Gardens. Europe's largest book celebration. Tickets £5-10.

International Film Festival (☎0131 228 4051; www.edfilmfest.org.uk), during the last 2 weeks of Aug. at The Filmhouse, 88 Lothian Rd. Box office sells tickets in late July.

THE GRAND FINALE FOR POCKET CHANGE. The closing fireworks ceremony of the Edinburgh International Festival (opposite page), accompanied by the Scottish Chamber Orchestra, is not to be missed. Tickets to watch the concert in Princes St. Gardens are notoriously hard to come by. While you can see the fireworks from pretty much anywhere in the city, the best spot is **Inverleith Park,** by the Botanic Gardens. In addition to its unobstructed views of the lit sky, a big-screen TV and giant speakers are set up to broadcast the concert live—and it's all free.

◪ DAYTRIPS FROM EDINBURGH

SOUTH QUEENSFERRY. Eight miles west of Edinburgh and easily accessible by the #43 bus, the town of South Queensferry lies at the narrowest part of the Firth of Forth, where two bridges—the **Forth Road Bridge** and the **Forth Rail Bridge**—cross the waterway. From Hawes Pier, under Forth Rail Bridge, the **Maid of the Forth** ferries visitors to Inchcolm Island. Float by colonies of seals to **Inchcolm Abbey,** the best-preserved 12th-century abbey in Scotland. *(Ferry ☎0131 331 5000; www.maidoftheforth.co.uk. Runs from mid-July to early Sept. daily; Oct. and Apr.-June Sa-Su. Round-trip ticket includes abbey admission. £14.70, concessions £12.70, children £6.)* Two miles west of South Queensferry stands the stately **Hopetoun House** and its 150 acres of sprawling land, including a wooded deer park. Begun around 1700 and designed by Sir William Bruce (who is also responsible for Holyroodhouse), it offers views of the Forth and is the setting for many British television shows. *(No public transportation runs to Hopetoun; take a taxi from South*

YOU'VE GOT GRAIL

The folks at Rosslyn Chapel may wish Dan Brown's novel *The Da Vinci Code* hadn't sold quite so many copies. Rosslyn was featured in the novel as a possible resting place for the Holy Grail, and its number of visitors has since increased from 40,000 per year to 175,000 in 2006.

This huge influx has created challenges for the small chapel. A new entrance has to be built. The parking lot and visitors center have to be expanded. Cameras, disguised as carvings of angels, were installed to protect against the greedy fingers of grail-hunters. Curators estimate that renovations will cost about £13 million.

The chapel itself seems to be taking on the hordes of visitors relatively well—for now. Rosslyn is made of soft sandstone, which will start to erode if the flow of visitors remains so high. "We might be the only attraction in existence that actually wants to get people to stop coming," joked Rosslyn Interpretation and Events Manager Simon Beattie.

Has the chapel seen any grail sleuthing? "We had one man try to steal the cross from the front of the chapel," Beattie says. "He didn't have a bag or anything, he just tried to walk out the front with it, but it's rather large. Needless to say, we caught him." Beware, souvenir hunters: the angels are watching you.

Queensferry. ☎0131 331 2451; www.hopetounhouse.com. Open from mid-Mar. to late Sept. daily 10:30am-5pm. Last entry 4pm. £8, concessions £7, children £4.25.)

ROSLIN. The Rosslyn Chapel, in the village of Roslin, 7 mi. south of Edinburgh, is one of the many British sites some suspect harbors the Holy Grail. The stone carvings filled with occult symbols raised eyebrows in 15th-century Scotland; check out the *danse macabre*, or "dance of death," an image in which skeletons meddle with people from all walks of life. The chapel found new popularity after its mention in Dan Brown's *The Da Vinci Code*. Thousands of recreational Grail hunters flock to its intricate walls. Outside the chapel, footpaths lead to the ruined Roslin Castle in Roslin Glen. *(From Edinburgh, take bus #15A from St. Andrew Sq. (40min.). ☎0131 440 2159; www.rosslynchapel.com. Open M-Sa 9:30am-6pm, Su noon-4:45pm. £7.50, concessions £6, children free. Renovations on the chapel began fall 2008; call for details before planning your visit.)*

THE BORDERS

From Roman occupation through Jacobean rebellion, for much of Britain's history the Borders were caught in a violent tug of war between Scotland and England. Present-day Borderers, however, suffer no crisis of identity—the blue-and-white cross of St. Andrew reigns over the Union Jack here. The Scottish land is dotted with fortified houses and ruined abbeys in Dryburgh, Jedburgh, Kelso, and Melrose. These grim reminders of warfare contrast with the gentle countryside, which inspired the poetry of Sir Walter Scott.

TRANSPORTATION

There are no trains in the Borders, but **buses** are frequent and inexpensive. **Galashiels,** or "Gala," has few visitor attractions of its own but is a travel hub for the surrounding towns. (Bus station open M-F 9am-5pm.) First (☎01896 752 237) runs most of the longer routes across the region, while Munro's (☎01835 862 253) operates many local services. TICs and Traveline (☎08706 082 608) have schedules. Bus #60 (M-F 10 per day, Sa-Su 8 per day) goes from Berwick to Galashiels (1¾hr.) via Melrose (1½hr.). Bus #62 goes from Melrose to Edinburgh via Galashiels and Peebles (2¼hr.; M-Sa 2 per hr., Su every hr.). To get to Edinburgh from Jedburgh, take bus #51/67 (2hr.; M-Sa every hr., Su 6 per day). Bus #52/68 runs to Edinburgh from Kelso (2hr.; M-Sa every hr., Su 6 per day). National

Express #383 (1 per day) heads from Edinburgh to Newcastle via Galashiels, Melrose, and Jedburgh. Bus #95/X95 (8 per day) travels the route from Carlisle to Edinburgh (3½hr.) via Galashiels (1¼hr.). Bus #68/71 goes to Jedburgh from Galashiels (1½hr.) via Melrose (15min.).

ACCOMMODATIONS

TICs can help you book a bed for £4 plus a 10% deposit. For advance bookings call Scottish Borders Customer Service Centre (☎08706 080 404). **SYHA** operates four hostels in the Borders area. All have a 10:30am-5pm lockout and are only open from April to September.

- 🏠 **Melrose** (☎01896 822 521), off High Rd., near the town center. From Market Pl., follow the footpath between Anderson fishmonger and the Ship Inn and bear right through the car park. Housed in a huge estate with views of the abbey, which is lit at night and makes a haunting spectacle as it looms behind the trees. A quiet atmosphere, popular with hikers and cyclists. Self-catering kitchen. Laundry £4. Internet £1 per 20min. Curfew 11:30pm. Dorms £13.25-14, under 18 £11. MC/V. ❶

- **Broadmeadows** (☎01750 763 72), 5 mi. west of Selkirk off the A708 and 1 mi. south of the Southern Upland Way. The first SYHA hostel (opened 1931), close to the Tweedsmuir Hills. 20 beds available. Dorms £13.50-14.50, under 18 £10.50-11. Cash only. ❶

- **Coldingham Sands** (☎08701 553 255), a 20min. walk from Coldingham at St. Abbs Head, 5min. from the ocean. 36 beds. Dorms £12.50-13, under 18 £9.25. MC/V. ❶

- **Kirk Yetholm** (☎08700 041 132), at the junction of the B6352 and B6401, near Kelso. 7 buses per day run from Kelso. Located at the end of the Pennine Way. Popular with hikers and cyclists. 22 beds. Dorms £14, under 16 £9.50. Cash only. ❶

THE GREAT OUTDOORS

Hikers of all levels enjoy the Borders for late afternoon strolls in the hills or more serious treks through the wilderness. The valley of the **River Tweed** offers many beautiful stretches for a day's hike. At the river's source in the west, the **Tweedsmuirs** make for difficult terrain. In the north, the **Moorfoots** and **Lammermuir Hills** are well suited to the country rambler. Two long-distance paths cross the Borders. Marked by a thistle in a hexagonal symbol, the challenging **Southern Upland Way** winds through the region for 82 mi., passing near Galashiels and Melrose on its route to the sea. **Saint Cuthbert's Way** runs 62 mi. from Melrose to Holy Island on the English coast and is marked by a white cross on a green sign. The Borders are covered extensively by Ordnance Survey Landranger (#72-75, 79, and 80; £6.50) and Explorer (#330, 331, 336-340, and 346; £7.50) maps. Upon arriving in the Borders, grab a free copy of the superb *Walking the Scottish Borders*, which details 30 day-long walks, at any TIC or look for *Short Walks on the Eastern Section of the Upland Way* (£2.50). The Borders also cater to on- and off-trail bikers. Excellent **mountain biking** can be found near Peebles on trails at Glentress and Innerleithen, part of the award-winning 7stanes project (www.7stanes.gov.uk). A number of well-marked trails traverse the region, including the **Tweed Cycleway,** a 90 mi. route that hugs the River Tweed from Biggar to Berwick, and the **Four Abbeys Cycle Route,** which connects the abbeys at Melrose, Dryburgh, Jedburgh, and Kelso. The 250 mi. **Borderloop** offers more strenuous trails. *Cycling in the Scottish Borders* (free at TICs) outlines these routes and 20 shorter trails, lists local cycle shops, and dispenses good advice. The *Scottish Borders* series also offers guides to golfing and fishing.

TOP TEN LIST

GRUESOME GLOSSARY

Border towns like Melrose and Peebles bore centuries of feuding between the English and Scottish. All that pillaging, burning, and killing left its mark on the region, especially its language. Here's a guide to help you learn Border Reiver lingo and to see how much of today's criminal jargon comes from this bad blood.

1. Reive: to forcibly steal.
2. Reiver: a raider, robber, or bandit. The bad guys.
3. Bereaved: to be reived of a loved one, either by death or by kidnap for ransom to the Reivers.
4. Blackmail: tribute paid by Border residents so that the reivers wouldn't raid their homes. Blackmail was usually paid in goods or labor, as opposed to "white mail," which was paid in silver.
5. Jeddart Justice: hang first, trial later. After Jedburgh (p. 569)
6. Trod: to follow someone.
7. Hot Trod: the lawful trailing of Reivers in response to a raid. A hot pursuit with flaming torches.
8. Pele Tower: a fortified stone house, like the ones found in every town in the Borders.
9. Fray: to frighten or alarm. Reivers would fray the wives of other Reivers when they knew the men were out at a pub.
10. Gear: goods stolen by Reivers during a Border raid.

MELROSE ☎(0)1896

Melrose is the prettiest of the region's towns, and most of its visitors come for its abbey. The town is within convenient reach of Dryburgh Abbey and Abbotsford, Sir Walter Scott's country home. A stop on the Four Abbeys Cycle Route, Melrose is also the start of St. Cuthbert's Way and lies near both the Southern Upland Way and Tweed Cycleway, making it the best base for outdoor activities in the Borders.

TRANSPORTATION AND PRACTICAL INFORMATION. Buses to Melrose stop in Market Sq.; another stop across the street from the abbey services Peebles. Active Sports, Annay Rd., beside the River Tweed, rents **bikes** and leads river trips. Take the road going out of town past the abbey and bear left at the fork, heading toward the footbridge over the river. (☎01896 822 452. Bikes £17 per day; 24hr. rental. Call ahead. Open daily 9:30am-9:30pm.) The **Tourist Information Centre** is across from the abbey on Abbey St. (☎08706 080 404. Open July-Aug. M-Sa 9:30am-5pm, Su 10am-4pm; Sept. and June M-Sa 9:30am-5pm, Su 10am-2pm; Oct. M-Sa 10am-4pm, Su 10am-2pm; Nov.-Mar. M-Sa 10am-2pm; Apr.-May M-Sa 10am-5pm, Su 10am-2pm.) Get free **Internet** access at the **Melrose Library,** Market Sq. (☎01896 823 052. Open M and W 10am-1pm and 2:30-5pm, F 2:30-5pm and 5:30-7pm.) The **post office** is on Buccleuch St. (☎01896 822 040. Open M-F 9am-1pm and 2-5:30pm, Sa 9am-noon.) **Postcode:** TD6 9LE.

ACCOMMODATIONS AND FOOD. Close to the town center, ⚑**SYHA Melrose ❶** (p. 565) is the best budget option in town. **Braidwood B&B ❸,** Buccleuch St., is comfortable and convenient, though on the pricey side. (☎01896 822 488; www.braidwoodmelrose.co.uk. No smoking. Singles £40; doubles and twins £55-60. Cash only.) **Gibson Park Caravan Club Site,** off High St., provides clean facilities within easy walking distance of the town center. (☎01896 822 969. £4.80-7.60 per person. MC/V.) The **Co-op** on Market Pl. sells basic groceries. (Open M-Sa 7am-10pm, Su 8am-10pm.)

SIGHTS. The fascinating ⚑**Melrose Abbey** dates to the 12th century, although it was later reconstructed in the Gothic and Romanesque styles after particularly harsh pillagings by the English. Search the grounds for the tombstone marking Robert the Bruce's embalmed heart. The abbey's famed gargoyles include a bagpipe-playing pig. The **Abbey Museum** displays objects unearthed from the abbey grounds and regional Roman forts. (☎01896 822 562. Open daily Apr.-Sept. 9:30am-5:30pm; Oct.-Mar. 9:30am-4:30pm. Last entry 30min. before close. £5.20, concessions £4.20.) A Roman fort once spanned the three volcanic summits of the **Eildon Hills,** which tower above Melrose. (Guided walks leave from the tiny Trimontium Museum on Market Sq. July-Aug. Tu and Th 1:30pm; Sept.-Oct. and Apr.-June Th 1:30pm. £3.) Legend has it that King Arthur and his knights lie asleep in a cavern beneath the hills—if they're not in Wales, Glastonbury, or anywhere else that makes similar claims. The bare peaks afford fabulous views of the town. The easy **Eildon Hills Walk** (4 mi.) leaves from the abbey and is marked on the town map available from the TIC.

▓ **DAYTRIP FROM MELROSE: ▓DRYBURGH ABBEY.** The peaceful grounds of Dryburgh Abbey host extensive ruins, views of the Tweed Valley, and the graves of Sir Walter Scott and Field Marshall Earl Haig, commander of the British Expeditionary Force in France during WWI. Built in 1150, the abbey was inhabited by Premonstratensian monks for nearly two centuries. When Edward II began removing his English troops from Scotland in 1322, the abbey's monks rang their bells in premature celebration. Angry soldiers retraced their steps and set the abbey on fire. *(From Melrose, take bus #67 or 68 (10min., frequent) to St. Boswell's, turn left from the bus station, cross the street, and follow the small green signs for St. Cuthbert's Way along the River Tweed, eventually crossing a metal footbridge and continuing up the hill to the right to reach the abbey (30min.). By car, take Scott's View, north of Dryburgh on the B635. The 4 Abbeys Cycle Route connects Melrose and Dryburgh. ☎01835 822 381. Open Apr.-Sept. daily 9:30am-5:30pm; Oct.-Mar. M-Sa 9:30am-4:30pm, Su 2-4:30pm. Last entry 30min. before close. £4.70, concessions £3.70, children £2.35.)*

▓ **DAYTRIP FROM MELROSE: ABBOTSFORD.** It's easy to picture Sir Walter Scott toiling away in the dark, romantic interior of this mock-Gothic estate 2 mi. west of Melrose. The libraries were the birthplace of most of Scott's *Waverley* novels, while the dining room was the place of his death in 1832. The house has 9000 rare books, a collection of weapons, Rob Roy's gun, a lock of Bonnie Prince Charlie's hair, and a piece of the gown worn by Mary, Queen of Scots, at her execution. The gardens extend toward the river. *(Frequent buses between Galashiels and Melrose stop nearby. Ask the driver to let you off at the 1st Tweedbank stop, walk back to the roundabout, and follow the sign to the house, which is ¼ mi. down the B6360. ☎01896 752 043; www.scottsabbotsford.co.uk. Open June-Sept. daily 9:30am-5pm; Oct. and Mar.-May M-Sa 9:30am-5pm, Su 2-5pm. £6.20, children £3.10.)*

▓ **DAYTRIP FROM MELROSE: THIRLESTANE CASTLE.** The ancient seat of the duke of Lauderdale, Thirlestane Castle stands 10 mi. north of Melrose on the A68, near Lauder. The defensive walls in the paneled room and library are 13 ft. thick. The beautiful restoration belies the castle's bloody history—jealous nobles hanged a host of King James III's supporters here in 1482. *(From Melrose or Galashiels, take bus #61 toward Lauder and ask to be let off at the castle. ☎01578 722 430; www.thirlestanecastle.co.uk. Open July-Aug. M-Th and Su 10am-3pm; Sept. and May-June W-Th and Su. Grounds close at 5pm. £7.50, concessions £6.50. Grounds without castle £3/3.)*

PEEBLES ☎(0)1721

The sleepy town of Peebles lies along the River Tweed 18 mi. west of Galashiels. There isn't much in the way of sights or attractions, but the town's cobblestone streets, pleasant shops, and excellent walks make it worth a visit.

⬛🌠 ORIENTATION AND PRACTICAL INFORMATION. Cobblestone High St., leading up to a small church at the end, is lined with small shops, fish-and-chips stands, and Indian restaurants, while several B&Bs and more upscale restaurants can be found on the adjacent streets. The helpful **Tourist Information Centre,** 23 High St., books rooms in town for $4 plus a 10% deposit. (☎08706 080 404. Open June M-Sa 9am-5:30pm, Su 11am-4pm; July-Aug. M-Sa 9am-6pm, Su 10am-4pm; Sept. M-Sa 9am-5pm, Su 11am-3pm; Oct. M-Sa 9:30am-5pm, Su 11am-3pm; Nov.-Dec. M-Sa 9:30am-4pm, Su 11am-3pm; Jan.-Mar. M-Sa 9:30am-4pm; Apr.-May M-Sa 9am-5pm, Su 11am-4pm.) Other services include free **Internet** at the **library,** High St. (open M, W, F 9:30am-5pm, Tu and Th 9:30am-7pm, Sa 9am-12:30pm) and the **post office,** 14 Eastgate (☎01721 720 119; open M-F 9am-5:30pm, Sa 9am-12:30pm). **Postcode:** EH45 8AA.

🌠🏠 ACCOMMODATIONS AND FOOD. Get a great night's rest in the spacious rooms of the inviting **Rowanbrae ❸,** 103 Northgate. (☎01721 721 630. No smoking. Rooms $25-$30 per person. Cash only.) At the **Victorian Viewfield ❷,** 1 Rosetta Rd., you can spend the evening relaxing in the garden. (☎08445 432 994. No smoking. Singles from $22; doubles from $38. Cash only.) Campers will feel at home at the **Rosetta Caravan Park ❶,** Rosetta Rd., 10min. from town. (☎01721 720 770; www.rosettacaravanpark.com. Open from mid-Mar. to Oct. $7.50 per person, children 50p. Cash only.) Grab your groceries at **Somerfield,** Northgate. (☎01721 724 518. Open M-Sa 8:30am-8pm, Su 9am-6pm.) The **Sunflower Restaurant ❸,** 4 Bridgegate, prepares modern Mediterranean cuisine (entrees $12-14) with a twist, such as duck with ginger and blackcurrants. Excellent vegetarian options available. (☎01721 722 420; www.thesunflower.net. Open M-W and Su 10-11:30am and noon-3pm, Th-Sa 10-11:30am, noon-3pm, 6-9pm. MC/V.)

🌠🏔 SIGHTS AND OUTDOOR ACTIVITIES. The **Tweed Cycleway** and many other bike trails pass through town and connect to the other Border towns. One excellent short walk departs from the Kingsmeadow car park and follows a 5 mi. circular route down and back along the River Tweed. **Neidpath Castle** is about 20min. into the walk on the town center side of the river. The 11 ft. thick walls have been breached only once in their long history. Today, visitors can explore its many preserved levels and admire the view from the top. Inside, batiks, artwork created by dripping wax on cloth, depict the life of Mary, Queen of Scots. (☎01721 720 333. Open May-Sept. W-Sa 10:30am-5pm, Su 12:30-5pm. $3, concessions $2.50, children $1.) Learn about the region's history in the free **Tweeddale Museum and Gallery,** in the Chambers Institute on High St. (☎01721 724 820. Open Apr.-Oct. M-F 10:30am-12:30pm and 1-4pm, Sa 10am-1pm and 2-4pm; Nov.-Mar. M-F 10:30am-12:30pm and 1-4pm.)

🌠 DAYTRIP FROM PEEBLES: 🏠TRAQUAIR HOUSE. Twelfth-century Traquair House (trar-KWEER), the oldest inhabited house in Scotland, stands 6 mi. east of Peebles and about 1 mi. south of the A72. The interior is a maze of low-ceilinged rooms and spiral staircases, but it's no challenge compared to the famed **hedge labyrinth** outside. Celebrate finding your way out of either maze with a free sample of Traquair Ale, from the house's own 300-year-old **brewery,** and try dinner at the 1745 **Cottage Restaurant** downstairs. *(From Peebles, take bus #62 toward Galashiels to Innerleithen and walk 1 mi. There is also a scenic back road running 7 mi. from Peebles to the house; biking is a good option. For a taxi, call Alba Taxis at ☎01896 831 333 (approx. £9). Traquair House ☎01896 830 323; www.traquair.co.uk. Open June-Aug. daily*

10:30am-5pm; Sept. and May daily noon-5pm; Oct. daily 11am-3pm; Nov. Sa-Su 11am-3pm; from mid-Mar. to Apr. Sa-Su noon-5pm. £6.50, children £3.50; grounds without house £3.50/2.50.

JEDBURGH   ☎(0)1835

Jedburgh (known to locals as "Jethart"), 13 mi. south of Melrose, takes its name from Jed Water, the small tributary river on whose banks it sits. In the 12th century, King David I of Scotland founded Jedburgh Abbey, the ruins of which still tower over the small town.

🖪🖪 **TRANSPORTATION AND PRACTICAL INFORMATION. Buses** stop on Canongate, near the abbey and next to the **TIC.** The TIC sells National Express tickets, books rooms for £4 plus a 10% deposit, and has a commission-free **bureau de change.** (☎08706 080 404. Open July-Aug. M-Sa 9am-6:30pm, Su 10am-5pm; Sept. and June M-Sa 9am-5pm, Su 10am-4pm; Oct. M-Sa 9:15am-4:30pm, Su 11am-4pm; Nov.-Mar. M-Sa 9:15am-4:30pm.) Free **Internet** access is available at the **library,** Castlegate. (Open M and F 10am-7pm, Tu-Th 10am-5pm.) The **police station** is at 14 Castlegate Rd. The **post office** is at 37 High St. (☎01835 862 268. Open M-F 9am-5:30pm, Sa 9am-12:30pm.) **Postcode:** TD8 6DG.

🖪🖪 **ACCOMMODATIONS AND FOOD.** B&Bs are scattered throughout town. Family-friendly **Meadhon House ❸,** 48 Castlegate, has a secluded garden and a room with a view of the abbey. (☎01835 862 504; www.meadhon.com. All rooms ensuite. Singles £36; doubles £56; triple £84. Cash only.) Fun-loving campers can head to **Jedwater Caravan Park ❶,** 4 mi. south of the town center off the A68, for clean facilities and a recreational atmosphere, complete with a game room and trampoline. The site also offers access to fishing, hiking, and other outdoor pursuits. (☎01835 840 219; www.jedwater.co.uk. Hair dryers, showers, and laundry. Open Mar.-Oct. 2-person site with car £12. Cash only.) For groceries, try **Co-op Superstore,** at the corner of Jewellers Wynd and High St. (☎01835 862 944. Open M-Sa 8am-10pm, Su 9am-6pm. MC/V.) At **Simply Scottish ❷,** 6-8 High St., enjoy traditional Scottish fare and meaty dishes like venison for reasonable prices. (☎01835 864 696. Entrees £7.50-10.45. Open M-Th 10am-8:30pm, F-Sa 10am-9pm, Su 11am-9pm.)

🖪 **SIGHTS.** Although pillaging Englishmen were successful in sacking **Jedburgh Abbey** on numerous occasions, much of the magnificent 12th-century structure still stands. A very narrow spiral staircase at the end of the nave leads to great views of the site; the modern exhibition room at the entrance to the abbey gives interesting background and displays several impressive artifacts. (☎01835 863 925. Open daily Apr.-Sept. 9:30am-5:30pm; Oct.-Mar. 9:30am-4:30pm. Last entry 30min. before close. £5.20, concessions £4.20, children £2.60. Free audio tour.) For the best free view of the abbey, walk along Abbey Close, off Castlegate. The **Mary, Queen of Scots, House,** down Smith's Wynd on Queen St., tells the story of the queen's life through paintings, tapestries, and artifacts (including a lock of Mary's hair); the audio tour helps bring the queen's tale to life. The house itself is a rare example of a 16th-century structure fortified against border conflict. (☎01835 863 331. Open Mar.-Nov. M-Sa 10am-5pm, Su 11am-4:30pm. Free.) The 19th-century **Jedburgh Castle Jail and Museum** looms atop a hill on Castlegate. The jail was built on the site of the original Jethart Castle, which was destroyed in 1409. (☎01835 864 750. Open Mar.-Oct. M-Sa 10am-4:30pm, Su 1-4pm. Last entry 30min. before close. Free admission; audio tour extra.) Walkers may enjoy the circular route leaving from the TIC, which temporarily follows **Dere Street,** an old Roman road, before tracing Jed Water back to town (roughly 5 mi.). Cyclists can join the **Four Abbeys Cycle Route** in town or pedal out to the **Borderloop.** Both routes offer views of all the historic sights you could ever wish to see from behind bars—handlebars, that is.

KELSO

☎(0)1573

Described by Sir Walter Scott as "the most beautiful, if not the most romantic, town in Scotland," Kelso (pop. 6000) sits at the meeting of the Rivers Tweed and Teviot, near the English border.

▆▌ TRANSPORTATION AND PRACTICAL INFORMATION. Buses stop on Woodmarket. The **Tourist Information Centre,** Market Sq., books rooms for £4 plus a 10% deposit. (☎08706 080 404. Open July-Aug. M-Sa 10am-5pm, Su 10am-2pm; Sept.-Oct. and Apr.-June M-Sa 10am-5pm, Su 10am-2pm; Nov.-Mar. M-Sa 10am-4pm.) Get free **Internet** access at the **library,** Bowmont St. (Open M and F 10am-1pm and 2-5pm, Tu and Th 10am-1pm, 2-5pm, 5:30-7pm, W 10am-1pm, Sa 9:30am-12:30pm.) The **police** are located on Coalmarket (☎01573 223 434). The **post office** is at 13 Woodmarket. (☎01573 224 795. Open M-F 9am-5:30pm, Sa 9am-12:30pm.) **Postcode:** TD5 7AT.

▐▣ ACCOMMODATIONS AND FOOD. The **SYHA Kirk Yetholm ❶** (p. 565) is 6 mi. southeast of Kelso. Near town, the spacious **Bellevue Guest House ❸,** Bowmont St., makes a great base for touring the city. (☎01573 224 588. Singles £35; doubles £58. MC/V.) Restock at **Somerfield** grocery, Roxburgh St. (☎01573 225 641. Open M-Sa 7am-9pm, Su 9am-9pm.) If you're hungry for a good steak, **Oscar's ❷,** 35-37 Horsemarket, can satisfy your craving. Lively music and an early-bird menu (entrees £10 until 7pm) are the best deal in town. (☎01573 224 008. Open M-Sa noon-2:30pm and 5-10pm, Su 5-10pm.) Cheerful **Coffee Nouvelle ❶,** 61 Housemarket St., serves up everything from panini and jacket potatoes to eggs and scones (£1.35-6.50) and even has used books for sale. (☎01573 225 423. Paperbacks £1.50, hardcovers £2. Open daily 8am-9pm. MC/V.)

◨ SIGHTS. One mile from the town center along the Tweed, the duke and duchess of Roxburgh reside in the palatial **◪Floors Castle.** The largest inhabited castle in Scotland, Floors has vast grounds, stately rooms, and a window for each day of the year—really. James II of Scotland met his end while inspecting a cannon in the yard, and Queen Victoria once took her afternoon tea in the gardens. (☎01573 223 333. Open Easter-Oct. daily 11am-5pm. Last entry 4:30pm. £7, concessions £6, children £3.50, families £17.) The oncegrand **Kelso Abbey,** another victim of English invasion, is now a shadow of its former self, but the remaining stone ruins of beautiful arches and moss-covered columns merit a visit. (Open Apr.-Sept. daily 9:30am-6:30pm; Oct.-Mar. M-W and Sa-Su 9:30am-4:30pm. Free.) A farther option available to those with their own transportation is **Mellerstain House,** one of Scotland's finest Georgian homes, 6 mi. northwest of Kelso on the A6089. Begun in 1725 by William Adam and completed by his son Robert, the house is noted for its art collection, which includes paintings by Gainsborough and Van Dyke, among others. (☎01573 410 225; www.mellerstain.com. Open July-Aug. M, W-Th, Su 12:30-5pm; Sept. and May-June W and Su 12:30-5pm; Oct. Su 12:30-5pm. Last entry 4:15pm. Grounds open 11:30am-5:30pm.) Serious walkers can try the 13 mi. section of the **Borders Abbeys Way,** which runs alongside the River Teviot and links Kelso to Jedburgh. Cyclists can pedal onto the **Four Abbeys Cycle Route** and the **Borderloop** from Kelso (p. 569).

DUMFRIES AND GALLOWAY

Although Dumfries and Galloway see less tourism than other parts of the country do, this corner of Scotland has historic attractions and beautiful landscapes. JM Barrie created *Peter Pan*'s Neverland while watching schoolboys play in the region's famous gardens, and most sights are devoted to local heroes like Robert the Bruce and Robert Burns. Wise visitors head for the country, where mountains, forest, and 200 mi. of coastline supply rewarding scenery.

ACCOMMODATIONS

B&Bs and hotels are listed in individual towns. Of the region's two SYHA hostels, only Minnigaff is easily reached by public transport.

Kendoon (☎01644 460 268). Bus #520 can stop on the A713 opposite the hostel. Ask the driver to let you off at Kendoon. Rustic hostel near Loch Doon and the Southern Upland Way. Open Apr.-Sept. Dorms £12.50-14, under 18 £9.50-10. Cash only. ●

Minnigaff, Minnigaff village (☎01671 402 211), across the bridge, ½ mi. from Newton Stewart. Accessible by bus from Dumfries, Stranraer, and Kirkcudbright. Basic dorms and a comfortable common room. Popular with hikers and anglers, with an ideal location and knowledgeable staff. 36 beds. Open Apr.-Sept. Dorms £14. MC/V. ●

THE GREAT OUTDOORS

The best of Dumfries and Galloway lies outdoors, and, with some 1300 mi. of marked trails, there is something for everyone. **Merrick** (2765 ft.) in the **Galloway Hills** and **White Coomb** (2696 ft.) in the **Moffat Hills** provide a challenge for seasoned hikers, along with the region's main draw—the **Southern Upland Way.** Beginning in Portpatrick on the coast of the Irish Sea and snaking 212 mi. across Scotland, this tough long-distance route cuts through Dumfries and Galloway, passing near the region's two SYHA hostels. The official *Southern Upland Way* guide (£18) breaks the route into 15 sections and includes a complete Ordnance Survey map of its course. In the west, the **Galloway Forest Park** is Britain's largest at over 300 sq. mi., although its excellent walking, cycling, and horseback-riding trails can be difficult to reach without a car. The park has three visitors centers: **Clatteringshaws** (☎01644 420 285), 6 mi. west of New Galloway; **Glen Trool** (☎01671 402 420), 12 mi. north of Newton Stewart; and **Kirroughtree** (☎01671 402 165), 3 mi. east of Newton Stewart. (All open daily July-Aug. 10am-5:30pm; Apr.-June 10:30am-5pm; Oct. 10:30am-4:30pm.) Guides from the *Walks In and Around* series sell for £1 and detail day outings and afternoon walks. Alternatively, pick up the free *Twelve Walks in Dumfries and Galloway* from area TICs. Along the coasts and inland, the region is popular with serious birdwatchers, particularly around the **Mull of Galloway,** Scotland's southernmost coast—its sea cliffs are home to thousands of marine birds. **Mountain bikers** will be in heaven in six award-winning trail parks, part of the 7stanes project. See www.7stanes.gov.uk for further details, including bike rental near the trails. Touring cyclists will find *Cycling in Dumfries and Galloway* (free at TICs) useful. The #7 and 74 **National Cycle Routes** cross Dumfries and Galloway, and the **KM Cycle Trail** runs from Drumlanrig down to Dumfries.

DUMFRIES   ☎(0)1387

Dumfries (DUM-freez; pop. 37,000) boasts little but the tales of two Roberts. Robert the Bruce proclaimed himself king of Scotland after stabbing Red Comyn at Greyfriars in 1306. A few centuries later, Robert Burns immortalized the town's local women in verse—hopefully he included the mothers of his 13 mostly illegitimate children. The beloved writer made Dumfries his home from 1791 until his death in 1796, and the town devotes many (many) a site to him.

TRANSPORTATION AND PRACTICAL INFORMATION. The **train station** is on Station Rd. (☎01387 255 115. Open M-Sa 6:35am-7:30pm, Su 10:30am-7:55pm.) **Trains** (☎08457 484 950) depart to Carlisle (40min., every hr., £4.70), Glasgow (2hr.; M-Sa 8 per day, Su 2 per day; £12.20), and Stranraer via Ayr (3hr., 4 per day, £25.20). **Buses** arrive and depart along Whitesands, and #974 runs to Glasgow (2hr.; M-Sa 4 per day, Su 2 per day). Bus #100 travels to Edinburgh (2hr.; M-Sa 3 per day, Su 2 per day; £6.50) via Penicuik (2hr.), while #500/X75 connects Dumfries to Carlisle (1hr., 2 per day, £2.40) and Stranraer (2hr., 8 per day, £5). A **Day Discoverer Ticket,** available on buses, allows unlimited travel in Dumfries and Galloway (£6, children £3, families £12).

The **Tourist Information Centre,** 64 Whitesands Rd., books beds for £4 plus a 10% deposit and sells bus tickets. (☎01387 253 862. Open July-Aug. M-Sa 9am-6pm, Su 11am-4:30pm; Sept.-Oct. M-Sa 9:30am-5pm, Su 10:30am-3pm; Nov.-Easter M-F 9:30am-5pm, Sa 9:30am-4pm. Other services include: **banks** along High St.; free **Internet** access at **Ewart Library,** Catherine St. (☎01387 253 820; open M-W and F 9:15am-7:30pm, Th and Sa 9:15am-5pm); **police** on Loreburn St. (☎01387 250 484); and the **post office,** 73 Whitesands (☎01387 269 058; open M 8am-5:30pm, Tu 9:30am-5.30pm, W-Sa 9am-5:30pm). **Postcode:** DG1 1AA.

ACCOMMODATIONS AND FOOD. A number of B&Bs line Lover's Walk, steps from the train station, including welcoming **Torbay Lodge ❸,** 31 Lover's Walk. (☎01387 253 922; www.torbaylodge.co.uk. From £25 per person. AmEx/ MC/V.) Find groceries at **Morrisons** on Brooms Rd. (☎01387 266 952. Open M-W 8:30am-8pm, Th-F 8:30am-10pm, Sa 8am-8pm, Su 9am-8pm.) Top off a Burns-filled day with a pint at **The Globe Inn,** 56 High St., one of the poet's favorite haunts. (☎01387 252 335; www.globeinndumfries.co.uk. Open M-W 10am-11pm, Th 10am-midnight, F-Sa 10am-1am, Su 11:30am-midnight. Kitchen open M-Th and Su 10am-3pm, F-Sa 10am-3pm and 7-9pm.)

SIGHTS. Robert Burns fans, rejoice! Every sight in town pays homage to Dumfries's favorite son. Pick up a free copy of *Dumfries: A Burns Trail* at the TIC for an easy-to-follow Burns walking tour. Across the river, the **Robert Burns Centre,** Mill Rd., attempts to explain the phenomena that surround Scotland's national poet. Visit **Burns House,** Burns St., where Burns scratched his autograph into the upstairs study windows with his diamond ring. Memorabilia on display include a snuffbox made with wood from the bed where the poet died at the young age of 37. (☎01387 255 297. Open Apr.-Sept. M-Sa 10am-5pm, Su 2-5pm; Oct.-Mar. Tu-Sa 10am-1pm and 2-5pm. Free.) Complete your pilgrimage at the **Burns Mausoleum** in St. Michael's Kirkyard, where a marble Burns leans on a plow and gazes at the attractive muse hovering overhead. (Guided tours available through the Robert Burns House. Free.) On the top floor of the **Dumfries Museum,** Rotchell Rd., check out the town through the lens of Britain's oldest camera obscura. (☎01387 253 374; www.dumgal.gov.uk. Open Apr.-Sept. M-Sa 10am-5pm, Su 2-5pm; Oct.-Mar. Tu-Sa 10am-1pm and 2-5pm. Museum free. Camera obscura £2.10, concessions £1.05. The TIC has vouchers for 2-for-1 admission.) To escape the Burns-fest, try a relaxing walk through **The Crichton,** a parkland 1 mi. south of Dumfries town center, which has huge rock gardens and an arboretum. (Follow posted signs. Accessible 24hr. Free.)

▶ DAYTRIP FROM DUMFRIES: ▦CAERLAVEROCK CASTLE.

Eight miles southeast of Dumfries, on the B725 just beyond Glencaple, Caerlaverock Castle (car-LAV-rick) is one of Scotland's finest medieval ruins. Although no one is sure whether this strategic marvel was built for Scottish defense or English offense, it was seized by England's Edward I in 1300 and passed around like a hot kipper thereafter. A short video in the entrance building relives the details of the 1300 seige and explains some medieval weaponry. Beyond the castle is a path that runs down to the shore of the **Solway Firth** (10min.). The mountains of the Lake District rise up in the distance beyond the firth, which at low tide is nothing but sand for 20 mi. *(Stagecoach Western Bus #371 runs to the castle from the Loreburn Shopping Centre, off Irish St. in Dumfries (20min.; M-Sa 12 per day, Su 2 per day; roundtrip £3).* ☎01387 770 244. *Open daily Apr.-Sept. 9:30am-6:30pm; Oct.-Mar. 9:30am-4:30pm. Last entry 30min. before close. £5.20, concessions £4.20, children £2.60.)*

▶ DAYTRIP FROM DUMFRIES: ▦DRUMLANRIG CASTLE.

Eighteen miles north of Dumfries off the A76, Drumlanrig Castle is the home of the duke of Buccleuch. Surrounded by formal gardens and a large country park, the castle's noted art collection includes works by Rembrandt and Leonardo da Vinci as well as a tapestry made by Mary, Queen of Scots, that shows her rival Queen Elizabeth with a beard. *(☎01848 331 555; www.buccleuch.com. Castle open by guided tour May-Aug. daily 11am-4pm. Grounds open Easter-Sept. daily 11am-5pm. £7, concessions £6, children £4. Grounds without castle £4/3.50/3.)*

▶ DAYTRIP FROM DUMFRIES: SWEETHEART ABBEY.

They say the way to a man's heart is through his stomach, but in the case of John Balliol you're better off trying his wife's casket. After her husband's death, Lady Devorguilla Balliol carried around his heart in an ivory and silver box and upon her death was buried with the embalmed organ in the abbey she founded in 1275. The line between romantic and creepy is very thin. Now a well-preserved ruin, the abbey still has high arches and a central spire that stand as a testament to their love. *(Take MacEwan's bus #372 to New Abbey from Dumfries. 20min.; M-Sa 1-2 every 2hr., Su 2 per day. ☎01387 850 397. Open Apr.-Sept. daily 9:30am-6:30pm; Oct.-Mar. M-W and Sa-Su 9:30am-4:30pm. £3, concessions £2.50.)*

CASTLE DOUGLAS   ☎(0)1556

Between Dumfries and Kirkcudbright, Castle Douglas resembles most other towns in Scotland's southwest, with its gray stone storefronts and windows lined with flower pots. One mile west, however, the 60-acre **Threave Garden** deserves a visit, with native and exotic blooms pruned by students of the nearby School of Gardening. Buses #501 and 502 (10min., every hr.) between Kirkcudbright and Castle Douglas pass the garden turnoff; ask the driver to stop, then walk 15min. (☎01556 502 575. Garden open daily 9:30am-sunset. Walled garden and greenhouses open daily 9:30am-5pm. £6, concessions £5.) The **Threave Estate Walk** (2-7 mi.) meanders through the countryside. Leaving from the garden car park, it leads hikers to good birdwatching spots as well as the scenic ruins of 14th-century **Threave Castle.** A stronghold of the earls of Douglas and built by Archibald the Grim, this massive tower-castle sits on an island in the River Dee. The Kirkcudbright bus can drop you off at the roundabout on the A75. From there, follow the signs for 1 mi. along a one-lane road and then a marked footpath. Once at the river, ring the ship's bell and a boatman will appear to ferry you across to the castle. (Open Apr.-Sept. daily 9:30am-6:30pm. Last boat 5:30pm. £4.20, concessions £3.20; includes return ferry.)

The best-priced accommodation in town is at **The Craig ❸**, 44 Abercromby Rd., with spacious rooms near the golf course. (☎01556 504 840. No smoking.

Singles £25-30; doubles and twins £46-54. Cash only.) Castle Douglas proclaims itself Galloway's "Food Town" thanks to the number of cafes and delis that line **King Street**. Beneath an art gallery, ▤**Designs** ❷ serves sandwiches on home-baked ciabatta and has great specials noon-3pm. (☎01556 504 552. Open 9:30am-5pm. MC/V.) For groceries, the **Co-op Superstore** is on Cotton St. (Open M-Sa 8am-10pm, Su 9am-6pm.)

Buses #501 and 502 stop in Castle Douglas along their route between Dumfries to Kirkcudbright (from Dumfries 40min., from Kirkcudbright 20min.; 2 per hr.; £3.70). For local lodgings, ask at the **Tourist Information Centre.** (☎01556 502 611. Open July-Aug. M-Sa 9:30am-6pm, Su 10am-4pm; Sept. M-Sa 10am-4pm, Su 11am-4pm; Oct. M-Sa 10am-4pm; Apr.-June M-Sa 10am-5pm, Su 11am-4pm.) **Banks** with **ATMs** can be found on King St. The **post office** is at 100 King St. (☎01556 502 577. Open M-F 9am-5:30pm, Sa 9am-4:30pm.) **Postcode:** DG7 1LU.

KIRKCUDBRIGHT ☎(0)1557

Established as a royal burgh in 1455, Kirkcudbright (ker-COO-bree) is a quiet fishing town situated at the mouth of the River Dee, with wide streets lined with pastel houses. In the 1880s, the town attracted a group of artists known as the Glasgow Boys, and Kirkcudbright still fancies itself an artists' colony.

▣▨ TRANSPORTATION AND PRACTICAL INFORMATION. Buses #501 and 502 travel to Dumfries (every hr., £3.70), and bus #431 travels to Gatehouse of Fleet (20min.; M-Sa 12 per day, Su 6 per day). The **TIC**, Harbour Sq., books rooms for £4. (☎01557 330 494. Open July-Aug. M-Sa 9:30am-6pm, Su 10am-5pm; Sept.-Nov. and Feb.-June M-Sa 10am-5pm, Su 11am-4pm.) Other services include: free **Internet** access at the **library,** High St. (☎01557 331 240; open M 2-7:30pm, Tu and F 10am-7:30pm, W noon-7:30pm, Th and Sa 10am-5pm); **Shirley's** launderette, 20 St. Cuthbert St. (☎01557 332 047; open M-F 9am-4pm, Sa 9am-1pm); and the **post office,** 5 St. Cuthbert's Pl. (☎01557 330 578; open M-F 9am-5:30pm, Sa 9am-12:30pm). **Postcode:** DG6 4DH.

▨▢ ACCOMMODATIONS AND FOOD. One Gordon Place ❸, High St., is a cozy and cheap option right in the middle of the "action" on historic High St. (☎01557 330 472. Singles from £25. Cash only.) Family-run **Castle Restaurant ❸,** 5 Castle St., has a variety of options including fish, vegetarian fare, and plates piled high with meat. (☎01557 330 569. Open daily 11:30am-2:30pm and 6:30-9pm. MC/V.) Get groceries at **Somerfield,** 52 St. Cuthbert St., at Millburn St. (☎01557 330 516. Open M-Sa 8:30am-6pm, Su 10am-5pm.)

▨ SIGHTS. The former home of the turn-of-the-century artist EA Hornel, **Broughton House and Garden,** 12 High St., contains a library filled with the painter's impressive personal collections and a beautiful garden influenced by his trips to Japan. (☎01557 330 437. House open July-Aug. daily noon-5pm; Sept.-Oct. and Apr.-June M and Th-Su noon-5pm. Garden open July-Aug. daily noon-5pm; Sept.-Oct. and Apr.-June M and Th-Su noon-5pm; Feb.-Mar. M-F 11am-4pm. £8, concessions £5, families £20.) The **Tollbooth Art Centre,** High St., explains the artist migration to Kircudbright in the 1880s and displays the work of local artists. (☎01557 331 556. Open June-Sept. M-Sa 11am-4pm, Su 2-5pm; Oct.-May M-Sa 11am-4pm. Free.) **MacLellan's Castle,** a 16th-century tower house, dominates the town on Castle St. Sneak into the "Laird's Lug," a secret chamber behind a fireplace from which the lord could eavesdrop on conversations in the Great Hall. (☎01557 331 856. Open Apr.-Sept. daily 9:30am-1pm and 2-6:30pm. £3.20, concessions £2.50, children £1.50.) One fine walk in the area departs from the

TIC and runs along the coastal headland to **Torrs Point** (8½ mi. round-trip). Pick up a guide (20p) from the TIC before you head out.

STRANRAER AND THE RHINS OF GALLOWAY   ☎(0)1776

Scottish Gaelic for "the fat nose," an Sron Reamhar, or Stranraer (stran-RAHR), and the hammerhead peninsula known as "the Rhins" hang off the southwestern tip of Scotland. It's a short ride over to Northern Ireland, so Stranraer plays host to many tourists taking daytrips to Belfast or staying the night before catching the morning ferry. Locals have a unique accent, and, as most early residents came from Ireland, they are often referred to as the Galloway Irish.

TRANSPORTATION AND PRACTICAL INFORMATION. The **train station,** by the ferry pier, is open daily 9:30am-3pm and 4-6:30pm. Trains (☎08457 484 950) depart to Ayr (1hr.; M-Sa 7 per day, Su 2 per day; £11.70) and Glasgow (2hr.; M-Sa 4-7 per day, Su 3 per day; £17). **Buses** leave from Port Rodie in Stranraer to Ayr (#358, 1hr., 2 per day, £5.10) and Dumfries (#500/X75; 2hr.; M-Sa 12 per day, Su 3 per day; £4.50). National Express (☎08705 808 080) runs to Carlisle (2hr., £17), London (10hr., 1 per day, £42), and Manchester (6hr., 2 per day, £32). Buses #358, 367, and 411 serve Portpatrick from Stranraer (25min.; M-Sa 16 per day, Su 3 per day; £3). **Ferries** travel from Northern Ireland across the North Channel. Stena Line (☎08705 707 070; www.stenaline.co.uk) sails between Belfast and Stranraer (1-3hr.; 5-7 per day; £15-25, concessions £11-20). Five miles up the coast at **Cairnyan,** P&O Ferries (☎08702 424 777; www.poirishsea.com) provides access to Larne (1-1½hr., 5-8 per day, £20-29). Discounts are available when booking sea passage with a connecting bus or train.

The **Tourist Information Centre,** 28 Harbour St., sells bus and ferry tickets and books rooms for £4 plus a 10% deposit. (☎01776 702 595. Open July-Aug. M-Sa 9:30am-5pm, Su 11am-3pm; Sept.-Mar. M-Sa 10am-4pm; Mar.-June daily 10am-4pm.) Other services in town include: free **Internet** access at the **Stranraer Library,** 2-10 N. Strand St. (☎01776 707 400; open M-F 9:15am-7:30pm, Sa 9:15am-1pm and 2-5pm); **Boots** pharmacy, across from the castle (☎01776 707 224; open M-Sa 9:30am-5pm); and the **post office,** in Tesco on Charlotte St. (☎01776 702 587; open M-F 7am-6pm, Sa 7am-5pm). **Postcode:** DG9 7EF.

ACCOMMODATIONS AND FOOD. There are a number of hotels and B&Bs in Stranraer and Portpatrick, with a scattering of other options across the Rhins. Feel like a part of the family at the **Balyett B&B ❸,** Cairnyarn Rd., possibly the most welcoming B&B in Scotland. The seaside farm has ensuite rooms and runs a small five-bed **hostel ❶** in a caravan. Call ahead, and the owner will pick you up from the ferry, bus, or train station. (☎01776 703 395. Breakfast included. Dorms £15; B&B singles £30-35; doubles and twins £50. MC/V.) **Lakeview Guest House ❸,** 19 Agnew Crescent, near the town center, has seafront accommodations run by a friendly young couple. (☎01776 703 472; www.lakeviewguesthouse.co.uk. £25 per person. MC/V.) Catch a plate of fresh fish at one of the waterfront **fish shops** on Charlotte St. or pick up groceries at **Tesco,** on Charlotte St. (Open M-Sa 7am-8pm, Su 10am-6pm.)

SIGHTS. The town of Stranraer itself provides ferry access to Northern Ireland—and that's about it. Four miles east on the A75, however, the **Castle Kennedy Gardens** include 75 acres of lovely landscaping between a pair of lochs and castles. From Stranraer, buses (#430, 416, and 500) pass the castles; ask the driver to let you off and walk 1 mi. from the main road. (☎01776 702 024. Open

Apr.-Sept. daily 10am-5pm. £4, concessions £3, children £1.) Back in town, the tiny **Castle of Saint John,** George St., is a 1510 edifice with fantastic views. Its rooftop was once the exercise yard of the town prison. (☎01776 705 088. Open from Easter to mid-Sept. M-Sa 10am-1pm and 2-5pm. Free.)

If you've come this far west, it's worth traveling to the small seaside town of **Portpatrick,** where pastel houses look across to Northern Ireland. Bus #367 (20min.; M-Sa 16-17 per day, Su 3 per day) will get you there. The coast-to-coast **Southern Upland Way** (p. 565) begins here, and there's also a coastal path leading back to Stranraer. Another path runs along the cliffs to the ruins of ▨**Dunskey Castle,** an empty shell sitting high above the pounding surf. At the **Mull of Galloway,** the southernmost point in Scotland, a lighthouse and thousands of sea birds teeter atop cliffs. On a clear day, you can see all the way to Northern Ireland and the Isle of Man.

AYRSHIRE

AYR   ☎(0)1292

The pleasant seaside town of Ayr (AIR) is little more than a base for exploring surrounding Ayrshire. Racing fans head to Scotland's top horse track, which hosts the **Scottish Grand National** in April and the **Ayr Gold Cup** in September. (☎01292 264 179. Tickets £10-25.) The world's only remaining ocean paddle steamer, the *Waverley*, departs from Ayr's harbor during July and August, touring many of the nearby islands, including the Isle of Arran. (☎0845 130 4647; www.waverleyexcursions.co.uk. Cruises July-Aug. M-W. £17-33.)

Craggallan Guest House ❹, 8 Queens Terr., has a pool table and access to the Ayrshire golf courses. (☎01292 264 998; www.craggallan.com. Singles from £28; doubles and twins from £56; triples £60-65. AmEx/MC/V.) Among the many B&Bs near the beach, **Eglinton Guest House ❸,** 23 Eglinton Terr., certainly isn't the flashiest, but it is the cheapest. (☎01292 264 623. £22 per person. Cash only.) Across from the train station on Castlehill Rd., **Morrisons** supermarket has everything you need. (☎01292 283 906. Open M-W 8:30am-8pm, Th-F 8:30am-9pm, Sa 8am-8pm, Su 9am-5pm.) **Kando ❷,** 9-13 S. Harbour St., serves up everything from fajitas to burgers and pasta right beside the harbor. (☎01292 291 200. Sandwiches and entrees £4.25-17. MC/V.)

Ayr's **train station** is a 10min. walk from the town center at the crossroads of Station Rd., Holmston Rd., and Castle Hill Rd. (Open M-Sa 5:30am-11:10pm, Su 8:30am-11:10pm.) Trains (☎08457 484 950) run to Glasgow (1hr., 2 per hr., £6.40) and Stranraer (1hr.; M-Sa 4 per day, Su 3 per day; £11.70). The **bus station** is on Fullerton St. off Sandgate. It sends Stagecoach Western (☎01292 613 500) buses to Glasgow (1hr.; M-Sa every 25min., Su every hr.; £3.15) and Stranraer (1hr.; M-Sa every 2hr., Su 4 per day; £6.20). The **Tourist Information Centre** is at 22 Sandgate. (☎0845 225 512. Open July-Aug. M-Sa 9am-6pm, Su 10am-5pm; Sept. M-Sa 9am-5pm, Su 11am-4pm; Oct.-June M-Sa 9am-5pm.) Other services include: **banks** on High St.; free **Internet** access at the **Carnegie Library,** 12 Main St. (☎01292 286 385; open M-F 10am-7:30pm, Sa 10am-5pm); and the **post office,** inside WHSmith on High St. **Postcode:** KA7 1AA.

▨CULZEAN CASTLE   ☎(0)1655

Twelve miles south of Ayr along the A719, romantic Culzean Castle (cul-LANE) commands panoramic views of the Ayrshire coast from its clifftop setting. According to legend, one of the cliff's caves holds the Phantom Piper, who plays to his lost flock when the moon is full; search for his lair yourself if you're willing to scramble along the rocky coastline. (☎08701 181 945; www.culzeancastle.net. Open Apr.-Oct. daily 10:30am-5pm. Last entry 4pm.) The people of Scotland gave the building's top floor to Dwight D. Eisenhower for use during his stays in the country—with a presidential budget you can rent his digs for the night. (£375; other castle accommodations from £225. MC/V.) Popular during the summer, the castle is surrounded by a 560-acre **country park** that includes one of the nation's finest walled gardens, a swan pond, and miles of wooded walkways. (Open 9:30am-sunset. £12, concessions £8, families £30. Park without castle £8/5/20.) At the entrance to the castle and country park, close to the **bus** stop, the **Glenside Culzean Caravan and Camping Park ❷** is a great place to pitch your tent, with fresh sea air and views of the Isle of Arran. (☎01655 760 627. Showers and laundry. Open from mid-Mar. to Oct. 2 nonmembers with car £15-20. MC/V.) The nearest bus stop is on the main road, about 1 mi. away from the castle. Bus #60 (30min., 2 per hr.) runs to Ayr.

ISLE OF ARRAN

The glorious Isle of Arran (AH-ren; pop. 4750) justifiably bills itself as "Scotland in miniature." Gentle lowland hills, majestic highland peaks, and dense forests crowd into an island fewer than 20 mi. long. The crags of Goatfell and the Caisteal range dominate the north. Near the western coast, prehistoric stone circles rise out of boggy grass. The eastern coastline winds south from Brodick Castle past Holy Island into meadows and white beaches.

◨ TRANSPORTATION

Transportation between the mainland and Arran is available from CalMac **ferries** (☎08705 650 000), which cross the Firth of Clyde between Brodick and Ardrossan (55min.; M-Sa 5-6 per day, Su 4 per day; £6.40, bikes £2). Reach Ardrossan by First ScotRail's **train** service from Glasgow (1hr., every hr., £5.65). There's also a summer ferry service between Lochranza and Claonaig on the Kintyre Peninsula (30min.; from mid-Apr. to mid-Oct. 8-9 per day; £5.20, bikes £1.60). Bus #448 takes travelers from Kennacraig to the Claonaig ferry landing (15min., M-Sa 3 per day). Arran has a very reliable local **bus** service operated by Stagecoach Western (☎01770 302 000; office at Brodick pier). A connection to and from every part of the island meets each Ardrossan-Brodick ferry, and frequent buses also meet the Lochranza ferry (fares up to £3). The

FROM THE ROAD

SHEEP CROSSING

On Scotland's famously tranquil southern isles, I didn't expect traffic jams to be a regular problem. So when my bus driver on the Isle of Arran explained that he was running 40min. late because of road congestion, I was surprised; I hadn't seen a single car pass during my wait at the bus stop.

Twenty minutes later, I was stuck in a traffic jam you will never find on a highway: the bus was inching slowly forward behind five sheep that were ambling down the street. The narrow one-lane roads made passing impossible, and so the bus deferred to the slow fluffy animals' right of way.

This experience repeated itself several times, the details varying only in the type of animal that happened to be hogging the road. Later on Arran, my bus had to reverse 15 ft. for a deer that was blithely strolling down the middle of the street. On Mull, a family of pheasants halted traffic while they preened in the dust.

Yes, these feathered and furred travelers slowed down the human transportation on the islands. At first I found the bus delays somewhat irritating, throwing off my carefully scheduled travel plans. But life on these islands moves at different pace from the mainland's, a pace dictated just as much by the natural as by the human inhabitants. At least in these traffic jams you don't have to worry about road rage.

—Leslie Lee

Arran Area Transport Guide, distributed free at the TIC and on the ferry, contains transportation information and all bus schedules for the island. Additional services are run by the Royal Mail **postbus** (☎01770 302 507). Available on board, the **Day Rover Ticket** grants a full day of travel on Stagecoach and postbus services (£4.40, children £2.20). From April to October, Stagecoach offers half- and full-day island tours departing from Brodick pier (½-day £5, full-day £8). **Car rental** is available at the Brodick pier. (☎01770 302 121. From £25.) To put foot to pedal, Arran Adventure rents **bikes.** (☎01770 302 244; www.arranadventure.com. Bikes £15 per day, £45 per week; includes safety equipment. Open Apr.-Sept. daily 9am-5:30pm.) For bike rental elsewhere on Arran, try Blackwaterfoot Garage, in Blackwaterfoot. (☎01770 860 277. £8 per day, £20 per week. Open M-F and Su 8:30am-5:30pm, Sa 9am-5pm.)

ORIENTATION AND PRACTICAL INFORMATION

The A841 completes a 56 mi. circuit around the Isle of Arran. Ferries from Ardrossan arrive at **Brodick,** on the eastern shore; those from Claonaig arrive at **Lochranza,** in the north. The villages of Lamlash and Whiting Bay line the picturesque southeastern coast. **Blackwaterfoot** is the largest town on the sparsely populated western shore. Home to green hills, deep valleys, and pine forests, the interior of the island is practically uninhabited. Brodick has the widest range of services, including Arran's only **TIC,** across from the ferry pier. It books B&Bs for £4 plus a 10% deposit. (☎01770 303 774. Open M-Th and Sa 9am-5pm, F 9am-7:30pm, Su 10am-5pm.) From May to September, a tourist information desk on the Ardrossan-Brodick ferry answers questions. The island's **police** station (☎01770 302 574) is located on Shore Rd. in Lamlash.

HIKING AND OUTDOORS

Although geographically close to Glasgow, the wilderness in the north and southwest of Arran feels far from the city bustle. Ordnance Survey Landranger #69 (£7) and Explorer #361 (£8) maps, available at the TIC in Brodick, cover the island in extraordinary detail. Among the available literature, the Forestry Commission produces the small, popular *A Guide to the Forest Walks of the Isle of Arran* (£1) and the more comprehensive *Walking on The Isle of Arran* (£11), available at bookstores. The TIC has free leaflets for all area walks. Highlights include the path up **⬛Goatfell,** Arran's highest peak (2866 ft.). Beginning on the road between Brodick and Brodick Castle, this hike passes forests, heather, and mountain streams before the final rocky ascent into the clouds (7 mi. round-trip). The route takes around 5hr. and only becomes challenging in the last 300 ft. The view from the cold, windy peak (on a clear day, all the way to Ireland) is worth the final scramble. **Glen Rosa** offers some great scenery without the mountain climb. The terrain remains mostly flat as the walk follows the glen into the heart of Arran's peaks. From Brodick, head about 1 mi. north, turn left onto "The String" road toward Blackwaterfoot, and take the first right. Another fine walk is the 8 mi. **Cock of Arran** route, which departs from the ruins of **Lochranza Castle,** following the coastline along rocky stretches of beach and intriguing cliffside caves. Well-marked shorter walks depart from Whiting Bay and north of Blackwaterfoot.

Biking on the hilly island is a rewarding challenge. Pedaling all or part of the 56 mi. circuit ringing the island affords splendid views, and traffic is light in most stretches, except at the height of summer. Adrenaline junkies will want to try one of the off-road routes that leave from Brodick and Whiting Bay, listed in the free *Mountain Biking and Cycling* brochure available in bike shops and at the TIC. Located 900 ft. from Brodick pier along Shore Rd., **Arran Adventure** has expedition leaders who tackle everything from rock climbing to gorge walking and offer mountain-bike rental (opposite page).

DON'T GET SHOT. Deer-hunting season on Arran runs from August to February (peak Aug.-Sept.), when hunting parties trek through estates in the northern part of the island. To avoid unfortunate run-ins with hunter or hunted, pick up the free leaflet from the TIC (available starting in late July) for a list of areas to avoid each day or call **Hillphones** (☎01770 302 363).

BRODICK   ☎(0)1770

Most travelers who visit Arran will pass through Brodick, with its numerous amenities and busy ferry port. North of town, the **Brodick Castle and Country Park** overlooks the harbor, with a backdrop of rugged mountains and a small sweep of beach. Built on the site of an old Viking fort, the castle resembles a Victorian manor and contains a collection of paintings and deer-hunting trophies. Giant rhododendrons bloom in the garden. If you can't manage a visit, look on the back of a Scottish £20 note. Walk 30min. from the Brodick ferry or take bus #324 or 327. (☎01770 302 202. Castle open daily Easter-Sept. 11am-4:30pm; Oct. 11am-3:30pm. Garden open daily 9:30am-sunset. Castle and gardens £10, concessions £7, families £25. Gardens without castle £5/4/14.)

As the hub of island transportation, Brodick has many options if you're looking to spend the night. Upscale and close to the ferry is ⊠**Dunvegan House ❸**, Shore Rd., where you can enjoy beach views from the elegant dining room. (☎01770 302 811; www.dunveganhouse.co.uk. No smoking. Dinner £18. No singles. £30 per person. Cash only.) Five minutes uphill from the ferry pier, the **Strathwhillan House ❸** has comfy beds with lots of perks, like hair dryers, bathrobes, and tasty breakfast. (☎01770 302 331. From £15 per person. MC/V with £2 surcharge.) **Glen Rosa Farm ❶**, just over 2 mi. north of Brodick pier, provides basic camping facilities and a lush valley. (☎01770 302 380. Toilets and cold water. £4 per person. Cash only.) You can pick up groceries at either of Brodick's two **Co-ops**, one across from the ferry; a smaller one is at the other end of Shore Rd., next to the library. (☎01770 302 515. Open M-Sa 8am-10pm, Su 9am-7pm.) A number of bars and restaurants line Shore Rd.

Brodick's **Shore Road** has almost all services on the island, including the only **banks** and **ATMs**. Free **Internet** access can be found at the **Arran Library,** Shore Rd. (Open Tu 10am-5pm, Th and F 10am-7:30pm, Sa 10am-1pm.) The **post office** is set back from Shore Rd. on Mayish Rd. (☎01770 303 578. Open M-F 9am-5pm, Sa 9am-12:45pm.) **Postcode:** KA27 8AA.

LAMLASH AND WHITING BAY   ☎(0)1770

The popular sailing center of **Lamlash Bay** is dominated by the sacred site of **Holy Island.** Home to St. Molaise in the sixth century, the island is cared for today by a group of Tibetan Buddhist monks, whose rock carvings and gardens share the hills with herds of wild ponies. The island also has a number of walking paths, including one up **Mulloch Mor** (1030 ft.), the highest point on the island, with splendid views of Arran's mountains and the bright blue sea below. The southern end of the island is closed off to the public as a cloistered private space for 12 women completing a three-year, three-month Tibetan Buddhist retreat. Holy Island requests that you respect their spiritual study by avoiding this area; pick up the free *Holy Island* leaflet that maps out acceptable walking routes from the TIC. A regular ferry (☎01770 600 349) departs Lamlash for Holy Island (15min.; May-Sept. 8 per day, depending on tides; £9), although prior arrangements must be made in winter. Farther south, Whiting Bay is a sleepy seaside village stretched along the A841. From a trailhead toward the southern end of town, two easy walks lead to the **Glenashdale Falls** (1 mi.) and the megalithic stone structures at **Giant's Graves.**

In Lamlash, a small **Co-op** sells groceries along the A841. (Open M-Sa 8am-10pm, Su 10am-6pm.) Just past where the A841 veers from the coast toward Brodick, the **Shore B&B ❸**, Shore Rd., has Scandinavian-style lodgings with fantastic views of Holy Island. (☎01770 600 764. Doubles £60. MC/V.) Several hotels also serve food. ⊠**The Coffee Pot ❶**, toward the southern end of Whiting Bay on the coastal road, is a picturesque spot for afternoon tea (£1.40-2.20) or a bowl of scrumptious homemade soup for £2.50. (☎01770 700 382. Open daily 10am-5pm. Kitchen open until 4pm. Cash only.)

NORTHERN ARRAN AND LOCHRANZA   ☎(0)1770

Northern Arran is a land of green hills, bare peaks, and rocky coast. Sheep roam the streets and the remains of a **13th-century castle** in peaceful Lochranza. (Open 24hr. Free.) The whisky produced in the **Isle of Arran Distillery,** on the road to Brodick, is less peaty than other malts and is thus more palatable to the uninitiated; "Arran Gold," a sweet cream liquor, tastes like dessert and gives a warm glow. (☎01770 830 264; www.arranwhisky.com. Open Mar.-Oct. daily 10am-6pm; Nov.-Feb. reduced hours; call for details. 7 tours per day 10:30am-4:30pm. £4, concessions £3, under 12 free.) One mile down the coast, the fishing village of Catacol Bay harbors the **Twelve Apostles,** a dozen connected white houses that differ only in the shapes of their windows. A number of the northern peaks, including Caisteal Abhail (2817 ft.), are within a day's walk.

Toward the southern end on the main road to Brodick, the quiet **SYHA Lochranza ❶** has 64 beds and a fence to keep the sheep out. Question: if a sheep falls on Arran and nobody shears it, does it make a sound? (☎08700 041 140. Laundry and Internet. Lockout 10:30am-5pm. Curfew 11:30pm. Open Mar.-Oct. Dorms £12.50-15, under 18 £9.50-12. MC/V.) Housed in a century-old former church across from the castle, the **Castlekirk B&B ❸** has high ceilings and a lounge with stained-glass windows. (☎01770 830 202; www.castlekirk.co.uk. £22.50-27.50 per person. Cash only.) Campers can pitch at the **Lochranza Golf Course Caravan and Camping Site ❶,** also home to the only shop in the village. (☎01770 830 273. Toilets, showers, and laundry. Open Apr.-Oct. £5 per person; £3.60 per tent. Cash only.) The restaurant at the **Isle of Arran Distillery ❷** serves sandwiches, more substantial meals (£4.75-6.50), and tempting desserts, including homemade ice cream. (Open Mar.-Oct. M-Sa 10am-5pm, Su 11am-5pm; Nov.-Feb. F-Su 10am-4pm. MC/V.) For cheap and ready-to-go fare, stop by **The Sandwich Station ❶,** across from the pier and to the right. Call in advance for picnic lunches. (☎07917 671 913. Open M-Tu and Th-Su 8am-5pm. Cash only.)

WESTERN ARRAN AND BLACKWATERFOOT   ☎(0)1770

The western shore of Arran harbors a handful of tiny settlements separated by miles of coastline. The **Machrie Moor Stone Circle,** a mysterious Bronze Age arrangement of standing stones and boulders, lies at the end of an easy 3 mi. walk. According to legend, the standing stone with the hole in it was where the mythical giant Fingal tethered his giant dog, Bran. Follow the farm path 1 mi. south of Machrie village along the A841. Another mile south, the trail leading to the **King's Cave** (3 mi.) begins in a Forestry Commission car park. Passing along coastal cliffs, the walk terminates at the caves where Robert the Bruce learned a lesson in perseverance from a spider; legend has it that, when he witnessed the spider finally rebuild its web after falling many times, the famous Scot decided to retry his fight for the crown.

Another 2 mi. to the south lies Blackwaterfoot, the largest town on the western side of the island. The **Blackwaterfoot Lodge ❸** has comfortable rooms and a cozy lounge with a fireplace. (☎01770 860 202; www.blackwaterfoot-lodge. co.uk. Breakfast included. Singles £28; doubles and twins £72.) The **Mariner's Restaurant ❸** in the lodge serves sandwiches (£2.75-3.50) and entrees like Arran beef and fish pie (£11.50-17.50). Buses to Brodick and the remainder of the island leave across the parking lot from the Kinloch Hotel. Just up the street, the **A&C Cameron Store** has groceries and a **post office** (☎01770 860 220).

GLASGOW   ☎(0)141

Glasgow (pop. 579,000), once a dreary industrial shipyard, has transformed into a destination city for the young and hip. Fueled by a large student population, the West End's chic pubs and restaurants complement the sweaty after-hours party scene in the city center. Glasgow University's classic Gothic architecture stands across the River Clyde from the futuristic multi-million-dollar Science Centre, representing an ever-changing vision of Scotland's biggest city. In the summer months, Glasgow buzzes with festivals full of cutting-edge art, performances, and music (yes, bagpipes too).

◼ INTERCITY TRANSPORTATION

Glasgow lies along the River Clyde, 40 mi. west of Edinburgh along the M8. The city marks the northern end of the M74, which runs to England.

Flights: Glasgow is served by 2 international airports.

Glasgow International Airport (GLA; ☎08700 400 008; www.glasgowairport.com), 8 mi. west in Abbotsinch. Scotland's major airport, served by **KLM, British Airways,** and local airlines. Fairline (www.glasgowairportlink.com) bus #905 runs from the airport to downtown Buchanan Station. Hop on or off at any point along the route. 25min.; 5:40am-6pm every 10min., 6pm-midnight every 15-30min.; £5, one-way £3.

Prestwick International Airport (PIK; ☎08712 230 700; www.gpia.co.uk), 32 mi. southwest of the city center. **Ryanair** flies to London and other major European cities. Trains from PIK to Central Station (50min.; M-Sa 6am-11pm, Su 9am-11pm every 30min.; £5.20, with Ryanair printout £2.60). Express bus #X77 runs from the terminal to Buchanan St. (50min., every hr., £7).

Trains: A 5-10min. walk separates Glasgow's 2 main stations. Book in advance online (www.nationalrail.co.uk) for discounts.

Central Station, Gordon St. U: St. Enoch. Toilets 20p; shower with soap and towel £2. Open daily 5:30am-midnight. Ticket office open M-Sa 6am-9:30pm, Su 7:10am-11pm. Trains to: **Ardrossan** (1hr., 10-12 per day, £5.70); **Carlisle** (1hr., every hr., £33.50); **Dumfries** (2hr.; M-Sa 7 per day, Su 2 per day; £12.20); **London King's Cross** (6hr., 1-2 per hr., £100); **Manchester** (4hr., every hr., £50); **Stranraer Harbor** (2hr.; M-Sa 5 per day, Su 3 per day; £18.30).

Queen Street Station, George Sq. (☎0845 748 4950). U: Buchanan St. Serves trains from the north and east. Toilets 20p. Lockers £3-5 per day. Open M-Sa 5:10am-11:55pm, Su 7:10am-11:55pm. Travel center open M-Sa 6:15am-9:45pm, Su 7am-10pm. Trains to: **Aberdeen** (2hr.; M-Sa every hr., Su 7 per day; £38); **Edinburgh** (50min., 4 per hr., £10); **Fort William** (4hr., 2-4 per day, £23); **Inverness** (3hr.; M-Sa 7 per day, Su 4 per day; £38).

Buses: Buchanan Station, Killermont St. (☎0141 331 3708), 2 blocks north of Queen St. Station. National Express and Scottish Citylink buses. Toilets 20p. Luggage storage £3-5. Open M-Sa 9am-5pm; ticket office daily 7am-9:30pm; lockers daily 6:30am-10:30pm. Scottish Citylink (☎08705 505 050) to: **Aberdeen** (3hr., every hr., £22); **Edinburgh** (1hr., every 15min., £5.10); **Perth** (1hr., every hr., £9); **Inverness** (3-4hr., every hr., £21); **Oban** (3hr., 8 per day, £13.55). National Express (☎08705 808 080) runs to **London** (9hr., 5 per day, £18).

ORIENTATION

George Square is the center of town; the train and bus stations and TIC are all within three blocks. Sections of **Sauchiehall** (Sawkey-HALL), **Argyle,** and **Buchanan Streets** are lined with stores and open only to pedestrians, forming an L-shaped outdoor shopping district in the center of the city. The vibrant, upscale **West End** revolves around **Byres Road** and **Glasgow University,** 1 mi. northwest of George Sq. The city extends south of the **River Clyde** toward Pollok Country Park and southeast toward the Science Centre.

> **TIP** **WATCH THE ONE-WAYS.** When driving in Glasgow, beware of unmarked one-way streets. Often, one-way signs often don't show up until after you need them.

LOCAL TRANSPORTATION

Strathclyde Passenger Transport (SPT) Authority, St. Enoch's Sq., just two blocks from Central Station, is a travel center that dispenses advice, passes, and Underground maps. (☎0870 608 2608; www.spt.co.uk.)

Public Transportation: Glasgow's transportation system includes suburban rail, private local bus services, and the small, circular **Underground (U)** subway line, a.k.a. the "Clockwork Orange" (☎0845 748 4950; www.spt.co.uk). U trains (£1.10 one-way, children 55p) run every 4-8min. M-Sa 6:30am-11pm, Su 11am-5:30pm. New "Nightrider" bus service (every 20min.; F-Sa midnight-6:30am, Su 6pm-midnight; £2) at marked bus stops near U stations. Several stations provide locker facilities, secure bike facilities, and park and ride service. **Underground Journey** and **Season Tickets** are a good deal (10 trips £9, children £4.50; 20 trips £17/8.50; 7 days £10/5). The **Discovery Ticket** (£1.90) for 1 day of unlimited travel is valid on the Underground M-Sa after 9:30am and Su all day. The **Traveline** service (☎08706 082 608; www.traveline.org.uk) helps travelers coordinate bus, train, and ferry trips in Scotland.

Taxis: Airport Taxi Services (☎0141 848 4900) provides 24hr. service from Glasgow International Airport. Wheelchair-accessible services available. **Glasgow Taxis LTD** (☎0141 429 7070). 1-3hr. tours for £30-50.

Bike Rental: Some brave bikers venture onto Glasgow's busy streets. Bike paths run along both sides of the River Clyde and through Glasgow Green and Kelvingrove Park. **Alpine Bikes,** 50 Couper St. (☎0141 552 8575; www.alpinebikes.com), in Tiso Glasgow Outdoor Experience. £20 per day.

PRACTICAL INFORMATION

TOURIST AND FINANCIAL SERVICES

Tourist Information Centre: Visit Scotland, 11 George Sq. (☎0141 204 4400; www.visitscotland.com), off George Sq. south of Queen St. Station. U: Buchanan St. Books accommodations for £4 plus a 10% deposit, sells CalMac ferry tickets, and arranges car rentals. Contains a bookshop, Western Union, **bureau de change,** and a wide selection of maps. Pick up the free *Essential Guide to Glasgow* and a stack of pamphlets promoting upcoming shows and festivals. Open July-Aug. M-Sa 9am-8pm, Su 10am-6pm; June M-Sa 9am-7pm, Su 10am-6pm; Sept.-Apr. M-Sa 9am-6pm. MC/V.

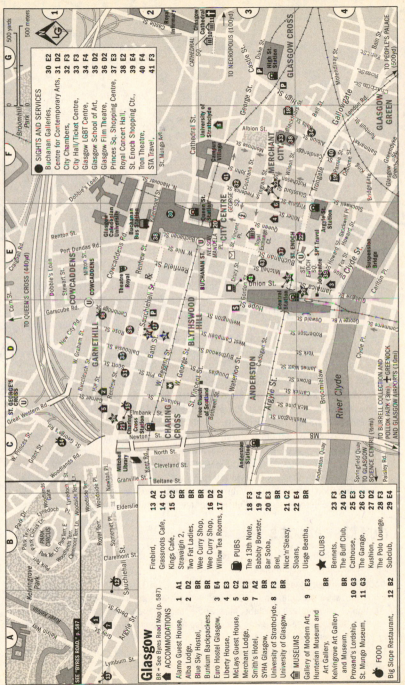

SIGHTS AND SERVICES

Buchanan Galleries,	30 E2
Centre for Contemporary Arts,	31 D2
City Chambers,	32 F3
City Hall/Ticket Centre,	33 F3
Glasgow LGBT Centre,	34 F4
Glasgow School of Art,	35 D2
Glasgow Film Theatre,	36 D2
Princes Sq. Shopping Centre,	37 E3
Royal Concert Hall,	38 E4
St. Enoch Shopping Ctr.,	39 F4
Tron Theatre,	40 F4
STA Travel,	41 F3

Glasgow

BR = See Byres Road Map (p. 587)

ACCOMMODATIONS

Alamo Guest House,	1 A1
Alba Lodge,	2 D2
Blue Sky Hostel,	BR
Bunkum Backpackers,	BR
Euro Hostel Glasgow,	3 E4
Liberty House,	4 E3
McLays Guest House,	5 C2
Merchant Lodge,	6 E3
Smith's Hotel,	7 A2
SYHA Glasgow,	8 F3
University of Strathclyde,	BR
University of Glasgow,	BR

MUSEUMS

Gallery of Modern Art,	9 E3
Hunterian Museum and Art Gallery,	BR
Kelvingrove Art Gallery and Museum,	BR
Provand's Lordship,	10 G3
St. Mungo Museum,	11 G3

FOOD

Big Slope Restaurant,	12 B2
Firebird,	13 A2
Grassroots Cafe,	14 C1
Kings Cafe,	15 C2
Stravaigin 2,	BR
Two Fat Ladies,	BR
Wee Curry Shop,	16 D2
Wee Curry Shop,	BR
Willow Tea Rooms,	17 D2

PUBS

The 13th Note,	18 F3
Babbity Bowster,	19 F4
Bar Soba,	20 E3
Brel,	BR
Nice'n'Sleazy,	21 C2
Sloans,	22 E4
Uisge Beatha,	BR

CLUBS

Bennets,	23 F3
The Buff Club,	24 D2
Cathouse,	25 E3
The Garage,	26 C2
Kushion,	27 D2
The Polo Lounge,	28 F3
Subclub,	29 E4

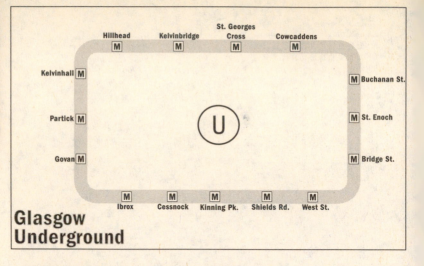

Glasgow Underground

Tours: City Sightseeing (☎0141 204 0444; www.scotguide.com). Tickets (£9, concessions £7) can be purchased at the TIC and allow 2 days of unlimited hop-on, hop-off access to tours on big red buses. Look for the bus stop signs or board in George Sq. Wheelchair-accessible. Book online for discounts. Phoning the **Glasgow City Rangers** (☎0141 946 4542) ahead of time can get you free Glasgow Green tours as well as tours of the Necropolis. Through **Glasgow City Walk** (☎0141 946 4542), members of the Scottish Tour Guides Association give historically rich group tours (£40 per group).

Budget Travel: STA Travel, 122 George St. (☎08714 680 622; www.statravel.co.uk). Branch at 184 Byres Rd. (☎08714 680 621). Open M-Sa 10am-6pm.

Banks: Barclays, 90 St. Vincent St. (☎08457 555 5555). Open M-F 9:30am-4:30pm. **American Express,** 115 Hope St. (☎0870 600 1060). Open M-Tu and Th-F 8:30am-5:30pm, W 9:30am-5:30pm, Sa 9am-noon. **ATMs** are on many corners.

Beyond Tourism: Glasgow's TIC accepts job applications up to 1 year before high season; knowledge of Scotland preferred. Other work in Scotland can be found by visiting www.s1jobs.com or the Glasgow **Central Job Centre,** 50-58 Jamaica St. (☎0856 060 234; www.jobcentreplus.gov.uk). The **Volunteer Centre,** 84 Miller St., 4th fl. (☎0141 226 3431; www.volunteerglasgow.org) lists volunteer opportunities and contact information.

LOCAL SERVICES

Library: Mitchell Library, North St. (☎0141 287 2999; www.mitchelllibrary.org). Free Internet. Open M-Th 9am-8pm, F-Sa 9am-5pm.

GLBT Resources: Glasgow LGBT Centre, 84 Bell St. (☎0141 552 4958; www.glgbt.org. uk). The 1st center of its kind in Scotland with support groups, get-togethers, and information on gay and lesbian clubs, bars, and activities. Brand new on-site coffee shop is open to all, providing a safe and open space for conversation and community. Karaoke F and Sa. Open daily 11am-midnight.

Launderette: Bank Street Laundry, 39 Bank St. (☎0141 339 5568). U: Kelvinbridge. Wash £2, dry 20p per 5min. Open M-Sa 8am-8pm, Su 10am-7pm.

EMERGENCY AND COMMUNICATIONS

Police: 173 Pitt St. (☎0141 532 2000).

Pharmacy: Boots, 200 Sauchiehall St. (☎0141 332 1925). Open M-W and F-Sa 8am-6pm, Th 8am-7pm, Su 8:30am-5:30pm.

Hospitals: Glasgow Royal Infirmary, 84 Castle St. (☎0141 211 4000). **Western Infirmary,** Church St. (☎0141 211 1000).

Internet Access: Free at **Mitchell Library** (see **Library**). Also free at **Gallery of Modern Art,** Royal Exchange Sq. (☎0141 229 1996). Internet cafes line Great Western Rd.

Post Office: Post offices are everywhere. 47 St. Vincent St. (☎08457 223 344) has a **bureau de change.** Open M-F 8:30am-5:45pm, Sa 9am-5:30pm. Branches at Hope St. and Bothwell St. **Postcode:** G2 5QX.

⚑ ACCOMMODATIONS

Glasgow has hostels, B&Bs, and hotels to suit any budget. The best places fill up quickly during the summer; book well ahead. Those on a tight budget need not worry—hostels start at £12-14 per night. Many of Glasgow's B&Bs are scattered on **Argyle Street** in the university area or near **Renfrew Street.** The major universities offer summer housing, and plenty of long-term residents rent apartments, often at summer or student discounts.

HOSTELS

▨ **SYHA Glasgow,** 7-8 Park Terr. (☎0141 332 3004). U: Kelvinbridge. Take bus #44 from Central Station, ask for the 1st stop on Woodlands Rd., and follow the signs to Park Terr. Overlooks Kelvingrove Park from a quiet street in the heart of the West End. Once the residence of a nobleman, later an upscale hotel, and now the best hostel in town. Low-key atmosphere with children and families to balance a steady stream of 20-somethings. Coffeehouse in the basement with Internet and light eats. All rooms (4-8 beds) ensuite. Bike shed, kitchen, and TV and game rooms. Laundry available. Dorms June-Sept. £16, under 18 £12; Oct.-May prices vary but start at £12. MC/V. ❶

Euro Hostel Glasgow (☎0141 222 2828; www.euro-hostels.co.uk), at the corner of Clyde St. and Jamaica St., near Central Station. U: St. Enoch. Screams "student-friendly" but caters to everyone from globetrotting backpackers to families on holiday. Located near some of Glasgow's hippest clubs, the hostel itself feels like a destination, satisfying a late-night crowd with its own bar and big-screen TVs. Breakfast included. Laundry £2. Free Wi-Fi. Internet. Wheelchair-accessible. Dorms £13-19; singles £40. MC/V. ❷

Bunkum Backpackers, 26 Hillhead St. (☎0141 581 4481; www.bunkumglasgow.co.uk), up the hill from Glasgow University and the West End. U: Hillhead. Half-hidden on a small residential street. The busy kitchen and common areas fill with a mix of itinerant backpackers and long-term residents who have discovered a home away from home in this refurbished Victorian house. Lockers £10 deposit. Laundry £2.50. Free parking. Dorms £12, £60 per week; twins £16. MC/V. ❷

Blue Sky Hostel, 3 Bank St. (☎0141 337 7000; www.blueskyhostel.com). U: Kelvinbridge. Offers crowded but clean facilities for the lowest price in town. TVs in common area. Ensuite bathrooms. Light breakfast included. Dorms £13; singles £38. ❶

UNIVERSITY DORMS

University of Glasgow, 73 Great George St. (☎0141 330 4116; www.cvso.co.uk). Off Hillhead St. in the Queen Margaret Bldg. Summer housing at several dorms. Office open daily 9am-5pm. Cairncross House, 20 Kelvinhaugh Pl., has self-catering rooms off Argyle St. near Kelvingrove Park. Soap, towels, and linens provided. Dorms £17-32. MC/V. ❷

University of Strathclyde, Office of Sales and Marketing, 50 Richmond St. (☎0141 553 4148; www.rescat.strath.ac.uk). On the hill, between Cathedral and George St. Dorm-style rooms and apartments available in summer. 1 kitchen per floor. Laundry and towels provided. Book well in advance. Open from mid-June to mid-Sept. Singles £75 per week, students £65; 4-6 person apartments £330 per week. MC/V. ❸

Liberty House, 59 Miller St. (☎0141 248 9949; www.libertystudents.com). Dorm-style rooms for students, behind Queen St. near the shopping district. Rooms include ensuite bathroom and communal kitchen. Secure facility and good rates for long-term stays. Open June-Sept. Singles £95 per week; doubles £145 per week. AmEx/MC/V. ❸

B&BS

⬛ **Alamo Guest House,** 46 Gray St. (☎0141 339 2395; www.alamoguesthouse.com). On a quiet street with access to the West End and Sauchiehall St. A family feel and a surplus of helpful services make this luxurious Victorian house the absolute best deal in Glasgow. Newly refurbished rooms include elegant baths and large windows overlooking Kelvingrove Park. Pet the cat, chat with the owners, and enjoy the fresh continental breakfast. Most rooms have DVD players for use with movie collection of over 300 movies and free temporary local gym membership. Pets allowed by arrangement. Free Wi-Fi. Book far ahead. Singles from £32; doubles from £48. MC/V. ❸

Merchant Lodge, 52 Virginia St. (☎0141 552 2424). U: Buchanan St. A quiet haven among the hubbub of the city center. The building still boasts the original stone spiral staircase from its days as a tobacco store in the 1800s. All rooms ensuite. Full Scottish breakfast included. Singles £48; doubles £58; triples £90. AmEx/MC/V. ❹

Alba Lodge, 232 Renfrew St. (☎0141 332 2588). U: Cowcaddens. Only recently opened, Alba offers spacious rooms and clean furnishings with soothing, pastel-toned decor. Centrally located, tucked away behind Sauchiehall St., yet quiet and secluded. Most rooms ensuite. Full Scottish breakfast included. Free WiFi. Singles £28; doubles £45; family rooms £70. MC/V. ❸

McLays Guest House, 260-276 Renfrew St. (☎0141 332 4796; www.mclays.com). U: Cowcaddens. With 3 elegant dining rooms, satellite TV, and a phone in each room, this posh B&B looks and feels like a hotel. Modern rooms in an old house create an air of trendy dignity. Most rooms ensuite. Full Scottish breakfast included. Internet £2 per hr. Book ahead, especially for singles. Singles from £28; ensuite £36; doubles £48/56; family (1 double bed, 2 singles) £70/80. AmEx/MC/V. ❸

Smith's Hotel, 963 Sauchiehall St. (☎0141 339 7674; www.thesmithshotel.com), 1 block east of Kelvingrove Park in the West End. Near the pub-packed action of upper Sauchiehall, Smith's provides a welcome respite from the city's racket. Decent value for larger groups looking for long-term budget rooms, but book in advance. Breakfast included. Singles from £60; doubles from £70; ensuite triples from £80. MC/V. ❸

◘ FOOD

Annual competitions repeatedly crown Glasgow as the curry capital of Britain, and with good reason. The city's West End brims with kebab and curry joints. In the past few years, the organic-food and fair-trade movements have begun to change the focus of many of Glasgow's restaurants toward more inventive menu options made with locally produced ingredients. **Byres Road** and the trendy **Ashton Lane** thrive with cafes, bars, and bistros. Groceries are

Byres Road

🏠 ACCOMMODATIONS
Blue Sky Hostel, **7**
Bunkum Backpackers, **6**
SYHA Glasgow, **8**
University of Glasgow, **5**

🍴 FOOD
Stravaigin 2, **2**
Two Fat Ladies, **1**
Wee Curry Shop, **4**
🍺 PUBS
Brel, **3**
Uisge Beatha, **9**

available at **Sainsbury's**, 236-240 Buchanan Galleries. (☎0141 332 1480; www.
sainsburys.co.uk. Open M-Sa 7am-10pm, Su 7am-9pm.)

🎨 **Willow Tea Rooms,** 217 Sauchiehall St. (☎0141 332 0521; www.willowtearooms.
co.uk). U: Cowcaddens, upstairs from Henderson Jewellers. Branch at 97 Buchanan St.
(☎0141 204 5242). U: Buchanan St. Light streams through the windows of this 3-story
ode to architect Charles Rennie Mackintosh. A Glasgow landmark, the building's facade
was designed by Mackintosh himself, and the cozy upstairs tearoom features handsome
chairs in the classic "Glasgow style." Sample over 20 teas (£2 per pot) or indulge in
3-course afternoon tea (£12). Open M-Sa 9am-4:30pm, Su 11am-4:15pm. MC/V. ❷

🎨 **Grassroots Cafe,** 97 St. George's Rd. (☎0141 333 0534). U: St. George's Cross. Roughly
carved wood tables and chairs reflect the cuisine of this vegetarian restaurant: organic
with a twist. Ethnic-inspired dishes tempt the adventurous. Try the Haloumi salad (fried
cheese with chickpeas and balsamic vinegar; £6). A mecca for Glasgow veggie culture,
with Green Party offices upstairs. Open daily 10am-9:45pm. AmEx/MC/V. ❷

Wee Curry Shop, 7 Buccleuch St. (☎0141 353 0777). U: Cowcaddens. Branch at 23
Ashton Ln. (☎0141 357 5280) takes MC/V. U: Hillhead. The best bang for your buck
in a town full of *pakora* and *puri*. The portions are as large as the dining area is small.
2-course lunch £5.25. Open M-Sa noon-2pm and 5:30-10pm. Cash only. ❶

Kings Cafe, 71 Elmbank St. (☎0141 332 3247), on a small alleyway off Sauchiehall
St. This tiny diner offers authentically cheap, greasy, and satisfying meals and snacks
for the Scottish palate. Family-owned, serving everything from haggis to pizza. Try the
homemade lentil soup (£1.40) or fill up on a stuffed roll for just £1. Fried Mars Bars
and Irn Bru round out the experience and the stomach. Takeaway available. Most items
£1-3. Open daily 7am-4am. Cash only. ❶

Big Slope, 36A Kelvingrove St. (☎0141 564 5201). U: Kelvingrove. Imposing racks of
deer antlers are mounted on the walls of Big Slope's underground bar and booths, a
great place for a relaxing meal. Ample outdoor tables. Specialty pizzas and moderately
priced game meats in traditional pub dishes (beef and rabbit lasagna £7.50) make it
worth a look. Open daily noon-midnight. AmEx/MC/V. ❷

Stravaigin 2, 8 Ruthven Ln. (☎0141 334 7165; www.stravaigin.com), off Byres Rd. U:
Hillhead. Less formal and less pricey than the original Stravaigin, 28 Gibson St. (☎0141

334 2665). The mantra "think globally, eat locally" inspires international cuisine show-casing fresh Scottish seafood, game, and produce. Those who dare to sample haggis can find no better than Stravaigin's, voted best in Scotland. The menu also includes a selection of Thai- and Middle Eastern-inspired dishes (£8-14). Open for lunch M-F noon-7pm, Sa-Su 11am-5pm; dinner M-F 7-11pm, Sa-Su 5-11pm. AmEx/MC/V. ❸

Firebird, 1321 Argyle St. (☎0141 334 0594; www.firebirdglasgow.com). U: Kelvinhall. Treats a diverse crowd to daily specials and locally famous pizzas (£9.50). Try the sage pork with caramelized apples (£13) and enjoy the friendly company. Free Wi-Fi. DJ F-Sa night. Open M-Th and Su 11am-midnight, F-Sa 11am-1am. MC/V. ❸

Two Fat Ladies, 88 Dumbarton Rd. (☎0141 339 1944; www.twofatladiesrestaurant. com). An open kitchen and bronze facade welcome epicures to this small, well-known West End restaurant. Serves gourmet seafood in a casual atmosphere. The delicious Two Fat's fish platter (£16) changes daily, but leave room for desserts like the signature Trio of Crème Brûlée (£5). Open for lunch daily noon-3pm; dinner daily 5:30-10:30pm. ❹

◉ SIGHTS

Glasgow is a paradise for the budget traveler. Many of the best sights are part of the Glasgow Museums network (www.glasgowmuseums.com), whose free collections are scattered across the city. Don't shy away from trekking a mile or two out of town for gorgeous city views and attractions. *The List* (www. list.co.uk; £2.50), available from newsstands, is an essential review of current exhibitions, galleries, music, and nightlife.

CITY CENTER

▨GLASGOW CATHEDRAL AND NECROPOLIS. Glasgow Cathedral is a humbling example of 13th-century Gothic architecture. Descend the stairs to visit the tomb of St. Mungo, patron saint of Glasgow. *(Castle St. ☎0141 552 6891. Open Apr.-Sept. M-Sa 9:30am-5:30pm, Su 1-5pm; Oct.-Mar. M-Sa 9:30am-4pm, Su 1-4pm. Organ recitals and concerts July-Aug. Tu 7:30pm; £7. Free personal tours by enthusiastic guides.)* A statue of Reformation leader John Knox looks over the Necropolis. Climb up the hill for a view of the city in near-solitude amid tombstones, statues, and obelisks. *(Behind the Cathedral over the Bridge of Sighs. Open 24hr. Free.)*

GEORGE SQUARE. This grand, red-paved landmark has always been the physical, cultural, commercial, and historical center of Glasgow. Filled with couples, tourists, and pigeon feeders, the square is frequently the site of citywide displays and events. Although named for George III, the square's 80 ft. central column features a statue of Sir Walter Scott, Scottish novelist and poet. The **City Chambers,** on the east side of George Sq., house an elaborate Italian Renaissance interior with mosaic floors and marble columns and staircases. *(☎0141 287 4017. Free 45min. tours M-F 10:30am, 2:30pm.)* The eclectic **Gallery of Modern Art (GoMA),** Queens St., south of George Sq., displays cutting-edge but occasionally inscrutable installations. *(☎0141 229 1996. Open M-W and Sa 10am-5pm, Th 10am-8pm, F and Su 11am-5pm. Guided tours Sa-Su noon, 2pm. Free)*

ST. MUNGO MUSEUM OF RELIGIOUS LIFE AND ART. Home to Britain's first Japanese Zen garden, the museum houses artifacts and information about hundreds of religions and cultural traditions. The third floor surveys Scotland's own religious history. *(2 Castle St. ☎0141 553 2557. Open M-Th and Sa 10am-5pm, F and Su 11am-5pm. Wheelchair-accessible. Free.)*

CENTRE FOR CONTEMPORARY ARTS (CCA). Three free galleries, a theater, artists' residences, a cafe, and a cinema make up this avant-garde mecca, which houses the prestigious Beck's Futures prize (the UK's top prize for contemporary visual art) every June and July. Exhibits are increasingly focused on computer art, and student shows display the work of Glasgow's up-and-coming artists. *(350 Sauchiehall St. ☎0141 352 4900; www.cca-glasgow.com. Open Tu-W 11am-11pm, Th 11am-midnight, F 11am-1am, Sa 10am-1am. Free galleries. Film prices vary.)*

OTHER CENTRAL SIGHTS. Duck down low to enter the small rooms of **Provand's Lordship,** the oldest house in Glasgow. Visitors are greeted by mannequins of monks in musty red robes. Antique furnishings and a third floor dedicated to Scottish cartoons and photos round out this eclectic walk through Glasgow's past. *(3-7 Castle St. ☎0141 552 8819. Open M-Th and Sa 10am-5pm, F and Su 11am-5pm. Free.)* Originally built for Glasgow's working class community, the **People's Palace** on Glasgow Green features rotating exhibits that focus on social trends and the "common man" in the last 250 years of the city's history. In the adjacent "winter gardens," visitors relax in a greenhouse and chat in the cafe. *(☎0141 271 2951. Open M-Th and Sa 10am-5pm, F and Su 11am-5pm. Gardens open daily 10am-6pm. Free.)*

WEST END

KELVINGROVE PARK, MUSEUM, AND ART GALLERY. Along the River Kelvin, **Kelvingrove Park** furnishes green space for walkers and bikers along with fountains and statues of obscure but influential Glaswegians. The park also houses recreational tennis courts, a skate park, playground, and lawn bowling green. Don't be surprised to hear bagpipes played by shirtless, bearded college students. City-sponsored festivals often fill the park with more official traditional music. Spires of the Kelvingrove Art Gallery and Museum rise from the park's southwest corner. The museum features everything from tastefully taxidermied animals to a large recreation of homes designed by Charles Rennie Mackintosh. *(Argyle St. ☎0141 276 9599; www.glasgowmuseums. com. U: Kelvinhall. Bus #9, 16, 18, 18A, 42, 42A, 62. Open M-Th and Sa 10am-5pm, F and Su 11am-5pm. Free.)* Across the street from the Kelvingrove Museum, the **Museum of Transport** is full of interactive and kid-friendly exhibits tracing the history of getting around in Scotland. *(1 Bunhouse Rd. ☎0141 287 2720. U: Kelvinhall. Open M-Th and Sa 10am-5pm, F and Su 11am-5pm. Free.)*

UNIVERSITY OF GLASGOW. The central spire of the neo-Gothic university towers over University Ave. Stately archways lead to the different wings of campus from a series of central quads. Pick up *Welcome to the University of Glasgow,* free at the TIC, or stop by the **Visitor Centre** for a free map and self-guided tour. *(☎0141 330 5511. U: Hillhead. Open M-Sa 9:30am-5pm. Tours Th-Sa 2pm; £4.50.)* Up a red-carpeted staircase is the ▨**Hunterian Museum,** the oldest museum in Scotland. The newly renovated halls house the personal collections of William Hunter, which include such varied and charmingly random attractions as an ancient elephant skeleton, human organs preserved in formaldehyde, and the penis bones of a whale and a weasel, displayed side by side for comparison. The upper level features the prolific inventions of the 19th-century physicist Lord Kelvin. *(☎0141 330 4221; www.hunterian.gla.ac.uk. Open M-Sa 9:30am-5pm, Su 2-5pm. Free.)* Across University St. on Hillhead St., the **Hunterian Art Gallery** displays 19th-century Scottish art, the world's largest Whistler collection, and a variety of Rembrandts and Pissarros. *(☎0141 330 5431. Open M-Sa 9:30am-5pm. Gallery free. House £3, students free; W after 2pm free for all.)*

BOTANIC GARDENS. Creatively landscaped gardens cover the stretch of the River Kelvin along Byres Rd. On sunny days, it feels as though all of Glasgow comes here (with their dogs) before heading to the beer gardens on nearby Ashton Ln. Look for the wall of carnivorous plants as well as the national collection of tree ferns, orchids, and begonias in the **Main Range** hothouse. Wander around the herb, rose, and vegetable gardens outside. The newly renovated **Kibble Palace** is a gleaming glass structure containing an international collection of plants from temperate climates. *(730 Great Western Rd. and Byres Rd. ☎0141 334 2422. U: Hillhead. Gardens open daily 7:30am-sunset. Kibble Palace and Main Range open daily Apr. to early Oct. 10am-6pm; late Oct. to Mar. 10am-4:15pm. Tours available by reservation. Free.)*

SOUTH OF THE CLYDE

◙POLLOK COUNTRY PARK AND BURRELL COLLECTION. The Pollok Country Park is a beautifully integrated expanse of darkened forest paths, art galleries, grazing highland cattle, and lots of native Scottish flora. The famous **Burrell Collection** can be found in a glass building in the middle of the park. Once the private stash of ship magnate William Burrell, the collection includes paintings by Cézanne and Degas, Egyptian and Buddhist sculptures, medieval armor and tapestries, Persian textiles, and fine china. *(☎0141 287 2550. Open M-Th and Sa 10am-5pm, F and Su 11am-5pm. Tours daily 1, 2pm. Free.)* Also in the park is **Pollok House,** a mansion with the collection of the Maxwell family, who lived in the area for 700 years. The artwork includes works by El Greco, Goya, and William Blake. The former servants' quarters have been converted into a cafe serving soups and sandwiches. *(☎0141 616 6410. Take bus #45, 47, or 57 from Jamaica St. 15min., £1.30. Open daily 10am-5pm. £5, students £3.75; Nov.-Mar. free.)*

GLASGOW SCIENCE CENTRE. Like a glittering eye on the river, the UK's only titanium-clad exterior is covered in glass panes overlooking the Clyde. The three buildings require three tickets. The first houses Scotland's only **IMAX theater.** *(Open daily 10am-6pm.)* The second contains hundreds of interactive exhibits. *(Open daily 10am-5pm.)* Lastly, the 417 ft. **Glasgow Tower** is the only building in the world that rotates 360° from the ground up. Climb the 523 steps to the top or follow the crowd to the lift. Offering the very best views of Glasgow, the building is a cone whose weight rests on a base of just a few centimeters. *(50 Pacific Quay. ☎0141 420 5010; www.gsc.org.uk. U: Cessnock, accessible by Bells Bridge. Open daily 10am-5pm. Each building £7-8, concessions £5-6; any 2 buildings £10/8.)*

♫ ENTERTAINMENT

The city's dynamic student population ensures countless film, food, and music events from October to April. **Ticket Centre,** City Hall, Candleriggs, has information on plays, films, and concerts taking place at Glasgow's dozen-odd theaters. (☎0141 287 5511. Open M-Sa 9:30am-9pm.) Theaters include **Theatre Royal,** Hope St. (☎0141 332 9000), the **Tron Theatre,** 63 Trongate (☎0141 552 4267), and the **Citizens' Theatre,** 119 Gorbals St. (☎0141 429 0022). The **Cottier Theatre,** 935 Hyndland St., features a variety of theatrical events, from avant-garde to opera. (☎0141 357 3868.) The **Glasgow ABC,** 300 Sauchiehall St., hosts bands and events throughout the year in a building that housed Glasgow's first cinema. (☎0870 4000 818.) **The Royal Concert Hall,** Sauchiehall St., is a frequent venue for the Royal Scottish National Orchestra. (☎0141 353 8000. Box office open M-Sa 10am-6pm.) The **Glasgow Film Theatre,** 12 Rose St., screens both mainstream and sleeper hits and hosts the traveling London Lesbian and Gay Film Festival in September. (☎0141 332 6535; www.gft.org.uk. Box office open M-F noon-9pm, Sa-Su 30min. before 1st film. £5, concessions £4.)

SHOPPING

You'll pass kilted mannequins and Charles Rennie Mackintosh jewelry for blocks on end as you make your way up **Sauchiehall Street** and down **Buchanan Street.** The two streets form a pedestrian-only zone and boast excellent shopping. Shops stay open late on Thursdays but close early on the weekends. The three main indoor shopping centers are **Princes Square,** 48 Buchanan St., a high-end shopping mall; **Saint Enoch Centre,** 55 St. Enoch Sq.; and the **Buchanan Galleries** at the north end of Buchanan St. The West End's **Byres Road** is full of boutiques, often with a focus on fair trade and organic products. A cross between a farmers' market and a flea market, **The Barrows** is an escape from the higher prices of elsewhere in Glasgow. Located at the intersection of Argyle and Trungate St. (under the sign marked "Barrowland"), The Barrows offers a dizzying array of commodities at bargain prices. (Open Sa-Su 10am-5pm.)

NIGHTLIFE

Glaswegians have a reputation for partying hard. Three universities and the highest student-to-resident ratio in Britain guarantee a kinetic after-hours vibe. *The List* (www.list.co.uk; £2.50), available from newsstands, has detailed nightlife and entertainment listings, while *The Gig* (free) highlights what's happening in the live music scene.

PUBS

You'll never find yourself far from a frothy pint in this city of beer gardens. Students from the University of Glasgow mingle with 20-somethings on **Ashton Lane** and **Byres Road.** In the East End, the University of Strathclyde and the Glasgow School of Art are well supplied by the more lively **Buchanan Street.**

- **Babbity Bowster,** 16-18 Blackfriars St. (☎0141 552 5055). U: St. Enoch. An authentic Glaswegian experience: few kilts and little Gaelic music, but you are likely to hear the sound of a pint hitting the bar and a jubilant patron asking for another. Small patio on a quiet street. Offerings range from the unique cauliflower and mung bean moussaka (£7.70) to the traditional fish soup (£7). Open M-Sa 11am-midnight, Su 10am-midnight. Kitchen open until 10pm. Upstairs restaurant open Tu-Sa until 6pm. MC/V.

- **Uisge Beatha,** 232 Woodlands Rd. (☎0141 564 1596). U: Kelvinbridge. Uisge Beatha (ISH-keh VAH-ha) is Gaelic for "water of life" (whiskey), and this pub has over 100 malts (from £2.50). The dark interior and tra-

ON KNIFE'S EDGE

In 2005, Scotland received a dubious honor—a United Nations report named it the most violent country in the developed world. Four years later, fighting knife crime remains a priority for the Scottish, a battle that has proven difficult to win outright.

The 2005 UN report found that over 3% of Scottish citizens had been victims of violent assault, compared with 1.2% of Americans, and that the blade is the weapon of choice. Glasgow alone witnessed 3000 assaults in 2007, and various organizations ranging from national charities to notorious tabloids have waged campaigns to draw attention to the stories of innocent victims murdered by drunk, drugged-up, knife-carrying hooligans.

Overall, knife crime rates have fallen by 15% in the past year in the UK, but debate rages over the best method of tackling the "booze and blade" culture after a recent spate of fatal stabbings. Some politicians have called for stronger measures against carrying knives, including automatic prison sentences. Others have criticized such policies as impractical to enforce (jail space is finite) and possibly counterproductive in the long term (youths could become even more resentful of police if they were randomly searched). At times, it seems that the sole point of agreement between the Labour and Tory parties is that violent assault incurs steep, sometimes irrecoverable social costs.

SCOTSPEAK

The Scots love to talk, to anyone and about anything. But, despite their sociable overtures, sometimes you may find that you just can't understand the words that are coming out of their mouths. To help with some of that accent interpretation, here are some words that may sound familiar but that take on a different meaning in bonnie Scotland.

Dinna is not your evening meal but rather a replacement for the contraction "do not." For example, you might hear the phrase, "I *dinna* have your dinner ready."

A *bairn* is not where you keep your cows. It's a little child.

Lug means "ear," not to carry—unless you're being dragged around by your ear, which we hope won't happen to you during your travels in Scotland.

Wee is not something you do in the bathroom. It means small.

Braw may sound like an undergarment with a twang, but it just means something good. A day with fine weather is a *braw day*.

Far from a gently bubbling river, a *Reiver* was a member of the violent clans that terrorized the Borders towns from the 13th to the 16th centuries.

If someone asks you for a *smuirich*, pucker up! True, it does sound like drunken request for a "smooch," but its connotation is less bold: it's just a simple, common word for a kiss.

ditional decor adds an authentic feel without seeming cheesy. Irish tunes Th after 8pm; live Scottish music Su. Happy hour daily 4-7pm. Open daily noon-midnight. Light snacks served noon-5pm. MC/V.

The 13th Note, 50-60 King St. (☎0141 553 1638, www.13thnote.co.uk). U: St. Enoch. A reasonably priced all-organic, all-vegetarian menu and excellent local music ranging from electro-hardcore to folk (starts daily 9pm; cover £3-5). Open daily noon-midnight. Kitchen open noon-10pm.

Brel, Ashton Ln. (☎0141 342 4966; www.brelbarrestaurant.com). Named for the singer-songwriter, Brel specializes in Belgian beer and undiscovered local bands. Simple wood booths and outdoor patio seating. The restaurant menu includes sandwiches (£5) and mussel pots (small £6, large £11). Entrees £7-11. Open daily noon-midnight. MC/V.

Sloans, 108 Argyll St. (☎0141 221 8886; www.sloansglasgow.com). U: St. Enoch. Glasgow's oldest bar and restaurant, the recently reopened Sloans is kitschy but charming nonetheless. Entrees £6-8. Ceilidh dancing in the grand ballroom F 7:30pm-1am. Open M-Th noon-midnight, F-Su noon-1am. MC/V.

Bar Soba, 11 Mitchell Ln. (☎0141 204 2404; www.barsoba.co.uk). U: Buchanan St. Tucked down an alleyway off Buchanan St. Perfect for quiet conversation over drinks. Thai-inspired dishes like prawn with pumpkin (£10) complement an impressive selection of beers, wines, and mixed drinks. Open M-Sa 11am-midnight, Su noon-midnight.

Nice'n'Sleazy, 421 Sauchiehall St. (☎0141 333 0900; www.nicensleazy.com). U: Charing Cross. Sleazy's, as it is known to hipster Glaswegians, is one of many local venues that features up-and-coming local bands on its cavernous underground stage nearly every night. More nice than sleazy, this colorful hotbed of funk and punk serves food and alcohol upstairs. Open M-Th and Su 11:30am-11:45pm, F-Sa 11:30am-3am.

CLUBS

With loads of options for picky clubbers and giant venues to house everyone else, Glasgow parties hard every night of the week. On weekday nights, check *The List* for open clubs. Weekends see long stretches of Sauchiehall and Buchanan Streets awake and buzzing.

Kushion, 158-166 Bath St. (☎08451 666 031). A long line of well-heeled and well-dressed Glaswegians stretches out the door of this Thai-themed club. Fog machines and gleaming wood statues evoke the mysteries of a rainforest. Tu student night. F-Sa mix of indie, soul, and funk. Cover £3-5. Open M 9pm-1am, Tu-Su 11pm-3am.

The Buff Club, 142 Bath Ln. (☎0141 248 1777; www.thebuffclub.com), behind Bath St. A wee club and hard to find, but packed every night of the week. 2 dance floors and an attached bar. Floral wallpaper, disco balls, and enthusiastic crowd of all ages. Music ranges from indie to funky house music. Sa salsa. Cover M-Th and Su £3-5, F-Sa £6. Su students free. Open M-Th and Su 11pm-3am, F-Sa 10:30pm-3am.

The Polo Lounge, 84 Wilson St. (☎0141 553 1221). Behind gold colored curtains, this long-standing gay and lesbian club heats up early. 80s music and mainstream pop in a space that feels classy and casual. W all drinks £1. Cover £5. Chill out with a martini in the adjoining cocktail bar, **Moda,** 62 Virginia St. Both open W and F-Su 5pm-3:30am.

Subclub, 22 Jamaica St. (☎0141 248 4600; www.subclub.co.uk). The smooth, silver exterior is impossibly cool. Mostly hired out at night by different promoters. Local musicians performing at Subclub range from laptop composers to the Glasgow School of Guitar Bands. Sa-Su cover £6-7. Open Sa-Su 11:30pm-3am. Other nights vary.

Bennets, 90 Glassford St. (☎0141 552 5761; www.bennets.co.uk). Bennets is a staple of the gay and lesbian cruising scene. Music varies by room, and decor is simple but rarely noticed by the energetic crowd. Cover £6. Open Tu and Th-Su 11:30pm-3am.

The Garage, 490 Sauchiehall St. (☎0141 332 1120; www.garageglasgow.co.uk). Look for the yellow truck hanging over the door. Supposedly Scotland's biggest club, The Garage helps over 3000 frenetic dancers get their fill on weekends. Flashing neon signs stud the staircases and 5 dance floors blast everything from indie to pop. VIP lounge hosts after parties and the occasional celebrity. Cover £3-7; frequent student discounts. M-F free entry before 11:30pm. Open M-F and Su 11pm-3am, Sa 10:30pm-3am.

Cathouse, 15 Union St. (☎0141 248 6606; www.cathouseglasgow.co.uk). Grunge, goth, and indie please a younger crowd in this 3-floor club. Frequently hosts live acts, including a few big name groups. Under-18 rockers can headbang downstairs in the Voodoo Room (Sa 5-9:30pm). Th and Sa free entry; Th drinks starting at £1. Cover F-Sa £5-6, students £4. Open Th-Su 11pm-3am.

TIP — HARD-CORE. Although most clubs are open until 3am, Glasgow police maintain the authority to order large and potentially disruptive groups in public to disperse after 2am.

FESTIVALS

The year kicks off with a month-long Scottish ceilidh (folk or traditional dance party) at the **Celtic Connections** (www.celticconnections.com) festival in January. The fun continues with the three-year-old **Glasgow Film Festival** (www.glasgowfilmfestival.org.uk) in the middle of February. If the city already seems saturated with art, it gets completely drunk on it for one weekend in early April with the **Glasgow Art Fair** (www.glasgowartfair.com). Summer is the real festival season, bringing tourists from around the globe. During the **West End Festival** (www.westendfestival.co.uk) in June, the city comes alive with longer bar hours and guest musicians. The **Glasgow International Jazz Festival** (☎0141 552 3552; www.jazzfest.co.uk), in late June, draws international jazz greats to venues scattered across the city. The **Glasgow River Festival,** in mid-July, celebrates the nautical history of the city with music and activities on the Clyde. **Bard in the Botanics** (www.bardinthebotanics.org), or "Shakespeare in the Park," takes place in the West End Botanic Gardens during June and July. Take advantage of the fine dining during **Gourmet Glasgow,** when for two weeks in August over 50

SOUTHERN SCOTLAND

restaurants and bars offer fixed-price meals and free tastings. Pick up *Gourmet Glasgow*, free at the TIC. On the second Saturday of August, over 100 bagpipe bands compete on the Glasgow Green for the **World Pipe Championships** (☎0141 221 5414). One weekend in early September brings **Whisky Live** (www.whisky-live.com), an extravaganza surrounding the much-vaunted national drink.

▣ DAYTRIP FROM GLASGOW

NEW LANARK

Bus #240X (1hr., every hr.) runs from Glasgow to the nearby town of Lanark, where you can catch Stuart bus #135 connecting Lanark and New Lanark—ask at the TIC or Visitor Centre for times. Purchase tickets at the Visitor Centre (☎01555 661 345; www.newlanark.org). Open daily June-Aug. 10:30am-5pm, Sept.-May 11am-5pm. £7, concessions £6, families £22. Guided tours £1 per person; call ahead to book.

The restored mill town of New Lanark gained international notoriety during its heyday in the 19th century, when social pioneer Robert Owen implemented radical reforms to the management of the mills here, limiting child labor and providing free health care, education, and better housing for workers. Today, the town is a UNESCO World Heritage site. Inside the Visitor Centre is the entrance to the **New Millennium Experience,** which, besides a 19th-century steam engine, also houses a theme-park-style ride with videos and high tech displays about Robert Owen's vision of a society "without crime, without poverty, and with intelligence and happiness increased a hundredfold." The commands to continue Owen's work in today's society grow a little heavy-handed, but the exhibit does score some poignant reminders that the child labor Owen tried to abolish still exists in the modern world. Check out the rooftop garden and viewing platform for views of stern mill buildings along the lush riverbank.

Footpaths along the River Clyde make for serene strolling along the peaceful bank. The **Dundaff Linn** waterfall is just beyond the heritage site, and a 30min. walk will lead you to the **Corra Linn** waterfall (1km from New Lanark). A further 25min. walk will bring you to the gushing **Bonnington Linn** waterfall (2km from New Lanark). These walks can be muddy in winter, so come prepared, and always stick to the paths, as the hydroelectric power station close can cause sudden changes in the river's water level.

CENTRAL SCOTLAND

Less rugged than the Highlands to the north and more subdued than the cities to the south, central Scotland has draws all of its own. The eastern shoulder, curving from Fife to the Highland Boundary Fault along the North Sea, has centuries-old communities and historical landmarks. To the west, the landscape flattens from snow-covered peaks into the plains of the Central Lowlands. Escape Celts and kilts in the remote Inner Hebrides, where palm trees, stucco homes, and sandy beaches offer a relaxing change from the mainland.

HIGHLIGHTS OF CENTRAL SCOTLAND

ADMIRE the 5 ft. sword of William Wallace and one of Britain's grandest castles in **Stirling,** the historic royal seat of Scotland.

RELAX on the bonnie, bonnie banks of **Loch Lomond** before exploring the **Trossachs**, Scotland's first national park (p. 601).

DRINK famous **Islay** whisky at one of the island's many distilleries (p. 622).

STIRLING   ☎ (0)1786

Located between Edinburgh and Glasgow at the narrowest point of the Firth of Forth, Stirling controlled the flow of goods in and out of Scotland for centuries. The city has thus been the site of many political struggles. At the 1297 Battle of Stirling Bridge, William Wallace overpowered the English army. Despite modern development, this former royal capital hasn't forgotten its heroes: Stirling swarms with *Braveheart* fans searching for the Scotland of old.

▬ TRANSPORTATION

Trains: The station is in the town center on Goosecroft Rd. (☎08457 484 950). Travel Centre open M-F 6am-9pm, Sa 6am-8pm, Su 8:50am-10pm. Trains to: **Aberdeen** (2hr.; M-Sa every hr., Su 6 per day; £36.60); **Edinburgh** (50min., 2 per hr., £6.50); **Glasgow** (40min.; M-Sa 2-3 per hr., Su every hr.; £6.70); **Inverness** (3hr.; M-Sa 4 per day, Su 3 per day; £56.30); **London King's Cross** (5½hr., 1 per day, £134.50).

Buses: The bus station is also on Goosecroft Rd. (☎01786 446 474). Ticket office open M-Sa 9am-5pm. Station open M-Sa 6:45am-10pm, Su 10:15am-5:45pm. Scottish Citylink (☎0870 505 050) buses run to **Glasgow** (40min., 1 per hr., £5.40) and **Inverness** via **Perth** (3¾hr., 4-6 per day, £17.80). First (☎01324 613 777) bus #38 runs to **Edinburgh** (1¼hr., every hr., £5.50).

⚡ PRACTICAL INFORMATION

Tourist Information Centre: 41 Dumbarton Rd. (☎01786 475 019). Internet £1 per 12min. Open July-Aug. M-Sa 9am-7pm, Su 9:30am-6pm; from mid-Sept. to mid-Oct. M-Sa 9:30am-5pm; from mid-Oct. to Mar. M-F 10am-5pm, Sa 10am-4pm; from Apr. to early June M-Sa 9am-5pm; early Sept. and mid-June. M-Sa 9am-6pm.

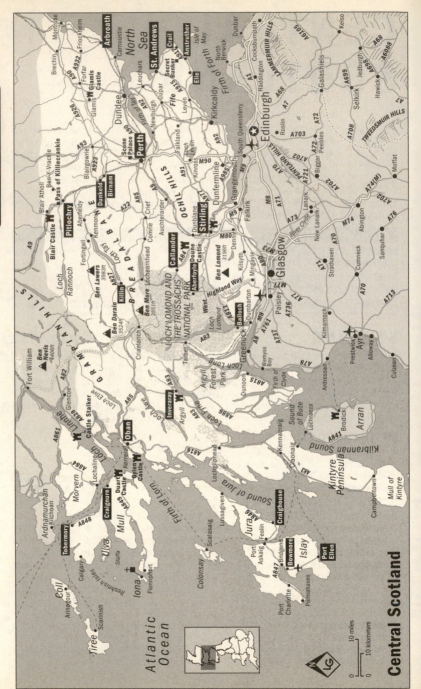

Central Scotland

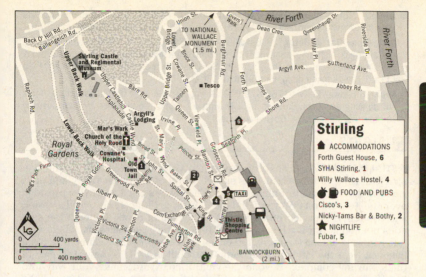

CENTRAL SCOTLAND

Tours: City Sightseeing Stirling (☎01786 446 611). Runs a hop-on, hop-off tour that departs directly from the train station, traveling on to Bannockburn, Stirling Castle, the Wallace Monument, and Stirling University. £7.50, concessions £5, children £3.

Library: Corn Exchange (☎01786 432 107). Free Internet. Open M, W, F 9:30am-5:30pm, Tu and Th 9:30am-7pm, Sa 9:30am-5pm.

Launderette: 9 Barnsdale Rd. (☎01786 473 540). Open M-F 8:15am-7pm, Sa 9am-6pm, Su 10am-5pm.

Police: Randolphfield (☎01786 456 000).

Internet Access: At the TIC and the library (above).

Post Office: Inside the WHSmith in the Thistles Shopping Centre (☎01786 465 392). **Bureau de change.** Open M-F 9am-5:30pm, Sa 9am-12:30pm. **Postcode:** FK8 2BP.

ACCOMMODATIONS

Willy Wallace Hostel, 77 Murray Pl. (☎01786 446 773), in the center of town. A party atmosphere prevails in the bright, colorful, high-ceilinged rooms. 54 beds. 1 all-female dorm. No lockable dorms. Self-catering kitchen. No lockers. Laundry. Internet £1 per hr.; Wi-Fi £2 for 24hr. Dorms £15. MC/V. ❶

SYHA Stirling, St. John St. (☎01786 473 442), halfway up the hill to the castle. Occupies an old Separatist church. 126 beds in 2- to 6-bed dorms. Self-catering kitchen, laundry, and Internet. Curfew 2am. Dorms £15-17.25. MC/V. ❷

Forth Guest House, 23 Forth Pl. (☎01786 471 020; www.forthguesthouse.co.uk), near the station. A Georgian house with meticulously decorated ensuite rooms. Singles £28-45; doubles and twins £40-50. MC/V. ❸

FOOD AND NIGHTLIFE

A huge **Tesco** on Burghmuir Rd. has groceries as well as beach umbrellas and barbecue grills, in case you find yourself in need. (☎0845 677 9658. Open M-F 8am-10pm, Sa 7:30am-9pm, Su 9am-8pm.)

Cisco's, 70 Port St. (☎01786 445 900). Find every sandwich combination under the sun for unbeatable prices (£2.10-4.25). Open M-Sa 10am-4pm. MC/V. ❶

Nicky-Tams Bar & Bothy, 29 Baker St. (☎01786 472 194; www.nickytams.co.uk). A laid-back nighttime hangout with student drink discounts and live music on W and most weekends. DJs Th. Quiz night Su. Open M-Th and Su 11am-midnight, F-Sa 11am-1am. Kitchen open noon-9pm. MC/V. ❶

Fubar, 6 Maxwell Pl. (☎01786 472 619). A popular late-night destination with 2 floors of dancing and bars. Student night Th with £2 drinks. Cover varies by night, usually around £5, students £4. Open 11pm-3am.

◉ SIGHTS

STIRLING CASTLE. From atop a dormant volcano surrounded by the scenic Ochil Hills, Stirling Castle has superb views of the Forth Valley and prim gardens that belie its turbulent history. The castle's regal gargoyles presided over the 14th-century Wars of Independence, a 15th-century royal murder, and the 16th-century coronation of Mary, Queen of Scots. Beneath the cannons pointed at Stirling Bridge lie the 16th-century **great kitchens,** where visitors can walk among the recreated chaos of cooks preparing game for a royal banquet. Near the kitchens, the **North Gate,** built in 1381, is the oldest part of the sprawling complex. Beyond the central courtyard, make your way into **Douglas Garden,** named for the earl of Douglas, who was murdered in 1452 by James II before his body was dumped here. Free 45min. guided tours leave twice per hour from inside the castle gates. (☎01786 450 000. Open daily Apr.-Sept. 9:30am-6pm; Oct.-Mar. 9:30am-5pm. Last entry 45min. before close. £8.50, concessions £6.50, children £4.25. Audio tour £2, concessions £1.50, children £1.) The castle also contains the **Regimental Museum of the Argyll and Sutherland Highlanders,** which follows the regiments based at Stirling Castle. (Open daily Easter-Sept. 9:30am-5pm; Oct.-Easter 10am-4:15pm. Last admission 15min. before close. Free.) Many consider **Argyll's Lodging,** the 17th-century earl's mansion below the castle, to be the most important surviving Renaissance mansion in Scotland. It has been impressively restored, with the original staircases and fireplaces intact. (Open daily Apr.-Oct. 9:30am-6pm; Nov.-Mar. 9:30am-5pm. By guided tour only. Tours 2-4 times per day; register with a member of the castle staff. £4, concessions £3, children £1.60. Free with castle admission.)

NATIONAL WALLACE MONUMENT. This 19th-century tower affords incredible views to those determined enough to climb its 246-step, wind-whipped spiral staircase. Halfway up, catch your breath and admire William Wallace's actual 5 ft. sword. One can't help but wonder how he lugged that thing around all the time. (Hillfoots Rd. 1 mi. from Stirling proper. Sightseeing Stirling runs here, as do local buses #62 and 63 from Murray Pl. ☎01786 472 140; www.nationalwallacemonument.com. Open daily June 10am-6pm; July-Aug. 9am-6pm; Sept. 9:30am-5:30pm; Mar.-May and Oct. 10am-5pm; Nov.-Feb. 10:30am-4pm. £6.70, concessions £5, children £4, families £17.)

OLD TOWN. On Mar's Walk, **Castle Wynd** is an elaborate Renaissance facade, all that was completed of a 16th-century townhouse before its wealthy patron died. Next door is the **Church of the Holy Rood,** which hosted the coronation of James VI and shook under the fire and brimstone of Presbyterian minister John Knox. Check out the stained-glass windows and the organ, each considered among the finest in the UK. (Open May-Sept. daily 11am-4pm. Service Su July-Dec. 10am; Jan.-June 11:30am. Organ recitals May-Sept. W 1pm.) Down the driveway lies 17th-century **Cowane's Hospital,** built as an almshouse for members of the merchant guild. (Open M-Sa 9am-5pm, Su 1-5pm. Free.) The **Old Town Jail,** St. John St., features lively reenactments of 19th-century prison life. The roof has an exhibit on prisons today and views of the Forth Valley. (☎01786 450 050. Open daily June-Sept. 9:30am-5:30pm; Oct. and Apr.-May 10am-5pm; Nov.-Mar 10am-4pm. Last entry 1hr. before close. £6, concessions £4.50, children £3.80, families £15.70. MC/V.) Stirling's **town walls** are some of the best preserved in Scotland; follow them along the **Back Walk.**

BANNOCKBURN. Two miles south of Stirling at Bannockburn, a statue of **Robert the Bruce** overlooks the field where his men defeated the English in 1314, initiating 393 years of Scottish independence. The cry "Bannockburn" still inspires Scottish nationalist sentiment to this day. In mid-September, the site fills with falcons and archers for the annual reenactment of the Battle of Bannockburn. The Heritage Centre describes the historical context of the battle, gives a detailed account of the fighting, and displays some interesting items, including a reconstruction of Robert the Bruce's leprosied head. (☎01786 812 664. Heritage Centre and Shop open Mar.-Oct. daily 10:30am-5:30pm. Sightseeing Stirling stops here, as do First buses #52, X39, and 139.)

▶ DAYTRIP FROM STIRLING

DOUNE CASTLE. Above a bend in the River Teith is the 14th-century fortress Doune Castle. Many of the castle's original rooms are intact, most notably the great hall and the kitchen, with a fireplace large enough to roast a cow. Today, scholars of medieval architecture share the castle with Monty Python fans—many scenes from *Monty Python and the Holy Grail* were filmed here, including the ▓**Knights Who Say Ni!** The ticket desk provides coconut shells for reenactors. (From Stirling, First bus #59 stops in Doune on its way to Callander (25min., every hr.). The castle is a 5min. walk from town. ☎01786 841 742. Open daily Apr.-Sept. 9:30am-5:30pm; Oct.-Mar. 9:30am-4:30pm. £4.20, concessions £3.20, children £2.10.)

LOCH LOMOND AND BALLOCH   ☎(0)1389

Immortalized by a famous 19th-century ballad, Loch Lomond and its surrounding wilderness continue to awe visitors. Britain's largest lake is dotted by 38 islands, and its proximity to Glasgow makes it the perfect destination for a daytrip. The bonnie banks get crowded, especially during summer, when daytrippers pour into the area's largest town. A short walk from the southern tip of the loch, Balloch is a good transportation hub beside the River Leven.

▐▐ TRANSPORTATION AND PRACTICAL INFORMATION. The Balloch **train station** is on Balloch Rd., across from the TIC. Trains (☎08457 484 950) depart to Glasgow Queen St. Monday through Saturday and to Glasgow Central on Sunday (45min., 2 per hr., £4). Scottish Citylink (☎08705 505 050) runs frequent **buses** between Glasgow and Balloch (45min., 7 per day, £5.10), leaving about 1 mi. from the town center, north of the Balloch roundabout. These buses continue along the loch's western shore to Luss and Tarbet. Bus #976 from Glasgow to Oban stops at the Loch Lomond Youth Hostel (below; 45min., 4 per day). First runs #204, 205, and 215 from Glassford St. between Glasgow and Balloch Town Center (1hr., frequent, £4.10). To reach the eastern side of the loch, take bus #309 from Balloch to Balmaha (25min., 5-7 per day, £2). Bus #305 heads for Luss (15min., 7-9 per day, £1.70). MacFarlane's **mail boat** takes passengers between the lake's four inhabited islands, leaving Balmaha at 11:30am (10:50am in winter) with a 1hr. stop on Inchmurrin (2hr.; July-Aug. M and W-Sa; Sept. and May-June M, Th, Sa; Oct.-Apr. M and Th; weather permitting; £8).

Balloch's **Tourist Information Centre,** Balloch Rd., is in the Old Station Building, across the street from the end of the platform. (☎08707 200 607. Open daily June-Sept. 9:30am-6pm; Apr.-May 10am-6pm.) The larger **National Park Gateway**

Loch Lomond and The Trossachs National Park

▲▲ ACCOMMODATIONS

Lomond Woods Holiday Park, **2**
Station Cottages, **5**
SYHA Inveraray, **1**
SYHA Loch Lomond, **4**
SYHA Rowardennan, **3**
Trossachs Backpackers, **7**
Trossachs Holiday Park, **6**

Forest Areas

Centre sits 1 mi. to the north at the Loch Lomond Shores complex. (☎01389 722 199. Open daily Apr.-Sept. 9:30am-6:30pm; Oct.-Mar. 10am-5pm.)

⌐ ACCOMMODATIONS. Hostels don't get much grander than ⬛**SYHA Loch Lomond ❷**, a turreted 19th-century tobacco baron's mansion 2 mi. north of Balloch on the A85. Citylink buses to Oban and Cambelltown stop right outside, as do buses #305 and 306 from Balloch—just be sure to tell the driver where to let you off. From the train station, turn left and follow the main road three-quarters of a mile to the second roundabout. Turn right, continue 1 mi., and turn left at the sign for the hostel; it's a short walk up the hill. Adventure-seekers can ask for the haunted room, while aesthetes can take the one with the stained-glass window. (☎01389 850 226. Self-catering kitchen; be sure to stock up before you get here. Laundry and Internet access. Dorms £15.75-17.75, under 18 £12-12.75. MC/V.) On Loch Lomond's eastern shore, the **SYHA Rowardennan ❶**, the first hostel along the West Highland Way, overlooks the lake and is convenient for exploring the region. From Balloch, take the bus to Balmaha and walk 8 mi. along the well-marked path. (☎01360 870 259. 75 beds. Basic groceries and laundry. Curfew 11:30pm. Open Apr.-Oct. Dorms £13.50-15.50, under 18 £9.50-10.50.) Several B&Bs are on Balloch Rd., close to the TIC. Across from the train station, **Station Cottages ❸**, Balloch Rd., provides a peaceful and luxurious environment. (☎01389 750 759. ₤30-50 per person. MC/V.) The **Lomond Woods Holiday Park ❶**, Old Luss Rd., up Balloch Rd. from the TIC, is a convenient place to park your caravan. Self-catering holiday homes are also available for rent and are popular with groups. (☎01389 755 000. Pool table, table tennis, and laundry. July-Aug. ₤20; Sept.-June ₤15-17. MC/V.)

◙ ▟ **SIGHTS AND OUTDOOR ACTIVITIES.** Stock up on supplies and information at the TIC or Gateway Centre. Ordnance Survey Explorer maps #347 and 364 (₤7.50) chart the south and north of the loch, respectively, while Landranger map #56 (₤6.50) gives a broader view of the entire region. The **West Highland Way** runs 95 mi. from Milngavie to Fort William and skirts Loch Lomond's eastern shore, allowing for long walks. *The West Highland Way* official guide (₤15) includes maps for each section of the route. Rising above all, **Ben Lomond** (3195 ft.) is the southernmost of Scotland's 284 Munros (peaks over 3000 ft.). A popular walk departs from the 19th-century **Balloch Castle and Country Park,** across the River Leven from the train station, where you will find both a visitors center and a park ranger station. (Castle closed to the public.) Outside of **Balmaha,** the strenuous 5 mi. hike up **Conic Hill** rewards hikers with magnificent views of the loch. Visitors can arrange a short boat ride with MacFarlane's mailboat (☎01360 870 214) from Balmaha to the island of **Inchcailloch,** where a 1 mi. walk circles around a nature preserve. The **Glasgow-Loch Lomond Cycleway** runs 20 mi. from the city to the lake along mostly traffic-free paths. At Balloch, where the route ends, **National Cycle Route #7** heads east to the Trossachs; the smaller **West Loch Lomond Cycle Path** follows the lake to the west.

 Loch Lomond Shores is the region's lakeside visitor complex, full of eateries and gift shops designed to ensure that tourists leave with empty wallets. Its centerpiece, **Drumkinnon Tower,** is home to the new **Loch Lomond Aquarium.** (☎01389 721 500. Open daily 10am-5pm. ₤11, concessions ₤10, children ₤8, families ₤33.) Across from the Shores, rent bikes or paddle boats from **Can You Experience,** which also offers guided paddling and cycling tours. (☎01389 602 576; www.canyouexperience.com. Bikes ₤12 per 4hr., ₤17 per day. Canoes and paddle boats ₤12 per 30min., ₤17 per 1hr. MC/V.) **Sweeney's Cruises** provides one of the best introductions to the area with 1-2hr. tours departing from the Balloch TIC on the River Leven and from Loch Lomond Shores in the summer. (☎01389 752 376; www.sweeneyscruises.com. 1hr. tours daily every hr. 10:30am-4:30pm; ₤6.50, children ₤4, families ₤19.50. 2hr. tours daily 1, 3pm; ₤12, children ₤6, families ₤32. 1½hr. evening tours daily 7:30pm; ₤9.50, children ₤5, families ₤26.) Avert your eyes (or don't) from the nudist colony on one of the islands.

THE TROSSACHS   ☎ (0)1877

The lush tranquility of the Lowlands meets the rugged beauty of the Highlands in the Trossachs, Scotland's first national park. The most accessible tract of Scotland's wilderness, the Trossachs are popular for their moderate hikes amid dramatic scenery. Here you will find cycle routes winding through dense forest, the glassy tranquility of Loch Katrine, and Scotland's most manageable peaks.

▛ **TRANSPORTATION.** Accessing the Trossachs is easiest from Stirling. First (☎01324 613 777) **bus** connects the region's main towns, running buses #59 and M59 between Stirling and Callander (45min., 12 per day, ₤3.20) and bus #11 between Stirling and Aberfoyle (45min., 4 per day, ₤2.70). Scottish Citylink runs a bus to Edinburgh and Callander via Stirling (1hr., 1 per day, ₤9.60). Bus service between Aberfoyle and Glasgow requires a change at Balfron. During the summer, the useful Trossachs Trundler (☎01786 442 707) loops between

Callander, Aberfoyle, and the Trossachs Pier at Loch Katrine. One daily trip begins in Stirling and is the only public transportation that connects the Trossachs towns (July-Sept. M-Tu and Th-Su 4 per day; Day Rover £5, concessions £4, children £2; with travel from Stirling £8/6/2.50). **Postbuses** reach some remote areas of the region; find timetables at TICs or call the **Stirling Council Public Transport Helpline** (☎01786 442 707). At the Trossachs Pier on Loch Katrine, rent **bikes** from **Katrinewheelz**. (☎01877 376 316. £10 per ½-day, £15 per day.) Another rental option is **Cycle Hire Callander**, Ancaster Sq., beside the Callender TIC. (☎01877 331 052. £8 per ½-day, £12 per day. Open daily 9am-6pm. MC/V.)

 TRAVELING IN THE TROSSACHS. Public transportation can be nearly impossible in the Trossachs, with ever-changing bus schedules and seasonal closings. Even the word "seasonal" is subjective—some summer routes don't begin until mid-July. Plan your route carefully and ask the TIC which buses are running during your visit.

ACCOMMODATIONS AND FOOD. For lodgings and hiking, the star of the region is ⬛**Trossachs Backpackers ❷**, Invertrossachs Rd. A TV lounge, barbecue, kitchen, and cycle hire await visitors, making it worth the 1 mi. walk from Callander's town center. (☎01877 331 200, bike hire 331 100. 32 beds in 2- to 8-bed rooms. Breakfast included. Laundry. Bikes £8 per ½-day, £13 per day. Dorms £17.50-20. MC/V.) In Callander's center, **White Shutters B&B ❷**, 6 S. Church St., is just steps from the main road. There are no ensuite rooms, but the owners make a delicious hot breakfast. (☎01877 330 442. £18.50 per person, £17.50 for subsequent nights. Cash only.) Limited camping is available at the well-equipped **Trossachs Holiday Park ❶**, 2 mi. south of Aberfoyle on the A81, with a game room and TV lounge that are nicer than those at most hostels. (☎01877 382 614; www.trossachsholidays.co.uk. Toilets, showers, laundry, and bike rental. Open Mar.-Oct. £14-20 per person. AmEx/MC/V.)

Co-op grocery stores are easily found in both Callander and Aberfoyle, as well are number of bakeries and eateries whose delicious aromas fill the town centers. **Munchy's Restaurant ❷**, Main St., Callander, has wholesome, home-cooked vittles like haddock and chips. (☎01877 331 090. Entrees £3.20-6.75.Open in summer M and W-Sa 10:30am-7pm, Su noon-7pm. Cash only.) On the same street, **Ciro's Italian Restaurant ❷**, 114 Main St., serves affordable entrees in a classy atmosphere. (☎01877 331 070. Entrees £5.95-8.50. Open M-Tu and Th-F 10am-5pm, Sa-Su 11am-5pm. MC/V.)

OUTDOOR ACTIVITIES. Get the scenic layout of the area by taking a drive or a ride on the Trossachs Trundler down the Trossachs Trail. Really just the A821, the road offers fantastic views of the majestic **Loch Katrine**, the setting of Sir Walter Scott's *The Lady of the Lake*. The popular **Steamship Sir Walter Scott** cruises Loch Katrine from Trossachs Pier, stopping at Stronachlachar on the northwest bank in the mornings. (☎01877 332 002. From mid-June to mid-Sept. at 10:30am, 1:30, 3pm; call ahead to check sailing times and for advance bookings. £8, concessions £7, children £6.) For a good daytrip, take the ferry to Stronachlachar and then walk or ride back along the 14 mi. wooded shore road to the pier. Above the loch hulks **Ben A'an** (1187 ft.), a reasonable 2.5 mi. ascent beginning from a car park 1 mi. down the A821.

Set beside the quiet River Teith, the town of **Callander** makes a good base for exploring the Trossachs and lies close to outdoor attractions. Dominating the horizon, **Ben Ledi** (2883 ft.) is a manageable trek. A 6 mi. trail up the mountain begins just north of town along the A84. A number of walks depart from Callander itself: **The Crags** (6½ mi.) heads up through the woods to the ridge above town, while the popular walk to **Bracklinn Falls** (5 mi.) wanders along a picturesque glen. In Callander, cyclists can join **The Lowland Highland Trail,** a lovely stretch running north to Strathyre along an old railway line. Passing through forest and beside Loch Lubnaig, a sidetrack from the route runs to **Balquhidder,** where the Scottish folk hero Rob Roy and his family are buried. The renegade's surname, MacGregor, was outlawed in Scotland, but his grave is marked by a stone reading, "MacGregor Despite Them." Callander's **Rob Roy and Trossachs Visitor Centre,** Main St., is a combined TIC and exhibit on the 17th-century local hero. Pick up Ordnance Survey maps, Explorer #378 (£8), or Landranger #57 (£7). Walkers will find the *Callander Walks and Fort Trails* pamphlet (£2) useful, and cyclists can consult *Rides Around The Trossachs.* (☎01877 330 342. Open daily July-Aug. 10am-6pm; Sept.-Oct. and Mar.-June 10am-5pm; Nov.-Feb. 10am-4pm. Exhibit £3.60, concessions and children £2.40, families £9.60.)

Aberfoyle is another springboard into the surrounding wilderness. The **Queen Elizabeth Forest Park** covers a vast stretch of territory from the shore of Loch Lomond to the slopes of the Strathyre Mountains, with Aberfoyle at its center. For more information on trails, visit the Trossachs Discovery Centre, a TIC in town. (☎01877 382 352. Open July-Aug. daily 9:30am-6pm; Sept.-Oct. and Apr.-June daily 10am-5pm.) Aberfoyle is also the self-proclaimed "Faerie Capital of Scotland," thanks to the Reverend Robert Kirk, who wrote *The Secret Commonwealth* in 1691, claiming to expose the world of elves and pixies. Legend has it that members of the spirit world took revenge on the reverend for revealing their secrets by trapping him inside a giant pine tree on top of **Doon Hill.** A 2.5 mi. walk from town leads to the top of the hill, where the ancient tree still stands (faerie sightings have been scarce since Kirk's disappearance).

NORTH SEA COAST

ST. ANDREWS   ☎ (0)1334

St. Andrews is the unquestioned homeland of golf. The game's rules were formally established here in 1764, and its courses draw giddy amateurs from around the world as well as pros seeking British Open acclaim. Although plaid pants and shiny golf shoes are common around town, St. Andrews is full of attractions for those whose idea of the game is limited to putters and windmills. The town is home to Scotland's oldest university, a number of medieval sights, and the highest concentration of pubs in the UK.

▐ TRANSPORTATION

Drivers can take the A917 (Fife Coastal Tourist Route) or the faster M90 to A91 to Edinburgh. All **trains** (☎08457 484 950) stop 5 mi. away in Leuchars (LU-cars). Most trains from Leuchars travel to Edinburgh (1hr., 1-2 per hr., £10.60) or Perth (1hr., every hr., £9.10), a transfer point for trains to Aberdeen, Inverness, and London. From Leuchars, **buses** #94, 96, and 99 run to St. Andrews (5 per hr. 6am-10:30pm, £2). The **bus station** (☎01334 474 238) is on City Rd. Scottish Citylink (☎08705 505 050) bus #X60 runs to Edinburgh (2hr., M-Sa 1-2 per hr., £7); the X24 runs to Glasgow (2hr., M-Sa every hr., £7). Buses run reduced service in the evenings and on Sundays. Call Traveline (☎08712 002 233) for info.

⚡ 🛈 ORIENTATION AND PRACTICAL INFORMATION

The three main streets—**North Street, Market Street,** and **South Street**—run nearly parallel to each other, terminating by the cathedral at the town's east end.

Tourist Information Centre: 70 Market St. (☎01334 472 021). Ask for the free *St. Andrews Town Map and Guide* and the extremely useful *Essential Guide to Fife.* Books accommodations for £4 plus a 10% deposit. **Bureau de change.** Open July-Sept. M-Sa 9:15am-7pm, Su 10am-5pm; Oct.-Mar. M-Sa 10:15am-5pm; Apr.-June M-Sa 9:30am-5:30pm, Su 11am-4pm.

Banks: Royal Bank of Scotland, 113-115 South St. (☎01334 472 181). **Bureau de change.** Open M-Tu and Th-F 9:15am-4:45pm, W 9:45am-4:45pm.

Library: St. Andrews Library (☎01334 659 378). Free Internet with free library membership. Open M and F-Su 9:30am-5pm, Tu-Th 9:30am-7pm.

Police: 100 North St. (☎08456 005 700).

Hospital: St. Andrews Memorial, Abbey Walk (☎01334 472 327), southeast of town. 24hr. care also available at the **Health Centre,** 68 Pipeland Rd. (☎01334 476 840).

Internet Access: Free with library membership at **St. Andrews Library** (above) and at **Costa Coffee,** 83 Market St. Open M-F 7am-7pm, Sa 8am-6pm, Su 9am-6pm.

Post Office: 90-92 South St. Open M-Sa 9am-5:30pm. **Postcode:** KY16 9QD.

🏠 ACCOMMODATIONS

St. Andrews makes a plausible daytrip from Edinburgh and is also an ideal base for visiting the Fife Seaside. The town has only one year-round hostel but is packed with B&Bs; over 20 separate establishments line **Murray Park** and **Murray Place** alone. Prices are often lower during term time, from October to May.

St. Andrews Tourist Hostel, St. Mary's Pl. (☎01334 479 911), above the Grill House restaurant. From the bus station, turn right on City Rd., then turn left on St. Mary's Pl. Colorful, spacious rooms make for a comfortable place to stay between rounds. Laundry £6. Internet £1 per 30min. Free Wi-Fi. Golf club rental £5 per day. Reception 8am-3pm and 6-10pm. Dorms £12-16. MC/V. ●

SYHA St. Andrews, Buchanan Gardens (☎01334 476 726), in the David Russell Apartments. From City Rd., turn right onto Argyle St., continue on Hepburn Gardens, and take the right fork at Buchanan Gardens. New hostel in university housing 20min. walk from town center. Upscale, hotel-style ensuite rooms with TVs suit the high prices. Open from mid-July to Sept. Singles £26; doubles £39. MC/V. ❸

Brownlees, 7 Murray Pl. (☎01334 473 868; www.brownlees.co.uk). A 19th-century Victorian house. Huge beds and TV. Plaid decor in 5 ensuite rooms. Full Scottish breakfast included. £36-48 per person. MC/V. ❹

Cameron House, 11 Murray Park (☎01334 472 306). Soft crimson-hued decor and golf enthusiast owners. Walk out the front door for a sweeping view of the ocean. TVs in rooms. Free Wi-Fi. £35-40 per person. MC/V. ❹

🍴 FOOD

Sandwich shops, juice bars, and ethnic eateries are sprinkled along the three main streets. With a variety of high-end cuisine and plenty of late-night takeaways, you won't go hungry. **Tesco** supermarket is at 138-140 Market St. (☎08456 779 631. Open M-Sa 7:30am-midnight, Su 10am-10pm.)

Northpoint, 24 North St. (☎01334 473 997). The consummate student cafe. Hardwood tables and a steady stream of intellectual conversation complement soups (from

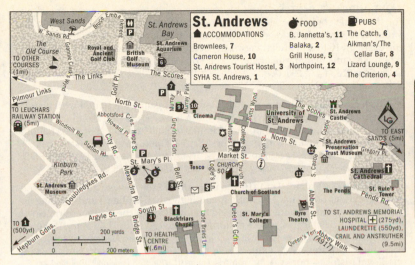

St. Andrews

FOOD | **PUBS**

ACCOMMODATIONS
Brownlees, **7**
Cameron House, **10**
St. Andrews Tourist Hostel, **3**
SYHA St. Andrews, **1**

B. Jannetta's, **11**
Balaka, **2**
Grill House, **5**
Northpoint, **12**

The Catch, **6**
Aikman's/The
Cellar Bar, **8**
Lizard Lounge, **9**
The Criterion, **4**

£1.80) and sandwiches (from £4). Stacks of fluffy pancakes with maple syrup, bacon, or banana and toffee make a tasty snack any time of day. Happy hour 8-10am, when all hot beverages are £1. Open daily 8am-4:30pm. MC/V. ❶

Balaka, 3 Alexandra Pl. (☎01334 474 825), on the lower level. This house of incredible South Asian cuisine pleases everyone from the university debate team to celebrities and royals, including Sean Connery and the king of Malaysia. Romantic tables and fantastic chicken tikka masala (£11). Open M-Th noon-3pm and 5pm-12:30am, F-Sa noon-1am, Su 5pm-12:30am. AmEx/MC/V. ❸

B. Jannetta's, 31 South St. (☎01334 473 285). 52 flavors of ice cream, frozen yogurt, and sorbet made from local ingredients. Tourists shoulder up alongside hungry locals to sample a 100-year-old St. Andrews institution. Outdoor seating available. Open M-Sa 9am-9:30pm, Su 1-4pm. MC/V. ❶

Grill House Restaurant, St. Mary's Pl. (☎01334 470 500), between Alexandra Pl. and Bell St. Conveniently situated downstairs from the St. Andrews Tourist Hostel. Cheerful, bright dining area and a large Mexican-inspired menu. 2-course dinner with drink daily 5-6:30pm (£11). AmEx/MC/V. ❸

👁 SIGHTS

SAINT ANDREWS CATHEDRAL. The haunting, romantic ruin of what was Scotland's largest building is still the heart and soul of St. Andrews, especially since its stones make up most of the facades along South St. The old cemetery has overtaken the inside, so the ruins now enclose a field of graves. The stones are beautiful in dim light, so dawn and dusk are the best times to see the cathedral and contemplate the religious turmoil leading to its destruction. The square **Saint Rule's Tower** still stands above the site where the Greek monk St. Rule buried the relics of St. Andrew. Climb the steep stairs in the tower for spectacular views of the sea and countryside. The **Saint Andrews Cathedral Museum** houses ancient Pictish carvings and modern tombs. (☎01334 472 563. Open daily Apr.-Sept. 9:30am-5:30pm; Oct.-Mar. 9:30am-4:30pm. Cathedral free. Museum and tower £4.20, concessions £3.20, children £2.10. Joint ticket with castle £7.20, concessions £5.20, children £3.60.)

CENTRAL SCOTLAND

SAINT ANDREWS CASTLE. The 14th century castle features siege tunnels (not for the claustrophobic) and bottle-shaped dungeons (not for anyone). The walls were designed to keep out religious heretics, who nevertheless stormed the castle in 1546. For stellar views, descend the path south of the castle fence, where seagulls nest in the crags; watch your step. *(On the water at the end of North Castle St. ☎01334 477 196. Open daily Apr.-Sept. 9:30am-5:30pm; Oct.-Mar. 9:30am-4:30pm. Tours leave daily 11:30am, 3:30pm. £5.20, concessions £4.20, children £2.60.)*

BRITISH GOLF MUSEUM. A huge display of golf gear punctuated with historical artifacts and mannequins, this collection holds some of the earliest spoons (clubs) and feathers (balls). Modern tributes include the sweat-stained hat that Tiger Woods wore while winning his first British Open. *(Bruce Embankment. ☎01334 460 046. Open Apr.-Oct. M-Sa 9:30am-5:30pm, Su 10am-5pm; Nov.-Mar. daily 10am-4pm. £5.50, concessions £4.80. Combined museum ticket and tour of Old Course £5.)*

OTHER SIGHTS. Founded in 1410, the **University of Saint Andrews** maintains a well-heeled student body (until recently including Prince William) and a strong liberal arts program. Meander into placid quads through the entrances on North St., including **Saint Mary's,** where a thorn tree planted in 1563 by Mary, Queen of Scots, still grows. *(Between North St. and The Scores.)* The **Saint Andrews Museum,** with its main "St. Andrews A-Z" exhibit, keeps its focus off golf and on fairly obscure medieval history—not even "g" stands for golf. *(Kinburn Park, down Doubledykes Rd. ☎01334 659 380. Open daily Apr.-Sept. 10am-5pm; Oct.-Mar. 10:30am-4pm. Free.)* An olde chemist's shoppe and painful-looking dentistry tools are among artifacts in the tiny **Saint Andrews Preservation Trust Museum.** *(North St. ☎01334 477 629. Open daily May-Sept. 2-5pm. Donations welcome.)* The **Saint Andrews Aquarium** houses over 100 species of wildlife and overlooks the ocean where their relatives swim free. *(The Scores. ☎01334 474 786. Open in summer daily 10am-5:30pm; call for winter hours. Seal feeding noon, 3pm. £6.80, concessions £5.50.)* From Shakespeare to off-Broadway hits, **Byre Theatre** puts on plays year-round. *(Abbey St. ☎01334 475 000; www.byretheatre. com. Ticket prices vary, usually £12.50, concessions £8.50. Student discounts available.)*

🎱 GOLF

If you love golf, play golf, or think that you might ever want to play golf, this is your town. It was such a popular pastime in St. Andrews that Scotland's rulers outlawed the sport three times just to get people off the links. At the northwest edge of town, the **Old Course** stretches along the **West Sands,** a beach as well manicured as the greens. Mary, Queen of Scots, supposedly played here just days after her husband was murdered. Nonmembers must present a handicap certificate or letter of introduction from a golf club. Book at least a year or two in advance, enter your name into a near-impossible lottery by 2pm the day before you hope to play, or get in line before dawn by the caddie master's hut as a single. *(☎01334 466 666; www.standrews.org.uk. Apr.-Oct. £90-130 per round; Nov.-Mar. £64.)* Tee times are easier to obtain at the less revered but still excellent **New, Jubilee, Eden,** and **Strathtyrum** courses. *(£25-65 per round.)* The budget option is the nine-hole **Balgove Course.** *(£12 per round.)*

🍺 PUBS

After a long day of golf, it's the 19th hole that's most important, and St. Andrews has plenty of options to choose from.

Aikman's/The Cellar Bar, 32 Bell St. *(☎01334 477 425; www.aikmans.co.uk or www. cellarbar.co.uk).* Dark, well-worn, and comfortable. Techno beats pound upstairs, while the basement fills with specialty continental beer and good company; town-gown relations couldn't be better. Open M-Sa 11am-1am, Su noon-1am.

The Lizard Lounge, 127 North St. (☎01334 473 387), in the basement of the Oak Rooms Bar. A good place to sink into the oversized furniture, down a pint (£3), and while away an afternoon with friends. Open M-Tu and Su 6pm-midnight, W-Sa 6pm-1am.

The Criterion, 99 South St. (☎01334 474 543). Tiny neighborhood pub with comfortable leather chairs and booths. Indulge in malt whiskies, steak pies (£4), and all things Scottish. Open M-W and Su 8am-midnight, Th-Sa 8am-1am. Cash only.

The Catch (☎01334 477 470), tucked beside the St. Andrews Aquarium. Arguably the best location in town. The outdoor patio is a stone's throw from waves lapping at the shore. Open M-W and Su 5pm-midnight, Th-Sa 5pm-1am.

⚡ DAYTRIP FROM ST. ANDREWS: FIFE SEASIDE

"A fringe of gold on a beggar's mantle" is how James II of Scotland described these burghs, built among the sheltered bays of the Kingdom of Fife. The tidy gardens and gabled roofs of fishing villages stretch from St. Andrews to Edinburgh. The coastal road A917 (Fife Coastal Tourist Route) links the small villages, each with its own harbor attractions. Non-drivers need not worry: take a bumpy ride on the double-decker Stagecoach #95 from St. Andrews to Leven for the full coastline experience. The **Fife Coastal Walk** runs along the shore and allows for walking, hiking, and biking within and between towns.

CRAIL. The oldest of Fife's villages, Crail developed around a 12th-century castle and presents a maze of streets and stone cottages. Crail's **Tourist Information Centre,** 62-64 Marketgate, adjoins a small local history museum. (☎01333 450 869. Open Apr.-Sept. M-Sa 10am-1pm and 2-5pm, Su 2-5pm.) Guided historical walks leave from the museum. (1-2hr.; July-Aug. Su 2:30pm; £2, children £1.)

ANSTRUTHER. The largest of the seaside towns, Anstruther lies 5 mi. west of Crail on the A917 and 9 mi. southeast of St. Andrews on the B9131. The excellent **Scottish Fisheries Museum,** Shore St., uses artifacts to tell the 1000-year-long story of fishing and smuggling in Fife. (☎01333 310 628. Open Apr.-Sept. M-Sa 10am-5:30pm, Su 11am-5pm; Oct.-Mar. M-Sa 10am-4:30pm, Su noon-4:30pm. Last entry 1hr. before close. £5, concessions £4.) Six miles off the coast, the stunning mile-long **Isle of May Nature Reserve** is home to a large population of puffins, kittiwakes, razorbills, guillemots, shags, seals, and, sometimes, dolphins and whales. Inland from the towering cliffs stand the ruins of Scotland's first lighthouse and the haunted 12th-century **Saint Adrian's Chapel,** named after a monk murdered here by the Danes in AD 875. From June to August, weather and tide permitting, the *May Princess* sails from Anstruther to the isle. (☎01333 310 103; www.isleofmayferry.com. 5hr. round-trip, including time ashore. Runs May-Sept. £17, concessions £15, children £8. Cash only.) Call ahead for times or check with Anstruther's **Tourist Information Centre,** beside the museum. (☎01333 311 073. Open Apr.-Sept. M-Sa 10am-5pm, Su 11am-4pm; Oct. M-Sa 10am-4pm, Su 11am-4pm.) On the way back from the bay and lighthouse, the **Anstruther Fish Bar and Restaurant ❷,** 44 Shore St., has repeatedly won the award for Scotland's best fish and chips (£6.30, takeaway £4.10). To avoid a long queue, eat in the restaurant for faster service or do as the locals do and try one of the less celebrated but equally tasty chippies along the waterfront. Watch out for crafty seagulls, who will conspire to steal your food. (☎01333 310 518. Open daily 11:30am-10pm. MC/V.)

SECRET BUNKER. In the 1950s, the British government built a subterranean shelter halfway between Anstruther and St. Andrews (off the A917) to house British leaders in case of a nuclear war. Over 20,000 sq. ft. of strategy rooms, sensory equipment, and weapons-launching systems lie 100 ft. below a Scottish farmhouse. Locals claimed knowledge of the bunker long before the "secret" broke in 1993. Take bus #61 Anstruther-St. Andrews, ask to get off near the Bunker, walk 1 mi. east on B940, then follow a winding road for half a mile. (☎01333 310 301; www.secretbunker.co.uk. Open Apr.-Oct. daily 10am-5pm. Free Internet access. £7.50, concessions £6. Group discounts available.)

ELIE. On sunny summer days, every person in Elie is either wearing a bathing suit, eating ice cream, riding a bike, or managing all three at once. The town boasts an ancient granary on its rebuilt 15th-century pier. The 18th-century **Lady's Tower** is worth the short walk. Lady Janet Anstruther built a stone changing room on the cliffs here and sent a bell-ringing servant to warn villagers to keep away when she was swimming, lest some commoner spot her skinny-dipping. Elie's sweeping beachfront is an ideal spot for watersports, walks, and pleasant, if chilly, swims. The picturesque **Ruby Bay,** named for the garnets occasionally found on its red-tinted sands, is a great place to turn yourself into a floating ice cube. **Elie Watersports,** down Stenton Row, at the end of The Toft, gives instruction on watersports. (☎01333 330 962; www. eliewatersports.com. Bikes £8 per ½-day, £12 per day, £35 per week. Wetsuits £10 per day. Windsurfers, canoes, dinghies, and paddle boats £18-25 per hr.; windsurfing and sailing lessons from £25 per hr. Waterskiing £20, water tube ride £8, banana boat rides £8.)

ARBROATH   ☎(0)1241

Once a booming fishing port, Arbroath now attracts tourists with its picturesque harbor and the magnificent ■**Arbroath Abbey,** Abbey St., from which followers of Robert the Bruce issued a famous Scottish independence edict in 1320. Today, after several fires and raids, the abbey is a ruin of its former self, although the impressive vaulted chambers of the abbot's house remain largely intact. The visitors center has an audio-visual walkthrough of the abbey's history. (☎01241 878 756. Open daily May-Sept. 9:30am-5:30pm; Oct.-Apr. 9:30am-4:30pm. Wheelchair-accessible. Last entry 30min. before closing. £4.70.)

An abundance of pricey B&Bs welcomes summertime visitors. The elegant velvet curtains of **Blairdene Guest House ❸,** 216 High St., shut out the commotion of the main shopping area below. (☎01241 872 872 380; www.blairdene.co.uk. £30-35 per person. Cash only.) The **Towerbank Guest House ❸,** 9 James St. just off High St., provides ensuite rooms with TVs and a vegetarian breakfast option next door to the abbey. (☎01241 431 343. £30 per person. MC/V.)

Arbroath's maritime heritage lives on in the form of the delectable smoked haddock—take a deep breath anywhere near the waterfront to get a fishy whiff of the smokehouses. Enjoy an Arbroath smokie (as the haddock is known), a pint, and a view of the waterfront at the family-friendly **Old Brewhouse ❷,** at Danger Point. The pub's seafood entrees (£8-13) are fresh from the fish market. (☎01241 879 945. Open M-Sa 11am-9pm, Su noon-9pm. MC/V.) **Sugar & Spice ❷,** 9-13 High St., a Victorian-style tearoom complete with waitresses in lacy aprons, serves delectable sandwiches (£6-9), pastries, and floral beverages. (☎01241 437 500. Open M-Sa 10am-4pm, Su noon-4pm. MC/V.) Buy groceries from the **Co-op** in the Abbeygate Shopping Centre, High St. (☎01241 870 588. Open M-F 8am-8pm, Sa 8am-7pm, Su 9am-6pm.)

Trains go to nearby Dundee (20min., every 30min., £4.10), Edinburgh (1½hr., every hr., £22.60), and Aberdeen (1hr., every 30min.). Stagecoach and Citylink **buses** run to Dundee (40min., every 30min., £4). The **Tourist Information Centre** is on Fish Market Quay. From the bus or train station, walk south until reaching the harbor. (☎01241 872 609. Open June-Sept. M-Sa 9:30am-5:30pm, Su 10am-4pm; Oct.-May M-Sa 10:30am-4pm.) Other services include: several **banks**

on Commerce St.; free **Internet** access at the **library,** on the corner of Academy St. and Hill Terr. (☎01241 872 248; open M and W 9:30am-8pm, Tu 10am-6pm, Th 9:30am-6pm; F-Sa 9:30am-5pm); **Boots** pharmacy, 142-146 High St. (☎01241 870 451; open M-Sa 9am-5:30pm); and a **post office** in the Abbeygate Shopping Centre on High St. (open M-Sa 9am-5:30pm). **Postcode:** DD11 1HY.

PERTH AND KINROSS

PERTH   ☎(0)1738

Scotland's capital until 1452, today's Perth is a transportation and shopping hub with a residential feel. Situated on the River Tay, the city offers pleasant city walks, historical sights, and hikes in nearby Kinnoull Hill Wood.

☐ TRANSPORTATION. The **train station** is on Leonard St. (Ticket office open M-F 6:45am-7:30pm, Sa 7:15am-7:15pm, Su 8:15am-7:15pm.) Trains (☎08457 484 950) go to: Aberdeen (1hr., every hr., £25.50); Edinburgh (1hr., 7 per day, £11.60); Glasgow (1hr., every hr., £11.60); Inverness (2hr., 7 per day, £19.50). The **bus station** is a block away on Leonard St. (Ticket office open M-F 7:45am-5:30pm, Sa 8am-1:30pm.) Scottish Citylink (☎08705 505 050) buses go to: Aberdeen (2hr., 8 per day, £18.30); Dundee (35min., every hr., £5.40); Edinburgh (1hr., every hr., £8.50); Glasgow (1hr., every hr., £8.70); Inverness (2hr., every 2hr., £16.40); Pitlochry (40min., every 2hr., £7.60).

🏠 PRACTICAL INFORMATION. The **Tourist Information Centre,** W. Mill St., Lower City Mills, books local rooms for £4 plus a 10% deposit. From either station, turn right on Leonard St., bear right onto County Pl., and take a left on S. Methven St. (☎01738 450 600; www.perthshire.co.uk. Open July-Aug. M-Sa 9:30am-6pm, Su 10:30am-4pm; Sept.-Oct. and Apr.-June M-Sa 9:30am-4:30pm, Su 11am-3pm; Nov.-Mar. M-Sa 10am-4pm.) Other services include: free **Internet** access at the **library,** York Pl., with free membership (☎01738 444 949; open M, W, F 9:30am-5pm, Tu and Th 9:30am-8pm, Sa 9:30am-4pm); **Fair City** launderette, 44 N. Methven St. (☎01738 631 653; open M-F 8:30am-5:30pm, Sa 9am-5pm); **police,** Barrack St. (☎01738 621 141); **Superdrug** pharmacy, 100 High St. (☎01738 639 746; open M-Sa 8:30am-5:30pm, Su 1:30-4:30pm); **Perth Royal Infirmary,** Taymount Terr. (☎01738 623 311); and the **post office,** 109 South St. (☎01738 624 413. Open M and W-Sa 9am-5:30pm, Tu 9:30am-5:30pm.) **Postcode:** PH2 8AF.

🏠🍴 ACCOMMODATIONS AND FOOD. Perth has slim pickings for the budget traveler. Plenty of B&Bs line **Glasgow Road,** a 10min. walk from the city center, and **Pitcullen Crescent,** across the river. **Hazeldene Guest House ❸,** Strathmore St., is chock-full of amenities, including a flatscreen TV and Wi-Fi. (☎01738 623 550; www.hazeldeneguesthouse.com. £30 per person. MC/V.) **Dunallan House ❹,** 10 Pitcullen Crescent, has ensuite rooms with TV and old-fashioned but charming lacy decor. (☎01738 622 551; www.dunallan.co.uk. Free Wi-Fi. £30 per person. AmEx/MC/V.) **Heidl Guest House,** 43 York Pl., is located less than a 5min. walk from the train and bus stations. The owner also offers massages and other alternative physical therapies. (☎01738 635 031; www.guesthouse-perth.co.uk. £25-27 per person. MC/V.) Those on a tighter budget can camp at **Scone Camping and Caravanning ❶,** 4 mi. from the city center, next to the racetrack. Head to Scone Palace and then follow signs for the racetrack or take bus #58 to Old Scone. (☎01738 552 323. Laundry. £4-6 per tent. MC/V.)

An enormous **Morrison's** supermarket is located on Caledonian Rd. (☎01738 442 422. Open M-W and Sa 8am-8pm, Th-F 8am-9pm, Su 9am-8pm.) Restaurants crowd the city's main streets. **Scaramouche ❶**, 103 South St., is worn in and homey, serving up cheap portions of classic pub grub. Grab an afternoon pint or stay into the evening for dancing. (☎01738 637 479. Open M-W noon-11pm, Th-Sa noon-12:30am, Su 12:30-11pm. Kitchen open daily noon-8pm. MC/V.) Tucked behind the vintage facade of Perth Theatre, **Redrooms ❷**, 185 High St., satisfies a theatergoing crowd with well-made sandwiches and panini (£5). Glass chandeliers hanging over sleek black booths add a glamorous touch. (☎01738 472 709; www.horsecross.co.uk. Entrees around £7. Open M-Sa 10am-5pm, performance days 10am-8:30pm. MC/V.)

SIGHTS AND HIKING. Try on 17th-century clothing at the **Perth Museum and Art Gallery,** at the intersection of Tay St. and Perth Bridge. The old, stately museum chronicles city life and hosts exhibits by local artists. (☎01738 632 488. Open M-Sa 10am-5pm. Free.) In 1559, John Knox delivered a fiery sermon from the pulpit of **Saint John's Kirk,** on St. John's Pl., sparking the Scottish Reformation. (☎01738 638 482. Open for Su services 9:30, 11am. Open to visitors daily 10am-4pm.) **The Perth Theatre,** 185 High St., hosts shows and concerts year-round. (☎01738 472 700; www.horsecross.co.uk. Box office open M-Sa 10am-6pm, performance days 10am-8pm.) The 16th-century home of the earls of Kinnoull, **Balhousie Castle,** off Hay St., north of the city, now functions as a regimental headquarters and houses the **Black Watch Regimental Museum.** The museum traces the history of Scottish military involvement in several wars and includes many memorials to former officers. (☎01313 108 530. Open May-Sept. M-Sa 10am-4:30pm; Oct.-Apr. M-F 10am-3:30pm. Free.)

A 20min. walk across the **Perth Bridge** leads to **Kinnoull Hill Woodland Park** and its four nature walks, all of which finish at a magnificent summit with views of the countryside and river. Beginners can try the **Tower Walk,** while experienced hikers might choose the **Nature Walk,** which winds through the thick of the forest. The Kinnoull Hill bus runs up the hill from South St. (every hr., £1). Across the Queen's Bridge, near the Fergusson Gallery, the 1 mi. **Perth Sculpture Trail** begins in the Rodney Gardens and surveys 24 pieces of modern art along the river. **Bell's Cherrybank Gardens** provide a beautifully sculpted place to stroll amid over 700 types of heather. Take bus #7 from South St. (every 20min.) or walk 20min. uphill along Glasgow Rd. (☎01738 472 818; www.thecalyx.co.uk. Open Mar.-Oct. M-Sa 10am-5pm, Su noon-5pm; Nov.-Dec. M-Sa 10am-4pm, Su noon-4pm. £3.75, concessions £3.40, children £2.50, under 12 free.)

DAYTRIP FROM PERTH: SCONE PALACE. Scone (SKOON) Palace, 3 mi. northeast of Perth on the A93, is still occupied by the Earl of Mansfield and his family. The regal, extravagantly decorated halls are lined with an impressive collection of china, portraits, ivories, and furniture as well as the earl of Mansfield's spectacular orchid collection. Macbeth, Robert the Bruce, and Charles II were crowned at Moot Hill on the humble Stone of Scone, now on display in Edinburgh Castle. Every year in late July, the **Highlander Challenge World Championship** resurrects the martial traditions of the ancient Scots as 16 nationally ranked athletes from all over the world compete in jousting, wrestling, and hammer-throwing. Peacocks roam the grounds, which include the challenging **Murray Star Maze,** with a fountain at its center. The attached cafe makes a mean scone for £1.60. *(Directly off the A94. Take bus #3 or 58 from South St. (every hr., £1.30) and tell the driver where you're going. ☎01738 552 300; www.scone-palace.co.uk. Open Apr.-Oct. daily 9:30am-5:30pm. £8, concessions £7, under 16 £5. Grounds without palace £4.50/4/3.)*

DUNKELD AND BIRNAM ☎(0)1350

The towns of Dunkeld (dun-KELD) and Birnam, separated by a small bridge over the River Tay, together represent the essence of the Scottish small town. The region is known for the towering forests that line the river, and both towns boast famous past residents, from the 14th-century supervillain Wolf of Badenoch to the cuddly children's author Beatrix Potter. Enjoy a pint at some of the most musical pubs in Scotland or explore the woods on one of a dozen local walks.

TRANSPORTATION. The unstaffed train station in Birnam is on the Edinburgh-Inverness line. **Trains** (☎08457 484 950) run to: Edinburgh (2hr., 7 per day, £12.20); Glasgow (2hr., 7 per day, £12.20); Inverness (1hr., 8 per day, £20.40); Perth (20min., 7 per day, £5.80). Scottish Citylink **buses** (☎08705 505 050) leave the Birnam House Hotel to: Edinburgh (1hr., 5 per day, £13); Glasgow (2hr., 5 per day, £13); Inverness (2hr., 5 per day, £15); Perth (20min., 5 per day, £7.40); Pitlochry (20min., 5 per day, £7.10). Grab the *Highland Perthshire and Stanley Area Local Public Transportation Guide.*

PRACTICAL INFORMATION. Nearly all public transportation arrives in Birnam (a popular Victorian vacation spot), but most tourist amenities are in more historic Dunkeld. The Dunkeld **Tourist Information Centre,** in the town center, 1 mi. from the train station, books beds for £4 plus a 10% deposit. (☎01350 727 688. Open July-Aug. M-Sa 9am-5:30pm, Su 10:30am-4pm; Sept.-Oct. and Apr.-June M-Sa 10am-4pm, Su 10:30am-3:30pm; Nov.-Mar. F-Su 11am-4pm.) Other services include: a **Bank of Scotland,** High St. (☎01350 727 415; open M-W and F 9:15am-12:30pm and 1:30-4:30pm; Th 9:15am-12:30pm); free **Internet** access at the **Birnam Library,** Station Rd., in the Birnam Institute (☎01350 727 971; reserve a slot; open M 6-8pm, W 2-4pm and 6-8pm, F-Sa 10am-noon); **Davidson's Chemists,** 1 Bridge St. (☎01350 727 210; open M-F 9am-1pm and 2-5:30pm, Sa 9am-1pm and 2-5pm); and the **post office,** Bridge St. (☎01350 727 257; open M-W and F 9am-1pm and 2-5:30pm, Th 9am-1pm, Sa 9am-12:30pm). **Postcode:** PH8 0AH.

ACCOMMODATIONS AND FOOD. The closest hostel is 4 mi. away from Dunkeld, but quiet B&Bs are easy to find throughout the two towns—the TIC has a handy list outside its office. The cozy **Wester Caputh Hostel ❷** has a nice countryside

ON THE MENU

HAGGIS FOR THE FAINT OF HEART

Perhaps the best known of Scotland's national delicacies, haggis can look and sound none too appetizing in spite of its renown. Traditional recipes vary, but all require that assorted organs of a sheep be minced and spiced, then stuffed in the animal's stomach and boiled for several hours. The end result is a dark, steaming mash that can intimidate even the most adventurous epicures. If you have a difficult time stomaching the thought of boiled stomach but still want to engage in a national tradition, here are a few alternative ways of enjoying haggis:

Battered and deep-fried in your local pub. Deep-frying makes everything better, so why not sheep liver in sheep stomach?

Hurled (but not vomited). Haggis-hurling is a real sport, and the truly talented can enter the world championships, held annually. The present world record was set in 1984 by Alan Pettigrew, who threw a haggis over 180 ft.

On a bun. Just think of it as a fancy Scottish hamburger.

Hunted down. Some (primarily American) visitors to Scotland believe that a haggis is a small, furry, and notoriously shy creature whose uneven legs are perfect for darting up and down mountains. Laboring under this impression, they have been known to set out on missions to capture this elusive animal, often assisted by indulging and amused Scottish guides.

location, a garden with roses and raspberries, and instruments adorning the walls. From Dunkeld, head east on the A984, turn right toward Murthly/Stanley, and find the hostel on the left, past a churchyard and a raspberry field. (☎01738 710 449. Bikes £6-10 per day. Dorms £15. Cash only.)

The **Co-op** supermarket, 13 Bridge St., is in Dunkeld. (Open M-Sa 8am-9pm, Su 9am-6pm.) Don't miss out on a "session" (a wee dram of something local and a song) at the **Taybank Hotel pub ❷**, where visitors snack on "stovies" (potatoes mashed with meat or veggies; £5.40) while enjoying casual gatherings of musicians. (☎01350 727 340. Open M-Th 11am-11pm, F-Sa 11am-midnight, Su noon-11pm. MC/V.) For lunch, head to the **Palmerston's Coffee House and Bistro ❶**, 20 Atholl St., for freshly prepared contemporary Scottish cuisine (baguette with poached Orkney salmon £4.75) or have your tea with a freshly made scone for £1.70. (☎01350 727 231. Open M-Sa 10am-4:15pm, Su 11am-4:15pm. Cash only.)

🌀 ⚠ SIGHTS AND OUTDOOR ACTIVITIES. Carefully maintained 18th-century houses line the way to the towns' main attraction, **🔲Dunkeld Cathedral,** High St., just steps from the TIC. A peaceful spot on the grand banks of the River Tay, the cathedral still holds services and events. Its oldest sections are postcardworthy ruins. The notorious Alexander Stewart (known as the Wolf of Badenoch) rests inside, despite having been excommunicated after he burned down Elgin Cathedral in a fit of rage in 1390. (☎01350 727 614. Open Apr.-Sept. M-Sa 9:30am-6:30pm, Su 2-6:30pm; Oct.-Mar. M-Sa 9:30am-4pm, Su 2-4pm. Free.) Beatrix Potter spent most of her childhood holidays in Birnam; walk among sculptures of her most beloved characters at the **Beatrix Potter Garden** at the **Birnam Institute.** (☎01350 727 674; www.birnaminstitute.com. Open daily Apr.-Sept. 10am-5pm; Oct.-Mar. 10am-4:30pm. Free.)

Pick up *Dunkeld & Birnam Walks* (£1) at the TIC for a guide to the many area rambles. Paths lead north from Birnam to the great **Birnam Oak,** the sole remnant of the Birnam Wood made famous by *Macbeth*. A well-marked 1 mi. path passes through designated photo ops, including the roaring **Black Linn Waterfall.** The **Birnam Hill Walk** ascends 1000 ft. and rewards dedicated climbers with vast views. To **fish,** obtain a license (from £3-5 per day) from the Spar Shop, 2-3 Murthly Terr. (☎01350 727 395. Open M-F 6:30am-8pm, Sa 7am-8pm, Su 7:30am-6pm.) Trout season lasts from mid-March to mid-October.

PITLOCHRY ☎(0)1796

The small, Victorian town of Pitlochry, the "gateway to the Highlands," sits at the intersection of the Lowlands and the mountains. More than just a travel hub, it offers two distilleries, several famous pubs, and boundless hospitality.

🚊 TRANSPORTATION. Trains (☎08457 484 950) leave from near the town center to: Edinburgh (2hr., 7 per day, £24); Glasgow (2hr., 7 per day, £24.10); Inverness (1hr., 9 per day, £17.40); Perth (30min., 9 per day, £10). Scottish Citylink **buses** (☎08705 505 050) leave from outside the Fishers Hotel on Atholl Rd. to: Edinburgh (2hr., 10 per day, £12); Glasgow (2hr., 5 per day, £12); Inverness (2hr., 5 per day, £12.30); Perth (40min., 5 per day, £7.60). From Perth, Pitlochry is accessible by local buses; call Traveline (☎08712 002 233) for information. Call ahead to rent **bikes** at Escape Route, 3 Atholl Rd. (☎01796 473 859. Open M-Sa 9am-5:30pm, Su 10am-5pm. £10 per ½-day, £18 per day.) Pitlochry Backpackers (below) also rents at a lower rate.

🛈 PRACTICAL INFORMATION. The **Tourist Information Centre,** 22 Atholl Rd., stocks *Pitlochry Walks* (£1) and has a **bureau de change.** (☎01796 472 215.

Open July-Aug. M-Sa 9am-7pm, Su 9:30am-5pm; Sept.-Oct. and May-June M-Sa 9:30am-5:30pm, Su 10am-4pm; Nov.-Apr. M-Sa 10am-4pm.) Other services include: a **Royal Bank of Scotland,** 84 Atholl Rd. (☎01796 472 771; open M-Tu and Th-F 9:15am-12:30pm and 1:30-4:45pm, W 9:45am-12:30pm and 1:30-4:45pm); a **launderette,** 3 W. Moulin Rd. (☎01796 474 044; wash £3, dry £2; open M-Sa 8am-5pm); **Lloyds** pharmacy, 122-124 Atholl Rd. (☎01796 472 414; open M-F 9am-5:30pm, Sa 9am-5pm); **Internet** access at the **Computer Services Centre,** 67 Atholl Rd. (☎01796 473 711; 5p per min., £2.75 per hr.; open M-F 9am-5:30pm, Sa 9am-12:30pm), or at the **Pitlochry Library,** 26 Atholl Rd. (☎01796 474 919; free; open Tu 4-6pm, W 10am-noon and 2-5pm, Th 2-4pm and 6-8pm, F 2-5pm, Sa 9:30am-12:30pm; call ahead); and a **post office,** 92 Atholl Rd. (open M-F 9am5:30pm, Sa 9am-12:30pm). **Postcode:** PH16 5BL.

⬛◨ ACCOMMODATIONS AND FOOD. ◨**Pitlochry Backpackers Hotel ❶,** 134 Atholl Rd., in the center of town, has handwritten tips for exploring the area lining the walls. Rooms can be cramped, but lively common rooms, a selection of movies, and a friendly staff compensate. (☎01796 470 044. Bike rentals from £8 per ½-day, £13 per day. Curfew M-Th and Su 1am, F-Sa 2am. Open Apr.-Oct. Dorms £13-15; doubles and twins £35-50. AmEx/MC/V.) Across from the TIC, **Atholl Villa ❸,** 29 Atholl Rd., rents 10 airy ensuite rooms of different sizes along with TVs, spacious family areas, and free parking. (☎01796 473 820. Singles £25-55; doubles £50-65. MC/V.) Orange curtains spice up the ensuite rooms of **SYHA Pitlochry ❷,** at Knockard and Well Brae Rd., on a hill with great views of town. From the train station, turn right on Atholl Rd. and left onto Bonnethill Rd., from which the hostel is signposted. (☎01796 472 308. Laundry £2. Internet access £1 per 20min. Reception 7am-11pm. Curfew 11:45pm. Dorms £14-17, under 16 £10-12.50. AmEx/MC/V.)

On W. Moulin Rd., the **Pitlochry Co-op** provides groceries. (☎01796 474 088. Open daily 8am-10pm.) The microbrewery attached to the 300-year-old **Moulin Inn ❷,** Moulin Sq., in the wee village of Moulin just north of Pitlochry, consistently wins brewing awards. Try the signature "Braveheart Ale" (souvenir bottles available) and chow with the locals on the pub fare. (☎01796 472 196. Entrees £8-10. Free brewery tours M-F noon-3pm. Open M-Th and Su noon-11pm, F-Sa noon-midnight. Kitchen open noon-9:30pm.) For Mediterranean food ranging from tagliatelle to *tzatziki*, head to the romantic, upscale **Fern Cottage Restaurant and Tea Room ❸,** Ferry Rd., just off Atholl Rd. Exotic Turkish- and Greek-style (£11-14) dishes include spicy lamb güveçs and whole stuffed vegetables. (☎01796 473 840. Open daily 10:30am-9pm. MC/V.) End the night at **McKays ❷,** 138 Atholl Rd., the pub next door to Pitlochry Backpackers. Long benches at large tables are great for groups. Mediocre pub grub (entrees £8-15) makes it better for seeing live Scottish music on weekends than for grabbing a meal. (☎01796 473 888; www.mckayshotel.co.uk. Open M 11am-11pm, Tu-W 11am-12:30am, Th 11am-1am, F-Sa 11am-1:30am, Su 9am-midnight. MC/V.)

◧⚠ SIGHTS AND OUTDOOR ACTIVITIES. Pitlochry stands on the cusp of the Cairngorms and serves as an entrance point to the endless miles of trails in the area. For local jaunts, **hikers** should arm themselves with *Pitlochry Walks* (£1), available at the TIC. For a quick walk around town, take the path over the suspension footbridge or the road behind the train station to the **Pitlochry Dam and Salmon Ladder.** Cross over the dam to the observation chamber, where fish struggle ceaselessly against the current as an electronic fish counter keeps tally. (☎01796 473 152. Open July-Aug. daily 10am-5:30pm; Sept.-Oct.

and Apr.-June M-F 10am-5:30pm. Free.) Fishing permits (£3-5 per day; from £20 for salmon fishing) are available at the TIC.

If whisky is the water of life, Pitlochry just might live forever. At the polished **Blair Athol Distillery**, half a mile from the TIC down the main road, kilted guides lead tours of the leading contributor to the famous Bell's blend. (☎01796 482 003. Open June-Oct. M-Sa 9:30am-5pm, Su noon-5pm; Nov.-Easter M-F 10am-4pm; Easter-May M-Sa 9:30am-5pm. Tours Easter-Oct. every 30min.; Nov.-Easter 11am, 1, 3pm. £3; includes dram and discount voucher. MC/V.) Just 3 mi. away on a pristine lawn, **Edradour**, Scotland's smallest distillery, produces only 40 bottles per day and uses methods straight out of ancient whisky-making tradition. Enjoy the folksy video and tour and try a handmade sample. Edradour is a 2 mi. walk from Pitlochry, past Moulin along the A924. (☎01796 472 095; www.edradour.co.uk. Open Mar.-Oct. M-Sa 9:30am-6pm, Su 11:30am-5pm; Nov.-Dec. M-Sa 9:30am-4pm, Su 11:30am-4pm; Jan.-Feb. M-Sa 10am-4pm, Su noon-4pm. Distilling ends at 3pm. Free.)

⬛ ENTERTAINMENT. The **Pitlochry Festival Theatre**, over the Aldour Bridge, hosts traveling theater productions from larger cities at affordable prices. (☎01796 484 626; www.pitlochry.org.uk. Ticket prices vary; concessions available.) In the recreation fields southwest of town, near Tummel Crescent, **Highland Nights** feature local pipe bands and traditional folk dancing. (May-Sept. M 8pm. Tickets available at the gate. £5, concessions £4, children £1.) Pick up the free *What's On in Perthshire* at the TIC for other entertainment ideas.

▶ DAYTRIP FROM PITLOCHRY: ▩BLAIR CASTLE. The gleaming white turrets of Blair Castle burst from the wooded landscape 7 mi. north of Pitlochry on the A9. The longtime residence of the dukes of Atholl, its 30 furnished rooms are some of the most elegant and best-preserved in Scotland, brimming with paintings and weapons used by the Atholl Highlanders, the only legal private army in Europe. The grounds regularly host international equestrian trials, featuring some of the world's most talented riders. *(Take the train to Blair Atholl and walk 10min. or hop on bus #87 from the West End Car Park. ☎ 01796 481 207; www.blair-castle.co.uk. Open Apr.-Oct. daily 9:30am-4:30pm. £8, concessions £7. Grounds only £2.70.)*

▶ DAYTRIP FROM PITLOCHRY: BEN-Y-VRACKIE. The views from 2757 ft. Ben-y-Vrackie stretch all the way to Edinburgh on a clear day. Turn left onto the road directly behind the Moulin Inn and follow the curve until you reach a fork. At the fork, the **Dane's Stone**, a solitary standing stone, will be in the field right in front of you. Take the right-hand road to Ben-y-Vrackie. The left-hand road leads to **Craigower Hill** for a western view from Loch Tommel and Loch Rannoch to the Glencoe Mountains.

▶ DAYTRIP FROM PITLOCHRY: PASS OF KILLIECRANKIE. A few miles north of Pitlochry, right off the A9, the valley of the River Garry narrows into a deep gorge. Stop at the **National Trust Visitors Centre** down the path to learn more about the unique wildflowers that line the walk. In 1689, a Jacobite army slaughtered William III's troops here in an attempt to reinstall James VII of Scotland to the English throne. One fleeing soldier, Donald MacBean, decided to risk falling down the gorge rather than facing certain death at the hands of the Highlanders. He successfully vaulted 18 ft. across **Soldier's Leap.** The area is also home to an array of wildlife. *(Elizabeth Yule bus #87 runs from the West End Car Park to the pass in summer. ☎08444 932 194. Open Apr.-Oct. daily 10am-5:30pm.)*

KILLIN AND LOCH TAY   ☎(0)1567

The pristine Loch Tay lies southwest of Pitlochry and acts as the eastern gateway to Trossachs. The Loch is bookended by the villages of Kenmore to the north and Killin to the south, with the A827 winding from end to end. Although difficult to reach without a car, Loch Tay serves as a welcome relief from more heavily touristed nearby areas. Killin is the best base for exploring the loch.

TRANSPORTATION. Public transportation around Loch Tay is challenging at best, as many buses only run on certain days of the week. Pick up a copy of *Highland Perthshire and Stanley Area Buses* from the Aberfeldy TIC and inquire about services that are currently running. One **postbus** per day circles Loch Tay, passing through Killin and Aberfeldy (#213, 3hr.); another travels from Crianlarich (#25, 45min., 1 per day). Postbuses do not run on Sunday, and coverage of the villages can be inconsistent. Scottish Citylink **bus** #973 from Oban to Aberdeen stops at the south end of Killin's Main St. (2 per day).

PRACTICAL INFORMATION. The **Tourist Information Centre**, by the Falls of Douchart on Main St., dispenses information on countless local walks. (☎01567 820 254. Open daily July-Aug. 10am-5:30pm; Sept.-Oct. and Apr.-June 10am-5pm.) Other services in Killin include: a **Bank of Scotland** (☎01877 302 000; open M-Tu and Th-F 10am-12:30pm and 1:30-4pm, W 10:30am-12:30pm and 1:30-4pm); **Internet** access at the **Killin Library,** Main St. (☎01567 820 571; open M 10am-1pm and 2-5pm, Tu and F 10am-1pm and 3-7pm, W 2-5pm); **Grant's Launderette** (☎01567 820 235; open M-Sa 9am-10pm, Su 11am-10pm); **police** on Main St. (☎01567 820 222); and the **post office** (open M-Tu and Th-F 8:30am-5pm, W 8:30am-2pm, Sa 8:30am-1pm). **Postcode:** FK21 8UH.

ACCOMMODATIONS AND FOOD. A warm and welcoming, if occasionally disorganized, atmosphere awaits at **Braveheart Backpackers ❶**, Main St., behind the Killin Hotel. The kitchen and dining area are in the same open room as a working fireplace circled by leather couches. (☎07796 886 899. Internet £1 per 30min. Dorms £15; singles from £45.) Pick up groceries at the **Co-op,** Main St. (☎01567 820 255. Open M-Sa 8am-10pm, Su 8am-8pm.) Grab homemade food from the **Coach House ❷**, Lochay Rd., half a mile north of the town center. With tartan cushions, local music, and a small beer garden, this pub provides a lively night for locals and visitors alike. (☎01567 820 349. Entrees £7-9. Open M-Th and Su 11am-midnight, F-Sa 11am-1am. Kitchen open daily 11am-8pm. MC/V.) The warm, fragrant **Shutters Restaurant ❷**, Main St. serves a homemade farmhouse breakfast for £7 and has delicious soups for £3. (☎01567 820 314. Open M-Sa 10am-8pm, Su 11am-8pm. MC/V.)

SIGHTS AND OUTDOOR ACTIVITIES. About 5 mi. past Aberfeldy on the southern shore of Loch Tay (A827) resides the **Scottish Crannog Centre,** where a reconstruction of an Iron Age crannog offers a look into the water-based dwellings and life as it was 2600 years ago. Tunic-clad guides explain why researchers think Iron Age Scots may have worn hair gel and enjoyed cheese toasties. After the tour, visitors have the chance to use Iron Age tools. (☎01887 830 583; www.crannog.co.uk. 1hr. tour every hr. Open from mid-Mar. to Oct. daily 10am-5:30pm. Last tour at 4:15pm. Booking recommended. £5.75, concessions £4.75.) In Killin, visit the two-room **Breadalbane Folklore Centre,** Main St., above the TIC, in a mill built before written records. There, discover the legends that surround St. Fillan and view his famous healing stones. (Open daily July-Aug. 10am-5:30pm; Sept.-Oct. and Apr.-June 10am-5pm. £3, concessions £2.50.) A free 2hr. hike starts from behind the schoolyard on Main St. and travels past the

Falls of Dochart, the supposed burial place of the Celtic hero Fingal. The views of the loch from here are, well, killin'. Just outside town, follow signs to the **Moirlanich Longhouse** and explore the preserved mid-19th-century home and the surrounding meadow. (☎01567 820 988. Open May-Sept. W and Su 2-5pm. £3, concessions £2.) Circling Loch Tay on the A87 and A827 by foot or car makes an excellent daytrip. As you head north on the western shore of the lake, a spectacular single-track road takes you off the A827 for a scenic route up the side of mighty **Ben Lawers** to its **Visitor Centre.** The center offers information about hiking Ben Lawers, weather updates, and a small audio-visual display. (☎01567 820 397. Open daily 10am-5pm. £2, concessions £1.) The tiny village of **Fortingall,** on the northern end of Loch Tay, is the supposed birthplace of Pontius Pilate. It is also home to an ancient **yew tree,** the oldest living organism in Europe. The Fortingall yew reached over 50 ft. in girth in the 18th century, but since then souvenir-seekers have hacked away pieces from its trunk, preventing experts from pinpointing its exact age (between 2000 and 5000 years). At **Dewar's World of Whisky,** half a mile north of Aberfeldy on the A827, take a guided tour through the distillery, which includes an interactive, audio-guided whisky exhibit and a recreated blender's lab. (☎01887 822 010; www.dewarsworldofwhisky.com. Open Apr.-Oct. M-Sa 10am-6pm, Su noon-4pm; Nov.-Mar. M-Sa 10am-4pm. £6.50, concessions £4.50.) Beginning just north of Killin, the 60 mi. **Lowland Highland Trail** leads ambitious cyclers over the famous **Highland Boundary Fault** to the south and passes through the varied landscapes ot the Trossachs and Loch Lomond. Pick up a trail map at the TIC in Killin.

ARGYLL AND BUTE

INVERARAY   ☎(0)1499

In the 18th century, the duke of Argyll tore down and rebuilt the town of Inveraray to make room for his very own lakefront castle. The resulting village retains a regal air, with pristine whitewashed houses overlooking the silvery **Loch Fyne,** the area's main attraction. Today, palatial **Inveraray Castle** is still home to the duke and duchess of Argyll. The third duke of Argyll built the castle as a sign of a more peaceful era in Scottish history, although it still bristles with an array of weapons. (☎01499 302 203; www.inverary-castle.com. Open Apr.-Oct. M-Sa 10am-5:45pm, Su noon-5:45pm. Last entry 5pm. £6.80, concessions £5.70. Grounds free.) *Five Walks in Inveraray Estate* (£1), available from the TIC or castle, details short walks (1-2 mi.) that leave from the castle car park, touring the forest and the top of **Dun na Cuaiche.** The morbid **Inveraray Jail** welcomes visitors with an exhibit on Torture, Death, and Damnation. Guests can try out the Whipping Table, sit in on a 19th-century court scene, or try to stop the wax figures from branding (melting) each other with hot irons. (☎01499 302 381. Open daily Apr.-Oct. 9:30am-6pm; Nov.-Mar. 10am-5pm. Last entry 1hr. before close. £7.25, concessions £5.50, children £4.25, families £16.)

Relax in the privacy of two- to four-bed dorms in the small, basic **SYHA Inveraray ❷,** on the northern edge of town on Dalmally Rd. From the bus stop, take a left through the arch next to the Inveraray Woollen Mill onto Oban Rd.; the hostel is on the left-hand side, past the gas station. (☎08700 041 125. Self-catering kitchen. Internet £1 per 20min. Lockout 11am-5pm. Curfew 11:30pm. Open Apr.-Sept. Dorms £13.25-15, under 18 £10-15. MC/V.)

Scottish Citylink **buses** (☎08705 505 050) connect Inveraray with Glasgow (1hr., 6 per day, £5) and Oban (1hr., 3 per day, £5). The **Tourist Information Centre,** Front St., has Internet access (£1 per 15min.) and books accommodations for

£4 plus a 10% deposit. (☎01499 302 063. Open July-Aug. daily 9am-6pm; Sept.-Oct. and early Apr. M-Sa 10am-5pm, Su noon-5pm; Nov.-Mar. daily 10am-3pm; from late Apr. to June M-Sa 9am-5pm, Su 11am-5pm.) The **post office** is on Main St. S. (☎01499 302 062. Open M-Tu and Th-F 9am-1pm and 2-5:30pm, W 9am-1pm, Sa 9am-12:30pm.) **Postcode:** PA32 8UD.

OBAN   ☎(0)1631

The saltiest ferry port on Scotland's west coast, Oban (OH-ben) welcomes thousands of visitors bound for the Inner Hebrides every summer, making the colorful town a fine base for exploring the islands and Argyll countryside.

⌇ TRANSPORTATION. The **train station** (☎08457 484 950) is on Railway Pier. Trains run to Glasgow Queen St. (3hr., 3 per day, £18.30). Scottish Citylink **buses** (☎08705 505 050) leave from the train station to Fort William (1hr., M-Sa 4 per day, £11.40) and Glasgow (3hr.; M-Sa 6 per day, Su 5 per day; £13.40). Caledonian MacBrayne **ferries** sail from Railway Pier to the Inner Hebrides and the southern Outer Hebrides. Pick up an *Explorer* timetable at the ferry terminal or TIC. Ferries go to: Craignure, Mull (45min.; M-Sa 7 per day, Su 5 per day; extra sailings July-Aug.; £4.25); Lismore (50min., M-Sa 2-4 per day, £3); Colonsay (2hr., M and W-Su 1 per day, £12); Tiree (3hr., 1 per day, £13) via Coll (2hr.); South Uist (7hr., 4 per week, £20.30) via Barra (5hr.). Passengers with cars should book ahead. (☎01631 566 688, reservations 08705 650 000. Terminal open M 6am-6pm, Tu and Th 6:45am-6pm, W 4:45am-8pm, F 4:45am-10:30pm, Sa 5:45am-8pm, Su 7:45am-6pm.) Rent bikes at **Evobikes,** 29 Lochside St., across from the Tesco. (☎01631 566 996. £10 per ½-day, £15 per day. Open Feb.-Oct. M-Sa 9am-5:30pm; Nov.-Mar. M-Tu and Th-Sa 9am-5pm.)

▉🗹 ORIENTATION AND PRACTICAL INFORMATION. Corran Esplanade runs along the coast north of town, **Gallanach Road** along the coast to the south. Fronting the harbor, **George Street** is the heart of Oban. A block inland, **Argyll Square** is actually a misleadingly named roundabout. The **Tourist Information Centre,** Argyll Sq., inhabits the vaulted interior of an old church and books beds for £4 plus a 10% deposit. (☎01631 563 122. Open from late June to Aug. M-Sa 9am-8pm, Su 9am-7pm; Sept.-Oct. M-Sa 9am-5:30pm, Su 10am-4pm; Nov.-Mar. M-F 9:30am-5pm, Sa 10am-4pm, Su noon-4pm; from late Apr. to mid-June M-F 9am-5:30pm, Sa-Su 10am-5pm.) Several operators offer day **tours** to the isles of Mull, Iona, and Staffa. From April to October, Bowman's Tours, across from Railway Pier, runs daily to Mull, Iona, and Staffa. (☎01631 566 809. Mull and Iona £31.40, children £17; including Staffa £44/23.) **Internet** access is available at the **Oban Library,** Albany St. (free; open M and W 10am-1pm and 2-7pm, Th 10am-1pm and 2-6pm, F 10am-1pm and 2-5pm, Sa 10am-1pm), and at the TIC (£1 per 20min.). **Boots** pharmacy, 34-38 George St., is on the north harbor. (Open M-Sa 8:45am-5:30pm.) There are **post offices** in the Tesco, Lochside St. (☎01631 510 450; open M-Sa 8am-6pm, Su 10am-1pm) and on Corran Esplanade across town (open M-F 9am-5:30pm, Sa 9am-1pm). **Postcode:** PA34 4HP.

▛ ACCOMMODATIONS. The waterfront ▨**SYHA Oban ❶,** Corran Esplanade, lies three-quarters of a mile north of the train station, just past St. Columba's Cathedral. Enjoy spacious dorms and sea views from bay windows but be aware of the strict no-alcohol policy. (☎01631 562 025. 128 beds in 6- to 10-bed dorms plus 42 beds in 4-bed ensuite rooms. Laundry and Internet access. Wheelchair-accessible. Reception until 11:30pm. Curfew 2am. Dorms £13.50-16.75, under 18 £10-14; private rooms from £30. MC/V.) Definitely not just for teetotalers, a more lively atmosphere prevails at ◪**Oban Backpackers ❶**, 21 Breadalbane St., part of the Scotland's Top Backpackers chain and often filled with enthusiastic MacBackpackers groups. You'll still sleep soundly in the blissfully soft beds. Take George St. away from Railway Pier and bear right at the first fork; the hostel is on the right. (☎01631 562 107. 48 beds in 6- to 12-bed single-sex dorms. Self-catering kitchen. Breakfast £2. No lockable dorms, no lockers. Safe at reception. Laundry £2.50. Internet 80p per 30min. Free Wi-Fi. Curfew M-Th and Su 12:30am, F-Sa 2am. Dorms £13.50. AmEx/ MC/V.) **Corran House ❷**, 1-2 Victoria Crescent, sits near the water north of the train station, affiliated with (and located on top of) Markie Dan's Ale House. (☎01631 566 040. 36 beds in 2- to 6-bed dorms and 11 private rooms with TVs. Self-catering kitchen. Breakfast £2. No lockable dorms, no lockers. Laundry £5. Dorms £14-16; private rooms £25-35. MC/V.) Several **B&Bs** populate the hills near the pier—call the TIC for the cheapest available options.

⌂◪ FOOD AND PUBS. Pick up groceries at **Tesco**, Lochside St. (Open M-Sa 8am-10pm, Su 9am-6pm.) Abundant fish-and-chips shops line the pier area, proving that seafood is what Oban does best. Splurge on fine food and finer wine at **Ee'Usk ❸**, on the North Pier, Oban's best seafood restaurant. (☎01631 565 666. Entrees £13-20. Open daily noon-3pm and 6-10pm. MC/V.) The interior of **O'Donnell's Irish Pub ❶**, Breadalbane St., across the street from Oban Backpackers, is a cross between the American Wild West and the Highlands, with antlers on the wall, tartan curtains, and occasional live bluegrass music. (☎01631 566 159. Open M-W 4pm-1am, Th 4pm-2am, F and Su 2pm-2am, Sa noon-2am; reduced low-season hours.) **Markie Dan's ❶**, Victoria Crescent, off Corran Esplanade under Corran House, has live music, drink specials, and a jovial bar staff. (☎01631 564 448. Open daily 11am-1am.)

◪ SIGHTS. If your feet are hurting from a long day of wandering the pier, a stop at the renowned ◪**Oban Distillery,** Stafford St., will cure all your aches and pains with a free sample of the local malt whisky following a 1hr. tour. (☎01631 572 004; www.discovering-distilleries.com. Open July-Sept. M-F 9:30am-7:30pm, Sa 9:30am-5pm, Su noon-5pm; Oct. and Apr.-June M-Sa 9:30am-5pm; Nov. and Mar. M-F 10am-5pm; M-F Dec.-Feb. 12:30-4pm. Tours every 20min. in summer, less frequent in low season; call ahead for reservations. Last tour 1¼hr. before close. £6, children £3.) The Colosseum-esque structure dominating Oban's skyline is **McCaig's Tower.** Commissioned at the end of the 19th century by John Stuart McCaig, it was intended as an art gallery, but construction was abandoned when McCaig died. Take the steep stairway at the end of Argyll St., then turn left along Ardconnel Rd. and right up Laurel St. (Open 24hr. Free.) Perfect for hide and seek, the ivy-covered ruins of seventh-century **Dunollie Castle,** Oban's oldest building, sit atop a cliff north of town. From town, walk 20min. north along the water until you've curved around the castle, then take the overgrown path up the hill. (Open 24hr. Free.)

▣ DAYTRIP FROM OBAN: KERRERA. Across the bay from Oban is the beautiful, nearly deserted isle of Kerrera (CARE-er-uh), where a no-car policy (the only motor vehicles are owned by the 30 residents) guarantees a peaceful habitat for seals and eagles. Ringed by a network of gravel roads, Kerrera makes for great walking and mountain biking. From the ferry landing, turn left and follow the road for 2 mi. to the southern tip of the isle, where tiny **Gylen Castle** stands atop the cliffs in an isolated spot overlooking the sea. Enjoy a hearty meal made with homegrown veggies or spend the night in the cozy ◪**Kerrera Bunkhouse and Tea Garden ❶**, 2 mi. from the pier near the castle. (☎01631 570

223. Tea Garden open Easter-Oct. W-Su 10:30am-4:30pm. 7 beds. Self-catering kitchen with free tea and coffee. Dorms £12. Cash only.) A **ferry** crosses to Kerrera from a pier 2 mi. south of Oban along Gallanach Rd. Turn the board to the black side to signal that you wish to cross. The ferryman also dispenses helpful maps of the island. (☎01631 563 665. *Easter-Oct. daily 2 per hr. 10:30am-12:30pm and 2-6pm, also M-Sa 8:45am; Nov.-Easter 5-6 per day. Round-trip £4.50, children £2; bikes 50p.)*

ISLE OF MULL

Never thought you'd see palm trees in Scotland? Welcome to Mull, the largest (pop. a whopping 3000) and most accessible of the Inner Hebrides. Towering mountains, remote glens, and pristine coastline reward explorers who venture beyond the well-trodden routes. Much of Mull's Gaelic heritage has yielded to the pressure of English settlers, who now comprise over two-thirds of the population, but lifelong locals keep tradition alive. Mull's main hubs, **Tobermory** (northwest tip), **Craignure** (east tip), and **Fionnphort** (FINN-a-furt; southwest tip), form a triangle bounded by the A849 and A848. A left turn off the **Craignure Pier** leads 35 mi. along the southern arm of the island to Fionnphort. There, the ferry leaves for **Iona**, a tiny island to the southwest.

▐ TRANSPORTATION

CalMac (Craignure Office ☎01680 812 343) runs a **ferry** to Oban from Craignure (45min.; M-Sa 7 per day, Su 5 per day; more July-Aug.; £4.25). Smaller ferries run from Lochaline on the Morvern Peninsula, north of Mull, to Fishnish, on the east coast 6 mi. northwest of Craignure (15min.; M-Sa 13-14 per day, Su 9 per day; £2.60), and from Kilchoan on the Ardnamurchan peninsula to Tobermory (35min.; June-Aug. M-Sa 7 per day, Su 5 per day, Oct.-May M-Sa 7 per day; £4). Day **tours** run to Mull, Iona, Staffa, and the Treshnish Isles from Oban (p. 617). Stop by area TICs or the Oban ferry terminal to pick up a free copy of the *Explorer CalMac* timetable for comprehensive listings.

Check the sometimes erratic **bus** times to avoid stranding yourself. Bowman Coaches (☎01680 812 313) operates the main routes. Bus #496 meets the Oban ferry at Craignure and goes to Fionnphort (70min.; M-F 4 per day, Sa 3 per day, Su 1 per day; round-trip £10). Bus #495 runs between Craignure and Tobermory via Fishnish (50min.; M-F 6 per day, Sa 4 per day, Su 3-4 per day; round-trip £7.30). RN Carmichael (☎01688 302 220) #494 links Tobermory and Calgary (45min.; M-F 4 per day, Sa 2 per day; round-trip £3.80). TICs stock copies of the comprehensive *Mull and Iona Area Transport Guide*.

▣ ▨ HIKING AND OUTDOOR ACTIVITIES

The Isle of Mull features a range of terrain for hikers, from headland treks to sea-to-summit ascents to gentle forest strolls. Ordnance Survey Landranger Maps #47-49 (£6) cover Mull, while *Walking in North Mull* and *Walking in South Mull and Iona* (£4 each) highlight individual trails. From Tobermory, a 2 mi. walk departs from the Royal Lifeboat Station at the end of Main St. and follows the shore to a **lighthouse.** Outside of Craignure, the Dun da Ghaoithe Ridge walk begins just past the entrance to **Torosay Castle** on the A849. This 11 mi. route ascends 2513 ft., follows a ridge with views over the Sound of Mull, and finishes on the A848 on the bus route. Popular climbs up **Ben More** (3169 ft.) and **Ben Buie** (2526 ft.) start from the sea. You can also take the bus along the road to ▧**Calgary Bay**, where stretches of white sand beach and rocky headland border the water. Short-term camping is permitted in the bay, which has toilets but no drinking water. In Tobermory, **Tackle and Books,** 10 Main St., runs 3hr.

fishing trips suited to experienced anglers and first-timers alike. (☎01688 302 336. Trips Apr.-Oct. 2-5pm. Call in advance to arrange a sailing. £30, children £20. Store open M-Sa 9am-5:30pm, Su 11am-4pm.) Tobermory is also a home base for wildlife tours. The boats of **Sea Life Surveys,** on Main St. by the bus stop, head out in search of whales, seals, and basking sharks. (☎01688 302 916; www. sealifesurveys.com. 3-6 trips per day. Call ahead. £12-80, children £6-35.)

CRAIGNURE   ☎(0)1680

Craignure, Mull's main ferry port, is a tiny town with one main street. From the pier, turn left and take the first left again to reach **Mull Rail,** where you can ride a vintage narrow-gauge toy of a train that will make you feel like a giant. (☎01680 812 494; www.mullrail.co.uk. From mid-Mar. to mid-Oct. 4-12 per day, £4.75. MC/V.) Farther along the coast, spectacular ▨**Duart Castle,** a 700-year-old stronghold 4 mi. from Craignure, remains the seat of the MacLean clan chief. It is the most widely photographed attraction on Mull, with its ancient keep and dungeons still intact. The bus runs to the end of Duart Rd., 2 mi. from the castle. (☎01680 812 309; www.duartcastle.com. Open May-Oct. daily 10:30am-5:30pm; Apr. M-Th and Su 11am-4pm. £5, concessions £4.50.) The Duart Castle Coach meets the ferry from Oban, and the driver gives a brief history of the island and castle. (May-Oct. £9 for coach and castle.)

Every tent has sea views at ▨**Shieling Holidays Campsite ❶,** a short walk from the ferry terminal. Super-clean toilet and shower facilities, a TV lounge, and several permanent tents with gas cookers provide hostel-like accommodations. (☎01680 812 496; www.shielingholidays.co.uk. Linen £2.50. Open from late Mar. to Oct. Tent sites from £14.50, with car from £16.50. Dorms £11.50. MC/V.) **Aon a'Dha ❷,** 1-2 Kirk Terr., half a mile from the ferry, has beds at bargain prices. (☎01680 812 318. Breakfast £3. Singles £22. Cash only.)

Across from the ferry, the **TIC** books rooms for £4 plus a 10% deposit. (☎01680 812 377. Open July-Aug. M-F 8:30am-7pm, Sa-Su 10am-6:30pm; Sept.-Oct. and Apr.-June M-F 8:30am-5:15pm, Sa-Su 10:30am-5:30pm; Nov.-Mar. M-Sa 9am-5pm, Su 10:30am-noon and 3:30-5pm.) The adjoining CalMac ferry office is Mull's largest. Although the closest **bank** is in Tobermory, get cash back at **Spar** on the main street, which also has a **post office.** (☎01631 812 301. Store open M 7:30am-7pm, Tu-Sa 8am-7pm, Su 10am-7pm. Post office open M-W and F 9am-1pm and 2-5pm, Th and Sa 9am-1pm.) **Postcode:** PA65 6AY.

TOBERMORY   ☎(0)1688

Bright buildings surround a leisurely fishing harbor in Mull's largest town. Just across from the bus stop is the **Tobermory Distillery,** which conducts 30min. tours and offers samples of the so-called "water of life." (☎01688 302 647. Open M-F 10am-5pm. Tours every hr. 11am-4pm. Reservations recommended. £3.50, children and seniors £1.50.) Farther along Main St., the tiny **Mull Museum** chronicles the island's history with local artifacts. (Open Easter-Oct. M-F 10am-4pm. £1, children 20p.) During the last weekend of April, Tobermory hosts the **Mull Music Festival,** and late July brings the **Mull Highland Games,** with caber-tossing, hammer-throwing, and bagpipes.

The pink-painted **SYHA Tobermory ❶,** on the far end of Main St. from the bus stop, has bright rooms with bonnie sea views. (☎01688 302 481. 39 beds. Internet 5p per min. Reception 7:30-10am and 5-10pm. Curfew midnight. Open Apr.-Oct. Dorms £12.50-15, under 16 £9-15. MC/V.) Moderately-priced B&Bs line Breadalbane St. above the bay. **Failte Guest House ❸** is one option on waterfront Main St. (☎01688 302 495. Singles £32; doubles and twins £64. MC/V.) The **Co-op** supermarket, Main St., sits opposite Fisherman's Pier. (☎01688 302 004. Open M-Sa 8am-8pm, Su 12:30-7pm.) The **Island Bakery and Delicatessen ❶,** 26 Main St., sells a variety of sandwiches (£2.65-4), tempting pastries, and local cheeses. (☎01688 302 225. Open Apr.-Oct. M-W 9am-5:30pm, Th-Sa 9am-7:30pm, Su noon-4pm; Nov.-Mar. M-Sa 9am-5:30pm. Cash only.)

Tobermory's **Tourist Information Centre,** on the pier near the bus stop, sells tour tickets and books rooms for £4 plus a 10% deposit. (☎01688 302 182.) Other services include: a CalMac office next to the TIC (☎01688 302 517; open M-F 9am-5:30pm, Sa 9am-1pm and 2-4pm); **bike rental** at Archibald Brown & Son, 21 Main St. (☎01688 302 020; £10 per ½-day, 15 per day; open M-Sa 8:45am-1pm and 2-5:30pm); **Clydesdale Bank,** Main St. (open M-Tu and Th-F 9:15am-4:45pm, W 9:45am-4:45pm); **Internet** access with printer- and webcam-equipped computers at **Posh Nosh Cafe/Restaurant,** on Main St. next to the Co-op (☎01688 302 499; 75p per 15min.; min. 30min.; open daily in summer 10am-10pm; in winter 10am-4pm); and the **post office,** 36 Main St. (open M-Tu and Th-F 9am-1pm and 2-5:30pm, Sa 9am-1pm). **Postcode:** PA75 6NT.

IONA   ☎(0)1681

Just 1 mi. off the coast of Mull, the Isle of Iona (pop. 150) beckons travelers with white sand beaches, brilliant blue waters, and rugged hills. For nearly two centuries after the Irish monk St. Columba landed on this island in AD 563, Iona was one of Europe's cradles of Christianity. A 13th-century **nunnery,** one of the better-preserved medieval convents in Britain, faces visitors as soon as they step off the ferry. Signs lead to the **Iona Heritage Centre,** which traces the history of the island from St. Columba through WWII. (☎01681 700 576. Open Easter-Oct. M-Sa 10:30am-4:30pm. £2.50, concessions and children £1 50.) The centerpiece of the island is **Iona Abbey,** a 13th-century structure on the site of St. Columba's original monastery. Follow signs from the pier to the abbey. (☎01681 700 512. Open daily Apr.-Sept. 9:30am-6:30pm; Oct.-Mar. 9:30am-5pm. Services M-Sa 9am, 2, 9pm, Su 10:30am, 9pm. £4.70.) Next to the abbey, the 12th-century **Saint Oran's Chapel** is the oldest ecclesiastical building on the isle. The burial ground supposedly holds 48 kings, including the infamous Macbeth.

On the isle's north end, the isolated ▣**Iona Hostel ②,** on a working croft 1 mi. from the pier along the road past the abbey, seeks to reunite its guests with nature. There is no TV, radio, or Internet, but postcard-perfect beaches nearby are ideal for contemplative walks. (☎01681 700 781; www.ionahostel.co.uk. 21 beds. Dorms £17.50. Cash only.) The island has scattered **B&Bs** by the pier; call the Tobermory TIC to book ahead, as the small number of rooms fill up fast. The restaurant at the **Argyll Hotel ③** serves fine cuisine with ingredients straight from the organic garden outside. (☎01681 703 334; www.argyllhoteliona.co.uk. Entrees £8.50-12.50. Kitchen open 8-10am, 12:30-1:30pm, 7-8pm. MC/V.)

CalMac **ferries** (☎01681 700 559) sail between Iona and Fionnphort, Mull (5min., round-trip £3.75). Left of the pier, **Finlay Ross** rents **bikes** and runs a **launderette.** (☎01681 700 357. £8 per day; £10 deposit. Open M-Sa 10am-5:15pm, Su 11am-4:30pm.) The **post office** is near the pier. (☎01681 700 515. Open M-Tu and Th-F 9am-1pm and 2-5pm, Sa 9am-12:30pm.) **Postcode:** PA76 6SJ.

STAFFA AND THE TRESHNISH ISLES

The isolation and rugged beauty of these tiny, uninhabited islands off Mull's west coast make them worth the effort it takes to get there. Sixty million years ago, lava was cooled by the sea and formed the towering, hexagonal basalt columns that have made Staffa famous. Ringed by treacherous cliffs, the 80 acres of soil that blanket the stone were inhabited by a handful of hardy folk as recently as the late 18th century. The only residents these days are a colony of puffins, but seals and sharks are also often seen in the area. At low tide, enter ▣**Fingal's Cave** and marvel at its natural basalt cathedral. When rough seas roar into the cavern,

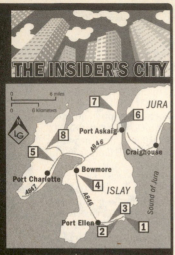

THE INSIDER'S CITY

THE WHISKY TRAIL

Islay is renowned for its malt whiskys and boasts eight distilleries. The island's malts are known for their peaty flavor—not surprising given that half of Islay is a peat bog. What gives each malt its distinctive flavor? Water supply, air quality, temperature, the barley—even the shape of the pot still (distilling structure). Pick up the *Islay and Jura Whisky Trail* brochure, free at TICs.

1. Ardbeg (☎01496·302 244), on the southeast coast, 4 mi. from Port Ellen. The peatiest of the island's malts, Ardbeg is rapidly emerging as one of Islay's best. Tours M-Sa. £2.

2. Lagavulin (☎01496 302 400), 3 mi. from Port Ellen. Check out the massive washbacks that overflow with foam during the fermenting process. Tours M-F. £4.

3. Laphroaig (☎01496 302 418), 2 mi. from Port Ellen. In Gaelic, its name means "beautiful

the noise echoes off the walls. The pounding waves inspired one of Felix Mendelssohn's most famous works, the *Hebrides Overture*.

The Treshnish Isles teem with rare birds and other wildlife. Unthreatened by humans, the animals tolerate up-close examination on these isolated islands, which require a bit of rock-scrambling to explore. Along the cliffs of Lunga, birds perch on one of the only remnants of human habitation, a 13th-century **chapel**. Legend has it that monks from Iona buried their library on one of the Isles to save it from pillage during the Reformation. Many have tried digging for it, so far without luck.

Both Staffa and the Treshnish Isles are only accessible by tours. During the summer, **Gordon Grant Tours** (☎01681 700 338; www.staffatours.com) leaves Oban's ferry port to Iona (previous page), Staffa, and the Treshnish Isles (£45). The **Kirkpatricks** (☎01681 700 358) send daily cruises to Staffa from Fionnphort, Mull (3hr.; £20, children £10). **Turus Mara** operates tours that leave from the town of Ulva Ferry on Mull. (☎08000 858 786; www.turusmara.com. £45,.) Day tours to the islands also operate from Oban (p. 617).

ISLE OF ISLAY

Although it may be known to many as "Whisky Island," the Isle of Islay (EYE-luh) has more to offer than its famed "liquid sunshine." Birdwatchers, walkers, and cyclists are greeted by sweeps of empty coastline and woodland paths. The island's eight distilleries are home to some of the world's finest single malts.

TRANSPORTATION

British Airways Express (☎08705 444 000) **planes** fly from Glasgow Airport to the Islay Airport (45min., 1-3 per day, £40), located between Port Ellen and Bowmore. For **taxis,** contact Carol's Cabs (☎01496 302 155, mobile 0777 578 2155; www.carols-cabs.co.uk), which provides 24hr. service and island tours. CalMac **ferries** (☎01496 302 209) leave from **Kennacraig Ferry Terminal,** 7 mi. south of Tarbert on the mainland Kintyre Peninsula, and sail to Port Askaig and Port Ellen (Port Askaig 2hr.; Port Ellen 2hr., 1-4 per day; £8.45). To reach Kennacraig, take Scottish Citylink (☎08705 505 050) **bus** #926 running between Glasgow and Campbeltown (Kennacraig to Glasgow 3hr.; M-Sa 4 per day, Su 1-2 per day; £8). On Wednesdays in summer, a ferry leaves Oban, stops on Colonsay, and continues to Port Askaig (4hr., £12.15). The comprehensive

Islay and Jura Area Transport Guide, available free at TICs, has more on these services and island bus timetables. Islay Coaches (☎01496 840 273) operates a few daily buses between Islay towns. Bus #451 connects Port Ellen and Port Askaig via Bowmore (M-Sa 5-6 per day); bus #450 and **postbus** #196 (☎01246 546 329) run from Port Ellen to Port Charlotte via Bowmore (M-Sa 5-6 per day). Many bus times apply to school days only, so read schedules carefully. **Hitchhikers** may find more success here than on the mainland, although only on main roads. Elsewhere, traffic is too sparse to find a ride. *Let's Go* does not recommend hitchhiking.

PORT ELLEN ☎(0)1496

Port Ellen lacks the usual bustle of a ferry town. Its white houses and empty streets are quieter than the island's other main villages, but it serves as a base for many pleasant walks and bicycle journeys. To the west, the windswept coast **Oa** (OH-uh) drops dramatically into the sea. A walk along the Oa road leads to the crescent-shaped **Traigh Bhan**, a favorite beach of many locals who frequent its "singing sands" in the summer heat. As you head east along the A846, you will find three of Islay's finest distilleries, all of which recommend advance booking for tours: ◪**Laphroaig** (2 mi.; ☎01496 302 418; www.laphroaig.com; tours June-Sept. M-F 10:15, 11:45am, 2:15, 3:30pm; reduced in low season; $2, under 18 free; includes sample); **Lagavulin** (3 mi.; ☎01496 302 730; www.malts.com; guided tours M-F 9:30, 11:15am, 2:30pm); and **Ardbeg** (4 mi.; ☎01496 302 244; www.ardbeg.com; tours June-Aug. M-F 10:30am, noon, 1:30, and 3pm; Oct.-Easter open daily 10:30am-3pm; $4, under 18 free). Ardbeg distillery also has a **cafe ❶** where you can grab some tasty sustenance while you sober up. (Open June-Aug. daily noon-4pm; Sept.-May M-F noon-4pm.) They're all easy to get to by bus—hop on the #451 between Port Ellen and Ardbeg and tell the driver where you're headed. Getting between the distilleries is also easy on foot or by bike (unless you've enjoyed too many whisky samples). Behind Lagavulin, the grass-covered rubble of 16th-century **Dunyvaig Castle** looms beside the sea. Just past Ardbeg you will come across the **Loch an t-Sailein,** known as Seal Bay for its breeding colonies. Another 3 mi. east along the A846 from Ardbeg, 12th-century **Kildalton Chapel** holds the ◪**Kildalton High Cross,** a carved Celtic blue stone thought to date from the mid-eighth century.

In town, Mr. and Mrs. Hedley's ◪**Trout Fly Guest House ❸,** 8 Charlotte St., has tartan carpets and rooms across from the ferry. (☎01496 302 204. $32

hollow by the broad bay." Considered by many to be Islay's finest malt; judge for yourself through free samples. Tours M-F 2 per day. Closes for 4 weeks in July or August. Call ahead. £2. Info center open M-F 9am-5pm.

4. Bowmore (☎01496 810 441), in town. The oldest of Islay's distilleries in full operation (est. 1779) and one of the last to malt its own barley; a favorite of many throughout the UK. Tours M-F 4 per day, Sa 1-4 per day. £4.

5. Bruichladdich (brook-LAD-dee; ☎01496 850 190), 2 mi. from Port Charlotte. A smoother malt, produced with 19th-century equipment. The only one on Islay that bottles its own product. Tours M-F 3 per day, Sa 2 per day. £4.

6. Caol Ila (cool-EE-la; ☎01496 302 760), 1 mi. from Port Askaig. Fine views across the sound and a complimentary swig. Tours Apr.-Sept. by appointment. £4.

7. Bunnahabhain (bun-na-HAV-en; ☎01496 840 646). Home to the "Black Bottle," containing all 7 of Islay's malts. Tours M-F 3 per day. Free.

8. Kilchoman (☎01496 850 011). Islay's newest distillery is at Rockside Farm, 4 mi. from Port Charlotte. But don't expect a dram—bottles won't be out until 2011. Tours daily 2 per day. £2.

per person. Cash only.) The **Mactaggart Community Cyber Cafe ❶**, 30 Mansfield Pl., offers diner-style meals, satellite TV, and a pool table. (☎01496 302 693. Internet £1 per 30min. Open daily noon-7pm. Kitchen open until 6:30pm.) **Bike rental** is available from **Port Ellen Playing Fields,** at the edge of town on the B846. (☎01496 302 349 or 07831 246 911. £5 per ½-day, £8 per day. Open May-Sept. daily noon-4pm and 6-9pm.) There is a **bank** in town, but no ATM.

BOWMORE   ☎(0)1496

Located 10 mi. from both Port Ellen and Port Askaig, the small town of Bowmore is a convenient transportation base, and the colorfully trimmed white-washed houses look out on the sandy bay. The town is arranged in a grid centering on Main St., with the 18th-century **Bowmore Round Church** at the top. The church was built perfectly circular to keep Satan from hiding in corners. (Open daily 9am-6pm. Free.) Across from the TIC, **Bowmore Distillery** is the island's oldest. (☎01496 810 441; www.bowmore.com. Open from July to mid-Sept. daily 9am-5pm; from mid-Sept. to Easter M-F 9am-5pm, Sa 9am-noon; Easter-June M-Sa 9am-5pm. Tours M-F 10, 11am, 2, 3pm, Sa 10am. £4, under 18 free.) **The Big Strand,** 7 mi. of white sand beach with waves perfect for bodysurfing (if you can stand the cold), lines the coast between Bowmore and Port Ellen.

Among a flock of similarly priced B&Bs, the friendly proprietors of the **Lambeth Guest House ❸**, Jamieson St., offer decent lodgings supplemented by good conversation. (☎01496 810 597. No singles. From £28 per person. AmEx/MC/V.) A quick 5min. walk from the TIC, the **Meadow House B&B ❸** has no ensuite rooms but comfortable beds and tasty breakfasts galore. (Singles £35; doubles and twins £60.) A small **Co-op** sells groceries on Main St. (☎01496 810 201. Open M-Sa 8am-8pm, Su 12:30-7pm.) The **Harbour Inn Restaurant ❹** serves excellent local seafood. (www.harbour-inn.com. Entrees £14-26. Kitchen open daily noon-2pm and 6-9pm. Bar open M-Sa 11am-1am, Su noon-1am. MC/V.)

Islay's **Tourist Information Centre,** Main St., books accommodations for £4 plus a 10% deposit and furnishes travelers with useful maps of the area. Ordnance Survey Explorer #352 and 353 (£8) and Landranger #60 (£7) maps cover Islay. *The Isles of Islay, Jura and Colonsay Walks* (£2) details hikes. (☎01496 810 254. Open July-Aug. M-Sa 9:30am-5:30pm, Su 2-5pm; Sept.-Oct. M-Sa 10am-4pm; Nov.-Mar. M-F 10am-4pm; Apr. M-Sa 10am-5pm; May-June M-Sa 9:30am-5pm, Su 2-5pm.) Other services include: a **launderette** in the **Mactaggart Leisure Centre,** School St. (☎01496 810 767; open W-Th 10:30am-9:30pm, F 10:30am-9pm, Sa-Su 10:30am-5:30pm); free **Internet** at the Servicepoint on Jamieson St., just beyond the gas station (☎01496 301 301; open M-F 9am-5pm); and the **post office,** Main St. (☎01496 810 366; open M-W and F 9am-5:30pm, Th 9am-1pm, Sa 9am-12:30pm), which also rents **bikes** (£10 per day). **Postcode:** PA43 7JH.

ISLE OF JURA

Separated from Islay by a narrow strait, the Isle of Jura (Deer Island) has grown wilder and more and isolated during the past century. A census in 1841 found 2299 people; today, fewer than 200 call the island home. Living in scattered houses along a single-track road on the eastern shore, these hardy folk are outnumbered by deer 30 to one. The isle was remote enough to satisfy novelist George Orwell, who escaped to Jura while penning *1984*. The entire western coast and center of the island are uninhabited. Its great hiking country includes a series of tough ascents up the three **Paps of Jura** (all over 2400 ft.), scaled by runners in the annual Jura Fells Race in May. The land surrounding **Loch Tarbet** is harsh but beautiful. At the island's northern tip, the **Corryvreckan Whirlpool**—the second largest in the world—churns violently. Ordnance Survey Explorer

#353 (£8) and Landranger #361 and 61 maps cover the island, and *Jura: A Guide for Walkers* (£3.50) details various hikes. More conservative walkers will enjoy the rare plant species that inhabit the **Jura House Walled Garden.**

Although the distance between Islay and Jura is short, do not attempt the swim, as tidal currents are powerful. The Jura **ferry** (☎01496 840 681) takes cars and passengers across the Sound of Islay from Port Askaig to Feolin (5min.; in summer M-Sa 13-16 per day, Su 6 per day, in winter schedules more limited; £3.10). During the summer and on weekdays during the school year, the Jura bus service meets the ferry by request (☎01496 820 314 or 820 221).

CRAIGHOUSE ☎(0)1496

Jura's only village is a tiny, one-road settlement 10 mi. north of the ferry landing. At the center of Craighouse, the **Isle of Jura Distillery** employs 5% of the island's population and offers tours by appointment. (☎01496 820 385. Shop open Easter-Oct. M-F 10am-4pm.) Nearby, a small, unstaffed **information center** has walking and wildlife guides. More detailed information and free **Internet** can be found a 5min. walk down the street from the distillery, heading away from the ferry, at the **Jura Service Point.** (☎01496 820 161. Open M-F 10am-1pm.) Craighouse is home to one hotel and a couple of B&Bs. The only **restaurant ❷** in town is in the **Jura Hotel ❶,** where bar lunches (noon-2pm) and evening meals (7-9pm) average £6.50-13. (☎01496 820 243; www.jurahotel.co.uk. Toilets, showers, and laundry available for a fee. Hotel from £35 per person. AmEx/MC/V.) Jura has no banks, but the hotel will give cash back on purchases. There's also a van run by the **Royal Bank of Scotland** that functions as a bank on wheels and is in town around 1-3pm on Wednesdays. Across from the distillery, **Jura Stores** sells groceries and houses a **post office.** (☎01496 820 231. Store open M-Th 9am-1pm and 2-5pm, F-Sa 9am-1pm and 2-4:30pm. Post office open M-Tu and Th-F 9am-12:30pm, W 9-9:30am, Sa 9am-1pm and 2-4:30pm.) **Postcode:** PA60 7XS.

HIGHLANDS AND ISLANDS

Misty and remote, the untamed wilds of the Scottish Highlands have long been the stuff of legend and fantasy. These sheep-dotted moors, sliced by the narrow lochs of the Great Glen and framed by stoic granite mountain ranges, have endured for thousands of years. Once home to kilted clans, the Highlands' current residents include some of Scotland's last Gaelic-speaking Scots, artisans, and crofters. Raging winds and ocean currents can be forbidding, but the land's unparalleled beauty draws thousands of visitors every year.

HIGHLIGHTS OF THE HIGHLANDS AND ISLANDS

CLIMB Ben Nevis, the highest mountain in Britain, whose 4406 ft. peak hides behind a layer of clouds. On a clear day, you can see all the way to Ireland (p. 635).

DISCOVER an unsurpassed wealth of ancient ruins set amid sheep, sky, and ocean in the **Orkney** and **Shetland Islands** (p. 671).

TREK through the Cuillin Mountains and misty waters of the **Isle of Skye** (p. 655).

TRANSPORTATION

Although it's possible to travel by public transportation through the Highlands in the summer months, advance planning is essential, as bus and train schedules seem to shift with the winds. In winter, treacherous weather conditions and many fewer buses and trains make travel even more difficult. The essential *Public Transport Travel Guides*, free from TICs, are region-specific and up-to-date. **Trains** (☎08457 484 950) travel to major destinations and shipping areas, and Scottish Citylink **buses** (☎08705 505 050) often connect train travelers to smaller towns. Citylink offers an **Explorer Pass** (3 consecutive days £35, 5 days in 10 £59, 8 days in 16 £79), which includes 50% off on CalMac ferries. The Royal Mail operates a **postbus** service (www.postbus.royalmail.com) that is often the best way to access remote areas in summer months. **Driving** in the Highlands is more convenient but involves navigating single-lane roads, icy winter conditions, and sheep with a death wish (see **By Car,** p. 37). Most **ferries,** especially on the west coast, are operated by Caledonian MacBrayne (CalMac; ☎08000 665 000; www.calmac.co.uk). Peruse the website for the combination ticket ("Island Hopscotch" pass) that best suits your trip.

NORTHEAST SCOTLAND

ABERDEEN   ☎(0)1224

From the stately granite buildings of its Old Town to the leafy avenues of its upscale West End to the crowded shopping streets of the city center, Aberdeen combines a dignified, old-fashioned elegance with an energetic vibe fueled by

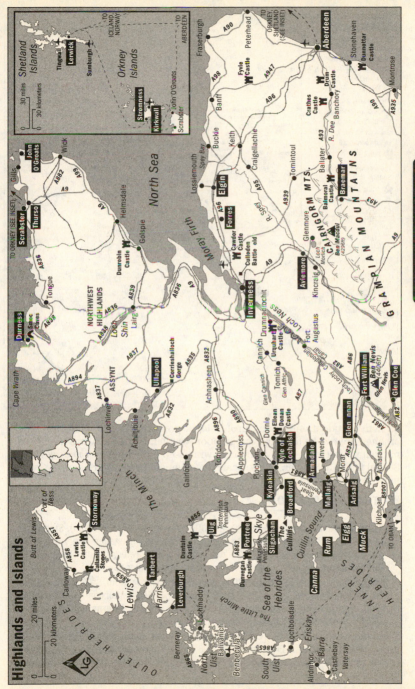

Highlands and Islands

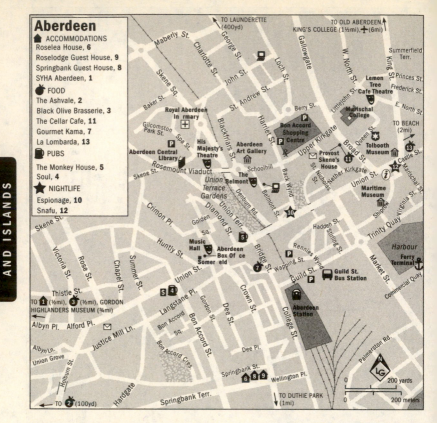

Aberdeen

⌂ ACCOMMODATIONS
Roselea House, **6**
Roselodge Guest House, **9**
Springbank Guest House, **8**
SYHA Aberdeen, **1**

🍴 FOOD
The Ashvale, **2**
Black Olive Brasserie, **3**
The Cellar Cafe, **11**
Gourmet Kama, **7**
La Lombarda, **13**

🍺 PUBS
The Monkey House, **5**
Soul, **4**

★ NIGHTLIFE
Espionage, **10**
Snafu, **12**

its active student and young professional populations. The uniformly gray architecture can be discouraging in poor weather, but the city has a real cosmopolitan bustle. Recent years have witnessed a boom due to nearby North Sea oil fields, and several large-scale development projects are in progress to move the city away from and beyond its industrial and shipping roots.

▌▛ TRANSPORTATION

Flights: Aberdeen Airport (☎08700 400 006; www.aberdeenairport.com). Stagecoach Bluebird #10, 307, and 737 run to the airport from the bus station (every hr., £1.30) and First (☎01224 650 065) #27 runs from Guild St. (every hr. until 8pm, £1.80). **British Airways** (☎08457 733 377) flies to **London** (11 per day, £100-160).

Trains: Station on Guild St. Ticket office open M-F 6:30am-7:30pm, Sa 6:15am-7:30pm, Su 8:45am-6pm. Trains (☎08457 484 950; www.firstscotrail.com) to: **Edinburgh** (2hr., every hr., £38.20); **Glasgow** (2hr., every hr., £38.20); **Inverness** (2hr., every hr., £23.50); **London King's Cross** (7hr., 6 per day, £148).

Buses: Station on Guild St. (☎01224 212 266). Ticket office open M-F 8am-6pm, Sa 8:30am-5pm. National Express (☎08717 818 181) to **London** (2 per day, £43). Megabus (☎08705 505 050) to **London** (2 per day, £19). Scottish Citylink (☎08705 505

050) to **Edinburgh** and **Glasgow** (both 4hr., every hr., £21.70). Stagecoach Bluebird (☎01224 212 266) #10 to **Inverness** (4hr., every hr., £8.10).

Ferries: Aberdeen Ferry Terminal, Jamieson's Quay (☎08456 000 449; www.northlink-ferries.co.uk). Turn left at the traffic light off Market St. onto Commercial Quay. Open M, W, F 7am-7pm, Tu, Th, Sa-Su 7am-5pm. Northlink Ferries run to **Kirkwall, Orkney** (6hr.; Tu, Th, Sa-Su 5pm; round-trip from £32.60), and **Lerwick, Shetland** (12-14hr.; M, W, F, Su 7pm, Tu, Th, Sa 5pm; round-trip from £42.80).

Public Transportation: First Aberdeen, 47 Union St. (☎01224 650 065), runs public buses. Office open M-Sa 8:45am-5:30pm. Unlimited day travel £3.70.

Taxis: Com Cabs (☎01224 353 535).

Car Rental: Arnold Clark Car Hire (☎01224 249 159; www.arnoldclarke.com). Open M-F 8am-8pm, Sa 8am-5pm, Su 9am-5pm. From £19 per day, £99 per week. 23+.

PRACTICAL INFORMATION

Tourist Information Centre: 23 Union St. (☎01224 288 828; www.agtb.org). From the bus station, turn right on Guild St., then go left on Market St.; take the 2nd right on Union St. Books rooms for £4 plus a 10% deposit. Internet £1 per 20min. Open July-Aug. M-Sa 9am-6:30pm, Su 10am-4pm; Oct.-June M-Sa 9:30am-5pm.

Tours: Grampian Coaches (☎01224 650 024; www.firstgroup.com) runs various day tours to nearby castles, Royal Deeside, the Whisky Trail, Loch Ness, and beyond. June-Sept. £15-20, concessions £11-14.

Banks: Ubiquitous. **Thomas Cook,** 335-337 Union St. (☎08453 089 101). Open M-W and F-Sa 9am-5:30pm, Th 10am-5:30pm.

Beyond Tourism: Volunteer Service Aberdeen, 38 Castle St. (☎01224 212 021; www.vsa.org.uk or www.volunteerscotland.org).

Library: Aberdeen Central Library (☎01224 652 532), on Rosemount Viaduct. Free Internet in the Media Centre. Open M-Th 9am-8pm, F-Sa 9am-5pm.

Launderette: A1, 555 George St. (☎01224 621 211). £10.50. Open daily 9am-5pm.

Police: Queen St. (☎08456 005 700).

Pharmacy: Boots, Bon Accord Shopping Centre (☎01224 626 080). Open M-W and F-Su 8:30am-6pm, Th 8:30am-8pm.

Hospital: Aberdeen Royal Infirmary, on Foresterhill Rd. (☎08454 566 000).

Internet Access: Free at the **library** (above). **The Hub,** 22 John St. (☎01224 658 844). £1.50 per 30min. Open M-F 8am-5pm, Sa-Su 11am-5pm. **Books and Beans,** 22 Belmont St. (☎01224 652 511). £3 per hr. Open M-Sa 10am-5pm, Su 11am-4pm.

Post Office: 489 Union St. **Bureau de change.** Open M-F 9am-5:30pm, Sa 9am-12:30pm. **Postcode:** AB11 6AZ.

ACCOMMODATIONS

With only one hostel convenient to the city, Aberdeen has few budget accommodations. B&Bs, many of them housed in nearly identical townhouses, pepper **Bon Accord** and **Springbank Terrace,** near the train station. From the bus and train stations, turn south from Guild St. on College St., then west on Wellington Pl., which melds into Springbank Terr. Generally, the farther away from Union St., the cheaper the accommodation is.

SYHA Aberdeen, 8 Queens Rd. (☎01224 646 988). A 30min. walk on Union St. and Albyn Pl. or a 5-10min. ride on bus #13, 14, or 27. In an old stone house, with a large dining room. Laundry £4. Internet £1 per 20min. Reception 7am-11pm. Curfew 2:30am. Seasonal dorms £13.50-17, under 18 £12-13. AmEx/MC/V. ❷

Roselodge Guest House, 3 Springbank Terr. (☎01224 586 794). Vegetarian breakfasts and rooms with a few housecats. Singles and doubles £25-35. Cash only. ❸

Roselea House, 12 Springbank Terr. (☎01224 583 060; www.roseleahouse.co.uk). Family-owned with large roses outside. Singles from £32; doubles from £44. MC/V. ❸

Springbank Guest House, 6 Springbank Terr. (☎01224 592 048). Family-owned B&B with comfortable furniture. Singles £30-35; doubles £40-45. Cash only. ❸

 BIG OIL. The weekend is the best time for a stopover in Aberdeen. During the week, oil-rig workers fill up hotel and B&B rooms, driving up prices. When the workers leave the city, many rates drop significantly.

🍴 FOOD

Save money at **Somerfield** supermarket, 204 Union St. (☎01224 645 583. Open M-Sa 7am-9pm, Su 8am-9pm.) **Union Street** and its branches feature dozens of restaurants serving international cuisine.

Black Olive Brasserie, 32 Queens Rd. (☎01224 208 877), up the street from the SYHA Hostel. Modern European food served in a glass-enclosed sunroom decked out in contemporary black and white. The tomato and black olive gnocchi (£8) is a great taste of the sunny Mediterranean flavors that the bistro evokes. Entrees £7-16. Open in summer M-Sa 10am-10pm; Su 11:30-6:45; in winter M-Sa 10am-10pm. AmEx/MC/V. ❷

La Lombarda, 2-8 King St. (☎01224 640 916). The oldest Italian restaurant in Britain, located in the pedestrian-only district. Romantically lit. Pasta and pizza (£8-10), meat and fish (£11-17), and lunch entrees (£5). Outdoor seating available. Open M-Th and Su 10am-2pm and 5-9:30pm, F-Sa 10am-2pm and 5-10pm. MC/V. ❷

The Ashvale, 42-48 Great Western Rd. (☎01224 596 981). The award-winning Ashvale serves up the best fish and chips around (£7-9). By finishing the signature Ashvale Whale, a 1 lb. fried haddock (£10.70), the hungriest diners can win a free dessert or a 2nd Ashvale Whale. Open daily 11:45am-11pm. MC/V. ❷

The Cellar Cafe, Provost Skene's House (☎01224 522 743). After touring the reconstructed rooms in the house, enjoy the cafe fare in the fortified basement. Tall windows keep it pleasantly bright. Lunch £5; muffins 1.30. Open M-Sa 10am-5pm. MC/V. ❶

Gourmet Kama, 20 Bridge St. (☎01224 575 754; www.gourmetkama.co.uk). Hole in the wall serving delectable fare straight from Delhi. Sit-down and takeaway. Entrees £7-10. Lunch buffet W-Sa noon-3pm (£6-8). Open daily noon-11pm. AmEx/MC/V. ❷

👁 SIGHTS

TOLBOOTH MUSEUM. Jailbird mannequins strike uncomfortable poses in the Tolbooth Museum, which displays prison artifacts and police equipment in the Tolbooth, a renovated 17th-century jail. It's fun if you have an interest in tools of barbaric punishment or a slightly macabre sense of humor. (☎01224 523 666. Open July-Sept. Tu-Sa 10am-4pm, Su 12:30-3pm.)

MARITIME MUSEUM. Great for families, the Maritime Museum has interactive exhibits and a huge collection of navigation tools and instruments in a sleek facility. It provides a comprehensive history of Aberdeen's long affair with the sea, from whaling to drilling for oil. The preserved deep sea creatures on display include unidentifiably bizarre and grotesque specimens. (On Shiprow. ☎01224 337 700. Open M-Sa 10am-5pm, Su noon-3pm. Free.)

OLD ABERDEEN. The northern part of Aberdeen is known as Old Aberdeen and includes the **University of Aberdeen.** For a complete tour of the stately, Gothic buildings that constitute this neighborhood, pick up the free *Old Aberdeen Trail* guide at the TIC. Stop at the Chapel of **King's College** to see the 16th-century "misery seats"—students were forced to sit on the un-orthopedic chairs for hours. *(From the city center, take bus #1, 2, 13, or 40 from the city center or walk some distance along King St. ☎01224 272 137. Open daily 9am-4:30pm. Tours July-Aug. Su 2-5pm. Free.)* The **Cruikshank Botanic Gardens** are a well-documented collection of plants managed by the University of Aberdeen. *(St. Machar Dr. ☎01224 493 288. Open May-Sept. M-F 9am-4:30pm, Sa-Su 2-5pm; Oct.-Apr. M-F 9am-4:30pm. Free.)*

DUTHIE PARK. A flowering expanse on the south side of the city, Duthie (DA-thee) sports an extensive rose garden and the **Winter Gardens Hothouse,** home to enormous bougainvillea, hibiscus, and thistle. *(By the River Dee at Polmuir Rd. and Riverside Dr. Take bus #17 or 21. ☎01224 523 201. Park open daily from 8am to 1hr. before dusk. Hothouse open daily Apr.-Oct. 9:30am-6:30pm; Nov.-Mar. 9:30am-3:30pm. Free.)*

OTHER SIGHTS IN THE CITY CENTER. The columned **Aberdeen Art Gallery** features traveling exhibits and stately rooms with a focus on Scottish contemporary art. *(On Schoolhill. ☎01224 523 700; www.aagm.co.uk. Open M-Sa 10am-5pm, Su 2-5pm. Free.)* The rooms of the castle-like **Provost Skene's House** have been decorated to recall its 17th-century roots. *(45 Guestrow, just up Broad St. from the Maritime Museum. ☎01224 641 086. Open M-Sa 10am-5pm, Su 1-4pm. Free.)*

🎵 ENTERTAINMENT

Seagulls aren't the only things to listen to in Aberdeen; the city sways to the rhythms of performers seven nights a week. Find out about the latest events from the **Aberdeen Box Office,** on Union St. (☎01224 641 122; www.boxofficeaberdeen.com. Open M-Sa 9:30am-6pm.)

Lemon Tree Cafe Theatre, 5 W. North St. (☎01224 337 688; www.boxofficeaberdeen.com), near Queen St. Small venue serving homemade food and drink in front of its main stage. Hours vary depending on event; check website or pick up a copy of *The Lemon Tree Magazine* for the latest showtimes. Buy tickets from the Aberdeen Box Office.

The Music Hall, Union St. (☎01224 641 122; www.musichallaberdeen.com), next to the Aberdeen Box Office. Features pop bands, musicals, and orchestra recitals. Buy tickets through the Aberdeen Box Office.

His Majesty's Theatre, Rosemount Viaduct (☎01224 641 122; www.hmtaberdeen.com). Presents drama with a classical focus. Tickets through the Aberdeen Box Office.

Aberdeen Arts Centre, 33 King St. (☎01224 635 208; www.aberdeenartscentre.org.uk). Stages avant-garde and traditional plays.

Belmont Picture House, 49 Belmont St. (☎01224 343 536). The Belmont screens independent films. Tickets £6-8.

📍 NIGHTLIFE

Soul, 333 Union St. (☎01224 211 150). Pub/club combo in an old cathedral packed with trendy Aberdonians all week. Stained-glass windows and a DJ in the pulpit create an ironic environment. Free Wi-Fi. Entrees £8-11. Happy hour F 4-7pm with £4 mixed drinks. Open M-Th and Su 10am-midnight, F-Sa 10am-1am. Turns into club at 10pm. Kitchen open noon-9:30pm. MC/V.

Espionage, 120 Union St. (☎01224 561 006; www.espionage007.co.uk). Great theme nights that are often Bond-focused, with large dance spaces and occasional live music.

Martinis (shaken or stirred) are available (£5), and beer flows faster than a chase scene (£3.50). No cover. Open M-Th and Su 9pm-2am, F-Sa 9pm-3am.

Snafu, 1 Union St. (☎01224 596 111; www.clubsnafu.com). Intimate underground venue for an eclectic assortment of performers. Frequent live comedy on weeknights and live music on weekends. Open M-Th 10pm-2am, F-Sa 10pm-3am.

The Monkey House, 1 Union Terr. (☎01224 251 120). Kid-friendly restaurant that transitions into an upscale candlelit lounge bar at 10pm. Burgers and fish entrees attract hungry Union St. shopping hordes. Entrees £8-13. Open M-Th and Su noon-midnight, F-Sa 11am-1am. Kitchen open M-F noon-8:30pm, Sa-Su noon-9:30pm. MC/V.

⯈ DAYTRIPS FROM ABERDEEN

▨DUNNOTTAR CASTLE. The lawn surrounding 14th-century Dunnottar Castle (dun-AHT-ur) drops off into a sheer rock face, framing the cliffside ruins. One of Scotland's best-defended castles, Dunnottar has been the site of many bloody battles. Here, Presbyterians were imprisoned during the Reformation, the crown jewels of Scotland were stolen during Cromwell's reign, and an English garrison was burned by William Wallace. *(Trains (20min., 1-2 per hr.) and Bluebird Northern buses #107 and 117 (1hr., 2 per hr.) connect Aberdeen to Stonehaven. Walk 30min. south from Stonehaven along the main road or via the footpath along the cliffs; follow signs. ☎01569 762 173. Open Easter-Oct. M-Sa 9am-6pm, Su 2-5pm; Nov.-Easter M-F 9am-dusk. £5.)*

FYVIE CASTLE. Northwest on the A947, 25 mi. from Aberdeen, 13th-century Fyvie Castle is as picturesque as any postcard and has found its way onto many. The castle is plagued by a ghost called the Green Lady who taps visitors on the shoulder (and appears in about 10 other Scottish castles). The grounds include fruit and vegetable gardens along with the requisite sculpted gardens. Among the castle's painting collection are several iconic Sir Henry Raeburn portraits of its former residents. *(Stagecoach Bluebird (☎01224 212 266) #305 runs from Aberdeen to Fyvie village (1hr., every hr.), a 1½ mi. walk from the castle. Castle ☎01651 891 266. Open July-Aug. daily 11am-5pm; Sept. and Easter-June Sa-Su noon-5pm. Last entry 4:15pm. Grounds open daily 9:30am-dusk. £8, concessions £5, families £20.)*

DRUM CASTLE. The oldest of the preserved castles in Scotland, Drum was continuously occupied from 1323 to 1975. Although the castle is less dramatic than some of its peers are, the large rose garden and grounds make for a lovely walk, while the castle rooms contain their share of impressive art and preserved knick-knacks. *(10 mi. west of Aberdeen on the A93. ☎08444 932 161. Open July-Aug. daily 11am-5pm; Sept.-Oct. and Apr.-June M, W-Th, Sa-Su 12:30-5pm. Grounds open daily 9:30am-dusk. £8, concessions £5. Grounds and garden without castle £2.50/2.)*

BRAEMAR   ☎(0)1339

Sixty miles west of Aberdeen on the A93, Braemar serves as an excellent base for seeing the Royal Deeside and trekking into the Cairngorms.

⯈❼ TRANSPORTATION AND PRACTICAL INFORMATION. The only ways into and out of Braemar by public transportation are Stagecoach **bus** #201 from Aberdeen (2hr., 6-7 per day, £11), which stops at Crathie for Balmoral Castle 15min. away, and Heather Hopper buses #501 and 502, which stop in Braemar en route to Pitlochry. Drivers can reach Braemar from Perth or Aberdeen on the A93. In Braemar, rent **bikes** from the Mountain Sports Shop, Invercauld Rd., at the eastern edge of town. (☎01339 741 242. Bikes £10 per ½-day, £16 per day. Skis £16. Open daily 9am-6pm.)

The **Tourist Information Centre,** on Mar Rd., at the Mews, books accommodations and provides information about local hikes and walks. (☎01339 741 600. Open July-Aug. daily 9am-6pm; Sept. and Mar.-June daily 10am-5pm; Nov.-Feb. M-Sa 10:30am-4:30pm, Su 1-4pm.) The **post office** can be found in the **Alldays Co-op,** across from the TIC. (☎01339 741 201. Open M-W and F 9am-noon and 1-5:30pm, Th and Sa 9am-1pm.) **Postcode:** AB35 5YL.

⬛⬛ ACCOMMODATIONS AND FOOD. The rugged **Rucksacks Bunkhouse ❶,** 15 Mar Rd., behind the TIC, is welcoming and warm, with cozy bunks and a large kitchen. (☎01339 741 517. Laundry £2. Internet £2 per hr. Dorms £12-15; unheated alpine hut bunks £7. Cash only.) The 64-bed **SYHA Braemar ❶,** 21 Glenshee Rd., is located in a sheltered stand of trees. The large stone house has a common room and standard bunks. (☎01338 741 659. Laundry £2. Internet £1 per 20min. Reception 7:30-10:30am and 5-11pm. Dorms £15; twins £18 per person, under 18 £10. AmEx/MC/V.) Attached to the Braemar Hotel, the **Braemar Lodge Bunkhouse ❶,** 6 Glenshee Rd., rents rooms in a comfortable, rustic wood bunkhouse and serves a huge breakfast at the hotel ($6), located just up from SYHA on the southern side of town. (☎01338 741 627. Dorms £13. MC/V.) **SYHA Inverey ❶,** Linn of Dee Rd. 4 mi. from Braemar, offers few amenities but is located in a gorgeous field at the foot Ben Macdui. The daily postbus stops at the hostel before swinging by the Linn. (☎01339 741 017. No showers. Open May-Aug. Dorms £12.50-13.50, under 18 £9.50. AmEx/MC/V.)

Braemar has several teashops and plenty of gift shops that sell packaged haggis. Grab groceries at the **Alldays Co-op** (open M-Th 7:30am-8:30pm, F-Sa 7:30am-9pm, Su 9am-6pm; MC/V) or enjoy the locally renowned burgers ($4.20) at **The Hungry Highlander ❶,** 14 Invercauld Rd. (☎01339 741 556. Open M and Th 10am-8pm, W noon-8pm, F-Sa 10am-9pm, Su 9am-8pm.)

⬛⬛ FESTIVALS AND HIKING. On the first Saturday in September, the town hosts the ⬛**Braemar Gathering,** part of the Highland Games. In this 900-year-old tradition, pipers entertain, buff Highland athletes compete in events like caber-tossing, and Her Majesty's military forces vie for glory and honor in a tug of war. (☎01339 741 089. Seats £14-20; field admission £8.)

> **TIP**
>
> **TRUST US.** If you are visiting many sights in Scotland, consider becoming a member of the National Trust for Scotland. **NTS membership** grants free admission at any National Trust sight. At £44 (under 25 £15), it's a good deal. The three-, seven-, or 14-day **Discovery Tickets** are a bargain. (☎08444 932 100; www.nts.org.uk.)

The area around Braemar has hikes for all skill levels, centering on the frothy **Linn of Dee.** The area's best-known hike traverses the steep **Ben Macdui** (21 mi., 3100 ft.) and should be attempted only by the fit and well prepared. Begin at the car park at the Linn of Dee and follow the signs, although eventually a map is needed for the steepest part of the climb. For a more leisurely day, try the 2hr. round-trip **Derry Lodge Walk** around the river. This walk also begins at the Linn of Dee and passes through the forests around the Cairngorms. Signposts often stop short of the end of hikes; don't be caught without a map (Ordnance Survey #43; £6.50; ask for other applicable maps at the TIC). To get to the Linn, drive 10min. west of Braemar on the Linn of Dee Rd. or catch the daily **postbus** from the Braemar post office between 1:30 and 2:30pm. Otherwise, walk or bike the scenic 7 mi. alongside the Linn of Dee Rd.

HIGHLANDS AND ISLANDS

DAYTRIP FROM BRAEMAR: BALMORAL CASTLE. An hour west along the A93 from Braemar, Balmoral Castle and Estate rests on the southern side of the River Dee. As a current palace used by the royal family, Balmoral is a popular tourist destination. Walking and riding trails snake through 50,000 acres of hills and woodlands, passing monuments that commemorate royal marriages and deaths. Large formal gardens and greenhouses brighten up the landscape. A tractor awaits visitors at the entrance and takes them to the beginning of the self-guided audio-visual tour. Inside the castle, only the ballroom and exhibition are open to the public. *(Stagecoach bus #201.* ☎ *01339 742 534; www.balmoral-castle.com. Open Apr.-July daily 10am-5pm. £7, under 16 £3, seniors £6.)*

CAIRNGORM MOUNTAINS   ☎(0)1479

Cairngorm National Park is Britain's largest, and its mountains tower well above the treeline, providing one of Europe's sweetest ski spots and views stretching as far as Ben Hope, 96 mi. to the north. Temperatures on the mountains dip low even in the warmest months, providing challenging hikes for seasoned climbers and chilly walks for casual view-seekers.

TRANSPORTATION

The largest town in the Cairngorms, Aviemore (p. 636) is located on the main Inverness-Edinburgh rail and bus lines. The **train station** is on Grampian Rd., just south of the TIC. (☎01780 784 404. Open M-F 7:30am-9:25pm, Sa 8am-2:40pm, Su 10am-5:35pm.) **Trains** serve Edinburgh and Glasgow (both 2hr., 8-9 per day, £37.40) and Inverness (45min., £9.10). Southbound **buses** stop at the shopping center north of the train station, while northbound buses stop at the Cairngorm Hotel. Scottish Citylink (☎08705 505 050) runs every hour to Edinburgh (3hr., £20), Glasgow (3hr., £20), and Inverness (40min., £8.10). **Kincraig,** 6 mi. south of Aviemore on the A9, is accessible by Scottish Citylink M91 from Perth (6 per day). For updates and detailed information, call Traveline (☎08712 002 233).

The principal path into Glenmore Forest Park, the **Ski Road,** begins south of Aviemore (on the B970) and heads eastward. The road passes the sandy beaches of Loch Morlich before carrying on to Glenmore and ending at the base of Cairn Gorm. From Aviemore's train station, Highland Country bus #34 travels the same route (every hr.). The Cairngorm Service Station, on Aviemore's Main St., rents **cars.** (☎01479 810 596. Open M-F 8:30am-5pm. £36-42 per day, £190-210 per week.) For **bike** rental, head to Bothy Bikes, Grampian Rd. (☎01479 810 111. Open daily 9am-5:30pm. £15 per ½-day, £20 per day; includes helmet and map. MC/V.) Ellis Brigham, on Grampian Rd., rents **skis** during the winter and climbing equipment during the summer. (☎01479 810 175. Open daily 9am-6pm.) The Glenmore Shop and Cafe, opposite the SYHA Cairngorm in Glenmore, rents bikes, skis, **snowboards,** and **mountainboards.** (☎01479 861 253. Bikes £15 per ½-day, £20 per day. Open daily 9am-5pm.)

ORIENTATION AND PRACTICAL INFORMATION

Britain's most popular ski village in winter, **Aviemore** (p. 636) stays busy in summer, when tourists come to hike, bike, sail, surf, and swim. The areas surrounding Aviemore provide endless opportunities for outdoor activities. Many companies organize adventure sports packages, but the independent traveler can also enjoy the region's natural riches. **Glenmore** offers an up-close view of the range, and **Kincraig,** to the south, sustains visitors with a welcome breath of non-touristed air on the tranquil shores of **Loch Insh.** Smaller towns like **Boat-of-Garten** or **Grantown** are also packed with places to stay, often at lower rates.

The **Rothiemurchus Estate Visitors Centre,** near Inverdruie, 1 mi. east on the Ski Rd. from Aviemore, has info on tours and activities in the area. (☎01479 812 345. Open daily 9:30am-5:30pm.) **Glenmore Forest Park Visitors Centre,** at the end of the Ski Rd. in Glenmore, gives out maps and advice on walks west of the mountains. (☎01479 861 220. Open daily 9am-5:30pm.)

ACCOMMODATIONS AND CAMPING

Lazy Duck Hostel (☎01479 821 642; www.lazyduck.co.uk), in Nethy Bridge. Catch Highland Country bus #15 or 34 from Aviemore (20min., 6-9 per day) to the Nethy Bridge Causer and follow the signs. 6-8 beds, wood-burning stove, sauna, and resident egg-laying waterfowl. Free Internet. Call ahead. Dorms £10. MC/V online only. ❶

Slochd Mhor Lodge (SLOKT-moor; ☎01479 841 666; www.slochd.co.uk). From Carrbridge, turn left off the A9 to Slochd Mhor. Gorgeous wood lodge perfect for getting away from it all. Bike and ski rentals and Nordic and downhill ski lessons in winter. Wheelchair-accessible. Dorms from £15; twins from £36. ❷

Fraoch Lodge (☎01479 831 331; www.scotmountain.co.uk), on Deshar Rd. in Boat-of-Garten, 6 mi. northeast of Aviemore on the A95. Ask at the Aviemore bus station to be let off in Boat-of-Garten. Cozy lounge with working fireplace and exceptional meals. Owner leads area hikes in summer and larger winter mountaineering expeditions. Free continental breakfast; cooked breakfast £3; packed lunch £5; 2-course dinner £12. Book ahead. Family rooms and twins from £16 per person. MC/V. ❶

Ardenbeg Bunkhouse (☎01479 872 824; www.ardenbeg.co.uk). Take the A9 to Grant-own on Spey, turn off High St. keeping the bank on the left and the Co-op on the right, and turn left onto Grant St.; the hostel is on the right. Accessible by Highland Country bus from Aviemore. Owners can arrange outdoor instruction and equipment rental for guests. Laundry £1.50. Free Wi-Fi. Alpine-style bunks £14.50. MC/V. ❶

Insh Hall Lodge (☎01540 651 272; www.lochinsh.com), 1 mi. downhill from Kincraig on Loch Insh; take Highland Country bus #35 or 38 from Aviemore (15min., M-F 3 per day). From watersports with instructors in summer to ski school in winter, Insh Hall is like a lakeside camp. Rooms sufficient for outdoors enthusiasts looking for a comfortable bed for the night. Daily wildlife tours £8. Watersport equipment available (kayaks from £24 per day). Call ahead. Dorms from £12.50; B&B £25.50 per person. MC/V. ❷

SYHA Cairngorm Lodge (☎01479 861 238) in Glenmore. Catch Highland Country bus #34 or 36 from the Cairngorm Hotel opposite the rail station and ask to be dropped off. Loch Morlich beach across the road. Located in a former hunting lodge 7 mi. from Aviemore, 2 mi. from Cairn Gorm ski area. Beautiful mountain backdrop. Optional 2-course dinner £9.50. Doubles, dorms, and family rooms. £14-17 per person, under 18 £11.50-12.50. AmEx/MC/V. ❷

Glenmore Forest Camping and Caravan Park (☎08451 308 224), opposite the SYHA Cairngorm Lodge. At the base of the peaks with ample space and good facilities. £19.30-19.80 per 2-person tent, Extra person £6.30. MC/V. ❶

OUTDOOR ACTIVITIES

The Cairngorms have Scotland's highest concentration of ski resorts. Outdoor enthusiasts and snowbunnies converge at **CairnGorm Mountain** (on the mountain of **Cairn Gorm**) for skiing in winter and panoramic vistas in summer. On the funicular, or inclined railway, visitors can sit facing down the mountain for great views on the ride up to **Ptarmigan Centre,** Britain's highest train station (3600 ft.). Catch the peak of **Ben Nevis** to the west from the observation deck. Due to conservation concerns, riders may not set foot outside the station. The only way to explore the peak is to hike from the bottom. The hike

(3hr. round-trip) is not difficult on the main path, the **Coire Cas.** The **Windy Ridge** trail (3-4hr. round-trip) is shorter and more direct but also more strenuous and requires a map and navigation skills. Highland County bus #34 runs to Cairn Gorm from Aviemore. Trains run every 15-30min. (☎01479 861 261; www. cairngormmountain.org.uk. Ticket office opens 9:30am. Funicular £9.25.)

To reach the peak of **Ben Macdui,** Britain's second-highest at 4296 ft., take the **Northern Corries Path** from the car park to its terminus and navigate the unmarked route using the Ordnance Survey Landranger Map (£7). The mountain should only be attempted by the well prepared (7hr. round-trip). Before setting out, consult the helpful **Cairngorm Rangers** about trail and weather conditions and fill out a route plan sheet. The office is next to the Cairn Gorm Mountain car park. (☎01479 861 703. Open daily 9am-5pm, weather permitting.)

The Cairngorm Rangers also host free **guided hikes.** For forest walks, **Glenmore Visitors Centre** has several trails; the most popular is the easygoing 3hr. **Ryovan Trek** through the woods and along **Green Lochen.** Closer to Aviemore, the renowned **Lairig Ghru** trail heads south through 20 mi. of lush valley to Braemar. Be ready for an all-day trek. **Loch an Eilein** has paths that circle the lake through the woods, with gorgeous views of the castle at its center.

For **skiers,** a day ticket with a railpass at Cairngorm costs £29 (concessions £20). Several companies run ski schools and rent equipment; pick up a copy of *Ski Scotland* at the Aviemore TIC for details. Three miles west of the funicular, the interactive **Cairngorm Reindeer Centre** is home to dozens of the majestic creatures—the only remaining herd in Britain. Visit them in the pen attached to the center or take the trek to the hillside at 11am or 2:30pm to hand-feed the free-rangers. (☎01479 861 228. Open daily 10am-5pm. Paddock viewing £2.50, concessions £1.50; trek to the herd £9, concessions £6.50, families £27.) At **Working Sheepdogs** on Leault farm, just south of Kincraig on the A95, watch one of the only remaining Cairngorm shepherds command eight enthusiastic dogs at once. (☎01540 651 310. Demonstrations at 4pm and often at other times, depending on demand. Reservations welcome. £4.) The 269 acres of **Highland Wildlife Park,** in Kincraig, provide lots of kid-friendly opportunities to see local wildlife. (☎01540 651 270; www.highlandwildlifepark.org. Open daily July-Aug. 10am-6pm; Sept.-Oct. and Apr.-June 10am-5pm; Nov.-Mar. 10am-4pm. Last entry 1hr. before close. £10.50, concessions £8.50.) **Strathspey Highland Ponies,** by the Rothiemurchus visitors center, organizes treks for all ages and abilities on pedigree Highland ponies through the heart of virgin forests. (☎01479 812 345. Open Mar.-Nov daily 9am-5pm. Treks last 30-90min. Book ahead.)

> **❗ SAFETY PRECAUTIONS.** Although the Cairngorms rise only 4000 ft., the region can have the weather patterns of the Arctic tundra. Many trails are not posted or blazed, and trekkers must rely on a map, compass, and good navigational skills. Make sure to use an Ordnance Survey map (Landranger #35 and 36), available at the TIC. Leave a description of your intended route with the police or at the mountain station and learn the locations of the shelters (known as bothies) along your trail.

AVIEMORE
☎(0)1479

The largest town in Cairngorm National Park, Aviemore is a popular ski resort and a good base for exploring the surrounding mountains. The new and conveniently located **Aviemore Bunkhouse ❶,** Dalfaber Rd., near the town center by the Old Bridge Inn., has wood bunks, storage lockers, and free Wi-Fi. (☎01479 811 181; www.aviemore-bunkhouse.com. Dorms £15; doubles £40. Cash only.) The ranch-style **SYHA Aviemore ②**, 25 Grampian Rd., south of the TIC, has the usual SYHA amenities. (☎01479 810 345. 106 beds, 4-8 per room. Internet £1 per 20min. Curfew 2am. Dorms £14-17, under 18 £11.50-12.50. AmEx/MC/V. Campers will find cheap lodgings at **Rothiemurchus Camp and Caravan Park ❶**, 1 mi. south of Aviemore on the Ski Rd. (☎01479 812 800. £5 per person. MC/V.)

Grampian Road is lined with pubs and cafes to suit any budget. For groceries, the local **Tesco** is north of the train station. (☎08456 779 017. Open M-Sa 8am-10pm, Su 9am-8pm.) The menu at the ☒**Mountain Cafe ②**, 111 Grampian Rd. above Cairngorm Mountain Sports, features local produce in innovative entrees (£7-10) including many New Zealand-inspired and vegetarian options. (☎01479 812 473. Open daily 8:30am-5:30pm. MC/V.) The modern **Cafe Mambo ②**, 12-13 Grampian Rd., serves delicious burgers (£7-8.50) and soothing hot chocolate (£2) by day and transforms into a bar by night. (☎01479 811 670. Free Wi-Fi with a coffee order. Open daily noon-1am. Kitchen open M-Th and Su until 8:30pm, F-Sa until 7:30pm. MC/V.)

The **Aviemore and Spey Valley Tourist Information Centre**, on Grampian Rd., stocks free copies of the *Cairngorms Explorer* bus and train timetables, exchanges currency, and books B&Bs for £4 plus a 10% deposit. (☎01479 810 363. Open from July to mid-Sept. M-Sa 9am-6pm, Su 10am-4pm; from mid-Sept. to June M-Sa 9am-5pm, Su 10am-4pm.) Other services include: a **Bank of Scotland**, on Grampian Rd., across from Tesco (☎01479 887 000; open M-Tu and Th-F 9am-5pm, W 9:30am-5pm); free **Internet** access at **Aviemore Library**, Grampian Rd. (☎01479 811 113; 1hr. slots; open Tu 2-5pm and 6-8pm, W 10am-12:30pm, 2-5pm, 6-8pm, F 10am-12:30pm and 2-5pm); **police**, Grampian Rd. (☎01479 810 222); and the **post office**, Grampian Rd. (☎01479 811 056; open M-F 9am-5:30pm, Sa 9am-12:30pm). **Postcode:** PH22 1RH.

ELGIN ☎(0)1343

A visit to Elgin (EL-ghin; pop. 26,000) provides a look at the prototypical Highland town. The magnificent ruined arches of Elgin Cathedral, nicknamed the "Lantern of the North," warrant a stopover in the town, located between Aberdeen and Inverness on the A96.

▮▮ TRANSPORTATION AND PRACTICAL INFORMATION. The **train station** is 5min. south of the city center, at the end of South Guildry St. (Ticket office open M-Sa 6:30am-7:30pm, Su 10:30am-5:30pm.) Trains (☎08457 484 950; www.firstscotrail.com) run to Aberdeen (1hr., 10 per day, £14) and Inverness (45min., 11 per day, £9.40). **Buses** stop behind High St. and the St. Giles Centre. Stagecoach Bluebird (☎01343 544 222) buses #10 and 305 leave the bus station, on Alexandra Rd., across from the town hall, to Aberdeen (2hr., every hr., £8.10) and Inverness (1hr., 2 per hr., £8.10). Call Traveline (☎0871 200 2233) for complete schedules and information. Rent bikes at **Bike and Bowl,** 7 High St. (☎01343 549 656. £10 per day. Open M-Sa 9am-5pm.) The **Tourist Information Centre,** 17 High St., books accommodations for £4 plus a 10% deposit. (☎01343 542 666. Open July-Aug. M-Sa 9am-6pm, Su 11am-4pm; Sept. and May-June M-Sa 10am-5pm, Su 11am-3pm; Oct. and Mar.-Apr. M-Sa 10am-5pm; Nov.-Feb. M-Sa 10am-4pm.) Other services include free **Internet** at **Elgin Library** in Cooper Park (☎01343 562 600; open M-F 10am-8pm, Sa 10am-4pm) and the **post office,** 19 Batchen St. (☎01343 546 466; open M-F 8:30am-6pm, Sa 8:30am-4pm). **Postcode:** IV30 1BH.

▮▮ ACCOMMODATIONS AND FOOD. With lots of B&Bs catering to the Whisky Trail crowd (p. 638), Elgin has few options for the budget traveler. The owners of the Thunderton House Pub (below) operate the recently opened **Thunderton Backpackers ❷** upstairs, the only hostel in town. (☎07968 416 508. Free Wi-Fi. Dorms £20 per person. AmEx/MC/V.) North of High St., **Richmond Bed & Breakfast ❸**, 48 Moss St., has vegetarian breakfast options, ensuite rooms, and garden-side seating. (☎01343 542 561. Singles £30-35; doubles £50. Cash only.) Next to the Elgin Bowling Club, the high ceilings of the **Auchmillan Guest House ❸**, 12 Reidhaven St., give its rooms a regal feel. (☎01343 549 077. Singles £35; doubles £50. MC/V.) Camp in a caravan at **Riverside Caravan Park ❶**, West Rd. (☎01343 542 813. Open Apr.-Oct. £14-16 per caravan. Cash only.)

Pick up groceries at **Tesco,** Blackfriars Rd., near the bus station. (☎01343 527 300. Open 24hr. AmEx/MC/V.) **Thunderton House Pub ❶**, off High St., sells filling bargain lunches (£4). Locals come in droves for quiz night on Sundays. (☎01343 554 921; www.thundertonhouse.co.uk. Open M-Th and Su 10am-11pm, F-Sa 10pm-1am. Kitchen open M-Th and Su 10am-2:30pm, F-Sa 10am-5:45pm. AmEx/MC/V.) **Scribbles ❶**, 154 High St., fills with a Saturday crowd enjoying the assortment of thin-crust pizzas (£5-8) made from scratch. (☎01343 542 835. Open M-Sa 9am-10pm, Su noon-10pm. MC/V.) Indian and Pakistani cuisine make their peace at **Qismat ❷**, 202-204 High St., which features a mix of classic tandoori dishes and more unusual curries. (☎01343 541 461. Entrees £8-13. Open M-Sa noon-2pm and 5-11:30pm. AmEx/MC/V.)

◪ **SIGHTS.** Once the largest church in Scotland, **Elgin Cathedral** was burned twice in its 800-year history, reducing it to a scattered graveyard and two 90 ft. towers. (☎01343 547 171. Open Apr.-Sept. daily 9:30am-5:30pm; Oct.-Mar. M-W and Sa-Su 9:30am-12:30pm and 1:30-5:30pm. £4.70, children £2.35.) Next door, all 104 plants mentioned in the Good Book thrive in the **Biblical Garden.** (Open daily May-Sept. 10am-7:30pm. Free.) The **Elgin Museum,** 1 High St., boasts a fossil collection and Roman coins. (☎01343 543 675; www.elginmuseum.org.uk. Open Apr.-Oct. M-F 10am-5pm, Sa 11am-4pm. £3, concessions £1.50.)

▌ **DAYTRIP FROM ELGIN: ◪MALT WHISKY TRAIL.** Enticing smells hang in the air above the eight distilleries on the world-famous Malt Whisky Trail in the Speyside area around Elgin. *(Stagecoach Bluebird bus #10 covers Keith, Elgin, and Forres. Always tell the driver where you want to go. Day Rover ticket £14.)* The trail begins at the **Strathisla Distillery** in Keith, the oldest in the Highlands, offering guided tours and two different drams to willing tasters. *(A 5min. walk from the bus and train stations in Keith.* ☎*01542 783 044; www.chivas.com. Open from mid-Mar. to Nov. M-Sa 9:30am-4pm, Su noon-4pm. £5. No charge—and no drinking—for those under 18.)* Follow the marked trail along the A941 south to **Glenfiddich,** whose well-known whisky is doled out on the free "Original Tour" of the facility. If you have deeper pockets and a discerning nose, opt for the Connoisseurs' Tour (£20), which offers a tutored nosing of at least five of Glenfiddich's offerings. *(17 mi. south of Elgin. Take Stagecoach Bluebird bus #336 from Elgin to the distillery. 40min., every hr.* ☎*01340 820 373; www.glenfiddich.com. Open from Easter to mid-Oct. M-Sa 9:30am-4:30pm, Su noon-4:30pm; from mid-Oct. to mid-Dec. and Jan.-Easter M-F 9:30am-4:30pm.)* Stagecoach bus #336 to Glenfiddich (glen-FID-ick) will stop on request at the **Speyside Cooperage,** which repairs over 100,000 casks every year and displays the process. *(¼ mi. south of Craigellachie, 4 mi. north of Dufftown on the A941.* ☎*01340 871 108; www.speysidecooperage.co.uk. Open M-F 9am-4:30pm. Last entry 4pm. £3.10, concessions £2.50.)*

THE GREAT GLEN

INVERNESS   ☎(0)1463

The only city in the Highlands, Inverness retains an appealing mix of Highland hospitality and urban hustle. Split by the River Ness, the city's amenities cater to tourists returning from daytrips to nearby Loch Ness or heading farther afield to explore the most remote glens and footpaths of the Highlands.

📧 TRANSPORTATION

Flights: Inverness Airport (☎01667 464 000; www.hial.co.uk), 9 mi. east of the city and accessible by bus (M-Sa every hr.). **British Airways** (☎08444 930 787; www.britishairways.com) flies to **Dublin, Edinburgh, Glasgow, London, Orkney, and Shetland. EasyJet** (☎08706 000 000; www.easyjet.co.uk) flies to **London** and **Bristol.**

Trains: Station on Academy St., in Station Sq. Travel center open M-F 6:30am-8:30pm, Sa 6:30am-6:30pm, Su 9:15am-8:30pm. Luggage storage £3-5. Trains (☎08456 015 929) to: **Aberdeen** (2hr., 10 per day, £23.50); **Edinburgh** (3hr., 8 per day, £38.20); **Glasgow** (3hr., 8 per day, £38.20); **Kyle of Lochalsh** (2hr., 4 per day, £17.30); **London** (9hr., 6 per day, £149); **Thurso** (3hr., 3 per day, £15.30).

Buses: Farraline Park Bus Station (☎01463 233 371), off Academy St. Scottish Omnibuses sells tickets for most companies. Office open M-Sa 8:30am-5:30pm, Su 9am-5:30pm. National Express (☎08705 808 080) to **London** (13hr., 1 per day, £39). Scottish Citylink (☎08705 505 050) to: **Edinburgh** (4hr., every hr., £22.20); **Glasgow** (4hr., every hr., £22.20); **Kyle of Lochalsh** (2hr., 6 per day, £16.20); **Perth** (3hr., every hr., £16.40); **Thurso** (3hr., 4-5 per day, £17.50). Both Citylink and Rapsons Coaches (☎01463 222 244) to **Ullapool** (1hr., M-Sa 2 per day, £10.80).

Public Transportation: Buses travel around Inverness throughout the day; pick up the *Travel Times* brochure at the TIC or bus station.

Taxis: Inverness Taxis (☎01463 222 900). Taxis queue by the Eastgate Shopping Centre or at the train station in Station Sq.

Car Rental: Budget (☎01463 713 333; www.albacarhire.com) is on Railway Terr., behind the station. **Europcar** (☎01463 235 525; www.northernvehiclehire.co.uk) has a Telfer St. office, although rates may be higher. **Thrifty,** 33 Harbour Rd. (☎01463 224 466; www.thrifty.co.uk), has a fleet of automatic vehicles and delivery service to airport.

Bike Rental: Barney's, 35 Castle St. (☎01463 232 249). £12 per day. Open daily 7:30am-11pm.

🔷🔢 ORIENTATION AND PRACTICAL INFORMATION

The **River Ness** divides Inverness. Most attractions and restaurants lie on the east bank (Old Town), where **Castle Road, Church Street,** and **Academy Street** are connected by pedestrian-only **High Street.**

Tourist Information Centre: Castle Wynd (☎01463 234 353), up the steps toward the castle. The friendly staff helps track Nessie by bus, boat, and brochure and stocks a wealth of information on transportation and sights. Books CalMac ferry tickets, local tours (£1 per party), and non-hostel beds (£4 plus a 10% deposit). Internet £3 per hr. Open Apr.-July and Sept.-Oct. M-Sa 9am-6pm, Su 9:30am-4pm; Aug. M-Sa 9am-6pm, Su 9:30am-5pm; Nov.-Mar. M-Sa 9am-5pm, Su 10am-4pm.

Tours: Puffin Express (☎01463 717 181; www.puffinexpress.co.uk) runs daily summer minibus tours to John O'Groats and several Scottish Isles (£30-100). **CitySightseeing**

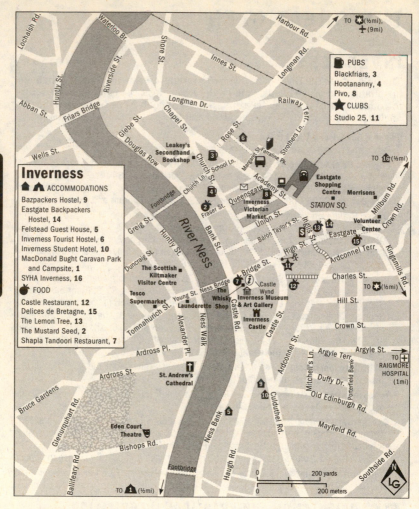

Inverness

■ ♠ ACCOMMODATIONS
Bazpackers Hostel, **9**
Eastgate Backpackers Hostel, **14**
Felstead Guest House, **5**
Inverness Tourist Hostel, **6**
Inverness Student Hotel, **10**
MacDonald Bught Caravan Park and Campsite, **1**
SYHA Inverness, **16**
♦ FOOD
Castle Restaurant, **12**
Delices de Bretagne, **15**
The Lemon Tree, **13**
The Mustard Seed, **2**
Shapla Tandoori Restaurant, **7**

■ PUBS
Blackfriars, **3**
Hootananny, **4**
Pivo, **8**
★ CLUBS
Studio 25, **11**

(☎01708 866 000; www.city-sightseeing.com) buses allow hop-on, hop-off service to major historical sights (depart bus station every hr.). Numerous tours hit Loch Ness (p. 644). **MacBackpackers** (☎01315 589 900; www.macbackpackers.com) offers a day tour of Inverness geared toward 20-somethings, departing from the Inverness Student Hotel about once per week. Office open daily 9am-6pm. £15.

Beyond Tourism: Open M-Tu and Th-F 9am-5pm, W 10am-5pm. **Volunteering Highland,** 1 Millburn Rd. (☎01463 711 393), across from Morrisons. Places volunteers in and around Inverness; call in advance for an appointment. In summer, the best bet for jobs is to go knocking on hostel, restaurant, and tourist-attraction doors.

Luggage Storage: At the bus station. £3-5.

Library: Farraline Park (☎01463 236 463). Photo ID required. Free Internet. Open M and F 9am-7:30pm, Tu and Th 9am-6:30pm, W 10am-5pm, Sa 9am-5pm.

Launderette: New City, 17 Young St. (☎01463 235 522). Wash £3, dry £1 per 15min. Internet £1 per 20min. Open Apr.-Sept. M-F 8am-8pm, Sa 8am-6pm, Su 10am-4pm; Oct.-Mar. M-F 8am-6pm, Sa 10am-4pm. Last wash 1hr. before close.

Police: Burnett Rd. (☎01463 715 555).

Hospital: Raigmore Hospital, Old Perth Rd. (☎01463 704 000).

Internet Access: Free at the **library** (above). **New City** (see **Launedrette**).

Post Office: 14-16 Queensgate (☎01463 243 574). Open M and W-Sa 9am-5:30pm, Tu 9:30am-5:30pm. **Postcode:** IV1 1AX.

ACCOMMODATIONS AND CAMPING

Inverness boasts a variety of accommodations for any budget. Well-maintained hostels with plenty of facilities are scattered throughout the city. For more privacy and waterfront views, B&Bs and guesthouses line either side of the Ness beginning just south of the castle.

- **Bazpackers Hostel,** 4 Culduthel Rd. (☎01463 717 663; www. bazpackershostel.co.uk). Homey, laid-back vibe. Working fireplace, comfortable armchairs and couches, and a brightly lit dining room. Just a few minutes from the city center. Lockers with £5 deposit. Laundry £5. Internet £1 per 30min. Free Wi-Fi. Dorms £13; doubles £32. MC/V. ❶

- **Inverness Student Hotel,** 8 Culduthel Rd. (☎01463 236 556). Funky riverside hangout playing loud music with cozy, quiet rooms. Houses a mix of backpackers, long-term residents, and MacBackpackers tour groups. Breakfast £2. Laundry £2.50. Internet 80p per 30min. Free Wi-Fi. Dorms £12-13.50. MC/V. ❶

- **Eastgate Backpackers Hostel,** 38 Eastgate (☎01463 718 756; www.eastgateback-packers.com), in the pedestrian Eastgate Precinct. Climb the stairs in the street-level bar. 38 beds. Urban hostel with a social crowd and murals taking gentle jabs at national stereotypes. Laundry £4. Free Wi-Fi. Dorms £10-13; twins £27-32. MC/V. ❶

- **Inverness Tourist Hostel (Backpackers Hostel),** 24 Rose St. (☎01463 241 962), in the alleyway behind the bus station. Cheapest hostel in the city provides solid amenities. Simple bunk beds, satellite TV, and leather couches. Internet £1 per hr. Free Wi-Fi. Dorms £8-10. MC/V. ❶

- **SYHA Inverness,** Victoria Dr. (☎01463 231 771). From the station, turn left on Academy St., go up Millburn Rd., and turn right on Victoria Dr. Industrial facilities, hotel-style hallways, and large numbers of guests create an impersonal feel. Comfortable beds, free parking, and great security compensate. Laundry £2. Internet and Wi-Fi £1 per 20min. Lockout 10am-2pm. Curfew 2am. Dorms £14-18, under 16 £10-12. AmEx/MC/V. ❷

- **Felstead Guest House,** 19 Ness Bank (☎01463 230 065), ½ mi. south of the city center. Large bay windows overlook the river and blossoming yard at this B&B. Check in at the Waterside Hotel next door. From £52 per person. MC/V. ❹

- **MacDonald Bught Caravan Park and Campsite,** Bught Ln. (☎01463 236 920). By the River Ness; easy to access from the A82. Well-kept campground full of amenities. Laundry available. Internet £1 per 30min. Open Apr.-Sept. £6 per 1- or 2-person tent; £6 per additional person. MC/V. ❶

FOOD

Inverness is full of international food options and some of the best traditional cuisine the Highlands has to offer. Buy groceries from **Morrisons,** Millburn Rd., near the train station; follow Academy St. east and then north. (☎01463 250 260. Open M-W and Sa 8am-8pm, Th-F 8am-10pm, Su 9am-8pm. MC/V.)

- **The Mustard Seed,** 16 Fraser St. (☎01463 220 220; www.themustardseedrestaurant. co.uk). One of the most popular restaurants in town. Elegant entrees like halibut with chorizo and basil (£15) served in dining area with mustard yellow walls. Early evening menu includes 2 courses and wine for £12. Excellent river views. Entrees from £10. 2-course lunch £6. Open daily noon-3pm and 5:30-10pm. AmEx/MC/V. ❸

Shapla Tandoori Restaurant, 2 Castle Rd. (☎01463 241 919). Climb the mirror-lined stairway to reach an expansive, elegant dining room overlooking the river. Generous portions of specialty curries and *baltis* at fair prices. 3-course lunch £6. Open daily 11am-11:30pm. AmEx/MC/V. ❷

The Lemon Tree, 18 Inglis St. (☎01463 241 114), north of High St. Contagiously cheerful staff and delicious homemade food. Cakes and scones (£2) come fresh from the oven daily, and the warm, comforting Thai soup (£2.50) is popular with lunchtime crowds. Open M-Sa 8:30am-5:30pm. Cash only. ❶

Delices de Bretagne, 4A-6 Stephen Brae (☎01463 712 422), on a small hill by High St., across from Eastgate Centre. Sweet and savory crepes (£3-6) in an airy cafe with wicker chairs and vintage posters. Open M-Sa 9am-5:30pm. MC/V. ❶

Castle Restaurant, 41 Castle St. (☎01463 230 925). Packed with families chowing on home-cooked American food. Great macaroni and cheese (£5.25) and a bustling diner backdrop. Entrees £5-9. Open M-Sa 9am-8:30pm. Cash only. ❷

⑤ SIGHTS

INVERNESS CASTLE. The pink sandstone Inverness Castle and its meticulously landscaped grounds dominate the city's skyline—its monumental facade is worth a closer look. Although it was built in the 12th century and used as a fortress for the vindictive Mary, Queen of Scots, the castle now serves as the city's courthouse. Unfortunately, the interior is closed to tourists.

LEAKEY'S SECONDHAND BOOKSHOP. The tall shelves of Leakey's hold over 100,000 volumes. Trade in an old favorite and enjoy a cup of tea with your new old read at the cushy balcony cafe. *(At the northern end of Church St. in Greyfriars Hall. ☎01463 239 947. Open M-Sa 10am-5:30pm. Cafe open M-Sa 10am-4:30pm. MC/V.)*

WHISKY SHOP. A standout among Inverness's many souvenir shops, the Whisky Shop features over 500 single-malt whiskies and offers free tastings. Knowledgeable staff can help select the perfect bottle as a gift for your family, friends, or yourself. *(17 Bridge St. ☎01463 710 525; www.whiskyshop.com. Open July-Aug. M-Sa 9am-10pm, Su 12:30pm-5pm; Sept.-Dec. and Easter-June M-Sa 9am-5:30pm, Su 12:30-4pm; Jan.-Easter M-Sa 9am-5:30pm. 18+.)*

SCOTTISH KILTMAKER VISITOR CENTRE. Inverness's kiltmakers have designed kilts for movies such as *Braveheart* and *Rob Roy*. Tour the museum, which features hunky mannequins in kilts, a video musical medley of kilts in the media, and kiltmakers live in action. *(4-9 Huntly St. ☎01463 222 781; www.highlandhouseof-fraser.com. Open from mid-May to Sept. M-Sa 9am-9pm, Su 10am-5pm; from Oct. to mid-May M-Sa 9am-5pm. £2, concessions £1. Made-to-measure kilts £300-450.)*

INVERNESS DOLPHIN CRUISES. Boarding a cruise into the Moray Firth offers a chance to see dolphins and a sure-fire way to enjoy Inverness by sea. Sightings are especially common 3hr. before high tide. Boats leave from the Shore St. quay, downstream from the city center. *(☎01463 717 900; www.inverness-dolphin-cruises.co.uk. 1hr. Mar.-Oct. 6 per day. £12.50, concessions £10.)*

⑥ PUBS AND NIGHTLIFE

The bar and club scenes blend together in Inverness, where the party begins and ends on the early side. An odd law states that all patrons must be inside a bar or club by midnight if they want to stay later, forcing full capacity earlier in the evening. The city's pubs are full of select local whiskies, and it's almost too easy to find that good, old-fashioned Scottish pint.

Hootananny, 67 Church St. (☎01463 233 651; www.hootananny.co.uk). A feisty, wood-studded bar combining authentic Scottish song and dance with a mouthwatering Thai restaurant downstairs (entrees £6-7). Upstairs Mad Hatter Club open W-Th 8pm-1am, F-Sa 8pm-3am. Downstairs open daily noon-1am. MC/V. ●

Studio 25, 9-21 Castle St. (☎01463 233 322). Students and fashionable 20-somethings line up for drinks at the padded white bar and frenzied dancing under a flashing disco ball. Chart-toppers on lower level, commercial dance music on upper level. Cover £5-7. Open Th-F and Su 10pm-3am, Sa 9pm-3am.

Blackfriars, 93-95 Academy St. (☎01463 233 881). Feel like a lad or lass at this foot-stomping bar. Scottish beer, Scotch whisky, Scottish food, Scottish music, and Scottish Scottishness. Live music all week. Ceilidh Night M-W. Open M-Th and Sa 11am-12:30am, F 11am-1am, Su 12:30pm-midnight. Kitchen open noon-3pm and 5-9pm.

Pivo, 38-40 Academy St. (☎01463 713 307). Czech-themed bar serving solid, upscale burgers with a selection of hard-to-find Eastern European beers. Later on, Pivo hosts a cutting-edge bar scene with leather lounge areas and white formica tables. Entrees £6-8. Open M-Th 11am-11pm, F-Sa 11am-2am, Su noon-11am.

FESTIVALS

Inverness Highland Games (☎01463 724 262; www.invernesshighlandgames.com), in late July. Enjoy Highland machismo and endless kilts. Tickets from £2.

Inverness Tattoo Festival (☎01463 242 915; www.tattooinverness.org.uk), for 1 week at the end of July. At the Northern Meeting Park, Ardross St. An epic military salute to Scotland and its history. £8-10.

Marymas Fair (☎01463 715 760), in Aug. Begins with a horse and carriage parade and recreates medieval life with craft stalls and performances.

DAYTRIPS FROM INVERNESS

The Highland Country Tourist Trail **Day Rover** ticket (☎01463 222 244; £9) is great for those who wish to see multiple sights. It allows one day of unlimited bus travel between Inverness, Culloden Battlefield, Cawdor Castle, and other sights. Buses leave from the Inverness bus station or Queensgate. Car rental is a pricier but more flexible option (p. 37). Don't try to squeeze more than two daytrips into one day without a car.

CAWDOR CASTLE. The fairy-tale-like castle sits on manicured grounds alongside a minigolf course, putting green, restaurant, and 5 mi. of hiking trails. Made famous by its role in Shakespeare's *Macbeth*, the castle's draw-bridge and garden maze enhance its billing as Scotland's most romantic castle. Built around a sacred (and long-dead) holly tree, it has been the residence of the thane of Cawdor's descendants since the 15th century and is still inhabited for much of the year. (*Between Inverness and Nairn on the B9090, off the A96. Highland Country bus #12 (30min., M-Sa every hr., round-trip £5) departs from the post office at Queensgate. ☎01667 404 401; www.cawdorcastle.com. Open May-Oct. daily 10am-5:30pm. Last entry 5pm. £7, concessions £6. Golf £12 per day.*)

DUNROBIN CASTLE. Dunrobin is one of the few castles still occupied (part-time) by its original owners, the Sutherland family. A tour of the castle provides a look at numerous additions as well as plenty of rumors about mysteries and ghosts in the walls. The castle gardens are an exhibit to themselves, modeled after those at Versailles. The twice daily **Falconry Display** draws crowds to see birds of prey fly close overhead. *(900 ft. north of Dunrobin station, 1 mi. north of Golspie. Train from Inverness (2hr., 4 per day, £16). Castle ☎ 01408 633 177; www.dunrobin-castle.co.uk. Open June-Aug. daily 10:30am-5:30pm; from Sept. to mid-Oct. and Apr.-May M-Sa 10:30am-4:30pm, Su noon-4:30pm. Last entry 30min. before close. £7.50, concessions £6.)*

CULLODEN BATTLEFIELD. The large field sits just east of Inverness on the B9006. Wander around the barren heath where well-trained English muske-teers decimated Bonnie Prince Charlie's men, killing 1200 Scots in 40min. as they charged at their enemy brandishing broadswords and leather shields. Gravestones commemorate the losses suffered by several major clans in the 1746 battle, the last to be fought on Scottish ground. The visitors center houses artifacts from the battle and 360° theater that runs a short clip reliving the fateful events. One scenic mile south, a grove hides the stone circles of the Bronze Age **Cairns of Clava.** *(Highland Country bus #12 (15min., every hr., round-trip £3). Visitors center ☎ 01463 790 607. Open daily Apr.-Oct. 9:30am-6pm; Nov.-Dec. and Feb.-Mar. 11am-4pm. Fields free. Visitors center £4. Guided tour £4.)*

LOCH NESS   ☎(0)1456

The Loch Ness Monster has captivated the world for hundreds of years, and even with a 24hr. webcam trained on the loch (www.lochness.co.uk), thou-sands of tourists make the trip each year to ponder its secrets. The tales began in AD 565, when St. Columba repelled a savage sea creature as it attacked a monk. Whether a prehistoric leftover, giant sea snake, or product of an overac-tive imagination, the monster and its lair remain a mystery to date. Just 70 ft. from its edge, the loch is 700 ft. deep, and no one has definitively determined how vast the loch really is or what life exists at its bottom.

TRANSPORTATION AND PRACTICAL INFORMATION. Scottish Citylink **buses** running from Inverness to the Isle of Skye (#917, 3-5hr., 3 per day); stop at Drumnadrochit and Urquhart Castle. The Drumnadrochit **Tourist Information Centre,** located on the main road, has its own take on the loch's mysteries and provides travel specifics. (☎01456 459 086. Open June-Oct. M-Sa 9am-5:30pm, Su 10am-4pm; Nov.-Mar. M-Sa 10am-1:30pm.)

ACCOMMODATIONS AND FOOD. Within walking distance of Loch Ness, the homey **Loch Ness Backpackers Lodge ❶,** Coiltie Farm House, East Lewiston, has a lively outdoor courtyard with a house band, frequent bonfires, and par-ties. Continue along the A82 from Drumnadrochit 1 mi. south to Lewiston, turn left at the sign beyond the gas station, and look for the white building with a gigantic Nessie mural. The lodge provides an entire wall of maps to get you to pubs and vistas, including to the 100 ft. **Divach Falls,** a 1hr. walk from the hostel. (☎01456 450 807; www.lochness-backpackers.com. Continental breakfast £3. Laundry £3.80. Internet and Wi-Fi £1. Dorms £14; family rooms £17 per person.) The more remote **SYHA Loch Ness ❷** stands alone on the loch's western shore, 7 mi. south of the castle. (☎01320 351 274. Laundry £2. Internet £1 per 20min. Book in advance July-Aug. Open Apr.-Oct. Dorms £13-15, under 16 from £10-11.) Both hostels lie on the Scottish Citylink bus routes between Inverness and Fort William (#919 and 917, every 2hr., £5 from Inverness). **Fid-dler's ❷,** the Village Green, opposite the Drumnadrochit TIC, has patio seating, a huge selection of whisky lining the walls (£3-6), and entrees (£8-15) one step above the usual pub fare. Try the boozy ice cream for £4.50. (☎01456 450 678. Open daily 12:30-2:30pm and 6-8:30pm. MC/V.)

◉ SIGHTS. The easiest way to see the loch is with one of the dime-a-dozen tour groups. **Jacobite Cruises,** Glenurquhart Rd., offers a variety of bus and boat trips. (☎01463 233 999; www.jacobite.co.uk. £10-25; includes castle admission.) Many cruises leave Drumnadrochit or Inverness and tour Loch Ness for £9-20, including **Castle Cruises Loch Ness** (☎01456 450 695), in the Clansman Gift Shop, and **Loch Ness Cruises** (☎01456 450 395), in the Original Loch Ness Visitor Centre, whose boats are equipped with underwater cameras.

In tiny Drumnadrochit, 13 mi. south of Inverness, two visitors centers examine the Nessie legend. For diehard believers, the **Original Loch Ness Visitors Centre** offers current footage of the loch and recent monster sightings. It also has a *Braveheart* center, focusing on Robert the Bruce's famous battle at Bannockburn. (☎01456 450 342. Open daily 9am-9pm. £5, students £4.25.) The **Official Loch Ness Exhibition Centre,** with its 40min. visual display (available in 11 languages), uses science to dispel the hoaxes. The dramatic sound effects create a spooky, live-action version of a sixth-grade textbook. Both centers have monstrous gift shops. (☎01456 450 573; www.lochness.com. Open daily July-Aug. 9am-6:30pm; Sept. and June 9am-6pm; Oct. and Feb.-May 9:30am-5pm; Nov.-Jan. 10am-3:30pm. £6.50, concessions £5.) **⬛Urquhart Castle** (URK-hart) was one of the largest castles in Scotland before it was blown up in 1692 to prevent Jacobite occupation. A video boils down 1000 years of history into a 10min. viewing and culminates in an unveiling of a panoramic castle view. Tours from Inverness stop at the ruins. (☎01456 450 551. Open Apr.-Sept. daily 9:30am-6pm; Oct. daily 9:30am-5pm; Nov.-Mar. M-Sa 9:30am-4:30pm. £6.50, concessions £5.) The **Abriachan Wood** paths (www.wildaboutswoods.org.uk), off the A82, provide a view of the loch and a hidden picnic spot. The **Great Glen Cycle Route** passes the loch on its way to Fort William. The River Foyers empties into the loch in a series of waterfalls 18 mi. down.

FORT WILLIAM AND BEN NEVIS ☎(0)1397

In 1654, General Monck founded the town of Fort William among Britain's highest peaks to keep out "savage clans and roving barbarians." But the town's location on the banks of Loch Linnhe caused his plan to backfire; today thousands of Highlands-bound hikers invade Fort William. Despite the tourists, the town makes an excellent base for exploring the impressive wilderness, including Ben Nevis, the highest peak in Great Britain.

▐ TRANSPORTATION

The **train station** is just beyond the north end of High St. Walk under the overpass to the right of the supermarket. **Trains** (☎08457 484 950) run to Glasgow Queen St. (3hr.; M-Sa 4 per day, Su 2 per day; £19.50) and Mallaig (1hr.; M-Sa 4 per day, Su 1-3 per day; £8.10). Many opt for the incredible **◼West Highland Railway** (☎01524 737 751; www.westcoastrailway.co.uk) Jacobite Steam train, which travels from Fort William to Mallaig through some of the Highland's most pristine wilderness, including vistas used in the *Harry Potter* films. (Runs July-Aug. M-F and Su; June and Sept.-Oct. M-F. Departs Fort William at 10:20am and Mallaig at 2:10pm. £29, one-way £22.) The Caledonian sleeper train runs to London Euston (12hr., 1 per day, £99). **Buses** arrive next to the Morrison's supermarket by the train station. Scottish Citylink (☎08705 505 050; www.citylink.co.uk) travels to: Edinburgh (4hr., 3 per day, £21); Glasgow (3hr., 4 per day, £14.70); **Inverness** (2hr., 7-8 per day, £9.20); Kyle of Lochalsh (2hr., 3 per day, £13.30); Oban (1hr., M-Sa 2-4 per day, £8.40). Scottish Citylink/Shiel sends a bus to Mallaig (1hr., M-F 1 per day, £5).

HIGHLANDS AND ISLANDS

Locally, Highland Country Buses (☎01397 702 373) travel around Fort William and the surrounding area. From June to September, #42 departs from the bus station and heads to the Nevis Range, and another bus takes visitors to the SYHA Glen Nevis and the Ben Nevis trailhead (10min.; M-Sa 7 per day, Su 4 per day; £1.30). An unnamed shuttle runs between the Glen Nevis town center and Lower Falls (£1.30). Bus #45 runs to Corpach from the car park behind the post office (15min.; M-Sa 3 per hr., Su every hr.; £1). **Taxis** queue outside the Tesco on High St.; try Al's Tours & Taxi (☎01397 700 700). Rent **bicycles** at Offbeat Bikes, 117 High St. (☎01397 704 008. £10 per ½-day, £15 per day. Open M-Sa 9am-5:30pm, Su 10am-5pm. AmEx/MC/V.)

◼️ 🚺 ORIENTATION AND PRACTICAL INFORMATION

From the bus and train stations, an underpass leads to **High Street,** Fort William's main pedestrian avenue.

Tourist Information Centre: High St. (☎01397 701 801). Books accommodations for a £4 charge plus a 10% deposit. Open July-Aug. M-Sa 9am-7pm, Su 9:30am-5pm; Apr.-June and Sept.-Oct. M-Sa 9am-6pm, Su 10am-4pm; Nov.-Mar. M-Sa 9am-5pm.

Banks: All along High St. **Royal Bank of Scotland,** 6 High St. (☎01397 705 191). Open M-F 9:15am-4:45pm, Sa 9:15am-2pm.

Outdoors Shops: Nevisport, Airds Crossing (☎01397 704 921), at the north end of High St. Hiking boots £9 per day plus deposit. Crampons and ice axes also available. Open M-Sa 9am-5:30pm, Su 9:30am-5pm and occasionally until 10pm on weekends in the high season. MC/V.

Library: High St., across from Nevisport (☎01397 703 552). Open M and Th 10am-8pm, Tu and F 10am-6pm, W and Sa 10am-1pm.

Police: High St. (☎01397 702 361).

Pharmacy: Boots, High St. (☎01397 705 143). Open M-F 9am-6pm, Sa 9am-5:30pm.

Hospital: Belford Rd. (☎01397 702 481).

Internet Access: One World, 123 High St. (☎01397 702 673). £3 per hr. Open daily 9:30am-9pm. Cash only.

Post Office: 5 High St. (☎01397 702 827), with a **bureau de change**. Open M-Sa 9am-5:30pm. **Postcode:** PH33 6AR.

🏠 🏕️ ACCOMMODATIONS AND CAMPING

Take care to reserve accommodations early on weekends, especially on rainy days when sensitive backpackers run for cover. Fort William's B&Bs might outnumber their local residents, but "no vacancy" signs are a common sight in the summer months. Follow the A82 into Glen Nevis for accommodations closer to the mountain trails and farther from the "city lights" of Fort William.

▨ **Calt William Backpackers,** 6 Alma Rd. (☎01397 700 711; www.scotlandstophostels. com). From the train station, turn left on Belford Rd., head right on Alma Rd., and bear left at the split. Rugged, welcoming atmosphere and facilities geared toward hikers. Watch the sun setting over Loch Linnhe from the back deck. 38 beds in 6- to 8-bed co-ed dorms; single-sex arrangements available. Self-catering kitchen. Breakfast £2. Laundry £2.50. Internet access £1 per 20min. Bike rental £12 per day. Lockout 1:30-4pm. Curfew 2am. Dorms £12.50-13.50; twins £28-33. AmEx/MC/V. ❶

▨ **Calluna,** Connochie Rd. (☎01397 700 451; www.fortwilliamholiday.co.uk), past the West End Roundabout, off Lundavara Rd.; call for a lift. Flower gardens surround this self-catering, spacious lodge. The owner, a local guide, rents equipment (hiking boots

£5 per day), leads expeditions, and gives lessons. 22 beds in 2- to 4-bed rooms. Drying rooms. Laundry £3. Internet £1 per 15min. Dorms £12-14. AmEx/MC/V. ❶

Farr Cottage Lodge (☎01397 772 315; www.farrcottage.com), on the A830 in Corpach. Take Highland Country bus #45 from Fort William. A licensed bar, affordable food service, and easy access to outdoor adventures make Farr Cottage worth the 10min. drive. Full or continental breakfast (£2.50-4), bagged lunches for climbers (£4.50), and dinner by request (£5). Dorms £13; private rooms from £17 per person. MC/V. ❶

Achintee Farm B&B and Hostel, Achintee Farm (☎01397 702 240; www.achinteefarm.com), across the river from the Glen Nevis Visitor Centre, 2 mi. from town on the Glen Nevis Rd. Walk across the footbridge or call for a lift. Ideal for exploring Glen Nevis, with large, comfortable rooms and a self-catering kitchen. 14 beds in 2- to 5-bed dorms. Laundry. Dorms £12-14; private rooms £30 per person. MC/V. ❶

SYHA Glen Nevis (☎01397 702 336), 3 mi. from town on the Glen Nevis Rd. Walk or take a Highland Country Bus. Backpackers' hub with ideal location—the front door opens onto the trail to Ben Nevis. 88 beds in 6- to 8-bed single-sex dorms. Self-catering kitchen. Laundry available. Wi-Fi and Internet access £1 per 20min. Dorms £16, under 16 £13; doubles £40-50; triples £60. AmEx/MC/V. ❶

Bank Street Lodge, Bank St. (☎01397 700 070; www.bankstreetlodge.co.uk), just off High St. opposite the post office, above the Stables Restaurant. Comfortable wood bunks with kitchen and TV lounge. 43 beds in 5- to 7-bed dorms. Laundry £3 for wash and dry. Dorms £14; doubles £45-55. AmEx/MC/V. ❶

Distillery House, North Rd. (☎01397 700 103; www.stayinfortwilliam.co.uk). From the train station, turn left on Belford Rd. and continue to the roundabout. Set of large white houses less than 1 mi. from the famous distillery. Whisky barrel tables stand in the lobby. Relax with complimentary whisky and shortbread served in the lounge. No smoking. Singles £45; doubles £76-90. AmEx/MC/V. ❹

Glen Nevis Caravan and Camping Park (☎01397 702 191), 2 mi. from town on the Glen Nevis Rd. Ben Nevis towers nearby, but your view is likely to include trailer-owning neighbors. Toilets, showers, electricity, and laundry. Reservations July-Aug. Open from mid-Mar. to Oct. £1.60-2.50 per person; £5.40-9 per tent. MC/V. ❶

FOOD AND PUBS

High St. offers classic Scottish food in addition to a smorgasbord of international fare with questionable authenticity but plenty of character. At the north end of High St., **Tesco** sells groceries. (Open M-Sa 8am-8pm, Su 10am-5pm.)

Grog & Gruel, 66 High St. (☎01397 705 078). The lively and always packed Grog has an odd mix of Cajun and Tex-Mex along with the requisite haggis. Kelp Seaweed Ale (£1.50) made from fresh ingredients straight from the loch. Entrees £8-13. Food served at the bar noon-9pm, in the restaurant 5-9:30pm. Open daily noon-10pm. MC/V. ❷

Nevis Bakery, 49 High St. (☎01397 704 101). The lowest prices in town, award-winning Scotch pies served cold or heated (£1.50), and packed lunches (£3) perfect for a day on the mountain. Open M-F 8am-5pm, Sa 8am-4pm. Cash only. ❶

Everest Indian Restaurant, 141B High St. (☎01397 700 919). Escape the crowds down a small alleyway at this hole-in-the-wall restaurant overlooking the loch. Light, buttery naan, plenty of vegetarian options, and attentive servers. Entrees £6-11. Open daily noon-2pm and 5:30-11pm. MC/V. ❷

Crannog Seafood Restaurant (☎01397 705 589), on the pier. Fresh fish practically flop into the dining room, which is fashioned out of Fort William's pier. Try the Scottish Cheese Board with traditional "Brammle" whisky (£7.50). Entrees £10-17. Open M-Sa noon-2:30pm and 6-9:30pm, Su 12:30-2:30pm, and 6:30-9:30pm. MC/V. ❸

GIVING BACK

UPKEEP OF A SECRET

Many budget travelers rely on hostels for cheap places to spend the night but fail to realize that free accommodation can be found in many parts of the Highlands. Bothies—simple shelters in the most remote corners of the country—are left unlocked by their owners for the use of hikers passing through the area. Their locations are not well publicized due to fears of overuse and vandalism.

Despite efforts to keep locations secret, some bothies have already experienced problems with garbage and human waste buildup as more people explore rural Scotland. The Bothy Code requests that users leave the bothy in the same or better condition as they found it, but the sheer number of hikers seeking shelter has strained the honor system. To repair damage to the bothies, the **Mountain Bothies Association** organizes regular work parties of volunteers to perform tasks ranging from repainting walls to rebuilding ruins. Bothy work does not require special skills, and volunteers can participate for as long or as short a time as they wish.

The Mountain Bothies Association recommends that volunteers become members. Annual membership costs £15, with reduced rates of £7.50 for people under 16, over 60, or unemployed. Members receive a quarterly newsletter listing planned work parties and projects. For more information, visit www.mountainbothies.org.

Crofter Bar, High St. (☎01397 704 899). All the elements of a traditional British pub, including a dartboard, a selection of beers and real ales on tap, and a TV screen showing the current football match. Filled with locals as well as the odd climber straight off the paths of Ben Nevis. Open daily noon-1am. MC/V. ❶

👁 SIGHTS

While the magnificent vistas of the surrounding glens and highlands are Fort William's main draw, the pedestrian-only **High Street** also teems with shoppers searching for that perfect swatch of Scottish plaid. ◪**The Jacobite,** a.k.a. the Harry Potter train, is a vintage steam-powered locomotive that travels 42 mi. to Mallaig as part of the scenic **West Highland Railway.** (☎01463 239 026. Runs July-Aug. M-F and Su; June and Sept.-Oct. M-F. Departs Fort William at 10:20am. £29, round-trip £22.) The **West Highland Museum,** most famous for its Jacobite college, houses paintings and artifacts from the area in an old house next to the visitors center. (☎01397 702 169; www.westhighlandmuseum.org.uk. Open M-Sa 10am-5pm. £3, children 50p.) Two miles outside of town, on the A82 to Inverness, the **Ben Nevis Distillery** leads tours that include free samples and discounts on select whisky. (☎01397 700 200; www.bennevisdistillery.com. Open July-Aug. M-F 9am-5pm, Sa 10am-4pm, Su noon-4pm; Easter-June and Sept. M-F 9am-5pm, Sa 10am-4pm; Oct.-Easter M-F 9am-5pm. Last tour 1hr. before close. £4, children £2.) Hop aboard **Crannog Cruises** to scope out a local seal colony. Boat trips along Loch Linnhe leave from the town pier. (☎01397 703 919; www.crannog.net. 1hr. cruises depart from Mar. to mid-May 11am, 2pm; from mid-May to mid-Sept. 10am, noon, 2, 4pm. £8, children £4. MC/V.) In nearby Corpach, **Treasures of the Earth** has an unexpectedly large collection of gems on display, including local stones and fossils. Tours are available for larger groups. (☎01397 772 283. Open daily July-Sept. 9:30am-7pm; Feb.-June 10am-5pm. £4.)

🏔 OUTDOOR ACTIVITIES

The **West Highland Way** completes its 95 mi. track in Fort William. Hikers or cyclists hungry for more can venture another 60-odd miles along the **Great Glen Way,** which runs north to Inverness Castle. The 75p *Cycling in the Forest—The Great Glen* pamphlet breaks the route into 11 manageable sections and includes maps. Numerous adventure sports are practiced around Fort William, from canyoning, abseiling (rappelling), and kayaking around the unreal **Inchree Falls** to rafting and hang gliding in the glen. In Corpach, **Rock Hopper Sea Kayaking** rents gear, sells lessons, and leads trips. (☎07739 834 344; www.rockhopperscotland.co.uk. Activities from £40.) **Vertical Descents** furnishes gear to outfit a variety of adventure sports. (☎01855 821 593; www.verticaldescents.com.)

Glen Nevis: South of Fort William. Serves as a jumping-off point for outdoor enthusiasts.Spectacular views of mountains, gorges, rivers, and waterfalls. The drive up the glacial valley brings you to some fine day hikes. At the end of Glen Nevis Rd., a popular 3 mi. walk heads to **Nevis Gorge** and **Steall Falls.** Head to the **Glen Nevis Visitor Centre** (☎01397 705 922) to stock up on info, get the latest weather report, and acquire a nifty ecological history of the area. Open daily Easter-Oct. 9am-5pm. Pick up the Pathfinder Guide #7 (£11) for walks and the Ordnance Survey Explorer #392 or Landranger #41 (both £8) for area-wide maps.

Ben Nevis (4406 ft.). Britain's tallest mountain and by far the biggest draw to the region. A challenging but manageable hike. The 10 mi. ascent typically takes 6-8hr. round-trip. The record, set in 1984 during the annual **Ben Nevis Race** (www.bennevisrace.co.uk), is an incomprehensible 85min. up and back. For the most beautiful views, pause at **Lochan Mull,** a stunningly clear lake about halfway up.

Aonach Mòr (4006 ft.), 7 mi. northeast of Fort William along the A82. On the mountain, the **Nevis Range** (☎01397 705 825; www.nevisrange.co.uk) is Scotland's highest ski area. Journey beyond the clouds up 2150 ft. on the resort's gondola. Open daily July-Aug. 9:30am-6pm; from Sept. to mid-Nov. and from mid-Dec. to June 10am-5pm. Weather permitting. £8.75. Highland Country buses #41 and 42 (15min.; M-Sa 8 per day, Su 4 per day) travel to Aonach Mor from Fort William's bus station. Nevis Range hosts the World Cup in downhill mountain-bike racing in early June on its famous 2100 ft. downhill track. Pick up a mountain-bike racing kit from **Off Beat Bikes** (☎01397 704 008; www.offbeatbikes.co.uk) at the Nevis Range. £25; includes bike, helmet, body armor, and ticket for Nevis Range track.

GLEN COE ☎(0)1855

The Glen Coe valley seems to rise from nowhere to enfold the unsuspecting traveler in jaw-dropping mountains on all sides. The glen's two tiny, peaceful villages belie a bloody history. In 1692, the MacDonald clan was massacred here by the Campbells in the wake of the Glorious Revolution. Today, Glen Coe offers outdoor adventure to suit all types and temperaments as well as a hefty dose of Highland merriment and music.

TRANSPORTATION AND PRACTICAL INFORMATION. The Glen Coe valley comprises the villages of **Glencoe** and **Ballachulish,** which rest near the edge of Loch Leven, at the mouth of the River Coe. The A82 runs the length of the valley. Food and accommodations lie on a parallel road that winds from Ballachulish through Glencoe. Scottish Citylink (☎08705 505 050) **buses** travel from Fort William to Glasgow (4 per day, £4.50) and provide direct access to the valley. Rapsons Highland Country bus #44 serves Glencoe Village from Fort William (35min., M-Sa 9 per day). Some travelers find that buses will pick them up anywhere if they motion with their arms in a place where the bus can pull over safely; buses may also drop them off along the road.

South of Glencoe Village, you'll find the **Tourist Information Centre** just off the A82 in Ballachulish. (☎01855 811 866. Open Apr.-Sept. daily 9am-6pm; Oct.-Mar. M-Sa 9am-5pm, Su 10am-5pm.) Along the A82 in the opposite direction, 1 mi. southeast of Glencoe Village, the **Glen Coe Visitor Centre** provides succinct, detailed information on a dozen mountain trails. To walk from the village to the center and avoid the highway, take the Woodland Trail, a short hike that passes by the ruins of one of the massacre homesteads. The center also features extensive displays on the history and topography of the area along with practical weather and gear information for climbers and backpackers. The adjacent cafe serves simple soups and sandwiches. (☎01855 811 307. Open Apr.-Aug. daily 9:30am-5:30pm; Sept.-Oct. daily 10am-5pm; Nov.-Feb. M and F-Su 10am-4pm; Mar. daily 10am-4pm. Last entry 30min. before closing. Exhibit £5, concessions £4.) The **post office** can be found along the parallel road, just beyond the TIC. (Open M-Tu and Th-F 9am-1:30pm.) **Postcode:** PH49 4HS.

HIGHLANDS AND ISLANDS

ACCOMMODATIONS AND CAMPING. Many of Glen Coe's accommodations are situated along or just off a minor riverside road that runs 4 mi. up the valley to Glencoe Village, roughly parallel to the A82. Turn right on this road to access the **SYHA Glencoe ❶**, 1 mi. southeast of Glencoe Village. (☎01855 811 219. 60 beds in 6- to 8-bed dorms. Self-catering kitchen. Laundry and drying room. Internet £1 per 20min. Book in advance. Curfew M-Th and Su 11:45pm, F-Sa 12:30am. Dorms £16, under 18 £12. AmEx/MC/V.) The **Glencoe Independent Hostel ❶**, halfway between Glencoe Village and the A82, provides homey accommodations in the middle of renovations. (☎01855 811 906; www.glencoehostel.co.uk. 16-bed bunkhouse £9.50; 8-bed dorms £12. Log cabin for 2 £32.) Glencoe Village is full of B&Bs, most of which tend to fill quickly in the summer. With a front lawn at the base of a mountain, the family-run **Clachaig Inn ❹** furnishes comfortable rooms with spectacular views of nearby summits. From the A82, turn right onto the riverside road; the inn is less than a mile down on the left. (☎01855 811 252; www.clachaig.com. Dogs allowed by prior arrangement. £38-42 per person. Self-catering cottages June-Aug. £545 per week; Sept.-May £400 per week. MC/V.) The **Glen Coe Caravan and Camping Site ❶**, next to the visitors center, is well maintained, secure, and ideal as a hiking base. (☎01855 811 397. Toilets, showers, laundry, and cooking shelters. Open Apr.-Oct. £4.20-6.40 per person. Cash only.) Beside the River Coe, the **Red Squirrel Campsite ❶**, 1 mi. along the riverside road off the A82, just beyond the Clachaig Inn, provides flat campsites and views of both sides of the valley. (☎01855 811 256; www.redsquirrelcampsite.com. Showers 50p. £7 per person. Cash only.)

FOOD. The **Spar** market sits along the parallel road, across from the post office. (☎01855 811 367. Open in summer daily 7:30am-8pm; reduced winter hours.) The **Clachaig Inn ❷** is the place to go for food and entertainment. This social restaurant serves Scottish fare such as steak pie and venison burgers (£6-10). Most of the meat comes from local game. The inn also sells packed lunches (from £4.45). The lively **public bar ❷**, a traditional trail's-end pub, serves 15 beers and real ales on tap and hosts live local music Saturdays after 9pm. Look for special package deals in October and May for Glencoe's two beer festivals. (☎01855 811 252. Open M-Th and Su 11am-11pm, F 11am-midnight, Sa 11am-11:30pm. Kitchen open noon-9pm. MC/V.) In the village, **Carnoch ❶** serves soups, sandwiches, and other simple but well-prepared traditional dishes for £4-8. (☎01855 811 140. Open in summer daily 11am-9pm. MC/V.)

OUTDOOR ACTIVITIES. Glen Coe offers some of Scotland's most spectacular outdoor experiences for visitors of all ability levels. Walkers stroll the floor of the valley, climbers head for the cliffs, skiers race down the slopes, and ice-climbers ascend frozen waterfalls. Although it seems a shame not to take advantage of the surrounding scenery, The Ice Factor mountaineering center, 5 mi. away off B863 Kinlochleven, features the UK's largest indoor **ice wall** as well as hiking and climbing lessons. (☎01855 831 100; www.ice-factor.co.uk. Open M and F-Su 9am-7pm, Tu-Th 9am-10pm.) Many of the **trailheads**

lie several miles beyond Glencoe. With the right timing, you can use the Scottish Citylink buses that travel up the A82. For a small fee, most area hostels will shuttle hikers to the trailheads. Always bring a map; Landranger #41 (£7), Pathfinder Guide #7 (£11), and Short Walks #30 (£6) detail the area. Short but challenging daytrips abound. At the Glencoe Lachon Hiking Area just through Glencoe Village, the 45min. Woodland Walk provides an easy introduction to the area. Pick up a trout-fishing pass at Scorrybreac Guest House just beyond and **fish** on the Lachan trail, which runs about 1 mi. around the lake. In the upper valley, the Two Passes route (9 mi.) climbs some 2100 ft., passing through two U-shaped glacial scars. For serious backpackers, the Three Sisters, Glen Coe's signature triumvirate of peaks along the Aonach Eagach Ridge, takes hikers along narrow paths with 2000 ft. drops on either side and past the nearly concealed Hanging Valley, where the MacDonalds are thought to have hidden their cattle during the 1692 massacre. Over the Pass of Glen Coe just off the A82, find **ski** fields and the Glen Coe Ski Centre Chairlift. During the winter, daily lift passes (£20-25) are available. (☎01855 851 226. Open June-Aug. 9:30am-4pm, weather permitting. £6.) When the weather behaves, Glencoe Cruises and Fishing Trips (☎01855 811 658) scuttles across Loch Leven, leaving from the pier in Ballachulish. Glencoe Safaris travels from the visitors center into the wilderness with guides who discuss Glencoe's wildlife and the famous MacDonald massacre. (☎01855 811 307. Apr., July-Aug., and Oct. £3 per person. Massacre Tour at 10:15am, Wildlife Tour at dusk.)

ROAD TO THE ISLES

The A830 travels from Fort William to Mallaig, following the historic Road to the Isles route (Rathad Iarainn nan Eilean). The winding drive to the coast captures the many landscapes of Scotland—stark mountain faces, dense forests, and sparkling lochs. Still single-lane in parts, the road often requires as much attention as the scenery. The **West Highland Railway** (originating in Glasgow; p. 583) runs alongside the road, offering sublime views at a fast clip (4-5 per day, £9.20). In summer, **"The Jacobite"** steam train (p. 645) runs from Fort William to Mallaig (via Glenfinnan and the 21-arch viaduct) in the morning and back in the afternoon. (June and Sept.-Oct. M-F; July-Aug. M-F and Su. Departs Fort William at 10:20am and Mallaig at 2:10pm. £29, one-way £22.) Buses make the same trip. (1½hr.; July-Sept. M-Sa 3 per day, Oct.-June M-F 1 per day; £5.50.)

 DRIVING IN THE HIGHLANDS. Many single-lane roads in the Highlands widen at regular intervals to form passing places for cars approaching head on or overtaking a slower vehicle from behind.

GLENFINNAN ☎(0)1397

The road runs westward from Fort William along Loch Eil, arriving after 12 mi. at Glenfinnan, on **Loch Shiel**. Trains often stop on trestle-bridged **Glenfinnan Viaduct**. A towering monument recalls Bonnie Prince Charlie's row up Loch Shiel to rally the clans around the **Stewart Standard** (see **The Jacobite Rebellion,** p. 74). For a panoramic view of the loch and the viaduct, visitors can climb a narrow (read: friggin' tiny) spiral staircase and stand atop the monument next to the statue of the Young Pretender. Purchase tickets (£3) in the **Visitor Centre**. Look for gliding golden eagles as you drift on 2hr. **Loch Shiel Cruises** as far as **Acharacle,** at the loch's far shore. Trips depart from the Glenfinnan House Hotel. (☎01687 470 322; www.highlandcruises.co.uk. £13-15. AmEx/MC/V.)

🅜**Glenfinnan Sleeping Car ●**, a red railway car that has been bolted down and converted into a hostel, furnishes unique, if cramped, lodgings near the train station. There are two bunks in each of the four compartments. (☎01397 722 295. Food served from 8:30am with adequate demand. Linens £2. Dorms £12. Cash only.) Take a self-guided tour of the adjacent train station museum for just 50p. For a twilight loch view, opt for pub grub at the **Glenfinnan House Hotel ❷**. (☎01397 722 235. Open daily noon-9pm. AmEx/MC/V.) The Visitor Centre has pamphlets on local history, which you can read with a slice of homemade gingerbread (£1.50) in the **cafe ❷**. (☎08444 932 221. Open daily July-Aug. 9:30am-5:30pm; Apr.-June and Sept.-Oct. 10am-5pm.)

By **train**, Glenfinnan is 30min. from Fort William (£4.80) and 50min. from Mallaig (£6); by Scottish Citylink **bus**, the trips are both 30min. (£5.50).

ARISAIG AND LOCH MORAR   ☎(0)1687

The road meets the west coast at the sprawling settlement of Arisaig. A popular spot for caravans and camping, Arisaig has patches of rocky beach with striking views of the outer islands. Stop at the **Land, Sea and Islands Centre**, 7 New Buildings, for tide tables and other outdoor information as well as exhibits about area wildlife. (☎01687 450 263. Open M-F 10am-4pm, Su 1-4pm.) **Arisaig Marine Ltd.** operates regular **day cruises** from Arisaig to Rum, Eigg, and Muck from £17. (☎01687 450 224. Departs daily 11am.) Compact white beaches with hidden coves are 3 mi. south of town on the A830; from the Camusdarach campsite, follow the signposted path. A winding 5 mi. walk west of the town center follows the banks of Loch Morar, Britain's deepest freshwater loch (1017 ft.) and home to Morag, Nessie's lesser-known but no less formidable cousin.

Three miles north on the A830 from Arisaig, the placid **Camusdarach campsite ●**, as well groomed as the golf course around the corner, overlooks the beach. (☎01687 450 221. Showers included with £5 key deposit. Laundry £1. Book ahead. £12 per tent. MC/V.) The **Spar** on Main St. is the only supermarket between Fort William and Mallaig; inside is an **ATM.** (☎01687 450 226. Open M-Th 8:30am-8pm, F-Sa 8:30am-6pm, Su 9:30am-6pm.) Dine on homemade pastries (from £1.50) as you surf the Internet at the **Rhu Cafe ●** in Arisaig. (☎01687 450 707. Internet £1 per 30min. Open Tu-Su 10am-4pm. MC/V.)

Down the street from the Rhu is the **post office.** (☎01687 223 344. Open M and W-F 9am-1pm and 2-5:30pm; Tu and Sa 9am-1pm.) **Postcode:** PH39 4NR.

MALLAIG   ☎(0)1687

The scenic A830 ends in Mallaig (MAL-egg). The port provides pretty views of the inner isles but not a whole lot to do. Fishermen and travelers fill the streets on weekends, waiting to depart for their next destination and feasting on the town's ample seafood offerings in the meantime.

🄵🄽 **TRANSPORTATION AND PRACTICAL INFORMATION.** CalMac **ferries** (☎08000 665 000; www.calmac.co.uk) sail from Mallaig to Armadale, Skye (May-Sept. M-Sa 8 per day, Su 6 per day, Oct.-Apr. M-Sa 6 per day; £3.50, 5-day round-trip £6, car £18.75/32.50), and to the Small Isles. North of the pier, the Water's Edge **Tourist Information Centre** books accommodations along the Road to the Isles. (☎07876 518 042; www.thewatersedgetic.co.uk. Open June-Aug. M-F 10:15am-5:30pm, Sa 10:15am-3:30pm, Su 11am-3pm; Sept.-May M-F 10:15am-5:50pm, Su 10:15am-3:30pm.) Other services include: a **Bank of Scotland** (☎01687 462 265; open M-Tu and Th-F 9:15am-1pm and 2-4:45pm, W

9:30am-1pm and 2-4:45pm); a **library** with free **Internet** across the tracks from the Heritage Centre in the Mallaig Community Centre (☎01687 460 097; open M 1-5pm, Tu 10:30am-2pm, W 9:30am-1:30pm and Th 5-8pm, Sa 10am-noon); and the **post office,** located in the Spar up the hill from the TIC. (☎01687 460 257. Open M-Tu, Th-F 9am-3pm, W 9am-1pm, Sa 9am-12:30pm. Spar open M-Sa 8am-10pm, Su 9:30am-9pm.) **Postcode:** PH41 4PZ.

▓▓ ACCOMMODATIONS AND FOOD. Family-owned **Sheena's Backpackers Lodge ❶,** on the right after the station, above the Tea Garden restaurant, provides a common room spruced up with plants and flowers. Book ahead. (☎01687 462 764. Dorms £13. MC/V.) Check out the view of the harbor from the bright and clean **Moorings Guest House ❸,** East Bay (☎01687 462 225. £25 per person. Cash only.) Closest to the pier, the **Marine Hotel ❹,** Station Rd., fills its bar with rowdy locals at night and has slightly shabby but comfortable accommodations. (☎01687 462 217. Single £35; double £50; triple £75. MC/V.) Groceries can be found at the **Co-op,** in the center of town. (Open M-Sa 8am-10pm, Su 9am-9pm.) The **Fishmarket Restaurant ❷** serves up bountiful portions of the best fish in town, with views of fishing boats docked in the bay. Large starters and soups begin at £3. (☎01687 462 299. Open daily noon-2:30pm and 6-9pm. Entrees £8-17. MC/V.) The **Tea Garden ❸** at Sheena's Backpackers serves upscale seafood and local game with great views of the hanging garden and harbor. (Entrees £9-15. MC/V.) The **Fisherman's Mission ❶** contains a muted cafeteria with rich, inexpensive food popular with fishermen on weeklong breaks from the sea. Grab a homemade sugar-filled donut (85p) and enjoy the big-screen TV and fishermen's stories. (☎01687 462 086. Open M-F 8:30am-9pm, Sa 8:30am-noon. Kitchen open M-F 8:30am-1:45pm and 5:30-9pm, Sa 8:30am-noon. Cash only.)

THE SMALL ISLES

The small isles of Rum, Eigg, Muck and Canna make stunning daytrips from the mainland. They offer everything from tours of a working Highland farm to Celtic music festivals to 2000 ft. mountain hikes. Small communities of islanders shower travelers with information about their beloved homes, but be sure to set aside plenty of time to explore the islands' remote beauty on your own.

GIVING BACK
A RUM DEAL

The Isle of Rum is a land of craggy mountains, hidden waterfalls, deserted stretches of sandy beach, and some of the most intimate volunteer opportunities in Scotland. The **Scottish Natural Heritage (SNH)** owns the island and oversees a variety of upkeep projects. These projects are open to public volunteers, who can arrange work and job training with the island manager.

Despite Rum's small size, the tasks are surprisingly varied. Volunteers can survey the local bird and otter populations, garden, round up the island's cattle herd, care for farm animals, repair fences, plant trees, and work with Rum's herd of 19 domesticated horses. Four days of service will earn you an entire week's worth of free accommodation. If you're lucky, your bed could even be in **Kinloch Castle** (next page).

Volunteering on Rum is especially enjoyable because of the welcoming island community and the varied nature of the jobs. While regular traveling can expose many aspects of a country, working to care for some part of it can show you a different side—one that is infinitely more satisfying. On Rum, it will also earn you a free bed with time to explore one of Scotland's most beautiful islands, blissfully out of reach of the tourist horde.

Island Manager ☎01687 462 026. Info at www.snh.org.uk.

GETTING THERE

CalMac **ferries** (☎01687 462 403) sail from Mallaig to Rum (£8.50, 5-day round-trip £15), Eigg (£5.75/10.10), Muck (£8.70/15.40), and Canna (£10.75/18.60); call for schedules. Ferries require that cars have governmental permission to board, but many find that having a car registered in Scotland will suffice. They are timed to connect with trains from Glasgow and Fort William and charge £2.30 per bicycle. Gaming the ferry schedules so that you get to all of the isles can be difficult. A more convenient and expensive option is the *MV Shearwater*, operated by Arisaig Marine Ltd. (☎01687 450 224; www.arisaig. co.uk), which sails at 11am from Arisaig (p. 652) to Rum (June-Aug. Tu, Th, Sa; Sept. and Easter-June Tu and Th; round-trip £23), Eigg (M-W and F-Su; £17), and Muck (M, W, F, Su; £17).

 TIP **FERRY ANNOYING.** Don't assume that ferries to the Small Isles will return to pick you up after your visit. Schedules vary and many assume an overnight excursion on the isle. Come prepared with schedule information and, if needed, camping gear.

RUM   ☎(0)1687

Rum's miles of pristine trails and uneven coastline make for gorgeous hiking and camping. The largest of the four isles, Rum is managed by Scottish National Heritage, whose staff helps protect and preserve the island's elusive Manx shearwaters, red deer, and sea eagles. The only island residents are 24 Scottish National Heritage researchers and family members. At the ferry landing, pick up a self-guided tour of the **Loch Scresort Trail** (2hr. round-trip), a straightforward path that runs along the coast and allows for the occasional seal sighting. To the left of the trail lies the sprawling red-stone **Kinloch Castle** (☎01687 462 037). Built in 1897 as the plaything of George Bullough, a former owner of the isle, the castle's rooms are cluttered with animal skins and imported tapestries. Scottish National Heritage staffers lead daily tours timed with the arrival of the CalMac ferries. (M 1:15pm, Tu-Th and Sa-Su 2pm, F 2:30pm. £6.) The adjacent **Community Hall Tea Shop** sells snacks (from £1.50).

With ferries arriving in the middle of the day, a night spent on Rum leaves time for plenty of exploring. Spend the night in the **Kinloch Castle Hostel ❷**, whose rooms overlook the lake. The double rooms with antique four-poster beds are worth the splurge. (☎01687 462 037. Kitchen. Breakfast £7, packed lunch £5, 3-course dinner £13.50. Showers £2. Laundry £2. Free Wi-Fi. Advance booking required. Dorms £14; B&B double £55. MC/V.) For information on camping or using either of the two bothies (small, basic shelters) on Rum, contact the Island Manager, Scottish Natural Heritage, Isle of Rum, PH43 4RR. (☎01687 462 026. Tent or bothy by donation.) In the morning, take the rugged **Ridgewalk trail** up over 2000 ft. to the island's highest point and enjoy one of the most spectacular views in the region.

EIGG   ☎(0)1687

With a population of 78, Eigg is home to the largest and youngest community of the small isles, but travelers who are uninterested in the island's hopping pub scene can drink up the landscape on several well-marked trails instead. The island has been privately owned for many years, but in 1997 Eigg's community successfully bought it from a German artist. The **Sgurr of Eigg** (1290 ft.), a massive lava cliff that juts up from island's center, makes Eigg easily recognizable. Ranger John Chester offers guided historical and wildlife walks. (☎01687 482

477. £3. Call in advance to schedule a tour.) A minibus (3-4 per day, £4) meets each ferry for a trip to the **Singing Sands,** named for the squeaking sound the beach makes when trod upon. The hike to 🏴Massacre Caves (1.7 mi.) winds down the face of a cliff along a sheep path to a hidden set of caves where the entire island's population was slaughtered by a rival clan in the 16th century.

Glebe Barn ❶ rents cozy beds in a building with a wood-burning stove and views of Rum and Muck. The hostel is 1 mi. from the pier. (☎01687 482 417. Book ahead. Open Apr.-Oct. Dorms £11-14. Cash only.) For bicycles, look for the shed just north of the grocery store. (☎01687 482 432. £12 per day.)

MUCK   ☎(0)1687

Three generations of the McEwen family have lived and farmed on Muck over the past 100 years. The small island (2 mi. long) is a sprawling farm with cows sleeping on the beach, horses roaming the hills, and sheep lining up to be sheared in early summer. Take a tractor tour of the isle for £1 or venture down to the beach and explore beds of iridescent seaweed.

Stay at the refinished **Port Mor House Hotel ❹** (☎01687 462 365; full board £42.50; cash only) or the cozy **Isle of Muck Bunkhouse ❶**. (☎01687 462 042. Linens £1. £10.50 per person. Cash only.) **The Yurt ❶**, a circular canvas tent that sleeps from three to five people, is a good value option for intrepid travelers (☎01687 462 362. Bring sleeping bags. Stove for cooking and heating provided. Showers at hotel. Yurt £15.) Visit the **Tea Room and Restaurant ❶** for savory leek and potato soup or the signature lamb burger, starting at £2. (☎01687 462 362. Open daily 11am-5pm, or call ahead to book a dinner.) The adjoining craft shop features handmade wool items (from £3).

CANNA   ☎(0)1687

On Wednesdays and Saturdays, the CalMac ferry gives travelers time to spend a few hours on the isle of Canna (Gaelic for "porpoise"), home to 16 residents and owned by the National Trust for Scotland. Walk the harbor road to find two chapels and the **Harbor View Tearoom ❶**, which has a snack menu and dinner options. (☎01687 462 465. Open Mar.-Oct. M-Sa noon-2pm and 6-9pm; book before 5pm. AmEx/MC/V.) When the tide is out, ambitious power walkers can access the ruins of **Saint Columba's Chapel,** a 7th-century nunnery.

ISLE OF SKYE

Nicknamed the Misty Isle for the swirling clouds that obscure its mountain peaks, Skye and its hills, peninsulas, and seaside paths hold many secrets for the savvy traveler. Crofts and cottages pepper the island, providing glimpses into Highland culture and Gaelic traditions. Because visitors tend to stick to major roads, many of Skye's landscapes lie virtually undisturbed—a far cry from the island's revived castles and their summer crowds.

TRANSPORTATION

GETTING THERE

The tradition of ferries that carried passengers "over the sea to Skye" ended with the construction of the Skye Bridge, which links Kyleakin to the mainland's Kyle of Lochalsh 3 mi. away. Pedestrians can take either the bridge's 1½ mi. **footpath** or the **shuttle bus** (every hr.). **Trains** (☎08457 484 950) run from Kyle to Inverness (2hr.; M-Sa 4 per day, Su 2 per day; £17.30). Scottish Citylink buses travel daily to Fort William (2hr., 3 per day, £17), Glasgow (5hr., 3 per day, £28), and Inverness (2hr., 6 per day, £15). From the Outer Hebrides, CalMac **ferries** (☎08000 665 000) sail from Uig to Tarbert, Harris, and Lochmaddy, North Uist (1hr.; M-Sa 1-2 per day; £10, 5-day round-trip £17.10, cars £48/82). Ferries also run from Armadale in southwest Skye to Mallaig on the mainland (30min.; June-Aug. daily 8-9 per day, Sept.-May M-Sa 8-9 per day; £3.50, 5-day round-trip £6, cars £18.75/32.50). From Aros or Portree, take an On the Wing guided bus tour through Skye. (☎01478 613 649; www.aros.co.uk.)

GETTING AROUND

To avoid headaches, pick up the handy *Public Transport Map: The Highlands, Orkney, Shetland and Western Isles* at any TIC. On Sunday, buses run infrequently and mostly to meet the Raasay and Armadale ferries (June-Aug.). Prices listed below are often estimates—fares can change rapidly and often depend on the driver of the bus. For the eager and intrepid, the stellar █MacBackpackers Skye Trekker Tour (☎01599 534 510; www.macbackpackers.com) departs from the hostel in Kyleakin and offers a three-day tour emphasizing the mythology and history of the island (£79; weekly departure F 9am).

Buses: Rapsons Highland Country buses traverse Skye. They are not always timed to connect with ferries or even other buses, and a bus's route may change suddenly. It is best to let the driver know your plans. The most reliable service is Scottish Citylink, which runs regular buses from **Kyleakin** to **Broadford** to **Portree** on the A87. The **Skye Rover** ticket offers unlimited bus travel on Skye and can be purchased on any local bus (1-day £6, 3-day £15). For a traveler planning more than 2 bus rides in a day, the Rover is likely a good deal, as fares tend to be surprisingly high.

Car Rental: Kyle Taxi Company (☎01599 534 323). 23+. £40 per day.

Bike Rental: Cycling is common and enjoyable on Skye, but be prepared for steep hills, nonexistent shoulders, and rain. Most buses will not carry bikes. Rent bikes in Broadford at **Fairwinds Cycle Hire** (☎01471 822 270), in Broadford. £8 per day. £5 deposit for 1-day rentals, £10 for overnight. **Island Cycles** (☎01478 613 121), in Portree. £14 per day. Discounts for longer rentals. Reserve ahead, especially in summer.

HOLIDAYS AND FESTIVALS

Cultural life on Skye is vibrant, engaging tourists and locals alike. Snag a copy of the seasonal newspaper *The Visitor* at the TIC for a list of special events on the island or in nearby Lochalsh. The **Skye Music Festival** (www.skyemusicfestival.co.uk) draws bands and fans from across the UK in late May. In mid-July, **Feis an Eilein** (☎01471 844 207; www.skyefestival.com), on the Sleat Peninsula, is a two-week celebration of Gaelic culture, featuring concerts, ceilidhs, workshops, and films. Additional revelry can be found at the **Highland Games** (☎01478 612 540; www.skye-highland-games.com), a day of bagpipes and merriment in Portree on the first Wednesday in August, and **Skye Scene,** with ceilidhs and other musical events, also in Portree (July-Aug. Tu-W; £8, concessions £6).

KYLE AND KYLEAKIN   ☎(0)1599

Kyle of Lochalsh ("Kyle" for short) and Kyleakin (Ky-LAACK-in) bookend the Skye Bridge, both serving as hubs for tired backpackers headed to and from the island. Kyle's upscale accommodations and restaurants cater to a different crowd than does Kyleakin's buzzing backpacker nightlife.

█ █ TRANSPORTATION AND PRACTICAL INFORMATION. The Kyle **train station** is near the pier; the **bus stop** is just to the west. Highland Country buses meet incoming trains and go to Kyleakin (every hr.). The Kyle **Tourist Information Centre (TIC)**, by the pier, has a phone for booking accommodations (open May-Oct. M-F 9:30am-5pm, Sa-Su 10am-4pm). Other services include: a **Bank of Scotland** with ATM, Main St. (☎01599 534 220; open M-Tu and Th-F 9am-5pm, W 9:30am-5pm), free **Internet** access at the **Kyle Library** (☎01599 534 146; open M and W-F 9am-5pm, Tu 1:30-8pm), and a **post office** (☎01599 534 246; open M-Sa 9am-12:30pm, 1:30-5:30pm). **Postcode:** IV40 8AA.

█ ACCOMMODATIONS. In Kyle of Lochalsh, **Cu'chulainn's Backpackers Hostel ❶**, Station Rd., rents basic hostel bunks with easy access to the pub and restaurant that shares its name. (☎01599 534 492. Laundry £2.50. Internet £2 per hr. Key deposit £5. Dorms £12.50-15. Cash only.) For a more luxurious and expensive option, follow the sign to the **Kyle Hotel ❹**, Main St., which has elegant plaid bedspreads and views of the main drag. (☎01599 534 204; www.kylehotel. co.uk. Singles £40-52; doubles £80-120. AmEx/MC/V.)

Kyleakin serves as the hostel hub of the area. The laid-back staff and whimsical rooms (with themes such as "the solar system" and "fairies") contribute to the lighthearted atmosphere at **Skye Backpackers ❶**. (☎01599 534 510; www. scotlandstophostels.com. Continental breakfast £2. Laundry £2.50. Internet access 80p per hr. Free Wi-Fi. Dorms £10-13. AmEx/MC/V.) **Dun-Caan Hostel ❶** is a 200-year-old renovated cottage overlooking the bay. A sparkling clean kitchen and quiet, secure dorms make it ideal for travelers seeking a good night's rest. (☎01599 534 087; www.skyerover.co.uk. Dorms £13. MC/V.) On the village green, two doors down from the large white building that used to house an SYHA hostel, **Saucy Mary's ❷** operates a small hostel and B&B adjacent to its bar, the liveliest in town. (☎01599 534 845; www.saucymarys.com. Optional breakfast and Wi-Fi £2.50. Dorms £15.50; B&B rooms from £30. AmEx/MC/V.)

█ █ FOOD AND PUBS. In Kyle, grab groceries at the **Co-op,** up the hill to the west of the Kyle bus station. (☎01599 530 190. Open M-Sa 8am-10pm, Su 10am-6pm.) **Cu'chulainn's ❶** sells pub fare with an emphasis on local seafood at its bar and restaurant. (☎01599 534 492. Open M-Sa 11am-midnight. Kitchen open 11am-2pm. MC/V.) By the pier, **Hector's ❶** serves takeaway and homemade ice cream. (☎01599 534 248. Open M-Sa noon-10pm, Su noon-9pm.)

In Kyleakin, **Saucy Mary's,** named after a Norse seductress, packs in pints, crowds, and occasional live music. (Open M-Th 5pm-midnight, F 5pm-1am, Sa 5-11:30pm, Su 5-11pm. AmEx/MC/V.) The large **King Haakon Bar,** at the east end of the village green, serves delicious seafood in a room ripe for dancing. (☎01599 534 164. 18+ after 8:30pm. Open M-Th 12:30pm-midnight, F 12:30pm-1am, Sa 12:30pm-12:30am, Su 12:30-11:30pm. Kitchen open 12:30-7:30pm. MC/V.)

█ SIGHTS. The child-oriented **Bright Water Visitor Centre,** on the pier in Kyleakin, boasts interactive exhibits on local wildlife. (☎01599 530 040; www.eileanban. org. Open Mar.-Oct. M-F 10am-4pm. Free.) The center runs 1hr. walking tours to **Eilean Ban,** the island under the Skye Bridge. Departure times vary and are limited, so call ahead. (M-F 1-2 per day; £6, concessions £5.) The colorful boats in **Kyleakin Harbor** make for a calm walk around the pier, especially at sunset. For views of the village, scramble up the hill across the harbor to reach the small ruins of **Castle Maol.** Look for tiles that mark the way and the foreboding "Beware the Tides" stone. Heed its warning——the ruins are accessible only when the tide is out. According to legend, Norwegian princess "Saucy Mary" built the original castle and stretched a chain across the water, charging a toll to ships. She supposedly flashed those who paid the toll—hence her colorful moniker. (Open 24hr. Free.) In Kyle, the **Seaprobe Atlantis** is a glass-bottomed boat that affords close-up views of the ocean, which teems with sea life. (☎0800 980 4846; www.seaprobeatlantis.com. £12.50 for a 1hr. trip.)

ARMADALE AND THE SLEAT PENINSULA   ☎(0)1471

Two miles south of Broadford, the A851 leaves the clouds behind, revealing lush green gardens and glimmering sea views. Seventeen winding miles later, it reaches the scattered town of Armadale. Follow the sprawling nature paths through the **Armadale Castle Gardens** near the ruins of the former MacDonald stronghold. The **Museum of the Isles** is a beautifully displayed walkthrough of 1500 years of Scottish history. The adjacent study center is one of the best places in Scotland for **genealogical research.** (☎01471 844 305; www.clandonald. com. Open daily Apr.-Oct. 9:30am-5:30pm. Last entry 5pm. £5.60, concessions £4, families £16. Research is an additional £12 per ½-day.) North of Armadale at **Ostaig,** the famous Gaelic college **Sabhal Mòr Ostaig** offers language courses for a few hours or a week, many of which cater to tourists. (☎01471 888 000; www.smo.uhi.ac.uk. Courses £140 for 1 week. MC/V.) The panoramas of the Sleat Peninsula include dense woodlands, views of nearby isles Rum, Muck, and Eigg, and the dramatic backdrop of the Cuillins. A short footpath beginning at the shore of Loch Eishort (west off the A851) leads to little-known **Dunscaith Castle** ruins (1 mi.). A longer hike (4-5hr. round-trip) reaches Skye's southernmost tip, the **Point of Sleat,** with a lighthouse and views of the Cuillins to the north. The trailhead begins at the end of the A851, south of **Ardvasar** at the **Aird of Sleat.** An hour's walk is rewarded with spectacular views of **Rum** from the inlet of **Acairseid an Rubha.** Near the bus stop, a gallery displays and sells paintings of local landscapes by Nigel Grounds. (☎01471 844 439; www.nigelgrounds.com. Open Apr.-Oct. M-F 10am-6pm, Sa-Su noon-6pm.)

The **Flora MacDonald Hostel ❶,** 3 mi. north of Armadale, is a rustic lodge surrounded by Eriskay ponies. (☎01471 844 272 or 844 440. Kitchen and TV. Laundry £5. Dorms £12. Cash only.) In the building that used to keep the MacDonalds' horses, ◪**Stables Cafe ❶** makes exceptional homemade soups (from £3) and overlooks the gardens. (☎01471 844 305. Open daily 9:30am-5pm.)

Ferries run from Armadale to Mallaig (8 per day; single £3.50, 5-day roundtrip £6, cars £18.75/32.50). Highland Country **buses** run between Armadale and Broadford (1 per hr.); ask the bus driver to drop you off.

CENTRAL SKYE   ☎(0)1478

The dominant Cuillin Hills (COO-leen) are the highest peaks in the Hebrides and can be seen from all over Skye. The Kyleakin-Portree road winds its way through the Red Cuillins, which beckon to hikers through the misty clouds. Tiny Sligachan (SLIG-a-han), at the junction of the A87 to Portree and the A863 to Dunvegan, serves as an excellent base for exploring the hills. The famous trail through Glen Sligachan (opposite page) begins in Sligachan.

⌐⌐ **ACCOMMODATIONS AND FOOD.** A 5min. walk from the bus station, the **Sligachan Bunkhouse ❶** is a red cabin in the woods—perfect for a quiet night. (☎01478 650 204. Linens £3. Dorms £12. MC/V.) The **Sligachan Hotel ❹** has rooms with soft beds and plush chairs where weary hikers can rest their legs. (☎01478 650 204. £54 per person. Breakfast included. MC/V.) The **Sligachan Campsite ❶** is just across the road. (Open May-Sept. £4 per person. Cash only.) Several miles south of Sligachan on Loch Brittle, the wooden **SYHA Glenbrittle ❶** stands against the wind. (☎01478 640 278. Open Apr.-Sept. Dorms £13-14, under 18 £9.50-11.

MC/V.) Glenbrittle cannot be reached by public transportation; hearty back-packers with time on their hands should take the bus to Carbost and then walk 7 mi. down a single-lane track lined with evergreens. The **Glenbrittle Campsite** ❶ lies at the foot of the Black Cuillins and overlooks the loch. (☎01478 640 404. Reception 8am-7pm. Open Apr.-Oct. £4.50 per person. MC/V.)

The Sligachan Hotel's **Seumas' Bar** ❷ is the only pub around, offering a broad selection of beers and malts, including several from the attached Cuillin Brewery. (Live music F-Sa. Open daily 8am-11:30pm. MC/V.)

HIKING AND OUTDOOR ACTIVITIES. The Cuillin Hills are great for experienced hikers but can be risky for beginners. TICs, campgrounds, and hostels are well stocked with maps and books for walks throughout the region (see **Wilderness Safety**, p. 51). For a list of current guided walks, pick up a free copy of *Ranger Guided Walks and Events* from a TIC. The pitted peat of the Cuillins is always drenched and summer temperatures dip low—expect wet, frigid feet. A short, scenic path follows the stream from Sligachan to the head of **Loch Sligachan**. After crossing the old bridge, fork right off the main path and walk upstream along the right-hand bank. The narrow, boggy path leads past pools and waterfalls, in some places tracing the top of a small cliff (2 mi. round-trip). The 2537 ft. **Glamaig** proves a steep, challenging 3hr. hike. A smaller trail branches off after 1 mi. and leads up the ridge.

The daunting **Sgurr nan Gillean**, to the southwest of Glamaig, provides an all-day hike into the clouds, towering 3167 ft. above a tiny lake. For more level terrain, take the 8 mi. walk down **Glen Sligachan** through the heart of the Cuillins to the beach of **Camasunary**, with views of the isles of Rum and Muck. From Camasunary, you can hike 5 mi. along the coast to **Elgol**. From there, a sailing trip to **Loch Coriusk** with **Bella Jane Boat Trips** grants a different view of Skye and the surrounding isles. (☎01471 866 244; www.bellajane.co.uk. Runs Apr.-Oct. M-Sa; call for reservations 7:30-10am. £20-30. MC/V.) Elgol is 14 mi. southwest of Broadford on the B8083; Highland Country **buses** #50 and 52 travel to Broadford and Portree (M-Sa 1 per hr., Su 2 per day). Scottish Citylink buses also travel between Kyle and Portree via Broadford and Sligachan (M-Sa 6 per day, Su 4 per day.) Eight miles from Sligachan, the staff of **Cuillin Trail Riding** offers guided horseback rides for all ability levels. (☎07789 714 106; www.cuillintrailriding.co.uk. Open M-Sa dawn to dusk.)

THE MINGINISH PENINSULA   ☎(0)1478

The Minginish Peninsula is the road less traveled on Skye, but the serene sea-side towns are full of lovely ocean views and places to stay. In **Carbost,** on the road to Talisker, the **Talisker Distillery** sits on Loch Harport and offers straightfor-ward tours of its processes. The 45min. distillery tour is not nearly as memo-rable as its denouement: a wee dram of Skye's only malt at the end of the tour packs a fiery finish. (☎01478 614 308. Open July-Aug. daily 9:30am-4:30pm; Sept.-Oct. and Apr.-June M-Sa 9:30am-4:30pm; Nov.-Mar. M-F 2-4:30pm. £5.)

Four miles past Sligachan toward Dunvegan, **The Old Inn** ❶ has nautical-themed rooms overlooking the water and a giant kitchen and common area. (☎01478 640 205; www.carbost.f9.co.uk. Laundry £4.50. Dorms £13. MC/V.) Four miles up the road in Portnalong, the stylish **Taigh Ailean's** ❸ plaid furniture creates a homey atmosphere for its B&B crowd. (☎01478 640 271; www.taigh-ailean-hotel.co.uk. £25-30 per person. MC/V.) The **Skyewalker Hostel** ❶, Fiskavaig Rd., Portnalong, has decent accommodations and operates the best (and only) **cafe** ❶ on the peninsula. (☎01478 640 250; www.skyewalkerhostel.com. Dorms £13-15. MC/V.) **Croft Bunkhouse** ❶ sits in a sunny field and rents cheap, comfortable beds. (☎01478 640 254; www.skye-hostels.com. Campsites in adjacent field £7. Dorms and bothies £10. MC/V.)

Highland Country **buses** #53 and 54 travel to Portree and Sligachan (M-F 4 per day, Sa 1-2 per day), stopping at Carbost and the Talisker Distillery and continuing to Portnalong. The **post office** is in the hostel. (Open M and W-Th 9-11am.) **Postcode:** IV47 8SL.

PORTREE   ☎(0)1478

Most visitors to Skye end up in Portree at one point or another. It's the island's largest town and best transportation hub, with colorful buildings and harbor crowds that create a center for cultural life.

🖥 📱 TRANSPORTATION AND PRACTICAL INFORMATION. Scottish Citylink and Highland Country **buses** travel from Somerled Sq. to Kyle and Kyleakin (M-Sa 8-10 per day, Su 5 per day). To reach the **Tourist Information Centre,** Bayfield Rd., from the square, face the Bank of Scotland, turn left down the lane, and go left again onto Bridge Rd. The staff books lodgings for £4 plus a 10% deposit. (☎01478 612 137. Open June-Aug. M-Sa 9am-6pm, Su 10am-4pm; Sept.-Oct. and Apr.-June M-F 9am-5pm, Su 10am-4pm; Nov.-Mar. M-F 9am-5pm, Sa 10am-4pm.) Other services include: a **Royal Bank of Scotland** with ATM, Bank St. (☎01478 612 822; open M-Tu and Th-F 9:15am-4:45pm, W 9:45am-4:45pm); a **launderette,** underneath the Independent Hostel (☎01478 613 737; open M-Sa 9am-9pm); **Internet** access at the TIC (£3 per hr.) or at the library in the new school (☎01478 612 697; free, but book ahead; open M, W, F 9am-5pm, Tu and Th 9am-8pm, Sa 10am-4pm); and the **post office,** Wentworth St. (☎01478 612 533; open M-Sa 9am-5:30pm). **Postcode:** IV51 9EJ.

🛏 🍴 ACCOMMODATIONS AND FOOD. The bright yellow 🏠**Portree Independent Hostel ❶,** in the center of town, has spacious rooms, a colorful staff, and plenty of amenities, including a well-stocked kitchen and a large selection of movies for the common room TV. (☎01478 613 737. Dorms £12-13. MC/V.) Right as you enter Portree, the **Easdale B&B ❷,** Bridge Rd., is hidden up a stone pathway, behind a garden complete with old iron farm tools and garden gnomes. (☎01478 613 244. £28 per person. Cash only.) For higher-end lodgings, the **Portree Hotel ❹,** Somerled Sq., has occupied its castle-like building in the square since 1865. (☎01478 612 511. Free Wi-Fi. £45-50 per person. MC/V.)

The Somerfield **supermarket** is on Bank St. (☎01478 612 855. Open M-Sa 8am-9pm, Su 9am-6pm.) To satisfy cosmopolitan tastes, head to 🏠**Cafe Arriba ❷,** on Quay Brae, and sample the wide variety of fusion cuisine. (☎01478 611 830. Entrees £8-12. Open daily 7am-10pm. MC/V.) Vegetarian options and warm bread make the **Granary ❶,** Somerled Sq., a snacker's heaven. (☎01478 612 873. Open Apr.-Oct. daily 8am-5pm; Nov.-Mar. M-Sa 9am-5pm. MC/V.) Feast on delicate entrees at **Bosville Hotel ❸,** Bank St. (☎01478 612 846; www.macleodhotels.co.uk/bosville. Entrees £12-20. Open daily noon-9pm. AmEx/MC/V.) The **Caledonian Hotel** pub, upstairs on Wentworth St., is removed from the buzz of the main square. On weekends, it's the place to be for dancing. (☎01478 612 641. Live music F-Su. Open M-F noon-midnight, Sa noon-12:30am, Su 12:30-11:30pm.) **The Isles Inn,** Somerled Sq., is a refurbished croft house that features frequent live music and a large selection of ales. (☎01478 612 129. Open M-Sa 11am-midnight, Su 11am-11:30pm. MC/V.)

📱 DAYTRIP FROM PORTREE: TROTTERNISH PENINSULA. Many of the cliffs, waterfalls, and ancient standing stones that dot the Trotternish Peninsula remain seemingly untouched. A steep hike (1hr. round-trip) leads to the **Old Man of Storr**, a 165 ft. basalt stone at the top of the highest peak in Trotternish (2358 ft.), located north of Portree on the A855. Begin from the car park to attempt this ascent. North of Staffin, a footpath leads through the **Quiraing rocks**, a stark and otherworldly group of geological formations (3hr. round-trip). Nearby **Staffin Bay** abounds with Jurassic fossils and pottery artifacts from more recent settlers. South of Staffin, **Kilt Rock** boasts "pleated" lava columns above a rocky base crumbling into the sea. Climb to the top of nearby **Mealt Falls** (300 ft.) for the best view. The challenging 12 mi. hike along the Trotternish Ridge encompasses many of the sights on the peninsula. Begin at the Old Man of Storr car park and follow the signs to Staffin. On a bluff 5 mi. north of Staffin, the **Dun Flodigarry Hostel ❶** has a huge, colorful kitchen and overlooks the cliffs and ocean. Take the Staffin bus from Portree and ask to be let off. (☎01470 552 212; www.hostelflodigarry.co.uk. Camping £6.50 per person. Dorms £12.50.)

❷ DAYTRIP FROM PORTREE: DUNTULM. At the northern tip of the peninsula, the ruins of the former MacDonald stronghold **Duntulm Castle** stand at the edge of the sea. According to legend, the house was cursed when a nurse dropped the chief's child from a window. Be careful of the edge. (Open 24hr. Free.) Near Duntulm at Kilmuir, iron tools dot the yard of the **Skye Museum of Island Life**, a preserved crofter village of 18th-century black houses. (☎01470 552 206; www.skyemuseum.co.uk. Open Easter-Oct. M-Sa 9:30am-5pm. £2.50.) Down the road from the museum is the **Kilvaxter Iron Age Farmstead and Souterrain**, which dates back to 300 BC. Crawl down the narrow tunnel at your own risk.

❷ DAYTRIP FROM PORTREE: DUNVEGAN CASTLE. Off the A850, Dunvegan Castle is the longest-inhabited castle in Scotland, occupied since the 13th century. Elegantly restored rooms, a vast set of sculptured gardens, and a video about the MacLeod clan await visitors. Arrive early or late in the day to avoid hordes of summer tourists. For a free view of the castle and grounds, try the **Two Churches walk,** a few miles north of Dunvegan on the A850. *(From Portree, Highland Country buses run to the various sights. M-Sa 3-8 per day. #56 runs straight to the castle. M-Sa 4 per day. ☎01470 521 206; www.dunvegancastle.com. Open daily from mid-Mar. to Oct. 10am-5:30pm; from Nov. to mid-Mar. 11am-4pm. £7.50. Gardens without castle £5.)*

UIG   ☎(0)1470

Serving as little more than a sleepy stepping stone for island travelers, Uig (YOU-ig) has a calm harbor and sound accommodations. While waiting for a ferry, stop by the **Isle of Skye Brewery,** next to the pier. Employees give brief tours when they're not busy brewing. (☎01470 542 477; www.skyebrewery.co.uk. Open M-F 10am-6pm, Su noon-4pm. £2. Advance booking requested.)

The **SYHA Uig ❶**, a 30min. walk from the ferry dock, has rooms that will block out the pervasive early summer light as well as a knowledgeable staff that can suggest short walks and hikes in the area. Turn right on the winding road from the ferry dock and walk around the bay. (☎01470 542 211. Reception open 5pm-10am. Open Apr.-Oct. Dorms from £12, under 18 from £9. AmEx/MC/V.) Navigate colorful yard decor to reach **Orasay B&B ❷**, next to the pier, where all rooms are ensuite. (☎01470 542 316; www.holiday-skye.co.uk. £27 per person. Cash only.) The **Pub at the Pier ❷** doubles as a restaurant and bar, with classic offerings (burger £6, entrees £9-14), fresh seafood, and the occasional local band. (☎01470 542 212. Open M-F 11am-1am, Sa 11am-12:30am, Su 12:30-11pm. Kitchen open 11:30am-4:45pm and 6-9pm. MC/V.)

CalMac runs a **ferry** connecting Uig to Tarbert, Lewis, and to Lochmaddy, North Uist (1hr.; M-Sa 1-2 per day; £10, 5-day round-trip £17.10, with car

£48/82). Highland Country **buses** #57A and 57C and Scottish Citylink buses also run to Portree (M-F 6 per day, Sa 4 per day).

THE OUTER HEBRIDES

Ancient history comes to life in the Outer Hebrides, where thatched-roof houses, standing stones, and relics from generations past sit amid a landscape of exposed rock. The islands are so steeped in tradition that you're more likely to get an earful of Gaelic here than anywhere else in Scotland. On the Calvinist islands of Lewis and Harris, almost all establishments close and public transportation ceases on Sundays, although one or two places may assist lost souls with a pint. The extreme seclusion and quiet of the islands make the Western Isles some of Scotland's most undisturbed, unforgettable realms.

TRANSPORTATION

CalMac (☎08000 665 000) has a near monopoly on passenger and car **ferries** along major routes. It runs from Ullapool to Stornoway, Lewis (2hr.; 2-3 per day; £15, 5-day round-trip £26, car £75/127), from Uig, Skye to Lochmaddy, North Uist (1hr.; 1-2 per day; £10, 5-day round-trip £17.10, car £48/82), and to Tarbert, Harris (1hr.; 1-2 per day; £10, 5-day round-trip £17.10, car £48/82), and from Oban to Castlebay, Barra and Lochboisdale, South Uist (6hr.; 1 per day; £22, 5-day round-trip £50, car £81/137). Call ahead if you wish to take a car.

In the archipelago, ferries brave rough sounds and infrequent buses cross causeways connecting the islands. TICs carry the invaluable, free *Discover Scotland's Islands with Caledonian MacBrayne, Lewis and Harris Bus Timetables*. Inexpensive **car rental** (from £25 per day) is available. Road signs are in Gaelic first and English second, if at all. Although many names are similar in English, TICs often carry translation keys, and *Let's Go* lists Gaelic equivalents after English place names where appropriate. For more on Scottish Gaelic words, see the **Appendix, p. 719**. **Cycling** is popular, although windy hills and sudden rains often wipe out novice riders. Traffic is light, but hitchhikers report frequent lifts on all the islands. *Let's Go* does not recommend hitchhiking.

LEWIS (LEODHAS)

The sloping moors of Lewis make for spectacular walking and biking trips, and its historical artifacts are among the most celebrated in Scotland. Stornoway, the capital city, offers a splash of world culture while the smaller surrounding communities, preserve a traditions of craftsmanship and sustainable farming.

Galson Motors (☎01851 840 269) offers a day pass on the west coast of Lewis (£6.50), or a round-trip ticket to see one, two, or three of the major sights from May to October (£4-5). Alternatively, travel with **Out and About Tours.** (☎01851 612 288; www.hebridean-holidays.co.uk. Harris full day tour £120, Lewis full day tour £140.) **Albannach Guided Tours** offers personalized excursions. (☎01851 830 433; www.albannachtours.co.uk. From £10 per hr. per person.)

STORNOWAY (STEORNOBHAIGH)   ☎(0)1851

The urban feel of Stornoway comes as a shock after any exploration of the remote Outer Hebrides. Home to nearly a third of the population of the Western Isles, Stornoway bustles with surprising energy during the week, which contrasts sharply with its strict observance of the Sabbath. Parks and museums make the town well worth the visit, and lively traditional music flows through its pubs on weekends.

🖪🔁 TRANSPORTATION AND PRACTICAL INFORMATION. CalMac **ferries** sail to Ullapool (2hr.; M-Sa 2-3 per day; £15.30, 5-day round-trip £26.60, car £75/127). **Buses** operated by Western Isles depart from the Beach St. station; pick up a free *Lewis and Harris Bus and Ferry Services Timetable.* (☎01851 704 327. Luggage storage 20p-£1. Station open M-Sa 8am-5:45pm.) Destinations include Callanish (*Calanais;* 1hr., M-Sa 4-6 per day), Port of Ness (*Nis;* 1hr., M-Sa 6-8 per day), and Tarbert (An Tairbeart; M-Sa 3-7 per day, £4.50). **Car rental** is cheaper here than on the mainland. Try Lewis Car Rentals, 52 Bayhead St. (☎01851 703 760. £30-50 per day. 21+. Open M-Sa 9am-6pm. AmEx/MC/V.) Rent **bikes** at Alex Dan's Cycle Centre, 67 Kenneth St. (☎01851 704 025. £12 per day. Open M-Sa 9am-5:30pm. AmEx/MC/V.)

The **Tourist Information Centre** is at 26 Cromwell St. From the ferry terminal, turn left onto South Beach and right on Cromwell St. (☎01851 703 088. Open Apr.-Oct. M-F 9am-6pm and 8-9pm; Nov.-Mar. M-F 9am-5pm.) Other services include: a **Bank of Scotland,** across from the TIC (☎01851 705 252; open M-Tu and Th-F 9am-5pm, W 9:30am-5pm); free **Internet** at the **Stornoway Library** (☎01851 708 631; open M-W and Sa 10am-5pm, Th-F 10am-6pm); and the **post office,** 16 Francis St. (open M-F 9am-5:30pm, Sa 9am-12:30pm). **Postcode:** HS1 2AA.

🛏🍴 ACCOMMODATIONS AND FOOD. Hands down the best place to stay in Stornoway, the immaculate 🗷**Heb Hostel ❶,** 25 Kenneth St., offers exceptional amenities, including stand-alone bathtubs and an impressive variety of free continental breakfast items. (☎01851 709 889; www.hebhostel.co.uk. Laundry £5. Internet £1 per 30min. £15 per person. Cash only.) **The Laxdale Bunkhouse ❶,** off Bayhead Rd., sleeps 16 in four modern rooms on the Laxdale Holiday Park campgrounds, 1½ mi. from downtown. (☎01851 706 966; www.laxdaleholiday-park.com. £2 per person; £5 per tent. Dorms £12-13. Cash only.) For higher-end digs, the family-owned **Park Guest House ❹,** 30 James St., is a recently renovated Victorian townhouse that gives a taste of historic Stornoway. (☎01851 702 485; www.theparkguesthouse.co.uk. £42 per person. MC/V.)

Cheap chow is plentiful in takeaway-heavy Stornoway. Stock up on groceries at the **Co-op** on Cromwell St. (☎01851 702 703. Open M-Sa 8am-8pm.) Feast on classic dishes in the green-curtained glow of the 🗷**Thai Cafe ❷,** 27 Church St., which serves inexpensive, mouthwatering entrees and a whole section of vegetarian dishes (£5-7) on silk tablecloths and rattan mats. (☎01851 701 811. Open M-Sa noon-2:30pm and 5-11pm. MC/V.) The cosmopolitan **HS-1 ❷,** Cromwell St., is the only restaurant in Stornoway open on Sunday and sells innovative fusion cuisine. (☎01851 702 109. Entrees £8-12. Open daily noon-4pm and 5-9pm. AmEx/MC/V.) The **library cafe ❶,** attached to the library on Cromwell St., satisfies large lunchtime crowds with its homemade soups and sandwiches starting at £2. (☎01851 708 632. Open M-Sa 10am-4pm.)

◩ SIGHTS. The **An Lanntair Arts Centre,** on Kenneth St., runs a year-round program of visual and performing arts, a plush bar and restaurant, and an evening film series. (☎01851 703 307; www.lanntair.com. Open M-Sa 10am-11pm. Free; film series prices vary.) The **Museum nan Eilean,** Francis St., hosts fascinating exhibits on 9000 years of Hebridean history. (☎01851 709 266; www. cne-siar.gov.uk. Open Apr.-Sept. M-Sa 10am-5:30pm; Oct.-Mar. Tu-F 10am-5pm, Sa 10am-1pm. Free.) The woods surrounding the mock-Tudor **Lewis Castle** provide shaded walks along the water. The castle itself was built in the 19th century and stands overlooking the town, adjacent to the golf course. The entrance is on Cromwell St., but turn left after the footbridge from New St. to admire it from across the water on N. Beach St.

NIGHTLIFE AND FESTIVALS. Stornoway livens up unexpectedly on weekend nights. Pubs and clubs crowd the area between Point St., Castle St., and the two waterfronts. Formerly a center that offered alternatives to alcohol, **McNeill's** has returned to its roots as a classic pub that serves a solid pint. (☎01851 703 330. Live music W. Open M-W 11am-11pm, Th-Sa 11am-1am. Cash only.) The big-screen TV at the **Lewis Bar,** N. Beach St., attracts pub-goers on nights of big sporting events. Behind the counter, look for the large collection of malt whiskies and Matchbox cars on display. (☎01851 704 567. M-W 11am-11pm, Th 11am-midnight, F 11am-2am, Sa 11am-1am. Cash only.) The popular **Crown Inn,** Castle St., features live music and a traditional pub atmosphere for unwinding after a long day. (☎01851 703 181. Open M-W 11am-11pm, Th-F 11am-midnight, Sa 11am-11:30pm. Cash only.) The **Hebridean Celtic Festival** (☎01851 621 234; www.hebceltfest.com) in mid-July draws top musical talent from Scotland and all over the world. The main acts sell out far in advance.

GETTING AROUND LEWIS. Traveling up the **west coast** of Lewis allows a glimpse of thousands of years of the island's history preserved in ruins, museums, and reconstructed villages. But transportation can be tough. The W2 bus operates on a circuit beginning at the Stornoway bus station (M-Sa 4-6 per day). The trick with the W2 is that it runs in both directions, so if you time it properly, you can travel back and forth along the circuit and visit more places than you could if you just took it all the way around one way. The information desk at the bus station can help plan a route to maximize the number of sights visited. Alternatively, a number of touring companies offer packages that will bring you to most of the major sights (p. 662).

DAYTRIP FROM STORNOWAY: CALLANISH STONES (CALANAIS). The gargantuan Callanish Stones, 14 mi. west of Stornoway on the A858, are second only to Stonehenge in grandeur and are less overrun with tourists. The largest group of stones, dubbed Callanish 1, consists of dozens of crystalline slabs arranged in a cross. Some archaeologists believe that prehistoric peoples used Callanish and two nearby circles to track the movements of the heavens. The Visitor Centre has a comprehensive exhibit and a short video. (☎01851 621 422. Open Apr.-Sept. M-Sa 10am-6pm; Oct.-Mar. W-Sa 10am-4pm. Stones free; exhibit and film £2, concessions £1.35.) Nibble scones at the newly renovated **Callanish Tea House ❶,** the only privately owned black house (below) on the island. (Open M-Sa 9am-6pm. Cash only.) A mile south of Callanish, the W3 bus makes its way across the bridge to the stark, white beaches of the island of **Great Bernera**.

DAYTRIP FROM STORNOWAY: CARLOWAY BROCH. Five miles north of Callanish along the A858 lies the crofting settlement of Carloway (*Charlabhaigh*), dominated by the Iron Age ruins of the Carloway Broch. Dating from the first century BC, this double-walled stone tower would have been home to a powerful community leader and is one of the largest remaining brochs. Since then, half the wall has crumbled, and some visitors find that climbing inside allows them to view a cross section of the building. The visitors center provides a tour revealing what life would have been like in a broch. (☎01851 643 338. Visitor Centre open May-Oct. M-Sa 10am-4pm. Broch always open. Free.)

▶ DAYTRIP FROM STORNOWAY: GEARRANNAN VILLAGE. Up the road in Carloway proper is a restored community of traditional black houses. Occupied as recently as the 1960s, some have been converted into a hostel and holiday cottages, but one remains a museum that offers a glimpse into the changing Hebridean lifestyle. These houses had no chimneys, and peat fires constantly burned in the center of the stone floors. Tar from the smoke coated the thatched roofs, helping to hold them together, but also turned the interiors of the houses a sooty black. A local weaver works in the houses and tells the history of the community. Half-hour guided historical walks leave from the settlement. (☎01851 643 416. Open M-Sa 9:30am-5:30pm. £2.40, concessions £2. Guided walks £2.50; call for hours.) Farther north on the A858, in Arnol beyond Shawbost, lies a restored crofter's cottage known as the **Arnol Black House.** A more modern "white house" stands nearby, abandoned once the original owners discovered that its newfangled construction also made it intolerably damp inside. Walk along the beach near the black house to find pieces of pottery from surrounding communities. (☎01851 710 395. Open Apr.-Sept. M-Sa 9:30am-5pm; Oct.-Mar. M-Sa 9:30am-4pm. Last entry 30min. before close. £4.50.)

▶ DAYTRIP FROM STORNOWAY: BUTT OF LEWIS. Besides being the butt of terrible puns, the Butt of Lewis has an enormous natural stone arch that stands where the Atlantic crashes into the cliffs with deafening ferocity. Legend has it that the Vikings attached a chain to the arch and tried to pull the Hebrides back to Norway with them, causing the islands to split apart into the formation they have today. To the north you'll pass the village of Galson and the quiet **Galson Farm Guesthouse and Bunkhouse ❶**. Be sure to call ahead. (Butt of Lewis always open. Free. Galston Farm ☎01851 850 492; www.galsonfarm.freeserve.co.uk. Dorms £12. MC/V.)

▶ DAYTRIP FROM STORNOWAY: DALMORE BEACH AND SURF SPOTS. Several beaches on Lewis and Harris are quickly becoming known as world-class (if chilly) surf spots. In Lewis, competitors flock to **Dalmore Beach,** near the town of Dalbeg, as well as to the beaches of **Valtos** and **Europie,** farther down the western coast. Amateur archaeologists and shell hunters search for Neolithic artifacts and the pink shells fabled to be mermaid fingernails. With its rip-tide currents, the **Port of Ness** is a dangerous place to surf—only the experienced should head there. **Hebridean Surf Holidays,** on the corner of Keith and Francis St. in Stornoway, leads all-inclusive surfing lessons, rents equipment, and shuttles surfers to the beach. (☎07939 194 880; www.lewissurftrek.com. Lessons from £35 per day; board and ride to beach from £20. The W2 bus route (M-Sa 6-10 per day) runs past Dalbeg and Dalmor Beach, while W4 buses (M-Sa 2-4 per day) from Stornoway pass other ideal surf spots farther down the coast. The W1 bus (M-F 8-9 per day, Sa 6 per day) travels along the northwest coast to the Butt and the Port of Ness.)

HARRIS (NA HEARADH)

Harris shares an island with Lewis, but the two regions are different worlds—when the ruling MacLeod clan split, so did the isle. The rugged peaks of Harris in the north stand in stark contrast to the deserted flatlands of Lewis. Tufts of grass protruding from cracks in ancient boulders give the landscape an eerie appearance, like the surface of the moon. Toward the west coast, the Forest of Harris (in fact a treeless, heather-splotched mountain range) descends onto brilliant crescents of white sand bordered by cerulean waters and *machair* (coastal meadows). The A859, or "Golden Road" (named for the king's ransom spent blasting it from the rock), winds to Harris's southern tip—it's a trip for seasoned cyclists or bus travelers ready for a bumpy ride.

TARBERT (AN TAIRBEART)   ☎(0)1859

As the largest town on Harris, Tarbert serves both as a ferry port for traveling to the Isle of Skye and as a good base for walks and hikes around Harris.

⊟🛈 TRANSPORTATION AND PRACTICAL INFORMATION. Hebridean Transport runs **buses** (☎01851 502 441) from Leverburgh and Stornoway (bus W10; 1hr., M-Sa 3-7 per day, £4.50). CalMac (☎08000 665 000) **ferries** sail from Tarbert to Uig, Skye (M-Tu, Th, Sa 2 per day, W and F 1 per day; £10, 5-day round-trip £17.10). Check at the pier in Tarbert for timetables. Rent **bicycles** from the grocery store in Ardhasaig, 3 mi north of Tarbert, or from Paula Williams in Leverburgh. (☎01859 520 319. £10-12 per day.) The **Tourist Information Centre** is on Pier Rd., and Tarbert's only **ATM** is located at the back of the building. (☎01859 502 011. Open from Apr. to mid-Oct. M, W, F 9am-5pm, Tu, Th, Sa 9am-5pm and 7-8pm, depending on ferry arrivals.) A **Bank of Scotland** is uphill from the pier. (☎01859 502 453. Open M-Tu and Th-F 10am-12:30pm and 1:30-4pm, W 11:15am-12:30pm and 1:30-4pm.) Free **Internet** access is available in the **public library** in Sir E. Scott School, a cream-colored building 10min. along the A859 to Stornoway. (☎01859 502 926. Open M 9:30am-6pm, Tu and Th-F 9:30am-4:20pm, W 9:30am-4:20pm and 7-9pm, Sa 10am-12:30pm.) The **post office** is on Main St. (☎01859 502 211. Open M-Tu and Th-F 9am-1pm and 2-5:30pm, W 9am-1pm, Sa 9am-12:30pm.) **Postcode:** HS3 3DB.

🛏🍴 ACCOMMODATIONS AND FOOD. The homey **Drinishader Hostel ❶** is located 6 mi. from Tarbert. Get there by going south on the A859 and following signs to Drinishader. (☎01859 511 255. Dorms £10. Cash only.) For those stuck in Tarbert for the night, the sparsely decorated **Rockview Bunkhouse ❶** is less than a 5min. walk from the pier on Main St. It's run by two postal clerks—you can check in at the post office. (☎01859 502 211. Dorms £10. MC/V.) Up the road from the ferry terminal, the **Harris Hotel ❹** sits among sculptured gardens and proudly displays the signature of *Peter Pan* creator JM Barrie etched into a window, now encased in a glass frame. Guests can request rooms with traditional tartan decor. (☎01859 502 154. £35-65 per person, with dinner £68-88. MC/V.) **AD Munro,** Main St., serves Tarbert as grocer, butcher, and baker. (☎01859 502 016. Open M-Sa 7:30am-7:30pm. MC/V.) Nestled behind fragrant flowering bushes, the hugely popular **Firstfruits Tearoom ❶**, across from the TIC, pours hot drinks in a homey setting. (☎01859 502 439. Open Apr.-Sept. daily 10:30am-4:30pm and 7-9pm. Book ahead. Cash only.) The **Harris Hotel Restaurant and Bar ❹** serves Hebridean shellfish and Scottish beef (£14-18) in the main building's upscale dining room. (☎01859 502 154. Bar open M-Sa 11am-11pm, Su 12:30-2:30pm and 6:30-10:30pm. MC/V.)

🏔🥾 SIGHTS AND HIKING. Some of Harris's most impressive sights, including miles of pristine beaches, lie only a few miles away from Tarbert and inspire awe even on gray days. The **Harris Walkway** runs north from Clisham to Scaladal, passing through Tarbert in the middle. The tallest peaks lie in the **Forest of Harris,** whose main entrances are off the B887 to Huishinish Point, at Glen Meavaig, and farther west at 19th-century **Amhuinnsuidhe Castle,** 15 mi. from Tarbert. The infrequent summertime W12 bus from Tarbert serves these points (3 per day). If you don't have much time, use one of the unmarked eastern trails to hike up **Gillaval** (1554 ft.; at least 1hr.) or take a coastal stroll from Taobh Tuath to Horgabost. Ordnance Survey maps for these areas are available in the TIC. Tarbert itself has few attractions, but it is a good place to buy swatches and teddy bears made of the world-famous Harris tweed. Pick up a copy of *The Heb* (£4), which lists upcoming events and festivals.

ROCK THE TWEED. Buying tweed in larger towns and shops ensures a high-quality product from a Highland source. Look for the Harris Tweed authenticity patch to verify that your item was made by a crofter on Harris.

RODEL AND LEVERBURGH ☎(0)1859

Rodel (Roghadal), at Harris's southern tip, is the site of **Saint Clement's Church,** which houses three MacLeod tombs from the 16th century, including one of the best-preserved examples of medieval stone carvings. Climb the wood ladders and squeeze through hatches to reach the top of the church for sweeping views of the isle. Three miles up the road is Leverburgh, a small port. Colorful anchors and coiled rope decorate the lawn of the **Am Bothan Bunkhouse ❷,** a funky, comfortable hostel in town, half a mile from the Leverburgh pier. The owner can also arrange boat rides. (☎01859 520 251; www.ambothan.com. Laundry £5. Camping £10. Dorms £15. MC/V.) The straightforward **Anchorage Restaurant ❷** serves classic seafood dishes on Leverburgh's pier. Enjoy a casual dinner (entrees £8-14) or a full breakfast for £6. (☎01859 520 225. Open M-Sa 11am-9pm. AmEx/MC/V.) CalMac (☎08000 665 000) **ferries** sail to Leverburgh from Ardmaree, Berneray (M-Sa 3-4 per day; £5.75, 5-day round-trip £9.75). **Buses** W10 and W13 run from Tarbert (1hr., M-Sa 3-7 per day, £4.15).

NORTHWEST HIGHLANDS

Removed from the tourist hordes that pass through the islands, the Northwest Highlands remain largely unexplored. The scree-covered Torridon Mountains challenge the most seasoned climbers, while harbor towns preserve the fishing and farming lifestyles that have fueled their existence for thousands of years. Easiest to tour by foot or car, the Northwest Highlands straddle the line between wilderness and civilization with awe-inspiring beauty.

TRANSPORTATION

Without a car, traversing the Northwest Highlands is tricky in summer and nearly impossible in winter. Scotrail (☎08457 484 950) runs **trains** from Inverness to Thurso (4hr., 3 per day, £15.30). Scottish Citylink (☎08705 505 050) and Rapson **buses** travel from Inverness to Thurso (3hr., 5 per day, £16.50) and Ullapool (1hr., M-Sa 2-4 per day, £9.80) to connect with ferries from Stornoway, Lewis. From April to October, the **Northern Explorer Ticket,** available at bus stations, provides unlimited travel between Inverness and Thurso (3 consecutive days £35; 5 of 10 £59; 8 of 16 £79). Postbuses are another option; consult the public transportation guide. Caution: the narrow roads are full of fast-moving locals and tentative visitors.

ULLAPOOL ☎(0)1854

Ullapool stands as a center of transportation and activity in the middle of the Highlands. With a rich seafaring heritage, the town has retained plenty of charm and personality even as its herring fishing industry died away. Its summer stream of ferry-riding tourists enhances business at its several restaurants and cafes, while its proximity to some of the most pristine wilderness of Scotland make it a favored stopping place for more rough-and-tumble hikers.

⬛🔲 TRANSPORTATION AND PRACTICAL INFORMATION. Except for the 1am arrivals, **ferries** from Stornoway, Lewis (M-F 2-3 per day; £15, 5-day round-trip £26, with car £73/125) are met simultaneously by Scottish Citylink and Rapsons Coaches **buses** (☎01463 222 244). Buses run to Inverness (1hr., 2 per day, £7.70), including one with an attachment for bicycles (☎01349 883 585; 1hr., 1 per day, £8.50). The **Tourist Information Centre** is on Argyle St. (☎01854 612 486. Open July-Aug. M-Sa 9am-5:30pm, Su 10am-4pm; Sept.-Oct. and Apr.-June M-Sa 10am-5pm, Su 10am-4pm; Nov.-Mar. M-Sa 10am-4pm.) An **ATM** can be found at the **Bank of Scotland** on W. Argyle St. (☎01854 612 643. Open M-Tu and Th-F 9am-12:30pm and 1:30-5pm, W 9:30am-12:30pm and 1:30-5pm.) The **library,** Mill St., has free computer terminals. (☎01854 612 543. Open during the school year M, W, F 9am-5pm, Tu and Th 9am-8pm; in summer Tu 2-8pm, Th-F 10am-5pm. Book ahead.) Access free **Wi-Fi** above Northwest Outdoors, W. Argyle St., in the coffee shop. (Open M-Sa 9:30am-4:30pm.) The **post office** is at 4 W. Argyle St. (☎01854 612 228. Open M-Tu and Th-F 9am-1pm and 2-5:30pm, W and Sa 9am-1pm.) **Postcode:** IV26 2TY.

⬛🔲 ACCOMMODATIONS AND FOOD. The bright common spaces of the **SYHA Ullapool ❶,** Shore St., overlook the harbor in the front and a small garden out back. (☎01854 612 254. Laundry £2. Lockout 10:30am-5pm. Curfew M-W and Su 11:30pm, Th-Sa midnight. Dorms £14, under 18 £9-10. AmEx/MC/V.) The social **Scotpackers West House ❷,** W. Argyle St., has an open kitchen, a computer room, and a hipster feel. (☎01854 613 126; www.scotpackers-hostels.co.uk. Internet £1 per 30min. Dorms £14. Cash only.) For more privacy, the affiliated **Crofton House ❸** sleeps nine in a self-catering cottage with a sloping ceiling and a loft bedroom. (☎01854 613 126. Book far ahead. £750 per week. Cash or check only.) Camping is available at **Broomfield Holiday Grounds,** a large field on W. Argyle St. (☎01854 612 664. £14 per tent.)

Tesco, Latheron Ln. off Quay St., supplies groceries. (Open M-Sa 8am-8pm, Su 9am-6pm.) **Costcutter,** across from the post office, has a smaller selection. (☎01854 612 661. Open M-F 7am-8pm, Sa-Su 8am-8pm.) Several award-winning pubs line W. Argyle St. ⬛**The Seaforth ❷,** named UK seafood pub of 2008, makes classic fish and chips with mushy peas (£8.50) in a diner-style kitchen. (☎01854 612 122; www.theseaforth.com. Entrees £5-13. Open M-F 9am-1am, Sa 9am-midnight, Su noon-midnight. MC/V.) Rambler roses and flowering vines soften the outline of the stark white building that houses **The Ceilidh Place ❸,** a hotel, cafe, bar, bookstore, and art gallery. (☎01854 612 103; www.theceilidh-place.com. Entrees £8-14. Open daily 8:30am-9pm. Rooms from £48. AmEx/MC/V.) The fragrant **Jasmine Tandoori ❶,** West Ln., is Ullapool's only Indian restaurant, offering a selection of curry and balti dishes. (☎01854 613 331. Entrees £8-12. Open daily noon-2pm and 5-11pm. MC/V.)

⬛🔲 SIGHTS AND HIKING. Although many come to Ullapool for a rest from hiking, a local, well-trodden walk up **Ullapool Hill** offers great views of the area without too much effort. Follow the signs from North Rd., near the school. The SYHA hostel (above) provides free leaflets detailing longer walks that traverse Scots Pine and the Inverpolly Nature Reserve. Situated in a former parliamentary church, the **Ullapool Museum,** 7-8 W. Argyle St., has a genealogical research facility and an impressive collection of artifacts and maps detailing the history of the area. (☎01854 612 987. Open Apr.-Oct. M-Sa 10am-5pm; Nov.-Mar. by arrangement. £3, concessions £2, children 50p.) Look for seals and puffins on the remote but nearby **Summer Isles** on a powerboat trip with Seascape Expeditions (☎01854 633 708; £23) or opt for a longer trip aboard the *Summer Queen* (☎04854 612 472; www.summerqueen.co.uk).

DAYTRIP FROM ULLAPOOL: CORRIESHALLOCH GORGE. On the A835, 12 mi. south of Ullapool, the River Broom cascades 150 ft. down the **Falls of Measach** into a deep, dramatic gorge. Turn right on the footpath across from the bus stop and follow the path to the jutting overlook for gorgeous views. A suspension bridge allows the brave to sway in the breeze overlooking the 40m drop to the icy water. The gorge has been intermittently closed for repairs to the bridge; check at a TIC. It is easily accessible by most Ullapool-Inverness buses; check that a return exists before you set out.

DURNESS
☎(0)1971

One of the northernmost settlements in mainland Scotland, the seaside village of Durness caters to surfers with its big waves and small-town vibes.

TRANSPORTATION AND PRACTICAL INFORMATION. To reach Durness, Rapsons Highland Country **buses** roll in from Lairg at 3pm (M-Sa 1-2 per day). Tim Dearman Coaches also run to Inverness (5hr., 1 per day, round-trip £21) and Ullapool (3hr., 1 per day, round-trip £18.50). The **TIC** books B&Bs for £4 plus a 10% deposit. (☎01971 511 368. Open daily Apr.-Oct. 10am-5pm; Nov.-Mar. 10am-1:30pm.) The **post office** is up the road in the Spar store. (☎01971 511 209. Store open M-F 8am-6pm, Sa 9am-6pm, Su 10am-6pm. The store's staff can open the post office if it appears closed.) **Postcode:** IV27 4PN.

ACCOMMODATIONS AND FOOD. In the center of town, the **Lazycrofter Bunkhouse** ❸ promotes a relaxed atmosphere with unlocked, mixed-sex dorms. Guests can relax on leather couches or on the porch outside during spells of sunshine. (☎01971 511 202; www.durnesshostel.com. Check in at Mackay's Hotel next door. Dorms £14.) The two-building complex of **SYHA Durness** ❶, 1 mi. north of town along the A838, affords easy access to the Smoo Caves. Amenities include a coal-burning stove, outdoor picnic tables, a barbecue, and a small garden. (☎01971 511 264. Reception 7-10:30am and 5-11pm. Open March-Sept. Dorms £12-14, under 16 £9-10. AmEx/MC/V.) Next to the visitors center, the **Sango Sands Camping Site** ❶ is basically beachside. (☎01971 511 726. Reception 9-9:30am and 6-6:30pm. £4.75 per tent. Cash only.)

The nearby **Sango Sands Oasis Bar and Restaurant** ❷ supplies comfort foods like pies and burgers in a dim but welcoming dining area. (☎01971 511 222. Open daily noon-2:30pm and 6-9pm. MC/V.) In the nearby **Balnakeil Craft Village,** half a mile west of Durness, sample rich, delectable, and expensive French truffles (9 for £7) made by hand with West Highland cream in the open kitchen of Cocoa Mountain. (☎01971 511 233; www.cocoamountain.co.uk. Open daily June-Aug. 9am-6pm; Sept.-May 10am-5pm. MC/V.)

SIGHTS. The **Smoo Caves** draw tourists in for a look at the deep holes in the limestone, rumored to have been used to dispose of the bodies of over 20 murder victims. During the 17th and 18th centuries, superstitious locals avoided the cavern, believing that the devil resided inside. Take a tour and float via rubber dinghy past the interior waterfall. (☎01971 511 704. Tours depart from cave entrance Apr.-Sept. daily every 20min. 10am-5pm. £3.) Stop in the hamlet of Blairmore on the northwestern coast to walk the 4 mi. path to **Sandwood Bay,** a pristine bit of coast home to rare ferns and colorful legends. **Cape Wrath's** cliffs, 12 mi. west of Durness, are the tallest on mainland Britian. From the Cape Wrath Hotel, 2 mi. west of the town center, a ferry crosses to Kyle of Durness (☎01971 511 376; 3-4 per day, round-trip £5), where it's met by a minibus that completes the trip to Cape Wrath (☎01971 511 287; round-trip £9).

Ferries and buses operate on demand May-Sept. from 9:30am. The cape may be closed for live military exercises; call the range to check (☎01971 511 242).

THURSO AND SCRABSTER   ☎(0)1847

Thurso (pop. 10,000) is considered a veritable metropolis by the crofters and fishermen of Scotland's desolate north coast. The town offers little in the way of cultural sights but has plenty of amenities that cater to travelers on their way to nearby destinations. On the east side of town, **castle ruins** sparkle against miles of coastline, where one of the best **surf spots** in the world awaits enthusiasts willing to brave the icy waters. Rent wetsuits (£10 per day) and surfboards (£10 per day) from **Tempest Surf,** Thurso Harbor, on the waterfront. (☎01847 892 500. Open daily 10am-5pm. MC/V.) Scrabster, 2 mi. east of Thurso, is a ferry port for Orkney and little else.

🛏**Sandra's Backpackers Hostel ❶,** at 26 Princes St. above a snack shop, sometimes smells of deep-fried takeaway but is centrally located with 30 bunks in ensuite dorms. The owners provide lifts to Scrabster for noon ferry connections. (☎01847 894 575; www.sandras-backpackers.co.uk. Continental breakfast included. Internet £1 per 30min. Free Wi-Fi in the snack shop downstairs. Dorms £13. Cash only.) **Sandra's Snack Bar and Takeaway ❶,** beneath the hostel, is filled with locals looking for a quick bite and is happy to serve a hearty breakfast to backpackers from the hostel. (☎01847 894 575. Open M-F 10am-11pm, Sa 10am-midnight, Su 11am-10:30pm. Cash only.) For fancy but affordable dining, try the newly refurbished **Red Pepper Restaurant and Bar ❸,** 16 Princes St. Locals get dressed up to enjoy the locally raised steaks (£11-14) and classy ambience. (☎01847 892 771. Open M-Sa noon-2pm and 5:30-8:30pm, Su 12:30-2:30pm and 5:30-8:30pm. Book ahead.) In Scrabster, grab morning eats at **The Fisherman's Mission ❶.** (☎01847 892 402. Breakfast from £2.50. Open M-F 7:30am-5pm, Sa 7:30am-noon.)

Highland Country **bus** #78 links Thurso to Scrabster (M-F 5 per day, Sa-Su 3 per day). Scottish Citylink buses travel to Inverness (M-Sa 6 per day, Su 4 per day), as do ScotRail **trains** (3 per day). Highland Country bus #80 runs to John O'Groats (M-F 6 per day, Sa 3 per day). Schedules change frequently; check in at the TIC or call ☎0871 200 2233. A **Tourist Information Centre,** Riverside Rd., treats Thurso's few sights with casual indifference but its visitors with warmth. (☎08452 255 121. Open June M-Sa 10am-5pm, Su 10am-4pm; July-Aug. M-Sa 9:30am-5:30pm, Su 10am-5pm; Sept.-Oct and Apr.-May M-Sa 10am-5pm.) Other services include a **Bank of Scotland** on Trail St. with an **ATM** (open M-Tu and Th-F 9:15am-4:45pm, W 9:30am-4:45 pm) and a **post office** inside the **Co-op** supermarket on Grove Ln. (☎01847 893 117; Co-op open M-W and Sa 8am-8pm, Th-F 8am-9pm, Su 9am-7pm; post office open M-Sa 9:30am-5pm). **Postcode:** KW14.

JOHN O'GROATS   ☎(0)1955

Named for the first man to arrange ferries to the islands (Jan de Groot, a Dutchman), John O'Groats proudly proclaims its position as mainland Britain's northernmost town. Scores of walkers and cyclists arrive in the town each year to complete the trek from the Land's End to John O'Groats, but the islands to the north are the real destination. While in town, have a professional photographer take a photo of you at the personalizable Land's End sign by the ferry dock (from £7). **Wildlife Cruises,** run by John O'Groats Ferries, cruise the waters of Pentland Firth, home to kittiwakes and great black-backed gulls. (☎01955 611 353; www.jogferry.co.uk. Runs daily June-Aug. 2:30pm. 1hr. tours £15. AmEx/MC/V.) **Dunnet Head,** halfway from John O'Groats to Thurso, is the northernmost point on the Isle of Great Britain. If stuck on the mainland, make your way 2 mi. west to Canisbay and the quaint **SYHA John O'Groats ❶.** (☎01955

611 761. Reception 7-10am and 5-10pm. Curfew 11pm. Open Easter-Oct. Dorms from £12, under 18 £9. AmEx/MC/V.) To reach town from the Wick train station, take Highland Country **bus** #77 (40min., 4-5 per day), which also runs to Thurso (1hr.; M-F 9 per day, Sa 3 per day) and passes the hostel. From May to August, John O'Groats Ferries's Orkney Bus runs from Inverness (daily June-Aug. 7:30am, 2:20pm, Sept-May 2:20pm; £15). The **Tourist Information Centre,** County Rd., by the pier, helps plan escapes to surrounding areas and can arrange accommodations if you miss a ferry. (☎01955 611 373. Open daily June-Aug. 9am-6pm; Sept.-Oct. and Apr.-May 10am-5pm.)

ORKNEY ISLANDS

The remote Orkney Islands are a mix of beaches, docile farmland, and archaeological wonders. In Orkney, sheep feast on seaweed, seagulls roost in hay fields, and football pitches are carved from cow pastures. Here, Nordic traditions have battled Celtic customs for centuries, creating a distinct Orcadian dialect and vocabulary. From the fishing boats at the capital city of Kirkwall to miraculous sunsets on the virtually abandoned far northern isles, Orkney's wild beauty is not soon forgotten.

TRANSPORTATION

GETTING THERE

Ferries are the main mode of transportation between Orkney and mainland Scotland. The affordable Pentland Ferry (☎01856 831 226; www.pentlandferries.co.uk) runs from Gills Bay, west of John O'Groats on the A836 (1hr.; 3-4 per day; £12, children £6, cars £28; MC/V). Ferries land at St. Margaret's Hope on Orkney and connect with Orkney Coaches buses heading to Kirkwall. John O'Groats Ferries (☎01955 611 353; www.jogferry.co.uk) travels from John O'Groats to Burwick, Orkney, where a free bus plays rousing accordion tunes as it takes passengers to Kirkwall (ferry 40min., bus 35min.; May 2 per day, June-Aug. 4 per day, Sept. 2 per day; round-trip £26-28). John O'Groats Ferries offers several **ferry-tour packages.** Its Maxi Day Tour makes stops at major sights and includes a 2hr. break in Kirkwall (May-Sept. daily 9am-7:45pm; last boarding 8:50am; £40; book ahead). The Highlights Day Tour hits the same sights but stops in Kirkwall for only 1hr. (10:30am-6pm; £37). Northlink Ferries (☎08456 000 449) sails from Scrabster to Stromness on the plush Hamnavoe with an ensuite B&B on board the ship (1hr.; M-F 3 per day, Sa-Su 2 per day; round-trip £26.60-31). A bus departs from the Thurso rail station for Scrabster before each crossing. Northlink also sails from Aberdeen to Kirkwall (6-8hr.; departs Aberdeen Tu, Th, Sa-Su; round-trip from £32.60).

 WATCH YOUR MOUTH. For locals, the terms "Orkneys" and "Shetlands" hold a strong taboo. To avoid ruffling feathers, use "Orkney" and "Shetland" when referring to the islands as a group. For example: "I took a ferry to Orkney, where I met the love of my life. We will be honeymooning in the Shetland Islands, which I sometimes refer to as 'Shetland,' since I am savvy."

GETTING AROUND

Orkney Coaches (☎01856 870 555; www.rapsons.co.uk) runs **buses** between Kirkwall bus station and Stromness Pier Head (30min., M-Sa every hr., round-trip £4). The staff at Orkney Ferries (☎01856 872 044; www.orkneyferries. co.uk), based on Shore St. at the Kirkwall harbor, can help travelers island-hop. Some ferries are foot-passenger only, all ferries offer student discounts, and schedules are likely to change; call ahead. **Ferries** (£7.30-9, concessions £3.40-4, cars £20-22.30) depart from Kirkwall to: Eday (1hr.); North Ronaldsay (2hr.); Papa Westray (2hr.); Sanday (1hr.); Shapinsay (25min.); Stronsay (1hr.); Westray (1hr.). Ferries also depart Tingwall to Rousay, Egilsay, and Wyre (30-60min.). Ferries leave Houton (30min. west of Kirkwall on the A964) to Flotta (45min.) and Lyness in the south of Hoy (20-45min.). A passenger-only ferry runs from Stromness to Moaness in the north of Hoy (15min.).

Car rental is by far the most convenient way of getting around Orkney. Try **WR Tullock,** Castle St., Kirkwall Airport. (☎01856 876 262. From £32 per day. 21+.) **Orkney Car Hire,** Junction Rd., Kirkwall (☎01856 872 866; www.orkneycarhire.co.uk; from £35 per day; 21+) and **Stromness Car Hire,** John St., Stromness (☎01856 850 973; from £30 per day with a UK license, £35 per day otherwise; 21+) also rent cars. **Biking** is an alternative, although fast-changing weather conditions make rain gear essential and winds can easily reach over 50 mph. Rent wheels in Kirkwall from **Cycle Orkney,** Tankerness Ln., off Broad St. (☎01856 875 777; www.cycleorkney.co.uk; open M-Tu and Th-Sa 9am-5:30pm, W 9am-1pm, 2-5:30pm) or in Stromness at **Orkney Cycle Hire,** 54 Dundas St. (☎01856 850 255; from £6 per day; open daily 8:30am-late).

KIRKWALL
☎(0)1856

The buzzing center of Orkney swells with people during the long summer days as cars and shoppers meander through town, making plans to see the islands, peeking in store windows, and enjoying Orkney's famously rich ice cream. With ferries headed for the smaller isles virtually every hour, Kirkwall makes the perfect starting place for exploring the wilds of Orkney.

🛈 **PRACTICAL INFORMATION.** The Kirkwall **Tourist Information Centre,** 6 Broad St., books B&Bs for £4 plus a 10% deposit. (☎01856 872 856. Open June-Sept. daily 8:30am-8pm; Oct.-May M-F 9am-5pm.) Guidebooks are also available at **The Orcadian Bookshop** on Albert St. (☎01856 878 888). Inter-island ferries can be booked at **Orkney Ferries,** Shore St. (☎01856 872 044; www.orkneyferries. co.uk.) Other services include: a **Bank of Scotland** with an **ATM,** 56 Albert St. (☎01856 682 000; open M-Tu and Th-F 9:15am-5pm, W 9:30am-5pm); **Volunteer Centre Kirkwall,** 12 Bridge St. (☎01856 872 897; www.orkneycommunities.co.uk/vc; wash £4, dry £1 per 5min.; soap 20p; open M-F 9am-5pm); **Kelvinator** launderette, 47 Albert St. (☎01856 872 982; open M-F 8:30am-5:30pm, Sa 9am-5pm); **police,** Great Western Rd. (☎01856 872 241); **Boots** pharmacy, 49-51 Albert St. (☎01856 872 097; open M-Sa 9am-5:30pm); **Internet** access at **Support Training Limited,** 2 W. Tankerness Ln. (☎01856 873 582; £1 per 10min., £5 per hr.; open M-F 8:30am-7:30pm, Sa 10am-5pm) or next door at the **public library** (☎01856 873 166; free Internet 1hr. per day; open M-Th 9am-7pm, F-Sa 9am-5pm); and the **post office,** 15 Junction Rd. (☎01856 874 249; open M-Tu and Th-F 9am-5pm, W 9am-4pm, Sa 9:30am-12:30pm). **Postcode:** KW15 1AA.

🏠 **ACCOMMODATIONS AND CAMPING.** A number of hostels, B&Bs, and croft houses can be found in the Tourist Board's free annual visitor's guide, available around town and at the TIC. Keep in mind that sometimes the best budget accommodations are in the most remote areas. Ten cozy beds fill up quickly in the **Peedie Hostel ❶,** 1 Ayre Rd., across from the pier. (☎01856 875 477. All rooms have TVs. Book far in advance. Dorms £10. Cash only.) Kirkwall's

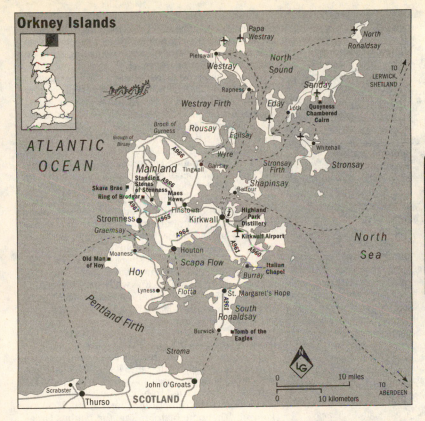

Orkney Islands

ATLANTIC
OCEAN

North
Sound

Papa
Westray

Pierowall

North
Ronaldsay

Westray

TO
LERWICK,
SHETLAND

Rapness

Sanday

Westray Firth

Eday

Loth

Quoyness
Chambered
Cairn

Broch of
Gurness

Rousay

Egilsay

Brough of
Birsay

Wyre

Whitehall

Mainland

Tingwall

Garrsay

Stronsay
Firth

Stronsay

Standing
Stones
of Stenness

Shapinsay

Skara Brae
Ring of Brodgar

Maes
Howe

Balfour

Finstown

Kirkwall

Highland
Park
Distillery

Stromness

A965

North
Sea

Graemsay

Kirkwall Airport

Houton

Moaness

Old Man
of Hoy

Scapa Flow

Italian
Chapel

Hoy

Burray

Lyness

Flotta

St. Margaret's Hope

Pentland Firth

South
Ronaldsay

Stroma

Burwick

Tomb of the
Eagles

0   10 miles

0   10 kilometers

TO
ABERDEEN

Scrabster

Thurson

John O'Groats

SCOTLAND

HIGHLANDS
AND ISLANDS

dimly lit **SYHA hostel ❶** is on Old Skapa Rd. Follow Junction St. south for 1 mi. and turn right on Wellington St.; follow the signs to the hostel, partially hidden by a pile of rubble. (☎01856 872 243. Reception 8-10:30am and 5pm-12:30am. Curfew 12:30am. Open Apr.-Oct. Dorms ₤13, under 18 ₤10.50. AmEx/MC/V.) At the **Cumliebank B&B ❷**, Cromwell Rd., stay at the top of a ship's staircase and get to know the fishermen who often check in on weekends. (☎01856 873 160. ₤20 per person.) The **West End Hotel ❹**, Main St., sits just out of the way of pedestrian traffic, providing soft beds in its ensuite rooms. (☎01856 872 368. Breakfast included. Singles ₤46; doubles ₤76. MC/V.) Camp at the **Pickaquoy Centre Caravan & Camping Site ❶**, on Pickaquoy Rd. just south of the A965. (☎01856 879 900; www.pickaquoy.com. ₤4-7.20 per tent; ₤7.50 per caravan.) You can pitch a tent almost anywhere on the islands, but always ask the landowner first.

◪◧ FOOD AND NIGHTLIFE. Before a trip to the islands, stock up on groceries at the **Co-op** on the corner of Broad St. and Great Western Rd. (☎01856 873 056. Open M-F 9am-8pm, Sa 9am-7pm, Su 10am-6pm.) **Trenabies Cafe ❶**, 16 Albert St., imports ice cream from Shetland (from ₤2) and serves fresh cafe fare. (☎01856 874 336. Sandwiches ₤4-5. Open M-F 9am-7pm, Sa 11am-4pm, Su noon-4pm. MC/V.) Across the street, the homemade soup at **Peppermill Deli's ❶**, 21 Albert St., is a steal at ₤1. Browse for the freshest locally grown veggies

NO WORK, ALL PLAY

UPPIES AND DOONIES

Orcadians may be famed for their hospitality, but when the Ba' game starts, visitors should leave the playing to those who know which way is Up and which is Down. Part street football, part anything goes, Ba' is contested every Christmas and New Year in the streets of Kirkwall. Between 200 and 300 players are divided into two teams, "Up-the-Gates" and "Down-the-Gates," and their mission is to move a cork-filled leather ball, the Ba', to their respective goal—the harbor, for the Doonies, or a wall on Junction Rd., for the Uppies.

The game begins on the green opposite St. Magnus Cathedral, where a community leader or Ba' veteran throws up the Ba'. Creativity is an asset in Ba', played without uniforms and almost without rules. In the past, the Ba' has been smuggled into cars, hidden in buildings, and sneaked over rooftops. Many businesses erect Ba' barriers to prevent damage to their shops as the mob rushes through the streets. To the casual observer, the game can appear to be a confused, disorderly riot—until the ball suddenly emerges from the crowd and hundreds of men dash down a narrow, winding alleyway to follow it.

Hours later, when the Ba' is either Up or Doon, the players elect an individual as the winner of the Ba' game. His house then acts as a rest to players seeking refreshment, and he receives the ultimate prize—the Ba' itself, hanging in a sitting-room window.

and meats or pick up exotic spices from all over the world. (☎01856 878 878. Open M-F 9am-5pm, Sa 9am-9pm, Su 11am-4pm. MC/V.) An American flag and the front end of a Ford Mustang hang on the walls of **Buster's Diner ❶**, 1 Mounthoolie Pl., which cooks up pizza and burgers for less than £5. (☎01856 876 717. Open May-Sept. Tu-Sa noon-2pm and 4:30-9pm. Cash only.) At **Indian Garden ❷**, 37 Junction St., grab tasty classic dishes and take-away late into the night. (☎01856 875 575. Entrees from £7. Open daily 5pm-midnight. MC/V.)

The **Bothy Bar ❶**, on Mounthoolie Pl. across from Buster's, has expanded its seating to accommodate the crowds of locals and travelers who come to dance and drink the night away. (☎01856 876 000. Live folk music Su night. Open M-W 11am-midnight, Th-Sa 11am-1am, Su noon-midnight. Kitchen open noon-midnight.) Imitation flames burn in a mock fireplace at **The Shore Bar,** a contemporary pub with a flatscreen TV for watching sporting events. (☎01856 872 200; www.theshore.co.uk. Open M-Th and Su noon-11pm, F-Sa noon-midnight.) Cut a rug at **Fusion,** 10-12 Ayre Rd., Kirkwall's only nightclub. (☎01856 879 489; www.fusionclub.co.uk. Cover £3. Open Th 10pm-1:30am, F-Sa 10pm-2:30am. Last entry 11:45pm. Cash only.)

◨ ❄ SIGHTS AND FESTIVALS. Nicknamed "The Light in the North" and famous for the red and yellow sandstone bands that line its walls, **Saint Magnus Cathedral** is the town's central landmark. The cathedral was created to honor Earl Magnus, who was killed at the direction of his cousin, Haakon Paulson. The tomb of John Rae, the famous Orcadian Arctic explorer, lies in the rear of the building. (Open Apr.-Sept. M-Sa 9am-6pm, Su 2-6pm; Oct.-Mar. M-Sa 9am-12:30pm and 1:30-5pm. Free.) Across Palace Rd. from the cathedral, the **Bishop's and Earl's Palaces** once housed the bishop of Orkney and his enemy, the wicked Earl Patrick Stewart. The houses were joined when the earl was executed for treason. Climb a spiral staircase to the top of the Bishop's Palace for a sweeping view of Kirkwall. The beautiful palace gardens and lawn are also perfect for enjoying a picnic or waiting for the bus. (☎01856 871 918. Both open Apr.-Sept. daily 9:30am-5:30pm. £3.70, concessions £3. Ticket for all 6 Historic Scotland Orkney sights £16, students £11.50, children £6.) For a thorough history lesson, check out the **Orkney Museum,** Broad St., in the center of town, across from the chapel. (☎01856 873 535. Open Apr.-Sept. M-Sa 10:30am-5pm, Su 2-5pm; Oct.-Mar. M-Sa 10:30am-12:30pm and 1:30-5pm. Free.) The 200-year-old **Highland Park Distillery,** a

20min. walk to the south of town on Holm Rd., is the world's northernmost Scotch whisky distillery and the largest of the three distilleries on Orkney. Originally the sight of an illicit smuggling operation, it now offers samples of its acclaimed single malts, a tour, and a melodramatic informational video. Walk to the southern end of Broad St., turn west on Clay Loan, head south on Bignold Park Rd., and take the right fork on Holm Rd. (☎01595 874 619; www.highlandpark.co.uk. Open May-Aug. M-Sa 10am-5pm, Su noon-5pm; Sept. and Apr. M-F 10am-5pm; Oct.-Mar. daily 1-5pm. Tours every hr.; last tour 4pm. Prices depend on number of whiskies sampled. From £5.)

Every schoolchild in Kirkwall learns to play a musical instrument, and the city shares its music with thousands of visitors during the **Saint Magnus Festival** in late June. Ranging from folk singers to the BBC Philharmonic, musicians from all over the world descend upon Kirkwall for the festival. The St. Magnus Festival Office, 60 Victoria St., has further information on the festivities. (☎01856 871 445; www.stmagnusfestival.com.)

STROMNESS   ☎(0)1856

The Vikings originally named Stromness "Hamnavoe," meaning "The Haven Inside the Bay," and the town is rich in maritime history. Cars clank down the narrow stone streets past historic buildings, giving Stromness a distinct charm complete with beautiful bay views.

◪✒ ORIENTATION AND PRACTICAL INFORMATION. Almost everything you'll need is on **Victoria Street,** which runs parallel to the harbor. The **Tourist Information Centre,** in an 18th-century warehouse on the pier, gives out free maps. (☎01856 850 716. Open May-Sept. daily 9am-5pm; Oct. and Apr. M-Sa 9:30am-3:30pm.) The **Bank of Scotland,** 99 Victoria St., has an **ATM.** (☎01856 851 230. Open M-Tu and Th-F 9:45am-4:15pm, W 10:45am-4:15pm.) Find free **Internet** access at the **library,** 2 Hellihole Rd. (☎01856 850 907. Open M-Th 2-7pm, F 2-5pm, Sa 10am-5pm.) The **post office** is at 37 Victoria St. (☎01865 850 225. Open M-F 9am-1pm and 2-5:15pm, Sa 9am-12:30pm.) **Postcode:** KW6 3BS.

◪◪ ACCOMMODATIONS AND FOOD. ◪**Brown's Hostel ❷,** 45-47 Victoria St., spans two stories and offers single, double, and triple rooms for a bargain, along with laundry and free Wi-Fi. The brightly lit upstairs rooms feature comfortable wood frame beds, while the downstairs rooms are slightly smaller. (☎01856 850 661. Dorms upstairs £13, downstairs £12. Cash only.) The **Orca Hotel ❸,** tucked into an alleyway at 76 Victoria St., offers B&B-style service in the middle of town and keeps an unpretentious restaurant, **Bistro 76 ❸,** below. Enjoy the fresh catch of the day amid romantic, nautical decor. (Hotel ☎01856 850 447; www.orcahotel.com. Free laundry. £25-30 per person. MC/V. Restaurant ☎01856 851 803. Entrees £9-14. Open Th-Sa 7-10pm. Cash only.) A bastion of Stromness history, the century-old **Stromness Hotel ❹,** at the Pier Head on Victoria St., has a collection of 100 malt whiskies, which it serves in its two bars and restaurant. (☎01856 850 298; www.stromnesshotel.com. Laundry £5. May-Sept. £49 per person; Oct.-Mar. £32 per person; Apr. £38 per person. MC/V.) One mile south of town on Victoria St., the **Point of Ness Caravan and Camping Site ❶** sits on a lawn overlooking the placid bay. (☎01856 851 235. Showers 20p. Open from May to mid-Sept. £5-8 per tent; £12.50 per caravan. Cash only.)

Across from the pier, the bustling **Julia's Cafe & Bistro ❶,** 20 Ferry Rd., has baked goods, vegetarian options (£5-8), and a clear view of Stromness ferry arrivals. (☎01856 850 904. Open Apr.-Sept. M-Sa 9am-5pm, Su 10am-5pm; Oct.-Mar. daily 10am-5pm. MC/V.)

◙ **SIGHTS.** The **Pier Arts Centre,** Victoria St., houses the work of contemporary Scottish artists and a brilliant collection of 20th-century British artists, all in a sparkling new facility. (☎01856 850 209; www.pierartscentre.com. Open July-Sept. M-Sa 10:30am-5pm and Su noon-4pm; Oct.-June M-Sa 10:30am-5pm. Free.) The **Stromness Museum,** 52 Alfred St., was founded in 1837 and has built an impressive collection of artifacts from Stromness's nautical past and stuffed Orkney birds of all shapes and sizes. (☎01856 850 025. Open Apr.-Sept. daily 10am-5pm; Oct.-Mar. M-Sa 11am-3:30pm. £3.50, concessions £2.50.)

ELSEWHERE ON THE ORKNEY MAINLAND

The Orkney Mainland contains a treasure trove of Iron and Stone Age relics that have gradually come to light, representing over 5000 years of archaeological history. As site excavations on the isles continue, artifacts and stone formations add to researchers' understandings of these ancient, long-lost societies. In addition to the service bus #98 that runs between Kirkwall and Stromness (£4 round-trip), multiple tour buses service the four main archaeological sites between Kirkwall and Stromness.

◙ **SIGHTS**

▨**SKARA BRAE.** Five thousand years ago, Skara Brae was a Stone Age village; today it is an archaeological marvel, representing the best-preserved and oldest Neolithic village in the world. Sand covered the village until 1850, when a storm revealed the first remnants of nine houses, a workshop, and covered town roads. Today, visitors can walk around the village on a small, grassy path. The **Skail House,** home of the unsuspecting gentleman who "discovered" Skara Brae in his backyard, sheds light on Orcadian lifestyles during the more accessible 18th and 19th centuries after Scottish customs took root. *(19 mi. northwest of Kirkwall on the B9056; take the A965 from Kirkwall to Stromness and turn right at the sign after Maes Howe. Continue along the road until the signs for Skara Brae or Skail House. ☎01856 841 815. Open daily Apr.-Sept. 9:30am-5:30pm; Oct.-Mar. 9:30am-4:30pm. Last entry 45min. before close. In summer £6.70, concessions £5.20; in winter £5.70/4.70.)*

RING OF BRODGAR. Six miles east of Skara Brae and 5 mi. northeast of Stromness on the B9055 stands a group of giant stones arranged in a perfect circle. Thought to have been built in 2500 BC, the Ring of Brodgar may once have witnessed gatherings of local chieftains or burial ceremonies. In a year, the stones witness more sunlight than almost any other spot on the island, revealing the builders' deep understanding of solar and lunar patterns. On the summer solstice, neopagan worshippers arrive in droves to use the sacred circle. The 60 stones (only 27 of which still stand) draw large crowds in the middle of the day; arrive early in the morning for a more private viewing. *(Open 24hr. Free.)*

STANDING STONES OF STENNESS. One mile east of the Ring on the B9055, the Standing Stones of Stenness have been reduced over time to a humble few. The oldest remaining archaeological artifacts on the island, the gargantuan stones were probably once used with the Brodgar stones in the same ceremonies. By 1760, only four of the original 12 stones remained—the others were likely knocked down by locals angered by the monument's pagan origins. *(Open 24hr. Free.)* After a visit to the standing stones, visit the tiny **Gerrie's Ice Cream** in Stenness, which features stone-themed treats and ice cream made on Orkney. *(Open May-Sept. daily about 11am-5pm.)*

MAES HOWE TOMB. Between Kirkwall and Stromness on the A965, this tomb may have held the bones of the area's earliest settlers (from 2700 BC). On the winter solstice, the setting sun shines through a long tunnel to illuminate the back wall of the tomb. Tour guides lead groups into the mound to view the largest collection of runic inscriptions in the world, created by the plundering Vikings in the mid-12th century. In recent years, linguists cracked the runic alphabet here, translating the following profound statements: "This was carved by the greatest rune carver" and "Ingigerth is the most exquisite of women." (☎01856 761 606; www.maeshowe.co.uk. Open daily Apr.-Sept. 10am-4pm; Oct.-Mar. 10am-3pm. Tours every hr., with additional tours June-Aug. 6-8pm. Last tour 1hr. before close. £5.20, concessions £4.20. Call ahead.)

BROCH OF GURNESS. Off the A966, on the north coast of the Evie section of Mainland, this broch is the site of a preserved Iron Age village, fortuitously unearthed in 1929 by the ultimate Orcadian Renaissance man, Robert Rendall, a poet, historian, and theologian. The reconstructed Pictish and Viking settlements are worth a stop on the way between towns. (☎01856 751 414. Open daily Apr.-Sept. 9:30am-12:30pm and 1:30-5:30pm; Oct. 9:30am-12:30pm and 1:30-4:30pm. £4.70, students £3.70, children £2.35.)

SCAPA FLOW. At the end of WWII, German Admiral von Reuter ordered all 74 of his ships to be scuttled rather than remain in British hands. The ships sank at Scapa Flow, the bay south of Houton on Mainland. To the delight of scuba divers worldwide, seven of the wrecks remain. **Scapa Scuba,** in the red Lifeboat House on Dundas St., Stromness, offers non-certified "try-a-dive" lessons, equipment, and a dive to the wrecks. (☎01856 851 218; www.scapascuba.co.uk. £70 per ½-day.) For those who don't want to get wet, **Roving Eye Enterprises** does the marine work for you via a roaming underwater camera. The boat leaves from Houton Pier and stops on Hoy during its 3hr. cruise. (☎01856 811 360; www.orknet.co.uk/rov. Tours daily 1:20pm. £28, children £14.)

SMALLER ISLANDS

The smaller islands, most accessible by car or ferry from Kirkwall or Stromness, are full of historical and natural sights. Take particular care when traveling; erratic ferry schedules dependent upon tides and scant public transportation on the islands mean that you could end up sleeping with the seals and birds. Make sure to tell someone where you're going and to bring warm clothing and rain gear with you.

ISLAND FLIGHTS FOR POCKET CHANGE. Spending the night on one of Orkney's smaller islands can cut the cost of your plane ticket by more than half. For example, if you spend the night on North Ronaldsay, the price of a round-trip Loganair flight drops from the normal price of £30 to £12 because the government wants to support local tourism. The discount will factor automatically into the price of round-trip tickets during booking.

HOY ☎(0)1856

Hoy, the second-largest of the Orkney Islands (57 sq. mi.), gets its name from the Norse word "Haey," meaning "high island." Northern Hoy is spectacularly hilly, while the south is lower and more fertile. Its most famous landmark, the ▓**Old Man of Hoy,** is a 450 ft. sea stack of sandstone off the west coast of the island. Hikers can take the steep footpath from the partially abandoned crofting village of Rackwick, 2 mi. away (3hr. round-trip). The **North Hoy Bird Reserve** offers respite for guillemots and a host of other species. Puffins roost during breeding season, from late June to early July. The **SYHA Hoy ❶**, near the pier, and the eight beds of the simple **SYHA Rackwick ❶**, at the start of the path toward the Old Man, offer places to sleep. Visitors must bring a sleeping bag. (☎01856 873 535. Hoy open all year. Rackwick open Apr.-Sept. Hoy dorms £13, under 18 £10. Rackwick dorms £10.25, under 18 £9.) If you plan to stay overnight on Hoy, bring adequate provisions, since the only shops are located at the southern end of the island and there is no public transportation. For a taxi or minibus, call **North Hoy Transport** (☎01856 971 315).

SHAPINSAY ☎(0)1856

Only 25min. from Kirkwall, with frequent ferry services, Shapinsay is the most accessible of the outer isles. **Ward Hill,** the island's highest point at 210 ft., slopes gently above the island's flat ground. From its "peak" on a rare clear day, you can see almost all the islands. **Burroughston Broch,** an Iron Age shelter, lies 5 mi. north of the ferry pier and is a good place to spot seals. An excellent example of the Victorian Baronial style, 19th-century **Balfour Castle ❺**, near the ferry dock on the southwestern side of the isle, was once home to the influential lairds of Balfour. The last laird died in 1960, leaving four wives but no heirs, and the castle has since been converted to a posh guesthouse. Guided tours of the castle depart from Kirkwall pier and include the ferry ride and tea. (☎01856 711 282; www.balfourcastle.com. Tours May-Sept. Su 2:15pm. £20. Meals included. Rooms from £110 per person.) There are no hostels on Shapinsay, but the award-winning **Girnigoe B&B ❹**, near the beach, has two rooms in a converted 200-year-old farmhouse. For those looking to get hitched in a quiet place, the owner can also conduct weddings. (☎01856 711 256; www.girnigoe. net. Twins and doubles from £50. Cash only.)

ROUSAY ☎(0)1856

Many argue that Orkney's finest archaeological sights lie not on Mainland but on Rousay. The **Midhowe Broch and Cairn** has Stone, Bronze, and Iron Age relics. The **Knowe of Yarso Cairn** stands on a cliff overlooking Eynhallow Sound, and the **Westness Walk,** once called the most important archaeological mile in Scotland, winds past sites from the Neolithic, Pictish, Viking, and medieval eras. Above the ferry terminal, a visitors center has an exhibition on the points of interest in Rousay and nearby Egilsay and Wyre (☎01856 821 359). Stay at the **Rousay Hostel ❶** on Trumland Farm near the pier; turn left from the ferry port and walk 5min. down the main road. (☎01856 821 252. Dorms £10. Cash only.)

STRONSAY ☎(0)1856

Seven miles long, this island is a collection of bays and beaches. Along the east coast, between Lamb Ness and Odiness, is the stunning **Vat of Kirbister,** an opening ("gloup") spanned by a dramatic natural stone arch. There are Pictish settlements and an Iron Age fort on the southeastern bay. Stay at **Stronsay Fishmart ❶**, a former herring-boning station in Whitehall Village, which also has a cafe. (☎01857 616 386. Laundry £2. £13 per person. Cash only.)

EDAY ☎(0)1856

Home to tales of captured pirates and tombs of the ancients, Eday's peat-covered hills remain home to a handful of crofters and hundreds of species of birds. One of the quieter, smaller islands, Eday contains chambered tombs like the **Vinquoy and Huntersquoy Cairns,** the towering **Stone of Setter,** and, on the **Calf of Eday,** the remnants of an Iron Age roundhouse. The newly renovated **SYHA Hostel ❶** is located on the main north-south road, 4 mi. from the pier. (☎01857 622 206. Camping from £5 per person. Dorms £12, under 16 £10. Cash only.)

SANDAY ☎(0)1856

Home to the elusive Sanday Vole and the vast beaches that give the island its name, Sanday offers more than just one day of island exploration; plan to stay overnight. The island is 87 mi. long, and beachside and inland walks traverse the isle. Tina meets ferries in her **bus** and drops passengers wherever they want to go; call for a pickup (☎01857 600 284). Rangers also meet ferry arrivals on select "Sanday Sundays" for island tours. Check the Kirkwall TIC for details. Seal pups can be seen swimming at Otterswick in June, and gray seals are born on the beaches in November. On the south side of the island, turn south off the main road and follow the signs to the **Quoyness Chambered Cairn.** The cairn, accessible by foot via a spectacular beachside walk, is worth the 40min. trip. It held the remains of at least 15 people and dates back to 2900 BC. Take the torch by the door and crawl into the well-preserved rooms. The **Orkney Angora Craft Shop,** in Upper Breckan, features incredibly soft wool from Angora rabbits. Ask the owner for a tour of the workshop. (☎01856 600 421; www.orkney-angora.co.uk. Open daily 1:30-5:30pm or by arrangement.)

At **Ayre's Rock Hostel and Campsite ❶**, about 7 mi. from the ferry on the main road, find a spotless bunkhouse with two double rooms, a family room, a kitchen, and sunsets over the ocean. (☎01857 600 410. Laundry £1.50. Internet access 50p per hr. Free Wi-Fi. Dorms from £12. Cash only.)

WESTRAY ☎(0)1856

The northern island of Westray features ruined **Noltland Castle,** the **Knowe O'Burristae Broch,** ancient rubble, and magnificent cliffs. Legend holds that the windowless 16th-century castle, marked by over 60 gun holes, is linked underground to the **Gentlemen's Cave,** which hid supporters of Bonnie Prince Charlie. The castle's first owner, Gilbert Balfour, was implicated in two royal assassination plots, the second of which got him executed. Birdwatchers rejoice on **Noup Head Reserve** and on the opposite end of the island, where thousands of puffins congregate. You'll feel like one of the family at **The Barn ❶**, Chalmersquoy, at the southern end of Pierowall village, in a converted stone barn. (☎01857 677 214; www.thebarnwestray.com. £13 per person, children £9. Cash only.) **Bis Geos Hostel ❶**, 2 mi. west of Pierowall, is a croft ruin turned hostel, complete with heated floors and a gorgeous room overlooking the cliffs. (☎01857 677 420; www.bisgeos.co.uk. Open Apr.-Oct. Dorms £12. MC/V.)

NORTH RONALDSAY ☎(0)1856

Due to the warm Gulf Stream, this northernmost Orkney is an average of 10°F warmer than its latitudinal neighbors. The smell of seaweed greets visitors as they step off the ferry, and the island's famous wool-producing **sheep** wander the beaches munching on kelp. The small community is one of the few remaining to practice collective herding, or "punding," during the shearing season. North Ronaldsay also offers archaeological wonders, like the **Broch of Burrian,** an unusual standing stone with a hole through it, and two weathered lighthouses. The lighthouse keeper gives excellent tours. (☎07703 112 224. £6, children £3.) Viciously protective nesting birds are all over—take a cue from them and stay at the solar- and wind-powered **North Ronaldsay Bird Observatory Hostel ❶**. (☎01857 633 200. Free Internet. Call ahead for a ride from the airport. Dorms £12, full board £27. Cash only.)

SOUTHEAST ISLANDS   ☎(0)1856

Accessible by road from Mainland, this string of islands, including **Lamb Holm, Burray,** and **South Ronaldsay,** is quiet and full of wonderful craft shops and an organic farm hostel. On Lamb Holm, the ▩**Italian Chapel** is all that remains of Camp 60, a WWII prison that held hundreds of Italian POWs who used food cans for sacred lighting and transformed their bare cement hut into a beautiful house of worship that is still in use today. (Open daily Apr.-Sept. 9am-10pm; Oct.-Mar. 9am-4:30pm. Occasionally closed F afternoons, the traditional time for Orkney weddings. Services 1st Su of the month. Free.) During the summer, buses (3-4 per day) run from Kirkwall to the pier at St. Margaret's Hope, on the larger isle of South Ronaldsay.

The greatest treasure to be found on South Ronaldsay is the family-run ▩**Tomb of the Eagles,** south of St. Margaret's Hope and east of the Burwick ferry terminal in Isbister. The tomb was discovered by the farmer Ronald Simison in 1958, and his family now operates a visitors center where you can handle 5000-year-old artifacts including marvelously intact human skulls and sea-eagle talons. A quarter of a mile from the visitors center is a Bronze Age burnt mound, a stone dwelling with a plumbing system, the dramatic sea cliffs, and the spectacular Stone Age tomb after which the property is named. (☎01856 831 339; www.tomboftheeagles.co.uk. Open daily Apr.-Oct. 9:30am-5:30pm; Nov.-Feb. by appointment; Mar. 10am-noon. £6, students £5.) A hostel and organic farm, **Wheems Bothy ❶** stands on the blustery promontory of South Ronaldsay. Fresh produce is available. Call ahead for pickup. (☎01856 831 537. Open Apr.-Oct.)

SHETLAND ISLANDS

Closer to Norway than to mainland Britain, Shetland was part of Norway until the 15th century. Its people and landscapes have a rich dual heritage. The islands' peat-covered hills give them a rougher appeal than beach-studded Orkney. Best suited for the traveler with plenty of time to explore, the islands are full of archaeological marvels, rare wildlife, and stark, brutal landscapes.

TRANSPORTATION

GETTING THERE

Air travel is the fastest, most expensive way to Shetland. Flights are usually cheaper if you stay over a Saturday night. British Airways (☎08457 733 377) flies from: Aberdeen (1hr.; M-F 3 per day, Sa-Su 2 per day; £130-200); Edinburgh (1hr., 1 per day, £181-250); Glasgow (2hr.; M-F 2 per day, Sa-Su 1 per day; £120-270); Inverness (1hr., 1 per day, round-trip £120-180); Kirkwall, Orkney (35min., 1 per day, round-trip £90-150). Travel agents **Shetland Travelscope** (☎01595 696 644) and **John Leask & Son** (☎01595 693 162; www.leaskstravel. co.uk) purchase tickets and organize trips. All flights land at **Sumburgh Airport,** on the southern tip of Shetland's Mainland, which also has a visitors center with Internet access, Wi-Fi (£1 per 20min.), and a knowledgeable staff. The airport is 25 mi. (and a hefty £30-35 taxi ride) from Lerwick, the islands' capital and largest town. John Leask & Son **buses** make the journey from the airport to Lerwick (1hr.; M-Sa 5 per day, Su 3 per day; £3), and an alternative express bus meets midday flights (30min., 2-3 per day, £5). Buses arrive at the **Viking Bus Station** (☎01595 694 100), 5min. from the city center on Commercial Rd.

Ferries are the other means of travel to Shetland. Though cheaper, they take far longer than flights. Most ferries arrive at **Holmsgarth Terminal,** a 20min. walk

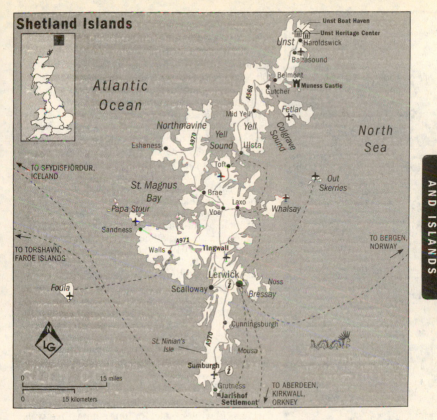

Shetland Islands

Atlantic Ocean

North Sea

Unst Boat Haven
Unst Heritage Center
Unst • Haroldswick
Baltasound
Belmont
Muness Castle
A968
Gutcher
Fetlar
Mid Yell
Yell
Northmavine
A970
Yell
Sound
Ulsta
Colgrave Sound
Eshaness
Toft
Out
Skerries
TO SEYDISFJÖRDUR,
ICELAND
St. Magnus
Bay
Brae
Papa Stour
Laxo
Voe
Whalsay
Sandness
A971
TO BERGEN,
NORWAY
Walls
Tingwall
TO TORSHAVN,
FAROE ISLANDS
Lerwick
Noss
Foula
Scalloway
Bressay
Cunningsburgh
St. Ninian's
Isle
A970
Mousa
N
LG
Sumburgh
0   15 miles
0   15 kilometers
Grutness
Jarlshof
Settlement
TO ABERDEEN,
KIRKWALL,
ORKNEY

northwest of Lerwick's town center, or the smaller **Victoria Pier,** across from the TIC. Northlink Ferries (☎08456 000 449; www.northlinkferries.co.uk) arrive from Aberdeen (12-14hr.; M, W, F 7pm, Tu, Th, Sa-Su 5pm; £22-32) and Kirkwall, Orkney (7hr.; Tu, Th, Sa-Su 11:45pm; £14-19.70). Arrive 30min. in advance. P&O Smyril Line (☎02075 543 530; www.smyril-line.com) runs in summer from Lerwick to Bergen, Norway (12hr., M 11:30pm, £77.50) and to Iceland (30hr.; W 2am; £150, with car from £184) via the Faroe Islands. (13hr., £77.50. Arrive 1hr. in advance.) Call ahead for prices and times from mid-September to April.

GETTING AROUND

Infrequent public transportation makes getting around Shetland difficult without a car. **Car-rental** companies include John Leask & Son (☎01595 693 162; £31-42 per day), the more extensive Bolts Car Hire, 26 North Rd. (☎01595 693 636, airport branch 01950 460 777; www.boltscarhire.co.uk; £35-49 per day; 21+), and Grantfield Garage, North Rd. (☎01595 692 709; www.grantfieldgarage.co.uk; £24-30 per day; 23+).

Travel between the islands is heavily subsidized. Ferries sail to the larger islands nearly every hour and to the smaller islands at least once per day; no trip costs more than £5. Shetland's main **bus** provider is John Leask & Son (☎01595 693 162). Whites Coaches (☎01595 809 443) handles the North

LOCAL LEGEND

SEEING ISN'T BELIEVING

The Shetland Islands boast a rich lore of unearthly creatures that share the isles with humans, sometimes peaceably and sometimes not. If you encounter any of the following sights, think twice about what you've seen—or thought you saw.

If you see a beautiful Shetland pony. Don't jump on its back! You might have spotted a njuggle, a water horse infamous for luring travelers to take a ride and then diving into the nearest loch to drown its passengers.

If you see a seal on the beach. You might be looking at a selkie, a creature that can shed its sealskin to take human form. Many tragic Shetland love stories tell of doomed romances between selkies and humans.

If you see "wee folk" darting in and out of the hillside. Listen for fiddle music—trows, Shetland's hill folk, are thought to be musicians and are known to invite humans to play at their wedding feasts. Don't linger, though—mere hours spent in the company of trows can be equivalent to years passing above ground.

If you see something big with fins. The waters around Shetland supposedly teem with enormous and powerful creatures. The strongest among them is the Finn, which can row 50 mi. with a single stroke of the oars. The Finns can also overturn and sink fishing boats, but throwing a handful of coins will distract them long enough for you to make your getaway.

Mainland services. In general, bus service is patchy—pick up the *Shetland Transport Timetable* (£1) with bus, ferry, and plane schedules. Eric Brown's Cycle Hire, on the second floor of Grantfield Garage, offers **bike rentals.** (☎01595 692 709. £5 per day, £30 per week. Open M-W 8am-9pm, Th-Sa 8am-10pm, Su 11am-9pm.) High winds and steep hills can make biking difficult.

Tour companies offer convenient ways of seeing Shetland. Puffins are a dime a dozen on **Seabirds-and-Seals,** a 3hr. tour, which consistently yields close encounters with seals and features an underwater camera that reveals Shetland's submerged kelp forest. Tea and coffee are served on board. Trips depart from Victoria Pier, Lerwick. (☎01595 693 434; www.seabirds-and-seals.com. Daily from mid-Apr. to mid-Sept. 10am, 2pm. £40.) Walking tours include the **Shetland Ranger Service's** guided treks across the islands, which are great for birdwatching (☎01957 711 528 or 01950 694 688; May-Aug. £2.50), **Geo Tours's** daylong geology and landscape expeditions (☎01595 859 218; www.shetlandgeotours.com), and the folklore-oriented **Island Trails** with locals Elma Johnson and Douglas Sinclair. (☎01950 422 408. May-Sept. 2hr. tour £10-15, children £4.) For the more adventurous, Tom Smith leads introductory (£20), half-day (£35), and full-day (£60) **kayaking trips** around the islands. (☎01595 859 647; www.seakyakshetland.co.uk.)

HOLIDAYS AND FESTIVALS

Shetland's endless daylight in summer and endless darkness in winter make for long summer festivals and fiery winter ones. The annual **Shetland Folk Festival** (☎01595 694 757; www.shetlandfolkfestival.com), from April 30 to May 3 in 2009, celebrates Shetland's music and lures fiddlers from around the world, while the **Shetland Accordion and Fiddle Festival** (☎01595 693 162; www.shetlandaccordionand-fiddle.com) takes place in Lerwick in mid-October. **Johnsmas Foy,** a two-week festival around the summer solstice, showcases Shetland food, music, and history. The first four days features the **Flavour of Shetland on Victoria Pier,** where visitors can sample island cuisines (☎01595 744 940; www.johnsmasfoy.com). Shetland's Viking heritage is never more apparent than in the annual **Up Helly Aa** festival (www.uphellyaa.com), held in several towns from January to March. During Lerwick's dramatic celebration, Europe's largest fire festival, hundreds of torch-bearing men set a replica of a Viking galley alight, and the whole community parties through the long winter night until the next morning.

LERWICK ☎(0)1595

⬛🔳 ORIENTATION AND PRACTICAL INFORMATION. On the eastern coast of Mainland, Lerwick sits on the island's central artery, the A970. The **Tourist Information Centre,** Market Cross, books beds for £4 plus a 10% deposit. (☎01595 693 434; www.visitshetland.com. Internet access £1 per 30min; Wi-Fi available. Open Apr.-Oct. M-F 8am-6pm, Sa-Su 8am-4pm; Nov.-Mar. M-F 9am-5pm, Sa 8am-4pm.) Other services include: the **Royal Bank of Scotland,** 81 Commercial St. (☎01595 694 520; open M-Tu and Th-F 9:15am-4:45pm, W 9:45am-4:45pm); free **Internet** access in the Learning Centre adjacent to the **Shetland Library,** on Lower Hillhead (☎01595 693 868; open M and Th 9:30am-8pm, Tu-W and F-Sa 9:30am-5pm); and the **post office,** 46-50 Commercial St. (☎08457 223 344; open M and W-F 9am-5pm, Tu 9:30am-5pm, Sa 9am-12:30pm). **Postcode:** ZE1 0EH.

🔳🔳 ACCOMMODATIONS AND CAMPING. The community-run ⬛SYHA Lerwick ❷, at King Harald and Union St., is an expansive hostel with a large dining room, excellent facilities, well-furnished common spaces, and gardens. The four rotating wardens love to talk about Shetland. (☎01595 692 114. Laundry £2. Wheelchair-accessible. Reception 9-9:30am, 4-4:30pm, 9:45-10:15pm; at other times, go to the Community Centre across the street. Curfew 11:45pm. Open Apr.-Sept. Dorms £15.50, under 18 £13. AmEx/MC/V.) At the **Glen Orchy Guest House ❹,** 20 Knab Rd., dine on homemade Thai cuisine and enjoy lovely aqua-colored rooms with views of Lerwick. Rooms include TVs, complimentary fresh fruit, and full Scottish breakfasts. (☎01595 692 031. Meals available with advance reservation; dinner £18. Free laundry and Wi-Fi. MC/V. Singles £47-50; doubles £74-80.) There are three campgrounds on Mainland, but you can pitch almost anywhere with the landowner's permission. **Clickimin Caravan and Camp Site ❶** is closest to the Lerwick ferry terminal. Turn left on Holmsgarth Rd. (A970), go through the roundabout, and merge onto North Lochside; it's on the right. (☎01595 741 000. Pool, bar, cafe, and showers. Laundry £3. Reception 8:45am-10:30pm. Open May-Sept. £7.30-9.90 per tent. MC/V.)

🔳🔳 FOOD AND PUBS. Stock up on groceries at the **Co-op,** Holmsgarth Rd., one block from the ferry station. (☎01595 693 419. Open M-W and Sa 8am-8pm, Th-F 8am-9pm, Su 9am-6pm.) On the Esplanade, the two-story ⬛**Peerie Shop Cafe ❶** packs in hungry locals and visitors and serves fresh sandwiches, baked goods, organic cider, and a sinful hot chocolate (£1.25, with rum £3.10). The affiliated shop next door sells funky woolens. (☎01595 692 817. Open M-Sa 9am-6pm. Cash only.) For modern cuisine made with traditional Shetland produce, look no farther than **Monty's ❸,** 5 Mounthooly St. Local salmon and seafood (£9-12) are served in an intimate brick-walled dining room. (☎01595 696 555. Open Tu-Sa noon-2pm and 6:30-10pm. MC/V.) **Osla's Cafe ❷,** 88 Commercial St., specializes in pancakes, pizzas, and pastas. (☎01595 696 005. Entrees £7-10. Open June-Aug. daily 10am-10pm; Sept.-May M-Sa 10am-10pm, Su 10am-5pm. AmEx/MC/V.) **Raba ❸,** 26 Commercial St., offers traditional Indian cuisine and atmosphere. (☎01595 695 554. All-you-can-eat Su buffet £9.50; 3-course business lunch £6. Open M-Sa noon-2pm and 5pm-midnight, Su noon-midnight. MC/V.) For hostelers, the city's most convenient food awaits at the **Blue Rock Cafe ❶,** next door at the Community Centre. (☎01595 692 114. Open M-Sa 9:45am-9pm, Su noon-4pm and 6:30-9pm. Cash only.)

The Lounge, 4 Mounthooly St., welcomes visitors and local pub-goers into its small, packed rooms. The upstairs bar fills with Shetland fiddle music and dancing on Wednesday and Thursday nights in summer. (☎01595 692 231. Open

M-Sa 11am-1am.) **Captain Flint's,** in Market Cross, stays busy well into the night and has great harbor views. (☎01595 692 249. Occasional live music. Happy hour F 5-7pm. Open M-Sa 8am-1am, Su 12:30pm-midnight. Kitchen open M-Sa noon-2:15pm, Su 12:30-2:15pm. MC/V.) Rack 'em up on the pool tables and chat with the Shetland locals at **Thule Bar** (THOO-lee) on the Esplanade near Victoria Pier. (☎01595 692 508. Open M-Sa 11am-1am, Su 12:30pm-1am.)

◻ **SIGHTS.** Lerwick is a souvenir shopper's paradise. Take home some famous ▨**Shetland wool,** which can be found in all forms, from freshly sheared to mittens and handbags, in stores throughout town. Observe a local weaver at work and buy local wares at the **Spider's Web,** 51 Commercial St., across from the Queen's Hotel. (☎01595 695 246. Open M-Sa 10am-5pm.) Weather permitting, you can cruise around the bay on the ▨**Dim Riv,** a full-scale replica of a Viking longship. (☎07970 864 189. Open May-Sept. usually M 7pm; call ahead for times. Book in advance. £5.) The newly opened **Shetland Museum,** Hay's Dock, contains all kinds of geographic and historical information on the isles, as well as sheep's wool displays and rotating exhibits, all in an old Böd with a modern addition. (☎01595 695 057. Open M and Sa 10am-5pm, Tu-Th 10am-6pm, F 10am-7pm, Su noon-5pm. 40min. tours daily at 2:30pm. Free.) Don't miss the **Up-Helly-Aa Exhibition** in the Galley Shed, St. Sunniva St., where costumes and elaborate party regalia from the last 50 years are on display. (Open from mid-May to mid-Sept. Tu 2-4pm and 7-9pm, F 7-9pm, Sa 2-4pm. £3, concessions £1.) The **Islesburgh Exhibition,** in the Islesburgh Community Centre, showcases traditional music, dance, crafts, and a replica of a 1920s croft house. (☎01595 692 114. Open June-Aug. M and W-Th 7-9:30pm. £4, concessions £2.) For a great view of Lerwick and the ferry boats rocking in the water, climb the giant pentagonal **Fort Charlotte,** just off Commercial St. at the north end of town. (Open daily 9am-10pm. Free.) **The Knab,** a small, impressive promontory at the end of Knab Rd., is a short coastal walk from **Clickimin Broch,** 1 mi. west of the city center. The broch was built in a stronghold from 400 BC and stands in the middle of a loch. Climb to the grassy top for a great view. (Open 24hr. Free.)

I WANT YOUR BÖD. Outside Lerwick, the best budget accommodations come in the form of **Böds** ❶ (Old Norse for "barns"; www.camping-bods. com). In various states of repair, these converted fishing cottages now serve as camping barns. Bring a sleeping bag, camping stove, cooking utensils, and coins for electricity (when available). Böds are available from April to September. All Böds cost £6-8 per night and must be booked in advance through the Lerwick TIC or the Shetland Amenity Trust (☎01595 694 688).

SCALLOWAY   ☎(0)1595

Scalloway, the ancient capital of Shetland, 7 mi. west of Lerwick, provides an authentic taste of the fishing industry on the islands. Crumbling **Scalloway Castle** looms large over the harbor and was once home to the hated and tyrannical Earl Patrick Stewart. Get the key from the Scalloway Hotel. (☎01595 880 444. Castle always open, within reason. Free.) The popular ▨**Da Haaf Restaurant** ❶, located within the North Atlantic Fisheries College, serves the best fish—fried, baked, or grilled—on the island in a family-friendly dining area. The Shetland salmon is £6. Call ahead to reserve a table. (☎01595 880 747. Open daily 8:30am-4:30pm. MC/V.) John Leask & Son sends buses from Lerwick (☎01595 693 162; M-Sa 10 per day, round-trip £3.40).

HIGHLANDS AND ISLANDS

JARLSHOF AND SOUTH MAINLAND ☎(0)1595

At the southern tip of Mainland, southwest of Sumburgh Airport, **Jarlshof** is one of Shetland's most remarkable archaeological sites. In 1896, a storm uncovered stone walls and artifacts from different stages in Shetland's history, some over 4000 years old. (☎01950 460 112. Open daily Apr.-Sept. 9:30am-5:30pm. Last entry 5pm. £4.70, concessions £3.70.) A mile up the road, the **Old Scatness Broch** is the site of ongoing excavation. Remains were discovered in 1975 during airport construction; since then, an entire Iron Age village and over 20,000 artifacts have surfaced. Guided tours include reenactments of life in the broch and info on the ongoing excavation. (☎01595 461 869. Open Apr.-Sept. M-Th and Su 10am-5:30pm. £4, concessions £3.) On nearby **Sumburgh Head,** gulls, guillemots, and puffins rear their young on steep cliff walls. Four miles north of the airport at Voe, the ▓**Croft House Museum,** signposted off the A970, is a restored working croft house, barn, watermill, and byre from the 19th century. (☎01950 460 557. Open daily May-Sept. 10am-1pm and 2-5pm. Free.) Next door to Old Scatness, **Betty Mouat's Böd ❶** has hot water and showers. All South Mainland sights can be reached by the Leask bus that runs to Sumburgh Airport from Lerwick (☎01595 693 162; 5 per day).

NORTHMAVINE ☎(0)1595

A drive north across Mavis Grind, a 300 ft. wide isthmus, reveals the stark cliffs and jutting rocks of Northmavine, the northeastern tip of the Shetland Mainland. Begin at the **Eshaness Lighthouse** and walk with the sea at your left to the majestic cliffs of Eshaness, which provide shelter for rare sea birds and are a great place to spot seals. To the east of the lighthouse, the **Dore Holm** natural arch is one of the most impressive in the world. The **Tangwick Haa Museum** serves free tea and coffee and has CDs of Shetland natives recalling their lives on the island. (☎01806 503 389. Open May-Sept. daily 11am-5pm. Free.) Johnson Transport runs one bus per day from Lerwick to Hillswick. For an overnight stay in Northmarvine, try **Johnnie Notions Böd ❶**, in Hamnavoe. Explore the rocky shore with only the sheep for company. ▓**Da Böd Cafe ❷,** on the waterfront in Hillswick, serves outstanding organic vegetarian food and donates all proceeds to the seal and otter sanctuary. (☎01806 503 348. Menu changes daily. Open May-Sept. Sa-Su 11am-6pm.)

SMALLER ISLANDS

BRESSAY AND NOSS ☎(0)1595

Hike to the summit of the conical **Ward of Bressay,** locally called "Da Wart" (742 ft.), for an open view of the sea. From Bressay's east coast, 3 mi. past the Lerwick ferry port (follow the "To Noss" signs), inflatable dinghies go to the Isle of Noss. Stand at the "Wait Here" sign and wave to flag one down. Great and Arctic skuas dive-bomb visitors at the bird sanctuary—wave a hat or stick over your head to ward them off. The best views of Bressay, Noss, and the bird sanctuary are from the ocean. (National Nature Reserve ☎01595 693 345. Open May-Sept. Tu-W and F-Su 10am-5pm. Round-trip £3.20, concessions £2.60. Noss open Tu-W and F-Su 10am-5pm. Overnight stays forbidden.) Ferries (☎01595 743 974; 7min.; every hr.; £3.30, cars £8) sail from Lerwick to Bressay.

MOUSA ☎(0)1595

The tiny, uninhabited island of Mousa, just off the east coast of Mainland, is famous for its 6000 pairs of the miniscule nocturnal storm petrels. It also holds the world's best-preserved Iron Age broch, a 50 ft. dry-stone fortress that has endured 1000 years of Arctic storms. Catch a Sumburgh-bound Leask bus in Lerwick and ask the driver to let you off at the Setter Junction for Sandsayre (round-trip £5); it's a 15min. walk from there to the ferry. (☎01950 431 367. Ferry departs June-Aug. M, W-F, Su 12:30, 2pm, Tu and Sa 2pm; Sept. and Apr.-May M-Th and Sa 2pm, F and Su 12:30, 2pm. £9.30.) **Trips to Mousa** also provides, well, trips to Mousa, departing from Sandwick. (☎01950 431 367; www.mousa-boattrips.co.uk. Call ahead for schedules. £12, concessions £10.)

YELL   ☎(0)1595

The soft peat of Yell (ahhh!) adds spring to walks on the island, but for most it passes in a blur on the way to the Unst ferry. Aptly named Otterswick, on the southeastern side of the island, is the best place to spot otters, which can sometimes wander up to the road; watch out if you're driving. In the center of the isle, the haunted ruins of the Windhouse date back 5000 years. Next door, the **Windhouse Lodge Böd ❶** provides shelter from the wind and a place to stay the night. At the ferry terminal, the **◪Wind Dog Cafe** features folklore posters, stuffed animals by the piano, and well-made food. Try the crofter's lunch of ham, cheese, homemade oatcakes, and a pickle (£3) for a literal taste of Highland life. (☎01957 744 321. Internet access £1 per 30min. Open M-F 9am-7pm, Sa-Su 10am-7pm. Cash only.) Killer whales are occasionally spotted in Bluemull Sound between Yell and Unst. **Ferries** run from Toft, Mainland, to Ulsta, Yell (20min.; 1-2 per hr.; £3.20, cars £7.60).

ST. NINIAN'S ISLE

Off the southwest coast of Mainland, an unusual **tombolo**—a beach surrounded on both sides by the sea—links St. Ninian's Isle to Mainland, just outside of Bigton. Inhabited from the Iron Age to the 18th century and the site of an early monastery, the isle is now home to a ruined church, rabbits, and sheep. It achieved brief fame in 1958 when a hoard of silver was discovered. In order to visit St. Ninian's in a day—necessary, since there are no accommodations—take the noon Sumburgh-bound bus from Lerwick to Bigton and the 1:30pm bus back from Bigton to Lerwick, allowing 1hr. to explore the island.

UNST

Unst (www.unst.org), the northernmost inhabited region in Britain, is home to impressive bird life, quirky museums and shops, and walks that lead to the end of the earth and back again. At the **◪Hermaness National Nature Reserve,** puffins and gannets nest by the thousands on the inner faces of giant cliffs. Beginning at the **Visitors Centre,** a 3hr. loop around the top of the isle travels past insect-eating plants. Follow the path to the north and touch the tip of Britian, gazing at spectacular views of the **Muckle Flugga Lighthouse** and the ocean. At the center of the isle off the A968 is the roofless **Muness Castle,** built in the late 16th century and often raided by pirates. Grab a key and torch from the nearby cottage to explore the dark rooms. (Open all year. Free.) In Haroldswick, the former Royal Air Force station at **Saxa Vord** has been renovated and re-opened as the **Sergeant's Mess Bunkhouse ❶,** which contains 26 single, double, and twin rooms. (☎01957 711 711; www.saxavord.com. Free Wi-Fi. £15 per person; B&B from £21.50 per person. MC/V.) Just outside the compound, stop by **◪Foords Chocolates and Tearoom ❶** for a taste of some of Britian's finest handmade chocolates in the unlikeliest of locations. Ask for a tour of the two-room shop and grab homemade cake (£2) in the tearoom. (☎01957 711 438; www.foordschocolates. com. Open M-Sa 1-5pm.) To get to Unst, take a ferry from Gutcher to Belmont (10min.; 1-2 per hr.; £3, cars £7). A Leask bus leaves Lerwick (2hr.; M-W 2 per day, Th-F 3 per day; £4.80) and connects with ferries and minibuses running as far north as Haroldswick on Unst. If stuck, call a **taxi** at ☎01957 711 666. The Baltasound **post office** (☎01957 711 655; open M-Tu and F 9am-1pm and 2-5:30pm, W 9am-1pm and 2-4:30pm, Th and Sa 9am-1pm) features Britain's northernmost **postcode:** ZE2 9DP.

OTHER ISLANDS

Shetland's outer islands are perfect for the traveler looking to leave civilization and head out into remote landscapes. Plan to stay overnight, as ferry schedules can be erratic and ferries do not operate in inclement weather. **Planes** depart for the islands from Tingwall on Mainland, but **ferries** are cheaper. Many run from Walls, Vidlin, and Laxo on Mainland, which can be reached by bus from Lerwick (generally under 1hr.; consult the *Shetland Transport Timetable*).

Whalsay ("whale island" in Norse; pop. 1000) is the center of Shetland's fishing industry. The prosperous isle is accessible by bus and ferry from Lerwick and is home to coastal walks and Stone Age relics. **Symbister House,** an impressive example of Georgian architecture, bankrupted its owners. The **Out Skerries** settlement supports 80 hardy fishermen. Stay at **The Grieve House Böd ❶** (former home of poet Christopher Grieve, alias Hugh MacDiarmid). Planes (☎840 246; M and W-Th 1-2 per day, £27) arrive from Tingwall, while ferries come from Lerwick (2hr.; 2 per week; £3, cars £4) and Vidlin (1hr., 10 per week). Ferries depart Laxo every hour (30min.; £3.30, cars £7.80).

Papa Stour's (pop. 24) coastline features sea-flooded cliff arches and used to house a colony of "lepers" on the southwest side of the isle. As it turns out, the poor folk simply suffered from terrible malnutrition and vitamin deficiencies. Backpackers can camp and use the toilet facilities at the ferry terminal. To get to Papa Stour, fly (Tu only, £27) from Tingwall or sail (☎810 460; 8 per week; £3, cars £4; book ahead) from West Burrafirth.

NORTHERN IRELAND

 The calm tenor of everyday life in Northern Ireland has long been overshadowed by headlines about riots and bombs. While the violence has subsided and the Irish Republican Army (IRA) and Ulster Volunteer Force (UVF) have agreed to total disarmament, the divisions in civil society continue. Protestants and Catholics usually live in separate neighborhoods, attend separate schools, patronize different stores and pubs, and even play different sports (while Protestant schools play rugby and cricket, Catholic schools tend toward Gaelic football and hurling). The 1998 Good Friday Agreement, designed by leaders of Northern Ireland, Great Britain, and the Republic of Ireland to end the Troubles, began a slow march to peace. All sides have renewed their efforts to make their country as peaceful as it is beautiful.

NORTHERN IRELAND HIGHLIGHTS

BEHOLD ballet at Belfast's historic **Grand Opera House** (p. 697).

EXPLORE the geological wonder of the **Giant's Causeway** in County Antrim (p. 717).

GET TIPSY at the **Bushmills Distillery,** the oldest licensed whiskey producer in the world (p. 718).

MONEY. The pound sterling is legal tender in Northern Ireland. Northern Ireland has its own bank notes, which are identical in value to English and Scottish notes of the same denominations but are sometimes not accepted outside Northern Ireland. Both English and Scottish notes, however, are accepted. Euro are generally not accepted, except in some border towns.

SAFETY AND SECURITY. Although sectarian violence is at an all-time low since the height of the Troubles, some neighborhoods and towns still experience unrest during sensitive political times. It's best to remain alert and cautious while traveling in Northern Ireland, especially during **Marching Season,** which reaches its peak July 4-12. August 12, when the **Apprentice Boys** march in Derry/Londonderry, is also a testy period. Despite these concerns, Northern Ireland has one of the lowest tourist-related crime rates in the world. Unattended luggage is always considered suspicious and is often confiscated. It is generally unsafe to hitch a ride in Northern Ireland.

LIFE AND TIMES

Since the partition of 1920, the people of Northern Ireland have retained their individual cultural and political identities. Many continue to defend the lines that define their differences, whether ideological divisions across the chambers of Parliament or actual streets marking the end of one culture and the beginning of the next. Generally speaking, the 950,000 Protestants are **Unionists,** who want the six counties of Northern Ireland to remain in the UK. Of the

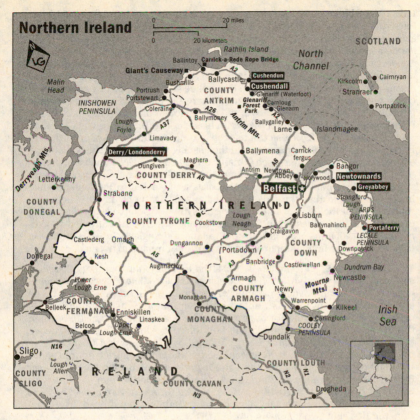

Northern Ireland

650,000 Catholics in Northern Ireland, most tend to identify with the Republic of Ireland, not Britain. Many are **Nationalists,** who crave to be integrated into the Republic. The more extreme (generally working-class) members of either side are known, respectively, as **Loyalists** and **Republicans.** These groups have historically defended their turf with rocks and gas bombs.

A DIVIDED ISLAND. In the 12th century, the English took control of Ireland, and King Henry VIII declared himself King of Ireland in 1541. Irish uprisings encouraged King James I to begin a series of plantations in six of the nine counties of **Ulster** in the 17th century. In 1688 the gates of Derry were shut against the troops of the Catholic James II, and in 1690 William III defeated James II at the **Battle of the Boyne.** The **Orange Order** (named after the uniforms of Protestant William III's army) formed in County Armagh in 1795 and provided explosive opposition to the first **Home Rule Bill** in 1886. After the **Easter Rising** in the Republic in 1916, the 1920 **Government of Ireland Act** split Ireland into two self-governing units: 28 counties in the south and six counties in northeast Ireland. In 1949, the Republic was officially established, and the **Ireland Act** recognized Northern Ireland's right to autonomy; violence (barring the occasional border skirmish) diminished. Between 1956 and 1962, the IRA launched attacks on the border, but this ended due to lack of support.

THE TROUBLES. In 1966, Protestant Unionists founded the **Ulster Volunteer Force (UVF),** which was declared illegal. The UVF and the IRA actively bombed each other (and civilians) throughout 1966. In response, the religiously mixed **Northern Ireland Civil Rights Association (NICRA)** sponsored a march in Derry/Londonderry in 1968. The march became a bloody mess, eventually broken up by the **Royal Ulster Constabulary (RUC)** with several water cannons. Violent rioting during parades became so common that police stopped entering parts of some cities, particularly Derry/Londonderry, where the slogan **"Free Derry"** became famous. The IRA later split in two; the more violent and extreme faction, the **Provisional IRA** (or **Provos**), took over with less ideology and more guns.

On January 30, 1972, British troops fired into a peaceful crowd of protesters in Derry/Londonderry. **Bloody Sunday,** and the ensuing reluctance of the British government to investigate, increased Catholic outrage. In 1978, Nationalist prisoners in the **Maze Prison** began a campaign for political prisoner status, going on a **hunger strike** in 1981. Republican leader **Bobby Sands** was elected to Parliament while imprisoned and leading the strike. He died at age 26 after 66 days of fasting; he remains one of the conflict's most powerful symbols. Bombings and factioning continued on both sides throughout the 80s and 90s. The IRA attained an estimated 30 tons of arms, used in Northern Ireland and England. In 1991, the **Brooke Initiative** led to the first multiparty talks in Northern Ireland in over a decade.

1994 CEASEFIRE. On August 31, 1994, the IRA announced a "complete cessation of military activities." The **Combined Loyalist Military Command,** speaking on behalf of all Loyalist paramilitary organizations, offered "to the loved ones of all innocent victims…abject and true remorse" as it announced its ceasefire. The peace held for over a year. The ceasefire ended in 1996, when the IRA bombed an office building in London's Docklands. The stalled peace talks, chaired by US Senator **George Mitchell,** were scheduled to reconvene but fell apart when a blast in a Manchester shopping district injured more than 200 people. In May 1997, the Labour party swept British elections. **Tony Blair** became prime minister, and the government ended its ban on talks with **Sinn Féin** (the political party of the IRA). Hopes for a renewed ceasefire were dashed when the UVF bombed the car of a prominent Republican. In retaliation, the IRA shot two members of the RUC.

GOOD FRIDAY AGREEMENT. After long negotiations between politicians and paramilitaries from Northern Ireland, the Republic of Ireland, and Britain (Blair blocked a door to prevent participants from walking out), the delegates approved a draft of the 1998 Northern Ireland Peace Agreement—better known as the **Good Friday Agreement.** The pact emphasized that change in Northern Ireland could come only with majority will and the recognition of "birthright," allowing citizens of to adopt British, Irish, or dual citizenship.

On May 22, 1998, in the first island-wide vote since 1918, residents of Northern Ireland and the Republic voted the agreement into law; 71% of Northern Ireland and 94% of the Republic voted to reform **Northern Ireland's government.** As per the agreement, the main body, a 108-member Northern Ireland Assembly, assigns committee posts and chairs proportionately to the parties' representation and is headed by a first minister. The second strand of the new government, a **North-South Ministerial Council,** serves as a cross-border authority. The final strand, the **British-Irish Council,** controls governance across the isles.

But shortly after these leaps forward, Marching Season began. The July 4 **Drumcree parade** was forbidden from marching down war-torn Garvaghy Rd., spurring a standoff between Republican and Loyalist paramilitaries. On the night of July 11, three young boys died in a firebombing of a Catholic home.

The attack was universally condemned, and the paramilitaries of the **Drumcree Standoff** lost support from both sides. On August 15, a bombing in **Omagh**, intended to undermine the Good Friday Agreement, left 29 dead and 382 injured; a splinter group called the **Real IRA** claimed responsibility.

CURRENT EVENTS. At midnight on May 29, 2000, Britain restored a power-sharing Northern Irish government (as outlined in the Good Friday Agreement) after the IRA promised to begin disarming. In 2001, the RUC became **Police Service of Northern Ireland.** On July 28, 2005, the IRA ordered a formal paramilitary disarmament, announcing that it would pursue its political ends only through peaceful means. The **Bloody Sunday Inquiry** records testimonies from British military and IRA figures. All sides are now making efforts to reconcile the past. In May 2007, the UVF finally responded to the IRA's disarmament by unofficially renouncing violence. The Northern Ireland Assembly has since been reconvened, and Ian Paisley (of the Democratic Unionist Party) and Martin McGuinness (of Sinn Féin) occupied the first minister and deputy first minister posts. As Paisley announced his resignation in March of 2008, it is anticipated that the party's deputy leader Peter Robinson will take his place as first minister. There is hope that the joint government will lead to a lasting peace.

BELFAST (BÉAL FEIRSTE)   ☎(0)28

The second-largest city on the island, Belfast (pop. 276,000) is the focus of Northern Ireland's cultural, commercial, and political activity. Queen's University testifies to the city's rich academic history—luminaries such as Nobel Laureate Seamus Heaney and Lord Kelvin (of chemistry fame) once roamed the halls of Queen's, and Samuel Beckett taught the young men of Campbell College. The Belfast pub scene ranks among the best in the world, combining the historical appeal of old-fashioned watering holes with more modern bars and clubs.While Belfast has suffered from the stigma of its violent past, it has rebuilt itself and now surprises most visitors with its neighborly, urbane feel. This is true for most of the city, with the exception of the still-divided West Belfast area, home to separate communities of Protestants and Catholics.

✈ INTERCITY TRANSPORTATION

Flights: Belfast is served by 2 airports.

Belfast International Airport (☎028 9448 4848; www.belfastairport.com) in Aldergrove. **Aer Lingus** (☎087 0876 5000), **Air Transat** (☎028 9031 2312), **BMI** (☎087 0264 2229), **Continental** (☎012 9377 6464), **easyJet** (☎087 1244 2366), **Flyglobespan** (☎087 0556 1522), **Jet2** (☎087 1226 1737), **Manx2** (☎087 0242 2226), and **Wizz Air** (☎+48 22 351 94 99) operate from here. **Translink Bus 300** has 24hr. service from the airport to Europa bus station in the city center (M-F every 10min. 6:50am-6:15pm, every 15-40min. otherwise; Sa every 20min. 7:35am-6:40pm, at least once per hr. otherwise; Su every 30min. 8:15am-10:40pm, at least once per hr. otherwise; call ☎028 9066 6630 or visit www.translink.co.uk for full timetables). £6, round-trip £9 if you return within 1 month. Taxis (☎028 9448 4353) get you there for £25-30.

Belfast City Airport (☎028 9093 9093; www.belfastcityairport.com), at the harbor. **Flybe** (☎087 1700 0535), **BMI** (☎087 0607 0555), **Ryanair** (☎00353 1249 7791), **Aer Arann** (☎080 0587 2324), and **Manx2** (☎087 0242 2226) operate from here. To get from City Airport to Europa bus station, take **Translink Bus 600** (M-F every 20min. 8:35am-10:05pm, every 30min. 5:30-8:35am; Sa every 20min. 8:05am-9:50pm, every 30min. 5:30-8:05am; Su every 45 min. 7:30am-9:50pm). £1.30, round-trip £2.20.

Trains: For train and bus info, contact Translink (☎028 9066 6630; www.translink.co.uk; inquiries daily 7am-8pm). Trains leave **Central Station,** E. Bridge St., to **Dublin** (2hr.; M-Sa 8 per day, Su 5 per day; £25, round-trip £36). Trains call at several of Belfast's

NORTHERN IRELAND

TO SHANKILL RD. (100m)

Peter's Hill

WEST BELFAST

TO FALLS RD. AND IRISH CULTURAL CENTRE (100m)

Smithfield Market
Life Cycles
West St.
Castlecourt Shopping Centre
Old Museum Arts Centre
St. Mary's
Bank St.
Tesco
US

University of Ulster
St. Anne's Cathedral
First Presbyterian Church
Jackson Sports
Albert Memorial Clock
Custom House
Lagan Lookout
Laganside Bus Center

TO SINCLAIR SEAMAN'S (150m)

TO ODYSSEY (350yd)

Linen Hall Library
Thomas Cook
Belfast Opera House
Great Victoria St. Rail Station
Europa Bus Station
Belfast Superbowl

Donegall Sq.
Belfast Wheel
City Hall
Ulster Hall

General Register's Office
Laganside Courts
Royal Courts
Victoria Sq.

Ormeau Baths Gallery

TO LYRIC THEATRE (1km)

PUBS
The Botanic Inn, 7
The Duke of York, 27
The John Hewitt, 24
Katy Daly's Pub, 23
The Kremlin, 22
McHugh's, 30
Mynt, 28
The Crown, 14
Kelly's Cellar, 19
Madden's Bar, 13
The Black Box, 26

TO BELFAST CASTLE (1.7km)

City Hospital
City Hospital Rail Station
Fenderesky Gallery
Launderette
Botanic Rail Station

TO McCONVEY CYCLES (200m)

Queen's University

0   150 yards
0   150 meters

Belfast

ACCOMMODATIONS
The Ark (IHH), 21
Arnie's Backpackers (IHH), 6
Avenue Guest House, 1
Belfast Hostel (HINI), 9
Camera Guesthouse, 3
The Linen House Youth Hostel (IHH), 18
Marine House, 4
Paddy's Palace, 5
Windermere Guest House, 2

FOOD
Archana, 16
Benedict's, 10
Bookfinders, 8
The Other Place, 17
O'Brien's, 25
Café Carberry, 29
Little Italy, 15
ToJo's, 12
Foo-Kin Noodle Bar, 11
Windsor Dairy, 20

stations (Great Victoria St., City Hospital, Botanic, Central) for **Derry/Londonderry** (2hr.; M-F 9 per day, Sa 8 per day, Su 4 per day; £10.50, round-trip £15).

Buses: Europa Bus Terminal, off Great Victoria St., behind the Europa Hotel (☎028 9043 4424; ticket office open M-Sa 7:35am-8:05pm, Su 9:15am-6:15pm). Buses to **Derry/Londonderry** (1¾hr.; M-F 39 per day, Sa 20 per day, Su 11 per day; £10, round-trip £15) and **Dublin** (3hr.; 24 per day; £10, round-trip £14). The **Centrelink** bus connects the station with the city center. **Metro** buses are free with rail tickets.

Ferries: Norfolk Ferries (www.norfolkline-ferries.co.uk) operates out of the SeaCat terminal and cross the Irish Sea to **Liverpool** (8hr.; fares seasonal, from £20). Book online before the day of travel to avoid a £10 booking fee. Stena Line (☎087 0570 7070; www.stenaline.com), up the Lagan River, has the quickest service to Scotland, docking in **Stranraer** (1hr.; fares seasonal, from £55). Book online.

ORIENTATION

Buses arrive at the Europa Bus Station on **Great Victoria Street.** To the northeast is **City Hall** in **Donegall Square.** Donegall Pl. turns into **Royal Avenue** and runs from Donegall Sq. through the shopping area. To the east, in **Cornmarket,** pubs in narrow **entries** (small alleyways) offer an escape. The stretch of Great Victoria St. between the bus station and Shaftesbury Sq. is known as the **Golden Mile** for its high-brow establishments and Victorian architecture. **Botanic Avenue** and **Bradbury Place** (which becomes **University Road**) extend south from Shaftesbury Sq. into **Queen's University** turf.

Westlink Motorway divides working-class **West Belfast,** more politically volatile than the city center, from the rest of Belfast. The Protestant district stretches along Shankill Rd., just north of the Catholic neighborhood, centered on Falls Rd. The **River Lagan** splits industrial **East Belfast** from Belfast proper. The shipyards and docks extend north on both sides of the river as it turns into **Belfast Lough.** During the week, the area north of City Hall is essentially deserted after 6pm. Streets remain quiet even during the weekend, belying the boisterous club scene. Although muggings are infrequent in Belfast, it's wise to use taxis after dark, particularly near pubs and clubs in the northeast.

LOCAL TRANSPORTATION

Transportation cards and tickets are available at the pink Metro kiosk in Donegall Sq. W. (open M-F 8am-5:25pm, Sa 9am-5:20pm) and around the city.

Buses: Belfast has 2 bus services. Many local bus routes connect through Europa Bus Station, Great Victoria St., and Laganside Bus Station, Queen's Sq.

Metro buses (☎028 9066 6630; www.translink.co.uk) gather in Donegall Sq. and cover Belfast.

Ulsterbus "blue buses" cover the suburbs. Day passes £3.50. Travel within the city center £1.10 (£1.40 beyond the city center), under 16 55p.

Taxis: Value Cabs (☎028 9080 9080). **City Cab** (☎028 9024 2000). Both 24hr.

Bike Rental: McConvey Cycles, 183 Ormeau Rd. (☎028 9033 0322). £15-20 per day, £60 per week; £50 deposit. Lock and helmet supplied. Pannier £8 per week. Open M-Sa 9am-6pm, Th 9am-8pm. **Life Cycles,** 36-37 Smithfield Market (☎028 9043 9959; www.lifecycles.co.uk). £9 per day. Bicycle city tours available (see **Tours,** below).

PRACTICAL INFORMATION

Tourist Information Centre: Belfast Welcome Centre, 47 Donegall Pl. (☎028 9024 6609; www.gotobelfast.com). Gives out booklets on Belfast and info on surrounding areas. Books reservations in Northern Ireland (£2) and the Republic (£3). Open June-Sept. M-Sa 9am-7pm, Su 11am-4pm; Oct.-May M-Sa 9am-5:30pm, Su 11am-4pm.

Tours: Multiple groups lead different themed tours of Belfast and environs:

■ Black Cab Tours (☎077 2106 7752 or 0797 481 4002). Commentary on the murals and sights on both sides of the peace line. Most drivers have been personally affected by the Troubles, but they remain impartial. The 5 Protestant and 5 Catholic drivers give impassioned yet even-handed commentary. 1hr. £30 for the individual, £10 for each additional person.

Bailey's Historical Pub Tours of Belfast (☎028 9268 3665; www.belfastpubtours.com). Guides visitors through Belfast's oldest and best pubs with a little sightseeing and city history served on the side. Tumbler of Bailey's Irish Cream included. 2hr. Departs from Crown Dining Rooms, above the Crown Liquor Saloon, May-Oct. Th 7pm, Sa 4pm. £6, £5 for members of groups of 10+.

Bike Tours. Life Cycles (see **Bike Rental,** p.693) and **Irish Cycle Tours,** 27 Belvoir View Park (☎028 9064 2222; www.irishcycletours.com), give tours for £12-16 per day.

Mini-Coach (☎028 9031 5333). Conducts bus tours of Belfast (1hr.; departs M-F noon; £10, children £5) and the Giant's Causeway (daily 9:45am-6:45pm; £25, students £22). Tours depart from the Belfast International Youth Hostel. Tickets available at Belfast Welcome Centre.

Currency Exchange: ATMs at: **Ulster Bank,** 140 Great Victoria St. (☎028 9024 2686); **Ulster Bank,** 11 Donegall Sq. E. (☎028 9024 4112); **Alliance and Leicester,** 63 Royal Ave., (☎028 9024 1957); **First Trust,** 92 Ann St. (☎028 9032 5599); **Northern Bank,** 14 Donegall Sq. W. (☎028 9024 5277). Most banks open M-F 9am-4:30pm.

Library: Belfast Central Library, 122 Royal Ave. (☎028 9050 9150). Internet £1.50 per 30min. for nonmembers. Open M-Th 9am-8pm, F 9am-5:30pm, Sa 9am-4:30pm.

Launderette: Globe Drycleaners & Launderers, 37-39 Botanic Ave. (☎028 9024 3956). £5 per load. Open M-F 8am-9pm, Sa 8am-6pm, Su noon-6pm.

Police: 6-18 Donegall Pass and 65 Knock Rd. (☎028 9065 0222).

Hospitals: Belfast City Hospital, 91 Lisburn Rd. (☎028 9032 9241). From Shaftesbury Sq., follow Bradbury Pl. and take a right at the fork for Lisburn Rd. **Royal Victoria Hospital,** 12 Grosvenor Rd. (☎028 9024 0503). From Donegall Sq., take Howard St. west to Grosvenor Rd.

Internet Access: At **Belfast Welcome Centre** (above). £1 per 20 min. Also at **Belfast Central Library** (above).

Post Office: Central Post Office, on the corner of High St. and Bridge St. (☎084 5722 3344). Open M-Sa 10am-5:30pm. **Postcode:** BT2 7FD.

■ ACCOMMODATIONS

Despite fluctuating tourism and rising rents, Belfast boasts a solid lineup of hostels. Almost all are near Queen's University, close to the city's pubs and restaurants, and a short walk or bus to the city center. This area is by far the best place to stay in Belfast. If you are hindered by baggage, catch Metro Bus #8A, 8B, 8C, 9A, 9B, or 9C from Donegall Sq. or from Europa on Great Victoria St.

HOSTELS

■ Arnie's Backpackers, 63 Fitzwilliam St. (☎028 9024 2867; www.arniesbackpackers.co.uk). Look for a cutout sign of a sky-gazing backpacker. Arnie, the hostel's jovial owner, may greet you with a cup of tea. Bunked beds in bright, clean rooms. Kitchen, fireplace, common room with TV, and back garden. Shared bathrooms are immaculate. Library of travel info includes bus and train timetables, bulletin board in entryway posts work opportunities, and friendly staff can answer questions. Reception 8:30am-9pm. 8-bed dorms £9; 4-bed £11. ❶

The Belfast Palace (Paddy's Palace), 68 Lisburn Rd. (☎028 9033 3367; www.paddyspalace.com). Call it The Belfast Palace in public: Paddy has Catholic associations and could cause upset. Sociable new hostel offers free satellite TV and videos in the lounge. Kitchen. Breakfast (cereal, toast, tea, coffee) included. Laundry. Free Wi-Fi daily 8am-11:30pm. Dorms from £9.50-13.50. MC/V. ❶

The Ark, 44 University St. (☎028 9032 9626; www.arkhostel.com). Spacious, sunny dorms and a kitchen stocked with staples, free tea, and coffee. Helpful staff provides info on work opportunities. Dining room and TV area. Lockers and weekend luggage storage available. Compete for free laundry on 1 machine. Internet £3 per hr. Reception daily 8am-2am. Curfew 2am. 4- to 15-bed dorms (co-ed) £11. MC/V. ❶

Belfast Hostel, 22 Donegall Rd. (☎028 9031 5435; www.hini.org.uk), off Shaftesbury Sq. A large, modern hostel. Groups socialize in the large common room and kitchen. The **Causeway Cafe** serves breakfast (£4) daily 8-11am. Laundry £3.50 per load. Wi-Fi and Internet access £1 per 20min. Wheelchair-accessible. Reception 24hr. 4- to 6-bed dorms £9.50 M-Th and Su, F-Sa £10.50; ensuite £10.50/11.50. MC/V. ❶

The Linen House Youth Hostel, 18-20 Kent St. (☎028 9058 6400; www.belfasthostel. com). Converted 19th-century linen factory, bordering West Belfast. Kitchen and common room. Luggage storage 50p. Towels 50p. Laundry. Internet £2 per hr. Dorms £6.50-12; singles M-Th and Su £20, F-Sa £25; doubles £15/20. MC/V. ❶

BED AND BREAKFASTS

B&Bs cluster south of Queen's University between **Malone** and **Lisburn Road.**

Windermere Guest House, 60 Wellington Park (☎028 9066 2693; www.windermereguesthouse.co.uk). Leather couches provide comfy seating in the living room. Singles £31-42; doubles £56-60. Cash only. ❸

Camera Guesthouse, 44 Wellington Park (☎028 9066 0026; www.cameraguesthouse. com). Quiet, pristine Victorian house. Breakfasts offer wide selection of organic foods and herbal teas that cater to specific dietary concerns. Singles £34, with bath £48; doubles £45/52. MC/V with 3% surcharge. ❹

Avenue Guest House, 23 Eglantine Ave. (☎028 9066 5904; www.avenueguesthouse. com). 4 large, airy rooms equipped with TVs and Wi-Fi. Comfortable living room has free DVDs and books. £27.50-30 per person. ❸

Marine House, 30 Eglantine Ave. (☎028 9066 2828). Mansion with high ceilings and wonderful housekeeping. All rooms with TVs, bath, and phones. Breakfast included. Singles £45; doubles £60; family rooms £85-100. ❹

◖ FOOD

Dublin Road, Botanic Avenue, and the **Golden Mile** around **Shaftesbury Square** have the highest concentration of restaurants. The huge **Tesco** supermarket, 2 Royal Ave., is in an old bank building. (☎028 9032 3270. Open M-W and Sa 8am-7pm, Th 8am-9pm, F 8am-8pm, Su 1-5pm.)

Little Italy, 13 Amelia St. (☎028 9031 4914). A warm Mediterranean kitchen in Belfast's city center. Customers watch at the brick counter as the industrious staff make their pizzas to order. Find a seat on the sidewalk—there are no tables here. Call ahead to avoid a wait or savor the oven's aromas with the crowd. Italiano, Vege, Fabio, and Hawaiian are a few of several options. 9 in. £3.30-5.80, 10 in. £4-7, 12 in. £5-8. MC/V. ❶

Tojo's, Smithfield Market (☎028 9032 4122). There is nothing pretentious about Tojo's, which offers some of Belfast's lowest prices for honest food. Friendly staff, mismatched furniture, and a chalkboard full of sandwich options (£3) fulfill its promise of "homemade food with a modern twist." Try a hearty fried breakfast (£3-4). Cash only. ❶

Bookfinders, 47 University Rd. (☎028 9032 8269), 1 block from the university, on the corner of Camden St. and University Rd. Read, eat, and surf free Wi-Fi amid cluttered bookshelves. A favorite with the university crowd because of its proximity, low prices, and character. Hosts occasional poetry readings and features student art upstairs. Vegan soup and bread £3; sandwiches £3. Open M-Sa 10am-5:30pm. ❶

Windsor Dairy, 4 College St. (☎028 9032 7157). Family-run bakery doles out piles of pastries (under £1), pies (£1.30-2), and satisfying daily specials (£2-3). Come early before locals gobble up the best batches. Open M-Sa 7:30am-5:30pm. ❶

Cafe Carberry, 153 Victoria St. (☎028 9023 4020). A stylish urban oasis for the crowd-weary traveler. Refuel with daily specials (£3-5) or enjoy a selection of standard and exotic coffees and teas (£1.60-3). MC/V. ❶

Foo-Kin Noodle Bar, 38 Bradbury Pl. (☎028 9023 2889). Choose among buffet options like chili chicken and vegetable chow mein or order a Cantonese specialty from the menu (£7-9). Lunch buffet £7, students £6; dinner buffet £10/9. Open M-F noon-2pm and 5-10pm, Sa 5-10pm, Su 1-10pm. MC/V. ❷

Benedict's, 7-21 Bradbury Pl. (☎028 9059 1999; www.benedictshotel.co.uk). Swanky hotel restaurant is an upscale break from nearby sandwiches and pizza. Meat, chicken, pasta, and vegetarian entrees. Lunches £7.50-12. Dinners £12-16. "Beat the Clock" meal deal offers reduced-price menu selections (£5-10) daily 5-7:30pm. Open M-Sa noon-2:30pm and 5-10pm, Su noon-9pm. ❸

The Other Place, 79 Botanic Ave. (☎028 9020 7200). Bustling eatery serves fried breakfasts (£3) until 5pm. Hearty specials and ethnic entrees. Try the "bang bang chicken," with spicy soy sweet chili and peanut sauce. Steak special M £8. Open in summer M-Th and Su 8am-4pm, F-Sa 8am-10pm; from fall to spring daily 8am-10pm. ❷

◉ SIGHTS

CENTRAL BELFAST

BELFAST CITY HALL. The most dramatic and impressive piece of architecture in Belfast is also its administrative and geographic center. Dominating the grassy square that serves as the locus of downtown Belfast, its green copper dome is visible from nearly any point in the city. Inside, a grand staircase ascends to the second floor, where portraits of the city's lord mayors line the halls. The city council's oak-paneled chambers, used only once per month, are deceptively austere, considering the council's reputation for rowdy meetings (fists have been known to fly). The interior of City Hall is only accessible by guided tour. (*☎028 9027 0477. No tours until late 2009.*)

BELFAST WHEEL. The city's oversized Ferris wheel offers unrivaled views of Belfast and the surrounding countryside. A seat in the wheel's VIP capsule—reserved for celebrities and spendthrifts—is a whimsical £55 ride. (*Open M-Th and Su 10am-9pm, F 10am-10pm, Sa 9am-10pm. £6.50, children £4.50, toddlers £1.*)

QUEEN'S UNIVERSITY BELFAST. Charles Lanyon designed the beautiful Tudor Gothic brick campus in 1849, modeling it after Magdalen College in Oxford. The **Visitors Centre,** in the Lanyon Room to the left of the main entrance, offers Queen's-related exhibits and merchandise as well as a free pamphlet detailing a walking tour of the grounds. Upstairs, the **Naughton Gallery** displays rotating exhibits of contemporary art. (*University Rd. ☎028 9097 5252; www.qub.ac.uk/vcentre. Wheelchair-accessible. Open May-Sept. M-Sa 10am-4pm; Oct.-Mar. M-F 10am-4pm. Gallery open M-Sa 11am-4pm. Tours May-Sept. Sa noon; Oct-Mar. by request. £5, children free. Gallery free.*)

ODYSSEY. The poster child of Belfast's riverfront revival, this attraction packs five distinct sights into one entertainment center. (*2 Queen's Quay. ☎028 9045 1055; www.theodyssey.co.uk.*) The **Odyssey Arena,** with 10,000 seats, is the largest indoor arena in Ireland. When the Belfast Giants ice hockey team isn't on the ice, big-name performers heat up the stage. *(Box office ☎ 028 9073 9074; www.odysseyarena. com. Hockey arena ☎ 028 9059 1111; www.belfastgiants.com.)* The **W5 Discovery Centre** (short for "whowhatwherewhenwhy?") is a playground for curious minds and hyperactive schoolchildren. Design your own racecar, waltz up the musical stairs, build a wind turbine, or stage a space rescue mission. *(☎ 028 9046 7700; www.w5online.co.uk. Open M-Sa 10am-6pm, Su noon-6pm. Last entry 1hr. before closing. Wheelchair-accessible. £7, children £5. Family discounts available.)* The **Sherbidan IMAX Cinema** plays both 2D and 3D films on its enormous 62 ft. by 82 ft. screen, while **Warner Village Cinemas** shows Hollywood blockbusters on its own 12 screens. *(IMAX ☎ 028 9046 7014; www.belfastimax.com. £5, students £4.50, children £4. Warner Village Cinemas ☎ 028 9073 9134; www.stormcinemas.co.uk/belfast. £6/4/3.80. Tu tickets £2.50.)* The **Pavilion** contains shops, bars, and restaurants—including that tourist mecca, the **Hard Rock Cafe** *(Hard Rock Cafe ☎ 028 9076 6990. Open M-Sa noon-1am, Su noon-midnight.)*

GRAND OPERA HOUSE. The opera house was bombed by the IRA, restored to its original splendor at enormous cost, and then bombed again. Visitors today enjoy its second restoration, and tours offer a look behind the ornate facade and include a complimentary coffee and pastry at the cafe, **Luciano's.** *(☎ 028 9023 1919; www.goh.co.uk. Open M-F 8:30am-9pm, Sa 8:30am-6pm. Tours begin across the street at the office W-Sa 11am. £3, concessions £2.)*

BELFAST CASTLE. Built in 1870 by the third marquis of Donegall, the castle sits atop **Cave Hill,** long the seat of Ulster rulers, and offers the best panoramas of the Belfast port—on a clear day views extend as far as Scotland and the Isle of Man. The ancient King Matudan had his McArt's Fort here, where the more modern United Irishmen plotted rebellion in 1795. These days, the castle sees more weddings than skirmishes. Marked trails lead north from the fort to five caves in the area that historians postulate are ancient mines. Only the lowest is accessible to tourists. For those on foot, the small path to the right of the gate makes for a far shorter and prettier walk than the road. *(☎ 028 9077 6925; www. belfastcastle.co.uk. Open M-Sa 9am-10pm, Su 9am-5:30pm. Free.)*

SAINT ANNE'S CATHEDRAL. This Church of Ireland cathedral was begun in 1899, but, to keep from disturbing regular worship, it was built around a smaller church already on the site. Upon completion of the new exterior, builders extracted the earlier church brick by brick. Each of the cathedral's 10 interior pillars names one of Belfast's professional fields: science, industry, healing, agriculture, music, theology, shipbuilding, freemasonry, art, and womanhood. In an enclave called the **Chapel of Unity,** visitors pray for understanding among Christians of all denominations. *(Donegall St., a few blocks from the city center. Open M-Sa 10am-4pm, Su before and after services at 10am, 11am, 3:30pm.)*

SINCLAIR SEAMEN'S CHURCH. Designed to accommodate the hordes of sinning sailors landing in Belfast port, this quirky church does things its own way—the minister delivers his sermons from a pulpit carved in the shape of a ship's prow, collections are taken in miniature lifeboats, and the choir uses an organ from a Guinness barge with port and starboard lights. *(Corporation St., down from the SeaCat terminal. ☎ 028 9071 5997. Open W 2-5pm; Su services at 11:30am, 7pm.)*

SIR THOMAS AND LADY DIXON PARK. The most stunning of the city's parks sits a short remove from the center of Belfast, on Upper Malone Rd. Rambling paths and 20,000 flowering rose bushes occlude the proximity to the city. The gardens were founded in 1836 and include stud China roses, imported betwee~ 1792 and 1824. They now feature a prodigious trial collection of other intern~ tional varieties. *(☎ 028 9091 8768. Open M-Sa 7:30am-dusk, Su 9am-dusk.)*

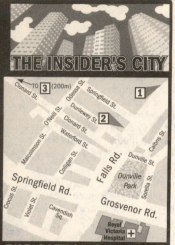

THE CATHOLIC MURALS

The murals of West Belfast are a powerful testament to the volatile past and fierce loyalties of the divided neighborhoods. Many of the most famous Catholic murals are on Falls Rd., an area that saw some of the worst of the Troubles.

1. Mural illustrating protestors during the **Hunger Strikes of 1981,** in which Catholics fasted for the right to be considered political prisoners.

2. Portrayal of **Bobby Sands,** the first hunger striker to die, is located on the side of the Sinn Féin Office, Sevastopol St. Sands was elected as a member of the British Parliament under a "political prisoner" ticket during this time and is remembered as the North's most famous martyr.

. The **Clonard Martyrs Memorial rden** on Bombay St. commemo-**s** the attack there—Bombay St. **he** first to be bombed during **ubles**—and lists the names **ead.**

BELFAST ZOO. Set in the hills alongside Cave Hill Forest Park, the zoo's best attribute is its natural setting—catching sight of a lumbering elephant against the backdrop of Belfast lough can be a surreal experience. The recommended route highlights the standard lineup of tigers, giraffes, camels, zebras, and the acrobatic spider monkey. *(4 mi. north of the city on Antrim Rd. Take Metro bus #1A, 1B, 1C, 1D, 1E, 1F, 1G, or 2A from city center. ☎028 9077 6277. Open daily Apr.-Sept. 10am-7pm, last entry 5pm; Oct.-Mar. 10am-4pm, last entry 2:30pm. Apr.-Sept. £8.10, children £4.30; Oct.-Mar. £6.70/3.40.)*

WEST BELFAST AND THE MURALS

West Belfast has historically been at the heart of political tensions in the North. The Troubles reached their peak in the 1970s; the particularly violent year of 1972 saw 1000 bomb explosions and over 400 murders. While there have not been any large-scale outbreaks of violence in recent years, tensions remain high. The Catholic area (centered on **Falls Road**) and the Protestant neighborhood (centered on the **Shankill**) are separated by the **peace line,** a grim, gray wall with a number of gates that close at nightfall. Along the wall, scorch marks, abandoned buildings, and barricaded homes testify to a tumultuous history and an uneasy future. One bit of the peace line, near Lanark Way, connecting the Falls and Springfield Rd., contains symbolic paintings and signatures—left mostly by visitors—promoting hope for peaceable relations. West Belfast is not a tourist site in the traditional sense; the walls and houses along the streets speak to a religious and political divide that is living as well as historical.

Those traveling to these sectarian neighborhoods often take **black taxis,** community shuttles that whisk community residents to the city center along set routes. Some black taxis can also be booked for tours of the Falls or Shankill (below). *Let's Go* offers two neighborhood maps (see **Catholic** and **Protestant Murals,** sidebars) of the murals and memorials for a self-guided tour.

It's safest to visit the Falls and Shankill during the day, when the neighborhoods are full of locals and the murals are visible. It's best to stay away from the area altogether during Marching Season (the weeks around July 12), when the parades are underscored by mutual antagonism that can lead to violence (see **Life and Times,** p. 688). Be wary of visiting outside daylight hours, and don't wander from one neighborhood to the other. Instead, return to the city center between visits to Shankill and the Falls. New murals in the Falls and Shankill are constantly produced, so the descriptions below and the neighborhood maps describe only a fraction of what is there. Before taking a camera, ask about the current political climate. Photography is ill-advised during Marching Season but generally acceptable on black cab tours, as drivers have agreements with the communities.

SHANKILL. Shankill Rd. begins at the Westlink and turns into **Woodvale Road** as it crosses Cambrai St. Woodvale Rd. intersects Crumlin Rd. at the Ardoyne roundabout and leads back to the city center. The **Shankill Memorial Garden,** Shankills Rd., facing Berlin St., honors 10 people who died in a bomb attack on Fizzel's Fish Shop in October 1993. On Shankill Rd., farther toward the city center, is a mural of James Buchanan, the 15th president of the United States, who was a descendant of Ulster Scots (known in the US as the Scots-Irish). Other cultural murals, near the Rex Bar, depict the 50th Jubilee of the coronation of Queen Elizabeth II (crowned in 1952) and the death of the queen mother in 2002. Historical murals include a memorial to the UVF who fought at the Battle of the Somme during WWI. Outside of the **Shankill Estate,** murals represent Cromwell suppressing the 1741 rebellion against Protestant plantation owners. The **Orange Hall** sits on the left at Brookmount St. **McClean's Wallpaper** on the right is where Fizzel's Fish Shop stood before the blast. Through the estate, Crumlin Rd. heads back to the city center, passing an army base, the courthouse, and the jail.

THE FALLS. This Catholic and Republican neighborhood is larger than Shankill, following Castle St. west from the city center. As Castle St. continues across A12/Westlink, it becomes **Divis Street.** A high-rise building marks **Divis Tower,** an ill-fated housing development built by optimistic social planners in the 1960s. The project soon became an IRA stronghold and saw some of the worst of Belfast's Troubles during the 1970s. The British Army still occupies the top floors.

Continuing west, Divis St. turns into **Falls Road.** The office of Sinn Féin (the political party of the IRA) is easily spotted: one side of it is covered with a portrait of Bobby Sands (see **The Troubles, p. 690**) and an advertisement for the Sinn Féin newspaper, *An Phoblacht.* Continuing down Falls Rd., murals appear on the side streets. In the past, both the Falls and the Shankill contained many militaristic representations of the past, but newer murals, which sometimes replace the old ones, feature less charged historical and cultural themes. The newest Falls murals recall Celtic myths and legends and depict the Great Hunger, the phrase Northern

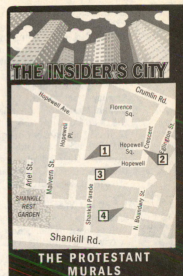

THE INSIDER'S CITY

THE PROTESTANT MURALS

The Protestant murals, in the Shankill area of West Belfast, tend to be overtly militant. Most are found near Hopewell St. and Hopewell Crescent, to the north of Shankill Rd., or down Shankill Parade and are accessed by traveling south from Crumlin Rd.

1. Commemoration of the **Red Hand Commando,** a militant Loyalist group.

2. Mural of the **Battle of the Boyne,** commemorating William of Orange's 1690 victory over James II.

3. The **Marksman's** gun seems to follow you as you pass by.

4. Portrait of the infamous **Top Gun,** a man responsible for the deaths of many high-ranki Republicans.

Catholics use to refer to the famine of 1845-52. Earlier militant murals still exist, including some that depict the Republican armed struggle.

Falls Rd. soon splits into **Andersonstown Road** and **Glen Road,** one of the few urban areas with a predominant Irish-speaking population. On the left are the Celtic crosses of **Milltown Cemetery,** the resting place of many fallen Republicans. Inside the entrance, a memorial to Republican casualties is bordered by a low, green fence on the right; the grave of Bobby Sands lies here. Nearby, **Bombay Street** was the first street to be burned down during the Troubles. There, **Clonard Martyrs Memorial Garden** commemorates the event and lists the names of the dead. Another mile along Andersontown Rd. lies a housing project that was formerly a wealthy Catholic neighborhood—and more murals. The Springfield Rd. Police Service of Northern Ireland station, previously named the RUC station, was the most attacked police station in Ireland and the UK. It was recently demolished. The **Andersonstown Barracks,** at the corner of Glen and Andersonstown Rd., are still heavily fortified.

BEYOND WEST BELFAST

This area's Protestant population is growing steadily, partly due to the redevelopment of the **Sandy Row** area and because many working-class residents are leaving the Shankill. This stretch is a turn off Donegall Rd. at Shaftesbury Sq. An orange arch topped with King William once marked its start. Nearby murals show the Red Hand of Ulster, a bulldog, and William crossing the Boyne. East Belfast is a secure, growing Protestant enclave. Murals line **Newtownards Road.** One depicts the economic importance of the shipyard to the city's history. On the Ballymacart road, which runs parallel to Newtownards Rd., is a mural of local son CS Lewis's *The Lion, the Witch, and the Wardrobe.*

🏛 MUSEUMS

In addition to the listings below, several theater venues in Belfast double as spaces for visual art exhibits. See **Entertainment** (below) for additional listings.

FENDERESKY GALLERY. Inside the Crescent Arts building, the Fenderesky hosts contemporary shows and sells local artists' work. *(2 University Rd. ☎ 028 9023 5245. Open Tu-Sa 11:30am-5pm.)*

OLD MUSEUM ARTS CENTRE. Affectionately called OMAC, it's one of the largest venues in the North for contemporary artwork. A small gallery hosts rotating exhibits, but its focus is performance art. Pick up a booklet detailing upcoming workshops and a variety of dance, theater, and music performances. *(7 College Sq. N. ☎ 028 9023 5053, tickets 9023 3332; www.oldmuseumartscentre.org. Tickets £6-9, concessions £3. Open M-Sa 9:30am-5:30pm.)*

🎵 ENTERTAINMENT

Belfast's many cultural events and performances are covered in the monthly *Arts Council Artslink,* free at the tourist office, while the bimonthly *Arts Listings* covers arts and entertainment throughout Northern Ireland. Listings appear daily in the *Belfast Telegraph* (which also has a Friday "Arts" supplement) and in Thursday's issue of the *Irish News.* July and August are slow months for arts as the city shuts down for Marching Season, but check *What About?, The Big List,* and *Fate* for summer events and concerts. In addition to the listings below, check out the **Old Museum Arts Centre** (above), which houses theatrical performances as well as visual art.

▩ **The Black Box,** 18-22 Hill St. (☎ 028 9024 4400; www.blackboxbelfast.com). Hip and vibrant arts venue. A space for plays, music, comedy, burlesque shows, and balls. The

Black Box cafe hosts exhibitions, book signings, seminars, film screenings, and free music. Box office open M-F 9:30am-4:30pm. Cafe open M-F 10am-5pm.

The Crescent Arts Centre, 2 University Rd. (☎028 9024 2338). Hosts concerts and art exhibits. Also supplies some general Belfast arts info. Classes £40-60, children £24-32. Open in term time M-F 10am-10pm, Sa 10am-7pm; otherwise M-Sa 10am-5pm.

The Grand Opera House, 4 Great Victoria St. (☎028 9024 0411, tickets 9024 1919; www.goh.co.uk). Presents opera, ballet, musicals, and drama. Tickets £9-27. Open M-F 8:30am-9pm, Sa 8:30am-6pm.

The Lyric Theatre, 55 Ridgeway St. (☎028 9038 5685; www.lyrictheatre.co.uk). Puts up a mix of classical and contemporary plays with an emphasis on Irish productions. Counts Liam Neeson among its esteemed alums. Tickets M-W £14, concessions £11; Th-Sa £17. Open M-Sa 10am-7pm.

Waterfront Hall, 2 Lanyon Pl. (☎028 9066 8798; www.ulster-orchestra.org.uk). One of Belfast's newest concert centers, hosting a variety of performances throughout the year. Its concourse features visual arts exhibitions. The Ulster Orchestra plays concerts at Waterfront Hall. Tickets £8-24; student discounts available.

SPORTS

Take a cab to the **Odyssey Arena** to catch the **Coors Belfast Giants** battle it out on the ice with county competitors (☎028 9073 9074; www.belfastgiants.com). Football (soccer) fanatics can catch a game at the **Windsor Park** pitch on Donegall Ave. (☎028 9024 4198). Gaelic footballers run to **Andersonstown,** West Belfast, to enjoy Sunday afternoon matches. (Contact the Gaelic Athletic Association at ☎028 9038 3815; www.gaa.ie.) Belfast is crazy about horse racing; see the action down at the **Maze** (☎028 9262 1256; www.downroyal.com) in Lisburn. Just 10 mi. from Belfast, the racecourse has events throughout the year, including **Mirror May Day** and the **Ulster Harp Derby** in June. Ulster Rugby, former winners of the European Cup, play at **Ravenhill Stadium** (☎028 9049 3222).

PUBS AND NIGHTLIFE

Pubs in Belfast are the place to experience the city's *craic* (fun and spirit) and meet its colorful characters. Pubs were targets for sectarian violence at the height of the Troubles, so most are new or restored, although many retain their historic charm. Those in the city center and university area are now relatively safe. *Bushmills Irish Pub Guide*, by Sybil Taylor, relates the history of Belfast pubs (£7; available at local bookstores). For a full list of entertainment options, grab a free copy of *The Big List* or *Fate*, available in tourist centers, hostels, and certain restaurants and pubs.

The Duke of York, 7-11 Commercial Ct. (☎028 9024 1062). Old boxing venue turned Communist printing press; rebuilt after it was bombed by the IRA in the 60s. Now home to the city's largest selection of Irish whiskeys. Traditional Irish Th. Acoustic guitar F. Disco Sa. 18+. Cover Sa £5. Open M 11:30am-11pm, Tu-F 11:30am-1am, Sa 11:30am-2am, Su 2-9pm. Kitchen serves sandwiches and toasties daily until 2:30pm.

Madden's Bar, 74 Berry St. (☎028 9024 4114; www.maddensbarbelfast.com). You might hear Gaelic, and you'll definitely hear live music--if none is scheduled, a local musician or group will likely strike up. Beginners' language class W 8:30pm, followed by beginners' Irish step dancing 9:30pm. Beginners' piping class and open-mike pipers' session Th. Folk night downstairs, trad upstairs F. Blues, jazz, or electric folk downstairs, trad upstairs Sa. Open daily 11am-1am. Kitchen open M-F noon-2pm.

Katy Daly's Pub, 17 Ormeau Ave. (☎028 9032 5942; www.the-limelight.co.uk). Behind City Hall, head toward Queen's and take a left on Ormeau Ave. A stalwart of the Belfast music and nightlife scene. Students and young people, tourists included, congregate in the high-ceilinged, wood-paneled venue—a combined performance space and party spot. Pub quiz M. Student night and disco Tu. Headbangers' ball 1st Th of the month, school disco 2nd Th, live local act 3rd Th. Disco or rock/current F. Bar open M-F noon-1am, Sa 3pm-1am, Su 8pm-midnight. Kitchen open M-F noon-2:30pm.

Kelly's Cellars, 30 Bank St. (☎028 9024 6058). Turn right at St. Mary's Chapel, and you'll find Kelly's, the pub that the others are emulating. Its mottled plaster walls, sloping floors, and arched doorways give away its 1720 pedigree; Kelly's is Belfast's oldest pub. The bar is set up in a series of old casks, and there are several beers on tap. You'll never find it empty; locals and tourists, young and old, drink here together. When the stereo's off, it's because an impromptu performance has begun. Open daily 11:30am-11pm, until 1am on performance nights. MC/V.

The Botanic Inn, 23 Malone Rd. (☎028 9050 9740). Standing in as the unofficial student union, the hugely popular "Bot" is packed nightly with raucous groups of friends and diehard sports fans. Live music M. Choose-your-music Sa. 19+. Open M-Sa 11:30am-1am, Su noon-midnight. Kitchen open noon-8pm. MC/V.

The John Hewitt, 51 Lower Donegall St. (☎028 9023 3768; www.thejohnhewitt.com), around the corner from the Duke of York. Named after the late Ulster poet and run by the Unemployment Resource Centre. Half the profits go to the Centre, so drink up. Open-mike M. 18+. Open M-F 11:30am-1am, Sa noon-1am, Su 7pm-midnight.

The Crown, 46 Great Victoria St. (☎028 9027 9901). Interior shows off fine craftsmanship: gargoyles atop snug posts, stained-glass windows, etched mirrors behind the bar, lanterns, and scaly pillars. Long, granite bar is well-stocked. Open M-Sa 11:30am-midnight, Su 12:30-10:30pm. Kitchen open M-Sa noon-3pm, Su 12:30-5pm.

McHugh's, 29-31 Queen's Sq. (☎028 9050 9999; www.mchughsbar.com), across from the Custom House. Wrought-iron banisters, contemporary art, and a chess set of caricatured politicians are a few of the attractions of this historic pub, open since 1711. Local Belfast ale. Kick your party up a level by heading downstairs; basement events include Blackout and DJ Radio K on weekends. Trad W and Sa. Iggy and Paddy (guitar and keyboard) F and Su. 18+. Cover £5 for basement events. Open M and Su noon-midnight, Tu-Sa noon-1am. Kitchen open M-Sa 5-10pm, Su 5-9pm.

Mynt, 2-16 Dunbar St. (☎028 9023 4520; www.myntbelfast.com). Sleek, mod club. Casual cafe-bar in front leads to 2 floors of clubbing. £2 drinks M 9pm-midnight. Karaoke W. 2-for-1 drinks 9pm-midnight and gameshow F. 2-for-1 drinks 6-9pm and DJ Sa. Open M-Tu noon-1am, W-F and Su noon-3am, Sa noon-6am.

◢ DAYTRIP FROM BELFAST

▨ULSTER FOLK MUSEUM. Established by an act of Parliament in 1958, the Folk Museum aims to preserve the way of life of Ulster's farmers, weavers, and craftspeople. The museum contains over 30 buildings from the past three centuries divided into a town and rural area, the latter containing cottages from all nine Ulster counties, including the usually overlooked Monaghan, Cavan, and Donegal in the Republic. All but two of the buildings are transplanted originals. They have been artfully integrated into a landscape befitting their rural origins; the size of the property and the natural surroundings provide full immersion in the lost-in-time wonderland, creating a remarkable air of authenticity. Unobtrusive attendants in period costume stand nearby to answer questions. In Ballydugan Weaver's House, John the Weaver, a fourth-generation practitioner of his craft, operates the only working linen loom in Ireland. A fully functional printer's press still runs on Main St. Along with a corn mill and a sawmill from Fermanagh, the town is currently in the process of recreating a silent film

NORTHERN IRELAND

house from County Down. The museum hosts special events, including trad sessions, dance performances and workshops, storytelling festivals, and textile exhibitions. Call ahead for details. Go on a sunny day and leave time to wander. *(The museum stretches across 170 acres in the town of Holywood. Take the Bangor road (A2) 7 mi. east of Belfast. Buses and trains stop here on the way to Bangor. ☎028 9042 8428; www.uftm. org.uk. Open July-Sept. M-Sa 10am-6pm; Su 11am-6pm; Oct.-Feb. M-F 10am-4pm, Sa 10am-5pm; Su 11am-5pm; Mar.-June M-F 10am-5pm, Sa 10am-6pm, Su 11am-6pm. Each museum £5.50, concessions and children £3.50, families £11-15.50, disabled free. Combined admission £7, concessions and children £4, families £13-19. Group discounts and season passes available.)*

ARDS PENINSULA

NEWTOWNARDS   ☎(0)28

At the head of the Strangford Lough lies Newtownards, Ards Borough's capital city. This relatively quiet town, in the shadows of the iconic Scrabo Tower, serves as a convenient base for further exploration of the Ards Penninsula.

⌐ TRANSPORTATION

Buses: Station at 33 Regent St. (☎028 9181 2391; www.translink.co.uk), next to the tourist office. To **Belfast** (35min.; M-F every 10-30min., Sa-Su at least 1 per hr.; £2.40), **Bangor** (M-F every 15-30min., Sa every 30min., Su every 2hr.; £2.10), and **Ards Penin-sula** towns, including **Portaferry** (50min.; M-F 16 per day, Sa 12 per day, Su 5 per day; £4.70). A bus to **Comber, Downpatrick, Killyleagh,** and **Newcastle** runs July-Aug. All buses stop at Gibsons Ln. between Regent St. and Mill St.

Taxis: Rosevale Taxis (☎028 9182 1111). Wheelchair-accessible. **Ards Cabs** (☎028 9181 1617). Taxis also operate from the bus station on Regent St.

✦ ⁊ ORIENTATION AND PRACTICAL INFORMATION

Conway Square is home to the town hall and a small pedestrian area. Running north to south on either side of the square are **Church Street,** which becomes **Regent Street** and then **Frances Street** as it progresses southeast to Donaghadee, and **Mill Street,** which becomes **High Street.** Between the two main streets toward the tourist office is **Gibsons Lane,** where all buses stop and leave.

Tourist Information Centre: 31 Regent St. (☎028 9182 6846; www.ards-council.gov. uk). Books accommodations for £2 plus a 10% deposit. Stays open year-round and has ample information on all destinations in Northern Ireland. The office is also home to the **Ards Crafts** store, which sells the work of local artisans. Open July-Aug. M-Th 9am-5:15pm, F-Sa 9am-5:30pm; Sept.-June M-F 9:15am-5pm, Sa 9:30-5pm.

Banks: Northern Bank, 35 High St. (☎028 9004 5510). Open M 10am-5pm, Tu-W and F 10am-3:30pm, Th 9:30am-3:30pm, Sa 9:30am-12:30pm. **Ulster Bank,** 22 Frances St. (☎028 9181 3120). Open M-Tu and Th-F 9:30am-4:30pm, W 10am-4:30pm.

Beyond Tourism: Grafton Recruitment, 13 High St. (☎028 9182 6353).

Library and Internet Access: Newtownards Library, Regent St. (☎028 9181 4732), in Queen's Hall, a few doors from the tourist office. £1.50 per 30min. Open M-W 9:30am-8pm, Th 10am-5pm, F 9:30am-5pm, Sa 10am-4pm.

Police: John St. (☎028 9181 8080).

Pharmacy: Boots, 12-14 Regent St. (☎028 9181 3359). Open M-Sa 9am-6pm.

Hospital: Ards Community Hospital, Church St. (☎028 9181 2661), treats minor injuries. Open daily 9am-5pm. Emergencies and children under 4 go to **Ulster Hospital,** Upper Newtownards Rd. (☎028 9048 4511), in Dondonald.

Post Office: 8 Frances St. (☎084 5722 3344). Open M-F 9am-5:30pm, Sa 9am-12:30pm. **Bureau de change.** Also in the Asda supermarket at Ards Shopping Center (☎028 9182 0203). Open M-F 9am-5:30pm, Sa 9am-1pm. **Postcode:** BT23.

ACCOMMODATIONS

Despite its centrality and accessibility to the rest of the Ards, Newtownards itself does not have many places to stay. There is only one hotel in town, but a 5-10min. taxi or car ride outside the city yields a variety of B&Bs.

Woodview B&B, 8 Ballywalter Rd. (☎028 4278 8242; www.kingdomsofdown.com/woodview), in Greyabbey. Follow signs for Ballywalter; after passing the abbey, the easily missed driveway is on the left where the church wall ends. Peaceful B&B surrounded by farmland. Kind Mrs. Carson welcomes visitors to her home with a cup of tea and biscuits with homemade jam. Singles £25; doubles £50. Discount for stays of 3+ nights. ❸

Strangford Arms Hotel, 92 Church St. (☎028 9181 4141; www.strangfordhotel.com). A legitimate reason to indulge: the town's only hotel is sleek, lively, and centrally located. Singles £79; doubles £99. AmEx/MC/V. ❺

Rockhaven B&B, 79 Mountain Rd. (☎028 9182 3987; www.kingdomsofdown.com/rockhaven), a short drive toward Crawfordsburn (A2): pass the Leisure Centre and the subsequent traffic light, then make a right on Mountain Rd. Rockhaven is ½ mi. on the right. Secluded modern home with world art and 2 comfortable rooms. Laundry and free Wi-Fi. Book in advance during the summer. Singles £40; doubles £60. ❹

FOOD AND PUBS

For groceries, visit **Tesco** (☎028 9181 5290; open M-F 8am-9pm, Sa 8am-8pm, Su noon-6pm) or **Asda** (☎028 9181 5577; open M-Sa 8am-10pm, Su 1-6pm), in the **Ards Shopping Centre** off Church St. after the Strangford Arms Hotel. **Bakeries** and **fruit stands** line Regent St. between Frances St. and Conway Sq.

Shaw's Home Bakery, 26 Frances St. Indulgent treats are also wholesome: granary and wheat loaves (£1-3.50), filled soda farls (from 50p), apple squares, and wagon wheels (50p). Lunch specials like lasagna and meat pies £3. ❶

Regency Restaurant, 5A Regent St. (☎028 9181 4347). Family-oriented bakery and restaurant features grill options (£2.50-3.50) and sandwiches (£2-2.50) for takeaway. Try the "Ulster Fry" breakfast special—sausage, bacon, eggs, and bread (8-10:45am £2, 10:45am-4pm £4). Open M-F 8am-5pm, Sa 8am-6:15pm. ❶

Cafe Mocha, 23 High St. (☎028 9181 2616). Tranquil (and delicious) haven amid town square's bustle. Breakfasts £3-5; sandwiches £2.50-3.65; lunches £3.50-6.50. Open M-F 9am-4:30pm, Sa 9am-5pm, Su 9am-3pm. ❶

SIGHTS

The Ards Tourist Information Centre organizes occasional tours from Easter through September, ranging from historical guided walking tours of Newtownards to folklore-themed jaunts. Contact the tourist board or pick up the booklet *Experience Ards* for schedules.

MOUNT STEWART. Budget travelers needn't forswear luxury altogether. Soak up the grandeur of Mt. Stewart, most recently the estate of Lady Londonderry and Viscount Castlereagh and now a National Trust property. The home and gardens bear the mark of Lady Londonderry's decided and singular tastes: dessert plates each embossed with a flower from her garden, a crystal galleon chandelier floating above the window with a view to the lough, and a tribute garden to her youngest daughter, who used to be wheeled there in her pram for naps. History buffs will delight in the set of chairs used by participants of the 1814-15 Vienna Congress, and art lovers will marvel at John Singer Sargent portraits and a magnificent George Stubbs tribute to the family's prize-winning horse. Lady Londonderry spent days mapping and executing her extensive formal gardens to dramatic effect, and the lakeside gardens are just as scenic. *(Head away from Newtownards center on Frances St. At the roundabout, take the 2nd exit for the A21. After less than ½ mi., turn right for the A20. Follow the A20 for 5 mi. Mt. Stewart is signposted and will appear on your left. The bus to Portaferry stops at Mt. Stewart on request (£2.10). ☎028 4278 8387. Grounds and 1st floor of house wheelchair-accessible; video of upstairs tour available. House open Mar. and July.-Aug. daily noon-6pm; Apr. and Oct F-Su noon-6pm; May M and W-F 1-6pm, F-Su noon-6pm; June M-Th 1-6pm, F-Su noon-6pm; Sept. M and W-F noon-6pm. Formal Gardens open May-Sept. daily 10am-8pm; Oct. and Apr. daily 10am-6pm; from mid- to late Mar. Sa-Su and holidays 10am-4pm. Lakeside Gardens open daily 10am-sunset. Gardens and house £7, children £3.50, families £17.50. Gardens without house £5.35/2.70/13.40.)*

SCRABO TOWER AND COUNTRY PARK. This 200 ft. tower was erected in 1857. It was a memorial to Charles William Steward, third marquis of Londonderry (1778-1854), in commemoration of the struggles his tenants faced during the Great Famine. Although Charles Lanyon's elaborate plan for the tower was never realized due to lack of funding, it is one of Northern Ireland's most recognizable landmarks. Visitors enjoy exhibits on the tower's history and the park as well as an audio-visual presentation. Those who brave the steep spiral staircase leading to the top are rewarded with panoramic views. The adjoining park's quarries supplied the stone for **Greyabbey,** down the road (next page), and the Albert Memorial Clock in Belfast. Ramblers are welcome at Killynether Wood, home to many tree-lined walks. *(203A Scrabo Rd. Head north out of Newtownards, taking Blair Maine Rd. from the Newtownards Shopping Centre roundabout, then make a right at Scrabo Rd. and the 2nd left on that road. The bus to Comber also stops near the tower upon request (£2.10), but the walk is roughly 2 mi.; a taxi might be your best bet. ☎028 9181 1491. Tower open Apr.-Sept. M-Th and Sa-Su 10:30am-6pm. Grounds open year-round. Free.)*

🎵 🎭 ENTERTAINMENT AND FESTIVALS

Pick up a copy of the *Ards Arts Guide* at the tourist office or town hall and check out the season's performances, classes, and exhibitions. Throughout the year, the Newtownards Town Hall showcases artists' and craftsmen's work in upstairs and dowstairs galleries at the **Ards Arts Centre.** (☎028 9182 3131. Open M-Th 9am-5pm, F 9am-4:30pm, Sa 10am-4pm.) Festivals are common throughout the peninsula. For four days around mid-October, the **Ards International Guitar Festival** fills local cafes, bars, and halls with six-string sounds ranging from folk to flamenco. Late September presents the Ards-wide **Festival of the Peninsula,** when musicians, dramatists, dancers, and other performers come from Donegal, Scotland, and all over Ireland to entertain visitors.

🏞 OUTDOOR ACTIVITIES

In addition to the listings below, check out **Scrabo Tower and Country Park** (above), which includes wilderness walks in the surrounding grounds.

Castle Espie, 78 Ballydrain Rd. (☎028 9187 4146; www.wwt.org.uk), 6 mi. fror Newtownards (12 mi. from Belfast). From Newtownards, take the C2 toward Comb then the A22 toward Killyleagh. Take the 1st left at Ballydrain Rd. A wetlands prese that protects endangered birds and has the largest population of ducks, geese swans in Ireland. An emphasis on conservation and environmental education govern the site's woodland walks, children's activities, sustainable garden, and art gallery. Activity is especially high in fall and winter, when flocks migrate from the Arctic. Open July-Aug. M-F 10:30am-5:30pm, Sa-Su 11am-5:30pm; Sept.-Oct. M-F 10:30am-5pm, Sa-Su 11am-5:30pm; Nov.-Feb. M-F 11am-4pm, Sa-Su 11am-4:30pm; Mar.-June M-F 10:30am-5pm, Sa-Su 11am-5pm. £6, concessions £4.50, children £3, under 4 free.

Ark Open Farm (☎028 9182 0445; www.thearkopenfarm.co.uk). Visitors are encouraged to return to their agrarian roots. Milk a cow, feed red deer, pet a llama, or ride a pony. The working farm specializes in caring for over 80 rare species of domestic animals, including White Bud cows, which are believed to have been brought to Britain by the Romans. Open Apr.-Oct. M-Sa 10am-6pm, Su 2-6pm; Nov.-Mar. M-Sa 10am-5pm, Su 2-5pm. £4.20, concessions and children £3.20, under 3 free, families £15.

Movilla Trout Fishery (☎028 9181 3334; www.movillatroutfishery.co.uk), on Movilla Lake. 4 mi. down Donaghadee Rd. (B172) from Newtownards, on Movilla Rd.; make a right after Movilla HS; after 2 mi., the fishery will be signposted. Practice a little catch and release. 1 fish £12, 2 fish £14; catch and release £10. Open in summer daily 9am-dusk; in winter Th-Su 9am-dusk. Note that a rod license is necessary and can be purchased at **Country Sports** (☎028 9181 2585), across from the bus station at 48 Regent St. Open M-Th 9:30am-5:30pm, F 9:30am-7pm, Sa 9:30am-5pm.

Ards Leisure Centre, William St. (☎028 9181 2837; www.leisureards.org.uk). From Regent St., heading away from town hall, make a right on William St. and walk ¼ mi. to the compound. Go for a swim, play some badminton or ping-pong, or opt for one of the fitness classes (£4.50, concessions £2.70). Pool £2.80, concessions and children £1.80. Open M, W, F 9am-10pm, Tu and Th 7:30am-10pm, Sa 9am-6pm, Su 1-6pm.

DV Diving, 138 Mt. Stewart Rd. (Bangor office ☎028 9146 4671, dive center ☎9186 1686; www.dvdiving.co.uk). Leave Newtownards on Portaferry Rd. (E4), pass Ards Sailing Club after 3 mi., and make a left onto Mt. Stewart Rd.; it is 2 mi. down on the left. Leads dives in Belfast, Strangford Lough, and around the peninsula. Certified instructors provide equipment and offer diving qualification courses. £25 per dive; £40 full-equipment hire for the day. 1hr. introductory lessons £25.

Mike the Bike, 53 Frances St. (☎028 9181 1311). Land and lough lovers alike delight in Newtownards's double-whammy bike and kayak rental. Bikes £15 per day; kayaks £40 per day. Open M-W and F 9am-5pm.

DAYTRIP FROM NEWTOWNARDS

GREYABBEY. A few miles down from Mt. Stewart through the tiny town of Greyabbey lies its famous ruined **Cistercian abbey.** Founded in AD 1193 by Affreca, wife of Norman conqueror John de Courcey, the abbey was the first fully Gothic building in Ireland. The beautiful ruins have an adjoining cemetery and a medieval **Physic Garden,** where healing plants were cultivated to cure such common monastic ailments as flatulence, melancholy, and lunacy. Visitors can touch and taste the plants—and often take some home as well. A medieval vegetable garden grows elephant garlic, kale, and white carrots, which seasoned monks' meals before their orange counterparts came into existence 1500. (*#10 bus from Belfast's Oxford St. Bus Station to Portaferry goes via Greyabbey. A few ⋯ks from the town's crossroads at the bend in the road on Church St. ☎028 9181 1491. Open ⋯ept. M-Sa 9am-6pm, Su 1-6pm; Oct.-Mar. Sa 10am-4pm and by appointment. Free.*)

PORTAFERRY (PORT AN PHEIRE) ☎(0)28

Portaferry lies on the Ards Peninsula's southern tip, across the waters of Strangford Lough from the town of Strangford. Tourists stop in this seaside town to relax, explore the Ards, and enjoy Northern Ireland's largest aquarium.

🔲 TRANSPORTATION

Buses: Ulsterbuses from Belfast drop off visitors at The Square in the center of town (1½hr.; M-F 10 per day, Sa 9 per day, Su 4 per day; £5.70).

Ferries: Strangford Ferry (☎028 4488 1637) leaves Portaferry's waterfront at 15 and 45min. past the hour for **Strangford** (10min., £1.10), returning every 30min. Open M-F 7:45am-10:45pm, Sa 8:15am-11:15pm, Su 9:45am-10:45pm.

Taxis: JCS Taxis (☎077 6293 3210) or **Abbeydale Taxis** (☎028 9186 8181).

🔲🔲 ORIENTATION AND PRACTICAL INFORMATION

Tourist Information Centre: Castle St. (☎028 4272 9882). Beyond brochures and accommodations bookings (£2 plus 10% deposit), it also has a 12min. video on the medieval tower houses of County Down, precursors of the grand estates. Open July-Aug. M-Sa 10am-5:30pm, Su 1-6pm; Sept. and Easter-June M-Sa 10am-5pm, Su 2-6pm.

Library and Internet Access: 45 High St. (☎028 4272 8194). £1.50 per 30min. Open M and W 2-8pm, F 10am-1pm and 2-5pm, Sa 10am-1pm.

Launderette: Full Steam Ahead, 80-82 Church St. (☎028 4272 9333). Open M-W and F 9am-5pm, Th 9am-8pm, Sa 10am-12:30pm.

Hospital: Portaferry Health Centre, 10 High St. (☎028 4272 8429, after hours 275 511). Open M-F 8:30am-6pm.

Post Office: 28 The Square (☎028 4272 8201). **ATM** and **bureau de change.** Open M-W and F 9am-1pm and 2-5:30pm, Th 9am-1pm and 2-4:30pm, Sa 9am-12:30pm. **Postcode:** BT22.

🔲 ACCOMMODATIONS

🔲 **Portaferry Barholm Youth Hostel,** 11 The Strand (☎028 4272 9598), across from the ferry dock. With both hotel- and hostel-style accommodations, Barholm is a cut above standard hostels and is ideally located right on Strangford Lough, with a kitchen, conservatory dining room, and excellent views. Laundry. Free Wi-Fi. Wheelchair-accessible. Weekend reservations are necessary. Dorms £14; singles £18; doubles £40. ❷

Fiddler's Green B&B (☎028 4272 8393; info@fiddlersgreenportaferry.com), located above the pub on Church St. Hardwood floors, private baths, and airy rooms with matching bedsheets and curtains. Fills up on weekends; call ahead. Singles £22-25. ❸

Adair's Bed and Breakfast, 22 The Square (☎028 4272 8412). Rents sunny, tidy rooms in a 2-story house on The Square. The lounge has a TV, and breakfast is cooked to order. Singles £20; doubles £36. Cash only. ❷

🔲🔲 FOOD AND PUBS

Numerous fresh produce markets, butchers, and convenience stores are scattered around **High Street** and **The Square.** For opening hours, you can't beat **Spar,** 16 The Square. (☎028 4272 8957. Open M-Sa 6:30am-9pm, Su 7:30am-9pm.) Every Saturday from Easter to September, **Market House** in The Square welcomes a country market (9:30am-noon).

◪ **Fiddler's Green,** 10-14 Church St. (☎028 4272 8393). Publican Frank and his sons lead rowdy sing-alongs on weekends. As the wall proclaims, "There are no strangers here. Just friends who have not yet met." Quiz Night and supper Th 9:30pm (£2). Live folk, trad, rock, or pop F-Su. Open daily 11:30am-1:30am. ●

Ferry Grill, 3 High St. (☎028 4272 8448), across from Spar. Great for a quick bite: burgers and fries or fish and chips for under £3.50. Open M-Th noon-2pm and 4:30-8pm, F noon-9:30pm, Sa noon-2pm and 4:30-9:30pm, Su 4:30-9pm. ●

Rock Bakery, 24 The Square (☎028 4272 1239 or 4272 8239). Will send you off with pastries (from 50p), soda and wheaten farls (50p), and several varieties of loaves (£1-1.20). Open M-Sa 8:30am-5:30pm. ●

White Satin, 2-8 Castle St. (☎028 4272 9000), before Exploris and Portaferry Castle. Chinese food, including a wide selection of beef, chicken, duck, and seafood dishes. Entrees £5-7. Open M-Th 5-11pm, F-Su noon-11pm. ❷

Deli-licious, 1A Castle St. (☎028 4272 9911). A warm interior despite the generous heaps of ice cream (cones 80p-£1.70). Hot breakfasts (£3-5) and lunches (£3-6). Open daily 9am-3pm; during Gala Week 8am-8pm. ●

The Milestone, 1-3 Church St. (☎028 4272 9629). Locals gather for booze and billiards. Open daily 11:30am-12:30am. ●

The Coach Inn, 1-3 Anne St. Walk down Church St. away from The Square, and it's on your right. Pool table upstairs. Pints £2.50. Live folk 1st Su of the month 3-6pm, 2nd and 4th Tu 9:15pm. Open M-Sa 11:30am-11:30pm, Su 12:30pm-12:30am. ●

⊙ SIGHTS

◪**EXPLORIS.** Portaferry's pride and joy is Northern Ireland's only public aquarium and one of the UK's best. The journey begins in the shallow waters of Strangford Lough, proceeds through the Narrows, and ends in the depths of the Irish Sea, where one of Europe's largest tanks houses sharks and other large fish. The aquarium is renowned for its seal sanctuary, which rehabilitates injured or orphaned seals along the coastline. Outside Exploris, October through December is the best time for seal sightings; check out **Ballyquinton Point** and **Cloughy Rocks** or ask at the aquarium for the best spots. (☎028 4272 8062; www.exploris.org.uk. Open Apr.-Aug. M-F 10am-6pm, Sa 11am-6pm, Su noon-6pm; Sept.-Mar. M-F 10am-5pm, Sa 11am-5pm, Su 1-5pm. £7, concessions and children £4, under 4 free.)

WINDMILL HILL. Ascend Windmill Hill to see Portaferry's oldest windmill. At the top, a tablet points out items of interest on the horizon; on a clear day, you can see to Scotland and the Isle of Man as well as the pastureland and drumlins (hills created by glacier) surrounding Portaferry. (From The Square, take Meetinghouse St. until it turns into Windmill Hill. Climb until you see the windmill, about a 10min. walk.)

PORTAFERRY CASTLE. Much of the stone masonry of this 16th-century castle remains intact, although it's hard to imagine the castle in its previous incarnation: weeds and flowers grow out of the walls. Built to house the Savages, a prominent Ards family, the castle was occupied for nearly three centuries until 1765. (Down from The Square on Castle St. Open July-Aug. M-Sa 10am-5:30pm, Su 1-6pm; Sept. and Easter-June M-Sa 10am-5pm, Su 2-6pm.)

❉ FESTIVALS

The second or third week of July brings the town-wide celebration **Gala Week:** a festival of floats, football matches, and paper boat races. Crowds, performers, and general revelry fill the streets (www.portaferrygala.com). From Easter to September, the tourist office opens the attic for **Art in the Loft,** displaying local art from expert crafts to elementary-school sketches. Free children's workshops take place during Easter and Gala Week.

DAYTRIP FROM PORTAFERRY

CASTLE WARD. Across the lough in Strangford is 18th-century Castle Ward, a stone mansion set among trees. Its grounds, now maintained by the National Trust, include a farmyard, a children's Victorian play center, and the surrounding forest. (Take the ferry across the lough. From Strangford, take the main road, the A25 to Downpatrick, by car or on foot. Castle Ward is signposted about 1 mi. away. ☎028 4488 1204; www.nationaltrust.org.uk. Open Mar.-Sept. daily 1-6pm. Hours variable; call or check online for details. Grounds open Apr.-Sept. daily 10am-8pm; Oct.-Mar. 10am-4pm. £2.70. Grounds £4.80.)

GLENS OF ANTRIM

During the Ice Age, glaciers plowed through the coastline northeast of Antrim, leaving nine deep scars in the mountains. Over the years, water collected in these valleys, nourishing trees, ferns, and other flora not usually found in Ireland. The A2 coastal road connects the mouths of these glens and provides entry to roads inland. Still relatively unspoiled and much less touristed than the northern coast, the nine glens are rich in lore and distinct in character. While the road offers stunning coastal vistas, the glens are best explored on daytrips inland from the coastal villages of Glenarm, Waterfoot, and Cushendall.

TRANSPORTATION

Most visitors travel the glens by car, but two **Ulsterbus** routes serve the area year-round (Belfast ☎028 9032 0011; Larne ☎028 2827 2345). Bus #150 runs between Ballymena and Cushendun (M-F 6 per day, Sa 4 per day; £5.70) with intermediate stops at Waterfoot and Cushendall (M-F 6 per day, Sa 3 per day; £4.70). The **Antrim Coaster** (#252) runs year-round, stopping at every town on the road from Belfast to Coleraine (July-Sept. M-Sa 2 per day, Su 1 per day; Nov.-June M-Sa 2 per day; £4.10 to Larne, £9.50 to Coleraine). Cycling the glens is scenic and rewarding. G. McAlister Cycles, 16 Glenleary Rd., in Coleraine, rents **bikes** for £10 per day. (☎028 7035 8443. Open M-Sa 9am-6pm. Cash only.) The coastal road from Ballygally to Cushendun is relatively flat. Once the road passes Cushendun, however, it becomes hilly enough to make even motorists groan, not to mention bikers. Crossroads are reportedly the best places to find a lift, although *Let's Go* never recommends hitchhiking.

CUSHENDALL (BUN ABHANN DALLA) ☎(0)28

Cushendall is nicknamed the "Capital of the Glens," thanks to its natural wonders. The four streets in the town center house a variety of goods, services, and pubs unavailable anywhere else in the region. The town's proximity to Glenaan, Glenariff, Glenballyeamon, Glencorp, and Glendun reinforces its importance as a commercial center. Unfortunately, the closing of its only hostel means that budget travelers are diverted to the camping barn outside of town.

TRANSPORTATION. Ulsterbus (☎028 9066 6630) stops at the Mill St. tourist office, where current bus times are posted. Bus #252 (a.k.a. the **Antrim Coaster**) goes coastal from Belfast to Coleraine, stopping in Cushendall and most everywhere else. (July-Sept. daily 1 per day; Oct.-June M-Sa 1 per day). Bus #150 stops in Cushendall along its route between Cushendun and Ballyman, also servicing Glenariff and Waterfoot (M-F 6 per day, Sa 4 per day; £4.70-5.70).

███ **ORIENTATION AND PRACTICAL INFORMATION.** The busiest section of Cushendall is its crossroads. From the center of town, **Mill Street** turns into **Chapel Road** and heads northwest toward Ballycastle; **Shore Road** extends south toward Glenarm and Larne. On the north side of town, **High Street** leads uphill from **Bridge Road,** a section of the Coast Road (an extension of the A2) that continues toward the sea at Waterfoot.

The **tourist office,** 25 Mill St., is near the bus stop at the northern (Cushendun) end of town. (☎028 2177 1180. Open from mid-June to mid-Sept. M-F 10am-1pm and 2-5pm, Sa 10am-1pm; Oct.-May Tu-Su 10am-1pm.) **Northern Bank,** 5 Shore Rd., has a 24hr. **ATM.** (☎0845 602 6521. Open M 9:30am-12:30pm and 1:30-5pm, Tu-F 10am-12:30pm and 1:30-3:30pm.) **O'Neill's,** 25 Mill St., sells fishing and hiking gear. (☎028 2177 2009. Open July-Aug. M-Sa 9:30am-6pm, Su 12:30-4pm; Sept.-June M and W-Sa 9:30am-6pm, Tu 9:30am-1pm.) The **library** across from the tourist office has Internet access for £1.50 per 30min. (☎028 2177 1297. Open Tu 2-8pm, Th and Sa 10am-1pm and 2-5pm). **Numark Pharmacist** is on 8 Mill St. (☎028 2177 1523. Open M-Sa 9am-6pm.) The **post office** is inside the Spar on Coast Rd. (☎028 2177 1201. Open M and W-F 9am-1pm and 2-5:30pm, Tu and Sa 9am-12:30pm.) **Postcode:** BT44.

███ **ACCOMMODATIONS AND CAMPING.** ▓**Ballyeamon Barn ❶,** 6 mi. south of town on the B14 at 127 Ballyeamon Rd., is Cushendall's last bastion of budget travel. The barn has views of Glenariff Forest Park, and owner Liz is a professional storyteller happy to regale visitors with ghost stories and fairy tales. A happy community of guests cooks together in the kitchen, shares one large partitioned dormitory, and makes its own evening fun at the barn or in the village. It's far from town but near the Moyle Way and well worth the trip. Bus #150 coming from Cargan will stop across the field. (☎028 2175 8451 or 2175 8699; www.ballyeamonbarn.com. Internet £1 per 30min. Call for pickup. Dorms £12.) A bevy of B&Bs surrounds Cushendall, but the majority are just south of town. Overlooking the sea and surrounded by grazing cows, **Glendale ❸,** 46 Coast Rd., has huge rooms and colorful company. Tea, coffee, candy, and biscuits are in each room. (☎028 2177 1495. Internet access. Singles £25; doubles £40. MC/V.) **Mountain View ❸,** 1 Kilnadore Rd., a few minutes' walk out of town, has four smallish but comfortable rooms with bath. (☎028 2177 1246. Doubles £45.) The **Central B&B ❸,** 7 Bridge St., is the most central choice. (☎028 2177 1730. All rooms with bath. Singles £25; doubles £50. Cash only.) The town's caravan parks aren't particularly well suited to tents, but campers in need can find a bit of earth at **Cushendall Caravan Park ❶,** 62 Coast Rd. (☎028 2177 1699. No showers. Laundry. Open Apr.-Oct. £9; caravan sites with electricity £17.50.)

███ **FOOD AND PUBS.** **Arthur's Tea and Coffee Warehouse ❶,** 6 Shore Rd., is much cheerier than its name portends. The cafe serves simple, fresh sandwiches for £4 and full breakfasts for £2.75. (☎028 2177 1627. Open daily July-Aug. 9am-5pm; Oct.-June 9am-4pm.) Renowned throughout the Glens for its big portions of delicious fish and meat dishes, **Harry's Restaurant ❷,** 10-12 Mill St., serves upscale pub grub (£4-8) by day and big dinners by night. (☎028 2177 2022. Dinner entrees £10-12.50. Kitchen open daily noon-9pm.) One of the Isles' best pubs for Irish music, ▓**Joe McCollam's (Johnny Joe's),** 23 Mill St., packs in crowds for ballads, fiddle-playing, and slurred limerick recitals. (☎028 2177 1992. Opens between 3 and 7pm; last call at midnight; drinkers get booted out at 1:30am.) **An Camán** ("hurling bat"), 5 Bridge St., at the foot of the bridge, is marked on one side of the building by a giant mural of a hurler. (☎028 2177 1293. Live music or disco W and F-Su. Open daily 11:30am-1:30am.)

⊡ 🏃 SIGHTS AND OUTDOOR ACTIVITIES. The sandstone **Curfew Tower** in the center of town, on the corner of Mill St. and High St., was built in 1817 by the eccentric, slightly paranoid Francis Turley. This Cushendall landlord made a fortune in China; when he returned to Ireland, he built the tower based on a Chinese design, complete with openings for pouring boiling oil onto would-be robbers. The bell on the tower was co-opted by the British forces during the Irish Revolution and sounded at the designated curfew, at which time Catholics were confined indoors and under surveillance—hence the tower's name. Today, the structure is privately owned and closed to the public. The austere ruins of **Layde Church,** a medieval friary, lie along Layde Rd. Its ruins are noteworthy for their sprawling burial ground, which extends to the edge of the cliff. The misplaced dirt for burials has raised the ground by about a meter, evident in the church's low portals and windows. The graveyard includes **Cross Na Nagan,** an unusual pagan rai stone used for marriage ceremonies and later Christianized into a Celtic cross. Sloping down toward the cliffside, the site has spectacular seaviews of Scotland, as do the seaside walks that begin at its car park. (Open 24hr. Free.) **Tieveragh Hill,** half a mile up High St., is known locally as Faery Hill, inspired by the otherworldly "little people" who supposedly reside in the area. Although it would make a fine patch of farmland, locals have honored the "wee folk" and let the hedgerows grow. The summit of similarly supernatural **Lurige-than Hill,** more commonly "Lurig Mountain," flattens out 1153 ft. over town. **Oisín's Grave** (OH-shans) is a few miles away on the lower slopes of Tievebul-liagh Mountain. Actually a Neolithic burial cairn dating from around 4000 BC, it is linked by tradition with the Ulster warrior-bard Oisín, who was buried here around AD 300. The A2 leads north from Cushendall toward Ballymoney and the lower slopes of Tievebulliagh, where a sign points to the grave.

The steep walk up the southern slope of **Glenaan** rewards travelers with views of the lush valley. **Ardclinis Outdoor Adventure,** in back of the house at 11 High St., rents outdoor equipment and gives advice for canoeing, rafting, and other outdoor pursuits. Besides leading group outings in kayaking and rock climbing, they also guide coasteering trips (May-Oct.), which involve jump-ing, climbing, swimming, and negotiating the coastline by any means neces-sary. (☎028 2177 1340; www.ardclinis.com. Wetsuits £5-10 per day. Coasteer-ing about £18 per person; requires a group of 10.) The **Walk the Glens** group leads occasional (usually monthly) walks around the area for a nominal fee. (Contact the Development Office at ☎028 2177 1378.) The second week of June hails the **Glens Walking Festival,** when the Walk the Glens group leads cheerful ramblers in a series of Glens treks for about £5. The second week of August brings the **Heart of the Glens** festival, a 10-day affair with parades, sporting events, performances and workshops. The festival also sponsors the **Lurig Run,** during which locals have clocked records of 26min. (men) and 34min. (women) racing up the hill—the less eager amble up in about 45min.

CUSHENDUN (COIS ABHAINN DUINE)   ☎(0)28

In 1954, the National Trust bought the minuscule seaside village of Cushendun, 5 mi. north of Cushendall on the A2, to preserve its unusual whitewashed, black-shuttered buildings. The **Maud Cottages** lining the main street were built by Lord Cushendun for his wife in 1925. Along with its Cornish architecture, the town also harbors some natural structures of note—murky **caves** carved into the red cliffs can be explored along the beach. (Head past Mace over the bridge and tal the first right. Walk past the large condominium block and find the caves on yo right.) The less intrepid will enjoy a relaxing meander around the historic monuments in town and in nearby Glendun, a preserved village and another fine example of Cornish architecture. The **riverside footpath,** marked from the Tea Room car park and the bridge, follows the River Dun for a stretch before depositing visitors at Church Ln. Watch for otters, kingfishers, and herons. During the second week of July, Cushendun swarms with sports fans for the annual **Sports Week.** In the fields northwest of town (toward Ballycastle), various games are played all week; the highlight is the big hurling match that takes place on the last day.

The large rooms at **Cloneymore B&B ❸,** 103 Knocknacarry Rd., are ensuite and wheelchair-accessible. The house itself borders a sheep pasture. (☎028 2176 1443 or 077 4061 3604. Singles £35; doubles £50. Cash only.) **Cushendun Caravan Park ❶,** 14 Glendun Rd., 150 ft. from the end of the beach, will soon open a game room with a TV and DVD player. (☎028 2176 1254. Laundry. Open Apr.-Oct. Tent sites for 2 £9; family sites £13; caravan site with electricity £17.50.) The town's most popular attraction is also its only real pub: **Mary McBride's,** 2 Main St., used to be in the *Guinness Book of World Records* as the smallest bar in Europe. The original wee bar (where there's a portrait of Mary herself looking rather fierce) has been expanded to create a lounge for viewing sports matches. Cushendun's characters leave the bar only to move to the lounge, where musicians play. (☎028 2176 1511. Music Su. Bar open July-Aug. daily noon-1am; Sept.-Oct and Apr. M-Th noon-11pm, F-Su noon-1am; Nov.-Mar. M-Th 5pm-1am, F-Su noon-1am. Kitchen open July-Aug. daily 12:30-8:30pm; Nov.-Mar. F-Su 12:30-7pm; Apr.-June daily 12:30-7pm.) **Cushendun Tea Rooms ❷,** across the street, serves cafe fare while patrons relax on a green lawn. (☎028 2176 1506. Sandwiches £2.50. Entrees £6-10. Open Apr.-Sept. daily 10am-6pm; Oct.-Mar. F-Su 10am-6pm.) **Bus** #150 (M-F 6 per day, Sa 4 per day) pauses on the coast road at Cushendun's **Mace** grocery shop, which houses a **post office** and an **ATM,** on its way to Waterfoot via Cushendall. (☎028 2176 1355.)

CAUSEWAY COAST ☎(0)28

The coastline between Cushendun and Ballycastle is one of the most famous stretches in Ireland. Although motorists and other travelers seeking a speedy trip between the two towns opt for the wide A2, this road seems tame compared with its coastal counterpart, the scenic (read: occasionally terrifying) **Torr Road.** This narrow coastal road affords incomparable views and sheer cliffs but also demands tricky maneuvers around steep corners and tight squeezes with oncoming traffic. The most famous vista is **Torr Head,** the site of many ancient forts and the closest point on the isle to the Scottish coast, 12 mi. away. Past Torr Head is **Murlough Bay,** protected by the National Trust, where a stunning landscape hides the remains of the medieval church **Drumnakill,** once a pagan holy site. A small gravel car park above the bay leads to the north and east vistas. The east vista is accessible by car and thus more crowded than the pedestrian-only north vista. The road then bumps on to **Fair Head,** 7 mi. north of Cushendun and 3 mi. east of Ballycastle. This rocky, heather-covered headland winds past several lakes, including **Lough na Cranagh;** in its middle sits a crannog, an island built by Bronze Age Celts as a fortified dwelling for elite chieftains. Bikes should be left at the hostel: the area is steep and slippery, and it's only a 1hr. hike from Ballycastle.

The more direct A2, the official bus route, does have its advantages—the road passes its own set of attractions and is more manageable for cyclists, with only one long climb and an even longer descent from the boggy plain. Sparse traffic makes hitching impossible. A few miles northeast of Cushendun, a high hollow contains a vanishing lake called **Loughareema** (or **Faery Lough**), which during the summer can appear and disappear into the bog in less than a day. When it's full, the lake teems with fish. When it empties, the fish take refuge in caverns beneath the limestone. Locals claim that the lough is still haunted by the ghost of a coachman named Colonel McNeill, who misjudged the shifting water levels and drowned along with his horses. Farther along, part of the plain was drained and planted with evergreens. The result is the secluded **Ballypatrick Forest,** with a scenic drive and pleasant, pine-scented walks. Before Ballycastle town and roughly 1 mi. into the woods, **Ballycastle Forest** contains the eminently climbable 1695 ft. **Knocklayde Mountain.**

RATHLIN ISLAND   ☎(0)28

Six miles off the coast of Ballycastle lies Rathlin Island (Reachlainn, "Fort of the Sea"), famous for its flower-covered cliffs and undulating hills. Head south to **Rue Lighthouse** for views of seals on the rocks by New Quay or to see the large expanse of rock that is **Fair Head.** Walking eastward takes you to the island's Protestant and Catholic churches or to the **East Lighthouse.** Another lighthouse watches over the west side of the island, where the **Seabird Centre** is Rathlin's main attraction. Offshore sea stacks and monolithic rock formations are home to thousands of seabirds like puffins, guillemots, razorbills, kittiwakes, and fulmars. (☎028 9049 1547. Open Apr.-Aug. Free.)

    Kinramer Cottage Camping Barn ❶, 2 mi. west from the harbor, can tuck 14 people into two sleeping areas, but bring your own linens. Pillows and pillowcases are provided. (☎028 2076 3948. £5 per person.) **Bruce's Kitchen ❶,** across the street from the island's boathouse, caters to hungry, chilly visitors with sandwiches (£2), toasties (£2), burgers (£1.90-2.20), and chips for £1.20. (☎028 2076 3981. Open in summer daily 10:30am-8pm.)

    Ferries, operated by Rathlin Ballycastle Ferry, 18 Bayview Rd., run between the island and Ballycastle on the mainland. (☎028 2076 9299; www.rathlinballycastleferry.com. Reserve ahead. 5 per day; £10, ages 5-16 £5, under 5 free, bicycle £2.60.) To reach Ballycastle, take Antrim Coaster #131 from southern towns, #178 from western towns, or #252 from either direction. **Buses,** like the **Bird Bus,** meet tourists at the ferry slip for a run to the West Lighthouse and Seabird Centre and occasionally for other routes. (Apr.-Oct. £3.) The **Boathouse Visitor Center** is housed in a 19th-century boathouse signposted a quarter-mile east of the harbor. (☎028 2076 3951. Open May-Aug. daily 10:30am-4pm.)

COUNTY DERRY   ☎(0)28

The A2 coastal road connects Counties Antrim and Derry, providing an easily accessible journey for visitors. Seaside novelties replace natural wonders with the carnival lights of Portrush and Portstewart, and the road finally terminates at Derry/Londonderry, the North's second-largest city.

DERRY/LONDONDERRY

Modern Derry/Londonderry is trying to cast off the legacy of its political Troubles with much success. Although the landscape was razed by years of bombings, recent years have been relatively peaceful. Today's rebuilt city is beautiful and intimate with a cosmopolitan vibe.

▣ TRANSPORTATION

Flights: Eglinton/Derry Airport, Eglinton (☎028 7181 0784). 4 mi. from Derry. to **Bristol, Dublin, Edinburgh, Glasgow, Liverpool, London-Stansted,** and **Man**

The **AIRporter** (☎028 7126 9996; www.airporter.co.uk) runs from Quayside Shopping Centre to Belfast International and Belfast City airports. M-F 12 per day, Sa-Su 7 per day. £17.50, under 16 £8.75, seniors free, couples £27.50, families £40.

Trains: Duke St., Waterside (☎028 7134 2228), on the east bank. A free **Rail-Link bus** connects the bus station to the train station; call the rail or bus station to find the corresponding bus. Trains from Derry go to: **Belfast** via **Ballymena, Ballymoney, Castlerock,** and **Coleraine** (2hr.; M-Sa 9 per day, Su 4 per day; £10.50, children £5.25). Connections may be made from Coleraine to **Portrush** (Derry to Portrush £8.40, children £4.20). Bus and train combo passes £15 per day, July-Aug. families £18.50 per day.

Buses: Most stop at the Ulsterbus depot on Foyle St., between the walled city and the river. Office open M-Sa 5:30am-6pm, Su 8am-7pm. Ulsterbus (☎028 7126 2261) serves destinations in the North and a few in the Republic. #212 and 273 to **Belfast** (1-3hr., at least every 2hr., £9.40). Translink help line ☎028 9066 6630.

Cabs: Derry Taxis (☎028 7126 0247). **Quayside Taxis** (☎028 7136 3636).

> **?** **TROUBLED LANGUAGE.** Originally christened Doire, meaning "oak grove," the city's name was anglicized to Derry and finally to Londonderry. The city's label remains a source of contention, as the minority Protestant population uses the official title, while many Republicans and informal Protestants refer to the city as Derry. Even in the city center, some signs refer to Derry or Londonderry without any consistency.

🛈 PRACTICAL INFORMATION

Tourist Information Centre: 44 Foyle St. (☎028 7126 7284; www.derryvisitor.com), inside the Derry Visitor and Convention Bureau. Ask for the free *Derry Visitor's Guide* and *Derry Visitor's Map.* Books accommodations (£2 plus a 10% deposit), exchanges currency, and runs guided walking tours of the city. 24hr. computerized info kiosk. Open July-Sept. M-F 9am-7pm, Sa 10am-6pm, Su 10am-5pm; Oct. and Mar.-June M-F 9am-5pm, Sa 10am-5pm; Nov.-Feb. M-F 9am-5pm.

Tours: Multiple companies lead tours of Derry/Londonderry:

■**Free Derry Tours** (☎077 9328 5972; www.freederry.net). Cover the monuments and murals of the Bogside, the city walls, and the Fountain area. Local Republicans who have been affected by the city's conflicts introduce visitors to Derry/Londonderry's fraught politics. Tours depart the Museum of Free Derry on Rossville St. daily at 10am, 2pm, sometimes 4pm. Special interest tours can be arranged. Book ahead in summer. From £5, concessions £4.

The Derry Visitor and Convention Bureau Guided Tours (☎028 7126 7284; www.derryvisitor.com). Take visitors around the city walls, stopping at various sights like St. Columb's Cathedral. Other tours follow narratives ranging from the 1689 siege to emigration. Tours leave from the TIC July-Aug. M-F 11:15am, 2:30pm; Sept.-June M-F 11:15am. 1hr. £6, students and seniors £5.

City Tours, 11 Carlisle Rd. (☎028 7127 1996; www.irishtourguides.com). Lace your walking shoes and pound the pavement for a 2hr. historical tour. Literary tours or tours of the Sperrins (the city's natural surroundings) can be arranged. Tours depart daily at 10am, noon, 2pm. From £4.

Banks: Bank of Ireland, Shipquay St. (☎028 7126 4992). Open M-Tu and Th-F 9:30am-4:30pm, W 10am-4:30pm. **Northern Bank,** Guildhall Sq. (☎028 7126 5333). Open M-W and F 10am-3:30pm, Th 9:30am-5pm, Sa 9:30am-12:30pm. 24hr. **ATMs.**

Libraries and Internet Access: Central Library, 35 Foyle St. (☎028 7127 2310). Internet £3 per hr. Open M and Th 8:30am-8pm, Tu-W 8:30am-5:30pm, Sa 9:15am-5pm. ^ame rate at **Waterside Library,** 23 Glendermot Rd. (☎028 7134 2963). Open M and 9:15am-8pm, Tu and Th 9:15am-5:30pm, Sa 9:15am-1pm.

e: Strand Rd. (☎028 7136 7337).

Hospital: Altnagelvin Hospital, Glenshane Rd. (☎028 7134 5171). Cross the bridge to the Waterside and follow the signs.

Post Office: 3 Custom House St. (☎028 7136 2563). Open M-F 9am-5:30pm, Sa 9am-12:30pm. Another is at The Diamond, inside the city wall. Unless addressed to 3 Custom House St., Poste Restante letters will go to the **Postal Sorting Office** (☎028 7136 2577), on the corner of Great James and Little James St. **Postcode:** BT48.

ACCOMMODATIONS

Derry City Independent Hostel, 44 Great James St. (☎028 7137 7989 or 7128 0280). With so much imagination and expense invested in the decor of the 2 buildings, it's little wonder so many hostelers flock to fill Steve and Kylie's 70 beds year after year. Friendly staffers greet the crowds with a rundown of Derry's offerings, inspiring a laid-back, sociable vibe. Breakfast included; all-you-can-eat barbecues for £3. Free Internet. Dorms £12; doubles £36. 5 nights for the price of 4. ❶

Paddy's Palace, 1 Woodleigh Terr. (☎028 7130 9051; www.paddyspalace.com). Cheap stay and clean facilities near the city center. Pool table in lounge. Continental breakfast included. Laundry. Free Internet. Aug. 6-bed dorms £15; Sept.-July £12. Cash only. ❶

The Saddler's House, 36 Great James St. (☎028 7126 9691; www.thesaddlershouse.com). Kind, knowledgeable owners welcome guests into their lovely Victorian home. Breakfast included. Free Internet. Singles £30-45; doubles £50-60. MC/V. ❸

Abbey B&B, 4 Abbey St. (☎028 7127 9000 or 077 2527 7864; www.abbeyaccommodation.com). In the heart of the Bogside neighborhood near the murals. Greets visitors with coffee and spacious peach rooms. Ensuite rooms. Free Wi-Fi. Wheelchair-accessible. Singles £45; doubles £60; family rooms £80. MC/V. ❹

FOOD

Groceries are available at **Tesco,** in the Quayside Shopping Centre (☎028 7137 4400. Open M-F 9am-9pm, Sa 8:30am-8pm, Su 1-6pm.) The first Saturday of each month brings a local and organic foods market to **Guildhall Square** (9am-3pm).

Love Olive, 41 William St. (☎028 7126 7459). 90-100 varieties of cheese and 15-20 types of olives. Daily lunch specials like salads and panini run £2.50-3. Lasagna (£2.20), soups (£1.20), and gluten-free items. Open M-Sa 9am-6pm. MC/V. ❶

The Sandwich Co., The Diamond (☎028 7137 2500), 61 Strand Rd., (☎028 7126 6771), and 33 Spencer Rd., Waterside (☎028 7131 3171). Trio of eateries lets customers design their own from a selection of breads and fillings. Eat at the Strand location to avoid queues. Sandwiches £2.25-4.70. Open M-F 8am-5pm, Sa 8:30-5pm. ❶

Ice Wharf/Lloyd's No. 1 Bar, 22-24 Strand Rd., across from The Strand nightclub. Part of the Wetherspoon's pub chain. Plenty of food and drink promos: 2 meals for £7 all day; burger, chips, and beer £4 all day; carvery roast £6 Su noon-9pm. Breakfast £2 before noon. Open M-W and Su 9am-midnight, Th-Sa 9am-1am. ❶

Danano, 2-4 Lower Clarendon St. (☎028 7126 6646). Watch chefs shove tasty pizzas and confused lobsters into the only wood-burning oven in Northern Ireland at this modern Italian eatery. Adjoining takeaway offers pizzas (£3.80-5.70), pastas (£4.20-6), and salads (£2.40-4) for slightly less. Open daily 5-11pm. ❶

Exchange, Queens Quay (☎028 7127 3990), down Great James St. toward the River Foyle, right at the Derry City Hotel. Trendy eatery with private booths. Lunch dishes (like *chicken escalope*) £6-7. Dinner (like grilled sea bass) £11-18. Many vegetarian options. Open M-Sa noon-2:30pm and 5:30-10pm, Su 4-9pm. ❸

Spice, 162 Spencer Rd. (☎028 7134 4875), on the east bank. Cross Craigavon Bridge and continue as it turns into Spencer. Try sea bass with herby lentils and lemon yogurt.

NORTHERN IRELAND

Appetizers £3-7; lunch £4-8; dinner £11-19. Vegetarian and vegan menu has £4 appetizers and £12 entrees. Open Tu-F 12:30-2:30pm and 5:30-10pm, Sa 5-10:30pm. ❷

👁 SIGHTS

🏛CITY WALLS. Derry's city walls, 18 ft. high and 20 ft. thick, were erected between 1614 and 1619. The mile-long periphery has never been breached, hence the Protestant nickname "the Maiden City." However, such resilience did not save the city from danger; during the Siege of 1689, 600 mortar bombs sent from the nearby hills by fleeing English King James II and his brigade of Catholic Frenchmen went over what they could not go through, decimating the 30,000 Protestants crowded inside. Seven **cannons**—donated by Queen Elizabeth I and the London Guilds who "acquired" the city during the Ulster Plantation—stand along the northeast wall between Magazine and Shipquay Gates. A plaque marks the water level in the days when the Foyle ran along the walls (it now flows 300 ft. away). The 1½ mi. walk around the city walls leads past most of Derry's best-known sights, including the raised portion of the stone wall past New Gate that shields St. Columb's Cathedral, the symbolic focus of the city's Protestant defenders. The same area also affords a perfect view of the red-, white-, and blue-painted Unionist **Fountain** neighborhood. Stuck in the center of the southwest wall, **Bishop's Gate** received an ornate face-lift in 1789, commemorating the victory of Protestant William of Orange 100 years earlier. The southwest corner supports **Roaring Meg,** a massive cannon donated by London fishmongers in 1642 and used in the 1689 siege. This corner commands a sprawling view of the **Bogside** neighborhood and a look at some of the murals, which are best accessed from **Butcher's Gate.** Just south of Butcher's Gate, the **Memorial Hall** is the traditional clubhouse of the Apprentice Boys, a prominent Protestant fraternity that aims to commemorate the seige of Derry.

TOWER MUSEUM. Just inside the City Walls,, the Tower Museum tells Derry's history from monastic settlement to trade capital by way of a winding tour. Descend the floors of the tower itself to track the demise of a Spanish ship in the Armada fleet that sank off Derry's coast and was recently excavated by archaeologists. *(Union Hall Pl. ☎028 7137 2411. Open June-Sept. M-Sa 10am-5pm, Su 10am-noon; Oct.-May Tu-Sa 10am-5pm. £4, concessions and children £2.50, families £9.)*

MUSEUM OF FREE DERRY. Covering the Catholic civil-rights struggle in Northern Ireland up until Bloody Sunday, the museum displays artifacts from civil-rights marches, the Battle of the Bogside, internment, Free Derry, and of course Bloody Sunday. The Free Derry tours depart from here (see **Tours,** p. 694). The museum is across Rossville St. from the Bloody Sunday monument. *(55 Glenfada Park ☎028 7136 0880; www.museumoffreederry.org. Open Apr.-Sept. M-F 9:30am-4:30pm, Sa-Su 1-4pm; Sept.-Mar. M-F 9:30am-4:30pm. £3, concessions and children £2)*

SAINT COLUMB'S CATHEDRAL. Named after St. Columb, whose monastery was the foundation on which Derry was built, the cathedral was constructed between 1628 and 1633 and was the first Protestant cathedral in Britain or Ireland (all older ones were confiscated Catholic cathedrals). The original wood steeple burned down after being struck by lightning, while the second (a leaden and rounded replacement) was smelted into bullets and cannonballs during the Great Siege of 1689. The same fate did not befall the cathedral itself, as it was designed to double as a fort with 6 in. thick walls and a walkway for musketeers to shoot from the spire. The foyer still holds the mortar shell that delivered the terms of surrender directly to the courtyard. The roughly hewn stone interior holds an exquisite Killybegs altar carpet, an extravagant bishop's chair dating from 1630, and 214 hand-carved Derry-oak pews, no two of which are the same. A small museum in the **chapter house** displays the original locks along with keys of the four main city gates and other relics. The tombstones lying flat on the ground in the **graveyard** outside were leveled during the siege to protect the graves from Jacobite cannonballs. The small **Mound of Martyrs,** in the back left corner toward the walls, contains the 5000 dead previously buried in the cellars of the nearby houses, transplanted here during the city's redesigning efforts. *(London St., off Bishop St. in the southwest corner of the city. ☎028 7126 7313; www.stcolumbscathedral.org. Open M-Sa 9am-5pm. Tours 30-60min. Services July-Aug. M-F 10:30am, Su 8, 11am; Sept.-June M-F 10:30am, Su 8, 11am, 4pm. £3.)*

PUBS AND CLUBS

Most pubs line Waterloo St. and the Strand, although new ones are popping up within the city walls. Trad and rock are available almost any night of the week, and pubs stay lively until the 1am closing time.

Peadar O'Donnell's, 53 Waterloo St. (☎028 7137 2138). Named for the Donegal socialist who organized the Irish Transport and General Workers Union. Celtic and Orangeman paraphernalia hang beside chalkboards of drink specials. Live music Tu-F 11pm. Trad Su 10pm. Open M-Sa 11am-2am (last call 1am), Su 1pm-midnight.

The Gweedore, 59-61 Waterloo St. (☎028 7137 2138). Back door has connected to Peadar's since Famine times. Handles overflow from Peader's and caters to a slightly younger set with rock, bluegrass, and funk bands nightly. Live music Tu-Sa. Open M-Th 6:30pm-1am, F-Sa 2pm-1am, Su 6pm-midnight.

Sandino's Cafe Bar, 1 Water St. (☎028 7130 9297; www.sandinos.com), next to the bus station. Named after Nicaraguan guerrilla leader Augusto Sandino, this left-wing watering hole is plastered with pictures of Che and Fidel. Venue for poetry readings, local up-and-coming bands, and international music artists. Performances £5-10. Open M-Sa 11am-1am, Su 1pm-midnight. Nightclub upstairs opens at 10pm.

Bound for Boston, 27-31 Waterloo St. (☎028 7127 1315). Young crowd relaxes in oversized leather booths by day and rocks out to alternative bands by night. Upstairs, pool sharks and their prey watch sports at Club Q. 3-level beer garden. Live music Tu and Th-Sa. Quiz night W. Karaoke Su. Open M-Sa 11:30am-1am, Su 1pm-midnight.

The Strand Bar, 31-35 Strand Rd. (☎028 7126 0494). Young revelers fill bars on the ground, basement, and mezzanine levels. Karaoke Tu. Bands Th. DJs F-Sa. Main bar open daily noon-12:30am. Basement and mezzanine open F-Sa noon-12:30am.

DAYTRIPS FROM DERRY

THE GIANT'S CAUSEWAY. Geologists believe that the unique rock formations found at Giant's Causeway were created some 60 million years ago by lava outpourings that left curiously shaped cracks in their wake. Although locals have different ideas, everyone agrees that the causeway is an awesome sight to behold. Comprising more than 40,000 symmetrical hexagonal basalt columns, it resembles a descending staircase leading from the cliffs to the ocean's floor. Several other formations stand within the causeway: the **Giant's Organ,** the **Wishing Chair,** the **Granny,** the **Camel,** and the **Giant's Boot.** Advertised as the eighth natural wonder of the world, the Giant's Causeway is Northern Ireland's most famous natural sight, so don't be surprised if 2000 others pick the same day to visit. Visit early in the morning or after the center closes to avoid crowds.

Once travelers reach the Visitors Centre, they have two trail options: the more popular low road, which directly swoops down to the Causeway (20min.), or the more rewarding high road, which takes visitors 4½ mi. up a sea cliff to the romantic Iron Age ruins of **Dunseverick Castle.** Bus #172 and the 252 "Antrim

Coaster" stop in front of the castle, from which it's 4½ mi. farther to Ballintoy. The trail is well marked and easy to follow, but you can also consult the free map available at the Visitors Centre. The center also offers a 12min. film about the legend of Finn McCool and speculates on the geological explanation for the formations. *(The causeway is always open and free to pedestrians. Ulsterbus #172 to Bally-castle, the 252 Antrim Coaster, and the Ulsterbus Causeway Rambler (June-Sept.) all drop visitors at Giant's Causeway Visitors Centre, in the shop next to the car park. The Causeway Coaster minibus runs to the columns. ☎028 9066 6630; www.translink.co.uk. 2min.; every 15min.; £1, round-trip £2, children 50p/£1. Visitors Centre ☎028 2073 1855; www.giantscausewaycentre.com. Open daily July-Aug. 10am-7pm; Sept.-Mar. 10am-4pm; June 10am-6pm. Movie every 15min.; £1, child £0.50. Parking £5. To avoid the fee, park at nearby Heritage Railway Centre's free car park, a 2min. walk away, or behind the Causeway Hotel.)*

DUNLUCE CASTLE. On top of a craggy sea cliff, the remarkably intact ruins of this 16th-century fortress seem to merge seamlessly with their rocky foundation. Indeed, the castle is built so close to the cliff's edge that the kitchen once fell into the sea during a grand banquet, resulting in the arrest of the host and the relocation of the lady of the house (who despised the sound of the sea) to an inland residence. Built as the seat of the MacDonnell family, the castle was considered unbreachable by any army, and it can only be accessed across a small bridge, which was originally a narrow, rocky pass. The east wall has cannons from the *Girona*, a Spanish Armada vessel that sank nearby. Beneath the castle, a covert **sea cave** offered a quick escape route toward Rathlin Island or Scotland; climbing down can be slippery, but adventurers are rewarded with a different perspective of the castle's cliffside location. While a small fee is required to get up close and personal with the castle, the most spectacular views are along the A2 coming from Bushmills. From mid-June until mid-September, a free "living history" exhibit shows the castle as it would have been before it was ruined. *(The castle is located along the A2, between Bushmills and Portrush. The Antrim Coaster (☎028 9066 6630; www.translink.co.uk) stops by the castle on request (M-Sa leaves Coleraine 9:35am, 3:40pm). Castle ☎028 2073 1938. Open daily Apr.-Sept. 10am-6pm; Oct.-Mar. 10am-5pm. £2, under 16 and seniors £1, under 4 free.)*

BUSHMILLS DISTILLERY. Ardently Protestant Bushmills has been home to the Old Bushmills Distillery, creator of Bushmills Irish Whiskey, since 1608, when a nod from King James I established it as the oldest licensed whiskey producer in the world. Travelers have been stopping at the distillery since ancient days, when it lay on the route to Tara from castles Dunluce and Dunseverick. In those days, the whiskey's strength was determined by gunpowder's ability to ignite when doused with the fiery liquid. When the plant is operating, the tour shows the various stages involved in the production of Irish whiskey. During the three weeks in July when production stops for maintenance, the less interesting experience is redeemed by the free sample at its end. *(The distillery and Bushmills are at the intersection of the A2 and the B17, 3 mi. east of Portrush and 2 mi. west of the causeway; served by the Causeway Rambler bus (☎028 7032 5400 or 9066 6630; www.trans-link.co.uk). June-Sept. daily 7 per day 10:15am-5pm. The Giant's Causeway and Bushmills Railway connect the 2. ☎028 2073 2844; www.discovernorthernireland.com. July-Aug. daily 7 per day 11am-5pm; Sept.-Oct. and Apr.-June Sa-Su 7 per day 11am-5pm. £5.25, children £3.25. Distillery ☎028 2073 3272; www.bushmills.com. Open July-Aug. M-Sa 9:15am-5pm, Su 11:30am-5pm; Sept.-Oct. and Mar.-June M-Sa 9:15am-5pm, Su noon-5pm. Tours leave every 10-30min.; last tour 1hr. before close. £6, students and seniors £5, ages 8-17 £3, families £17.)*

APPENDIX

CLIMATE

Winds from the Atlantic mix with seas surrounding the island country to produce the dense fog and low clouds characteristic of Britain's land- and city-scapes. Though notorious for a wet and variable climate, weather in Britain is highly variable. Days are cool to mild with frequent cloud and rain and occasional calm spells. Visitors are often surprised by the long summer days, a happy consequence of Britain's northern latitude. Summers in Britain are cooler than in continental Europe, though winters are milder.

AVG. TEMP. (LOW/HIGH), PRECIP.	JANUARY			APRIL			JULY			OCTOBER		
	°C	°F	mm	°C	°F	mm	°C	°F	mm	°C	°F	mm
London	2/6	36/43	54	6/13	43/55	37	14/22	57/72	57	8/14	46/57	57
Cardiff	2/7	36/45	108	5/13	41/55	65	12/20	54/68	89	8/14	46/57	109
Edinburgh	1/6	34/43	57	4/11	39/52	39	11/18	52/65	86	6/13	43/55	66
Belfast	2/6	36/43	80	4/12	39/54	48	11/18	52/65	94	7/13	45/55	83

To convert from degrees Fahrenheit to degrees Celsius, subtract 32 and multiply by 5/9. To convert from Celsius to Fahrenheit, multiply by 9/5 and add 32.

°CELSIUS	-5	0	5	10	15	20	25	30	35	40
°FAHRENHEIT	23	32	41	50	59	68	77	86	95	104

MEASUREMENTS

Like the rest of the rational world, Britain uses the metric system. The basic unit of length is the meter (m), which is divided into 100 centimeters (cm) or 1000 millimeters (mm). One thousand meters make up one kilometer (km). Fluids are measured in liters (L), each divided into 1000 milliliters (mL). A liter of pure water weighs one kilogram (kg), the unit of mass that is divided into 1000 grams (g). One metric ton is 1000kg. Gallons in the US and those in Britain are not identical: one US gallon equals 0.83 Imperial gallons. You'll notice that Britain's longtime conversion to the metric system is still in progress—road signs indicate distances in miles.

MEASUREMENT CONVERSIONS	
1 inch (in.) = 25.4mm	1 millimeter (mm) = 0.039 in.
1 foot (ft.) = 0.305m	1 meter (m) = 3.28 ft.
1 yard (yd.) = 0.914m	1 meter (m) = 1.094 yd.
1 mile (mi.) = 1.609km	1 kilometer (km) = 0.621 mi.
1 ounce (oz.) = 28.35g	1 gram (g) = 0.035 oz.
1 pound (lb.) = 0.454kg	1 kilogram (kg) = 2.205 lb.
1 fluid ounce (fl. oz.) = 29.57mL	1 milliliter (mL) = 0.034 fl. oz.
1 gallon (gal.) = 3.785L	1 liter (L) = 0.264 gal.

LANGUAGE

BRITISH ENGLISH

Who says Britain has no foreign language? As a traveler to Britain, you find yourself in a country where biscuit means cookie, vest means undershirt, and football means soccer (and soccer means serious business). Below is a list of British words for the linguistically lost. Use this guide to find the best nosh in town and the best place to kip when you're knackered.

BRITISH ENGLISH	AMERICAN ENGLISH	BRITISH ENGLISH	AMERICAN ENGLISH
augerbine	eggplant	give a bollocking to	shout at
bap	soft bun	grotty	grungy
barmy	insane, erratic	high street	main street
bed-sit, bed-sitter	studio apartment	hire	rental, to rent
beer mat	coaster	holiday	vacation
biro	ballpoint pen	hoover	vacuum cleaner
biscuit	cookie or cracker	ice-lolly	popsicle
bonnet	car hood	interval	intermission
boot	car trunk	in a street	"on" a street
braces	suspenders	jam	jelly
brilliant, brill	awesome, cool	jelly	Jell-O
campy	effeminate	jumper	sweater
caravan	trailer, mobile home	kip	sleep, nap
car park	parking lot	kit	sports team uniform
cheeky	mischievous	knackered	tired, worn out
cheerio	goodbye	knickers	underwear
cheers	thank you	lavatory, lav	restroom
chemist/chemist's	pharmacist/pharmacy	lay-by	roadside turnout
chips	french fries	legless	intoxicated
chuffed	pleased	lemonade	lemon soda
coach	intercity bus	let	to rent
concession	discount on admission	lift	elevator
courgette	zucchini	loo	restroom
crisps	potato chips	lorry	truck
dear	expensive	mashed	extremely intoxicated
dicey, dodgy	sketchy	mate	pal
the dog's bollocks	the best	minger	an ugly person
dual carriageway	divided highway	motorway	highway
dustbin	trash can	naff	unfashionable
ensuite	with attached bathroom	nosh	food
fag	cigarette	pants	underwear
fanny	vagina	petrol	gasoline
first floor	second floor	pissed	drunk
fortnight	two weeks	plaster	Band-Aid
full stop	period (punctuation)	prat	stupid person
get knocked up	get woken up	geezer	adult male
pull	hit on, seduce	sweet(s)	candy
public school	private school	swish	swanky
punter	average person	take the piss out of	to make fun of
queue up, queue	line up	toilet	restroom

BRITISH ENGLISH	AMERICAN ENGLISH	BRITISH ENGLISH	AMERICAN ENGLISH
quid	pound (in money)	torch	flashlight
roundabout	rotary road intersection	tosser	term of abuse; see prat
rubber	eraser, condom	trainers	sneakers
self-catering	with kitchen facilities	trousers	pants
self-drive	car rental	twat	idiot, vagina
serviette	napkin	vest	undershirt
a shag, to shag	sex, to have sex	waistcoat (weskit)	men's vest
single carriageway	non-divided highway	wanker	masturbator
sod it	forget it	way out	exit
snogging	making out	WC (water closet)	toilet, restroom
pudding	dessert	zed	the letter Z

BRITISH PRONUNCIATION

Berkeley	BARK-lee	Magdalen	MAUD-lin
Berkshire	BARK-sher	Norwich	NOR-ich
Birmingham	BIRM-ing-um	Salisbury	SAULS-bree
Derby	DAR-bee	Shrewsbury	SHREWS-bree
Dulwich	DULL-idge	Southwark	SUTH-uk
Edinburgh	ED-in-bur-ra	Thames	Tems
Gloucester	GLOS-ter	Woolwich	WOOL-ich
Greenwich	GREN-ich	Worcester	WOO-ster
Hertfordshire	HART-ford-sher	gaol	jail
Grosvenor	GROV-nor	quay	key
Leicester	LES-ter	scones	skons

WELSH WORDS AND PHRASES

Consult **Language,** p. 465, for the basic rules of Welsh pronunciation. Listed below are some words and phrases you may encounter on the road. Note that the pronunciation of these words may vary depending on regional dialect.

WORD/PHRASE	PRONUNCIATION	MEANING
allan	ahl-LAN	exit
ar agor	ahr AG-or	open
ar gau	ahr GUY	closed
bore da	boh-re DAH	good morning, hello
cariad	CARRY-ad	darling
croeso	CROY-so	welcome
Cymorth!	CUH-morth!	Help!
diolch	dee-OLCH	thank you
dw i'n dy garu di	doo een duh GAR-ee dee	I love you
dwn i ddim	dun ee thim	I don't know
dwr	doorr	water
dydd da	DEETH dah	good day
Fy eny yw	vu E-noo you	My name is...
Ga i peint o cwrw?	Gah-ee PAINT oh coo-roo?	Can I have a pint of beer?
gwerin	GUEH-rin	men
hwyl/hwyl fawr	huh-will/huh-will vour	goodbye
ia	eeah	yes

WORD/PHRASE	PRONUNCIATION	MEANING
iawn	eeawn	well, fine
lechyd da	YE-chid dah	cheers
llwybr cyhoeddus	hlooee-BIR cuh-HOY-this	public footpath
merched	mehrch-ED	women
na, nage	nah, nah-GE	no
nos da	nos dah	good night
noswaith dda	nos-WAYTHE tha	good evening
os gwelwch yn dda	ohs gwell-OOCH uhn tha	please
perygl	pehr-UHGL	danger
prefait	PRAY-vat	private
safle'r bws	savlehr boos	bus stop
siaradwch yn araf	sha-RA-dooch un arav	speak more slowly
stryd fawr	streed VOUR	high street

IRISH WORDS AND PHRASES

You may come across the following words and phrases in your travels in Northern Ireland. Spelling conventions almost never match English pronunciations: "mh" sounds like "v," and "dh" sounds like a soft "g."

WORD/PHRASE	PRONUNCIATION	MEANING
an lár	on lahr	city center
Conas tá tú?	CUNN-us thaw too?	How are you?
dia dhuit	JEE-a dich	good day, hello
dia's muire dhuit	JEE-as MWUR-a dich	reply to "good day"
Eire	AIR-uh	Ireland; official name of the Republic of Ireland
fáilte	FAWLT-cha	welcome
go raibh maith agat	guh roh moh UG-ut	thank you
ní hea	nee hah	no (literally, "it is not")
oíche mhaith dhuit	EE-ha woh ditch	good night
Oifig an Phoist	UFF-ig un Fwisht	Post Office
sea	shah	yes
sláinte	SLAWN-che	cheers, to your health
slán agat	slawn UG-ut	goodbye
sraid	shrawd	street
Tá mé are meisce.	Taw may air mesh-keh.	I am very drunk.
Tá tu go halainn.	Taw two guh haul-inn.	You are beautiful.

GAELIC WORDS AND PHRASES

Consult **Language,** p. 541, for information on Scottish Gaelic. Listed below are a number of words and phrases you may encounter on the road.

WORD/PHRASE	PRONUNCIATION	MEANING
allt	ALT	stream
An toir thu dhomh póg?	Un TUH-r ooghawnh pawk?	Will you give me a kiss?
baile	BAL-eh	town
einn	BEN	mountain
mar a tha sibh?	KI-mer a HA shiv?	How are you?
n t-ainm a th'oirbh?	JAY an TEN-im a HO-riv?	What's your name?

WORD/PHRASE	PRONUNCIATION	MEANING
Failte gu...	FAL-chuh goo...	Welcome to...
gleann	GLAY-ahn	valley
gle mhath	GLAY va	very well
gabh mo leisgeul	GAV mo LESH-kul	excuse me
Is mise...	ISH MISH-uh...	My name is...
latha ma	LA-huh-MA	good day
ionad	EE-nud	place, visitors center
madainn mhath	MA-ting VA	good morning
oidhche mhath	a-HOY chuh VA	good night
ratha	RAH-hud	road
Slàinte! Mhòr agad!	SLAHN-tchuh! VORR AH-kut!	Cheers! Good health to you!
sraid	SRAHJ	street
tapadh leibh	TA-pa LEEV	thank you
Tha gaol agam ort.	Hah GEUL AH-kum orsht.	I love you.
Tha gu math.	HA gu MA.	I'm fine.

SCOTS WORDS AND PHRASES

Consult **Language,** p. 541, for more info on Scots, a distinct dialect of English. Listed below are a few of the many Scots words and phrases used in standard Scottish English and their pronunciation, if applicable.

WORD/PHRASE	MEANING	WORD/PHRASE	MEANING
aye	yes	kirk	church
ben	mountain	lad	man, boy
blether, guide blether	talk idly, chat (good BLA-ther)	lass	woman, girl
breeks	pants	nae	no (nay)
bonnie	beautiful	nicht	night
brae	hill near water (bray)	sassenach	Lowlander (SAS-uh-nach)
braw	bright, strong, great	strath	broad valley
burn	stream	tatty	potato
cannae	cannot (CAN-eye)	thane	minor noble
eejit	idiot	tipple	a drink
gye	very	weegie	Glaswegian (WEE-gee)

APPENDIX

INDEX

INDEX

INDEX

SMART TRAVELERS KNOW:
GET YOUR CARD BEFORE YOU GO

An HI USA membership card gives you access to friendly and affordable accommodations at over 4,000 hostels in more than 85 countries around the world.

HI USA Members receive complementary travel insurance, airline discounts, free stay vouchers, long distance calling card bonus, so its a good idea to get your membership while you're still planning your trip.

Hostelling International USA

JENNIFER BURKE
8401 COLESVILLE ROAD
SILVER SPRING, MD 20910

060-0010001
02/01/10
Expires
Signature   *Jennifer Burke*

ADULT
10/18/84
Date of Birth

Get your card online toda

hiusa.or

MAP INDEX

MAP LEGEND

✛	Hospital
✚	Police
✉	Post Office
ⓘ	Tourist Information Centre
⬤	National Park Information Centre
$	Bank
	Pharmacy
	Site or Point of Interest
	Embassy or Consulate
	...ry
	...t Cafe
	.../Landing

✈	Airport
🚌	Bus Station
🚆	Train Station
⊖	London Tube Station
U M	Subway Station
TAXI	Taxi Stand
🏖	Beach
⛪	Church/Cathedral
⌒	Gate/Entrance
⚓	Ship/Submarine
🦌	Wildlife Reserve
⬭	Surfing
🏛	Stone Monument
♜	Castle

🏠	Hotel/Hostel
▲	Camping
🍎	Restaurant
★	Nightlife/Clubs
🍺	Nightlife/Pubs
🎭	Theatre
🏛	Museum
≋	Mountain Pass
⛰	Observatory
∫	Waterfall
∩	Cave
🗼	Lighthouse
⬛	Pedestrian Zone
▤	Stairs

▲ 0-3280 ft. / 3280-6560 ft. / >6560 ft.	Mountain
≈	Mountain Range
‖‖‖‖‖	Contour Lines
⬡	Tunnel
··········	Footpaths/Trails
┼┼┼┼	Railroads
	Park
	Beach
	Water
	Buildings
▬▬	City Walls

The Let's Go compass always points NORTH.